DATE DUE

BRODART, CO.   Cat. No. 23-221

D1029081

The University of Chicago Spanish–English Dictionary

Diccionario Universidad de Chicago Inglés-Español

The University of Chicago Spanish–English Dictionary

Diccionario Universidad de Chicago Inglés–Español

Originally Compiled by Carlos Castillo and Otto F. Bond
Compilación original de Carlos Castillo y Otto F. Bond

SIXTH EDITION · *SEXTA EDICIÓN*

David A. Pharies
Editor in Chief · *Director*

María Irene Moyna
Editor · *Editora*

Gary K. Baker
Assistant Editor · *Redactor*

Meagan M. Day
Editorial Assistant · *Redactora*

The University of Chicago Press
Chicago & London

DAVID A. PHARIES is associate dean for humanities in the College of Liberal Arts and Sciences and professor of Spanish at the University of Florida. He is the author of *A Brief History of the Spanish Language* and *Breve historia de la lengua española*, both published by the University of Chicago Press.

The University of Chicago Press, Chicago 60637
The University of Chicago Press, Ltd., London
© 2012 by The University of Chicago
All rights reserved. Published 2012.
First Edition published 1948
Printed in the United States of America

21 20 19 18 17 16 15 14 13 12   1 2 3 4 5

ISBN-13: 978-0-226-66695-2 (cloth)
ISBN-13: 978-0-226-66696-9 (paper)
ISBN-10: 0-226-66695-6 (cloth)
ISBN-10: 0-226-66696-4 (paper)

Library of Congress Cataloging-in-Publication Data

The University of Chicago Spanish-English dictionary / originally compiled by Carlos Castillo and Otto F. Bond ; David A. Pharies, editor in chief ; María Irene Moyna, editor ; Gary K. Baker, assistant editor ; Meagan M. Day, editorial assistant. — Sixth edition.
     pages ; cm
     Added t.p. title: Diccionario Universidad de Chicago inglés-español.
     Includes bibliographical references.
     ISBN 978-0-226-66695-2 (cloth : alkaline paper) — ISBN 0-226-66695-6 (cloth : alkaline paper) — ISBN 978-0-226-66696-9 (paperback : alkaline paper) — ISBN 0-226-66696-4 (paperback : alkaline paper) 1. Spanish language—Dictionaries—English. 2. English language—Dictionaries—Spanish. I. Castillo, Carlos, 1890–, compiler. II. Bond, Otto Ferdinand, 1885–, compiler. III. Pharies, David A., editor. IV. Moyna, María Irene, editor. V. Title: Diccionario Universidad de Chicago inglés-español.
     PC4640.U5 2012
     463'.21—dc23
                                                            2012005113

♾ This paper meets the requirements of the ANSI/NISO Z39.48-1992 (Permanence of Paper).

Contents

Preface to the Sixth Edition

The *University of Chicago Spanish–English Dictionary* has been compiled for the general use of Spanish-speaking learners of American English and American English-speaking learners of Spanish. In step with the rapid pace of cultural and linguistic change at the beginning of the twenty-first century, we have thoroughly revised the *Dictionary* for its sixth edition to reflect the most current vocabulary and usage in both languages.

Since our goal is to ensure that users will always find the words and phrases they seek, the greatest change for this new edition is the addition of some six thousand words and meanings. In choosing among possible additions, we have paid particular attention to frequency of use in written and spoken contexts, since a user is more likely to seek a word that appears frequently (e.g., *libertad* 'liberty', number 540 in frequency according to the extensive list available at www.wordfrequency.info) than one that appears infrequently (e.g., *verdolaga* 'purslane', number 19,705).

Frequency of use cannot serve as the sole criterion for new material, however, for three reasons. First, some words become current so quickly that no frequency list can possibly capture them. Digital terminology offers good examples of this trend, such as the word *app*, which has risen from obscurity to universal acceptance in very little time. Second, some of the changes that a dictionary should reflect occur at a semantic or phrasal level not captured by frequencies. Current expressions such as *to go off on* 'to scold' and *to be down with* 'to be in agreement with' consist of extremely frequent words used in novel ways. Finally, a word can be essential without being frequent. Medical terms, for example, can be vitally important to anyone negotiating another nation's health system, even if they are used infrequently outside of medical contexts.

Medicine is in fact one of four cultural and technical areas of increasing global importance for which we have specially enhanced our coverage for this edition. Along with the 600 new words and meanings that have been added in this field, the sixth edition incorporates 750 new items from the field of business, 500 relating to digital technology, and over 400 relating to the terminology of several globally popular sports, including basketball, baseball, soccer, tennis, and golf.

In many cases, the additions in these four areas warranted completely new entries, as in the case of *allergen* (Sp. *alérgeno*), *auditing* (*auditoría*), *adapter* (*adaptador*), and *unplayable* (*injugable*). In many others, we added a meaning or an equivalent to an existing entry, as in the case of *pinza* (to whose entry was added Eng. [*medical*] *clamp*), *fraudulento* (adding *bogus*), *descifrar* (*to decrypt*), and *abanicar* (*to swing and miss*). On the English side, many additions take the form of compounds attached to existing entries—for example, *clubfoot* (*pie zambo*), added to the *club* entry; *business agreement* (*con-*

venio comercial), added to the *business* entry; *copy protection* (*protección contra copias*) added to *copy*; and *corner kick* (*córner*) added to *corner*.

To further increase the utility of the *Dictionary* for beginning learners of both Spanish and English, we have added "blind" or reference entries for irregular verb forms that differ markedly from their citation forms. These entries take the following form: *quepa, quepo*: ver *caber* (Spanish–English) and *frozen*: see *freeze* (English–Spanish).

Finally, we have invested considerable effort in expanding and perfecting the already well-developed set of semantic delimiters or disambiguators whose purpose is to help users differentiate among meanings in polysemic words. The English word *easy*, for example, has different Spanish equivalents according to whether it means 'simple' (*fácil, sencillo*), 'compliant' (*fácil*), 'comfortable' (*cómodo*), 'informal' (*desenvuelto*), or 'unworried' (*tranquilo*). Similarly, the Spanish word *gusto* has different equivalents for its several meanings: 'sentido', 'sabor', 'sentido estético' (*taste*), 'agrado' (*pleasure*), and 'preferencia personal' (*like*).

Preámbulo a la sexta edición

El *Diccionario Universidad de Chicago Inglés–Español* se ha compilado para el uso general de estudiantes hispanoparlantes que aprenden el inglés de los Estados Unidos y para estudiantes angloparlantes de los Estados Unidos que estudian español. Para acompasarse a los rápidos cambios culturales y lingüísticos que se vienen sucediendo desde comienzos del siglo XXI, se ha hecho una revisión profunda del *Diccionario* con el fin de reflejar el vocabulario y los usos más actualizados en ambas lenguas.

Ya que nuestro propósito es asegurar que los usuarios siempre encuentren los términos y expresiones que buscan, el cambio más sustancial de esta nueva edición es la inclusión de unos seis mil términos y significados nuevos. Para elegir entre las muchas posibles adiciones, se le prestó mucha atención a la frecuencia de uso en el medio escrito y oral, ya que es más probable que un usuario se encuentre con una palabra que aparece con frecuencia (v.g., *libertad*, que ocupa el puesto 540 en frecuencia según la exhaustiva lista de frecuencias disponible en www.wordfrequency.info) que con otra palabra que aparece con baja frecuencia (v.g., *verdolaga*, que ocupa el puesto 19.705 en la misma lista).

Sin embargo, la frecuencia de uso no puede ser el único criterio empleado para incluir material nuevo, por tres razones. En primer lugar, algunas palabras se generalizan tan rápidamente que no alcanzan a ser incluidas en listas de frecuencia. Un buen ejemplo de esta tendencia lo constituye la terminología digital; considérese la palabra inglesa *app* 'aplicación informática', que en muy poco tiempo ha pasado de ser casi desconocida a tener aceptación general. En segundo lugar, algunos de los cambios que debe reflejar un diccionario suceden al nivel de la frase, y estos cambios no se pueden registrar meramente a partir de las frecuencias de los términos. Algunas expresiones actuales tales como *to go off on* 'regañar' y *to be down with* 'estar de acuerdo con' están constituidas por palabras de alta frecuencia empleadas en combinaciones novedosas. Por último, una palabra puede ser esencial sin por ello ser muy frecuente. Por ejemplo, la terminología médica puede ser de importancia vital para alguien que está tratando de resolver un problema de salud mientras se encuentra en un país extranjero. Por lo tanto, esas palabras deben figurar en el *Diccionario* aunque sean de poca frecuencia fuera de los contextos médicos.

De hecho, la medicina es una de las cuatro áreas culturales y técnicas cuya cobertura se ha aumentado en esta edición, debido a su importancia cada vez mayor en el contexto internacional. Además de 600 nuevos términos y significados del área médica, la presente edición incorpora 750 nuevos términos del campo de los negocios, 500 relacionados con el mundo de la informática y la tecnología digital y más de 400 relacionados con varios deportes de popularidad mundial, incluyendo el baloncesto, el béisbol, el fútbol, el tenis y el golf.

En muchos casos, las incorporaciones a estos cuatro campos nos llevaron a crear entradas completamente nuevas, como es el caso de *alérgeno* (ing. *allergen*), *auditoría* (*auditing*), *adaptador* (*adapter*) e *injugable* (*unplayable*). En muchos otros casos, se agregó un significado o un equivalente nuevo a una entrada preexistente. Tal es el caso de *pinza* (a cuya entrada se le agregó el significado inglés de [*medical*] *clamp*), *fraudulento* (*bogus*), *descifrar* (*decrypt*) y *abanicar* (con el significado en béisbol de *to swing and miss*). En el lado inglés, se incorporaron muchos términos compuestos a entradas ya existentes, tales como *clubfoot* (*pie zambo*), que fue agregado a la entrada de *club*; *business agreement* (*convenio comercial*), que fue agregado a la entrada de *business*; *copy protection* (*protección contra copias*) agregado a *copy*; y *corner kick* (*córner*) agregado a *corner*.

Para hacer todavía más útil el *Diccionario* para los estudiantes principiantes tanto de español como de inglés, se han agregado entradas "ciegas" o de referencia, para las formas verbales irregulares que son muy diferentes de sus formas infinitivas. Estas entradas tienen la siguiente estructura: *quepa, quepo*: ver *caber* (español–inglés) y *frozen*: see *freeze* (inglés–español).

Por último, se ha hecho un esfuerzo considerable para expandir y perfeccionar todavía más los delimitadores semánticos o desambiguadores, que tienen como propósito asistir a los usuarios a distinguir entre los diversos significados de palabras polisémicas. Por ejemplo, la palabra inglesa *easy* tiene diferentes equivalentes en español según signifique 'simple' (*fácil* o *sencillo*), 'compliant' (*fácil*), 'comfortable' (*cómodo*), 'informal' (*desenvuelto*) o 'unworried' (*tranquilo*). Del mismo modo, la palabra española *gusto* tiene diferentes equivalentes ingleses para sus múltiples significados: *taste* para 'sentido', 'sabor', 'sentido estético', *pleasure* para 'agrado' y *like* para 'preferencia personal'.

How to Use *The University of Chicago Spanish–English Dictionary*

Order of Entries

Alphabetical order is observed irrespective of hyphens or spaces, such that *air conditioner* precedes *aircraft* and *middle school* precedes *middle-sized*. Homographs are placed under a single entry (*lie* 'to prevaricate', *lie* 'to recline', both pronounced [laɪ]), unless they are pronounced differently (e.g., *bow* [baʊ] 'forward end of a vessel', *bow* [bo] 'bend, curve'). Regarding Spanish, according to the current policy of the Spanish Royal Academy,[1] *ch* and *ll* are no longer recognized as separate letters, such that *ch* now follows *ce* and precedes *ci*, and *ll* follows *li* and precedes *lo* in alphabetization.

Compounds listed within entries are also alphabetized. However, the need to list compounds under their first element sometimes interferes with alphabetization, as when *slumlord*, a compound listed under *slum*, comes before the next headword, *slumber*, even though strict alphabetization would require the reverse.

Spelling

Spelling of English words reflects common American usage, variants being noted where applicable (*ax, axe; sulfur, sulphur; stymie, stymy*). The spelling of Spanish words, where possible, follows the conventions of the Spanish Royal Academy. For the orthography of problematic Spanish words such as recent borrowings (*escáner, scooter*), country names (*Malí, Irak*) and adjectives of nationality (*zimbabuo*), a variety of authorities were consulted, including the *Diccionario del español actual*, the *Diccionario de dudas*, the *Libro de estilo* published by the Madrid newspaper *El País*, and various Internet sources.[2] It should be noted that there is vacillation in some cases, such as *Bahrain*, which is listed as *Bahrein* in the *Libro de estilo* and as *Bahráin* or *Bahréin* in the *Diccionario de dudas*. In these cases, we either opt for the form that appears to be most generally accepted or provide multiple equivalents.

---

1. Real Academia Española, *Ortografía de la lengua española* (Madrid: Espasa-Calpe, 1999), 2.
2. Manuel Seco, Olimpia Andrés, and Gabino Ramos, *Diccionario del español actual* (Madrid: Aguilar, 1999); Manuel Seco, *Diccionario de dudas y dificultades de la lengua española*, 10th ed. (Madrid: Espasa-Calpe, 1998); *El País: Libro de estilo*, 9th ed. (Madrid: Ediciones El País, 1990).

Omissions

Some categories of words are systematically omitted from the vocabulary entries. Adverbial forms ending in -ly (English) and -mente (Spanish) are included only when their usage and meaning are not transparently derivable from their adjectival bases. Thus, *clearly* is omitted, as its usage is predictable from its adjectival base ('in a clear way'), while *surely* is included, since in addition to 'in a sure way', it means 'undoubtedly' or 'without fail'. Similarly, *claramente* 'clearly' is omitted, while *atentamente* is retained, since the latter, in addition to meaning 'in an attentive manner', is used as a farewell, equivalent to 'yours truly'. Also, English nouns ending in -ing and adjectives in -ed, which may appear as glosses of Spanish words, are not always accorded separate entries on the English–Spanish side, due to their derivational regularity and to considerations of space.

Structure of Entries

1. HEADWORD. Spelling variants, if any, follow the most frequent form, which appears first. In Spanish, occupational designations, titles, and kinship terms are shown in both masculine and feminine forms, as in *abogado -da*.

2. PRONUNCIATION. Pronunciation of English words is indicated through a modified version of the International Phonetic Alphabet, whose conventions are explained on pp. 294–95. No individual transcription of Spanish words is required, given the simplicity and consistency of the Spanish orthographic system. See "The Spanish Spelling System and the Sounds Represented" (p. 2) for an explanation.

3. GRAMMATICAL CATEGORY. Meanings are marked according to whether they reflect usage as a noun (N), adjective (ADJ), adverb (ADV), conjunction (CONJ), preposition (PREP), pronoun (PRON), interjection (INTERJ), transitive verb (VT), or intransitive verb (VI). The exception to this rule is that nouns on the Spanish–English side are marked only by gender, M (masculine noun) or F (feminine noun).

   Order of meanings within an entry reflects frequency of usage. Where more than one grammatical category can be rendered by the same gloss, the two are listed together, cf. Eng. *red*, which can be glossed as Sp. *rojo* in both its adjective and noun meanings.

   Traditionally, Spanish adjectives are listed in their masculine form only. However, where the adjective normally functions as a noun as well, it is shown with both masculine and feminine forms if both are possible, cf. the case of *africano -na*, which can mean *African* in the adjectival sense as well as *African (man)* and *African (woman)*.

   Special mention must be made of the combination "VI/VT." Occasionally, a single verb form may function both transitively and intransitively, e.g., both *to eat* and its Spanish equivalent *comer*. Not infrequently, however, Spanish glosses of English intransitives require the addition of the pronominal particle -se. Thus, in cases such as *to bathe*, marked "VI/VT" and glossed *bañar(se)*, it should be understood that the bare form is transitive and the -se form intransitive. Finally, where transitivity differs between a headword and its equivalent in the second language, particles must be added to reflect this, as in the case of the transitive English verb *to regret*, which is glossed in Spanish as *arrepentirse de*, since *arrepentirse* alone is intransitive. Where an English verb can be used both transitively and intransitively and its Spanish equivalent is only intransitive, the latter may sometimes be made transitive through the addition of a preposition, which appears in brackets. Thus, English *fight* is glossed as *pelear* [con] to show that its intransitive equivalent is *pelear*, whereas its transitive equivalent is *pelear con*.

Again for reasons of economy, pronominal forms of Spanish verbs are omitted in two cases: first, when the particle -se functions as a direct object, either reflexive or reciprocal, cf. *mirarse*, which can mean both *to look at oneself* and *to look at each other*, and second, when the addition of -se does not affect the English translation, cf. *bañar(se)*, glossed in both meanings as *to bathe*. In contrast, pronominal forms of verbs are included when they differ substantially in meaning from the bare forms, cf. *ir*, glossed as *to go*, vs. *irse*, which means *to leave*.

4. DELIMITERS. Whenever a word, within a grammatical category, is considered to have two or more meanings, these are differentiated by means of delimiters, that is, explanatory markers. Most commonly, synonyms are used, cf. *retort*, which in the meaning 'reply' is glossed as *réplica* and in the meaning 'vessel' as *retorta*. On occasion, however, other strategies may be adopted. Thus, transitive verbs are sometimes best differentiated according to the objects they take, cf. *to negotiate* (a contract), which is glossed *negociar*, while *to negotiate* (an obstacle) is glossed *salvar*. Similarly, adjectives may be most easily distinguished by showing the referents to which they regularly apply, cf. *refreshing*, which applied to drink is *refrescante*, to sleep is *reparador*, and to honesty is *amable*. Not infrequently, a single equivalent covers almost all meanings of a headword in a single grammatical category. In such cases, only the "exceptional" meaning, placed second, is delimited. For example, the equivalent of Eng. *net* in almost all its meanings is Sp. *red*, but when it refers specifically to a hairnet it is *redecilla*. Although delimiters typically precede the gloss they are meant to distinguish, occasionally they are placed afterward. In these cases they are meant to erase doubts about the applicability of a given gloss in a specific secondary context, cf. *site*, whose gloss *sitio* is followed by the delimiter "also Internet."

5. GLOSSES. Insofar as is possible, glosses are intended to match the headword in terms of meaning, register, and frequency. Thus, *cop* is glossed as *poli* rather than the more formal *policía*. Similarly, *orinar* is glossed as *to urinate* rather than the informal and vulgar *to piss*. Glosses separated by a comma are to be considered interchangeable, if not perfectly synonymous. Semicolons, on the other hand, indicate separate meanings.

6. REGIONAL USAGE. No systematic attempt has been made to reflect regional usage in either English or Spanish, since in the great majority of cases a word of more general currency is available as a gloss. Thus, among the many Spanish equivalents of Eng. *peasant*, Sp. *campesino* is understood everywhere, even where a local term also exists, such as Puerto Rican *jíbaro*, Cuban *guajiro*, and Chilean

guaso. However, Spanish regional usage is marked where any of the following conditions are met: (1) there is no term of international currency, or it might not be understood in a given location (cf. the various regional Spanish equivalents of Eng. *bean*), (2) the use of a given term in a given region could cause embarrassment or misunderstanding, as in the case of *coger*, which means 'to catch' or 'to get' in Spain and Cuba, but is a vulgar term meaning 'to have sexual relations with' in large parts of Spanish America, or (3) a specific regionalism is known throughout the Spanish-speaking world to be typical of a given dialect, cf. River Plate *che* 'hey!', Mexican *ándale* 'come on!', *cuate* 'pal'.

7. STYLISTIC MARKERS. Because, as mentioned earlier, equivalents are chosen in order to match headwords in all aspects of their meaning, including register and frequency, stylistic markers are only infrequently employed. They are included, redundantly, in the case of taboo or offensive words, in order to provide a second level of warning to potential users. Thus, whereas there is no need to mark the Spanish gloss *tonto* as familiar, since it is meant to be equivalent to the equally familiar Eng. *fool*, the gloss of Eng. *whore*, viz., *puta*, is marked "offensive," on the chance that a given user might not realize that this is also true of *whore*. Only five register markers are employed: literary (*lit*), which also includes poetic and formal language; familiar (*fam*), which designates words used among family and friends; vulgar (*vulg*), for words whose use is socially censured; pejorative (*pej*), which implies a negative evaluation; and *offensive* (not abbreviated), for words meant to insult people.

Taboo and offensive words are included in this dictionary because of its purely descriptive rather than prescriptive nature; that is, this dictionary is intended to reflect how the vocabularies of English and Spanish are actually used by their speakers, rather than how we or other people may feel that they should be used. The inclusion of vulgar and offensive words here should not be construed as an indication that we condone or encourage their use.

8. COMPOUNDS. Ease of usage would dictate that each lexical item receive its own entry, but for reasons of economy this is not possible in a concise dictionary. This explains why compound words, which are composed of two or more preexisting words, are listed in almost all cases under the entry of their initial constituent, at the end of the corresponding grammatical category. Thus, *doghouse* is listed as —*house*, under *dog*. There are certain exceptions to this convention, however. First, compounds are listed under the headword of their second constituent when the first is extremely frequent, as are the so-called empty verbs such as Eng. *keep*, *take*, *turn*, Sp. *hacer*, *tener*, *tomar*. Thus, *to have a good time*, glossed *divertirse*, is listed under *time* rather than *have*, and *tener paciencia*, glossed *to be patient*, is under *paciencia* rather than *tener*. Second, English compounds whose first element is a preposition (*offsides*, *outcast*, *overcome*) are listed as separate headwords, chiefly because of their frequent grammatical complexity, cf. *overhead*, which can be an adverb (*it flew overhead*), an adjective (*overhead projector*), or a noun (*overhead from grant money*). Conversely, derived words, that is, words that contain one or more affixes (e.g., *antiabortion*, composed of the prefix *anti-* plus *abortion*, and *kingdom*, composed of *king* plus the suffix -*dom*), are listed as separate headwords.

9. ILLUSTRATIVE PHRASES. Appearing together with the compound words perti-
    nent to any given grammatical category are illustrative phrases, a category de-
    fined so as to include idioms, collocations, proverbs, and, especially, sentences
    required to clarify usage in some way, as when the usage of *gustarle a uno* as a gloss
    of *to like* is illustrated by the phrase *he likes dogs*, with the translation *le gustan los
    perros*.

Cómo usar el *Diccionario Universidad de Chicago Inglés-Español*

Orden de las entradas

Se respeta el orden alfabético, independientemente de la presencia de guiones o espacios, de tal manera que *air conditioning* precede a *aircraft* y *middle school* precede a *middle-sized*. Los homógrafos se ubican en una sola entrada (*lie* 'mentir' y *lie* 'yacer', ambos con la pronunciación [laɪ]), a no ser que se pronuncien de forma diferente (e.g., *bow* [baʊ] 'proa' y *bow* [bo] 'curva'). En cuanto al español y siguiendo la política oficial de la Real Academia Española,[1] *ch* y *ll* ya no se reconocen como letras independientes, de tal manera que *ch* ahora sigue a *ce* y precede a *ci*, y *ll* sigue a *li* y precede a *lo* en el orden alfabético.

Asimismo, los compuestos incluidos dentro de una entrada determinada aparecen en orden alfabético a continuación de su primer elemento, lo cual a veces interfiere con el orden alfabético general. Así, por ejemplo, *rompeolas* aparece a continuación de *romper*, porque se trata de un compuesto de dicho verbo, si bien el orden alfabético requeriría lo contrario.

Ortografía

La ortografía de los vocablos ingleses refleja el uso general en inglés americano, y las variantes se incluyen en los casos pertinentes (*ax, axe; sulfur, sulphur; stymie, stymy*). La ortografía española sigue las convenciones de la Real Academia Española. Para la grafía española de palabras problemáticas, tales como préstamos recientes (*escáner, scooter*), nombres de países (*Malí, Irak*) y gentilicios (*zimbabuo*), se consultaron fuentes tales como el *Diccionario del español actual*, el *Diccionario de dudas*, el *Libro de estilo* de *El País* de Madrid y varios sitios en el internet.[2] Corresponde hacer notar que la grafía de algunos términos vacila entre varias posibles, cf. la versión española de *Bahrain*, que aparece como *Bahrein* en el *Libro de estilo* y como *Bahráin* o *Bahréin* en el *Diccionario de dudas*, en cuyo caso damos la forma que parece más generalmente aceptada u ofrecemos varias.

---

1. Real Academia Española, *Ortografía de la lengua española* (Madrid: Espasa-Calpe, 1999), 2.

2. Manuel Seco, Olimpia Andrés y Gabino Ramos, *Diccionario del español actual* (Madrid: Aguilar, 1999); Manuel Seco, *Diccionario de dudas y dificultades de la lengua española*, 10ª ed. (Madrid: Espasa-Calpe, 1998); *El País: Libro de estilo*, 9ª ed. (Madrid: Ediciones El País, 1990).

Omisiones

Algunas categorías de palabras se omiten sistemáticamente de las entradas del diccionario. Las formas adverbiales que terminan en -*mente* (español) y en -*ly* (inglés) se incluyen solamente cuando su uso y significado no pueden deducirse claramente de sus bases adjetivas. De esta forma, *claramente* se omite, ya que su significado es predecible a partir de su base adjetiva ('de manera clara'), mientras que *atentamente* se incluye, ya que además de significar 'de manera atenta', también se usa como fórmula de despedida epistolar. Del mismo modo, se omite *clearly*, porque su equivalente, 'de manera clara', se deduce de su base adjetiva, mientras que se incluye *surely* porque además de significar 'de forma segura' también quiere decir 'sin duda'. Debe notarse también que los sustantivos ingleses terminados en -*ing* y los adjetivos en -*ed*, que pueden aparecer como traducción de palabras españolas en la parte español–inglés, no figuran siempre como cabezas de artículo en la parte inglés–español debido a la total regularidad de su formación y a consideraciones de espacio.

Estructura de las entradas

1. PALABRAS CABEZA DE ARTÍCULO. Las variantes ortográficas, si las hay, siguen a la forma más frecuente, que aparece en primer término. En español, las designaciones de profesiones y oficios, los títulos y las relaciones de parentesco aparecen tanto en la forma masculina como en la femenina, como por ejemplo, *abogado -da*.

2. PRONUNCIACIÓN. La pronunciación de las palabras inglesas se indica mediante una versión modificada del Alfabético Fonético Internacional, cuyas convenciones se explican en las pgs. 294–95. No se requiere transcripción individual de las palabras españolas, gracias a la simplicidad y sistematicidad de la ortografía española. Para detalles, ver la sección titulada "The Spanish Spelling System" en la p. 2.

3. CATEGORÍA GRAMATICAL. Los significados se marcan según reflejen el uso de la palabra como sustantivo masculino (*m*), sustantivo femenino (*f*), adjetivo (*adj*), adverbio (*adv*), conjunción (*conj*), preposición (*prep*), pronombre (*pron*), interjección (*interj*), verbo transitivo (*vt*) o verbo intransitivo (*vi*). En inglés, en cambio, los sustantivos se marcan con *n*, abreviación de *noun*.

   Los significados dentro de una entrada aparecen ordenados de manera que el más frecuente figure primero. Cuando la misma traducción cubre el significado de dos categorías gramaticales, ambas aparecen juntas, cf. el inglés *red*, que puede traducirse como *rojo* tanto en su significado sustantivo como en el adjetivo.

   Siguiendo la tradición, los adjetivos españoles aparecen exclusivamente en su forma masculina. Sin embargo, cuando el adjetivo frecuentemente funciona además como sustantivo, se muestra tanto en la forma masculina como en la femenina si ambas son posibles, cf. el caso de *africano -na*, traducido al inglés como *African*, forma adecuada para todos sus usos.

   La combinación *vi/vt* merece mención especial. En ocasiones, una única forma verbal funciona tanto transitiva como intransitivamente, v.g., tanto *comer* como su equivalente inglés *to eat*. Sin embargo, es también frecuente que las traducciones españolas de verbos intransitivos ingleses requieran el agregado de una partícula pronominal *-se*. Así, en casos tales como *to bathe*, que se marca "vi/vt" y se traduce como *bañar(se)*, debe entenderse que la forma no pronominalizada es transitiva y la forma con *-se* es intransitiva. En aquellos casos cuando la palabra cabeza de artículo y su equivalente en la otra lengua difieren en transitividad, se deben agregar partículas para reflejar esta diferencia. Tal es el caso del verbo *aprobar*, que se traduce al inglés como *to approve of* en algunos de sus significados, ya que *to approve* es intransitivo si no va acompañado de preposición. Finalmente, en los casos en los que un verbo español puede usarse tanto intransitiva como transitivamente y su equivalente inglés es exclusivamente intransitivo, este último puede a veces volverse transitivo mediante el agregado de una preposición entre corchetes. Así, el esp. *chivar* se traduce como *to snitch* [*on*] para mostrar que su forma intransitiva en inglés es *to snitch* mientras que el equivalente transitivo es *to snitch on*.

Por razones de espacio se omiten las formas pronominales de los verbos españoles en dos casos. En primer lugar, se omiten si la partícula pronominal hace las veces de complemento directo reflexivo o recíproco, cf. *mirarse* (a sí mismo o el uno al otro). En segundo lugar no se incluyen tampoco si la partícula pronominal no afecta la traducción al inglés, como en el caso de *bañar* y *bañarse*, ambos *to bathe*. Sí se incluyen aquellas formas pronominales que difieren semánticamente de sus verbos de base, cf. *ir* vs. *irse*.

4.   INDICADORES SEMÁNTICOS. En aquellos casos en los que una palabra, dentro de una misma categoría gramatical, tiene dos o más acepciones, estas se distinguen por medio de indicadores semánticos, o sea, explicaciones parentéticas. Lo más frecuente es que se empleen sinónimos, cf. *arco*, que se traduce *arc* cuando se trata de una curva, como *arch* cuando se refiere a una estructura arquitectónica, y como *bow* cuando se trata de un arma, aunque en otras ocasiones se adoptan otras estrategias. Así, los verbos transitivos a veces se distinguen con mayor facilidad mediante los tipos de complementos directos que los acompañan, cf. *acordonar* (un zapato) *to lace*, (un lugar) *to rope off*, (una moneda) *to mill*, mientras que la forma más sencilla de distinguir adjetivos es mostrar los tipos de referentes a los cuales se aplican con mayor frecuencia, cf. *inseguro*, que aplicado a una personalidad se traduce por *insecure*, a un vehículo por *unsafe*, y al andar por *unsteady*. Es frecuente que un único equivalente abarque casi todas las acepciones de una palabra cabeza de artículo dentro de una categoría gramatical determinada. En esos casos, solamente el significado "excepcional", que aparece en segundo lugar, se acompaña de un indicador semántico. Por ejemplo, el equivalente de *acceso* en casi todas sus acepciones es *access*, excepto cuando se refiere a un ataque de tos o rabia, en cuyo caso se traduce como *fit*. Aunque los indicadores semánticos normalmente preceden a la traducción que les corresponde, en ocasiones se ubican después. En estos casos tienen como objetivo eliminar dudas acerca del empleo de una traducción determinada en un contexto secundario específico, cf. *acompañar*, cuya traducción *to accompany* va seguida de un indicador semántico "también en música" para confirmar al lector su aplicación a ese contexto.

5. TRADUCCIONES. En la medida de lo posible, se ha tratado de que las traducciones sean equivalentes a la palabra cabeza de artículo en cuanto a su significado, registro y frecuencia. Así, *poli* se traduce como *cop* y no como *policeman*, palabra más formal. De la misma forma, *to urinate* se traduce como *orinar* y no como *mear*, palabra más familiar. Las traducciones separadas por una coma deben considerarse equivalentes, aunque no sean exactamente sinónimas. El uso del punto y coma indica acepciones distintas.

6. USO REGIONAL. No se ha hecho ningún esfuerzo sistemático por reflejar usos regionales, ni en inglés ni en español, ya que en la gran mayoría de los casos existe una palabra de uso general. Así, entre los muchos equivalentes españoles de la palabra inglesa *peasant*, su equivalente español *campesino* se entiende en todo el mundo de habla hispana, aun cuando existan términos locales, tales como *jíbaro* en Puerto Rico, *guajiro* en Cuba y *guaso* en Chile. Sin embargo, el uso regional se indica para el español en tres casos específicos. En primer lugar se encuentran los casos en los que una palabra determinada podría resultar desconocida en una región dada, como los varios equivalentes españoles del ingl. *bean*. En segundo lugar, hay casos en que el empleo de una palabra podría dar lugar a situaciones bochornosas o equívocas. Tal es el caso de *coger*, que significa 'tomar' u 'obtener' en España y Cuba, pero es un vulgarismo para 'tener relaciones sexuales con' en gran parte de Hispanoamérica. En tercer término, se han incluido regionalismos que se reconocen en todo el mundo de habla hispana como típicos de un dialecto determinado, cf. español rioplatense *che*, mexicano *ándale, cuate*.

7. INDICADORES DE ESTILO. Ya que, como se mencionó anteriormente, los equivalentes se eligen para que correspondan a las palabras cabeza de artículo en todos los aspectos de su significado, incluyendo nivel de lengua y frecuencia, los indicadores de estilo se usan poco. Aunque son redundantes, se incluyen en los casos de palabras tabú o términos ofensivos para reforzar la advertencia a los usuarios potenciales del término. Así, aunque no hay necesidad de indicar que la palabra inglesa *fool* es familiar, ya que figura como equivalente del español *tonto*, la traducción de *puta* como *whore* va acompañada del indicador *ofensivo* por si el usuario ignora las connotaciones de la palabra española. Se han empleado cinco indicadores de estilo: literario (*lit*), que incluye lenguaje poético y formal, familiar (*fam*), que designa palabras que se usan en situaciones de intimidad, vulgar (*vulg*), que designa términos cuyo uso está censurado socialmente, peyorativo (*pey*), que designa palabras que tienen una carga connotativa negativa hacia el referente, y *ofensivo* (sin abreviar), que designa insultos. Las palabras tabú y los términos ofensivos se incluyen en el diccionario debido a la naturaleza descriptiva y no prescriptiva del mismo. Es decir, el diccionario tiene como objetivo reflejar el uso que los hablantes nativos dan a los términos y no las opiniones nuestras o ajenas de cómo deberían usarse, de manera que la inclusión de estas palabras no debe interpretarse como una indicación de que preconizamos su empleo.

8. COMPUESTOS. El criterio de facilidad de uso requeriría que cada palabra recibiera su propia entrada, pero por razones de economía de espacio esto no es posible en un diccionario conciso. Por lo tanto, las palabras compuestas, formadas por dos o más vocablos preexistentes, aparecen en casi todos los casos en la entrada de su

primer constituyente, al final de la categoría gramatical correspondiente. De tal forma, *hombre rana* aparece como — *rana*, en la entrada de *hombre*. Hay ciertas excepciones a esta regla, sin embargo. En primer lugar, los compuestos aparecen bajo la cabeza de artículo de su segundo constituyente cuando el primero es extremadamente frecuente, tal como lo son los verbos semánticamente "vacíos" como el español *hacer, tener, tomar* y el inglés *to keep, to take, to turn.* De este modo, *tener paciencia* aparece en la entrada de *paciencia* y no en la de *tener*, y *to have a good time* figura bajo *time* y no bajo *to have.* En segundo lugar, los compuestos ingleses cuyo primer elemento es una preposición (*offsides, overcome, outcast*) aparecen como cabezas de artículo independientes, sobre todo debido a su complejidad gramatical, cf. *overhead*, que puede ser adverbio (*it flew overhead*, que equivale a *voló en lo alto*), adjetivo (*overhead projector*, es decir, *retroproyector*) y sustantivo (*overhead from grant money*, o sea, *gastos generales de una subvención*). No obstante, las palabras derivadas, i.e., aquellas que contienen uno o más afijos (e.g., *anticuerpo*, compuesta del prefijo *anti-* y *cuerpo*, y *cabezón*, compuesta por *cabeza* y el sufijo -*ón*), figuran como cabezas de artículo independientes.

9.   FRASES ILUSTRATIVAS. Junto con las palabras compuestas de una determinada categoría gramatical figuran las frases ilustrativas, una categoría que incluye expresiones idiomáticas, colocaciones típicas, refranes y, especialmente, oraciones necesarias para aclarar el uso de alguna palabra, como cuando el uso de *like* como traducción de *gustar* se ilustra con la frase *he likes dogs*, que se traduce *le gustan los perros.*

Spanish–English · Español–Inglés

List of Abbreviations / Lista de abreviaturas

adj	adjective	adjetivo
adv	adverb, adverbial	adverbio, adverbial
Am	America	América
art	article	artículo
Carib	Caribbean	Caribe
conj	conjunction	conjunción
def	definite	definido
dem	demonstrative	demostrativo
Esp	Spain, Spanish	España, español
f	feminine	femenino
fam	familiar	familiar
indef	indefinite	indefinido
interj	interjection	interjección
interr	interrogative	interrogativo
inv	invariable	invariable
lit	literary	literario
loc	locution	locución
m	masculine	masculino
Méx	Mexico	México
num	numeral	numeral
pej, pey	pejorative	peyorativo
pers	personal	personal
pl	plural	plural
pos	possessive	posesivo
prep	preposition, prepositional	preposición, preposicional
pron	pronoun	pronombre
rel	relative	relativo
RP	River Plate	Río de la Plata
sg	singular	singular
Sp	Spain, Spanish	España, español
v aux	auxiliary verb	verbo auxiliar
vi	intransitive verb	verbo intransitivo
vt	transitive verb	verbo transitivo
vulg	vulgar	vulgar

Spanish Pronunciation

Spanish orthography very closely mirrors Spanish pronunciation, much more so than is the case in English. This explains why, in bilingual dictionaries such as this, each English entry must be accompanied by a phonetic representation, while Spanish pronunciation may be presented in synoptic form.

This synopsis is meant only as an introduction, however. In spite of the clarity of the orthographical system of Spanish, the individual sounds of the language are difficult for adult native speakers of English to pronounce, and this difficulty is compounded by the syllabic structure of the language. For these reasons, readers who wish to perfect their pronunciation of Spanish are strongly advised to seek the help of a competent teacher.

To say that orthography mirrors pronunciation means that there is a close correlation between letters and sounds. Thus, most Spanish letters correspond to a single sound, or to a single family of closely related sounds, as is the case for all vowels and the consonants *f*, *l*, *m*, *n*, *p*, *t*, and *s*. In a few cases a single letter represents two very different sounds, as *c*, which is pronounced as *k* before *a*, *o*, and *u*, but *th* (as in *thin*, in parts of Spain, or as *s* in America) before *e* or *i*. Rarely, two letters represent a single sound, as in the case of *ch*.

The overarching differences between Spanish and English pronunciation are tenseness of articulation and syllabification within the breath group. Due to the tenseness of their articulation, for example, all Spanish vowels have a clear nondiphthongal character, unlike English long vowels, which tend to be bipartite (e.g., *late*, pronounced [leⁱt]). Syllabification is a problem for English speakers because in Spanish, syllables are formed without respect to word boundaries, such that *el hado* 'fate' and *helado* 'ice cream' are both pronounced as e-la-do, and the phrase *tus otras hermanas* 'your other sisters' is syllabified as tu-so-tra-ser-ma-nas. In fast speech, vowels may combine, as in *lo ofendiste* 'you offended him', pronounced lo-fen-dis-te. Finally, when Spanish consonants occur in clusters, very often the articulation of the second influences that of the first, as when *un peso* 'one peso' is pronounced um-pe-so, and *en que* 'in which' is pronounced eŋ ke, where ŋ represents the sound of the letters *ng* in English.

The Spanish Spelling System and the Sounds Represented

I. VOWELS

i as a single vowel always represents a sound similar to the second vowel of *police*. Examples: **hilo, camino, piso.** As a part of a diphthong, it sounds like the *y* of English *yes, year.* Examples: **bien, baile, reina.**

e is similar to the vowel of *late* ([leⁱt]), but without the diphthong. Examples: **mesa, hablé, tres.**

a is similar to the vowel of *pod*. Examples: **casa, mala, América.** Notably, **a** is always pronounced this way, even when not stressed. This contrasts with the English tendency to reduce unstressed vowels to schwa ([ə]), as in *America*, pronounced in English as [ə-mɛ́-rɪ-kə].

o has a value similar to that of the vowel in Eng. *coat* [koʷt], but without the diphthong. Examples: **no, modo, amó.**

u has a value similar to that of English *oo*, as in *boot* [buʷt], but without the diphthong. Examples: **cura, agudo, uno.** Note that the letter **u** is not pronounced in the syllables **qui, que, gui,** and **gue** (unless spelled with dieresis, as in *bilingüe*). When **u** occurs in diphthongs such as those of **cuida, cuento, deuda,** it has the sound of *w* (as in *way*).

II. CONSONANTS

b and **v** represent the same sounds in Spanish. At the beginning of a breath group or when preceded by the *m* sound (which may be spelled *n*), they are both pronounced like English *b*. Examples: **bomba, en vez de, vine, invierno.** In other environments, especially between vowels, both letters are pronounced as a very relaxed *b*, in which the lips do not completely touch and the air is not completely stopped. This sound has no equivalent in English. Examples: **haba, uva, la vaca, la banda.**

c represents a *k* sound before **a, o, u, l,** and **r.** However, this sound is not accompanied by a puff of air as it is in Eng. *can* and *coat* (compare the *c* in *scan*, which is more similar to the Spanish sound). Examples: **casa, cosa, cuna, crudo, aclamar.** In contrast, when appearing before the vowels **e** and **i,** **c** is pronounced as *s* in Spanish America and the southwest of Spain, and as *th* (as in *thin*) in other parts of Spain (see **s** for more information).

ch is no longer considered to be a separate letter in the Spanish alphabet. However, it represents a single sound, which is similar to the English *ch* in *church* and *cheek*. Examples: **chato, chaleco, mucho.**

d is phonetically complex in Spanish. In terms of articulation, it is pronounced by the tongue touching the teeth rather than the alveolar ridge as in English. Second, it is represented by two variants. The first of these, which is similar to that of English *dame* and *did*, occurs at the beginning of breath groups or after **n** and **l.** Examples: **donde, falda, conde.** In all other situations the letter represents a sound similar to the *th* of English *then*. Examples: **hado, cuerda, cuadro, usted.** This sound tends to be very relaxed, to the point of disappearing in certain environments, such as word-final and intervocalic.

f is very similar to the English *f* sound. Examples: **faro, elefante, alfalfa.**

g is phonetically complex. Before the vowels **e** and **i,** it is pronounced as *h* in many American dialects, while in northern Spain it is realized like the *ch* in the German word *Bach*. Examples: **gente, giro.** At the beginning of breath groups and after nasals before the vowels **a, o, u,** and the consonants **l** and **r,** it is pronounced like the **g** of English *go*. Examples: **ganga, globo, grada.** In all other environments it is pronounced as a very relaxed *g*. Examples: **lago, la goma, agrado.**

h is silent. Examples: **hoja, humo, harto.**

j is realized in most American dialects as *h*, while in northern Spain it is pronounced like the *ch* in the German word *Bach*. Examples: **jamás, jugo, jota.**

k sounds like Eng. *k*, but without the accompanying puff of air. Examples: **kilo, keroseno.**

l is pronounced forward in the mouth, as the *l* in *leaf, leak*, never in the back, as in *bell, full*. Examples: **lado, ala, sol.**

ll is no longer considered to be a separate letter in the Spanish alphabet. However, it does represent a single sound, which differs widely in pronunciation throughout the Spanish-speaking world. In most areas, it is pronounced like the *y* of Eng. *yes*, though with greater tension. In extreme northern Spain and in parts of the Andes, it sounds like the *lli* in Eng. *million*. In the River Plate area it is pronounced like the *g* in *beige* or the *sh* in *ship*. Examples: **calle, llano, olla.**

m is essentially the same as in English. Examples: **madre, mano, cama.** However, in final position, as in **álbum** 'album', it is pronounced as [ŋ], the final sound of Eng. *sing*.

n is normally pronounced like Eng. *n*. Examples: **no, mano, hablan.** There are exceptions, however. For example, before **b, v, p,** and **m,** it is pronounced *m*, as in **en Barcelona, en vez de, un peso,** while before **k, g, j, ge-,** and **gi-,** it is realized as [ŋ], the final sound of Eng. *sing*, as in **anca, tengo, naranja, engendrar.**

ñ is similar to but more tense than the *ny* of Eng. *canyon*. Examples: **cañón, año, ñato.**

p is like English *p* except that it is not accompanied by a puff of air, as it is in Eng. *pill* and *papa* (compare the *p* in *spot*, which is more similar to the Spanish sound). Examples: **padre, capa, apuro.**

q combined with **u** has the sound of *k*. Examples: **queso, aquí, quien.**

r usually represents a sound similar to that of the *tt* in Eng. *kitty* and the *dd* in *ladder*. Examples: **caro, tren, comer.** In contrast, at the beginning of words and after **n, l, s,** the letter **r** is realized as a trill, as in **rosa, Enrique, alrededor, Israel.** The double letter **rr** always represents a trill, as in **carro, correr, guerrero.**

s is pronounced the same as in standard American English in most parts of Spanish America and in parts of southern Spain. In most of Spain, in contrast, it is realized with the tip of the tongue against the alveolar ridge, producing a whistling sound that is sometimes heard in southern dialects of American English. Examples: **solo, casa, es.** In the Caribbean and in coastal Spanish generally, there is a strong tendency to pronounce **s** in certain environments (usually preconsonantal) as *h*, or to eliminate it entirely. In these dialects, *esta* may be pronounced as *ehta* or *eta*.

t differs from English *t* in two respects: first, it is articulated by the tongue touching the teeth rather than the alveolar ridge, and second, it is not accompanied by a puff of air, as it is in English *too* and *titillate* (compare the *t* in *stop*, which is more similar to the Spanish sound). Examples: **tela, tino, tinta.**

x has a wide range of phonetic realizations. Between vowels, it is usually pronounced *ks* or *gs* (but never *gz*), as in **examen, próximo,** though in a few words it is pronounced as *s*, e.g., *exacto, auxilio*. Before a consonant, **x** is almost always pronounced *s*, as in **extranjero, experiencia.** In many Mexican and Central American words of indigenous origin, **x** represents *h*, as in **México.**

y varies regionally in its pronunciation. In most areas it is pronounced like the *y* of Eng. *yes*, though with greater tension. In the River Plate area it is pronounced like the *g* in *beige* or the *sh* in *ship*. Examples: **yo, ayer.**

z is subject to dialectal variation as well. In most parts of Spain, except the southwest, it is pronounced as the *th* in Eng. *thin, cloth*. In southwestern Spain and all of Spanish America, in contrast, it is pronounced *s*. Examples: **zagal, hallazgo, luz.**

Stress Assignment in Spanish and the Use of the Written Accent

Spanish words are normally stressed on the next-to-last syllable when they end in a vowel or the consonants **n** or **s**. Examples: **mesa, zapato, acontecimiento, hablan, mujeres.** Words whose pronunciation does not conform to this rule are considered exceptions, and their stressed syllable is indicated with an accent mark. Examples: **lámpara, estómago, género, acá, varón, además.**

Conversely, Spanish words are normally stressed on the final syllable when they end in a consonant other than **n** or **s**. Examples: **mujer, actualidad, pedal, voraz.** Words whose pronunciation does not conform to this rule are considered exceptions, and their stressed syllable is indicated with an accent mark. Examples: **nácar, volátil, lápiz.**

For the purposes of stress assignment, diphthongs are considered the same as simple vowels. Thus, **arduo** and **industria** are considered to have two and three syllables respectively, with regular stress on the penultimate syllable. However, some sequences of vowels are not considered diphthongs. For example, **alegría** and **continúo** are both considered to have four syllables, with the stress mark indicating the absence of a diphthong.

Until recently certain words received written accents in order to differentiate functions, even though they are pronounced identically (this is still true in certain cases, such as **de** 'of', **dé** 'give'). Thus, the orthography **esta** was assigned to the demonstrative adjective ('this', fem.), while the demonstrative pronoun ('this one', fem.) was written **ésta.** This convention is no longer observed by most writers.

Notes on Spanish Grammar

The Noun

Gender. All Spanish nouns, not just those that denote male or female beings, are assigned either masculine or feminine gender. As a general rule, male beings (**muchacho** 'boy', **toro** 'bull') and all nouns ending in -**o** (**lodo** 'mud') are assigned masculine gender (exceptions: **mano** 'hand', **foto** 'photo', both feminine). Similarly, female beings (**mujer** 'woman', **vaca** 'cow') and nouns ending in -**a** (**envidia** 'envy') tend to be assigned feminine gender (exceptions: **mapa** 'map', **drama** 'drama', **día** 'day', all masculine). In addition, nouns ending in -**ción, -tad, -dad, -tud,** and -**umbre** are always feminine: **canción** 'song', **facultad** 'college', **ciudad** 'city', **virtud** 'virtue', and **muchedumbre** 'crowd'. Otherwise, nouns ending in consonants and vowels other than -**o** and -**a** are of unpredictable gender. Some are feminine (**barbarie** 'savagery', **clase** 'class', **nariz** 'nose', **tribu** 'tribe'), while others are masculine (**antílope** 'antelope', **corte** 'cut', **mesón** 'lodge', **nácar** 'mother of pearl').

Nouns in -**o** that denote human beings (and to some extent, animals) form the feminine by replacing -**o** with -**a**, as in **tío** 'uncle' / **tía** 'aunt', **niño** 'boy' / **niña** 'girl', **oso** 'bear' / **osa** 'she-bear'. Where the masculine noun does not end in -**o**, the rules of formation are more complex. For example, nouns ending in -**ón, -or,** and -**án** require the addition of -**a**, as in the pairs **patrón** / **patrona** 'patron', **pastor** / **pastora** 'shepherd', **holgazán** / **holgazana** 'lazy person'. In other cases the difference is more unpredictable: **emperador** 'emperor' / **emperatriz** 'empress', **abad** 'abbot' / **abadesa** 'abbess'.

Some nouns have different genders according to their meanings: **corte** (m) 'cut', (f) 'court', **capital** (m) 'money capital', (f) 'capital city', while others have invariable endings which are used for both the masculine and the feminine: **artista** 'artist' (and all nouns ending in -**ista**), **amante** 'lover', **aristócrata** 'aristocrat', **homicida** 'murderer', **cliente** 'customer'. Finally, some words vacillate as to gender, e.g., **mar** 'sea', which is normally masculine but is feminine in certain expressions (**en alta mar** 'on the high seas') and in poetic contexts, and **arte,** which is masculine in the singular but feminine in the plural. Some words, such as **armazón** and **esperma,** can be both masculine and feminine.

Pluralization. Nouns ending in an unaccented vowel and **-é** add **-s** to form the plural: **libro / libros, casa / casas, café / cafés.** Nouns ending in a consonant, in **-y,** or in an accented vowel other than **-é** add **-es: papel / papeles, canción / canciones, ley / leyes, rubí / rubíes.** Exceptions to this rule include the words **papá / papás** and **mamá / mamás,** as well as the small group of nouns ending in unaccented **-es** or **-is,** which do not change in the plural: **lunes** 'Monday', 'Mondays', **tesis** 'thesis', 'theses'.

Articles

Definite Article. The equivalent of English **the** is as follows: masculine singular, **el;** feminine singular, **la;** masculine plural, **los;** feminine plural, **las.** Feminine words beginning with stressed **a** or **ha** take **el** in the singular and **las** in the plural: **el alma** 'the soul' / **las almas** 'the souls', **el hacha** 'the hatchet' / **las hachas** 'the hatchets'. In spite of this, these nouns remain feminine in the singular, as shown by adjective agreement: **el alma bendita** 'the blessed soul'. When preceded by the prepositions **a** and **de,** the masculine singular article **el** forms the contractions **al** and **del.**

Indefinite Article. The equivalent of English **a, an** is as follows: masculine singular, **un;** feminine singular, **una.** In the plural, masculine **unos** and feminine **unas** are equivalent to English **some.** Feminine words beginning with stressed **a** or **ha** take **un** in the singular and **unas** in the plural: **un alma** 'a soul' / **unas almas** 'some souls', **un hacha** 'a hatchet' / **unas hachas** 'some hatchets'.

Adjectives

Agreement. The adjective in Spanish agrees in gender and number with the noun it modifies: **el lápiz rojo** 'the red pencil', **la casa blanca** 'the white house', **los libros interesantes** 'the interesting books', **las flores hermosas** 'the beautiful flowers'.

Formation of the Plural. Adjectives follow the same rules as nouns for the formation of the plural: **pálido, pálidos** 'pale', **fácil, fáciles** 'easy', **cortés, corteses** 'courteous', **capaz, capaces** 'capable'.

Formation of the Feminine. Adjectives ending in **-o** change to **-a: blanco, blanca** 'white'. Adjectives ending in other vowels are invariable: **verde** 'green', **fuerte** 'strong', **indígena** 'indigenous, native', **pesimista** 'pessimistic', **baladí** 'trivial', as are adjectives ending in a consonant: **fácil** 'easy', **cortés** 'courteous', **mayor** 'older', 'larger'. Some cases are more complex: (a) adjectives ending in **-ón, -án, -or** (except comparatives like **mayor**) add **-a** to form the feminine: **holgazán, holgazana** 'lazy', **preguntón, preguntona** 'inquisitive', **hablador, habladora** 'talkative'; (b) adjectives of nationality ending in a consonant add -**a** to form the feminine: **francés, francesa** 'French', **español, española** 'Spanish', **alemán, alemana** 'German'.

Adverbs

Most adverbs are formed by adding -**mente** to the feminine form of the adjective: **clara** 'clear' / **claramente** 'clearly', **fácil** 'easy' / **fácilmente** 'easily'.

Comparison of Inequality in Adjectives and Adverbs

The comparative of inequality is formed by placing **más** or **menos** before the positive form of the adjective or adverb: **más rico que** 'richer than', **menos rico que** 'less rich than', **más tarde** 'later', **menos tarde** 'less late'. The superlative is formed by placing the definite article **el** before the comparative: **el más rico** 'the richest', **el menos rico** 'the least rich'.

The following adjectives and adverbs have irregular forms of comparison:

Positive	Comparative	Superlative
bueno	mejor	el (la) mejor
malo	peor	el (la) peor
grande	mayor	el (la) mayor
pequeño	menor	el (la) menor

Common Spanish Suffixes

-aco   is a pejorative suffix: **pajarraco** 'ugly bird' (from **pájaro** 'bird'), **libraco** 'large, bulky book' (**libro** 'book')

-ada *a.* attaches to verbal stems to indicate an action: **mirada** 'look' (**mirar** 'to look'), **empujada** 'push' (**empujar** 'to push')

b. attaches to noun stems to indicate a blow: **cachetada** 'blow on the cheek' (**cachete** 'cheek'), **puñalada** 'stab with a dagger' (**puñal** 'dagger')

c. attaches to nominal stems to indicate an action characteristic of a person or group: **bobada** 'foolish act' (**bobo** 'fool'), **niñada** 'childish act' (**niño** 'child')

-al, -ar   attach to nouns indicating trees to form nouns that denote a grove: **naranjal** 'orange grove' (from **naranjo** 'orange tree'), **pinar** 'pine grove' (**pino** 'pine tree')

-azo   attaches to noun stems, forming nouns that indicate

a. augmentation: **hombrazo** 'big man' (**hombre** 'man'), **marranazo** 'large hog' (**marrano** 'hog')

	b.	a blow or explosion: **porrazo** 'blow with a club' (**porra** 'club'), **cañonazo** 'cannon shot' (**cañón** 'cannon')

-cito is a diminutive suffix: **cochecito** 'a little car' (**coche** 'car'), **mujercita** 'little woman' (**mujer** 'woman')

-dor forms agent nouns from verbs: **hablador** 'talker' (**hablar** 'to talk'), **regulador** 'regulator' (**regular** 'to regulate'), which are sometimes used as adjectives: **hablador** 'talkative', **regulador** 'regulating'

-ejo is a pejorative suffix: **librejo** 'worthless book' (**libro** 'book'), **lugarejo** 'Podunk' (**lugar** 'place')

-ería attaches to noun stems to denote
- *a.* a place where something is made or sold: **zapatería** 'shoestore' (**zapato** 'shoe'), **pastelería** 'pastry shop' (**pastel** 'pastry')
- *b.* a profession, business, or occupation: **carpintería** 'carpentry' (**carpintero** 'carpenter'), **ingeniería** 'engineering' (**ingeniero** 'engineer')
- *c.* a group: **chiquillería** 'bunch of children' (**chiquillo** 'little kid')

-ero
- *a.* attaches to nouns to indicate a person who makes, sells, or is in charge of something: **librero** 'bookseller' (**libro** 'book'), **zapatero** 'shoemaker' (**zapato** 'shoe'), **carcelero** 'jailer' (**cárcel** 'jail')
- *b.* attaches to nominal stems to form adjectives: **guerrero** 'warlike' (**guerra** 'war'), **conejero** 'for hunting rabbits' (**conejo** 'rabbit')

-ez, -eza are used to make abstract nouns from adjectival bases: **vejez** 'old age' (**viejo** 'old'), **niñez** 'childhood' (**niño** 'child'), **grandeza** 'greatness' (**grande** 'large, great'), **rareza** 'rarity' (**raro** 'rare')

-ía forms abstract nouns from adjectival bases: **valentía** 'courage' (**valiente** 'brave'), **cobardía** 'cowardice' (**cobarde** 'coward')

-ico is a diminutive suffix: **ratico** 'little while' (**rato** 'while'), **momentico** 'brief moment' (**momento** 'moment')

-(i)ento attaches to adjectives to indicate attenuation, as in **amarillento** 'yellowish' (**amarillo** 'yellow'), or an undesirable quality, as in **hambriento** 'hungry' (**hambre** 'hunger')

-illo is sometimes a diminutive suffix: **politiquillo** 'insignificant politician' (**político** 'politician'), **chiquillo** 'little kid' (**chico** 'child')

-ísimo attaches to adjectives to indicate an extreme degree of a quality: **hermosísimo** 'very beautiful' (**hermoso** 'beautiful')

-ito		is a diminutive suffix: **librito** 'small book' (**libro** 'book'), **casita** 'little house' (**casa** 'house')
-izo		forms adjectives from nominal stems, indicating a tendency or attenuation: **rojizo** 'reddish' (**rojo** 'red'), **olvidadizo** 'forgetful' (**olvidar** 'to forget')
-mente		is the adverbial ending attached to the feminine form of the adjective: **generosamente** 'generously' (**generoso** 'generous'), **claramente** 'clearly' (**claro** 'clear')
-ón	*a.*	is an augmentative adjectival suffix: **barrigón** 'potbellied' (**barriga** 'belly'), **cabezón** 'large-headed' (**cabeza** 'head')
	b.	attaches to verb stems to denote sudden actions: **tirón** 'pull, jerk' (**tirar** 'to pull'), **apretón** 'push' (**apretar** 'to push')
-oso		forms adjectives from nouns, indicating abundance or character: **rocoso** 'rocky' (**roca** 'rock'), **tormentoso** 'stormy' (**tormenta** 'storm')
-ote, -ota		is an augmentative and pejorative suffix attached to nouns: **discursote** 'long, boring speech' (**discurso** 'speech'), **narizota** 'big ugly nose' (**nariz** 'nose')
-udo		forms adjectives from nouns, indicating an excess: **peludo** 'hairy' (**pelo** 'hair'), **panzudo** 'big-bellied' (**panza** 'belly')
-ura		forms abstract nouns from adjectives: **negrura** 'blackness' (**negro** 'black'), **altura** 'height' (**alto** 'high')
-uzco		forms adjectives from other adjectives, indicating attenuation: **blancuzco** 'whitish' (**blanco** 'white'), **negruzco** 'blackish' (**negro** 'black')

Spanish Regular Verbs

First Conjugation

infinitive	**hablar**
pres. indic.	hablo, hablas, habla, hablamos, habláis, hablan
pres. subj.	hable, hables, hable, hablemos, habléis, hablen
pret. indic.	hablé, hablaste, habló, hablamos, hablasteis, hablaron
imp. indic.	hablaba, hablabas, hablaba, hablábamos, hablabais, hablaban

imp. subj.	hablara, hablaras, hablara, habláramos, hablarais, hablaran, *or*
	hablase, hablases, hablase, hablásemos, hablaseis, hablasen
fut. indic.	hablaré, hablarás, hablará, hablaremos, hablaréis, hablarán
cond.	hablaría, hablarías, hablaría, hablaríamos, hablaríais, hablarían
imper.	habla (tú), hable (usted), hablemos (nosotros), hablad (vosotros), hablen (ustedes)
pres. part.	hablando
past part.	hablado

Second Conjugation

infinitive	**comer**
pres. indic.	como, comes, come, comemos, coméis, comen
pres. subj.	coma, comas, coma, comamos, comáis, coman
pret. indic.	comí, comiste, comió, comimos, comisteis, comieron
imp. indic.	comía, comías, comía, comíamos, comíais, comían
imp. subj.	comiera, comieras, comiera, comiéramos, comierais, comieran, *or*
	comiese, comieses, comiese, comiésemos, comieseis, comiesen
fut. indic.	comeré, comerás, comerá, comeremos, comeréis, comerán
cond.	comería, comerías, comería, comeríamos, comeríais, comerían
imper.	come (tú), coma (usted), comamos (nosotros), comed (vosotros), coman (ustedes)
pres. part.	comiendo
past part.	comido

Third Conjugation

infinitive	**vivir**
pres. indic.	vivo, vives, vive, vivimos, vivís, viven
pres. subj.	viva, vivas, viva, vivamos, viváis, vivan
pret. indic.	viví, viviste, vivió, vivimos, vivisteis, vivieron
imp. indic.	vivía, vivías, vivía, vivíamos, vivíais, vivían
imp. subj.	viviera, vivieras, viviera, viviéramos, vivierais, vivieran, *or*
	viviese, vivieses, viviese, viviésemos, vivieseis, viviesen
fut. indic.	viviré, vivirás, vivirá, viviremos, viviréis, vivirán
cond.	viviría, vivirías, viviría, viviríamos, viviríais, vivirían
imper.	vive (tú), viva (usted), vivamos (nosotros), vivid (vosotros), vivan (ustedes)
pres. part.	viviendo
past part.	vivido

Spanish Irregular and Orthographic Changing Verbs

The superscript number or numbers listed as part of a verb entry indicate that the verb is to be conjugated like the model verb in this section that has the corresponding number. Only the tenses that have irregular forms or spelling changes are given, and these irregular forms and spelling changes are shown in boldface type.

1. **pensar**
   pres. indic.   **pienso, piensas, piensa,** pensamos, pensáis, **piensan**
   pres. subj.   **piense, pienses, piense,** pensemos, penséis, **piensen**
   imper.   **piensa** (tú), **piense** (usted), pensemos (nosotros), pensad (vosotros), **piensen** (ustedes)

2. **perder**
   pres. indic.   **pierdo, pierdes, pierde,** perdemos, perdéis, **pierden**
   pres. subj.   **pierda, pierdas, pierda,** perdamos, perdáis, **pierdan**
   imper.   **pierde** (tú), **pierda** (usted), perdamos (nosotros), perded (vosotros), **pierdan** (ustedes)

3. **discernir**
   pres. indic.   **discierno, disciernes, discierne,** discernimos, discernís, **disciernen**
   pres. subj.   **discierna, disciernas, discierna,** discernamos, discernáis, **disciernan**
   imper.   **discierne** (tú), **discierna** (usted), discernamos (nosotros), discernid (vosotros), **disciernan** (ustedes)

4. **adquirir**
   pres. indic.   **adquiero, adquieres, adquiere,** adquirimos, adquirís, **adquieren**
   pres. subj.   **adquiera, adquieras, adquiera,** adquiramos, adquiráis, **adquieran**
   imper.   **adquiere** (tú), **adquiera** (usted), adquiramos (nosotros), adquirid (vosotros), **adquieran** (ustedes)

5. **contar**
   pres. indic.   **cuento, cuentas, cuenta,** contamos, contáis, **cuentan**
   pres. subj.   **cuente, cuentes, cuente,** contemos, contéis, **cuenten**
   imper.   **cuenta** (tú), **cuente** (usted), contemos (nosotros), contad (vosotros), **cuenten** (ustedes)

6. **volver**
   pres. indic.   **vuelvo, vuelves, vuelve,** volvemos, volvéis, **vuelven**
   pres. subj.   **vuelva, vuelvas, vuelva,** volvamos, volváis, **vuelvan**

imper.	**vuelve** (tú), **vuelva** (usted), volvamos (nosotros) volved (vosotros), **vuelvan** (ustedes)
past part.	**vuelto**

7. dormir

pres. indic.	**duermo, duermes, duerme,** dormimos, dormís, **duermen**
pres. subj.	**duerma, duermas, duerma, durmamos, durmáis, duerman**
pret. indic.	dormí, dormiste, **durmió,** dormimos, dormisteis, **durmieron**
imp. subj.	**durmiera, durmieras, durmiera, durmiéramos, durmierais, durmieran,** or **durmiese, durmieses, durmiese, durmiésemos, durmieseis, durmiesen**
imper.	**duerme** (tú), **duerma** (usted), **durmamos** (nosotros), dormid (vosotros), **duerman** (ustedes)
pres. part.	**durmiendo**

8. sentir

pres. indic.	**siento, sientes, siente,** sentimos, sentís, **sienten**
pres. subj.	**sienta, sientas, sienta, sintamos, sintáis, sientan**
pret. indic.	sentí, sentiste, **sintió,** sentimos, sentisteis, **sintieron**
imp. subj.	**sintiera, sintieras, sintiera, sintiéramos, sintierais, sintieran,** or **sintiese, sintieses, sintiese, sintiésemos, sintieseis, sintiesen**
imper.	**siente** (tú), **sienta** (usted), **sintamos** (nosotros), sentid (vosotros), **sientan** (ustedes)
pres. part.	**sintiendo**

9. pedir

pres. indic.	**pido, pides, pide,** pedimos, pedís, **piden**
pres. subj.	**pida, pidas, pida, pidamos, pidáis, pidan**
pret. indic.	pedí, pediste, **pidió,** pedimos, pedisteis, **pidieron**
imp. subj.	**pidiera, pidieras, pidiera, pidiéramos, pidierais, pidieran,** or **pidiese, pidieses, pidiese, pidiésemos, pidieseis, pidiesen**
imper.	**pide** (tú), **pida** (usted), **pidamos** (nosotros), pedid (vosotros), **pidan** (ustedes)
pres. part.	**pidiendo**

10. reír

pres. indic.	**río, ríes, ríe,** reímos, reís, **ríen**
pres. subj.	**ría, rías, ría, riamos, riáis, rían**
pret. indic.	reí, reíste, **rió,** reímos, reísteis, **rieron**

imp. subj.	**riera, rieras, riera, riéramos, rierais, rieran,** or **riese, rieses, riese, riésemos, rieseis, riesen**
imper.	**ríe** (tú), **ría** (usted), **riamos** (nosotros), reíd (vosotros), **rían** (ustedes)
pres. part.	**riendo**
past part.	**reído**

11. **reñir**

pres. indic.	**riño, riñes, riñe,** reñimos, reñís, **riñen**
pres. subj.	**riña, riñas, riña, riñamos, riñáis, riñan**
pret. indic.	reñí, reñiste, **riñó,** reñimos, reñisteis, **riñeron**
imp. subj.	**riñera, riñeras, riñera, riñéramos, riñerais, riñeran,** or **riñese, riñeses, riñese, riñésemos, riñeseis, riñesen**
imper.	**riñe** (tú), **riña** (usted), **riñamos** (nosotros), reñid (vosotros), **riñan** (ustedes)
pres. part.	**riñendo**

12. **seguir**

pres. indic.	**sigo, sigues, sigue,** seguimos, seguís, **siguen**
pres. subj.	**siga, sigas, siga, sigamos, sigáis, sigan**
pret. indic.	seguí, seguiste, **siguió,** seguimos, seguisteis, **siguieron**
imp. subj.	**siguiera, siguieras, siguiera, siguiéramos, siguierais, siguieran,** or **siguiese, siguieses, siguiese, siguiésemos, siguieses, siguiesen**
imper.	**sigue** (tú), **siga** (usted), **sigamos** (nosotros), seguid (vosotros), **sigan** (ustedes)
pres. part.	**siguiendo**

13. **erguir**

pres. indic.	**yergo, yergues, yergue,** erguimos, erguís, **yerguen** or **irgo, irgues, irgue,** erguimos, erguís, **irguen**
pres. subj.	**yerga, yergas, yerga, irgamos, irgáis, yergan** or **irga, irgas, irga, irgamos, irgáis, irgan**
pret. indic.	erguí, erguiste, **irguió,** erguimos, erguisteis, **irguieron**
imp. subj.	**irguiera, irguieras, irguiera, irguiéramos, irguierais, irguieran,** or **irguiese, irguieses, irguiese, irguiésemos, irguieseis, irguiesen**
imper.	**yergue** or **irgue** (tú), **yerga** or **irga** (usted), **irgamos** (nosotros), erguid (vosotros), **yergan** or **irgan** (ustedes)
pres. part.	**irguiendo**

14. **elegir**

pres. indic.	**elijo, eliges, elige,** elegimos, elegís, **eligen**
pres. subj.	**elija, elijas, elija, elijamos, elijáis, elijan**

pret. indic.	elegí, elegiste, **eligió,** elegimos, elegisteis, **eligieron**
imp. subj.	**eligiera, eligieras, eligiera, eligiéramos, eligierais, eligieran,** or **eligiese, eligieses, eligiese, eligiésemos, eligieseis, eligiesen**
imper.	**elige** (tú), **elija** (usted), **elijamos** (nosotros), elegid (vosotros), **elijan** (ustedes)
pres. part.	**eligiendo**

15. **tañer**

pret. indic.	tañí, tañiste, **tañó,** tañimos, tañisteis, **tañeron**
imp. subj.	**tañera, tañeras, tañera, tañéramos, tañerais, tañeran,** or **tañese, tañeses, tañese, tañésemos, tañeseis, tañesen**
pres. part.	**tañendo**

16. **bullir**

pret. indic.	bullí, bulliste, **bulló,** bullimos, bullisteis, **bulleron**
imp. subj.	**bullera, bulleras, bullera, bulléramos, bullerais, bulleran,** or **bullese, bulleses, bullese, bullésemos, bulleseis, bullesen**
pres. part.	**bullendo**

17. **gruñir**

pret. indic.	gruñí, gruñiste, **gruñó,** gruñisteis, **gruñeron**
imp. subj.	**gruñera, gruñeras, gruñera, gruñéramos, gruñerais, gruñeran,** or **gruñese, gruñeses, gruñese, gruñésemos, gruñeseis, gruñesen**
pres. part.	**gruñendo**

18. **creer**

pret. indic.	creí, creíste, **creyó,** creímos, creísteis, **creyeron**
imp. subj.	**creyera, creyeras, creyera, creyéramos, creyerais, creyeran,** or **creyese, creyeses, creyese, creyésemos, creyeseis, creyesen**
pres. part.	**creyendo**
past part.	**creído**

19. **huir**

pres. indic.	**huyo, huyes, huye,** huimos, huís, **huyen**
pres. subj.	**huya, huyas, huya, huyamos, huyáis, huyan**
pret. indic.	hui, huiste, **huyó,** huimos, huisteis, **huyeron**
imp. subj.	**huyera, huyeras, huyera, huyéramos, huyerais, huyeran,** or **huyese, huyeses, huyese, huyésemos, huyeseis, huyesen**

imper.		**huye** (tú), **huya** (usted), **huyamos** (nosotros), huid (vosotros), **huyan** (ustedes)
pres. part.		**huyendo**

20. **argüir**

pres. indic.	**arguyo, arguyes, arguye,** argüimos, argüís, **arguyen**
pres. subj.	**arguya, arguyas, arguya, arguyamos, arguyáis, arguyan**
pret. indic.	argüí, argüiste, **arguyó,** argüimos, argüisteis, **arguyeron**
imp. subj.	**arguyera, arguyeras, arguyera, arguyéramos, arguyerais, arguyeran,** or **arguyese, arguyeses, arguyese, arguyésemos, arguyeseis, arguyesen**
imper.	**arguye** (tú), **arguya** (usted), **arguyamos** (nosotros), argüid (vosotros), **arguyan** (ustedes)
pres. part.	**arguyendo**

21. **errar**

pres. indic.	**yerro, yerras, yerra,** erramos, erráis, **yerran**
pres. subj.	**yerre, yerres, yerre,** erremos, erréis, **yerren**
imper.	**yerra** (tú), **yerre** (usted), erremos (nosotros), errad (vosotros), **yerren** (ustedes)

22. **oler**

pres. indic.	**huelo, hueles, huele,** olemos, oléis, **huelen**
pres. subj.	**huela, huelas, huela,** olamos, oláis, **huelan**
imper.	**huele** (tú), **huela** (usted), oled (vosotros), **huelan** (ustedes)

23. **avergonzar**

pres. indic.	**avergüenzo, avergüenzas, avergüenza,** avergonzamos, avergonzáis, **avergüenzan**
pres. subj.	**avergüence, avergüences, avergüence, avergoncemos, avergoncéis, avergüencen**
pret. indic.	**avergoncé,** avergonzaste, avergonzó, avergonzamos, avergonzasteis, avergonzaron
imper.	**avergüenza** (tú), **avergüence** (usted), **avergoncemos** (nosotros), avergonzad (vosotros), **avergüencen** (ustedes)

24. **degollar**

pres. indic.	**degüello, degüellas, degüella,** degollamos, degolláis, **degüellan**
pres. subj.	**degüelle, degüelles, degüelle,** degollemos, degolléis, **degüellen**
imper.	**degüella** (tú), **degüelle** (usted), degollemos (nosotros), degollad (vosotros), **degüellen** (ustedes)

25. **averiguar**
    pres. subj.   **averigüe, averigües, averigüe, averigüemos,**
         averigüéis, averigüen
    pres. indic.   **averigüé,** averiguaste, averiguó, averiguamos,
         averiguasteis, averiguaron
    imper.   averigua (tú), **averigüe** (usted), **averigüemos**
         (nosotros), averiguad (vosotros), **averigüen** (ustedes)

26. **continuar**
    pres. indic.   **continúo, continúas, continúa,** continuamos,
         continuáis, **continúan**
    pres. subj.   **continúe, continúes, continúe,** continuemos,
         continuéis, **continúen**
    imper.   **continúa** (tú), **continúe** (usted), continuemos
         (nosotros), continuad (vosotros), **continúen** (ustedes)

27. **reunir**
    pres. indic.   **reúno, reúnes, reúne,** reunimos, reunís, **reúnen**
    pres. subj.   **reúna, reúnas, reúna,** reunamos, reunáis, **reúnan**
    imper.   **reúne** (tú), **reúna** (usted), reunamos (nosotros), reunid
         (vosotros), **reúnan** (ustedes)

28. **enviar**
    pres. indic.   **envío, envías, envía,** enviamos, enviáis, **envían**
    pres. subj.   **envíe, envíes, envíe,** enviemos, enviéis, **envíen**
    imper.   **envía** (tú), **envíe** (usted), enviemos (nosotros), enviad
         (vosotros), **envíen** (ustedes)

29. **prohibir**
    pres. indic.   **prohíbo, prohíbes, prohíbe,** prohibimos, prohibís,
         prohíben
    pres. subj.   **prohíba, prohíbas, prohíba,** prohibamos, prohibáis,
         prohíban
    imper.   **prohíbe** (tú), **prohíba** (usted), prohibamos (nosotros),
         prohibid (vosotros), **prohíban** (ustedes)

30. **buscar**
    pres. subj.   **busque, busques, busque, busquemos, busquéis,**
         busquen
    pret. indic.   **busqué,** buscaste, buscó, buscamos, buscasteis, buscaron
    imper.   busca (tú), **busque** (usted), **busquemos** (nosotros),
         buscad (vosotros), **busquen** (ustedes)

31. **trocar**
    pres. indic. **trueco, truecas, trueca,** trocamos, trocáis, **truecan**
    pres. subj. **trueque, trueques, trueque, troquemos, troquéis, truequen**
    pret. indic. **troqué,** trocaste, trocó, trocamos, trocasteis, trocaron
    imper. **trueca** (tú), **trueque** (usted), **troquemos** (nosotros), trocad (vosotros), **truequen** (ustedes)

32. **convencer**
    pres. indic. **convenzo,** convences, convence, convencemos, convencéis, convencen
    pres. subj. **convenza, convenzas, convenza, convenzamos, convenzáis, convenzan**
    imper. convence (tú), **convenza** (usted), **convenzamos** (nosotros), convenced (vosotros), **convenzan** (ustedes)

33. **esparcir**
    pres. indic. **esparzo,** esparces, esparce, esparcimos, esparcís, esparcen
    pres. subj. **esparza, esparzas, esparza, esparzamos, esparzáis, esparzan**
    imper. esparce (tú), **esparza** (usted), **esparzamos** (nosotros), esparcid (vosotros), **esparzan** (ustedes)

34. **cocer**
    pres. indic. **cuezo, cueces, cuece,** cocemos, cocéis, **cuecen**
    pres. subj. **cueza, cuezas, cueza, cozamos, cozáis, cuezan**
    imper. **cuece** (tú), **cueza** (usted), **cozamos** (nosotros), coced (vosotros), **cuezan** (ustedes)

35. **conocer**
    pres. indic. **conozco,** conoces, conoce, conocemos, conocéis, conocen
    pres. subj. **conozca, conozcas, conozca, conozcamos, conozcáis, conozcan**
    imper. conoce (tú), **conozca** (usted), **conozcamos** (nosotros), conoced (vosotros), **conozcan** (ustedes)

36. **placer**
    pres. indic. **plazco,** places, place, placemos, placéis, placen
    pres. subj. **plazca, plazcas, plazca, plazcamos, plazcáis, plazcan**
    imper. place (tú), **plazca** (usted), **plazcamos** (nosotros), placed (vosotros), **plazcan** (ustedes)

37. **yacer**

pres. indic.   **yazco** or **yazgo** or **yago,** yaces, yace, yacemos, yacéis, yacen

pres. subj.   **yazca, yazcas, yazca, yazcamos, yazcáis, yazcan,** or **yazga, yazgas, yazga, yazgamos, yazgáis, yazgan** or **yaga, yagas, yaga, yagamos, yagáis, yagan**

imper.   yace or **yaz** (tú), **yazca** or **yazga** or **yaga** (usted), **yazcamos** or **yazgamos** or **yagamos** (nosotros), yaced (vosotros), **yazcan** or **yazgan** or **yagan** (ustedes)

38. **conducir**

pres. indic.   **conduzco,** conduces, conduce, conducimos, conducís, conducen

pres. subj.   **conduzca, conduzcas, conduzca, conduzcamos, conduzcáis, conduzcan**

pret. indic.   **conduje, condujiste, condujo, condujimos, condujisteis, condujeron**

imp. subj.   **condujera, condujeras, condujera, condujéramos, condujerais, condujeran,** or **condujese, condujeses, condujese, condujésemos, condujeseis, condujesen**

imper.   conduce (tú), **conduzca** (usted), **conduzcamos** (nosotros), conducid (vosotros), **conduzcan** (ustedes)

39. **lucir**

pres. indic.   **luzco,** luces, luce, lucimos, lucís, lucen

pres. subj.   **luzca, luzcas, luzca, luzcamos, luzcáis, luzcan**

imper.   luce (tú), **luzca** (usted), **luzcamos** (nosotros), lucid (vosotros), **luzcan** (ustedes)

40. **llegar**

pres. subj.   **llegue, llegues, llegue, lleguemos, lleguéis, lleguen**

pret. indic.   **llegué,** llegaste, llegó, llegamos, llegasteis, llegaron

imper.   llega (tú), **llegue** (usted), **lleguemos** (nosotros), llegad (vosotros), **lleguen** (ustedes)

41. **negar**

pres. indic.   **niego, niegas, niega,** negamos, negáis, **niegan**

pres. subj.   **niegue, niegues, niegue, neguemos, neguéis, nieguen**

pret. indic.   **negué,** negaste, negó, negamos, negasteis, negaron

imper.   **niega** (tú), **niegue** (usted), **neguemos** (nosotros), negad (vosotros), **nieguen** (ustedes)

42. **colgar**
    pres. indic. **cuelgo, cuelgas, cuelga,** colgamos, colgáis, **cuelgan**
    pres. subj. **cuelgue, cuelgues, cuelgue, colguemos, colguéis, cuelguen**
    pret. indic. **colgué,** colgaste, colgó, colgamos, colgasteis, colgaron
    imper. **cuelga** (tú), **cuelgue** (usted), **colguemos** (nosotros), colgad (vosotros), **cuelguen** (ustedes)

43. **jugar**
    pres. indic. **juego, juegas, juega,** jugamos, jugáis, **juegan**
    pres. subj. **juegue, juegues, juegue, juguemos, juguéis, jueguen**
    pret. indic. **jugué,** jugaste, jugó, jugamos, jugasteis, jugaron
    imper. **juega** (tú), **juegue** (usted), **juguemos** (nosotros), jugad (vosotros), **jueguen** (ustedes)

44. **distinguir**
    pres. indic. **distingo,** distingues, distingue, distinguimos, distinguís, distinguen
    pres. subj. **distinga, distingas, distinga, distingamos, distingáis, distingan**
    imper. distingue (tú), **distinga** (usted), **distingamos** (nosotros), distinguid (vosotros), **distingan** (ustedes)

45. **coger**
    pres. indic. **cojo,** coges, coge, cogemos, cogéis, cogen
    pres. subj. **coja, cojas, coja, cojamos, cojáis, cojan**
    imper. coge (tú), **coja** (usted), **cojamos** (nosotros), coged (vosotros), **cojan** (ustedes)

46. **dirigir**
    pres. indic. **dirijo,** diriges, dirige, dirigimos, dirigís, dirigen
    pres. subj. **dirija, dirijas, dirija, dirijamos, dirijáis, dirijan**
    imper. dirige (tú), **dirija** (usted), **dirijamos** (nosotros), dirigid (vosotros), **dirijan** (ustedes)

47. **abrazar**
    pres. subj. **abrace, abraces, abrace, abracemos, abracéis, abracen**
    pret. indic. **abracé,** abrazaste, abrazó, abrazamos, abrazasteis, abrazaron
    imper. abraza (tú), **abrace** (usted), **abracemos** (nosotros), abrazad (vosotros), **abracen** (ustedes)

48. **empezar**
   pres. indic. **empiezo, empiezas, empieza,** empezamos, empezáis, **empiezan**
   pres. subj. **empiece, empieces, empiece, empecemos, empecéis, empiecen**
   pret. indic. **empecé,** empezaste, empezó, empezamos, empezasteis, empezaron
   imper. **empieza** (tú), **empiece** (usted), **empecemos** (nosotros), empezad (vosotros), **empiecen** (ustedes)

49. **forzar**
   pres. indic. **fuerzo, fuerzas, fuerza,** forzamos, forzáis, **fuerzan**
   pres. subj. **fuerce, fuerces, fuerce, forcemos, forcéis, fuercen**
   pret. indic. **forcé,** forzaste, forzó, forzamos, forzasteis, forzaron
   imper. **fuerza** (tú), **fuerce** (usted), **forcemos** (nosotros), forzad (vosotros), **fuercen** (ustedes)

50. **asir**
   pres. indic. **asgo,** ases, ase, asimos, asís, asen
   pres. subj. **asga, asgas, asga, asgamos, asgáis, asgan**
   imper. ase (tú), **asga** (usted), **asgamos** (nosotros), asid (vosotros), **asgan** (ustedes)

51. **bendecir**
   pres. indic. **bendigo, bendices, bendice,** bendecimos, bendecís, **bendicen**
   pres. subj. **bendiga, bendigas, bendiga, bendigamos, bendigáis, bendigan**
   pret. indic.. **bendije, bendijiste, bendijo, bendijimos, bendijisteis, bendijeron**
   imp. subj. **bendijera, bendijeras, bendijera, bendijéramos, bendijerais, bendijeran** or **bendijese, bendijeses, bendijese, bendijésemos, bendijeseis, bendijesen**
   fut. indic. bendeciré, bendecirás, bendecirá, bendeciremos, bendeciréis, bendecirán
   cond. bendeciría, bendecirías, bendeciría, bendeciríamos, bendeciríais, bendecirían
   imper. **bendice** (tú), **bendiga** (usted), **bendigamos** (nosotros), bendecid (vosotros), **bendigan** (ustedes)
   pres. part. **bendiciendo**
   past part. bendecido

52. **caer**
   pres. indic. **caigo,** caes, cae, caemos, caéis, caen
   pres. subj. **caiga, caigas, caiga, caigamos, caigáis, caigan**

pret. indic.	caí, caíste, **cayó,** caímos, caísteis, **cayeron**
imp. subj.	**cayera, cayeras, cayera, cayéramos, cayerais, cayeran,** or **cayese, cayeses, cayese, cayésemos, cayeseis, cayesen**
imper.	cae (tú), **caiga** (usted), **caigamos** (nosotros), caed (vosotros), **caigan** (ustedes)
pres. part.	**cayendo**
past part.	**caído**

53. **decir**[1]

pres. indic.	**digo, dices, dice,** decimos, decís, **dicen**
pres. subj.	**diga, digas, diga, digamos, digáis, digan**
pret. indic.	**dije, dijiste, dijo, dijimos, dijisteis, dijeron**
imp. subj.	**dijera, dijeras, dijera, dijéramos, dijerais, dijeran,** or **dijese, dijeses, dijese, dijésemos, dijeseis, dijesen**
fut. indic.	**diré, dirás, dirá, diremos, diréis, dirán**
cond.	**diría, dirías, diría, diríamos, diríais, dirían**
imper.	**di** (tú), **diga** (usted), **digamos** (nosotros), decid (vosotros), **digan** (ustedes)
pres. part.	**diciendo**
past part.	**dicho**

54. **hacer**

pres. indic.	**hago,** haces, hace, hacemos, hacéis, hacen
pres. subj.	**haga, hagas, haga, hagamos, hagáis, hagan**
pret. indic.	**hice, hiciste, hizo, hicimos, hicisteis, hicieron**
imp. subj.	**hiciera, hicieras, hiciera, hiciéramos, hicierais, hicieran,** or **hiciese, hicieses, hiciese, hiciésemos, hicieseis, hiciesen**
fut. indic.	**haré, harás, hará, haremos, haréis, harán**
cond.	**haría, harías, haría, haríamos, haríais, harían**
imper.	**haz** (tú), **haga** (usted), **hagamos** (nosotros), haced (vosotros), **hagan** (ustedes)
past part.	**hecho**

55. **oír**

pres. indic.	**oigo, oyes, oye,** oímos, oís, **oyen**
pres. subj.	**oiga, oigas, oiga, oigamos, oigáis, oigan**
pret. indic.	oí, oíste, **oyó,** oímos, oísteis, **oyeron**

1. The compound verbs of *decir* have the same irregularities with the exception of the following: The future and conditional forms of the compound verbs *contradecir, desdecir,* and *predecir* are used interchangeably in both their irregular and regular forms (see 51 **bendecir**). However, their past participles are always irregular (see 74 **Irregular Past Participles**).

imp. subj.	**oyera, oyeras, oyera, oyéramos, oyerais, oyeran,** or **oyese, oyeses, oyese, oyésemos, oyeseis, oyesen**
imper.	**oye** (tú), **oiga** (usted), **oigamos** (nosotros), oíd (vosotros), **oigan** (ustedes)
pres. part.	**oyendo**
past part.	**oído**

56. poner

pres. indic.	**pongo,** pones, pone, ponemos, ponéis, ponen
pres. subj.	**ponga, pongas, ponga, pongamos, pongáis, pongan**
pret. indic.	**puse, pusiste, puso, pusimos, pusisteis, pusieron**
imp. subj.	**pusiera, pusieras, pusiera, pusiéramos, pusierais, pusieran,** or **pusiese, pusieses, pusiese, pusiésemos, pusieseis, pusiesen**
fut. indic.	**pondré, pondrás, pondrá, pondremos, pondréis, pondrán**
cond.	**pondría, pondrías, pondría, pondríamos, pondríais, pondrían**
imper.	**pon** (tú), **ponga** (usted), **pongamos** (nosotros), poned (vosotros), **pongan** (ustedes)
past part.	**puesto**

57. salir

pres. indic.	**salgo,** sales, sale, salimos, salís, salen
pres. subj.	**salga, salgas, salga, salgamos, salgáis, salgan**
fut. indic.	**saldré, saldrás, saldrá, saldremos, saldréis, saldrán**
cond.	**saldría, saldrías, saldría, saldríamos, saldríais, saldrían**
imper.	**sal** (tú),[2] **salga** (usted), **salgamos** (nosotros), salid (vosotros), **salgan** (ustedes)

58. tener

pres. indic.	**tengo, tienes, tiene,** tenemos, tenéis, **tienen**
pres. subj.	**tenga, tengas, tenga, tengamos, tengáis, tengan**
pret. indic.	**tuve, tuviste, tuvo, tuvimos, tuvisteis, tuvieron**
imp. subj.	**tuviera, tuvieras, tuviera, tuviéramos, tuvierais, tuvieran,** or **tuviese, tuvieses, tuviese, tuviésemos, tuvieseis, tuviesen**
fut. indic.	**tendré, tendrás, tendrá, tendremos, tendréis, tendrán**

2. The compound *sobresalir* is regular in the familiar imperative: *sobresale.*

cond.	**tendría, tendrías, tendría, tendríamos, tendríais, tendrían**
imper.	**ten** (tú), **tenga** (usted), **tengamos** (nosotros), tened (vosotros), **tengan** (ustedes)

59. **traer**

pres. indic.	**traigo,** traes, trae, traemos, traéis, traen
pres. subj.	**traiga, traigas, traiga, traigamos, traigáis, traigan**
pret. indic.	**traje, trajiste, trajo, trajimos, trajisteis, trajeron**
imp. subj.	**trajera, trajeras, trajera, trajéramos, trajerais, trajeran,** or **trajese, trajeses, trajese, trajésemos, trajeseis, trajesen**
imper.	trae (tú), **traiga** (usted), **traigamos** (nosotros), traed (vosotros), **traigan** (ustedes)
pres. part.	**trayendo**
past part.	**traído**

60. **valer**

pres. indic.	**valgo,** vales, vale, valemos, valéis, valen
pres. subj.	**valga, valgas, valga, valgamos, valgáis, valgan**
fut. indic.	**valdré, valdrás, valdrá, valdremos, valdréis, valdrán**
cond.	**valdría, valdrías, valdría, valdríamos, valdríais, valdrían**
imper.	**val** or vale (tú), **valga** (usted), **valgamos** (nosotros), valed (vosotros), **valgan** (ustedes)

61. **venir**

pres. indic.	**vengo, vienes, viene,** venimos, venís, **vienen**
pres. subj.	**venga, vengas, venga, vengamos, vengáis, vengan**
pret. indic.	**vine, viniste, vino, vinimos, vinisteis, vinieron**
imp. subj.	**viniera, vinieras, viniera, viniéramos, vinierais, vinieran,** or **viniese, vinieses, viniese, viniésemos, vinieseis, viniesen**
fut. indic.	**vendré, vendrás, vendrá, vendremos, vendréis, vendrán**
cond.	**vendría, vendrías, vendría, vendríamos, vendríais, vendrían**
imper.	**ven** (tú), **venga** (usted), **vengamos** (nosotros), venid (vosotros), **vengan** (ustedes)
pres. part.	**viniendo**

62. **dar**

pres. indic.	**doy,** das, da, damos, dais, dan

pres. subj.	**dé,** des, **dé,** demos, deis, den
pret. indic.	**di, diste, dio, dimos, disteis, dieron**
imp. subj.	**diera, dieras, diera, diéramos, dierais, dieran,** or
	diese, dieses, diese, diésemos, dieseis, diesen
imper.	da (tú), **dé** (usted), demos (nosotros), dad (vosotros), den (ustedes)

63. **estar**

pres. indic.	**estoy, estás, está,** estamos, estáis, **están**
pres. subj.	**esté, estés, esté,** estemos, estéis, **estén**
pret. indic.	**estuve, estuviste, estuvo, estuvimos, estuvisteis, estuvieron**
imp. subj.	**estuviera, estuvieras, estuviera, estuviéramos, estuvierais, estuvieran,** or **estuviese, estuvieses, estuviese, estuviésemos, estuvieseis, estuviesen**
imper.	**está** (tú), **esté** (usted), estemos (nosotros), estad (vosotros), **estén** (ustedes)

64. **ir**

pres. indic.	**voy, vas, va, vamos, vais, van**
pres. subj.	**vaya, vayas, vaya, vayamos, vayáis, vayan**
imp. indic.	**iba, ibas, iba, íbamos, ibais, iban**
pret. indic.	**fui, fuiste, fue, fuimos, fuisteis, fueron**
imp. subj.	**fuera, fueras, fuera, fuéramos, fuerais, fueran,** or **fuese, fueses, fuese, fuésemos, fueseis, fuesen**
imper.	**ve** (tú), **vaya** (usted), **vayamos** (nosotros), id (vosotros), **vayan** (ustedes)
pres. part.	**yendo**

65. **ser**

pres. indic.	**soy, eres, es, somos, sois, son**
pres. subj.	**sea, seas, sea, seamos, seáis, sean**
imp. indic.	**era, eras, era, éramos, erais, eran**
pret. indic.	**fui, fuiste, fue, fuimos, fuisteis, fueron**
imp. subj.	**fuera, fueras, fuera, fuéramos, fuerais, fueran,** or **fuese, fueses, fuese, fuésemos, fueseis, fuesen**
imper.	**sé** (tú), **sea** (usted), **seamos** (nosotros), sed (vosotros), **sean** (ustedes)

66. **andar**

pret. indic.	**anduve, anduviste, anduvo, anduvimos, anduvisteis, anduvieron**

imp. subj.	**anduviera, anduvieras, anduviera, anduviéramos, anduvierais, anduvieran,** or **anduviese, anduvieses, anduviese, anduviésemos, anduvieseis, anduviesen**

67. **caber**

pres. indic.	**quepo,** cabes, cabe, cabemos, cabéis, caben
pres. subj.	**quepa, quepas, quepa, quepamos, quepáis, quepan**
pret. indic.	**cupe, cupiste, cupo, cupimos, cupisteis, cupieron**
imp. subj.	**cupiera, cupieras, cupiera, cupiéramos, cupierais, cupieran,** or **cupiese, cupieses, cupiese, cupiésemos, cupieseis, cupiesen**
fut. indic.	**cabré, cabrás, cabrá, cabremos, cabréis, cabrán**
cond.	**cabría, cabrías, cabría, cabríamos, cabríais, cabrían**
imper.	cabe (tú), **quepa** (usted), **quepamos** (nosotros), cabed (vosotros), **quepan** (ustedes)

68. **haber**

pres. indic.	**he, has, ha, hemos,** habéis, **han**
pres. subj.	**haya, hayas, haya, hayamos, hayáis, hayan**
pret. indic.	**hube, hubiste, hubo, hubimos, hubisteis, hubieron**
imp. subj.	**hubiera, hubieras, hubiera, hubiéramos, hubierais, hubieran,** or **hubiese, hubieses, hubiese, hubiésemos, hubieseis, hubiesen**
fut. indic.	**habré, habrás, habrá, habremos, habréis, habrán**
cond.	**habría, habrías, habría, habríamos, habríais, habrían**

69. **poder**

pres. indic.	**puedo, puedes, puede,** podemos, podéis, **pueden**
pres. subj.	**pueda, puedas, pueda,** podamos, podáis, **puedan**
pret. indic.	**pude, pudiste, pudo, pudimos, pudisteis, pudieron**
imp. subj.	**pudiera, pudieras, pudiera, pudiéramos, pudierais, pudieran,** or **pudiese, pudieses, pudiese, pudiésemos, pudieseis, pudiesen**
fut. indic.	**podré, podrás, podrá, podremos, podréis, podrán**
cond.	**podría, podrías, podría, podríamos, podríais, podrían**
pres. part.	**pudiendo**

70. **querer**

pres. indic.	**quiero, quieres, quiere,** queremos, queréis, **quieren**
pres. subj.	**quiera, quieras, quiera,** queramos, queráis, **quieran**
pret. indic.	**quise, quisiste, quiso, quisimos, quisisteis, quisieron**
imp. subj.	**quisiera, quisieras, quisiera, quisiéramos, quisierais, quisieran,** or **quisiese, quisieses, quisiese, quisiémos, quisieseis, quisiesen**
fut. indic.	**querré, querrás, querrá, querremos, querréis, querrán**
cond.	**querría, querrías, querría, querríamos, querríais, querrían**
imper.	**quiere** (tú), **quiera** (usted), queramos (nosotros), quered (vosotros), **quieran** (ustedes)

71. **saber**

pres. indic.	**sé,** sabes, sabe, sabemos, sabéis, saben
pres. subj.	**sepa, sepas, sepa, sepamos, sepáis, sepan**
pret. indic.	**supe, supiste, supo, supimos, supisteis, supieron**
imp. subj.	**supiera, supieras, supiera, supiéramos, supierais, supieran,** or **supiese, supieses, supiese, supiésemos, supieseis, supiesen**
fut. indic.	**sabré, sabrás, sabrá, sabremos, sabréis, sabrán**
cond.	**sabría, sabrías, sabría, sabríamos, sabríais, sabrían**
imper.	sabe (tú), **sepa** (usted), **sepamos** (nosotros), sabed (vosotros), **sepan** (ustedes)

72. **ver**[3]

pres. indic.	**veo,** ves, ve, vemos, veis, ven
pres. subj.	**vea, veas, vea, veamos, veáis, vean**
pret. indic.	**vi, viste, vio, vimos, visteis, vieron**
imp. indic.	**veía, veías, veía, veíamos, veíais, veían**
imp. subj.	**viera, vieras, viera, viéramos, vierais, vieran** or **viese, vieses, viese, viésemos, vieseis, viesen**
imper.	ve (tú), **vea** (usted), **veamos** (nosotros), ved (vosotros), **vean** (ustedes)
past part.	**visto**

---

3. The verb *prever* differs orthographically in the second- and third-person forms of the present indicative (*prevés, prevéis, prevé, prevén*), the first- and third-person singular forms of the preterit indicative (*preví, previó*), and the familiar imperative form (*prevé*).

73. Defective Verbs

The following verbs are used only in the forms that have an **i** in the ending: **abolir, agredir, aterirse, empedernirse, transgredir.**

The verb **atañer** is used only in the third person, most frequently in the present indicative: atañe, atañen.

The verb **concernir** is used only in the third person of the following tenses:

pres. indic.	**concierne, conciernen**
pres. subj.	**concierna, conciernan**
imp. indic.	concernía, concernían
imp. subj.	concerniera *or* concerniese, concernieran *or* concerniesen
fut. indic	concernirá, concernirán
cond.	concerniría, concernirían

The verb **roer** (also **corroer**) has three forms in the first person of the present indicative: **roo, royo, roigo,** all of which are infrequently used. In the present subjunctive the preferable form is **roa, roas, roa,** etc., although the forms **roya** and **roiga** are found.

The verb **soler** is used most frequently in the present and imperfect indicative. It is less frequently used in the present subjunctive.

pres. indic.	**suelo, sueles, suele,** solemos, soléis, **suelen**
pres. subj.	**suela, suelas, suela,** solamos, soláis, **suelan**
imp. indic.	solía, solías, solía, solíamos, solíais, solían

74. Additional Irregular Past Participles
absolver—**absuelto**
abrir—**abierto**
anteponer—**antepuesto**
circunscribir—**circunscrito**
componer—**compuesto**
contradecir—**contradicho**
cubrir—**cubierto**
decir—**dicho**
deponer—**depuesto**
descomponer—**descompuesto**
describir—**descrito**
descubrir—**descubierto**
desdecir—**desdicho**
desenvolver—**desenvuelto**
deshacer—**deshecho**
devolver—**devuelto**
disolver—**disuelto**

disponer—**dispuesto**
encubrir—**encubierto**
entreabrir—**entreabierto**
entrever—**entrevisto**
envolver—**envuelto**
escribir—**escrito**
exponer—**expuesto**
freír—**frito** (often regular, **freído**)
hacer—**hecho**
imponer—**impuesto**
imprimir—**impreso** (often regular, **imprimido**)
indisponer—**indispuesto**
inscribir—**inscrito**
interponer—**interpuesto**
morir—**muerto**
oponer—**opuesto**
poner—**puesto**
posponer—**pospuesto**
predecir—**predicho**
predisponer—**predispuesto**
prescribir—**prescrito**
presuponer—**presupuesto**
prever—**previsto**
proponer—**propuesto**
proscribir—**proscrito**
proveer—**provisto** (often regular, **proveído**)
pudrir—**podrido**
reabrir—**reabierto**
recubrir—**recubierto**
reescribir—**reescrito**
rehacer—**rehecho**
reponer—**repuesto**
resolver—**resuelto**
revolver—**revuelto**
romper—**roto**
satisfacer—**satisfecho**
sobreponer—**sobrepuesto**
suscribir—**suscrito**
superponer—**superpuesto**
suponer—**supuesto**
transcribir—**transcrito**
trasponer—**traspuesto**
ver—**visto**
volver—**vuelto**
yuxtaponer—**yuxtapuesto**

Aa

a PREP **voy — Londres** I'm going to London; **te lo doy — ti** I'm giving it to you; **se sentó — la sombra** she sat down in the shade; **tumbarse —l sol** to lie down in the sun; **una soga —l cuello** a rope around his neck; **lo miraba — la luz de una vela** she looked at him by the light of a candle; **— dos pesetas cada uno** at two pesetas each; **— las tres y media** at three-thirty; **sentarse — la mesa** to sit down at the table; **prestar dinero —l 15%** to lend money at 15%; **en grupos de — cinco** in groups of five; **cocina — gas** gas cooker; **fotos — todo color** full-color photos; **nadie le gana — testaruda** no one touches her for stubbornness; **terminaron — puñetazos** they ended up fighting; **¡— jugar!** let's play! **¿— qué vienen?** what are they coming for? **veo — mi mamá** I see my mother

AA [Alcohólicos Anónimos] F AA

abacá M manila

abad -esa M abbot; F abbess

abadejo M cod

abadía F abbey

abajo ADV (dirección) down; (posición relativa) below; **mirar para —** to look down; **el piso de —** the apartment below; **véase —** see below; **— de** under, underneath; **Stefan está — del coche** Stefan is under/ underneath the car; **¡— el rey!** down with the king! **— firmante** undersigned; **echar —** to knock down; **río —** downstream; **venirse —** to go to ruin

abalanzarse[47] VI **— sobre** to lunge at, to swoop down upon

abanderado -da MF standard-bearer

abandonado ADJ abandoned; **es una persona muy abandonada** she's very unkempt

abandonar VT (a una persona, a una familia) to leave, to desert; (el hogar, un partido) to abandon; (una competencia, el poder) to give up; (una competencia, a un enamorado, el hábito de fumar) to quit; (en los naipes) to fold; (un curso) to drop out of

abandono M (descuido) neglect; (acción de abandonar, condición de abandonado) abandonment; **— de funciones** dereliction of duties

abanicar[30] VT (contra el calor) to fan; (en béisbol) to swing and miss

abanico M (accesorio) fan; (rango) array; (en béisbol) swing and a miss; **abrirse en —** to fan out

abaratar VT (bajar el precio) to lower the price of; (desprestigiar) to cheapen

abarcar[30] VT (categorías) to embrace, to encompass; (tiempo) to span

abarrotería F *Méx* grocery store

abarrotero -ra MF *Méx* grocer

abarrotes M PL *Méx* groceries; **tienda de —** *Méx* grocery store

abastecedor -ora MF supplier

abastecer[35] VT (un ejército, una ciudad) to supply; (una tienda) to stock

abastecimiento M supply

abasto M supply; **mercado de —s** farmers' market; **yo sola no doy —** I can't cope alone

abatido ADJ dejected, despondent, downcast

abatimiento M dejection, despondency

abatir VT (bajar) to lower; (derribar) to knock down; (desanimar) to depress; (matar a tiros) to shoot; **—se** to swoop down

abdicar[30] VI/VT to abdicate

abdomen M abdomen

abdominal ADJ abdominal; M sit-up

abecedario M alphabet

abedul M birch

abeja F bee; **— asesina** killer bee

abejón M bumblebee

abejorro M bumblebee

aberración F aberration

abertura F (acción) opening; (cualidad) openness

abeto M fir

abierto ADJ (no cerrado, no determinado, destapado) open; (franco) frank; **— de par en par** wide open

abierto *ver* abrir

abigarrado ADJ motley

abigeato M cattle rustling

abismal ADJ abysmal

abismo M abyss, chasm; **— generacional** generation gap

ablandar VT to soften

abnegación F self-denial

abobado ADJ silly

abocar[30] VI to turn onto; **—se a** to devote oneself to

abochornar VT (avergonzar) to embarrass; **—se** to become embarrassed

abocinar VT to flare

abofetear VT to slap

abogacía F legal profession; **estudiar —** to study law

abogado -da MF lawyer, attorney; **— tributarista** tax attorney, tax lawyer

abogar[40] VI **— por** to advocate, to plead for

abolengo M ancestry

abolición F abolition

abolir[73] VT to abolish

abollado ADJ dented

abolladura F dent

abollar VT to dent; —**se** to become dented
abolsarse VI to sag
abombar VT to make bulge
abominable ADJ abominable, loathsome
abominación F abomination
abominar VI to detest
abonado -da MF subscriber
abonar VT (suscribir) to subscribe; (pagar) to make a payment; (poner fertilizante) to fertilize; —**se** to subscribe; — **a una cuenta** credit an account
abono M (a una revista) subscription; (para una temporada deportiva) season ticket; (de autobús) pass; (para la tierra) fertilizer; (de dinero) payment
abordar VT (un avión, un buque) to board; (un problema) to tackle, to approach; (a una persona) to accost
aborigen ADJ aboriginal; MF native inhabitant; — **australiano** Australian aborigine
aborrascarse[30] VI to become stormy
aborrecer[35] VT to abhor, to loathe
aborrecible ADJ hateful, abhorrent
aborrecimiento M abhorrence
abortador -ora MF abortionist
abortar VI (naturalmente) to miscarry, to have a miscarriage; VI/VT (intencionadamente) to abort
abortero -ra MF abortionist
aborto M (espontáneo) miscarriage; (provocado) abortion; — **espontáneo** spontaneous abortion
abotargarse[40] VI to bloat
abotonar VT to button; —**se** to button up
abovedar VT (una iglesia) to vault, to cover with a vault; (una calle) to arch, to cover as a vault
abozalar VT to muzzle
abracadabra M abracadabra
abrasador ADJ burning
abrasar VT to burn; —**se** to be consumed
abrasión F abrasion; — **cutánea** dermabrasion
abrasivo ADJ abrasive
abrazadera F clamp
abrazar[47] VT (rodear con los brazos) to hug, to embrace; (rodear una cosa sujetando) to clasp; (una opinión) to espouse
abrazo M hug, embrace
abrevadero M trough
abrevar VT (dar de beber) to water; (beber) to drink
abreviación F abbreviation
abreviar VT to abbreviate, to abridge
abreviatura F abbreviation
abridor M opener
abrigado ADJ (ropa) warm; (lugar) sheltered
abrigar[40] VT (refugiados) to shelter; (emociones) to harbor; —**se** to bundle up
abrigo M (refugio) shelter; (prenda de vestir) coat, wrap; — **impositivo** tax shelter

abril M April
abrillantar VT to make shiny
abrir[74] VI/VT (una puerta) to open; VT (un candado) to unlock; (un grifo) to turn on; — **el apetito** to whet one's appetite; — **la sesión** call a meeting to order; — **paso** to make way; M SG **abrebotellas** bottle opener; M SG **abrelatas** can opener; VI (el cielo) to clear up; —**se** to open up; —**se paso** to press through; **en un** — **y cerrar de ojos** in the twinkle of an eye
abrochar VT to fasten; —**se** to buckle [up]
abrogación F repeal
abrogar[40] VT to repeal
abrojo M bur, sticker
abrumador ADJ overwhelming, overpowering
abrumar VT to overwhelm, to weigh down; —**se** to become foggy
abrupto ADJ abrupt
absceso M abscess
absolución F acquittal
absolutamente ADV, INTERJ absolutely
absoluto ADJ absolute; **en** — absolutely not
absolver[6,74] VT to absolve, to acquit
absorbente ADJ absorbent
absorber VT to absorb
absorción F absorption
absorto ADJ absorbed, engrossed
abstemio -mia ADJ abstemious; MF teetotaler
abstención F abstention
abstenerse[58] VI to abstain; — **de** to abstain from, to refrain from, to forego
abstinencia F abstinence
abstracción F abstraction
abstracto ADJ abstract
abstraer[59] VT to abstract
abstraído ADJ lost in thought
absurdo ADJ absurd, preposterous; M absurdity
abuchear VI/VT to boo, to jeer
abucheo M boo, jeer
abuelo -la M grandfather; F grandmother; —**s** grandparents
abulia F apathy
abultado ADJ bulgy
abultar VI to bulge
abundancia F abundance, plenty
abundante ADJ abundant, plentiful
abundar VI to abound; — **en** to abound in
aburrido ADJ (sin entretenimiento) bored; (pesado) boring, tiresome
aburrimiento M boredom
aburrir VT to bore; —**se** to become bored
abusar VT — **de** to abuse; (sexualmente) to molest
abuso M abuse; — **conyugal** spousal abuse; — **de confianza** breach of trust; — **de drogas** drug abuse; — **de sustancias** substance abuse
abyecto ADJ abject

acá ADV (en este lugar) here; (hacia este lugar) over here, *lit* hither; **— y allá** here and there

acabado ADJ finished; M finish

acabar VT to finish; VI to end; (llegar al orgasmo) *vulg* to come; **— de comer** to have just eaten; **— por** to end up by; **— con** (la corrupción) to put an end to; (las cucarachas) to get rid of; **él y yo hemos acabado** he and I are through; **se acabaron los dulces** the candy is all gone; **se nos acabaron las ideas** we ran out of ideas; **y se acabó** and that's that

academia F (corporación, escuela militar) academy; (centro privado de enseñanza) private school

académico ADJ academic

acallar VT to silence, to quiet

acalorado ADJ heated

acaloramiento M **sufrió un —** he got too hot

acalorarse VI/VT (sofocarse) to overheat; (emocionarse) to get excited

acampada F camping trip

acampante MF camper

acampar VT to camp

acanalar VT to groove

acantilado ADJ sheer, steep; M bluff, cliff

acantonarse VT to be quartered

acaparar VT (productos) to hoard; (atención) to capture; (monopolizar) *fam* to hog; **— el mercado** to corner the market

acaramelar VT to candy

acariciar VT to caress; **— una esperanza** to harbor a hope

ácaro M mite

acarrear VT (transportar) to transport; (transportar en carro) to cart; (ocasionar) to bring about

acarreo M transport

acaso ADV perhaps; **por si —** just in case

acatamiento M compliance

acatar VT to abide by, to comply with

acatarrar VI to chill; **—se** to catch cold

acaudalado ADJ wealthy

acceder VI **— a** (un pedido) to accede to; VI (una invitación) to accept

accesibilidad F accessibility

accesible ADJ accessible, convenient

acceso M (entrada) access; (de ira) fit; **— a internet** Internet access; **— denegado** access denied; **— remoto** remote access, remote login; **de — prohibido** off limits

accesorio ADJ & M accessory

accidentado -da ADJ (viaje) eventful; (terreno) uneven; MF accident victim

accidental ADJ accidental

accidentarse VI to have an accident

accidente M (suceso imprevisto) accident; (del terreno) feature; (automovilístico) wreck; **— de tránsito** traffic accident; **por —** by accident

acción F (acto) action; (valor de bolsa) share of stock; **— de gracias** thanksgiving; **buenas acciones** good deeds; **acciones preferenciales** preferred stock; **acciones ordinarias** common stock

accionable ADJ actionable

accionar VT to operate

accionista MF shareholder, stockholder

acebo M holly

acechar VT (emboscar) to lie in ambush; (amenazar) to stalk

acecho M **rondar en —** to prowl; **estar al —** to lie in wait

aceitar VT to oil

aceite M oil; **— de linaza** linseed oil; **— de oliva** olive oil; **— de ricino** castor oil; **— vegetal** vegetable oil

aceitera F (recipiente) oilcan; (fábrica) oil factory

aceitoso ADJ oily

aceituna F olive

aceleración F acceleration

acelerador M accelerator

acelerar VT to accelerate, to speed up; VI to accelerate, to step on the gas; **— en vacío** to rev, to race; **—se** *Am* to get nervous

acémila F pack animal

acento M (pronunciación, signo) accent; (intensidad mayor, de voz) stress

acentuar[26] VT (aumentar) to accentuate; (poner tilde) to accent; (reforzar la voz) to stress; **—se** to accentuate

acepción F gloss, meaning

aceptable ADJ acceptable

aceptación F acceptance

aceptar VT to accept; **— entrega** to take delivery

acequia F irrigation ditch

acera F sidewalk

acerado ADJ made of steel

acerar VT to steel

acerca PREP **— de** about, concerning

acercamiento M approach

acercar[30] VT to bring near; **os acerco a la estación** I'll give you a ride to the station; **—se** to come near, to approach

acería F steel mill

acero M steel; **— inoxidable** stainless steel

acérrimo ADJ bitter

acertado ADJ right

acertar[1] VT to hit; VI to be right; **— con** to hit upon; **— a pasar** to happen to go by; **no —** to miss the mark

acertijo M riddle, conundrum

acervo M heritage

acetaminofén M acetaminophen

acetona F acetone

achacar[30] VI to blame

achacoso ADJ infirm, ailing

achaparrado ADJ (planta) stunted; (persona) squat

achaque M affliction, ailment; —s aches and pains

achicado ADJ weak-kneed

achicar[30] VT (de tamaño) to make small; (un vestido) to take in; (agua) to bail; —se (acobardarse) to feel intimidated; (empequeñecerse) to get smaller

achicoria F chicory

aciago ADJ unlucky

acicalado ADJ clean-cut

acicalarse VI to dress up

acicate M incentive

acidez F (de una solución) acidity; (del vinagre) sourness; — **de estómago** heartburn

ácido M acid; —**s grasos** fatty acids; ADJ (propio del ácido) acidic; (fruta) sour, tart

acierto M (contestación) right answer; (elección) felicitous choice

aclamación F acclamation, acclaim; **por** — by acclamation

aclamar VT to acclaim, to hail

aclaración F clarification

aclarar VT (con explicaciones) to clarify; (con agua) to rinse; (la voz) to clear; VI to dawn; **aclaró después de la tormenta** it cleared up after the storm; —**se** to lighten

aclimatar VT to acclimate

acné M acne

acobardar VT to intimidate

acogedor ADJ (persona) hospitable; (cuarto) cozy

acoger[45] VT (una sugerencia) to receive; (a un refugiado) to shelter; —**se** to take refuge; —**se a la ley** to have recourse to the law

acogida F reception

acogimiento M reception

acolchar VT to pad

acollarar VT to collar

acometer VT (atacar) to attack; (emprender) to undertake

acometida F attack

acomodado ADJ well-off

acomodador -ora MF usher

acomodar VT (arreglar) to arrange; (ajustar) to adjust; (adaptar) to adapt; —**se** (ponerse cómodo) to make oneself comfortable; (adaptarse) to adapt oneself

acomodo M position; **no tengo** — I can't find a comfortable position

acompañamiento M (acción, música) accompaniment; (grupo de personas que acompaña) retinue; (comida) side dish; (tenis) follow-through

acompañante ADJ accompanying; MF (compañero) companion; (en música) accompanist

acompañar VI/VT to accompany (también en música); (escoltar) to escort; (en una carta) to enclose; —**se de** to be accompanied by; **esperemos que el tiempo acompañe** let's hope the weather cooperates; **te acompaño en el sentimiento** my thoughts are with you

acompasado ADJ (rítmico) rhythmical; (mesurado) measured

acomplejado ADJ self-conscious

acondicionar VT to prepare

acongojado ADJ grief-stricken

acongojar VT to distress; —**se** to become distressed

aconsejable ADJ advisable

aconsejar VT to advise, to counsel

acontecer[35] VI to take place

acontecimiento M event; **todo un** — quite a happening; **a esta altura de los** —**s** at this point in the proceedings

acopiar VT to stockpile

acopio M (acción de guardar) storing; (cosas guardadas) stockpile

acoplamiento M coupling; — **universal de cardán** universal joint

acoplar VT to couple; —**se** (piezas complementarias, partes) to couple, to join; (altavoces) to have feedback

acople M coupling, connection

acorazado ADJ armored; M battleship, warship

acorazar[47] VT to armor

acordado VI agreed-upon

acordar[5] VT to agree; VI — **en** to arrange to; —**se [de]** to remember

acorde M chord; ADJ in agreement; **en** — **con** in agreement with

acordeón M accordion

acordonar VT (un zapato) to lace; (un lugar) to rope off, to seal off; (una moneda) to mill

acorralar VT (meter en un corral) to corral; (arrinconar) to corner

acortamiento M shortening

acortar VT to shorten

acosar VT (perseguir) to harry; (atacar) to beset; (atormentar) to badger; (importunar sexualmente) to harass

acoso M (de presa) hunting down, pursuit; (de una persona) harassment, hounding

acostar[5] VT to put to bed; —**se** to go to bed; —**se con** to sleep with

acostumbrado ADJ (normal) accustomed; (habitual) customary; **estar** — **a** to be used / accustomed to

acostumbrar VT to accustom; (soler) to be accustomed to; —**se [a]** to get accustomed [to]; **acostumbraban ir al teatro** they used to go to the theater

acotación F (anotación) marginal note; (en una obra de teatro) stage directions

acotar VT (un terreno) to mark off; (un texto) to

make marginal notes on

acre ADJ acrid, pungent, sharp; M acre

acrecentamiento M growth, increase

acrecentar[1] VT to grow; **—se** to grow

acreditar VT (una cuenta) to credit; (a un profesional) to accredit; **— a una cuenta** to credit an account; **a quien pueda — ser el dueño de** to whoever can prove to be the owner of

acreedor -ora ADJ deserving; **saldo —** positive balance; MF creditor

acribillar VI (a balazos) to riddle [with]; (a pedradas) to pelt

acrílico ADJ & M acrylic

acritud F acrimony

acrobacia F (arte) acrobatics; (pirueta) stunt

acróbata MF acrobat

acrobático ADJ acrobatic

acrofobia F acrophobia

acrónimo M acronym

acta F (de nacimiento) certificate; (de una reunión) minutes; (de un congreso) proceedings

actitud F attitude, mind-set

activar VT to activate

actividad F activity

activismo M activism

activista MF activist

activo ADJ active; **en —** working; M assets; **— líquido** liquid assets; **— convertible** convertible assets

acto M (solemne, sexual, dramático) act; (acción) action; **— seguido** immediately after; **— fallido** Freudian slip; **en el —** on the spot; **hacer — de presencia** to show up

actor M actor, performer; **— de carácter** character actor

actriz F actor, actress, performer

actuación F (acción) acting; (rendimiento, desempeño) performance

actual ADJ current, present

actualidad F present time; **—es** latest news; **de — ** up-to-date

actualización F (de información) update; (de ordenador) upgrade

actualizado ADJ (al día) up-to-date; (al minuto) up-to-the-minute

actualizar[47] VT to update; (programa de ordenador) to upgrade; (pantalla de ordenador) to refresh

actualmente ADV presently, currently

actuar[26] VI (comportarse) to act; (dar una representación) to perform

actuario -ria MF (judicial) clerk; (de seguros) actuary

acuarela F watercolor

acuario M aquarium

acuartelar VT to quarter

acuático ADJ aquatic

acuchillar VT (penetrar) to stab; (cortar) to slash

acuclillado ADJ squatting

acuclillarse VI to squat

acudir VI (ir) to go; (asistir) to attend; **— a** to turn to; **— al llamado** to respond to the call; **— al socorro de** to go to the rescue of; **— en masa** to flock

acueducto M aqueduct

acuerda, acuerde ver acordar

acuerdo M agreement; **— comercial** trade agreement; **— contractual** contractual agreement; **— global** package deal agreement; **estar de —** to be in agreement; **ponerse de —** to come to an agreement; **de — con** in accordance with

acumulación F (de dinero) accumulation; (de tensión) buildup

acumulador M storage battery

acumular VT (desperdicios) to accumulate; (fortuna) to amass; (deudas) to accumulate, to run up; **—se** to collect; **rabia acumulada** pent-up rage

acumulativo ADJ cumulative

acuñación F coinage, minting

acuñar VT (monedas, una expresión) to coin; (meter cuñas) to wedge

acuoso ADJ watery

acupuntor -ora MF acupuncturist

acupuntura F acupuncture

acurrucarse[30] VI to nestle, to huddle

acusación F accusation, charge

acusado -da MF accused; (en un juicio) defendant

acusador -ora MF accuser

acusar VT (culpabilizar) to accuse; (detectar) to detect; (revelar) to betray; (entre niños) to tattle, to tell; **— el golpe** to feel the blow; **— recibo** to acknowledge receipt

acuse M acknowledgment

acusetas MF SG tattletale

acusica MF tattletale

acústica F acoustics

acústico ADJ acoustic

adagio M adage

adaptabilidad F resilience, adaptability

adaptación F adaptation

adaptador M adapter

adaptar VT to adapt

adecuado ADJ appropriate

adecuar VT to adapt; **—se a** to be suitable for

adefesio M sight, hideous thing

adelantado ADJ (economía, alumno) advanced; (reloj) fast; (tren) ahead of time, ahead of schedule; **por —** in advance

adelantamiento M (de una fecha) bringing forward; (de un coche) overtaking

adelantar VT (una fecha, dinero) to advance; (la mano) to move forward; (un coche) to pass; (una noticia) to have a scoop; VI (un reloj) to gain; — **en** to make progress in; —**se** (sacar ventaja) to get ahead; (actuar antes) to go first; (innovar) to be ahead; (hablar antes de tiempo) to get ahead of oneself

adelante ADV forward; — **con los faroles** let's get started; — **de mí** in front of me; **de aquí en** — from now on; **hacia** — forward; **ir** — to go ahead; **más** — later; **sacar** — to make prosper; **seguir** — to go on; INTERJ go for it!

adelanto M (de la ciencia) advance, breakthrough; (de un coche) passing; (pago) advance; **el** — **de los relojes** setting the clocks forward

adelfa F oleander

adelgazar[47] VI to lose weight; VT to lose; (hacer perder peso) to make one lose weight; (hacer menos espeso) to thin; (hacer parecer delgado) to make one look thinner; — **cinco kilos** to lose five kilos; —**se** to get thinner

ademán M gesture; **hacer un** — **a alguien** to motion to someone

además ADV moreover, besides, in addition; — **de deberme dinero** besides / in addition to owing me money

adentrarse VI — **en** (un asunto) to go deeply into; (un lugar) to go deep into, to penetrate into; (una edad) to enter

adentro ADV inside; **ir para/hacia** — to go inside; **hablar para sus** —**s** to talk to oneself; **con lo de** — **para afuera** inside out

aderezar[47] VT (embellecer) to adorn; (condimentar) to season, to garnish

aderezo M (adorno) adornment; (de un alimento) seasoning; (de una ensalada) dressing

adeudar VT (deber) to owe; — **una cuenta** to debit an account

adeudo M (endeudamiento) indebtedness; (a una cuenta) debit

adherencia F adhesion

adherir[8] VI to adhere; —**se a** (una cosa) to stick to; (una huelga) to join; (una idea) to subscribe to

adhesión F (a una cosa) adhesion; (a una doctrina) adherence

adhesivo ADJ adhesive; M (pegamento) cement, adhesive; (calcomanía) sticker

adicción F addiction

adición F addition

adicional ADJ additional

adictivo ADJ addictive, habit-forming

adicto -ta ADJ addicted; MF addict; — **al trabajo** workaholic

adiestramiento M training

adiestrar VT to train

adinerado ADJ wealthy, well-to-do, moneyed

adiós INTERJ good-bye; **hacer** — **con la mano** to wave good-bye

adiposo ADJ fatty

aditivo M additive

adivinanza F riddle

adivinar VT to guess

adivino -na MF fortune-teller

adjetivo ADJ & M adjective

adjudicación F award

adjudicar[30] VT to award; —**se** to be awarded

adjuntar VT (incluir en una carta) to enclose; (añadir) to add, to attach, to append

adjunto ADJ (unido) attached; (incluido) enclosed; (asistente) adjunct; ADV herewith; M attachment

adminículo M gadget

administración F administration, management; — **pública** civil service; — **intermedia** middle management

administrador -ora MF administrator, manager; — **de cuentas** account manager; — **de un sitio web** webmaster

administrar VT (un medicamento) to administer; (una empresa) to administer, to manage; (justicia) to dispense; —**se** to budget

administrativo ADJ administrative

admirable ADJ admirable

admiración F admiration

admirador -ora MF admirer; (de una estrella de cine) fan

admirar VT to admire; —**se** to be amazed; —**se de** to wonder at

admisible ADJ admissible, allowable

admisión F (aceptación) admission; (reconocimiento) acknowledgment

admitir VT (dejar entrar, reconocer) to admit; (aceptar) to accept; (permitir) to allow

ADN [ácido desoxirribonucleico] M DNA

adobar VT (aderezar carne) to season; (curtir una piel) to tan; (encurtir) to pickle

adobe M adobe

adobo M sauce for seasoning

adoctrinar VT to indoctrinate

adolecer[35] VI — **de** to suffer from

adolescencia F adolescence

adolescente ADJ adolescent; MF adolescent, teenager

adonde ADV REL **esa es la casa** — **vamos** that's the house [that] we're going to, that's the house where we're going

adónde ADV INTERR & PRON where

adopción F adoption

adoptar VT to adopt

adoptivo ADJ adoptive

adoquín M cobblestone

adorable ADJ adorable

adoración F (a una persona) adoration; (a un dios) worship

adorador -ora MF worshiper

adorar VT (a una persona) to adore; (a un dios) to worship

adormecer[35] VT (dar sueño) to make drowsy;

(entumecer) to numb; **—se** (de sueño) to become drowsy; (de frío) to go numb

adormilado ADJ sleepy

adornar VT to adorn, to embellish

adorno M adornment, ornament, decoration

adquirir[4] VT (un bien) to acquire; (una característica) to take on

adquisición F (compra) acquisition; (nuevo miembro) addition; (compra de una compañía) takeover

adquisitivo ADJ purchasing

adrede ADV on purpose

adrenalina F adrenaline

aduana F (control) customs; (edificio) customshouse

aduanero -ra ADJ customs; **control —** customs control; MF customs officer

aducir[38] VT to adduce

adueñarse VI to take possession

adulación F flattery

adulador -ora ADJ flattering; MF flatterer

adular VI/VT to flatter

adulón -ona ADJ flattering; MF *fam* brown-noser

adulterar VT to adulterate

adulterio M adultery

adúltero -ra MF adulterer

adulto -ta ADJ & MF adult

adusto ADJ stern

advenedizo ADJ upstart

advenimiento M advent

adverbio M adverb

adversario -ria MF adversary, opponent

adversidad F adversity

adverso ADJ adverse

advertencia F (aviso) notice; (amonestación) warning, admonition

advertir[8] VT (avisar) to warn; (notar) to notice; (notificar) to advise, to tip off

Adviento M Advent

advierta, advierte *ver* advertir

adyacente ADJ adjacent

aéreo ADJ aerial; **correo —** airmail

aeróbico ADJ aerobic

aeróbic M aerobics

aerobio ADJ aerobic

aerodeslizador M hovercraft

aerodinámica F aerodynamics

aerodinámico ADJ aerodynamic, streamlined

aeródromo M airport

aeroespacial ADJ aerospace

aerolínea F airline

aeronáutica F aeronautics

aeronave F aircraft

aeropuerto M airport

aerosol M (suspensión) aerosol; (aparato) spray can

aerotransportado ADJ airborne

aerotransportar VT to airlift

afabilidad F affability, friendliness

afable ADJ affable, friendly

afamado ADJ famed

afán M eagerness

afanar VT *fam* to swipe; VI **—se** to work hard

afanoso ADJ hardworking

afasia F aphasia

afear VT to make ugly; **—se** to become ugly

afección F condition

afectación F affectation

afectado ADJ (dañado, lastimado) affected, stricken; (artificial) affected, unnatural

afectar VT to affect

afecto M affection, fondness; **— a** fond of

afectuoso ADJ affectionate, loving

afeitado -da ADJ clean-shaven; M shave

afeitadora F shaver

afeitar VT to shave

afelpado ADJ & M plush

afeminado ADJ effeminate, sissy

aferrado ADJ stubborn, obstinate

aferrar VT (agarrar) to grasp; (atar) to grapple; **—se** to cling

affaire M affair

Afganistán M Afghanistan

afgano -na ADJ & MF Afghan, Afghani

afianzado ADJ (garantizado) bonded; (apuntalado, amarrado) secured, firmed up

afianzar[47] VT (una pared) to secure; (un préstamo) to secure, to guarantee; (una amistad) to build up

afiche M poster

afición F (inclinación) inclination; (afecto) fondness; (hinchada) fans

aficionado -da ADJ **— a** fond of; MF (no profesional) amateur; (hincha) fan

aficionarse VI **— a** to become fond of

afilado ADJ sharp; M sharpening

afilador -ora MF grinder, sharpener

afilar VT to sharpen, to grind

afiliación F affiliation; **sin — política** nonpartisan

afiliarse VI **— con** to affiliate oneself with

afín ADJ kindred, related

afinación F tune-up

afinado ADJ in tune

afinador -ora MF tuner

afinar VT (una destreza) to perfect; (un plan) to fine-tune; (un piano) to tune; **—se** to become thinner

afinidad F (afecto) affinity; (parentesco) kinship

afirmación F (aseveración) assertion; (aseveración positiva) affirmation

afirmar VT (decir) to assert, to declare; (aseverar) to affirm; (sujetar) to secure; **—se** to steady oneself

afirmativa F affirmative answer

afirmativo ADJ affirmative

aflicción F affliction, woe

afligir[46] VT (dar dolor) to afflict; (entristecer) to distress

aflojar VT (una soga) to slacken, to loosen; (la vigilancia) to relax; — **el dinero** to hand over the money; VI to ease up, to slack off; —**se** to work loose, to loosen up

afluencia F influx

afluente M tributary

afluir[19] VI (río) to flow [into]; (turistas) to flock

afortunadamente ADV fortunately, luckily

afortunado ADJ fortunate, lucky

afrecho M bran

afrenta F affront

afrentar VT to offend

África F Africa

africano-na ADJ & MF African

afroamericano-na ADJ & MF African American

afrodisíaco M aphrodisiac

afrontar VT to face

afuera ADV (de un edificio) outdoors; (de un recipiente) outside; F PL **las —s** outskirts

agachar VT to lower; —**se** to crouch, to stoop

agalla F (de pez) gill; (de roble) gallnut; **tener —s** to have guts/spunk

agarrado ADJ tight-fisted

agarrar VT (sujetar) to seize, to grasp, to grab; (capturar) to catch; (adherirse) to grip; — **por sorpresa** to catch by surprise; —**le la onda a algo** to get the swing of something; —**se una neumonía** to catch a case of pneumonia; —**se** to hold on; —**se de** to latch onto; **agarré por la calle ocho** I took Eighth Street; **agarró y se fue** he up and went

agarre M (también golf) grip

agarrón M grab

agarrotarse VI (el cuerpo) to stiffen up; (un motor) to seize [up]

agasajar VT to entertain

agasajo M (acogida) welcome; (regalo) gift

agazaparse VI to crouch

agencia F agency, bureau; — **de empleo** employment agency; — **de publicidad** advertising agency; — **de viajes** travel agency; — **gubernamental** government agency

agenciar VT to wrangle

agenda F (cuaderno) daily planner; (orden del día) agenda

agente MF (representante) agent; (espía) operative; — **de policía** police officer; — **de compras** purchasing agent

ágil ADJ agile, nimble

agilidad F agility

agilizar VT to expedite

agitación F (acción de agitar, nerviosismo) agitation; (protesta) turmoil, unrest

agitado ADJ (estado) agitated; (vida) eventful, hectic; (mar) choppy; (sueño) uneasy

agitador-ora M (aparato) agitator; MF (rebelde) agitator, troublemaker

agitar VT (sacudir) to agitate, to shake up; (incitar a la protesta) to agitate; —**se** (ponerse nervioso) to get worked up; (moverse) to thrash around

aglomeración F crowd

aglomerado M particle board

aglomerarse VI to crowd together

agnóstico-ca ADJ & MF agnostic

agobiado ADJ (por los enemigos) embattled; (por el trabajo) overwhelmed

agobiante ADJ overwhelming

agobiar VT (con una carga excesiva) to weigh down; (con trabajo) to overwhelm; (con impuestos) to burden

agolparse VI to crowd together

agonía F throes of death; **ser un —s** to be a whiner

agonizante ADJ dying

agonizar[47] VI to be in the throes of death

agorafobia F agoraphobia

agorero-ra ADJ ominous; MF soothsayer

agosto M August; **hacer su —** to make hay while the sun shines

agotado ADJ (persona) worn-out, tired out; (libro) out-of-print; (mercancía) out-of-stock

agotador ADJ exhausting

agotamiento M (de una persona) exhaustion; (de un recurso) depletion

agotar VT (recurso) to exhaust, to use up, to deplete; (energía) to sap; (a una persona) to wear down; —**se** (acabarse) to be all gone; (venderse) to sell out; (secarse) to dry up; (libro) to go out of print

agraciado ADJ attractive

agraciar VT to grace

agradable ADJ (persona) agreeable, pleasant, congenial; (situación) pleasant, enjoyable

agradar VT to please

agradecer[35] VT (dar gracias) to thank; (sentir gratitud) to be grateful for; **se agradece** thank you

agradecido ADJ thankful, grateful

agradecimiento M thankfulness, appreciation; (en un libro) acknowledgment

agradezca, agradezco ver agradecer

agrado M pleasure; **de su —** to his liking

agrandamiento M enlargement

agrandar VT to enlarge

agrario ADJ agrarian

agravar VT to aggravate, to make worse; —**se** to get worse

agraviar VT to outrage

agravio M outrage

agredir[73] VT to assault

agregado-da MF (funcionario de embajada) attaché; (profesor) adjunct; M (mezcla) aggregate

agregar[40] VT to add

agresión F (violencia) aggression; (ataque) assault; — **con lesiones** assault and battery

agresividad F (actitud) aggressiveness; (propensión violenta) aggression

agresivo ADJ aggressive

agresor -ora MF aggressor, assailant

agreste ADJ (recio) rough; (silvestre) wild

agriar[28] VT to make sour; —**se** to go sour

agrícola ADJ agricultural

agricultor -ora MF agriculturist, farmer

agricultura F agriculture, farming

agridulce ADJ (sabor) sweet-and-sour; (memoria) bittersweet

agrietarse VI (cristales) to crack; (los labios) to chap

agrimensor -ora MF surveyor

agrimensura F surveying

agrio ADJ sour

agrisarse VI to gray

agropecuario ADJ agricultural

agrumarse VI to lump

agrupación F group

agrupamiento M grouping

agrupar VT (objetos, personas) to group; (documentos digitales) to queue

agua F water; — **con gas** sparkling water; — **corriente** running water; — **de colonia** cologne; — **de grifo** tap water; — **de manantial** spring water; — **dulce** fresh water; —**marina** aquamarine; — **mineral** mineral water; — **oxigenada** hydrogen peroxide; — **potable** drinking water; — **salada** salt water; —**s abajo** downstream; —**s arriba** upstream; —**s negras** sewer water; **hacer** — *fam* to take a leak; **se me hace** — **la boca** my mouth is watering

aguacate M avocado

aguacero M shower, cloudburst, downpour

aguada F watering hole

aguadero M watering hole

aguado ADJ (fruta) watery; (vino, sopa) watered-down

aguantar VT (miserias) to endure; (a una persona molesta) to bear, to stand; (un peso) to bear; (la respiración) to hold; VI (mantenerse) to stand; (durar) to last; (esperar) to wait; (no pudrirse) to keep; **aguántate** grin and bear it

aguante M (para el trabajo) endurance, stamina; (para el vino) tolerance

aguar[25] VT (añadir agua, despojar de fuerza) to water down; (estropear) to spoil; — **una fiesta** to ruin a party; —**se** to become diluted; MF SG **aguafiestas** killjoy, wet blanket

aguardar VI to wait; VT to wait for, to await

aguardentoso ADJ hoarse

aguardiente M brandy

aguarrás M turpentine

agudeza F (visual) sharpness, keenness; (del ingenio) quickness; (para los negocios) acumen; (dicho agudo) witticism

agudo ADJ (dolor, enfermedad, ángulo) acute; (vista, mente) sharp, keen; (mentón) pointed; (voz) high-pitched; (chiste) witty

agüero M portent, omen; **de mal** — portentous

aguijada F goad

aguijar VT to goad

aguijón M (de planta) spur; (de insecto) sting, stinger

aguijonear VT (a un buey) to goad, to prod; (insecto) to sting

águila F eagle; **es un** — he is sharp

aguilucho M eaglet

aguinaldo M Christmas bonus

aguja F (de coser, tejer, tocadiscos, pino, velocímetro) needle; (de reloj) hand; (riel móvil) railroad switch; (chapitel) steeple, spire; — **de croché** crochet hook; — **de punto** knitting needle; — **de zurcir** darning needle; — **hipodérmica** hypodermic needle; **como una** — **en un pajar** like a needle in a haystack

agujerear VT to pierce

agujero M (orificio) hole; (vacío legal) loophole; (déficit) shortfall; — **negro** black hole; **tapar** —**s** (reparar orificios) to plug holes; (pagar deudas) to pay debts

aguzar[47] VT to sharpen; — **el oído** to prick up one's ears

ahechaduras F PL chaff

ahí ADV there; **por** — over there, thereabouts; **de** — hence; — **te quiero ver** I want to see you in that situation

ahijado -da M godson; F goddaughter

ahínco M **trabajar con** — to work hard

ahogamiento M drowning

ahogar[40] VT (asfixiar en agua) to drown; (inundar con combustible) to flood; (asfixiar por falta de aire) to smother; (reprimir) to stifle; (asfixiar por presión al cuello) to throttle, to strangle, to choke; — **las penas bebiendo** to drown one's sorrows in drink; —**se** (en agua) to drown; (por falta de aire) to asphyxiate

ahogo M (por calor, falta de aire) suffocation; (por un esfuerzo) breathlessness; **vivir sin** —**s** to live a comfortable life

ahondar VT (hoyo) to deepen; (asunto) to dig deeper into; —**se** to become deeper

ahora ADV now; — **bien** now then; — **mismo** right now; — **sí** now we're cooking; **por** — for the present, for now; **hasta** — to date, up to now, so far

ahorcar[30] VT to hang; *fam* to string up

ahorita ADV (ahora mismo) right now; (dentro de poco) in a second

ahorrar VT (dinero) to save; (molestias) to spare
ahorrativo ADJ frugal, thrifty
ahorro M thriftiness; —**s** savings; —**s de toda la vida** life savings
ahuecar[30] VT to hollow out; — **la voz** to speak in a hollow voice
ahumado ADJ smoked; M smoking
ahumar VT to smoke
ahuyentar VT to drive away, to scare away; —**se** to get scared
airado ADJ irate
airarse VI to get angry
airbag M airbag
aire M air; (melodía) tune; (manera de ser) manner; — **acondicionado** air conditioning; — **libre** outdoors; **al** — **libre** outdoors; **andar con el culo al** — to walk around buck naked; **cambiar de** —**s** to change surroundings; **darse** —**s** to posture; **en el** — up in the air; **estar en el** — to be on the air; **tener** — **de** to look like; **tomar** — to breathe in, to get some air
airear VT to air out
airoso ADJ graceful; **salir** — to come out smelling like a rose
aislacionismo M isolationism
aislado ADJ (persona) isolated; (lugar) secluded
aislador M insulator; ADJ insulating
aislamiento M (acción de aislarse) isolation; (cosa que aísla) insulation; (soledad) seclusion
aislante M insulator
aislar[28] VT (separar) to isolate; (envolver) to insulate; (rechazar socialmente) to ostracize
ajar VT (una planta) to wither; (las manos) to make rough; (la piel) to age
ajedrez M chess
ajeno ADJ (de otro) belonging to someone else; (extraño) alien; — **a un peligro** oblivious to a danger; — **a mi voluntad** beyond my control; — **a mi experiencia** foreign to my experience
ajetrearse VI to bustle about
ajetreo M bustle, hustle and bustle
ají M chile
ajo M garlic
ajonjolí M sesame
ajuar M (de novia) trousseau; (mobiliario) furnishings
ajustado ADJ tight, snug; — **a la ley** in accordance with the law
ajustar VT (una prenda) to adjust; (un contrato) to tweak; (una tuerca) to tighten; — **cuentas** to settle accounts; VI to fit tight; —**se a derecho** to be in accordance with the law
ajuste M (de horarios, planes) adjustment; (del cinturón) tightening; (de una máquina) fine-tuning; (de cuentas) settlement; (de una prenda) alteration; **hacer** —**s** to tinker with
ala F (de ave) wing; (de sombrero) brim; (en

fútbol) winger; **cortarle las** —**s a alguien** to clip someone's wings
alabanza F praise
alabar VT to praise
alabeo M warp
alacena F pantry
alacrán M scorpion
alamar M (adorno) frog; (presilla) clasp
alambique M still
alambrada F wire fence
alambrado M (barrera) wire fence; (acción de alambrar) wiring
alambrar VT to wire
alambre M wire; — **de púas** barbed wire
alameda F poplar grove
álamo M poplar tree
alancear VT to wound with a lance, to spear
alano M mastiff
alarde M show; **hacer** — **de** to boast of, to show off
alardear VI — **de** to boast about
alargar[40] VT (hacer más largo) to lengthen; (un brazo, un guiso) to stretch [out]; — **la vista** to peer into the distance; —**se** to go on [longer than expected]
alargue M (fútbol) extra time
alarido M scream, howl
alarma F alarm; — **antirrobo** burglar alarm; — **contra incendios** fire alarm
alarmante ADJ alarming
alarmar VT to alarm
alba F dawn
albacea MF executor
albanés -esa ADJ & MF Albanian
Albania F Albania
albañal M sewer
albañil M mason, bricklayer
albañilería F masonry
albaricoque M apricot
albatros M albatross
alberca F (depósito) reservoir; (piscina) *Méx* swimming pool
albergar[40] VT (refugiar) to shelter; (hospedar) to lodge; (ser sede de) to house; (guardar rencor, un secreto) to harbor; —**se** (protegerse) to take shelter; (alojarse) to lodge
albergue M lodging; **dar** — (a un refugiado) to give refuge; (a un criminal) to harbor
albinismo M albinism
albino -na MF albino
albóndiga F meatball
albor M dawn
alborada F dawn
albornoz M bathrobe
alborotador -ora ADJ rowdy; MF troublemaker
alborotar VT (el pelo) to muss; (la casa) to mess up; (una turba) to rouse; (a los niños) to excite; —**se** to get excited
alboroto M hubbub, fuss

alborozado ADJ joyful
alborozar[47] VT to gladden; **—se** to rejoice
alborozo M joy
albricias F PL & INTERJ congratulations
álbum M album
alcachofa F artichoke
alcahuete -ta MF (soplón) tattletale; (mediador, encubridor) procurer
alcaide M warden
alcalde -esa MF mayor
alcaldía F (edificio) city hall; (oficio) mayoralty
álcali M alkali
alcalino ADJ alkaline
alcance M (de una persona) reach; (de los deseos) attainment; (de un misil) range; (de una ley) scope; **de corto[s] —[s]** of meager intellect; **al —** at hand, within reach; **a su —** within his reach; **al — del oído** within hearing; **dar — a** to catch up with; **de gran —** far-reaching; **de largo —** long-range
alcancía F piggybank
alcanfor M camphor
alcantarilla F (para agua sucia) sewer; (para lluvias) gully, gutter
alcantarillado M sewage system
alcanzar[47] VT (llegar, cumplir) to reach; (igualar) to catch up with; (pasar, poner en la mano) to pass; (herir a balazos) to get; **no alcanzo a verlo** I can't quite see it; **no me alcanza el dinero** I don't have enough money; **alcancé a conocer a mi abuela** I was born soon enough to meet my grandmother
alcaparra F caper
alcaucil M artichoke
alcázar M fortress
alce M (europeo, asiático) elk; (norteamericano) moose
alcoba F bedroom
alcohol M alcohol; **— etílico** ethyl alcohol; **— para fricciones** rubbing alcohol
alcohólico -ca ADJ & MF alcoholic
alcoholismo M alcoholism
alcornoque M (árbol) cork tree; (persona) blockhead
alcuza F oilcan
aldaba F (para llamar) knocker; (para cerrar) bolt
aldabón M large knocker
aldea F village, hamlet
aldeano -na MF villager; ADJ **joven aldeana** village girl
aleación F alloy
alear VT (metales) to alloy; VI (aves) to flap wings
aleatorio ADJ random
aleatorizar VT to randomize
aleccionar VT to teach a lesson
aledaños M PL vicinity
alegar[40] VT (aducir) to adduce; (pretender) to claim

alegato M (a favor de) plea; (en contra de) allegation
alegoría F allegory
alegrar VT (a una persona) to gladden; (una fiesta) to brighten up; **—se** to be glad; (por efecto del alcohol) to get tipsy
alegre ADJ (contento) joyful, cheerful, lighthearted; (ebrio) tipsy, lit
alegría F joy, merriment, cheer
alejamiento M (distanciamiento) withdrawal; (separacion de un cargo) dismissal
alejar VT (distanciar) to move away; (ahuyentar) to scare off; **—se** (físicamente) to move away; (emocionalmente) to withdraw
alelar VT to stupefy
alemán -ana ADJ & MF German; M (lengua) German
Alemania F Germany
alentador ADJ encouraging
alentar[1] VT (animar) to encourage, to cheer up; VI to breathe
alergeno/alérgeno M allergen
alergia F allergy
alérgico ADJ allergic
alergólogo -ga MF allergist
alero -ra MF (baloncesto) forward; M eaves
alerón M (de avión) aileron, flap; (de coche) spoiler
alerta ADJ & F alert
alertar VT to alert
aleta F (de pez) fin; (de ballena) fluke; (de buceador, delfín) flipper
aletargado ADJ sluggish, lethargic
aletargarse[40] VI to fall into lethargy, to become lethargic
aletazo M flap of a wing
aletear VI to flap, to flutter
aleteo M flapping, flutter
alevín M small fry
alevosía F treachery
alevoso ADJ treacherous
alfabetismo M literacy; **— digital** computer literacy
alfabetización F literacy; **— digital** computer literacy
alfabetizar[47] VI (enseñar) to teach to read and write; VT (ordenar) alphabetize
alfabeto M alphabet
alfalfa F alfalfa
alfanumérico ADJ alphanumeric
alfarería F pottery
alfarero -ra MF potter
alféizar M windowsill
alfeñique M (golosina) sugar paste; (persona) weakling
alférez MF second lieutenant; **— de fragata** ensign
alfil M bishop

alfiler M pin; — **de corbata** tie tack; **no cabe un** — it's totally full

alfiletero M pincushion

alfombra F (de pared a pared) carpet; (suelta) rug

alfombrar VT to carpet

alfombrilla F (en el suelo) mat; (para ordenador) mouse pad

alforja F saddlebag

alga F seaweed; —**s** algae

algarabía F uproar

algarrobo M locust tree

algazara F merriment

álgebra F algebra

algo PRON something; — **es** — something is better than nothing; **por** — **será** there must be reason; ADV somewhat, slightly

algodón M cotton; — **de azúcar** cotton candy; **se crió entre algodones** he had a protected childhood

algoritmo M algorithm

alguacil M (de policía) sheriff, marshal; (en un tribunal) bailiff

alguien PRON INDEF somebody, someone; **vino** — **a hablarte** someone came to talk to you; (en preguntas) anybody, anyone; **¿— lo vio?** did anyone see him?

alguno ADJ some; —**s** some, a few; **sin ruido** — without a sound; **en alguna parte** somewhere; **de alguna manera** somehow; **en algún momento** sometime; **¿lo has visto alguna vez?** have you ever seen him? **¿hay alguna forma de hacer esto?** is there any way to do this? PRON someone, something

alhaja F jewel (también persona); —**s** jewelry

alhajero M jewelry box

alharaca F fuss

alhelí M wallflower

aliado -da ADJ allied; MF ally

alianza F (con aliados, socios) alliance

aliar[28] VT to ally

alias M alias, assumed name; (uso policial) a k a

alicaído ADJ crestfallen

alicates M PL pliers

aliciente M inducement

aliento M (aire respirado) breath; (ánimo) encouragement; **cobrar** — to catch one's breath; **contener el** — to hold one's breath; **sin** — out of breath, breathless

aligerar VT to lighten; — **el paso** to quicken one's pace

alijo M cache, stash

alimentación F (comida) nourishment, food; (acción de dar de comer) feeding; — **intravenosa** intravenous feeding

alimentador M feeder; — **de hojas** paper feeder; — **de impresora** printer feeder

alimentar VT (a una persona) to feed, to

nourish; (un fuego) to stoke

alimentario ADJ alimentary; **canal** — alimentary canal

alimenticio ADJ (nutritivo) nutritious, nourishing; (relativo a los alimentos) alimentary; **industria alimenticia** food industry; **pensión alimenticia** alimony

alimento M food, nourishment

alineación F (deportes) lineup; (coche) alignment; — **a la derecha** right justification; — **a la izquierda** left justification

alinear VT (objetos) to line up; (a un deportista) to put in the lineup; —**se con** to align oneself with

aliño M condiment, seasoning

alisar VT (tela) to smooth; (pelo) to straighten

alistamiento M enlistment

alistar VT to enlist

aliviar VT (aligerar) to lighten; (mitigar) to alleviate, to relieve; (tranquilizar) to relieve; —**se** (mejorarse) to get better; (hacer sus necesidades) to relieve oneself

alivio M relief (también golf); — **de la deuda** debt relief

aljaba F quiver

aljibe M cistern

allá ADV there, over there; **más** — farther, beyond; **el más** — the hereafter; — **tú** that's your problem

allanamiento M raid; — **de morada** forcible entry

allanar VT (la tierra) to level, to smooth; (una dificultad) to iron out; (una casa) to raid; — **el camino** to smooth the way

allegado -da ADJ close to; MF relative

allegar[40] VT to gather; —**se** to arrive

allí ADV (espacial) there; (temporal) then; **por** — through there

alma F soul; **con toda el** — from the bottom of one's heart; **hasta el** — to the bone; **ni un** — not a soul; **no me cabía el** — **en el cuerpo** I was overjoyed; **se me fue el** — **al piso** my heart sank

almacén M (depósito) warehouse, storehouse, depot; (negocio) department store; **grandes almacenes** department store

almacenaje M storage

almacenamiento M storage; — **de datos** data storage; — **masivo** mass storage, bulk storage

almacenar VT to store, to stock up on; — **como** to save as

almacenista MF wholesaler

almáciga F nursery

almádena F sledgehammer

almanaque M (anuario) almanac; (calendario) calendar

almeja F clam

almendra F almond
almendro M almond tree
almiar M haystack
almíbar M syrup
almidón M starch
almidonado ADJ (persona) stiff; (camisa) starched
almidonar VT to starch
almirante M admiral
almohada F pillow; **consultarlo con la —** to sleep on it
almohadilla F (para sellos) cushion; (en las patas de los perros) pad; **— eléctrica** heating pad
almohadón M cushion
almohaza F currycomb
almohazar[47] VT to groom
almorranas F PL piles, hemorrhoids
almorzar[49] VT to lunch, to eat lunch
almuerzo M lunch
alocado ADJ wild
áloe M aloe vera
alojamiento M (residencia) lodging, accommodations; (militar) quarters; **— web** web hosting
alojar VT (a un invitado) to lodge, to accommodate; (a unos huérfanos) to house; (a las tropas) to quarter; **—se** (una bala) to lodge; (una persona) to board, to room
alondra F lark
alpaca F alpaca
alpinismo M mountain climbing
alpinista MF mountain climber, mountaineer
alpino ADJ alpine
alpiste M birdseed
alquería F farmhouse
alquilar VT to rent; **se alquila** for rent
alquiler M (pago mensual) rent; (acción de alquilar) renting; **coche de —** rental car; **dar en —** to hire out
alquitrán M tar
alquitranar VT to tar
alrededor ADV around; **— de la casa** around the house; M **—es** (de un área) surroundings; (de una ciudad) outskirts
alta F discharge; **dar de —** to discharge
altamente ADV highly
altanería F haughtiness
altanero ADJ haughty
altar M altar
alteración F alteration; **alteraciones al orden público** public disturbances
alterar VT to alter; **— el ánimo** to upset; **—se** to get upset
altercado M altercation
altercar[30] VT **— con** to quarrel with
alternador M alternator
alternancia F alternation
alternar VT to alternate; **— con** to rub elbows with
alternativa F alternative
alternativo ADJ (cambiante) alternating; (optativo) alternative
alterno ADJ alternate; **alterna y continua** AC/DC
alteza F highness
altibajos M PL ups and downs
altillo M attic
altímetro M altimeter
altiplano M high plateau
altisonante ADJ high-sounding
altitud F altitude
altivez F haughtiness
altivo ADJ haughty
alto ADJ (que está arriba) high; (que tiene altura vertical) tall; **altas finanzas** high finance; **— contraste** high contrast; **de alta calidad** high-quality; **de alta fidelidad** high-fidelity; **de — nivel** high-level; **de alta potencia** high-powered; **de — riesgo** high-risk; **de alta velocidad** high-speed; **en voz alta** aloud; **en — grado** to a great extent; **en alta mar** on the high seas; M **altavoz** loudspeaker; M **altoparlante** loudspeaker; M (altura) height; (piso) upper story; **— el fuego** cease-fire; ADV loud; **hablar —** to talk loud; **cotizarse —** to be set high; INTERJ halt!
altruismo M altruism
altura F (de persona, edificio, ola, epidemia) height; (de avión) altitude; (sobre el nivel del mar, lugar alto) elevation; **a estas —s** at this stage; **a la — de la calle ocho** at Eighth Street; **a la — de las circunstancias** equal to the circumstances
alubia F bean
alucinación F hallucination
alucinar VT (causar alucinaciones) to hallucinate; (fascinar) to fascinate; (deslumbrar) to bowl over; VI (sufrir alucinaciones) to hallucinate
alucinógeno M hallucinogen
alud M avalanche
aludir VI **— a** to allude to, to refer to
alumbrado M lighting; **— público** street lighting; ADJ lit
alumbramiento M childbirth
alumbrar VT encender, to light up; (dar a luz) to give birth to
aluminio M aluminum
alumnado M student body
alumno -na MF (de enseñanza primaria) pupil; (de enseñanza secundaria) student
alusión F allusion
aluvión M (de preguntas, pedidos) barrage; (de personas) flood
alza F appreciation; **— de precios** boost in prices

alzado ADJ elevated; MF insurgent
alzamiento M (acción de alzar) raising; (insurrección) uprising
alzaprima F crowbar
alzar[47] VT (la mano, la voz, una casa) to raise; (a un niño) to lift up; — **la vista** to look up; —**se** to rise up in rebellion; —**se con** to make off with
amabilidad F kindness; ¿**tendría la** — **de ...?** would you mind ...?
amable ADJ kind, nice
amado -da MF beloved
amaestrador -ora MF trainer
amaestramiento M training
amaestrar VT to train
amagar[40] VI/VT threaten; **amagó que iba a llover** it looked like it was going to rain; **amagó con golpearla** he made as if he was going to hit her
amago M **hacer** — to make as if
amague M (baloncesto) fake, juke
amalgamar VT to amalgamate
amamantar VT to nurse, to breast-feed
amanecer[35] VI to dawn; — **enfermo** to wake up ill; **amanecí en Londres** I woke up in London; M dawn, sunrise, daybreak
amanerado ADJ effete
amansar VT to tame
amante MF lover; — **de** fond of
amañar VT (una elección) to rig; (un documento) to tamper with
amapola F poppy
amar VT to love
amargar[40] VT to embitter
amargo ADJ bitter
amargor M bitterness
amargura F bitterness
amarillear VI/VT to yellow, to turn yellow
amarillento ADJ yellowish
amarillo -lla ADJ yellow; MF (esquirol) scab
amarra F cable, rope; —**s** moorings; **soltar** —**s** to cast off
amarrar VT (un barco) to moor; (una cosa) to secure, to tie down
amartillar VT (pegar con martillo) to hammer; (un arma) to cock
amasar VT (masa) to knead; (una fortuna) to amass
amateur ADJ INV & MF amateur
amatista F amethyst
Amazonas M Amazon River
Amazonia M Amazon Forest
ambages M PL **hablar sin** — to not mince words, to speak plainly
ámbar M amber
ambición F ambition
ambicionar VT to have the ambition to
ambicioso ADJ (emprendedor) ambitious; (codicioso) overambitious

ambidiestro ADJ ambidextrous
ambiental ADJ (limpieza) environmental; (temperatura) ambient
ambiente ADJ ambient; M (condiciones biológicas) environment; (atmósfera) atmosphere, ambience, ambiance; (sector social) milieu
ambigüedad F ambiguity
ambiguo ADJ ambiguous
ámbito M (ambiente) scene; (alcance) scope; (esfera) sphere
ambivalente ADJ ambivalent
ambos ADJ & PRON both
ambulancia F ambulance
ambulante ADJ itinerant
ambulatorio ADJ ambulatory
ameba F amoeba
amedrentar VT to scare
amén INTERJ amen; **decir** — to approve without discussion; — **de** besides
amenaza F threat, menace
amenazador ADJ threatening
amenazante ADJ threatening
amenazar[47] VT to threaten; — **con** to threaten to
amenidad F (cualidad de ameno) pleasantness
amenizar[47] VI to make entertaining
ameno ADJ enjoyable, entertaining
América F America
americano -na ADJ & MF American; F sport coat
ametrallador -ora MF gunner; F machine gun
ametrallar VT to strafe, to machine-gun
amianto M asbestos
amigable ADJ friendly
amígdala F (faríngea) tonsil; (cerebral) amygdala
amigdalitis F tonsillitis
amigo -ga ADJ friendly; — **de** fond of; — **de lo ajeno** thieving; MF friend
amiguismo M cronyism
aminoácido M amino acid
aminorar VT to lessen
amistad F (relación) friendship; (amigo) friend; **trabar** — to strike up a friendship
amistoso ADJ friendly, amicable
amnesia F amnesia
amniocentesis F amniocentesis
amnistía F amnesty
amo -ma M (de esclavo, sirviente) master; (de animal) owner; F (de esclavo, de sirviente) mistress; (de animal) owner; **ama de leche** wet nurse; **ama de llaves** housekeeper; **ama de casa** homemaker
amodorrado ADJ drowsy
amodorrar VI to make drowsy; —**se** to become drowsy
amolar[5] VT to annoy
amoldar VT to mold
amonestación F admonition, warning

amonestar VT to admonish, to warn
amoníaco M ammonia
amontonamiento M pile
amontonar VT to pile up
amor M love; — **propio** self-esteem; **de mil** —**es** gladly; **hacerle el** — **a** to make love to; **por el** — **de Dios** for God's sake; **por** — **al arte** unremunerated
amoral ADJ amoral
amoratado ADJ (de golpes) black-and-blue; (de frío, por falta de oxígeno) blue
amordazar^{47} VT (a una persona) to gag; (a un perro, a los críticos) to muzzle
amorfo ADJ amorphous
amorío M love affair
amoroso ADJ loving, amorous
amortajar VT to shroud
amortiguador M shock absorber
amortiguar^{25} VT (un sonido) to muffle, to absorb; (un golpe) to cushion, to absorb; (un dolor) to deaden, to dull
amortización F (desvalorización periódica) depreciation; (recuperación de una inversión) recovery; (reembolso gradual) amortization, paying off
amortizar^{47} VT (recuperar a plazos) to amortize; (depreciar) to depreciate
amoscarse^{30} VI to get peeved
amostazarse^{47} VI to get peeved
amotinarse VI (en un barco) to mutiny; (en una cárcel) to riot
amparar VT (proteger) to protect; (refugiar) to shelter; —**se** to protect oneself
amparo M (protección) protection; (refugio) shelter; **al** — **de** under the protection of
amperio M ampere
ampicilina F ampicillin
ampliación F (de una foto) enlargement; (de una casa) extension
ampliar^{28} VT (una foto) to enlarge; (una calle) to extend; (una explicación) to expand; (un volumen) to amplify; — **una imagen** to zoom in
amplificador M amplifier
amplificar^{30} VT (un sonido) to amplify; (una imagen) to magnify
amplio ADJ (información, tiempo) ample; (piso) spacious, roomy; (región, resonancia, sonrisa) broad; (vestido) full; **de amplias miras** open-minded
amplitud F (de comprensión) breadth; (de onda) amplitude
ampolla F (de la epidermis) blister; (vasija) vial
ampollar VT to blister
ampuloso ADJ bombastic
amputar VT to amputate
amueblar VT to furnish
amuleto M amulet, charm
anacronismo M anachronism

ánade M duck
anadear VI to waddle
anadeo M waddle
anaerobio ADJ anaerobic
anal ADJ anal
anales M PL annals
analfabetismo M illiteracy
analfabeto -ta ADJ & MF illiterate
analgésico ADJ & M analgesic
análisis M analysis; — **costo-beneficio** cost-benefit analysis; — **de mercado** market analysis; — **de orina** urinalysis
analista MF analyst
anotación F (béisbol) run; (básquetbol) point; (fútbol americano) touchdown; (glosa) note
analítico ADJ analytical, analytic
analizador M parser
analizar^{47} VT (datos) to analyze; (secuencia) to parse
analogía F analogy
analógico ADJ (relativo a la analogía) analogical; (no digital) analog
análogo ADJ analogous
ananá[s] M SG pineapple
anaquel M shelf
anaranjado ADJ & M (color) orange
anarquía F anarchy
anarquista MF anarchist
anatema M anathema
anatomía F anatomy
anatómico ADJ anatomical
anca F haunch, rump
ancho ADJ wide, broad; **a sus anchas** at his ease; **me viene** — it's too wide for me; M width, breadth; **a lo** — widthwise; **tiene un metro de** — it's one meter wide
anchoa F anchovy
anchura F width, breadth
ancianidad F old age
anciano -na ADJ elderly, aged; MF old person
ancla F anchor
anclar VI/VT to anchor
andada F **volver a las** —**s** to backslide
andador -ora MF walker
Andalucía F Andalusia
andaluz -za ADJ & MF Andalusian; M (dialecto) Andalusian
andamiaje M (para construcción) scaffolding; (fundamento) framework
andamio M scaffold
andanada F broadside; **una** — **de insultos** a barrage of insults
andante ADJ walking
andanzas F PL adventures
andar^{66} VI to walk; (coche, motor, reloj) to run; (el tiempo) to pass; (un aparato) to work; — **con cuidado** to be careful; — **en coche** to travel by car, to ride in a car; — **mal** to be in bad shape, to be a mess; — **mal del corazón**

to have heart trouble; **—se por las ramas / con vueltas** to beat around the bush; **no —se con rodeos** to make no bones about it; **en eso ando** that's what I'm up to; **¡andando!** move on! **¿dónde anda a estas horas?** where is he at this hour? **¡ándale!** *Méx* (apresúrate) come on! (de acuerdo) OK; M gait

andariego ADJ fond of walking

andas F **llevar en —** *RP* to carry on one's shoulders

andén M (de tren) platform; (para peatones) sidewalk

Andes M PL Andes

andino ADJ Andean

Andorra F Andorra

andorrano -na ADJ & MF Andorran

andrajo M rag, tatter

andrajoso ADJ ragged, tattered

andrógino ADJ androgynous

anduve, anduviera, anduviese *ver* andar

anécdota F anecdote

anegar[40] VT to flood

anejo ADJ attached; M accompanying volume

anemia F anemia; **— falciforme** sickle cell anemia; **— por deficiencia de hierro** iron deficiency anemia

anémico ADJ anemic

anestesia F (acción de anestesiar) anesthesia; (sustancia) anesthetic

anestesiar VT to anesthetize

anestésico ADJ & M anesthetic

anestesiología F anesthesiology

anestesiólogo -ga MF anesthesiologist

anestesista MF anesthesiologist

aneurisma M aneurysm

anexar VT (un territorio) to annex; (con una carta) to enclose

anexión F annexation

anexo ADJ attached; M (de un edificio) annex, extension; (a una ley) rider

anfeta F *fam* speed

anfetamina F amphetamine

anfibio ADJ & M amphibian

anfiteatro M amphitheater

anfitrión -ona M host (también informático); F hostess

ángel M angel; **— de la guarda** guardian angel

angelical ADJ angelic

angélico ADJ angelic

angina F **—s** tonsillitis; **— del pecho** angina pectoris; **— laríngea** laryngeal angina

angiocardiografía F angiocardiography

angiograma M angiogram

angioplastia F angioplasty

anglosajón -ona ADJ & MF Anglo-Saxon

Angola F Angola

angolano -na, angoleño -ña, angolés -esa ADJ & MF Angolan

angostar VT to narrow, to contract

angosto ADJ narrow

angostura F (cualidad de angosto) narrowness; (desfiladero) narrows

anguila F eel; **— eléctrica** electric eel

angular ADJ angular

ángulo M (figura geométrica, enfoque) angle; (rincón, esquina) corner; **— muerto** blind spot; **— recto** right angle

anguloso ADJ angular

angustia F (desasosiego) anguish, anxiety, distress; (congoja) heartache; (desazón existencial) angst

angustiado ADJ (desasosegado) anguished, anxious; (acongojado) distraught

angustiante ADJ nerve-wracking

angustiar VT to distress; **—se** to feel distressed

angustioso ADJ distressing

anhelante ADJ longing

anhelar VT to long for, to yearn for

anhelo M longing, yearning

anidar VI to nest

anillas F PL gymnastics rings

anillo M ring; **— de boda** wedding ring; **me queda como — al dedo** it fits me like a glove

ánima F soul of the departed

animación F (viveza) animation, liveliness; (en películas) animation

animado ADJ (vivo) animate; (bullicioso) lively

animador -ora MF (de un espectáculo) host; (de un equipo) cheerleader

animal ADJ & M animal

animar VT (dar vida) to animate, to enliven; (incitar) to encourage, to urge on; (dar aliento) to cheer up; **—se** (alegrarse) to cheer up; (atreverse) to gather courage

ánimo M (espíritu) spirit; (aliento) encouragement; (humor) mood; (intención) intention; **no estoy de — para eso** I'm not in the mood for that; INTERJ hang in there!

animosidad F animosity

animoso ADJ spirited

aniñado ADJ childlike

aniquilar VT to annihilate, to wipe out

anís M anise

aniversario M anniversary

ano M anus

anoche ADV last night

anochecer[35] VI to get dark; **anochecimos en París** night found us in Paris; M nightfall, dusk

anomalía F anomaly

anómalo ADJ anomalous

anonadado ADJ dumbfounded

anonadar VT (aniquilar) to annihilate; (vencer) overwhelm; (desconcertar) to dumbfound; **—se** to become dumbfounded

anónimo ADJ anonymous, nameless; M

anonymous letter
anorak M anorak
anorexia F anorexia
anoréxico ADJ anorexic
anormal ADJ abnormal; MF freak
anotación F (nota) annotation, notation; (en fútbol) goal
anotar VT (apuntar) to note; (marcar un tanto) to score; —**se** to sign up
anquilosarse VT (las articulaciones) to become stiff; (una institución) to become stagnant
ansia F (deseo) eagerness; (congoja) anguish
ansiar[28] VT to covet
ansiedad F anxiety
ansioso ADJ (ávido) anxious, eager; (inquieto) fretful
antagonismo M antagonism
antagonista MF antagonist
antagonizar[47] VT to antagonize
antaño ADV in the old days
antártico ADJ antarctic
Antártida F Antarctica
ante PREP before; — **este problema** in the face of this problem; — **todo** above all; M suede
anteanoche ADV night before last
anteayer ADV day before yesterday
antebrazo M forearm
antecedente ADJ & M antecedent; —**s** (profesionales) background; (criminales) record; —**s delictivos** criminal record
antecesor -ora MF (antepasado) ancestor; (predecesor) predecessor
antedatar VT to backdate
antedicho ADJ aforesaid
antelación LOC ADV **con** — beforehand
antemano LOC ADV **de** — beforehand
antena F (de radio) antenna, aerial; (de insecto) antenna, feeler
anteojera F blinder
anteojos M PL glasses, spectacles; — **de sol** sunglasses; — **bifocales** bifocals
antepasado -da MF ancestor, forebear
antepecho M sill
anteponer[56, 74] VT (poner delante, poner antes) to place before; (dar preferencia) to give priority to
anterior ADJ (en el tiempo) previous; (en el espacio) anterior, front; — **a** prior to
anterioridad F **con** — before
anteriormente ADV (antes) previously, formerly; (en la parte delantera) in front
antes ADV (previamente) before, formerly; (más temprano) sooner; **llegó** — he arrived sooner; — **de** before; — **la muerte** I'd rather die; — **bien** rather; — **de impuestos** pretax; — **del cierre** before closing; **lo** — **posible** ASAP, as soon as possible
antesala F (habitación) anteroom; (preludio) prelude; (béisbol) third base

antesalista MF third baseman
antiaborto ADJ INV antiabortion, right-to-life
antiácido ADJ & M antacid
antiaéreo ADJ antiaircraft
antialérgico ADJ antiallergic
antibacteriano ADJ antibacterial
antibalas ADJ INV bulletproof
antibalístico ADJ (misil) antiballistic; (chaqueta) bulletproof
antibiótico ADJ & M antibiotic; — **de amplio espectro** broad-spectrum antibiotic
antibloqueo ADJ INV antilock
anticipación LOC ADV **con** — in advance
anticipado LOC ADV **por** — in advance
anticipar VT (una fecha) to move up; (dinero) to advance; (el porvenir) to anticipate; —**se a los acontecimientos** to jump the gun
anticipo M advance, deposit
anticoagulante M anticoagulant
anticoncepción F contraception
anticonceptivo ADJ & M contraceptive
anticongelante M antifreeze
anticonvulsivo M anticonvulsant
anticuado ADJ antiquated, out-of-date
anticuerpo M antibody
antideportivo ADJ unsportsmanlike
antidepresivo ADJ & M antidepressant
antidiarreico M antidiarrheal
antidiurético M antidiuretic
antídoto M antidote
antieconómico ADJ wasteful
antiespasmódico M antispasmodic
antiestético ADJ unsightly
antígeno M antigen
antigualla F old piece of junk
antiguano -na ADJ & MF Antiguan
Antigua y Barbuda F Antigua and Barbuda
antigüedad F (cualidad de antiguo) antiquity; (objeto) antique; (tiempo en un cargo) seniority
antiguo ADJ (era, historia) ancient; (ropa) old; (mueble) antique; **a la antigua** in the old style; **la antigua capital** the former capital; **más** — with more seniority
antihigiénico ADJ unsanitary
antihistamínico M antihistamine
antiinflamatorio ADJ & M anti-inflammatory
Antillas F PL West Indies
antílope M antelope
antimonio M antimony
antimonopolio ADJ INV antitrust
antioxidante ADJ & M antioxidant
antiparras F PL goggles
antipatía F antipathy
antipático ADJ unfriendly, unkind
antipoliomielítico ADJ antipolio
antipsicótico M antipsychotic
antirreflejante ADJ anti-glare
antisemitismo M anti-Semitism

antiséptico ADJ & M antiseptic
antisocial ADJ antisocial
antítesis F antithesis
antitoxina F antitoxin
antitranspirante M antiperspirant
antitrust ADJ INV antitrust
antiviral M antiviral
antojadizo ADJ whimsical
antojarse VI **se le antojó comer salchicha** he took a notion to eat sausage; **esa tarea se me antoja difícil** that task seems hard to me
antojo M (deseo) whim, craving; (mancha de nacimiento) birthmark
antología F anthology, reader
antónimo M antonym
antorcha F torch
antracita F anthracite
ántrax M anthrax
antro M (bar) dive, joint; **— de perdición** den of iniquity
antropología F anthropology
antropólogo -ga MF anthropologist
anual ADJ annual, yearly
anualidad F annuity; **— variable** variable annuity
anuario ADJ annual; M yearbook
anudar VT to knot; **se le anudó la garganta** he got all choked up
anulación F (de un contrato) cancellation; (de un matrimonio) annulment
anular VT (un matrimonio) to annul; (un contrato, un evento) to cancel; (una sentencia) to overrule, to overturn; (un talón) to void; (un comando de computadora) to undo; **— una selección previa** to deselect; M ring finger
anunciador -ora MF announcer
anunciante MF advertiser
anunciar VT (información) to announce; (un producto) to advertise
anuncio M (de información) announcement; (de un producto) advertisement; **— clasificado** classified advertisement, want ad; **— publicitario** advertisement, ad; **poner un —** to place an ad
anzuelo M fishhook; **morder/picar el —** to take the bait
añadidura F addition; **por —** in addition
añadir VT to add
añejo ADJ aged, vintage
añicos M **hacerse —** to break into a thousand pieces
añil M indigo, bluing
año M year; (de la escuela) grade; (de vino) vintage; **— bisiesto** leap year; **— luz** light-year; **de cuarenta —s** aged forty; **del — hasta la fecha** year-to-date; **el — en curso** the current year; **el — pasado** last

year; **en los —s veinte** in the 1920s; **entrado en —s** getting on in years; **¿cuántos —s tienes?** how old are you?
añojo -ja MF yearling
añoranza F longing; (del hogar) homesickness
añorar VT to long for, to be homesick for
añoso ADJ old
añublo M blight
aorta F aorta
apabullar VT (impresionar) to bowl over; (derrotar) to crush
apacentar[1] VI to graze, to pasture
apacible ADJ good-natured, laid-back
apaciguar[25] VT (pacificar) to pacify; (aplacar) to mollify, to appease; **—se** to calm down
apadrinar VT to sponsor; (en un bautismo) to act as godfather to; (en una boda) to act as best man for; (en un duelo) to second
apagado ADJ (no llamativo) flat; (no intenso) dull
apagar[40] VT (un fuego) to put out, to extinguish; (una luz) to turn off, to turn out; (motor) to turn off, to kill; (una computadora) to power down; (una vida) to kill, to snuff out; (la sed) to quench; **—se** (luz) to go out; (un color) to fade; (una voz) to trail off; (un volcán) to become extinct
apagón M blackout, outage
apalabrarse VI **— con** to make a verbal agreement with
apalancamiento M leverage
apalear VT to thrash
aparador M sideboard, buffet, cupboard
aparato M (de gimnasia artística) apparatus; (para ejercicio) machine; (de cocina) appliance; (de teléfono) telephone; (máquina, dirigencia política) machine; (boato) pomp; **— circulatorio** circulatory system; **— de televisión** television set; **— ortodóntico** braces; **— ortopédico** leg brace
aparatoso ADJ pompous
aparcamiento M (lugar para aparcar) parking lot; (acción de aparcar) parking
aparcar[30] VI/VT to park; MF SG **aparcacoches** valet
aparcero -ra MF sharecropper
aparear VT (animales) to mate; (calcetines) to match, to pair; **—se** (animales) to mate; (en un baile) to pair off
aparecer[35] VI (ponerse a la vista, publicarse) to appear; (hacer acto de presencia) to show up; **se me apareció un ángel** an angel appeared to me
aparejar VT (un cuarto, un ejército) to prepare; (problemas) to entail; (una embarcación) to rig
aparejo M (de caballo) harness; (de buque) rigging; (para pescar) tackle; **—s** equipment
aparentar VT to feign; VI to show off; **aparenta**

la edad que tiene she looks her age
aparente ADJ apparent
aparezca, aparezco ver aparecer
aparición F (fantasma) apparition; (acción de aparecer) appearance
apariencia F (aspecto) appearance; (fingimiento) pretense, semblance; **las —s engañan** appearances are deceiving; **guardar las —s** to keep up appearances
apartado M section; **— postal** post office box; ADJ (recóndito) secluded; (distante) distant; **muy —** far apart
apartamento M apartment
apartamiento M separation
apartar VT (separar) sort out; **aparta las monedas de veinticinco centavos** set aside the quarters; (mover) to move away; **apartó la silla de la pared** he moved the chair away from the wall; (empujar) to push away/aside; **lo apartó de un empujón** she pushed him away; (aislar) to take aside; **lo aparté para hablarle** I took him aside to talk to him; (retirar) to take off; **apartó la cacerola del fuego** she took the pan off the fire; (alejar del cargo) to remove from office; **apartaron al ministro de su cargo** they removed the minister from his post; **apartó la vista** he looked away; VI **—se** to stray; **se apartaron del buen camino** they strayed from the straight and narrow; **los resultados se apartan de lo esperado** the results depart/deviate from the norm; **se apartó para que no lo atropellara el coche** he got out of the way so the car wouldn't hit him
aparte ADJ separate; ADV **bromas —** kidding aside; **dejar —** to exclude; **punto y —** new paragraph; M aside; PREP **— de** (además de) besides; (salvo) except for
apasionado ADJ (amor, hombre) passionate; (defensa, comentario) impassioned
apasionante ADJ exciting
apasionar VT **eso me apasiona** I love that; **—se por** to be passionate about
apatía F apathy
apático ADJ apathetic
apear VT to get down; **—se** to dismount
apechugar[40] VI **— con** to put up with
apedrear VT to stone
apegado ADJ attached
apegarse[40] VI to become attached
apego M attachment
apelación F appeal
apelar VI/VT to appeal
apellidarse VI to have the surname of
apellido M surname, last name
apelotonarse VI (una almohada) to ball up; (gente) to bunch together
apenado ADJ (dolorido) grieved; (avergonzado) embarrassed
apenar VT to grieve, to pain; **—se** to be grieved
apenas ADV hardly, scarcely, barely; **— llegó, se desmayó** no sooner had he arrived than he fainted; **— comienza la reunión** the meeting is just starting
apéndice M (órgano, parte de un libro) appendix; (añadido) appendage
apendicectomía F appendectomy
apendicitis F appendicitis
apercibir VT to warn; **—se de** to notice
aperitivo M appetizer
apero M farm implement
apertura F (transparencia) openness; (oportunidad) opening; **a la —** at the opening
apesadumbrado ADJ doleful
apestar VT (hacer heder) to stink up; (causar la peste) to plague; VI to stink, to reek
apestoso ADJ (hediondo) smelly; (apestado) pestilent
apetecer[35] VI **no me apetece ir contigo** I don't feel like going with you
apetecible ADJ appetizing
apetito M appetite
apetitoso ADJ appetizing
apiadarse VI **— de** to pity, to take pity on
ápice M apex; (de la lengua) tip; **no apartarse ni un —** not to diverge a jot
apio M celery
apisonadora F steamroller
apisonar VT to pack down
aplacamiento M appeasement
aplacar[30] VT (a una persona) to appease, to mollify; (miedo) to allay; (sed, pasión) to quench; **—se** to relent
aplanadora F steamroller
aplanamiento M flattening, leveling
aplanar VT (un terreno) to level, to flatten; (con una aplanadora) to roll
aplastado ADJ flattened
aplastamiento M crushing
aplastante ADJ (derrota) crushing; (victoria) sweeping
aplastar VT (achatar) to squash, to crush; (derrotar) to plaster, to stomp; (una revolución) to squelch, to smash, to crush; **—se** to crumple
aplaudir VI/VT to applaud
aplauso[s] M SG/PL applause
aplazamiento M postponement, deferral; (de un proceso legal) continuance
aplazar[47] VT to postpone, to put off
aplicable ADJ applicable
aplicación F (acción de aplicarse) application; (de un castigo) administration; (de computadora) application, app; **— de fondo** background application
aplicado ADJ (conocimiento, ciencia) applied; (trabajador) industrious

aplicador M applicator
aplicar[30] VT to apply; **—se** to work hard, to apply oneself
aplomado ADJ (equilibrado) poised; (vertical) plumb
aplomar VT to plumb
aplomo M poise
apnea M apnea; **— obstructiva del sueño** sleep apnea
apocado ADJ timid
apocalipsis MF (desastre) apocalypse; (Biblia) Revelation
apocamiento M timidity
apocarse[30] VI to become intimidated
apodar VT to nickname
apoderado -da MF proxy, agent
apoderarse VI **— de** to take possession of, to seize
apodo M nickname
apogeo M apogee; **en su —** (una fiesta) in full swing; (un estilo) in its heyday, at its peak
apolillado ADJ (comido por las polillas) moth-eaten; (anticuado) antiquated
apología F apology
apoplejía F apoplexy
aporrear VT to club, to cudgel
aportación F contribution
aportar VT (evidencia) to provide; (dinero) to contribute
aporte M contribution
aposento M chamber
apostador -ora MF bettor
apostar[5] VI/VT (a los caballos) to bet, to wager; (a un centinela) to station, to post; **— por** (caballo) to bet on; (cambio) to commit to
apóstol M apostle
apóstrofe MF apostrophe, invocation
apóstrofo M (ortografía) apostrophe
apostura F bearing
apoyar VT (sostener) to rest; (respaldar) to support, to back; (votar por) to second; (respaldar un argumento) to buttress; **—se en** (recostarse contra) to lean on, to prop against; (basarse en) to be based on; M SG **apoyabrazos** armrest
apoyo M support
apreciable ADJ (digno de aprecio) esteemed; (perceptible) noticeable; (registrable) appreciable
apreciablemente ADV significantly
apreciación F appreciation
apreciado ADJ (amigo) dear; (tesoro) valued, prized
apreciar VT (valorar) to appreciate; (percibir) to notice; (registrar) to measure; (considerar) to take into consideration; (sentir afecto) to cherish; **—se** (un fenómeno) to be noticeable; (moneda) to appreciate
aprecio M appreciation

aprehender VT (a un delincuente) to apprehend; (contrabando) to seize; (una idea) to grasp
aprehensión F (arresto) apprehension; (incautación) seizure
apremiante ADJ pressing
apremiar VT to pressure
apremio M pressure
aprender VI/VT to learn; **— de memoria** to memorize, to learn by heart
aprendiz -za MF (de un oficio) apprentice, trainee; (de una lengua, canto) learner
aprendizaje M (de un oficio) apprenticeship; (acto de aprender) learning
aprensión F apprehension, misgivings
aprensivo ADJ apprehensive
apresar VT (aprisionar) to imprison; (incautar) to seize
aprestar VT to prepare; **—se a** to get ready to
apresurado ADJ hasty, hurried
apresurar VT to hurry, to hasten
apretado ADJ (zapato) tight; (beso) hard; (racimo) compact; (síntesis) succinct; (jornada) busy; (situación) difficult, dangerous
apretar[1] VT (un botón) to press; (un gatillo) to squeeze; (un tornillo) to tighten; (los dientes, puños) to clench; (a un bebé) to clasp; **me apretó para que le diera dinero** he pressured me to give him money; **ese profesor nos aprieta mucho** that teacher demands a lot of us; VI (zapatos) to be tight, to pinch; (sol) to be intense; (esforzarse) to try hard, to bear down; **—se** to crowd together
apretón M squeeze; **— de manos** handshake
aprieta, apriete ver apretar
aprieto M jam, fix, predicament; **en —s** in need, hard-pressed, in dire straits; **estar en un —** to be in a tight spot, to be in trouble, to be in a pickle; **poner en —s** to embarrass
aprisa ADV quickly
aprisco M (para el ganado) fold
aprisionar VT to trap
aprobación F (aceptación) approval; (adopción, promulgación) passage, adoption; (calificación) passing grade; **— de crédito** credit approval
aprobar[5] VT (una medida, una opinión) to approve of; (una ley) to pass, to approve; (un examen) to pass; (un crédito) to sign off on; VI to pass
aprontar VT to ready
apropiación F appropriation; **— indebida** embezzlement
apropiadamente ADV properly, appropriately
apropiado ADJ appropriate, suitable
apropiarse VT **— de** to appropriate
aprovechable ADJ usable
aprovechado ADJ opportunistic

aprovechamiento M use

aprovechar VT (una ocasión) to take advantage of; (el espacio) to utilize; (la enseñanza) to profit from; VI to be useful; —**se de** to take advantage of; INTERJ ¡**que aproveche!** enjoy your meal!

aproximación F (acercamiento) approach; (estimado) rough estimate

aproximado ADJ approximate

aproximar VT to bring near; —**se** to approach; —**a** to approximate

aprueba, apruebe ver aprobar

aptitud F aptitude; —**es musicales** musical aptitude

apto ADJ apt, suitable; — **para menores** for general audiences

apuesta F bet, wager

apuesto ADJ good-looking

apuntalar VT to prop up, to shore up

apuntar VT (señalar) to point out; (dirigir sobre un blanco) to aim; (matricular) to enroll; (escribir) to write down, to note; (ayudar a un actor) to prompt; (marcar puntos) to score; VI (una flecha) to point; (canas) to sprout; — **a un blanco** to aim at a target; **me apunto para ir con vosotros** I'm game to go with you

apunte M notation; —**s** notes; **tomar**—**s** to take notes; **llevar el** — **a alguien** to pay attention to someone

apuñalar VT to stab

apurado ADJ (situación) difficult; (persona) in dire straits; (apresurado) in a hurry

apurar VT (consumir) to drink up; (apremiar) to put under pressure; —**se** Am to hurry

apuro M predicament, fix; (prisa) hurry; **estar en**—**s** to be in distress

aquejado ADJ stricken

aquejar VT to afflict, to trouble

aquel ADJ that; **aquella chica se llama María** that girl is named María; **aquellas ciudades son antiguas** those cities are old; PRON that one; — **es el mayor** that one is the oldest; **aquellos son mis hijos** those are my children; **de mis dos hijos, Juan y Pedro, este es gordo y** — **es flaco** of my two sons, Juan and Pedro, the latter is fat and the former is thin; **en/por** — **entonces** back then

aquí ADV here; **está por** — it is around here; **ven por** — come this way; **hasta** — this far; **de** — **a cuatro horas** four hours from now; **de** — **en adelante** from now on; **de** — **para allá** to and fro, back and forth; — **y ahora** here and now

aquietar VT to quiet; —**se** (los nervios) to calm down; (una tormenta) to subside

ara LOC ADV **en**—**s de** for the sake of

árabe MF (persona) Arab; M (caballo) Arabian; (lengua) Arabic; ADJ (caballo) Arabian; (costumbre, arte) Arab

Arabia Saudí, Arabia Saudita F Saudi Arabia

arácnido M arachnid

arado M plow

Aragón M Aragon

aragonés -esa ADJ Aragonese; MF (persona) Aragonese; M (dialecto) Aragonese

arancel M (impuesto) tariff; (lista de honorarios) list of fees

arancelario ADJ **acuerdo** — tariff agreement

arándano M blueberry; — **rojo** cranberry

arandela F washer

araña F (arácnido) spider; (candelabro) chandelier

arañar VT (rayar) to scratch; (herir con garras) to claw, to scratch; (raspar) to scrape, to score

arañazo M scratch

arañero M warbler

arar VI/VT to plow, to till

arbitraje M arbitration

arbitrar VT (un desacuerdo) to arbitrate; (un partido) to referee, to officiate; (un partido de béisbol) to umpire

arbitrariedad F (acción) arbitrary action; (cualidad) arbitrariness

arbitrario ADJ arbitrary

arbitrio M (libre albedrío) free will; (capricho) whim; (decisión) discretion; (deseos) wishes

árbitro -tra MF (del buen gusto) arbiter; (de conflictos) arbitrator; (de encuentros deportivos) referee

árbol M tree; (mástil) mast; — **de Navidad** Christmas tree; — **de levas** camshaft; — **genealógico** family tree

arbolado ADJ woody, wooded

arboleda F grove, clump

arbóreo ADJ arboreal

arbusto M shrub, bush

arca F ark; — **de Noé** Noah's ark; **las** —**s municipales** municipal coffers

arcada F arcade, archway; **tener/dar**—**s** to gag

arcaico ADJ archaic

arcaísmo M archaism

arcano ADJ arcane

arce M maple [tree]

arcén M shoulder of a road

archienemigo -ga MF archenemy

archipiélago M archipelago

archisabido ADJ very well-known

archivado ADJ on file

archivador M filing cabinet

archivar VT (guardar en un archivo) to file; (arrumbar) to shelve

archivo M (repositorio de documentos) archive; (fichero de ordenador) file; (acción de archivar) filing; — **comprimido** compressed file; — **cookie** cookie; — **corrupto** corrupted file; — **de datos** data

file; — **de lectura/escritura** read/write file
arcilla F clay
arco M (geométrico, eléctrico) arc; (estructura arquitectónica) arch; (arma, varilla de violín) bow; — **iris** rainbow
arder VT to burn; **la cosa está que arde** things are really getting hot; **el trigo se ardió** the wheat spoiled
ardid M scheme, artifice
ardiente ADJ (deseo) ardent; (calor, fuego, deseo) burning
ardilla F squirrel; — **de tierra** gopher; — **listada** chipmunk
ardite M **no valer un** — not to be worth a penny
ardor M (de pasión) ardor; (de fuego) heat; (por ácido) burning; — **de estómago** heartburn
arduo ADJ arduous, grueling
área F area; — **de penales** (fútbol) penalty area, box
arena F (tierra) sand; (plaza) arena; — **movediza** quicksand
arenero M sandbox
arenga F harangue
arengar[40] VT to harangue
arenisca F sandstone
arenisco ADJ sandy
arenoso ADJ sandy
arenque M herring
arete M earring
argamasa F mortar
Argelia F Algeria
argelino -na ADJ & MF Algerian
Argentina F Argentina
argentino -na ADJ Argentine, Argentinian; (como la plata) silvery; MF Argentine, Argentinian
argolla F iron ring
argón M argon
argot M slang
argucias F PL trickery
argüir[20] VT to argue
argumentar VT to argue
argumento M (razonamiento) argument; (conjunto de sucesos) plot
aridez F dryness
árido ADJ (seco) arid, dry, barren; (aburrido) dry; —**s** dry goods
ariete M (militar) battering ram; (fútbol) center forward
arisco ADJ surly
arista F (borde) edge; (de trigo) beard; **limar** —**s** to overcome difficulties
aristocracia F aristocracy
aristócrata MF aristocrat
aristocrático ADJ aristocratic
aritmética F arithmetic
aritmético ADJ arithmetical
arma F (instrumento bélico) arm, weapon; (división del ejército) branch; — **blanca** sharp weapon; — **de fuego** firearm; **a las** —**s** to arms; **de** —**s tomar** resolute; **tomar las** —**s** to take up arms
armada F armada, fleet
armado ADJ armed; **a mano armada** at gunpoint; M assembly, putting together
armador -ora MF (naviero) shipowner; (en fútbol) playmaker; (en vóleibol) setter
armadura F (cobertura de hierro) armor; (de un edificio) framework; (de gafas) frame; (de música) key signature
armamento M armament
armar VT (proveer de armas) to arm; (abastecer una embarcación) to equip; (reforzar) to reinforce; (ensamblar) to assemble, to put together; (levantar una tienda de campaña) to pitch; — **jaleo** to whoop it up; — **relajo** to make a mess; —**se de** to arm oneself with; — **una pendencia** to pick a fight, to start a quarrel
armario M (de ropa) wardrobe, closet; (de cocina) cabinet, armoire
armatoste M unwieldy object
armazón MF framework, skeleton
Armenia F Armenia
armenio -nia ADJ & MF Armenian
armería F (depósito) armory; (tienda) gun shop
armiño M ermine
armisticio M armistice
armonía F harmony
armónico ADJ & M harmonic
armonioso ADJ harmonious
armonizar[47] VI/VT to harmonize, to blend
ARN [ácido ribonucleico] M RNA
arnés M harness
aro M (de rueda) rim; (de baloncesto) hoop; **no tocó ni** — it was an airball
aroma M (olor agradable) aroma; (del vino) bouquet
aromático ADJ aromatic
arpa F harp
arpía F shrew
arpillera F burlap
arpón M harpoon
arponear VT to harpoon
arqueado ADJ arched
arquear VT to arch
arqueología F archaeology
arqueológico ADJ archaeological
arquero -ra MF (tirador de flechas) archer; (guardametas) goalkeeper
arquetipo M archetype
arquitecto -ta MF architect
arquitectónico ADJ architectural
arquitectura F architecture
arrabal M outlying slum
arraigar[40] VT to take root
arrancar[30] VT (una planta) to uproot; (el pelo) to

tear out; (un diente) to pull; (un vicio) to eradicate; (una flor) to pick; (una confesión) to extract; — **de** to wrest from; VI/VT (un vehículo) to start; **arrancó para el valle** he took off for the valley; **arrancó a sudar** he began to sweat; **sus problemas arrancan de su niñez** his problems are rooted in his childhood; **—se los cabellos** to tear one's hair [out]

arranque M (proceso de arrancar) starting; (dispositivo para arrancar) starter; (decisión, empuje) gumption; — **de ira** fit of rage

arrasar VT (destruir) to level, to raze; (derrotar) to crush; — **con** to obliterate; VI to win

arrastrado ADJ wretched

arrastrar VT (mover por el suelo) to drag; (llevarse consigo) to sweep away; (atraer) to draw; (soportar) to bear; (pronunciar lentamente) to draw out; — **los pies** (moverse con dificultades) to shuffle; (ser renuente) to stall; VI (cortinas) to hang down to the floor; **—se** (una serpiente) to slither; (una lagartija, un insecto) to crawl; (una persona) to grovel; — **y soltar** to drag and drop, to drag and release; M SG **arrastrapiés** shuffle

array M array

arrayán M myrtle

arrear VT to drive, to herd

arrebatar VT (quitar) to snatch away, to wrest away; (quemar) to burn on the outside; **—se** to have a fit

arrebatiña F mad scramble

arrebato M fit, outburst

arreciar VI to increase in intensity

arrecife M reef

arreglar VT (poner en orden, concertar, adaptar música) to arrange; (ordenar) to tidy up; (reparar) to fix, to repair; (resolver) to settle; — **cuentas** to settle accounts; **ya te arreglo** I'll fix you; **—se** (embellecerse) to fix oneself up; (llevarse bien con) to get along with; (entablar relaciones amorosas) to start dating; (reconciliarse) to make up; (conformarse) to make do; (despejarse) to clear up; **arreglárselas** to cope, to manage

arreglo M arrangement; **con — a** in accordance with; **no tiene —** it can't be helped; **llegar a un —** to settle; **—s** alterations

arrellanarse VI to lounge, to loll

arremangado ADJ turned up, rolled up

arremangar[40] VT to roll up; **—se** to roll up one's sleeves, to knuckle down

arremeter VI to attack; — **contra** to lunge at

arremetida F thrust, lunge

arremolinarse VT (viento) to whirl around; (agua) to eddy

arrendajo M bluejay

arrendamiento M rental

arrendar VI/VT to rent, to lease; **se arrienda** for lease

arrendatario -ria MF tenant

arreo M adornment; **—s** tack, harness

arrepentido ADJ repentant, rueful

arrepentimiento M (contrición) repentance; (disgusto) regret

arrepentirse[8] VI (de los pecados) to repent; (de los errores) to regret

arrestar VT to arrest

arresto M arrest

arriar[28] VT (la bandera) to lower; (un cabo) to slacken

arriate M flower bed

arriba ADV above; ¡—! get up! ¡— **las manos!** stick 'em up! ¡— **Juan!** long live Juan! **de — abajo** from top to bottom; **lleno hasta —** full to the brim; **te vas para —** you are doing well; **viven —** they live upstairs

arribar VI LIT to arrive; (buque) to put into port

arribista MF social climber

arribo M LIT arrival

arriendo M leasing, rental

arriero -ra MF animal driver

arriesgado ADJ (peligroso) risky; (valiente) daring

arriesgar[40] VT to risk; **—se** to take a chance

arrimar VT (acercar) to bring near; (golpear) to strike; **—se a** (apoyarse) to lean on; (acercarse) to get near

arrinconar VT (acorralar) to corner; (poner en un rincón) to put in a corner; (abandonar) to abandon

arritmia F arrhythmia

arrobamiento M rapture

arrobarse VI to be enraptured

arrodillarse VI to kneel

arrogancia F arrogance

arrogante ADJ arrogant

arrogarse[40] VT to claim

arrojadizo ADJ for throwing

arrojar VT (lanzar) to throw, to hurl; (expulsar) to throw out; (botar) to throw away; (vomitar) to throw up, to vomit; (proyectar una luz) to shed, to throw; — **un saldo de** to show a balance of; **—se** to hurl oneself

arrojo M boldness, daring

arrollador ADJ overwhelming

arrollar VT (enrollar) to roll up; (arrastrar) to run over; (derrotar) to defeat

arropar VT (con ropa) to wrap up; (en la cama) to tuck in; **—se** to pull up the covers

arroyo M stream, creek

arroz M rice; — **integral** brown rice

arrozal M rice field

arruga F wrinkle

arrugar[40] VT to wrinkle; — **el ceño** to knit one's brow; **—se** (pasar a tener arrugas) to get wrinkles; (asustarse) to be afraid

arruinar VT (estropear) to ruin; (destruir) to destroy, to ravage; (aguar) to spoil; (dejar en la quiebra) to bankrupt, to ruin; —**se** to go to ruin

arrullar VI (una paloma) to coo; VT (a un enamorado) to whisper sweet nothings to; (a un niño) to rock to sleep, to lull to sleep

arrullo M (de la tórtola) cooing; (del agua) babbling

arrumbar VT (arrinconar) to put aside; (marginalizar) to marginalize

arsenal M (depósito) arsenal; (astillero) navy yard

arsénico M arsenic

arte M SG art; F PL arts; M (destreza) skill, ability; (actividad manual) craft; **bellas —s** fine arts; **el — por el —** art for art's sake; **malas —s** wiles; **no tener ni — ni parte en algo** to have nothing to do with something; **por — de** by means of; **por — de magia** by magic

artefacto M (aparato) contrivance, device; (bomba) bomb

arteria F artery

arterial ADJ arterial

arteriosclerosis F arteriosclerosis

artero ADJ artful, wily

artesanía F (trabajo, obra) craft; (habilidad) craftsmanship

artesano -na MF artisan; M craftsman; F craftswoman

ártico ADJ arctic

articulación F (acción de articular) articulation; (juntura) joint

articular VT (pronunciar) to articulate, to enunciate; (unir) to join

artículo M (de revista) article; (de diccionario) article, entry; **— de fondo** editorial; **— definido** definite article; **hacer el —** to give a sales pitch

artífice MF (autor) architect; M (artesano) craftsman; F craftswoman

artificial ADJ artificial

artificio M artifice

artificioso ADJ affected, contrived

artillería F artillery

artillero -ra MF (militar) gunner; (en fútbol) striker

artimaña F trick, wile

artista MF (plástica) artist; (drama, música) performer

artístico ADJ artistic

artritis F arthritis

artroscopia F arthroscopy

artroscópico ADJ arthroscopic

artrosis F degenerative joint disease

Aruba F Aruba

arveja F pea

arzobispo M archbishop

arzón M saddletree

as M ace (también atleta)

asa F handle

asado ADJ roasted; M (carne asada) roast; (carne asada al aire libre) barbecue; (acción de asar) roasting

asador -ora M spit; MF barbecue cook

asalariado -da MF wage earner

asaltante MF mugger

asaltar VT (a una persona) to assault, to assail; (un banco) to hold up; (con preguntas) to assail; **—le a uno una idea** to be struck by an idea

asalto M (ataque) assault; (de un banco) holdup, stickup; **tomar por —** to storm

asamblea F assembly, gathering

asar VT to roast; **— a la parrilla** to grill; **— con adobo** to barbecue

asbesto M asbestos

ascendencia F ancestry

ascendente ADJ (que incrementa) ascending, rising; (que sube) upward

ascender[2] VT (a un empleado) to promote; (una montaña) to climb; VI to ascend; **— a** to amount to

ascendiente MF ancestor

ascenso M (acción de ascender) ascent; (en el trabajo) promotion

ascensor M elevator

asceta MF ascetic

ascético ADJ ascetic

ascienda, asciende ver ascender

asco M disgust, revulsion; **hacer —s a** to reject; **me da —** it makes me sick, it disgusts me; **ese hombre está hecho un —** that man is a mess; **su acné me da —** his acne is a turnoff

ascórbico ADJ ascorbic; **ácido —** ascorbic acid

ascua F ember; **estar en —s** to be on pins and needles; **tener a alguien en —s** to string someone along

aseado ADJ well-groomed

asear VT to clean up

asediar VT to besiege

asedio M siege

asegurable ADJ insurable

asegurador -ora MF underwriter

asegurar VT (una victoria) to assure; (una frontera, una cerradura) to secure; (con un contrato de seguros) to insure; **—se [de]** to make sure [of]; **te lo aseguro** I assure you

asemejarse VI **— a** to resemble

asentaderas F PL buttocks

asentamiento M (de una comunidad) settlement; (de un edificio) settling

asentar VT (datos) to enter; (una población) to establish; **—se** (posarse) to settle; (madurar) to settle down

asentimiento M assent, acquiescence

asentir[8] VI to assent, to acquiesce; **— con la cabeza** to nod

aseo M (acción de asearse) cleaning; (cualidad de aseado) cleanliness; (cuarto de baño) bathroom; (servicio) toilet, restroom

aséptico ADJ aseptic

asequible ADJ (disponible) available; (barato, económico) affordable

aserción F assertion

aserradero M sawmill, lumber mill

aserrado ADJ serrated; M sawing

aserrar[1] VT to saw

aserrín M sawdust

aserto M assertion

asesinar VT to murder; (a una figura pública) to assassinate

asesinato M murder, killing; (de una figura pública) assassination

asesino -na ADJ murderous; MF killer, murderer; (de una figura pública) assassin; **— en serie** serial killer

asesor -ora MF consultant, advisor/adviser

asesoramiento M (profesional, legal) consulting, advising; (académico) counseling; **— de crédito** credit counseling

asesorar VT to advise

asesor -ora MF aide

asestar VT **— un golpe** to inflict/deal a blow

aseveración F assertion

aseverar VT to assert

asexual ADJ asexual

asfalto M asphalt

asfixia F suffocation, asphyxiation, asphyxia

asfixiar VT to suffocate, to smother

así ADV so, thus, like this; **— —** so-so; **— como** in the same way that; **— de grande** that big; **— que** so that; **¿— que no vienes?** so you're not coming?

Asia F Asia

asiático -ca ADJ & MF Asian

asidero M hold; **eso no tiene — en la realidad** that has no basis in reality

asiduo ADJ (lector) assiduous; (cliente) steady

asiento M (lugar donde sentarse, parte de una silla, válvula) seat; (de nóminas) entry, record; **tomar —** to take a seat

asignación F (acción de asignar) assignment; (acción de dar fondos) appropriation; (lo asignado) allotment; (pago) allowance

asignar VT (una tarea) to assign; (fondos) to allot, to allocate, to earmark

asignatura F subject

asilado -da MF inmate; **— político -ca** political refugee

asilar VT (a un político) to give asylum to; (un animal) to shelter

asilo M (para los perseguidos) asylum; (para huérfanos, ancianos) home

asimétrico ADJ asymmetric, asymmetrical

asimilar VT (vitaminas, un grupo étnico) to assimilate; (información) to absorb

asimismo ADV likewise

asintomático ADJ asymptomatic

asir[50] VT to grasp, to grip; **—se a** to hold onto

asistencia F (presencia, personas presentes) attendance; (ayuda) assistance, aid; (servicio de averías) roadside assistance; (deporte) assist; **— médica** health care; **— social** (ayuda) welfare; (profesión) social work

asistente -ta ADJ assistant; MF assistant, helper; **— social** social worker

asistir VT **— a** (estar presente) to attend; (ayudar) to help, to assist

asma F asthma

asmático ADJ asthmatic

asno M ass, donkey

asociación F association; **— de propietarios** homeowners' association

asociado -da MF associate

asociar VT to associate; **—se** to join; **—se con** to fall in with

asolamiento M desolation

asolar VT to desolate, to devastate

asomar VI to show; VT to poke out, to stick out; **—se a** to look out

asombrar VT to astonish, to amaze, to astound; **—se** to be astonished

asombro M astonishment, amazement

asombroso ADJ astonishing, amazing

asomo LOC ADV **ni por —** by no means

asonancia F assonance

aspa F (de hélice) blade; (de ventilador) vane

aspartamo M aspartame

aspecto M (faceta) aspect, feature; (apariencia) looks

aspereza F roughness, harshness; **con —** sharply; **limar —s** to smooth over disagreements

áspero ADJ (terreno, mano) rough; (lucha) bitter; (tiempo, voz) harsh

aspiración F (ambición) aspiration, ambition; (respiración) breathing in; (succión) suction

aspiradora F vacuum cleaner

aspirante MF applicant, candidate

aspirar VT (inhalar) to breathe in, to inhale; (a un empleo) to apply for; **— a** to aspire to

aspirina F aspirin

asqueado ADJ disgusted

asquear VT to disgust

asquerosidad F nastiness; **¡estás hecho una —!** you're gross!

asqueroso ADJ nasty, disgusting, gross

asta F (de toro) horn; (de ciervo) antler; (de bandera) flagpole; (de lanza) shaft; **a media —** at half mast

asterisco M asterisk, star

asteroide M asteroid

astigmatismo M astigmatism

astilla F (de madera) chip, splinter; (de vidrio) sliver; **—s** kindling

astillar VT to chip, to splinter
astillero M shipyard
astringente ADJ & M astringent
astro M (del cielo) celestial body; (de cine) movie star
astrofísica F astrophysics
astrología F astrology
astronauta MF astronaut
astronáutica F astronautics
astronomía F astronomy
astronómico ADJ (relativo a las estrellas) astronomical; (muy elevado) astronomic, astronomical
astrónomo -ma MF astronomer
astucia F (listeza) cunning, guile; (treta) trick
asturiano -na ADJ & MF Asturian; (dialecto) Asturian
Asturias F SG Asturias
astuto ADJ shrewd, wily, cunning
asueto M (día libre) day off; (licencia) time off
asumir VT (una responsabilidad) to assume, to shoulder; (una mala noticia) to accept; — **un cargo** to take office
asunción F assumption; — **presidencial** presidential inauguration
asunto M (cuestión) matter; (tema de una obra) theme
asustadizo ADJ easily frightened, jumpy
asustado ADJ frightened, scared
asustar VT to frighten, to scare; —**se** to become frightened
atacante ADJ attacking; MF assailant
atacar[30] VT to attack, to assault; —**se de risa** to have a laughing fit
atado M bundle
atadura F **sin** —**s** with no strings attached
atajador M tackle
atajar VT (interrumpir) to cut off; VI (cortar camino) to take a shortcut
atajo M shortcut
atalaya F watchtower
atañer[15, 73] VI to concern, to pertain to
ataque M (de violencia, asma) attack; (de rabia, de tos) fit; (de epilepsia) seizure; (en fútbol americano) offensive series; — **cardíaco** heart attack; — **de nervios** nervous breakdown; — **relámpago** blitz
atar VT (sujetar) to tie, to bind; — **cabos** to put two and two together; —**se los zapatos** to tie one's shoes
atardecer[35] VI to get dark; M late afternoon, dusk, evening; **al** — at dusk
atareado ADJ busy
atarearse VI to busy oneself
atascadero M (lodazal) quagmire; (de tránsito) bottleneck
atascado ADJ stuck
atascar[30] VT (un tubo) to stop up; (una máquina) to jam; (el tráfico) to obstruct; —**se** (un

vehículo) to get stuck; (una máquina) to get jammed
ataúd M coffin, casket
ataviar[28] VT to attire, to array; —**se** to dress up
atavío M attire, garb
ateísmo M atheism
atemorizar[47] VT to frighten
atención F attention; (médica) care; (acto de cortesía) courtesy; — **al cliente** customer care; — **médica a largo plazo** long-term care; — **prenatal** prenatal care; — **primaria** primary care; **a la** — **de** to the attention of; **llamar la** — (hacer notar) to call attention; (ser llamativo) to attract attention; (interesar) to interest; INTERJ watch out!
atender[2] VT (a un enfermo) to take care of, to look after; (una súplica) to heed; (a un cliente) to serve; (el trabajo) to attend to, to take care of; VI — **a** to pay attention to
atenerse[58] VI — **a los hechos** to bear the facts in mind, to limit oneself to the facts; — **a la ley** to abide by the law
atentado M (asesinato) assassination; (ataque fracasado) assassination attempt; (con bomba) bombing; **un** — **contra** an affront to
atentamente ADV (con atención) attentively; (despedida en cartas) yours truly / yours sincerely
atentar[1] VI — **contra la vida de alguien** to make an attempt on someone's life
atento ADJ (que presta atención) attentive; (amable) thoughtful
atenuar[26] VT (la violencia) to attenuate; (una luz) to dim; —**se** to abate
ateo -a MF atheist
aterciopelado ADJ velvety
aterido ADJ stiff with cold
aterirse[73] VI to become stiff with cold
aterrador ADJ terrifying
aterrar VT to terrify
aterrizaje M landing; — **forzoso** crash landing
aterrizar[47] VI/VT to land
aterrorizar[47] VT (intimidar) to terrorize; (dar miedo) to terrify
atesorar VT (memorias) to treasure; (dinero) to hoard
atestado ADJ crowded, crammed
atestar VT (certificar) to attest to; (llenar) to jam, to pack
atestiguar[25] VT to bear witness, to testify
atiborrar VT to stuff; —**se** to stuff one's face
atienda, atiende ver atender
atiesar VT to stiffen
atildado ADJ spruced up
atinar VT (acertar) to hit the mark; (adivinar) to guess right; **no** — **a decir palabra** not to manage to get a word out
atípico ADJ atypical

atisbar VT (mirar con disimulo) to peek at, to peep at; (vislumbrar) to catch a glimpse of; VI to peek

atisbo M glimpse, hint

atizar[47] VT (fuego) to poke, to stoke; (pasiones) to stir up, to stoke

atlántico ADJ Atlantic; M **Océano Atlántico** Atlantic Ocean

atlas M atlas

atleta MF athlete

atlético ADJ athletic

atletismo M track and field

atmósfera F atmosphere

atmosférico ADJ atmospheric

atolladero M quagmire

atolondrado ADJ scatterbrained; (muchacha) ditsy

atómico ADJ atomic

atomizador M atomizer

atomizar[47] VT to atomize

átomo M atom

atónito ADJ dumbfounded

atontado ADJ stupefied

atontar VT to stupefy

atorar VT to jam; —**se** to choke

atormentar VT to torment; —**se por** to agonize over

atornillar VT to bolt

atracadero M dock

atracar[30] VT (amarrar) to dock; (robar) to hold up, to mug; —**se** to gorge oneself

atracción F attraction

atraco M holdup, stickup

atracón M **darse un** — to gorge

atractivo ADJ attractive, fetching; M (capacidad de atraer) attractiveness, appeal; (cosa que atrae) attraction; — **sexual** sex appeal

atraer[59] VT to attract

atragantarse VI to choke

atraiga, atraigo, atrajo, atrajera, atrajese ver atraer

atrancar[30] VT to bolt, to bar

atrapada F catch

atrapar VT (en una trampa) to trap, to ensnare, to catch; (una pelota, el interés) to catch

atrás ADV — **de la casa** behind the house; **cuatro años** — four years back; **hacia** — backward; **para** — back/backwards; **quedarse** — to fall behind

atrasado ADJ (de tiempo) late; (en el pago) in arrears, behind; (país) backward; (un libro de biblioteca) overdue; **tengo sueño** — I'm behind in my sleep; **el reloj anda** — the clock is slow; **feliz cumpleaños** — belated happy birthday

atrasar VT (un plazo) to delay; (un objeto) to push back; (un reloj) to turn back; VI (un reloj) to run slow; —**se** to fall behind, to lag

atraso M (condición de atrasado) backwardness;

(pago) back payment; (de trabajo) backlog; **con dos meses de** — two months in arrears

atravesar[1] VT (cruzar) to cross; (estar tendido) to span; (penetrar) to impale, to run through; — **un momento difícil** to go through a difficult moment; **se me atravesó un caballo** a horse crossed in front of me; —**se en la cama** to lie crossways in bed

atraviesa, atraviese ver atravesar

atrayendo ver atraer

atreverse VI to dare, to go for it; ¡**atrévete!** go for it!

atrevido ADJ (audaz) bold, daring; (insolente) insolent

atrevimiento M (cualidad de atrevido) boldness, daring, audacity; (acción atrevida) daring act

atribución F attribution; **atribuciones** powers

atribuir[19] VT (imputar) to attribute, to ascribe; (conferir) to confer; VI —**se** to claim

atribular VT to distress; —**se** to be distressed

atributo M attribute

atribuya, atribuye, atribuyendo, atribuyera, atribuyese ver atribuir

atril M stand

atrincherar VT to entrench

atrio M atrium

atrocidad F atrocity

atrofia F atrophy

atrofiar VT to atrophy, to stunt

atronador ADJ thunderous, deafening

atronar[5] VI to make a racket

atropellar VT (a un peatón) to run over, to run down; (los derechos de alguien) to trample upon

atropello M (arrollamiento) running over; (ultraje) outrage; (abuso) trampling

atroz ADJ (modales, crimen) atrocious; (dolor) excruciating; (ofensa) grievous

atuendo M getup

atún M tuna

aturdido ADJ bewildered; **estar** — to be in a daze

aturdimiento M bewilderment

aturdir VT to bewilder, to daze

atusar VT to smooth, to fix

audacia F audacity, boldness

audaz ADJ audacious, bold

audible ADJ audible

audición F audition; — **radial** radio program

audiencia F (tribunal) court; (público) audience; (en un pleito, proceso legal) hearing

audífono M (para sordos) earphone; (para música) headphone

audio M audio; —**libro** audio book

audiología F audiology

audiovisual ADJ audiovisual; M audiovisual presentation

auditar VI/VT to audit

auditivo ADJ auditory
auditor-ora MF auditor
auditoría F (revisión) audit; (trabajo de auditor) auditing
auditorio M (público) audience; (local) auditorium
auge M (del mercado) boom; (de una moda) heyday; (de una carrera) peak
augurar VT to foretell; **no — nada bueno** not to bode well
aula F (de clase) classroom; (de conferencia) lecture hall
aullar VI to howl
aullido M howl
aumentar VT to augment, to increase; **— los salarios** to raise pay; VI (precios) to rise, to escalate; (población) to grow; (violencia) to escalate
aumento M increase; (de expectativas) buildup; (de población) growth; (de precios) rise, upturn; (de peso) gain; **— por mérito** merit raise; **— salarial / de sueldo** pay raise
aun ADV even; **— así** even so; **— cuando** even though/if
aún ADV still
aunque CONJ though, although
aura F aura
áureo ADJ golden
aureola F halo
auricular M (de teléfono) receiver; **—es** headphones, earphones
aurora F dawn, aurora; **— boreal** aurora borealis, northern lights
auscultar VT to listen to with a stethoscope
ausencia F absence
ausentarse VT to absent oneself
ausente ADJ absent, missing
ausentismo M absenteeism
auspicios M PL auspices
austeridad F austerity
austero ADJ austere, stern
Australia F Australia
australiano-na ADJ & MF Australian
Austria F Austria
austríaco-ca ADJ & MF Austrian
autenticar[30] VT to authenticate
autenticidad F authenticity
auténtico ADJ authentic
autismo M autism
autista ADJ autistic
auto M (coche) auto; (orden judicial) writ; **— de choques** bumper car
autoadhesivo M decal; (para el parachoques) bumper sticker
autoayuda F self-help
autobiografía F autobiography
autobomba M RP fire engine
autobús M bus
autocine M drive-in movie theater

autocompasión F self-pity
autocontrol M self-control
autócrata MF autocrat
autóctono ADJ indigenous
autodestructivo ADJ self-destructive
autodeterminación F self-determination
autodisciplina F self-discipline
autoedición F desktop publishing
autoescuela F driving school
autoestima F self-esteem
autogobierno M self-government
autogol M own goal
autógrafo M autograph
autoimagen F self-image
automático ADJ automatic
automatización F automation
automatizar[47] VT (mecanizar) to automate; (hacer automáticamente) to do automatically
automóvil M automobile
automovilista MF motorist
automovilístico ADJ automotive
autonomía F autonomy; (de un vehículo) range
autonómico ADJ autonomic
autónomo ADJ (independiente) autonomous, independent; (que trabaja por su cuenta) self-employed; (que se presenta solo) stand-alone
autopista F freeway, turnpike; **— de la información** information superhighway
autopropulsado ADJ self-propelled
autopsia F autopsy
autor-ora MF author
autoridad F authority
autoritario ADJ (tiránico) authoritarian; (respetado) authoritative
autorización F authorization
autorizar[47] VT (permitir) to authorize; (dar propiedad intelectual) to license
autosatisfacción F self-satisfaction
autoservicio M (sistema de venta) self-service; (tienda) convenience store
autosuficiencia F self-reliance
autosuficiente ADJ (independiente) self-sufficient; (presumido) smug
autovía F freeway
auxiliar VT to help; ADJ auxiliary; MF assistant; **— de vuelo** flight attendant
auxilio M help
avalancha F avalanche
avalar VT to guarantee, to cosign
avaluar[26] VT to appraise
avalúo M appraisal
avance M (acción de avanzar, adelanto) advance, headway; (sinopsis de película) trailer
avanzada F scouting party
avanzado ADJ advanced
avanzar[47] VI (ir hacia adelante) to advance; (progresar) to make headway; **a medida que avanzaba la mañana** as the morning

progressed; VT (un vehículo) to move forward; (una grabación) to fast-forward

avaricia F avarice

avariento ADJ avaricious, miserly

avaro ADJ miserly, avaricious

avasallar VT to subjugate

avatar M (vicisitud) vicissitude; (encarnación de un dios, personaje digital) avatar

ave F bird; — **de corral** poultry; — **de rapiña** bird of prey; — **canora** songbird; — **zancuda** wading bird

avecindarse VI to take up residence

avellana F hazelnut

avellano M hazel

avena F oats

avenencia F agreement

avenida F avenue

avenir[61] VI to reconcile; —**se a** to come around to; —**se bien** to get along

aventadora F fan, blower

aventajar VT (ser mejor) to be superior to; (sobrepasar) to get ahead of

aventón M **dar un** — *Méx* to give a lift

aventura F (suceso) adventure; (relación amorosa) fling, affair

aventurado ADJ (arriesgado) risky; (atrevido) daring

aventurar VT (arriesgar) to risk; (sugerir) to venture; —**se a** to dare to

aventurero -ra ADJ adventurous; MF adventurer

avergonzado ADJ (tímido) abashed; (arrepentido) ashamed, embarrassed

avergonzar[23] VT to shame, to embarrass; —**se** to be ashamed/embarrassed

avería F (de frutas) damage, bruise; (de coche) breakdown, mechanical trouble

averiado ADJ (un coche) broken-down; (un televisor) on the blink; (un ascensor) out of service; (fruta) bruised, damaged

averiarse[28] VI (fruta) to become damaged; (un coche) to break down

averiguar[25] VT to find out, to ascertain

aversión F aversion, dislike

avestruz MF ostrich

avezado ADJ seasoned

aviación F aviation

aviador -ora MF aviator

aviar[28] VT to fix

avidez F eagerness

ávido ADJ eager, avid

avinagrado ADJ sour

avinagrar VT to sour; —**se** to become sour

avío M tidying up; —**s de pescar** fishing tackle

avión M (máquina) airplane; (ave) martin; — **comercial** airliner; — **a reacción** jet airplane; — **caza** fighter airplane

avisar VT (notificar) to advise; (alertar) to alert

aviso M notice; — **publicitario** advertisement;

estar sobre — to be forewarned; **poner sobre** — to forewarn; **sin previo** — without warning

avispa F wasp

avispado ADJ (despierto) lively; (inteligente) smart

avisparse VI to wise up

avispero M wasp's nest; **alborotar el** — to stir up a wasp's nest

avispón M hornet

avistar VT to catch sight of

avivar VT (una llama) to fan; (una fiesta) to enliven; (un fuego, un debate) to fuel

avizorar VT to spy on

axila F underarm

ay INTERJ (de dolor) ouch; (de decepción) oh, no; (de sorpresa desagradable) oh; ¡— **de mí!** poor me; ¡**ay, no!** oh, no!

ayer ADV yesterday

ayuda F (asistencia) help; (después de una catástrofe) relief; — **en línea** online help

ayudante -ta MF assistant, helper, aide; — **de médico** physician's assistant

ayudantía F assistantship

ayudar VT to help, to aid

ayunar VI to fast

ayunas F PL **en** — (antes de comer) without having eaten; (despistado) clueless; **estoy en** — I am fasting

ayuno M fast, fasting

ayuntamiento M (gobierno) municipal government; (edificio) city hall

azabache M jet; ADJ jet-black, raven

azada F hoe

azadón M hoe

azafato -ta MF (en aviones) flight attendant; (en ferias) host

azafrán M saffron

azahar M orange blossom

azar M chance; **al** — by chance, at random

azaroso ADJ (arriesgado) risky; (aleatorio) random

azerbaiyano -na, azerbaijano -na ADJ & MF Azerbaijani, Azerbaijanian

Azerbaiyán F Azerbaijan

azogar[40] VT to silver

azogue M (sustancia) quicksilver, mercury; (niño inquieto) restless child; **tener** — **en el cuerpo** to be restless

azorar VT (alarmar) to alarm; (avergonzar) to embarrass

azotaina F flogging

azotar VT (con azote) to whip, to lash, to flog; VI/VT (el viento) to whip, to buffet; (el sol) to beat down; (la lluvia) to sting

azote M (instrumento) whip; (golpe) lash; (aflicción) scourge; (golpe de viento) buffet

azotea F flat roof

azteca ADJ, MF Aztec

azúcar MF sugar; — **moreno -na** brown sugar
azucarar VT to sugar
azucarera F (fábrica) sugar mill; *Am* (recipiente) sugar bowl
azucarero M sugar bowl
azucena F white lily
azufre M sulfur, sulphur
azul ADJ blue; — **acero** steel blue; — **celeste** sky blue; — **claro** light blue; — **marino** navy blue
azulado ADJ bluish
azular VT to color blue
azulear VI (tener color azul) to be blue; (ponerse azul) to become blue; VT (dar color azul) to color blue
azulejar VT to tile
azulejo M tile
azuzar[47] VT (a un perro) to sic; (a una persona) to egg on

Bb

baba F drivel, drool, slobber; (de un caracol, de agua estancada) slime; **se le cae la — por el coche nuevo** he's drooling over the new car
babear VI to drivel, to drool
babero M bib
babor M portside
babosa F slug
babosear VI/VT to slobber [on]
baboso ADJ (caracol) slimy; (persona que babea) driveling; (persona tonta) idiotic; (adulador) fawning
babuino M baboon
baca F luggage rack
bacalao M cod
bache M (pozo) pothole; (momento) bad time; (de aire) air pocket
bacheado ADJ bumpy
bachiller -ra M (graduado) high school graduate; (alumno) high school student
bachillerato M baccalaureate
bacilo M bacillus
backgammon M backgammon
bacteria F bacteria
bacteriano ADJ bacterial
bacteriología F bacteriology
badajo M bell clapper
badana F sheepskin
bagaje M baggage
bagatela F trifle
bagazo M pulp
Bahamas F PL Bahamas
bahameño -ña ADJ & MF Bahamian

bahía F (geography) bay; (computer) slot
Bahrein M Bahrain
bahreiní ADJ & MF Bahraini
bailador -ora MF folk dancer; ADJ dancing
bailar VI/VT to dance; **me bailan los pantalones** my pants are falling off; **me tocó — con la más fea** I was left holding the bag; **que me quiten lo bailado** I enjoyed it anyway
bailarín -ina MF dancer
baile M (actividad) dance; (fiesta) dance, ball; — **aeróbico** aerobic dance; — **de máscaras** masked ball; — **folklórico** folk dance; — **zapateado** clog dance
bailongo M hop
bailotear VI to dance around
baivel M bevel
baja F (de temperatura, presión) drop; (de precios) decline; (de guerra) casualty; (del ejército) discharge, dismissal; (del trabajo) leave; **dar de —** to discharge; **darse de —** to call in sick
bajada F (acción de bajar, pendiente) descent; (de un caballo) dismount; — **contra-reloj** downhill ski race
bajar VI (descender) to go down; (correr) to run down; (de un árbol) to climb down; (de un caballo) to get down; (de un ómnibus) to step off, to get off; (en calidad) to worsen; (la marea) to ebb; (una creciente) to subside; VT (las escaleras) to go down; (un avión de un tiro) to shoot down; (comida con agua) to wash down; (la cabeza) to lower; (un cargamento) to let down; (el volumen) to turn down; (focos) to dim; (la voz) to lower, to soften; (los precios) to cut; — **de categoría** to demote; — **el cursor** to scroll down; — **en picado** to dive; —**se los pantalones** to pull down one's pants
bajeza F (cualidad) baseness; (acción) vile act
bajío M shoal
bajista ADJ (bolsa) bearish; MF (músico) bassist
bajo ADJ (nubes, estante, precio, voz grave) low; (persona) short; (voz débil) soft; (río) lower; (vista, persianas) lowered; (acto) base; **baja espalda** small of the back; **de baja calidad** low-end; **de baja ley** base; **de — precio** low-cost; **de — presupuesto** low-budget; **de —s ingresos** low-income; PREP under; — **contrato** under contract; — **control** under control, in hand; — **cuerda** under-the-table; — **fianza** on bail; — **fuego** under fire; — **sospecha** under a cloud; — **tierra** underground; **poner — llave** to lock up; **por lo —** under one's breath; M (en un coro, contrabajo) bass; (de pantalón) cuff; **hacer los —s** to cuff; ADV low
bala F (de pistola) bullet; (atletismo) shot; (de cañón) ball

balada F ballad
baladí ADJ trivial
balance M (cálculo) balance; (documento) balance sheet; (número de víctimas) toll; (movimiento) sway; **hacer un —** to take stock
balancear VT to swing; VI to sway; **—se** to sway
balanceo M (de un cuerpo) swinging, swing; (de un barco) rolling, roll
balancín M seesaw
balanza F scale; **— comercial** balance of trade; **— de pagos** balance of payments
balar VI to bleat
balasto M ballast
balazo M (disparo) shot; (herida) bullet wound
balbucear VI (un adulto) to stammer; (un bebé) to babble
balbuceo M (tartamudeo) stammer; stammering; (de bebé) babble, babbling
balcón M balcony
balde M pail, bucket; **de —** gratis; **en —** in vain
baldear VT to flush
baldío ADJ (terreno) fallow; (acción) useless
baldosa F (en una casa) floor tile; (en una calle) flagstone
balido M bleat, bleating
balística F ballistics
balístico ADJ ballistic
ballena F (animal) whale; (para corsé) whalebone
ballenato M whale calf
ballet M ballet
balneario M (de veraneo) seaside resort; (con aguas medicinales) spa
balón M ball; **baloncesto** basketball; **balonmano** handball; **— de angioplastia** angioplasty balloon; **se le fue el —** (fútbol americano) he fumbled; (fútbol) he lost the ball; M **balonvolea** volleyball
balsa F (embarcación) raft, balsa; (lago) pond
bálsamo M balsam, balm
baluarte M bulwark, stronghold
bambolear VT to sway, to swing; **—se** to sway, to swing
bamboleo M swinging, swaying
bambú M bamboo
banal ADJ banal; **una respuesta —** a pat answer
banana F banana
banano M (tree) banana tree; (fruit) banana
banca F (industria) banking; (en el juego) bank; **— electrónica** e-banking; **— en línea** online banking; **— por internet** Internet banking
bancario -ria ADJ bank, banking; MF banker
bancarrota F bankruptcy
banco M (establecimiento) bank; (asiento) bench; (de peces) school; (de arena) shoal, spit; (de suplentes) bench; **— de datos** data

bank; **— de niebla** fog bank; **Banco Mundial** World Bank
banda F (de músicos) band; (cinta ancha, también de computadora) band; (cinta de vestido) sash; (de delincuentes) gang, band, ring; (dibujo) stripe; (de neumático) tread; (lindero) side, edge, border; (de un barco) side; (en deporte) sideline; **— ancha** broadband; **— de frecuencia** frequency band; **— horaria** time slot; **— magnética** magnetic strip; **— sonora** soundtrack
bandada F (de aves) flock, flight; (de peces) school
bandeja F tray; **me lo sirvieron en — [de plata]** they served it to me on a silver platter
bandera F flag; **jurar la —** to pledge allegiance to the flag
banderín M pennant
banderola F pennant
bandido -da MF (delincuente) bandit, outlaw; (niño terrible) rascal
bando M (decreto) edict; (partido) camp
bandolero -ra MF bandit
Bangladesh M Bangladesh
bangladeshí, bangladesí ADJ & MF Bangladeshi
banjo M banjo
banquero -ra MF banker
banqueta F (taburete) stool; (acera) *Méx* sidewalk
banquete M banquet
banquetearse VI to feast
banquillo M bench (también en fútbol)
bañar VT (a un bebé) to bathe; (una torta) to ice, to frost; **—se** (en una bañera) to take a bath; (en el mar) to swim
bañera F bathtub
bañista MF bather
baño M (acción) bath; (cuarto) bathroom, lavatory; (de torta) icing, frosting; **darse un —** (bañarse) to take a bath; (nadar) to take a swim; **— de asiento** sitz bath; **— de esponja** sponge bath; **— [de] María** double boiler; **— de remolino** whirlpool bath; **— de sangre** bloodbath
bar M bar
barahúnda F ruckus, racket
baraja F pack/deck of cards
barajada F shuffle
barajar VI/VT (naipes) to shuffle; (alternativas) to weigh
baranda F railing, guard rail
barandal M banister
barandilla F rail, railing
barata F *Méx* sale
baratear VT to sell cheap
baratija F trinket, knickknack
barato ADJ cheap
baratura F cheapness

barba F beard; **—s** whiskers; **hacer algo en las —s de alguien** to do something right under someone's nose
barbacoa F barbecue
barbadense ADJ & MF Barbadian
barbado ADJ bearded
Barbados M Barbados
barbaridad F atrocity; **una — de** a lot of; **¡qué —!** what nonsense!
barbarie F savagery
bárbaro -ra ADJ (salvaje) barbarous, barbaric; (estupendo) cool, super; MF barbarian
barbecho M fallow land
barbería F barbershop
barbero -ra MF barber
barbilla F chin
barbitúrico M barbiturate
barbudo ADJ bearded
barca F rowboat
barcaza F barge
barco M boat; **— petrolero** oil tanker
bardo M bard
bario M barium
barítono ADJ & M baritone
barlovento M windward
barniz M (para madera) varnish; (para cerámica) glaze; (de cultura) veneer
barnizar[47] VT (madera) to varnish; (cerámica) to glaze
barómetro M barometer
barón M baron
barquero -era M boatman; F boatwoman
barquillo M rolled wafer
barquinazo M **dar —s** to lurch
barra F (de hierro, arena, chocolate, en un bar) bar; (en gimnasia) crossbar; (signo ortográfico) slash; **— de estado** status bar; **— de herramientas** toolbar; **— de jabón** bar of soap; **— de menú** menu bar; **— de tareas** task bar; **— espaciadora** space bar; **— invertida** backslash
barrabasada F mischief
barraca F (de feria) stall, stand; (casucha) hovel; (depósito) shed
barracuda F barracuda
barranca M ravine
barranco M gully, ravine
barrena F (de un taladro) bit; (de un avión) tailspin; **entrar en —** to go into a tailspin
barrenar VT to drill
barredora F sweeper
barrendero -ra MF street sweeper
barrer VI/VT (pasar escoba) to sweep; (derrotar) to defeat decisively; M SG **barreminas** minesweeper
barrera F (protección) barrier; (valla) barrier, bar; **— arancelaria** tariff barrier; **— comercial** trade barrier; **— de coral** barrier reef; **— del sonido** sound barrier

barrica F vat
barricada F barricade
barrida F sweep
barrido M (acción de barrer) sweeping; (movimiento) sweep
barriga F (abdomen) belly; (panza) paunch; **rascarse la —** to do nothing
barrigón ADJ potbellied
barril M barrel, keg, drum
barrio M neighborhood, quarter; **— residencial** residential neighborhood; **—s bajos** slums
barritar VI to trumpet
barro M (lodo) mud; (arcilla) clay; (acné) pimple; **de —** earthen
barroco ADJ & M baroque
barroso ADJ muddy
barrote M bar
barruntar VT to suspect
barrunto M suspicion
bártulos M PL stuff
barullo M hubbub
basal ADJ basal
basalto M basalt
basar VT to base; **—se en** (depender de) to rely on; (fundamentar en) to be based on
basca F nausea
báscula F scale
base F (apoyo, área militar, en química, en béisbol) base; (punto de partida) basis; (de maquillaje) foundation; (de una campaña) plank; MF (baloncesto) point guard; **—s de concurso** contest rules; **— de datos** database; **— de lanzamiento** launching pad; **con — en** on the basis of; **en — a** on the basis of; **las —s** (de un partido) base, grass roots; (de un sindicato) rank and file; **salario — base** salary; **tener una — sólida** to be on a strong footing; **—s llenas** (béisbol) bases loaded; **— por bolas [intencional]** [intentional] base on balls
basic M (lenguaje de programación) BASIC
básico ADJ (fundamental) basic; (sin lujos) no-frills, bare-bones
básquet M basketball
básquetbol M basketball
bastante ADJ & PRON enough, sufficient; **tiene bastante dinero como para ser feliz** she has enough money to be happy; ADV (suficientemente) enough; **me lo has dicho bastante** you've told me that enough times; (mucho) quite a lot; **la herida me duele bastante** my injury is hurting a lot; (algo) quite, pretty; **la película estuvo bastante bien** the movie was quite good
bastar VI to be enough, to suffice; **¡basta!** enough!
bastardilla F italics
bastardo -da ADJ & MF *ofensivo* bastard

bastedad F coarseness
bastidor M (de teatro) wing; (para bordado) frame; (de coche) chassis; (de ventana) sash; **entre —es** (en teatro) offstage; (en privado) behind the scenes
bastimentos M PL provisions
basto ADJ coarse, crude; M suit in the Spanish deck of cards
bastón M cane, walking stick; **— de esquí** ski pole
basura F rubbish, garbage, trash
basural M *Am* dump
basurero -ra MF (persona) garbage collector; M (lugar) dump
bata F (para llevar en casa) robe, housecoat; (de laboratorio) lab coat; (de pacientes) hospital gown; **— de baño** bathrobe
batahola F racket, din
batalla F battle; (de un carro) wheelbase; **— naval** sea battle; **ropa de —** everyday clothing; **trabar —** to engage in battle
batallar VI to battle
batallón M battalion
batata F sweet potato
bate M baseball bat; **al —** at bat
batea F tray
bateador -ora MF batter; **— ambidiestro -ra** switch hitter; **— designado -da** designated hitter; **— emergente** pinch hitter
batear VT to bat, to hit; **— un jonrón** to hit a homerun; **— un sencillo** to hit a single
batería F (de coche, artillería, béisbol) battery; (de cocina) pots and pans; (musical) drums; **— de iones de litio** lithium-ion battery
baterista MF drummer
batiburrillo M hodgepodge
batido M shake, milk shake
batidor M whisk, beater
batidora F mixer
batintín M gong
batir VT (una alfombra) to beat; (un terreno) to comb; (mantequilla) to cream, to churn; (un récord) to break; (huevos) to beat; (crema) to whip; (alas) to flap, to beat; **— palmas** to clap, to applaud; **—se en duelo** to duel; **—se en retirada** to retreat
batuta F baton; **llevar la —** to call the shots
baudio M baud
baúl M trunk
bautismo M baptism, christening; **— de fuego** baptism of fire
bautizar[47] VT to baptize, to christen
bautizo M christening, baptism
baya F berry
bayeta F cleaning cloth
bayo ADJ bay
bayoneta F bayonet
baza F card trick; **meter — en una conversación** to participate in a

conversation
bazar M bazaar
bazo M spleen
bazofia F slop
bazuca F bazooka
beagle M beagle
beato ADJ (bendito) blessed; (piadoso) beatified; (santurrón) overly pious
bebé M baby, infant
bebedero M (en un corral) drinking trough; (en el campo) watering hole; (para personas) water fountain
bebedor -ora MF drinker
beber VI/VT to drink
bebercio M *fam* booze
bebida F drink, beverage
beca F scholarship, fellowship
becario -ria MF scholar, fellow
becerro M (animal) calf; (piel) calfskin
becuadro M natural sign
befa F jeer
befar VT to jeer at
beicon M *Esp* bacon
beige ADJ & M beige
béisbol M baseball
beisbolista M baseball player
beldad F beauty
belga ADJ & MF Belgian
Bélgica F Belgium
Belice M Belize
beliceño -ña ADJ & MF Belizean
bélico ADJ warlike
belicoso ADJ (guerrero) bellicose; (peleador) feisty
beligerante ADJ & MF belligerent
bellaco M rascal, scoundrel
bellaquería F mischief
belleza F beauty
bello ADJ beautiful
bellota F acorn
bemol M (música) flat; **tener —es** to be tricky
bencina F benzine
bendecir[51] VT to bless
bendición F (parte de la misa) benediction; (acción de bendecir) blessing; (beneficio) boon, blessing
bendito ADJ (agua) holy; (alma) blessed; **— sea** may he be blessed; **dormir como un —** to sleep like a log; **es un —** he is a saint
benefactor -ora MF benefactor, patron
beneficencia F charity; **— pública** welfare
beneficiar VT to benefit; **—se de** to benefit from
beneficiario -ria MF (de una herencia, perdón, acto de bondad) beneficiary; (de un cheque) payee
beneficio M benefit (también espectáculo); **—s adicionales** perks; **—s por fallecimiento** death benefits

beneficioso ADJ beneficial
benéfico ADJ beneficent
benemérito ADJ worthy of esteem
benevolencia F benevolence
benévolo ADJ benevolent
bengala F flare
bengalés -esa ADJ & MF Bangladeshi
benigno ADJ benign
Benín M Benin
beninés -esa ADJ & MF Beninese
benjamín -ina MF youngest child
beodo ADJ drunk
berbiquí M carpenter's brace
berenjena F eggplant
bermejo ADJ reddish
bermellón M vermilion
berrear VI (animal) to bellow, to bawl; (bebé) to squall
berrido M (de animal) bellowing, bawling; (de bebé) squall, squalling
berrinche M tantrum
berro M watercress
berza F cabbage
besar VT to kiss
beso M kiss
bestia F beast
bestial ADJ bestial
best-seller M best seller
besuquear VT to kiss repeatedly; **—se** to make out
betabel M *Méx* beet
betabloqueador M beta blocker
betabloqueante M beta blocker
betún M shoe polish
Biblia F Bible
bíblico ADJ biblical
bibliografía F bibliography
biblioteca F (edificio) library; (anaquel) bookcase
bibliotecario -ria MF librarian
bicarbonato M bicarbonate; **— de sosa/soda** bicarbonate of soda
bíceps M SG bicep[s]
bicho M (insecto) bug (también en informática); (animal) *fam* critter; **— raro** odd bird; **mal —** creep; **¿qué — te ha picado?** what's gotten into you? **—s** vermin
bici F bike
bicicleta F bicycle; **— de montaña** mountain bike; **— estática** stationary bike
bicúspide ADJ bicuspid
biela F connecting rod
Bielorrusia F Belarus
bien ADV well; **—aventurado** blessed; **— arreglado** well-groomed; **— conocido** well-known; **— hecho** well-made, well-done; **— poco** very little; **agarrarse —** to hold on tight; **ahora —** now then; **apretar —** to press hard; **está —** she is fine;

más — rather; **me doy — cuenta** I'm perfectly aware; **pues —** now; **qué —** how wonderful; **si —** although; **ya está —** that's enough; M good; **—es** property, assets; **—es consumibles** consumable goods; **—es inmuebles** real estate; **—es muebles** personal property; **—es raíces** real estate; **—estar** well-being, welfare; **—hechor** benefactor; **persona de —** a good person; INTERJ OK!
bienio M biennium
bienvenida F welcome
bienvenido ADJ welcome
bifurcación F (en un camino) fork, forking; (en un programa de computadora) branch
bifurcarse[30] VI to fork, to branch off
bigamia F bigamy
bigote M (de hombre) mustache; (de animal) whisker
bikini M bikini
bilateral ADJ bilateral
bilingüe ADJ & MF bilingual
bilingüismo M bilingualism
bilis F bile
billar M (juego) billiards, pool; (mesa) pool table
billete M (de viaje, para espectáculos) ticket; (de banco) bill, banknote; (financiero) note; **— de ida solo** one-way ticket; **— de ida y vuelta** return ticket
billetera F billfold
billón M trillion
bimestral ADJ bimonthly
bimestre M two-month period
binario ADJ binary
bingo M bingo
binomial ADJ binomial
binomio M binomial
biodegradable ADJ biodegradable
biofeedback M biofeedback
biografía F biography
bioingeniería F bioengineering
biología F biology
biológico ADJ biological
biólogo -ga MF biologist
biombo M folding screen
biopsia F biopsy
bioquímica F biochemistry
biorritmo M biorhythm
biotecnología F biotechnology
bipartidista ADJ bipartisan
bipolar ADJ bipolar
birlar VT *fam* to pinch, to swipe
Birmania F Burma
birmano -na ADJ & MF Burmese, from Myanmar
birrete M mortarboard
bis M encore
bisabuelo -la M great-grandfather; F great-grandmother

bisagra F hinge
bisecar[30] VT to bisect
biselado ADJ beveled
biselar VT to bevel
bisemanal ADV biweekly
bisexual ADJ bisexual, *fam* switch-hitter
bisiesto ADJ **año** — leap year
bisnieto -ta M great-grandson; F
  great-granddaughter
bisonte M bison, buffalo
bistec M beefsteak
bisturí M scalpel
bisutería F costume jewelry
bit M bit
bizarría F gallantry
bizarro ADJ gallant
bizco ADJ cross-eyed
bizcocho M (pastel) sponge cake; (pastelillo)
  pastry
bizcochuelo M sponge cake
bizquear VI to be cross-eyed
black-jack M blackjack
blanca ADJ half note
blanco ADJ (color) white; (tez) fair; M (color)
  white (también clara de huevos, ojos); (de
  tiro) target; (de una burla) butt; — **fácil**
  sitting duck; **dar en el** — to hit the target; **en**
  — (hoja de papel, mente) blank; (sin dormir)
  sleepless; **en** — **y negro** in black and white
blancura F whiteness; (de tez) fairness
blancuzco ADJ whitish
blandir VT to brandish, to wield
blando ADJ (sin dureza, sin rigor) soft;
  (sensiblero) mushy
blandura F softness
blanqueador ADJ whitening; M bleach,
  whitener
blanquear VT (una pared) to whitewash;
  (dinero) to launder; (verduras) to blanch;
  —**se** to whiten
blanquecino ADJ whitish
blanqueo M whitening
blasfemar VI to blaspheme
blasfemia F blasphemy
blasón M coat of arms
blasonar VI to boast
blazer M blazer
blindado ADJ armored
blindaje M armor
blindar VT to armor
bloc M writing tablet, pad of paper
blog M blog
bloguear VI to blog
bloguero -ra MF blogger
bloque M block (también de motor, político);
  (edificio) building; **en** — together
bloquear VT (carretera, asalto, pase, virus
  digital) to block; (puerto) to blockade;
  (cuentas bancarias) to freeze; —**se** to choke

bloqueo M (deporte) block; (computadoras)
  block, blocking; (militar) blockade
blues M PL blues
bluff M bluff
blusa F blouse, top
boa F boa constrictor
boato M pomp
bobada F (tontería) foolish act; (fruslería) trifle
bobalicón -ona ADJ goofy; MF nincompoop
bobear VI to fool around, to monkey around
bobería F (cualidad) foolishness; (dicho) foolish
  remark; (hecho) foolish act
bobina F (de hilo) bobbin; (de alambre, de
  coche) coil; (de película) reel
bobinar VT to reel
bobo -ba ADJ (tonto) dumb, dimwitted, silly;
  (estupefacto) flabbergasted; MF dimwit,
  booby, fool
boca F mouth (también de río); (de un arma de
  fuego) muzzle; (del estómago) pit; (de una
  cueva) opening; —**calle** intersection; — **a** —
  mouth-to-mouth; — **abajo** face down; —
  arriba face up; **a** — **de jarro** at close range;
  callarse la — to shut up
bocadillo M snack; *Esp* sandwich
bocado M (de comida) bite, morsel, mouthful;
  (de una brida) bit
bocanada F (de líquido) mouthful; (de humo)
  puff; (de aire) sniff
bocazas MF SG loudmouth
boceto M sketch
bochorno M (calor) oppressive heat;
  (vergüenza) embarrassment
bochornoso ADJ (caluroso) sultry, oppressive,
  muggy; (vergonzoso) embarrassing
bocina F (de coche) horn; (megáfono)
  megaphone
bocinazo M honk, toot
bocio M goiter
boda F wedding; —**s de oro** golden anniversary;
  —**s de plata** silver anniversary
bodega F (despensa subterránea) cellar; (para
  vinos) wine cellar; (vinería) winery; (espacio
  en un barco, avión) hold; (tienda de
  comestibles) *Carib, Am Central* grocery store
bodeguero -ra MF (viñatero) wine producer;
  (almacenero) *Carib, Am Central* grocer
bofe M [de animal] lung; **echar los** —**s** to tire
  oneself out
bofetada F slap
boga LOC ADV **en** — in vogue, fashion
bogar[40] VI/VT to row
bogey M bogey
bohemio -mia ADJ & MF (nacionalidad)
  Bohemian; (estilo) bohemian
boicot M boycott
boicotear VT to boycott
boicoteo M boycott
boina F beret

bol M bowl

bola F (golf, tenis, béisbol) ball; (canica) marble; (de helado) dip; (de algodón) wad; (jugada de béisbol) ball; — **blanca** cue ball; **en —s** in the buff; **no dar pie con —** to be lost; **no dar ni —** not to pay attention; — **de nudillos** knuckleball; **darle una base por —s** to walk someone; **sacar una base por —s** to walk; — **de break** break point; — **de partido** match-ball; — **de ruptura** break point

bolera F bowling alley

boleta F (de lotería) ticket; (de votación) *Méx* ballot

boletín M bulletin

boleto M ticket; — **de ida solo** one-way ticket; — **de ida y vuelta** return ticket

boliche M (juego) bowling; (bolera) bowling alley

bolígrafo M ballpoint pen; — **computadora portátil** pen computer; — **ordenador portátil** pen computer

bolita F pellet

Bolivia F Bolivia

boliviano -na ADJ & MF Bolivian

bollo M bun, roll

bolo M bowling pin; **jugar a los —s** to bowl

bolsa F (saco) bag; (cartera) purse; (órgano) sac; (marsupio) pouch; — **de valores** stock market; — **de aire** airbag; — **de estudio** scholarship; — **de miseria** pocket of poverty; **hace —s** it pooches out

bolsillo M pocket; **de —** pocket-sized

bolsista MF stockbroker

bolso M (grande) bag; (pequeño) purse

bomba F (para agua, gasolina) pump; (artefacto explosivo) bomb; (noticia, mujer) *fam* bombshell; — **atómica** atomic bomb; — **de hidrógeno** hydrogen bomb; — **de neutrones** neutron bomb; — **de tiempo** time bomb; — **fétida** stink bomb; — **incendiaria** incendiary bomb; — **inteligente** smart bomb; **lo pasamos —** we had a blast

bombacha F *RP* panties, underpants

bombardear VT to bombard

bombardeo M bombardment, bombing

bombardero -ra MF (tripulante) bombardier; M (avión) bomber

bombear VT to pump

bombero -ra MF firefighter

bombilla F lightbulb

bombo M (en música) bass drum; (en béisbol) fly ball; **dar —** to extol; **con —s y platillos** with great fanfare

bombón M (chocolate) bonbon; (mujer atractiva) *fam* dish

bombonería F candy store

bonachón ADJ (amable) good-natured; (inocente) naive

bonaerense ADJ from the city of Buenos Aires; MF person from Buenos Aires

bonanza F (buen tiempo) fair weather; (prosperidad) prosperity

bondad F goodness, kindness; **—es** virtues; **tenga la — de** would you please

bondadoso ADJ kind, kindly

boniato M sweet potato

bonito ADJ pretty; M tuna

bono M (título de deuda) bond; (vale) voucher

boñiga F dung

boqueada F gasp

boquear VI to gasp

boquete M opening

boquiabierto ADJ (de boca abierta) openmouthed; (asombrado) astonished

boquilla F (para cigarros) cigarette holder; (para trompeta) mouthpiece; **defender de —** to pay lip service to

bórax M borax

borbollar VI to bubble

borbollón M (burbujeo) bubbling; (alboroto) commotion; **a borbollones** bubbling over

borbotar VI to bubble, to gurgle

borboteo M bubbling, gurgling

bordado M embroidery, needlework

bordar VI/VT to embroider

borde M (de una superficie) edge, border; (de un vaso) rim, brim; (de un desastre) brink; (de una calle) *Méx* curb

bordear VT (rodear) to skirt, to go along the edge of; (adornar) to trim

bordillo M curb

bordo LOC ADV **a —** on board

bordó, bordeaux ADJ INV & M maroon

borla F (de birrete) tassel; (de algodón) powder puff

boro M boron

borra F dregs

borrachera F (estado) drunkenness; (juerga) drunken spree

borrachín -ina M drunkard

borracho -cha ADJ drunk, wasted; **no lo hago ni —** I would never do such a thing; MF drunkard, wino

borrado M erasure

borrador M (bosquejo) rough draft; (goma) eraser

borrar VT (texto escrito) to erase; (texto digital) to cut, to erase; **—se de un club** to withdraw from a club

borrasca F squall

borrego M lamb

borrico M (asno) donkey; (persona) *pey* ass

borrón M blot, blotch, smudge; **hacer — y cuenta nueva** to start over at square one

borronear VT to smudge

borroso ADJ (imagen) blurry, blurred;

(memoria) fuzzy
boscaje M thicket
Bosnia-Herzegovina F Bosnia and Herzegovina
bosnio -nia ADJ & MF Bosnian
bosque M forest, woods
bosquecillo M grove
bosquejar VT to sketch, to outline
bosquejo M sketch, outline
bosta F dung
bostezar[47] VI to yawn
bostezo M yawn
bota F (calzado) boot; (para vino) leather wine bag
botadura F launch
botánica F botany
botánico ADJ botanical
botar VT (una pelota) to bounce; (un buque) to launch; (basura) to throw out
botarate M fool
bote M (jarro) can; (embarcación) boat; (rebote) bounce; — **de basura** garbage can; — **de remos** rowboat; — **de salvamento** lifeboat; **de** — **en / a** — filled to overflowing; (tenis) — **pronto** half volley
botella F bottle
botero -ra M boatman; F boatwoman
botija F earthen jug
botijo M earthen jar
botín M (de guerra) booty, plunder; (de ladrón) loot, haul
botiquín M (en el baño) medicine cabinet; (de primeros auxilios) first-aid kit
botón M (de aparato, de camisa) button; (remache) stud; (de planta) bud; **botones** bellboy, page; — **de inicio** start button
bótox M botox
Botsuana F Botswana
botsuano -na MF Botswanan
botulismo M botulism
bouquet M bouquet
boutique F boutique
bóveda F (techo) arched roof, vault; — **celeste** the vault of heaven
bowling M bowling
box M (para coches de carrera) pit
boxeador -ora MF boxer, prizefighter
boxear VI/VT to box
boxeo M boxing
bóxer M boxer
boya F (en el mar) buoy; (corcho) float
boyante ADJ buoyant
boyar VI to buoy
bozal M muzzle
bozo M fuzz on the lip
bracear VI to move one's arms
bracero -ra MF migrant worker
bragas F PL underpants, panties
bragueta F fly

brainstorming M brainstorming
bramar VI (ciervo, cochino) to bellow; (león, viento) to roar
bramido M (de ciervo, cochino) bellow; (de león, viento) roar
brandy M brandy
brasa F ember
brasero M brazier
Brasil M Brazil
brasileño -ña ADJ & MF Brazilian
brasilero -ra ADJ & MF Brazilian
bravata F act of bravado
bravío ADJ wild
bravo ADJ (animal, río) wild; (terreno) rugged; (persona) brave; (barrio) tough; INTERJ bravo!
bravucón -ona ADJ bullying; MF bully
bravuconería F bullying
bravura F (de bestia) fierceness; (de persona) courage
braza F fathom
brazada F (cantidad) armful; (en natación) stroke
brazalete M bracelet
brazo M arm (también de silla); (de cornamenta) branch; (de balanza) beam; — **de mar** sound; — **derecho** right-hand man; —**s day** laborers; **con los** —**s abiertos** with open arms; **con los** —**s cruzados** with crossed arms; **ir del** — to go arm in arm; **luchar a** — **partido** to fight to the end
brea F pitch, tar
brecha F (en un muro) breach, gap; (entre generaciones) gap
brécol M broccoli
bregar[40] VI to struggle, to toil
breña F scrub
breve ADJ (cuento) brief, short; (bikini) scanty; **en** — shortly
brevedad F brevity, shortness; **a la** — as soon as possible
bribón -ona ADJ roguish; MF rascal, rogue, scoundrel
brida F bridle
brigada F brigade
brillante ADJ brilliant, bright; M diamond, gem
brillantez F brilliance
brillantina F glitter
brillar VI (oro) to shine; (ojos) to sparkle, to twinkle; (nieve) to glisten; — **por su ausencia** to be conspicuous by its absence
brillo M (de metal, piedras preciosas) shine, luster, sparkle; (de los ojos) twinkle; (de nieve) glistening; (del pelo, plumas) sheen; (de diamantes) sparkle; (de una pantalla) brightness; **dar** — to give luster; **sacar** — to polish
brilloso ADJ shiny
brincar[30] VI to hop, to skip
brinco M hop, skip

brindar VI (beber) to toast; (proporcionar) to provide; — **por alguien** to toast someone; **—se a hacer algo** to volunteer to do something

brindis M toast

brío M spirit

brioso ADJ spirited

brisa F breeze

británico ADJ British

brizna F blade of grass

broca F drill bit

brocado M brocade

brocal M (borde) rim; (boca de pozo) curb

brocha F paintbrush; **de — gorda** coarse

broche M (alhaja) brooch; (sujetador) clasp, clip; (para el pelo) barrette; **— de oro** grand finale

brocheta F skewer

brócoli, bróculi M broccoli

broma F (chiste) joke; (réplica) jest, wisecrack; — **pesada** practical joke; **—s aparte** kidding aside; **en —** in jest; **gastar una —** to play a joke; **ni en —** no way; **no estoy para —s** I'm not in the mood for kidding

bromear VI to joke, to kid

bromista MF wag, joker

bromo M bromine

bromuro M bromide

bronca F row; **armar una —** to cause a disturbance, to raise a rumpus; **echarle la — a alguien** to bawl someone out; **tener —** to be angry

bronce M bronze

bronceado ADJ (cubierto de bronce) bronzed; (tostado) tanned; (de color bronce) bronze; M suntan

broncear VT (un objeto) to bronze; **—se** to get a tan

bronco ADJ (voz) gruff; (terreno) rough; (caballo) wild

bronquial ADJ bronchial

bronquio M bronchial tube

bronquitis F bronchitis

brotar VI (planta) to sprout; (enfermedad eruptiva) to break out; (agua) to gush, to flow, to issue

brote M (de una enfermedad) outbreak; (retoño) sprout, spear

broza F brushwood

bruces LOC ADV **de —** face down

brujería F witchcraft, devilry

brujo -ja M wizard, sorcerer; F witch

brújula F compass

bruma F mist

brumoso ADJ misty

brunch M brunch

bruneano -na ADJ & MF Bruneian

Brunéi M Brunei

bruñir[17] VT to burnish

bruscamente ADV (girar, responder) sharply; (hablar) brusquely

brusco ADJ (descortés) brusque, curt; (repentino) sudden

brusquedad F (descortesía) brusqueness; (lo repentino) suddenness

brutal ADJ brutal

brutalidad F brutality

bruto -ta ADJ (ignorante) ignorant; (maleducado, burdo) uncouth; (violento) brutish; (sin descuentos) gross; **a lo —** roughly; **en —** in the rough; **recaudar en —** to gross; MF (ignorante) blockhead; (persona violenta) brute; (mal educado) lout, brute

bucal ADJ oral

bucear VI (sumergirse) to scuba dive; (indagar) to explore

buceo M scuba diving

buche M (en las aves) crop; (bocado) mouthful

bucle M (de pelo) curl, ringlet; (en informática) loop

budín M pudding

budismo M Buddhism

budista ADJ, MF Buddhist

bueno ADJ good; **buena fe** good faith; **a la buena de Dios** haphazardly; **de buenas a primeras** out of the blue; **estar —** to be sexy; **hace buen tiempo** it is fine weather; **lo —** the good thing; **por las buenas o por las malas** by hook or by crook; **ser — con los números** to be good at figures; INTERJ OK! **—s días** good day/morning; **buenas noches** good night/evening; **buenas tardes** good afternoon

buey M ox, steer

búfalo M buffalo, bison

bufanda F scarf, muffler

bufar VI to snort; **está que bufa** he is incensed

bufete M (despacho) lawyer's office; (negocio) practice

buffet M buffet

bufido M snort

bufón -ona MF buffoon, jester

bufonear VI to clown

buhardilla F (desván) attic, garret

búho M owl

buhonero -ra MF peddler

buitre M vulture, buzzard

buje M bushing

bujía F spark plug

bulbo M bulb

bulldog M bulldog

bulevar M boulevard

Bulgaria F Bulgaria

búlgaro -ra ADJ & MF Bulgarian

bulimia F bulimia

bulla F uproar, fuss, bustle

bulldozer M bulldozer

bullicio M uproar, racket, bustle

bullicioso ADJ boisterous, rowdy

bullir[16] VI (hervir) to boil; (hacer burbujas) to bubble; (ajetrearse) to bustle; (moverse) to stir

bullón M puff

bullpen M bullpen

bulto M (paquete) bundle; (tumor) lump, growth; (silueta) shape; (saliente) bulge; **a —** approximately; **escurrir el —** to slack off

bungaló M bungalow

bungee M bungee jumping

búnker M bunker

buñuelo M fritter

buque M ship; **— de carga** freighter

burbuja F bubble

burdel M brothel, *fam* whorehouse

burdo ADJ coarse

burgués ADJ bourgeois

burguesía F bourgeoisie, middle class

burla F ridicule, mockery; **hacer — a alguien** to mock someone

burlar VT to mock; **—se de** to scoff at, to make fun of

burlesco ADJ burlesque

burlón ADJ mocking

burocracia F bureaucracy

burócrata MF bureaucrat

burrez F stupidity

burro M (animal) donkey, ass; (persona) dunce; ADJ dense

bursátil ADJ **mercado —** stock market

bursitis F bursitis

burundés -esa ADJ & MF Burundian

Burundi M Burundi

bus M bus; **— en serie** serial bus

busca LOC ADV **en — de** in search of

buscar[30] VT (objetos perdidos) to seek, to look for, to search for; (datos, palabras) to look up; (provocar) to provoke; (la verdad) to seek after; (minerales) to prospect for; (talento) to scout for; **—se problemas** to invite trouble; **— y reemplazar** to search and replace; **tú te lo buscaste** you asked for it; **ir a —** to fetch; M SG **buscapersonas** beeper, pager

búsqueda F search; **— del tesoro** treasure hunt; **— hacia atrás** backward search; **— por palabra clave** keyword search

busto M bust

butaca F (en la casa) armchair; (en el teatro) seat

Bután M Bhutan

butanés -esa ADJ & MF Bhutanese

butano M butane

buzo M diver

buzón M mailbox; **— de sugerencias** suggestion box

bypass M bypass operation, coronary bypass

byte M byte

Cc

cabal ADJ (completo) complete; (exacto) exact; (honrado) upright; **estar uno en sus —es** to be in one's right mind

cabalgar[40] VI to ride horseback

caballa F mackerel

caballada F herd of horses

caballejo M nag

caballeresco ADJ chivalrous

caballería F (tropas) cavalry; (equino) equine; (condición de caballero) knighthood

caballeriza F stable

caballerizo M groom

caballero M (señor) gentleman; (hidalgo) knight; **— andante** knight errant; ADJ gentlemanly

caballerosidad F chivalry

caballeroso ADJ chivalrous, gentlemanly

caballete M (soporte de madera) sawhorse; (de la nariz) bridge; (de pintor) easel; (de tejado) ridge

caballo M (animal) horse; (en ajedrez) knight; (heroína) *fam* smack; **a —** on horseback; **— de carreras** racehorse; **— de batalla** hobbyhorse; **— de fuerza** horsepower; **— de Troya** Trojan horse

cabaña F (casucha) hovel; (casa de campo) cabin, cottage; (conjunto de ganado) livestock

cabaret M cabaret

cabecear VI (mover la cabeza) to nod; (dormirse) to nod off; (un barco) to bob, to pitch; VT (balón) to head

cabeceo M (de la cabeza) nodding; (de un barco) pitching

cabecera F (de cama) headboard; (de mesa) head

cabecilla MF ringleader

cabellera F head of hair

cabello M hair; **traido por los —s** far-fetched

caber[67] VI to fit; **no cabe duda** there is no doubt; **no cabe nadie más** there is no room for anybody else; **no — uno en sí** to be puffed up with pride; **no cabe en lo posible** it is absolutely impossible; **¿en qué cabeza cabe?** who would believe that?

cabestrillo M sling

cabestro M halter

cabeza F head; **— de chorlito** scatterbrain, airhead; **— de playa** beachhead; **— de puente** bridgehead; **— de turco** scapegoat, fall guy; **— de serie** seed; **— rapada** skinhead; **a la —** at the forefront; **caerse de —** to fall head first; **echarse de —** to plunge headlong; **ir a la —** to lead the way; **por —** each; **romperse la —** to rack one's brains; **la**

fama se le fue a la — fame went to his head; **sentar** — to settle down; **tiene la** — **cuadrada** she's a square

cabezada F nod; **dar —s** to nod off

cabezal M magnetic head

cabezazo M (golpe) head butt; (jugada de fútbol) header

cabezón ADJ (de cabeza grande) big-headed; (testarudo) pig-headed; (con mucho alcohol) strong

cabezudo ADJ (de cabeza grande) big-headed; (testarudo) pig-headed

cabida F capacity; **dar** — to include; **tener** — **en** to fit in

cabina F (de pasajeros) cabin; (de piloto) cockpit; (de camión) cab; (de teléfono, control) booth

cabizbajo ADJ crestfallen, downcast

cable M cable; — **coaxial** coaxial cable; **—s del ordenador / de la computadora** media

cableado M wiring

cablevisión F cable television

cabo M (parte extrema) end; (hilo) thread; (cuerda) rope; (saliente de la costa) cape; MF (rango militar) corporal; — **suelto** loose end; **al — de** at the end of; **atar —s** to put two and two together; **de — a rabo** from beginning to end; **llevar a** — to carry out

cabotaje M coastal trade

Cabo Verde M Cape Verde

caboverdiano -na ADJ & MF Cape Verdean

cabra F goat; — **montés** mountain goat; **[loco] como una** — completely crazy

cabrá, cabría ver caber

cabrearse VI to get mad

cabrestante M winch

cabrillas F PL whitecaps

cabrio M rafter

cabrío ADJ **macho** — he-goat

cabriola F caper

cabriolar VI to cavort

cabritilla F kid [leather]

cabrito M kid [goat]

cabrón -ona M (macho de cabra) he-goat; (cornudo) cuckold; (hijo de puta) *ofensivo* bastard; F (hija de puta) *ofensivo* bitch; MF (cobarde) wimp

caca F poop; **hacer** — to poop

cacahuate M *Méx* peanut

cacahuete M *Esp* peanut

cacao M cocoa

cacarear VI to cackle, to squawk

cacareo M cackling, squawking

cacatúa F cockatoo

cacería F hunt; — **de brujas** witch hunt

cacerola F saucepan

cacha F (de navaja) handle; (nalga) thigh, butt; **hasta la** — completely

cachalote M sperm whale

cacharro M (vasija) earthen pot; (coche viejo)

clunker, jalopy

cachaza F slowness

cachazudo ADJ slow

caché M (en informática) cache; (distinción) cachet; — **de memoria** memory cache

cachear VT to body-search, to frisk

cachet M artist's fee

cachetada F slap

cachete M cheek

cachiporra F blackjack

cachivaches M PL stuff, odds and ends

cacho M hunk

cachondo ADJ *fam* horny

cachorro M (de oso, lobo, tigre, león) cub; (de perro) puppy

cacique -ca M (de indios) chief, chieftain; MF (caudillo) political boss

cacofonía F cacophony

cacto/cactus M cactus

cada ADJ each; — **uno** each one; — **vez más** more and more; — **vez menos gente** fewer and fewer people; — **vez menos harina** less and less flour; — **vez peor** worse and worse; **doscientas pesetas** — **una** two hundred pesetas each/apiece

cadalso M gallows

cadáver M (para enterrar) corpse; (para disecar) cadaver

cadavérico ADJ ghastly

caddie, caddy MF caddie

cadena F (serie de piezas) chain; (de televisión) network; (cordillera) mountain range; — **alimenticia** food chain; — **de montaje** assembly line; — **perpetua** life sentence; **—s** shackles; **tirar la** — to flush

cadencia F cadence

cadera F hip

cadete M cadet

cadmio M cadmium

caducar[30] VI to lapse, to expire

caducidad F expiration

caduco ADJ (deciduo) deciduous; (decrépito) decrepit

caer[52] VI to fall; (desplomarse) to fall down; (colgar) to hang; (ir a parar) to end up; **al** — **la noche** at nightfall; — **en desgracia** to fall into disfavor, to fall out of favor; — **en desuso** to fall into disuse; — **en cama** to fall ill; — **en cuenta** to catch on; — **en ruina** to fall into disrepair; **—le bien/mal a uno** (una persona) to make a good/bad impression; (una comida) to agree with; **—le en suerte a uno** to fall to one's lot; — **tan bajo** to fall so low; **caiga quien caiga** let fall who may; **dejar** — to drop; **está al** — he's about to show up; **—se** (persona) to fall down; (computadora, ordenador) to crash; **se cayó el sistema** the system crashed; **—se de culo** to fall on one's bottom

café M (bebida) coffee; (color) brown; (establecimiento) coffee shop, café
cafeína F caffeine
cafetal M coffee plantation
cafetera F coffeepot
cafetería F snack bar, cafeteria, diner
cafetero -ra MF coffee dealer; ADJ **industria cafetera** coffee industry
cafeto M coffee bush
cagada F (acción de cagar) *vulg* dump; (desacierto) *vulg* screw-up; **este libro es una —** *fam* this book sucks
cagalera F *vulg* the trots, the shits
cagar[40] VI/VT *vulg* to shit, to take a crap; **—la** *vulg* to screw up, to fuck up; **me cago en diez / la mar** *fam* I'll be damned; **me cago en tu madre** *ofensivo* fuck you! **me cagué la chaqueta** *vulg* I fucked up my jacket; **—se de miedo** *vulg* to shit a brick, to be scared shitless
caída F (acción de caer) fall, tumble, spill; (de presión arterial) drop; (de un ordenador) crash; (de una cortina) hang; (de precios) drop; **— libre** free fall; **— del sol** sunset; **— en picado** nosedive; **—s del sistema** system crashes
caído ADJ (orejas) floppy; (arco del pie) fallen; **los —s** the fallen
caiga, caigo *ver* caer
caimán M alligator
caja F box; **— boba** *fam* boob tube; **— chica** petty cash; **— de ahorros** savings bank; **— de bateo** batter's box; **— de cambios** transmission; **— de escalera** stairwell; **— de fusibles** fuse box; **— de herramientas** toolkit; **— de jubilaciones** pension fund; **— de música** music box; **— de seguridad** safe deposit box; **— de reloj** watchcase; **— fuerte** safe; **— negra** flight recorder; **— registradora** (aparato) cash register, till; (mostrador) checkout counter; **— tonta** idiot box; **— torácica** rib cage; **entrar en —** (comenzar) to get going; (establecerse) to settle down
cajero -ra MF cashier; (en un banco) teller; **— automático** ATM
cajetilla F pack [of cigarettes]
cajilla F pack [of cigarettes]
cajón M (para transportes) crate; (parte de un mueble) drawer; **eso es de —** that's a foregone conclusion
cajuela F *Méx* car trunk
cal F lime; **cerrar a — y canto** to close hermetically
calabacín M zucchini
calabaza F (grande y redonda) pumpkin; (pequeña y/o alargada) squash; (vaciada) gourd; **dar —s** to turn down
calabozo M dungeon

calado M draft
calamar M squid
calambre M cramp
calamidad F calamity
calamina F calamine
calandria F lark
calar VT (agujerear) to perforate; (empapar) to soak, to drench; **— a alguien** to see through someone; **— hondo** to resonate; **—se** to get drenched
calavera F skull; M libertine
calcar[30] VT (sobre papel) to trace; (imitar) to copy
calcetería F hosiery
calcetín M sock
calcinar VT to bake
calcio M calcium
calco M (acción de calcar) tracing; **es el — de su padre** he's the spitting image of his father
calcomanía F decal
calculador ADJ calculating
calculadora F calculator
calcular VT (computar) to calculate, to figure; (sopesar) to weigh; (prever) to reckon
cálculo M (cómputo) calculation; (aritmética) arithmetic; (integral, diferencial) calculus; **— biliar** gallstone; **— renal** kidney stone
caldear VT to warm up; **— los ánimos** to get everyone upset
caldera F (en una máquina de vapor) boiler; (recipiente con asas) kettle; (de calefacción) furnace
calderón M hold
caldo M broth, stock; **— de cultivo** culture medium
calefacción F heat, heating; **— central** central heating
calendario M calendar
caléndula F marigold
calentador M heater; **— de agua** water heater
calentamiento M warming; (en deportes) warm-up; **— global** global warming
calentar[1] VI/VT (poner caliente) to warm, to heat; **—se** (ponerse caliente, prepararse para un partido) to warm up, to heat up; (excitarse sexualmente) *fam* to get horny
calentura F (fiebre) fever; (excitación sexual) *fam* horniness
calesa F buggy
caletre M **no tener —** to have no brains
calibrador M caliper
calibrar VT to gauge, to calibrate
calibre M (de pistola, tubo) caliber; (de alambre) gauge; (calibrador) caliper
calicó M calico
calidad F quality; **baja —** low quality; **de —** of good quality; **de — inferior** substandard; **estoy aquí en — de representante** I'm here in my capacity as representative

cálido ADJ warm

caliente ADJ (agradable) warm; (excesivo) hot; (excitado sexualmente) *fam* horny

calificación F (nota) grade, mark; (acción de asignar notas) grading; (comparación) rating; — **crediticia** credit rating; **le dieron la — de genio** they called him a genius

calificar[30] VT (juzgar la calidad) to rate, to adjudge; (asignar nota) to grade; —**se como** to be characterized as

calificativo ADJ qualifying; M label

caligrafía F (letra) penmanship; (arte) calligraphy

calina F haze

callado ADJ silent, quiet; **estarse** — to keep quiet

callar VT (no manifestar, no dejar decir) to quiet; VI (no hablar) to remain silent; (dejar de hablar) to go quiet; —**se la boca** to shut up, to pipe down

calle F (de ciudad) street; (golf) fairway; — **abajo** down the street; — **arriba** up the street; — **de sentido único** one-way street; **hacer la** — *fam* to cruise for johns, to turn tricks; **no pisar la** — to stay home

calleja F narrow street

callejear VI to walk the streets

callejero ADJ **perro** — stray dog; **caos** — chaos in the streets

callejón M alley; — **sin salida** blind alley, dead end

callo M callus, corn

calloso ADJ callous

calma F calm; — **chicha** absolute calm; **mantener la** — (no enojarse) to keep one's temper; (no ponerse nervioso) to stay calm; **tomar las cosas con** — to take things easy

calmante ADJ & M sedative

calmar VT (nervios) to calm; (dolor) to sooth; (miedo) to allay, to quell; (sed) to quench; —**se** (una persona) to calm down; (una tormenta, la ira) to subside, to abate

calmo ADJ calm

calmoso ADJ easygoing

calor M (temperatura alta) heat; (temperatura templada) warmth; (actitud acogedora) warmth; **hace** — **hoy** it's hot today; **los —es** hot flashes; **tengo** — I'm hot

caloría F calorie

calumnia F calumny, slander

calumniar VT to slander, to malign

calumnioso ADJ slanderous

caluroso ADJ (día) hot; (recepción) warm

calva F bald spot

calvario M **mi vida es un** — *fam* my life is hell

calvicie F baldness

calvo ADJ bald, baldheaded; **ni tanto ni tan** — *fam* it ain't necessarily so; **quedarse** — to go bald

calza F long sock

calzada F pavement

calzado M footwear

calzador M shoehorn

calzar[47] VT (poner zapatos) to shoe; (hacer zapatos para) to make shoes for; — **a la familia** to buy shoes for the family; **calzo 42** I take size 10; —**se** to put on shoes

calzones M PL (de mujer) panties; (de hombre) shorts

calzonazos M SG henpecked man

calzoncillos M PL underpants, briefs; — **largos** long johns

cama F bed; — **de agua** waterbed; — **doble** double bed; — **elástica** trampoline; — **individual** twin bed; **guardar** — to be confined to bed; **meterse en la** — **con** to sleep with

camada F litter

camafeo M cameo

camaleón M chameleon

cámara F (espacio) chamber; (de neumático) inner tube; (fotográfica) camera; — **de comercio** chamber of commerce; — **de diputados** lower house; — **de gas** gas chamber; — **digital** digital camera; — **de oxígeno** oxygen tent; — **frigorífica** cold-storage locker; — **legislativa** legislature; — **hiperbárica** hyperbaric chamber; **en** — **lenta** in slow motion; MF (persona que maneja una cámara) camera operator

camarada MF comrade

camarero -ra M (restaurante) waiter, server; (coche cama) steward; F (restaurante) waitress, server; (coche cama) stewardess; (hotel) maid; MF (béisbol) second baseman

camarilla F clique

camarógrafo -fa M cameraman; F camerawoman

camarón M shrimp

camarote M cabin, stateroom

cambalache M (intercambio) fraudulent swap; (tienda) secondhand store

cambalachear VI/VT to swap fraudulently

cambiante ADJ (que cambia) changing; (propenso a cambiar) changeable; (temperamento) volatile

cambiar VI/VT to change; VT (una cosa por otra) to exchange, to swap, to trade; — **de marcha** to shift gears; — **de opinión/parecer** to change one's mind; — **de sitio** to move places

cambiario ADJ **sistema** — foreign exchange system

cambio M (acción de cambiar) change; (marcha) gear; (cotización) exchange rate; (de ferrocarril) railway switch; (béisbol) changeup; — **de velocidad** (en béisbol)

change-up; — **de lado** (tenis) changeover; —
de divisas foreign exchange; — **para peor**
a turn for the worse; — **y fuera** over and out;
a — **[de]** in return [for]; **en** — on the other
hand

cambista MF money changer

Camboya F Cambodia

camboyano -na ADJ & MF Cambodian

camellear VT to push [drugs]

camello -lla MF (animal) camel; (vendedor de
droga) pusher

camerino M dressing room

Camerún M Cameroon

camerunés -esa ADJ & MF Cameroonian

camilla F stretcher, litter

camillero -ra MF hospital orderly

caminante MF walker, wayfarer

caminar VI/VT to walk; (baloncesto) to travel

caminata F long walk; (por un lugar agreste)
hike

camino M (carretera) road; (itinerario, dirección
a seguir) way; — **de** on the way to; — **de
mesa** table runner; — **de rosas** bed of roses;
abrirse — to make way; **a medio** —
halfway; **en** — **[a]** on the way [to]; **llevar por
mal** — to lead astray; **mostrar el** — to lead
the way; **ponerse en** — to set out; **señalar
el** — to show the way

camión M (de cargas) truck; (para transporte de
personas) *Méx* bus; — **de la basura** garbage
truck; — **de mudanzas** moving van; — **de
remolque** tow truck, wrecker; — **de
reparto** delivery truck; — **volteador** dump
truck

camionero -ra MF truck driver; *Méx* bus driver

camioneta F (furgoneta) van, minivan;
(camioncito) pickup truck; (coche sin
maletero) station wagon

camisa F shirt; — **de fuerza** straitjacket;
meterse en — **de once varas** to get into a
jam

camiseta F (exterior) T-shirt; (interior)
undershirt

camisón M nightgown

camorrista MF hell-raiser; ADJ rowdy

campamento M (de refugiados, exploradores)
camp; (recreativo) campground

campana F bell; **tocar una** — to ring a bell

campanario M belfry, bell tower

campanilla F (campana pequeña) small bell;
(flor) bluebell; (órgano en la boca) uvula

campanilleo M ringing

campánula F bellflower

campaña F campaign; — **publicitaria**
advertising campaign; **hacer** — to campaign;
el ejército estaba de — the army was on
the front

campechano ADJ straightforward

campeón -ona MF champion

campeonato M championship; — **Mundial de
Fútbol** Soccer World Cup

campero ADJ **hombre** — a man from the
country

campesino -na MF peasant; ADJ **casa
campesina** peasant house

campestre ADJ rural

camping M (lugar) campground; (actividad)
camping

campiña F open country

campista MF camper

campo M (fuera de la ciudad) country,
countryside; (para cultivos, deportes, ámbito
del saber) field; (grupo en un conflicto) camp;
— **abierto** range; MF —**corto** (béisbol)
shortstop; — **de acción** field of action; — **de
batalla** battlefield; — **de concentración**
concentration camp; — **de golf** golf course;
— **de juego** athletic field; — **de tiro**
shooting range; — **libre** free rein; —
magnético magnetic field; — **minado**
minefield; — **petrolífero** oil field; — **visual**
visual field; **a** — **traviesa** cross-country;
—**santo** churchyard

campus M campus

camuflaje M camouflage

camuflar VT to camouflage

can M dog

cana F white hair; **echar una** — **al aire** to go
out for a good time

Canadá M Canada

canadiense ADJ & MF Canadian

canal M (cauce artificial de agua) canal; (estrecho
marítimo, banda de frecuencia) channel;
(emisora) station; — **de parto** birth canal; —
radicular root canal

canalé M ribbed fabric

canalizar[47] VT to channel

canalla MF *ofensivo* scum, lowlife

canalón M spout

canana F cartridge belt

canapé M (mueble) divan; (aperitivo) canape,
starter

canario -ria M canary; ADJ of/from the Canary
Islands; MF Canary Islander

canasta F basket (también en baloncesto)

canasto M hamper

cancelación F cancellation

cancelar VT (contrato, sello) to cancel; (deuda)
to pay off; (evento) to call off

cáncer M cancer; — **de mama** breast cancer; —
de colon colorectal cancer

cancerígeno ADJ carcinogen

canceroso -sa MF cancer patient; ADJ cancerous

cancha F (de baloncesto, tenis) court; (de fútbol)
field; **¡abran** —**!** gangway! **falta** — there's no
room

canciller MF (de Alemania, de universidades)
chancellor; (de EEUU) secretary of state

canción F song; — **de cuna** lullaby
candado M padlock
candela F (vela) candle; (fuego) fire
candelabro M candelabrum
candelero M candlestick; **en el** — in the limelight
candente ADJ red-hot
candidato -ta MF candidate
candidatura F (hecho de ser candidato) candidacy; (conjunto de candidatos) ticket
candidez F innocence
cándido ADJ naive
candil M oil lamp
candilejas F PL footlights
candor M innocence
canela F (especia) cinnamon; (árbol) cinnamon tree
canesú M yoke of a shirt
cangrejo M crab
canguro M kangaroo; MF *Esp* baby-sitter
caníbal ADJ & MF cannibal
canica F toy marble
caniche M poodle; — **enano** toy poodle
canilla F (espinilla) shin; (pantorrilla) calf; (grifo) faucet
canino ADJ canine; **tener un hambre canina** to be ravenous; M canine [tooth]
canje M exchange
canjear VT (prisioneros, libros) to exchange; (un cupón) to redeem
cano ADJ gray-haired
canoa F canoe
canon M (regla, modelo) canon; (canción) round
canónigo M canon
canoso ADJ gray-haired
cansado ADJ (fatigado) tired, weary; (fatigoso) wearing, tiring
cansancio M weariness
cansar VT (fatigar) to tire, to tire out; (aburrir) to bore; —**se** to get tired
cantante MF singer
cantar VI/VT (hacer música) to sing; VT (anunciar) to call out; (revelar secretos) to squeal; — **a tono** to sing on key; —**le a alguien las cuarenta** to give someone a piece of one's mind; — **victoria** to declare victory; **en menos que canta un gallo** before you can say Jack Robinson; M epic poem; **eso es otro** — that's another story
cántaro M pitcher; **llover a** —**s** to rain cats and dogs
cantera F quarry
cantero M *RP* flower bed
cántico M chant
cantidad F quantity, amount; (de dinero) amount, sum; — **a pagar** amount payable; — **debida** amount due; — **pagada** amount paid; — **de gente** a lot of people
cantimplora F canteen, water bottle

cantina F (lugar donde comer) mess hall, mess, canteen; (bar) tavern
cantinela F chant
cantinero -ra MF bartender
canto M (cosa cantada) song; (piedra) pebble; — **de cisne** swan song; — **llano** chant; — **rodado** rounded pebble; **de** — on edge
cantor -ora MF singer
canturrear VI to hum
canturreo M hum, humming
caña F (planta gramínea) reed; (de azúcar) cane; (cerveza) *Esp* beer; (vaso) *Esp* beer glass; — **de pescar** fishing pole; **dale** — floor it
cañada F (barranco) ravine; (arroyo) brook
cáñamo M hemp
cañaveral M reed patch
cañería F (en la calle) piping; (en la casa) plumbing
caño M (tubo) pipe; (grifo) spout; (de arma) barrel; **de doble** — double-barreled
cañón M (arma) cannon; (pieza hueca) barrel; (cañada profunda) canyon; (de pluma, bolígrafo) shaft
cañonero M gunboat
caoba F mahogany
caos M chaos
caótico ADJ chaotic
capa F (prenda) cape, cloak; (de pintura, animal) coat; (de tierra) layer; (de hielo) sheet; — **de ozono** ozone layer; — **freática** water table; **de** — **y espada** cloak and dagger
capacidad F capacity; —**es** aptitude, ability, capability; — **de almacenamiento de disco** disk capacity
capacitación F training; — **para empleados** in-service training
capacitar VT (entrenar) to train; (habilitar) to qualify
capar VT to castrate
caparazón M shell
capataz -za MF boss, overseer
capaz ADJ (habilidoso) capable, able; (apto) apt; (espacioso) spacious, roomy; (competente) competent
capear VT to ride out, to weather
capellán M chaplain
caperuza F pointed hood
capilar ADJ & M capillary
capilla F chapel; **estar en** — (castigado) to be in the doghouse; (en ascuas) to be on pins and needles
capital M (dinero) capital; (de préstamo) principal; — **de riesgo** venture capital; — **inicial** start-up funds; **el gran** — big business; F capital [city]; ADJ main
capitalino ADJ **atmósfera capitalina** capital city atmosphere
capitalismo M capitalism
capitalista MF capitalist; ADJ capitalistic

capitalización F capitalization
capitalizar[47] VT (aportar capital) to capitalize; (aprovechar) to capitalize on
capitán -ana MF captain
capitanear VT to captain
capitel M capital
capitolio M capitol
capitulación F (militar) capitulation, surrender; **capitulaciones matrimoniales** prenuptial agreement
capitular VI to capitulate
capítulo M chapter
capó M hood [of a car]
capo M mafia boss
capota F top [of a car]
capote M cloak; (de coche) *Méx* hood; **decir para su — to** say under one's breath
capricho M caprice, whim, notion
caprichoso ADJ (impredecible) capricious; (impulsivo) whimsical, fanciful; (malcriado) willful
cápsula F capsule
captación F (de agua) collection; (de clientes) attraction; (de inversiones, fondos) raising
captar VT (un concepto) to grasp; (atención, interés) to capture; (una emisión) to receive; (una indirecta) to get; **— la onda** to get the drift
captor -ora MF captor
captura F (acción de capturar) capture; (pesca capturada) catch; (fútbol americano) sack; **— de video/vídeo** video capture
capturar VT to capture; (pescado) to catch
capucha F (de cabeza) hood, cowl; (de lapicero) cap
capuchina F nasturtium
capuchino M cappuccino
capullo M (de insecto) cocoon; (de flor) bud; (tonto) *vulg* dickhead
caqui M khaki
cara F (rostro) face; (de cubo) surface; (de papel, moneda) side; (morro) nerve; **— a —** face to face; **— o cruz** heads or tails; **dar la —** to face up to things; **de — al sur** facing south; **decir en la —** to tell to one's face; **de dos —s** two-sided; **la otra — de la moneda** the other side of the coin; **poner buena —** to put on a good face; **se le ve en la —** it's written all over his face; **tener — [dura]** to have a lot of nerve; **un ojo de la —** an arm and a leg; **volverle la — a** to snub
carabinero -ra MF (oficial de aduana) border patrol officer; (agente de policía) police officer; M (crustáceo) red prawn
caracol M (molusco) snail; (concha) snail shell; INTERJ **¡—es!** *fam* darn!
carácter M (temperamento, signo) character; (rasgo) characteristic; (índole) kind
característica F characteristic, feature; (en informática) feature
característico ADJ characteristic
caracterización F (descripción) characterization, description; (retrato) portrayal
caracterizar[47] VT to characterize
carajo INTERJ *vulg* shit! **irse al —** *vulg* to go to hell; **no sabe un —** *vulg* he doesn't know shit; **¿qué — quieres?** *vulg* what the fuck do you want? **un artista del —** *vulg* a shitty artist; M *Esp vulg* dick
caramba INTERJ *fam* darn! good grief! heck!
carámbano M icicle
carambola F carom; **por —** indirectly
caramelo M (azúcar fundido) caramel; (dulce pequeño) bonbon
caramillo M reed pipe
carátula F (máscara) mask; (portada) title page
caravana F (en el desierto, convoy) caravan; (remolque) trailer
caray INTERJ *fam* shoot! darn!
carbohidrato M carbohydrate
carbón M (sustancia) coal; (pedazo) piece of coal; **— de leña** charcoal
carboncillo M charcoal drawing
carbonera F coal bin
carbono M carbon
carburador M carburetor
carburante M fuel
carca ADJ old-fashioned; MF *fam* fossil, old fogey
carcaj M quiver
carcajada F burst of laughter, guffaw
carcamal M *fam* fossil, old fogey
cárcel F jail, prison
carcelero -ra MF jailer
carcinógeno M carcinogen
carcinoma M carcinoma; **— de célula basal** basal cell carcinoma
carcomido ADJ worm-eaten
carda F card, comb
cardán M universal joint
cardar VT (lana) to card, to comb; (pelo) to rat, to tease
cardenal M (pájaro, prelado) cardinal; (moretón) bruise
cardíaco -ca ADJ cardiac; MF heart patient
cardinal ADJ cardinal
cardioangiograma M cardioangiogram
cardiograma M cardiogram
cardiología F cardiology
cardiólogo -ga MF cardiologist
cardiopulmonar ADJ cardiopulmonary
cardiovascular ADJ cardiovascular
cardo M thistle
cardumen M school of fish
carear VT to bring face to face; **—se** to meet face to face
carecer[35] VI **— de** to lack
carencia F (falta) lack; (deficiencia alimenticia)

deficiency

carenciado ADJ disadvantaged

carente ADJ lacking; **— de** lacking in

carero ADJ expensive

carestía F (escasez) scarcity; (costo alto) high cost

careta F mask

carezca, carezco *ver* carecer

carga F (cosa cargada) load, freight; (de la prueba, impuesto) burden; (hipoteca) lien; (de encendedor) refill; (de explosivo, electricidad) charge; (de programas) upload; **— de municiones** round of ammunition; **— útil** payload; **volver a la —** to insist

cargado ADJ (bebida) stiff; (pausa) pregnant; (cartucho) live; **— de deudas** deep in debt; **— de espaldas** stooping

cargador M (de batería) charger; (de arma de fuego) clip, magazine

cargamento M cargo, load, shipment

cargar⁴⁰ VT (cargamentos, dados, arma, programa de ordenador) to load; (batería, a una cuenta, en baloncesto) to charge; (de obligaciones) to burden with; (a un niño) to carry; (a un estudiante) *Esp* to flunk; (molestar) to bother; **— a alguien de responsabilidades** to saddle someone with responsibilities; **— al hombro** to shoulder; **— de combustible** to fuel; **— un programa** to upload; VI to charge; **— con la culpa** to be saddled with blame; **— sobre** to charge, to attack

cargo M (función en una empresa) position; (en una factura, a una cuenta) charge; (acusación) count, charge; **— de conciencia** guilt feelings; **—s atrasados** back charges; **— de tramitación** handling charges; **a mi —** under my charge; **hacerse — de** (responsabilizarse de) to take charge of; (ser consciente de) to understand; **investir de un —** to induct into office; **los niños están a — de la maestra** the children are under the care of the teacher; **la maestra está a[l] — de los niños** the teacher is in charge of the children

cargoso ADJ fussy

carguero ADJ freight-carrying

cariado ADJ decayed

caribeño ADJ Caribbean

caricatura F (dibujo) caricature; (con texto) cartoon

caricaturista MF cartoonist

caricaturizar⁴⁷ VT to caricature

caricia F caress

caridad F charity

caries F INV cavity, tooth decay

carillón M chimes

cariño M (amor) affection, fondness; (apodo) honey; **darle —s a alguien** to send love to

someone; **ella y el perro se hacen —s** she and the dog nuzzle each other; **hacer algo con —** to do something with great care; **tenerle — a alguien** to be fond of someone

cariñoso ADJ affectionate, loving

carisma M charisma

caritativo ADJ charitable

cariz M complexion; **no me gusta el — que está tomando la situación** I don't like the look of this

carmesí ADJ INV & M crimson

carmín M (carmesí) crimson; (lápiz de labios) lipstick

carnal ADJ carnal

carnaval M carnival

carne F (para comer) meat; (de animal vivo, de persona, de tomate) flesh; **— de cañón** cannon fodder; **— de cerdo** pork; **— de cordero** mutton; **— de gallina** (comida) chicken; (reacción de la piel) goose bumps; **— de res** beef; **— de venado** venison; **— y hueso** flesh and blood; **como — y uña** *fam* thick as thieves; **en — viva** raw; **metido en —s** overweight

carnear VT to butcher

carnero M ram

carnet/carné M **— de conducir** driver's license; **— de identidad** ID

carnicería F (tienda) butcher's shop; (matanza) carnage, bloodbath

carnicero -ra MF butcher; ADJ (carnívoro) carnivorous; (cruel) cruel

carnívoro ADJ carnivorous

carnoso ADJ fleshy

caro ADJ expensive, high-priced, *fam* pricey; ADV at a high price

carona F saddle pad

carótida F carotid artery

carozo M RP pit, stone

carpa F (pez) carp; (tienda) tent

carpeta F (para documentos, también de ordenador) folder; (cartera) portfolio

carpintería F (oficio) carpentry; (taller) carpenter's shop

carpintero -ra MF carpenter

carraspear VI to clear one's throat

carraspera F scratchy throat

carrera F (conjunto de estudios) major; (trayectoria profesional) career; (competición) race; (en las medias) run; (recorrido corto) run, dash; (en fútbol americano, béisbol) run; (de pistón) stroke; **— a pie** footrace; **— de caballos** horse race; **— de relevos** relay race; **a la —** running; **hacer —** to succeed in a profession; **tomar —** to get a running start; **— impulsada** (en béisbol) run batted in; **— limpia** (en béisbol) earned run; **— sucia** (en béisbol) unearned run

carreta F wagon

carrete M (de película) reel; (de hilo) bobbin; (de alambre) spool

carretera F highway; — **de circunvalación** bypass; — **de peaje** toll road

carretero ADJ **sistema** — highway system

carretilla F (de una rueda) wheelbarrow; (de más de una rueda) dolly; **de** — by memory

carretón M large wagon

carril M (de ferrocarril) rail; (de calle) lane

carrillo M cheek, jowl; **a dos/cuatro** —**s** voraciously

carrillón M chimes

carrizo M reed

carro M (automóvil) car; (vehículo de dos ruedas, de golf) cart; (de máquina de escribir) roll; — **alegórico** parade float; — **blindado** armored car; — **de guerra** chariot; **poner el** — **delante de los bueyes** to put the cart before the horse; **subirse al** — to get on the bandwagon

carrocería F auto body

carroña F carrion

carroza F (de caballos) coach; (de desfile) parade float; (fúnebre) hearse

carruaje M carriage, coach

carta F (misiva) letter; (naipe) card; (de restaurante) menu; (constitución) charter; (mapa) chart; — **blanca** freehand; — **con anexos** cover letter; — **de agradecimiento** thank-you letter; — **de remisión** cover letter; — **de renuncia** resignation letter; **a la** — à la carte; **echarle las** —**s a alguien** to do a card-reading for someone; **tomar** —**s en la situación** to take charge of a situation

cartearse VI to correspond

cartel M poster, placard; **en** — showing; — **de la droga** drug cartel

cartelera F (de periódico) entertainment section; (publicitaria) billboard; (tablón para anuncios) bulletin board

cárter M oil pan

cartera F (para dinero) wallet, billfold; (para papeles) briefcase; (escolar) satchel; (bolsa) handbag; (de valores) portfolio

carterista MF pickpocket

cartero -ra MF letter carrier; M mailman, postman

cartílago M cartilage

cartilla F (para aprender a leer) reader; (de información) booklet; — **de racionamiento** ration book; — **de examen de vista** eye chart

cartografiar[28] VT to chart

cartón M cardboard, pasteboard; — **de cigarrillos** carton of cigarettes

cartuchera F cartridge belt

cartucho M (de pistola) cartridge, shell; (de monedas) roll; (de dinamita) stick; — **de fogueo** blank cartridge; — **de tinta / tóner** toner cartridge; **quemar el último** — to exhaust one's resources

cartulina F thin cardboard

casa F (edificio) house; (hogar) home; (negocio) business firm; — **de ancianos** old folks' home; — **de citas** cheap motel for rendezvous; — **de empeños** pawnshop; — **de la moneda** mint; — **de muñecas** dollhouse; — **de pompas fúnebres** funeral home; — **de putas** *vulg* whorehouse; — **de reposo** rest home; — **de rehabilitación** halfway house; — **de subastas** auction house; — **embrujada** haunted house; — **rodante** house trailer; — **solariega** manor house; **de** — **en** — from house to house; **en** — at home; **entró como Perico por su** — he made himself right at home; **estás en tu** — make yourself at home; **ir a** — to go home; **la** — **paga** on the house; **poner una** — to set up a household; **quedarse en** — to stay home; **tirar la** — **por la ventana** to live it up

casaca F riding jacket

casadero ADJ marriageable

casado ADJ married

casamentero -ra MF matchmaker

casamiento M wedding, marriage ceremony

casar VT to marry off; —**se** to get married, to wed; —**se con** to get married to; **no** —**se con nadie** to remain independent

cascabel M (campanita) jingle bell; (de víbora) rattle; **ser un** — to be lively; **ponerle el** — **al gato** to stick one's neck out

cascada F cascade, waterfall

cascajo M old wreck

cascar[30] VT (quebrar) to crack; (dar bofetadas) to slap around; —**se** to crack open; M SG

cascanueces nutcracker; MF SG

cascarrabias crab, grouch; ADJ INV grouchy

cáscara F (de huevo, fruto seco) shell; (de granos, arvejas) husk; (de fruto seco) hull; (de fruta) rind; (de naranja, manzana) peel

casco M (de ciclista, militar) helmet; (de obrero) hard hat; (de barco) hull; (de naranja) shell; (uña del pie de caballería) hoof; — **urbano** built-up area

cascote M rubble

caserío M (aldea) hamlet; (casa) *Esp* farmhouse

casero -ra ADJ (doméstico) domestic; (hecho en casa) homemade; MF (cuidador) caretaker; M (propietario) landlord; F landlady

caseta F (en un mercado) booth, stall; (de guardia) guardhouse; (de perro) doghouse

casete MF cassette

casi ADV almost, nearly; — **diez mil** almost/ nearly ten thousand; — **lo hago** I almost did it; — **siempre** almost always; — **nadie**

hardly anyone; — **nunca** hardly ever

casilla F (en el tablero de ajedrez) square; (en una tabla) box; (en un casillero) pigeonhole, cubbyhole; — **de perro** doghouse; **sacarle a alguien de sus —s** to drive someone up the wall

casino M (club) men's club; (lugar de apuestas) casino

caso M case; — **de fuerza mayor** act of God; — **perdido** (persona incapacitada) basket case; (persona incorregible) lost cause; **en — de** in the event of; **en — de que** in case that; **el — es que** the deal is that; **en todo** — in any case, at any rate; **en último** — as a last resort; **eso no viene al** — that is beside the point; **hacer** — **[de]** to pay attention [to]; **hacer — omiso de** to disregard; **no hay** — there's no point; **pongamos por** — let's suppose that; **venir al** — to come to the point

caspa F dandruff

casquillo M (de bala) case; (de lámpara) socket

cassette MF cassette

casta F caste

castaña F chestnut; — **de cajú** cashew

castañetear VI to chatter; — **con los dedos** to snap one's fingers

castañeteo M (de dientes) chattering; (de dedos) snapping

castaño M (árbol) chestnut tree; (color, madera) chestnut; ADJ chestnut-colored, brown

castañuela F castanet

castellano ADJ & MF Castilian; M (lengua) Castilian

castidad F chastity

castigar⁴⁰ VT to chastise, to punish

castigo M chastisement, punishment; ¡**qué** —! what a nuisance!

Castilla F Castile

castillo M castle; — **de arena** sandcastle; —**s en el aire** *fam* pie in the sky

casting M casting

castizo ADJ traditional

casto ADJ chaste

castor M beaver

castrar VT (a un hombre, animal) to castrate; (a una mascota) to neuter, to fix; (a mascotas hembras) to spay

casual ADJ chance, accidental

casualidad F chance, coincidence; **da la** — **que** it so happens that; **oír por** — to overhear; **por** — by chance

casucha F shack

cata F — **de vinos** wine-tasting

catalán -**ana** ADJ (del catalán) Catalan; (de Cataluña) Catalonian; MF Catalan; M (lengua) Catalan

catalejo M spyglass

catalizador M catalyst

catalogar⁴⁰ VT to catalog/catalogue

catálogo M catalog, catalogue

Cataluña F Catalonia

catar VT to taste

catarata F (cascada) cataract, waterfall; (de los ojos) cataract

catarí ADJ & MF Qatari

catarro M cold

catástrofe F catastrophe

catatonia F catatonia

catecismo M catechism

cátedra F (puesto de profesor) chair, professorship; (enseñanza) teaching; (división académica) department; **sentar** — to hold forth, to pontificate

catedral F cathedral

catedrático -**ca** MF [full] professor

categoría F category; **de** — important; **de** — **mundial** world-class; **de poca** — third-rate

caterpillar M caterpillar

catéter M catheter

cateterización F catheterization

cateterizar VT to catheterize

cátodo M cathode

catolicismo M Catholicism

católico -**ca** ADJ Catholic; MF Catholic

catorce NUM fourteen

catre M cot

cátsup M catsup, ketchup

cauce M channel; — **de río** riverbed

cauchero -**ra** MF rubber gatherer; ADJ **industria cauchera** rubber industry

caucho M rubber; — **sintético** synthetic rubber

caución F security payment

caudal M (de bienes) wealth; (de agua) volume of water

caudaloso ADJ mighty

caudillo M leader

causa F (motivo) cause; (proceso) case; — **noble** worthy cause; — **perdida** lost cause; **a** — **de** on account of, because of; **con conocimiento de** — wittingly; **hacer** — **común** to work together

causante ADJ causing; MF instigator

causar VT to cause; — **problemas** to make trouble

cáustico ADJ caustic

cautela F caution

cautelar ADJ preventive

cauteloso ADJ cautious, wary

cauterizar⁴⁷ VT to cauterize

cautivar VT (capturar) to capture; (atraer) to captivate

cautiverio M captivity

cautivo -**va** MF captive

cauto ADJ cautious, wary

cava F (acción de cavar) digging; (sótano) cellar; (vino) cava

cavar VT to dig

caverna F cavern, cave

cavidad F cavity
cavilar VI to muse
cayado M shepherd's crook, staff
cayendo, cayera, cayese, cayeron *ver* caer
cayo M key
caza F (acción de cazar) hunt, hunting; (conjunto de animales) wild game; — **mayor** big game; — **menor** small game; **andar a la — de** to hunt for; **dar — a** to hunt down; M (avión) fighter
cazador -ora ADJ hunting; MF hunter; F Windbreaker™
cazar[47] VI/VT (buscar presas) to hunt; (matar presas) to shoot, to bag; (atrapar presas) to trap; MF SG **cazatalentos** talent scout, headhunter; M **cazatorpedero** destroyer, torpedo boat
cazo M (cacerola) pan; (cucharón) ladle, dipper
cazoleta F pipe bowl
cazuela F (recipiente) casserole; (cazo) pan
CD M CD; — **ROM** CD-ROM
cebada F barley
cebador M pump primer
cebar VT (un animal) to fatten; (bombas) to prime; (anzuelos) to bait; —**se** to vent one's anger
cebo M (para peces) bait, lure; (para animales) feed
cebolla F onion
cebollar M onion patch
cebollino M scallion
cebra F (animal) zebra; (paso) crosswalk
cecear VI to lisp
ceceo M lisp
cecina F jerky
cedazo M sieve
ceder VT (propiedad) to cede, to assign; (un sitio) to yield, to give up; VI (el frío) to diminish; (la resistencia) to give way
cedro M cedar
cédula F document; — **de identidad** identification card
céfiro M zephyr
cegar[41] VT to blind
ceguera F blindness; — **cromática** color blindness
ceja F (sobre el ojo) eyebrow; (en una encuadernación) tab; **quemarse las —s** to cram for an exam; **cejijunto** with thick eyebrows
cejar VI to back down
celada F ambush
celador -ora MF (en una escuela) school monitor; (en un barrio) security officer
celar VT to guard
celda F cell
celebración F (fiesta) celebration; (acto solemne) performance
celebrar VT (una fiesta) to celebrate; (una

reunión) to hold; (un rito) to perform
célebre ADJ famous, noted
celebridad F celebrity
celeste ADJ (relativo al firmamento) celestial; (del color del cielo) azure, light blue
celestial ADJ celestial, heavenly
célibe ADJ celibate; MF unmarried person
cellisca F sleet; **caer** — to sleet
celo M (diligencia) zeal; (excitación sexual) heat; **estar en** — to be in heat; —**s** jealousy; **tener** —**s** to be jealous
celofán M cellophane
celosía F window lattice
celoso ADJ (que tiene celos) jealous; (diligente) zealous
célula F cell; — **adiposa** fat cell; — **estaminal embrional** stem cell
celular ADJ cellular; M mobile phone
celulitis F cellulite
celuloide M celluloid
celulosa F cellulose
cementar VT to cement
cementerio M cemetery, graveyard
cemento M cement; — **armado** reinforced concrete
cena F supper, dinner
cenagal M quagmire, swamp
cenagoso ADJ marshy, swampy
cenar VI to eat supper, to eat dinner; **vamos a — pescado** we're having fish for dinner
cencerro M cowbell
cenicero M ashtray
ceniciento ADJ ashen
cenit M zenith
cenizas F PL ashes, cinders
censar VI/VT to take a census [of]
censo M census
censor -ora MF censor; — **de cuentas** auditor
censura F (reprobación) censure; (control) censorship
censurador ADJ censuring
censurar VT (criticar) to censure; (examinar) to censor
centavo M cent
centella F sparkle; **pasar como una —** to go by in a flash
centelleante ADJ sparkling
centellear VI to sparkle, to scintillate
centelleo M sparkle
centenar M group of a hundred; —**es** hundreds
centenario M centennial; ADJ centenarian
centeno M rye
centésimo ADJ & M hundredth
centígrado ADJ centigrade
centímetro M centimeter
céntimo M cent
centinela MF sentry, sentinel
centrado ADJ (un tablón) true; (un cuadro) centered; (una persona) focused; M truing

central ADJ central; F plant; — **de teléfonos** telephone exchange; — **eléctrica** power plant; — **lechera** milk processing plant; — **nuclear** nuclear power plant

centralita F switchboard

centralizar[47] VT to centralize; —**se** to become centralized

centrar VT to center; —**se** to focus, to be focused

céntrico ADJ central

centrífugo ADJ centrifugal

centrípeto ADJ centripetal

centro M center (también de baloncesto); (de ciudad) downtown; — **comercial** shopping center; — **de gravedad** center of gravity; — **de mesa** centerpiece; MF —**campista** (fútbol) midfield player

Centroamérica F Central America

centroamericano -na M Central American

ceñido ADJ tight

ceñir[11] VT (rodear) to gird; (abrazar) to encircle; — **la corona** to be crowned; VI (estar apretado) to be tight; —**se a** (limitarse) to limit oneself to; (arrimarse) to get close to

ceño M **fruncir el** — to frown, to scowl

cepa F (de árbol) stump; (de viña) stock; (de bacteria) strain; **de pura** — of good stock

cepillar VT (dientes, pelo) to brush; (madera) to plane, to shave

cepillo M (para pelo, dientes) brush; (para madera) carpenter's plane; — **de dientes** toothbrush

cepo M (para cazar) trap; (para inmovilizar coches) boot

cera F wax; — **de oídos** earwax; — **para muebles** polish

cerámica F (arte) ceramics; (conjunto de artículos) pottery, earthenware

cerámico ADJ ceramic

cerbatana F blowpipe

cerca ADV near, nearby, close; — **de** near, close to; **de** — close up; F fence

cercado M (terreno cercado) enclosure; (cerca) fence

cercanía F proximity, nearness, closeness

cercano ADJ (lugar) near, nearby; (pariente) close; — **Oriente** Near East

cercar[30] VT (rodear con una cerca) to fence, to enclose; (sitiar) to besiege

cercenar VT (cortar) to chop off; (reducir) to curtail, to encroach upon

cerciorarse VI — **[de]** to make sure [of]

cerco M (sitio) siege; (cerca) fence

cerdo -da M (animal, persona sucia) hog, pig; (carne) pork; F (puerca) sow; (de cepillo) bristle

cerdoso ADJ bristly

cereal M cereal; —**es** breakfast cereal; **cultivo** — cereal crop

cerebral ADJ cerebral

cerebro M (órgano, genio) brain; (organizador de un plan) mastermind; **lavarle el** — **a** to brainwash

ceremonia F ceremony

ceremonial ADJ & M ceremonial

ceremonioso ADJ ceremonious

cereza F cherry

cerezo M cherry tree

cerilla F match

cerner[2] VT to sift; —**se** (un ave) to hover; (un desastre) to loom

cernícalo M kestrel

cero M (cifra) zero; (en deportes) nothing, goose egg, zip; (en tenis) love; — **absoluto** absolute zero; **partir de** — to start from scratch; **ser un** — **a la izquierda** to be a nobody

cerrado ADJ (no abierto) closed; (tonto) dense; (poco comunicativo) reserved; (intransigente) closed-minded; (anguloso) sharp; M enclosure

cerrador -ora MF closer

cerradura F lock; — **de combinación** combination lock

cerrajería F locksmith's shop

cerrajero -ra MF locksmith

cerrar[1] VT (la puerta, un cajón) to close, to shut; (un trato) to close, to clinch; (un terreno) to enclose; (el gas, un grifo) to turn off; (una fábrica) to shut down, to close; — **filas** to close ranks; — **el paso** to block passage; VI to close; —**se** (una flor, una tienda) to close; (un plazo) to end; —**se el cielo** to become overcast

cerrazón F (de la mente) closed-mindedness; (del cielo) stormy skies

cerro M hill

cerrojo M bolt

certamen M contest; — **de belleza** beauty contest

certero ADJ sure

certeza F certainty

certidumbre F certainty

certificación F certification

certificado ADJ certified; M certificate; — **de nacimiento** birth certificate

certificar[30] VT (la autenticidad) to certify; (una carta) to register

cervatillo M fawn

cervecera F brewery

cervecería F bar

cerveza F beer; — **de barril** draft beer

cervical ADJ cervical

cérvix M cervix

cerviz F cervix

cesar VI to cease; — **de trabajar** to stop working; — **en un cargo** to resign from a position; — **a** to dismiss

cesárea F cesarean [section]

cese M cessation; — **el fuego** ceasefire; — **de actividades** shutdown

cesión F (de propiedad) assignment; (de derechos) waiver

césped M (ante una casa) lawn; (hierba, también para tenis) grass

cesta F basket

cestería F basketry

cesto M (cesta) basket; (para ropa) hamper

cetrino ADJ olive-colored

chabacano ADJ (modales) crude; (gustos) tacky; M *Méx* apricot

chacal M jackal

chacha F servant girl

cháchara F small talk

chacota F joke; **tomarse algo a la** — to take lightly

chacra F (establecimiento agrícola) small farm; (terreno) small plot

Chad M Chad

chadiano -na ADJ & MF Chadian

chal M shawl, wrap

chala F *Am* husk; **quitar la** — to husk

chalán M horse trader

chalé M cottage

chaleco M waistcoat, vest; — **antibalas** bulletproof vest; — **de fuerza** straitjacket; — **salvavidas** life jacket

chalupa F small canoe; *Méx* tortilla with sauce

chamaco -ca M *Méx* boy; F *Méx* girl

chamarra F sheepskin jacket

chambergo M wide-brimmed hat

chambón ADJ clumsy

champán/champaña M champagne

champiñón M mushroom

champú M shampoo

chamuscadura F scorch

chamuscar[30] VT to scorch, to singe; —**se** to get scorched, to get singed

chamusquina F scorching, singeing

chance MF chance

chancearse VI — **de** to make fun of

chancho M hog

chanchullo M *fam* monkey business

chancleta F thong, flipflop; **tirar la** — to kick up one's heels

chanclo M galosh, overshoe; —**s** rubbers

chándal M sweatsuit

chantaje M blackmail

chantajear VT to blackmail

chanza F jest

chao INTERJ bye-bye

chapa F (de metal) sheet metal; (de policía) badge; (de botella) bottle top; (de prostituta) trick; (de madera) veneer; — **en la puerta** shingle on the door; **hacer** —**s** to turn tricks; **hacerle** — **y pintura a un coche** to fix the bodywork and paint of a car

chapado ADJ — **a la antigua** old-fashioned

chapalear VI to splash

chapar VT to plate

chaparral M dry rangeland, chaparral

chaparro M scrub oak; ADJ *Méx* short

chaparrón M cloudburst

chaperón -ona MF chaperon[e]; **ir de** — to chaperon[e]

chapitel M spire, steeple

chapotear VI to splash

chapoteo M splash, splashing

chapucear VT to botch, to bungle

chapucería F (trabajo, obra) botched job; (cualidad) sloppiness

chapucero ADJ shoddy, slipshod

chapurrear VT to speak a language poorly

chapuz M dive

chapuza F botched job

chapuzar[47] VI to dive

chaqueta F jacket; — **de sport** sport jacket

charada F charades

charca F pond

charco M puddle, pool; **cruzar el** — to cross the ocean

charcutería F (tienda) delicatessen; (industria) sausage-making

charla F chat, talk

charlar VI to chat, to gab

charlatán -ana ADJ talkative; MF (parlanchín) chatterbox, windbag; (curandero) charlatan, quack

charlotear VI to chatter, to jabber

charloteo M chatter, jabber

charol M (barniz) varnish; (cuero barnizado) patent leather

charolar VT to varnish

charqui M beef jerky

charro ADJ flashy, tawdry

chárter M charter flight

chascar VT (los nudillos, un hueso) to crack; (los labios) to smack; (la lengua) to click

chascarrillo M funny anecdote

chasco M (broma) prank, practical joke; (decepción) dud; **llevarse un** — to be disappointed

chasis M frame, chassis

chasquear VT (decepcionar) to disappoint; (una cerradura, la lengua) to click; (un látigo) to crack; (los labios) to smack; (los dedos) to snap; —**se** to be disappointed

chasquido M (de látigo, madera, articulaciones) crack; (de labios) smack; (de la lengua, una cerradura) click; (de los dedos) snap

chata F bedpan

chatarra F scrap iron

chatarrería F junkyard

chatear VI to chat

chato ADJ (nariz) snub-nosed; (zapatos, pecho) flat; — **como una tabla** as flat as a pancake

chaucha F green bean

chaval -la M *Esp* boy; F *Esp* girl
chaveta F cotter pin; **perder la** — *fam* to go bonkers
che INTERJ *RP* say! hey!
checo -ca ADJ & MF Czech
chef MF chef
cheque M check; — **de viajero** traveler's check; — **de caja** bank check; — **sin fondos** bad check, worthless check
chequear VT to check
checar VT to check
chequera F checkbook
chic ADJ INV & M chic
chicha F (bebida alcohólica) *Am* corn liquor; (carne) *Esp fam* meat; **de** — **y nabo** two-bit; **ni** — **ni limonada** neither fish nor fowl
chicharra F (insecto) cicada; (timbre) buzzer
chiche M *Am vulg* tit, boob
chichi M *Am vulg* tit, boob; *Esp vulg* beaver, cunt
chichón M bump, lump, knot
chicle M chewing gum; — **de globo** bubblegum
chico -ca ADJ small, little; M boy; F girl; **mis** —**s** my kids
chicote M *Am* whip
chicotear VT *Am* to whip
chicoteo M *Am* whipping
chiflado ADJ *fam* nuts, cuckoo, loony; MF (persona loca) *fam* basket case, loon
chifladura F craziness
chiflar VI (silbar) to whistle; VT (volver loco) to drive crazy; —**se** to go crazy
chiflido M whistle
chifón M chiffon
chile M chile
Chile M Chile
chileno -na ADJ & MF Chilean
chillar VI (persona) to shriek; (puerta, ratón) to squeak; (cerdo) to squeal
chillido M (de persona) shriek; (de puerta, ratón) squeak; (de cerdo) squeal
chillón ADJ (sonido) shrill; (color) loud, gaudy, flashy
chimenea F (salida de humo) chimney; (hogar) fireplace; (de volcán, baño, mina) vent; (de fábrica) smokestack
chimpancé M chimpanzee
china F (porcelana) china; (piedra) pebble
China F China
chinche F (insecto) bedbug; (chincheta) thumbtack; MF (persona molesta) pain
chinchilla F chinchilla
chinchorro M rowboat
chingar[40] VT (fastidiar) *vulg* to screw with; (estropear) *vulg* to screw up; VI/VT *Méx vulg* to fuck
chino -na ADJ Chinese; M (lengua) Chinese; MF Chinese; **vi a un chino** I saw a Chinese person; **los chinos no están de acuerdo** the Chinese don't agree; **eso es** — that's

Greek to me
chip M (de ordenador, en golf) chip; (de papa/ patata) potato chip; — **de silicio** silicon chip
Chipre M Cyprus
chipriota ADJ & MF Cypriot[e]
chiquilín -ina M little boy; F little girl
chiquito ADJ tiny, wee
chiripa F stroke of good luck; **por/de** — by a fluke
chirivía F parsnip
chirona F jail
chirriante ADJ squeaky
chirriar[28] VI (puerta, freno) to squeak; (ave, freno) to screech
chirrido M (de puerta, freno) squeak; (de ave, freno) screech
chisgarabís M pipsqueak
chisguete M squirt
chisme M (rumor) gossip, piece of gossip; (objeto) *fam* gizmo, thingamajig
chismear VI to gossip
chismoso -sa ADJ gossipy; MF gossip
chispa F (partícula incandescente) spark; (ingenio) wit; **echar** —**s** to be furious; **pasar echando** —**s** to whiz by
chispeante ADJ (que echa chispas) sparkling; (ingenioso) witty
chispear VI (echar chispas) to spark; (lloviznar) to sprinkle
chisporrotear VI (fuego) to sputter; (cigarrillo) to fizzle; (carne) to sizzle
chisporroteo M (de fuego) sputter; (de carne) sizzle
chiste M (verbal) joke; (visual) cartoon; (ocurrencia) wisecrack; — **verde** dirty joke; **no le veo el** — I don't see the humor in it
chistera F top hat
chistoso ADJ funny, amusing, humorous
chivar VI/VT to snitch [on], to rat [on]
chivatar VI/VT to squeal [on], to snitch [on]
chivato -ta MF (delator) informer, snitch, stool pigeon; (chivito) kid
chivo M kid; — **expiatorio** scapegoat; **estar como un** — to be crazy as a loon
chocante ADJ shocking, jarring
chocar[30] VI (golpearse) to bump, to collide; (antagonizar) to clash; VT (sorprender) to shock; (destrozar) to wreck; — **los cinco** to shake hands
chocarrería F coarseness
chochear VI to be in one's dotage
chochera F senility, dotage
chochez F senility, dotage
chocho ADJ senile; **estar** — to be in one's dotage; **estar** — **con** to dote on; M *vulg* cunt
choclo M ear of corn
chocolate M (planta, dulce) chocolate; (bebida) cocoa, drinking chocolate; (hachís) *Esp* pot
chocolatera F chocolate pot

chocolatina F chocolate bar
chófer, chofer MF chauffeur, driver
cholo -la MF (mestizo) person of mixed race; (indio) Europeanized Indian
chopo M poplar
choque M (de objetos móviles) collision, bump, crash; (eléctrico, emocional, cultural) shock; **— insulínico** insulin shock
chorizo M sausage
chorlito M plover
chorrear VI/VT (poco) to drip; (mucho) to gush
chorro M spurt, jet; **a —s** in buckets
chotearse VI **— de** to make fun of
choteo M mocking
chovinismo M chauvinism
choza F hut, shack, hovel
chubasco M squall, shower
chuchería F trinket, knickknack
chueco ADJ *Am* crooked
chuleta F (papel para copiar) cheat sheet; (golf) divot; **— de cerdo** pork chop; **— de ternera** veal cutlet
chulo -la M (proxeneta) pimp; (dandi) dandy, dude; (bravucón) tough guy; MF working-class resident of Madrid; ADJ (fanfarrón) boastful; (bonito) cute
chupada F (de cigarro) puff; (de bebida) sip
chupar VI/VT (succionar) to suck; (fumar) to puff [on]; VT (absorber) to absorb; (vivir a costa de) to sponge off; **chupársela** *vulg* to suck off; **chúpate esa** put that in your pipe and smoke it; M SG **chupasangre** leech
chupete M pacifier
chupetín M *RP* lollipop, sucker
churrasco M *Am* barbecued steak
churro M fritter
chusma F rabble, riffraff
chut M hard shot
chutar VI (drogas) to shoot up; VT (un balón) to shoot; *Esp* **— la bola** to kick the ball hard
chute M narcotic fix
chuzo M watchman's pike
CIA F CIA
cianotipo M blueprint
cianuro M cyanide
cibercafé M cybercafe
ciberespacio M cyberspace
cibernética F cybernetics
ciberpunk MF cyberpunk
cicatero ADJ stingy
cicatriz F scar
cicatrizar VI (formar cicatriz) to form a scar; (curarse) to heal up
cíclico ADJ cyclical
ciclista MF bicycle rider, cyclist, biker
ciclo M cycle; **—motor** moped; **— vital** life cycle; **— de auditoría** audit cycle; **— de facturación** billing cycle; **— presupuestario** budget cycle

ciclón M cyclone
ciclotrón M cyclotron
cicuta F hemlock
ciego ADJ (no vidente) blind; (por borrachera) plastered; (por drogas) high; **quedarse —** to go blind; **a ciegas** blindly
cielo M (firmamento) sky; (paraíso) heaven; **a — abierto** under the open sky; **minería a — abierto** open pit mining; **— raso** ceiling; **¡—s!** good heavens! **estar en el séptimo —** to be in seventh heaven; **me cayó del —** it's a godsend; **poner el grito en el —** *fam* to hit the ceiling
ciempiés M centipede
cien, ciento NUM hundred; **por ciento** percent
ciénaga F swamp, mire, marsh
ciencia F (campo de investigación) science; (conocimiento) knowledge; (arte) art; **— ficción** science fiction; **—s políticas** political science; **a — cierta** with certainty; **las —s ocultas** the occult; **no tiene —** there's nothing to it
cieno M mud, mire
científico -ca ADJ scientific; MF scientist
cierre, cierre *ver* cerrar
cierre M (traba) clasp, fastener; (cremallera) zipper; (acción de cerrar) closing, closure; **— patronal** lockout; **al —** (noticias) at press time; (acciones) at the close
ciertamente ADV certainly
cierto ADJ certain; (verdadero) true; (seguro) sure; **en — sentido** in a sense; **hasta — punto** to a certain extent; **por —** by the way; INTERJ you're right!
ciervo -va M (animal) deer; (macho) stag; **— volante** stag beetle; F (hembra) doe, hind
cierzo M north wind
cifra F (numeral) digit; (número) figure; (clave) cipher, key; **— aproximada** ballpark estimate; **poner en —** to encode
cifrado M encryption; **— de datos** data encryption
cifrar VT to write in code, to encrypt; **— las esperanzas en** to place one's hopes on; **el monto se cifra en veinte millones de pesos** the figure amounts to twenty million pesos
cigarra F cicada
cigarrera F cigar case, cigarette case
cigarrillo M cigarette
cigarro M (cigarrillo) cigarette; (puro) cigar
cigoto M zygote
cigüeña F stork
cigüeñal M crankshaft
cilíndrico ADJ cylindrical
cilindro M cylinder
cima F summit
cimarrón -ona ADJ wild; MF runaway slave
címbalo M cymbal

cimbel M decoy
cimbrar VT to sway, to vibrate
cimentar VT (una casa) to lay the foundation of; (una victoria) to secure
cimiento M foundation
cinc M zinc
cincel M chisel
cincelar VT to chisel
cincha F cinch, girth
cinchar VT to cinch, to girth
cinco NUM five
cincuenta NUM fifty
cine M cinema, movies
cineasta MF filmmaker
cinematografía F cinematography, movie-making
cinematografiar[28] VI/VT to film
cinematográfico ADJ cinematographic; **industria cinematográfica** motion-picture industry
cinestesia F kinesthesia
cingalés-esa ADJ & MF Sri Lankan
cínico-ca ADJ cynical; MF cynic
cinismo M cynicism
cinta F (de adorno) ribbon; (adhesiva) tape; (cinematográfica) film; — **aislante** electrical tape; — **de vídeo** videotape; — **magnetofónica** recording tape; — **métrica** tape measure; — **rodante** treadmill; — **transportadora** conveyor belt
cinto M belt
cintura F (de persona) waist; (de cosa) middle
cinturón M belt; — **de seguridad** safety belt
ciprés M cypress
circo M circus
circonio M zirconium
circuitería F circuitry
circuito M circuit; — **cerrado** closed circuit; — **impreso** circuit board; — **integrado** integrated circuit
circulación F (de sangre, de bienes) circulation; (de vehículos) traffic; **poner en** — to circulate
circular VI to circulate; **hay que** — **por la derecha** you have to drive on the right; F circular letter
circulatorio ADJ circulatory; **problemas —s** cardiovascular problems; **atasco** — traffic jam
círculo M circle; — **vicioso** vicious circle
circuncidar VT to circumcise
circundante ADJ surrounding
circundar VT to surround
circunferencia F circumference
circunlocución F circumlocution
circunscribir[74] VT to circumscribe
circunspecto ADJ circumspect
circunstancia F circumstance
circunstancial ADJ circumstantial

cirio M candle
cirro M cirrus
cirrosis F cirrhosis
ciruela F plum; — **pasa** prune
ciruelo M plum tree
cirugía F surgery; — **de corazón abierto** open-heart surgery; — **plástica/estética** plastic surgery, cosmetic surgery
cirujano-na MF surgeon
cisne M swan
cisterna F cistern
cita F (romántica) date; (con el médico) appointment; (textual) quotation, quote; — **a ciegas** blind date; **darse** — to meet
citación F citation, summons
citar VT (a un testigo) to summon; (a un autor) to cite, to quote; —**se con** (el médico) to make an appointment with; (un amigo) to make a date with
citología F (ciencia) cell biology, cytology; (toma de células vaginales) pap smear
cítrico ADJ citric; M citrus
ciudad F city
ciudadanía F citizenship
ciudadano-na MF citizen
Ciudad del Vaticano F Vatican City
ciudadela F citadel
cívico ADJ civic
civil ADJ (no criminal, no religioso) civil; (no militar) civilian
civilidad F civility
civilización F civilization
civilizador ADJ civilizing
civilizar[47] VT to civilize; —**se** to become civilized
cizalla F metal shears
cizaña F **sembrar** — to sow discord
clamar VT/VI to demand; — **por** to clamor for
clamor M clamor, outcry
clamorear VI/VT to shout
clamoreo M shouting
clamoroso ADJ clamorous
clan M clan
clandestino ADJ clandestine
claqué M tap dance
clara F egg white; — **de huevo** egg white
claraboya F skylight
clarear VI (aclararse) to become clear; (amanecer) to grow light; (desenturbiarse) to thin; VT to illuminate; —**se** to grow light
claridad F (de ideas) clarity; (de la luz) brightness, lightness
clarificar[30] VT to clarify, to clear
clarín M bugle
clarinete M clarinet
clarividente MF & ADJ clairvoyant
claro ADJ clear; (franco) straightforward; (iluminado) light, bright; **azul** — light blue; **a las claras** clearly; ADV clearly; INTERJ of

course! M (espacio) gap; (en un bosque) clearing; — **de luna** moonlight

clase F (tipo) kind, sort; (grupo social, sesión docente, alumnado) class; (aula) classroom; — **alta** upper class; — **media** middle class; — **obrera** working class; — **turista** economy class; **dar** — to teach a class; **toda** — **de** all sorts of

clasicismo M classicism

clásico ADJ (destacado, consabido) classic; (de un período histórico) classical; M classic

clasificación F (taxonómica) classification; (deportiva) qualification; — **descendiente** descending sort

clasificado M want ad

clasificar[30] VT (ordenar) to classify; (en deportes) to qualify; —**se para** to qualify for; —**se segundo** to come in second

claustro M cloister; — **de profesores** university faculty

claustrofobia F claustrophobia

claustrofóbico ADJ claustrophobic

cláusula F clause

clausura F closing

clausurar VT (una sesión) to bring to a close, to conclude; (una tienda) to close [down]

clavadista MF diver

clavado ADV exactly; M (de clavos) nailing; (en una piscina) dive; **tirarse un** — to dive

clavar VT (perforar con un clavo) to nail, to drive a nail into; (pinchar) to stick, to poke; —**le la mirada / los ojos a alguien** to stare at someone; — **los frenos** to stomp on the brakes; **me clavaron** I got a raw deal

clave F (sistema de signos) code; (tabla de correspondencias) key; (signo musical) clef; (clavicémbalo) harpsichord; (de mapa) legend; — **de fa** bass clef; — **de seguridad** password; — **de sol** treble clef; ADJ key

clavel M carnation

clavetear VT to put pegs on

clavicémbalo M harpsichord

clavícula F collarbone, clavicle

clavija F (de guitarra) peg; (de enchufe) pin

clavo M (pieza de metal) nail; (capullo) clove; (de zapato) spike; **dar en el** — to hit the nail on the head

claxon M car horn

clearing M clearing

clemencia F clemency, mercy

clemente ADJ forgiving, merciful

cleptomanía F kleptomania

cleptómano -na MF kleptomaniac

clerecía F (funciones) ministry; (clérigos) clergy

clerical ADJ clerical

clérigo M clergyman, minister

clero M clergy

clic M click; **hacer** — to click; **hacer doble** — to double-click

cliché M (placa fotográfica) photographic plate; (expresión muy usada) cliché

cliente MF, **clienta** F (de un profesional) client; (de un negocio) customer; (de un restaurante) patron; (de un hotel) guest

clientela F clientele, customer base

clientelismo M patronage

clima M climate

climático ADJ climatic; **cambio** — climate change

climatización F air conditioning

clímax M climax

clinch M clinch

clínica F clinic

clínico ADJ clinical

clip M paper clip

clítoris M clitoris

cloaca F sewer

clon M clone

clonación F cloning

clonaje M cloning

clonar VT to clone

cloquear VI to cluck

cloqueo M cluck, clucking

clorhidrato M hydrochloride; — **de Ritalina** Ritalin hydrochloride

cloro M chlorine

clorofila F chlorophyll

cloroformo M chloroform

cloruro M chloride

club M club (también palo de golf); — **nocturno** nightclub

coacción F compulsion, coercion; **bajo** — under duress

coagulación F (de sangre) clotting; (por productos químicos) coagulation

coagulante M coagulant

coagular VI (con productos químicos) to coagulate; (sangre) to clot

coágulo M clot

coalición F coalition

coartada F alibi

coartar VT (una libertad) to restrict; (a una persona) to inhibit; (la creatividad) to strangle

cobalto M cobalt

cobarde ADJ cowardly; MF coward

cobardía F cowardice

cobertizo M shed

cobertor M cover

cobertura F (de nieve, aérea) cover; (de seguros, noticias, televisión) coverage; — **extendida** extended coverage

cobija F (cubierta) cover; (manta) blanket

cobijar VT to shelter; —**se** to seek shelter

cobra F cobra

cobrador -ora MF (persona) collector; M (perro) retriever

cobranza F collection

cobrar VT (impuestos) to collect; (una factura) to

charge; (un cheque) to cash; (el sueldo) to earn; (víctimas) to claim; **— al entregar** to collect on delivery; **— ánimo** to take heart; **— caro** to charge a lot; **— de más** to overcharge; **— de menos** to undercharge; **— valor** to gain importance; **a —** receivable; **vas a —** you're in for it

cobre M (elemento) copper; (utensilios) copper utensils

cobrizo ADJ copper-colored

cobro M collection, charge; **— excesivo** overcharge

coca F (planta, hoja) coca; (cocaína) *fam* coke

cocaína F cocaine

cóccix M coccyx

cocear VI/VT to kick

cocer[34] VI/VT (huevos) to boil; (verduras) to cook; (cerámica) to fire; **— al vapor** to steam; **a medio —** half-cooked; **romper a —** to break into a boil; **¿qué se cuece aquí?** what's up?

coche M (automóvil, vagón) car; (autobús) coach; (vehículo tirado por caballerías) carriage; **— bomba** car bomb; **— cama** sleeper; **—-comedor** dining car; **— de bebé** stroller, baby carriage; **— de bomberos** fire engine; **— de choque** bumper car; **— de golf** golf cart; **— de línea** city bus; **— deportivo** sports car; **— fúnebre** hearse; **ir en —** to go by car, to drive; **pasear en —** to go on a drive

cochera F carport

cochinada F (asquerosidad) filthy action; (maldad) dirty trick

cochinilla F woodlouse

cochino -na ADJ filthy; MF pig

cocido M stew

cociente M quotient; **— intelectual** IQ

cocina F (habitación) kitchen; (electrodoméstico) range, stove; (arte) cuisine, cookery

cocinar VI/VT to cook; (tramar) to cook up

cocinero -ra MF cook

cócker MF cocker spaniel

coco M (fruto) coconut; (cabeza) *fam* dome; (fantasma) bogeyman; **comerse el —** to get all worked up

cocodrilo M crocodile

cóctel M (bebida) cocktail, mixed drink; (fiesta) cocktail party

codazo M jab with the elbow; **dar —s** to elbow

codear VI/VT to elbow, to jab; **—se** to nudge one another; **—se con** to rub elbows with

codeína F codeine

codicia F (avaricia) greed; (deseo sexual) lust

codiciar VT (una cosa) to covet; (a una persona) to lust after

codicioso ADJ covetous, greedy

codificación F coding, encoding

codificar[30] VT (mensaje) to codify, to encrypt; (programa de computadora) to code

código M code; **— abierto** open code; **— de acceso** access code; **— de barras** bar code; **— de país** country code; **— fuente** source code; **— genético** genetic code; **— impositivo** tax code; **— postal** zip code

codo M elbow; **— a —** side by side; **— de tenista** tennis elbow; **empinar el —** to drink too much; **hablar por los —s** to talk one's head off; **hasta los —s** up to one's elbows

codorniz F quail

coeficiente M coefficient; **— de inteligencia** intelligence quotient

coerción F coercion

coetáneo ADJ contemporary

coexistencia F coexistence; **— pacífica** peaceful coexistence

cofre M coffer

coger[45] VT (a un criminal, una pelota) to catch; (con las manos) to grasp; (flores) to gather; to pick; (a un empleado) to hire; (una emisora) to receive; (cosas del suelo) to pick up; (espacio) to take up; (un pez) to land, to catch; (un camino, tren, curso) to take; (poseer sexualmente) *Am vulg* to screw, to fuck; **— por/de sorpresa** to catch by surprise; **— el sueño** to fall asleep; **— hacia el castillo** to turn toward the castle; **—le miedo a algo** to become scared of something; **—le el tranquillo a algo** to get into the swing of things; **—se un resfriado** to come down with a cold; **coge y le dice** he up and says

cognado ADJ & M cognate

cognitivo ADJ cognitive

cogollo M heart

cogote M neck

cohabitar VI (amigos) to live [with]; (una pareja) to cohabitate

cohecho M bribe

coheredero -ra MF joint heir

coherencia F (consecuencia) consistency; (lógica) coherence

coherente ADJ (consecuente) consistent; (lógico) coherent; (con significado) meaningful; **lo que dices no es —** you're not making any sense

cohesión F cohesion

cohesivo ADJ coherent

cohete M rocket

cohetería F rocketry

cohibición F inhibition

cohibido ADJ inhibited, self-conscious

cohibir VT to inhibit

coincidencia F coincidence

coincidir VI to coincide

coito M coitus

cojear VI to limp; **saber de qué pie cojea alguien** to know someone's weaknesses

cojera F limp

cojín M cushion

cojinete M bushing; **— de bolas** ball bearing

cojo ADJ lame, crippled

cojones M PL (testículos) *vulg* balls, nuts; (valor) guts, grit; **estoy hasta los —** I've had it; **¿qué — quieres?** *vulg* what the hell do you want? **tener —** to be brave; **tu doctorado me lo paso por los —** *vulg* I don't give a shit about your doctorate

cojonudo ADJ (estupendo) cool; (valeroso) gutsy

cok M coke

col F cabbage; **—es de Bruselas** Brussels sprouts

cola F (de perro, ave, avión) tail; (de vestido) train; (hilera de gente) line; (secuencia de datos o programas) queue; (pegamento) glue; **— de caballo** ponytail; **hacer —** to stand in line; **no pegar ni con —** not to go together; **traer —** to have consequences

colaboración F collaboration

colaborador -ora MF (con el gobierno) collaborator; (de periódico) contributor

colaborar VI to collaborate; (con un periódico) to contribute

colación F **sacar a —** to bring up

colacionar VT to collate

colador M (para té) strainer; (para verduras) colander

colágeno M collagen

colapso M (de puente, edificio) collapse; (de nervios) breakdown; (de mercado) crash

colar[5] VT (té) to strain; (metal líquido) to pour; VI to go through, to slip through; **esa excusa no va a —** that excuse won't wash; **—se en una fiesta** to crash a party

colateral ADJ collateral

colcha F bedspread

colchón M (para dormir) mattress; (para emergencias) cushion

colchoneta F mat

colear VI (un perro) to wag the tail; (un tema) to be pending; (un auto) to fishtail

colección F collection

coleccionar VT to collect

coleccionista MF collector

colecta F charity collection

colectividad F collective, community

colectivo M (grupo) collective; (autobús) *Am* bus

colector M (de aguas negras) sewer; (eléctrico) collector; (de coche) manifold

colega MF colleague

colegio M (escuela privada) private school; (escuela primaria) elementary school; (centro de educación secundaria) high school; (asociación profesional) association, college

colegir[14] VI to gather

cólera F rage, wrath; **montar en —** to fly into a rage; M cholera

colérico ADJ irritable, choleric

colesterol M cholesterol

coleta F pigtail

coletilla F tag

coleto M **decir para su —** to say to oneself

colgadero M hanger; ADJ hanging

colgado ADJ high and dry

colgadura F drapery; **—s** hangings

colgante ADJ hanging; M pendant

colgar[42] VT (suspender, ahorcar) to hang; (un teléfono, un abrigo) to hang up; VI (un espejo) to hang; (un andrajo) to dangle; (un asunto) to be pending; **esa falda te cuelga por atrás** that dress hangs down in the back; **—se [un ordenador]** to crash; **—se de** to get hooked on; **—se del teléfono** to tarry on the phone

colibrí M hummingbird

cólico M colic

coliflor F cauliflower

colilla F cigarette butt

colina F hill, knoll

colindante ADJ neighboring

colindar VI **— con** to border [on], to adjoin

colirio M eyedrops

coliseo M coliseum

colisión F collision

collage M collage

collar M (de perlas) necklace; (de perro) collar; **— antipulgas** flea collar

collera F horse collar

collie M collie

colmar VT (un vaso) to fill; (una demanda) to satisfy; **— de alabanzas** to lavish praise upon

colmena F beehive

colmillo M (de persona) eyetooth, cuspid; (de elefante) tusk; (de víbora) fang

colmo M **— de la locura** height of folly; **¡eso es el —!** that takes the cake; **para —** to top it all

colocación F (ubicación) placement; (puesto) position

colocar[30] VT (poner, encontrar lugar para) to place; (casar) to marry off; (invertir) to invest; **—se** (drogarse) to get stoned; (encontrar empleo) to get a job; (ubicarse) to place oneself

coloide M colloid

Colombia F Colombia

colombiano -na ADJ & MF Colombian

colon M colon

colón M (moneda) colon

colonia F (territorio, grupo de insectos) colony; (comunidad de inmigrantes) community, settlement; (vivienda) development; (perfume) cologne

colonial ADJ colonial

colonización F colonization

colonizador -ora MF colonist

colonizar[47] VT to colonize, to settle
colono -na MF (habitante de una colonia) colonist, settler; (arrendatario) tenant farmer
colonoscopia F colonoscopy
coloquial ADJ colloquial
coloquio M colloquium
color M (tono) color; (pintura) paint; (maquillaje) rouge; (de naipes) flush; **—es primarios** primary colors; **a todo —** full color; **persona de —** person of color
coloración F coloring
colorado ADJ & M red; **ponerse —** to blush
colorante ADJ & M coloring
coloreado ADJ colored; M coloring
colorear VT to color
colorete M rouge
colorido M (de un caballo) coloring; (de un comentario, paisaje) color; ADJ colorful
colosal ADJ (grande) colossal; (estupendo) wonderful
colostomía F colostomy
columbrar VT to glimpse
columna F column; **— de dirección** steering column; **— vertebral** spinal column, backbone
columnista MF columnist
columpiar VI/VT to swing
columpio M swing
colza F (planta) rape; (aceite) rapeseed oil
coma F (signo) comma; M (falta de conciencia) coma
comadre F (mujer chismosa) gossip; (partera) midwife; (parienta) godmother of one's child
comadreja F weasel
comadrona F (mujer chismosa) gossip; (partera) midwife
comandancia F command
comandante MF (rango militar) major; (militar que ejerce el mando) commander; **— en jefe** commander in chief
comandar VT to command; **— un avión** to pilot an airplane
comando M (grupo militar) commando; (orden dada al ordenador) command
comarca F district
comatoso ADJ comatose
comba F (de una pared) bulge; (de madera) warp; **saltar a la —** to jump rope
combar VI (una pared) to sag; (madera) to warp; (trayectoria de pelota) to curve
combate M combat, fight; **fuera de —** out of combat / the competition
combatiente MF combatant
combatir VI/VT to combat
combativo ADJ combative
combinación F (mezcla) combination; (billete) transfer ticket
combinar VT to combine; **—se para hacer algo** to agree to do something; **esos colores no combinan** those colors don't match
combo M combo
combustible ADJ combustible; M fuel
combustión F combustion
comedero M trough
comedia F (obra teatral) comedy; (farsa) farce; **— de situación** situation comedy, sitcom; **hacer la — de** to play the part of
comediante MF comedian
comedido ADJ moderate; Am obliging
comedirse[9] VI to show restraint; **— a hacer algo** RP to volunteer to do something
comedor M (habitación) dining room; (de empresa) cafeteria
comensal MF [fellow] diner
comentador -ora MF commentator
comentar VI/VT to comment [on], to remark [on]
comentario M (análisis) commentary; (observación) comment, remark
comentarista MF commentator
comenzar[48] VI/VT to begin, to start; **— a comer** to begin to eat; **— preguntando** to begin by asking
comer VI/VT to eat; (al mediodía) to have lunch; (en ajedrez) to take; (en el juego de damas) to jump; **dar de —** to feed; **sin —lo ni beberlo** through no fault of one's own; **—se** (corroer) to eat away; (terminar la comida) to eat up; **—se las eses** to drop one's esses; **—se las palabras** to eat one's words; **—se un semáforo en rojo** to run a red light
comercial ADJ & M commercial
comercialización F marketing, merchandising
comercializar[47] VT (volver comercial) to commercialize; (vender) to market, to merchandise
comerciante MF merchant, trader, dealer
comerciar VI to trade
comercio M commerce, trade; **— electrónico** e-business; **— exterior** foreign trade; **— minorista** retail trade; **— mayorista** wholesaler
comestible ADJ edible; M PL groceries
cometa M (cuerpo celeste) comet; F (juguete) kite
cometer VT to commit
cometido M purpose, objective
comezón F itch, itching; **tener —** to itch
cómic M comic book
comicios M PL polls
cómico -ca ADJ comic, comical; MF comedian
comida F (ocasión) meal; (alimento) food; (al mediodía) lunch; **— basura** junk food; **— macrobiótica** health food; **— rápida** fast food
comience, comienza ver comenzar
comienzo M beginning; **a —s de** toward the beginning of; **al —** at first, initially; **desde un/el —** from the start

comilla F quotation mark; **entre —s** in quotes
comilón -ona MF big eater; F binge
comino M cumin; **me importa un —** *fam* I don't give a hoot; **no vale un —** *fam* it's not worth a hoot
comisaría F **— de policía** police station, precinct
comisario -ria MF (comisionado) commissioner; (jefe de policía) police chief
comisión F (acción de cometer, porcentaje ganado) commission; (comité) committee
comisionar VT to commission
comistrajo M bad food
comisura F **— de los labios** corner of the mouth
comité M committee
comitiva F retinue
como ADV (del mismo modo que) as, like; **ella pinta — yo** she paints like I do; (aproximadamente) about; **pesa — diez kilos** it weighs about ten kilos; CONJ (puesto que) since; **— no tenemos dinero** since we have no money; **— no me pagues** if you don't pay me; **era — que muy viejo** he was, like, real old; **— que te voy a permitir** as if I would let you; **— quieras** as you please; **— si** as if; **¡— si me lo fuera a creer!** a likely story!
cómo ADV INTERR & PRON (de qué manera) how; (¿perdón?) excuse me? what? **¡— brillan las estrellas!** how the stars are shining! **¡— no!** of course! **¿a — me lo vende?** what does that cost?
cómoda F chest of drawers, dresser, bureau
comodidad F (cualidad) comfort; (cosa cómoda) convenience; **—es** amenities
comodín M joker, wild card
cómodo ADJ (mueble) comfortable; (horario) convenient; (persona) lazy
Comoras F PL Comoros
compactar VT to compact
compacto ADJ compact
compadecer[35] VT to pity; **—se de** to take pity on
compadre M (amigo) pal, crony; (pariente) godfather of one's child
compañero -ra MF (camarada) companion; (de un zapato) mate; **— de clase** classmate; **— de cuarto** roommate; **— de equipo** teammate
compañía F company; **— de importación y exportación** import-export company; **— fantasma** bogus company; **— recién establecida** start-up; **en — de** in the company of
comparable ADJ comparable
comparación F comparison
comparar VI/VT to compare; **—se con** to compare [oneself] with
comparativo ADJ comparative

comparecencia F appearance
comparecer[35] VI to appear
compartimiento M compartment
compartir VT (bienes) to share; (tiempo) to divide
compás M (instrumento de geometría) compass; (ritmo) beat; (espacio entre barras) measure, bar; (división de música) time signature; **marcar el —** to beat time
compasión F compassion
compasivo ADJ compassionate, sympathetic
compatibilidad F compatibility
compatible ADJ compatible
compatriota MF compatriot
compeler VT to compel
compendiar VT to summarize
compendio M digest, condensation
compenetración F bonding
compensación F compensation
compensar VT (un daño) to compensate; (un gasto) to offset; **compensa su falta de inteligencia con mucha disciplina** he makes up for his lack of intelligence with a lot of discipline; **te voy a — por esto** I'll make it up to you
competencia F (pugna, competición, competidores) competition; (cualidad de competente) competence
competente ADJ competent
competición F athletic competition, meet
competidor -ora ADJ competing; MF (comercial) competitor; (deportivo) athlete, participant
competir[9] VI to compete, to vie
competitividad F competitiveness
competitivo ADJ competitive
compilador M compiler
compilar VT to compile
compinche M chum, crony
compita, compite, compitiendo, compitiera, compitiese *ver* competir
complacencia F satisfaction
complacer[36] VT to please, to gratify; **—se [en]** to take pleasure [in]
complaciente ADJ (que complace) obliging; (que consiente) indulgent
complejidad F complexity
complejo ADJ complex; M complex; **— de inferioridad** inferiority complex
complementar VT to complement, to supplement
complementario ADJ complementary
complemento M complement; **— alimenticio** dietary supplement; **— directo** direct object; **— indirecto** indirect object; **—s** fringe benefits
completar VT (terminar) to complete; (en fútbol americano) to complete [passes]; **—se** to be completed

completo ADJ (terminado) complete; (lleno) full; **hoy tenemos el —** today we have a full house; **por —** completely

complexión F build

complicación F complication

complicado ADJ complicated

complicar[30] VT to complicate; **—le a alguien la vida** to give someone trouble

cómplice MF accomplice

complicidad F complicity

complot M plot

compondrá, compondría ver componer

componenda F (arreglo provisional) quick fix; (arreglo ilegal) shady deal

componente ADJ & M component

componer[56, 74] VT (un grupo) to compose, to make up; (imprenta) to set; (un coche descompuesto) to fix; (música) to compose; **—se de** to be composed of; **componérselas** to deal with one's problems alone

componga, compongo ver componer

comportamiento M conduct, behavior

comportarse VI/VT to conduct oneself, to behave

composición F composition

compositor -ora MF composer

compostura F (arreglo) repair; (dignidad) composure

compra F purchase; **— apalancada** LBO; **ir de —s** to go shopping; **— hostil** hostile takeover

comprador -ora MF (comercial) buyer, purchaser; (en una tienda) shopper

comprar VT to buy, to purchase; **compró su silencio** he gave her hush money

comprender VT (entender) to understand, to comprehend; (abarcar) to cover, to include

comprensible ADJ comprehensible, understandable

comprensión F (intelectual) understanding, comprehension; (emocional) sympathy, understanding

comprensivo ADJ understanding

compresa F compress

compresión F compression; **— de archivos** file compression

comprimido ADJ compressed; M tablet

comprimir VT to compress

comprobación F verification, check

comprobante M proof; **— de compra** proof of purchase

comprobar[5] VT (verificar) to verify, to check; (probar) to prove; (darse cuenta) to realize

comprometer VT (obligar) to commit; (poner en peligro) to jeopardize, to compromise; **—se** (prometer) to promise; (tomar partido) to commit oneself; (para casarse) to get engaged

comprometido ADJ (obligado) obligated; (arriesgado) risky; (implicado) compromised; (con planes de casarse) engaged; (entregado, dedicado) committed, engaged

compromiso M (ideología, obligación, promesa) commitment; (acuerdo) agreement; (cita) appointment, engagement; (de matrimonio) engagement; (solución negociada) compromise; **no me pongas en —** don't compromise me; **sin — de compra** without obligation to buy

comprueba, compruebe ver comprobar

compuerta F sluice gate, floodgate

compuesto ADJ (ojos, tiempo, interés) compound; **estar — de** to be composed of; M compound

compuesto ver componer

compulsión F compulsion

compulsivo ADJ compulsive

compungirse[46] VI to feel sorry

computación F computing

computadora F computer; **— personal** personal computer; **— de escritorio** desktop computer; **— de mano** palmtop, handheld computer; **— digital** digital computer; **— portátil** laptop computer; **— torre** tower model

computar VT to compute

computarizar[47] VT to computerize

cómputo M computation

comulgar[40] VI (recibir el sacramento) to take Communion; (estar de acuerdo) to agree

común ADJ common; **en —** in common; **por lo —** generally; **el — de las gentes** the majority of the people

comuna F commune

comunicable ADJ communicable

comunicación F (interacción) communication; (ponencia) presentation; **se nos cortó la —** we got disconnected

comunicado M communiqué, report

comunicar[30] VI/VT to communicate; **—se con** (entenderse) to communicate with; (ponerse en contacto con) to reach; (desembocar en) to open into

comunicativo ADJ communicative

comunidad F community; **— internauta** Internet community; **— virtual** virtual community

comunión F communion

comunismo M communism

comunista ADJ & MF communist

comunitario ADJ (en común) communal; **espíritu —** community spirit; **presupuesto —** European Union budget

con PREP with; **— lo que come, tendría que estar obesa** given what she eats, she should be obese; **— mucho** by far; **— que le digas alcanza** just telling him is enough; **— tal [de] que** provided that; **— todo** all things considered

conato M attempt
concavidad F hollow
cóncavo ADJ concave
concebible ADJ conceivable
concebir[9] VT (engendrar) to conceive; (entender) to conceive of
conceder VT (dar) to grant; (admitir) to concede, to allow
concejal MF councilor
concejo M council
concentración F (densidad, atencíon, cantidad) concentration; (manifestación) rally, demonstration
concentrar VT to concentrate; **—se** (prestar atención) to concentrate, to focus; (manifestar) to rally
concepción F conception
concepto M (idea) concept; (artificio) conceit
conceptual ADJ conceptual
concernir[73] VT to concern
concertación F agreement
concertar[1] VT (arreglar) to arrange; (concretar) to finalize; (planear) to concert; **—se** to agree
concesión F (admisión) concession; (otorgamiento) grant; (permiso comercial) franchise
concesionario M dealership
concha F (de molusco) shell; (genitales femeninos) *Am vulg* pussy
conchabarse VI to conspire
conciba, concibe, concibiendo, concibiera, concibiese *ver* concebir
conciencia F (moral) conscience; (mental) consciousness, awareness; **tomar — de** to come to grips with; **— de marca** brand awareness
concienzudo ADJ conscientious, thorough
concierto M (música) concert; (armonía) harmony; (acuerdo) agreement
conciliación F conciliation
conciliar VT (personas) to conciliate; (ideas) to reconcile; **— el sueño** to fall sleep
concilio M council
concisión F conciseness
conciso ADJ concise, brief
conciudadano -na MF fellow citizen
concluir[19] VI/VT to conclude
conclusión F conclusion
concluya, concluye, concluyendo, concluyera, concluyese *ver* concluir
concluyente ADJ conclusive
concomitante ADJ attendant
concordancia F agreement
concordar[5] VI to agree
concordia F concord
concretamente ADV specifically; **tiene un perro, — un chihuahua** he has a dog, a chihuahua, to be precise
concretar VT (cerrar) to finalize; (especificar) to

be specific about; (realizar) to realize; **—se a** to focus on
concreto ADJ concrete; **en —** specifically; M *Am* concrete
concubina F concubine
concurrencia F (reunión) gathering; (asistencia) attendance
concurrido ADJ well-attended
concurrir VI (confluir) to come together; (asistir) to attend
concursante MF contestant
concurso M (para un premio) contest; (en una licitación) call for bids; (para un puesto de trabajo) competitive examination; **— de belleza** beauty pageant
concusión F graft
concusionario -ria MF grafter
condado M county
conde M count
condecoración F decoration
condecorar VT to decorate
condena F (castigo) sentence; (crítica) condemnation; **¡qué —!** what a pain!
condenación F condemnation
condenado ADJ (perdido) damned; (sentenciado) sentenced; **está — a muerte** he's on death row
condenar VT (criticar) to condemn; (sentenciar) to sentence; **eso le condenó al fracaso** that doomed him to failure; **—se** to go to hell
condensación F condensation
condensar VI to condense
condesa F countess
condescendencia F (tolerancia) acquiescence; (superioridad) condescension
condescender[2] VI (acomodarse) to acquiesce; (dignarse) to condescend
condición F condition; **— social** social station; **a — de que** on the condition that; **condiciones** (físicas) condition; (de un contrato) terms, provisos
condicional ADJ & M conditional
condicionamiento M conditioning
condicionar VT to condition
condimentar VT to season
condimento M condiment, seasoning
condiscípulo -la MF classmate
condolencias F PL condolences; **dar las —** to offer one's condolences
condolerse[6] VI to offer one's condolences
condominio M condominium
condón M condom, rubber
cóndor M condor
conducción F (de electricidad) conduction; (de un difunto o prisionero) transport
conducente ADJ conducive
conducir[38] VT (a un grupo) to lead; (una orquesta, electricidad) to conduct; (un coche) to drive, to steer; **—se** to behave

conducta F (moral) conduct, behavior; (biológica) behavior; **— de alto riesgo** high-risk behavior

conducto M (de agua) conduit; (anatómico) duct; **— de aire** airway; **por — de** through

conductor -ora ADJ (de electricidad) conductive; M (de electricidad) conductor; MF (de coches) driver; (en baloncesto) point guard

conductual ADJ behavioral

conduje, condujera, condujese *ver* conducir

conectar VI/VT to connect

conectividad F connectivity

conector M connector; **— en serie** serial connector

conejillo M **— de Indias** guinea pig

conejo M rabbit; (genitales femeninos) *Esp vulg* pussy

conexión F connection

confabulación F collusion

confección F (fabricación de ropa) dressmaking, tailoring; (calidad) workmanship; **de —** ready-made

confeccionar VT (productos) to manufacture; (ropa) to tailor, to sew

confederación F confederation

confederado -da ADJ & MF confederate

confederar VI to form a confederacy

conferencia F (discurso) lecture; (reunión) conference; **— de prensa** press conference; **dar una —** to give a lecture

conferenciante MF lecturer, speaker

conferenciar VI to confer

conferencista MF lecturer, speaker

conferir[8] VT to confer, to bestow; (un título) to confer

confesar[1] VI/VT to confess

confesión F confession

confesionario M confessional

confesor -ora MF confessor

confiabilidad F reliability

confiable ADJ reliable

confiado ADJ (seguro de sí) confident; (crédulo) trusting

confianza F confidence, trust; **en —** in confidence; **tener —** to be confident; **tener — en** to have confidence in; **tomar —s** to be overly familiar with

confianzudo ADJ overfamiliar

confiar[28] VT (un secreto) to confide; (un valor, bien) to entrust; **— en** to rely on; **confío que Dios me proteja** I trust that God will protect me

confidencia F confidence

confidencial ADJ confidential; **altamente —** top-secret

confidente MF (amigo) confidant; M (mueble) love seat

confiesa, confiese *ver* confesar

configuración F configuration

configurar VT to configure (también computadoras); **—se** to take shape

confinamiento M confinement

confinar VT to confine

confines M PL bounds, confines

confirmación F confirmation

confirmar VT to confirm

confiscación F (de una propiedad) confiscation, seizure; (de un monto) forfeiture

confiscar[30] VT to confiscate

confitar VT to candy

confite M candy

confitería F confectionery

confitura F confection

conflictivo ADJ (persona, tema) contentious; (región) volatile

conflicto M conflict

confluencia F (de calles) junction; (de ríos) confluence

conformación F creation, establishment

conformar VT to adapt; **—se** to go along; **—se con** to settle for

conforme ADJ in agreement, content; **— a** in accordance with; CONJ **— amanece** as dawn breaks

conformidad F conformity, agreement; **estar de/en — con** to be in accordance with

conformismo M conformity

confort M comfort

confortable ADJ comfortable

confortar VT to comfort

confraternidad F fraternity, fellowship

confraternizar[47] VI to fraternize

confrontación F confrontation

confrontar VT (a un enemigo) to confront; (dos listas) to compare

confundido ADJ confused, mixed-up

confundir VT to confuse, to perplex, to baffle; **—se** (personas) to become confused; (cosas) to mingle

confusión F (mental) confusion; (de cosas) clutter, disarray

confuso ADJ (que no comprende, desordenado) confused; (difícil de comprender) confusing

congelación F freezing; **— salarial** pay freeze

congelado ADJ frozen

congelador M freezer

congelar VT to freeze

congeniar VI **— con** to get along with

congénito ADJ congenital

congestión F congestion

conglomeración F conglomeration

conglomerado M conglomeration

Congo M Congo

congoja F anguish, grief

congoleño -ña ADJ & MF Congolese

congregación F (feligreses) congregation; (orden) order

congregar[40] VI to congregate
congresista MF (legislador) member of Congress; (asistente a un congreso) conference attendee, conventioneer
congreso M (cuerpo legislativo, edificio) congress; (reunión periódica) conference, convention
congresual ADJ congressional
congruencia F congruence
conífera F conifer
conjetura F conjecture, surmise
conjeturar VT to conjecture, to surmise
conjugación F conjugation
conjugar[40] VT to conjugate
conjunción F conjunction
conjuntamente ADV jointly
conjuntivitis F conjunctivitis, pinkeye
conjunto M (grupo de cosas) set; (totalidad) total, aggregate; (de ropa) outfit; — **musical** ensemble; **en** — as a whole, all told; ADJ joint
conjuración F conspiracy
conjurado-da MF conspirator
conjurar VT (conspirar) to conspire, to plot; (evitar, cancelar) to ward off
conjuro M incantation, spell
conllevar VT to entail, to involve
conmemoración F commemoration
conmemorar VT to commemorate
conmemorativo ADJ commemorative, memorial
conmigo PRON with me
conmiseración F commiseration
conmoción F commotion; — **cerebral** brain concussion, cerebral concussion
conmovedor ADJ moving, touching
conmover[6] VT to move, to touch
conmovido ADJ moved, touched
conmutador M switch
conmutar VT to commute
connatural ADJ inborn
connotación F connotation
cono M cone
conocedor-ora ADJ who know[s], aware; **muy** — **de la situación** well aware of the situation; MF connoisseur, expert
conocer[35] VT to know (también en sentido carnal); (reconocer) to recognize; (tratar por primera vez) to meet; — **el paño** to know the ropes; **se conoce que** it is clear that
conocido-da ADJ well-known; MF acquaintance
conocimiento M knowledge, acquaintance; — **de embarque** bill of lading; **perder el** — to lose consciousness; **poner en** — to inform; —**s** knowledge
conozca, conozco ver conocer
conque CONJ so
conquista F conquest
conquistador-ora MF conqueror; ADJ conquering

conquistar VT (un terreno) to conquer; (el amor de alguien) to win
consabido ADJ habitual
consagración F consecration
consagrar VT (declarar consagrado) to consecrate; (dedicar) to devote
consciente ADJ conscious; — **del problema** aware of the problem
conscribir VT to draft
consecución F attainment, achievement
consecuencia F (hecho que resulta de otro) consequence; (cualidad de consecuente) consistency; **a** — **de** as a result of
consecuente ADJ (que se sigue de) consequent, logical; (fiel en sus actos) consistent
consecutivo ADJ consecutive
conseguible ADJ obtainable
conseguir[12] VT (un derecho) to attain, to get; (un objetivo) to achieve; (un puesto de trabajo) to land, to get; — **hacer algo** to manage to do something
consejero-ra MF (asesor) adviser; (miembro del consejo) board member; **consejero-ra delegado-da** Esp CEO
consejo M (opinión) counsel, advice; (comité) council; — **de guerra** court-martial
consenso M consensus
consentimiento M consent, acquiescence
consentir[8] VT (permitir) to consent to, to acquiesce to; (mimar) to pamper, to indulge; — **en** to permit
conserje MF (limpiador) janitor; (portero) superintendent; (recepcionista) hotel clerk
conserva F canned food; **en** — canned
conservación F conservation, preservation
conservador-ora MF (en política) conservative; (de museo) curator; ADJ (de tradiciones) conservative; (de alimentos) preservative
conservadurismo M conservatism
conservante M preservative
conservar VT (guardar) to keep; (mantener) to retain; (preservar) to preserve; (ahorrar) to conserve
conservatorio M conservatory
considerable ADJ considerable
considerablemente ADV significantly
consideración F consideration; **de** — considerable; **tomar/tener en** — to take into consideration
considerado ADJ considerate, thoughtful
considerar VT to consider
consiga ver conseguir
consigna F (eslogan) motto, watchword; (orden) order
consignación F consignment; **a/en** — on consignment
consignar VT to consign
consignatario-ria MF consignee

consigo PRON with oneself/himself/herself/themselves

consigo, consiguiendo, consiguiera, consiguiese *ver* conseguir

consiguiente ADJ consequent; **por —** consequently

consistencia F consistency

consistente ADJ (firme) consistent; **— de** consisting of

consistir VI **— en** to consist of

consocio -cia MF fellow member

consola F console; **— de juegos** game console

consolación F consolation

consolar[5] VT to console

consolidación F consolidation

consolidar VT to consolidate

consonante ADJ & F consonant

consorcio M consortium

consorte MF consort

conspicuo ADJ conspicuous

conspiración F conspiracy, plot

conspirador -ora MF conspirator, plotter

conspirar VI to conspire, to plot

constancia F (en el amor) constancy; (en el esfuerzo) perseverance; (en el trabajo) steadiness; (prueba) documentary proof

constante ADJ & F constant; **—s vitales** vital signs

constar VI to be stated; **aquí consta que me debes cien dólares** here it states that you owe me a hundred dollars; **— de** to consist of, to be composed of; **hacer —** to mention; **me consta que** I am aware that; **que conste** let it be known

constatar VT to verify

constelación F constellation

consternación F consternation, dismay

consternar VT to dismay

constipación F constipation

constipado ADJ *Esp* (resfriado) suffering from a cold; *Am* (seco de vientre) constipated; M *Esp* head cold

constitución F constitution

constitucional ADJ constitutional

constituir[19] VT to constitute

constitutivo ADJ (constituyente) constituent; (inherente) inherent; **— de un delito** which constitutes a crime

constituya, constituye *ver* constituir

constituyente ADJ constituent

constreñimiento M constraint

constreñir[11] VT (limitar) to constrain; (apretar) to constrict, to constrain

constricción F constriction

construcción F (actividad de construir, cosa construida) construction, building; (gramatical) construction

constructivo ADJ constructive

constructor -ora MF builder; F construction company

construir[19] VI/VT to construct, to build

construye, construyendo, construyera, construyese *ver* construir

consuelo M consolation, comfort, solace

consuetudinario ADJ (acción) habitual; (derecho) common

cónsul MF consul

consulado M consulate

consulta F (acción de consultar) consultation; (pregunta) question; (consultorio) doctor's office

consultar VT to consult; **—lo con la almohada** to sleep on it

consultivo ADJ consultative

consultor ADJ consulting

consultoría F consulting firm

consultorio M doctor's office

consumado ADJ consummate, accomplished

consumar VT to consummate

consumidor -ora MF consumer; ADJ consuming

consumir VT to consume; **—se** (agua) to boil off; (neumático) to wear out; **—se de** to be consumed by

consumismo M consumerism

consumo M consumption

consunción F consumption

contabilidad F accounting, bookkeeping

contable MF accountant, bookkeeper

contactar VI/VT to contact; **—[se] con** to get in contact/touch with

contacto M contact; **— visual** eye contact; **en — con** in touch with

contado M **al —** in cash; ADJ **—s** few

contador -ora ADJ counting; M (de dinero) counter; (de electricidad) meter; **— Geiger** Geiger counter; MF accountant; **— público -ca** CPA

contaduría F accountant's office

contagiar VT to infect

contagio M (de enfermedad) contagion; (de ordenador) infection

contagioso ADJ contagious, catching, infectious

contaminación F (del agua, de la comida) contamination; (del medio ambiente) pollution; **— sonora** noise pollution

contaminante M contaminate

contaminar VT (agua, alimentos, cultura) to contaminate; (el medio ambiente) to pollute; **—se** (agua) to become contaminated; (medio ambiente) to become polluted

contar[5] VI/VT (medir una cantidad) to count; (decir historias) to tell; **el hotel cuenta con una piscina** the hotel has a swimming pool; **cuento con mi hermano** I count on my brother; **esto no cuenta** this doesn't count; **¿me lo vas a contar a mí?** you can say that again; **tienes que — el tiempo** you have to

watch the time; M SG **cuentakilómetros**
(marcador de kilómetros) odometer;
(velocímetro) speedometer
contemplación F contemplation
contemplar VT (mirar, tener en cuenta) to
contemplate; (consentir) to spoil; VI to
contemplate
contemporáneo ADJ contemporary
contención F containment
contender[2] VI to contend
contendrá, contendría ver contener
contenedor M container
contenedorizar VT containerize
contener[58] VT (un líquido) to contain; (risa,
lágrimas) to hold back; (entusiasmo) to
restrain; (el aliento) to hold
contenga, contengo ver contener
contenido ADJ restrained; M content[s]
contentar VT to satisfy; **—se** to be satisfied
contento ADJ (conforme) content, contented;
(feliz) happy; M contentment
conteo M count
contera F (de paraguas) tip; (de bolígrafo) cap
contestación F answer, reply
contestador M answering machine
contestar VT to answer; VI to talk back, to
mouth off
contexto M context
contextura F (de un objeto) makeup; (de
persona) build
contienda F (guerra) conflict; (encuentro
deportivo) competition
contiene, contienes ver contener
contigo PRON with you
contiguo ADJ contiguous; **estar — a** to adjoin
continental ADJ continental
continente M (masa geográfica) continent;
(opuesto a isla) mainland; ADJ continent
contingencia F contingency
contingente ADJ & M contingent
continuación F (de una acción) continuation;
(de una película) sequel; (tenis)
follow-through; **a —** after that; **a — hubo
una guerra** there ensued a war
continuado ADJ continuing
continuar[26] VI/VT to continue
continuidad F continuity
continuo ADJ (ininterrumpido) continuous;
(repetido) continual
contonearse VI (mujer) to swing one's hips;
(hombre) to swagger
contoneo M (de mujer) swinging of the hips; (de
hombre) swagger
contorno M (forma) outline, contour; (tamaño
de árbol, persona) girth
contorsión F contortion
contra PREP against; M **los pro y los —** the pros
and cons; **en —** against; F drawback; **llevarle
la — a alguien** to contradict someone

contraatacar[30] VI/VT to counterattack
contraataque M (militar) counterattack; (en
baloncesto) fast break
contrabajo M double bass; MF double bass
player
contrabandear VI/VT to smuggle
contrabandista MF smuggler
contrabando M (actividad) smuggling;
(mercancías) contraband; **hacer —** to
smuggle
contracción F contraction
contrachapado M plywood
contractual ADJ contractual
contracultura F counterculture
contradecir[53, 74] VT to contradict
contradicción F contradiction
contradictorio ADJ contradictory
contraejemplo M counterexample
contraer[59] VT (enfermedad) to contract;
(derechos) to limit; (deudas) to incur; **—
matrimonio** to get married
contraespionaje M counterespionage
contrafuerte M (de muro) buttress; (de zapato)
counter
contrahecho ADJ deformed
contralor M (control) comptroller, controller;
(auditor) auditor
contralto M (voz) alto; MF (persona) alto
contramandar VT to countermand
contramedida F countermeasure
contraoferta F counteroffer
contraorden F countermand
contrapartida F compensation
contrapelo LOC ADV **a —** against the grain
contrapesar VT to counterbalance
contrapeso M counterbalance
contraproducente ADJ counterproductive
contrariar[28] VT to annoy; **—se** to get annoyed
contrariedad F (fastidio) annoyance;
(dificultad) snag
contrario ADJ (opuesto) opposite; (discrepante)
conflicting; **al —** on the contrary; **de lo —**
otherwise; **llevar la contraria** to be
contrary; **por el —** on the contrary; **soy — al
doblaje de películas** I'm against the
dubbing of films; **todo lo —** just the opposite
contrarrestar VT to counteract
contrarrevolución F counterrevolution
contraseña F password, watchword
contrastar VI/VT to contrast
contraste M contrast
contrata F contract
contratación F hiring; **— externa** outsourcing
contratar VT (a un empleado) to hire; (un
servicio) to contract for; **—se** to be hired; **— y
despedir** hire and fire
contratiempo M mishap
contratista MF contractor, builder
contrato M contract; **— de alquiler** rental

agreement; **por** — by contract
contravenir[61] VT to contravene
contraventana F shutter
contribución F (regalo, participación) contribution; (impuesto) tax; — **alternativa mínima** alternative minimum tax
contribuir[19] VT to contribute
contribuya, contribuye, contribuyendo, contribuyera, contribuyese *ver* contribuir
contribuyente MF taxpayer
contrincante MF opponent
contrito ADJ contrite
control M (dominio, dirección) control; (contralor médico) checkup; (vigilancia) check; (puesto) checkpoint; — **de calidad** quality control; — **de daños** damage control; — **de la natalidad** birth control; — **fronterizo** border control; — **paternal** parental control; — **remoto** remote control; **bajo** — under control
controlador -ora MF comptroller; M driver; — **de impresora** printer driver
controlar VT (restringir) to control; (vigilar) to check on
controversia F controversy
controvertido ADJ controversial
contumacia F obstinacy
contumaz ADJ stubborn
contundente ADJ (argumento) forceful; (objeto) blunt; (prueba) convincing; (victoria) resounding
contusión F bruise, contusion
contuve, contuviera, contuviese *ver* contener
convalecencia F convalescence
convalecer[35] VI to convalesce
convaleciente MF convalescent
convección F convection
convencer[32] VT (por lógica) to convince; (por insistencia) to persuade
convencimiento M (creencia) conviction; (acción) convincing
convención F convention
convencional ADJ conventional
convendrá, convendría, convenga, convengo *ver* convenir
convenido ADJ agreed-upon
conveniencia F (algo cómodo) convenience; (algo aconsejable) desirability; **a su** — at your convenience
conveniente ADJ (cómodo) convenient; (aconsejable) advisable
convenio M agreement; — **colectivo** collective bargaining; — **comercial** business agreement
convenir[61] VI (ser apropiado) to be suitable; (llegar a un acuerdo) to agree
convento M convent

convergencia F convergence
converger[45] VI to converge
conversación F conversation; **trabar** — **con** to engage in a conversation with
conversar VI to converse
conversión F conversion; — **de dos puntos** two-point conversion
converso -sa MF convert
convertible ADJ convertible
convertidor M converter
convertir[8] VT to convert; —**se en** to become
convexo ADJ convex
convicción F conviction
convicto -ta ADJ convicted; MF convict
convidar VT to invite; *Am* to offer
convierta, convierte *ver* convertir
convincente ADJ convincing, compelling
convine, conviniendo, conviniera, conviniese *ver* convenir
convirtiendo, convirtiera, convirtiese *ver* convertir
convite M (invitación) invitation; (banquete) banquet
convivencia F (coexistencia) coexistence; (cohabitación) cohabitation, living together
convivir VI (coexistir) to coexist; (cohabitar) to cohabitate, to live together
convocación F convocation
convocar[30] VT to convoke, to call together; (una reunión, un concurso) to convene
convocatoria F (anuncio) announcement; (llamamiento) call
convoy M convoy
convoyar VT to convoy
convulsión F convulsion
conyugal ADJ conjugal, marital
cónyuge MF spouse
coñac M cognac, brandy
coñazo M (molestia) *vulg* pain in the butt
coño M *vulg* pussy, cunt; **en el quinto** — in the boondocks; INTERJ *fam* damn!
cooperación F cooperation
cooperar VI to cooperate
cooperativa F cooperative, co-op
cooperativista MF member of a cooperative
cooperativo ADJ cooperative
coordenada F coordinate
coordinación F coordination
coordinado ADJ coordinate
coordinador -ora MF coordinator; ADJ coordinating
coordinar VT to coordinate
copa F (vaso) goblet, wineglass; (de árbol) top; (de sombrero) crown; (palo de la baraja) card in the suit of *copas*; (trofeo, parte de un sujetador) cup; **ir de** —**s** to go for a drink; — **del Mundo** World Cup
copago M copayment
copete M (de pelo) tuft; (de plumas) crest; **estar**

hasta el — to be fed up
copia F (réplica) copy; (de foto) print; — **de respaldo** backup copy; — **de respaldo automático** automatic backup copy; — **de seguridad** backup copy; — **en papel** hard copy; — **impresa** hard copy
copiadora F copy machine
copiar VT (reproducir) to copy; (en un examen) to cheat
copión -ona MF copycat
copioso ADJ copious, plentiful
copla F (canción) popular song; (estrofa) stanza
copo M (de nieve) snowflake; (de lana, algodón) wad; —**s de maíz** cornflakes
copropietario -ria MF joint owner
coprotagonista MF costar
cópula F (acto sexual) coupling, mating; (verbo) copula
copulación F copulation
copular VI to copulate
copyright M copyright
coque M coke
coqueta F (mujer) coquette; (mueble) dressing table
coquetear VI to flirt, to dally
coquetería F flirtation
coqueto ADJ flirtatious
coraje M (valentía) courage; (enojo) anger
coral M (marino) coral; (musical) chorale
coralino ADJ coral
coraza F armor
corazón M (órgano) heart; (de manzana) core; (vocativo) honey; **con el — en la boca** (cansado) really tired; (nervioso) on edge; **de buen** — kindhearted; **de todo** — wholeheartedly; **romperle el — a alguien** to break someone's heart
corazonada F hunch
corbata F necktie, tie, cravat
corcel M charger, steed
corchea F eighth note; — **con puntillo** dotted eighth note
corchete M (en costura) hook and eye; (paréntesis recto) square bracket; (llave) brace
corcho M (para botella) cork; (para pescar) float
corcova F hump, hunchback
corcovear VI to buck
cordaje M strings
cordel M string
cordero M (animal) lamb; (piel, cuero) lambskin
cordial ADJ cordial
cordillera F mountain range
cordobés -esa ADJ from Cordoba; MF person from Cordoba
cordón M (cinta) cord; (al borde de la calle) *Am* curb; — **de apertura** ripcord; — **de zapatos** shoelace, shoestring; — **policial** police cordon; — **umbilical** umbilical cord
cordoncillo M ridge, rib

cordura F sanity
Corea F Korea; — **del Norte** North Korea; — **del Sur** South Korea
coreano -na ADJ & MF Korean
corear VI/VT to chant
coreografía F choreography
cornada F goring
cornear VT to gore
corneja F crow
córner M corner kick
corneta F cornet; MF bugler
cornisa F cornice, ledge
corno M horn; — **francés** French horn
cornudo ADJ horned; M cuckold
coro M (cantantes) choir, chorus; (música) chorus; (parte de la iglesia) loft; **cantar a** — to sing in unison
corolario M corollary
corona F crown
coronación F coronation
coronar VT to crown
coronario ADJ coronary
coronel M colonel
coronilla F crown of the head; **estar hasta la** — to be fed up
corpiño M (almilla) bodice; (sujetador) *Am* bra
corporación F guild
corporal ADJ corporal, bodily
corporativo ADJ corporate
corpus M corpus
corpúsculo M corpuscle
corral M (de granja) barnyard, farmyard; (para ganado) corral, pen
correa F (de cuero) leather strap; (de ventilador) belt; (de perro) leash
corrección F (acción de corregir) correction; (cualidad de correcto) correctness
correctamente ADV correctly, properly
correcto ADJ (apropiado) correct, proper; (acertado) right
corrector -ora MF editor; — **de pruebas** proofreader
corredizo ADJ sliding
corredor -ora ADJ running; MF (persona que corre, también en deportes) runner; (deportista automovilístico, ciclista) racer; (intermediario) broker, agent; M (pasillo) hallway, corridor
correduría F brokerage
corregir[14] VT (errores) to correct; (exámenes) to grade; —**se** (en lo moral) to mend one's ways; (en los errores) to correct oneself
correlación F correlation
correlacionar VT to correlate
correlato M correlate
correo M mail; (edificio) post office; — **aéreo** air mail; — **certificado** certified mail; — **de voz** voice mail; — **electrónico** e-mail; —

electrónico basura junk e-mail, spam;
echar al — to mail
correoso ADJ tough
correr VI (persona, agua, calle) to run; (coche) to
go fast; (una puerta) to slide; (dinero, tiempo)
to pass; **— con los gastos** to take on the
costs; VT (una cortina) to draw; (una carrera,
un riesgo) to run; **—se** (moverse) to scoot
over; (desteñir) to run, to bleed; (manchar) to
smear; (tener orgasmo) *Esp fam* to come
correría F foray
correspondencia F correspondence
corresponder VI (ser adecuado, estar en
consonancia) to correspond; (pertenecer) to
belong; VT (amor, favores) to reciprocate; **a
mí me corresponde llamarla** it's up to me
to call her, it behooves me to call her
correspondiente ADJ corresponding; MF
correspondent
corresponsal MF correspondent
corretaje M broker's/agent's commission
corretear VI to run around
corrida F (acción de correr) running;
(competición) race; (orgasmo) *Esp* orgasm;
(de banco) run; **— de toros** bullfight; **de —**
without stopping
corrido ADJ (experimentado) worldly;
(continuo) uninterrupted; **de —** without
stopping; M ballad
corriente ADJ (que corre) running; (común)
usual; (franco) frank; **el — mes** the current
month; **estar al —** to be up to date; F (de
agua, electricidad) current; (de dinero) flow;
(de pesimismo) wave; (de aire) draft; (de
computadora) streaming; **— alterna**
alternating current; **— continua** direct
current; **— del Golfo** Gulf Stream; **al —** in
the loop; **dejarse llevar por la —** to
conform; **llevarle la — a alguien** to humor
someone
**corrija, corrijo, corrigiendo, corrigiera,
corrigiese, corrigió** *ver* corregir
corrillo M group of gossips
corro M circle of people
corroborar VT to corroborate
corroer[73] VT to corrode
corromper VT (a una persona) to corrupt; (un
alimento) to rot; **—se** (una persona) to
become corrupt; (un alimento) to rot
corrompido ADJ corrupt
corrosión F corrosion
corrupción F corruption
corrupto ADJ corrupt
corsé M corset
cortada F shortcut
cortado ADJ (abreviado, sucinto) clipped;
(tímido) shy; M (café) coffee with some milk;
(desnivel) slope; (tenis) backspin, slice
cortador -ora MF (persona) cutter; F (aparato)

cutter; **cortadora de césped** lawn mower
cortadura M cut
cortante ADJ (comentario, instrumento)
cutting; (frío, viento) biting; (tono,
instrumento) sharp
cortar VT to cut (también un texto digital); (un
vestido, el uso de algo) to cut out; (a un
locutor, una rama, el gas) to cut off; (un árbol)
to cut down; (las uñas) to clip; (el césped) to
mow; **— el paso** to block; **— por lo sano** to
take drastic action; M SG **cortacésped** lawn
mower; M SG **cortacircuitos** circuit
breaker; M SG **cortafuego** fire line; M SG
cortafuegos firewall; M SG **cortapapeles**
paper cutter; M SG **cortaplumas** penknife;
M SG **cortauñas** nail clipper; VI (el frío) to
bite; (la piel) to crack; **—se** (lastimarse) to cut
oneself; (intimidarse) to be intimidated;
(cuajarse) to curdle, to sour; **—se el pelo** to
get a haircut; **— y pegar** cut and paste
corte M (de un traje, herida) cut; (acción de
cortar) cutting; (de televisión) commercial
break; (estilo) style; **— de pelo** haircut; **—
transversal** cross section; **— y confección**
dressmaking; **eso me da —** that embarrasses
me; F (real, judicial) court; (séquito) retinue;
las —s Spanish parliament; **hacer la —** to
court
cortedad F shortness
cortejar VT to court, to woo
cortejo M (séquito) entourage; (acción de
cortejar) courtship
cortés ADJ courteous, polite
cortesano -na MF courtier
cortesía F courtesy, politeness
córtex M cortex
corteza F (de árbol) bark; (de pan, de la Tierra)
crust; (de queso, fruta) rind; **— cerebral**
cerebral cortex
corticoesteroide M corticosteriod
cortijo M country house
cortina F (de ventana) curtain; (de lluvia) sheet;
— de humo smoke screen
cortisona F cortisone
corto ADJ (breve) short; (tonto) short on brains;
(encogido) bashful; **— de vista**
short-sighted; **a — plazo** in the short run, in
the short term; **quedarse —** to come up
short; **vestirse de —** to wear a short dress; M
short [film]; M **—circuito** short circuit
cosa F thing; **como quien no quiere la —**
without realizing it; **como si tal —** as cool as
a cucumber; **¡cómo son las —s!** what a
surprise; **decir una — por otra** to tell a lie;
esperamos — de cinco minutos we
waited about five minutes; **las —s como son**
let's be honest; **las —s de la vida** that's life;
no es gran — it's no big deal; **otra —**
something else

cosecha F crop, harvest; **de su** — of his invention; **vino** — **1975** wine of 1975 vintage

cosechadora F combine

cosechar VT (cultivos) to harvest; (resultados) to reap

coser VI/VT to sew

cosignatario -ria MF cosigner

cosmético ADJ & M cosmetic

cósmico ADJ cosmic

cosmología F cosmology

cosmonauta MF cosmonaut

cosmopolita ADJ cosmopolitan

cosmos M cosmos

cosmovisión F worldview

coso M doodad

cosquillas F **hacer** — to tickle; **tener** — to be ticklish

cosquillear VT to tickle

cosquilleo M tickle

cosquilloso ADJ ticklish

costa F (del mar) coast, shore; **a toda** — at all costs; —**s** costs

Costa de Marfil F Ivory Coast

costado M side; **al** — alongside; **de** — edgewise; **por los cuatro** —**s** from all sides

costal M sack

costanero ADJ coastal

costar[5] VI/VT to cost; — **trabajo** to be difficult; — **un dineral** to cost a fortune; — **un ojo de la cara** to cost an arm and a leg

Costa Rica F Costa Rica

costarricense, costarriqueño -ña ADJ & MF Costa Rican

coste M cost; — **de [la] vida** cost of living; **al** — at cost

costear VT to defray costs; VI to sail along the coast

costero ADJ coastal

costilla F rib; **lo hizo a** —**s de su padre** he did it at his father's expense

costo M cost; — **adicional** added cost, extra cost; — **de [la] vida** cost of living; **al** — at cost; — **de mantenimiento** maintenance cost; — **de operación** operating cost

costoso ADJ costly

costra F (de pan) crust; (de herida) scab

costroso ADJ (pan) crusty; (heridas) scabby

costumbre F (hábito) habit; (tradición) custom; **de** — habitual; **tener la** — **de** to have the habit of; **está más cansado que de** — he's especially tired today

costura F (acción de coser) sewing; (línea de puntadas) stitching; (unión de dos piezas) seam; **alta** — high fashion, haute couture

costurero -ra M (caja) sewing box; (sastre) tailor; F seamstress

costurón M (puntada) large stitch; (cicatriz) large scar

cota F (nivel del agua) height above sea level; (estándar) benchmark

cotejar VT to check against

cotejo M comparison

cotidiano ADJ everyday

cotización F price quote, price quotation

cotizar[47] VT to quote

coto M — **de caza** game preserve; **poner** — **a** to put an end to

cotorra F (loro) parrot; (persona) chatterbox

cotorrear VI to chatter

covacha F small cave

coyote M coyote

coyuntura F (articulación) joint; (situación) juncture; **aprovechar la** — to take advantage of the situation

coz F kick; **dar coces** to kick

crack M (cocaína) crack; (deportista) ace

cráneo M cranium, skull

craso ADJ crass

cráter M crater

crayola® F crayon

creación F creation

creacionismo M creationism

creador -ora MF creator; ADJ creative

crear VI/VT to create

creatividad F creativity

creativo ADJ creative

crecer[35] VI (un niño) to grow; (masa, río) to rise; (madera, mar) to swell; (la luna) to wax

crecida F rise of a river

crecido ADJ (adulto) grown; (grande) large; (demasiado alto) overgrown

creciente ADJ (que crece) growing; (luna) crescent; M (luna) crescent; (marea) high tide; (de un río) flood

crecimiento M growth

credencial F credential

credibilidad F credibility

crédito M (solvencia, unidad de estudios) credit; (hecho de creer) credence; (fama) reputation; (préstamo) loan; — **al consumidor** consumer credit; — **rotativo** revolving credit; **dar** — **a** to believe; —**s** film credits; **vender a** — to sell on credit

credo M creed

crédulo ADJ credulous, gullible

creencia F belief

creer[18] VI/VT (tomar como cierto) to believe; (opinar) to think, to feel; —**se** to fall for; **¿quién se cree que es?** who does he think he is? **se cree artista** he fancies himself an artist; **¡ya lo creo!** I should say so!

creíble ADJ credible, believable

crema F cream (también cosmético); — **de espárragos** cream of asparagus; — **para [los] labios** lip balm, Chapstick®

cremallera F (de coche) rack; (de prenda) zipper; — **y piñón** rack and pinion

cremar VT to cremate

cremoso ADJ creamy
creosota F creosote
crepitación F crackle
crepitar VI to crackle
crepúsculo M twilight
crespo ADJ wiry, kinky
crespón M crepe
cresta F (de ola, montaña) crest; (de ave) tuft; (de gallo) comb
creyendo, creyera, creyese, creyó ver creer
creyente MF believer; ADJ believing
crezca, crezco ver crecer
cría F (acción de criar) breeding; (camada) litter; (animal joven) young
criada ver criado
criadero M — **de peces** hatchery; — **de pollos** chicken farm
criado -da MF servant; F maid
criador -ora MF breeder
crianza F (de animales) breeding; (de hijos) upbringing; (modales) manners
criar[28] VT (animales) to breed; (hijos) to bring up, to rear, to raise; **estar criando malvas** fam to be pushing up daisies; —**se** to grow up
criatura F (ser extraño) creature; (bebé) baby
criba F sieve
cribar VT to sift
crimen M (delito grave) serious crime, felony; (asesinato) murder; — **de guerra** war crime
criminal ADJ & MF criminal
criminalidad F serious crime
crin F mane
criogénico ADJ cryogenic
criollo ADJ (nacido en América) born in Spanish America; (tradicionalmente americano) traditionally Spanish American; M (lengua) creole
críquet M cricket
crisálida F chrysalis
crisantemo M chrysanthemum
crisis F crisis; — **de la edad madura** midlife crisis
crisma F crown of the head
crisol M crucible, melting pot
crisparse VI (un músculo) to contract; (los puños) to clench; (los nervios) to be on edge
cristal M (mineral, vidrio fino) crystal; (vidrio de ventana) Esp glass, pane; (lente) lens; — **labrado** cut glass
cristalería F (objetos) glassware; (establecimiento) glassware store; (fábrica) glassworks
cristalino ADJ (de cristal) crystalline; (transparente) crystal-clear; M lens of the eye
cristalizar[47] VI/VT to crystallize
cristiandad F Christendom
cristianismo M Christianity
cristiano -na ADJ & MF Christian; **hablar en** — (claramente) to speak clearly; (español) to speak Spanish
criterio M criterion
crítica F criticism; (de un libro) review
criticar[30] VT to criticize
crítico -ca ADJ critical; MF critic; (de un libro) reviewer
criticón -ona ADJ critical; MF faultfinder
Croacia F Croatia
croar VI to croak
croata ADJ & MF Croatian
crocante ADJ crisp, crunchy
croché, crochet M crochet; **hacer** — to crochet
croissant M croissant
crol M (estilo de natación) crawl, freestyle
cromado ADJ chroming
cromo M chromium, chrome
cromosoma M chromosome
crónica F (narración de eventos) chronicle; (reportaje) feature; — **policial** police report
crónico ADJ chronic
cronista MF (deportivo) reporter; (histórico) chronicler
cronología F chronology
cronológico ADJ chronological
cronometrador -ora MF timer, timekeeper
cronometraje M timing
cronometrar VT to time
cronómetro M chronometer, stopwatch
croquet M croquet
croquis M rough sketch
cross M cross-country race
cruasán M croissant
cruce M (acción, lugar) crossing; (de dos calles) crossroads, intersection; (de razas) crossbreeding; (de palabras) blend; (animal híbrido) cross; — **peatonal** crosswalk
crucero M (buque de guerra) cruiser; (viaje de placer) cruise
cruceta F crosspiece
crucial ADJ crucial
crucificar[30] VT to crucify
crucifijo M crucifix
crucigrama M crossword puzzle
crudo ADJ (comida, seda) raw; (tiempo, invierno, imágenes) harsh; (petróleo, lenguaje) crude; **agua cruda** hard water; **color** — yellowish white
cruel ADJ cruel, mean
crueldad F cruelty, meanness
cruento ADJ grisly, gruesome
crujido M (de puerta, piso) creak; (de un tallo al quebrarse) crack; (de hojas) rustle; (de un fuego) crackle
crujiente ADJ (manzana, tocino) crisp, crispy; (nueces) crunchy
crujir VI (puerta, piso) to creak; (dientes) to grate; (hojas) to rustle; (nueces) to crunch; (fuego) to crackle
cruz F (cristiana) cross; (de moneda) tails;

hacerse cruces to dread
cruzada F crusade
cruzado M (soldado) crusader; ADJ (tenis) crosscourt; (boxeo) cross; (traje) double-breasted
cruzamiento M (de piernas, razas) crossing; (de calles) crossroads; (de razas) cross
cruzar[47] VT (la calle) to cross; (un cheque) to write across; **—le la cara a alguien** to backhand someone's face; **cruzo los dedos** I'll keep my fingers crossed; **—se con alguien** to bump into someone; **—se de brazos** to fold one's arms; **se me cruzó un ciervo** a deer crossed in front of me
cuaderno M notebook; **— de bitácora** logbook; **— de espiral** spiral notebook
cuadra F (establo) stable; (distancia) *Am* block
cuadrado ADJ square; **estar —** to be fat; M square; **es |un| —** he's a square; **dos al —** two squared; **elevar al —** to square
cuadrangular ADJ (geometría) quadrangular; M (béisbol) home run
cuadrar VT (estar en ángulo recto) to square; VI (corresponder) to fit; (ser conveniente) to be convenient; (ser iguales) to balance, to add up; **— con** to be in agreement with
cuadricular VT to divide into squares
cuadrilátero ADJ quadrilateral; M (en boxeo) ring; (polígono) quadrilateral
cuadrilla F (de ladrones) gang; (de obreros) crew; (baile) square dance
cuadro M (cuadrado) square; (pintura) picture; (de bicicleta) frame; (de jardín) bed; (en tela) checker; (de fútbol) team; **— clínico** symptoms; **— interior** (béisbol) infield; **— sinóptico** summary table; **a/de —s** checked
cuadrúpedo ADJ & M quadruped
cuajada F curd
cuajar VI (leche) to curdle; (queso, cemento) to set; (gelatina) to jell; (un grupo, una organización) to come about; **—se** to curdle; **la cosa no cuajó** that didn't pan out
cuajarón M clot
cual PRON REL which; **el/la —** (cosa) which; (persona) who; **lo —** which; **sea — sea** whichever it may be; ADV like; **— hoja al viento** like a leaf in the wind
cuál PRON INTERR which; **¿cuáles son los tuyos?** which ones are yours?
cualidad F quality, trait
cualitativo ADJ qualitative
cualquiera ADJ INDEF any; **de cualquier manera/forma** anyhow; **en cualquier lado** anywhere; PRON INDEF (cosa) any; (persona) anyone; **— que sea su nacionalidad** whatever his nationality may be; **— que elijas** whichever one you choose; **— podría hacer eso** anyone could do that
cuando ADV REL when; **— menos** at least; **—**

mucho at most; **se rompió — lo usaba** it broke while she was using it; PREP **— la guerra** during the war
cuándo ADV INTERR & PRON when
cuantía F (cantidad) quantity; (importancia) importance
cuántico ADJ quantum
cuantificar[30] VT to quantify
cuantioso ADJ considerable
cuantitativo ADJ quantitative
cuanto ADJ REL any; **lee — libro ve** she reads any book she sees; PRON REL **unos —s** a few; CONJ **hice — pude** I did as much as I could; ADV **— antes** as soon as possible; **— más trabajo, menos consigo** the more I work, the less I accomplish; **en —** as soon as possible; **en — a** regarding; **en — que** as
cuánto ADJ, ADV & PRON INTERR (dinero, agua) how much; (personas, libros) how many; **¿cada —?** how often? **¿— piensas quedarte?** how long do you plan to stay?
cuarenta NUM forty; **cantarle las — a alguien** to bawl someone out; **— iguales** (tenis) deuce
cuarentena F quarantine; **una — de libros** forty-odd books
cuarentón -ona MF person in his or her forties
cuaresma F Lent
cuarta F (marcha) fourth gear; (palmo) span of a hand
cuartear VT (una res) to quarter; (los labios) to chap; **—se** to chap
cuartel M barracks; **— general** headquarters; **no dar —** to give no quarter
cuartelada F military coup
cuartelazo M military coup
cuarteto M quartet
cuartilla F sheet of paper
cuarto ADJ one-fourth, quarter; M (habitación) room; (cantidad) quarter, one-fourth; **— de baño** bathroom; **— de estar** living room; **— de final** quarter finals; **— oscuro** darkroom; **¡ni que ocho —s!** no way! **tres —s** three-fourths
cuarzo M quartz
cuásar M quasar
cuate M *Méx* pal, buddy
cuatrero -ra MF cattle rustler
cuatrillizo -za MF quadruplet
cuatro NUM four; **— ojos** four-eyes; **más de — ** a good number
cuba F (barril) cask, barrel; (tina) tub, vat
Cuba F Cuba
cubano -na ADJ & MF Cuban
cubeta F (recipiente rectangular) tray; (balde) pail; **— de hielo** ice tray
cúbico ADJ cubic
cubículo M cubicle
cubierta F (de libro) cover; (cosa para cubrir)

covering; (neumático) tire; (de buque) deck

cubierto M place setting; — **de plata** silverware; **a** — sheltered

cubierto *ver* cubrir

cubismo M cubism

cúbito M ulna

cubo M (cuerpo geométrico, tercera potencia) cube; (balde) bucket; (de rueda) hub; (juguete) building block; — **de basura** trash can

cubrir[74] VT (con una manta) to cover; (con carteles) to plaster; (una vacante) to fill; (con pintura) to coat; (con crema batida) to smother; (de niebla) to shroud; —**se** (nublarse) to fog up; (ponerse el sombrero) to put on one's hat

cucaracha F cockroach

cuchara F (cubierto) spoon; (de excavadora) bucket; (para helado) scoop; — **sopera** soup spoon; **meter la** — to butt in

cucharada F (lo que cabe en una cuchara) spoonful; (medida) tablespoonful; (de helado) dip

cucharadita F teaspoonful

cucharear VT to spoon

cucharita F teaspoon

cucharón M (para helado) scoop, dipper; (para sopa) ladle

cuchichear VI/VT to whisper

cuchicheo M whisper

cuchilla F (cuchillo grande) large knife, cleaver; (de afeitar, de licuadora) blade; (de patín) runner

cuchillada F (golpe) stab, slash; (herida) stab wound, gash

cuchillería F (conjunto de cuchillos) cutlery; (tienda) cutlery store

cuchillo M knife; **pasar a** — to kill with a knife

cuclillas LOC ADV **en** — squatting; **sentarse en** — to squat

cuclillo M cuckoo

cuco ADJ cute

cucú INTERJ cuckoo

cucurucho M (de papel) paper cone; (para helado) ice-cream cone; (capirote) hood

cuelga, cuelgue *ver* colgar

cuello M (del cuerpo) neck; (de una prenda) collar; — **de botella** bottleneck; — **uterino** cervix; — **vuelto** turtleneck; **estoy hasta el** — **en deudas** I'm up to my neck in debts

cuenca F (de un río) basin; (del ojo) eye socket

cuenco M earthen bowl

cuenta F (cálculo) count, calculation; (factura) bill, check; (relación de ingresos y gastos) account; (bolita) bead; (depósito bancario) bank account; — **conjunta** joint account; — **corriente** checking account; — **de ahorros** savings account; — **de contrapartida** contra account; — **de crédito** charge account; — **de depósito en garantía** charge account; — **de gastos** expense account; — **de mercado monetario** escrow account; — **en un paraíso fiscal** offshore account; —**s por/a cobrar** accounts receivable; —**s por/a pagar** accounts payable; — **regresiva/atrás** countdown; **abrir/cerrar una** — to open/close an account; **a fin de** —**s** when all is said and done; **ajustar** —**s** to settle old scores; **caí en [la]** — **de que** it just dawned on me that; **dar** — **de** to finish off; **dar** —**s** to give an accounting; **darse** — to realize; **en** — **de margen** on margin; **en resumidas** —**s** in short; **eso corre por mí** — that is my responsibility; **habida** — **de** bearing in mind; **más de la** — more than necessary; **pasar la** — to call in a favor; **tomar/tener en** — to take into account; **trabajar por** — **propia** to freelance; M SG **cuentagotas** eyedropper

cuenta, cuente *ver* contar

cuento M story, tale; — **chino** tall tale; — **de hadas** fairy tale; — **de nunca acabar** never-ending story; **déjese de** —**s** come to the point; **traer a** — to bring up; **venir a** — to be to the point

cuerda F (soga) cord, rope; (de arco) bowstring; (de guitarra) string; (de reloj) spring; — **floja** tightrope; —**s vocales** vocal cords; **bajo** — under the table; **contra las** —**s** on the ropes; **dar** — **a** to wind; **no le des** — don't get him started

cuerdo ADJ sane

cuerno M horn (también instrumento de viento); (de caracol) feeler; (de ciervo) antler; — **de la abundancia** horn of plenty; **coger el toro por los** —**s** to take the bull by the horns; **irse al** — *vulg* to go to hell; **poner** —**s a** to be unfaithful to

cuero M (piel de animal) hide; (piel curtida) leather; — **cabelludo** scalp; **en** —**s** naked

cuerpo M body; (torso) torso; **¡** — **a tierra!** hit the deck! — **de bomberos** fire department; — **de policía** police force; — **de prensa** press corps; — **docente** teaching staff; **a** — **de rey** in great luxury; — **extraño** foreign body; **dar** — **a** to flesh out; **de** — **entero** through and through; **ganó por tres** —**s ventaja** he won by three lengths; **ir de** — to have a bowel movement

cuervo M crow, raven

cuesta F slope; — **abajo** downhill; — **arriba** uphill; **a** —**s** piggyback

cuesta, cueste *ver* costar

cuestión F question; **en** — **de segundos** in a matter of seconds; **poner en** — to question; **ser** — **de** to be a matter of

cuestionable ADJ questionable

cuestionador ADJ questioning

cuestionar VT to question
cuestionario M questionnaire
cueva F cave
cuidado M (atención) care; (preocupación) worry; — **con el perro** beware of the dog; — **de la casa** housekeeping; — **dental** dental care; — **posparto** postnatal care; — **prenatal** prenatal care; — **terminal** end-of-life care; **al** — **de** under the care of; **con** — carefully; **eso me trae sin** — I don't care about that; **tener** — to be careful; **un enfermo de** — a severely ill patient; INTERJ look out!
cuidador -ora MF caregiver, caretaker
cuidadoso ADJ careful
cuidar VT to take care of, to look after; — **de** to take care of; — **la casa** to keep house; — **niños** to babysit; —**se de** to beware of
culata F (anca) haunch; (de rifle) butt; (de motor) cylinder head
culatazo M (golpe) blow with the butt of a rifle; (rebote al disparar) recoil
culear VI/VT *Am vulg* to fuck, to screw
culebra F snake
culebrear VI to slither
culebrilla F shingles
culinario ADJ culinary
culminación F (de carrera, ceremonia) culmination, high point; (de un sueño) fulfillment
culminante ADJ climactic
culminar VI to culminate
culo M (trasero) *vulg* ass, butt; (ano) anus; — **de botella** bottle bottom; — **del mundo** boondocks; — **veo,** — **quiero** I want everything I see; **caerse de** — (desplomarse) to fall on one's butt; (sorprenderse) to be astounded; **dar por el** — (fastidiar) to bother; (sodomizar) to sodomize; **nacer de** — to be lucky; **lamer** —**s** *fam* to suck up to someone, *vulg* to brown-nose; **rascarse el** — *vulg* to fart around; **romperse el** — *vulg* to bust one's ass
culpa F (responsabilidad) fault, blame; (sentimiento) guilt; **echar la** — **a** to blame; **por** — **de** because of; **tener la** — to be to blame
culpabilidad F guilt
culpable ADJ guilty; MF culprit
culpar VT to blame
cultivable ADJ (planta) cultivable; (tierra) arable
cultivado ADJ (tierra) cultivated; (perlas, persona) cultured
cultivador -ora MF (persona) cultivator; F (aparato) cultivator
cultivar VT (cosecha) to grow, to raise; (la tierra) to farm; (relaciones, inteligencia) to cultivate; (microbios) to culture
cultivo M (de plantas) growing; (de la tierra) farming; (de microbios) culture; (de relaciones) cultivation; **de** — cultured
culto ADJ educated, cultured; M worship; **libertad de** — freedom of religion
cultura F culture; — **general** general knowledge
cultural ADJ cultural
culturismo M body-building
cumbre F summit
cumpleaños M SG birthday
cumplido ADJ (cortés) polite; (perfecto) perfect; M compliment; **hacer algo de** — to do something out of duty; **hacer un** — to pay a compliment
cumplimiento M (de un contrato) performance; (de una promesa, obligación) fulfillment; (de un plazo) expiration
cumplir VT (una obligación) to fulfill, to discharge; (una promesa) to keep, to honor; (una condena) to complete, to serve; — **diez años** to turn ten; **hacer** — to enforce; VI (vencer) to expire; — **con** to meet [a goal]; **me cumple informarle que** it is my duty to inform you that
cúmulo M (grupo) host; (tipo de nube) cumulus
cuna F (que se mece) cradle; (con barandas) crib
cundir VI (extenderse) to spread; (rendir) to go a long way
cuneta F roadside ditch; **en la** — out to pasture
cunilinguo M cunnilingus
cuña F (pieza para hender) wedge; (bacinilla) bedpan
cuñado -da M brother-in-law; F sister-in-law
cuño M die-stamp; **de** — **hispano** with a Hispanic stamp
cuota F (cantidad que le corresponde a uno) quota, allotment; (cantidad que hay que pagar) dues; (mensualidad) installment; —**s del coche** car payments; —**s sindicales** union dues
cupé M coupé
cupe, cupiera, cupiese *ver* caber
cupo M (cantidad) quota; (capacidad) *Am* room
cupón M coupon
cúpula F dome
cura F cure, remedy; M priest
curable ADJ curable
curación F cure
curanderismo M faith healing
curandero -ra MF healer
curar VT (una enfermedad, carne) to cure; (una herida) to heal; —**se** to heal; —**se en salud** to take precautionary measures
curiosear VI to look around; (en asuntos ajenos) to pry
curiosidad F curiosity
curioso ADJ curious
Curita® F *Am* adhesive bandage, Band-aid®
currículo/currículum M résumé; — **vitae** CV

curro M *Esp* job

curruca F warbler

curry M curry

cursar VT (estudios) to take; (mensaje, invitación) to send

cursi ADJ (afectado) affected; (de mal gusto) tacky

cursillo M (individual) tutorial; (corto) short course

cursivo ADJ cursive; **escribir en cursiva** to write in cursive

curso M (de río, enfermedad, acontecimientos, moneda) course; (período docente) academic year; (grupo de estudiantes) class; (libro) textbook; — **legal** legal currency; **el mes en** — the current month

cursor M cursor

curtiduría F tannery

curtiembre F tannery

curtir VT (cuero) to tan; (cutis) to weather; (el carácter) to harden; —**se** (envejecerse) to get weathered; (acostumbrarse) to become accustomed to hardships

curva F curve (también béisbol); — **de campana** bell curve

curvatura F curvature

curvo ADJ curved

cúspide F summit

custodia F custody, keeping; **en** — (un monto de dinero) in escrow; (un prisionero) in custody

custodiar VT to guard

custodio -dia MF guardian

cutáneo ADJ cutaneous

cutícula F cuticle

cutis M facial skin

cuyo ADJ REL whose

cyborg M cyborg

Dd

dádiva F gift

dadivoso ADJ generous

dado ADJ given; M die; **jugar a los** —**s** to throw dice

dador -ora MF giver; — **de sangre** blood donor

daga F dagger

dalia F dahlia

daltónico ADJ color-blind

dama F lady; (en el juego de mesa) king; **jugar a las** —**s** to play checkers; — **de honor** bridesmaid

damajuana F demijohn

damasco M (fruta) apricot; (árbol) apricot tree

damisela F damsel

dandi M dandy

danés -esa ADJ Danish; MF Dane; M (lengua) Danish

danza F dance; — **del vientre** belly dance; **en** — in action

danzante MF dancer

danzar[47] VI/VT to dance

dañar VT to harm, to damage; —**se** to suffer harm

dañino ADJ harmful

daño M damage, harm; — **colateral** collateral damage; — **emergente** actual damage; — **físico** bodily harm; —**s materiales** property damage; —**s y perjuicios** damages; **hacer** — to harm

dañoso ADJ harmful

dar[62] VT (un regalo) to give; (un golpe, naipes) to deal; (sal) to add; (una fiesta) to throw; (la hora) to strike; (un olor) to give off; (la alarma) to raise; (un paseo) to take; — **a** (un edificio) to face; (una calle) to lead to; — **a conocer** to announce; — **a entender** to intimate; — **con** to hit upon, to find; — **de alta** to discharge, to release from the hospital; — **de baja** to discharge; — **de comer** to feed; — **de sí** to perform at capacity; **esta tela da de sí** this fabric gives; — **en la pared** to hit the wall; —**le con** to scrub with; **lo misma da** it makes no difference; **¿qué más da?** what difference does it make? **dale que dale** on and on; **hoy no doy una** today I can't get anything right; **le doy cincuenta años** he must be about fifty; **me da rabia/miedo** that makes me angry/afraid; **no me da el tiempo para ir al cine** I don't have time to go to the movies; **que no le dé el sol** don't let the sun shine on it; **y dale** enough already; —**se a la bebida** to indulge in drinking; —**se por conforme** to be satisfied; —**se prisa** to hurry; **dárselas de** to boast of being; **en este lugar se dan las flores silvestres** in this location wildflowers are found

dardo M dart

dársena F dock

datar VT to date; — **de** to date from

dátil M date

dato M piece of information; —**s** data

d.C. ADV AD

de PREP — **la familia** of the family; — **Madrid** from Madrid; **habló** — **la guerra** he talked about the war; **el hombre** — **gafas** the man with glasses; **el mejor estudiante** — **la clase** the best student in the class; **fácil** — **hacer** easy to do; **más** — **tres** more than three; **llevar** — **la mano** to lead by the hand; — **regreso a España** upon returning to Spain; — **venta en farmacias** on sale in pharmacies; **ancianos** — **respeto** older people to be respected; — **lo más lindo**

really pretty; **tonto — mí** silly me

dé *ver* dar

deambular VI to amble, to saunter; **— por** (el bosque) to wander about; (el internet) to surf

deán M dean

debacle M debacle

debajo ADV under, underneath; PREP **— de** under, below; **por — de** under

debate M debate

debatir VT to debate; **—se** to struggle

debe M debit

deber VT **deben apoyarme** they should support me; **debe de ser** it must be; **deberías sentarte** you should sit down; VT to owe; **me debes una** you owe me one; **me debo a mis alumnos** I'm devoted to my students; M duty; **—es** homework

debidamente ADV duly

debido ADJ due; **— a** due to, owing to; **a su — tiempo** in due time

débil ADJ (sin fuerza) weak; (endeble) frail, feeble; (sonido) faint

debilidad F (falta de fuerza) weakness; (cualidad de endeble) frailty; (de un sonido) faintness

debilitamiento M weakening

debilitante ADJ debilitating

debilitar VT to weaken, to debilitate

débito M debit

debutar VI to make a debut

década F decade

decadencia F (moral) decadence, decay; (cultural, económica) decline

decadente ADJ decadent

decaer[52] VI (fuerza) to weaken; (energía) to ebb; (salud) to fail; (ánimo) to flag

decaimiento M (decadencia) decline; (debilidad) weakness

decano -na ADJ senior; MF dean

decapitar VT to behead, to decapitate

decatlón M decathlon

decena F **—s de candidatos** tens of candidates

decencia F decency

decenio M decade

decente ADJ decent; **muy —** rather good

decepción F disappointment

decepcionante ADJ disappointing

decepcionar VT to disappoint

decibelio M decibel

decidido ADJ resolute, determined; **una decidida preferencia** a decided preference

decidir VI/VT to decide; **—se** to make up one's mind; **—se a** to resolve to

deciduo ADJ deciduous

décima F tenth

decimal ADJ decimal

décimo ADJ & M tenth

decir[53, 74] VT (palabras, oraciones) to say; (una mentira, un chiste, la verdad) to tell; **— tonterías** to talk nonsense; **con —te que**

suffice it to say that; **este tipo no me dice nada** this guy leaves me cold; **¡que me lo digan a mí!** you're telling me that? VI to say; **diga** hello (al contestar el teléfono); **es —** that is to say; **he dicho** I have spoken; **no es prometedor que digamos** it's hardly promising; **no me digas** you don't say; **querer —** to mean; M saying

decisión F decision; **tomar una —** to make a decision

decisivo ADJ decisive

declaración F (de amor, independencia, guerra) declaration; (de un hecho) statement; (de un testigo) deposition; **— de derechos** bill of rights; **— de impuestos / de la renta** tax return; **— de impuestos sobre la renta** income tax return; **— jurada** affidavit; **— de la misión** mission statement; **— errónea/ falsa** misstatement; **— sobre la privacidad** privacy statement

declarar VT (amor, independencia, ingresos) to declare; (un hecho) to state; **— culpable** to find guilty; **os declaro marido y mujer** I pronounce you man and wife; VI (como testigo) to testify; **—se** (un amante) to declare one's love; **—se culpable** to plead guilty; **—se en huelga** to go on strike; **—se en quiebra** to declare bankruptcy

declinar VI/VT to decline

declive M (pendiente) slope, drop; (decadencia) decline

decoración F decoration; **— de interiores** interior decorating

decorado M (de casa) decoration; (de escenario) scenery

decorar VT to decorate

decorativo ADJ decorative

decoro M decorum, propriety

decorosamente ADV decorously, properly

decoroso ADJ decorous, proper

decrépito ADJ decrepit

decrepitud F decrepitude

decretar VT to decree

decreto M (disposición ejecutiva) decree; (ley) act

dedal M thimble

dedicación F dedication

dedicar[30] VT (la vida) to dedicate, to devote; (un libro) to dedicate; **—se** to dedicate oneself; (a los estudios) to apply oneself

dedicatoria F dedication

dedo M (de la mano) finger; (del pie) toe; **— anular** ring finger; **— índice** index finger; **— mayor / del corazón** middle finger; **— meñique** little finger; **— pulgar** thumb; **chuparse el —** to be a fool; **chuparse los —s** to lick one's fingers; **cruzar los —s** to keep one's fingers crossed; **elegir a —** to appoint directly; **hacer —** to hitch a ride; **no**

mover un — not to lift a finger
deducción F deduction; **— impositiva** tax deduction
deducible ADJ deductible
deducir[38] VT (concluir) to deduce, to conclude; (descontar) to deduct
defecación F bowel movement
defecar[30] VI/VT to defecate
defección F defection
defecto M defect, flaw; **por —** by default
defectuoso ADJ defective, faulty
defender[2] VT (un fuerte) to defend; (una causa) to champion; (los derechos) to stand up for, to stick up for; **se defiende en francés** he can hold his own in French
defendible ADJ defensible
defensa F defense (también deportes); MF (fútbol) defender; **— individual** man-to-man defense; **— en zonas** zone defense; **aprende — personal** he's learning self-defense; **lo dijo en — propia** he said it in self-defense
defensivo ADJ defensive; **a la defensiva** on the defensive
defensor -ora MF (en la guerra) defender; (de una causa) champion
deferencia F deference
deficiencia F deficiency
deficiente ADJ deficient
déficit M deficit, shortfall; **— presupuestario** budget deficit
defienda, defiende ver defender
definición F definition; **— por penales** penalty shoot-out
definido ADJ definite
definir VT to define
definitivamente ADV definitely; once and for all; **— voy a comprar una impresora** I am definitely going to buy a printer; **lo arreglaremos todo —** we will take care of everything once and for all
definitivo ADJ (superior) definitive; (final) final; **en definitiva** all things considered
deflación F deflation
deflector M baffle
deforestación F deforestation
deformación F deformation
deformar VT to deform; **—se** to become deformed
deforme ADJ deformed, misshapen
deformidad F deformity
defraudar VT (cometer fraude) to defraud; (decepcionar) to disappoint
defunción F death
degenerado -da ADJ & MF degenerate
degenerar VI to degenerate
degenerativo ADJ degenerative
deglución F swallowing
degollar[24] VT to slash someone's throat

degradación F degradation
degradar VT (envilecer) to degrade, to debase; (rebajar el rango) to demote; **—se** to degrade
degüello M throat-slashing; **lucha a —** fight to the death
dehesa F pasture
deidad F deity
dejada F **— de volea** drop shot, stop-volley
dejadez F slovenliness
dejado ADJ slovenly
dejar VT (abandonar, no comer, legar) to leave; (a un enamorado) to leave, to dump; (permitir) to let; (soltar) to let go; **— de** to stop; **— caer** to drop; **— pasar** to pass up; **déjame en paz** leave me alone; **me dejó atónito** it left/rendered me speechless; **no dejes de venir** don't fail to come; **te lo dejo en mil dólares** I'll sell it to you for one thousand dollars; **—se** to let oneself go; **—se crecer la barba** to grow a beard; **déjate de joder** give me a break
deje M slight accent
dejo M (sabor) aftertaste; (acento) slight accent; (toque) hint; **tener un — de** to smack of
delantal M apron
delante ADV in front; **— de** in front of, ahead of
delantera F (de carrera) lead; (de vestido) front; **llevar la —** to be in the lead; **tomar la —** to take the lead
delantero -ra ADJ (pata) front; MF (línea, deportista) forward; M front
delatar VT to inform against, to squeal on; **— la edad** to betray one's age
delator -ora MF accuser, informer
delegación F delegation
delegado -da MF delegate
delegar[40] VT to delegate
deleitar VT to delight; **—se en algo** to revel in something; **—se la vista con** to feast one's eyes on
deleite M delight
deletrear VT to spell; **— mal** to misspell
deleznable ADJ despicable
delfín M dolphin
delgadez F thinness
delgado ADJ thin, slender, slim
deliberación F deliberation
deliberadamente ADV deliberately
deliberado ADJ deliberate
deliberar VI/VT to deliberate
delicadeza F (tacto) gentleness; (fineza) delicacy; **con —** gently; **tuvo la — de llamar** he was kind enough to call
delicado ADJ (suave, frágil, controvertido) delicate; (enfermizo) frail; (exquisito) dainty; (quisquilloso) squeamish
delicatessen F PL delicacies
delicia F delight
delicioso ADJ delicious, delectable

delimitar VT to delimit
delincuencia F crime
delincuente ADJ & MF delinquent, criminal; — **juvenil** juvenile delinquent
delineador M eyeliner
delinear VT to delineate, to outline
delirante ADJ delirious, raving
delirar VI to be delirious, to rave
delirio M delirium; — **paranoico** paranoid delusion; —**s de grandeza** delusions of grandeur
delito M crime, offense
deltoides M SG deltoids
demacrado ADJ drawn, gaunt, haggard
demagogo -ga MF demagogue
demanda F (de mercancías) demand; (de seguros) insurance claim; (pleito) lawsuit; **por** — on demand; **entablar una** — to file a lawsuit
demandado -da MF (en un pleito) defendant; (en un arbitraje) respondent
demandante MF plaintiff
demandar VT (pedir) to ask for; (poner pleito) to sue, to file a suit against
demarcar[30] VT to demarcate
demás ADJ (restante) remaining; PRON the others, the rest; **lo** — the rest; **y** — and whatnot; ADV **por lo** — moreover; **por** — useless
demasía LOC ADV **en** — excessively
demasiado ADV too; too much; **eso es** — **para mí** that's too much for me; **él es** — **alto** he's too tall; ADJ too much; too many; — **dinero** too much money; **demasiadas cosas** too many things
demencia F (locura) insanity; (senilidad) senility; (enfermedad mental) dementia
demente ADJ demented, insane, deranged
democracia F democracy
demócrata MF democrat; **Partido** — Democratic Party
democrático ADJ democratic; (del Partido —) Democrat, Democratic
democratización F democratization
demografía F demographics
demográfico ADJ demographic
demoler[6] VT to demolish, to tear down
demonio M demon; **al** — **con los libros** *vulg* to hell with books; **mandar al** — *vulg* to tell someone to go to hell; **¿qué** —**s haces?** what the heck are you doing? **un frío del** — bitter cold
demora F delay
demorar VT to delay; —**se** to linger
demostración F (prueba) demonstration; (de un programa digital) demo; — **de fuerza** show of force
demostrar[5] VT (mostrar) to demonstrate, to show; (comprobar) to prove, to demonstrate

demostrativo ADJ demonstrative
demudar VT to change, to alter
demuestra, demuestre *ver* demostrar
denegación F (de una petición) denial
dengue M dengue fever
denigrar VT to denigrate, to disparage
denodado ADJ untiring
denominación F (valor) denomination; (nombre) designation
denominador M denominator; — **común** common denominator
denominar VT to designate, to term
denostar[5] VT to revile
denotación F denotation
denotar VT to denote
densidad F density; **alta** — high density
denso ADJ (sólido) dense; (líquido) heavy
dentado ADJ (rueda) toothed; (montaña) ragged
dentadura F set of teeth; — **postiza** false teeth
dental ADJ dental
dentellada F (mordedura) bite; (señal de diente) tooth mark; **a** —**s** biting
dentífrico M toothpaste, dentifrice
dentista MF dentist
dentro ADV inside; (tenis) in; PREP — **de la casa** inside the house; — **de la ley** within the law; — **de quince días** (en el plazo de) within two weeks; (al cabo de) in two weeks; **por** — within
denuncia F (acusación) denunciation; (de mina, de seguro) claim
denunciar VT (un hecho negativo) to denounce; (una mina) to claim; (un delito) to report
deparar VT (tener preparado) to have in store; (proporcionar) to afford; **el destino me deparaba una sorpresa** fate had a surprise in store for me
departamento M (división) department; (piso) small apartment; (provincia) province
departir VI *lit* to commune
dependencia F (hecho de depender) dependence; (habituación) dependency; (filial) branch office
depender VI to depend; — **de** to depend on
dependiente -ta ADJ dependent; MF sales clerk, salesperson
depilación F hair removal
depilar VT to remove hair; (con cera) to wax
depilatorio ADJ & M depilatory
deplorable ADJ deplorable
deplorar VT to deplore
deponer[56, 74] VT (las armas) to lay down; (a un ministro) to depose, to remove; VI to defecate
deportar VT to deport
deporte M sport; **me gusta el** — I like sports/ athletics
deportista ADJ athletic; MF athlete
deportivo ADJ athletic; **revista deportiva** sports magazine

deposición F (de un testigo) deposition; (de un ministro) removal; (movimiento de vientre) bowel movement

depositante MF depositor

depositar VT to deposit; **—se** to settle

depositario -ria MF repository

depósito M (en el banco) deposit; (de gasolina) tank; (de agua) reservoir; (de armas) depot, dump; (de mercancías) stock room, storehouse; **— de cadáveres** morgue; **— de garantía** security deposit; **hacer un —** to make a deposit; **en —** on consignment

depravado ADJ depraved

depreciar VI to depreciate

depredador -ora MF predator

depresión F depression

depresor M depressor; **— de lengua** tongue depressor

deprimente ADJ depressing

deprimido ADJ depressed

deprimir VT to depress

deprisa ADV quickly

depuración F (de agua) purification; (de un programa) debugging

depurador M debugger

depurar VT to purify; (un programa) to debug

derby M derby

derecha F (política) right wing; (tenis) forehand; **a la —** to the right; **de —s** right-wing

derechista ADJ right-wing; MF rightist

derecho ADJ (no izquierdo) right; (recto) straight; **ponerse —** to hold oneself erect, to stand up straight; ADV straight; **volver — a casa** to go straight home; **todo —** straight ahead; M (preceptos, disciplina) law; (prerrogativa) right; **— al trabajo** right to work; **— consuetudinario** common law; **— de admisión** fee; **—s del cliente** customer rights; **— internacional** international law; **—s fees; —s aduaneros** tax on imports; **—s civiles** civil rights; **—s de autor** royalties; **—s de la mujer** women's rights; **—s de los animales** animal rights; **—s mineros** mineral rights; **estar en su —** to be entitled; **poner al —** to put on right side out; **registrar los —s** to copyright

derechura F straightness

deriva F drift; **ir a la —** to be adrift

derivación F derivation

derivado M (subproducto) by-product; (palabra) derivative

derivar VT to derive

dermabrasión F dermabrasion

dermatología F dermatology

dermatólogo -ga MF dermatologist

derogación F repeal

derogar[40] VT to repeal

derramamiento M spill, spilling; **— de sangre** bloodshed

derramar VT (un líquido) to spill; (sangre, lágrimas) to shed; **—se** to spill over, to run over

derrame M spill; **— cerebral** stroke, cerebral hemorrhage

derredor LOC ADV **en —** all around

derrengar[40] VT (dañar la espalda) to sprain one's back; (cansar) to exhaust

derretir[9] VT to melt; **—se por alguien** to be crazy about someone

derribar VT (un edificio) to demolish, to tear down; (a una persona) to knock down; (un gobierno) to topple, to overthrow; (un avión) to shoot down, to down

derrocamiento M overthrow

derrocar[30] VT (un gobierno) to overthrow, to topple; (a un dictador) to depose

derrochador -ora ADJ extravagant; MF (de dinero) spendthrift; (de recursos) squanderer

derrochar VT (dinero) to squander; (salud) to radiate

derroche M (de recursos) waste, extravagance; (de color) profusion

derrota F defeat

derrotar VT to defeat

derrotero M course

derrubio M washout

derruido ADJ dilapidated

derrumbadero M precipice

derrumbamiento M collapse

derrumbar VT to demolish; **—se** (edificio) to collapse; (túnel, caverna) to cave in

derrumbe M (de tierra) landslide; (de un edificio) collapse

desabotonar VT to unbutton, to undo

desabrido ADJ (comida) tasteless; (persona) *Am* dull; *Esp* surly

desabrigado ADJ exposed; **no salgas tan —** put on some warm clothes before you go out

desabrochado ADJ undone, unfastened

desabrochar VT (botones) to undo; (ganchos) to unhook; (hebillas, cinturones) to unbuckle; (botones) to unbutton; **—se** to come undone

desacato M disrespect; **— al tribunal** contempt of court

desacelerar VI to decelerate

desacierto M mistake

desaconsejable ADJ inadvisable

desaconsejar VT to caution against

desacoplar VT to uncouple, to disconnect

desacostumbrado ADJ unusual

desacostumbrar VT to break of a habit; **—se** to lose a habit

desacreditar VT to discredit

desactivación F deactivation

desactivar VT (explosivo, situación) to defuse; (mecanismo) to disable; (virus) to deactivate

desacuerdo M disagreement; **estar en —** to be at odds

desafiante ADJ defiant
desafiar[28] VT (retar) to challenge, to dare;
(enfrentar) to defy
desafilado ADJ dull
desafilar VT to dull; —**se** to become dull
desafinado ADJ out of tune, off-key
desafinar VT to be out of tune
desafío M (reto) challenge; (desobediencia)
defiance
desafortunadamente ADV unfortunately
desafortunado ADJ unfortunate, unlucky
desafuero M (de un diputado) withdrawal of
immunity; (atropello) outrage
desagradable ADJ disagreeable, unpleasant
desagradar VT to displease
desagradecido ADJ ungrateful
desagrado M displeasure
desagraviar VI to make amends, to redress
desagravio M redress
desaguadero M drainpipe
desaguar[25] VI to drain
desagüe M (acción de desaguar) drainage; (de
lavabo) drain, drainpipe; (en la azotea) gutter
desaguisado M mess
desahogado ADJ (cómodo) comfortable;
(espacioso) spacious
desahogar[40] VT (aliviar) to relieve; —**se** to pour
out one's feelings
desahogo M relief; **vivir con** — to live an easy
life
desairar VT to slight, to snub, to rebuff
desaire M slight, snub, rebuff
desajustar VT to loosen; —**se** to come loose
desalentado ADJ despondent
desalentador ADJ disheartening
desalentar[1] VT to discourage, to dishearten;
—**se** to get discouraged
desaliento M discouragement, dismay
desaliñado ADJ disheveled, slovenly, unkempt
desaliño M slovenliness
desalmado ADJ heartless
desalojar VT (una piedra) to dislodge; (un
tribunal) to clear; (un edificio) to evacuate; (a
un inquilino) to evict; (una vivienda) to vacate
desamparado ADJ helpless, forlorn
desamparar VT to forsake
desamparo M abandonment, helplessness
desamueblado ADJ unfurnished
desangrar VT to bleed; —**se** to bleed to death
desanimado ADJ (persona) discouraged;
(jornada) dull
desanimar VT to discourage
desánimo M discouragement
desaparecer[35] VI (perderse) to disappear, to
vanish; (morir) to pass away
desaparezca, desaparezco ver desaparecer
desaparición F disappearance; (muerte) demise
desapasionado ADJ dispassionate
desapego M detachment

desapercibido ADJ unnoticed
desaprobación F disapproval
desaprobar[5] VT to disapprove of
desarmado ADJ unarmed
desarmar VT (quitar las armas) to disarm;
(desmontar) to take apart
desarme M disarmament
desarraigar[40] VT to uproot
desarreglar VT to disturb, to mess up
desarreglo M (trastorno, enfermedad) disorder;
(desorden) mess
desarrollador-ora MF developer
desarrollar VT (aumentar) to develop;
(extender algo enrollado) to unroll; (llevar a
cabo) to carry out; (aclarar) to elaborate, to
flesh out; —**se** to unfold
desarrollo M development; (de una ecuación)
expansion; **en** — developing
desarticulado ADJ disjointed
desaseado ADJ slovenly
desaseo M slovenliness
desasir[50] VT to let go of
desasosiego M uneasiness
desastrado ADJ (desaseado) untidy; (funesto)
ill-fated
desastre M disaster
desastroso ADJ disastrous
desatado ADJ (ambición) unfettered; (zapatos)
untied
desatar VT (un nudo) to untie, to loosen; (una
ola de violencia) to unleash; —**se** to come
untied; —**se en insultos** to let out a string of
insults
desatascador M plunger
desatascar[30] VT (un inodoro) to unclog; (un
objeto atrapado) to dislodge
desatención F lack of attention
desatender[2] VT (no ocuparse de algo) to
neglect; (ignorar) to ignore
desatendido ADJ (descuidado) neglected;
(ignorado) ignored
desatento ADJ inattentive
desatinado ADJ imprudent
desatornillar VT to unscrew
desatracar[30] VI/VT to cast off, to shove off
desavenencia F discord
desayunar VT **desayuné huevos** I had eggs for
breakfast; —**se** to have breakfast; —**se [con
que]** to find out [that]
desayuno M breakfast
desazón F uneasiness
desbandarse VI to disband
desbaratar VT (un plan) to disrupt; (un hechizo)
to break; —**se** to break down
desbocado ADJ (caballo) runaway; (collar) loose
desbordamiento M overflow
desbordante ADJ overflowing
desbordar VI (derramar) to overflow; VT
(abrumar) to overwhelm; —**se** to overflow, to

spill over
desbravar VT to break
descabalgar[40] VI to dismount
descabellado ADJ harebrained
descabezar[47] VT to behead; — **un sueño** to
take a nap
descafeinado ADJ decaffeinated
descalabrar VT (la cabeza) to split someone's
head open; (a una persona) to hurt
descalabro M disaster
descalcificación F decalcification
descalificar VT to disqualify
descalzar[47] VT to take off someone's shoes; —**se**
to take off one's shoes
descalzo ADJ barefoot
descaminado ADJ **andar/ir** — to be on the
wrong track
descamisado ADJ (sin camisa) shirtless; (pobre)
poor
descansar VI/VT to rest; — **en paz** to rest in
peace; —**se en** to rely on
descanso M (acción de descansar) rest; (de
escalera) landing; (intermisión, receso)
break; (en fútbol) halftime; **en** — at ease
descapotable ADJ & M convertible
descarado ADJ shameless, impudent, brazen; **a
la descarada** shamelessly
descarga F (de batería, agua, armas) discharge;
(de buques) unloading; (emocional)
outpouring; (de electricidad) shock; (de
internet) download
descargar[40] VT (una batería, agua) to discharge;
(un buque, un arma de fuego) to unload;
(bomba) to drop; (un programa de
computadora) to download; —**se** (una
batería) to drain; (ira) to vent
descargo M **en su** — in his defense
descarnado ADJ (realidad) stark; (cara)
emaciated
descaro M effrontery, impudence, nerve
descarriar[28] VT to lead astray; —**se** to go astray
descarrilarse VI to derail, to jump the track
descartar VT (un naipe) to discard; (una
posibilidad) to dismiss, to discard
descarte M discard; **por** — by elimination
descascararse VI (en jirones) to peel; (en
fragmentos) to chip, to flake
descendencia F (linaje) descent;
(descendientes) descendants
descendente ADJ descending, downward
descender[2] VI to descend; — **de** to descend
from
descendiente MF descendant
descenso M descent
descentralización F decentralization
descienda, desciende ver descender
descifrado M deciphering
descifrar VT to decipher
descodificación F decoding, decryption

descodificar[30] VT to decode, to decrypt
descolgar[42] VT (una cortina) to take down; (un
teléfono) to pick up; —**se con** to come up
with; —**se de** to come down from
descollar[5] VI to excel
descolorido ADJ (persona) pale; (cosa) colorless
descomponer[56, 74] VT (disgustar) to upset; (dar
diarrea) to give diarrhea; (dar náuseas) to
make nauseous; (separar) to break down;
(cadáveres) to decompose; (un reloj) to break;
— **en factores** to factor; —**se** (productos
químicos) to break down; (cadáveres) to
decompose; (un reloj) to break; (sentir
náuseas) to be nauseous; (tener diarrea) to
have diarrhea; (disgustarse) to go to pieces
descomposición F (de cadáveres)
decomposition; (de productos químicos)
breaking down; (diarrea) diarrhea
descomprimir VT to decompress
descompuesto ADJ (roto) broken; (caótico)
chaotic; (con diarrea) having diarrhea
descomunal ADJ enormous
desconcertado ADJ disconcerted
desconcertante ADJ disconcerting
desconcertar[1] VT to disconcert, to puzzle, to
baffle; —**se** to become disconcerted
desconchar VT to chip
desconcierto M confusion
desconectado ADJ disconnected
desconectar VT to disconnect
desconexión F (acción de desconectar)
disconnecting; (incomunicación) disconnect
desconfiado ADJ mistrustful, suspicious
desconfianza F mistrust
desconfiar[28] VT to distrust, to mistrust, to be
wary of
descongelación F thawing
descongestionante M decongestant
descongestionar VT to decongest
desconocer[35] VT (no reconocer) to fail to
recognize; (no saber) not to know; **te
desconozco** you are not acting like yourself
today
desconocido -da ADJ unknown; MF stranger
desconocimiento M ignorance
desconsideración F thoughtlessness
desconsiderado ADJ thoughtless,
inconsiderate
desconsolado ADJ disconsolate, dejected
desconsolador ADJ disheartening
desconsolar[5] VT to dishearten; —**se** to become
disheartened
desconsuelo M dejection
descontaminación F decontamination
descontaminar VT to decontaminate
descontar[5] VT (bajar el precio) to discount;
(excluir) to exclude; (quitar) to dock
descontentadizo ADJ hard to please
descontentar VT to displease

descontento ADJ & M discontent
descorazonado ADJ disheartened
descortés ADJ discourteous, impolite
descortesía F discourtesy, impoliteness
descortezar[47] VT to strip the bark from
descoser VT to rip; —**se** to come unsewn
descosido ADJ unsewn; M unsewn place;
 hablar como un — to talk one's head off
descostrar VT to remove the crust from
descoyuntado ADJ dislocated, out of joint
descoyuntar VT to dislocate; —**se** to become
 dislocated
descrédito M discredit
descreído -da ADJ unbelieving; MF unbeliever
descreimiento M unbelief
describir[74] VT to describe
descripción F description
descriptivo ADJ descriptive
descrito *ver* describir
descuartizar[47] VT to quarter
descubierto ADJ (destapado) uncovered; (sin
 sombrero) hatless; **al** — in the open; **estar al**
 — to be exposed; **poner al** — to expose, to
 lay bare; **en** — overdrawn; M overdraft
descubierto *ver* descubrir
descubridor -ora MF discoverer
descubrimiento M discovery
descubrir[74] VT (hallar) to discover; (destapar) to
 uncover; —**se** to take off one's hat; — **el**
 pastel to spill the beans
descuento M discount; — **por grupo** group
 discount; **con** — at a discount; **los** —**s** extra
 time, injury time
descuidado ADJ (en una tarea) careless,
 negligent; (en el aspecto personal) slovenly
descuidar VT to neglect; **descuida, yo me**
 ocupo de eso don't worry, I'll take care of
 that; —**se** to be negligent
descuido M (falta de cuidado) neglect; (acción
 descuidada) oversight; **al** — offhand; **por** —
 by chance
desde PREP (origen) from; (tiempo) since; —
 Madrid from Madrid; — **el martes** since
 Tuesday; — **luego** of course; — **el principio**
 from the start; — **el vamos** from the get-go;
 — **entonces** ever since
desdecirse[53, 74] VI (contradecirse) to contradict
 oneself; (retractarse) to retract
desdén M disdain, scorn
desdentado ADJ toothless
desdeñar VT to disdain, to scorn
desdeñoso ADJ disdainful, scornful
desdicha F misfortune; **por** — unfortunately
desdichado ADJ wretched
desdoblamiento M division
desdoblar VT (desplegar) to unfold; (dividir) to
 divide
deseabilidad F desirability
deseable ADJ desirable

desear VT to desire
desecación F drying
desecar[30] VT to dry, to desiccate; —**se** to dry up,
 to desiccate
desechable VT disposable, throwaway
desechar VT (ropa vieja) to discard; (una oferta)
 to refuse; (una posibilidad) to dismiss
desecho M waste material; —**s** refuse, waste
desembalar VT to unpack
desembarazar[47] VT to rid of; —**se** to get rid of
desembarcadero M dock
desembarcar[30] VI (de un buque) to disembark,
 to go ashore; (de un avión) to deplane
desembarco M landing
desembarque M landing
desembocadura F mouth
desembocar[30] VI to flow; — **en** to flow into; **la**
 calle Ocho desemboca en la avenida A
 Eighth Street feeds into Avenue A
desembolsar VT to disburse, to pay out
desembolso M disbursement, outlay
desembragar[40] VI/VT to disengage [the clutch]
desempacar[30] VT to unpack
desempañar VT to wipe clean
desempate M (tenis) tie-break; **[partido de]**
 desempate playoff [game]
desempeñar VT to redeem; — **un cargo** to
 perform the duties of a position; — **un papel**
 to play a part; —**se** to get out of debt
desempeño M (de un cargo o papel)
 performance; (de una cosa en prenda)
 redemption
desempleado ADJ unemployed
desempleo M unemployment
desempolvar VT to dust off
desencadenar VT (quitar las cadenas) to
 unchain; (provocar, causar) to trigger, to
 spark
desencajado ADJ (mandíbula) dislocated;
 (mirada) wild; **estaba** — **en el funeral** he
 was deeply disturbed at the funeral
desencajar VT (un cajón) to unstick; (la
 mandíbula) to dislocate
desencantar VT (desilusionar) to disillusion;
 (quitar un hechizo) to remove a spell from
desencanto M disillusion
desenchufar VI/VT to unplug
desenfadado ADJ uninhibited
desenfado M lack of inhibition
desenfrenadamente ADV with wild abandon
desenfrenado ADJ (sin moderación) unbridled,
 wanton, rampant; (muy rápido) reckless
desenganchar VT to unhook
desengañar VT to disabuse; —**se** (de un error)
 to become disabused; (de una ilusión) to
 become disillusioned
desengaño M disillusion
desengranar VT to take out of gear
desenlace M (de un libro) ending; (de un suceso)

outcome

desenmarañar VT to disentangle

desenmascarar VT to unmask, to expose

desenredar VT (el cabello) to disentangle; (una historia) to disentangle

desenrollar VT to unroll

desenroscar VT to untwist

desentenderse[2] VI to pay no attention

desentendido ADJ **hacerse el** — to pretend not to notice/know

desenterrar[1] VT (un tesoro) to unearth, to dig up; (un cadáver) to disinter

desentonado ADJ out of tune

desentonar VI (cantar mal) to sing off key; (estar fuera de lugar) to be out of place

desentrañar VT to unravel

desenvoltura F self-assurance

desenvolver[6, 74] VT (desenrollar) to unroll; (quitar la envoltura) to unwrap; **—se** to behave

desenvuelto ADJ self-assured

deseo M desire, wish; (sexual) desire; **pedir un** — to make a wish

deseoso ADJ desirous

desequilibrado -da ADJ unbalanced; MF unbalanced person

desequilibrar VT to unbalance

desequilibrio M imbalance

deserción F desertion; — **escolar** school dropout rate

desertar VI/VT to desert; — **de** to defect from

desértico ADJ desert

desertor -ora MF (militar) deserter; (escolar) drop-out

desesperación F desperation

desesperadamente ADV desperately

desesperado ADJ desperate

desesperanza F despair, hopelessness

desesperanzado ADJ hopeless

desesperanzar[47] VT to discourage, to deprive of hope; **—se** to despair

desesperar VI to despair; VT to drive crazy

desestabilizar[47] VT to destabilize

desestimación F rejection

desestimar VT to reject

desfachatez F audacity

desfalcar[30] VT to embezzle

desfalco M embezzlement

desfallecer[35] VI (debilitarse) to grow weak; (desmayarse) to faint

desfallecimiento M (debilidad) weakness; (desmayo) faint

desfavorable ADJ unfavorable

desfibrilación F defibrillation

desfibrilador M defibrillator

desfibrilar VT to defibrillate

desfigurar VT (el rostro) to disfigure; (una estatua) to deface

desfiladero M narrow passage

desfilar VI (coches) to file by; (soldados, modelos) to parade

desfile M parade

desgana F (falta de apetito) lack of appetite; (falta de entusiasmo) lack of enthusiasm

desganado ADJ apathetic, without enthusiasm

desgarbado ADJ ungainly, gawky

desgarrado ADJ (prenda, músculo) torn; (grito) heartrending

desgarradura F tear

desgarrar VT (rasgar) to tear; (un escándalo) to dredge up; **—le el corazón a alguien** to break someone's heart; **—se** to tear, to pull

desgarro M muscle pull

desgarrón M tear

desgastar VT to wear away; **—se** to get worn away

desgaste M wear and tear

desglosar VT (una suma) to itemize; (un tema) to break down

desglose M (de una suma) itemization; (de un tema) breakdown

desgracia F (infortunio) misfortune; (infelicidad) unhappiness; **—s personales** casualties; **caer en** — to fall into disgrace/ disfavor

desgraciadamente ADV unfortunately

desgraciado -da ADJ (desafortunado) unfortunate; (infeliz) unhappy; MF (persona desafortunada) unfortunate person; (hombre despreciable) *vulg* bastard; F (mujer desgraciada) *vulg* bitch

desgranar VT (granos) to thrash, to thresh; (guisantes) to shell

desgravable ADJ tax-deductible

desgreñado ADJ disheveled, unkempt

desgreñar VT to dishevel; **—se** to muss up one's hair

desguazar[47] VT to scrap

deshabitado ADJ (territorio) uninhabited; (casa) vacant

deshacer[54, 74] VT (una acción, comando a la computadora) to undo; (una cama) to strip; (un plato, un jarrón) to destroy; (un sólido en un líquido) to dissolve; (un nudo) to untie; — **la maleta** to unpack the suitcase; **—se de** to get rid of; **—se en elogios** to rave about

deshaga, deshago, deshará, desharía *ver* deshacer

desharrapado ADJ ragged

deshecho *ver* deshacer

deshelar[1] VT to thaw

desheredar VT to disinherit

deshice, deshiciera, deshiciese *ver* deshacer

deshielo M thaw

deshierbar VT to weed

deshilachar VT to unravel, to fray

deshojado ADJ leafless

deshojar VT to strip of leaves; **—se** (un árbol) to

shed leaves; (un libro) to lose pages

deshonestidad F (falta de honradez) dishonesty; (falta de recato) immodesty

deshonesto ADJ (no honrado) dishonest; (no modesto) immodest

deshonra F dishonor, disgrace

deshonrar VT to dishonor, to disgrace

deshonroso ADJ dishonorable

deshora LOC ADV a — at an inopportune time; **comer a** — to eat between meals

deshuesar VT (un fruto) to stone; (un animal) to bone

deshumanizar[47] VT to dehumanize

deshumidificador M dehumidifier

desidia F indolence

desierto ADJ (lugar) deserted; (premio) unawarded; M (región árida) desert; (región poco fértil y no habitada) wilderness

designación F (acción de designar, nombre) designation; (nombramiento) appointment

designar VT to designate; (a un funcionario) to appoint

designio M design

desigual ADJ (pelea) one-sided; (actuación) uneven; (números) not equal; (rango) unequal; (terreno) uneven

desigualdad F inequality; (del terreno) roughness

desilusión F disillusion, disappointment

desilusionar VT to disillusion, to disappoint; —**se** to become disillusioned/disappointed

desinencia F ending

desinfección F disinfection

desinfectante ADJ & M disinfectant

desinfectar VT to disinfect

desinfestación F disinfestation

desinflado ADJ (globo, persona) deflated; (neumático) flat; M flat tire

desinflar VT to deflate

desinformación F (falta de información) disinformation; (mala información) misinformation

desinformar VT to misinform

desinhibido ADJ uninhibited

desinstalar VT to uninstall

desintegración F disintegration; — **atómica** atomic decay

desintegrarse VI to disintegrate; (material radiactivo) to decay

desinterés M (falta de interés) lack of interest; (generosidad) unselfishness

desinteresado ADJ (apático) disinterested; (generoso) unselfish, selfless

desistir VI to desist

deslavado ADJ faded

deslavar VT (quitar color) to fade; (lavar ligeramente) to wash superficially

desleal ADJ (persona) disloyal, faithless; (competencia) unfair

desleír[10] VT to mix with a liquid

deslindar VT to mark off

desliz M slipup

deslizamiento M slide, glide

deslizar[47] VT (un patín) to slip, to slide, to glide; (una tarjeta) to swipe; —**se** (un patín) to slide, to glide; (un error) to slip by

deslucido ADJ (actuación) dull; (color) dingy

deslucir[39] VT (un espectáculo) to tarnish; (color) to make dingy

deslumbramiento M dazzle

deslumbrante ADJ dazzling

deslumbrar VT to dazzle; —**se** to be dazzled

deslustrar VT to tarnish

deslustre M tarnish

desmadejado ADJ (fatigado) exhausted; (desgarbado) ungainly

desmadejar VT to exhaust

desmán M abuse

desmantelar VT to dismantle

desmañado ADJ awkward, clumsy

desmayar VI to lose courage; —**se** to faint, to pass out

desmayo M faint, swoon; **peleó sin** — hc fought unflaggingly

desmedido ADJ excessive

desmejorar VI (empeorar el aspecto) to look worse; (debilitarse) to get worse

desmembrar VT to dismember

desmentido M denial

desmentir[8] VT to deny

desmenuzar[47] VT (pan) to crumble; (zanahorias) to mince

desmerecer[35] VI — **en valor** to not do justice; **no** — **de** to compare favorably with

desmesurado ADJ (esfuerzo) inordinate; (orejas) too large

desmigajar VT to crumb, to crumble

desmitificar[30] VT to debunk

desmochar VT to top, to cut the top off of

desmontar VT (limpiar un monte) to clear; (desarmar) to dismantle, to take apart; (derribar de una caballería) to throw; —**se** to dismount

desmoralizar[47] VT to demoralize; —**se** to become demoralized

desmoronar VT to crumble

desmovilizar[47] VT to demobilize

desnatar VT to skim

desnaturalizado ADJ (madre) unnatural; (aceite) denatured

desnudar VT to undress; —**se** to get undressed

desnudez F nakedness

desnudo ADJ nude, naked

desnutrición F malnutrition

desnutrido ADJ underfed, undernourished

desobedecer[35] VT to disobey

desobediencia F disobedience; — **civil** civil disobedience

desobediente ADJ disobedient

desocupación F (paro) unemployment; (abandono de vivienda) vacating

desocupado ADJ (asiento, casa) unoccupied, empty; (tiempo) idle; (que no trabaja) unemployed

desocupar VT to vacate; —**se** to become free

desodorante M deodorant

desodorizar VT to deodorize

desoír[55] VT to turn a deaf ear to

desolación F desolation

desolado ADJ desolate, bleak

desolar VT to lay waste to, to desolate; —**se** to be desolated

desollar[5] VT to skin; — **vivo** to skin alive

desorbitado ADJ (precio, reacción) out of proportion; (ojos) bulging

desorden M disorder, disarray; — **público** public disturbance; **en** — in disarray

desordenado ADJ (persona, situación) messy; (persona, estilo de vida) wild; (cuarto) untidy, disorderly; (archivo) disorganized

desordenar VT to mess up

desorganización F disorganization

desorganizado ADJ disorganized

desorientar VT (marear, hacer perder) to disorient; (confundir) to confuse; —**se** to lose one's bearings, to become disoriented

desovar VT to spawn

desoxidar VT to deoxidize

despabilado ADJ (despierto) wide-awake; (listo) on the ball

despabilar VT (cortar el pabilo) to trim the wick of; (despertar) to awaken; —**se** to wake up

despachar VT (problemas) to dispatch; (una carta) to mail; (a un cliente) to take care of; (mercancías) to ship; (a una víctima) to bump off; (un pedido) to fill; — **al público** to sell to the public; —**se a su gusto** to speak one's mind

despacho M (oficina) office; (comunicación) dispatch; (envío de cartas) mailing; (envío de mercancías) shipping

despachurrar VT to squash

despacio ADV slow, slowly

desparasitar VT to worm

desparejo ADJ uneven

desparpajo M (desenvoltura) ease; (descaro) impudence

desparramar VT to scatter; —**se** to be scattered

desparramo M (lío) commotion; (de libros) clutter

despatarrarse VT (caerse) to sprawl; (abrirse de piernas) to spread one's legs

despecho M spite; **por** — out of spite

despectivo ADJ derogatory, pejorative

despedazar[47] VT to tear to pieces

despedida F farewell; — **de soltero** bachelor party

despedir[9] VT (decir adiós) to see off; (echar de un empleo) to fire, to dismiss; (emitir un dolor) to emit, to give off; **despídeme de tus padres** say good-bye to your parents for me; —**se [de]** to take leave [of], to say good-bye [to]

despegar[40] VT (dos cosas pegadas) to detach; VI (un avión) to take off; (un cohete) to blast off; —**se** to become detached

despegue M (de avión) takeoff; (de cohete) blastoff, liftoff

despeinado ADJ unkempt

despejado ADJ (el cielo) clear, cloudless; (un camino) clear; (la frente) with one's hair pulled back; (una persona) bright

despejador M (fútbol americano) punter

despejar VT (el campo, una pelota) to clear; (en fútbol americano) to punt; VI (una duda, el cielo) to clear up; —**se** to sober up

despellejar VT to skin

despensa F pantry

despeñadero M cliff

despeñar VT to push off a precipice; —**se** to fall down a precipice

despepitar VT (una granada) to seed; (una manzana) to core; —**se por una cosa** to be crazy about something

desperdiciar VT to waste; —**se** to go to waste

desperdicio M waste; —**s** scraps

desperdigar[40] VT to scatter; —**se** to be scattered

desperezarse[47] VI to stretch

desperezo M stretch

desperfecto M damage; — **mecánico** mechanical breakdown

despertador M alarm clock

despertar[1] VT (a una persona) to awaken, to wake up; (sospecha) to arouse; (interés, deseo) to kindle; —**se** to wake up

despiadado ADJ merciless, heartless, ruthless

despida, despide, despidiendo, despidiera, despidiese *ver* despedir

despido M dismissal, termination; — **temporal de un empleado** layoff

despierta, despierte *ver* despertar

despierto ADJ (no dormido) awake; (vivaracho) alert

despilfarrador ADJ wasteful

despilfarrar VT to squander

despilfarro M waste

despistado ADJ absent-minded, out of it

despistar VT (confundir) to throw off the track; (deshacerse de) to lose; —**se** to get confused

desplantador M trowel

desplante M rude remark

desplazado -da MF displaced person

desplazamiento M (de tropas) movement; (de refugiados) displacement

desplazar[47] VT to displace; —**se** to move

desplegar[41] VT (papel plegado) to unfold; (una bandera) to unfurl; (tropas) to deploy; (interés) to display

despliegue M display

desplomarse VI (edificio, precios) to collapse; (una persona) to slump; (esperanzas) to be dashed

desplome M collapse

desplumar VT (un ave) to pluck; (a un incauto) to fleece

despoblado ADJ uninhabited; — de árboles treeless; M open country

despojar VT to despoil; —se to shed leaves

despojos M PL (de batalla) spoils; (mortales) remains

desportilladura F chip

desportillar VT to chip

desposeer VT to dispossess

déspota MF despot

despótico ADJ despotic

despotismo M despotism

despotricar[30] VI to rant

despreciable ADJ (vil) contemptible, despicable, worthless; (insignificante) negligible

despreciar VT (menospreciar) to despise, to look down on; (rechazar) to snub

desprecio M (menosprecio) contempt, disdain; (rechazo) snub

desprender VT (un cierre) to unfasten; (algo prendido) to detach; (gases) to give off; —se de algo to part with something; —se la ropa to undo one's clothes; **de lo dicho se desprende que** from what has been said it follows that

desprendimiento M (de retina) detachment; (de energía) release; (de tierra) landslide; (generosidad) generosity

despreocupado ADJ carefree

desprestigiar VT to discredit; —se to lose one's prestige

desprestigio M loss of prestige

desprevenido ADJ unprepared; **tomar** — to take by surprise

desproporcionado ADJ disproportionate, out of proportion

despropósito M nonsense

desprovisto ADJ — de lacking in

después ADV after, afterward; — de after; — de todo after all; — de horas hábiles after hours

despuntar VI/VT to blunt; —se to become blunt

desquiciar VT to unhinge; —se to come unhinged

desquitarse VI to get even

desquite M getting even, revenge

desregular VT to deregulate

destacable ADJ notable, noteworthy

destacado ADJ outstanding

destacamento M military detachment, military detail

destacar[30] VT (tropas) to detach; (una cualidad) to highlight, to accentuate; VI to stand out; —se to stand out

destajo LOC ADV **a** — by the job

destapar VT (una cacerola) to take the top off; (un plan, a un niño en cama) to uncover; —se (en la cama) to uncover; (desnudarse) to bare all

destartalado ADJ dilapidated

destellar VI to flash

destello M flash

destemplado ADJ (persona) feverish; (sonido) out of tune

desteñido ADJ washed-out

desteñir[11] VI/VT to fade; VI to run; —se to fade

desternillarse VI — de risa to dic laughing

desterrado -da ADJ exiled, banished; MF (persona) exile

desterrar[1] VT to exile, to banish

destetar VT to wean

destierro M exile, banishment

destilación F distillation

destilar VT to distill

destilería F distillery

destinar VT (determinar el destino) to destine; (dirigir) to address; (asignar) to commit

destinatario -ria MF addressee, recipient

destino M (hado) destiny, fate, lot; (uso) use; (final de viaje) destination

destitución F dismissal

destituir[19] VT to dismiss

destornillador M screwdriver

destoxificación F detoxification

destrabar VT to untie

destreza F dexterity, skill

destripar VT to gut

destronar VT to dethrone

destrozar[47] VT (estropear) to ruin; (causar grandes daños) to destroy; (derrotar) to rout

destrozo M damage

destrucción F destruction

destructible ADJ destructible

destructivo ADJ destructive

destructor -ra ADJ destructive; M (buque) destroyer; MF (persona) destroyer

destruir[19] VT (destrozar) to destroy, to obliterate; (estropear) to ruin

destruya, destruya, destruyendo, destruyera, destruyese ver destruir

desunir VT to divide; —se to come apart

desusado ADJ (no frecuente) unusual; (no usado) obsolete

desuso M disuse, obsolescence; **caer en** — to fall into disuse

desvaído ADJ faded

desvainar VT to hull, to husk

desvalido ADJ helpless

desvalijar VT (un cuarto) to ransack; (a una persona) to clean out

desvalimiento M helplessness

desván M attic

desvanecer[35] VT (un color) to fade; (un contorno) to blur; —**se** (una persona) to faint; (un color, arrugas) to fade; (un sonido) to trail off

desvanecido ADJ (una persona) fainted; (un color) faded; (un contorno) blurred

desvanecimiento M (de una persona) fainting; (de colores) fading; (de un contorno) blurring

desvariar[28] VI to rave

desvarío M raving

desvelado ADJ sleepless

desvelar VT to keep awake; —**se** to be sleepless

desvelo M (falta de sueño) sleeplessness; —**s** (esfuerzos) efforts

desvencijado ADJ dilapidated, rickety; **estoy —** I'm all beat up

desventaja F disadvantage; **estar en —** to be at a disadvantage

desventura F misfortune

desventurado ADJ unfortunate

desvergonzado ADJ shameless

desvergüenza F shamelessness

desvestir[9] VT to undress; —**se** to get undressed, to undress

desviación F (de una norma) deviation, divergence; (en ruta) detour; (de fondos) diversion; (de la columna vertebral) curvature; — **estándar** standard deviation

desviar[28] VT (la vista) to avert; (fondos, tráfico) to divert; (un golpe) to ward off; (una conversación) to steer; (un tren) to sidetrack; —**se de** (un camino) to stray from; (una norma) to deviate from

desvío M (camino secundario) side road; (desviación) detour

desvirtuar[26] VT to distort; —**se** to become distorted

desvivirse VI — **por hacer algo** to bend over backward to do something; — **por alguien** to go out of one's way for someone

detallado ADJ detailed

detallar VT to detail, to go into detail about

detalle M (pormenor) detail; (venta al por menor) retail; (lista) list; **¡qué —!** how thoughtful! **con/al/en —** in detail

detallista ADJ (cuidadoso) meticulous; (considerado) thoughtful; M (comercio) retail; MF retailer

detección F detection

detectar VT to detect

detective M detective; — **privado** private eye

detector M detector; — **de incendios** smoke detector; — **de mentiras** lie detector; — **de metales** metal detector

detención F (arresto) detention, arrest; (de un

vehículo) stop; — **domiciliaria** house arrest; — **ilegal** false arrest

detendrá, detendría ver detener

detener[58] VT (arrestar) to detain, to arrest; (parar) to stop; —**se** to stop; —**se en** to linger on; —**se a pensar** to stop to think

detenga, detengo ver detener

detenidamente ADV closely

detenido ADJ thorough

detenimiento LOC ADV **con —** with care

detergente ADJ & M detergent

deteriorado ADJ in disrepair

deteriorar VT to deteriorate

deterioro M deterioration, disrepair

determinación F determination; — **del grupo sanguíneo** blood typing

determinado ADJ (cierto) certain; **es lo que suponen determinadas personas** that is what certain people suppose; (específico) definite, specific; **pidió una cantidad determinada** he asked for a specific amount

determinante ADJ determining; M determiner

determinar VT to determine

detestable ADJ detestable

detestar VT to detest

detiene, detienes ver detener

detonación F detonation; **hacer detonaciones** to backfire

detonar VI/VT to detonate

detrás ADV behind; — **de** (en el espacio) behind; (en el tiempo) after; **por —** behind

detritus M INV debris

detuve, detuviera, detuviese ver detener

deuce M deuce

deuda F debt; — **incobrable** bad debt

deudor -ora ADJ & MF debtor; — **hipotecario** mortgagor

devaluación F devaluation

devanar VT to spool; —**se los sesos** to rack one's brain

devaneo M (pasatiempo) idle pursuit; (amorío) fling

devastador ADJ devastating

devastar VT to devastate

devengar[40] VT to earn

devoción F devotion

devolución F (de un producto) return; (de poder político) devolution

devolver[6, 74] VT (dar al dueño) to return; (enviar por correo) to send back; — **al remitente** to return to sender; — **la llamada** to call back; VI (vomitar) to throw up

devorar VT to devour

devoto ADJ (pío) devout; (que muestra devoción) devoted

devuelto, devuelva, devuelve ver devolver

dextrosa F dextrose

di ver dar, decir

día M day; — **a —** day-to-day; — **tras —** day after

day; **al** — up-to-date; **al otro** — on the next day; **de** — by day; **de todos los —s** everyday; **el** — **de mañana** in the future; **hoy** — nowadays; **no veo el** — I can't wait; **ponerse al** — to catch up; **por** — by the day; **todo el** — all day; **todos los —s** every day; **un** — **sí y otro no** every other day; **vivir al** — to live from hand to mouth

diabetes F SG diabetes

diablo M devil; **irse al** — *vulg* to go to hell; **pobre** — poor devil; **¿por qué —s dices eso?** *fam* why the heck are you saying that?

diablura F devilry, mischief

diabólico ADJ (ritual) diabolic, devilish; (perverso) diabolical

diácono M deacon

diacrítico ADJ & M diacritic

diafragma M diaphragm

diagnosis F diagnosis

diagnosticar[30] VT to diagnose

diagnóstico ADJ diagnostic; M diagnosis

diagonal ADJ & F diagonal

diagrama M diagram; — **de flujo** flow chart; — **de pastel** pie chart

dial M dial

dialéctica F dialectic

dialéctico ADJ dialectic

dialecto M dialect

dialectología F dialectology

diálisis F dialysis

dialogar[40] VI to dialogue, to hold talks

diálogo M dialogue, conversation; **fue un** — **de sordos** they talked past each other

diamante M diamond; — **en bruto** diamond in the rough

diámetro M diameter

diana F bull's-eye

diapasón M tuning fork

diapositiva F slide

diario ADJ daily; M (periódico) newspaper; (de sucesos personales) journal, diary; (de navegación) log; **a** — every day; **de** — everyday; **llevar un** — to keep a diary

diarrea F diarrhea

diastólico ADJ diastolic

diatriba F diatribe

dibujante MF illustrator

dibujar VT to draw; **—se** to appear, to loom

dibujo M (arte de dibujar, cosa dibujada) drawing; (diseño) design; — **al carbón** charcoal drawing; **—s animados** animated cartoon

dicción F diction

diccionario M dictionary

dice, dicen *ver* decir

dicha F happiness

dicharachero ADJ witty

dicho ADJ aforementioned; M saying

dicho *ver* decir

dichoso ADJ happy; **todo el** — **día** the whole blessed day

diciembre M December

diciendo *ver* decir

dicotomía F dichotomy

dictado M (ejercicio) dictation; (orden) dictate; **escribir al** — to take dictation

dictador -ora MF dictator

dictadura F dictatorship

dictamen M (opinión) report; (judicial) ruling

dictaminar VI (dar una opinión) to report; (fallar) to rule

dictar VT to dictate; — **clase** to teach class; — **sentencia** to rule

diecinueve NUM nineteen

dieciocho NUM eighteen

dieciséis NUM sixteen

diecisiete NUM seventeen

diente M (de persona, sierra) tooth; (de víbora) fang; (de rueda dentada) cog; (de tenedor) prong; — **de león** dandelion; — **de leche** baby tooth; **—s postizos** false teeth; **entre —s** under one's breath; **tener buen** — to have a good appetite

diera, diese *ver* dar

diesel M diesel

diestra F right hand

diestro -tra ADJ (habilidoso) skillful, deft; (no zurdo) right-handed; MF right-handed person; **a diestra y siniestra** on all sides

dieta F (ingesta) diet; (dinero para gastos) per diem; **estar a** — to be on a diet

dietético ADJ dietary

dietista MF dietitian

diez NUM ten

diezmar VT to decimate

diezmo M tithe; **pagar el** — to tithe

difamación F (oral) slander; (escrita) libel

difamar VT to defame, to malign; (oralmente) to slander; (por escrito) to libel

difamatorio ADJ slanderous

diferencia F difference; **a** — **de** unlike; **hacer —s entre** to treat differently; **partir la** — to split the difference

diferenciación F differentiation, distinction

diferencial ADJ & M (distancia, pieza de coche) differential; F (matemática) differential

diferenciar VT to differentiate; **—se de** to differ from

diferente ADJ different

diferir[8] VT (aplazar) to defer; VI (ser diferente) to differ

difícil ADJ difficult, hard

difícilmente ADV (apenas) hardly; (con dificultad) with difficulty

dificultad F difficulty

dificultar VT to make difficult

dificultoso ADJ difficult

difteria F diphtheria

difundir VT (luz) to diffuse; (noticias) to broadcast
difunto -ta ADJ & MF deceased
difusión F (de luz) diffusion; (de noticias) broadcasting
difuso ADJ diffuse
diga ver decir
digerible ADJ digestible
digerir[8] VT to digest
digestible ADJ digestible
digestión F digestion
digestivo ADJ digestive
digesto M digest
digital ADJ digital
digitalizar[47] VT to digitalize, to digitize
digitar VI/VT to type
dígito M digit
dignarse VI to deign
dignatario -ria MF dignitary
dignidad F dignity
digno ADJ (respetable) worthy; (orgulloso) dignified; **— de confianza** trustworthy; **— de elogio** praiseworthy
digo ver decir
digresión F digression
dije M charm
dije, dijera, dijese ver decir
dilación F delay; **sin —** without delay
dilatación F (de un metal, parte dilatada) expansion; (del ojo) dilation
dilatar VT (pupilas, capilares) to dilate; (metal, músculo) to expand; (tiempo, plazo) to defer; (prolongar) to prolong; **—se en un asunto** to dwell on a subject
dilema M dilemma
diletante MF dilettante
diligencia F (laboriosidad) diligence, industry; (vehículo) stagecoach; (tarea) errand; **— debida** due diligence
diligente ADJ diligent, industrious
dilucidar VT to elucidate
diluido ADJ dilute
diluir[19] VT (una solución) to dilute; (pintura, sopa) to thin
diluvio M deluge
dimensión F dimension
dimes M PL **— y diretes** gossip; **andar en — y diretes** to quibble
diminutivo ADJ & M diminutive
diminuto ADJ (tamaño) diminutive; (cantidad) minute
dimisión F resignation
dimitir VI to resign
Dinamarca F Denmark
dinámica F dynamics
dinámico ADJ dynamic
dinamismo M vigor
dinamita F dynamite
dinamitar VT to dynamite

dínamo M dynamo
dinastía F dynasty
dineral M fortune
dinero M money; **— contante y sonante** ready cash, hard cash; **— de plástico** plastic, credit card; **— sucio** dirty money
dinosaurio M dinosaur
diodo M diode; **— electroluminiscente** light-emitting diode
Dios M God; **dios** god; **— dirá** we'll see; **— los cría y ellos se juntan** birds of a feather flock together; **— mediante** God willing; **¡— mío!** my God! **— te lo pague** may God reward you; **— y su madre** everybody and their dog; **a la buena de —** any old way; **como — manda** as it should be; **¡por —!** oh, my! **que — te oiga** I hope you're right
diosa F goddess
diploma M diploma
diplomacia F diplomacy
diplomático -ca ADJ diplomatic; MF diplomat
diptongo M diphthong
diputación F council
diputado -da MF representative
dique M (presa) dike; (al lado de un río) levee; **— seco** dry dock
dirá ver decir
dirección F (sentido, rumbo) direction; (domicilio) address; (administración) management; (administración de una escuela) principal's office; (mecanismo, acción de conducir) steering; **— asistida** power steering; **— de correo electrónico** e-mail address
directiva F (orden) directive; (norma) guidelines; (junta de directores) board of directors
directrices F PL guidelines
directivo -va ADJ leadership; MF officer
directo ADJ (sin desviaciones, intermediarios) direct; (derecho) straight; **en —** live
director -ora MF (de una empresa) director, manager; (de una escuela) principal; (de orquesta) conductor; **— de correos** postmaster; **— general** CEO; **— técnico** coach
directorio M (índice) directory; (junta directiva) board of directors; **— [de] raíz** root directory; **— padre** parent directory
diría ver decir
dirigente MF leader; **— sindical** union leader
dirigible M dirigible
dirigir[46] VT (una obra teatral) to direct; (una empresa) to manage; (una orquesta) to conduct; (a un turista) to guide; (un saludo, una carta, una pregunta, una crítica) to address; **—se a** (hablar con) to address; (ir a) to go to; (tratar de) to be aimed at
discapacidad F disability

discapacitado ADJ disabled
discar[30] VI/VT *Am* to dial
discernimiento M discernment, insight
discernir[3] VT to discern
disciplina F discipline
disciplinar VT to discipline
discípulo -la MF disciple
disco M (cartílago, objeto plano y circular) disk;
  (fonográfico) record; — **compacto** compact
  disc; — **comprimido** compressed disk; —
  de iniciación boot disk; — **duro** hard disk;
  — **duro interno** internal hard disk; —
  volador Frisbee®; **es un — rayado** he's a
  broken record
díscolo ADJ unruly
disconforme ADJ dissatisfied
discontinuo ADJ discontinuous
discordancia F discord
discordia F discord
discoteca F (lugar donde bailar) discotheque;
  (colección de discos) record collection
discreción F discretion; **a** — at one's own
  discretion
discrepancia F discrepancy
discrepar VI to disagree; — **de** to take issue with
discreto ADJ (prudente) discreet; (separado)
  discrete; **un partido** — a sorry game
discriminación F discrimination; — **por edad**
  age discrimination; — **positiva** affirmative
  action; — **sexual** sexual discrimination
discriminar VI to discriminate; — **a** to
  discriminate against
disculpa F (excusa) excuse; (perdón) apology
disculpable ADJ excusable
disculpar VT (excusar) to excuse; (perdonar) to
  forgive, to pardon; —**se** to apologize
discurrir VI (transcurrir) to pass; (exponer) to
  discourse
discursear VI to make speeches
discurso M (enunciado) discourse; (disertacíon
  pública) speech, address; — **de apertura**
  keynote address
discusión F (charla) discussion; (riña) argument
discutible ADJ debatable, questionable
discutir VT (hablar sobre) to discuss; (oponerse
  a) to dispute; VI (reñir) to argue
disecar[30] VT (cortar) to dissect; (preparar para
  conservar) to stuff
diseminación F dissemination
diseminar VT to disseminate
disensión F dissension, dissent
disenso M dissent
disentería F dysentery
disentir[8] VI to dissent, to disagree
diseñador -ora MF designer
diseñar VT to design
diseño M design; — **de interiores** interior
  design; — **de página** page layout; —
  gráfico graphic design

disertación F lecture
disertar VI to lecture
disfraz M (para ocultarse) disguise; (de carnaval)
  costume
disfrazar[47] VT to disguise
disfrutar VI/VT to enjoy; — **de** to enjoy
disfrute M enjoyment
disfunción F dysfunction
disgustado ADJ (molesto) upset; (enojado)
  angry
disgustar VT to upset; —**se** (molestarse) to get
  upset; (enfadarse) to get angry
disgusto M (desagrado) unpleasantness;
  (discusión) quarrel; **a** — (con desgana) against
  one's will; (con incomodidad) uncomfortably;
  (en disconformidad) in conflict; **esa niña no
  da más que** —**s** that girl keeps us upset all
  the time
disidente ADJ & MF dissident
disimulado ADJ **hacerse el** — to pretend not to
  notice
disimular VI (fingir) to dissemble; (ocultar) to
  conceal
disimulo M (fingimiento) dissimulation;
  (ocultamiento) concealment
disipación F dissipation
disipar VT (niebla, calor) to dissipate; (dudas) to
  dispel; (miedo) to allay; (dinero) to squander;
  —**se** to dissipate; (miedo, dudas) to allay, to
  lift
dislexia F dyslexia
dislocación F dislocation
dislocar[30] VT to dislocate; —**se** to get dislocated
disminución F (acción de disminuir) decrease,
  lessening; (desprecio) belittling; (de ventas)
  dip, decrease
disminuir[19] VT (menguar) to diminish, to
  decrease, to lessen; (despreciar) to belittle
**disminuya, disminuye, disminuyendo,
  disminuyera, disminuyese** *ver* disminuir
disolución F dissolution
disoluto ADJ dissolute, loose
disolvente M solvent; — **de pintura** paint
  thinner
disolver[6, 74] VT (sal) to dissolve; (reunión) to
  break up
disonancia F discord
dispar ADJ disparate
disparar VT (un arma de fuego) to shoot, to fire;
  (una cámara) to click; (la inflación) to trigger;
  VI (en fútbol) to shoot; —**le a alguien** to
  shoot at someone; —**se** (aumentar) to take
  off; (salir) to shoot out
disparatado ADJ absurd
disparatar VI to talk nonsense
disparate M absurdity, nonsense; **decir** —**s** to
  talk nonsense; **un** — **de plata** a ton of
  money; **puros** —**s** *vulg* pure bullshit
disparo M (acción de disparar) shooting; (tiro,

herida) shot, gunshot; (tiro de fútbol) shot at goal

dispensa F dispensation

dispensación F dispensation

dispensar VT to dispense; — **de** to exempt from

dispensario M dispensary

dispersar VT to disperse

dispersión F dispersal

disperso ADJ (diseminado) dispersed, scattered; (distraído) absent-minded, distracted; (no concentrado) disperse

display M display

displicencia F flippancy

displicente ADJ (comportamiento) flippant; (actitud) cavalier

dispon, dispondrá, dispondría ver disponer

disponer[56, 74] VT (colocar) to arrange; (preparar) to prepare, to dispose; (mandar) to order; — **de** to have; —**se** to set about; —**se para** to get ready for

disponga, dispongo ver disponer

disponibilidad F availability

disponible ADJ (asiento, taxi) available; (dinero) on hand; (inventario) in stock

disposición F (voluntad) disposition; (colocación) arrangement; (de ánimo) mood; **a** — **de** at the disposal of

dispositivo M device; — **analógico** analog device; — **de almacenamiento** storage device; — **de salida** output device; — **intrauterino** intrauterine device

dispuesto ADJ ready; **bien** — willing; **no estar** — **a** to be unwilling to

dispuesto, dispuse, dispusiera, dispusiese ver disponer

disputa F (controversia) dispute; (riña) argument

disputar VI/VT to dispute; —**se el poder** to vie/ challenge/contend for power; —**se la posición** to jockey for position

disquete M floppy disk; — **de iniciación** bootable diskette

disquetera F disk drive

distancia F distance; **a** — at arm's length; **guardar** —**s** to keep at a distance; **¿a qué** — **está?** how far away is it?

distanciarse VT to distance oneself

distante ADJ distant

distar VI **dista mucho de** it's a far cry from; **dista diez kilómetros de** it's ten kilometers from

distender[2] VT (aflojar) to relax; (dilatar) to expand

distensión F distension; — **muscular** muscle strain

distinción F distinction

distinguido ADJ distinguished

distinguir[44] VT to distinguish

distintivo ADJ distinctive, distinguishing; M distinguishing characteristic

distinto ADJ (diferente) different; (claro) distinct

distorsión F distortion

distorsionar VT to distort

distracción F distraction

distraer[59] VT (la atención) to distract; (fondos, mano de obra) to divert; —**se** (divertirse) to entertain oneself; (dispersarse) to become distracted, fam to space out

distraído ADJ distracted, absent-minded; **hacerse el** — to play dumb

distribución F distribution

distribuidor -ora MF (persona) distributor; M (pieza de un motor) distributor

distribuir[19] VT to distribute

distrito M district

Distrito de Columbia M District of Columbia

distrofia F dystrophy; — **muscular** muscular dystrophy

disturbio M disturbance, trouble

disuadir VT (mediante palabras) to dissuade; (mediante acciones) to deter

DIU [dispositivo intrauterino] M IUD

diurético ADJ & M diuretic

diurno ADJ (actividad) daytime; (animal) diurnal

divagación F rambling

divagar[40] VI to ramble on, to digress

diván M divan; (de psiquiatra) couch

divergencia F divergence

divergir[46] VI to diverge

diversidad F diversity

diversión F (pasatiempo) amusement, entertainment, fun; (hecho de distraer la atención) diversion

diverso ADJ diverse; —**s** various

diverticulitis F diverticulitis

divertido ADJ amusing, entertaining

divertir[8] VT to amuse, to entertain; —**se** to have a good time, to have fun

dividendo M dividend

dividir VT to divide; (un territorio) to partition

divierta, divierte ver divertir

divieso M boil

divinidad F divinity

divino ADJ divine; **estuvo** — it was heavenly; **lo pasé** — I had a wonderful time

divirtiendo, divirtiera, divirtiese, divirtió ver divertir

divisa F (señal) emblem; (moneda) currency; (moneda extranjera) foreign currency

divisar VT to make out, to catch sight of

división F division; (de un territorio) partition

divisorio ADJ dividing

divorciar VT to divorce; —**se** to get divorced

divorcio M divorce

divulgación F dissemination; — **financiera** financial disclosure

divulgar[40] VT (un secreto) to divulge;

(información) to disseminate

dobladillo M hem; **hacer —s** to hem

doblado ADJ (hipócrita) hypocritical; M (de tela, papel) folding; (de tubos) bending

doblaje M dubbing

doblar VT (una sábana) to fold; (el capital) to double; (una esquina) to turn; (la voz de un actor) to dub; VI (un coche) to turn; (una campana) to knell; **—se** to bend over

doble ADJ double (también en tenis); **— agente** double agent; **— falta** double fault; **— indemnización** double indemnity; **— matanza** double play; **— pulsación** double click; **— personalidad** split personality; **— visión** double vision; **de — caño** double-barreled; **de — filo** double-edged; **de — sentido** two-way; MF (persona muy parecida, actor sustituto) double; M (repique) knell; **—s** doubles; **—s mixtos** mixed doubles; **el —** double

doblegar[40] VT to break

doblete M double

doblez M fold; F deceitfulness

doce NUM twelve

docena F dozen; **— del fraile** baker's dozen

docente ADJ teaching

dócil ADJ (persona, animal) docile, pliant; (pelo) manageable

docto ADJ learned

doctor -ora MF doctor; **— en medicina** MD

doctorado M doctorate

doctrina F doctrine

documentación F documentation (también para computadoras)

documental ADJ & M documentary

documentar VT to document

documento M document; **— de instrucciones previas** living will; **— de voluntad anticipada** living will

dogma M dogma

dogmático ADJ dogmatic

dogo M pug

dólar M dollar

dolencia F ailment

doler[6] VI to ache, to hurt; **me duele el brazo** my arm aches, my arm is sore; **—se de** (compadecerse) to feel sorry for; (arrepentirse) to regret

doliente ADJ aching; MF mourner

dolor M (físico) pain, ache; (espiritual) sorrow, pain; **— de barriga** bellyache; **— de cabeza** headache; **— de espalda** backache; **— de muela** toothache; **— de oídos** earache; **— de garganta** sore throat; **—es del crecimiento** growing pains; **— de garganta** sore throat; **—es de parto** labor pains

dolorido ADJ aching, sore

doloroso ADJ painful

doma F (de caballos) breaking; (de leones) taming

domado ADJ (caballo) broken; (león) tamed

domador -ora MF (de perros) trainer; (de leones) lion tamer

domar VT (caballos, personas) to break; (leones) to tame

domesticar[30] VT to domesticate, to tame

doméstico -ca ADJ domestic; MF servant

domiciliarse VI to take up residence; **¿dónde se domicilia usted?** where do you reside?

domicilio M (casa) dwelling; (dirección) address

dominación F domination

dominador ADJ (predominante) dominant; (tiránico) domineering, overbearing

dominante ADJ (predominante) dominant; (tiránico) domineering, overbearing

dominar VT (tener bajo su autoridad, ser más alto) to dominate; (reprimir) to control, to rein in; (tener sometido a su voluntad) to domineer

domingo M Sunday; **— de Ramos** Palm Sunday; **— de Pascua** Easter Sunday

Dominica F Dominica

dominicano -na ADJ & MF Dominican [de la República Dominicana]

dominio M (sobre una tierra, derecho de usar una cosa) dominion; (de sí mismo) control; (de una lengua) mastery, command; (hecho de dominar) domination; (ámbito, campo) domain; **— público** public domain

dominiqués -esa ADJ & MF Dominican [de Dominica]

dominó M (pieza) domino; (juego) dominoes

domo M dome

don M (gracia) gift; (título, jefe mafioso) don; **un — nadie** a nobody

dona F *Méx* doughnut, donut

donación F donation

donador -ora MF donor

donaire M grace

donante MF donor; **— universal** universal donor

donar MF to donate

doncella F *lit* maiden

donde ADV REL where; **de —** whence, from which; **ir — el herrero** to go to the blacksmith's shop; **— no** otherwise; **—quiera** wherever; **donde no comas, no te dejo salir a jugar** if you don't eat, I won't let you go out to play

dónde ADV INTERR where

donoso ADJ graceful

donut M *Esp* doughnut, donut

doña F doña

dopamina F dopamine

dopar VT to dope

dorado ADJ (cubierto de oro) gilt; (de color oro) golden; M dolphin fish

dorar VT to gild; — **la píldora** to sweeten the pill
dormido ADJ asleep
dormir[7] VI/VT to sleep; — **a** to put to bed; — **a un paciente** to anesthetize a patient; — **la mona** to sleep it off; — **la siesta** to take a nap; **se me ha dormido el brazo** my arm has fallen asleep; —**se** to fall asleep
dormitar VI to doze, to snooze
dormitorio M bedroom
dorso M back, reverse
dos NUM two; — **puntos** colon; — **veces** twice; **cada** — **por tres** constantly; **en un** — **por tres** in a jiffy; **los** — both of them
DOS M DOS
doscientos NUM two hundred
dosel M canopy
dosificar[30] VT to dose
dosis F (de medicamento) dose; (de droga) hit
dotación F (de fondos) endowment; (de personal) complement
dotar VT to endow
dote F dowry; —**s** talents
doy ver dar
draga F dredge
dragado M dredging
dragar[40] VT (para limpiar) to dredge; (para buscar objetos) to drag; M SG **dragaminas** minesweeper
dragón M (animal fantástico) dragon; (planta) snapdragon
drama M drama
dramático ADJ dramatic
dramatizar[47] VT to dramatize
dramaturgo -ga MF playwright, dramatist
drapear VI to drape
drástico ADJ drastic
drenaje M drainage
drenar VI/VT to drain
dribbling M dribble, dribbling
driblar VI/VT to dribble
drible M dribble
dril M drill
drive M drive
drive-in M drive-in
driver M driver
droga F drug; — **anticancerosa** anticancer drug; — **de recreo** recreational drug; —**s de diseño** designer drugs; **tomar** —**s** to do drugs; MF **drogadicto -ta** drug addict
drogar[40] VT to drug
drogata MF junkie
drogota MF junkie
droguería F (tienda) drugstore; (industria) drug industry
droguero -ra MF druggist
dropar VI to drop
ducado M dukedom
ducha F shower; — **vaginal** vaginal douche

ducharse VI to shower
ducho ADJ skillful
dúctil ADJ (metal) ductile; (persona) flexible, supple
duda F doubt; **en** — in doubt; **fuera de** — beyond doubt; **no cabe** — there's no doubt; **poner en** — to cast doubt on; **sin** — without a doubt, undoubtedly; **sin lugar a** —**s** without doubt; **tengo una** — I have a question
dudar VT (no creer) to doubt; (vacilar) to hesitate; — **de** to have doubts about
dudoso ADJ doubtful; **de dudosa honestidad** of dubious honesty
duela F stave
duela, duele ver doler
duelo M (combate) duel; (luto) mourning; (pena) grief; (dolientes) mourners; **estar de** — to be in mourning
duende M (gnomo) goblin, gremlin; (gracia) charm
dueño -ña MF owner; **me sentí** — **de la situación** I felt like I was in control of the situation; M landlord; F landlady
duerma, duerme ver dormir
dueto M duet
dulce ADJ (sabor, personalidad) sweet; (clima) pleasant; (agua) fresh; —**amargo** bittersweet; M (cosa dulce) sweet; (mermelada) preserves, conserve
dulcería F confectionery
dulcificar[30] VT to sweeten
dulzón ADJ unpleasantly sweet
dulzor M sweetness
dulzura F sweetness
duna F dune
dúo M duet; **decir a** — to say in unison
duodeno M duodenum
dúplex M duplex
duplicado ADJ & M duplicate; **por** — in duplicate
duplicar[30] VT to duplicate
duplicidad F duplicity
duque M duke
duquesa F duchess
durabilidad F durability
duración F duration; (de una película, vocal) length; — **de la vida** lifespan
duradero ADJ (ropa) durable, serviceable; (pilas) long-lasting
durante PREP during; — **el mandato de los Demócratas** under the Democrats; — **muchos años** for/over many years
durar VI/VT to last
duraznero M peach tree
durazno M (fruto) peach; (árbol) peach tree
dureza F (de metal) hardness; (del clima, de la expresión, de una tempestad) severity; (del invierno) harshness; (de un boxeador)

toughness; (del cuero) stiffness

durmamos, durmiendo *ver* dormir

durmiente ADJ sleeping; M railroad tie, sleeper

durmiera, durmiese *ver* dormir

duro ADJ (metal, golpe, droga, agua) hard; (clima, tormenta) severe; (invierno, expresión, sonido) harsh; (soldado) tough; (grifo) stuck; (viento) strong; (autoridad) inflexible; (pan) stale; (cuero) stiff; — **de corazón** hard-hearted; — **de entendederas** slow on the uptake; **a duras penas** barely; M five-peseta coin; **no tengo un** — I'm flat broke

DVD M DVD

Ee

e CONJ and

ebanista MF cabinetmaker

ébano M ebony

ebrio ADJ drunk, inebriated

ebullición F boiling

eccema M eczema

echar VT (una pelota, redes) to throw, to cast; (yemas, hojas) to sprout; (a un empleado) to fire; (humo, olor) to give off; (un líquido) to pour; (a un borracho) to throw out; — **abajo** to knock down; — **a la basura** to throw away; — **al mar** to put to sea; — **al correo** to mail; — **anclas** to drop anchor; — **a pique** to sink; — **carnes** to get fat; — **de menos** to miss; — **de ver** to notice; — **mano de** to seize upon; — **la culpa** to blame; — **por la borda** to jettison; — **raíces** to take root; — **sangre** to bleed; — **suertes** to draw lots; — **una carta** to mail a letter; — **una siesta** to take a nap; — **un vistazo a** to glance at, to take a look at; **te echo una carrera** I'll race you; —**le el muerto a alguien** to pass the buck to someone; —**se a** to lie down; —**se a** start to; —**se a correr** to bolt; —**se a perder** to spoil; —**se a reír** to burst out laughing; —**se a un lado** to dodge; —**se atrás** to back down/off; —**se para atrás** to lean back

ecléctico ADJ eclectic

eclesiástico ADJ & M ecclesiastic

eclipsar VT (ocultar) to eclipse; (superar) to eclipse, to outshine, to overshadow; —**se** to fade

eclipse M eclipse; — **de sol** solar eclipse; — **de luna** lunar eclipse

eco M echo; **hacer** — to echo; **hacerse** — **de** to repeat

ecocardiograma M echocardiogram

ecología F (medio ambiente) environment; (ciencia) ecology

ecológico ADJ (ambiental) environmental, ecological; (bueno para la naturaleza) eco-friendly

ecologista ADJ environmental; MF environmentalist

economato M commissary

economía F (actividades de producción) economy; (ciencia) economics; (familiar) finances; — **doméstica** home economics; —**s** savings; **hacer** —**s** to be thrifty

económico ADJ (relativo a la economía) economic; (frugal) frugal, thrifty; (barato) economical

economista MF economist

economizar[47] VT to economize, to save

ecosistema M ecosystem

ecuación F equation

ecuador M equator

Ecuador M Ecuador

ecualizar[47] VT to equalize

ecuatoriano -na ADJ & MF Ecuadorian

ecuménico ADJ ecumenical

edad F age; — **avanzada** ripe old age; — **de merecer** marriageable age; — **de Piedra** Stone Age; — **del consentimiento sexual** age of consent; — **Media** Middle Ages; — **mental** mental age

edición F (ejemplar) edition; (acción de editar) publication; — **de sobremesa** desktop publishing

edicto M edict

edificación F building

edificar[30] VT (construir) to build; (infundir sentimientos morales) to edify, to uplift

edificio M building

editar VT to edit, to publish

editor -ora ADJ publishing; MF editor

editorial ADJ publishing; F publishing house; M editorial

editorializar[47] VI to editorialize

edredón M comforter

educación F (escolar) education; (social) breeding; — **a distancia** distance learning; — **cívica** civics; — **especial** special education; — **en línea** e-learning; — **física** physical education; — **para adultos** continuing education; — **superior** higher education

educado ADJ (cortés) well-bred; (instruido) educated

educador -ora MF educator

educar[30] VT (desarrollar conocimientos) to educate; (entrenar) to train

educativo ADJ educational

edulcorante M sweetener

EEUU [Estados Unidos] M SG/PL USA

efectivamente ADV actually; **más de los que** — **encuentran** more than they actually find;

INTERJ exactly

efectividad F effectiveness; **tener** — to be valid, to become valid

efectivo ADJ (eficaz) effective; (real) actual; **hacer** — (un cheque) to cash; (una deuda) to pay off; (una amenaza) to make good on; M cash; **en** — in cash; **—s** troops

efecto M (resultado) effect, result; (letra comercial) bill of exchange; (rotación) English, spin; **en** — in fact; **llevar a** — to carry out; **surtir** — to work; — **invernadero** greenhouse effect; **—s especiales** special effects; **—s personales** personal effects; **perder** — to wear off; **rebotar con** — to glance off; **a estos —s** to this effect; **para los —s** to all intents and purposes; **por** — **de** as a consequence of

efectuar[26] VT to effect; **—se** to be carried out

eficacia F efficacy, effectiveness; — **de una ley** force of law

eficaz ADJ effective

eficiencia F efficiency

eficiente ADJ efficient

efigie F effigy; **quemar en** — to burn in effigy

efímero ADJ ephemeral, fleeting

efusivo ADJ effusive

egipcio -cia ADJ & MF Egyptian

Egipto M Egypt

égloga F pastoral

ego M ego

egocéntrico ADJ egocentric, self-centered

egoísmo M selfishness

egoísta ADJ selfish; MF selfish person

egotismo M egotism

egresado -da MF graduate

eje M (de la Tierra) axis; (de un vehículo) axle; — **del pistón** piston rod; **eso me parte por el** — that messes up my plans

ejecución F (de un condenado) execution; (de un plan, una orden) carrying out, execution; (de una tarea) performance; (de una propiedad) foreclosure

ejecutable ADJ executable

ejecutar VT (a un condenado) to execute; (un plan, una orden) to carry out; (una tarea, música) to perform; (una propiedad) to foreclose on

ejecutivo -va ADJ & MF executive; — **de empresa** corporate officer

ejemplar ADJ exemplary, model; M (libro) copy; (individuo) specimen

ejemplario M handout

ejemplificar[30] VT to exemplify

ejemplo M (cosa típica) example; (modelo) model; **a** — **de** on the example of; **dar** — to set an example; **por** — for example

ejercer[32] VT (una profesión) to practice; (influencia, fuerza) to exert; (poder) to wield

ejercicio M exercise; (de una profesión) practice;

hacer — to exercise; — **contable** accounting period; — **físico** physical exercise; **—s de Kegel** Kegel exercises; **en** — active

ejercitar VT (la vista, los músculos) to exercise; (a soldados) to drill; (a alumnos) to train; **—se** to train

ejército M army; **el** — the military

ejido M common

ejote M *Méx* green bean

el ART DEF M the; — **de la derecha** the one on the right; — **que** the one that; — **que sepa** whoever knows

él PRON PERS M SG (como sujeto) he; — **dijo** he said; (como objeto) him; **para** — for him; **le di el libro a** — I gave the book to him; **estamos hablando de** — we're talking about him; **el libro de** — his book

elaboración F (de miel, comida) making; (de un método) development; (de un informe) drafting

elaborado ADJ elaborate

elaborar VT (un método) to elaborate, to develop; (comida) to make; (un informe) to draft

elasticidad F elasticity

elástico ADJ (sustancia) elastic; (cuerpo) supple; (horario) flexible; M elastic

elección F (votación) election; (selección) choice, selection; **no tuve** — I had no choice

electo ADJ elect

elector -ora ADJ electoral; MF elector

electoral ADJ electoral

electricidad F electricity; — **estática** static electricity

electricista MF electrician

eléctrico ADJ (aparato) electric; (instalación, corriente) electrical

electrificar[30] VT to electrify

electrizado ADJ electrified

electrizante ADJ electrifying

electrizar[47] VT (suministrar electricidad) to electrify; (emocionar) to galvanize, to electrify

electrocardiograma M electrocardiogram

electrocutar VT to electrocute

electrodo M electrode

electrodoméstico M electrical appliance

electroencefalograma M electroencephalogram

electroimán M electromagnet

electrólisis F electrolysis

electromagnético ADJ electromagnetic

electrón M electron

electrónica F electronics

electrónico ADJ electronic

elefante M elephant

elegancia F elegance

elegante ADJ (armonioso) elegant; (bien

vestido) stylish, classy
elegibilidad F eligibility
elegible ADJ eligible
elegir[14] VT (seleccionar) to choose, to select; (votar) to elect
elemental ADJ (sencillo) elementary; (básico) elemental
elemento M element
elenco M cast
elevación F elevation; **tirar por —** to throw high in the air
elevado ADJ (pensamiento, estilo) elevated; (fiebre, montaña) high; (precios) high; M (béisbol) fly ball
elevador M elevator
elevar VT (en una jerarquía) to elevate; (precios, voz, objeto) to raise; (el espíritu) to uplift; — **la vista** to look up; — **al cuadrado** to square; — **al cubo** to cube; **—se a** to go up to, to rise to; **el rascacielos se eleva sobre la ciudad** the skyscraper towers over the city
elfo M elf
eliminación F elimination
eliminar VT to eliminate
eliminatoria F (atletismo, natación) heat; **—s** (fútbol) playoffs
elíptico ADJ elliptical
elite/élite F elite
elitista ADJ & MF elitist
ella PRON PERS F SG (como sujeto) she; — **dijo** she said; (como objeto) her; **para —** for her; **le di el libro a —** I gave the book to her; **el libro de —** her book
ellas PRON PERS F PL (como sujeto) they; — **dijeron** they said; (como objeto) them; **para — for** them; **les di el libro a —** I gave them the book; **el libro de —** their book
ello PRON NEUTRO it; — **es que** the fact is that
ellos PRON M PL (como sujeto) they; — **dijeron** they said; (como objeto) them; **para —** for them; **les di el libro a —** I gave them the book; **el libro de —** their book
elocuencia F eloquence
elocuente ADJ eloquent; **las estadísticas son —s** the statistics speak for themselves
elogiar VT to praise
elogio M praise
elote M *Méx* corn on the cob
elucidación F elucidation
elucidar VT to elucidate
eludir VT to elude, to avoid, to dodge
emanación F emanation, flow
emanar VI/VT to emanate
emancipación F emancipation
emancipar VT to emancipate; **—se** to become free
emascular VT to emasculate
embadurnar VT to daub
embajada F embassy

embajador -ora MF ambassador
embalador -ora MF packer
embalaje M packing, packaging
embalar VT to pack; VI to accelerate
embaldosar VT to tile
embalsamar VT (a un muerto) to embalm; (un animal) to stuff
embalse M reservoir
embanderar VT to adorn with flags
embarazada ADJ pregnant
embarazar[47] VT (impedir) to hamper; (fecundar) to make pregnant; **—se** to get pregnant
embarazo M (obstáculo) impediment; (estado de embarazada) pregnancy
embarazoso ADJ embarrassing, awkward
embarcación F boat, embarkation, craft
embarcadero M wharf, pier
embarcar[30] VT (pasajeros) to embark; (mercancías) to load; **—se** to embark, to go aboard; **—se en** to embark upon
embargar[40] VT to seize; **estar embargado de emoción** to be overcome with emotion
embargo M embargo; — **judicial** seizure; **imponer un —** to embargo; **sin —** nevertheless, however
embarque M (de mercancías) loading; (de pasajeros) embarkation
embarrado ADJ smeared with mud
embarrar VT to smear with mud, to muddy
embate M lashing
embaucador M confidence man
embaucar[30] VT to dupe
embeber VT to soak up; **—se** to be absorbed
embelesar VT to enrapture
embeleso M rapture
embellecer[35] VI/VT to beautify
embestida F charge
embestir[9] VI/VT to charge
embetunar VT to polish
emblanquecer[35] VI/VT to whiten
emblema M emblem
embobar VT to amaze; **—se** to be amazed
embolia F embolism; — **cerebral** cerebral embolism
émbolo M piston, plunger
embolsar VT (dinero) to pocket; (una compra) to bag
emborrachar VT (a una persona) to intoxicate; (el carburador) to flood; **—se** to get drunk
emborronar VT (manchar) to blot; (hacer impreciso) to blur
emboscada F ambush; **tender una —** to lie in ambush
emboscar[30] VT to ambush; **—se** to lie in ambush
embotamiento M (efecto de embotar) dullness, bluntness; (acción de embotar) dulling
embotar VT to dull
embotelladora F bottling plant

embotellamiento M (de cerveza) bottling; (de tráfico) traffic jam, bottleneck

embotellar VT (cerveza) to bottle; (tráfico) to bottle up

embozar[47] VT to conceal

embragar[40] VI to engage the clutch

embrague M clutch

embriagado ADJ drunken

embriagar[40] VT to intoxicate; —**se** to become intoxicated

embriaguez F intoxication, drunkenness

embridar VT to bridle

embrión M embryo

embrionario ADJ embryonic

embriónico ADJ embryonic

embrollar VT (involucrar) to embroil; (confundir) to muddle

embrollo M muddle

embromar VT to kid

embrujar VT to bewitch

embrujo M spell

embrutecer[35] VT to stupefy

embudo M funnel

embuste M lie

embustero -ra MF liar, trickster

embutido M sausage

embutir VT to cram, to jam

emergencia F emergency

emergente ADJ emergent, emerging

emerger[45] VI (surgir) to emerge; (salir del agua) to surface

emigración F (de personas) emigration; (de animales) migration

emigrante ADJ & MF emigrant

emigrar VI (personas) to emigrate; (animales) to migrate

eminencia F eminence; — **gris** gray eminence

eminente ADJ eminent

emisario -ria MF emissary; M outlet

emisión F (de acciones, billetes) issue; (de un olor) discharge; (de programas) broadcast; (de gas) emission

emisor ADJ emitting; M transmitter

emisora F radio/television station

emitir VT (un olor, vapor) to emit; (juicios) to pronounce; (dinero, acciones) to issue; VI/VT (programas) to broadcast; —**se** to be on the air; **el programa se emite en horas de la mañana** the program airs in the morning

emoción F emotion; ¡**qué —**! what a thrill!

emocional ADJ emotional

emocionante ADJ (conmovedor) touching; (apasionante) exciting

emocionar VT (apasionar) to excite; (conmover) to move, to touch; —**se** (estar ilusionado) to be excited; (estar conmovido) to be touched

emoticón M emoticon

emoticono M emoticon

emotivo ADJ emotional

empacador -ora MF packer

empacar[30] VT (regalos, mercancías) to pack; (algodón) to bale

empachar VI to cause indigestion; —**se** to suffer indigestion; —**se de** to get sick on, to stuff oneself with

empacho M (indigestión) indigestion; (cohibición) inhibition; **no tener — en** to have no qualms about

empalagar[40] VI/VT to cloy

empalagoso ADJ cloying, saccharine

empalar VT to impale

empalizada F stockade, palisade

empalmar VT to splice; — **con** to join

empalme M (de caminos) junction; (de cuerdas) splice; — **genético** gene splicing

empanada F turnover, pie

empanar VT to bread

empañado ADJ (vidrio) misty, foggy; (metal, reputación) tarnished

empañar VT (vidrio) to fog up; (metal, reputación) to tarnish

empapado ADJ soggy, sopping wet

empapamiento M soaking

empapar VT (mojar) to soak, to drench; (recoger con algo) to soak up; —**se** (mojarse) to get soaked; (enterarse) to find out all about

empapelado M wallpapering

empapelar VT to paper, to wallpaper; — **las calles** to plaster the streets

empaque M (acción de empacar) packing; (envoltorio) packaging

empaquetadura F gasket

empaquetar VT to pack, to package; —**se** to get dolled up

emparedado M sandwich

emparejar VT (una carga, un partido) to even up; VI/VT (los enamorados) to pair up; (calcetines, zapatos) to match up

emparentado ADJ akin, related

emparentar VT to relate by marriage; —**se** to become related by marriage

empastar VT to fill

empaste M filling

empatar VI to tie; — **una marca** to tie a record

empate M tie, draw

empatía F empathy

empecinado ADJ stubborn

empedernido ADJ (criminal) hardened; (mujeriego) incorrigible; (solterón) confirmed

empedernirse[73] VI to become hardened

empedrado M (acción) paving with stones; (cosa) cobblestone pavement; ADJ paved with stones

empedrar[1] VT to pave with stones

empeine M (del pie) instep; (del vientre) groin

empellón M shove; **a empellones** with shoves, shoving

empeñar VT to pawn; — **la palabra** to pledge; —**se** (endeudarse) to go into debt; (obstinarse) to insist; (esforzarse) to apply oneself; —**se en** to engage in

empeño M (prenda) pawn; (insistencia) insistence; (deseo) desire; (esfuerzo) exertion; **poner** — **en** to strive for

empeorar VT to make worse, to aggravate; VI to worsen; —**se** to get worse

empequeñecer[35] VT to make smaller; VI to get smaller

emperador -triz M emperor; F empress

emperifollarse VI to deck oneself out, to doll oneself up

empezar[48] VI/VT to begin, to start; — **a** to start to; — **de cero** to start from scratch; **para** — for starters; **no tengo ni para** — **con él** I can't touch him; — **por** to begin with; **empezamos mal** we got off to a bad start; **un paquete sin** — an unopened box; **por algo se empieza** you have to start somewhere

empinado ADJ steep

empinar VT to raise; — **el codo** to drink; —**se** (una persona) to stand on tiptoes; (un caballo) to rear; (una torre) to tower

empírico ADJ empirical

empizarrar VT to cover with slate

emplastar VT to plaster

emplasto M plaster

emplazamiento M (colocación) placement; (lugar) location

empleado -da MF employee; — **temporal** temp

emplear VT (usar) to employ, to use; (dar trabajo) to employ; —**se en** to be employed in

empleo M (ocupación) employment, work; (puesto de trabajo) job; (utilización) use

emplumado ADJ feathery

emplumar VT (adornar) to adorn with feathers; (pegar plumas en el cuerpo) to tar and feather; VI (echar plumas) to grow feathers

empobrecer[35] VI/VT to impoverish

empollar VT (huevos) to hatch, to brood; VI/VT (para un examen) to cram

empollón -ona MF *fam* egghead, overachiever

empolvar VT to cover with dust; —**se** (con cosméticos) to powder oneself; (con polvo) to get dirty

emponzoñar VT to poison

empotrado ADJ built-in

emprendedor ADJ enterprising

emprender VT (una tarea) to undertake; (un viaje) to embark on; —**la con alguien** to attack someone

empresa F (cosa que se emprende) undertaking; (compañía) company, enterprise; **libre** — free enterprise; — **privada** private

enterprise; — **pública** public company; — **tiburón** raider

empresarial ADJ —**es** business administration studies; **grupo** — business group

empresario -ria MF entrepreneur

empréstito M loan

empujar VT (mover) to push; (mover con violencia) to shove; (apresurar) to hurry

empuje M (ánimo) drive; (fuerza de propulsión) thrust; (fuerza hacia arriba) lift

empujón M shove, push; **dar empujones** to jostle

empuñadura F (espada) hilt; (cuchillo) handle; (palo de golf, raqueta) grip

empuñar VT to grasp

emular VT to emulate

en PREP in; — **Asturias** in Asturias; (sobre una superficie) on, upon; — **la mesa** on the table; **sentarse** — **el suelo** to sit down on the floor; **me lo vendió** — **mil pesetas** she sold it to me for a thousand pesetas; — **la parada del autobús** at the bus stop; — **la noche** at night; **ir** — **tren** to go by train

enaguas F PL petticoat

enajenación M (locura) insanity; (transferencia) transfer

enajenar VT (trasladar) to transfer; (alienar) to alienate; —**se** to become alienated

enaltecer[35] VT to extol

enamorado -da ADJ in love; MF lover

enamoramiento M crush

enamorar VT to make fall in love; —**se [de]** to fall in love [with]

enanismo M dwarfism

enano -na MF (personaje imaginario, persona deforme) dwarf; (persona pequeña bien proporcionada) midget

enarbolar VT (una bandera) to raise on high; (un garrote) to brandish

enardecer[35] VT to inflame; —**se** to become inflamed

enardecimiento M inflaming

encabezado M header

encabezamiento M heading

encabezar[47] VT (una carta, una obra, un gobierno) to head; (un desfile) to lead

encabritarse VI (un caballo) to rear [up]; (una persona) to get furious

encadenar VT (poner en cadenas) to chain; (unir) to link

encajar VI/VT (colocar) to fit; VI (un gol) to allow; **el policía me encajó una multa** the policeman stuck me with a fine; **tu historia no encaja** your story doesn't hold water

encaje M (tejido) lace; (reserva bancaria) reserve; (acción de encajar) fitting together

encajonar VT (meter en una caja) to box; (apretar) to squeeze in

encallar VI to run aground, to strand; (una

ballena) to beach; VT to ground

encamarse VI — **con** to go to bed with, to sleep with

encaminar VT to direct; **—se hacia** to head for

encanecer[35] VI to go gray; VT to cause to go gray

encanijado ADJ sickly

encanijarse VI to become sickly

encantado ADJ (contento) delighted; (hechizado) enchanted; **— de conocerla** pleased to meet you

encantador -ora ADJ charming, delightful; MF charmer

encantamiento M enchantment

encantar VT to enchant; **eso me encanta** I love that

encanto M (encantamiento) enchantment; (atractivo) charm; **un — de persona** a delightful person; **como por —** as if by magic

encapotado ADJ overcast

encapotarse VI to become overcast

encapricharse VI — **con/de/por** to become infatuated with

encapuchar VT (a una persona) to hood; (un bolígrafo) to put the top on

encaramar VT to raise; **—se** to climb up on; **—se al primer puesto** to rise to first place

encarar VT to face; **me encaró el fusil** he pointed the rifle at me; **—se con** to face

encarcelamiento M imprisonment

encarcelar VT to imprison, to jail, to incarcerate

encarecer[35] VI (subir de precio) to increase in price; VT (rogar) to beg

encarecidamente ADV earnestly

encargado -da ADJ on order; MF person in charge; **— de curso** lecturer

encargar[40] VT (responsabilizar) to put in charge; (pedir) to order; (mandar) to commission, to order; **— a alguien una tarea** to charge someone with a task; **—se de** to take care of

encargo M (pedido) order; (tarea) assignment, charge, errand; **construido por/de —** custom-built; **hecho por —** made to order

encariñarse VI — **de** to become fond of

encarnación F incarnation

encarnado ADJ (color) red; (uña) ingrown

encarnar VT (un ideal) to embody; (a un personaje) to play; **se me encarnó una uña** one of my nails got ingrown

encarnizado ADJ fierce

encarnizarse[47] VI — **con alguien** to attack someone viciously

encarte M insert

encasillar VT to pigeonhole

encauzamiento M channeling

encauzar[47] VT to channel

encefalitis F encephalitis; **— espongiforme bovina** mad cow disease

encendedor M cigarette lighter

encender[2] VT (un cigarro, fuego) to light; (un

fósforo) to strike; (una luz, radio) to switch on, to turn on; (una computadora) to power on, to power up; (pasión) to arouse; VI **—se** (una persona, sexualmente) to become aroused; (una lámpara) to turn on

encendido ADJ (rojo) bright; (excitado) aroused; M ignition

encerado M (pizarrón) blackboard; (acción de encerar) waxing; (capa de cera) wax coating; ADJ waxed

encerar VT to wax, to polish

encerrar[1] VT (palabras entre paréntesis) to enclose; (una oveja) to pen; (a una persona) to lock up; (un contenido) to contain; (un peligro) to involve; **—se** (aislarse) to isolate oneself; (obstinarse) to become fixated

encestar VI to make a basket

enchapar VT (metal) to plate; (madera) to veneer

enchilada F enchilada

enchufar VT (un aparato eléctrico) to plug in; (a un protegido) to fix up; **— un tubo con otro** to fit one pipe into another

enchufe M (entrada eléctrica) socket, plug-in, electrical outlet; (situación ventajosa) connection

encías F PL gums

enciclopedia F encyclopedia

encienda, enciende ver encender

encierra, encierre ver encerrar

encierro M (confinamiento) confinement; (lugar) enclosure

encima ADV (arriba) on top; (además) in addition; **— de** on top of, atop; **por — de** above; **sacarse de —** to get rid of; **orinarse —** to urinate on oneself; **ya tenía el coche —** the car was already on top of me; **no lleves tanto dinero —** don't carry so much money on you; **se nos vienen — los exámenes** the exams are upon us; **mi madre siempre me está —** my mother is always on me; **lo leí por —** I scanned it

encimera F counter

encina F oak

encinta ADJ pregnant

enclaustrar VT to cloister

enclavarse VI to be located

enclave M enclave

enclenque ADJ (endeble) sickly; (desvencijado) rickety

encoger[45] VI/VT to shrink; **—se** (una prenda) to shrink; (una persona) to be intimidated; **—se de hombros** to shrug one's shoulders

encogido ADJ (tímido) shy; M (encogimiento) shrinkage, shrinking

encogimiento M (acción de encoger) shrinkage, shrinking; **— de hombros** shrug

encolar VT to glue

encolerizar[47] VT to incense; **—se** to become

incensed, to lose one's temper

encomendar[1] VT to entrust; **—se** to commend oneself

encomienda F (encargo) assignment, task; (colonial) encomienda [colonial land grant]

enconar VT to inflame; VI **—se** (discusión) to become inflamed; (herida) to fester

encono M animosity

encontrado ADJ contrary, opposing

encontrar[5] VT (hallar) to find; (verse con) to meet; **— a** to run into; **—se** (estar ubicado) to be located; (hallarse) to feel; **—se con** (verse por acuerdo) to meet with; (verse, por coincidencia) to run into; (enterarse) to find out; **vas a encontrarte la casa en obras** you'll find the house under construction

encontronazo M collision

encordado M strings

encordar[5] VT to string

encorvado ADJ stoop-shouldered

encorvamiento M slouch, stoop

encorvar VT to stoop; **—se** to bend over

encostrarse VI to scab

encrespar VT (el pelo) to curl; (el mar) to make choppy; **—se** (el pelo) to get curly; (el mar) to get choppy

encrucijada F crossroads

encuadernación F (oficio) bookbinding; (producto) binding

encuadernar VT to bind

encuadrar VT to frame; **la pocsía de esta época se encuadra en tres tendencias** the poetry of this period can be classified into three tendencies

encubierto ADJ covert

encubrimiento ADJ (de un delincuente) concealment; (de un escándalo) cover-up

encubrir[74] VT (un secreto) to conceal; (un escándalo) to cover up, to hush up

encuentra, encuentre ver encontrar

encuentro M (casual) encounter; (planeado) meeting; (partido) game; (de atletismo) meet; **salir al — de** (ir a encontrar) to go out to meet; (contradecir) to counter

encuerar VT to strip

encuesta F survey, poll

encuestado -da MF respondent

encuestar VI/VT to survey, to poll

encumbrado ADJ elevated, lofty

encumbramiento M elevation

encumbrar VT to elevate

encurtido M pickle

encurtir VT to pickle

ende LOC ADV **por —** hence

endeble ADJ (persona) feeble; (material, argumento) flimsy; (mesa) rickety

endémico ADJ endemic

endemoniado ADJ (poseído por el diablo) possessed by the devil; (niño) devilish;

(pregunta) tough

enderezar[47] VT to straighten; **enderézate** stand up straight; **la niña se enderezó con los años** the girl straightened out after a few years

endeudamiento M indebtedness

endeudarse VI to get into debt

endiablado ADJ devilish

endocrino ADJ endocrine

endocrinología F endocrinology

endodermo M endoderm

endomingado ADJ dressed in one's Sunday best

endorfina F endorphin

endosante MF endorser

endosar VT to endorse

endoso M endorsement

endrogar VT to drug

endulzante M sweetener

endulzar[47] VT to sweeten; **se endulzó el tiempo** the weather became milder

endurecer[35] VT to harden, to stiffen; VI **—se** (músculos) to get hard; (pegamento) to set

endurecimiento M hardening

enebro M juniper

eneldo M dill

enema MF enema

enemigo -ga ADJ & MF enemy; **buques —s** enemy ships; **ser — de algo** to dislike something

enemistad F enmity

enemistar VT to cause enmity between; **—se con** to become an enemy of

energético ADJ **política energética** energy policy

energía F energy; **— eólica** wind power; **— hidráulica** water power; **— nuclear** nuclear energy; **— solar** solar energy; **— térmica** thermal energy

enérgicamente ADV strongly

enérgico ADJ (persona) energetic; (protesta, medida, tono) forceful

enero M January

enervar VT (debilitar) to enervate; (irritar) to irritate

enfadado ADJ angry

enfadar VT to anger; *fam* to piss off; VI **—se** to get angry

enfado M anger

enfadoso ADJ annoying

enfardar VT to bale

énfasis M emphasis

enfático ADJ emphatic

enfatizar[47] VT to emphasize

enfermar VT to sicken; VI to become sick; **—se** to become ill

enfermedad F (malestar) sickness, illness; (cardiovascular, de Parkinson) disease; (social) ill; **— contagiosa** contagious disease; **— coronaria** heart disease; **— de**

altura altitude sickness; — **de Alzheimer** Alzheimer's disease; — **de las vacas locas** mad cow disease; — **del legionario** legionnaire's disease; — **de Lou Gehrig** Lou Gehrig's disease; — **de Lyme** Lyme disease; — **de Parkinson** Parkinson's disease; — **degenerativa articular** degenerative joint disease; — **mental** mental illness; — **parasitaria** parasitic disease; — **por radiación** radiation sickness; — **venérea** venereal disease

enfermería F infirmary

enfermero -ra M male nurse; F nurse

enfermizo ADJ (persona) sickly, infirm; (obsesión, aspecto) unhealthy; (imaginación) sick

enfermo -ma ADJ sick, ill; **me tiene — que vengan tarde** I'm sick of them coming late; MF patient; — **del corazón** heart patient

enfisema M emphysema

enflaquecer[35] VI to get thin

enfocar[30] VT (los ojos) to focus; (un faro) to point; (una cámara) to train; (un tema) to approach

enfoque M (método) approach; (acción de enfocar) focusing

enfrentamiento M clash, confrontation

enfrentar VT (enemigos) to confront; (una dificultad) to face, to tackle; — **a dos personas** to pit two people against each other; —**se con** to clash with

enfrente ADV opposite; — **de** in front of, opposite

enfriamiento M (del aire) cooling; (de una persona) chill; (de la economía, las relaciones) cooling off

enfriar[28] VT to cool, to chill; VI —**se** to cool off

enfundar VT to sheathe

enfurecer[35] VT to infuriate, to enrage; VI —**se** to become enraged, to rage

enfurruñado ADJ sulky

enfurruñarse VI to sulk

engalanar VT (una mesa) to decorate; (a una muchacha) to dress up; —**se** to dress up

enganchar VT (bueyes) to hitch; (una red) to snag; (un teléfono) to hook up; (a los televidentes, a un adicto) to hook; VI —**se** to get hooked

enganche M (del gas, teléfono) connection, hookup; (de drogas) addictiveness; (de vagones) coupling; (de caballos) team; (primer pago) *Méx* down payment

enganchón M snag

engañador ADJ deceitful

engañar VT (mentir) to deceive; (ser infiel) to cheat on; — **el hambre** to ward off hunger; —**se** to deceive oneself

engaño M deceit, deception

engañoso ADJ (una persona) deceitful; (un

hecho) misleading

engastar VT to set

engaste M setting

engatusar VT to coax, to cajole

engendrar VT (emociones) to engender; (hijos) to father

englobar VT to encompass

engomar VT to glue

engordar VI to get fat, to put on weight; VT to make fat, to fatten; **esta semana he engordado dos kilos** I gained two kilos this week

engorroso ADJ irksome

engoznar VT to hinge

engranado ADJ meshed, interlocking; **estar —** to be in gear

engranaje M gears, gearing; **el — del partido** the party apparatus

engranar VT (meter una marcha) to put in gear, to throw into gear; (encajar) to mesh; — **la marcha atrás** to put [the car] in reverse

engrandecer[35] VT (a una persona) to aggrandize; (un palacio) to make more grandiose

engrapar VT to staple, to cramp

engrasar VT (untar) to grease; (manchar) to make greasy; (sobornar) to grease someone's palm; —**se** to get greasy

engrase M grease job

engreído ADJ conceited

engreírse[10] VI to become conceited

engrillar VT to shackle

engrosar VT (una manifestación) to swell; (un volumen) to grow; (una persona) to get fat

engrudo M paste

engullir[16] VT to gobble

enhebrar VT (un hilo) to thread; (cuentas) to string; — **idioteces** to string together a bunch of idiocies

enhorabuena F congratulation; INTERJ congratulations

enigma M (misterio) enigma, conundrum; (adivinanza) riddle; (problema) puzzle

enjabonar VT (poner jabón) to soap, to lather; (adular) to flatter

enjaezar[47] VT to harness

enjalbegar[40] VT to whitewash

enjambre M swarm

enjaular VT (un animal) to cage; (a una persona) to jail

enjuagar[40] VT to rinse; (ropa) to rinse out; (platos) to rinse off

enjuague M (limpieza) rinse, rinsing; (trama) scheme; — **bucal** mouthwash

enjugar[40] VT (la frente) to wipe; (lágrimas) to wipe away

enjuiciar VT to prosecute, to try

enjuto ADJ dry; (delgado) thin

enlace M (de trenes, web) link; (químico) bond;

(boda) marriage; (persona) liaison; —
muerto dead link
enladrillado M brick pavement
enladrillar VT to brick, to pave with bricks
enlatar VT to can
enlazar[47] VT (unir) to link (también en la web);
(sujetar con lazo) to rope, to lasso; VI to
connect; **—se** to connect
enlodar VT to muddy; **—se** to get muddy
enloquecedor ADJ maddening
enloquecer[35] VT to drive crazy; VI to go crazy;
—se to go crazy
enlosado M flagstone pavement
enlosar VT to pave with flagstones
enmantecar[30] VT to butter
enmarañar VT (pelo) to entangle; (problema) to
complicate
enmarcar[30] VT (un cuadro) to frame; **se
enmarca dentro de** it takes place in the
context of
enmascarar VT to mask
enmendar[1] VT (una ley) to amend; (un texto) to
revise; **— la situación** to mend matters; **no
me enmiendes la plana** don't correct me;
VI **—se** to mend one's ways
enmienda F (de una ley) amendment; (de un
texto) revision
enmohecer[35] VT to mold; **—se** to get moldy, to
mold
enmudecer[35] VT to silence; VI to go silent
ennegrecer[35] VI/VT to blacken
ennoblecer[35] VT to ennoble
enojadizo ADJ hotheaded
enojado ADJ angry, mad
enojar VT to anger; **—se** to get angry
enojo M anger
enojoso ADJ bothersome
enorgullecer[35] VT to fill with pride; **—se de** to
take pride in
enorme ADJ enormous
enormemente ADV vastly
enramada F bower
enrarecido ADJ thin, rare
enrarecimiento M rarity, thinness
enredadera F creeper
enredar VT (enmarañar) to entangle;
(complicar) to complicate; (involucrar) to mix
up; VI to cause trouble; **—se** to get tangled
up; **—se con** to become involved with
enredijo M tangle, snarl
enredo M (enredijo) snarl; (lío) mess;
(amancebamiento) affair
enredoso ADJ complicated
enrejado M (de metal) grating, grate; (de
varillas) lattice
enrejar VT to install a grate on
enrevesado ADJ involved
enriquecer[35] VT to enrich; **—se** to become rich
enriquecimiento M enrichment

enrojecer[35] VI/VT to redden
enrollar VT (manga, alfombra) to roll up; (hilo,
cuerda, cinta) to wind up; **—se con** to
become involved with
enronquecer[35] VT to make hoarse; VI to become
hoarse
enroscar[30] VT (soga) to coil, to roll up; (tuerca)
to screw in; (tapa) to screw on; **—se** (vid) to
twine; (serpiente) to coil up
ensacar[30] VT to sack
ensalada F salad
ensalzar[47] VT to extol
ensanchar VT to widen; **—se** (una calle) to
widen; (una falda) to flare
ensanche M (de una calle) widening; (de una
ciudad) expansion
ensangrentado ADJ gory, bloody
ensangrentar VT to smear blood on; **—se** to get
covered with blood
ensartar VT (cuentas) to string; (aguja) to
thread; (con un pincho) to pierce; (historias)
to rattle off
ensayar VT (probar) to try out; (intentar) to try;
(analizar un metal) to assay; (practicar una
obra teatral) to rehearse
ensayo M (intento) trial, attempt; (de teatro)
rehearsal; (obra literaria) essay; (nuclear)
testing; (de un metal) assay; **— clínico**
clinical trial; **— general** dress rehearsal; **por
— y error** by trial and error
enseguida ADV at once, immediately
ensenada F cove
enseña F ensign, flag
enseñanza F teaching, education; **—s** teachings
enseñar VT (mostrar) to show; (instruir) to
teach; **— a** to teach how to
enseres M PL household utensils
ensillar VT to saddle, to saddle up
ensimismarse VI to lose oneself in thought
ensoberbecer[35] VT to make haughty; **—se** to
become haughty
ensombrecer[35] VT (oscurecer) to make
shadowy; (entristecer) to sadden
ensoñación F dream
ensordecedor ADJ deafening
ensordecer[35] VT to deafen
ensortijar VT to curl
ensuciar VT to dirty, to sully; **—se** (mancharse)
to get dirty; (defecar) to soil oneself
ensueño M reverie, dream
entablar VT (relaciones) to establish; (un
conflicto) to start; (una conversación) to
strike up; (una demanda) to file; (una pelea)
to pick
entablillar VT to splint
entallar VT to take in
entarimar VT to floor with planks
ente M (ser) entity; (excéntrico) weirdo;
(agencia) agency

enteco ADJ sickly

entender[2] VT (comprender) to understand; (oír) to hear; (ser homosexual) *Esp* to be homosexual; — **de** to know about; —**se con** (comunicar) to communicate with; (llevarse bien) to get along with; **dar a** — to intimate; **yo me entiendo** I know what I'm doing; **se entiende** of course

entendido -da ADJ (comprendido) understood; (experto) expert; **tengo** — **que** I understand that; **caridad mal entendida** misguided charity; MF expert

entendimiento M understanding

enterado ADJ informed; **darse por** — to acknowledge; **estar** — **de** to be privy to

enterar VT to inform; —**se [de]** to find out [about]; **recién me entero** I just found out; **para que te enteres** just so you know

entereza F fortitude

enternecedor ADJ touching

enternecer[35] VT to touch; —**se** to be touched

entero ADJ (completo) entire, whole; (número) whole; **se mantuvo** — **durante el funeral** he held himself together during the funeral; M integer, whole number

enterramiento M (de un cable) burying; (de un difunto) burial

enterrar[1] VT (cable, muerto) to bury; (balón) to dunk

entibiar VT to make lukewarm; —**se** to become lukewarm

entidad F entity; **de** — significant; — **bancaria** banking institution

entienda, entiende *ver* entender

entierro M burial, funeral

entintar VT to stain with ink

entoldar VT to cover with an awning

entomología F entomology

entonación F intonation

entonar VT to sing; VI to sing in tune; — **con** to go well with; —**se** to get tipsy

entonces ADV then; **desde** — ever since; **hasta** — until then; **el** — **presidente** the then president; CONJ (así que) so

entornado ADJ half-open

entornar VT (una puerta) to leave ajar; (los ojos) to close partially

entorno M (lo que rodea) surroundings; (medio ambiente, informático) environment; — **de trabajo** work environment

entorpecer[35] VT (los sentidos) to dull; (el paso) to hinder; —**se** to become sluggish

entorpecimiento M (de los sentidos) dullness; (del paso) hindrance

entrada F (sitio por donde se entra, de un actor) entrance; (acción de entrar, artículo de diccionario) entry; (asistentes a un espectáculo) gate; (oportunidad para actuar) opening; (billete, derecho, precio de entrar) admission; (llegada) arrival; (primer plato) appetizer; (pago inicial) down payment; (tiempo en béisbol) inning; —**s** cash receipts; — **de coches** driveway; — **de datos** data input; — **por partida doble** double entry; **de** — from the start

entramado M lattice

entrante ADJ (alcalde) incoming; (año) next; M recess

entrañable ADJ (amistad) close; (persona) endearing

entrañas F PL (intestinos) entrails, *fam* guts; (sentimientos) heart, core; — **de la tierra** bowels of the earth; **de mis** — of my own flesh and blood

entrar VI (ir hacia adentro) to go in; (comenzar el día de trabajo) to come in; (caber) to fit; **dejar** — to let in; **hacer** — **en razón** to bring to reason; — **a medicina** to go into medicine; — **en calor** to warm up; — **en coma** to go into a coma; — **en/a un cuarto** to enter a room; — **en materia** to get to the meat of a matter; — **en vigencia/vigor** to go into effect; **me entró miedo** I became afraid; **me entró sueño** I got sleepy; **no sé cómo** —**le a esa chica** I don't know how to approach that girl; **la física no me entra** I can't learn physics; **no entra entre mis favoritos** it is not included among my favorites; **la semana que entra** next week; **este vestido no me entra** this dress doesn't fit me; **seis entra dos veces en doce** six goes into twelve two times; **hazle** — show him in; VT (datos) to enter, to input

entre PREP (dos) between; (muchos) among; — **vaso y vaso** between glasses; — **dientes** under one's breath

entreabierto ADJ ajar, half-open

entreabrir[74] VT (puerta) to crack open; (los ojos) to half-open

entreacto M intermission

entrecano ADJ graying

entrecejo M space between the eyebrows

entrecortado ADJ (voz) faltering; (respiración) irregular

entrecortarse VI to falter

entrecruzar[47] VT to interlace; —**se** to cross

entredicho LOC ADV **en** — in doubt

entrega F (de un paquete) delivery; (de un manuscrito) submission; (al vicio) surrender; (de una novela) installment; (de revista) issue; **a la** — on delivery; **por** —**s** serial; — **a domicilio** home delivery; — **de premios** presentation of awards; — **el mismo día** same-day delivery; — **gratuita** free delivery; — **inicial** down payment

entregar[40] VT (un paquete) to deliver; (a un rehén, prisionero) to hand over; (a un delincuente) to turn in; (a una hija en

matrimonio) to give; (premios) to hand out, to present; (tarea escolar) to hand in; (el coche) to trade in; —**se [a]** (la policía) to surrender [to]; (a una misión) to dedicate oneself to
entrelazar[47] VT to intertwine
entremés M (obra de teatro) interlude; (comida) hors d'oeuvre
entremeter VT to insert; —**se en** (meterse) to get mixed up in; (inmiscuirse) to meddle in
entremetido -da ADJ meddlesome, nosy; MF meddler, busybody
entremezclar VT to intermingle
entrenador -ora MF trainer, coach; — **en jefe** head coach
entrenamiento M training
entrenar VI/VT to train
entrepierna F (del cuerpo) crotch; (de pantalón) inseam
entrepiso M mezzanine
entresacar[30] VT (seleccionar) to cull; (adelgazar) to thin
entresuelo M (de hotel) mezzanine; (de cine) balcony
entretanto ADV meanwhile
entretejer VT (el pelo, una tela) to weave; (una historia) to weave together
entretener[58] VT (hacer atrasar) to delay; (distraer) to distract; (divertir) to entertain; —**se** (divertirse) to amuse oneself; (detenerse) to delay
entretenido ADJ entertaining
entretenimiento M entertainment, amusement
entrever[72, 74] VT (apenas) to catch a glimpse of; (a lo lejos) to make out
entreverar VT to mix, to intersperse; —**se** to meddle
entrevía F gauge
entrevista F interview; — **de salida** exit interview
entrevistar VT to interview; —**se con** to have an interview with
entristecer[35] VT to sadden; —**se** to become sad
entrometerse VI to meddle, to interfere
entrometido -da ADJ meddlesome, nosy; MF meddler, busybody
entronque M (ferroviario) junction; (parentesco) relationship
entropía F entropy
entumecido ADJ (dedo, diente) numb; (músculo) stiff
entumecimiento M (de los dedos, dientes) numbness; (de los músculos) stiffness
enturbiar VT (el agua) to muddy; (una decisión) to muddle; (el juicio, la alegría) to cloud; —**se** (agua) to get muddy; (alegría) to be marred
entusiasmado ADJ enthusiastic, excited
entusiasmar VT to excite; —**se** to be excited

entusiasmo M enthusiasm, excitement
entusiasta MF enthusiast; ADJ enthusiastic
enumerar VT to enumerate
enunciado M utterance
enunciar VT (palabras) to enunciate; (una teoría) to articulate, to enunciate
envainar VT to sheathe
envalentonar VT to embolden, to make bold; —**se** to become bold
envanecer[35] VT to make vain; —**se** to become vain
envarado ADJ stiff, staid
envaramiento M stiffness
envasar VT to package; — **al vacío** to vacuum-pack
envase M packaging
envejecer[35] VT to make old; **ese maquillaje te envejece** that makeup makes you look older; VI to grow old, to age
envejecimiento M aging
envenenamiento M poisoning
envenenar VT to poison
envergadura F (de un avión) wingspan; (de un ave) wingspread; (de un evento, proyecto) importance
envés M SG back
enviado -da MF (político) envoy; (periodístico) correspondent
enviar[28] VT to send; — **por fax** to fax
enviciar VT to corrupt; —**se con** to get hooked on
envidia F envy
envidiable ADJ enviable
envidiar VT to envy
envidioso ADJ envious, jealous
envilecer[35] VT to debase
envío M (acción) shipping; (mercancía) shipment; (manuscrito) submission; — **de anotación** touchdown pass; — **rápido** express delivery
envite M bet
envoltorio M (cosa envuelta) bundle; (envoltura) wrapper
envoltura F wrapping, wrapper; — **de plástico transparente** shrinkwrap
envolver[6, 74] VT (involucrar) to involve; (cubrir) to wrap; (atrapar) to entangle; (rodear) to surround; —**se** to become involved
envuelto, envuelva, envuelve ver envolver
enyesar VT (enlucir con yeso) to plaster; (escayolar) to put in a cast
enzima MF enzyme
épica F epic
epicentro M epicenter
épico ADJ epic
epidemia F epidemic
epidémico ADJ epidemic
epidermis F epidermis
epifanía F epiphany

epiglotis F epiglottis
epilepsia F epilepsy
epiléptico ADJ epileptic
epílogo M epilogue
episódico ADJ episodic
episodio M episode
epitafio M epitaph
epítome M epitome
época F (momento) time, period; (período histórico) age; (temporada) season; (período geológico) epoch
epopeya F epic poem
equidad F equity
equidistante ADJ equidistant
equilibrado ADJ balanced; M balancing
equilibrar VT to balance; — **un presupuesto** to balance a budget
equilibrio M equilibrium, balance; **perder el** — to lose one's balance; **hacer —s** to do a balancing act
equino ADJ & M equine
equinoccio M equinox
equipaje M baggage, luggage
equipamiento M equipment
equipar VT to equip, to outfit
equiparar VT to equate
equipo M (materiales) equipment; (grupo) team; — **de vida** life-support system; — **deportivo** sweatsuit; — **de esquí** ski gear
equitación F (arte) horsemanship; (actividad) riding
equitativo ADJ equitable
equivalente ADJ equivalent
equivaler[60] VI to be equivalent; **lo que equivale a decir** which amounts to saying
equivocación F mistake
equivocado ADJ mistaken, wrong; **estar —** to be wrong/mistaken
equivocar[30] VT to mistake; **—se** to be mistaken, to make a mistake, to miscalculate; **—se de sala** to choose the wrong room; **si no me equivoco** unless I'm mistaken; **me equivoqué de baño** I went into the wrong bathroom
equívoco ADJ (ambiguo) equivocal; (moralmente dudoso) questionable; M misunderstanding
era F (período) era, age; (lugar donde se trilla) threshing floor; (parcela) plot
era, eras *ver* ser
erario M treasury
erección F erection
eréctil ADJ erectile
erecto ADJ (cabeza) erect; (postura) upright
eres *ver* ser
ergonomía F ergonomics
ergonómico ADJ ergonomic
erguido ADJ erect, upright
erguir[13] VT to lift, to raise; **—se** to rise

erial M uncultivated land
erigir[46] VT (construir) to erect; (fundar) to found; **—se en** to set oneself up as
Eritrea F Eritrea
eritreo -a ADJ & MF Eritrean
erizado ADJ bristly; — **de** bristling with
erizar[47] VT to set on end; **—se** to bristle
erizo M hedgehog; — **de mar** sea urchin; **ser un** — to be a grouch
ermitaño -ña MF (persona) hermit; M (cangrejo) hermit crab
erógeno ADJ erogenous
erosión F erosion
erótico ADJ erotic
erotismo M eroticism
erradicación F eradication
erradicar[30] VT to eradicate, to root out
errado ADJ erroneous, in error
errante ADJ wandering
errar[21] VT to miss; — **el cálculo** to miscalculate; VI (estar equivocado) to be mistaken; (vagar) to roam, to rove, to wander
errata F misprint, typographical error
errático ADJ erratic
erróneo ADJ erroneous
error M error, mistake; — **de hecho** factual error; — **de imprenta** misprint; — **no forzado** unforced error; — **tipográfico** typo
eructar VI to belch, to burp
eructo M belch, burp
erudición F erudition, learning, scholarship
erudito -ta ADJ (persona) erudite; (obra) scholarly, learned; MF scholar
erupción F eruption; **hacer —** to erupt
es *ver* ser
esbelto ADJ slender
esbozar[47] VT to outline; — **una sonrisa** to give a hint of a smile
esbozo M sketch, outline; — **de una sonrisa** hint of a smile
escabechar VT to pickle
escabroso ADJ (agreste) rugged; (espinoso) thorny; (sórdido) lurid, sordid
escabullirse[16] VI (ladrones) to slip away, to steal away; (lagartijas) to scurry away/off; — **de** to wriggle out of
escafandra F (para el agua) scuba gear; (para el espacio) spacesuit
escala F (escalera, escalafón) ladder; (serie de grados, notas, serie ascendente) scale; (parada) stopover; — **de sueldos** salary range, wage scale; **hacer — en** to stop over at; — **salarial** wage scale, pay scale; **a — nacional** nationwide; **a/de gran —** large-scale; **sin —s** nonstop
escalada F (de una montaña) climb; (de violencia) escalation
escalador -ora MF climber

escalar VT (subir) to scale, to climb; (cambiar de tamaño) scale

escaldadura F scald

escaldar VT (la piel) to scald; (las verduras) to blanch; —**se** to get scalded

escalera F (en un edificio) stairs, staircase; (portátil) ladder; (de naipes) straight; — **mecánica** escalator; — **de caracol** spiral/ winding staircase; — **de color** straight flush; — **de incendios** fire escape; — **real** royal flush

escalfar VT to poach

escalinata F grand staircase

escalofriante ADJ chilling, hair-raising

escalofrío M chill; —**s** the shivers

escalón M (peldaño) step, stair; (de escalera de mano, de escalafón) rung; (terraza) rung; (formación militar) echelon

escalonar VT (distribuir) to stagger; (aterrazar) to terrace

escalope M scallop

escama F (de animal) scale; (de piel, corteza) flake

escamar VT to scale

escamoso ADJ (animal) scaly; (piel) flaky

escamotear VT (esconder) to palm; (robar) to snatch; (eludir) to shirk

escampar VI to clear up

escandalizar[47] VT (chocar) to scandalize; (causar escándalo) to cause a scandal; —**se** to be shocked

escándalo M (suceso vergonzoso) scandal; (riña) uproar

escandaloso ADJ (chocante) scandalous, shocking; (ruidoso) raucous

escandir VT *lit* to scan

escaneado M scanning

escanear VT to scan

escáner M scanner; — **color** color scanner

escaño M seat in parliament

escapada F (escape) escape

escapar VI (de un lugar, una situación) to escape; (de alguien, de una responsabilidad) to run away; —**se** (persona) to escape; (gas) to leak; **se me escapó una sonrisa** I inadvertently smiled; **Matilde se me está escapando de las manos** Matilde is getting out of hand

escaparate M shop window

escapatoria F (de un lugar) escape, way out; (legal) loophole

escape M (fantasía, escapatoria) escape; (de coche) exhaust; (de gas, agua) leak

escápula F scapula

escarabajo M beetle

escaramuza F skirmish

escaramuzar[47] VI to skirmish

escarbar VI/VT to dig, to scratch; — **en los archivos** to dig around in the files; —**se los dientes** to pick one's teeth

escarcha F frost

escarchar VI to frost

escardar VT to weed

escarlata ADJ INV & M (color) scarlet; F (enfermedad) scarlet fever

escarlatina F scarlet fever

escarmentar[1] VI to learn one's lesson; VT to teach a lesson

escarmiento M lesson; **que te sirva de —** let that be a lesson to you

escarnecer[35] VT to deride

escarnio M derision

escarpa F steep slope

escarpado ADJ steep, precipitous; M steep slope

escasear VI to be scarce

escasez F (falta) shortage; (carestía) scarcity, want

escaso ADJ sparse, scarce; **una docena escasa** a scant dozen; — **de** short on; — **de personal** short-handed

escatimar VT to skimp on; **no — gastos** to spare no expense

escena F (fragmento de una obra de teatro, episodio) scene; (escenario) stage; **montar una —** to make a scene; **en —** on stage; **poner en —** to stage; **entrar en —** to go on stage

escenario M stage

escénico ADJ **pánico —** stage fright

escenificación F staging

escepticismo M skepticism

escéptico -ca ADJ skeptical; MF skeptic

escisión F split

esclarecer[35] VT to elucidate

esclavitud F slavery

esclavizar[47] VT to enslave

esclavo -va MF slave

esclerosis F sclerosis; — **múltiple** multiple sclerosis

esclusa F (de un canal) lock; (de una presa) floodgate, sluice gate

escoba F broom

escobilla F whisk broom

escocer[34] VI to sting

escocés -esa ADJ Scottish; **[cuadros] escoceses** plaid; MF Scot; M (whisky) Scotch; (lengua) Scots

Escocia F Scotland

escoger[45] VT to choose

escolar MF pupil; ADJ **año —** school year

escoliosis F scoliosis

escollo M (arrecife) reef; (obstáculo) obstacle

escolta F (policial) escort; MF (persona) escort; (baloncesto) shooting guard

escoltar VT to escort

escombros M PL rubble, debris

esconder VT to hide; VI —**se** to hide

escondidas LOC ADV **a —** on the sly; **entrar a — to** sneak in; **meter algo a —** to sneak something in; **jugar a las** — to play hide and seek

escondite M (en un juego) hiding place; (de ladrón) hideout; (de cazador) blind; **jugar al** — to play hide and seek

escondrijo M hiding place

escopeta F shotgun

escoplo M chisel

escora F listing

escorar VI to list

escorbuto M scurvy

escoria F (de metales) slag; (de la sociedad) scum, dregs

escorpión M scorpion

escotado ADJ low-cut

escote M (parte del vestido) neckline; (parte del cuerpo) cleavage; **pagar a** — to go Dutch

escotilla F hatch

escozor M smarting sensation; — **vaginal** vaginal itching

escribiente MF clerk

escribir⁷⁴ VI/VT to write; **¿cómo se escribe?** how do you spell it? — **a máquina** to type

escrito ADJ written; — **a máquina** typewritten; **no** — unwritten; **por** — in writing; M document

escrito *ver* escribir

escritor-ora MF writer, author

escritorio M (mueble) desk; (oficina) office

escritura F (acción de escribir) writing; (certificado de propiedad) deed; — **de traspaso** conveyance; — **de venta** bill of sale

escroto M scrotum

escrúpulo M scruple, qualm; **sin** —**s** unscrupulous

escrupuloso ADJ scrupulous

escrutar VT (a una persona) to scrutinize; (el horizonte) to scan; (votos) to count

escrutinio M (examen) scrutiny; (recuento) vote count

escuadra F (de buques, soldados) squadron; (instrumento) square

escuadrilla F (de aviones) flight of aircraft; (de buques) squadron

escuadrón M squadron; — **de la muerte** death squad

escualidez F (delgadez) skinniness; (suciedad) squalor

escuálido ADJ (sucio) squalid; (delgado) thin

escuchar VT to listen to; (oír) to hear; VI to listen; — **a hurtadillas** to eavesdrop

escudar VT to shield

escudo M (arma defensiva) shield; (moneda de Portugal) escudo; — **de armas** coat of arms

escudriñar VT (a una persona) to scrutinize, to peer at; (el horizonte) to scan

escuela F school; — **industrial** trade school; — **normal** school of education; — **pública**

public school; — **primaria** elementary school; — **secundaria** secondary school; **tener** — to have good technique

escueto ADJ (explicación) succinct; (verdad) simple

esculpir VI/VT to sculpture, to sculpt

escultor-ora MF sculptor

escultura F sculpture

escupir VI/VT to spit

escupitajo M spit

escurridizo ADJ (acera) slippery; (ladrón) elusive, slippery

escurrir VI/VT (platos, verduras) to drain; (ropa) to wring out; —**se** to slink away

ese ADJ DEM that, those; **esa chica se llama Matilde** that girl is called Matilde; **esas ciudades son antiguas** those cities are old; PRON that one, those; **ese es el mayor** that one is the oldest; **esos son mis hijos** those are my children

esencia F essence

esencial ADJ essential; **lo** — the gist, the bottom line, the name of the game

esfera F (cuerpo sólido) sphere; (espacio, ámbito) realm, sphere; (de reloj) face, dial; — **de influencia** sphere of influence

esférico ADJ spherical; M soccer ball

esfínter M sphincter

esforzado ADJ valiant

esforzarse⁴⁹ VI to try hard, to exert oneself; — **por** to strive to, to make an effort to

esfuerzo M effort

esfumar VT to tone down; —**se** to vanish, to fizzle out

esgrima F fencing; **practicar** — to fence

esgrimir VT (armas) to brandish, to wield; (argumentos) to employ

eslabón M chain link; — **perdido** missing link

eslabonar VT to link

eslavo-va ADJ Slavic; MF Slav

eslogan M slogan

eslovaco ADJ & MF Slovakian; M (lengua) Slovakian

Eslovaquia F Slovakia

Eslovenia F Slovenia

esloveno-na ADJ & MF Slovene; M (lengua) Slovene

esmaltar VT to enamel

esmalte M enamel; — **de uñas** nail polish

esmeradamente ADV carefully

esmerado ADJ careful, painstaking

esmeralda F emerald

esmerarse VI to take pains

esmerilado ADJ frosted; M frosting

esmerilar VT to frost

esmero M care

esmirriado ADJ scrawny

esmoquin M tuxedo

esnifar VT to snort

esnob M snob

esnórquel M snorkel

eso PRON DEM that; — **es verdad** that's true; — **sí** granted; **a** — **de las tres** at about three o'clock; **de** —, **nada** no way! yeah, right! **en** — **llega y me dice** at that moment he arrives and says to me; **y** — **que le dije que viniese temprano** even when I told him to come early

esófago M esophagus

esotérico ADJ esoteric

espaciado M pitch, spacing; — **de palabras** word spacing

espacial ADJ spatial; **nave** — spaceship

espaciar VT to space; —**se** to space out

espacio M (capacidad) space, room; (superficie) expanse; (separación entre líneas) space, spacing; (en un formulario) blank space; (porción de tiempo) span; — **aéreo** aerospace; — **entre caracteres** letterspacing; — **exterior** outer space; — **noticioso** newscast; **a doble** — double-spaced; **a un** — single-spaced; **por** — **de una semana** for a week

espacioso ADJ spacious, roomy

espada F sword; —**s** (palo de naipes) swords; — **de doble filo** double-edged sword; **estar entre la** — **y la pared** to be between a rock and a hard place

espalda F back; — **mojada** *pey* wetback; **a** —**s de alguien** behind someone's back; **caerse de** —**s** to fall on one's back; **nadar [de]** — to do the backstroke; **tener las** —**s anchas** to take a lot of abuse; **volver las** —**s** to turn one's back

espaldar M chair back

espantadizo ADJ easily scared

espantado ADJ frightened

espantajo M scarecrow

espantar VT to frighten, to scare; (ahuyentar) to frighten away, to scare away; —**se** to get scared; M SG **espantapájaros** scarecrow

espanto M fright, dread; **estás hecho un** — you look a sight; **estoy curado de** — nothing surprises me anymore

espantoso ADJ frightful, dreadful

España F Spain

español -ola ADJ Spanish; MF Spaniard; M (lengua) Spanish

esparadrapo M surgical tape

esparcimiento M (recreo) relaxation; (reparto) spreading

esparcir[33] VT to scatter, to spread; —**se** to amuse oneself

espárrago M asparagus

espasmo M spasm, jerk

espasmódico ADJ spasmodic, jerky

espástico ADJ spastic

espátula F spatula

especia F spice

especial ADJ & M special; **en** — in particular, especially

especialidad F specialty, specialization

especialista MF specialist

especialización F specialization

especializar[47] VT to specialize; —**se en** to specialize in, to major in

especialmente ADV (de forma particular) specially; **esto lo hice** — **para ti** I made this specially for you; (en especial) especially; **este tipo es** — **bueno** this kind is especially good

especie F (clase) kind; (categoría biológica) species; —**s en peligro de extinción** endangered species; **pagar en** — to pay in kind; **una** — **de** a kind of

especiero M spice rack

especificar[30] VT to specify

específico ADJ & M specific

espécimen M specimen

espectacular ADJ spectacular

espectáculo M (escándalo) spectacle; (actuación pública) show; (vista) sight; **dar el** — to make a spectacle of oneself

espectador -ora MF (de un espectáculo) spectator; (de un suceso) onlooker

espectro M (fantasma) specter; (de la luz, de un antibiótico) spectrum

especulación F speculation

especulador -ora MF speculator

especular VT to speculate; ADJ mirror; **imagen** — mirror image

especulativo ADJ speculative

espejismo M (en el desierto) mirage; (ilusión) illusion

espejo M mirror; — **de cuerpo entero** full-length mirror; — **retrovisor** rearview mirror

espeluznante ADJ hair-raising

espeluznar VT to terrify; —**se** to be terrified

espera F (acción de esperar) wait; (aplazamiento) extension; **estar en** — **de** to be waiting for

esperanza F hope; — **de vida** life expectancy; **con una** — **de voto del 12,5%** expected to get 12.5% of the vote

esperanzado ADJ hopeful

esperanzador ADJ hopeful

esperanzar[47] VT to give hope to

esperar VT (tener esperanza) to hope; (estar embarazada, anticipar) to expect; (aguardar) to wait for; VI to wait; **como era de** — not surprisingly; **era de** — it was to be expected; **espera sentado** don't hold your breath; **estoy esperando un milagro** I'm hoping for a miracle; **todavía espera confirmación** it still awaits confirmation

esperma MF sperm

espermicida M spermicide

esperpento M fright, grotesque person or thing
espesar VT to thicken
espeso ADJ (pelo, sopa, niebla) thick; (cejas) bushy
espesor M thickness
espesura F (espesor) thickness; (lugar poblado de matorrales) thicket
espetar VT (decir bruscamente) to blurt out; (pinchar) to skewer
espeto, espetón M spit
espía MF spy
espiar[28] VI to spy; VT to spy on
espichar VI *fam* to croak, to bite the dust
espiga F spike
espigar[40] VT to glean; VI to grow spikes; **—se** to grow tall
espina F (de planta) thorn; (de pez) fish bone; **— dorsal** spinal column; **me quedé con la —** I was left wondering
espinaca F spinach
espinal ADJ spinal
espinazo M spine, backbone
espinilla F (en la pierna) shin; (de animal) shank; (acné, comedón) blackhead
espino M thorny shrub
espinoso ADJ thorny
espionaje M espionage
espiración F expiration
espiral ADJ & F spiral
espirar VI/VT to exhale, to breathe out, to expire
espíritu M (ánima, fantasma, intención de una ley) spirit; (alma) soul; **— fuerte** free spirit; **— deportivo** sportsmanship; **— emprendedor** can-do attitude, entrepreneurship; **— Santo** Holy Spirit
espiritual ADJ & M spiritual
espiritualidad F spirituality
espita F spigot
espléndido ADJ (estupendo) splendid; (dispendioso) lavish
esplendor M splendor
esplendoroso ADJ magnificent
espliego M lavender
espolear VT to spur
espoleta F bomb fuse
espolón M (de gallo, planta, estímulo) spur; (de buque) ram
espolvorear VT to dust, to sprinkle
esponja F (animal, utensilio) sponge; (borracho) souse
esponjado ADJ spongy
esponjar VT to make spongy; **—se** to become spongy
esponjoso ADJ spongy
esponsales M PL betrothal
espontaneidad F spontaneity
espontáneo ADJ spontaneous
espora F spore
esposar VT to handcuff

esposo -sa M husband; F wife; **esposas** handcuffs
espuela F spur
espulgar[40] VT to delouse
espuma F (de cerveza) froth; (de jabón) suds, lather; (de la boca) foam; (de colchón) foam rubber; (de mar) foam, spray; **echar — por la boca** to foam at the mouth; **hacer —** to make suds
espumar VT (quitar la espuma) to skim; (formar espuma) to foam
espumarajo M foam; **echar —s por la boca** to foam at the mouth
espumillón M tinsel
espumoso ADJ foamy
esputo M sputum
esquela F note; **— mortuoria** death notice
esquelético ADJ skeletal
esqueleto M (huesos) skeleton; (armazón) framework; **mover el —** (bailar) to dance; (moverse) to move
esquema M outline; **romperle los —s a alguien** (planes) to ruin one's plans; (conceptos) to shatter one's preconceptions
esquí M (tabla) ski; (deporte) skiing; **— acuático** (tabla) water ski; (deporte) waterskiing; **hacer — acuático** to water-ski
esquiar[28] VI to ski
esquila F (cencerro) cowbell; (acción de esquilar) shearing
esquilador -ora MF sheep shearer
esquilar VT to shear, to clip
esquileo M shearing
esquimal ADJ & MF Eskimo; M (lengua) Eskimo
esquina F corner; **en cada —** everywhere
esquinero ADJ **mesa esquinera** corner table; M cornerback
esquirol M strikebreaker; *pey* scab
esquivar VT (a una persona) to avoid; (un golpe) to dodge
esquivo ADV (tímido) shy, coy; (huraño) aloof; (reservado) elusive; (indirecto) evasive
esquizofrenia F schizophrenia
estabilidad F stability
estabilización F stabilization
estabilizar[47] VT to stabilize
estable ADJ (mesa) stable; (precio) firm; (huésped) long-term
establecer[35] VT to establish; (averiguar) to ascertain; **— una cita** to set up an appointment; **—se** to settle
establecimiento M establishment
establezca, establezco *ver* establecer
establishment M establishment
establo M stable
estaca F (con punta) stake; (gruesa) club
estacada F stockade; **dejar en la —** to leave in the lurch
estacar[30] VT (atar) to stake; (delimitar) to

stake off

estación F (de tren, autobús, radio) station; (del año) season; **— bípeda** bipedal stance; **— de bomberos** fire station; **— de esquí** ski resort; **— de servicio** gas/filling station; **— de trabajo** workstation; **— espacial** space station

estacional ADJ seasonal

estacionamiento M (acción) parking; (lugar) parking lot

estacionar VT (tropas) to station; (un vehículo) to park; **—se** (un coche) to park; (precios) to level off

estacionario ADJ stationary

estadía F stay

estadio M (recinto deportivo) stadium; (fase) stage

estadista M statesman; F stateswoman

estadística F (ciencia) statistics; **—s** (datos numéricos) statistics

estado M (situación, unidad política) state; **— civil** marital status; **— de cuenta** bank statement; **— de alarma** state of emergency; **— de ánimo** state of mind; **— de excepción** martial law; **— de guerra** state of war; **— de sitio** state of siege; **— mayor** chiefs of staff; **— policíaco** police state; **de — sólido** solid state; **en — interesante** expecting; **en — vegetativo** in a vegetative state, brain-dead

Estados Unidos M PL/SG United States

estadounidense ADJ & MF American

estafa F swindle, scam, racket

estafador -ora MF swindler, racketeer

estafar VT to swindle

estalactita F stalactite

estalagmita F stalagmite

estallar VI (una bomba) to explode; (un globo) to burst; (una guerra) to break out; (una persona) to snap; **— de risa** to burst out laughing; **— en una carcajada** to burst out laughing; **hacer —** to set off

estallido M (explosión) explosion; (ruido) bang, report

estampa F (de revista) illustration; (imagen) image; (apariencia) appearance; **de buena —** good-looking; **la viva — de la madre** the spitting image of her mother; **la viva — de la desolación** the very picture of desolation

estampado ADJ printed; M (tela) print; (acción) printing

estampar VT (en tela, papel) to print; (con un molde, en metal) to stamp; **—le un beso a alguien** to plant a kiss on someone

estampida F stampede

estampido M bang

estampilla F stamp

estampillar VT to stamp

estancado ADJ stagnant

estancamiento M stagnation (también económico)

estancar[30] VT to stem; to dam; to block; **—se** to stagnate

estancia F (estadía) stay; (habitación) hall; (hacienda) RP cattle ranch

estanco ADJ waterproof; M government store

estándar ADJ & M standard

estandarización F standardization

estandarizar[47] VT to standardize

estandarte M standard, banner

estanque M pond

estante M (tabla) shelf; (mueble) bookcase

estantería F (mueble) bookcase; (de biblioteca) stack

estañar VT to tin-plate

estaño M tin

estar[63] VI to be; **— a tres kilómetros de aquí** to be three kilometers from here; **— bien** to be all right; **— mal/enfermo del corazón** to have heart trouble; **— de más** to be unnecessary; **— para** to be about to; **— por** (a favor de) to be in favor of; (a punto de) to be about to; **— trabajando duro** to be working hard; **¿a cuántos estamos?** what day of the month is it? **ahí está** that's it; **¿está Alice?** is Alice there? **están muy buenos tus zapatos nuevos** your new shoes are nice; **estate tranquilo** don't worry; **no — to be out; cuarto de —** living room

estatal ADJ **compañía —** state-run company

estático ADJ static

estatua F statue

estatura F (importancia) stature; (altura física) height

estatutario ADJ statutory

estatuto M (ley) statute; (de una sociedad) bylaw; **— de quiebras** bankruptcy law

este ADJ DEM this, these; **esta chica se llama Hilary** this girl is called Hilary; **estas ciudades son antiguas** these cities are old; PRON DEM this one, these; **— es el mayor** this one is the oldest; **estos son mis hijos** these are my children; M & ADJ east; **hacia el —** eastward

estela F (de una embarcación) wake; (de humo, polvo) trail; **dejar una —** to leave a trail

estelar ADJ stellar

estenotipista MF court reporter

estentóreo ADJ booming

estepa F steppe

estera F mat

estercolar VT to fertilize with manure

estercolero M dunghill

estéreo ADJ & M stereo; **en —** in stereo

estereotipo M stereotype

estéril ADJ (gasa, esfuerzo) sterile; (mujer) barren

esterilidad F sterility

esterilizar[47] VT to sterilize

esternón M sternum, breastbone
esteroide M steroid; — **anabólico** anabolic
  steroid
estertor M death rattle
estética F aesthetics
estético ADJ aesthetic
estetoscopio M stethoscope
estibador M stevedore, longshoreman
estibar VT to stow
estiércol M manure
estigma M stigma
estigmatizar[47] VT to stigmatize
estilarse VI to be in style; **eso no se estila
  aquí** that's not done here
estilística F stylistics
estilístico ADJ stylistic
estilo M (literario, estético, caligráfico) style; (de
  natación) stroke; — **de vida** lifestyle; —
  espalda backstroke; — **indirecto** reported
  speech; — **libre** freestyle; — **mariposa**
  butterfly stroke; — **pecho** breaststroke; —
  perrito dog paddle; **cosas por el** — things
  like that
estima F esteem, regard
estimación F (cálculo) estimate; (estima)
  estimation
estimado ADJ esteemed; — **Sr.** Dear Sir
estimar VT (apreciar) to esteem; (determinar el
  valor) to estimate; (opinar) to think
estimulación F stimulation
estimulante ADJ stimulating; M stimulant
estimular VT (despertar, excitar) to stimulate;
  (alentar) to encourage
estímulo M stimulus
estío M *lit* summer
estipendio M stipend
estipulación F stipulation
estipular VT to stipulate
estirado ADJ stuck-up
estirar VT (alargar) to stretch; — **el cuello** to
  crane one's neck; — **la pata** *fam* to kick the
  bucket; (crecer) to grow; —**se** to stretch
estirón M growth spurt; **pegar un** — to have a
  growth spurt
estirpe F lineage
estival ADJ **vacaciones** —**es** summer vacation
esto PRON DEM this; — **es** that is to say; **a todo
  —** meanwhile; **en —** at this point
estocada F thrust; **lanzar una** — to thrust
estofa F type; **de baja** — low-class
estofado M stew
estofar VT to stew
estoico -ca ADJ & MF stoic
estolón M runner
estómago M stomach
Estonia F Estonia
estonio -nia ADJ & MF Estonian; M (lengua)
  Estonian
estopa F tow

estorbar VT (obstaculizar) to hinder, to impede;
  (molestar) to be a nuisance
estorbo M (obstáculo) hindrance, impediment;
  (molestia) nuisance
estornino M starling
estornudar VI to sneeze
estornudo M sneeze
estoy *ver* estar
estrado M bench
estrafalario ADJ bizarre, outlandish
estragar[40] VT (físicamente) to devastate;
  (moralmente) to corrupt
estrago M havoc; **hacer** —**s** to wreak havoc
estrangular VT to strangle
estratagema F stratagem
estrategia F strategy; (de negocios, deportes)
  game plan; — **de salida** exit strategy
estratégico ADJ strategic
estrato M stratum, layer; — **social** social class
estratosfera F stratosphere
estrechamente ADV closely
estrechamiento M constriction
estrechar VT (angostar) to narrow; (abrazar) to
  embrace; **la estrechó en sus brazos** he
  held her in his arms; —**se** to get narrower;
  —**se la mano** to shake hands
estrechez F (cualidad de estrecho) narrowness;
  (acción de estrechar) narrowing; (aprietos)
  dire straits
estrecho ADJ narrow; **la falda le quedaba
  estrecha** the skirt was too tight for her; M
  strait
estrella F star; — **binaria** binary star; — **de
  cine** movie star; — **de mar** starfish; —
  fugaz shooting star, falling star; **ver las** —**s**
  to see stars
estrellado ADJ (como una estrella) starlike;
  (cubierto de estrellas) starry
estrellar VT (aplastar) to smash; (romper) to
  crack; —**se** (avión) to crash; (intento) to fail;
  —**se contra** to smash into
estremecer[35] VT to make shudder; **el
  terremoto estremeció París** the
  earthquake rocked Paris; —**se** to shudder
estremecimiento M shudder
estrenar VT (un vestido) to wear for the first
  time; (una película, obra de teatro) to debut;
  (una bicicleta) to try out for the first time; (un
  título) to use for the first time; —**se** to debut
estreno M (de una película) premiere; (de un
  objeto) first use; (de una actividad) debut
estreñido ADJ (constipado) constipated;
  (antipático) uptight
estreñimiento M constipation
estreñir[11] VT to constipate; —**se** to become
  constipated
estrépito M racket, clatter; **causar** — to clatter
estrepitoso ADJ noisy
estrés M stress

estresante ADJ stressful, high-pressure
estresar VT to stress [out]
estría F (en la piel) stretch mark; (en una columna) flute; (en mármol) striation
estriado ADJ (piel) covered with stretch marks; (columna) fluted; (piedra) streaked
estriar[28] VT to flute; **—se** to get stretch marks
estribación F spur
estribar VI **— en** (apoyarse en) to lean on; (radicar en) to lie in
estribillo M refrain
estribo M (de silla, oído) stirrup; (de coche) running board; **perder los —s** to fly off the handle
estribor M starboard
estricnina F strychnine
estricto ADJ strict
estridente ADJ strident
estrofa F verse, stanza
estrógeno M estrogen
estropajo M scrubber; **tengo la boca que es un —** my mouth is as dry as a bone
estropajoso ADJ sinewy
estropear VT to ruin
estructura F structure
estructuración F structuring
estructural ADJ structural
estructurar VT to structure
estruendo M din, racket
estruendoso ADJ thunderous
estrujamiento M (para romper) crushing; (para sacar jugo) squeezing
estrujar VT (aplastar) to crush; (apretar) to squeeze
estrujón M squeeze
estuario M estuary
estucar[30] VT to stucco
estuche M (para joyas) jewelry box; (para pastillas) pill box; (para lentes) glasses case
estuco M stucco
estudiantado M student body
estudiante MF student
estudiantil ADJ **vida —** student life
estudiar VI/VT to study
estudio M (acción de estudiar, investigación, habitación) study; (taller de artista) studio; (apartamento pequeño) studio apartment; **en — under study; — del impacto ambiental** environmental impact study
estudioso -sa ADJ studious; MF scholar
estufa F (para calentar) heater, stove; (para cocinar) stove
estupefaciente ADJ & M narcotic
estupefacto ADJ stunned, speechless
estupendo ADJ stupendous, terrific; **me la pasé — en la casa de Hilary** I had a great time at Hilary's house
estupidez F stupidity; **estupideces** nonsense
estúpido ADJ stupid

estupor M stupor
estupro M statutory rape
estuve, estuviera, estuviese *ver* estar
etanol M ethanol
etapa F stage; **por —s** by stages
etcétera CONJ et cetera, and so forth
éter M ether
eternidad F eternity
eternizarse[47] VI to drag on
eterno ADJ eternal, everlasting
ética F ethics
ético ADJ ethical
etimología F etymology
etíope ADJ & MF Ethiopian
Etiopia F Ethiopía
etiqueta F (de comportamiento) etiquette; (en una lata, botella) label; (en una prenda) tag; **— adhesiva** sticker; **— de identificación** name tag; **— de precio** price tag; **nos trataron con —** they treated us very formally; **vestirse de —** to dress formally
etiquetar VT (latas, botellas, personas) to label; (prendas) to tag
etnicidad F ethnicity
étnico ADJ ethnic
etnografía F ethnography
etnología F ethnology
ETS [enfermedad de transmisión sexual] F STD
eucalipto M eucalyptus
eufemismo M euphemism
euforia F euphoria
eunuco M eunuch
euro M euro
Europa F Europe
europeo -a ADJ & MF European
euskera M Basque [language]
eutanasia F euthanasia
evacuación F (de un lugar) evacuation; (del vientre) bowel movement; (de agua) drainage
evacuar VT (un lugar, a una persona) to evacuate; (el vientre) to void; (agua) to drain; VI to defecate
evadir VT to evade; **—se** to escape
evaluación F evaluation; **— del rendimiento** performance review
evaluar[26] VT (analizar) to evaluate, to assess; (tasar) to estimate; (calificar) to test
evangélico ADJ evangelical
evangelio M gospel
evaporación F evaporation
evaporar VT to evaporate; **—se** to vanish
evasión F (fiscal) evasion; (de prisioneros, de la realidad) escape; **— de capitales** capital flight; **— de impuestos** tax evasion
evasiva F **salirse con —s** to beat around the bush
evasivo ADJ evasive
evasor -ora MF evader

evento M event

eventual ADJ (posible) possible; (temporal) temporary

evidencia F evidence; **dejar/poner en — a alguien** to show someone up; **quedar/ ponerse en —** to become apparent

evidenciar VT to make evident; **—se** to become evident

evidente ADJ evident, obvious

evidentemente ADV & INTERJ obviously

evitar VT (eludir) to avoid; (ahorrar) to spare

evocación F evocation

evocar[30] VT (una memoria) to evoke; (a los espíritus) to conjure up

evolución F evolution

evolucionar VI to evolve

evolutivo ADJ evolutionary

ex MF *fam* ex

exacerbar VT (intensificar) to exacerbate; (irritar) to aggravate

exactamente ADV & INTERJ exactly, precisely; **llegaron — a las tres** they arrived exactly at three

exactitud F accuracy, precision

exacto ADJ exact, precise, accurate; INTERJ exactly

exageración F exaggeration

exagerado ADJ exaggerated; **Jorge es un —** Jorge always exaggerates

exagerar VI/VT to exaggerate

exaltación F (elogio) praise; (excitación) excitement

exaltar VT to exalt; **—se** to get excited

examen M (inspección) examination; (prueba) examination, test, exam; **— de ingreso** entrance examination; **— dérmico de alergias** scratch test; **— final** final examination; **— físico** physical examination; **— médico** medical exam, checkup; **dar un —** to take a test; **poner un —** to give a test

examinar VT (inspeccionar) to examine; (someter a un examen) to test

exasperar VT to exasperate, to aggravate

excavación F (geológica) excavation; (arqueológica) dig

excavador -ora MF (persona) excavator; F (aparato) excavator, earthmover

excavar VT to excavate, to dig

excedente ADJ & M surplus

exceder VT (sobrepasar) to exceed; (superar) to surpass; **— de** to go beyond

excelencia F excellence; **por —** par excellence

excelente ADJ excellent, great

excentricidad F eccentricity

excéntrico ADJ eccentric

excepción F exception; **a — de** with the exception of

excepcional ADJ exceptional

excepto ADV & PREP except

exceptuar[26] VT to except

excesivo ADJ excessive

exceso M excess; **— de costos** overrun; **— de equipaje** excess baggage; **beber en —** to drink to excess; **comer en —** to overeat

excitación F (de músculos) excitement; (sexual) arousal

excitante ADJ stimulating

excitar VT (un nervio) to excite; (impulso sexual) to arouse; **—se** (sexualmente) to get aroused; (átomos) to be excited

exclamación F exclamation

exclamar VT to exclaim

excluir[19] VT to exclude

exclusión F exclusion

exclusivo ADJ exclusive

excomulgar[40] VT to excommunicate

excrecencia F excrescence

excreción F excretion

excremento M excrement

excretar VT to excrete

excursión F excursion, outing

excusa F excuse

excusable ADJ excusable

excusado M *Méx* toilet

excusar VT to excuse

exención F exemption

exento ADJ exempt; **— de impuestos** tax-exempt

exequias F PL funeral rites

exfoliación F exfoliation

exhalar VI/VT (aire) to exhale, to breathe out; (un olor) to give off; **— un suspiro** to sigh

exhaustivo ADJ exhaustive, thorough

exhausto ADJ exhausted

exhibición F (manifestación) exhibition; (despliegue) display

exhibicionismo M exhibitionism

exhibir VT (fotos) to exhibit; (mercancías) to display; (el carnet de identidad) to show; **—se** to show off; **le gusta exhibirse en traje de baño** she likes to show off in her bathing suit; **esa película ya no se exhibe** that movie is not showing anymore

exhortar VT to exhort, to urge

exhumación F exhumation

exigencia F demand

exigente ADJ demanding, exacting

exigir[46] VT to demand; **exigen a alguien que sepa inglés** they require someone who knows English

exiguo ADJ meager; **exigua mayoría** scant majority

exiliado -da MF exile

exiliar VT to exile

exilio M exile

eximido ADJ exempt; **— por la cláusula del abuelo** grandfathered

eximio ADJ illustrious

eximir VT (de impuestos) to exempt; (de sospecha) to clear; (de una responsabilidad) to excuse

existencia F existence; **complicarle la — a alguien** to cause someone trouble; **la lucha por la —** the fight for survival; **—s** stock on hand; **en —** in stock, on hand

existencial ADJ existential

existente ADJ extant, existing

existir VI to exist

éxito M success; (musical) hit; **— de taquilla** blockbuster; **tener —** to be successful; **tiene — con las mujeres** he's popular with women

exitoso ADJ successful

éxodo M exodus

exonerar VT to exonerate

exorbitante ADJ exorbitant

exorcisar VT to exorcise

exorcismo M exorcism

exótico ADJ exotic

expandir VT (dilatar) to expand, to spread; (propagar) to disseminate; **—se** to expand, to spread

expansión F (crecimiento) expansion; (diversión) relaxation

expansivo ADJ (que crece) expansive; (efusivo) effusive

expatriado -da MF expatriate

expatriar VT to expatriate, to exile

expectación F anticipation

expectativa F (esperanza) expectation; (posibilidad) prospect; **estar a la — de algo** to be on pins and needles; **— de vida** life expectancy

expectorante M expectorant

expectorar VI/VT to expectorate, to cough up

expedición F (viaje) expedition; (de documentos) issuing; (de mercancías) delivery

expedicionario -ria ADJ expeditionary; MF member of an expedition

expedidor -ora ADJ shipping; MF shipper

expediente M (administrativo) file, dossier; (policial, académico, médico) record

expedir[9] VT (enviar) to dispatch; (emitir) to issue

expeler VT to expel

expendedor -ora MF vendor; **— automático** vending machine

experiencia F experience

experimentación F experimentation

experimentado ADJ experienced

experimental ADJ experimental

experimentar VI (hacer experimentos) to experiment; VT (sufrir, tener experiencia) to experience

experimento M experiment

experto -ta ADJ & MF expert; **— en**

computación wizard, *fam* techie

expiación F atonement

expiar[28] VT to atone for

expirar VI to expire

explanada F (terreno junto al mar) esplanade; (terreno nivelado) leveled area

explayarse VI to become extended; **— sobre** to enlarge upon

explicable ADJ explainable, explicable

explicación F explanation

explicar[30] VT to explain; **—se** to make oneself clear; **no me explico por qué** I can't figure out why

explicativo ADJ explanatory

explícito ADJ explicit

exploración F exploration

explorador -ora ADJ exploring; MF (expedicionario) explorer; (militar) scout

explorar VI/VT to explore; (con fines diagnósticos) to scan; (con fines militares) to scout

exploratorio ADJ exploratory

explosión F explosion; **hacer —** to explode

explosivo ADJ & M explosive

explotación F exploitation

explotar VT (sacar provecho) to exploit; (hacer explosión) to explode

expondrá, expondría *ver* exponer

exponente M exponent

exponer[56, 74] VT (al sol, al peligro) to expose; (al público) to exhibit, to display; (explicar) to state, to set forth; **—se al peligro** to expose oneself to danger

exponga, expongo *ver* exponer

exportación F (acción) exportation, export; (cosa) export

exportador -ora ADJ exporting; MF exporter

exportar VI/VT to export

exposición F (feria) exposition; (de arte) exhibition; (explicación) explanation; (al sol, a una influencia, al peligro) exposure

expresar VT to express

expresión F expression; **valga la —** so to speak

expresividad F expressiveness

expresivo ADJ expressive

expreso ADJ (explícito) express; (rápido) fast; M express train; **café —** espresso

exprimidor M juicer

exprimir VT (naranjas) to squeeze; (zumo) to squeeze out

expropiar VT to expropriate

expuesto ADJ exposed; **lo —** what has been said

expuesto *ver* exponer

expulsar VT to expel; (de un bar) to throw out; (de un partido) to eject

expulsión F expulsion

expuse, expusiera, expusiese *ver* exponer

exquisito -ta ADJ (arte) exquisite; (comida) delicious

extasiado ADJ rapt
extasiarse[28] VI to be enraptured
éxtasis M ecstasy (también droga)
extender[2] VT (el brazo, radio de acción, gratitud) to extend; (un tapete, una masa, un idioma) to spread; (un cheque) to draw up; **—se** to extend; **la fiesta se extendió hasta las 3** the party lasted until 3 o'clock
extendido ADJ (brazos) outstretched; (costumbre) widespread
extensión F (del antebrazo, de significado, telefónica) extension; (de terreno) expanse; (de un texto) length; (eléctrica) extension cord; **por —** by extension; **tener mucha —** to be widespread
extensivo ADJ extensive; **hacer —** to extend
extenso ADJ (calendario, plan, grupo) extensive; (narración, programa de radio) extended
extenuado ADJ exhausted
exterior ADJ (de fuera) exterior, outer; (mundo) outside; (política) foreign; M (parte de afuera) exterior, outside; (aspecto) outward appearance; (fútbol americano) end; **en —es** on location
exteriorizar[47] VT to externalize
exterminación F extermination
exterminar VT to exterminate
exterminio M extermination
externo ADJ external
extienda, extiende *ver* extender
extinción F extinction
extinguidor M fire extinguisher
extinguir[44] VT (un fuego) to extinguish, to put out; (una especie) to make extinct, to wipe out; **—se** (animal, volcán) to go extinct
extinto ADJ extinct
extintor M fire extinguisher
extirpación F removal
extirpar VT to remove
extorsión F extortion
extorsionar VT to extort money from
extorsionista MF racketeer
extra ADJ extra; **horas —s** overtime; MF (actor) extra; M (cosa accesoria) extra; F (pago extraordinario) bonus
extrabursátil ADJ over-the-counter
extracción F extraction
extracto M (resumen) abstract; (de café) extract
extradición F extradition
extraditar VT to extradite
extraer[59] VT (esencia) to extract; (minerales) to mine; (un diente) to pull
extraiga, extraigo, extraje, extrajera, extrajese *ver* extraer
extrajudicial ADJ out-of-court
extramarital ADJ extramarital
extranjero -ra ADJ foreign; MF foreigner; **en el — abroad**
extrañar VT (sorprender) to surprise; (echar de menos) to miss; **no es de — que** it's no wonder that; **no me extraña** it doesn't surprise me; **—se** to be surprised
extrañeza F surprise
extraño -ña ADJ (persona, costumbre) strange; (partícula) foreign; MF stranger
extraoficial ADJ unofficial
extraordinario ADJ extraordinary
extrapolar VI/VT to extrapolate
extrasensorial ADJ extrasensory
extraterrestre ADJ & M alien, extraterrestrial
extravagancia F (cualidad de extravagante) extravagance; (comportamiento extravagante) outrageous behavior
extravagante ADJ flamboyant, outrageous
extraviar[28] VT (perder) to misplace; (confundir) to lead astray; **—se** to lose one's way, to get lost
extravío M loss
extrayendo *ver* extraer
extremadamente ADV extremely
extremado ADJ extreme
extremar VT to maximize
extremidad F extremity
extremo ADJ (máximo, mínimo, extraordinario) extreme; (más lejano) farthest; **con — cuidado** with utmost care; M (punto más alejado) extreme; (de una región) end; **llegar al — de** to go so far as to; **— Oriente** Far East; **extrema izquierda** far left; F **extrema unción** last rites
extrovertido -da ADJ extroverted; MF extrovert
exuberante ADJ (vegetación, jóvenes) exuberant; (mujer) voluptuous
exudar VI/VT to exude
exultante ADJ exhilarated, exultant
exultar VI to exult
eyacular VI/VT to ejaculate
eyectar VT to eject

Ff

fábrica F factory, plant; (de acero, textiles) mill
fabricación F manufacture, manufacturing
fabricante MF manufacturer; (de coches) maker
fabricar[30] VT (producir) to manufacture, to make; (construir) to build; (inventar) to concoct, to fabricate
fabril ADJ manufacturing
fábula F (relato) fable; (mentira) falsehood
fabuloso ADJ (imaginario) imaginary; (magnífico) awesome, fabulous
facción F faction; **facciones** facial features
faceta F facet
facha F **estaba hecho una —** he was a sight

fachada F facade
facial ADJ facial
fácil ADJ (sencillo) easy; (promiscuo) easy, loose; **— de entender** self-explanatory; **— de usar** user-friendly
facilidad F ease; (habilidad) facility, knack
facilitar VT (hacer más fácil) to facilitate; (proporcionar) to furnish
facsímil M fax
factible ADJ feasible
fáctico ADJ factual
factor M factor; **—es de riesgo** risk factors
factoría F trading post
factura F bill, invoice; **— detallada** itemized invoice
facturable ADJ billable
facturación F billing
facturar VT (importe) to invoice; (equipaje) to check
facultad F (habilidad) faculty; (autoridad) authority; (división de una universidad) college; **— de odontología** dental school
facundia F gift of gab
faena F (trabajo corporal) chore; (labor) task; (molestia) nuisance
fagot M bassoon
fairway M fairway
faisán M pheasant
faja F (cinta) sash; (prenda interior) girdle; (de tierra) ribbon, strip
fajar VT (ceñir) to gird; (envolver) to wrap up; (golpear) to thrash
fajo M (de dinero) wad; (de papel, paja) sheaf
falacia F fallacy
falaz ADJ fallacious
falda F (prenda de vestir) skirt (también mujeres); (de una montaña) slope
faldón M (de una camisa) tail, shirttail; (de un saco) coattail
falible ADJ fallible
falla F (en un argumento) flaw; (en un motor) miss; (de una máquina) failure; (geológica) fault; **las Fallas** Valencian holiday
fallar VI (no funcionar) to fail; (un motor) to miss; VI/VT (un juez) to find, to rule
fallecer[35] VI to pass away, to decease
fallecimiento M passing, decease
fallo M (de un programa) bug, glitch; (de la memoria) lapse; (de un juez) ruling, finding
falo M phallus
falsear VT to falsify
falsedad F (dicho falso) falsehood; (condición de falso) falseness
falsificación F (de dinero) counterfeit; (de un documento) forgery
falsificar[30] VT (documento) to falsify, to fake; (dinero) to counterfeit; (una firma) to forge; (libros de contabilidad) to cook
falso ADJ (dato) false, untrue; (sentimientos)

fake, phony; (dinero) counterfeit; (promesa) hollow; (amigo) faithless, two-faced; (excusa) made-up; **falsa alarma** false alarm; **jurar en —** to perjure oneself; **paso en —** a false step; **salida en —** false start
falta F (defecto) fault; (carencia) lack, want; (ausencia) absence, miss; (jugada ilícita) foul; (de ortografía) mistake; **— de aire** shortness of breath, breathlessness; **— de pago** default; **— de respeto** disrespect; **— personal** (baloncesto) personal foul; **— de pie** foot fault; **a — de** for want of, in the absence of; **cometer —** to commit a foul; **hacer —** to be necessary; **me haces —** I miss you; **sin —** without fail
faltar VI (ausentarse) to be absent; (no haber) to be lacking; **— a la palabra** to break a promise; **— a la verdad** to misstate oneself; **—le el respeto a** to disrespect; **— poco para las cinco** to be almost five o'clock; **me falta tiempo** I don't have enough time; **¡no faltaba más!** (con indignación) that's the last straw! (no hay de qué) don't mention it! (no te molestes) I wouldn't hear of it
falto ADJ lacking; **— de esperanza** devoid of hope
fama F (condición de conocido) fame; (reputación) reputation; **de — mundial** world-famous
famélico ADJ ravenous
familia F family; **— nuclear** nuclear family; **en — in** the family; **jefe de —** head of household; **la señora de Juan tuvo —** John's wife had a baby
familiar ADJ (muy conocido) familiar; (de familia) familial; **tamaño —** family-size; **coche —** family car; **vida —** family life; MF relative; **—es** next of kin
familiaridad F familiarity
familiarizar[47] VT to familiarize, to acquaint; **—se** to acquaint oneself, to become familiar with
famoso ADJ famous
fanático -ca ADJ fanatic; MF fanatic, zealot; (de deportes) freak
fanatismo M fanaticism
fanega F bushel
fanfarria F fanfare
fanfarrón -ona MF braggart, show-off; ADJ blustering
fanfarronear VI to bluster
fanfarronería F bluster, swagger
fango M mire
fangoso ADJ miry
fantasear VI to fantasize
fantasía F (imaginación) imagination; (imagen) fantasy; **de —** fake, artificial
fantasioso ADJ (niño) imaginative; (idea) fanciful

fantasma M ghost, phantom
fantasmagórico ADJ ghostly
fantástico ADJ fantastic
farándula F show business
fardo M (paquete) bundle; (de heno, algodón) bale
farfolla F husk
farfulla F jabber
farfullar VI to jabber
faringe F pharynx
faríngeo ADJ pharyngeal
farmacéutico -ca ADJ pharmaceutical; MF pharmacist, druggist
farmacia F pharmacy, drugstore
fármaco M medicine, pharmaceutical
farmacología F pharmacology
faro M (torre) lighthouse; (luz de alerta) beacon; (luz del coche) light; — **delantero** headlight
farol M (portátil) lantern; (del alumbrado público) street lamp, streetlight; (con pie de hierro) lamppost; (jactancia, envite) bluff; **darse** — to show off, to put on airs
farra F spree; **ir de** — to go on a spree
farsa F (engaño) sham, hoax; (obra teatral, imitación ridícula) farce, mockery
farsante MF fraud, fake
fascículo M installment
fascinación F fascination
fascinante ADJ fascinating, riveting
fascinar VI/VT to fascinate
fascismo M fascism
fascista ADJ & MF fascist
fase F phase
fastidiado ADJ irked
fastidiar VT to irk
fastidio M annoyance
fastidioso ADJ annoying, wearisome
fatal ADJ (mortal) fatal; (terrible) terrible; **mujer** — femme fatale; ADV very badly; **me fue** — **en el examen** I did very poorly on the exam
fatalidad F (desgracia) misfortune; (destino) destiny
fatídico ADJ ill-fated
fatiga F fatigue, exhaustion; — **ocular** eye strain; —**s** hardships
fatigado ADJ tired, weary
fatigar[40] VT to tire out
fatigoso ADJ (cansado) tiring; (aburrido) tiresome
fauces F PL jaws
faul M foul
fauna F fauna
favor M favor; **a** — **de** in favor of; **por** — please
favorable ADJ favorable
favorecer[35] VT to favor
favorezca, favorezco *ver* favorecer
favoritismo M favoritism
favorito -ta ADJ favorite; MF favorite; (en una

elección) front-runner; (de la maestra) pet
fax M fax
faxear VT to fax
faz F face
FBI M FBI
fe F faith; — **de bautismo** baptismal certificate; — **de erratas** list of errors; — **de nacimiento** birth certificate; **buena** — good faith; **de buena** — in good faith; **dar** — **de** to vouch for
fealdad F ugliness
febrero M February
febril ADJ (con fiebre) feverish; (actividad) feverish, hectic
fecal ADJ fecal
fecha F date; — **de vencimiento** date due, due date
fechado ADJ dated
fechar VT to date
fechoría F misdeed
fecundación F fertilization
fecundar VT (un huevo) to fertilize; (una hembra) to impregnate
fecundo ADJ fertile
federación F federation
federal ADJ federal
felación F fellatio
felicidad F happiness; ¡—**es!** congratulations
felicitación F congratulation; **¡felicitaciones!** congratulations!
felicitar VT to congratulate
feligrés -esa MF parishioner; **feligreses** congregation
felino ADJ feline; M cat
feliz ADJ happy
felizmente ADV happily
felpa F plush
felpudo M doormat
femenino ADJ (como una mujer, relativo al género gramatical) feminine; (de la mujer) female
feminidad F femininity
feminismo F feminism
feminista MF feminist
fémur M femur
fenómeno M phenomenon
feo ADJ (cara) ugly, homely; (dentadura) bad; (accidente) nasty
féretro M coffin
feria F (mercado) market; (exposición) fair; (espectáculo) carnival; (celebración) holiday
feriante MF trader at fairs, stallholder
fermentación F fermentation
fermentar VT (leche) to ferment; (cerveza) to brew
fermento M ferment
ferocidad F ferocity
feroz ADJ ferocious, fierce
férreo ADJ (puente) iron; (disciplina) harsh

ferretería F (tienda) hardware store; (artículos) hardware
ferrocarril M railroad, railway
ferroviario -ria ADJ railroad; MF railroad employee
ferry M ferryboat
fértil ADJ fertile
fertilidad F fertility
fertilización F fertilization
fertilizante M fertilizer
fertilizar[47] VT to fertilize
ferviente ADJ fervent
fervor M fervor, zeal
fervoroso ADJ zealous
festejar VT to celebrate
festejo M celebration
festín M feast; **darse un** — to treat oneself
festival M festival
festividad F festivity
festivo ADJ festive, celebratory; **día** — holiday
festón M scallop
festonear VT to scallop
fetal ADJ fetal
fetiche M fetish
fétido ADJ foul-smelling
feto M fetus
feudal ADJ feudal
feudo M manor
fiabilidad F reliability
fiable ADJ reliable
fiador -ora MF guarantor, voucher; (prestamista) backer; (de un preso) bondsman
fiambre M (carne) cold cut; (cadáver) *fam* stiff
fianza F (de un préstamo) security, guaranty; (de un preso) bail
fiar[28] VT (garantizar) to vouch for; **—se de** to trust
fiasco M fiasco
fibra F fiber; **— de vidrio** fiberglass; **— óptica** optical fiber
fibrosis F fibrosis; **— cística** cystic fibrosis
fibroso ADJ fibrous
ficción F fiction
ficha F (de teléfono) token; (de dominó) domino; (de damas) checker; (en poker, ruleta) chip; (tarjeta) index card; MF (delincuente) delinquent, criminal
fichar VT to open a file on; VI to punch in
fichero M (de computadora) file; (archivador) filing cabinet; **— de datos** data file
ficticio ADJ (no real) fictitious; (novelesco) fictional
fidedigno ADJ trustworthy
fideicomisario -ria MF trustee
fideicomiso M trusteeship
fidelidad F (de un amante) fidelity, faithfulness; (de una traducción) closeness; (a la bandera) allegiance
fideo M noodle

fiduciario -ria ADJ & MF fiduciary
fiebre F fever; **— aftosa** foot-and-mouth disease; **— amarilla** yellow fever; **— de candilejas** stage fright; **— del oro** gold rush; **— reumática** rheumatic fever; **— tifoidea** typhoid fever; **tener —** to run a fever
fiel ADJ (leal) faithful; (exacto) true, accurate; M pointer on a scale; **los —es** the congregation
fieltro M (tela) felt; (sombrero) felt hat
fiera F beast; **ponerse hecho una —** to go berserk
fiereza F ferocity
fiero ADJ (salvaje) fierce; (muy grande) huge
fiesta F (festejo) party; (día feriado) holiday; **aguar una —** to ruin a party
fiestero -ra ADJ fond of parties; MF merrymaker, party animal
figura F figure
figurado ADJ figurative
figurar VI (aparecer) to appear, to figure; (lucirse) to show off; **—se** to imagine; **¡figúrate!** imagine!
figurativo ADJ figurative
figurín M fashion plate
figurón M dummy
fijación F fixing; **— de precios** pricing
fijador M hairspray
fijar VT (un cartel) to fix, to fasten; (una fecha) to set; (precios) to peg; **—se en** (notar) to notice; (prestar atención) to pay attention to, to focus on
fijo ADJ (sujeto, incambiado) fixed; (inmóvil) fixed, stationary; (firme) firm; (definitivo) definite; (permanente) permanent
fila F (uno detrás del otro) row, file; (hombro a hombro) rank; (de espera) line; (de documentos) queue; **— india** single file; **cerrar —s** to close ranks; **romper —s** to break ranks
filamento M filament
filantropía F philanthropy
filarmónica F philharmonic
filarmónico ADJ philharmonic
fildear VT to field
fildeo M fielding
filete M (de carne) fillet; (de un plato) rim
filetear VT to fillet
filiación F (membresía) affiliation; (datos personales) personal information; (lazo de parentesco) filiation; **— política** political affiliation
filial ADJ filial; F affiliate, subsidiary
filibusterismo M filibustering
filigrana F filigree
Filipinas F Philippines
filipino -na ADJ & MF Filipino, Filipina
filme M film, movie
filmación F filming, shooting

filmar VT to film, to shoot
filo M (de una navaja) cutting edge; (biológico) phylum; **de doble** — two-edged; **al** — **de las dos** at around two o'clock
filón M seam, vein, pocket
filoso ADJ sharp
filosofía F philosophy
filosófico ADJ philosophical
filósofo -fa MF philosopher
filtración F (purificación) filtration; (pérdida) leak; (percolación) seepage
filtrar VT (purificar) to filter; (perder) to leak; (clasificar) to screen; —**se** (gotear) to leak through; (percolarse) to seep
filtro M filter; — **de aire** air filter; — **de amor** love potion
fin M (conclusión, objetivo) end; — **de año** New Year's Eve; **el** — **del mundo** (lugar apartado) boondocks; — **de semana** weekend; — **de siglo** turn of the century; **al** — at last; **al** — **y al cabo** at any rate; **a** — **de que** so that; **a** — **de mes** toward the end of the month; **de** — **de año** year-end; **en** — in conclusion; **poner** — **a** to put an end to; **por** — at last, finally; **sin** — (ilimitado) myriad; (continuo) endless
finado ADJ late
final ADJ final, last; F (deportiva) final; M (de una historia) ending; (de un terreno) end; (de una carrera) finish; (de una filmación) wrap
finalidad F objective, purpose
finalista MF finalist
finalización F completion
finalizar[47] VT to finish; — **una sesión** lo log off/out
finalmente ADV at last, finally
financiación F (para una compra) financing; (para un proyecto) funding
financiamiento M (para una compra) financing; (para un proyecto científico) funding; — **por el propietario** owner financing
financiar VT (una compra) to finance; (un proyecto) to underwrite, *fam* to bankroll
financiero -ra ADJ financial; MF financier
finanza F finance; —**s** finances
finca F (inmueble) property; (granja) farm, country estate
finés -esa MF Finn; M (lengua) Finnish; ADJ Finnish
fineza F (atención) courtesy; (suavidad) smoothness
fingir[46] VI/VT (sorpresa) to feign; (un ataque al corazón) to fake; **fingió que la quería** he pretended to love her
finiquito M settlement
finito ADJ finite
finlandés -esa MF Finn; M (lengua) Finnish; ADJ Finnish
Finlandia F Finland

fino ADJ (vino, arena, pelo, metal) fine; (sentidos) keen, sharp; (medias) sheer; (hielo, alambre, voz) thin; (modales) smooth, refined
finta F fake, juke
firma F (compañía) firm; (rúbrica) signature; — **consultora** consulting firm
firmamento M sky
firmante MF signer
firmar VI/VT (documento, carta) to sign; (contrato) to enter
firme ADJ (estructura) firm; (control) tight; (colores) fast; (amarras) secure; (mano) steady, sure; (resistencia) stiff; (apoyo, resistencia) strong, staunch, steadfast; **mantenerse** — to stand one's ground; **¡** —**s!** attention!
firmemente ADV firmly
firmeza F (de una estructura) firmness; (de la mano) steadiness; (de la resistencia) stiffness; (del apoyo) strength; **con** — firmly
fiscal ADJ fiscal; MF public prosecutor, district attorney
fiscalía F prosecution
fiscalización F (de comportamiento) supervision; (de gastos) oversight
fiscalizar[47] VT (comportamiento) to supervise; (gastos) to oversee
fisgar[40] VI to snoop
fisgón -ona ADJ snooping; MF snoop
fisgonear VI to snoop
físico -ca ADJ physical; MF (persona) physicist; M (cuerpo) physique; F physics
fisiología F physiology
fisiológico ADJ physiological
fisioterapia F physical therapy
fisonomía F features
fístula F fistula
fisura F fissure
fiyano ADJ Fijian
Fiyi M Fiji
flácido, fláccido ADJ (sin firmeza) limp, flaccid; (gordo) flabby
flaco ADJ thin, skinny; **su lado** — his weakness
flacura F thinness
flagrante ADJ gross; **en** — **delito** in the act
flamante ADJ brand-new
flamear VI (llamear) to flame; (ondear) to flap
flamenco -ca ADJ Flemish; MF Flemish person; M (lengua) Flemish; (ave) flamingo; (baile) flamenco
flamígero ADJ flaming
flan M caramel custard
flanco M (de un animal, ejército) flank; (de un neumático) sidewall
flanquear VT to flank
flaquear VI (intención) to waver; (salud) to wane
flaqueza F weakness
flash M (noticias, visión, memoria digital) flash;

(lámpara) flashbulb, flash
flashback M flashback
flatulencia F flatulence
flauta F flute; — **dulce** recorder
flautín M piccolo
flecha F arrow
flechar VT to wound with an arrow
flechazo M (herida) wound from an arrow; (enamoramiento) love at first sight
fleco M (de una alfombra) fringe; (de pelo) bangs
flema F phlegm
flequillo M bangs
fletamento M charter
fletar VT to charter
flete M (contratación) charter; (envío) transport; (precio de transporte) freight; (encuentro sexual) *Esp* one-night stand
flexibilidad F (ductilidad) flexibility; (libertad) latitude
flexible ADJ (material) flexible; (cuerpo humano) limber, supple; (opinión) pliant, pliable
flojear VT to slacken
flojedad F laxity, looseness; (debilidad) weakness
flojera F (debilidad) weakness; (pereza) laziness
flojo ADJ (suelto) loose, slack; (holgazán) lazy; (inferior) crummy; (débil) weak; (sin fundamento) flimsy
floppy M floppy disk
flor F flower, blossom, bloom; (cumplido) compliment; — **de la edad** prime of life; — **de Pascua** poinsettia; — **y nata** the cream of the crop; **a** — **de** flush with; **en** — in bloom
flora F flora (también bacteriana); — **intestinal** intestinal flora
floración F blooming, blossoming
floral ADJ flowery
floreado ADJ flowery
florear VT (adornar con flores) to decorate with flowers; (adornar) to adorn
florecer[35] VI (echar flores) to flower, to bloom; (prosperar) to flourish, to thrive
floreciente ADJ (próspero) flourishing, prosperous; (florecido) blooming
florecimiento M flourishing
floreo M flourish
florería F florist's shop
florero M flower vase
florete M fencing foil
florido ADJ flowery
florista MF florist
floritura F flourish
flota F fleet
flotador M (para nadar) float; (de un avión) pontoon; ADJ floating
flotante ADJ floating, buoyant
flotar VI (estar suspendido, variar en valor) to float; (moverse en la superficie) to drift; (ir

por el aire) to waft
flote M flotation; **a** — afloat; **poner a** — to set afloat
fluctuación F fluctuation; (amplitud de variación) range
fluctuar[26] VI to fluctuate
fluidez F (cualidad de fluido) fluency; (cualidad de diluido) thinness
fluido ADJ (que fluye) fluid, flowing; (no vacilante) fluent; M fluid
fluir[19] VI to flow
flujo M (de agua) flow; (vaginal) discharge; (de datos) streaming; — **continuo de datos de audio** audio streaming; — **continuo de datos de vídeo** video streaming; — **de caja** cash flow; — **de trabajo** work flow
flúor M (elemento gaseoso) fluorine; (sal) fluoride
fluorescente ADJ fluorescent
fluoruro M fluoride
fluvial ADJ **transporte** — river transportation
fluyente ADJ flowing
FMI [Fondo Monetario Internacional] M IMF
fobia F phobia
foca F seal
foco M (punto central) focus; (bombilla) bulb; (lámpara potente) spotlight
fofo ADJ mushy
fogata F (fuego abierto) bonfire; (en un campamento) campfire
fogonazo M flash
fogoso ADJ fiery, spirited
folclor, folclore M folklore
folclórico/folklórico ADJ folkloric; **cuento** — folktale
foliculitis F folliculitis
folículo M follicle
folio M folio
folíolo M leaflet
follaje M foliage
follar VT *vulg* to fuck, to screw
folleto M pamphlet, brochure
follón M (confusión) mess; (alboroto) ruckus
fomentar VT (estudio) to promote; (amistad) to foster; (discordia) to foment; (apoyo) to drum up
fomento M encouragement
fonda F inn
fondear VI to anchor
fondillos M PL seat of pants
fondista MF (posadero) innkeeper; (corredor) long-distance runner
fondo M (parte más profunda) bottom; (parte posterior) rear; (del mar) bed; (de un cuadro, foto) background; (de dinero) fund; (de una biblioteca) holdings; (de un jardín) backyard; — **común** pool; — **de contingencia** contingency fund; — **especulativo** hedge

fund; — **físico** endurance; — **musical** background music; — **mutuo** mutual fund; **—s** funds; **—s administrados** managed funds; — **sin comisión de entrada** no-load fund; **a —** in depth; **carrera de —** long-distance race; **de cuatro en —** four abreast; **de —** (exhaustivo) in depth; (subyacente) underlying; **sin —** bottomless; **tocar —** to hit rock bottom

fonética F phonetics

fonético ADJ phonetic

fonógrafo M phonograph

fonología F phonology

fontanería F plumbing

fontanero -ra MF plumber

footing M jogging

forajido -da MF outlaw

foráneo ADJ foreign; **influencia foránea** outside influence

forastero -ra MF stranger, outsider

forcejear VI to struggle

forcejeo M struggle

fórceps M PL forceps

forense ADJ forensic; MF forensic scientist

forestal ADJ forest; **división —** forestry division

forja F (fogón) forge; (acción de forjar) forging; (taller) blacksmith's shop

forjado ADJ wrought

forjar VT (metales, un acuerdo) to forge; (un acuerdo) to hammer out; (un documento) to frame

forma F (figura) form, shape; (manera) manner; **— de pago** mode of payment; **— de pensar** mind-set; **ponerse en —** to get in shape; **no hay —** no way; **dar — a** to shape

formación F formation

formal ADJ (que atañe a la forma) formal, serious; (fiable) reliable

formaldehído M formaldehyde

formalidad F (convencionalidad) formality; (fiabilidad) reliability

formalismo M formality

formalizar[47] VT to make official; **—se** to settle down

formar VT (crear) to form; (reunir tropas) to muster; (entrenar) to train; **—se** (montañas) to form; (estudiantes) to be educated

formatear VT to format

formateo M formatting

formativo ADJ formative

formato M format; **— de archivo/fichero** file format; **— de texto enriquecido** rich text format

formidable ADJ formidable

formón M wood chisel

fórmula F formula

formulación F (acción de formular) formulation; (fórmula) formula; (redacción) wording

formular VT to formulate; (un plan, una pregunta) to frame; (un documento) to word

formulario M form

fornicar[30] VI to fornicate

fornido ADJ stout, sturdy

foro M forum; (de un escenario) back

forrado ADJ (con un forro) lined; (bien provisto) flush

forraje M forage, fodder

forrajear VI to forage

forrar VT (un saco) to line; **—se** to line one's pockets

forro M lining; (de un libro) jacket

fortalecer[35] VT to fortify, to strengthen

fortalecimiento M strengthening

fortaleza F (construcción) fortress, fort; (fuerza) fortitude

fortificación F fortification

fortificar[30] VT to fortify

fortuito ADJ fortuitous, accidental

fortuna F fortune; **por —** fortunately; **probar —** to try one's luck; **hacer —** to become rich

forúnculo M boil

forzar[49] VT to force, to coerce; **— la entrada** to break into

forzoso ADJ (por la fuerza) forcible; (inevitable) necessary; (aterrizaje) forced

fosa F (sepultura) grave; (de la nariz) cavity; (en el fondo del mar) trench

fosfato M phosphate

fósforo M (sustancia) phosphorus; (cerilla) match

fósil ADJ & M fossil

foso M (de un castillo) moat; (de un taller, teatro) pit

foto F snapshot, photo

fotocopia F photocopy

fotocopiadora F photocopier

fotocopiar VI/VT to photocopy

fotoeléctrico ADJ photoelectric

fotogénico ADJ photogenic

fotografía F (foto) photograph; (arte) photography; **— digital** digital photography

fotografiar[28] VT to photograph

fotógrafo -fa MF photographer

fotón M photon

fotosíntesis F photosynthesis

foul M foul

frac M tails

fracasar VI (un proyecto) to fail; (de una película) to bomb; (una embarcación) to break up

fracaso M (de un proyecto) failure; (de una película) flop, bomb

fracción F fraction

fractura F fracture, break; **— fina** hairline fracture

fracturar VT to fracture, to break; **se fracturó**

la cadera she broke her hip
fragancia F fragrance
fragante ADJ fragrant; **en —** in the act
fragata F frigate
frágil ADJ (delicado) delicate; (quebradizo) fragile, brittle; (una paz) tenuous
fragilidad F (condición de quebradizo) brittleness, delicacy; (debilidad) frailty
fragmentación F fragmentation
fragmento M fragment; (de metal, piedra) scrap; (de una conversación) snatch; (de un texto) extract, excerpt
fragoso ADJ rugged
fragua F (fogón) forge; (taller) blacksmith's shop
fraguar²⁵ VT to forge; (una trama) to hatch; VI (cemento, yeso) to set
fraile M friar
frambuesa F raspberry
frambueso M raspberry bush
francamente ADV **—, me horroriza** frankly / to be honest, it horrifies me; **lo pasaban — bien** they were doing pretty well; **—, es ridículo** it is simply ridiculous
francés -esa ADJ French; M (lengua) French; (hombre) Frenchman; F (mujer) Frenchwoman
franchute -uta MF *pey* frog
Francia F France
franco ADJ (sincero) frank, candid; (exento) free; **una franca mayoría** a clear majority; **un tratado —-americano** a Franco-American treaty
francotirador -ora MF sniper
franela F flannel
franja F ribbon
franquear VT (una frontera) to cross; (una carta) to frank; **—se** to be frank
franqueo M postage
franqueza F (personal) frankness; (institucional) openness
franquicia F (concesión) franchise; (exención) exemption
frasco M (recipiente de vidrio) flask; (de medicina, perfume) bottle; (de mermelada) jar
frase F phrase
frasear VI/VT to phrase
fraternal ADJ fraternal, brotherly
fraternidad F fraternity
fraternizar⁴⁷ VI fraternize
fraterno ADJ fraternal
fraude M fraud
fraudulento ADJ fraudulent
frazada F blanket
frecuencia F frequency; **con —** frequently
frecuentar VT to frequent; (una tienda) to patronize
frecuente ADJ frequent
fregadero M sink

fregado M scrubbing
fregar⁴¹ VT to scour, to scrub
fregona F (persona) scrubwoman, drudge; (utensilio) mop
freír¹⁰,⁷⁴ VI/VT to fry
frenar VT (un coche) to brake; (la inmigración) to restrain; (los impulsos) to bridle; VI to brake, to apply the brakes
frenesí M frenzy; (de actividad) flurry
frenético ADJ frantic
freno M (de coche) brake; (de caballo) bit; (contra el contrabando) curb
frente F forehead; **el sudor de la —** the sweat of one's brow; M (parte delantera, zona de combate, zona meteorológica) front; (de un edificio) face; **— a** (ante) in the face of; (al otro lado) facing; **— a —** face to face; **de —** head-on; **en — de** in front of; **hacer —** to face; **pasar al —** to come to the fore
fresa F (fruta) strawberry; (herramienta) mill
fresadora F milling machine
fresar VT to mill
frescachona F buxom woman
fresco ADJ (reciente, descansado, insolente) fresh; (frío) cool, brisk; (poco abrigado) light; (no cocinado) raw; (pintura) wet; M (frío) coolness; (pintura) fresco
frescor M (de verduras) freshness; (del aire) coolness
frescura F (de verduras, de carácter) freshness; (del tiempo) coolness; (comentario) impudent remark
fresno M ash tree
friabilidad F looseness
frialdad F coldness, coolness
fricción F friction, rubbing
friccionar VT to rub
friega F rubbing, massage
frigidez F frigidity
frigorífico M (electrodoméstico) refrigerator; (cámara) refrigeration chamber
frijol M bean
frío ADJ (de temperatura, de temperamento) cold; (helado) frigid; M cold; **tener —** to be cold
friolento ADJ sensitive to cold
friolera F **la — de $50,000** a trifling $50,000
fritada F dish of fried food
frito ADJ fried; M dish of fried food
fritura F (acción de freír) frying; (comida frita) dish of fried food
frivolidad F frivolity
frívolo ADJ frivolous
fronda F foliage
frondoso ADJ leafy
frontal ADJ (ataque) frontal; (colisión) head-on
frontera F frontier, border
fronterizo ADJ frontier
frontón M (juego) jai alai; (pista) jai alai court

frotación F rubbing
frotar VI/VT to rub
frote M rub
frotis M smear
fructífero ADJ fruitful
fructificar[30] VI to bear fruit
fructosa F fructose
frugal ADJ frugal
frunce M (volante) ruffle; (defecto) pucker
fruncir[33] VT to gather; — **el ceño** to frown, to knit one's brow; — **los labios** to purse one's lips
fruslería F trifle
frustración F frustration
frustrar VT (los planes) to frustrate, to thwart, to foil; (las esperanzas) to shatter, to dash; —**se** to fail, to miscarry
fruta F fruit
frutero -era MF fruit vendor; M fruit dish
fruto M fruit; —**s del mar** seafood
fue *ver* ser, ir
fuego M fire; (para un cigarro) light; — **antiaéreo** antiartillery fire; —**s artificiales** fireworks; **abrir el** — to begin to fire; **alto el** — cease-fire; **bajo** — under fire; **arma de** — firearm; **entre dos** —**s** between a rock and a hard place; **hacer** — to fire; **prender/poner/pegar** — **a** to set fire to
fuelle M bellows
fuel-oil M fuel oil
fuente F (surtidor) fountain; (manantial, referencia) spring; (caracteres de imprenta) font; **de buena** — from the horse's mouth
fuera ADV (en el exterior) outside; (tenis) out; — **de** outside of; — **de borda** outboard; — **de combate** out of commission; — **de juego** (fútbol) offside; — **de límites** (golf) out of bounds; — **de línea** offline; — **de serie** one of a kind; — **de servicio** out of service; INTERJ out!
fuera, fuéramos *ver* ser, ir
fuero M (jurisdicción) jurisdiction; (privilegio) privilege, charter
fuerte ADJ (hombre, bebida) strong; (ruido) loud; (cuero) tough; (personalidad) forceful; (estantería) sturdy; (plato) hearty; M (castillo) fort; (talento especial) strong point; ADV (tirar) strongly; (respirar) heavily; (gritar) loud; **soplar** — to bluster; **pisar** — to stomp; **atar** — to tie tight
fuerza F (de una máquina) force; (de una persona, animal) strength; — **aérea** air force; — **bruta** brute force; — **de la naturaleza** force of nature; — **de tarea** task force; — **de voluntad** willpower; —**s armadas** armed forces; **a** — **de** by dint of; **con** — strongly; **hacer** — to press on; **por la** — by force; **sacar** — **de flaqueza** to pull oneself together

fuerza, fuerce *ver* forzar
fuese, fuésemos *ver* ser, ir
fuga F (escape) escape, flight; (de la cárcel) jailbreak; (de gas) leak; (de capitales) drain, flight
fugarse[40] VI to flee, to escape; — **con el dinero** to abscond with the money
fugaz ADJ fleeting
fugitivo -va ADJ fugitive; MF fugitive
fui, fuimos *ver* ser, ir
fulano -na MF so-and-so; —, **zutano y mengano** Tom, Dick, and Harry; F tart, tramp
fulgor M radiance
fulgurar VI to flash
full M full house
fullero -ra MF (tramposo) cheat; (en naipes) card sharp
fulminante M cap; ADJ devastating
fulminar VT to strike with lightning; to thunder; **lo fulminó con la mirada** she gave him a withering look
fumadero M crackhouse
fumador -ora MF smoker
fumar VI/VT to smoke; —**se mucho dinero** to blow a lot of money
fumigar[40] VT to fumigate, to fog
función F (uso) function; (representación) performance; (cargo) office; — **de búsqueda** search function
funcional ADJ functional; **una casa** — a practical/livable house
funcionamiento M operation, working
funcionar VI to function, to work; (motor) to run
funcionario -ria MF government employee, official; — **de préstamos** loan officer
funda F (de un mueble) cover; (de una almohada) pillowcase, slip; (de navaja) sheath
fundación F foundation
fundador -ora MF founder
fundamental ADJ (básico) fundamental; (importante) crucial
fundamentalmente ADV fundamentally, mainly
fundamentar VT to base, to support; —**se en/ sobre** to be based on, to be supported by
fundamento M foundation, basis; —**s** fundamentals
fundar VT (un instituto) to found, to establish; (un argumento) to base
fundición F (fábrica) foundry; (acción de fundirse) fusing
fundido ADJ molten; M (en cinematografía) fade-in/fade-out
fundidor -ora MF foundry worker
fundir VT (combinar) to fuse; (derretir) to melt; (moldear) to mold; —**se** (combinarse) to fuse;

(romperse una bombilla) to burn out
fúnebre ADJ (relativo a funerales) funeral; (lúgubre) funereal
funeral ADJ & M funeral
funerario -ria ADJ funeral; F funeral parlor; MF funeral director
funesto ADJ ill-fated, unlucky
fungible ADJ fungible
fungicida M fungicide
funicular M cable car
funky ADJ funky
furgón M (vagón) boxcar; (camioneta de policía) police van; — **blindado** armored vehicle; — **de cola** caboose
furia F fury
furibundo ADJ furious, livid
furioso ADJ (persona) furious; (tempestad) fierce
furor M fury; **hacer** — to be all the rage
furtivo ADJ furtive, stealthy
fuselaje M fuselage
fusible M electric fuse
fusil M rifle
fusilamiento M execution by firing squad
fusilar VT to execute with firearms
fusión F (de hielo) melting; (nuclear) fusion; (empresarial) merger; (de documentos digitales) merge; **fusiones y adquisiciones** mergers and acquisitions
fusionar VT (metales) to fuse; (compañías, documentos digitales) to merge
fusta F crop
fustigar[40] VT (golpear) to lash, to whip; (criticar) to lash out at
fútbol M soccer; — **americano** football
futbolista MF soccer player
fútil ADJ futile, trivial
futilidad F triviality
futuro ADJ future; M future; —**s** futures

Gg

gabacho -cha ADJ & MF (francés) *pey* frog; (americano) *pey* American
gabán M overcoat
gabardina F trench coat
gabinete M (ministerial) cabinet; (administrativo) office
Gabón M Gabon/Gabun
gabonés -esa ADJ & MF Gabonese
gacela F gazelle
gaceta F gazette
gacetilla F short news item
gachas F PL — **de avena** oatmeal
gachí F bimbo

gacho ADJ (orejas) drooping; (cabeza) bowed; (ojos) lowered
gachupín -ina MF *Méx pey* Spaniard
gafar VT to jinx
gafas F PL glasses
gafe M jinx
gaffe M gaffe, faux pas
gag M gag
gaita F bagpipe
gaje M —**s del oficio** occupational hazards
gajo M (de planta) branch; (de naranja) section
gala F (cena) banquet; —**s** finery; **hacer** — **de** to boast of, to flaunt; **vestirse de** — to dress up
galán M (pretendiente) gallant, suitor; (en cine) leading man
galante ADJ gallant
galantear VT to court
galanteo M courting
galantería F (caballerosidad) gallantry; (cumplido) compliment
galardón M award
galaxia F galaxy
galera F galley (también prueba de imprenta); *RP* top hat
galerada F galley proof
galería F (salón) gallery; (pasillo) corridor; (tiendas) mall, gallery; (de coro) loft; (subterráneo) tunnel; —**s** *Esp* department store
Gales M Wales
galés -esa ADJ & MF Welsh
galgo M greyhound
Galicia F Galicia
gallardete M pennant
gallardía F (elegancia) elegance; (valentía) bravery
gallardo ADJ (elegante) elegant; (valiente) brave
gallego -ga ADJ Galician; M (lengua) Galician; MF Galician
gallera F cockpit
galleta F (salada) cracker; (dulce) cookie
gallina F (pollo) chicken; (hembra adulta) hen; MF coward; — **ciega** blind man's bluff; **la** — **de los huevos de oro** the goose that laid the golden egg
gallinero M (de gallinas) chicken coop; (de teatro) gallery; **alborotar el** — to raise a ruckus
gallito ADJ cocksure, cocky; M braggart
gallo M cock, rooster; (de la voz) break; **tener** —**s en la garganta** to have a frog in one's throat; **en menos que canta un** — before you can say Jack Robinson
galón M (de líquido) gallon; (de tela) stripe
galopar VI/VT to gallop
galope M gallop; **al** — at a gallop
galvanizar[47] VT to galvanize
gama F gamut, range
gamba F large shrimp

gamberro -rra MF (rebelde, pandillero) punk, hoodlum; *Esp* (en fútbol) hooligan

Gambia F Gambia

gambiano -na ADJ & MF Gambian

gamo M buck

gamuza F (animal) chamois (también piel); (piel de venado) buckskin, deerskin; (piel de vaca) suede

gana F urge; **con —s** with a vengeance; **de buena —** willingly; **tener —s de** to feel like; **tengo —s [de ir al baño]** I have to go [to the bathroom]; **no me da la —** I just don't feel like it

ganadería F (cría) cattle breeding; (ganado) livestock

ganadero -ra M cattleman; F cattlewoman; ADJ **industria ganadera** cattle industry

ganado M livestock; **— ovino** sheep; **— porcino** swine; **— vacuno** cattle

ganador -ora MF winner; ADJ winning

ganancia F profit, gain, return; **—s** (recaudación de un evento) proceeds; (de un juego) winnings; (de un negocio) earnings; **—s pre-impositivas** before-tax earnings

ganapán M (obrero) menial worker; (trabajo) bread and butter

ganar VI/VT (una guerra, la lotería) to win; (kilos, eficacia) to gain; VT (un sueldo) to earn; (tiempo, espacio) to save; (tierra) to reclaim; **dejarse — por algo** to give in to something; **nos ganaron el partido** they beat us; **—se la vida** to make a living

ganchillo M crochet

gancho M hook (también en boxeo, baloncesto); (rama) snag; (para sujetar) clip; (atractivo) lure; **echar a uno el —** to hook someone; **tener —** to be attractive

gandul -la MF loafer

ganga F bargain, steal

gangoso ADJ twangy

gangrena F gangrene

gangrenarse VI to gangrene

gángster M gangster

ganguear VI to twang

ganso M (animal) goose; (macho) gander; (tonto) *fam* ding-a-ling

ganzúa F picklock

gañido M yelp

gañir[17] VI to yelp

garabatear VI/VT to scribble

garabato M scribble; **hacer —s** to scribble

garaje M garage

garante MF voucher

garantía F (de producto) guarantee, warranty; (de promesa) security, guaranty; (de un derecho) guarantee; (comercial) backing; **— de devolución de dinero** money-back guarantee; **— de préstamo** loan guarantee

garantizar[47] VT (producto) to guarantee, to warranty; (promesa) to warrant

garañón M stud, horse

garbanzo M chickpea

garbo M grace

garboso ADJ graceful

garfio M hook

garganta F (faringe) throat; (cuello) neck; (valle estrecho) gorge

gárgara F gargle; **hacer —s** to gargle

gargarismo M gargle

garita F sentry box

garito M gambling house

garra F (de ave) claw; (de león) paw with claws; **caer en las —s de alguien** to fall into someone's clutches

garrafa F decanter

garrapata F tick

garrapatear VI/VT to scribble

garrapiñar VT to candy

garrocha F pole

garrote M club

garrucha F pulley

gárrulo ADJ garrulous

garza F heron

gas M gas; **—es** (de motor) fumes; (de intestino) gas; **— ionizado** plasma; **— lacrimógeno** tear gas; **— mostaza** mustard gas; **— natural** natural gas; **— nervioso** nerve gas; **a todo —** at full speed

gasa F (tela) gauze; (para heridas) dressing

gaseosa F soda, soft drink

gaseoso ADJ gaseous

gasoducto M pipeline

gasolina F gasoline, gas

gasolinera F gas station

gastado ADJ (neumático) smooth; (ropa) worn-out, shabby

gastador -ora ADJ extravagant, wasteful; MF spendthrift

gastar VT (dinero, tiempo) to spend; (energía) to expend; (neumáticos, ropa) to wear out, to use up; **— una broma** to play a trick; **—se** to wear out

gasto M (desembolso) expense, expenditure; (desgaste) wear; **—s de desplazamiento** travel costs; **—s del hogar** household expenses; **—s de subsistencia** living expenses; **—s de viaje** travel expenses; **—s menores** incidentals

gástrico ADJ gastric

gastritis F gastritis

gastroenteritis F gastroenteritis

gastrointestinal ADJ gastrointestinal

gastronomía F gastronomy

gatas LOC ADV **a —** on all fours

gatear VI to creep, to crawl

gatillo M (de arma de fuego) trigger; (de dentista) forceps

gatito M kitten

gato M (felino) cat; (aparato para levantar) jack; — **montés** wildcat, mountain lion; **aquí hay— encerrado** I smell a rat; **a gatas** on all fours; **dar— por liebre** to sell someone a pig in a poke
gaucho M gaucho
gaveta F small drawer
gavilán M hawk
gavilla F (de maíz) sheaf; (de maleantes) gang
gaviota F seagull
gayola F *fam* big house
gazmoñería F prudery
gazmoño -ña MF prude; ADJ prudish
gaznate M gullet
gazpacho M *Esp* gazpacho
geco M gecko
géiser M geyser
gel M gel
gelatina F gelatin
gélido ADJ frigid
gema F gem, jewel
gemelo -la ADJ & MF identical twin; **—s** (mellizos) identical twins; (binoculares) binoculars, opera glasses; (botón) studs
gemido M (de dolor) moan, groan; (de queja) whine
gemir[9] VI (gruñir) to moan, to groan; (lloriquear) to whine
gen, gene M gene; — **recesivo** recessive gene
genealogía F genealogy
generación F generation
generador M generator
general ADJ & MF general; **por lo —** generally
generalidad F generality
generalización F (de un concepto) generalization; (de una moda) spreading
generalizar[47] VI/VT to generalize; **—se** to become widespread
generalmente ADV generally, usually
generar VT generate
genérico ADJ generic
género M (clase) kind; (gramatical) gender; (tela) material; (literario) genre; (biológico) genus; — **humano** human race; **—s** dry goods
generosidad F generosity
generoso ADJ generous
genética F genetics
genético ADJ genetic
genial ADJ brilliant
genio MF (persona inteligente) genius; M (inteligencia) genius, brilliance; (temperamento) temperament, nature; (mal humor) temper; **de mal —** mean; **de buen —** good-natured
genital ADJ genital; M PL **—es** genitals
geniudo ADJ quick-tempered
genocidio M genocide
genoma M genome

gente F people; — **de campo** country folk; — **de color** persons of color; — **en obra** men at work; — **joven** young people; — **menuda** small fry; **buena —** good person
gentil ADJ (cortés) gracious; (no judío) gentile; MF gentile
gentileza F graciousness
gentío M crowd
gentuza F rabble, riffraff
genuino ADJ genuine
geocéntrico ADJ geocentric
geoestacionario ADJ geostationary
geofísica F geophysics
geografía F geography
geográfico ADJ geographical
geología F geology
geológico ADJ geological
geometría F geometry
geométrico ADJ geometric
geopolítico ADJ geopolitical
Georgia F Georgia
georgiano -na ADJ & MF Georgian
geotérmico ADJ geothermal
geranio M geranium
gerencia F management
gerente MF manager
geriatría F geriatrics
geriátrico ADJ geriatric
germánico ADJ Germanic
germen M germ
germinar VI to germinate, to sprout
gerundio M gerund, present participle
gestación F gestation
gesticular VI (con ademanes) to gesture; (con movimientos exagerados) to gesticulate
gestión F (acción) step, measure; (dirección empresarial, digital) management; (administración política) administration; **—es** negotiations; — **de datos** data management; **hacer gestiones para** to take steps to
gestionar VT (negociar) to negotiate; (administrar) to administer, to manage
gesto M (con la cara) face; (con las manos) gesture; **hacerle —s a alguien** to make faces at someone
gestor -ora MF agent
Ghana F Ghana
ghanés -esa ADJ & MF Ghanaian
giba F hump, hunch
gibón M gibbon
Gibraltar M Gibraltar
gibraltareño -ña ADJ & MF Gibraltarian
giga F jig
gigabyte M gigabyte
gigahercio M gigahertz
gigante ADJ giant, gigantic; MF giant
gigantesco ADJ gigantic
gilipollas MF INV *ofensivo* idiot, schmuck

gimnasia F gymnastics
gimnasio M gymnasium, gym
gimotear VI to whimper
gimoteo M whimper
ginebra F gin
ginecología F gynecology
ginecólogo -ga MF gynecologist
gingivitis F gingivitis
gira F tour
girar VI/VT (una llave, un volante, un coche, a la derecha) to turn; VI (un trompo, un disco) to revolve, to spin, to whirl; VT (dinero) to wire
girasol M sunflower
giratorio ADJ rotary, revolving
giro M (movimiento circular) rotation, spin; (cambio de dirección) turn; (expresión) turn of phrase; (monetario) draft, remittance; — **de cheques sin fondos** check kiting; — **postal** money order
giroscopio M gyroscope
gitano -na ADJ & MF gypsy
glacial ADJ glacial, bitter
glaciar M glacier
gladiador M gladiator
glamoroso ADJ glamorous
glamour M glamour
glándula F gland; —**s sudoríparas** sweat glands
glandular ADJ glandular
glaseado M (de torta) glaze; ADJ (papel) glossy
glasear VT to glaze
glaucoma M glaucoma
glicerina F glycerin
global ADJ (mundial) global; (de conjunto) blanket, overall
globalización F globalization
globo M (esfera) globe; (de árbol de Navidad) ball; (lleno de gas) balloon; (en tenis) lob; — **ocular** eyeball; — **terráqueo** globe
globulina F globulin
glóbulo M globule; — **rojo** red cell; — **blanco** white cell
gloria F glory
glorieta F (pérgola) arbor; (rotonda) traffic circle
glorificar[30] VT to glorify
glorioso M glorious
glosa F gloss
glosar VT to gloss
glosario M glossary
glotal ADJ glottal
glótico ADJ glottal
glotis F glottis
glotón -ona ADJ gluttonous; MF glutton
glotonería F gluttony
glucosa F glucose
gluglutear VI to gobble
gluten M gluten
gobernabilidad F governability

gobernación F (acción de gobernar) governing; (entidad gubernamental) government
gobernador -ora ADJ governing; MF governor
gobernante ADJ governing; MF ruler
gobernar[1] VI/VT to govern, to rule; (un buque) to steer
gobierno M government
goce M enjoyment
gofre M waffle
gol M goal; — **de campo** (fútbol americano) field goal; — **del empate** (fútbol) equalizer; — **en contra** (fútbol) own goal
goleador -ora MF (artillero) shooter; (máximo anotador) top scorer
goleta F schooner
golf M golf
golfo -fa M (mar) gulf; (sinvergüenza) rascal; F pey tramp
gollería F delicacy
golondrina F swallow
golosina F sweet, goody, tidbit
goloso ADJ sweet-toothed
golpazo M bang, whack
golpe M (físico) blow, knock, whack; (emocional) blow; (estafa) sting; (robo) holdup; (golf) stroke; (de viento) buffet; (con el codo) jab; (con los nudillos) rap; — **bajo** low blow; — **cortado** (tenis) backspin, slice; — **cruzado** (tenis) crosscourt shot; — **de aproximación** (golf) approach shot; — **de calor** heat stroke; — **de derecha** (tenis) forehand; — **de estado** coup; — **de gracia** coup de grâce; — **de penalidad** (golf) penalty stroke; — **de sol** sunstroke; **de —** suddenly; **de un —** all at once
golpear VI/VT (pegar) to strike, to hit; (llamar) to knock, to rap; (dar una paliza) to beat, to batter; (patear) to kick; (codear) to jab
golpecito M tap
golpetear VI (dedos) to tap; (lluvia) to patter; (motor) to knock; (algo suelto) to rattle
golpeteo M (con los dedos) tap; (de lluvia) patter; (de un motor) knock; (de algo suelto) rattle
goma F (chicle) gum; (caucho) rubber; (neumático) tire; (en béisbol) home; — **de borrar** eraser; — **de mascar** chewing gum; — **elástica** rubber band; —**espuma** foam
gomero M rubber tree
gomoso ADJ slimy
gónada F gonad
góndola F gondola
gong M gong
gonorrea F gonorrhea, fam the clap
gordinflón ADJ pey fatso
gordito ADJ chubby
gordo ADJ fat; **se armó la gorda** all hell broke loose; **hacer la vista gorda** to turn a blind eye

gordura F (cualidad) fatness; (sebo) fat
gorgojo M weevil
gorila M (primate) gorilla; (portero) bouncer;
(guardaespaldas) bodyguard
gorjear VI (ave) to warble, to chirp, to twitter;
(niño) to gurgle
gorjeo M (de ave) warble, twitter, chirp; (de
niño) gurgle
gorra F cap; **de** — at someone else's expense;
vivir de — to sponge
gorrino M piglet
gorrión M sparrow
gorro M cap
gorrón M sponge, sponger
gorronear VI/VT to mooch, to freeload
gospel M gospel
gota F (de líquido) drop; (de sudor) bead;
(enfermedad) gout; — **a** — drop by drop; **—s**
oftálmicas eyedrops; **ser dos —s de agua**
to be like two peas in a pod; **sudar la —**
gorda (transpirar) to sweat profusely;
(trabajar) to work hard
gotear VI (caer gota a gota) to drip;
(rápidamente) to dribble, to trickle; (salirse)
to leak; (llover) to sprinkle
goteo M drip (también intravenoso); (rápido)
dribble, trickle
gotera F leak
gotero M dropper
gótico ADJ Gothic; M (lengua) Gothic
gourmet ADJ & MF gourmet
gozar⁴⁷ VT to enjoy; — **de** to enjoy
gozne M hinge
gozo M pleasure, enjoyment
gozoso ADJ enjoyable
grabación F recording
grabado M (en piedra) engraving; (con ácido)
etching
grabador-ora MF (persona) engraver; F
(aparato) tape recorder; (empresa) recording
company
grabar VI/VT (en piedra) to engrave; (con ácido)
to etch; (en cinta magnetográfica) to record,
to tape; (en computadora) to write; — **en la**
memoria to etch/imprint on one's memory
gracejo M wit
gracia F (garbo, desenvoltura) grace,
gracefulness; (humor) humor; (monería)
antic; (favor) favor; (indulto) pardon; **¡—s!**
thanks! thank you! **—s a Dios** thank God;
caer en — to please; **dar —s** to say the
blessing; **dar las —s** to thank; **hacer** — to
amuse; **tener** — to be funny
grácil ADJ supple, graceful
gracioso ADJ (chistoso) amusing, funny; (gentil)
gracious
grada F step, bleachers
gradación F gradation
graderías F PL bleachers

grado M (de temperatura, de parentesco, de un
ángulo, de universidad) degree; (militar)
rank; (de alcohol) proof; **de buen** —
willingly; **en alto** — to a great extent; **en
mayor o menor** — to some extent;
quemadura de primer — first-degree
burn
graduación F (de una escuela) graduation,
commencement; (militar) military rank; (de
alcohol) proof; (de un lente óptico) correction
graduado -da MF graduate
gradual ADJ gradual
graduar²⁶ VT (ajustar) to adjust; (regular) to
calibrate; **—se** to graduate, to get a degree
graffiti M graffiti
grafiar²⁸ VT to graph
gráfica F (arte) graphics; (representación)
graph, chart; — **de pastel** pie graph
graficar³⁰ VT to chart
gráfico -ca ADJ graphic; **acento** — written
accent; M (representación) graph, chart; MF
(empleado) printer
grafito M graphite
grama F lawn
gramática F grammar
gramatical ADJ grammatical
gramo M gram
grana ADJ & F scarlet
granada F (fruta) pomegranate; (proyectil)
grenade; — **de mano** hand grenade
Granada F Grenada
granadino -na ADJ & MF Grenadian
granado M pomegranate tree; ADJ notable
granate M garnet
Gran Bretaña F Great Britain
grande ADJ (de tamaño) large, big; (de
importancia) great; **un gran poeta** a great
poet; **divertirse en** — to have a whale of a
time; **a —s alturas** at high altitudes; **de
gran alcance** far-reaching; **de/a gran
escala** large-scale; **en gran parte** in large
measure, largely; **gran almacén**
department store
grandeza F greatness; **delirios de** — delusions
of grandeur
grandiosidad F grandeur
grandioso ADJ grandiose, grand
granero M (edificio) granary, grain barn;
(recipiente) bin, crib; **el** — **de América** the
breadbasket of America
granito M granite
granizada F hailstorm
granizar⁴⁷ VI to hail
granizo M hail
granja F farm
granjearse VI to win for oneself
granjero -ra MF farmer
grano M (de una foto, arena, semilla) grain;
(cereal) cereal, grain; (barrito) pimple; — **de**

café coffee bean; **ir al** — to come to the point
granuja MF ragamuffin
granular VT to granulate; **—se** to become granulated
granuloso ADJ granular
grapa F (para sujetar madera) clamp; (para sujetar papel) staple
grapadora F stapler
grasa F (aceite) grease; (animal) fat
grasiento ADJ greasy
graso ADJ (cutis) oily; (leche) fatty; (pelo) greasy
grasoso ADJ greasy
gratificación F bonus
gratificar[30] VT to gratify
gratis ADJ INV & ADV free
gratitud F gratitude, thankfulness
grato ADJ pleasant
gratuito ADJ (gratis) free; (arbitrario) wanton, gratuitous
grava F gravel
gravamen M (impuesto) tax, assessment; (carga sobre una propiedad) lien, encumbrance
gravar VT (con un impuesto) to tax, to assess; (con una carga) to encumber
grave ADJ (enfermedad, decisión) grave, serious; (sonido) low, deep; (injuria) grievous; (personalidad) earnest
gravedad F (fuerza de atracción) gravity; (de una situación) seriousness; (de una tormenta) severity; (de la voz) depth; (de una personalidad) earnestness
gravemente ADV (herido) seriously; (enfermo) seriously, gravely
gravitación F gravitation
gravitatorio ADJ gravitational
gravoso ADJ burdensome
graznar VI (cuervo) to caw, to croak; (pato) to quack; (ganso) to honk
graznido M (de cuervo) caw, croak; (de pato) quack; (de ganso) honk
Grecia F Greece
greda F clay
green M green
gregario ADJ gregarious
gremial ADJ **acuerdo** — union agreement
gremio M (conjunto de personas) trade; (asociación histórica) guild; (sindicato) trade union
greña F mop of hair
grey F flock, fold
griego -ga ADJ & MF Greek
grieta F crevice, crack
grifo M faucet, spigot, tap
grillete M fetter, shackle
grillo M (insecto) cricket; **—s** (grilletes) shackles
grima F uneasiness; **dar** — (disgustar) to be upsetting; (asquear) to be disgusting
gringo -ga ADJ & MF *pey* American
gripe, gripa F flu, influenza; — **asiática**

Asiatic flu
gris ADJ & M gray
grisáceo ADJ grayish
gritar VI/VT (vociferar) to shout, to yell; (chillar) to scream
gritería F shouting
grito M (voz alta) shout, cry; (chillido) scream; **el último** — the last word; **estar en un** — to be in agony; **pedir a —s** to clamor for; **poner el** — **en el cielo** to hit the ceiling
grosella F currant
grosellero M currant
grosería F (cualidad) rudeness; (hecho, dicho) profanity, something rude
grosero ADJ (descortés) rude, ill-mannered, boorish; (vulgar) vulgar, profane; (sin arte) coarse, unrefined
grosor M thickness
grotesco ADJ grotesque
grúa F (máquina) crane; (guinche, remolcadora) wrecker, tow truck
grueso -sa ADJ (persona) thick-set, heavy; (tabla) thick; (palabra, arena) coarse; M (grosor) thickness; (mayoría) majority; F gross
grulla F crane
grumo M lump
grumoso ADJ lumpy
gruñido M (de perro) growl, snarl; (de cerdo) grunt; (humano) grumble
gruñir[17] VI (el cerdo) to grunt; (el perro) to growl, to snarl; (el ser humano) to grumble
gruñón -ona ADJ grumpy; MF grumpy person
grupa F rump; **volver —s** to turn around
grupo M group; — **de apoyo** support group; — **de presión** lobby; — **étnico** ethnicity; — **paritario** peer group; — **sanguíneo** blood type; — **de usuarios** user group
gruta F grotto, cavern
guacal M crate
guacamole M *Méx* guacamole
guacho M (cría de ave) chick; *Am* (animal huérfano) orphan
guadaña F scythe
guagua F (fruslería) trifle; *Carib* bus; *Chile* baby; LOC ADV **de** — for nothing, free
guaje -ja MF urchin
guano M guano, bird dung
guantada F slap
guante M glove (también en deporte); **arrojar el** — to challenge; **echarle el** — **a alguien** to capture someone; **te queda como un** — it fits you like a glove
guantelete M gauntlet
guantera F glove compartment
guapetón -ona MF *fam* fox
guapo ADJ (hombre) good-looking, handsome; (mujer) good-looking, pretty; (valiente) brave; **¡hola —!** hey, good-looking!

guarapo M cane syrup
guarda MF (guardián) guard; F (almacenamiento) storage
guardameta MF (fútbol) goalkeeper
guardar VT (almacenar) to keep, to store; (observar) to observe; (datos) to save; (proteger) to guard; — **como** to save as; — **rencor** to hold a grudge; — **un secreto** to keep a secret; —**se de** to guard against; M SG **guardabarros** fender; M SG **guardacostas** Coast Guard cutter; MF SG **guardaespaldas** bodyguard; M SG **guardafangos** fender; M SG **guardapelo** locket; M SG **guardarropa** (armario, ropa) wardrobe; (en un local) cloakroom; MF SG **guardabosque[s]** forest ranger, forester; MF SG **guardafrenos** brake operator; MF SG **guardagujas** switch operator; MF SG **guardameta** goalie
guardería F nursery, day-care center
guardia MF (vigilante) guard; (en baloncesto) point guard; — **civil** civil guard; F (vigilancia) guard; **bajar la** — to let down one's guard; **de** — (militar) on duty, on watch; (médico) on call; **en** — en garde; **hacer/montar** — to stand guard
guardián -ana MF guardian, keeper
guarecerse[35] VT to take shelter
guarida F den, lair
guarismo M cipher
guarnecer[35] VT (un plato) to garnish; (un vestido) to trim; (una fortaleza) to man, to garrison
guarnición F (de tropas) garrison; (de comida) trimmings; **guarniciones** harness
guarro ADJ filthy; M pig
guasa LOC ADV **de/a** — in jest, as a joke
guasón -ona MF joker
guata F padding
Guatemala F Guatemala
guatemalteco -ca ADJ & MF Guatemalan
guau INTERJ woof
guay ADJ *Esp* cool, great
guayaba F guava
guayabera F tropical pleated shirt
gubernamental ADJ governmental
gubernativo ADJ governmental
gubia F gouge
guedeja F shock of hair
guepardo M cheetah
guerra F war, warfare; **dar** — to aggravate; **en pie de** — at war; — **fría** cold war
guerrear VI to war
guerrero -ra MF warrior; **operación guerrera** war operation; **espíritu** — warrior spirit
guerrilla F guerrilla army
guerrillero -ra MF guerrilla
gueto M ghetto
guía MF (persona) guide, leader; F (cosa o animal) guide; — **para padres** parenting guide; — **telefónica** telephone directory
guiar[28] VT to guide, to lead; —**se por** to follow
guijarro M pebble
guinche M *Am* (grúa) winch; (remolque) tow truck
guinda F cherry
guindilla F *Esp* small hot pepper
Guinea F Guinea
guineano -na ADJ & MF Guinean
guingán M gingham
guiñada F wink
guiñapo M rag
guiñar VI/VT to wink
guiño M wink
guión M (ortografía) hyphen; (libreto) script, screenplay
guionista MF screenwriter
guirnalda F garland; (de Navidad) tinsel
guisa F a — de by way of
guisado M stew, hash
guisante M pea
guisar VI/VT (cocer) to cook; (en olla) to stew
guiso M stew, casserole
guitarra F guitar
gula F gluttony
gusano M worm; — **de seda** silkworm
gustar VT (agradar) to be pleasing to; **ella me gusta** I like her; **le gustan los perros** he likes dogs; **no me gustan las fiestas** I dislike parties; **te guste o no te guste** whether you like it or not; **cuando gustes** whenever you want; — **de** (preferir) to be fond of; (saborear) to taste
gusto M (sentido, sabor, sentido estético) taste; (agrado) pleasure; (preferencia personal) like; **a** — at ease; **a mi** — to my liking; **dar** — to be a pleasure; **darle el** — **a alguien** to humor someone; **darse el** — to indulge oneself; **de mal** — in bad taste; **el** — **es mío** the pleasure is mine; **estar a** — to be comfortable; **mucho** — nice to meet you; **por** — for fun; **tener el** — **de** to have the pleasure of; **tomarle el** — **a una cosa** to become fond of something
gustoso ADJ (que gusta de) fond of; (agradable) pleasant; ADV willingly
Guyana F Guyana
guyanés -esa ADJ & MF Guyanese

Hh

ha, has *ver* haber
haba F (frijol) bean; (frijol verde) lima bean
habano M cigar

haber[68] V AUX to have; — **comido cuatro veces en un día** to have eaten four times in a day; **habérselas con** (un problema) to grapple with; (una persona) to have it out with; **ha de llegar mañana** he is to arrive tomorrow; **hay** there is, there are; **hay viento** it is windy; **hubo un problema** there was a problem; **había gente** there were people; **hay que** it is necessary to; **no hay de qué** don't mention it; **no hay forma** no way; **no hay problema** no problem; **¿qué hay?** what's up? **todo lo habido y por haber** everything possible; M (hacienda) assets; (columna en una cuenta) credit; —**es** earnings

habichuela F bean; — **verde** string bean

hábil ADJ adept, able; **día** — workday

habilidad F ability, skill

habilidoso ADJ deft, skillful

habilitar VT (equipar) to outfit; (autorizar) to authorize

habitación F (vivienda) dwelling; (cuarto) room

habitante MF (de un país, región) inhabitant; (de un barrio) resident

habitar VT to inhabit

hábitat M habitat

hábito M habit (también vestimenta religiosa); —**s de compra** buying habits

habitual ADJ habitual, usual

habituar[26] VT to accustom; —**se** to get used to

habla F (lenguaje) speech; (variedad local) dialect; — **infantil** baby talk; **al** — in communication with; **quedarse sin** — to be left speechless

hablador ADJ talkative

habladurías F idle talk, gossip

hablante ADJ speaking; **castellano**— Castilian-speaking; MF speaker; **castellano**— Castilian speaker

hablar VI/VT to talk; — **de política** to talk about politics; — **hasta por los codos** to talk one's head off; — **no cuesta nada** talk is cheap; — **por teléfono** to talk on the phone; — **solo / para sí** to talk to oneself; to speak; — **francés** to speak French; — **sin rodeos** to speak one's mind; — **por señas** to use sign language; **hablando mal y pronto** pardon my French; **no** —**se** not to be on speaking terms; **no me hagas** — don't get me started on it; **hablando en serio, ¿qué es lo que quieres?** seriously, what do you want?

hablilla F malicious tale

habrá, habría ver haber

hacedor -ora MF maker

hacendado -da MF landowner

hacendoso ADJ industrious, diligent

hacer[54, 74] VT (crear) to do, to make; (causar) to make; (resolver) to do; (decir) to go; **la vaca hace 'mu'** the cow goes moo; — **clic** to click; — **economías** to scrimp; — **frío/calor/ viento** to be cold/hot/windy; — **una oferta** make an offer; — **un pastel** to make a cake; — **un crucigrama** to do a crossword puzzle; — **un gol** to score a goal; **me hizo llorar** he made me cry; **hace mucho tiempo** a long time ago; **hace poco** a short while ago; **hizo como si estuvieras presente** he acted as if you were here; **a lo hecho, pecho** you've got to face the music; **la hiciste buena** you've really screwed up; **¿qué le vamos a hacer?** that's life; **¿qué se hizo de Juan?** whatever became of Juan? **haz el trabajo** do the work; **hecho a pedido** built to order; —**se rico** to become rich; —**se el tonto** to play the fool; —**se el listo** to pull a stunt; —**se pasar por el jefe** to pose as the boss; —**se a un lado** to step aside; —**se amigo de** to befriend; —**se a la oscuridad** to get used to the dark; —**se cargo** to take over; —**se [del] rogar** to play hard to get

hacha F (grande) ax[e]; (pequeña) hatchet

hachís M hashish

hacia PREP (en dirección a) toward; (aproximadamente) about; — **abajo** downward; — **adelante** forward; — **adentro** inward; — **afuera** outward; — **arriba** upward; — **atrás** backward; — **el este** eastward; — **la izquierda** to the left; **dar** — to face

hacienda F (bienes) estate; (establecimiento agropecuario) ranch; (impositiva) Internal Revenue Service

hacina F shock

hacinar VT (liar) to shock; (atestar) to crowd in

hada F fairy

hado M fate

haga, hago ver hacer

Haití M Haiti

haitiano -na ADJ & MF Haitian

halagar[40] VT to flatter, to compliment

halago M flattery, compliment

halagüeño ADJ (palabras) flattering; (perspectiva) promising

halcón M falcon

hálito M breath

halitosis F halitosis

hallar VT to find; —**se** to be; —**se en un aprieto** to be in a pickle; —**se mal de salud** to be in a bad way

hallazgo M finding; **ese documento fue un** — **sensacional** that document was a real find

halo M halo

halógeno ADJ & M halogen

halterofilia F weight training, weightlifting

hamaca F hammock

hambre F (deseo de comer) hunger; (hambruna) famine; **tener** — to be hungry; **pasar** — to go hungry; **morirse de** — to starve

hambrear VI/VT to starve
hambriento ADJ (con hambre) hungry; (famélico) famished, starving
hambruna F famine
hamburguesa F hamburger
hampa F underworld
hámster M hamster
hándicap M handicap
handicapar VT to handicap
hangar M hangar
hará, haría ver hacer
haragán -ana ADJ indolent; MF loafer
haraganear VI to loaf
haraganería F laziness
harapiento ADJ ragged, tattered
harapo M rag, tatter
hardware M hardware
harén M harem
harina F (fina) flour; (gruesa) meal; — **de avena** oat flour; — **de maíz** cornmeal; **es — de otro costal** that's another kettle of fish
hartar VT to satiate; —**se** (de comida) to have one's fill; (de aburrimiento) to get fed up
hartazgo M surfeit, excess
harto ADJ (satisfecho) full; **estar —** to be fed up; **ese asunto me tiene —** I'm sick and tired of the whole business
hasta PREP (temporal) till, until; (espacial) [up] to; — **ahora** to date / so far; — **cierto punto** to a certain extent; — **luego** good-bye, see you later; — **pronto** see you later; **caminó — la esquina** he walked to the corner; **lo llenó — el borde** he filled it up to brim; **estar — la coronilla** to be fed up; ADV even; — **mi madre lo notó** even my mother noticed it; — **que** until
hastiado ADJ jaded
hastial M gable
hastiar[28] VT to cloy, to tire; —**se** to grow weary of
hastío M tedium
hato M (envoltorio) bundle; (rebaño) herd
hay ver haber
haya F beech
haya, hayamos ver haber
hayuco M beechnut
haz[1] M (de leña) bundle; (de luz) beam; (de flechas) sheaf
haz[2] ver hacer
hazaña F deed, exploit, feat
hazmerreír M laughingstock
he VT IMPERSONAL **he aquí la lista** here's the list
he, hemos ver haber
hebilla F buckle
hebra F (de hilo) thread; (vegetal) fiber
hebreo -a ADJ & MF Hebrew
heces F PL (de vino, café) dregs; (excremento) feces

hechicería F enchantment
hechicero -ra ADJ bewitching; M sorcerer; F sorceress
hechizar[47] VT (embrujar) to bewitch, to enchant; (fascinar) to enthrall
hechizo M charm, spell
hecho M fact; **los —s de la noche del 17** the events of the night of the 17th; **de —** in fact
hecho ver hacer
hechura F cut
hectárea F hectare
heder[2] VI to stink, to reek
hediondez F stench
hediondo ADJ stinking, smelly
hedonismo M hedonism
hedor M stink, stench
hegemonía F hegemony
helada F (frente frío) freeze; (escarcha) frost
heladera F refrigerator
heladería F ice-cream parlor
helado ADJ (muy frío) frozen, freezing; (con hielo) icy; M ice cream
helar[1] VI/VT to freeze
helecho M fern
hélice F (espiral) helix; (de avión) propeller; (de barco) screw, propeller
helicóptero M helicopter
helio M helium
hematoma M hematoma
hembra F (de animal) female; (de venado) doe; (de ballena, foca) cow; (de ave) hen
hemisferio M hemisphere (también cerebral)
hemofilia F hemophilia
hemoglobina F hemoglobin
hemorragia F hemorrhage; — **cerebral** cerebral hemorrhage; — **vaginal** vaginal bleeding
hemorroide F hemorrhoid
henchir[9] VT to swell
hender[2] VI/VT to cleave, to split
hendido ADJ cleft, split
hendidura F (quebradura) crack; (geológica) fissure
henil M hayloft
heno M hay; **fiebre de —** hay fever
hepatitis F hepatitis
heraldo M herald
herbicida M weedkiller, herbicide
herbívoro ADJ herbivorous; M herbivore
herboso ADJ grassy
heredad F homestead
heredar VI/VT (recibir) to inherit; (dar) to bequeath
heredero -ra M heir; F heiress; —**s y cesionarios** heirs and assigns
hereditario ADJ hereditary
hereje MF heretic
herejía F heresy
herencia F (económica) inheritance; (cultural)

heritage; (genética) heredity

herida F (lastimadura) injury; (abierta) wound; — **de bala** gunshot wound; — **perforada** puncture wound; **respirar por la** — to reopen an old wound

herido ADJ (lastimado) injured; (con herida abierta) wounded

herir[8] VI/VT (lastimar) to injure; (con herida abierta) to wound; (sentimientos) to hurt

hermafrodita MF hermaphrodite

hermanastro -tra M stepbrother; F stepsister

hermandad F (de hombres) brotherhood; (de mujeres) sisterhood

hermanito -ta M little brother; F little sister

hermano -na MF sibling; M brother (también religioso); — **mayor** older brother; — **menor** younger brother; F sister (también religiosa); — **mayor** older sister; — **menor** younger sister

herméticamente ADV tight, tightly

hermético ADJ hermetic, airtight; (a prueba de agua) watertight; (que no revela secretos) secretive

hermosear VT to beautify

hermoso ADJ beautiful, lovely

hermosura F beauty

hernia F hernia

héroe M hero

heroico ADJ heroic

heroína F (droga) heroin; (personaje) heroine

heroísmo M heroism

herpes M (erupción) herpes; (en la boca) cold sore; — **febril** fever blister

herradura F horseshoe

herraje M ironwork

herramienta F tool

herrar[1] VT (un caballo) to shoe; (una vaca) to brand

herrería F blacksmith's shop

herrero -ra MF blacksmith

herrumbre F rust

hervidero M swarm

hervidor M kettle

hervir[8] VI/VT to boil; — **a fuego lento** to simmer; — **de** to be swarming with; **me hervía la sangre** I was seething

hervor M boiling; **levantar el** — to come to a boil

heterodoxo ADJ unorthodox

heterogéneo ADJ heterogeneous

heterosexual ADJ heterosexual; *fam* straight

hexágono M hexagon

hiato M hiatus

hibernar VI to hibernate

hibridación F hybridization

híbrido ADJ & M hybrid

hice, hiciera *ver* hacer

hidalgo M nobleman

hidalguía F (nobleza) nobility; (generosidad) generosity

hidrato M hydrate

hidráulico ADJ hydraulic

hidroavión M hydroplane, seaplane

hidrocarburo M hydrocarbon

hidroeléctrico ADJ hydroelectric

hidrofobia F hydrophobia

hidrógeno M hydrogen

hiedra F ivy

hiel F gall

hielo M ice; — **seco** dry ice; **romper el** — to break the ice

hiena F hyena

hierba F (pasto) grass; (especia) herb; (marihuana) *fam* weed; —**buena** mint; **mala** — weed; **y otras** —**s** and so on

hierro M iron (también de golf); — **corrugado** corrugated iron; — **forjado** wrought iron; — **fundido** cast iron; —**s** handcuffs

hígado M liver; **malos** —**s** ill will

higiene F hygiene

higiénico ADJ hygienic

higienista MF hygienist

higo M fig; **me importa un** — I couldn't care less

higuera F fig tree

hijastro -tra M stepson; F stepdaughter

hijo -ja M son; — **de perra** *ofensivo* son of a bitch; — **de puta** *ofensivo* son of a bitch; — **de su madre** *fam* son of a gun; **John Smith** — John Smith Jr.; **sin** —**s** childless; F daughter; **hija de puta** *ofensivo* bitch

hilachas F loose threads

hilado M spinning

hilandería F (fábrica) spinning mill; (técnica) spinning

hilandero -ra MF spinner

hilar VI/VT to spin; — **fino** to split hairs

hilaridad F mirth

hilera F row, line

hilo M (para coser) thread; (para tejer, hilar) yarn; (alambre) filament; — **de agua** trickle; — **de pensamiento** train of thought; — **de perlas** string of pearls; — **de voz** thin voice; — **dental** floss; **al** — in a row; **mover** —**s** to pull strings; **seguir el** — **de** to keep track of; **pender de un** — to be hanging by a thread; **perder el** — to lose track

hilván M basting

hilvanar VT to baste, to tack

himen M hymen

himno M (religioso) hymn; (patriótico) anthem

hincapié M emphasis; **hacer** — to emphasize

hincar[30] VT — **los dientes en** to sink one's teeth into; —**se** to kneel

hincha MF (aficionado) supporter; F (antipatía) *Esp* grudge

hinchado ADJ (inflamado) swollen, bloated; (exagerado) inflated

hinchar VT (un río) to swell; (un globo) to blow up; — **por el equipo de Uruguay** to pull for the Uruguayan team; —**se** (cuerpo) to swell; (pulmones) to inflate; (mejillas) to bulge; (de orgullo) to puff up; (el pan) to rise

hinchazón F swelling

hindi M Hindi

hindú ADJ & MF Hindu

hinojos LOC ADV **de** — on one's knees

hipar VI hiccup

hiperactivo ADJ hyperactive, overactive

hiperdocumento M hyperdocument

hiperenlace M hyperlink

hipermedia M hypermedia

hipermercado M superstore

hipermétrope ADJ farsighted

hipersensible ADJ (a la luz) hypersensitive; (a la crítica) touchy

hipertensión F hypertension, high blood pressure

hiperventilar VI to hyperventilate

hipervínculo M hyperlink

hipnosis F hypnosis

hipnoterapia F hypnotherapy

hipnotizar VI/VT to hypnotize, to mesmerize

hipo M (espasmo) hiccup; (sollozo) sob; **tengo** — I have the hiccups

hipoalérgico ADJ hypoallergenic

hipocondríaco -ca, hipocondriaco -ca ADJ & MF hypochondriac

hipocresía F hypocrisy

hipócrita ADJ hypocritical, two-faced; MF hypocrite

hipódromo M racetrack

hipogloso M halibut

hipoglucemia F hypoglycemia

hipopótamo M hippopotamus

hipoteca F mortgage; — **con tasa de interés ajustable** adjustable-rate mortgage; — **de tasa fija** fixed-rate mortgage

hipotecar[30] VT to mortgage

hipotecario ADJ **banco** — mortgage bank

hipótesis F hypothesis

hipotiroidismo M hypothyroidism

hiriente ADJ (comentario) catty, hurtful

hirviente ADJ boiling

hisopo M swab

hispánico -ca ADJ Hispanic

hispano -na ADJ Hispanic, Spanish-speaking; MF (por su lengua) Spanish-speaking person; (por su etnia) Hispanic

Hispanoamérica F Spanish America

hispanoamericano ADJ Spanish-American

histamina F histamine

histerectomía F hysterectomy

histérico ADJ hysterical

historia F (el pasado, estudio del pasado) history; (relato) story; — **clínica** case history, medical history; **dejarse de** —**s** to

stop fooling around; **esa es otra** — that's another story; **la** — **se repite** history repeats itself; **pasar a la** — to be a thing of the past

historiador -ora MF historian

historial M record; — **de crédito** credit history

histórico ADJ (de importancia histórica) historic; (pertinente a la historia) historical

historietas F PL funnies

histrionismo M histrionics

hito M landmark, milestone; **de** — **en** — fixedly; **marcar un** — to be a milestone

hobby M hobby

hocicar[30] VI/VT (un cerdo) to root; (un caballo) to nose

hocico M snout, muzzle

hockey M hockey

hogaño ADV *lit* nowadays

hogar M (lumbre) hearth, fireplace; (casa, asilo) home

hogareño ADJ domestic; **persona hogareña** homebody

hoguera F bonfire, campfire

hoja F (de planta) leaf; (de mesa plegable) flap; (de papel) sheet; (de libro) page; (de navaja) blade; — **clínica** medical chart; — **de afeitar** razor blade; — **de depósito** deposit slip; — **de ejercicios** worksheet; — **de metal** foil; **echar** —**s** to leaf; — **de servicio** record; F —**lata** tin plate

hojaldre M puff pastry

hojarasca F fallen leaves

hojear VT to page through, to flip through, to browse

hojuela F flake; —**s de maíz** cornflakes

hola INTERJ hello, hi

Holanda F Holland

holandés -esa ADJ Dutch; M (hombre) Dutchman; (lengua) Dutch; F Dutchwoman

holding M holding company

holgado ADJ (vida) comfortable; (pantalón) loose-fitting, baggy; (cuarto) roomy

holganza F (haraganería) idleness; (diversión) leisure

holgar[42] VI to loaf; **huelga decir** it is needless to say

holgazán -ana ADJ lazy, idle; MF idler, loafer, slouch

holgazanear VI to idle, to loaf

holgazanería F laziness

holgura F (de movimiento) ease; (financiera) comfort; (de la ropa) looseness

holístico ADJ holistic

hollejo M skin

hollín M soot, smut

holocausto M holocaust

hombre M man; — **anuncio** sandwich man; — **de bien** man of good will; — **de familia** family man; — **de las cavernas** caveman; — **de la calle** man on the street; — **de**

negocios businessman; — **del saco** bogeyman; — **de paja** straw man; — **lobo** werewolf; — **orquesta** one-man band; — **rana** frogman; **es bien** — he's a real he-man; INTERJ come on!

hombrera F shoulder pad

hombro M shoulder; **encogerse de —s** to shrug; **cargar al** — to shoulder; **en/a —s** piggyback; **poner el** — to lend a hand

hombruno ADJ mannish

home M home

homenaje M homage, tribute

homeopatía F homeopathy

homeopático ADJ homeopathic

homicida MF murderer

homicidio M homicide, murder; — **culposo/ involuntario** manslaughter; — **sin premeditación** manslaughter

homofobia F homophobia

homofóbico ADJ homophobic

homogeneizar[47] VT to homogenize

homogéneo ADJ homogeneous

homólogo -ga MF counterpart

homóplato M shoulder blade

homosexual ADJ homosexual; *fam* gay

honda F sling, slingshot

hondo ADJ deep; M hollow

hondonada F hollow, dell

hondura F depth; **meterse en —s** to get in over one's head

Honduras F Honduras

hondureño -ña ADJ & MF Honduran

honestidad F (castidad) chastity, modesty; (honradez) honesty

honesto ADJ (casto) chaste, modest; (honrado) honest, straightforward

hongo M (seta) mushroom; (moho) fungus; **aburrirse como un** — to be bored stiff

honor M honor; **con —es** with honors; **tener el** — **de** to have the honor of; **hacerle los —es a** to be appreciative of

honorable ADJ honorable

honorario ADJ honorary; M PL fee

honra F honor

honradez F honesty

honrado ADJ honest

honrar VT (respetar) to honor; (dignificar) to do credit to

honroso ADJ honorable

hora F hour; — **de dormir** bedtime; — **oficial** standard time; — **punta** rush hour; —**s extra[s]** overtime; **a esta** — at this time; **¿a qué —?** at what time? **a todas —s** at all hours; **a última** — at the last minute; **decir la** — to tell time; **en** — on time; **es** — **de** it is time to; **es** — **de que me vaya** it's time for me to go; **kilómetros por** — kilometers per hour; **no ver la** — **de** to be dying to; **por** — by the hour; **¿qué** — **es?** what time is it? **ya**

era — it was about time

horadar VT to bore

horario M (agenda) schedule, timetable; (manecilla del reloj) hour hand; — **de trabajo** work schedule

horca F (cadalso) gallows; (tridente) pitchfork; — **de ajos** string of garlic

horcajadas LOC ADV **a** — astraddle, astride

horda F horde

horizontal ADJ horizontal

horizonte M (del cielo) horizon; (de una ciudad) skyline

horma F (de zapato) shoe last; (de queso) wheel

hormiga F ant; — **blanca** termite

hormigón M concrete

hormigonera F cement mixer

hormiguear VI (moverse en grandes cantidades) to swarm; (dar sensación de hormigueo) to tingle

hormigueo M tingle

hormiguero M anthill

hormona F hormone; — **del crecimiento** growth hormone

hornada F batch

horneado M baking

hornear VI/VT to bake

hornilla F burner

horno M (industrial) furnace; (doméstico) oven; (para cerámica) kiln; — **de microondas** microwave oven; **alto** — blast furnace; **el** — **no está para bollos** it's not a good time; **recién salido del** — brand-new

horóscopo M horoscope

horquilla F (para el pelo) hairpin; (horca) pitchfork

horrendo ADJ (asesinato) horrific, ghastly; (vestido) hideous, ghastly

horrible ADJ horrible

horripilante ADJ gruesome, hair-raising

horror M (miedo, repulsión) horror; (monstruosidad) abomination; (espectáculo) sight; **tenerle** — **a** to be scared of

horrorizar[47] VT to horrify, to shock, to appall

horroroso ADJ appalling, awful

hortaliza F vegetable; —**s** produce

hortera ADJ tacky, uncool, cheesy

horticultura F horticulture

hosco ADJ sullen, surly

hospedaje M lodging

hospedar VT to lodge, to accommodate; —**se** to lodge, to room

hospicio M (para peregrinos) hospice; (para huérfanos) orphanage

hospital M hospital

hospitalario ADJ hospitable

hospitalidad F hospitality

hostal M hostel

hostería F inn, hostelry

hostia F (oblea) host, wafer; (golpe) whack; **¡—s!**

vulg shit! **me cago en la —** *vulg* goddammit!
hostigamiento M harassment
hostigar[40] VT to harass, to harry
hostil ADJ hostile
hostilidad F hostility
hotel M hotel
hotelero -ra MF hotel keeper
hoy ADV today; **— [en] día** nowadays; **de — en adelante** from now on; **— por —** at present
hoya F river basin
hoyo M hole (también de golf); (muy profundo) pit; **— en uno** (golf) hole in one
hoyuelo M dimple
hoz F sickle
hozar[47] VI to root
HTML M HTML
hube, hubiera, hubo *ver* haber
hucha F piggy bank
hueco ADJ (vacío) hollow; (vanidoso) vain, affected; **palabras huecas** empty words; M (entre los dientes) gap; (cavidad) hollow; (de ascensor) shaft
huelga F strike, work stoppage; **— de hambre** hunger strike; **declararse en —** to strike; **en — on** strike
huelguista MF striker
huella F (rastro) trace, trail; (de pie) footprint, track; (de rueda) track; **— dactilar/digital** fingerprint; **seguir las —s de alguien** to follow in someone's footsteps
huérfano -na ADJ & MF orphan
huerta F (de verduras) large vegetable garden; (de árboles frutales) large orchard; **la — valenciana** the farming region of Valencia
huerto M (de verduras) vegetable garden; (de árboles frutales) orchard
hueso M (de animal) bone; (de fruta) stone, pit; **calado hasta los —s** soaked to the bone; **la sin —** the tongue; **no dejarle un — sano a alguien** to break someone's bones; **un — duro de roer** a hard pill to swallow
huésped MF (invitado) guest; (anfitrión) host (también de parásitos)
hueste F host
huesudo ADJ bony
hueva F spawn
huevo M egg; **— de Pascua** Easter egg; **— duro** hard-boiled egg; **— estrellado/frito** fried egg; **— pasado por agua** soft-boiled egg; **—s** (testículos, valentía) *vulg* balls; **—s revueltos** scrambled eggs; **ir pisando —s** to walk on eggshells; **me importa un —** *vulg* I don't give a shit; **¡y un —!** *vulg* my ass!
huida F flight
huir[19] VI to flee, to fly
hule M oilcloth
hulla F soft coal; **— blanca** hydroelectric power
humanidad F (cualidad y condición) humanity; (conjunto de los seres humanos) humankind;

—es humanities
humanismo M humanism
humanitario ADJ (organización, ayuda) humanitarian; (generoso) humane
humano ADJ (del hombre) human; (generoso) humane; M human
humareda F cloud of smoke
humeante ADJ (hoguera) smoking; (sopa) steaming
humear VI (echar humo) to give off smoke; (echar vapor) to give off steam
humedad F (del aire) humidity; (de un paño) dampness; (en la tierra) moisture; (en una pared) moisture stain
humedal M wetland
humedecer[35] VT (sello, ojo) to moisten; (paño) to dampen; **se le humedecieron los ojos** his eyes grew teary
húmedo ADJ (trapo) damp; (aire) humid; (tierra) moist; (tiempo) wet, soggy
humero M flue, funnel
humidificar[30] VT to humidify
humildad F (actitud) humility; (condición) lowliness
humilde ADJ (actitud) humble; (condición) low, lowly, mean
humillación F humiliation
humillar VT (insultar) to humiliate; (disminuir) to humble; **—se** to grovel
humo M (de combustión) smoke; (de gases tóxicos) fume; (de agua) vapor, steam; **—s** conceitedness; **bajarle los —s a alguien** to cut someone down to size; **echar —** to put out smoke; **estar que echa —** to be fuming; **hacerse —** to vanish into thin air
humor M (actitud risueña) humor; (estado de ánimo) mood
humorada F witty remark
humorismo M (humor) humor; (profesión) comedy
humorista MF comedian
humorístico ADJ humorous
humoso ADJ smoky
hundimiento M (acción de hundirse) sinking; (hoyo) sinkhole
hundir VT (hacer naufragar) to sink, to scuttle; (arruinar) to destroy; (enterrar) to bury; **—se** (barco) to sink; (empresa, edificio, precios) to collapse; (tierra) to subside; (sol) to go down
húngaro -ra MF Hungarian
Hungría F Hungary
huracán M hurricane
huraño ADJ sullen, unsociable
hurgar[40] VI (en una bolsa) to rummage; (en la basura) to scavenge; **—se las narices** to pick one's nose
hurón M ferret
huronear VI to ferret out
hurra INTERJ hurrah

hurtadillas LOC ADV **a** — stealthily
hurtar VT to steal, to swipe; — **el cuerpo** to
dodge; —**se** to hide
hurto M (robo) theft, larceny; (robo en tiendas)
shoplifting; — **con escalo** break-in
husky M (perro) husky
husmear VT (un pedazo de carne) to sniff at; (a
un delincuente) to smell out; (peligro) to
smell; (en los asuntos ajenos) to nose around,
to poke around
husmeo M sniff
huso M spindle; — **horario** time zone
huy INTERJ (de sorpresa) wow; (de pena) oh
huya, huye, huyendo, huyera, huyese ver
huir

Ii

iba, ibas ver ir
ibérico ADJ Iberian
iberoamericano -na ADJ Ibero-American
ibuprofeno M ibuprofen
iceberg M iceberg
ictericia F jaundice
ictérico ADJ jaundiced
ID [investigación y desarrollo] F R&D
ida F outward journey; —**s y venidas** comings
and goings
idea F (reflexión) idea, thought; (intuición)
inkling
ideal ADJ & M ideal
idealismo M idealism
idealista ADJ idealistic; MF idealist
idear VT (un método) to devise, to think out, to
plan; (un plan) to conceive; (una solución) to
engineer; (un complot) to hatch
ídem PRON & ADV ditto
idéntico ADJ identical
identidad F identity
identificación F identification
identificar[30] VT to identify
ideología F ideology
ideológico ADJ ideological
idilio M idyll
idioma M language
idiosincrasia F idiosyncrasy
idiota ADJ idiotic, lamebrained; MF *fam* idiot,
dork, twerp
idiotez F idiocy
ido[1] ADJ out of it
ido[2] ver ir
idolatrar VT to idolize
idolatría F idolatry
ídolo M idol
idóneo ADJ (calificado) expert; (ideal) ideal
iglesia F church

iglú M igloo
ignición F ignition
ignifugar[40] VT to fireproof
ignorancia F ignorance
ignorante ADJ ignorant, uneducated; MF
ignoramus
ignorar VT (no saber) to be unaware of; (hacer
caso omiso de) to ignore, to disregard;
(despreciar) to shrug off, to discount
igual ADJ (idéntico) equal; (semejante) same,
alike; (derecho) even; **me da** — it's all the
same to me; **al** — **que** just like; M equal sign
igualar VT (alisar) to level; (ser igual a) to equal;
(hacer iguales) to equalize; (compararse con)
to match
igualdad F equality
igualmente ADV (de manera igual) equally;
quedaron — **sorprendidos** they were
similarly surprised; **¡que te vaya bien!** — I
hope things go well for you! likewise
ijada F loin
ijar M loin
ilegal ADJ illegal, unlawful, lawless
ilegítimo ADJ illegitimate
ileso ADJ unharmed, unhurt
ilícito ADJ illicit
ilimitado ADJ (crédito) unlimited; (energía)
boundless; (horizonte) limitless
iluminación F (luz) illumination, lighting;
(moral, académica) enlightenment
iluminado ADJ lit
iluminar VT (con luz) to illuminate, to brighten;
(con conocimiento) to enlighten; —**se** to light
up
ilusión F (idea o imagen falsa) illusion; (deseo)
dream, fond hope; (entusiasmo) thrill; —
óptica optical illusion; **me da** — I'm looking
forward to
ilusionado ADJ excited
iluso ADJ naive
ilusorio ADJ illusory
ilustración F illustration; **la** — the
Enlightenment
ilustrador -ora MF illustrator
ilustrar VT (dibujar) illustrate; (educar) to
enlighten
ilustre ADJ illustrious
imagen F (representación, reputación) image;
(foto, televisión) picture; (unidad de película
fotográfica) frame; — **especular** mirror
image; **la** — **del tacto** the soul of tact; — **por
resonancia magnética** magnetic
resonance imaging; **imágenes por
ultrasonido** ultrasound imaging
imaginable ADJ conceivable
imaginación F imagination
imaginar VT (crear una imagen mental) to
imagine, to picture; (idear) to dream up
imaginario ADJ imaginary

imaginativo ADJ imaginative
imán M magnet
imantar VT to magnetize
imbatible ADJ unbeatable
imbécil ADJ idiotic; MF *ofensivo* imbecile, moron
imbuir[19] VT to imbue
imitación F imitation
imitador -ora MF (copión) imitator; (mímico) mimic; **un — de Elvis** an Elvis impersonator
imitar VT (copiar) to imitate; (hacer mímica) to mimic; (representar a un personaje) to impersonate
impaciencia F impatience
impaciente ADJ impatient; *fam* antsy
impactar VI/VT to impact
impacto M impact
impagado ADJ unpaid
impala M impala
impar ADJ odd, uneven
imparcial ADJ (sin prejuicios) impartial, unbiased, neutral; (justo) evenhanded; (apartidario) nonpartisan
imparcialidad F impartiality
impartir VT to impart
impasible ADJ impassive
impasse M impasse
impávido ADJ undaunted
impeachment M impeachment
impecable ADJ (perfecto) flawless; (limpio) spick and span
impedimento M (obstáculo) impediment, hindrance; (incapacidad) handicap
impedir[9] VT to impede, to prevent, to hinder; (acceso) to bar
impeler VT (empujar) to impel; (inducir) to drive
impenetrable ADJ impenetrable
impensable ADJ unthinkable
imperante ADJ prevailing
imperar VI to prevail
imperativo ADJ & M imperative
imperceptible ADJ imperceptible
imperdible ADJ that shouldn't be missed; **una película —** a must-see movie; M safety pin
imperecedero ADJ undying
imperfecto ADJ & M imperfect
imperial ADJ imperial
imperialismo M imperialism
impericia F lack of skill
imperio M (organización política) empire; (gobierno) rule; **— industrial** manufacturing empire
imperioso ADJ (mandón) imperious; (necesario) imperative
impermeabilizar[47] VT to waterproof
impermeable ADJ (al agua) waterproof; (a la crítica) impervious; M raincoat, slicker
impersonal ADJ impersonal
impertinencia F (actitud) impertinence,

impudence; (réplica) backtalk
impertinente ADJ impertinent, impudent
impétigo M impetigo
ímpetu M impetus
impetuoso ADJ impetuous, brash
impida, impide, impidiendo, impidiera, impidiese *ver* impedir
impío ADJ godless
implacable ADJ implacable, relentless
implantación F (de un diente) implantation; (de una costumbre, sistema) establishment, introduction
implantar VT to implant
implante M implant; **— dental** dental implant
implementación F implementation
implementar VT to implement
implemento M implement
implicación F (lógica) implication; (en un delito) involvement
implicar[30] VT (involucrar) to implicate, to involve; (conllevar) to entail
implícitamente ADV implicitly, by implication
implícito ADJ implicit
implorar VI/VT to implore
impondrá, impondría *ver* imponer
imponente ADJ (impresionante) imposing; (espantoso) forbidding
imponer[56, 74] VT to impose, to force upon; (gravar) to assess; **—se** to get one's way
imponible ADJ taxable
impopular ADJ unpopular
importación F import
importancia F importance
importante ADJ (persona) important; (cantidad) substantial; (tema, asunto) weighty; (suceso, ocasión) momentous
importar VI (ser importante) to matter; **me importa un comino** I don't give a hoot; **no importa** it makes no difference; VT (introducir productos) to import
importe M amount
importunar VT to besiege
importuno ADJ inopportune
imposibilidad F impossibility
imposibilitar VT to make impossible
imposible ADJ impossible
imposición F (de ideas) imposition; (de impuestos) assessment
impositivo ADJ **sistema —** tax system
impostor -ora MF impostor, fraud
impotencia F impotence
impotente ADJ (sin poder) powerless; (sin libido) impotent
impreciso ADJ inaccurate
impredecible ADJ unpredictable
impregnar VT to impregnate
impremeditado ADJ unpremeditated
imprenta F (arte, oficio) printing; (máquina) press, printing press

imprescindible ADJ indispensable
impresión F (efecto en el ánimo) impression; (acción de imprimir) printing; (huella) imprint
impresionante ADJ (logro) impressive, imposing; (edificio) grand, imposing; (panorama) breathtaking
impresionar VT to impress; **—se** to be overwhelmed; **para—** for show
impreso M printed matter
impresor -ora MF (persona) printer; F (aparato) printer; **impresora de burbuja** bubble-jet printer; **impresora de inyección de tinta** ink-jet printer; **impresora en serie** serial printer; **impresora gráfica** plotter; **impresora láser** laser printer; **impresora local** local printer
imprevisible ADJ unpredictable
imprevisto ADJ unforeseen; M unforeseen event
imprimir[74] VI/VT (producir un impreso) to print; (marcar con presión) to imprint
improbable ADJ improbable, unlikely
improductivo ADJ unproductive
impromptu M impromptu
impropio ADJ (inadecuado) unbecoming; (atípico) atypical
improvisación F improvisation, role-playing
improvisado ADJ impromptu
improvisando ADV ad lib
improvisar VI/VT to improvise
improviso LOC ADV **de —** all of a sudden
imprudencia F (actitud) recklessness; (acción) reckless act
imprudente ADJ unwise, ill-advised
impublicable ADJ unprintable
impúdico ADJ immodest
impuesto M tax, duty; **—a la herencia** inheritance tax; **—s atrasados** back taxes; **— de tasa única** flat tax; **— de sucesión** inheritance tax; **—s** taxation; **— sobre ingresos** income tax; **— sobre las donaciones** gift tax; **— sobre las ventas** sales tax; **— sobre rentas** income tax
impuesto *ver* imponer
impugnar VT to contest, to dispute
impulsar VT (empujar) to propel, to drive; (estimular) to boost
impulsivo ADJ impulsive
impulso M (estímulo) boost; (deseo espontáneo) impulse, urge
impune ADJ unpunished
impunidad F impunity
impureza F impurity
impuro ADJ (sustancia) impure; (pensamiento) impure, unclean
impuse, impusiera, impusiese *ver* imponer
inacabado ADJ unfinished
inaccesible ADJ inaccessible

inaceptable ADJ (inadmisible) unacceptable; (insuficiente) inadequate
inacostumbrado ADJ unwonted
inactividad F inactivity
inactivo ADJ inactive
inadaptado -da ADJ maladjusted; MF misfit
inadecuado ADJ unsuitable
inadmisible ADJ (comportamiento) unacceptable; (pruebas) inadmissible
inadvertido ADJ unnoticed, unobserved
inagotable ADJ (recursos) inexhaustible; (optimismo) unfailing
inaguantable ADJ unbearable
inalámbrico ADJ cordless, wireless
inalterable ADJ unalterable, unchangeable
inalterado ADJ unchanged
inamovible ADJ immovable
inanición F starvation
inanimado ADJ inanimate
inapetencia F lack of appetite
inapreciable ADJ (invalorable) invaluable; (muy pequeño) too small to be seen
inapropiado ADJ unsuitable
inasequible ADJ inaccessible
inaudible ADJ inaudible
inaudito ADJ (historia, situación) unheard-of, unprecedented; (sufrimiento) untold
inauguración F (de un gobierno) inauguration; (de un monumento) dedication
inaugurar VT (un gobierno) to inaugurate; (un monumento) to dedicate
inca ADJ & MF Inca
incalculable ADJ untold
incandescencia F glow
incandescente ADJ incandescent, glowing
incansable ADJ untiring, tireless
incapacidad F inability
incapacitar VT to disable, to incapacitate
incapaz ADJ incapable
incautación F seizure
incauto ADJ unwary
incendiar VT to set fire to; VI/VT to burn; **—se** to catch fire, to burn down
incendiario -ria ADJ incendiary; MF arsonist
incendio M fire, blaze, conflagration; **— doloso** arson; **— forestal** forest fire
incentivo M incentive, inducement
incertidumbre F uncertainty, suspense
incesante ADJ incessant, ceaseless
incesto M incest
incestuoso ADJ incestuous
incidencia F incidence
incidental ADJ incidental
incidente M incident
incidir VI **— en un asunto** to affect/influence a situation
incienso M incense
incierto ADJ uncertain
incinerar VT to incinerate

incipiente ADJ incipient
incisión F incision
incisivo ADJ incisive; M incisor
incitar VT to incite, to whip up
incivilizado ADJ uncivilized
inclemencia F **las —s del tiempo** foul
    weather
inclemente ADJ inclement, foul
inclinación F (tendencia) inclination, bent,
    disposition; (acción de inclinar) tilting;
    (posición inclinada) tilt; (de un techo) slant;
    (del terreno) slope; (de opinión) bias
inclinar VT (ladear) to tilt; (bajar) to hang; **— la**
    cabeza to hang one's head; **—se** (doblarse en
    la cintura) to bend over; (tener tendencia a) to
    tend; (hacer una reverencia) to bow
incluido ADJ included; **con todo —** all-inclusive
incluir[19] VT (incorporar) to include; (abarcar) to
    include, to comprise; **incluyéndote a ti,**
    somos cuatro including you, there are four
    of us
inclusión F inclusion; **con — de** including
inclusive ADV even
inclusivo ADJ inclusive
incluso ADV even
incluya, incluye, incluyendo, incluyera,
    incluyese ver incluir
incobrable ADJ noncollectible, uncollectable
incógnita F unknown [quantity]
incógnito LOC ADV **de —** incognito
incoherente ADJ incoherent
incoloro ADJ colorless
incomestible ADJ inedible
incomformista ADJ & MF nonconformist
incomible ADJ inedible
incomodar VT to inconvenience
incomodidad F uneasiness
incómodo ADJ (silla) uncomfortable; (situación)
    awkward, inconvenient; (baúl) cumbersome;
    (silencio) uneasy; (que siente molestia) ill at
    ease
incomparable ADJ incomparable, peerless
incompatible ADJ incompatible
incompetente ADJ incompetent
incompleto ADJ incomplete
incomprensible ADJ incomprehensible
incomunicación F disconnect,
    miscommunication
inconcebible ADJ inconceivable
inconcluso ADJ unfinished
incondicional ADJ unconditional, unqualified
inconexo ADJ disconnected
inconformista MF nonconformist
inconfundible ADJ unmistakable
inconsciente ADJ (sin sentido) unconscious,
    senseless; (ignorante) unaware, oblivious
inconsecuencia F inconsistency
inconsecuente ADJ inconsistent
inconsolable ADJ heartbroken

inconstancia F inconstancy
inconstante ADJ inconstant, changeable
inconstitucional ADJ unconstitutional
incontable ADJ countless
incontenible ADJ uncontrollable
incontinente ADJ incontinent
incontrolable ADJ uncontrollable
incontrovertible ADJ incontrovertible
inconveniencia F inconvenience
inconveniente ADJ improper; M
    inconvenience, downside
incorporación F (inclusión) inclusion;
    (asimilación) incorporation
incorporado ADJ built-in
incorporar VT (incluir) to include; (asimilar) to
    incorporate; (agregar) to build into; **—se**
    (erguirse) to sit up
incorrectamente ADV incorrectly, wrongly
incorrecto ADJ incorrect, wrong
incorregible ADJ incorrigible
incredulidad F disbelief
incrédulo ADJ incredulous
increíble ADJ (inverosímil) incredible,
    unbelievable; (extraordinario) amazing
incrementar VT to augment
incremento M increment, increase
incriminar VT to incriminate
incrustación F inlay
incrustado ADJ (en piedra) embedded; (joyas)
    inlaid
incrustar VT (piedra) to embed; (oro) to inlay;
    —se en to become embedded in
incubadora F incubator
incuestionable ADJ unquestionable
inculcar[30] VT to inculcate, to instill
inculto ADJ (sin modales) uncultured,
    unrefined; (sin instrucción) uneducated
incumbencia F **no es de tu —** it's none of your
    business
incumplimiento M (de contrato) breach; (de
    deberes) nonperformance; (de deudas)
    default; (de metas) failure to accomplish; (de
    promesas) failure to keep
incumplir VT (contratos) to breach; (deberes) to
    fail to perform; (deudas) to default on;
    (metas) to fail to accomplish; (promesas) to
    renege on, to fail to keep
incurable ADJ incurable
incurrir VI **— en** (una deuda, un gasto) to incur;
    (un error) to fall into
incursión F raid, foray
incursionar VI to foray
indagación F investigation, probe
indagar[40] VI/VT to investigate, to inquire into
indebido ADJ improper
indecencia F indecency
indecente ADJ indecent
indecible ADJ unspeakable
indecisión F indecision

indeciso ADJ (que no ha decidido) undecided; (que suele vacilar) wishy-washy
indecoroso ADJ improper
indefendible ADJ indefensible
indefenso ADJ defenseless
indefinible ADJ indefinable
indefinido ADJ (plazo) indefinite; (silueta) undefined
indeleble ADJ indelible
indelicado ADJ indelicate
indemnización F (resarcimiento) indemnity; (de guerra) reparation; (de un pleito) recovery; — **por despido** severance pay
indemnizar[47] VT to indemnify
independencia F independence; (de un individuo) self-reliance
independiente ADJ independent
indescriptible ADJ indescribable
indeseable ADJ undesirable, unwelcome
indestructible ADJ indestructible
indeterminado ADJ indeterminate, undetermined
indexación F indexing
indexar VT to index
India F India
indicación F (señal) indication; (instrucción) instruction; **indicaciones** directions
indicador M pointer, indicator; — **clave** key indicator; —**es anticipados** leading indicators
indicar[30] VT (señalar) to indicate, to point out; (registrar) to read, to register; (mostrar) to show
indicativo ADJ & M indicative
índice M (lista alfabética) index; (tabla de materias) table of contents; (dedo) index finger; — **de confianza del consumidor** consumer confidence index; — **de mortalidad** mortality rate; — **de precios al consumidor** consumer price index
indicio M clue, sign
Indico M **Océano** — Indian Ocean
indiferencia F indifference; (frialdad) coolness
indiferente ADJ (apático) indifferent, unconcerned; (frío) cool; (sin entusiasmo) lukewarm; (no conmovido) unmoved; **esa chica me es** — I don't care about that girl
indígena ADJ indigenous; MF native
indigente ADJ destitute, indigent
indigestión F indigestion
indignación F indignation
indignado ADJ indignant
indignar VT to make indignant; —**se** to become indignant
indigno ADJ unworthy
índigo M indigo
indio -dia ADJ & MF Indian
indirecta F hint
indirecto ADJ (estilo, consecuencia) indirect;

(ruta) roundabout
indisciplinado ADJ unruly
indiscreción F indiscretion
indiscreto ADJ indiscreet
indiscutible ADJ unquestionable
indispensable ADJ indispensable
indisponer[56, 74] VT to indispose; —**se** to become indisposed
indispuesto ADJ (disgustado) upset; (enfermo) indisposed
indistinto ADJ indistinct, vague
individual ADJ (derechos) individual; (habitación) single; —**es** singles
individualidad F individuality
individualismo M individualism
individualista ADJ & MF individualist
individuo ADJ & M individual
indivisible ADJ indivisible
indiviso ADJ undivided
indocumentado -da ADJ (carta) undocumented; (persona) without identity papers; MF illegal immigrant
índole F type
indolencia F indolence
indolente ADJ indolent
indoloro ADJ painless
indomable ADJ indomitable
indomado ADJ unbroken
Indonesia F Indonesia
indonesio -sia ADJ & MF Indonesian
inducción F induction
inducir[38] VT to induce, to prompt
indudable ADJ undeniable; unquestionable
indudablemente ADV undoubtedly
indulgencia F indulgence
indulgente ADJ indulgent, lenient
indultar VT to pardon
indulto M pardon
indumentaria F apparel
industria F industry, trade; — **petrolera** oil industry
industrial ADJ industrial; MF industrialist
industrialización F industrialization
industrioso ADJ industrious
inédito ADJ unpublished
inefable ADJ ineffable
ineficaz ADJ ineffective, ineffectual
ineficiente ADJ inefficient
inelegible ADJ ineligible
ineludible ADJ inescapable, unavoidable
inempleable ADJ unemployable
inepto ADJ inept
inequívoco ADJ unequivocal
inercia F inertia
inerte ADJ inert
inescrutable ADJ inscrutable
inesperado ADJ unexpected
inestabilidad F instability
inestable ADJ (personalidad, estructura)

unstable; (andar) unsteady

inestimable ADJ inestimable, invaluable

inevitable ADJ (conclusión) inevitable; (accidente) unavoidable

inexacto ADJ inaccurate

inexcusable ADJ inexcusable

inexistente ADJ nonexistent

inexorable ADJ inexorable

inexperto ADJ (trabajador) inexperienced, unskilled; (ojo) untrained

inexplicable ADJ inexplicable

inexpresivo ADJ inexpressive, wooden

infalible ADJ (a toda prueba) infallible, foolproof; (confiable) unfailing

infame ADJ infamous

infamia F infamy

infancia F childhood

infante -ta MF (hijo -ja del rey) infante -ta; M (soldado) infantryman

infantería F infantry; — **de marina** marine corps

infantil ADJ (como niño) childlike; (aniñado) childish, infantile

infarto M infarction, heart attack; — **cardíaco** heart attack; — **cerebral** stroke, cerebral infarction; — **del miocardio** myocardial infarction

infección F infection; — **del tracto urinario** urinary tract infection; — **respiratoria alta** upper respiratory infection

infeccioso ADJ infectious

infectar VT to infect; —**se** to become infected

infecto ADJ foul, repugnant

infelicidad F misery

infeliz ADJ unhappy, wretched, miserable; MF poor wretch

inferencia F inference

inferior ADJ (en calidad) inferior, subpar; (en posición) lower

inferioridad F inferiority

inferir[8] VT to infer

infernal ADJ (calor) infernal; (ruido) unholy

infertilidad F infertility

infestación F infestation

infestar VT to infest

infiel ADJ unfaithful, faithless, untrue

infierno M (bíblico) hell; (lugar caliente) inferno; **en el quinto** — in the middle of nowhere

infinidad F infinity; **una** — **de** a large number of

infinitivo ADJ & M infinitive

infinito ADJ infinite; M infinity

inflación F inflation; — **básica** core inflation

inflado ADJ bloated; M pumping up

inflamable ADJ flammable

inflamación F inflammation

inflamar VT to inflame; —**se** to become inflamed

inflar VT (neumáticos) to inflate, to pump up; (globos) to blow up; (precios) to balloon

inflexible ADJ (rígido) inflexible; (testarudo) unbending, adamant

infligir[46] VT to inflict

influencia F influence, pull, clout; (sobre las masas) sway

influir[19] VI — **en/sobre** to influence; (las masas) to sway

influjo M influence

influya, influye, influyendo, influyera, influyese ver influir

influyente ADJ influential

infomercial M infomercial

información F information; (periodística) story

informal ADJ (no formal) informal, casual; (poco fiable) unreliable

informante MF (para un estudio) informant; (de la policía) informer

informar VT (enterar) to inform, to appraise; (un militar) to debrief; (un periodista) to report; (un abogado) to advise; —**se** to become informed

informática F computer science, information technology

informático -ca ADJ computing; MF computer specialist

informativo ADJ informative; M (televisión, radio) news program

informatizar[47] VT to computerize

informe M (de noticias) report; (militar) debriefing; — **de crédito** credit report; —**s de guía** information; ADJ shapeless

infortunio M misfortune

infracción F (de reglamentos) infraction, infringement; (de contrato) breach; (de tránsito) violation; (en deportes) penalty

infractor -ora MF lawbreaker

infraestructura F infrastructure

infrarrojo ADJ & M infrared

infrascrito -ta MF undersigned

infravalorado ADJ underrated, undervalued

infringir[46] VT to infringe, to breach, to violate

infructuoso ADJ fruitless, unsuccessful

ínfulas F PL airs; **darse** — to put on airs

infundado ADJ groundless, unfounded

infundir VT to infuse, to imbue

infusionar VT to steep

ingeniar VT to contrive; **ingeniárselas para** to contrive to

ingeniería F engineering; — **genética** genetic engineering; — **química** chemical engineering

ingeniero -ra MF engineer; — **civil** civil engineer; — **electricista** electrical engineer; — **en computación** computer engineer; — **informático** computer engineer

ingenio M (mental) ingenuity, cleverness; (verbal) wit; (artefacto) artifact; — **de azúcar**

(refinería) sugar refinery, sugar mill; (plantación) sugar plantation

ingeniosidad F ingenuity

ingenioso ADJ ingenious, resourceful

ingenuidad F ingenuousness, naiveté

ingenuo -nua ADJ (inocente) naive, ingenuous; (crédulo) gullible; MF dupe

ingerir VI/VT to ingest

ingestión F ingestion

ingle F groin

inglés -esa ADJ English; M Englishman; (lengua) English; F Englishwoman

ingobernable ADJ unruly

ingratitud F ingratitude

ingrato -ta ADJ thankless, ungrateful; MF ingrate

ingrávido ADJ weightless

ingrediente M ingredient; **ese libro tiene todos los —s de un éxito** that book has all the makings of a best seller

ingresar VT (datos) to input; (dinero en una cuenta) to deposit; VI (a un hospital) to be admitted; (a un sistema) to log in

ingreso M (permiso para entrar) entrance, entry; (depósito bancario) deposit; (renta) income; **—s** (de una firma) earnings; (del estado) revenue; **— bruto** gross income; **— neto ajustado** adjusted net income; **—s discrecionales** discretionary income; **—s disponibles** disposable income

inhábil ADJ unskilled

inhabilidad F inability

inhabilitar VT to disqualify

inhalación F inhalation; **— de humo** smoke inhalation

inhalar VI/VT to breathe in, to inhale

inherente ADJ inherent

inhibición F inhibition

inhibidor ADJ inhibiting; M inhibitor

inhibir VT to inhibit

inhospitalario ADJ inhospitable

inhóspito ADJ inhospitable

inhumano ADJ inhuman

iniciación M initiation, induction

inicial ADJ initial; (pago) up-front; F (letra) initial; (béisbol) first base

inicialista MF first baseman

inicializar[47] VT to initialize

inicialmente ADV initially

iniciar VT (conversaciones) to initiate; (en un grupo) to induct; (software) to launch; (computadora) to boot up; (negociaciones) to enter

iniciativa F initiative

inicio M beginning, start

inimitable ADJ inimitable

ininflamable ADJ fireproof

ininteligible ADJ unintelligible

ininterrumpido ADJ unbroken, uninterrupted

injerencia F interference

injertar VT to graft

injerto M graft; **— óseo** bone graft

injugable ADJ unplayable

injuria F (insulto) insult, verbal abuse; (daño) damage

injuriar VT to insult, to abuse verbally

injurioso ADJ insulting, injurious, verbally abusive

injustamente ADV unjustly, unfairly, wrongly

injusticia F (desigualdad) injustice; (acto injusto) wrong; (error judicial) miscarriage of justice

injustificable ADJ unjustifiable

injustificado ADJ uncalled-for, unwarranted

injusto ADJ unjust, unfair

inmaculado ADJ immaculate, spotless

inmaduro ADJ immature

inmanejable ADJ unmanageable

inmaterial ADJ immaterial

inmediaciones F PL vicinity

inmediato ADJ immediate, instant; **de —** at once

inmensidad F immensity, vastness

inmenso ADJ immense, vast

inmerso ADJ (en agua) submerged; (en el trabajo) absorbed; (en un tema, una situación) immersed

inmerecido ADJ unearned

inmigración F immigration

inmigrante ADJ & MF immigrant

inmigrar VI to immigrate

inminente ADJ imminent, impending

inmiscuir[19] VI to mix; **—se** to meddle

inmodestia F immodesty

inmodesto ADJ immodest

inmoral ADJ immoral

inmoralidad F immorality

inmortal ADJ & MF immortal

inmortalidad F immortality

inmóvil ADJ motionless, immobile

inmovilizar[47] VT (impedir los movimientos) to immobilize; (contra el suelo) to pin

inmueble M building

inmune ADJ immune

inmunidad F immunity

inmunodeficiencia F immunodeficiency

inmutable ADJ unchangeable, immutable

innato ADJ innate, inborn

innecesario ADJ unnecessary, needless

innegable ADJ undeniable

innoble ADJ ignoble

innocuo ADJ innocuous, harmless

innovación F innovation

innovador -ora ADJ innovating, innovative; MF innovator

innovar VI to innovate; VT to modernize

innumerable ADJ innumerable, countless

inocencia F innocence

inocente ADJ innocent, guiltless; MF dupe
inocuo ADJ innocuous, harmless
inodoro ADJ odorless; M toilet, commode
inofensivo ADJ inoffensive, harmless
inolvidable ADJ unforgettable
inoperable ADJ inoperable
inoportuno ADJ inopportune, untimely
inorgánico ADJ inorganic
inoxidable ADJ rustproof
inquietante ADJ distressing, worrisome
inquietar VT to worry
inquieto ADJ (movedizo) restless; (preocupado) uneasy
inquietud F (intranquilidad) restlessness; (preocupación) alarm, concern
inquilino -na MF (de un apartamento) tenant, renter; (de una pensión) lodger
inquina F spite
inquirir[4] VI/VT to inquire
inquisición F inquisition
inquisitivo ADJ inquisitive
insaciable ADJ insatiable
insalubre ADJ unhealthy, unsanitary
insatisfactorio ADJ unsatisfactory
insatisfecho ADJ dissatisfied, unhappy
inscribir[74] VT (grabar) to inscribe; (matricular) to register, to enroll; —**se** to register, to enroll
inscripción F (grabado) inscription; (matriculación) registration, enrollment
insecticida M insecticide
insectívoro ADJ insectivorous
insecto M insect
inseguridad F insecurity; **la — urbana** the lack of safety in cities / the city
inseguro ADJ (personalidad) insecure; (vehículo) unsafe; (andar) unsteady; (computadora) vulnerable to hacking
inseminación F insemination
insensato -ta ADJ foolish; MF fool
insensibilizar[47] VT to desensitize
insensible ADJ (cruel) insensitive, callous; (imperturbable) unfeeling, thick-skinned; (entumecido) numb
inseparable ADJ inseparable
inserción F insertion
insertar VT to insert
inservible ADJ useless
insidioso ADJ insidious
insigne ADJ famous
insignia F insignia, badge
insignificante ADJ insignificant, unimportant
insincero ADJ insincere
insinuación F (sugerencia) insinuation; (comentario sexual) innuendo
insinuante ADJ suggestive
insinuar[26] VT to insinuate, to suggest; —**se** to insinuate oneself
insípido ADJ insipid, flavorless

insistencia F (machaconería, testarudez) insistence; (perseverancia) persistence
insistente ADJ (testarudo, repetitivo) insistent; (perseverante) persistent
insistir VI/VT (repetir) to insist; (perseverar) to persist; — **en** to insist on; — **sobre** to harp on
insolación F (por sol) sunstroke; (por calor) heatstroke
insolencia F (falta de respeto) insolence; (comentario) smart remark
insolente ADJ insolent, sassy
insólito ADJ (situación) unusual; (accidente) freak, freakish
insoluble ADJ insoluble
insolvente ADJ insolvent
insomne ADJ wakeful, unable to sleep
insomnio M insomnia
insoportable ADJ (persona, conducta) unbearable, impossible; (dolor) excruciating, unbearable
insospechado ADJ unsuspected
insostenible ADJ untenable
inspección F (revisación) inspection; (encuesta) canvass
inspeccionar VT to inspect, to survey
inspector -ora MF inspector
inspiración F (idea) inspiration; (inhalación) inhalation
inspirar VI/VT to inspire; VI to inhale, to breathe in
instalación F (de programas, fontanería) installation; (de aparatos electrónicos) setup; **instalaciones** fixtures
instalar VT (programas, fontanería) to install; (aparatos electrónicos) to set up; —**se** to take up residence
instancia LOC ADV **a —s de** at the request of
instantánea F snapshot
instantáneo ADJ instantaneous
instante M instant; **al —** right away
instar VT to enjoin
instauración F establishment
instigador -ra MF instigator
instigar[40] VT to instigate, to abet
instintivo ADJ instinctive
instinto M instinct; **— suicida** death wish
institución F institution; **— benéfica** charity
institucional ADJ institutional
instituir[19] VT to institute
instituto M (institución, agencia) institute; (escuela secundaria) high school
institutriz F governess
instrucción F instruction, schooling
instructivo ADJ instructive
instructor -ora MF instructor
instruir[19] VT to instruct, to school
instrumental ADJ instrumental
instrumentar VT (un plan) to implement; (música) to do the instrumentation for

instrumento M instrument; **— de cuerda** string instrument; **— de metal** brass instrument; **— de percusión** percussion instrument; **— de viento** wind instrument; **—s quirúrgicos** surgical instruments

insubordinado ADJ insubordinate

insuficiencia F (incapacidad) insufficiency; (falla de los órganos) failure; **— cardíaca congestiva** congestive heart failure; **— coronaria** coronary failure; **— renal** kidney failure, renal failure; **— respiratoria** respiratory failure

insuficiente ADJ insufficient, inadequate

insufrible ADJ insufferable

insulina F insulin

insulso ADJ bland

insultar VT to insult

insulto M insult, put-down

insuperable ADJ (resultado) insuperable; (obstáculo) insurmountable

insurgente ADJ & MF insurgent

insurrección F insurrection

insurrecto -ta ADJ rebellious; MF rebel

intachable ADJ blameless

intacto ADJ intact, unbroken

intangible ADJ intangible

integración F (de razas) integration; (de elementos) incorporation

integral ADJ (parte) integral; ADJ (harina) whole-grain

integrante ADJ integral

integrar VT (crear) to form; (ser miembro de) to be a member of

integridad F integrity

íntegro ADJ (objeto) whole; (texto) unabridged; (comportamiento) upright

intelecto M intellect

intelectual ADJ & MF intellectual

inteligencia F intelligence (también militar); (persona) mind; **— artificial** artificial intelligence

inteligente ADJ intelligent, bright, smart

inteligible ADJ intelligible

intemperie LOC ADV **a la —** exposed to the weather

intención F intention, intent

intencional ADJ intentional

intendente MF (civil) administrator; (militar) quartermaster general

intensidad F intensity

intensificar[30] VT to intensify; **—se** (frío) to intensify; (violencia) to escalate

intensivo ADJ intensive

intenso ADJ (actividad) intense; (debate) fierce; (calor) severe

intentar VI/VT to try; VT to attempt

intento M (tentativa) try, attempt; (propósito) intention

interacción F interaction

interactivo ADJ interactive

interactuar[26] VI to interact

intercalación F insertion

intercalar VT to insert

intercambiador M interchange

intercambiar VI/VT to exchange

intercambio M exchange

interceder VI to intercede

interceptación F interception (también en fútbol americano)

interceptar VT intercept (también en fútbol americano)

intercesión F intercession

intercesor -ora MF advocate

interés M (intelectual, financiero) interest; (preocupación) concern; (participación comercial) stake; **— compuesto** compound interest; **— mutuo** mutual interest; **intereses ocultos** hidden agenda

interesado ADJ (atento) interested; (preocupado) concerned; (egoísta) self-serving

interesante ADJ interesting

interesar VT to interest; **—se por** to become interested in

interestatal ADJ interstate

interestelar ADJ interstellar

interface MF interface

interfaz MF interface; **— digital de instrumentos musicales** musical instrument digital interface

interferencia F (en los negocios ajenos) interference; (en una transmisión) interference, static; **— externa** outside interference

interferir[8] VT to jam; VI to interfere

interferón M interferon

ínterin M interim; **en el —** meanwhile

interino ADJ acting, interim

interior ADJ (habitación) inside; (mundo, vida) inner; (zona geográfica) inland; (mercado, comercio) domestic; M (parte) inside part, interior; **el — de la caja** the inside of the box; (de un país) the country, the provinces; **una ciudad del —** a provincial town

interiorizar[47] VT to internalize

interjección F interjection

interlineal ADJ interlinear

interlock M interlock

interlocutor -ora MF interlocutor

interludio M interlude

intermediario -ria M middleman; MF (mensajero) go-between; ADJ intermediary

intermediarista MF second baseman

intermedio -a ADJ intermediate; M intermission; **por — de** through; F (béisbol) second base

interminable ADJ interminable, unending, endless

intermitente ADJ intermittent; M turn signal
internación F inpatient care
internacional ADJ international
internado -da M (escuela) boarding school; (práctica) internship; MF (alumno) boarding student; (en un hospital) patient
internalizar[47] VT to internalize
internar VT (en una cárcel) to intern; (en un hospital) to admit, to hospitalize; (en un hospital psiquiátrico) to commit
internauta MF Internet user
internet M Internet, web; — **inalámbrico** wireless Internet; — **móvil** mobile Internet
internista MF internist
interno -na ADJ (correo) internal; (mercado) domestic; MF (persona que vive internada) inmate; (residente médico) intern
interpersonal ADJ interpersonal
interponer[56, 74] VT to interpose; —**se** to intervene
interpretación F (de un texto) interpretation; (artística) performance, rendition
interpretar VT (ideas) to interpret; (música) to perform; (intenciones) to construe
intérprete MF (traductor, explicador) interpreter; (músico) artist, performer
interracial ADJ interracial
interrelacionado ADJ interrelated
interrogación F interrogation
interrogador -ora MF questioner; ADJ questioning
interrogar[40] VI/VT (la policía) to interrogate; (con intensidad) to grill; (a un testigo) to question, to cross-examine
interrogativo ADJ interrogative
interrogatorio M interrogation, questioning
interrumpir VI/VT (cortar) to interrupt; VT (servicios) to disrupt, to cut off; (producción de un modelo) to discontinue; (en una conversación) to intrude, to cut in; (software) to abort
interrupción F interruption; (en una conversación) intrusion; (de producción) stoppage; (software) abort
interruptor M switch
intersección F intersection
intersticio M interstice
intervalo M (período) interval; (en el teatro) intermission, interlude
intervención F intervention; — **de teléfono** wiretap
intervendrá, intervendría, intervenga, intervengo ver intervenir
intervenir[61] VI to intervene; — **un teléfono** to wiretap
interventor -ora ADJ controlling, intervening; MF (en las elecciones) observer; (en lo fiscal) auditor
intervine, interviniendo, interviniera,

interviniese ver intervenir
interviú F interview
intestino ADJ & M intestine; — **delgado** small intestine; — **grueso** large intestine; —**s** bowels
intimar VI to become friendly
intimidad F intimacy
intimidar VT (una persona) to intimidate; (una tarea) to daunt
íntimo ADJ intimate, close
intitular VT to entitle; —**se** to be entitled
intolerable ADJ intolerable
intolerancia F intolerance, bigotry; — **a la lactosa** lactose intolerance
intolerante ADJ intolerant, narrow-minded
intoxicación F intoxication, poisoning; — **con plomo** lead poisoning; — **por alimentos** food poisoning
intoxicar[30] VT to poison, to intoxicate
intransigente ADJ intransigent, uncompromising
intransitivo ADJ intransitive
intravenoso ADJ IV [intravenous]
intrepidez F fearlessness
intrépido ADJ (sin miedo) intrepid, fearless; (aventurero) adventurous
intriga F intrigue
intrigante MF schemer; ADJ scheming
intrigar[40] VI/VT to intrigue, to scheme
intrincado ADJ intricate
intrínseco ADJ intrinsic
introducción F introduction
introducir[38] VT (incorporar) to introduce; (colocar) to put in, to insert
introduzca, introduzco ver introducir
introspección F introspection
introvertido -da ADJ introverted; MF introvert
intrusión F intrusion
intrusivo ADJ intrusive
intruso -sa ADJ intruding; MF intruder
intubación F intubation
intuición F intuition
intuir[19] VT to sense
intuitivo ADJ intuitive
inundación F flood
inundar VI/VT (de agua, de pedidos) to inundate, to flood; (de regalos) to shower
inusitado ADJ unusual
inútil ADJ (medida) useless, pointless; (esfuerzo) futile; (persona) worthless, good-for-nothing
inutilidad F uselessness; (de un esfuerzo) futility
inutilizar[47] VT to render useless, to put out of commission
invadir VI/VT to invade
invalidar VT to render invalid
inválido -da ADJ (discapacitado) invalid; (nulo) void; MF invalid
invalorable ADJ priceless, invaluable

invariable ADJ invariable
invasión F invasion
invasivo ADJ invasive
invasor-ora MF invader; ADJ invading
invencible ADJ invincible
invención F invention (también mentira); (mental) construct
inventar VT (un dispositivo) to invent; (una historia) to fabricate, to make up
inventariar[28] VT to inventory
inventario M inventory
inventiva F ingenuity
inventivo ADJ inventive
invento M invention
inventor-ora MF inventor
invernadero M greenhouse, hothouse; **efecto** — greenhouse effect
invernal ADJ wintry
invernar[1] VI to winter
inverosímil ADJ unlikely, farfetched
inversión F (trasposición) inversion; (financiera) investment
inversionista MF investor
inverso ADJ inverse, reverse; **a la inversa** the other way around
inversor-ora MF investor
invertir[8] VT (dar vuelta) to invert, to reverse; VI/VT (dinero) to invest
investidura F inauguration, investment
investigación F (policial) investigation, inquiry; (científica) research
investigador-ora MF investigator; (científico) researcher
investigar[40] VI/VT (policía) to investigate, to look into; (científico) to research
investir[9] VI/VT to invest; — **de un cargo** to induct into office
invicto ADJ unbeaten
invierno M winter
invierta, invierte, invirtiendo, invirtiera, invirtiese, invirtió *ver* invertir
invisible ADJ (no visible) invisible; (oculto) unseen
invitación F invitation
invitado-da MF guest
invitar VI/VT to invite
invocación F invocation
invocar[30] VT (razones, argumentos) to invoke; (espíritus) to conjure
involucrar VT (implicar) to implicate; (consistir de) to involve
involuntario ADJ (automático) involuntary; (accidental) inadvertent
inyección F (en medicina) injection, shot; (en coches) fuel injection
inyectado ADJ — **de sangre** bloodshot
inyectar VT to inject
ion, ión M ion
ionizar[47] VT to ionize

ir[64] VI to go; — **a caballo** to ride horseback; — **a pie** to walk; — **[a] por** to fetch; — **aprendiendo** to learn gradually; — **corriendo** to run; — **de mal en peor** to go from bad to worse; — **en coche** to drive/ride in a car; — **tirando** to scrape along; **no me va ni me viene** it's all the same to me; **¿cómo te va?** how are you? **los platos no van aquí** the plates don't belong here; **¡vaya!** well now! **¡vaya a saber uno!** go figure! **¡vamos!** let's go! come on! **¡vaya hombre!** what a man! **¡ve a freír espárragos!** take a hike! **va por dos años que me casé** it's going on two years since I got married; **voy a comer** I'm going to eat; **va y se come un hongo venenoso** she goes and eats a poisonous mushroom; **en lo que va del año** since the beginning of the year; **ya van siete veces que me lo dice** that makes seven times that she's told me; **voy a ir de rojo** I'm going dressed in red; **para que no vayas a creer** lest you should think; **no vayas a caerte** don't fall; **¡qué va!** no way! —**se** to go away, to leave; —**se a la quiebra** to go broke; —**se a las manos** to come to blows; —**se a pique** to founder; —**se de vacaciones** to take a vacation
ira F ire, wrath
Irak M Iraq
Irán M Iran
iraní ADJ & MF Iranian
iraquí ADJ & MF Iraqi
irascible ADJ irascible, quick-tempered
iridiscente ADJ iridescent
iris M iris
Irlanda F Ireland
irlandés-esa MF Irish; ADJ Irish
IRM [imagen por resonancia magnética] F MRI
ironía F irony
irónico ADJ ironic, wry
irracional ADJ irrational, unreasonable
irradiar VT to radiate, to irradiate
irreal ADJ unreal
irreconocible ADJ unrecognizable
irrecuperable ADJ irretrievable
irreflexivo ADJ thoughtless
irrefutable ADJ irrefutable
irregular ADJ (situación) irregular; (borde, filo) ragged; (pulso) unsteady; (superficie) rough, uneven; (comportamiento) erratic, haphazard
irregularidad F irregularity
irremediable ADJ hopeless
irremplazable ADJ irreplaceable
irreparable ADJ irreparable
irreprochable ADJ irreproachable, flawless
irresistible ADJ irresistible
irrespetuoso ADJ disrespectful

irresponsabilidad F irresponsibility
irresponsable ADJ irresponsible
irreverente ADJ irreverent
irreversible ADJ irreversible
irrevocable ADJ irrevocable
irrigación F irrigation
irrigar⁴⁰ VI/VT to irrigate
irritable ADJ irritable
irritación F irritation
irritante ADJ (molesto) irritating, grating; (agresivo) abrasive
irritar VI/VT to irritate, to aggravate
irrumpir VI to burst into
isla F island, isle; **—s Fiyi** Fiji Islands; **—s Malvinas** Falkland Islands; **—s Marshall** Marshall Islands; **—s Salomón** Solomon Islands; **—s Vírgenes** Virgin Islands
islam, Islam M Islam
islámico ADJ Islamic
islamismo M Islam
islandés -esa MF Icelander; ADJ Icelandic
Islandia F Iceland
isleño -ña MF islander
isobara F isobar
isométrico ADJ isometric
isótopo M isotope
Israel M Israel
israelí ADJ & MF Israeli
istmo M isthmus
Italia F Italy
italiano -na ADJ & MF Italian
itálico ADJ italic; F **itálica** italics
ítem M item
itinerante ADJ itinerant
itinerario M itinerary
IVA [impuesto al valor añadido/agregado] M sales tax, VAT
izar⁴⁷ VT to hoist, to raise
izquierda F left (también política); (mano) left hand; **a la —** to the left
izquierdista ADJ & MF leftist
izquierdo ADJ left

Jj

jab M jab
jabalí M [wild] boar
jabalina F javelin
jabón M soap
jabonera F soap dish
jabonoso ADJ soapy
jaca F nag
jacinto M hyacinth
jactancia F boastfulness
jactancioso ADJ boastful, blustering

jactarse VI to boast, to brag
jacuzzi M Jacuzzi™, hot tub
jade M jade
jadear VI to pant, to gasp
jadeo M panting, gasping
jaez M harness
jaguar M jaguar
jalar VI/VT to pull, to tug
jalea F jelly
jaleo M (lío) mess; (barahúnda) ruckus
jam M jam session
Jamaica F Jamaica
jamaicano -na ADJ & MF Jamaican
jamaiquino -na ADJ & MF Jamaican
jamás ADV never
jamelgo M hack
jamón M ham
jamona F buxom woman
Japón M Japan
japonés -esa ADJ & MF Japanese
jaque M check; **— mate** checkmate; **tener a uno en —** *fam* to have someone by the short hairs
jaqueca F migraine
jarabe M syrup; **— de ipecacuana** ipecac syrup
jarana F revelry; **ir de —** to paint the town red
jarcia F rigging
jardín M (de flores) garden; (de césped) yard; (béisbol) outfield; **— de niños** kindergarten; **— infantil** nursery
jardinero -ra MF (de oficio) gardener; (en béisbol) outfielder
jarra F (cántaro) jug, pitcher; (taza) mug; **en —s** akimbo
jarro M pitcher, jug
jarrón M vase
jaspe M (piedra silícea) jasper; (mármol) veined marble
jaula F cage, coop
jauría F pack
jazmín M jasmine
jazz M jazz
jeans M PL jeans
jefatura F headquarters
jefe MF, **jefa** F (laboral) boss; (militar) commander; (departamental) chair, head; (policial) chief; **— del estado mayor** chief of staff; **— de departamento** department head
jején M gnat
jengibre M ginger
jerarquía F hierarchy
jerez M sherry
jerga F jargon, slang
jerigonza F (sinsentido) gibberish, gobbledygook; (juego lingüístico) pig Latin
jeringa F syringe
jeringar⁴⁰ VT to annoy
jeroglífico ADJ & M hieroglyphic

jersey M sweater
jesuita ADJ & M Jesuit
Jesús INTERJ God bless you! gesundheit!
jeta F (hocico) snout; (cara) mug
jet-set M jet set
jilguero M goldfinch
jinete M rider
jinetear VI to ride horseback
jingle M jingle
jirafa F giraffe
jobar INTERJ holy cow! holy Moses! holy
   mackerel!
jóckey M jockey
jocoso ADJ jocular
joder VI/VT (tener relaciones sexuales) *vulg* to
   fuck; VT (dañar) *vulg* to fuck up; (fastidiar)
   vulg to jerk around; INTERJ *vulg* fuck! shit! ¡**no**
   jodas! (vete) buzz off! (¿en serio?) are you for
   real? no kidding! (no molestes) stop bothering
   me!
jodido ADJ (maldito) *vulg* fucking; (estropeado)
   vulg fucked up
jofaina F basin
jogging M jogging
jolgorio M rumpus
jonrón M home run
Jordania F Jordan
jordano -na ADJ & MF Jordanian
jornada F (día laboral) workday; (coloquio)
   colloquium
jornal M daily wage
jornalero -ra MF day laborer
joroba F hump
jorobado -da ADJ & MF hunchback
jorobar VT (molestar) to hassle; (estropear) to
   gum up
jota F jay; **no saber ni —** to know zilch
joven ADJ young; MF young person
jovial ADJ jolly
joya F jewel; (persona apreciada) gem; **—s**
   jewelry
joyería F jewelry store, jeweler's
joyero -ra MF jeweler
joystick M joystick
juanete M bunion
jubilación F (retiro) retirement; (pagos)
   pension; **— anticipada** early retirement
jubilado ADJ retired; MF retiree
jubilar VT to pension, to retire; **—se** to retire
jubileo M jubilee
júbilo M glee
jubiloso ADJ jubilant, joyous
judaísmo M Judaism
judicial ADJ judicial
judío -ía ADJ Jewish; MF Jew; F bean; **judía**
   blanca navy bean; **judía pinta** pinto bean;
   judía verde green bean
juego M (actividad recreativa) play; (deporte)
   game; (conjunto de piezas) set; (muebles)

suite; **— de apuestas** gambling; **— de**
   damas checkers; **— ofimático** office suite;
   — de palabras pun, play on words; **—s**
   Olímpicos Olympic Games; **estar en —** to
   be at stake; **hacer —** to match
juerga F binge; **irse de —** to go on a binge, to
   party
juerguista MF merrymaker
jueves M Thursday
juez M, **jueza** F (en un tribunal) judge; (en
   deportes) referee; **— de paz** justice of the
   peace; **— de línea** linesman; **— de silla**
   judge, umpire
jugada F play, move; **— de tres puntos**
   three-point play
jugador -ora MF (deportista) player; (apostador)
   gambler
jugar[43] VI to play; (apostar) to gamble; **— a la**
   baraja / a los naipes to play cards; **— con**
   fuego to play with fire; **— en casa** to play a
   home game; **— limpio** to play fair; **—se** to
   risk
jugarreta F bad turn
jugo M juice
jugoso ADJ juicy
juguete M plaything, toy
juguetear VI to toy with, to fiddle with
juguetón -ona ADJ playful
juicio M (criterio) judgment; (proceso) trial; **—**
   por quiebra bankruptcy proceedings;
   perder el — to lose one's mind; **a mi —** in
   my estimation
juicioso ADJ sensible, judicious
juke-box M jukebox
julio M July
jumbo ADJ jumbo; M jumbo jet
jumper M jumper
junco M (planta) rush, reed; (barco chino) junk
jungla F jungle
junio M June
junta F (reunión) meeting; (concejo) council;
   (juntura) joint; (pieza de motor) gasket; **—**
   directiva board of directors
juntar VT (tubos) to attach; (flores) to gather, to
   pick; (ganado) to round up, to wrangle; **—**
   polvo to gather dust; **— valor** to muster
   courage; **—se** (acumularse) to gather;
   (asociarse) to band together; (reunirse) to
   come together
junto ADJ together; LOC ADV **— a** next to; **— con**
   together with
juntura F (lugar) juncture; (articulación) joint
jurado -da MF (individuo) juror; M (grupo) jury
juramentar VI/VT to swear in; **—se** to be sworn
   in
juramento M oath; **— hipocrático** Hippocratic
   oath
jurar VI/VT to swear, to vow; **— en falso** to
   perjure oneself; **— la bandera** to pledge

allegiance to the flag
jurídico ADJ legal
jurisdicción F jurisdiction
jurisprudencia F (doctrina) jurisprudence; (derecho) law
justa F joust, tilt
justamente ADV (exactamente) precisely; (con justicia) fairly
justicia F justice
justificación F justification
justificar[30] VT to justify
justo ADJ (ecuánime) just; (equitativo) equitable; (pío) righteous, upright; ADV exactly, right; **— después de** right after; **— en ese momento** exactly at that moment
juvenil ADJ (inmaduro) juvenile; (de apariencia joven) youthful
juventud F youth
juzgado M court
juzgar[40] VI/VT to judge, to pass judgment [on]; **— mal** to misjudge

Kk

kaki M khaki
kart M go-cart
kayak M kayak
Kazajstán M Kazakhstan
kazako -ka ADJ & MF Kazak[h]
Kenia F Kenya
keniata ADJ & MF Kenyan
kermés F bazaar
keroseno M kerosene
ketchup M catsup, ketchup
kg ver kilogramo
kilo M kilo
kilobyte M kilobyte
kilogramo M kilogram
kilometraje M mileage
kilómetro M kilometer
kilovatio M kilowatt; F **-hora** kilowatt-hour
Kirguistán M Kyrgyzstan
Kiribati M Kiribati
kosher ADJ kosher
Kuwait M Kuwait
kuwaití ADJ & MF Kuwaiti

Ll

la ART DEF F the; **— del sombrero verde** the one with the green hat, that one with the

green hat; PRON PERS it, her; PRON REL **— que** she who, the one that
laberinto M labyrinth, maze
labia F gift of gab
labial ADJ labial
labihendido N harelipped
labio M (de la boca) lip; (de los genitales) labium; **—s agrietados** chapped lips; **— leporino** cleft lip, harelip; **con — leporino** harelipped
labor F (trabajo) labor; (tarea) task; (manualidad) handiwork
laboral ADJ work-related; **legislación —** labor legislation
laboratorio M laboratory
laborioso ADJ (trabajoso) laborious; (trabajador) hardworking
laborterapia F occupational therapy
labrado ADJ carved
labrador -ora MF (persona) farmhand; M (perro) labrador
labranza F plowing
labrar VT to till; **—se una carrera** to carve out a career
laca F lacquer
lacar[30] VT to lacquer
lacayo M lackey, flunky
laciar VT RP to straighten
lacio ADJ straight
lacónico ADJ (persona) laconic; (comentario) terse
lacra F (física) scar; (moral) blight
lacre M sealing wax
lacrimógeno ADJ tear-producing
lactancia F lactation; **— materna** breast-feeding
lactar VT to nurse
lácteo ADJ (como la leche) milky; (hecho de leche) dairy
lactosa F lactose
LAD [lipoproteína de alta densidad] F HDL
ladeado ADJ (torcido) awry, askew; (asimétrico) lopsided
ladear VT (una superficie) to tilt; (la cabeza) to cock; (un avión) to bank; (ignorar) to snub, to ignore; **—se** to tilt, to lean
ladeo M tilt
ladera F hillside
ladilla F crab louse
ladillo M sidebar
ladino ADJ artful
lado M side; **— a —** side by side; **al —** nearby; **¡a un —!** gangway! **de —** sideways; **hacerse a un —** to move over
ladrar VI (perro) to bark; VI/VT (persona) to snap [at]
ladrido M bark, barking
ladrillo M brick
ladrón -ona MF (de casas) burglar; (con violencia) robber; (con astucia) thief; (de

tiendas) shoplifter
lagartija F (animal) lizard; (ejercicio) push-up
lagarto M alligator; — **varano** monitor lizard
lago M lake
lágrima F tear, teardrop
lagrimear VI to weep
laguna F (de agua) lagoon; (de la memoria, conocimiento) gap; (legal) loophole
laico -ca MF layperson; ADJ lay
laja F slab
lamentable ADJ (desafortunado) lamentable, regrettable; (ruinoso) woeful
lamentablemente ADV unfortunately
lamentación F lamentation
lamentar VT (una acción) to lament, to regret; (una muerte) to grieve; —**se** to lament, to wail
lamento M lament, lamentation
lamer VT (pasar la lengua) to lick; (rozar) to lap; — **culos** *fam* to brownnose; MF SG
 lameculos brownnoser
lamida F lick
lámina F (de vidrio, metal) sheet; (de metal) plate; (grabado) print
laminar VT to laminate
lámpara F lamp
lamparilla F night-light
lampiño ADJ (sin pelo) hairless; (sin barba) beardless
lana F wool; — **de acero** steel wool
lanar ADJ wool-bearing
lance M incident
lancear VT to lance, to spear
lanceta F lancet, lance
lancha F launch, boat; — **a motor** motorboat
langosta F (crustáceo) lobster; (insecto) locust
langostino M prawn
languidecer[35] VI to languish, to wilt
languidez F languor
lánguido ADJ languid, listless
lanilla F flannel
lanolina F lanolin
lanudo ADJ wooly, shaggy
lanza F lance, spear; **romper una** — **por alguien** to stick one's neck out for someone
lanzadera F shuttle
lanzador -ora MF (beisbol) pitcher
lanzamiento M (de un cohete, producto) launch; (de suministros) drop; (de una roca grande) heave; (de una pelota, en béisbol) pitch; (en tenis) toss
lanzar[47] VT (un cohete) to launch; (un producto) to launch, to roll out; (una pelota) to throw; (una bala) to fire; (algo pesado) to heave; (lodo) to sling; VI/VT (vomitar) to puke; —**se** to launch forth/out; — **un tiro libre** to shoot a free throw; M SG —**llamas** flamethrower
lanzazo M thrust with a lance
Laos M Laos

laosiano -na ADJ & MF Laotian
lápida F (piedra) stone tablet; (de sepultura) gravestone, tombstone
lapidar VT to stone
lapidario ADJ & M lapidary
lápiz M pencil; — **de color** crayon; — **de labios** lipstick
lapso M lapse, span
lapsus M lapse, slip of the tongue
laptop M laptop
laquear VT to lacquer
largar[40] VT (soltar) to cough up; —**se** *fam* to scram, to buzz off, to shove off
largo ADJ (camino, cuento) long; (discurso) lengthy; **de** — **alcance** long-range; ¡— **de aquí!** scram! M —**metraje** feature film; **a la larga** in the long run; **a lo** — lengthwise; M length
larguero M crossbar
largueza F generosity
larguirucho ADJ lanky
largura F length
laringe F larynx
laringitis F laryngitis
larva F larva
lascivia F (deseo) lust; (perversión) lewdness
lascivo ADJ (pervertido) lascivious, lewd; (cachondo) *fam* horny
láser M laser
lástima F pity; ¡**qué** —! what a shame!
lastimadura F hurt
lastimar VT (herir) to hurt; (insultar) to hurt one's feelings; —**se** to get hurt
lastimoso ADJ pitiful
lastrar VT to ballast
lastre M ballast
lata F (envase) tin can, can; (con tapa) canister; (pesadez) bore; **dar la** — to be a nuisance
latente ADJ latent, dormant
lateral ADJ lateral, side
látex M latex
latido M (individual) beat, throb; (colectivo) beating; (del corazón) heartbeat
latifundio M large estate
latigazo M (golpe) lash; (chasquido) crack of a whip
látigo M whip
latín M Latin
latino -na ADJ (relativo a los hispanos) Latino; (relativo a la lengua latina) Latin; M Latino; F Latina
Latinoamérica F Latin America
latinoamericano ADJ Latin American
latir VI to beat, to throb
latitud F latitude (también flexibilidad)
latón M brass
latrocinio M larceny
laudable ADJ laudable
laurel M laurel; **dormirse sobre los** —**es** to

rest on one's laurels
lava F lava
lavable ADJ washable
lavabo M (retrete) lavatory, toilet; (recipiente) sink
lavadero M laundry; — **automático** Laundromat™
lavado M wash, washing; — **de cerebro** brainwashing; — **de dinero** money laundering; — **en seco** dry cleaning
lavadora F washing machine
lavanda F lavender
lavandera F washerwoman
lavandería F laundry
lavar VI/VT to wash; (ropa) to launder; —**se** to wash up; —**se las manos** to wash one's hands; M SG **lavaplatos/lavavajillas** dishwasher
lavativa F enema
lavatorio M washroom
laxante M laxative
laxitud F laxity
laxo ADJ lax
lazada F bowknot
lazar⁴⁷ VT to lasso
lazarillo M (persona) guide for the blind; (perro) guide dog
lazo M (soga) lasso, rope; (vuelta) loop; (nudo corredizo) noose; (relación) tie, bond
LBD [lipoproteína de baja densidad] F LDL
le PRON PERS — **dije** I told you/him/her; — **vi** *Esp* I saw him/you; **se** — **murió el perro** his/her dog died on him/her
leal ADJ loyal, trusty
lealtad F loyalty, allegiance; — **de marca** brand loyalty
lección F lesson, assignment; **darle una** — **a alguien** to teach someone a lesson
lechada F whitewash
leche F (de vaca) milk; (semen) *vulg* come; — **desnatada** skim milk; — **en polvo** powdered milk; — **entera** whole milk; — **homogeneizada** homogenized milk; — **malteada** malted milk; **¿qué** —**s quieres?** *Esp fam* what the hell do you want? **mala** — nasty disposition; **ir a toda** — to barrel along; **ese tío es la** — that guy's a case; **es un mala** — *fam* he's a nasty creep
lechería F dairy
lechero -ra ADJ dairy; M milkman; F milkmaid
lecho M bed (también de río)
lechón M suckling pig
lechoso ADJ milky
lechuga F lettuce
lechuza F screech owl, barn owl
lector -ora MF reader; — **de código de barras** bar code reader; M — **de tarjetas** card reader
lectura F (acción) reading; (material) reading matter

leer¹⁸ VI/VT to read
legación F legation
legado M legacy, bequest
legajo M file
legal ADJ legal, lawful
legalidad F (conjunto de normas) law; (cualidad de legal) legality
legalización F (de un documento) authentication; (de una actividad) legalization; — **de una validación testamentaria** probate
legalizar⁴⁷ VT to legalize
legar⁴⁰ VT to will, to bequeath
legendario ADJ legendary
leggings M PL leggings
legible ADJ (descifrable) legible; (fácil de leer) readable
legión F legion
legionario M legionnaire
legionelosis F legionnaire's disease
legislación F legislation
legislador -ora MF legislator, lawmaker
legislar VI/VT to legislate
legislativo ADJ legislative
legislatura F legislature
legitimidad F legitimacy
legítimo ADJ legitimate, lawful, rightful
lego -ga MF layperson; ADJ lay
legua F league
leguleyo -ya MF *pey* shyster
legumbre F legume
leído ADJ well-read
lejanía F distance
lejano ADJ (distancia) distant, faraway; (parentesco) remote
lejía F (producto de limpieza) bleach; (de sosa) lye
lejos ADV far away, far; **a lo** — in the distance; — **de** far from; **desde** — from afar
lelo ADJ silly
lema M (frase típica) motto; (propaganda política) slogan
lencería F lingerie
lengua F (órgano) tongue; (idioma) language; — **materna** mother tongue
lenguado M sole
lenguaje M language (también en informática); — **compilador** compiler language; — **corporal** body language; — **[de] máquina** machine language; — **de programación** programming language; — **de signos** sign language; — **ensamblador** assembly language
lenguaraz ADJ gossipy
lengüeta F (de un instrumento de viento) reed; (de un zapato) tongue
lengüetazo M lick
lentamente ADV slowly
lente MF lens; — **filtrador** filter lens; —**s**

eyeglasses; **—s de contacto** contact lenses;
—s negros/oscuros sunglasses, shades
lenteja F lentil
lentitud F slowness
lento ADJ (despacioso) slow; (tonto) dull;
(letárgico) sluggish; ADV slowly
leña F firewood
leñador -ora MF woodcutter, lumberjack
leñera F woodshed
leño M log
leñoso ADJ woody
león M lion; **— marino** sea lion
León M Leon
leona F lioness
leonés ADJ Leonese
leopardo M leopard
lepra F leprosy
lerdo ADJ slow
lesbiano -na ADJ lesbian; F lesbian
lesión F injury, lesion; **— ocular** eye injury
lesionar VT to injure; **—se** to get injured
Lesotho M Lesotho
letal ADJ lethal
letárgico ADJ lethargic
letargo M lethargy
letón -ona ADJ & MF Latvian
Letonia F Latvia
letra F (del alfabeto) letter; (caligrafía)
handwriting; (de una canción) lyrics, words;
— bastardilla/cursiva italics; **— chica**
fine print; **— de cambio** bill of exchange; **—
de imprenta** block letter; **— manuscrita**
longhand; **sin —s** uneducated
letrado ADJ learned, literate
letrero M sign
letrina F latrine
leucemia F leukemia
leudar VI to rise; VT to leaven
leva F (de tropas) levy; (de motor) cam
levadura F leaven, yeast
levantamiento M (revuelta) uprising;
(suspensión) suspension; **— de pesas**
weight-lifting
levantar VT (la mano) to raise; (una caja) to lift;
(un interruptor) to switch; (del piso) to pick
up; (perdices) to flush; (a un dormido) to
wake up, to rouse; (un edificio) to put up; **—
el campamento** to break camp; **— falso
testimonio** to bear false witness; **— la
mesa** to clear the table; **— la sesión** to
adjourn the meeting; **— vuelo** to take flight;
—se (de la cama) to get up, to rise, to arise;
(de una silla) to stand up, to get up; (un
edificio) to go up
levar VT **— anclas** to weigh anchor
leve ADJ (brisa) light; (resfrío) mild; (problema)
slight
levedad F (de una brisa) lightness; (de un resfrío)
mildness

levemente ADV lightly
léxico M lexicon, dictionary; ADJ lexical
lexicografía F lexicography
ley F law, statute; **— de prescripción** statute of
limitations; **— de [los] rendimientos
decrecientes** law of diminishing returns; **—
marcial** martial law; **de buena —** of good
quality
leyenda F (mitología) legend; (texto que
acompaña una figura) caption
leyendo, leyera, leyese, leyeron ver leer
liar[28] VT (paquetes) to bundle; (cigarros) to roll;
—se to get involved
libanés -esa ADJ & MF Lebanese
Líbano M Lebanon
libelo M libel
libélula F dragonfly
liberación F (de un país ocupado) liberation; (de
pecados) deliverance; (de presos) release
liberal ADJ & MF liberal
liberalidad F liberality
liberalismo M liberalism
liberalización F liberalization
liberar VT (de un deber) to relieve; (a un pueblo)
to liberate; (del sufrimiento) to deliver; (a un
preso) to free, to release
Liberia F Liberia
liberiano -na ADJ & MF Liberian
líbero M sweeper
libertad F liberty, freedom; **— condicional**
parole; **— de expresión** free speech; **poner
en —** to set free; **poner en — bajo fianza** to
let out on bail; **poner en — condicional** to
parole
libertador -ora MF liberator
libertar VT to liberate
libertinaje M licentiousness
libertino -na MF libertine
Libia F Libya
libidinoso ADJ libidinous
libido F libido
libio -bia ADJ & MF Libyan
libra F pound (también moneda)
librar VT (a un preso) to free, to set free; (de una
obligación) to release; (un cheque) to write;
(una letra de cambio) to draft; (una guerra) to
wage; **—se de** to get rid of
libre ADJ (persona) free; (asiento) vacant;
(camino) clear; (traducción) loose; (de una
obligación) exempt; **— albedrío** free will; **—
cambio/comercio** free trade; **— de cargos**
toll-free; **— de gravámenes** free and clear;
— de intereses interest-free; **— de
impuestos** duty-free, tax-free; **— de virus**
virus-free; **— pensador** freethinker
librería F bookstore
librero -ra MF bookseller
libresco ADJ bookish
libreta F small notebook; **— de direcciones**

address book
libreto M libretto
libro M book; — **de bolsa** pocket book; — **de cocina** cookbook; — **de texto** textbook; — **electrónico** e-book; — **en rústica** paperback; — **mayor** ledger
licencia F (carnet de conducir, libertad poética) license; (permiso) leave; (permiso para ausentarse) leave of absence; — **de sitio** site license; — **por maternidad** maternity leave
licenciado -da MF college graduate
licenciar VT to discharge; —**se** to graduate from college
licenciatura F bachelor's degree
licencioso ADJ licentious
liceo M high school
licitación F bid
lícito ADJ lawful, permissible
licor M liqueur, cordial
licuadora F blender
líder MF leader
liderar VT to head up
liderar VT to lead
liderazgo M (de una organización, condición de líder) leadership; (en una competencia) lead
lidiar VI/VT to contend, to grapple
liebre F hare; **levantar la** — to let the cat out of the bag
Liechtenstein M Liechtenstein
liechtensteiniano -na MF Liechtensteiner
lienzo M canvas
liftado M top spin
lifting M face-lift
liga F (alianza, grupo deportivo) league; (cinta elástica) garter; — **mayor** major league
ligado M slur
ligadura F ligature
ligamento M ligament
ligar[40] VT (atar) to bind; (conectar notas) to slur; VI (conquistar sexualmente) to score; —**se** to bind; —**se las trompas** to have one's tubes tied
ligeramente ADV lightly
ligereza F (de peso) lightness; (de temperamento) levity
ligero ADJ (poco pesado) light; (rápido) swift; (pequeño) slight; **a la ligera** lightly
ligue M (amistad casual) pickup; (conquista sexual) score
liguero M garter belt
lija F sandpaper
lijar VI/VT to sandpaper, to sand
lila ADJ & MF lilac
lima F (fruta) lime; (árbol) lime tree; — **de uñas** nail file
limar VI/VT to file
limero M lime tree
limitación F (restricción) limitation; (defecto) shortcoming

limitar VT (restringir) to limit; (gastos) to curb; —**se a** to limit oneself to
límite M (restricción) limit; (de una región) boundary; (de la paciencia) bounds; — **de edad** age limit; — **de tiempo** time limit; — **de velocidad** speed limit
limítrofe ADJ bordering
limo M slime
limón M lemon
limonada F lemonade
limonero M lemon tree
limosna F alms, handout
limpiador M cleanser
limpiar VI/VT to clean; VT (una superficie) to wipe; (la piel) to cleanse; (un camino, una pantalla de computadora, la reputación) to clear; (animales) to dress; (zapatos) to shine; (un derrame) to mop up, to wipe up; (dejar sin dinero) to clean out; M SG **limpiaparabrisas** windshield wiper; M SG **limpiavidrios** squeegee
límpido ADJ limpid
limpieza F (pulcritud) cleanliness, neatness; (operación militar) mop-up; — **étnica** ethnic cleansing
limpio ADJ (casa) clean, neat; (piel, conciencia) clear; (juego) fair; (sin dinero) broke; **pasar en** — to make a clean copy
limusina F limousine
linaje M lineage, ancestry
linaza F linseed
lince M (animal) lynx; (persona astuta) sly fox; **con ojos de** — sharp-eyed
linchar VT to lynch
lindante ADJ neighboring
lindar VI to border, to adjoin
linde MF boundary
lindero ADJ adjoining; M boundary
lindo ADJ pretty; **un día** — a nice day; **de lo** — a lot
línea F (raya, cola) line; (en béisbol) line drive; — **aérea** airline; — **de banda** (fútbol) sideline; — **de conducta** course of action; — **de crédito** credit line; — **de fondo** baseline; — **de golpeo** line of scrimmage; — **de meta** goal line; — **de montaje** assembly line; — **ofensiva** offensive line; **batear una** — to line out; **en** — online
lineal ADJ linear
linfa F lymph
linfocito M lymphocyte
linfoma M lymphoma
lingüista MF linguist
lingüística F linguistics
lingüístico ADJ linguistic
linimento M liniment
lino M (tela) linen; (fibra) flax
linóleo M linoleum
linterna F (a pilas, de bolsillo) flashlight; (de un

faro) lantern

lío M (bulto) bundle; (enredo, molestia) mess, hassle; (amorío) affair, fling; **armar un** — to raise a ruckus; **meterse en un** — to get oneself into a mess

liofilizar VI/VT to freeze-dry

liposucción F liposuction

liquidación F (ajuste de cuentas, de bienes) settlement, liquidation; (rebaja) sale, clearance sale; (pago completo) payment in full

liquidar VT (bienes, mercancías) to liquidate, to sell off; (una cuenta, herencia) to settle; (a una persona) *fam* to waste, to off, to whack

liquidez F liquidity

líquido ADJ & M liquid; — **amniótico** amniotic fluid

lira F (moneda) lira

lírica F lyric poetry

lírico ADJ lyric, lyrical

lirio M iris, lily; — **de los valles** lily of the valley

lirismo M lyricism

lisiado ADJ (descapacitado) handicapped; (lesionado) injured

lisiar VT to handicap

liso ADJ (neumático) bald; (camino) even, smooth; (terreno) flat; (pelo) straight; **azul** — solid blue

lisonja F flattery

lisonjear VI/VT to flatter

lisonjero -ra MF flatterer; ADJ flattering

lista F (de palabras) list; (de miembros) roster; (de alumnos) roll; (banda) stripe; (de precios) schedule, list; — **de control** checklist; — **de correo** mailing list; — **de espera** waiting list; — **negra** blacklist; **pasar** — to call the roll

listado ADJ striped; M listing, printout

listo ADJ (preparado) ready, set; (inteligente) clever, smart; **hacerse el** — to pull a stunt

listón M (tabla) board; (en salto de altura) crossbar

lisura F smoothness

litera F (cama en el tren, barco) berth; (cama superpuesta) bunk bed

literal ADJ literal

literario ADJ literary

literato -ta MF writer

literatura F literature

litigante MF litigant

litigio M (pleito) lawsuit; (acción de litigar) litigation

litio M lithium

litoral ADJ seaside; M seaboard, seacoast

litro M liter

Lituania F Lithuania

lituano -na ADJ & MF Lithuanian

liviano ADJ (leve) light; (promiscuo)

promiscuous

lívido ADJ livid

living M living room

llaga F sore

llama F (fuego) flame; (animal) llama

llamada F (de teléfono, a la acción) call; (grito) hail; (nota al pie) footnote; — **de cobro revertido / por cobrar** collect call

llamado M (acción de convocar) call; (petición) appeal

llamador M knocker

llamamiento M (conversación) call; (exhortación) appeal; **hacer un** — to appeal

llamar VT (un nombre, una huelga, por teléfono) to call; (a la puerta) to knock; (gritar) to hail; — **la atención** to call attention; **me llamo Juan** my name is Juan

llamarada F blaze, flare

llamativo ADJ (impactante) striking, bold; (chabacano) gaudy, flashy

llameante ADJ flaming

llamear VI to flare, to flame

llana F trowel

llano ADJ (sencillo) plain; (liso) flat, smooth, level; (de poca profundidad) shallow; M plain

llanta F (reborde metálico) rim; (neumático) tire

llanto M crying, weeping

llanura F plain, prairie

llave F (para puertas) key; (de armas de fuego) lock; (en lucha libre) lock, hold; (grifo) faucet, tap; (interruptor) light switch; (de gas) cock; — **de tuercas** wrench; — **inglesa** pipe wrench; — **maestra** master key

llavero M key ring

llegada F arrival

llegar[40] VI (arribar) to arrive, to get there/here; (alcanzar) to reach; — **a las manos** to come to blows; — **a ser** to become; — **a un acuerdo** to strike a deal; — **a un arreglo** to cut a deal; — **tarde** to be late

llenar VT (un recipiente) to fill; (un formulario) to fill out; — **el tanque** to tank up, to gas up; —**se** to fill up; —**se de** to get filled with; —**se de oro** to make a killing

lleno ADJ full; — **de** full of; **de** — totally; M **un** — **completo** a full house

llevadero ADJ bearable

llevar VT (transportar) to carry, to take; (transportar en coche) to drive; (tener puesto) to wear; (contener) to hold; (inducir) to lead, to drive; — **a cabo** to carry out; — **la cuenta** to keep score; — **la ventaja** to have an advantage; — **los libros** to keep the books; — **un mes aquí** to have been here one month; **le llevo dos años a mi hermano** I'm two years older than my brother; **llevo las de perder** the odds are against me; —**se** to carry away, to take away; —**se bien con** to get along with

llorar VI (con ruido) to cry, to bawl; (con lágrimas) to weep; VT (una pérdida) to lament; (una muerte) to mourn
lloriquear VI to whimper
lloriqueo M whimper
llorón -ona ADJ weeping; MF crybaby, whiner
lloroso ADJ tearful, weeping
llovedizo ADJ **agua llovediza** rainwater
llover[6] VI/VT to rain; **— a cántaros** to rain cats and dogs; **llueva o truene** rain or shine
llovizna F drizzle
lloviznar VI to drizzle, to mist
lluvia F (precipitación) rain; (de preguntas, críticas) barrage; (de protestas, flechas, piedras) volley; (de golpes, chispas) shower; **— ácida** acid rain; **— de ideas** brainstorming; **— torrencial** driving rain
lluvioso ADJ rainy
lo PRON PERS **— bueno** the good thing; **— de la protesta** the matter of the protest; **— que quiero** what I want; **sé — bueno que eres** I know how good you are; **yo — vi** I saw it/him/you
loable ADJ laudable, praiseworthy
loar VT to laud
lobato M wolf cub
lobbista, lobista MF lobbyist
lobby M lobby
lobezno M wolf cub
lobo M wolf
lobotomía F lobotomy
lóbrego ADJ gloomy
lóbulo M lobe
local ADJ local; M premises
localidad F (pueblo) town, locality; (en un teatro) seat
localización F location
localizar[47] VT (encontrar) to locate; (limitar) to localize
loción F lotion
loco -ca ADJ insane, mad, crazy; **— de remate** stark raving mad; MF lunatic, insane person; M madman
locomotora F locomotive, train engine
locuaz ADJ garrulous, loquacious
locura F madness, insanity
locutor -ora MF radio announcer
lodazal M quagmire
lodo M mud
lodoso ADJ muddy
logaritmo M logarithm
logia F lodge
lógica F logic
lógicamente ADV logically
lógico ADJ (razonado) logical; (bien fundado) sound
logística F logistics
lograr VT to achieve, to accomplish; **logré convencerle** I managed to / succeeded in

convincing him
logro M (lo conseguido) accomplishment, achievement; (hazaña) feat
lola F *fam* boob
loma F knoll
lombriz F (de tierra) earthworm; (de estómago) tapeworm
lomo M (de animal) back ridge; (corte de carne) loin
lona F canvas
longaniza F cured sausage
longevidad F longevity
longevo ADJ long-lived
longitud F (distancia angular) longitude; (largo) length; **— de onda** wavelength
lonja F (mercado) commodity exchange; (tajada) slice of meat
loquería F *fam* booby hatch, funny farm
loquero -ra MF (psiquiatra) *fam* shrink; M (manicomio) *fam* funny farm
lord M lord
loro M parrot
losa F (lápida) slab; (baldosa) flagstone
lote M lot
lotería F lottery
loza F (basta) crockery; (fina) china
lozanía F freshness, bloom
lozano ADJ fresh, blooming
LSD MF LSD
lubina F bass
lubricante ADJ & M lubricant
lubricar[30] VI/VT to lubricate
lucero M morning star; **— del alba** morning star
lucha F (pugna, contienda) struggle; (pelea) fight; **— libre** wrestling
luchador -ora MF fighter; (en lucha libre) wrestler
luchar VI/VT (contra un enemigo) to fight; (con un problema) to struggle; (en lucha libre) to wrestle; **— por** to strive for
lucidez F lucidity
lúcido ADJ lucid, clear-headed
luciérnaga F firefly, glowworm
lucio M pike
lucir[39] VI (mostrarse) to look; (favorecer, sentar bien) to look good on, to suit; VT (llevar) to model, to sport; (alardear de) to flaunt; **—se** (sobresalir) to excel; (ostentar) to show off
lucrativo ADJ lucrative, profitable
lucro M **sin fines de —** not for profit
luctuoso ADJ sad, mournful, dismal
luego ADV afterward, then, next; **— de** after; **desde —** of course; **hasta —** so long
lugar M place; **— común** platitude; **— de nacimiento** birthplace, place of birth; **— de trabajo** workplace; **dar — a** to give rise to; **no hay —** there's no room; **en — de** instead of

lúgubre ADJ mournful, gloomy
lujo M luxury; **darse un —** to indulge oneself; **con — de detalles** in great detail
lujoso ADJ (ropa) luxurious; (hotel) plush
lujuria F lust
lujurioso ADJ lustful
lumbago M lumbago
lumbar ADJ lumbar
lumbre F (fuego) fire; (luz) light
luminosidad F brilliance, luminosity
luminoso ADJ luminous
luna F (satélite) moon; (espejo) large mirror; **— de miel** honeymoon; **estar en la —** to be distracted; **— llena** full moon
lunar ADJ lunar; M (en la piel) mole; (en una tela) polka dot
lunático -ca ADJ & MF lunatic
lunes M Monday
lupa F magnifying glass
lúpulo M hops
lupus M lupus
lustrar VT to shine, to polish
lustre M luster, shine
lustroso ADJ (revista) glossy; (pelo) shiny, sleek
luto M mourning
luxación F dislocation
Luxemburgo M Luxembourg
luxemburgués -esa MF Luxembourger; ADJ Luxembourgian
luz F light (también aparato); (del sol) sunshine; (abertura) aperture; **— trasera** taillight; **— verde** green light; **dar a —** to give birth; **sacar a —** to disclose

Mm

macabro ADJ grim
macanudo ADJ cool
Macao M Macao
macarrones M PL macaroni
Macedonia F Macedonia
macedonio -nia ADJ & MF Macedonian
maceta F flower pot
machacar[30] VT (aplastar) to pound, to crush; (insistir) to harp on; (en baloncesto) to dunk
machacón ADJ persistent
machetazo M hack with a machete
machete M machete
machismo M [male] chauvinism
macho M (animal masculino) male; (mulo) he-mule; (varón) man; (hombre muy varonil) he-man; **— cabrío** he-goat; **— y hembra** hook and eye; ADJ (masculino) male; (fuerte) strong; INTERJ man!
machote ADJ butch

machucar[30] VT to bruise
macilento ADJ pale
macizo ADJ massive; M plateau
Madagascar M Madagascar
madama F madam
madeja F skein
madera F wood (también en golf); (árboles maderables) timber; (para construcción) lumber; **— contrachapada** plywood; **— flotante** driftwood; **— noble** hardwood; **—s** woodwinds; **tocar —** to knock on wood
maderaje M woodwork
madero M trunk
madrastra F stepmother
madre F mother; **— de alquiler** surrogate mother; **— patria** mother country; **—perla** mother-of-pearl; **— política** mother-in-law; **—selva** honeysuckle; **ciento y la —** everybody and their dog
madriguera F burrow, hole
madrileño -ña ADJ & MF [person] from Madrid
madrina F godmother
madrugada F early morning hours; **a las dos de la —** at two in the morning
madrugador -ra ADJ & MF early bird
madrugar VI to get up early; **— con gripe** to wake up with a cold
maduración F (animales, personas) maturation, maturing; (frutos) ripening; (vino) aging
madurar VI to mature, to grow up
madurez F (de persona) maturity; (de fruta) ripeness
maduro ADJ (persona) mature; (fruta) ripe
maestría F master's degree; **— en administración de empresas** master of business administration
maestro -tra MF (docente) [school]teacher; (artesano) master; (director) maestro
mafia F mafia
mafioso -sa MF mafioso
magia F magic
mágico ADJ magic, magical
magisterio M (actividad) teaching; (conjunto de los maestros) teachers; (profesión) teaching profession
magistrado -da MF magistrate
magistral ADJ masterful, masterly
magma M magma
magnánimo ADJ magnanimous
magnate MF magnate, tycoon
magnesia F magnesia
magnesio M magnesium
magnético ADJ magnetic
magnetismo M magnetism
magnetizar[47] VT to magnetize
magnificar[30] VT to magnify
magnificencia F magnificence
magnífico ADJ (palacio) magnificent; (día)

glorious
magnitud F magnitude
magno ADJ great
magnolia F magnolia
magnolio M magnolia tree
mago M magician, wizard
magro ADJ lean
magulladura F bruise, contusion
magullar VI/VT (machucar) to bruise; (mutilar) to mangle
mahonesa F mayonnaise
maicena® F cornstarch
maíz M corn, maize
maizal M cornfield
majadería F stupidity
majadero ADJ stupid
majar VT to pound
majestad F majesty
majestuoso ADJ majestic, stately
majo ADJ (atractivo) good-looking; (agradable) charming
mal M (maldad) evil; (enfermedad) malady, affliction; (daño) harm; — **de altura** altitude sickness; — **de ojo** evil eye; ADV wrong, badly; — **aconsejado** misguided; — **adquirido** ill-gotten; — **hablado** foulmouthed; **hablar — de alguien** to speak ill of someone; **hacer —** to do wrong; **lo hice mal** I did it badly
malabarista MF juggler
malandanza F misfortune
malaria F malaria
Malasia F Malaysia
malasio -sia ADJ & MF Malaysian
Malawi M Malawi
malawiano -na ADJ & MF Malawian
malbaratar VT to undersell
malcontento ADJ discontented
malcriado ADJ spoiled
malcriar VT to spoil
maldad F evil, wickedness
maldecir[51] VI/VT to curse
maldición F curse
maldito ADJ accursed; ¡— **sea!** *fam* damn it!
Maldivas F PL Maldives
maldivo -va ADJ & MF Maldivian
maleable ADJ malleable
maleante MF gangster, hoodlum
malear VT to corrupt
maleducado ADJ ill-mannered, ill-bred
maleficio M evil spell
maléfico ADJ evil
malentendido M misunderstanding
malestar M (de estómago) upset; (físico) discomfort; (espiritual) malaise; (social) unrest
maleta F suitcase, bag; **hacer la —** to pack one's suitcase
maletero M car trunk

maletín M briefcase
malévolo ADJ (persona) malevolent; (comentario) snide
maleza F (en el monte) underbrush, scrub; (en un jardín) weeds
malformación F malformation
malgache ADJ & MF Madagascan
malgastar VI/VT to waste, to throw away
malgasto M waste
malhechor -ora MF evildoer, criminal
malhumorado ADJ grumpy, ill-humored
Mali, Malí M Mali
malí ADJ & MF Malian
malicia F malice
malicioso ADJ malicious, spiteful
malignidad F malignancy
maligno ADJ (persona) vicious, evil; (tumor) malignant
malinterpretar VI/VT to misunderstand
malla F (de armadura) mail; (de metal) mesh
malo ADJ bad; (calidad, letra) poor; (enfermo) ill; **mal estado** disrepair; **mal humor** bad mood; **mala fama** ill repute; **mala fe** bad faith; **mala hierba** weed; **mala pasada** bad turn; **mala racha** slump; **mala suerte** bad luck
malograr VT to spoil, to ruin; —**se** to fail, to miscarry
malpagar[40] VI/VT to underpay
malparto M miscarriage
malsano ADJ unhealthy, unwholesome
malta F malt
Malta F Malta
maltés -esa ADJ & MF Maltese
maltratar VT to mistreat, to abuse
maltrato M mistreatment, abuse
maltrecho ADJ battered
malvado ADJ wicked, evil
malvavisco M marshmallow
malversación F misuse, misappropriation
malversar VT to misuse, to embezzle
mamá F mama, mamma, mom
mamada F suck; (felación) *vulg* blow job
mamado ADJ drunk
mamar VI (un bebé) to suckle, to nurse; VI/VT to suck; —**la** *vulg* to blow
mamario ADJ mammary
mamarracho M sight
mami F mommy
mamífero ADJ mammalian, mammal; M mammal
mamografía F mammography
mampara F partition
mamut M mammoth
manada F (de ballenas) pod; (de vacas) herd; (de lobos) pack
manantial M (naciente) spring; (fuente inagotable) wellspring
manar VI to stream out

mancha F (marca) stain, spot; (de tinta) blot; (cosa borrosa) blur; (aceitosa) smear, smudge; (menoscabo) tinge; (en la piel) blemish

manchado ADJ spotted

manchar VI/VT (ensuciar) to spot; (menoscabar) to stain, to blemish

manchón M large spot

mancilla F blemish

mancillar VT to defile, to sully

manco ADJ one-armed

mancuerna F dumbbell

mandado M errand

mandamás M *fam* big enchilada, big kahuna

mandamiento M commandment

mandante MF principal

mandar VI/VT (dar órdenes) to command, to order; (enviar) to send; — **buscar a** to send for; — **decir** to send word; ¿**quién manda?** who's in charge? —**se hacer un traje** to have a suit made; ¿**mande?** (hola) hello; (perdón) excuse me? what?

mandarina F tangerine

mandatario -ria MF (mediante contrato) agent; (abogado) attorney; (de estado) head of state

mandato M (orden) command, order; (cargo político) term, mandate

mandíbula F (quijada) jaw; (hueso) jawbone

mandil M apron

mandioca F manioc

mando M (de un estado) rule; (de un aparato) control; — **a distancia** remote control

mandolina F mandolin

mandón -ona ADJ bossy, domineering; MF bossy person, control freak

mandonear VI/VT to domineer, to boss around

manea F hobble

manear VT to hobble

manecilla F clock hand

manejable ADJ manageable

manejar VT (un vehículo) to drive, to steer; (un negocio) to run, to manage; (una máquina) to operate

manejo M (de un negocio) running, management; (de asuntos) handling; (de una máquina) operation

manera F manner, way; a — **de** like; **de alguna** — somehow; **de cualquier** — anyway; **de ninguna** — on no account; **de** — **que** so that

manga F (de una camisa) sleeve; (de una nave) beam; (de agua) hose; (tenis) set; — **de viento** windsock; **en** —**s de camisa** in shirtsleeves; **ser de** — **ancha** to be broad-minded; **sacar algo de la** — to pull something out of a hat

manganeso M manganese

mangle M mangrove

mango M (agarradera) handle, grip; (fruta, árbol) mango

mangosta F mongoose

manguera F hose

manguito M muff

maní M peanut

manía F (moda, estado patológico) mania; (hábito) bad habit; (tic) tic

maníaco -ca ADJ maniacal; MF maniac

maníaco-depresivo ADJ manic-depressive

maniatar VT to tie the hands; (manear) to hobble

maniático ADJ (que tiene manías) crotchety; (melindroso) fastidious

manicomio M *pey* insane asylum

manicura F manicure

manicurar VT to manicure

manido ADJ hackneyed

manifestación F (muestra) manifestation; (protesta) demonstration

manifestante MF demonstrator

manifestar[1] VI/VT to manifest, to show; (expresar) to air; (protestar en público) to demonstrate; (declarar) to state

manifiesta, manifieste *ver* manifestar

manifiesto ADJ & M manifest; **poner de** — to underscore; M (dogma) manifesto; — **de vuelo** manifest

manija F handle

maniobra F (militar) maneuver; (para llamar la atención) stunt; — **de Heimlich** Heimlich maneuver

maniobrar VI/VT to maneuver

manipulación F (de la opinión pública) manipulation; (de alimentos) handling

manipular VT (influir) to manipulate; (tocar con las manos) to handle

maniquí M (muñeco) mannequin; MF (modelo) model

manivela F crank

manjar M delicacy

mano F hand (también de naipes); (de pintura) coat; (fútbol) handball; — **a** — one on one; — **de obra** workforce; —**s a la obra** let's get to work; —**s de mantequilla** butterfingers; **a** — (presente) at hand; (con la mano) by hand; **a** — **armada** at gunpoint; **dar una** — to lend a hand; **dar una** — **de pintura** to put on a coat of paint; **darle una** — **a alguien** to lend someone a hand; **darse la** — (saludo) to shake hands; (señal de afecto) to hold hands; **de primera** — firsthand; **de segunda** — secondhand; **estar a** — **con alguien** to be even with someone; **hecho a** — handmade; **poner las** —**s en el fuego por alguien** to go out on a limb for someone; **quedar a** — to break even; **se le fue la** — he got carried away; **ser** — to lead [in a card game]; **tener buena** — **con/para algo** to have a knack for something; **tomarse de la** — to hold hands

manojo M (de monedas) handful; (de llaves) bunch

manómetro M pressure gauge

manopla F (guante) mitten; (en béisbol) glove

manosear VT (a una persona) to fondle, to grope; (tocar una cosa) to feel, to finger

manoseo M feel, grope

manotazo M swat; **tirarle un — a alguien** to take a swipe at someone

manotear VI to swat at

mansalva LOC ADV **a —** at will

mansedumbre F gentleness, meekness

mansión F mansion

manso ADJ (humilde) meek; (domesticado) tame; (apacible) gentle

manta F (gruesa) blanket, cover; (liviana) throw

manteca F lard, shortening; RP butter; **— de cacao** cocoa butter

mantecoso ADJ rich, buttery

mantel M tablecloth

mantendrá, mantendría ver mantener

mantener[58] VT (conservar, sostener) to maintain; (dejar prolongadamente) to keep; (alimentar, costear a alguien) to provide for; (apoyar a lo largo del tiempo) to sustain; **— a flote** to buoy up; **— el orden público** to keep the peace; **— en secreto** to keep under wraps; **— en suspenso** to keep in suspense; **— la calma** to remain calm; **—se** (quedarse) to remain; (ganarse la vida) to support oneself; **—se al corriente** to keep abreast; **—se al tanto** to stay informed; **—se en contacto** to keep in touch; **—se firme** to stand pat, to stick to one's guns

mantenga, mantengo ver mantener

mantenimiento M maintenance, upkeep

mantequera F (platillo) butter dish; (aparato para hacer mantequilla) churn

mantequilla F butter; **— de maní** peanut butter

mantiene, mantienes ver mantener

mantilla F mantilla

manto M mantle (también geológico); (de juez) robe

mantón M shawl

mantra M mantra

mantuve, mantuviera, mantuviese ver mantener

manual ADJ & M manual

manubrio M handlebar

manufactura F manufacture

manufacturar VT to manufacture

manufacturero -ra ADJ manufacturing; MF manufacturer

manuscrito ADJ written by hand; M manuscript

manutención F maintenance

manzana F (fruta) apple; (de ciudad) block; **— de la discordia** bone of contention

manzanar M apple orchard

manzano M apple tree

maña F (destreza) skill, knack; (artimaña) cunning

mañana F (división del día) morning; (futuro) tomorrow; ADV tomorrow; **— por la —** tomorrow morning

mañanero -ra MF early bird

mañoso ADJ tricky

mapa M map; **— de memoria** memory map; **— en relieve** relief map

mapache M raccoon

maple M maple

maqueta F mock-up

maquillaje M makeup

maquillar[se] VI/VT to put on makeup

máquina F (aparato) machine; (motor) engine; **— de búsqueda** search engine; **— de coser** sewing machine; **— de escribir** typewriter; **— de lavar** washing machine; **— de vapor** steam engine; **— expendedora** vending machine; **— fotográfica** camera

maquinación F scheming, plotting

maquinador -ora MF schemer

maquinal ADJ automatic

maquinar VI/VT to plot, to scheme

maquinaria F (aparato) machinery, apparatus; (del gobierno) machine

maquinilla F clipper; **— de afeitar** razor

maquinista M (de locomotora) locomotive engineer; (obrero) machinist

mar MF sea; **— de fondo** undercurrent; **llover a mares** to rain cats and dogs; **en alta —** on the high seas; **un — de cosas** a lot of things; **hacerse a la —** to put to sea

maraca F maraca

maraña F (de hilos) tangle, snarl; (de pelo) mat

marañón M cashew

maratón M marathon

maravilla F (portento) wonder, marvel; (flor) marigold; **a las mil —s** wonderfully

maravillar VT to amaze; **—se** to be amazed, to marvel

maravilloso ADJ marvelous, wonderful

marca F (récord) record; (de ganado) brand; (de producto) brand, brand name, label; (de coche) make; **— comercial** brand name; **— de nacimiento** birthmark; **— de fábrica** trademark; **— genérica** generic brand; **— registrada** registered trademark; **de —** name-brand

marcadamente ADV sharply

marcado ADJ (acento) thick; (contraste) sharp, stark; (descenso) steep; (parecido) strong

marcador M (lapicero) marker; (en deporte) scoreboard; **— de libros** bookmark; **— genético** genetic marker; **¿cómo va el —?** what's the score?

marcar[30] VT (una respuesta) to mark; (ganado) to brand; (el ritmo) to beat; (la hora) to say; (un tanto) to score; (medida) to read, to show; (un número telefónico) to dial; **— para**

seleccionar to highlight; **— un gol** to score a goal

marcha F (caminata, pieza musical) march; (partida) leaving; (progreso) course; (modo de andar) gait; (cambio en un coche) gear; (animación) nightlife; **— atrás** reverse; **ponerse en —** to get going; **puesta en —** beginning; **sobre la —** as you go

marchante MF (vendedor) art dealer; (cliente) customer

marchar VI (soldado) to march; (máquina, vehículo) to run; **—se** to go away

marchista MF walker

marchitar VT to wither; **—se** to wither, to shrivel up

marchito ADJ withered, shriveled up

marcial ADJ martial

marco M (de un cuadro, de una puerta, de referencia) frame; (moneda) mark

marea F tide; **— baja** low tide; **— alta** high tide

mareado ADJ (en un barco) seasick; (en un coche) carsick; (de alegría) giddy; (con vértigo) dizzy, lightheaded

marear VT (dar vértigo) to make dizzy; (en un barco) to make seasick; **—se** (tener vértigo) to get dizzy; (en un barco) to get seasick

marejada F tidal wave

maremoto M tidal wave

mareo M (en un barco) seasickness; (en un vehículo) motion sickness; (vértigo) dizziness

marfil M ivory

marfileño -ña ADJ & MF Ivorian

margarina F margarine

margarita F daisy; **echar —s a los cerdos** to cast pearls before swine

margen M (de un papel) margin; (de la sociedad) fringe; MF (de un río) bank; **— de error** margin of error; **— de ganancia** profit margin, markup; **— de seguridad** margin of safety; **al —** on the outside

marginación F (de un grupo) marginalization; (de un individuo) isolation; **hay cierta — entre entre los colegas** there is a certain distance among the colleagues; **la — de ciertos grupos minoritarios** the marginalization of certain minorities

marginado -da ADJ & MF outcast

marginal ADJ marginal

marginar VT to marginalize

mariachi M mariachi

marica ADJ (homosexual) *ofensivo* queer; (cobarde) sissy; M (homosexual) *ofensivo* queer, fruit; (cobarde) sissy, pansy

maricón ADJ (homosexual) *ofensivo* queer; (cobarde) sissy; M (homosexual) *ofensivo* queer, fruit; (cobarde) sissy

marido M husband

mariguana, marihuana F marijuana; *fam* grass, pot

marimacho ADJ (niña) tomboyish; (mujer) butch; MF (niña) tomboy; (mujer) butch

marimba F marimba

marina F navy; **— mercante** merchant marine

marinar VT to marinate

marinero -ra ADJ (buque) seaworthy; (nación) seafaring; MF sailor

marino -na ADJ marine; MF sailor; (oficial) naval officer

marioneta F marionette

mariposa F (insecto) butterfly (también en natación); (tuerca) wing nut; **— nocturna** moth

mariquita F ladybug

mariscal M marshal; **— de campo** (militar) field marshal; (fútbol americano) quarterback

mariscos M PL shellfish

marítimo ADJ maritime

marketing M marketing

marmita F pot

mármol M marble

marmóreo ADJ marble

marmota F groundhog

maroma F rope

marqués M marquis

marquesa F marquise

marrano M hog

marrón ADJ brown

marroquí ADJ & MF Moroccan

Marruecos M Morocco

marshalés -esa ADJ & MF Marshallese

marsopa F porpoise

martes M Tuesday

martillar VI/VT to hammer

martillo M hammer (también hueso del oído, pieza de revólver); (de juez) gavel; **— neumático** jackhammer

martinete M (martillo grande) pile driver; (pieza de piano) piano hammer

martini M martini

mártir MF martyr

martirio M martyrdom

martirizar[47] VT to martyr, to torment

marxismo M Marxism

marzo M March

mas CONJ but

más ADJ more; PREP plus; ADV more; (más tiempo) longer; **— allá de** beyond; **— bien** rather; **— de tres** more than three; **— o menos** more or less; **— que nada** primarily; **— que nunca** more than ever; **— que tú** more than you; **a lo —** at best; **a — tardar** at the latest; **de —** extra; **el — allá** the hereafter; **es de lo — simpático** he's really nice; **es —** furthermore; **está de —** it is superfluous; **otro —** yet another; **por — que** no matter how much; **y — todavía** and then some

masa F mass; (de agua) body; (de harina) batter;

(para amasar) dough; **en —** en masse, in large
numbers; **las —s** the masses; **— de hojaldre**
puff pastry
masacrar VT to massacre, to slaughter
masacre M massacre
masaje M massage
masajear VT to massage
masajista M masseur; F masseuse
mascar[30] VI/VT (chicle) to chew; (con ruido) to
crunch
máscara F mask; **— de gas** gas mask
mascarada F masquerade
mascota F (animal doméstico) pet; (emblema de
un equipo) mascot
masculino ADJ (como un hombre, género
gramatical) masculine; (del hombre) male
mascullar VI/VT to mumble
masilla F putty
masivo ADJ massive
masón M mason
masonería F masonry
masoquismo M masochism
mastectomía F mastectomy
máster M master; **— en administración de
empresas** master of business administration
masticar[30] VT to chew
mástil M (en un barco) mast; (para una bandera)
flagpole, flagstaff
mastín M mastiff
masturbarse VI to masturbate
mata F bush; **— de pelo** head of hair
matadero M slaughterhouse
matador ADJ horrendous; M bullfighter
matanza F slaughter, killing
matar VT to kill; (animales) to butcher, to
slaughter; **— a tiros** to gun down; **— de
hambre** to starve; VT **matasellar** to cancel
a stamp; M SG **matamoscas** flyswatter; M SG
matasellos postmark; M SG **matasanos**
quack [doctor]
mate M (en ajedrez) checkmate; (planta, bebida)
mate; ADJ (pintura) flat; **hacer un —**
(baloncesto) to dunk the ball
matemática, matemáticas F mathematics
matemático -ca ADJ mathematical; (exacto)
precise; MF mathematician
materia F (sustancia) matter; (tema de estudio)
school subject; (tema) topic; **— extraña**
extraneous matter; **— fecal** fecal matter; **—
gris** gray matter; **— prima** raw material
material ADJ (necesidades) material; (autor)
real; M material
materialismo M materialism
maternal ADJ (instinto) maternal; (amor)
motherly
maternidad F (relacionado con el nacimiento)
maternity; (estado de ser madre) motherhood
materno ADJ maternal
matiné M matinee

matiz M (de un color) tint, shade, hue; (de
ironía) tinge; (de sentido) nuance
matizar[47] VT (mezclar colores) to blend, to
tinge; (moderar) to qualify
matón -ona MF (persona que intimida a los
pequeños) bully; (pandillero, peleador) thug
matorral M (mata) thicket; (región) bush
matraz M flask
matriarca F matriarch
matrícula F (alumnado) enrollment,
matriculation; (de un coche) registration;
(placa) license plate; (costo de la universidad)
tuition fees
matriculación F matriculation
matricular VT to matriculate, to enroll
matrilineal ADJ matrilineal
matrimonial ADJ marital
matrimonio M (estado civil) matrimony,
marriage; (pareja) married couple
matriz F (en matemáticas) matrix;
(bidimensional) array; (útero) womb;
(plantilla) stencil; **casa —** main office
matrona ADJ frumpy, matronly; F matron
matutino ADJ of the morning
maullar VI to mew
maullido M mew
mauriciano -na ADJ & MF Mauritian
Mauricio M Mauritius
Mauritania F Mauritania
mauritano -na MF Mauritanian
maxilar M jawbone
máxima F maxim
maximizar VT to maximize
máximo ADJ & M maximum; (autoridad)
ultimate; (cuidado) utmost; **— histórico**
all-time high
maya ADJ & MF Maya, Mayan
mayo M (mes) May; (palo) maypole
mayonesa F mayonnaise
mayor ADJ (de tamaño) greater, larger; (de edad)
older, elder; (rango, clave) major; **al por —**
wholesale; **dedo —** middle finger; **el —
número de votos** the most votes; M (adulto)
adult
mayoral M boss
mayordomo M butler
mayoreo M wholesale
mayoría F majority; **— de edad** legal age,
majority; **en su —** largely
mayorista MF wholesale dealer
mayoritario ADJ majority
mayúsculo -la ADJ (letra) capital; (problema)
major; F capital letter
mazmorra F dungeon
mazo M mallet
mazorca F (con maíz) ear of corn; (sin maíz)
corncob
me PRON PERS **él — vio** he saw me; **él — habló**
he talked to me; **se — murió el perro** my

dog died on me

meadero M *fam* john

mear VI/VT *fam* to pee, to piss

mecánico -ca ADJ mechanical; MF mechanic; F mechanics

mecanismo M mechanism; — **de seguridad** safety device

mecanografía F typewriting

mecanografiar[28] VI/VT to type

mecanógrafo -fa MF typist

mecedora F rocking chair, rocker

mecenas MF SG/PL patron, sponsor

mecenazgo M patronage

mecer[32] VI/VT (cuna) to rock; (columpio) to swing

mecha F (de una vela) wick; (de explosivos) fuse; (de pelo) lock; —**s** (en el pelo) highlights

mechar VT (rellenar con tocino) to lard; (robar) to shoplift

mechero -ra MF shoplifter; M burner; — **Bunsen** Bunsen burner

mechón M lock, strand

medalla F medal

médano M dune

media F (hasta el muslo) stocking; (hasta la cintura) pantyhose; (calcetín) sock; (promedio) mean; M PL (medios de comunicación) media

mediación F mediation

mediador -ora MF mediator

mediados LOC ADV **a** — **de mayo** in mid-May

mediana F median

mediano ADJ (intermedio en tamaño) medium; (intermedio en calidad) average; **de tamaño** — middle-sized; **de mediana edad** middle-aged

medianoche F midnight

mediante PREP by means of

mediar VI (en un asunto) to mediate, to intervene; (tiempo) to intervene; **mediaba febrero** it was mid-February

medible ADJ measurable

medicación F medication

medicamento M medicine, drug

medicar VT to medicate; —**se** to self-medicate

medicina F medicine; — **defensiva** defensive medicine; — **familiar** family practice

medición F (de una cantidad) measurement; (de un terreno) survey

médico -ca MF doctor, physician; — **forense** coroner, medical examiner; — **general** general practitioner; — **tratante** attending physician; ADJ medical

medida F (dimensión) measure; (acto de medir) measurement; — **cautelar** restraining order; — **para áridos** dry measure; **a** — **que** as; **en la** — **en que** to the extent that; **hacer a la** — to make to measure; **hecho a la** — made-to-measure; **tomar** —**s** to take

measures; **tomarle las** —**s a alguien** to measure someone

medidor M gauge, meter

medieval ADJ medieval

medio ADJ (la mitad) half; — **pastel** half a cake; (promedio) average; **el ciudadano** — the average man; —**día** (hora) noon, midday; (hora de comer) lunch hour, noon hour; (punto cardinal) south; (territorio) the south; — **hermano** half-brother; **a media asta** at half-mast; **a** — **camino** halfway; **clase media** middle class; **el americano** — the average American; **media hora** half an hour; **mi media naranja** my better half; **temperatura media** mean temperature; — **tiempo** (fútbol) halftime; **de** — **tiempo** part-time; **media volea** (tenis) half-volley; **hacer una cosa a medias** to do something halfway; **ir a medias** to go halves; M (centro) middle; (ambiente) medium; —**s** means, resources; — **ambiente** environment; —**s de comunicación** media; — **de transporte** means of transport; **en [el]** — **de** in the middle of; **en** — **de la calle** in the middle of the street; **meterse de por** — to intervene; **por** — **de** by means of; **por todos los** —**s** by all possible means; ADV half; **a** — **derretir** half-melted

medioambiental ADJ environmental

mediocre ADJ mediocre; (actuación) lackluster

mediocridad F mediocrity

medir[9] VI/VT to measure; VT (consecuencias) to gauge; (terreno) to survey; — **a pasos** to step off; —**se** to be moderate

meditación F meditation

meditar VI to meditate, to ponder

mediterráneo ADJ Mediterranean

médium MF medium, psychic

medroso ADJ fearful

médula F marrow, pith; — **espinal** spinal cord; — **ósea** bone marrow

medusa F jellyfish, man-of-war

megabyte M megabyte

megáfono M megaphone

megahercio, megahertz M megahertz

megalomanía F megalomania

mejilla F cheek

mejor ADJ better; **el** — the best; **en el** — **de los casos** at best; **te deseo lo** — I wish you the best; ADV better; **a lo** — maybe; **tanto** — so much the better

mejora F improvement

mejoramiento M improvement

mejorar VT to improve, to improve upon; (software, aparato) to upgrade; (las posibilidades de uno) to better; VI (ventas) to pick up; —**se** to get better/well

mejoría F improvement

melancolía F melancholy, gloom

melancólico ADJ melancholy, gloomy
melanoma M melanoma
melaza F molasses
melena F mane
melindre M affectation
melindroso ADJ affected, finicky
mella F notch; **hacer —** to make a dent
mellar VT to notch
mellizo -za ADJ & MF twin
melocotón M peach
melocotonero M peach tree
melodía F melody
melódico ADJ (agradable al oído) melodious;
   (relativo a la melodía) melodic
melodioso ADJ melodious
melodrama M melodrama
melómano -na ADJ music-loving; MF music
   lover
melón M melon, cantaloupe
membrana F (en un órgano) membrane; (en las
   patas de los patos) web
membrete M letterhead
membrillo M (fruta) quince; (árbol) quince tree
membrudo ADJ stout
memorable ADJ memorable
memorándum M memorandum
memoria F (facultad de recordar, recuerdo)
   memory; (obra autobiográfica) memoir;
   (actas) proceedings; **— de acceso directo**
   random access memory [RAM]; **— de caché**
   cache memory; **— de ROM** read-only
   memory; **— de sólo lectura** read-only
   memory [ROM]; **— expandida** expanded
   memory; **— intermedia** buffer; **—**
   residente internal memory; **de —** by heart;
   hacer — to try to remember/recollect
memorial M memorial
memorizar[47] VI/VT to memorize
mención F mention
mencionar VT to mention
mendigar[40] VI to beg
mendigo -ga MF beggar
mendrugo M large crumb
menear VT (las caderas) to wiggle, to wriggle, to
   shake; (la cola) to wag
meneo M (de las caderas) wiggle; (de la cola) wag
menesteroso ADJ needy, destitute
mengua F diminution, waning
menguante ADJ waning
menguar[25] VI (luna) to wane; (energía) to flag;
   (provisiones) to dwindle
meningitis F meningitis
menjurje M concoction
menopausia F menopause
menor ADJ (de tamaño) smaller; (de cantidad)
   lesser, smaller; (de edad) younger; (de
   importancia, en música) minor; **el —** (de
   tamaño) the smallest; (de cantidad) the least,
   the smallest; (de edad) the youngest; MF **— de**

edad minor; **al por —** retail
menos ADV (no contables) less; (contables)
   fewer; **— de** less than, fewer than; **— de lo**
   que se esperaba less than expected, fewer
   than expected; **— mal** just as well; **a — que**
   unless; **al —** at least; **dar de —** to
   shortchange; **echar de —** to miss; **lo —** the
   least; **no es para —** there is good reason;
   por lo — at least; **signo de —** minus sign;
   venir a — to decline; **el que trabaja —** the
   one who works the least; **no puede — que**
   hacerlo he cannot help doing it; **tienes —**
   que yo you have less than I; **trabaja — que**
   yo she works less than I; PREP (salvo) except,
   but; **las cinco — cuarto** quarter to five; ADJ
   & PRON less, least; **— agua** less water; **—**
   problemas fewer problems; M minus
menoscabar VT to impair, to undermine
menoscabo M impairment
menospreciar VI/VT (despreciar) to despise; VT
   (burlarse de) to belittle, to demean
menosprecio M contempt
mensaje M message; **— de error** error
   message; **— de texto** text message
mensajería F carrier; **— instantánea** instant
   messaging
mensajero -ra MF messenger, courier
menstruación F menstruation
menstruar VI to menstruate
mensual ADJ monthly
mensualidad F (recibida) monthly allowance;
   (pagada) monthly installment
mensuario ADJ monthly
mensurable ADJ measurable
menta F mint, peppermint; **— verde** spearmint
mental ADJ mental
mentalidad F mentality
mente F mind
mentecato -ta ADJ foolish, simple; MF
   simpleton
mentir[8] VI to lie
mentira F lie, falsehood
mentirilla F fib, white lie
mentiroso -sa ADJ lying; MF liar
mentón M chin
mentor -ora MF mentor
menú M menu (también de computadoras); **—**
   abatible pull-down menu; **— del día** daily
   special; **— de inicio** start menu; **—**
   emergente pop-up menu
menudeo LOC ADV **al —** retail
menudo ADJ (pequeño) small; (insignificante)
   insignificant; **a —** often, frequently; **dinero**
   — small change; **— perro** that's some dog; M
   (entrañas) entrails
meñique ADJ & M little finger, *fam* pinkie; **dedo**
   — little finger
meollo M (médula) marrow; (parte sustancial de
   un asunto) marrow, pith, core; (seso) brain

mequetrefe M runt, pipsqueak
mercachifle M peddler, huckster
mercadear VT to market
mercadeo M merchandising; — **de nicho** niche marketing
mercader M merchant
mercadería F merchandise
mercado M market, marketplace; — **alcista** bull market; — **bajista** bear market; — **de divisas** currency exchange; — **de prueba** test market; — **de pulgas** flea market; — **de valores** stock market; — **extrabursátil** aftermarket; — **libre** free market; — **negro** black market; — **secundario** aftermarket
mercadotecnia F marketing
mercancía F merchandise, goods
mercante ADJ merchant
mercantil ADJ mercantile
merced LOC ADV — **a** thanks to; **a [la] — de** at the mercy of
mercenario -ria ADJ & MF mercenary
mercería F notions store
mercurio M mercury, quicksilver
merecedor ADJ deserving
merecer[35] VT to deserve, to merit
merecido M deserved punishment, due
merendar[1] VI to have a snack
merendero M picnic area
merezca, merezco *ver* merecer
meridiano ADJ & M meridian
meridional ADJ southern; MF southerner
merienda F afternoon snack
mérito M merit
meritorio ADJ meritorious, worthy
merluza F hake
merma F decrease
mermar VI/VT to decrease, to dwindle
mermelada F (de fresa, pera) jam; (de cítricos) marmalade
mero ADJ mere; **la mera idea** the very idea; M grouper
merodear VI to loiter
mes M month
mesa F (mueble) table; (consejo) board; (formación geológica) mesa; — **de noche** nightstand; **levantar la —** to clear the table; **poner la —** to set the table
mesada F monthly allowance
mesero -ra M waiter; F waitress
meseta F plateau
mesón M inn, lodge
mesonero -ra MF innkeeper
mestizo -za ADJ (persona de raza mezclada) *pey* half-breed; (perros) mongrel; MF (de raza mezclada) *pey* half-breed; (mezcla de europeo e india) mestizo; (perro de raza mezclada) mongrel
mesura F moderation
mesurado ADJ (persona, opinión) moderate;

(respuesta) measured
meta F (objetivo) goal; (en una carrera) finish line
metabólico ADJ metabolic
metabolismo M metabolism
metafísica F metaphysics
metafísico ADJ metaphysical
metáfora F metaphor
metafórico ADJ metaphorical
metal M metal; — **precioso** precious metal
metálico ADJ metallic; M cash
metalurgia F metallurgy
metamorfosis F metamorphosis
metano M methane
metástasis F metastasis
metastatizar VI to metastasize
meteorito M meteorite
meteoro M meteor
meteorología F meteorology
meteorológico ADJ meteorological; **parte —** weather report
meteorólogo -ga M weatherman; F weatherwoman
meter VT (en una bolsa) to put [into], to stick [into]; (un lío) to force [into]; (invertir) to invest; — **el estómago** to suck in one's stomach; — **la pata** to make a mistake; — **miedo** to scare; — **ruido** to make noise; — **un gol** to score a goal; **—se** to meddle; **—se a bailar** to begin to dance; **—se con** to mess with; **—se en camisa de once varas** to get oneself into a fix
metódico ADJ methodical
método M method
metodología F methodology
metralleta F portable machine gun
métrico ADJ metric
metro M (medida, ritmo poético) meter; (cinta de medir) measuring tape; (tren subterráneo) subway, metro
metrónomo M metronome
metrópoli F metropolis
metropolitano ADJ metropolitan; M subway
mexicano -na ADJ & MF Mexican
México M Mexico
mezcla F (de ingredientes) mixture, mix; (en albañilería) mortar; (de café, especias) blend
mezclador -ora MF (persona) mixer; F (aparato) mixer
mezclar VT (ingredientes) to mix, to blend; (naipes) to shuffle; (números) to scramble; **—se** (combinarse) to mix; (tener trato con) to mingle; (entrometerse) to meddle
mezcolanza F hodgepodge
mezquindad F (crueldad) meanness; (tacañería) stinginess
mezquino ADJ (cruel) mean, mean-spirited, petty; (insignificante) small, petty; (tacaño) tight, stingy

mezquita F mosque
mi ADJ POS my
mí PRON PERS me; **es para —** it's for me; **me vio a —** he saw me; **me la dio a —** he gave it to me
miau M meow
mico M long-tailed monkey
micra F micron
micro M (autobús) bus; (micrófono) microphone
microbio M microbe, germ
microbiología F microbiology
microcirugía F microsurgery
microcomputadora F microcomputer
microeconomía F microeconomics
microficha F microfiche
microfilm M microfilm
micrófono M microphone
Micronesia F Micronesia
micronesio -sia ADJ & MF Micronesian
microonda F microwave; M SG **—s** microwave oven
microordenador M microcomputer
microorganismo M microorganism
microprocesador M microprocessor
microscópico ADJ microscopic
microscopio M microscope; **— electrónico** electron microscope
mida, mide, midiendo, midiera, midiese ver medir
miedo M fear; **— al escenario** stage fright; **tener —** to be afraid
miedoso ADJ fearful
miel F honey
miembro M (integrante) member; (extremidad) limb; **— viril** penis
mienta, miente ver mentir
mientras CONJ (durante) while, as; (siempre y cuando) as long as; **— que** while; **— tanto** meanwhile; ADV in the meantime
miércoles M Wednesday
mierda F (excremento) vulg shit, crap; (droga) vulg shit; (persona o cosa despreciable) vulg piece of shit, piece of crap; **una — de coche** vulg a crappy/shitty car; **mandar a alguien a la —** vulg to tell somebody to go to hell; **¡—! ¡vete a la —!** vulg shit! go fuck yourself!
mies F grain; **—es** fields of grain
miga F crumb; **hacer buenas —s** to get along well
migaja F crumb
migración F migration
migrante ADJ migrant
migraña F migraine
migrar VI to migrate
migratorio ADJ migratory
mil NUM thousand; **— millones** billion; **llegamos a las — y quinientas** we got there very late
milagro M miracle, wonder

milagroso ADJ miraculous
milano M kite
milenio M millennium
milicia F militia
miligramo M milligram
mililitro M milliliter
milímetro M millimeter
militancia F (actitud) militance; (actitud) militancy
militante ADJ & MF militant
militar ADJ military; MF soldier; VI to militate
milla F mile
millaje M mileage
millar M thousand
millón M million
millonario -ria MF millionaire
millonésimo ADJ & M millionth
mimar VT to pamper, to spoil, to coddle
mimbre M wicker
mímico ADJ mimic; F mimicry
mimo M (trato cariñoso) caressing, cuddling; MF (actor) mime
mimoso ADJ cuddly
mina F (yacimiento) mine; (explosivo) [land] mine; (de un lápiz) lead; (fuente) storehouse
minado M mining
minar VT (sembrar minas) to mine; (socavar) to undermine; VI (cavar) to burrow
mineral M mineral; (de oro) ore; ADJ mineral
minería F mining
minero -ra MF miner; ADJ mining
mingitorio M urinal
miniatura F miniature
mini-break M (tenis) mini-break
minicomputadora F minicomputer
minifalda F miniskirt
minifundio M subsistence farm
minimizar[47] VT (gastos) to minimize; (a una persona) to belittle; VI (un incidente) to play down
mínimo ADJ (cantidad) least; (tamaño) smallest; M minimum; **como —** at least; **en lo más —** at all
minino M kitty
miniordenador M minicomputer
ministerial ADJ cabinet, ministerial
ministerio M (religioso) ministry; (gubernamental) ministry, department
ministro -tra MF minister, secretary; **— de justicia** attorney general
minoría F minority
minoridad F minority
minorista MF retailer
minoritario ADJ minority
mintiendo, mintiera, mintiese, mintió ver mentir
minucioso ADJ (detalle) minute; (trabajo) thorough; (persona) fastidious
minúsculo ADJ (tamaño) small, minuscule;

(cantidad) negligible; **letra minúscula** lowercase letter
minusvalía F disability
minusválido -da ADJ disabled; MF disabled person
minutas F (honorarios) lawyers' fees; (actas) minutes
minutero M minute hand
minuto M minute
mío ADJ & PRON mine; **este libro es —** this book is mine; **un amigo —** a friend of mine
miope ADJ shortsighted, nearsighted
miopía F nearsightedness, myopia
mira F (dispositivo de arma) gun sight; (intención) intention; **con —s a** with a view to
mirada F gaze, look; **— asesina** dirty look; **— de soslayo** side glance; **— fija** stare
mirador M vantage point, overlook
miramiento M consideration
mirar VI/VT to look [at]; (un partido, televisión) to watch; **— de soslayo** to look askance [at]; **— fijamente** to stare [at]; **¡mira [tú]!** you don't say!
miríada F myriad
mirilla F peephole
mirlo M blackbird
mirón M (curioso) onlooker; (erótico) voyeur
mirto M myrtle
misa F mass
misantropía F misanthropy
misántropo -pa MF misanthrope
misceláneo ADJ miscellaneous
miserable ADJ (vil, pobre) wretched, unhappy; (insignificante) paltry; (tacaño) miserly
miseria F (desgracia) misery; (pobreza) poverty, squalor; (cantidad despreciable) trifle
misericordia F mercy
misericordioso ADJ merciful, gracious
mísero ADJ miserable
misil M missile; **— balístico** ballistic missile; **— crucero** cruise missile
misión F mission (también religiosa)
misionero -ra MF missionary
mismo ADJ same; **ese — día** that very day; **se nombró a sí —** he named himself; **lo —** the same thing; **me da lo —** it's all the same to me; **yo —** I myself
misoginia F misogyny
misterio M mystery
misterioso ADJ mysterious
místico -ca ADJ mystical; MF mystic
mitad F half; **por la —** in half; **en la — de** in the middle of; **a — de[l] camino** midway
mítico ADJ mythic, mythical
mitigar[40] VT to mitigate
mitin M political meeting
mito M myth
mitocondria F mitochondria

mitología F mythology
mitológico ADJ mythological
mixto ADJ mixed; **escuela mixta** coed school
mobiliario M furniture
mocasín M (zapatilla, culebra) moccasin; (zapato sin cordones) loafer
mochar VT to chop off
mochila F backpack, knapsack
moción F motion
moco M (interno) mucus; (líquido) *fam* snot; (sólido) *fam* booger
mocoso -sa ADJ snotty; MF *fam* brat, punk
moda F fashion; **de —** fashionable, in style; **ponerse de —** to catch on
modales M PL manners
modalidad F form, variant; **ganó oro en la — de espalda** she won gold in the backstroke; **la — italiana es más conocida** the Italian form is better known
Moldavia F Moldova
modelar VI/VT to model
modelo ADJ & MF model
módem M modem
moderación F moderation, restraint
moderado -da ADJ (posición política) moderate; (invierno) mild; (precio) reasonable; (respuesta) measured; (clima) temperate; MF moderate
moderar VT (restringir) to moderate, to restrain; (presidir) to moderate
modernidad F (actualidad) modern age; (actualidad) modern world
modernismo M (cualidad de moderno) modernity, modernness; (tendencia artística) modernism
modernización F modernization
moderno ADJ modern
modestia F modesty
modesto ADJ modest
módico ADJ moderate, reasonable
modificación F modification
modificar[30] VT to modify
modismo M idiom
modista MF dressmaker
modo M (manera) mode, manner, way; (categoría gramatical) mood; (de computadora/ordenador) mode; **— a prueba de fallos/errores** safe mode; **— de ahorro** power-save mode; **— de dormir** sleep mode; **— de entrega** mode of delivery; **— de reescritura** overwrite mode; **a — de** by way of; **del mismo —** in like manner, similarly; **de ningún —** by no means; **de — que** so that; **de otro —** otherwise; **de ningún —** not at all; **de todos —s** anyway; **en cierto —** in a way; **ni —** no dice; **no hay —** no way
modorra F drowsiness
modulación F modulation
modular VT to modulate

módulo M (componente) module; (unidad) unit
mofa F jeer, ridicule
mofarse VI — dc to make fun of, to scoff at
mofeta F skunk
moflete M fat cheek, jowl
mohair M mohair
mohín M grimace
moho M mold, mildew
mohoso ADJ moldy
mojado -da ADJ wet; MF (inmigrante ilegal) *pey* wetback
mojadura F wetting
mojar VT (humedecer) to wet; (sumergir) to dip; —**se** to get wet; *vulg* to get laid
mojigatería F prudery
mojigato -ta ADJ prudish; MF prude
mojo M dip
mojón M (hito) landmark; (zurullo) turd
molar ADJ molar
moldavo -va ADJ & MF Moldovan
molde M (norma) mold, cast; (tortera) cake pan; (patrón) pattern; (de imprenta) die; **letras de** — block letters
moldeado M molding
moldear VT to mold, to cast
moldura F molding
mole F mass
molécula F molecule
molecular ADJ molecular
moler[6] VI/VT to mill, to grind; — **a palos** to beat thoroughly
molestar VT to bother, to pester; **no te molestes** don't bother
molestia F bother, nuisance; **no te tomes la** — don't go to the trouble
molesto ADJ (que molesta) bothersome, irksome; (que está molesto) uneasy, uncomfortable
molibdeno M molybdenum
molienda F grinding
molinero -ra MF miller
molinete M (puerta) turnstile; (juguete) pinwheel
molinillo M mill, grinder
molino M mill; — **de viento** windmill
mollete M muffin
molusco M mollusk
momentáneo ADJ momentary
momento M (tiempo) moment; (impulso) momentum; **al** — immediately; **a cada** — continually; **en todo** — all the time; **no veo el** — I can't wait
momia F mummy
Mónaco M Monaco
monada F (acción graciosa) antic; (persona atractiva) *fam* peach
monarca MF monarch
monarquía F monarchy
monárquico -ca MF monarchist; ADJ

monarchical
monasterio M monastery
mondar VT to pare; —**se los dientes** to pick one's teeth; M SG **mondadientes** toothpick
moneda F (dinero metálico) coin; (divisa) currency; — **corriente** common currency; — **de curso legal** legal tender; — **falsa** counterfeit money
monegasco -ca ADJ & MF Monegasque
monería F antic
monetario ADJ monetary
mongol -la ADJ & MF Mongolian
Mongolia F Mongolia
mongoloide ADJ mongoloid
monigote M puppet
monitor -ora M (aparato) monitor; — **[a] color** color monitor; MF (persona) monitor
monitorear VT to monitor
monitoreo M monitoring
monitorización F monitoring; — **fetal** fetal monitoring
monja F nun
monje M monk
mono -na MF (simio) monkey; — **araña** spider monkey; M (mimo) mimic; (prenda de trabajo) overalls, coverall; (síndrome de abstinencia) withdrawal symptoms; **dormir la mona** to sleep it off; ADJ cute
monogamia F monogamy
monokini M topless swimsuit
monólogo M monologue, monolog
mononucleosis F mononucleosis
monopatín M (tabla) skateboard; (con manillar) scooter; (de nieve) snowboard
monopolio M monopoly
monopolizar[47] VT (un producto) to monopolize; (un mercado) to corner
monotonía F monotony
monótono ADJ monotonous
monseñor M monsignor
monserga F nonsense
monstruo M (ser imaginario, persona perversa) monster; (persona grotesca) freak; ADJ INV monstrous
monstruosidad F monstrosity
monstruoso ADJ monstrous
monta F mount; **de poca** — of little value
montaje M (de un aparato) assembly, set up; (de una película) editing
montante M (total) total; (ventana de puerta) transom; (columna) upright
montaña F mountain; — **rusa** roller coaster
montañés -esa ADJ mountain; MF mountain dweller
montañismo M mountaineering
montañoso ADJ mountainous
montar VT (ir a caballo, en bicicleta) to ride; (un aparato) to assemble; (una película) to edit; (subirse al caballo) to mount, to get on; — **en**

cólera to fly into a rage; — **una escena** to make a scene; —**se a caballo** to mount a horse

montaraz ADJ coarse

monte M (montaña) mount; (zona agreste) wilderness; — **de piedad** pawnshop

montés ADJ (salvaje) wild; (de la montaña) of the mountains

montículo M mound; (béisbol) pitcher's mound

monto M amount; — **debido** amount due; — **pagado** amount paid

montón M (pila) pile, heap; (de papel) stack; (de nieve) drift; (de flores) basketful; (de gente) bunch; **a montones** in abundance; **del —** run-of-the-mill

montura F (animal) mount; (silla) saddle; (armazón de gafas) frame, rim

monumental ADJ monumental

monumento M monument

moño M (de pelo) bun; (adorno) bow

mopa F mop

moquearse VI to become snotty

moquillo M distemper

MOR [movimentos oculares rápidos] M PL REM

mora F (fruta) blackberry, mulberry; (tardanza) delay, delinquency; **en —** in default, past due

morada F dwelling, abode

morado ADJ purple; **ojo —** black eye

morador -ora MF dweller

moral ADJ moral; F (principios éticos) morals; (estado de ánimo) morale; M mulberry tree

moraleja F moral

moralidad F morality

moralista MF moralist

moralizar[47] VI/VT to moralize

morar VI to dwell, to abide

mórbido ADJ morbid

morbilidad F (predisposición a la enfermadad) morbidity

morbosidad F (que produce enfermedad) morbidity

morboso ADJ (mórbido) morbid; (atractivo) sexy

morcilla F blood sausage

mordacidad F sharpness

mordaz ADJ (comentario) cutting, sharp; (persona) sharp-tongued

mordaza F (de la boca) gag; (de un torno) vise jaw

mordedor ADJ biting, snappy

mordedura F bite

morder[6] VI/VT to bite; —**se la lengua** to bite one's tongue

mordida F (mordisco) bite; (soborno) bribe, kickback

mordiscar[30] VI/VT to nibble; to nip

mordisco M nibble, nip

mordisquear VI/VT to nip; to nibble

mordisqueo M nibble

moreno ADJ (piel) dark, dark-skinned, swarthy; (pelo) dark, brunette

moretón M bruise

morfina F morphine

morgue F morgue

moribundo ADJ dying, moribund

morir[7, 74] VI (persona, animal) to die; (calle) to end; —**se de envidia** to eat one's heart out; —**se de hambre** to starve; —**se de miedo** to die of fear; —**se de risa** to die laughing; —**se por algo** to crave something; —**se por alguien** to be crazy about someone

morisco ADJ Moorish

moro -ra ADJ Moorish; MF Moor; —**s y cristianos** (personas) Moors and Christians; (plato) beans and rice; **no hay —s en la costa** the coast is clear

morocho ADJ dark-haired, brunet, brunette

moroso ADJ delinquent, deadbeat

morrear VI to make out

morriña F homesickness

morro M (monte) knoll; (caradura) gall, nerve; (de un avión) nose; (de animal) snout

morrón M bell pepper

morsa F walrus

mortaja F shroud

mortal ADJ mortal, deadly; MF mortal

mortalidad F mortality

mortandad F death toll

mortecino ADJ fading

mortero M mortar

mortífero ADJ deadly

mortificación F mortification, chagrin

mortificar[30] VT to mortify, to chagrin

mortuorio ADJ mortuary; **casa mortuaria** funeral home

mosaico M mosaic

mosca F (insecto) fly; (dinero) dough; — **muerta** hypocrite; **no se oía volar una —** you could have heard a pin drop

mosquear VT (crear desconfianza) to cause distrust; (hacer enfadar) to enrage; —**se** (desconfiar) to distrust; (enfadarse) to become enraged

mosquitero M (pantalla de ventana) window screen; (red) mosquito net

mosquito M mosquito

mostacho M mustache, moustache

mostaza F mustard

mostrador M counter

mostrar[5] VT to show; —**se reticente** to appear reticent

mostrenco ADJ stray

mota F speck, speckle

mote M nickname

moteado ADJ speckled, spotted

motear VT to speck, to speckle

motejar VI — **de** to brand as

motel M motel

motín M (en un barco) mutiny; (de prisioneros) riot

motivación F motivation

motivar VT (impulsar) to motivate; (causar) to cause

motivo M (causa) motive, reason; (figura repetida) motif, theme; **con — de** on the occasion of

moto F bike, motorcycle

motocicleta F motorcycle

motociclista MF biker, motorcyclist

motor ADJ of motion; M motor, engine; **— de reacción** jet engine; **— de búsqueda** search engine; **— de combustión interna** internal combustion engine; **— fuera de borda** outboard engine

motriz ADJ **fuerza —** motive power

movedizo ADJ restless

mover[6] VT to move; **— palancas** to pull strings; **—se** to move, to budge

movible ADJ movable

movido ADJ (vida, fiesta) eventful; (foto) blurred; **— por gas** powered by gas

móvil M (motivo) motive; (teléfono) mobile telephone; (adorno, juguete) mobile; ADJ (que se mueve) mobile; (que puede ser movido) movable; **un blanco —** a moving target

movilidad F mobility

movilización F mobilization

movilizar[47] VI/VT to mobilize

movimiento M (cambio de posición) movement, motion; (organización, pieza de reloj) movement; (comercial) traffic; **—s oculares rápidos** REM [rapid eye movements]; **los rojos tienen poco —** the red ones don't sell well; **un cuerpo en —** a moving body

Mozambique M Mozambique

mozambiqueño -ña ADJ & MF Mozambican

mozárabe ADJ Mozarabic

mozo -za ADJ young; **en mis años —s** in my youth; M (joven) young man; (sirviente) servant; F (joven) young woman; (sirvienta) servant; **— de cordel** porter; **buen —** handsome man

mucama F chambermaid

muchacho -cha M boy, youngster; F (chica) girl; (de servicio) maid

muchedumbre F crowd, throng

mucho ADJ a lot of; (cosas contables) many; (cosas incontables, en oraciones interrogativas y/o negativas) much; **¿tienes — tiempo?** do you have much time? **no tenemos — tiempo** we don't have much time; **tenemos —s problemas** we have many problems; ADV much; (demasiado) too much; **hace — que no lo veo** I haven't seen

him for a long time; **ni con —** not by a long shot; **ni — menos** not by any means; **por — que** no matter how much; PRON a lot, many; (en preguntas y oraciones negativas) much; **¿había —s?** were there many?

mucoso ADJ mucous

muda F (de ropa, voz) change; (de plumas, piel de serpiente) molt

mudable ADJ fickle

mudanza F move

mudar VT (condiciones, clima) to change; (el pelo) to shed; (la piel, plumas) to molt; **—se [de casa]** to move [house]; **—se de ropa** to change clothes

mudez F dumbness, muteness

mudo -da ADJ (incapaz de hablar) mute, dumb; (por emoción) speechless; (película) silent; MF mute

mueble M piece of furniture; **—s** furniture

mueblería F (tienda) furniture store; (fábrica) furniture factory

mueca F grimace; **hacer —s** to grimace

muela F (diente) molar tooth; (piedra) grindstone; **— del juicio** wisdom tooth; **— impactada** impacted molar

muelle M (para embarcaciones) wharf, pier; (resorte) spring; **— en espiral** coil; **— real** mainspring

muera, muere ver morir

muérdago M mistletoe

muerte F death; **— cerebral** brain death; **— súbita** (fútbol) sudden death; (tenis) tie-break; **dar —** to kill; **sus clases son la —** his classes are unbearable; **de mala —** disreputable

muerto ADJ dead, lifeless; **— de cansancio** dead tired; **— de hambre** famished; **estoy — de sed** I'm parched; **echarle el — a uno** to pass the buck; **ni —** not in a million years

muerto ver morir

muesca F notch, indentation

muestra F (ejemplo) sample (también en computadoras); (señal) sign, token; **— de orina** urine specimen; **dar —s de impaciencia** to show impatience

muestra, muestre ver mostrar

muestrear VT to sample (también para computadoras)

muestreo M sampling

mueva, mueve ver mover

mugido M moo, lowing

mugir[46] VI to moo, to low

mugre F dirt, grime, crud

mugriento ADJ grimy, dirty

mujer F (género) woman; (esposa) wife; **— de negocios** businesswoman; **— de la vida** prostitute

mujeriego ADJ womanizing; M womanizer, *fam* player

mujerzuela F *pey* slut
mula *ver* mulo
mulato -ta ADJ & MF mulatto
muleta F crutch
muletilla F cliché
mullido ADJ fluffy
mullir[16] VT to fluff
mulo -la MF mule (también en el tráfico de drogas)
multa F fine, penalty; (de tránsito) ticket
multar VT to fine; (en tránsito) to ticket
multianual ADJ multiyear
multicultural ADJ multicultural
multilateral ADJ multilateral
multimedia M & ADJ INV multimedia
multipantalla ADJ multiscreen
múltiple ADJ multiple
multiplicación F multiplication
multiplicar[30] VI/VT to multiply; **—se** to breed
multiplicidad F multiplicity
múltiplo M multiple
multitarea F multitasking
multitud F multitude, throng
mundano ADJ mundane, worldly
mundial ADJ global, worldwide; **la guerra —** the world war
mundo M world; **todo el —** everybody; **tener — to** be worldly; **el tercer —** the third world; **el — al revés** the world upside-down
munición F ammunition, munition
municipal ADJ municipal; **servicios —es** city services
municipalidad F municipality
municipio M municipality; (ayuntamiento) city hall
muñeca F (juguete) doll; (articulación del brazo) wrist; **— de trapo** ragdoll
muñeco M (juguete) boy doll; (de ventrílocuo) dummy; **— de nieve** snowman
muñón M stump
mural ADJ & M mural
muralla F wall
murciélago M bat
muriendo, muriera, muriese *ver* morir
murmullo M (voz baja) murmur; (ruido de agua) babble
murmuración F gossip
murmurar VI/VT (voz) to murmur; VI (agua) to babble
muro M wall; **— de contención** retaining wall
murria F the blues; **tener —** to have the blues
musa F muse
musaraña F shrew
muscular ADJ muscular
músculo M muscle
musculoso ADJ muscular
muselina F muslin
museo M museum
musgo M moss

musgoso ADJ mossy
música F music; **— de cámara** chamber music; **— folclórica** folk music; **— incidental** incidental music
musical ADJ & M musical
músico -ca ADJ musical; MF musician
musitar VI to mutter
muslo M thigh
mustio ADJ (triste) sad, humble; (marchito) limp; (deslucido) faded
musulmán -ana ADJ & MF Muslim, Moslem
mutación F mutation
mutante ADJ & MF mutant
mutilar VT to mutilate, to mangle; (a un ser vivo) to maim, to mutilate; (una estatua) to deface
mutuo ADJ mutual
muy ADV very; **estás — grande para eso** you're too big for that
Myanmar M Myanmar

Nn

nabo M turnip
nácar M mother-of-pearl
nacarado ADJ pearly
nacer[35] VI (un bebé) to be born; (una calle) to begin; **— de** (río) to spring from; **— de nuevo** to have a new lease on life
naciente ADJ (tendencia) incipient; (sol) rising; M (de río) origin
nacimiento M (alumbramiento) birth; (pesebre) nativity scene; (naciente) origin [of a river]; **— del pelo** hairline
nación F nation
nacional ADJ & MF national
nacionalidad F nationality
nacionalismo M nationalism
nacionalista ADJ & MF nationalist
nacionalizar[47] VT to nationalize
nada PRON nothing; *fam* squat, zilch; **— del otro mundo** nothing special; **— en absoluto** nothing at all; **como si —** as if nothing had happened; **de —** you are welcome, don't mention it; **no es por —, pero** I hope you don't mind my saying this, but; **no sirve para —** it's useless; **no tener — que ver con** to have nothing to do with; **no tengo — de dinero** I don't have any money; **para —** in the least; **quedar en la —** to fall through; **salir de la —** to come out of nowhere; ADV not at all; **no me gusta [para] —** I don't like it at all; (tenis) **quince a —** forty love; F (existencial) nothingness
nadador -ora MF swimmer

nadar VI/VT to swim; — **en la abundancia** to be in the lap of luxury
nadería F trifle, nothing
nadie PRON nobody; — **más** no one else; **no vi a** — **en el parque** I didn't see anyone in the park; **un don** — a nobody
nafta F gasoline
nailon M nylon
naipe M playing card
nalgada F smack on the bottom
nalgas F PL buttocks
Namibia F Namibia
namibio -bia ADJ & MF Namibian
nana F (canción de cuna) lullaby; (lastimadura) boo-boo; (niñera) babysitter
nanosegundo M nanosecond
nanotecnología F nanotechnology
napalm M napalm
napias F PL *fam* snout
naranja F (fruta) orange; ADJ INV & M (color) orange; — **de ombligo** navel orange; **mi media** — my better half
naranjal M orange grove
naranjo M orange tree
narcisismo M narcissism
narciso M narcissus, daffodil
narcolepsia F narcolepsy
narcótico ADJ & M narcotic
narcotizar[47] VT to drug
narcotraficante MF drug trafficker
narcotráfico M drug trafficking
nariz F nose; — **chata** pug nose; **sonarse la** — to blow one's nose; F PL **narices** nostrils; **se dio de narices contra la ventana** he bumped his nose on the window; **estoy hasta las narices** I've had it up to here
narración F narration
narrador -ora MF narrator
narrar VT to narrate, to recount
narrativa F narrative
narrativo ADJ narrative
NASA F NASA
nasal ADJ nasal
nata F skin of boiled milk; *Esp* cream
natación F swimming
natal ADJ (relativo al nacimiento) natal; (suelo) native; **mi ciudad** — my hometown
natalidad F birth rate
natilla[s] F SG/PL custard
nativo -va ADJ & MF native
nato ADJ **es un músico** — he's a born musician
natural ADJ (no artificial) natural; (nacido en un lugar) native; (nacido fuera del matrimonio) illegitimate; (sin afectación) unaffected; M nature; **al** — unprocessed
naturaleza F nature; — **muerta** still life
naturalidad F naturalness
naturalista MF naturalist
naturalización F naturalization

naturalizar[47] VT to naturalize; —**se** to become naturalized
naturalmente ADV (de forma natural) naturally; (desde luego) of course
naufragar[40] VI (un barco) to shipwreck; (una empresa) to fail
naufragio M shipwreck
náufrago -ga MF shipwrecked person
Nauru M Nauru
nauruano -na ADJ & MF Nauruan
náusea F nausea; —**s** morning sickness; **dar** —**s** to nauseate; **hasta la** — ad nauseam; **tener** —**s** to be nauseated, to be sick to one's stomach
nauseabundo ADJ nauseating
nauseoso ADJ (que siente náuseas) nauseous, queasy; (que provoca náuseas) nauseating
náutica F navigation
náutico ADJ nautical
navaja F (de explorador) jackknife, pocketknife; (de barbero) razor
navajazo M (golpe) stab with a jackknife; (herida) stab wound
naval ADJ naval
navarro ADJ & MF Navarrese
nave F (embarcación) vessel; (parte de una catedral) nave; — **espacial** spaceship
navegable ADJ navigable
navegación F (de mar, río) navigation; (deportiva) boating; (en internet) surfing, browsing
navegador M browser; — **web** web browser
navegante MF navigator; ADJ navigating
navegar[40] VI/VT (buque) to navigate; (barco a vela) to sail; (en internet) to browse, to surf
Navidad F Christmas
navideño ADJ **fiesta navideña** Christmas party
navío M ship
nazi MF Nazi
neblina F mist
neblinoso ADJ misty
nebulosidad F cloudiness
nebuloso ADJ (poco claro) nebulous; (que tiene niebla) foggy
necesario ADJ necessary
neceser M toiletry bag
necesidad F (urgencia, sensación de falta) need; (cosa necesaria) necessity; **hacer sus** —**es** to relieve oneself; **de primera** — indispensable; **por** — out of necessity
necesitado ADJ needy
necesitar VT to need
necio -cia ADJ asinine, foolish; MF *pey* clod
necrología F necrology
necrosis F necrosis
néctar M nectar
nectarina F nectarine
nefasto ADJ unholy

nefritis F nephritis

negación F (partícula gramatical) negation; (rechazo) denial

negar[41] VT (decir que no es verdad) to deny; (no consentir) to refuse; (no reconocer) to disavow; —**se [a]** to refuse [to]

negativa F (rechazo verbal) denial; (falta de cooperación) refusal

negativo ADJ negative; **signo** — minus sign; M [photographic] negative

negligencia F (falta de atención) negligence, neglect; (médica) malpractice

negligente ADJ negligent, neglectful

negociación F negotiation; — **laboral** collective bargaining

negociador -ora MF negotiator; ADJ negotiating

negociante MF businessperson

negociar VI/VT (acordar) to negotiate; (comerciar) to trade

negocio M (tienda, actividad comercial) business; (transacción) business deal, business transaction; — **de ventas por correo** mail-order business; — **principal** core business; **hombre de —s** businessman; **mujer de —s** businesswoman; **hacer** — to make a profit

negrear VI to appear black; VT to blacken

negrilla F boldface

negritas F PL boldface type

negro -ra ADJ black (también café sin leche); (futuro) bleak; **pasarlas negras** to undergo hardships; F (nota) quarter-note; MF (persona) person of color, black person

negrura F blackness

negruzco ADJ blackish

némesis F nemesis

nene -na M baby boy; F baby girl

nenúfar M water lily

neologismo M neologism

neón M neon

neonatal ADJ neonatal

neozelandés -esa MF New Zealander

Nepal M Nepal

nepalés -esa ADJ & MF Nepali

nepalí ADJ & MF Nepalese

nepotismo M nepotism

nervado ADJ veined

nervio M nerve; — **pellizcado** pinched nerve; — **pinzado** pinched nerve; **perder los —s** to lose one's cool; **tener los —s de punta** to be on edge

nerviosismo M nervousness

nervioso ADJ (relativo a los nervios) nervous; (inquieto) nervous, jumpy

nervudo ADJ sinewy, wiry

neto ADJ (mejoría) distinct; (ganancia) net

neumático M tire; ADJ pneumatic

neural ADJ neural

neuralgia F neuralgia

neurastenia F neurasthenia

neurocirugía F neurosurgery

neurocirujano -na MF neurosurgeon

neurólogo -ga MF neurologist

neurona F neuron, nerve cell

neurosis F neurosis

neurótico -ca ADJ & MF neurotic

neurotransmisor M neurotransmitter

neutral ADJ neutral

neutralidad F neutrality

neutralizar[47] VT to neutralize

neutro ADJ neutral; (género) neuter

neutrón M neutron

nevada F snowfall

nevado ADJ snowy

nevar[1] VI to snow

nevera F icebox, refrigerator

nevisca F snow flurry

ni CONJ & ADV — **con mucho** not by a long shot; — **hablar** forget it; — **habló conmigo** he didn't even talk to me; — **idea** [it] beats me; — **modo** no way; — **que esto fuera un hotel** it's not like this is a hotel; — **siquiera** not even; — **soñar** fat chance; — **trabaja estudia** he neither works nor studies; — **una palabra** not a word; **no tiene amigos — enemigos** he has no friends nor enemies; **no es rico — mucho menos** he's not even close to being rich

Nicaragua F Nicaragua

nicaragüense ADJ & MF Nicaraguan

nicho M niche, recess

nicotina F nicotine

nidada F (huevos) nest of eggs; (crías) hatch, brood

nido M nest

niebla F fog

niega, niegue ver negar

nieto -ta M grandson; F granddaughter; —**s** grandchildren

nieve F snow (también droga en polvo)

Níger M Niger

Nigeria F Nigeria

nigeriano -na ADJ & MF Nigerian

nigerino -na ADJ & MF Nigerien

nigua F chigger

nihilismo M nihilism

nilón M nylon

nimio ADJ insignificant

ninguno ADJ & PRON **no tengo** — I have none / I don't have any; **ningún amigo mío** no friend of mine; **no tengo ningún libro** I don't have any books; — **de los dos** neither one; **de ningún modo** in no way

niñera F (ocasional) babysitter; (permanente) nanny

niñería F childish act

niñez F (infancia) childhood; (de niño) boyhood;

(de niña) girlhood
niño -ña M child, kid, boy; F child, kid, girl;
    niña del ojo pupil [of the eye]; ADJ childish
níquel M nickel
niquelado ADJ nickel-plated
níspero M loquat
nitidez F sharpness
nítido ADJ sharp
nitrato M nitrate
nitrógeno M nitrogen
nitroglicerina F nitroglycerine
nivel M level (también herramienta); (grado
    jerárquico) echelon; — **de cobertura**
    coverage level; — **de mar** sea level; — **de**
    vida standard of living; **a** — straight; **a** — **de**
    level with
nivelar VT (emparejar) to level; (aplanar) to
    grade
níveo ADJ snowy
no ADV no; — **quiero** I don't want to; —
    acreditado unlicensed; — **afiliado**
    unaffiliated; — **ajustado** unadjusted; —
    autorizado unauthorized; — **comercial**
    noncommercial; — **confirmado**
    unconfirmed; — **conforme** nonconforming;
    — **declarado** undeclared; — **disponible**
    unavailable; — **divulgado** undisclosed; —
    esencial nonessential; — **especificado**
    unspecified; — **ético** unethical; —
    gubernamental nongovernmental; —
    negociable nonnegotiable; —
    reembolsable nonrefundable; —
    relacionado unrelated; — **residente**
    nonresident; — **restringido** unrestricted; —
    solicitado unsolicited; — **tributable**
    nontaxable; — **bien llegaron** no sooner had
    they arrived; — **sólo** not only; — **sea que**
    lest; **a** — **ser que** unless
noble ADJ noble; M nobleman; F noblewoman
nobleza F nobility
nocaut M knockout
noche F (período sin luz) night; (horas de la
    noche) nighttime; —**buena** Christmas Eve;
    —**vieja** New Year's Eve; — **y día** day and
    night; **de** — at night; **de la** — **a la mañana**
    overnight; **esta** — tonight; **por la** — at night
noción F notion; **no tener ni** — to have no clue
nocivo ADJ harmful, noxious
nocturno ADJ (que actúa de noche) nocturnal;
    (que sucede todas las noches) nightly
nodo M node
nodriza F wet nurse
nódulo M node
nogal M walnut tree
nómada MF nomad
ningunear VT to dismiss
nomás ADV *Am* **aquí** — close by; **así** — just like
    that; **entre** — come right in
nombramiento M (civil) appointment;

(militar) commission
nombrar VT (a un funcionario) to name, to
    appoint; (a un oficial militar) to commission
nombre M name; — **completo** full name; — **de**
    acceso login name; — **de pila** first name; —
    de soltera maiden name; — **del usuario**
    username; **en** — **de** on behalf of; **eso no**
    tiene — that's unheard of; **hacerse un** — to
    make a name for oneself
nomenclatura F nomenclature
nomeolvides M SG forget-me-not
nómina F payroll
nominación F nomination
nominal ADJ nominal
nominar VT to nominate
non ADJ odd; M odd number
nopal M prickly pear
noquear VT to knock out
norcoreano -na ADJ & MF North Korean
nordeste ADJ & M northeast
nórdico ADJ Nordic
noreste ADJ & M northeast
norma F norm, standard; —**s industriales**
    industry standards
normal ADJ (estándar, común) normal,
    standard; F (escuela) teacher's college; (línea)
    perpendicular line
normalidad F normalcy, normality; **con toda**
    — normally; **todo volvió a la** — everything
    returned to normal
normalizar[47] VT to normalize
normalmente ADV normally, usually
normativa F norm
noroeste ADJ & M northwest
norte ADJ & M north
norteamericano -na ADJ & MF (de América del
    Norte) North American; (de EEUU) American
norteño -ña ADJ northern; MF northerner
Noruega F Norway
noruego -ga ADJ & MF Norwegian; M (lengua)
    Norwegian
nos PRON us; **él** — **vio** he saw us; — **dio el libro**
    he gave us the book, he gave the book to us
nosotros -as PRON we; **para** — for us
nostalgia F nostalgia
nostálgico ADJ nostalgic
nota F (musical) note; (anotación) annotation;
    (calificación) grade, mark; — **al pie de**
    página footnote; **de** — of note; **exagerar la**
    — to overdo something
notable ADJ notable, noteworthy, remarkable
notablemente ADV (destacadamente) notably;
    (visiblemente) noticeably
notación F notation
notar VT (percibir) to note, to notice; (señalar) to
    note
notariar VT to notarize
notario -ria MF notary
noticia F piece of news; —**s** news; **tener** —**s de**

alguien to hear from someone
noticiario M newscast, news bulletin
noticiero M newscast
notificación F (informe) notification; (policial) summons; **— de despido** pink slip
notificar[30] VT to notify
notorio ADJ (conocido públicamente) well-known; (evidente) obvious
novato -ta MF (profesional) novice; (policía, atleta) rookie
novecientos NUM nine hundred
novedad F novelty; **—es** news; **sin —** all's well
novedoso ADJ novel
novela F novel; **— policial** detective novel
novelesco ADJ fictional
novelista MF novelist
noveno ADJ ninth
noventa NUM ninety
noviazgo M engagement
novicio -cia MF novice
noviembre M November
novillo -lla M steer; **hacer —s** to play hooky; F heifer
novio -via M (comprometido) fiancé; (no formal) boyfriend; (de boda) bridegroom; F (comprometida) fiancée; (no formal) girlfriend; (de boda) bride
novocaína F novocaine
nubarrón M thunderhead
nube F (atmosférica) cloud; (de humo) billow; **poner por las —s** to praise to the skies; **está en las —s** his head is in the clouds; **los precios están por las —s** prices have gone through the roof
nublado ADJ (cielo) cloudy, overcast; (los ojos, de emoción) misty; (los ojos, por falta de sueño) bleary
nublar VT to blur; **—se** (el cielo) to become overcast; (los ojos) to cloud over
nubosidad F (de un concepto) nebulousness; (del cielo) cloudiness
nuboso ADJ cloudy
nuca F nape
nuclear ADJ nuclear
núcleo M (de célula, átomo) nucleus; (de reactor) core; (de sistema operativo) kernel
nudillo M knuckle
nudismo M nudism
nudista ADJ & MF nudist
nudo M knot (también en la madera, medida de velocidad); (de una obra teatral) turning point; (en el pelo) tangle; (en plantas) node; (en la garganta) lump; **— corredizo** slipknot; **— de rizo** square knot
nudoso ADJ knotty, gnarled
nuera F daughter-in-law
nuestro ADJ POS our; **— hijo** our son; PRON ours; **esto es —** this is ours
nuevamente ADV again

nueve NUM nine
nuevo ADJ new; **de —** again; **¿qué hay de —?** what's new?
nuez F walnut; **— de Adán** Adam's apple; **— moscada** nutmeg
nulidad F (legal) nullity; (persona) nonentity
nulo ADJ null and void, invalid
numeral ADJ & M numeral
numerar VT to number
numérico ADJ numerical
número M (dígito) number; (en un espectáculo) act; (de una revista) issue; (cifra) figure; **— de serie** serial number
numeroso ADJ numerous
nunca ADV never, not ever; **no viene —** he never comes, he doesn't ever come; **más que —** more than ever; **casi —** hardly ever; **peor que —** worse than ever
nupcial ADJ nuptial, bridal
nupcias F PL nuptials
nutria F otter
nutrición F nutrition
nutrido ADJ **el congreso tuvo una nutrida concurrencia** the conference was well attended
nutriente M nutrient
nutrir VT to nourish
nutritivo ADJ nutritious, nourishing

Ññ

ñandú M rhea
ñato ADJ *Am* pug-nosed
ñoño ADJ bland
ñu M gnu

Oo

o CONJ or; **— se casa — lo mato** either he gets married or I'll kill him; **— sea** that is
oasis M oasis
obedecer[35] VI/VT to obey; **esto obedece a que** this is due to the fact that
obedezca, obedezco *ver* obedecer
obediencia F obedience
obediente ADJ obedient
obertura F musical overture
obesidad F obesity
obeso ADJ obese
obispo M bishop
obituario M obituary

objeción F objection
objetable ADJ objectionable
objetar VI/VT to object, to take exception [to]
objetividad F objectivity
objetivo ADJ objective; M (lente) objective; (meta) aim, objective
objeto M object
oblea F wafer
oblicuo ADJ (inclinado) oblique; (sesgado) biased
obligación F (deber) obligation, duty; (deuda) obligation; (título financiero) bond
obligado ADJ (forzado) forced; (obligatorio) compulsory, obligatory; **me vi — a comprar otro coche** I was forced / had to buy another car
obligar[40] VT to force, to compel, to oblige; **—se [a]** to obligate oneself [to]
obligatorio ADJ obligatory, compulsory
oboe M oboe
obra F (artística, literaria, de construcción) work; (lugar de construcción) construction site; **— maestra** masterpiece; **en —s** under construction
obrar VI to act; **obra en nuestro poder** we acknowledge receipt of
obrero -ra MF worker; ADJ working
obscenidad F obscenity; **—es** filth
obsceno ADJ obscene
obscuridad ver oscuridad
obsequiar VT to present, to give; **me obsequió perfume** he gave me perfume
obsequio M gift
obsequioso ADJ obsequious
observación F (mirada) observation; (comentario) remark
observador -ora MF observer; ADJ observant
observancia F observance
observar VI/VT (mirar) to observe; (hacer un comentario) to remark, to observe
observatorio M observatory
obsesión F obsession
obsesionado ADJ obsessed
obsesionar VT to obsess; **—se con** to obsess over, to be obsessed with
obsesivo-compulsivo ADJ obsessive-compulsive
obstaculizar VT to impede
obstáculo M (impedimento) obstacle, hindrance, impediment; (en carreras) hurdle
obstante LOC PREP **no — tu oposición** notwithstanding your opposition; LOC ADV **no —, voy a ir** nevertheless, I am going to go
obstar VT to preclude
obstetra MF obstetrician
obstetricia F obstetrics
obstinación F obstinacy
obstinado ADJ obstinate, bullheaded
obstinarse VI to be obstinate
obstrucción F (de justicia, de un caño)

obstruction, blockage; (del intestino) obstruction, occlusion; **— intestinal** intestinal obstruction
obstruir[19] VT (un movimiento, procedimiento) to obstruct, to block; (un aparato) to jam; VI **—se** to get jammed
obtención F acquisition
obtendrá, obtendría ver obtener
obtener[58] VT (bienes) to obtain, to get; (permiso) to secure; (con dificultad) to procure
obtenga, obtengo, obtiene, obtienes ver obtener
obturador M (de una cámara fotográfica) shutter; (de un coche) choke
obtuve, obtuviera, obtuviese ver obtener
obviamente ADV obviously
obviar VT to obviate, to circumvent
obvio ADJ obvious
ocasión F (vez, instancia) occasion; (oportunidad) opportunity; (ganga) bargain; **de —** reduced
ocasional ADJ occasional
ocasionar VT to occasion, to cause
ocaso M sunset, twilight
occidental ADJ occidental, western; MF westerner
occidente M west
oceánico ADJ oceanic
océano M ocean
oceanografía F oceanography
ocelote M ocelot
ochenta NUM eighty
ocho NUM eight
ochocientos NUM eight hundred
ocio M (diversión) leisure; (inacción) idleness
ociosidad F idleness
ocioso ADJ (inactivo) idle; (no usado) unused
oclusión F occlusion
octágono M octagon
octano M octane
octava F octave
octavilla F tract
octavo ADJ & M eighth
octeto M byte
octógono M octagon
octubre M October
ocular M eyepiece; ADJ **infección —** eye infection
oculista MF oculist, eye doctor
ocultar VT to conceal; (información) to withhold
ocultismo M the occult
oculto ADJ (invisible) unseen; (sobrenatural) occult; (escondido) hidden, under wraps
ocupación F (trabajo) occupation; (capacidad) occupancy
ocupado ADJ (persona, teléfono) busy; (asiento, aseo) occupied
ocupante MF occupant

ocupar VT (usar) to occupy; (contratar) to employ; **—se de** to take care of, to address
ocurrencia F witticism, quip
ocurrente ADJ witty
ocurrir VI to occur
oda F ode
odiar VI/VT to hate
odio M hatred, hate
odioso ADJ (tarea) odious; (persona) hateful, obnoxious
odontología F dentistry
odre M wineskin
OEA [Organización de Estados Americanos] F OAS
oeste ADJ & M west
ofender VI/VT to offend; **—se** to get offended, to take offense
ofensa F offense
ofensiva F (militar) offensive; (deportiva) offense; (fútbol americano) offensive series
ofensivo ADJ offensive, obnoxious
oferta F (oportunidad) offer; (rebaja) special offer; **— de apertura** opening bid; **en —** on sale; **— de prueba** trial offer; **— pública inicial** initial public offering
offset M offset
oficial -la ADJ official; MF (militar) officer; (obrero calificado) skilled worker; **— general** high-ranking officer
oficialismo M party in power
oficialista ADJ in power
oficiar VI to officiate; **— de** to serve as
oficina F (despacho) office; (dependencia gubernamental) bureau; **— central** home office, headquarters; **— en el hogar** home office
oficinista MF office worker
oficio M (actividad laboral) trade, craft; (comunicación oficial) official communication; **tiene mucho —** he knows his stuff; **buenos —s** good offices
oficioso ADJ (entrometido) officious; (no oficial) unofficial, off-the-record
ofrecer[35] VT (un regalo) to offer; (en una subasta) to bid; (una cena) to give; **— resistencia** to put up resistance; **¿qué se le ofrece a usted?** how can I help you?
ofrecimiento M (acción de ofrecer) offering; (oferta) offer
ofrenda F offering
oftalmólogo -ga MF ophthalmologist
ofuscar[30] VT to bewilder
ogro M ogre
ohmio M ohm
oído M (facultad) hearing; (órgano) inner ear; (musical) ear; **— medio** middle ear; **al —** confidentially; **de —** by ear
oiga, oigo ver **oír**
oír[55] VI/VT (percibir) to hear; (atender) to listen; **— decir que** to hear that; **— hablar de** to hear about; **— misa** to attend mass; **¡oye!** listen! hey!
ojal M buttonhole
ojalá INTERJ **— estuviera aquí** I wish he were here; **— que venga** I hope that he comes
ojeada F glimpse
ojear VT to glimpse
ojera F dark circle under the eye
ojeriza F animosity
ojeroso ADJ with dark circles under the eyes
ojiva F (arco) pointed arch; (explosivo) warhead
ojo M (órgano, centro de huracán, instinto, yema de patata) eye; **¡—!** careful! look out! **a — de buen cubero** as a rule of thumb; **a —s vistas** clearly; **me costó un — de la cara** it cost me an arm and a leg; **¿no tienes —s en la cara?** are you blind? **dichosos los —s que te ven** you're a sight for sore eyes; **— de buey** porthole; **— de la cerradura** keyhole; **— de lince** eagle-eye; **— morado** black eye; **— por —** an eye for an eye
ola F wave; (de un olor) waft; (de protesta) storm
oleada F wave, surge
oleaje M swell, surge
óleo M oil painting
oleoducto M oil pipeline
oleoso ADJ oily
oler[22] VI/VT to smell (también sospechar); **— a** to smell of
olfatear VI/VT to scent, to sniff
olfateo M sniff, sniffing
olfato M (facultad) sense of smell; (instinto) nose
olfatorio ADJ olfactory
olimpíada F Olympiad; **—s** Olympic Games
olímpico ADJ Olympian
oliva F olive
olivar M olive grove
olivo M olive tree
olla F pot; **— de grillos** snake pit; **— podrida** stew of mixed vegetables and meat
olmo M elm
olor M smell, odor
oloroso ADJ odorous
olvidadizo ADJ forgetful
olvidar VI/VT to forget; **—se [de]** to forget; **se me olvidó algo** I forgot something
olvido M oblivion; **caer en el —** to be forgotten; **echar al —** to cast into oblivion; **tus —s** your forgetfulness
Omán M Oman
omaní ADJ & MF Omani
ombligo M navel
OMC [Organización Mundial del Comercio] F WTO
omisión F omission; **por —** by default
omiso ADJ **hacer caso — [de]** to ignore
omitir VT (eliminar) to omit, to leave out; (no notar) to overlook

ómnibus M bus
omnipotente ADJ omnipotent
omnisciencia F omniscience
omnisciente ADJ omniscient
omnívoro ADJ omnivorous
omóplato M scapula
OMS [Organización Mundial de la Salud] F
  WHO
once NUM eleven
oncología F oncology
onda F wave; — **corta** shortwave; — **expansiva**
  shock wave; — **sonora** sound wave;
  agarrarle la — a algo to get in the swing of
  things; **captar la —** to get the drift
ondeado ADJ wavy
ondeante ADJ flying
ondear VI to wave
ondulación F ripple, ruffle, roll
ondulado ADJ (pelo) wavy; (paisaje) rolling
ondulante ADJ undulating
ondular VI to undulate; VI/VT to wave
ónix M onyx
omnipotencia F omnipotence
onomatopeya F onomatopoeia
ONU [Organización de las Naciones Unidas]
  F UN
onza F ounce
opacar[30] VT (oscurecer) to dull; (eclipsar) to
  overshadow
opaco ADJ (no transparente) opaque; (no
  brillante) dull
ópalo M opal
opción F option; **opciones** stock options; — **de**
  venta put option
opcional ADJ optional
OPEP [Organización de Países
  Exportadores de Petróleo] F OPEC
ópera F (composición) opera; (teatro) opera
  house
operable ADJ operable
operación F operation
operador -ora M (en matemáticas) operator; MF
  (de teléfono) operator
operar VI/VT (usar maquinaria) to operate; VT
  (intervenir quirúrgicamente) to operate on;
  (llevar a cabo) to carry out; VI (hacer cuentas)
  to do mathematical operations
operario -ria MF operator, operative
operativo ADJ (que funciona) operative;
  (vigente) in effect; M *Am* — **policial** police
  operation
opiáceo M opiate
opinar VI/VT to hold an opinion, to think
opinión F opinion, view, feeling; **cambiar de**
  — to change one's mind
opio M opium
oponente MF (en un debate) opponent; (en una
  película) costar
oponer[56, 74] VT to oppose; —**se** to conflict; —**se**

a to oppose, to be against
oponga, opongo *ver* oponer
oporto M port wine
oportunidad F (chance) opportunity, chance;
  (pretexto) opening; (fútbol americano) down
oportunista ADJ & MF opportunistic
oportuno ADJ (conveniente) opportune, timely;
  (adecuado) appropriate
oposición F opposition; **oposiciones**
  competitive examinations
opositor -ora MF opponent
opresión F oppression
opresivo ADJ oppressive
opresor -ora MF oppressor
oprimir VT (al pueblo) to oppress; (un botón) to
  press; (un enlace digital) to click
optar VI to choose; — **por** to choose
optativo ADJ optional
óptico -ca ADJ optical; MF optician; F optics
optimismo M optimism
optimista ADJ optimistic; MF optimist
optimizar VT to optimize
óptimo ADJ optimal
optometría F optometry
optometrista MF optometrist
opuesto ADJ opposite, contrary; **se mostró —**
  al casamiento he was against the marriage;
  dos fuerzas opuestas two opposing forces;
  lo — the opposite; **dirección opuesta** the
  opposite/reverse direction
opulencia F opulence
opulento ADJ (decoración) opulent; (sociedad)
  affluent
opuse, opusiera, opusiese *ver* oponer
oración F (frase) sentence; (plegaria) prayer
oráculo M oracle
orador -ora MF orator, speaker
oral ADJ oral
orangután M orangutan
orar VI/VT to pray
oratoria F oratory
oratorio M oratory
órbita F (de los cuerpos celestes) orbit; (de los
  ojos) eye socket
orbitador M orbiter
orbital ADJ orbital
orbitar VI/VT to orbit
orca F killer whale
orden M (limpieza, secuencia) order; —
  ascendente ascending order; — **de**
  clasificación sort order; — **del día** order of
  the day; **perturbar el — público** to disturb
  the peace; **sin — ni concierto** haphazard; F
  (mando) command, order; (grupo religioso)
  order; — **de cateo** warrant; — **de compra**
  purchase order; — **judicial** court order; **a**
  sus órdenes at your service
ordenación F (arreglo) ordering, organization;
  (de un cura) ordination; (informatización)

computerization
ordenado ADJ orderly, neat
ordenador M *Esp* computer; — **de mano** palmtop; — **de sobremesa** desktop computer; — **digital** digital computer; — **portátil** laptop computer; — **torre** tower computer
ordenamiento M (arreglo) ordering, putting in order; (conjunto de leyes) legal code; — **territorial** land use
ordenanza F ordinance; MF orderly
ordenar VT (arreglar) to sort, to put in order; (mandar) to order, to command; (conferir órdenes religiosos) to ordain; —**se** to become ordained
ordeñar VT to milk
ordeño M milking
ordinal ADJ ordinal
ordinariez F vulgarity
ordinario ADJ (corriente) ordinary; (vulgar) vulgar
orear VT to air out
orégano M oregano
oreja F [outer] ear; (de un martillo) claw; (en un utensilio) flap; **aguzar la — ** to prick up one's ears; **sonreír de — a — ** to smile from ear to ear; **estar hasta las —s en algo** to be up to one's neck in something
orejera F earmuff
orfanato M orphanage
orfebre MF (con oro) goldsmith; (con plata) silversmith
orgánico ADJ organic
organigrama M organizational chart, flow chart
organismo M organism
organista MF organist
organización F organization
organizado ADJ organized
organizador -ora MF organizer
organizar[47] VT (una reunión, evento) to organize; (un ataque) to stage; (una fiesta) to give, to throw
organizativo ADJ organizational, organizing
órgano M organ
orgía F orgy
orgullo M pride; **es mi — ** she's my pride and joy
orgulloso ADJ proud
orientación F (vocacional, psicológica) orientation, guidance; (de velas) trim; (de estudios) track; (de un objeto) lie; (del terreno) lay; — **horizontal** landscape; — **vertical** portrait
orientado ADJ oriented; — **al cliente** customer-oriented
oriental ADJ oriental, eastern; MF oriental
orientar VT to orient; —**se** to get one's bearings
oriente M Orient, east
orificio M orifice

origen M origin; (de un problema, conflicto) source; (antecedentes familiares) birth
original ADJ original; M (de una pintura) original; (de una cinta magnética) master
originalidad F originality
originar VT to originate, to give rise to; —**se** to originate, to arise
originario ADJ (original) original; — **de** (de cierto origen) coming from, native of
orilla F (de un lago, mar) shore, bank; (de una cama) edge; (de una prenda) hem
orillar VT (una calle) to border; (una prenda) to hem
orín M rust; M PL **orines** urine
orina F urine
orinal M chamber pot
orinar VI/VT to urinate
oriundo ADJ ser — **de** (persona) to hail from; (cosa) to originate in
orla F (de un uniforme) trimming; (de una alfombra) fringe
orlar VT to fringe
orlón™ M Orlon™
ornamentación F ornamentation
ornamental ADJ ornamental
ornamentar VT to ornament, to embellish
ornamento M ornament
ornar VT to adorn
ornitología F ornithology
oro M gold; — **blanco** white gold; — **en lingotes** gold bullion; — **negro** black gold; — **puro** solid gold; **prometer el — y el moro** to promise the moon
orondo ADJ self-satisfied
oropel M tinsel
oropéndola F oriole
orquesta F orchestra
orquestar VT to orchestrate
orquídea F orchid
ortiga F nettle
ortodoncia F orthodontics
ortodoxo ADJ orthodox
ortografía F orthography, spelling
oruga F caterpillar
orujo M rape
orzuelo M sty
osadía F boldness, daring
osado ADJ bold, daring
osamenta F skeleton
osar VI/VT to dare
oscilación F oscillation
oscilar VI to oscillate, to seesaw; — **entre** to range between
oscurecer VI (ponerse oscuro) to get dark; VT (poner oscuro) to darken; (volver poco inteligible, ocultar) to obscure; —**se** to get darker
oscuridad F (lugar sin luz) dark, darkness; (condición de oscuro) darkness; (falta de

claridad conceptual, anonimato) obscurity
oscuro ADJ (sin luz) dark; (turbio) murky; (poco
claro, poco conocido) obscure; **lentes —s**
dark glasses; **gris —** dark gray; **a oscuras** in
the dark
óseo ADJ bony
osezno M bear cub
osificarse VI to ossify
ósmosis F osmosis
oso -sa M bear; F she-bear; **— blanco/polar**
polar bear; **— hormiguero** anteater
ostentación F ostentation, show, display;
hacer — de to flaunt
ostentar VI/VT to display, to show off, to flaunt
ostentoso ADJ ostentatious, showy
osteoartritis F osteoarthritis
osteoporosis F osteoporosis
ostión M large oyster
ostra F oyster
OTAN [Organización del Tratado del
Atlántico Norte] F NATO
otero M hillock
otitis F otitis; **— externa** swimmer's ear
otoñal ADJ autumnal
otoño M autumn, fall
otorgamiento M grant
otorgar[40] VT (permiso) to grant, to concede;
(premio) to award
otro ADJ (uno adicional) another; (uno diferente)
other; **otra vez** again; **otra cosa** something
else; **— más** another one; **al — día** the next
day; **de — modo** otherwise; **en otra parte**
somewhere else; **la otra cara de la**
moneda the flip side; **por otra parte** on
the other hand; PRON (uno más) another one;
(una persona diferente) someone else; (una
cosa diferente) something else
out ADV & M out; **— forzado** force out
ovación F ovation, acclaim
oval ADJ oval
ovalado ADJ oval
óvalo M oval
ovárico ADJ ovarian
ovario M ovary
oveja F (ovino) sheep; (hembra) ewe
ovejero M sheepdog
overoles M PL overalls
ovillar VT to ball; **—se** to curl up into a ball
ovillo M ball of yarn; **hacerse un —** to curl up
OVNI [objeto volador no identificado] M
UFO
ovoide N egg-shaped
ovulación F ovulation
ovular VI to ovulate
óvulo M egg
oxidación F oxidation, rusting
oxidado ADJ oxidized, rusty
oxidar VI/VT to oxidize, to rust
óxido M (compuesto químico) oxide;

(herrumbre) rust
oxígeno M oxygen
oye, oyendo, oyera, oyese ver oír
oyente MF (que oye) listener, hearer; (alumno
no oficial) auditor
ozono M ozone

Pp

pabellón M (puesto de feria) pavilion; (parte de
un edificio) wing; (bandera) flag; (sección de
hospital) ward; **— de la oreja** outer ear
pabilo M wick
paca F bale
pacana F (fruto) pecan; (árbol) pecan tree
pacer[35] VI to pasture, to graze; VT to crop, to
graze
paciencia F patience; **con —** patiently; **tener —**
to be patient
paciente ADJ & MF patient; **— ambulatorio**
-ria outpatient; **— externo -na** outpatient;
— de alto riesgo high-risk patient
pacificación F pacification
pacificar[30] VT to pacify
pacífico ADJ peaceful; M **Océano Pacífico**
Pacific Ocean
pacifismo M pacifism
pactar VT (hacer un pacto) to make a pact / an
agreement; (decidir de común acuerdo) to
agree; VI **— con el diablo** to sell one's soul to
the devil
pacto M pact, covenant
paddock M (de caballos) paddock; (de coches) pit
padecer[35] VI/VT to suffer; **— de cáncer** to
suffer from cancer
padecimiento M suffering
padezca, padezco ver padecer
padrastro M (marido de la madre) stepfather;
(uñero) hangnail
padre M father; **—s** parents, folks; **— de**
familia male head of the household;
—nuestro the Lord's Prayer; **John Smith,**
— John Smith Sr.; **ser —** to become a father;
ADJ **un lío —** a real mess
padrino M (de bautizo) godfather; (de boda) best
man; (en un duelo) second
paella F paella
paga F (salario) pay; (para un niño) allowance; **—**
de tiempo y medio time-and-a-half pay; **—**
por mérito merit pay
pagadero ADJ payable, due
pagado ADJ paid; **— de sí mismo** self-satisfied
pagador -ora MF payer
paganismo M paganism
pagano -na ADJ & MF pagan

pagar[40] VT (cuentas, deudas) to pay; (préstamo) to pay off; (mercancías) to pay for; —**se de** to be proud of; — **el pato** to be left holding the bag; **pagan justos por pecadores** the just pay for the sins of others; — **a plazos** to pay in installments; — **al contado** to pay cash; — **con la misma moneda** to pay in kind; — **en especie** to pay in kind

pagaré M promissory note

página F page; — **de estilo** stylesheet; — **web** web page

paginar VT to paginate

pago M payment; — **en efectivo** cash payment; ADJ paid

paila F large pan

país M country; — **de origen** country of origin; — **en desarrollo** developing country; — **exportador de petróleo** oil-exporting country

paisaje M landscape, scenery

paisajismo M landscape architecture

paisano -na M countryman; F countrywoman

paja F straw (también para beber de un vaso); **a humo de** —**s** thoughtlessly; **hacerse una** — *vulg* to jack off; **no caberle a alguien una** — **por el culo** to be self-satisfied; **por un quítame allá esas** —**s** for a trifle

pajar M hayloft

pájaro M bird; — **carpintero** woodpecker; — **pinto** cautious person; **un** — **francés** a French guy

paje M page

pajizo ADJ straw-colored

pajonal M *Am* grassland

pala F (para cavar) shovel; (para recoger basura) dustpan; (de hélice, remo) blade; (de zapato) upper; (para remar, de ping-pong) paddle; — **mecánica** power shovel; **lo tuvimos que recoger con** — he was exhausted

palabra F (unidad léxica) word; (facultad) speech; — **clave** key word; —**s mayores** a big deal; **cuatro** —**s** a few words; **cumplir con la** — to keep one's word; **dejar con la** — **en la boca** to cut someone off in midsentence; **en pocas** —**s** in a nutshell; **faltar a la** — to break a promise; **la última** — the final say; **ni una** — not a word; **no dijo** — he didn't breathe a word; **un hombre de** — a man of his word; **tener la** — to have the floor; **tomar la** — to take the floor; **traducción** — **por** — word-for-word translation; **tragarse/comerse las propias** —**s** to eat one's words

palabrerío M verbiage

palabrero ADJ long-winded

palabrota F curse word, four-letter word; —**s** profanity

palacio M palace

paladar M palate; — **hendido** cleft palate; —

óseo hard palate

paladear VT to relish

paladín M champion, crusader

palanca F (para levantar algo) lever; (para abrir algo) crowbar; (fuerza) leverage; — **de cambios** gearshift lever; — **de juegos** joystick; — **del regulador** throttle lever; **hacer** — to use leverage

palangana F basin

Paláu M Palau

palco M box

palenque M fence

paleontología F paleontology

Palestina F Palestine

palestino -na MF Palestinian; ADJ Palestinian

paleta F (de pintor) palette; (de albañil) trowel; (de ping-pong, para mezclar, batir) paddle; (hélice) blade; (de caramelo) lollipop, sucker; (de helado) Popsicle™

paletilla F shoulder

paleto -ta MF hayseed, hick

paliar VT to alleviate

paliativo M palliative

palidecer[35] VI to turn pale

palidez F pallor, paleness

pálido ADJ pallid, pale

palillo M (de dientes) toothpick; (de tambor) drumstick; (para comida china) chopstick; **tocar todos los** —**s** to try everything

palique M chitchat

paliza F beating, whipping; **dar una** — to beat, to whip

palma F (árbol) palm [tree]; (hoja) palm leaf; (de la mano) palm [of the hand]; **batir** —**s** to clap; **llevarse la** — to take the prize; **conocer como la** — **de la mano** to know like the back of one's hand

palmada F (en la espalda) slap; (aplauso) clap; (en el trasero) spank; **dar una** — (en la espalda) to slap; (en el trasero) to spank

palmear VT to slap on the back

palmera F palm tree

palmípedo M web-footed bird

palmo M span; — **a** — inch by inch

palmotear VT to slap on the back

palo M (de madera) stick; (de barco) mast; (de naipes) suit; (fútbol) goalpost; —**s** (fútbol americano) goalposts; — **de golf** golf club; — **de escoba** broomstick; **dar** —**s** to hit with a stick; **de tal** — **tal astilla** a chip off the old block

paloma F dove, pigeon

palomar M pigeon loft

palomilla F wing nut

palomita F (béisbol) fly ball; —**s** popcorn; **hacer** — to pop corn

palote M rolling pin

palpable ADJ palpable

palpar VT to feel

palpitación F palpitation
palpitante ADJ palpitating; **una cuestión —** a burning question
palpitar VI to palpitate
palta F *Am* avocado
paludismo M malaria
pampa F *Am* prairie
pamplinas F PL baloney, hogwash
pan M bread; (pieza) loaf of bread; **— comido** piece of cake, cinch; **— de cada día** everyday occurrence; **— rallado/molido** bread crumbs; **al —, — y al vino, vino** to call a spade a spade; **contigo, — y cebolla** love is all we need; **ganarse el —** to make a living
pana F corduroy
panacea F panacea, magic bullet
panadería F bakery
panadero -ra MF baker
panal M honeycomb
Panamá M Panama
panameño -ña ADJ & MF Panamanian
panamericano ADJ Pan-American
panceta F *RP* bacon
páncreas M SG pancreas
panda M panda bear
pandearse VT to buckle, to sag
pandemia F pandemic
pandémico M pandemic
pandeo M sag
pandereta F tambourine
pandilla F gang, band
panecillo M roll
panegírico M eulogy
panel M panel; **— de control** control panel
panera F breadbasket
panfleto M pamphlet
pánico ADJ & M panic
panoja F ear of corn
panorama M (paisaje) panorama; (horizonte) outlook
panorámico ADJ panoramic
panqueque M pancake
pantaletas F PL panties
pantalla F (de lámpara) lampshade; (para películas) screen; (de monitor) screen, display; (para actividades ilícitas) cover, front; **la — grande** the silver screen; **— dividida** split screen; **— táctil** touchscreen, touch-sensitive display
pantalón M pants, trousers; **— corto** shorts; **pantalones** pants, trousers; **llevar bien puestos los pantalones** to be master in one's own home
pantano M swamp, marsh
pantanoso ADJ swampy, marshy
panteón M vault
pantera F panther
pantomima F mime, pantomime
pantorrilla F calf

pantufla F slipper
panty M pantyhose
panza F paunch, belly
panzudo ADJ potbellied
pañal M diaper; **estar en —es** to be in its infancy
paño M (de tela) cloth; (de lana) woolen cloth; (para limpiar) rag; **— higiénico** sanitary napkin; **— mortuorio** pall; **— de manos** towel; **— de cocina** dishcloth; **— de mesa** tablecloth; **ella es mi — de lágrimas** I always cry on her shoulder; **—s menores** underwear
pañuelo M (de nariz) handkerchief; (de cuello) scarf
papa M pope; F *Am* potato; **no saber ni —** not to know a thing; **—s fritas** French fries
papá M papa, dad
papacito M (padre) daddy; (hombre apuesto) hunk
papada F double chin
papado M papacy
papagayo M parrot
papaíto M daddy
papal ADJ papal
papar VT to eat; MF SG **papamoscas** (pájaro) flycatcher; (tonto) half-wit; MF SG **papanatas** twerp
paparruchas F PL baloney, bull
papaya F papaya
papel M (para escribir) paper; (dramático) role, part; **— aluminio** aluminum foil; **— carbón** carbon paper; **— cuadriculado** graph paper; **— de cartas** stationery; **— de estaño** tinfoil; **— de estraza** brown paper; **— de lija** sandpaper; **— de seda** tissue paper; **— encerado** wax paper; **— higiénico** toilet paper; **— moneda** paper money; **— tisú** tissue paper; **desempeñar un —** to play a role; **en el —** on paper; **hacer buen —** to cut a good figure
papeleo M paperwork
papelera F (fábrica) paper factory; (cubo) wastepaper basket
papelería F stationery store
papeleta F (para escribir) slip of paper; (para votar) ballot
paperas F PL mumps
papito M daddy
páprika F paprika
papú ADJ & MF Papua New Guinean
paquete M (envuelto) package; (atado) bundle; (programas de ordenador) package; **— de programas de productividad** office suite; **— turístico** package tour
Paquistán M Pakistan
paquistano -na ADJ & MF Pakistani
par ADJ even; M (de cosas idénticas) pair; (de cosas diferentes) couple; (título nobiliario)

peer; (en golf) par; **a la** — at par; **sin** — peerless; **de** — **en** — wide-open

para PREP in order to, for; **lo hice** — **ganar dinero** I did it in order to earn money; **demasiado** — **mí** too much for me; **trabajo** — **mi padre** I work for my father; — **ser perro es inteligente** for a dog he's smart; — **mi sorpresa** to my surprise; **voy** — **Madrid** I'm going to Madrid; — **las dos** by two o'clock; — **atrás** backwards; — **empezar** for starters; — **llevar** to go; ¿— **qué?** what for? — **que** so that, so as to; — **siempre** forever; — **su información** FYI [for your information]; **habla** — **sí** he talks to himself; — **mis adentros** to myself; — **morirse de risa** hilarious; **no es** — **tanto** it's no big deal; **sin qué ni** — **qué** without rhyme or reason

parabién M congratulations; **dar el** — to congratulate

parada F (acción de parar) stop; (de perro de caza) point; (de taxis) stand; (militar) parade; (relevo de guardia) changing of the guard; (de balón) parry; (en fútbol americano) tackle

paradero M whereabouts

paradigma M paradigm

parado ADJ (inmóvil) stationary; (sin trabajo) unemployed, idle; **salir bien** — to come out on top

paradoja F paradox

paradójico ADJ paradoxical

parafernalia F paraphernalia

parafina F paraffin

parafrasear VI/VT to paraphrase

paráfrasis F paraphrase

paraguas M SG umbrella

Paraguay M Paraguay

paraguayo -ya ADJ & MF Paraguayan

paraíso M paradise

paraje M spot

paralelo -la ADJ & M parallel; F parallel line; **hacer** —**s** to draw parallels; **barras paralelas** parallel bars

parálisis F (inmovilidad física, espiritual) paralysis; (condición médica) paralysis, palsy; — **cerebral** cerebral palsy

paralítico -ca ADJ & MF paralytic

paralización F (de tránsito) gridlock; (del cuerpo) paralysis

paralizar[47] VT (movimiento) to paralyze; (negociaciones) to stall; —**se** to gridlock

paramédico -ca ADJ & MF paramedic

parámetro M parameter

paramilitar ADJ & MF paramilitary

páramo M cold highland, moor

parangón M comparison; **sin** — incomparable

parangonar VT to compare

paraninfo M auditorium

paranoia F paranoia

paranoico -ca ADJ & MF paranoid

paranormal ADJ paranormal

parapléjico -ca MF paraplegic

parapsicología F parapsychology

parar VI/VT (detener) to stop; (motor) to stall; VT (un pase de pelota) to block; (un golpe) to parry; — **de hacer algo** to stop doing something; **y para de contar** and that's it; — **en seco** to stop short; **ir a** — to end up; **habló sin** — he talked nonstop; —**se** (detenerse) to stop; (erguirse) *Am* to stand up; —**se a pensar** to stop to think; M SG **parabrisas** windshield; M SG **paracaídas** parachute; M SG **paracaídas dorado** golden parachute; M **paracaidismo** parachuting; M SG **parachoques** bumper; M SG **pararrayos** lightning rod; M **parasol** parasol; MF **paracaidista** parachutist

parasítico ADJ parasitic

parásito M parasite

parcela F parcel, plot

parcelación F subdivision

parcelar VT to parcel [out]

parche M (para remendar, informático) patch; (de tambor) drumhead; (médico) Band-aid®; — **de ojo** eye patch

parcial ADJ partial

pardillo M linnet

pardo ADJ (color) gray-brown; (mulato) mulatto

pareado M couplet

parear VT to match

parecer[35] VI to seem; — **que** to seem like, to look like; ¿**qué te parece?** what do you think? — **se a** to resemble, to look like; M (opinión) opinion; (aspecto) appearance; **al** — apparently; **a mi** — to my mind / way of thinking; **del mismo** — like-minded

parecido ADJ alike, similar; **bien** — good-looking; M similarity, resemblance

pared F wall; **poner a alguien contra la** — to corner; **subirse por las** —**es** to be furious; **de** — **a** — wall-to-wall; **reloj de** — wall clock

paredón M execution wall

pareja F (de personas) couple; (de cosas) [matching] pair; (compañero) partner

parejo ADJ (hermanos) alike; (carrera) even; (dientes) straight; **correr [al]** — to go hand in hand

parental ADJ parental

parentela F kin

parentesco M kinship, relation

paréntesis M parenthesis

parezca, parezco *ver* parecer

pargo M red snapper

paria MF pariah, outcast

paridad F parity

pariente MF, **parienta** F relative, relation; — **consanguíneo** blood relative

parir VI/VT to give birth [to]

parlamentar VI to parley
parlamentario -ria ADJ parliamentary; MF member of parliament
parlamento M (en una obra de teatro) speech; (negociación) parley; (cuerpo legislativo) parliament
parlanchín ADJ talkative; MF chatterbox
parlotear VI to chatter, to rattle on
parloteo M chatter
paro M (huelga breve) stoppage; (falta de trabajo) unemployment; (ave) tit; — **cardiaco** cardiac arrest; — **laboral** work stoppage
parodia F parody
parodiar VT to parody
parpadear VI (un ojo, pantalla) to blink; (una vela) to flicker; (una estrella) to twinkle
parpadeo M (del ojo) blink; (de una vela) flicker; (de una estrella) twinkle; (de una pantalla) blinking
párpado M eyelid
parque M park; — **automotor** fleet of cars; — **de atracciones** amusement park; — **zoológico** zoo
parra F grapevine
párrafo M paragraph; **echar un — con** to have a chat with
parral M grape arbor
parranda F binge, spree; **andar de —** to go out partying
parrandear VI to revel
parrandero -ra MF party animal
parrilla F (sobre el fuego) grill; (en el horno) broiler; (de calles) grid; (de coche) grille
parrillada F barbecue dish
párroco M parish priest
parroquia F (distrito) parish; (iglesia) parish church
parroquial ADJ parochial
parroquiano -na MF (de iglesia) parishioner; (de tienda) regular
parte F (sección) part; (lugar) place; (papel en una obra teatral) lines; (persona legal) party; — **integrante** built-in part; — **interesada** interested party; —**s pudendas** private parts, *fam* privates; **a otra —** somewhere else; **a —s iguales** fifty-fifty; **de un tiempo a esta —** for some time; **de — de** on behalf of; **de — a —** completely; **echar a mala —** to take amiss; **en —** partly; **en gran —** in large measure; **en otra —** elsewhere; **en/por todas —s** everywhere; **formar — de** to be part of; **ir por —s** to proceed by steps; **la mayor — de** most of; **la — del león** the lion's share; **no está en ninguna —** it's nowhere to be found; **no va a ninguna —** it's going nowhere; **por otra —** on the other hand; **tomar — en** to take part in; M report; **dar —** to report; **dar — de enfermo** to call

in sick; **dar — de un crimen** to report a crime
partera F midwife
partición F (of a country) partition; (of a cell) division
participación F (en un proyecto) participation, involvement; (en un negocio) interest; — **de nacimiento** birth announcement
participante MF (en un grupo) participant; (en una carrera) entrant; (en un concurso) contestant
participar VI to participate; VT to announce; — **de/en** to participate in, to share in
partícipe MF participant
participio M participle
partícula F particle
particular ADJ (específico) particular; (poco usual) peculiar; (privado) private; **en —** in particular; **clases —es** private lessons; M (detalle) particular; (asunto) matter; MF private citizen
partida F (fondos) appropriation; (grupo de personas) party; (cantidad de mercancía) parcel, lot; (de ajedrez) game; (acción de partir) departure; — **de nacimiento** birth record; **jugar una mala —** to play a mean trick; **por — doble** double-entry
partidario -ria MF (de una medida) supporter, advocate; (de un partido político) partisan
partidista ADJ & MF partisan
partido M (grupo político) party; (de golf) round; (de tenis, fútbol) game, match; **es un buen —** he's a good match; **sacar — de** to take advantage of; **tomar —** to take sides; **¿cómo va el —?** what's the score? ADJ split, cleft
partir VT (dividir) to divide; (repartir) to share; (quebrar) to break; **eso me parte por el eje** that screws me up; **que te parta un rayo** go jump in the lake; VI (salir) to depart, to leave; **a — de entonces** since then; **a — del lunes** starting Monday; —**se de risa** to die of laughter
partisano -na MF partisan
partitura F musical score
parto M childbirth, delivery; — **prematuro** premature birth; **estar en trabajo de —** to be in labor
parvulario M kindergarten, nursery
párvulo -la MF nursery school child
pasa F raisin
pasable ADJ passable
pasada F (acción de pasar) passing; (con una máquina) pass; **una mala —** a mean trick; **de — by the way
pasadizo M secret passage
pasado M past; ADJ (anterior) past; (demasiado maduro) overripe; — **mañana** day after tomorrow; **el año —** last year; **el — mes de**

septiembre last September

pasador M (de un cierre) pin; (de la puerta) latch

pasaje M (sitio por donde se pasa, fragmento de texto) passage; (billete) ticket; (precio de un viaje) fare; (conjunto de los pasajeros) passengers

pasajero -ra ADJ fleeting, transitory; MF (en un coche, tren) passenger; (en un taxi) fare

pasante M (tenis) passing shot; MF (compañía) intern

pasaporte M passport

pasar VI (no querer jugar, ir de un lado a otro, seguir su proceso, transcurrir) to pass; (ocurrir) to happen; — **a ser** to become; — **de moda** to go out of style; — **hambre** to go hungry; — **por** to pass by; — **por alto** to pass over; — **una tarjeta por un lector** to swipe a card; —**le por la cabeza a alguien** to occur to someone; **pasan de los 80 años** they're over 80 years old; **te pasaste de la casa** you missed the house; —**se** to spoil; —**se de la raya** to cross the line; —**se de sol** to get too much sun; —**se de listo** to outsmart oneself; **se me pasó ir a buscarte** I totally forgot to pick you up; **me la paso bien** I have a good time; VT (la sal, una prueba, la plancha, una pelota) to pass; (un sofocón) to endure; (una tarde) to spend; — **las de Caín** to go through hell; — **en limpio** to make a new copy; — **por alto** to overlook; — **los 50 kmh** to exceed 50 kmh; — **revista** to pass in review; **nos pasó un Volvo** a Volvo passed us; **no lo paso** I can't stand him; M **tienen un buen** — they have a comfortable life; M **pasamano** (de barco) guard rail, gangway; (de escalera) banister, railing; M **pasatiempo** pastime

pasarela F (en un barco) gangplank; (en un desfile de modas) runway

Pascua F (fiesta cristiana) Easter; (fiesta judía) Passover; — **Florida / de Resurrección** Easter Sunday; — **de Navidad** Christmas

pase M (deporte) pass; — **cruzado** cross; — **de anotación** touchdown pass; — **de cabeza** header; — **pantalla** screen pass

pasear VI (a pie) to take a walk; (en bici, a caballo) to go on a ride; (en coche) to go for a drive, to go on a ride; —**se** to parade, to take a walk; —**se a caballo** to go horseback riding; VT (un perro) to walk a dog

paseo M (a pie) walk, stroll; (a caballo, en bicicleta) ride; (en coche) drive, ride; (calle donde se pasea) mall; (recreativo) outing; **irse a** — to go jump in a lake; **dar un** — (a pie) to take a walk; (a caballo, en bicicleta) to go on a ride; (en coche) to go on a drive

pasillo M (de un teatro) aisle; (de un edificio) hallway, corridor; (para vuelo aéreo) corridor; — **de dobles** alley

pasión F passion

pasivo ADJ passive; **voz pasiva** passive voice; M (en un negocio) liabilities; (de una cuenta) debit side

pasmado ADJ astounded

pasmar VT to astound, to stun; —**se** to be astounded, to be stunned

pasmo M astonishment

pasmoso ADJ astonishing, stunning

paso M (acción de pasar, lugar donde pasar) pass; (de pie, de danza, distancia, de un proceso) step; (velocidad) pace; (de caballerías) walk; (de tornillo) pitch; (de coche) wheelbase; — **elevado** overpass; — **a nivel** grade crossing; — **de tortuga** snail's pace; — **a** — step by step; **dar** — (dejar pasar) to let pass; (dejar actuar) to make possible; **dar** —**s** to take steps; **hacer** —**s** to travel; **de** — by the way, in passing; **estar de** — to be passing through; **marcar el** — to set the pace; **al** — **que** while; **salir del** — to get out of a difficulty; **dicho sea de** — incidentally; **a cada** — at every turn; — **del tiempo** passage of time; **abrir** — **para** to make way for; **abrirse** — to plow through, to press through; **paso** dried

pasta F (de almidón) paste; (de harina) dough; (de fideos) pasta; (de libro) hard cover, binding; (dinero) *fam* dough; **de buena** — of good disposition; — **dentífrica/dental** toothpaste

pastar VI/VT to pasture, to graze

pastel M (torta) cake; (tarta) pie; (pintura, cuadro) pastel; — **de cumpleaños** birthday cake; — **de limón** lemon pie; — **de carne** meat pie; **descubrir el** — to spill the beans; ADJ pastel

pastelería F (establecimiento) pastry shop; (conjunto de pasteles) pastry

pastelero -ra M pastry cook

pasterizar, pasteurizar[9] VT to pasteurize

pastilla F (de medicina) tablet, pill; (para la tos) drop; (de jabón) bar

pastizal M grassland

pasto M (terreno) pasture, grassland; (hierba) grass; **ser** — **de** to be a victim of

pastor -ora MF (de ovejas) shepherd; (sacerdote protestante) pastor, minister; M — **alemán** German shepherd

pastoral ADJ pastoral; F pastoral letter

pastoril ADJ pastoral

pastoso ADJ pasty

pastura F feed

pat M putt

pata F (de animal, mueble) foot, leg; (de pollo) drumstick; (de un enchufe) pin; — **palmada** webfoot; — **de gallo** crow's feet; **en cuatro** —**s** on all fours; **a [la]** — **coja** skipping on one leg; **estirar la** — *fam* to kick the bucket; **mala** — bad luck; **metedura de** — faux pas;

meter la — to slip up; **—s arriba** upside down; ADJ **patihendido** cloven-hoofed; **patitieso** dumbfounded; **patizambo** (hacia adentro) knock-kneed; (hacia afuera) bow-legged

patada F kick (también en deportes); **libros a —s** tons of books; **en dos —s** in a jiffy; **dar —s** to kick; **echar a —s** to kick out; **— lateral** (fútbol americano) onside kick

patalear VI (en el aire) to kick; (en el suelo) to stamp

pataleo M (en el aire) kick; (en el suelo) stamp

pataleta F fit; **tener una** — to throw a fit

patán M boor

patata F *Esp* potato; **—s fritas** French fries; **— caliente** hot potato

pateador M kicker

patear VT (algo, a alguien) to kick; (el suelo) to stamp; VI to tramp around; VI/VT (en golf) to putt; VI to kick; **— al arco** to shoot at goal

patentar VT to patent

patente ADJ & F patent; **se hizo — su ignorancia** he betrayed his ignorance; **— en trámite** patent pending

paternal ADJ (del padre) paternal; (como un padre) fatherly

paternidad F paternity, fatherhood; **prueba de** — paternity test

paterno ADJ paternal

patético ADJ moving

patetismo M pathos

patíbulo M gallows scaffold, gallows

patilla F (de gafas) arm; **—s** (de pelo) sideburns

patín M (tabla) skate; (de trineo) runner; **— de ruedas** roller skate; **— de cuchilla / de hielo** ice skate

patinaje M skating

patinar VI (una persona) to skate; (un coche sobre hielo) to skid; (un embrague) to slip; (en un examen) to blank out

patinazo M (de embrague) slip; (de coche) skid

patio M (de casa) patio, courtyard; (de escuela) playground

pato M (ave) duck; (macho) drake; **pagar el** — to take the rap

patochada F blunder

patógeno M pathogen

patología F pathology

patológico ADJ pathological

patoso ADJ clumsy

patotero -ra MF *Am* hooligan

patraña F tall tale

patria F fatherland, homeland

patriarca M patriarch

patriarcal ADJ patriarchal

patrimonial ADJ inherited, patrimonial

patrimonio M patrimony; **— cultural** cultural heritage; **— neto** net worth; **— personal** personal assets

patriota MF patriot

patriótico ADJ patriotic

patriotismo M patriotism

patrocinador -ora MF sponsor

patrocinar VT to sponsor

patrocinio M sponsorship; **— empresarial** corporate backing

patrón -ona MF (protector) patron; (jefe) employer; (de navío) skipper; M (dueño de pensión) landlord; (de costura) pattern; (punto de referencia) yardstick, standard; (de planta) stock; (de un parásito) host; **— de oro** gold standard; F (dueña de pensión) landlady

patronal ADJ management; **asociación** — employers' association; F management

patronato M board of trustees

patrono -na MF patron

patrulla F (grupo de policías o soldados) patrol, squad; (coche) squad car

patrullar VI/VT to patrol

patrullero -ra M patrol car, squad car; MF patrol officer

pausa F (musical) pause, rest; **trabajar con** — to work slowly; **hacer** — to pause

pauta F guideline

pavimentar VT to pave

pavimento M pavement

pavo M turkey; **— real** peacock; ADJ silly

pavón M peacock

pavonearse VI to strut, to swagger

pavoneo M strut, swagger

pavor M dread

pavoroso ADJ frightful

payasada F clownish act or remark; **—s** antics, horseplay

payasear VI to clown around, to horse around

payaso M (de circo) clown; (persona poco seria) buffoon; **hacer el** — to clown around

paz F peace; **estamos en** — we are even; **[que] en — descanse** may she rest in peace; **hacer las paces** to make up; **dejar en** — to leave alone

PC M PC

peaje M (tasa) toll; (cabina donde se paga) tollbooth

peatón -ona MF pedestrian

peca F freckle

pecado M sin; **— mortal** mortal sin

pecador -ora MF sinner; ADJ sinful

pecaminoso ADJ sinful

pecar[30] VI to sin; **— contra** to transgress against; **— de bueno** to be too good; **— de generoso** to be generous to a fault; **— de oscuro** to be exceedingly unclear

pecera F (pequeña) fish tank, fishbowl; (grande) aquarium

pechera F (de camisa) front; (de delantal) bib

pecho M (parte del cuerpo) chest; (mama) breast; **dar el** — to nurse; **nadar** — to do the breaststroke; **tomar a —[s]** to take to heart; **sacar —** to puff out one's chest

pechuga F breast

pechugona ADJ buxom

pecio M flotsam and jetsam

pecoso ADJ freckled

pectoral ADJ & M pectoral

peculado M embezzlement

peculiar ADJ peculiar

peculiaridad F peculiarity

pedagogía F pedagogy, education

pedagógico ADJ pedagogical, teaching

pedagogo -ga MF pedagogue

pedal M pedal

pedalear VI/VT to pedal

pedante ADJ pedantic; MF pedant

pedazo M piece; **— de idiota** absolute idiot; **él es un — de pan** he's a saint; **hacer —s** to tear to pieces; **caerse a —s** to fall to pieces; **— por —** piece by piece

pederasta M pederast, pedophile

pedófilo -la MF pedophile

pederastia F pederasty

pedernal M flint

pedestal M pedestal

pedestre ADJ pedestrian

pediatra MF pediatrician

pediatría F pediatrics

pedido M (comercial) order; (petición) request; **hacer un —** to place an order; **— fijo** standing order; **— pendiente** back order; **— urgente** rush order

pedigrí M pedigree

pedigüeño -ña MF mooch, moocher; ADJ **no seas —** stop mooching

pedir[9] VT (requerir) to ask for, to request; (exigir) to demand; (encargar) to order, to requisition; **— limosna** to beg; **— prestado** to borrow; **— socorro** to cry for help; **— un deseo** to make a wish; **— que** to ask/pray that; **— la mano de una mujer** to ask a woman's hand in marriage; **— por alguien** to ask to speak to someone

pedo M fart; **tener/cogerse un —** to be drunk; **tirarse —s** to fart

pedofilia F pedophilia

pedrada F **dar una —** to hit with a stone; **matar a —s** to stone to death

pedregal M rocky ground

pedregoso ADJ stony

pedrería F precious stones

pedrusco M boulder

pedúnculo M stem

pega F snag

pegadizo ADJ catchy

pegado ADJ (adherido) stuck; (contiguo) adjoining, contiguous; **quedarse —** to get an electric shock; **— al televisor** glued to the television

pegajoso ADJ sticky, tacky

pegamento M glue

pegar[40] VT (con el puño) to hit, to strike; (algo con pegamento) to stick, to glue; (botones) to sew on; **— con** to match; **— contra** to touch; **— un cuadrangular** to hit a homerun; **— un grito** to yell; **— un sencillo** to hit a single; **— un susto** to give a scare; **— un salto** to jump; **—le a la bola** to hit the ball; **—le un tiro a alguien** to shoot someone; **—se** (adherir) to stick together, to cling; (contagiarse) to be contagious; **—se a** to latch onto; **no — un ojo** not to sleep a wink

pegote M glob

pegotear VT to gum up

peinado M (estilo) coiffure, hairdo; (acción) combing

peinador -ora MF hairdresser

peinar VT to comb (también registrar); (en una peluquería) to style; **— a contrapelo** to rub the wrong way

peine M comb

pelada F bald spot

pelado ADJ (sin pelo) hairless; (pobre) poor; (sin cáscara) peeled; (sin árboles) treeless; (sin plumas) plucked; (sin dinero) broke

pelador M peeler

pelaje M coat, fur

pelar VT (el pelo) to cut the hair of; (las plumas) to pluck the feathers from; (frutas, verduras, huevo) to peel; (a un jugador) to fleece; **duro de —** hard to deal with; **el agua está que pela** the water is really hot; **—se** to peel; M SG **pelagatos** nobody

peldaño M step, stair

pelea F (de palabra) fight, quarrel; (de obra) fight, scrape; (de boxeo) fight; **— a puñetazos** fistfight; **— de perros** dogfight

pelear VI (con palabras) to fight, to quarrel; (con obras) to fight, to scuffle; **—se con alguien** to have a fight with someone

pelechar VI (perder la piel) to shed; (mejorar) to get better

pelele M (persona sin carácter) wimp; (muñeca) straw doll

peletería F (tienda) fur store; (comercio) fur trade

pelícano M pelican

película F film (también membrana); (obra cinematográfica) motion picture, film, movie; **de —** extraordinary; **dar una —** to show a film; **— muda** silent film

peligrar VI to be in danger

peligro M danger, peril; **ese muchacho es un —** that boy is dangerous; **en —** in danger; **poner en —** to imperil/endanger/jeopardize

peligroso ADJ dangerous, perilous

pellejo M (piel de animal) hide, pelt; (odre) wineskin; **salvar el —** to save one's skin; **ser**

todo — to be skin and bones; **jugarse el** — to risk one's life

pellizcar[30] VT to pinch

pellizco M pinching

pelma MF jerk

pelo M (de persona) hair; (de animal) fur; (de alfombra) pile; **con —s y señales** with every possible detail; **de medio** — low-class; **eso me viene al** — that suits me perfectly; **montar en** — to ride bareback; **ni un** — not at all; **no tener —s en la lengua** not to mince words; **se le ponen los —s de punta** his hair stands on end; **se salvó por un** — he was saved by the skin of his teeth; **tomarle el — a alguien** to tease someone, to pull someone's leg; **traído de los —s** far-fetched; ADJ **pelirrojo** redheaded

pelón ADJ bald

pelota F (objeto) ball (también testículo); (juego) ballgame; — **vasca** jai-alai; **en —s** naked; **pasar la** — (dar el balón) to pass the ball; (dar la responsabilidad) to pass the buck

pelotear VI to rally

peloteo M rally

pelotera F brawl

pelotero -ra MF (jugador de béisbol) baseball player; (juego para niños) ball pit

pelotón M (pelota grande) large ball; (de tierra seca) clod; (de ciclistas) pack; (de soldados) platoon; (de fusilamiento) firing squad

peltre M pewter

peluca F wig

peludo ADJ (persona) hairy; (animal) furry; (perro) shaggy

peluquería F (para hombres) barbershop; (para mujeres) salon

peluquero -ra MF (de hombres) barber; (de mujeres) hairdresser

peluquín M toupee

pelusa F (de tela, ropa) lint, fluff; (de melocotón, de la piel) fuzz; (de plantas) hair; (de polvo) dust bunny

pelvis F pelvis

pena F (castigo) penalty; (tristeza) sorrow; (vergüenza) embarrassment; — **de muerte** death penalty, capital punishment; **—s** hardships; **a duras —s** with great difficulty; **me da** — it grieves me; **hecho una** — looking like a mess; **¡qué —!** what a shame! **sería una — perder** it would be a shame to lose; **so — de** on pain of; **valer la** — to be worthwhile

penacho M (de plumas) tuft, crest; (de humo) plume

penal ADJ penal; M penitentiary

penalidad F (penuria) hardship; (castigo) penalty

penalizar[47] VT to penalize

penalti, penalty M penalty kick

penar VI to suffer; VT to punish

penco M plug, nag

pendejo -ja M (pelo público) pubic hair; MF (persona licenciosa) *pey* swine; (persona tonta) *fam* dummy; M (hombre despreciable) *pey* schmuck

pendencia F wrangle, fight

pendenciero ADJ quarrelsome

pender VI to hang, to dangle

pendiente F slope, incline; M *Esp* earring; ADJ (aretes) dangling; (negocio) pending, unfinished; (pago) outstanding; **quedo — de tu llamada** I look forward to your call

pendón M banner

péndulo M pendulum

pene M penis

penetración F penetration

penetrante ADJ (mirada, sonido) penetrating, piercing; (frío) biting; (comentario) cutting; (inteligencia) keen

penetrar VT (pasar al interior) to penetrate, to pierce; (comprender) to comprehend

penicilina F penicillin

península F peninsula

peninsular ADJ peninsular

penitencia F (religiosa) penance; (castigo) detention; **¡estás en —!** you're grounded!

penitenciaría F penitentiary

penitente ADJ & MF penitent

penoso ADJ (triste) painful, grievous; (difícil) trying; (que da vergüenza) embarrassing

pensador -ora MF thinker; ADJ reflective

pensamiento M (facultad, acción, efecto) thought; (flor) pansy

pensante ADJ thinking

pensar[1] VI/VT to think; — **en** to think about/over; — **hacer algo** to intend to do something; **eso da que** — that seems questionable; **no lo pienses dos veces** don't think twice

pensativo ADJ pensive, thoughtful

pensión F (asignación periódica) pension, allowance; (comidas) board; (hostal) boardinghouse; — **completa** room and board; **tener en** — to have as a boarder

pensionado M boarding school

pensionar VT to pension

pensionista MF (que vive en una pensión) boarder; (que cobra una pensión) pensioner

pentágono M pentagon

pentagrama M musical staff

penthouse M penthouse

penúltimo ADJ next to the last, penultimate

penumbra F semi-darkness, dimness

penuria F (escasez) shortage; (pobreza) poverty

peña F boulder; — **folclórica** folklore club

peñasco M crag

peñascoso ADJ craggy

peñón M crag

peón -ona MF (obrero) unskilled laborer, farmhand; — **caminero** road worker; M (en ajedrez) pawn; (en damas) piece

peonada F gang of laborers

peonaje M gang of laborers

peonza F toy top

peor ADJ worse, worst; **este libro es** — this book is worse; **el** — **libro** the worst book; ADV worse; **trabaja** — he works worse; — **que** worse than; — **que nunca** worse than ever; **en el** — **de los casos** if worst comes to worst; **lo** — the worst [thing]; **tanto** — so much the worse

pepa F **es un viva la** — it's bedlam

pepino M cucumber

pepita F (simiente) seed; (tumor de gallina) pip; (masa de oro) nugget

pequeñez F (cualidad de pequeño) smallness; (cosa insignificante) trifle

pequeño -ña ADJ (de poco tamaño) small, little; (de corta edad) young; (de poca importancia) trivial

pera F pear; **pedirle** —**s al olmo** to ask the impossible

peral M pear tree

perca F perch; — **americana** black bass

percal M percale

percance M accident, mishap

percatarse VI (darse cuenta) to realize; (notar) to notice

percebe M barnacle

percepción F perception

perceptible ADJ perceptible, noticeable

perceptivo ADJ perceptive

percha F (para el armario) clothes hanger; (palo para colgar cosas) peg; (palo para aves) perch; (perchero) coat rack

perchero M coat rack

percibir VT (experimentar) to perceive, to sense; (recibir) to collect

percudir VT to make grimy; —**se** to get grimy

percusión F percussion

percutor M firing pin

perdedor -ora MF loser

perder[2] VT (dejar de tener algo, extraviar) to lose, to mislay, to misplace; (echar a perder) to spoil, to ruin; (ser derrotado) to lose; (no aprovechar) to waste; (no llegar a tiempo, no disfrutar) to miss; — **el conocimiento** to lose consciousness; — **el tiempo** to waste time; — **los estribos** to fly off the handle; — **hojas** to shed leaves; — **pie** to lose one's footing; — **terreno** to lose ground; **echarse a** — to spoil; **el vaso pierde agua** the glass leaks water; **llevo las de** — the odds are against me; —**se** (extraviarse) to lose one's way, to get lost; (apartarse del buen camino) to go astray, to stray; **se han perdido las llaves** the keys have gotten lost; —**se de**

vista to disappear; —**[se] una oportunidad** to pass up / miss an opportunity; — **el balón** (fútbol americano) to fumble; (fútbol) to lose the ball

perdición F perdition, damnation

pérdida F (acción de perder, cosa perdida) loss; (de dinero dado en prenda) forfeiture; **entrar en** — to nosedive; — **de tiempo** waste of time; — **de balón** (fútbol americano) fumble, turnover; (fútbol) loss of ball possession; —**s cubiertas** covered losses; —**s totales** total loss

perdido -da ADJ (extraviado) lost, missing; (aislado) isolated; (promiscuo) promiscuous; **un borracho** — an utter drunkard; **estar** — **por alguien** to be crazy about someone; M degenerate; F *pey* slut

perdigón M (pollo de perdiz) young partridge; (bolita de plomo) birdshot, buckshot

perdiz F partridge

perdón M (privado) forgiveness; (oficial) pardon; **con** — **de los presentes** present company excepted; **no tener** — to be unforgivable; INTERJ excuse me

perdonar VT (en privado) to forgive; (oficialmente) to pardon

perdurable ADJ lasting

perdurar VI to last

perecedero ADJ perishable

perecer[35] VI to perish

peregrinación F pilgrimage

peregrinar VI to go on a pilgrimage

peregrino -na MF pilgrim; ADJ far-fetched

perejil M parsley

perenne ADJ perennial

pereza F laziness, idleness, sloth

perezoso ADJ lazy, idle; M (animal) sloth

perfección F perfection; **a la** — to perfection, perfectly

perfeccionamiento M perfecting

perfeccionar VT to perfect

perfeccionista MF perfectionist

perfectamente ADV perfectly; **tú hablas español** — you speak Spanish quite well

perfecto ADJ perfect, flawless; **es un** — **tarado** he's an utter idiot; **es un** — **desconocido** he's a complete stranger

perfil M profile; **de** — from the side

perfilar VT to outline; —**se** (marcarse) to be outlined; (definirse) to become clear

perforación F (de una superficie) perforation; (de un pozo) drilling; (de la piel) piercing

perforar VT (agujerear) to perforate; (buscar petróleo) to drill

perfumar VT to perfume, to scent

perfume M perfume, scent

perfumería F perfumery

pergamino M parchment

pérgola F arbor

pericia F expertness, know-how
perico M (loro) parakeet; (cocaína) *fam* snow
periferia F periphery, fringe
periférico ADJ & M peripheral
perilla F (adorno, remate) knob; (pelo de barbilla) goatee; **me viene de —s** it's exactly what I need
perímetro M perimeter
periódico M newspaper; **— mensual** monthly periodical; ADJ periodic
periodismo M journalism
periodista MF journalist
periodístico ADJ journalistic
período M period (también menstruación); (de materia radiactiva) half-life; **— de prueba** (para un trabajo) probationary period; (para una mercancía) trial period; **— glaciar** ice age
peripecia F vicissitude
peripuesto ADJ dressed up, dolled up, decked out
periquito M parakeet
periscopio M periscope
perista MF fence
perito -ta ADJ expert, practiced; MF technician
peritonitis F peritonitis
perjudicar[30] VT to harm
perjudicial ADJ harmful, detrimental
perjuicio M harm
perjurar VT to swear; VI to commit perjury; **—se** to commit perjury
perjurio M perjury
perla F (de nácar) pearl; (persona) gem; (de sudor) bead; (de sabiduría) nugget; (frase inoportuna) blooper; **me viene de —s** it suits me perfectly
perlado ADJ pearly
permanecer[35] VI to remain, to stay
permanencia F (carácter de permanente) permanence; (acción de permanecer) stay
permanente ADJ permanent
permanezca, permanezco *ver* permanecer
permeable ADJ permeable
permear VT to permeate
permisible ADJ permissible
permisivo ADJ permissive
permiso M (para ir al baño) permission; (para faltar al servicio militar) furlough; (para faltar al trabajo) leave; (para casarse, conducir) license, permit; **— de trabajo** work permit; **con —** excuse me
permitir VT (dar permiso) to permit, to allow; (posibilitar) to enable; **—se** (una libertad) to take the liberty of; (un lujo) to allow oneself; **¿me permite?** may I?
permuta F exchange
permutación F permutation
permutar VT to exchange
pernetas LOC ADV **en —** barelegged

pernicioso ADJ pernicious
pernicorto ADJ short-legged
perno M bolt, pin
pero CONJ but; ADV **muy — muy lindo** very, very pretty; M objection; **no hay — que valga** there are no buts about it
perogrullada F platitude
perorar VI to hold forth
perorata F lecture
peróxido M peroxide
perpendicular ADJ perpendicular
perpetrar VT to perpetrate
perpetuar[26] VT to perpetuate
perpetuo ADJ perpetual
perplejidad F perplexity, bewilderment
perplejo ADJ perplexed, bewildered; VT **dejar — to** perplex
perrera F (lugar donde guardar perros) pound; (rabieta) tantrum
perrero -ra MF dogcatcher; ADJ dog-loving
perro M dog; **— caliente** hot dog; **— callejero** stray dog; **— cobrador** retriever; **— de caza** hunting dog; **— de lanas** poodle; **— esquimal** husky; **— faldero** lapdog; **— guía** guide dog; **— guardián** watchdog, guard dog; **— pastor** sheepdog; **— policía** police dog; **hijo de perra** *vulg* son of a bitch; ADJ miserable; **en la perra vida** never
perruno ADJ canine
persa ADJ & MF Persian; M (lengua) Persian
persecución F (religiosa) persecution; (policial) pursuit, chase
perseguidor -ora MF (que sigue) pursuer; (que acosa) persecutor
perseguir[12] VT (seguir para alcanzar) to pursue, to chase; (seguir para encontrar) to track down; (acosar) to hound; (tratar de destruir) to persecute
perseverancia F perseverance
perseverar VI to persevere
Persia F Persia
persiana F blind, shade
persiga, persigo, persigue, persiguiendo, persiguiera, persiguiese *ver* perseguir
persistencia F persistence
persistente ADJ persistent
persistir VI to persist
persona F person; **— influyente** player; **— legal** legal entity; **en —** in person; **— mayor** adult
personaje M (persona importante) personage; (de obra literaria) character; **es todo un —** he's quite a character
personal ADJ personal; M personnel, staff
personalidad F personality
personalmente ADV personally
personificar[30] VT to personify, to embody
perspectiva F (punto de vista, distancia, técnica de dibujo) perspective; (panorama) view,

vista; (posibilidad) prospect; **tener en —** to have planned

perspicacia F insight, sharpness

perspicaz ADJ perspicacious, perceptive

persuadir VT to persuade

persuasión F persuasion

persuasivo ADJ persuasive

pertenecer[35] VI to belong

perteneciente ADJ belonging

pertenencias F PL belongings

pertenezca, pertenezco *ver* pertenecer

pértiga F pole

pertinente ADJ pertinent, relevant

pertrechos M PL military supplies

perturbación F disturbance

perturbar VT to perturb, to disturb

Perú M Peru

peruano -na ADJ & MF Peruvian

perversidad F (distorsión) perversity; (maldad) wickedness

perversión F perversion

perverso ADJ (distorsionante) perverse; (malvado) wicked

pervertido -da MF pervert

pervertir[8] VT (enviciar) to pervert; (distorsionar) to distort; **—se** to become perverted

pesa F (para pesar) weight; (para hacer ejercicio) dumbbell; **—s y medidas** weights and measures

pesadez F (cualidad de pesado) heaviness; (tedio) tiresomeness; (persona pesada) tiresome person

pesadilla F nightmare

pesado -da ADJ (que pesa mucho, difícil de digerir) heavy; (aburrido) tiresome; (robusto) heavy-set; (tardo) slow; MF bore, pest

pesadumbre F grief, sorrow

pésame M condolence, expression of sympathy

pesar VT (apenar) to sadden; (medir el peso de) to weigh; (recaer sobre) to weight down; VI (tener peso, importancia) to weigh; M grief, sorrow; LOC ADV **a — de** in spite of

pesaroso ADJ (triste) sad; (arrepentido) repentant

pesca F (acción de pescar) fishing; (lo pescado) catch; **ir de —** to go fishing

pescadería F fish market

pescado M fish

pescador -ora MF fisherman

pescar[30] VI/VT (capturar peces) to fish; (sacar del agua, coger, comprender, sorprender, pillar) to catch; (obtener) to land, to nail

pescozón M blow to the back of the head

pescuezo M neck

pesebre M (para pienso) manger, crib; (belén) nativity scene

peseta F peseta

pesimismo M pessimism

pesimista MF pessimist

pésimo ADJ dismal, wretched

peso M (fuerza, importancia) weight; (cosa opresiva) burden; (cosa pesada) load; **vender al —** to sell by weight; **levantar en —** to lift off the ground

pesquería F fishery

pesquero ADJ fishing; M fishing boat

pesquisa F inquiry

pestaña F (del ojo) eyelash; (en costura) fringe; (de papel, texto) tab; **quemarse las —s** to burn the midnight oil

pestañear VI to blink; **sin —** unflinchingly

pestañeo M blink

peste F (enfermedad) plague; (persona molesta) pest; (hedor) stench; **— bubónica** bubonic plague; **— negra** black death; **hablar —s de alguien** to speak badly of someone

pestilencia F pestilence

pestillo M deadbolt, latch

petaca F (para tabaco) tobacco pouch; (para whisky) flask

pétalo M petal

petardear VI to backfire

petardeo M backfire

petate M bundle; **liar el —** to pack up and go

petición F petition, request

peticionar VT to petition

petirrojo M robin

pétreo ADJ stony

petróleo M petroleum, oil; **— crudo** crude oil

petrolero -ra ADJ oil, petroleum; **plataforma —** oil rig; M oil tanker; F oil company

petrolífero ADJ (que contiene petróleo) oil-bearing; (que produce petróleo) oil-producing; (relativo al petróleo) oil

petulancia F smugness

petulante ADJ smug

petunia F petunia

peyorativo ADJ pejorative

peyote M peyote

pez M fish; **— dorado** goldfish; **— espada** swordfish; **— gordo** *fam* fat cat, big shot; **— vela** sailfish; **— volador** flying fish; **como — en el agua** perfectly at ease; F pitch

pezón M nipple

pezuña F hoof

phishing M phishing

piadoso ADJ pious, saintly

piafar VI to stamp

pianista MF pianist, piano player

piano M piano; **— de cola** grand piano; **— vertical** upright piano

pianola F player piano

piar[28] VI to peep, to chirp

pica F (lanza) pike; (palo de baraja) spade

picada F (de insecto) bite; (de avión) nosedive; **caer en —** to dive

picadillo M meat [and vegetable] hash

picado ADJ (mar) rough, choppy; (carne) chopped; (de viruela) poked; M (de avión) nosedive; **caer en** — to dive

picador M picador; ADJ stinging

picadora F grinder; — **de carne** meat grinder

picadura F (de serpiente) bite; (de insecto) sting, bite

picante ADJ (especia) spicy, hot; (queso) sharp; (obsceno) risqué; M (especia fuerte) strong seasoning; (cualidad) spiciness

picar³⁰ VI/VT (un pez) to bite; (un ave) to peck; (comer en pequeñas cantidades) to nibble; VT (tomates) to chop up; (carne) to mince; (una vaca) to goad, to poke; (la curiosidad) to pique; (con espuelas) to spur; VI (una comida picante) to sting; (el sol) to burn; (la piel) to itch, to smart; (un avión) to dive; — **alto** to aim high; —**se** to spoil; —**se heroína** to shoot up heroin; **se pica el mar** the sea is getting rough; **se me picó un diente** I got a cavity; M SG **picapleitos** *pey* shyster; M **picaporte** latch

picardía F mischief

picaresco ADJ picaresque

pícaro -ra MF rogue, rascal; ADJ roguish, mischievous

picazón F (en la piel) itch; (en la garganta) tickle; **provoca** — it causes itching

picea F spruce

pichi M jumper

pichón M (paloma) pigeon; (cría de ave) chick

picnic M picnic

pico M (de ave) beak, bill; (de montaña) peak; (herramienta) pick; (de tetera) spout; **cuarenta y** — forty-odd; **cerrar el** — to shut one's mouth; **tener el** — **de oro** to be very eloquent

pícolo M piccolo

picotazo M peck

picotear VI/VT (aves) to peck; (personas) to nibble

pictórico ADJ pictorial

pida, pide, pidiendo, pidiera, pidiese *ver* pedir

pídola F leapfrog

pie M (del cuerpo, de calcetín, de cama, medida) foot; (de foto) caption; (de copa) stem; (de lámpara) stand; (de página) bottom; (para un actor) cue; (de árbol) trunk; (de mueble) leg; — **de atleta** athlete's foot; — **de autor** byline; — **de imprenta** printer's mark; — **zambo** clubfoot; **a** — on foot; **un soldado de a** — a footsoldier; — **de banco** silly remark; **a** — **juntillas** firmly; **al** — **de la letra** to the letter; **caer de** — to have good luck; **con un** — **en el estribo** with one foot out of the door; **dar** — (a una crítica) to give rise to; (a un actor) to cue; **de/en** — standing; **en** — **de guerra** (enojado) on the warpath;

(belicoso) on a war footing; **estar de** — to be standing; **estar en** — **de igualdad con** to be on a par with; **esto no tiene ni** —**s ni cabeza** I can't make heads or tails of this; **ir a** — to walk; **perder** — to lose one's footing; **ponerse de** — to stand up

piedad F (cualidad de pío) piety; (misericordia) mercy; **tener** — to show mercy

piedra F stone; — **angular** cornerstone, keystone; — **caliza** limestone; — **de afilar** whetstone; — **de toque** touchstone; — **pómez** pumice; — **preciosa** gemstone; **ser** — **de escándalo** to be an object of scandal

piel F (humana) skin; (animal) hide, pelt; (para confección) fur; — **de gallina** goosebumps; — **de naranja** cellulite

piensa, piense *ver* pensar

pienso M feed; **ni por** — no way

pierda, pierde *ver* perder

pierna F leg; — **de ternera** leg of lamb; **dormir a** — **suelta** to sleep like a log

pieza F (de artillería, de tela, de música, de teatro) piece; (habitación) room; — **de repuesto** replacement part; **de una** — astonished; **menuda** — a piece of work

pífano M fife

pifia F goof, miscue

pifiar VT to goof up, to miscue

pigmento M pigment

pigmeo -a MF pygmy

pija F *Mex vulg* cock, dick

pijama M pajamas

pila F (recipiente) basin; (bautismal) baptismal font; (cúmulo) pile, heap, stack; (generador) battery; — **atómica** atomic reactor

pilar M pillar

píldora F pill; —**s para dormir** sleeping pills

pillaje M pillage, plunder

pillar VT (saquear) to pillage, to plunder; (atrapar, coger) to catch; (en un juego infantil) to tag

pillo -lla ADJ (travieso) naughty; (taimado) sly; MF (adulto) scoundrel; (niño) scamp

pilluelo -la MF urchin

pilón M (fuente) large basin; (soporte) pylon

pilotar, pilotear VT to pilot, to fly

pilote M pile, stilt

piloto MF (conductor) pilot; (llama pequeña de gas) pilot light; — **automático** autopilot; — **de pruebas** test pilot

pimentar VT to pepper

pimentero M pepper shaker

pimentón M paprika

pimienta F pepper; — **blanca** white pepper; — **de cayena** red pepper; — **negra** black pepper

pimiento M pepper, bell pepper; — **verde** green pepper

pimpollo M (de rosa) rosebud; (de vid) shoot

PIN M PIN
pináculo M pinnacle
pinar M pine grove
pincel M artist's brush
pincelada F stroke; **dar las últimas —s** to put on the final touches
pinchadura F flat tire
pinchar VT (perforar) to prick, to puncture; (apuñalar) to poke; (inyectar) to inject; (intervenir un teléfono) to wiretap; (provocar) to needle; VI to have a flat; **ni corta ni pincha** he doesn't count; M SG **pinchadiscos** disk jockey, DJ
pinchazo M (acción de pinchar) puncture, prick; (neumático) flat tire; (puñalada) stab; (de teléfono) wiretap
pinche ADJ *Méx vulg* fucking
pincho M (palo afilado) spike; (de rotisería) spit
pingajo M (harapo) tatter; (harapiento) person dressed in rags
ping-pong M ping-pong
pingüe ADJ abundant
pingüino M penguin
pino M (árbol) pine; (ejercicio) handstand; **en el quinto —** in the boondocks
pinta F (mancha) dot; (aspecto) looks; (medida de líquidos) pint
pintada F grafitti
pintado ADJ (animales, plantas) colorful; **ese traje te queda —** you look great in that suit
pintar VT (colorear) to paint; (describir) to depict; **este marcador no pinta** this marker won't write; **no — nada** to count for nothing; **las cosas no pintaban bien** things did not look well; **—se** to put on makeup
pintarrajear VT to daub, to smear with paint; **—se** to put on too much makeup
pinto ADJ paint, dapple[d]
pintor -ora MF painter; **— de brocha gorda** house painter
pintoresco ADJ picturesque, colorful
pintorrear VT to smear with paint
pintura F (acción de pintar, obra) painting; (sustancia) paint; **— al óleo** oil painting; **— en aerosol** spray paint; **— fresca** wet paint
pinza F (de cangrejo) claw; (de médico) clamp; (de vestido) dart; (instrumento) clothespin; **—s** tweezers
piña F (fruto del pino) pinecone; (ananás) pineapple; (bomba) hand grenade
piñata F piñata
piñón M (semilla del pino) pine nut; (rueda del engranaje) pinion; (de bicicleta) sprocket
pío ADJ pious; INTERJ peep; **ni —** not a word
piojo M louse; **como —s en costura** like sardines
piojoso ADJ lousy
pionero -ra MF pioneer

pipa F (para fumar) pipe; (semilla) sunflower seed; **pasarlo —** to have a great time
pipí M pee; **hacer —** *fam* to pee
pipiolo -la MF novice
pique M (rivalidad) rivalry; (desavenencia) falling-out; **echar a —** to sink; **irse a —** to capsize
piquete M picket (también de huelga)
piquetear M to picket
piragua F dugout canoe
pirámide F pyramid
pirata MF pirate; **— informático -ca** hacker
piratear VT to pirate
piratería F piracy
piromanía F pyromania
pirómano -na MF pyromaniac
piropo M compliment
pirotecnia F pyrotechnics
pirulí M sucker, lollipop
pisada F (paso) footstep; (huella) footprint; **seguir las —s de** to follow in the footsteps of
pisar VT (oprimir con el pie) to step on, to tread on; (apisonar) to mash; **jamás pisó una plaza de toros** he never set foot in a bullring; **ir pisando huevos** to walk on eggshells; VI to step on; **— fuerte** to throw one's weight around; M SG **pisapapeles** paperweight
piscifactoría F fishery, fish farm
piscina F swimming pool
piso M (suelo) floor; (planta) story; (vivienda) apartment; **de — a techo** from the ground up
pisotear VT to tramp on, to trample, to stomp on
pisotón M stamp; **dar un —** to stamp, to step on
pista F (rastro) track, scent; (noticia) clue; (de aterrizaje) runway; (de circo) arena, ring; (de patinaje) skating ring; (de tenis) court; (de baile) floor; (de carreras) track, racetrack; **seguir la —** to track; **— para bicicletas** bike lane
pistola F (revólver) pistol; (para pintura) gun
pistolera F holster
pistolero MF gunner; M gunman; F gun woman
pistón M (válvula) piston; (explosivo) cap
pitada F drag, puff
pitar VI to toot, to whistle; VI/VT (rechiflar) to boo
pitazo M honk
pitido M (silbido) whistle, toot; (en deportes) whistle
pitillo M cigarette
pito M (silbato) whistle; (pene) *fam* dick; **no vale un —** *fam* it is not worth a damn; **entre —s y flautas** when all is said and done; **¿qué —s toca?** what's his role here?
pitón M (serpiente) python; (punta de cuerno)

tip of a bull's horn
pituitario ADJ pituitary
pivot MF *Am* (baloncesto) center
pivotar VI to pivot
pivote M pivot; — **central** kingpin
píxel M pixel
pizarra F (roca) slate; (pizarrón) blackboard, chalkboard
pizarrón M blackboard, chalkboard
pizca F (de sal) pinch, dash; (de evidencia) shred; (de verdad) grain; (de suciedad) speck; **no entiendo ni** — I don't understand a bit/jot
pizza F pizza
placa F (fotográfica) plate; (de policía) badge; (condecoración, sarro) plaque; (de coche) license plate; (de computadora/ordenador) board, card; — **lógica** logic board; — **madre** motherboard
placaje M tackle
placar[30] VI/VT to tackle
placebo M placebo
placenta F placenta, afterbirth
placentero ADJ pleasant
placer[36] M pleasure, enjoyment; VT *lit* to please
plácido ADJ placid
plaf INTERJ plop
plaga F (enfermedad) plague; (persona, insecto) pest
plagar[40] VT to infest; —**se de** to become infested with
plagio M plagiarism
plan M (proyecto) plan; (ligue) pickup; — **de estudios** curriculum; — **de juego** game plan; — **de salud administrado** managed care; **se vistió en** — **de vampiresa** she was dressed to kill
plana F newspaper page; — **mayor** top brass; **enmendar la** — **a uno** to correct a person's mistakes
plancha F (electrodoméstico) iron; (lámina) metal plate; (parrilla) griddle; **hacer la** — to float; **tirarse una** — to fall flat on one's face
planchado M ironing
planchar VT to iron, to press; **me dejó planchado** it left me speechless
plancton M plankton
planeador M glider
planeamiento M planning
planear VI/VT to plan; VI (volar) to glide, to plane; VT (madera) to plane
planeo M gliding
planeta M planet
planetario M planetarium
planificación F organization, planning; — **familiar** family planning; — **para contingencias** contingency planning
planificador M planner, scheduler; — **de rutas** trip planner
planificar[30] VI/VT to plan

planilla F (de sueldos) payroll; (digital) worksheet; *Am* — **de cálculo** spreadsheet
plano ADJ flat, even; M (superficie) plane; (de un edificio) plan; (de calles) map; — **inclinado** inclined plane; **caer de** — to fall flat; **de** — flatly; **primer** — foreground
planta F (vegetal) plant; (del pie) sole; — **baja** ground floor
plantación F plantation
plantar VT (una planta, cruz) to plant; (a un novio) to dump; (a un colega) to make wait; —**se** to stand firm, to refuse to move; — **una bofetada a alguien** to give someone a slap; **dejar plantado** to stand up
planteamiento M (enfoque) approach; (exposición) presentation; **es un** — **poco provechoso** it is not a very beneficial approach
plantear VT (presentar) to present; **me planteó sus planes** she explained her plans to me; (provocar) to give rise to; **eso plantea un problema** that gives rise to a problem; —**se** to occur to; **¿te has planteado lo que pasa si te quedas sin trabajo?** have you thought about what will happen if you become unemployed?
plantel M (personal) staff; (almáciga) nursery
plantilla F (pieza suelta) insole; (patrón para calcar) pattern, stencil; (digital) template
plantío M grove
plasma M plasma (también de pantalla)
plasmar VT (captar) to capture; (dar forma plástica o sensible) to mold, to shape; —**se** to materialize
plasta ADJ tiresome; F (cosa informe) lump; (persona) bore
plástico ADJ & M plastic
plata F (metal, color, objeto de plata) silver; *Am* (dinero) money; **hablar en** — to speak in plain language
plataforma F platform (también política y digital); — **de lanzamiento** launching pad; — **petrolífera** oil rig; — **continental** continental shelf
platanar M banana grove
plátano M (fruta) banana; (para cocinar) plantain; (bananero) banana tree; (árbol ornamental) plane tree
platea F main floor of a theater
plateado ADJ & M (color) silver; M (acción de platear) silver-plating
platear VT to silver-plate
platero-ra MF silversmith
plática F chat
platicar[30] VI to chat
platija F flounder
platillo M (plato pequeño) saucer; (instrumento musical) cymbal; — **volador** flying saucer
platino M platinum

plato M (recipiente) plate; (comida) dish; (béisbol) home plate; — **fuerte** main dish/course; — **hondo** bowl; — **sopero** soup dish

plausible ADJ plausible

playa F beach

playboy M playboy

plaza F (espacio amplio) plaza, public square; (puesto de trabajo) job; **de cuatro —s** four-seater; — **de toros** bullring; — **mayor** main square

plazo M term; **a corto —** short-term; **a largo —** long-term, long-range; **a — fijo** fixed-term; **a —s** on credit; **cumplir un —** to meet a deadline

plazoleta F court

plazuela F court

pleamar M high tide

plebe F rabble

plebeyo -ya ADJ & MF plebeian

plegable ADJ folding

plegadera F paper folder

plegadizo ADJ folding

plegar[41] VT to fold; **—se [a]** (ceder) to yield [to]; (unirse) to join

pleitesía F compliance

pleito M (pelea) dispute; (demanda judicial) litigation, lawsuit; **poner —** to sue

plenamente ADV fully

plenario ADJ & M plenary

plenitud F — **de la vida** prime of life

pleno ADJ complete; **en — día** in broad daylight; **en — invierno** in the dead of winter; **en — rostro** right on the face; **en — verano** in midsummer; **en plena vista** in plain sight; M full session

pliego M leaflet

pliegue M (en papel) fold; (en tela) pleat

plomada F plumb

plomería F plumbing

plomero -ra MF plumber

plomizo ADJ leaden

plomo M (metal, color) lead; (pesa) lead weight; (perdigón) shot; **a —** plumb; **caer a —** to fall vertically; **sin —** unleaded; ADJ INV tiresome

pluma F (de ave) feather, quill; (para escribir) pen; — **fuente** fountain pen

plumaje M plumage

plumero M dust mop, duster

plumífero ADJ feathery

plumón M down

plural ADJ & M plural

pluralidad F plurality

pluriempleo M moonlighting

pluscuamperfecto ADJ & N pluperfect

plutonio M plutonium

pluvial ADJ **aguas —es** rainwater

pluviómetro M rain gauge

PNB [producto nacional bruto] M GNP

población F (conjunto de personas) population; (acción de poblar) settlement; (pueblo) town

poblado M hamlet

poblador -ora MF settler

poblar[5] VT (habitar) to populate; (colonizar) to settle; **—se de** to become covered with

pobre ADJ poor; MF **los —s** the poor

pobrecito -ta MF poor thing

pobreza F (miseria) poverty; (escasez) scarcity

pocilga F pigsty, pigpen

pocillo M cup

poción F potion

poco ADJ (no mucho) little; **poca paciencia** little patience; **al — rato** after a little while; (no muchos) few; **—s pasajeros** few passengers; **al — tiempo** shortly; **a los —s meses** after a few months; **de pocas luces** stupid; **en pocas palabras** in a nutshell; ADV little; **trabaja —** he works little; — **caritativo** not very charitable; — **conocido** little known; — **a —** little by little; — **más o menos** about; **hace —** a short while ago; **por — me caigo** I almost fell; **tener en —** to hold in low esteem; PRON a little, a bit; **un —** a little bit, a little while; **como —** at least; **unos —s** a few

poda F trim

podadera F pruning hook

podar VT to prune, to trim

poder[69] VI to be able to; **no puedo llegar antes de las cinco** I can't get there before five; **¿puedo sentarme?** may I be seated? **puede que venga** she may come; **a más no —** to the utmost; **no puedo más** I can't go on; **nadie puede con ella** nobody can deal with her; **no puede menos que venir** he can't help but come; **no puede menos que hacerlo** he cannot help doing it; M (fuerza) power; (escrito que da autoridad) proxy, power of attorney; — **ejecutivo** executive branch; — **judicial** judiciary branch; — **legislativo** legislative branch; **por —** by proxy

poderío M power, might

poderoso ADJ powerful, mighty

podiatra MF podiatrist

podiatría F podiatry

podio M podium

podólogo -ga MF podiatrist

podrá, podría ver poder

podredumbre F rot

podrido ADJ rotten

podrir ver pudrir

poema M poem

poesía F (género lírico) poetry; (poema) poem

poeta MF, **poetisa** F poet

poética F poetics

poético ADJ poetic

polaco -ca ADJ Polish; M (lengua) Polish; MF Pole

polaina F legging
polar ADJ polar
polaridad F polarity
polarización F polarization
polca F polka
polea F pulley
polémica F polemic, controversy
polémico ADJ polemic
polen M pollen
poli MF cop; F *fam* cops
policía F (en conjunto) police; (mujer) policewoman; M policeman; MF police officer
policíaco ADJ police
policial ADJ police; **parte** — police report
poliéster M polyester
poliestireno M Styrofoam™
poligamia F polygamy
políglota ADJ & MF polyglot
polígrafo M polygraph
poliinsaturado ADJ polyunsaturated
polilla F moth
polímero M polymer
polinizar[47] VT to pollinate
polio F polio
pólipo M polyp
política F (actividad relativa al gobierno) politics; (conjunto de orientaciones) policy; — **exterior** foreign policy
político -ca ADJ (relativo a la política) political; (diplomático) politic; MF politician
poliuretano M polyurethane
póliza F policy; — **de seguros** insurance policy
polizón -ona MF stowaway
polizonte M *pey* cop
polla F (cría de ave) pullet; (pene) *vulg* cock, dick; **¡y una —!** *vulg* bullshit!
pollada F brood
pollera F (mujer) woman who raises and sells chickens; (falda) *Am* skirt
pollo M (cría de ave) young chicken; (carne) chicken
polo M (punto geográfico) pole; (juego) polo; — **acuático** water polo; — **de atención** focus of attention; — **Norte** North Pole
Polonia F Poland
poltrona F easy chair
polvareda F cloud of dust; **levantar una** — (causar escándalo) to raise a ruckus; (causar una nube de polvo) to kick up the dust
polvera F compact
polvo M (suciedad) dust; (partículas) powder; — **de hornear** baking powder; **echarse un** — *fam* to get laid; **juntar** — to gather dust; **limpio de** — **y paja** net
pólvora F gunpowder
polvoriento ADJ dusty
polvorín M (almacén de pólvora) magazine; (situación explosiva) powder keg
pomada F salve

pomelo M grapefruit
pómez F pumice
pomo M doorknob
pompa F (boato) pomp; (burbuja) soap bubble; — **s fúnebres** funeral ceremony
pomposo ADJ pompous
pómulo M cheekbone
pon *ver* poner
ponchado M (béisbol) strikeout
ponchar VT (un neumático) to puncture; — **a alguien** (en béisbol) to strike someone out; — **se** (un neumático) to become punctured; (en béisbol) to strike out
ponche M (bebida) punch; (en béisbol) strikeout
ponchera F punch bowl
poncho M poncho
ponderación F (acción de ponderar) pondering; (valor relativo) weighting
ponderar VT (considerar) to ponder, to consider; (exagerar) to exaggerate; (ajustar valores) to weight
pondrá, pondría *ver* poner
ponencia F presentation
poner[56, 74] VT to put, to place; (la mesa, un reloj) to set; (huevos) to lay; (azúcar) to add; (un examen) to give; (el televisor) to turn on; (un pleito) to file; — **a alguien a hacer algo** to assign someone to do something; — **en claro** to clarify; — **en limpio** to recopy, to make a clean copy; — **nombre a un niño** to name a child; — **sangre** to give a transfusion; **cada uno pone mil pesetas** each person contributes a thousand pesetas; **pongamos que** let us suppose that; **¿qué pone ahí?** what does it say there? —**se** (volverse) to become; (el sol) to set; (ropa) to put on; (sexualmente) to get turned on; —**se a** to begin to; —**se al corriente** to become informed; —**se de acuerdo** to come to an agreement; —**se de pie** to stand up; —**se por delante en el marcador** (deporte) to take the lead
póney M pony
ponga, pongo *ver* poner
poniente M (oeste) west; (viento del oeste) west wind
pontón M pontoon
ponzoña F poison
ponzoñoso ADJ poisonous
pool M pool
popa F poop, stern
populacho M mob
popular ADJ (conocido y citado) popular; (del pueblo) folk
popularidad F popularity
populoso ADJ populous
popurrí M (de perfume) potpourri; (musical) medley
poquito *ver* poco

por PREP — **barco** by boat; — **casualidad** by chance; — **Dios** by God; — **etapas** by stages; — **las buenas o** — **las malas** by hook or by crook; — **litro** by the liter; ¿— **qué?** why? for what reason? **multiplicar** — to multiply by; **lo agarró** — **la garganta** he grabbed him by the throat; **mi amor** — **ella** my love for her; — **poco tiempo** for a short time; — **primera vez** for the first time; — **vía de argumento** for the sake of argument; — **ejemplo** for instance; — **el momento** for the time being; **hazlo** — **mí** do it for my sake; **trabaja** — **mí** work on my behalf; **no me gustan** — **su olor** I don't like them because of their smell; **lo supe** — **él** I found out through him; **pasé** — **Londres** I passed through London; **un viaje** — **la costa** a trip along the coast; — **lo que cuentas** from what you're telling me; — **adelantado** in advance; — **escrito** in writing; — **la mañana** in the morning; — **lo general** in general; — **rachas** in spurts; **está** — **Badajoz** it's near Badajoz; — **fin** at last; — **el mes de marzo** around the month of March; — **ciento** percent; — **consiguiente** consequently; — **escrito** in writing; — **poco se muere** he almost died; **está** — **hacer** it is yet to be done; **él está** — **hacerlo** (a favor de) he is in favor of doing it; (a punto de) he is about to do it; **recibir** — **esposa** to take as a wife; **tener** — to consider, to think of as
porcelana F porcelain, china
porcentaje M percentage; — **de bateo** (béisbol) batting average
porche M porch, stoop
porcino ADJ **ganado** — swine; M pig
porción F (parte) portion, share; (de alimento) helping
pordiosear VT to panhandle
pordiosero -ra MF panhandler
porfía F obstinacy
porfiado ADJ willful
porfiar[28] VT to insist
pormenor M detail
pormenorizar[47] VT to detail, to go into detail about
porno M porn
pornografía F pornography
pornográfico ADJ pornographic
poro M pore
poroso ADJ porous
poroto M *Am* bean
porque CONJ because
porqué M reason; **el** — **de su tristeza** the reason for his sadness
porquería F (suciedad) filth; (acción despreciable) dirty trick; (cosa de mala calidad) crud; (comida de mala calidad) junk food; (persona despreciable) *pey* douchebag, dirtbag
porra F club, cudgel
porrista MF cheerleader
porro M joint
portada F (de un libro) title page; (de una revista) front cover
portador -ora MF (de enfermedad) carrier; (de cheque) bearer; — **del féretro** pallbearer
portal M portal, doorway; — **de videos/vídeos** video portal
portar VT to carry; —**se** to behave; —**se mal** to misbehave; M SG **portaaviones** aircraft carrier; M SG **portaequipajes** luggage bin; M **portaestandarte** standard-bearer; M **portafolio** briefcase; M SG **portalámparas** socket; M SG **portaligas** garter belt; M SG **portamonedas** coin purse; M **portaobjeto** slide; M SG **portapapeles** clipboard; MF **portavoz** spokesperson
portátil ADJ portable
portazo M slam; **dar un** — to slam the door
porte M (envío) freight; (por correo) postage; (aspecto) bearing, carriage; (capacidad de carga) capacity; (tamaño) size; — **de armas** the carrying of arms; **enviar** — **pagado** to send prepaid
portear VT to carry
portentoso ADJ portentous
porteño -ña MF (de Buenos Aires) person from Buenos Aires; (de un puerto) person from a port city; ADJ (de Buenos Aires) from Buenos Aires; (de un puerto) from a port city
portería F (de un edificio) entrance area; (en fútbol) goal
portero -ra MF (de un edificio) doorkeeper, superintendent; (en fútbol) goalkeeper; M — **automático** intercom
portón M gate
portuario ADJ harbor, port; **trabajador** — dockworker
Portugal M Portugal
portugués -esa ADJ & MF Portuguese; M (lengua) Portuguese
porvenir M future
pos LOC PREP **en** — **de** after
posada F inn, lodge
posaderas F PL *fam* rear end
posadero -ra MF innkeeper
posar VT (la mano, los ojos) to rest; VI (en el suelo) to sit down; (como modelo) to pose; —**se** (partículas) to settle; (mariposa) to alight; (pájaro) to perch
posdata F postscript
pose F pose
poseedor -ora MF possessor
poseer[18] VT to possess
poseído ADJ possessed
posesión F possession
posesivo ADJ & M possessive

poseyendo, poseyera, poseyese, poseyó *ver* poseer
posfechar VT to postdate
posguerra F postwar period
posibilidad F possibility
posibilitar VT (hacer posible) to make possible; (permitir) to allow, to permit
posible ADJ possible; **hacer lo** — to do one's best; **es** — it's possible
posición F (ubicación) position; (opinión) stance; (rango) standing; — **de negociación** bargaining position; — **del misionero** missionary position; — **fetal** fetal position
posicionamiento M (acción de posicionar, también de productos) placement, positioning; (actitud política) position, stance
posicionarse VI to position oneself
positivo ADJ & M positive
poso M (de vino) dregs; (de café) grounds
posparto M postpartum
posponer[56, 74] VT (aplazar) to postpone, to defer, to put off; (relegar) to put after
posta F (relevo) relay; (perdigón) buckshot
postal ADJ postal; F postcard
poste M (palo) post; (en fútbol) upright, goalpost
póster M poster
postergar[40] VT (para un ascenso) to pass over; (posponer) to postpone
posteridad F posterity; **eso quedará para la** — that will remain for all eternity
posterior ADJ (espacial) back, rear; (anatómico) posterior; (temporal) later; **nuestro divorcio fue** — **a la compra del negocio** our divorce came after we purchased the business
posterioridad LOC ADV **con** — later, subsequently
posteriormente ADV (atrás) in the back; (después) afterward[s]; **vocal pronunciada** — vowel pronounced in the back [of the mouth]
postigo M shutter
postizo ADJ false; **familia postiza** adoptive family; M hairpiece
postnasal ADJ postnasal
postrado ADJ prostrate, prone
postrar VT to prostrate
postre M dessert; **a la** — at last
postulado M postulate
postulante MF candidate
postular VT to postulate
póstumo ADJ posthumous
postura F posture (también opinión)
potable ADJ drinkable, potable
potasio M potassium
pote M (cilíndrico) jar; (panzudo) jug
potear VI/VT to putt
potencia F (sexual) potency; (de una fuerza, nación) power; **es un asesino en** — he's a

potential murderer; — **naval** sea power; **de alta** — high-powered; **segunda** — the second power
potencial ADJ & M potential
potenciar VT (a una persona) to empower; (proyectos, relaciones) to promote, to support
potentado -da MF potentate
potente ADJ potent, powerful
potranco -ca M colt; F filly
potrero M pasture; *Am* cattle ranch, stock farm
potro M (caballo) colt; (en gimnasia) vaulting horse; — **de tormento** rack
pozo M (de agua, petróleo) well; (hoyo profundo) pit; (minero) mine shaft; **sacar del** — to rescue; — **negro** sink; — **sin fondo** bottomless pit; — **séptico** septic tank
práctica F (repetición, costumbre) practice; (destreza) skill; **en la** — in practice; **poner en** — to put into practice; — **comercial desleal** deceptive practice
prácticamente ADV (casi) practically, virtually; (de forma práctica) practically; (en la práctica) in practice
practicante ADJ practicing; MF (que practica) practitioner; (asistente de médico) physician's assistant
practicar[30] VI/VT (una habilidad) to practice; (un agujero) to make
práctico ADJ (sencillo) practical; (adiestrado) skillful; M — **de puerto** harbor pilot
pradera F prairie, grassland
prado M meadow, pasture
pragmático ADJ pragmatic
preadolescente ADJ & MF preteen, preadolescent
preámbulo M preamble
preaprobado ADJ preapproved
precalentamiento M warmup
precanceroso ADJ precancerous
precario ADJ precarious, *fam* touch-and-go
precaución F precaution
precaverse VT to take precautions
precavido ADJ cautious
precedencia F precedence
precedente ADJ preceding; M precedent; **sin** — unprecedented; **sentar** — to set a precedent
preceder VI/VT to precede
precepto M precept
preciado ADJ (estimado) prized; (valioso) valuable
preciarse VI — **de** to be proud of
precintar VT to seal
precinto M seal
precio M price; **poner** — **a** to put a price on; **no tener** — to be priceless; — **de compra** purchase price; — **de lista** list price; — **de mercado** market price; — **de referencia** bench price; — **justo en el mercado** fair

market price; — **sugerido** suggested retail price; — **sugerido por el fabricante** manufacturer's suggested retail price; — **vigente** going price

preciosista ADJ precious

precioso ADJ (metal, piedra, objeto de gran valor) precious; (muy bonito) beautiful, adorable

precipicio M precipice, cliff

precipitación F precipitation (también atolondramiento)

precipitado ADJ precipitate, hasty, rash; M precipitate

precipitar VI to precipitate; VT to hurl; —**se** (apresurarse) to be hasty; (arrojarse) to plunge, to plummet; (depositarse) to precipitate; (adelantarse) to come to a head

precisamente ADV precisely, exactly, just; — **de eso te quería hablar** that is just what I wanted to talk to you about; (de hecho) as a matter of fact; —**, se alojó en este hotel** as a matter of fact he stayed in this hotel

precisar VT (determinar) to determine precisely; (necesitar) to need

precisión F precision, accuracy; **precisiones** clarifications

preciso ADJ precise, accurate; **es — que vengas** you must come; **en este — instante** at this very moment

precoz ADJ (niño) precocious; (diagnóstico) early

precursor -ora MF precursor, forerunner

predecesor -ora MF predecessor

predecir[53, 74] VT to predict, to foretell

predestinar VT to predestine

predeterminado ADJ predetermined

predicación F preaching

predicado ADJ & M predicate

predicador -ora MF preacher

predicar[30] VI/VT to preach

predicción F prediction

predilección F predilection

predilecto ADJ favorite, pet

predio M piece of land

predisponer[56, 74] VT to predispose

predisposición F predisposition

predominante ADJ predominant, prevailing

predominar VI to predominate

predominio M predominance

preeclampsia F preeclampsia

preeminente ADJ foremost

preempacado ADJ prepacked

preescolar ADJ nursery; MF nursery school child

preestablecido ADJ preset

preestreno M preview

preexistente ADJ preexisting

prefacio M preface

preferencia F preference; (en el tráfico) right of way; **de —** predominantly

preferente ADJ (tratamiento) preferential; (acciones) preferred

preferible ADJ preferable

preferido ADJ preferred, favorite

preferir[8] VT to prefer

prefiera, prefiere ver preferir

prefijar VT to prefix

prefijo M prefix

prefiriendo, prefiriera, prefiriese ver preferir

pregonar VT (noticias) to make public; (mercancías) to hawk

pregrabado ADJ prerecorded

pregunta F question; **hacer una —** to ask a question; —**s frecuentes** frequently asked questions

preguntar VI/VT to ask, to inquire; — **por** (pedir información) to inquire about; (pedir para hablar) to ask for; —**se** to wonder

preguntón ADJ inquisitive

prehistórico ADJ prehistoric

prejuicio M prejudice, bias

prejuzgar[40] VT to prejudge

preliminar ADJ & M preliminary

preludiar VT to prelude

preludio M prelude

prematrimonial ADJ premarital

prematuro ADJ (bebé) premature; (muerte) untimely

premeditado ADJ premeditated

premenstrual ADJ premenstrual

premiar VT to reward; **las obras premiadas** the award-winning works

première M premiere

premio M (galardón) prize, award; (de la moneda) appreciation; **Juan Pérez, — nacional de poesía** Juan Pérez, winner of the national poetry award; — **gordo** jackpot

premisa F premise

premonición F premonition

prenatal ADJ prenatal

prenda F (fianza) pawn, pledge; (de vestir) article of clothing, garment; **dejar en —** to pawn; **en — de** as a token of

prendar VT to charm; —**se de** to fall in love with

prendedor M brooch, pin

prender VT (agarrar) to grab; (sujetar) to clasp; (enganchar) to fasten; (detener) to arrest; (arraigar) to take root; (encender) to turn on, to switch on; — **fuego** to set on fire; **la vacuna no prendió** the vaccination didn't take

prensa F press; **tener mala —** to have bad press

prensar VT to press

prensil ADJ prehensile

prenupcial ADJ prenuptial

preñada ADJ pregnant

preñar VT (a una hembra animal) to impregnate;

(a una mujer) *vulg* to knock up

preñez F pregnancy

prcocupación F worry, concern

preocupado ADJ worried, concerned, anxious

preocupante ADJ worrisome

preocupar VT to worry, to concern; —**se de** to worry about; —**se por** to be concerned about

preocupón -ona MF worrywart

preparación F preparation

preparado ADJ ready; M preparation

preparar VT to prepare; —**se** to get ready, to brace oneself; — **el cuerpo de un difunto** to embalm a body

preparativo ADJ preparatory; M preparation

preparatorio ADJ preparatory; **escuela preparatoria** preparatory school

preponderancia F preponderance

preponderante ADJ preponderant

preponderar VI to predominate

preposición F preposition

prepucio M foreskin

prerrequisito M prerequisite

prerrogativa F prerogative

presa F (animal de caza) prey, quarry; (dique) dam

presagiar VT to forebode

presagio M omen, sign

présbita, présbite ADV & MF farsighted

prescindible ADJ dispensable

prescindir VI — **de** to dispense with, to do without

prescribir[74] VT to prescribe

prescripción F prescription

presencia F presence; — **de ánimo** presence of mind

presenciar VT to witness

presentable ADJ presentable

presentación F (de un tema) presentation; (de una persona) introduction

presentador -ora MF (de programa de televisión) host; (de noticiero) anchor

presentar VT (una idea) to present; (a una persona) to introduce; (la declaración de impuestos, una demanda) to file; (un informe) to submit; (documentos) to produce; (una queja) to lodge; (una renuncia) to tender; —**se** (aparecer) to appear; (hacerse conocer) to introduce oneself

presente ADJ present; M (tiempo) present; (regalo) present, gift; **al** — at the present time; **tener** — to bear in mind; **en el** — [contrato] herein; **por la** — [carta] hereby

presentimiento M presentiment, foreboding, hunch

presentir[8] VT to have a presentiment of

preservación F (protección) preservation; (ahorro) conservation

preservar VT (proteger) to preserve; (ahorrar) to conserve

preservativo M condom

presidencia F presidency

presidencial ADJ presidential

presidente MF, **presidenta** F (de un país) president; (de una reunión, junta) chair

presidiario -ria MF prisoner

presidio M prison

presidir VI to preside; VT to preside over

presilla F loop

presión F pressure; — **atmosférica** atmospheric pressure; — **arterial** blood pressure; — **arterial alta** high blood pressure, hypertension; — **de aire** air pressure

presionar VT (un botón) to press; (al gobierno) to lobby

preso -sa MF prisoner, inmate

prestación F provision; **prestaciones** benefits

prestador -ora MF lender

prestamista MF (de dinero) lender; (en un montepío) pawnbroker

préstamo M loan; — **convencional** conventional loan; — **garantizado** guaranteed loan

prestar VT to loan, to lend; — **ayuda** to give help; — **atención** to pay attention; — **juramento** to take an oath; — **servicio** to render service

prestatario -ria MF borrower

prestidigitación F sleight of hand

prestigio M prestige

prestigioso ADJ prestigious

presumido ADJ conceited, presumptuous

presumir VT (suponer) to presume; VI (ostentar) to show off; — **de valiente** to boast of one's valor

presunción F presumption

presuntamente ADV allegedly

presunto ADJ (dueño, autor de una obra) presumed; (autor de un crimen) alleged; — **heredero** heir apparent

presuntuoso ADJ presumptuous

presuponer[56, 74] VT to presuppose

presupuestación F budgeting

presupuestario ADJ budget, budgetary

presupuesto M (de gastos e ingresos) budget; (de costos) estimate; — **equilibrado** balanced budget

presuroso ADJ hasty

pretencioso ADJ pretentious

pretender VI (sostener) to claim, to purport; — **ser** to claim to be; — **al trono** to pretend to the throne; VT (intentar) to attempt

pretendiente MF, **pretendienta** F (al trono) pretender; (a un puesto) aspirant; M (de una mujer) suitor, admirer

pretensión F pretension

pretérito ADJ past; M past tense; — **perfecto** present perfect

pretexto M pretext, pretense; **so — de** under pretense of
pretil M railing
pretina F waistband
prevalecer[35] VI to prevail
prevaleciente ADJ prevalent
prevé, prevea, preveía *ver* prever
prevención F (protección) prevention; (recelo) caution
prevenido ADJ forewarned
prevenir[61] VT (precaver) to prevent; (prever) to foresee; (advertir) to warn; **— contra** to protect oneself against
preventivo ADJ preventive, precautionary
prever[72, 74] VT to foresee, to anticipate
previamente ADV previously
previo ADJ previous, prior; **— examen de salud** after undergoing a health examination
previsible ADJ foreseeable
previsión F foresight, anticipation
previsto *ver* prever
previsualización F previewing
prieto ADJ swarthy
prima F (cuota de seguro) premium; (recargo) surcharge; (pago extraordinario) bonus
primario ADJ primary
primate M primate
primavera F spring
primaveral ADJ springlike
primero ADJ & ADV first; **primer ministro** prime minister; **primer piso** second floor; **primer plano** foreground; **primera base** (posición) first base; (jugador) first baseman; **primera enseñanza** primary education; **primera persona** first person; **primer tiempo** first half; **—s auxilios** first aid; **a primera vista** at first sight; **de primer grado** first degree; **de primera** top-notch; **de primera mano** firsthand; **por primera vez** for the first time; **— del mes** first of the month; **Juan llegó —** Juan arrived first; F (marcha) first gear; (clase en un avión) first class
primicia F (fruto primero) first fruit; (noticia) scoop
primitivo ADJ primitive
primo -ma MF (hijo de tío) cousin; (persona incauta) sucker, dupe; **— hermano** first cousin; **— segundo** second cousin; ADJ prime
primogénito -ta ADJ & MF firstborn
primogenitura F birthright
primor M (esmero) care; (cosa fina) lovely thing
primordial ADJ primordial
primoroso ADJ exquisite
princesa F princess
principal ADJ principal, main; **la causa — de muerte** the leading cause of death; **el dormitorio —** the master bedroom

principalmente ADV mainly, principally
príncipe M prince
principesco ADJ princely
principiante MF beginner; ADJ beginning
principiar VT to commence
principio M (fundamento, regla de conducta) principle, tenet; (hecho de empezar, tiempo, lugar) beginning, start; **a —s de** toward the beginning of; **— activo** active ingredient; **al —** at the beginning, at first; **de — a fin** from beginning to end; **desde el —** from the beginning; **en —** in principle
pringar[40] VT (ensuciar) to get greasy; (mojar) to dip
pringoso ADJ greasy
pringue MF grease
prioridad F (autoridad, preferencia) priority, precedence; (en el tráfico) right of way
prioritario ADJ having priority, most important
prisa F haste, hurry; **a toda —** at full speed; **correr —** to be urgent; **darse —** to hurry; **las —s comienzan a la una** the rush starts at one; **tener —** to be in a hurry; **sin —** leisurely
prisión F prison; **— perpetua** life in prison
prisionero -ra MF prisoner; **— de guerra** prisoner of war
prisma M prism
prismáticos M PL binoculars
privacidad F privacy
privación F privation; **pasar privaciones** to suffer want
privado ADJ private; **en —** in private
privar VT to deprive; **—se de** to deprive oneself of
privativo ADJ exclusive
privatización F privatization
privatizar[47] VT to privatize
privilegiado ADJ privileged
privilegiar VT to favor, to give a privilege to
privilegio M privilege
pro M advantage; **en — de** in favor of; **en — y en contra** for and against
proa F prow, bow
proaborto ADJ INV pro-choice
probabilidad F (chance) likelihood; (en estadística) probability; **tienes pocas —es de ganar** you have little chance of winning; **¿qué —es tiene?** what are her odds?
probable ADJ probable, likely; **lo más — es que haya venido** in all likelihood he came
probador M dressing room
probar[5] VT (alimento, bebida) to taste, to try, to sample; (una hipótesis) to prove; (una guitarra) to try out; (un coche) to test-drive; **—se un vestido** to try on a dress; **— fortuna** to try one's luck; **prueba a venir más temprano** try to come earlier; **no — bocado** not to eat a bite

probatorio ADJ probationary
probeta F test tube
problema M problem; **él sólo da —s** he's nothing but trouble
problemático -ca ADJ problematic; F problems
procedencia F origin
procedente ADJ **— de** from
proceder VI to proceed; **— de** to come from; **— a** to proceed to; **— contra** to take action against
procedimiento M procedure; **—s** proceedings
procesable ADJ actionable
procesado -da MF accused; M processing
procesador ADJ processing; M processor; **— de textos** word processor
procesamiento M prosecution; **— de datos** data processing; **— de textos** word processing
procesar VT to prosecute, to try
procesión F procession; **la — va por dentro** he doesn't let it show
proceso M (etapas) process; (juicio) trial, legal proceedings
proclama F proclamation
proclamación F proclamation
proclamar VT to proclaim; **—se campeón** to be proclaimed winner
proclive ADJ prone
procrear VI/VT to procreate
proctología F proctology
procurador -ora MF attorney
procurar VT (intentar) to endeavor; (obtener) to procure, to obtain
prodigar[40] VT to lavish; **—se** to be lavish
prodigio M prodigy
prodigioso ADJ prodigious
pródigo -ga ADJ (derrochador) prodigal; (muy generoso) lavish; MF spendthrift
producción F (acción de producir) production; (cantidad producida) production, yield; **— masiva** mass production
producir[38] VT (efectos, mercancías, películas) to produce; (fruta, resultados) to yield, to bear; **—se** to happen
productividad F productivity
productivo ADJ (rendidor) productive; (exitoso) successful
producto M product; **— interno bruto** gross national product
productor -ora MF producer; ADJ **un país — de petróleo** an oil-producing country
produje, produjera, produjese ver producir
pro-elección ADJ INV pro-choice
proeza F exploit
profanación F desecration
profanar VT to profane, to desecrate
profano ADJ profane
profecía F prophecy
proferir[8] VT to utter

profesar VT to profess
profesión F profession
profesional ADJ & MF professional; **— de la salud** health care provider
profesionista MF *Méx* professional
profesor -ora MF (universitario) professor; (de enseñanza secundaria) teacher; (de tenis) instructor
profesorado M faculty
profeta MF prophet
profético ADJ prophetic
profetizar[47] VI/VT to prophesy
profilaxis F prevention
prófugo -ga ADJ & MF fugitive
profundidad F (del mar, de comprensión, de un armario) depth; (sabiduría) profundity
profundizar[47] VT to deepen; VI to go into deeply
profundo ADJ (idea, comentario, razonamiento) profound; (mar, pozo, armario, voz) deep
profuso ADJ profuse
progesterona F progesterone
programa M (de boxeo) card; (de televisión) show, program; (de un curso) syllabus; (de un congreso) program; **— antivirus** antivirus program, antivirus software; **— de protección contra virus** virus protection software; **— de instalación** setup program, install program; **— instalador** setup program, install program; **— para recuperar datos borrados** undelete utility; **—s almacenados en circuitos integrados** firmware
programable ADJ programmable
programación F programming
programador -ora MF programmer
programar VT (una computadora) to program; (un evento) to schedule
progresar VT to progress, to advance
progresión F progression
progresista ADJ & MF progressive
progresivo -va ADJ & MF progressive
progreso M progress
prohibición F prohibition, ban
prohibido ADJ forbidden; **prohibida la entrada** no admittance; **— el paso** no trespassing
prohibir[79] VT to prohibit, to ban; **se prohíbe fumar** no smoking
prohijar VT to adopt
prójimo -ma MF fellow human
prole F offspring
proletariado M proletariat
proletario -ria ADJ & MF proletarian
proliferación F proliferation, spread
prolífico ADJ prolific
prolijo ADJ (verboso) wordy; (esmerado) overly careful
prologar[40] VT to preface

prólogo M prologue, foreword, preface
prolongación F prolongation
prolongado ADJ extended
prolongar[40] VT to prolong; **—se** to wear on
promediar VT to average
promedio M average, mean; **de/en—** on average; **— de carreras limpias permitidas** earned run average
promesa F promise; **romper una —** to break a promise; **una joven —** a promising young player
prometedor ADJ promising
prometer VT to promise; VI to show promise
prometido-da ADJ engaged; M fiancé; F fiancée
prominente ADJ prominent
promiscuo ADJ promiscuous
promisorio ADJ promissory; **un futuro —** a promising future
promoción F (oferta comercial) promotion; (conjunto de personas) class
promocional ADJ promotional
promocionar VT to promote, to publicize
promontorio M promontory
promotor-ora MF (de un producto) promoter; (de bienes inmuebles) developer
promover[6] VT (ideas, producto, a un alumno) to promote; (la paz, una causa) to foster, to further
promulgación F enactment
promulgar[40] VT to promulgate, to enact
pronombre M pronoun
pronominal ADJ pronominal
pronosticar[30] VT to forecast
pronóstico M (del tiempo, de la economía) forecast; (de una enfermedad) prognosis
prontitud F promptness, dispatch
pronto ADJ (rápido) quick; (listo) ready; ADV soon, promptly; **de —** suddenly; **¡hasta —!** see you soon! **tan — como** as soon as
pronunciación F pronunciation
pronunciado ADJ pronounced
pronunciamiento M declaration, pronouncement
pronunciar VT (un sonido, una sentencia) to pronounce; (un discurso) to make, to deliver; **—se** (acusarse) to be pronounced; (expresarse) to declare one's opinion
propagación F propagation, spread
propaganda F (de ideas) propaganda; (de mercancías) advertising, publicity; **hacer —** to advertise
propagar[40] VT to propagate
propalar VT to spread
propano M propane
propasarse VI to go too far
propensión F propensity
propenso ADJ prone
propiciar VT to favor
propicio ADJ propitious, auspicious

propiedad F (cualidad, pertenencia, finca) property; (derecho de dueño) ownership; (corrección) precision; **— mayoritaria** majority ownership; **— privada** private property; **—es** estate; **—es colindantes** adjoining properties
propietario-ria M (de una tienda) proprietor, owner; (de un apartamento) landlord; F (de una tienda) owner; (de un apartamento) landlady; **— ausente** absentee landlord
propina F tip, gratuity; **dar [una] —** to tip
propinar VT **— una paliza** to give a beating
propio ADJ (correcto) proper; **el significado —** the proper meaning; (típico) like; **no es — de él quejarse así** it's not like him to complain like that; (conveniente) appropriate; **una expresión propia** an appropriate expression; (que le pertenece) own; **su — hijo** his own son; **un hijo —** a son of his own; **por tu — bien** for your own good; (mismo) same; **al — tiempo** at the same time
propondrá, propondría ver proponer
proponente MF proponent
proponer[56, 74] VT to propose; **—se** to set out to
proponga, propongo ver proponer
proporción F proportion, ratio; **proporciones** dimensions
proporcional ADJ proportional, proportionate
proporcionar VT (ajustar a proporción) to proportion; (brindar) to furnish, to provide
proposición F (lógica) proposition; (de matrimonio) proposal; **proposiciones deshonestas** indecent proposals
propósito M purpose, intent; **a —** (adecuado) apropos; (voluntariamente) on purpose, intentionally, deliberately; (además) by the way, incidentally; **a — de** apropos of
propuesta F proposal
propuesto ver proponer
propugnar VT to urge
propulsar VT to propel
propulsión F propulsion; **— a chorro** jet propulsion
propulsor-ora ADJ propelling; MF promoter
propuse, propusiera, propusiese ver proponer
prorratear VT to prorate
prórroga F (plazo) extension of time; (de un préstamo) renewal; (fútbol americano) overtime; (fútbol) extra time
prorrogar[40] VT (un pago) to put off, to defer; (un plazo) to extend; (un préstamo) to renew
prorrumpir VI to burst; **— en llanto** to burst into tears; **— en carcajadas** to burst out laughing
prosa F prose
prosaico ADJ prosaic
proscribir[74] VT to banish, to disenfranchise
proscripción F banishment

proseguir[12] VI to proceed
prosódico ADJ prosodic
prospectar VT to prospect
prospector-ora MF prospector
prosperar VI to prosper, to flourish, to thrive
prosperidad F prosperity
próspero ADJ prosperous
próstata F prostate [gland]
prostitución F prostitution
prostituir[19] VT to prostitute
prostituto-ta MF prostitute
protagonista MF protagonist
protagonizar[47] VT to star in
protección F protection; — **al consumidor** consumer protection; — **contra copias** copy protection; — **contra grabación** write protection; — **contra lectura** read protect; — **por contraseña** password protection
proteccionista ADJ & MF protectionist
protector-ora ADJ protective; MF protector; — **de pantalla** screen saver; — **de tensión** surge protector; — **sobrecargas de voltaje** surge protector; — **solar** sunblock
protectorado M protectorate
proteger[45] VT (a alguien vulnerable) to protect; (a un artista) to sponsor; — **contra grabación** to write-protect
protegido-da MF protégé[e]; — **por contraseña** password protected
proteína F protein
prótesis F prosthesis; — **de cadera** hip prosthesis
protesta F protest
protestante MF Protestant
protestar VI/VT to protest
protocolo M protocol
protón M proton
protoplasma M protoplasm
prototipo M prototype
protozoario M protozoan
protuberancia F protuberance, bulge, bump
protuberante ADJ bulging
provecho M (beneficio) benefit; (eructo) burp; **¡buen —!** bon appétit! **sacar — [de]** to benefit [from], to profit [from]
provechoso ADJ beneficial, advantageous
proveedor-ora MF (de un servicio) provider; (de un producto) supplier, vendor; — **de acceso** access provider; — **de acceso a internet** Internet access provider
proveer[18, 74] VT to provide; — **de** to provide with; —**se de** to provide oneself with
provenga, provengo ver provenir
proveniente ADJ — **de** coming from
provenir[61] VI to arise; — **de** to stem from
proverbio M proverb
providencia F providence
providencial ADJ providential
provincia F province

provincial ADJ provincial
provinciano-na ADJ & MF provincial
provine, proviniendo, proviniera, proviniese, provino ver provenir
provisión F provision, supply, store
provisional ADJ temporary, provisional
provisorio ADJ temporary
provocación F provocation
provocar[30] VT (ira) to provoke; (sexualmente) to excite; (un incendio) to start; (una respuesta) to elicit
provocativo ADJ provocative
proxeneta MF procurer, pimp, panderer
proximidad F proximity, nearness; **en las —es** in the vicinity
próximo ADJ (posterior) next; (cercano) near, nearby; **el lunes — pasado** last Monday; **de próxima aparición** forthcoming
proyección F projection
proyectar VT (un plan) to project; (una película) to screen; (una sombra) to cast; —**se** to overhang, to jut
proyectil M projectile
proyecto M (idea) project; (arquitectónico) plan; — **de ley** bill
proyector M (para películas) projector; (en el teatro) spotlight
prudencia F prudence
prudente ADJ prudent
prueba F (de imprenta, argumento irrefutable) proof; (argumento parcial) evidence; (intento, dificultad) trial, test; (examen) test, examination; (de ropa) fitting; — **beta** beta test; — **de detección** screening test; — **de doble incógnita** double-blind test; — **de embarazo** pregnancy test; — **de esfuerzo** stress test; — **de esfuerzo máximo** exercise electrocardiogram; — **de fuego** trial by fire; — **de ingresos** means test; — **de paternidad** paternity test; — **de Rorschach** Rorschach test; **a —** on approval; **a — de fallos** foolproof; **a — de incendio** fireproof; **poner a —** to put to the test
prueba, pruebe ver probar
psicoanálisis M psychoanalysis
psicodélico ADJ & M psychedelic
psicología F psychology
psicológico ADJ psychological
psicólogo-ga MF psychologist
psicópata MF psychopath
psicosis F psychosis
psicosomático ADJ psychosomatic
psicoterapia F psychotherapy
psicótico ADJ psychotic
psiquiatra MF psychiatrist
psiquiatría F psychiatry
psíquico ADJ psychic
psoriasis F psoriasis
púa F (con punta aguda) spike; (de alambre)

barb; (de guitarra) pick; (de erizo) quill; (de tridente) prong

puaf, puaj INTERJ yuck, ugh

pubertad F puberty

publicación F publication

publicar[30] VT to publish; (revelar) to divulge

publicidad F publicity, advertising; — **de cebo y anzuelo** bait-and-switch advertising; — **engañosa** false advertising; — **exterior** outdoor advertising; **hacer** — to advertise

publicitario -ria MF advertising agent; ADJ publicity

público ADJ public; M (testigo) public; (en un espectáculo) audience; **en** — in public

publirreportaje M infomercial

puchero M (vasija) pot; (guiso) stew; (gesto) pout; **hacer —s** to pout

puck M puck

pude, pudiendo, pudiera, pudiese ver poder

pudiente ADJ wealthy

pudín M pudding

pudor M (sexual) modesty; (emocional) reserve

pudrir[74] VI to rot

pueblerino ADJ provincial

pueblo M (población) town; (nación) people, folk

pueda, puede ver poder

puente M bridge (también dental, de gafas, de nariz); (fin de semana) long weekend; — **aéreo** (regular) shuttle; (de emergencia) airlift; — **cardiopulmonar** cardiopulmonary bypass, coronary bypass; — **colgante** suspension bridge; — **levadizo** drawbridge

puénting M bungee jumping

pueril ADJ childish

puerta F (de casa) door; (de aeropuerto, de ciudad) gate; (entrada) entrance; — **de acceso** gateway; **vender de** — **en** — to sell door to door; **dar a alguien con la** — **en las narices** to slam the door in someone's face; **llamar a la** — to knock on the door; — **trasera** back door; **a** — **cerrada** behind closed doors

puerto M port (también en informática); — **de acceso** gateway; — **de entrada** port of entry; — **de ratón** mouse port; — **paralelo** parallel port; — **serie/serial** serial port; — **USB** USB port; **llegar a buen** — to bring to a satisfactory conclusion

puertorriqueño -ña ADJ & MF Puerto Rican

pues CONJ (puesto que) since, for; ADV (entonces) then; — **bien** well then, now

puesta F — **al día** update; — **del sol** sunset, setting of the sun; — **en marcha** (de un proyecto) setting in motion; (de un coche) starting; — **en libertad** freeing

puestero -ra MF vendor, seller

puesto ADJ **bien** — (casa) well-appointed; (persona) well made-up; **llevar** — to have on; M (posición) place; (de venta) booth, stand; (de trabajo) post, position; — **de socorros** first-aid station; **quedarse con lo** — to be left with only the clothes on one's back; CONJ — **que** since

puesto ver poner

pugilato M boxing

pugilista MF boxer, prizefighter

pugna F struggle; **estar en** — **con** to be in conflict with

pugnaz ADJ feisty

puja F (del viento) push; (en una subasta) bid

pujanza F vigor

pujar VI (para dar a luz) to push; (en una subasta) to bid; — **por** to strive to

pujo M contraction

pulcritud F neatness

pulcro ADJ neat

pulga F flea; **tener malas** —s to be ill-tempered

pulgada F inch

pulgar M thumb

pulido ADJ polished; M polishing

pulimento M (de modales) refinement; (de metales) buffing; (polvo para pulir) scouring powder

pulir VT (metal, un discurso) to polish; (madera) to sand

pulla F taunt, dig

pulmón M lung; — **de acero** iron lung

pulmonar ADJ pulmonary; **capacidad** — lung capacity

pulmonía F pneumonia

pulpa F pulp

púlpito M pulpit

pulpo M octopus

pulque M *Méx* pulque

pulquería F *Méx* pulque bar

pulsación F (de corazón) pulse; (de ratón de computadora) click; (de tecla) keystroke

pulsar VT (una tecla) to press; (cuerdas de guitarra) to pluck; (la opinión pública) to gauge; — **y arrastrar** to click and drag

púlsar M pulsar

pulsera F (alhaja) bracelet; (de reloj) watchband; **reloj de** — wristwatch

pulso M (pulsación) pulse; (firmeza de mano) steadiness; **echar un** — to arm-wrestle; **tomar el** — to take the pulse; **a** — with great effort

pulular VI to swarm, to teem with

pulverizar[47] VT to pulverize

puma F mountain lion, cougar, puma

puna F cold, arid tableland of the Andes

punitivo ADJ punitive

punk ADJ & M punk

punkero -ra MF punk

punta F (de cuchillo) point; (de la lengua, de un

lápiz) tip; (de calcetín) toe; — **de lanza** spearhead; **una — de** a bunch of; **a — de cuchillo** at knifepoint; — **de flecha** arrowhead; **de —** on end; **iba caminando de —s** he was tiptoeing; **sacar — a un lápiz** to sharpen a pencil; **en la — de la lengua** on the tip of the tongue; **me pone los nervios de —** it makes me nervous; M **—pié** kick; ADJ **puntiagudo** sharp, pointed

puntada F stitch, prick

puntal M (de un edificio) prop; (de la economía) mainstay

puntear VT (una guitarra) to pluck; (un mapa) to make dots on; (una lista) to check off

puntería F aim; **tener buena —** to be a good shot

puntero M pointer

puntilla F point lace; **de —s** on tiptoe

punto M (puntuación) period; (de cinturón) notch; (marca, signo) point, dot; (anotación, tema, lugar) point; (puntada) stitch; — **álgido** fever pitch; — **culminante** (de una carrera) peak; (de una historia) climax; (de negociaciones) critical stage; — **de apoyo** foothold; — **de condensación** dewpoint; — **de congelación** freezing point; — **de ebullición** boiling point; — **de juego** game point; — **de manga** set point; — **de origen** point of origin; — **de partida** point of departure; — **de partido** match-point; — **de referencia** point of reference, benchmark; — **de vista** viewpoint, point of view; — **extra** (fútbol americano) point after touchdown; — **muerto** (en un negocio) stalemate, deadlock; (en un coche) neutral; — **y coma** semicolon; **al —** at once; **a —** ready; **a — de** on the point/verge of; **cogerle el —** to figure out; **dos —s** colon; **el — medio** the halfway mark; **en —** on the dot; **hacer —** to knit; **hasta cierto —** to a certain extent; **poner los —s sobre las íes** to dot one's i's and cross one's t's

puntuación F punctuation

puntual ADJ (en hora) punctual, prompt; (específico) specific

puntualidad F punctuality

puntualizar[47] VT to point out

puntuar[26] VT to punctuate

punzada F (de dolor) stab; (de remordimiento, hambre) pang, twinge

punzante ADJ sharp, piercing

punzar[47] VT to prick

punzón M (en papel) hole punch; (en cuero) awl

puñado M handful; **a —s** by the handful

puñal M dagger

puñalada F stab; **coser a —s** to stab to death

puñetazo M punch, slug; **dar un —** to punch; **dar un — en la mesa** to bang on the table

puño M (mano cerrada) fist; (en una manga) cuff;

(de espada) handle; **arreglarlo con los —s** to duke it out; **de mi — y letra** by my own hand

pupa F *Esp* boo-boo

pupila F pupil

pupilo -la MF ward

pupitre M school desk

puré M purée; — **de patatas/papas** mashed potatoes; **hacer —** to smash

pureza F purity

purga F (política) purge; (medicinal) purgative

purgación F atonement

purgante ADJ & M purgative, laxative

purgar[40] VT (el vientre, a un rival) to purge; (frenos) to bleed; (pecados) to atone for

purgatorio M purgatory

purificar[30] VT to purify

purista ADJ & MF purist

puritano ADJ puritanical

puro ADJ pure; **lo hizo de — bueno** he did it out of sheer kindness; **a pura fuerza** by sheer force; **la pura verdad** the plain truth; **son puras mentiras** that's a lot of bull; **de purasangre** thoroughbred; M cigar

púrpura ADJ & M purple

pus M pus

puse, pusiera, pusiese *ver* poner

puta F (prostituta) *ofensivo* whore, hooker; (mujer fácil) *ofensivo* slut; **de — madre** *vulg* very good; **de la gran —** *vulg* huge; **¡— madre!** *vulg* fuck! shit!

putañero M john

putón M *ofensivo* slut

putrefacto ADJ putrid, decayed

putter M putter

Qq

Qatar M Qatar

quásar M quasar

que PRON REL that; (con antecedente no humano) which; (con antecedente humano) who, whom; **el/la —** the one that; **lo — tú dices** what you say; **vino la suegra, lo — complicó la visita** the mother-in-law came, which complicated the visit; CONJ that; **no creo — haya tiempo** I don't think [that] there's time; **estoy — me muero** I feel like I'm about to die; **Carlos es más alto — Luis** Carlos is taller than Luis; **más/menos —** more/less than; **déjalo aquí — lo voy a necesitar después** leave it here because I will need it later; **por mucho —** no matter how much; **a — gana** I bet he'll win; — **yo sepa** as far as I know

qué ADJ INTERR & PRON what, which; **¿— libro**

vas a usar? what/which book are you going to use? **¿— dices?** what are you saying? **no sé — dijo** I don't know what he said; **¡— bonito!** how beautiful! **¡— de gente!** what a lot of people! **¿y eso —?** so what! **no hay de —** don't mention it; **¿— sé yo?** what do I know? **¿— tal?** how are you? **¡— más da!** what's the difference! **¡— va!** *fam* oh yeah? yeah right! **¡a mí —!** so what!

quebrada F (valle) ravine; (arroyo) creek

quebradizo ADJ breakable, brittle

quebrado ADJ (roto) broken; (rajado) cracked; (sin dinero) broke; M fraction

quebrantar VT (una casa, la salud) to weaken; (la ley) to violate

quebranto M weakening

quebrar[1] VT (romper) to break; (rajar) to crack; VI (irse a la bancarrota) to go bankrupt, to go under, to fail; **—se** to break [up]; **se quebró la muñeca** he broke his wrist; **—se uno la cabeza** to rack one's brain

queda F **toque de —** curfew

quedar VI (permanecer) to remain; (no haberse terminado) to be left; **queda leche en el vaso** there's milk in the glass; (estar ubicado) to be located; **la iglesia queda en la esquina** the church is located on the corner; (sentar bien la ropa) to suit; **— bien** to come out well; **— en** to agree to; **—se** to remain, to stay; **—se con una cosa** (comprar) to take/buy something; (llevarse) to take something

quehacer M chore, errand

queja F (protesta) complaint; (oficial) grievance

quejarse VI (protestar) to complain; (protestar ruidosamente) to gripe, to squawk; (protestar incesantemente) to whine

quejica ADJ whiny; MF nag, whiner

quejido M (de tono grave) moan, groan; (de tono agudo) squawk

quejoso ADJ whiny

quema F burning

quemado -da MF burn victim

quemador M burner

quemadura F (lugar quemado) burn; (sensación) burning; (enfermedad de plantas) blight

quemar VT to burn (también cedés); **—se** (un edificio) to burn up/down; (al sol) to sunburn

quemazón F burning sensation

quepa, quepamos *ver* caber

querella F lawsuit

querellante MF plaintiff

querellarse VI to file suit

querer[70] VI/VT (desear) to want; (amar) to love; **como quieras** as you please; **cuando quieras** whenever you want; **no quiso hacerlo** he refused to do it; **quiere llover** it is about to rain; **sin —** unwillingly; **— decir** to mean; **lo quiero mucho** I want it badly

querido -da ADJ beloved, dear; MF (enamorado) sweetheart; (como tratamiento) dear, darling

queroseno M kerosene

querrá, querría *ver* querer

quesería F dairy, cheese factory

queso M cheese; **— crema / de untar** cream cheese; **— suizo** swiss cheese

quiche M quiche

quicio M hinge; **sacar a uno de —** to drive someone up the wall

quiebra F bankruptcy (también moral); (de un mercado) crash; (de un comercio) failure; **— bancaria** bank failure

quiebra, quiebre *ver* quebrar

quiebre M break

quien PRON REL who, whom; **Juan, — recién cumplió cuarenta años** Juan, who just turned forty; **— hizo eso** whoever did that; **a — corresponda** to whom it may concern; **—quiera** whoever; **de —** whose; **con —** with whom

quién PRON INTERR & PRON who; **¿— es?** who is it? **no sé — entró** I don't know who came in; **¿a — se lo diste?** who did you give it to? to whom did you give it?

quiera, quiere *ver* querer

quieto ADJ still

quietud F stillness

quijada F jaw

quilate M carat

quilla F keel

química F chemistry

químico -ca ADJ chemical; MF chemist

quimioterapia F chemotherapy

quince NUM fifteen (también en tenis)

quincena F (de cosas) group of fifteen; (de días) two-week period

quincenal ADV biweekly

quincha F thatch

quinchar VT to thatch

quinesiología F kinesiology

quingombó M okra

quinientos NUM five hundred

quinina F quinine

quinqué M oil lamp

quinta F (casa) villa; (reclutamiento) draft

quinto ADJ, ADV, & M fifth

quiosco M kiosk, newsstand

quiquiriquí INTERJ cock-a-doodle-doo

quirófano M surgery, operating room

quiropráctico -ca ADJ chiropractic; MF chiropractor; F chiropractic

quirúrgico ADJ surgical

quise, quisiera, quisiese *ver* querer

quisquilloso ADJ particular, fussy

quiste M cyst

quitar VT (una mancha) to remove; (una prenda de vestir) to take off; (despojar de) to take away; M SG **quitaesmalte** nail polish

remover; M SG **quitanieves** snowplow; M SG
quitamanchas spot remover; VI **—se** to
take off; **—se a alguien de encima** to get
rid of someone; **quítate de ahí** move over
quite M **salir al — de** to go to the rescue of
quizá, quizás ADV perhaps, maybe

Rr

rabadilla F (coxis) tailbone; (de un ave) rump
rábano M radish; **me importa un —** I couldn't
care less
rabia F (enfermedad) rabies; (enojo) rage; **me
tiene —** he hates me; **dar —** to anger
rabiar VI to rage, to fume; **guapa a —**
drop-dead beautiful
rabieta F tantrum
rabino -na MF rabbi
rabioso ADJ (hidrofóbico, apasionado) rabid,
mad; (enojado) mad, furious
rabo M (cola) tail; (pene) *fam* dick; (cabo) stem;
mirar con el — del ojo to look out of the
corner of one's eye; **con el — entre las
piernas** with his tail between his legs
rabón ADJ bobtail
racha F (de suerte) streak; (de viento) gust
racial ADJ racial
racimo M (de plátanos, personas) bunch; (de
uvas) cluster
raciocinio M reasoning
ración F (de guerra) ration, allowance; (de
comida) portion
racional ADJ rational (también número)
racionalizado ADJ (justificado) rationalized;
(reestructurado) streamlined
racionalizar[47] VT (una acción) to rationalize;
(un negocio) to streamline
racionamiento M rationing
racionar VT to ration
racismo M racism
racista ADJ & MF racist
radar M radar
radiación F radiation
radiactivo ADJ radioactive
radiador M radiator
radial ADJ radial
radiante ADJ radiant
radiar VT (calor) to radiate; (por radio) to
broadcast
radical ADJ (extremo) radical; (células) root; M
(en química) radical; (en gramática) root
radicalismo M radicalism
radicar[30] VI to be located; **— en** to lie in; **—se** to
take up residence
radio M (hueso, segmento de un círculo) radius;

(elemento radiactivo) radium; F (aparato,
difusión) radio; (emisora) radio station; **— de
acción** sphere of influence
radiodifusión F broadcasting
radiodifusora F radio station
radioescucha MF radio listener
radiofónico ADJ radio
radiografía F x-ray
radiografiar[28] VT (hacer rayos x) to x-ray;
(examinar con cuidado) to examine carefully
radiología F radiology
radiólogo -ga MF radiologist
radiotelescopio M radio telescope
radioterapia F radiation therapy
radiotransmisor M radio transmitter
radón M radon
raer[52] VI/VT to scrape [off]; (un artículo de ropa)
to wear out
ráfaga F (de viento) gust, blast; (de luz) flash; (de
ametralladora) burst
raído ADJ threadbare
raigón M stump
raíz F root; **— cuadrada** square root; **a — de**
due to; **arrancar de —** to uproot; **cortar de
—** to nip in the bud; **echar raíces** to take
root
raja F (de melón) slice; (de falda) slit; (del
trasero) *vulg* crack; (de leña) stick
rajadura F (en piedra, metal) crack; (en tela)
rent, rip
rajar VT (una piedra) to crack; (un tronco) to
split; **—se** (partir) to split open; (acobardarse)
to chicken out, to blink; ADV **a rajatabla**
strictly
ralea F ilk
ralear VI to thin out
ralentización F (de la economía) slump; (de un
motor) idle
rallador M grater
rallar VT to grate, to shred
ralo ADJ sparse, thin
RAM M RAM
rama F branch, limb; (delgada) twig; **andarse
por las —s** to beat around the bush;
algodón en — raw cotton
ramaje M foliage
ramal M (de soga) strand; (de vía férrea) branch,
spur
ramera F *pey* whore
ramificarse[30] VI to divide into branches, to
branch off
ramillete M bouquet, bunch, spray
ramo M (de flores) bouquet; (de una ciencia)
branch; (de una actividad) line; **— de olivo**
olive branch
rampa F ramp
ramplón ADJ vulgar
rana F frog
ranchero -ra MF rancher; **música ranchera**

Mexican country music

rancho M (comida para soldados) mess; (comida mala) swill; (finca) ranch; (choza) hut; **hacer — aparte** to keep to oneself

rancio ADJ rancid; **de — abolengo** of ancient lineage

rango M (militar) rank; (categoría) standing

ranilla F frog [of a hoof]

ránking M (tenis) ranking

ranura F (corte) groove; (para insertar monedas, cartas) slot; **— para accesorios** accessory slot, expansion slot

rapar VT (pelo) to shave off; (cabeza) to shave

rapaz ADJ (animal) predatory; (destructivo) rapacious

rape M **cortar al —** to crop

rapé M snuff

rapear VI to rap

rápidamente ADV (con mucha velocidad) fast; (en poco tiempo) quickly

rapidez F (de un coche) speed; (de un movimiento) rapidity, quickness

rápido ADJ (con mucha velocidad) fast; (en poco tiempo) quick; M **—s** rapids; ADV (con mucha velocidad) fast; (en poco tiempo) quickly

rapiña F pillage

raptar VT to kidnap, to abduct

rapto M (secuestro) abduction, kidnapping; (arrebato) fit

raqueta F racket (también de tenis)

raquítico ADJ feeble, sickly

raramente ADV seldom, rarely

rareza F (escasez) rarity; (cosa rara) oddity; (cualidad de extraño) strangeness

raro ADJ (infrecuente) rare; (extraño) strange, funny; **rara vez** seldom, rarely; **sentirse —** to feel funny; **gas —** rare gas; **tierra rara** rare earth

ras LOC ADV **a — de la tierra** low to the ground

rascar[30] VT to scratch; **—se el culo** *vulg* to fart around; M SG **rascacielos** skyscraper

rasgado ADJ **ojos —s** slit eyes

rasgadura F tear, rip

rasgar[40] VT to tear, to rip

rasgo M (propiedad) trait, feature; **a grandes —s** in broad strokes

rasgón M tear

rasguñar VT to scratch

rasguño M scratch

raso ADJ (superficie) smooth; (cucharada) level; **al —** in the open air; M satin

raspado M scrape

raspador M scraper

raspadura F scrape

raspar VT to scrape

raspón M scrape

rastra F harrow; **a —s** dragging, pulling

rastrear VT (a un animal) to trail, to track, to trace; (un terreno) to search

rastreo M sweep, search

rastrero ADJ (planta) creeping; (persona) contemptible

rastrillar VT to rake

rastrillo M rake

rastro M (huella) track, trail; (olor) scent; (mercado) flea market; **ni —s** no trace

rastrojo M stubble

rasurado M shave

rasurador -ora MF razor

rasurar VT to shave

rata F rat

ratear VT to pilfer

ratería F petty larceny, pilferage

ratero -ra MF pickpocket

ratificación F ratification

ratificar[30] VT to ratify

rato M while; **—s perdidos** leisure hours; **a cada —** frequently; **a —s** from time to time; **pasar el —** to kill time; **pasar un buen —** (divertirse) to have a pleasant time; (permanecer) to spend a long time; **un largo —** a great while

ratón M mouse (también de computadora); **— almizclero** muskrat; **— en serie** serial mouse

ratonera F mousetrap

raudal LOC ADV **a —es** in great quantities

raudo ADJ swift

raya F (línea) line; (linde) boundary; (lista) stripe; (en el pelo) part; (en un pantalón) crease; (de ortografía) dash; (en un zapato) scuff; (pez marino) stingray; **tener a —** to hold in check; **pasarse de la —** to be out of line, to cross the line

rayado ADJ (papel) lined; (vestido) striped; **hablaba como disco —** he talked like a broken record

rayar VT (papel) to rule, to make lines on; (disco, espejo) to scratch; (zapatos) to scuff; **— el alba** to dawn; **— en** to border on

rayo M (de luz) ray, beam, streak; (de relámpago) flash of lightning; (de rueda) spoke; (de esperanza) ray, flicker; **— láser** laser beam; **—s infrarrojos** infrared rays; **—s X** x-rays

rayón M rayon

raza F (de personas) race; (de animal) breed

razón F (facultad) reason; (proporción) ratio; **— social** company name; **a — de** at the rate of; **¡con —!** no wonder! **entrar en —** to listen to reason; **te doy la —** I admit you're right; **perder la —** to lose one's mind; **tener —** to be right

razonable ADJ reasonable

razonamiento M reasoning

razonar VI (pensar) to reason; (arguir) to argue

reabastecer[35] VT to replenish

reabrir[74] VT to reopen

reacción F reaction; **— en cadena** chain

reaction; — **nuclear** nuclear reaction
reaccionar VI to react
reaccionario ADJ & MF reactionary
reacio ADJ averse, reluctant
reacondicionar VT to rebuild
reactivo M reagent
reactor M reactor; — **nuclear** nuclear reactor
readaptación F readjustment
readaptar VT to readjust
reafirmar VT to reaffirm; **—se** to reassert
reagrupar VT to regroup
reajustar VT to readjust
reajuste M readjustment
real ADJ (verdadero) real, actual; (del rey) royal; M fairground
realce M **dar—** to enhance
realeza F royalty
realidad F reality, actuality; **en —** really, actually; **en — no es abogado** he's not really a lawyer; — **virtual** virtual reality
realismo M realism
realista ADJ (auténtico) realistic; (partidario del rey) royalist; MF (no idealista) realist; (partidario del rey) royalist
realización F (de un sueño) realization, fulfillment; (de una tarea) completion; (de una película) production
realizador -ora MF (director) director; (productor) producer
realizar[47] VT (un sueño) to realize, to fulfill; (película) to produce
realmente ADV really
realzar[47] VT (mejorar) to enhance; (destacar) to accentuate; (intensificar) to heighten
reanimación F resuscitation; — **cardiopulmonar** cardiopulmonary resuscitation
reanimar VT (devolver fuerzas) to revive; (dar ánimos) to rally
reanudación F renewal; — **del juego** (fútbol) restart of play
reanudar VT (una amistad) to renew; (una reunión) to resume; (un partido del fútbol) to restart
reaparecer[35] VI to reappear
reasumir VT to resume
reata F lariat, lasso
reavivar VT to revive
rebaja F markdown, price cut; **con —** at a discount, on sale; **de —s** cut-rate
rebajado N on sale, reduced
rebajar VT (precios) to cut, to lower, to slash; (una bebida) to water down; (una crítica) to tone down; VI/VT (los cambios) to downshift; **—se** to lower oneself; **—se a** to stoop to
rebanada F slice
rebanar VT to slice
rebaño M flock, fold
rebasar VT (un coche) to overtake; (un límite) to

exceed
rebatir VT to refute
rebato M alarm
rebelarse VI to rebel, to revolt
rebelde ADJ (niño) rebellious; (pelo) unruly; MF rebel
rebeldía F rebelliousness, defiance; (no comparecencia) default
rebelión F rebellion
rebenque M whip
rebobinar VT to rewind
reborde M edge
rebosante ADJ (de líquido) brimming, overflowing; (de salud) flush, glowing; — **de alegría** overjoyed
rebosar VI (líquido) to overflow, to brim over; (de alegría) to bubble over; (de salud) to glow
rebotar VI/VT (en baloncesto) to rebound, to bounce; (chocar) to bounce; (cambiar de dirección una bala) to ricochet; (cambiar de dirección una pelota) to carom
rebote M (en baloncesto) rebound, bounce; (de bala) ricochet
rebotear VI (en baloncesto) to rebound
rebozar[47] VT to cover with batter; **—se** to muffle up
rebozo M shawl; **sin —** frankly
rebullir[16] VI to stir
rebuscado ADJ (estilo) overly elaborate; (persona) affected
rebuscar[30] VT (espigar) to glean; VI — **en** (la memoria) to search through; (un cajón) to rummage in
rebuznar VI to bray
rebuzno M bray, braying
recabar VT to raise
recado M (mensaje) message; (quehacer) errand; — **de escribir** writing materials
recaer[52] VI to relapse; — **sobre** to fall to
recaída F relapse
recalar VI to make a stop at
recalcar[30] VT to accentuate
recalcitrante ADJ obstinate
recalentar[1] VT (volver a calentar) to warm over; (calentar en exceso) to overheat
recamar VT to embroider
recámara F (de un arma de fuego) chamber; *Méx* (dormitorio) bedroom
recapitular VI/VT to recapitulate, to sum up
recargado ADJ busy
recargar[40] VT to overload, to burden
recargo M (emocional) burden; (de precio) surcharge, premium; — **por mora** late fee
recatado ADJ (cauteloso) cautious; (modesto) modest
recato M (cautela) caution; (modestia) modesty
recaudación F collection, levy; — **de fondos** fundraising
recaudador -ora MF tax collector

recaudar VT (impuestos) to collect, to levy; (fondos) to raise; — **en bruto** to gross; — **fondos** to raise funds; **lo recaudado** proceeds

recaudo M **estar a buen** — to be in a safe place

rección F government

recelar VT to suspect; — **de** to be suspicious of

recelo M misgivings

receloso ADJ mistrustful

recepción F reception

receptáculo M receptacle, holder

receptor M receiver (también en fútbol americano); (en béisbol) catcher; — **abierto** wide receiver; — **cerrado** tight end

recesión F recession

receta F (de cocina) recipe; (de médico) prescription

recetar VT to prescribe

rechazar[47] VT (una propuesta, un plan) to reject; (un ataque) to repel, to repulse; (una invitación) to decline, to turn down, to refuse; (una acusación) to deny; (a un amante) to spurn, to reject

rechazo M (de un amante) rejection; (de un ataque) repulse; (de una oferta) refusal; (de una acusación) denial

rechifla F whistling, booing

rechiflar VT to whistle, to boo

rechinamiento M (de una puerta) creaking, squeaking; (de los dientes) grinding

rechinante ADJ squeaky

rechinar VI (una puerta) to squeak, to creak; VI/VT (los dientes) to grind; **eso me rechina** that grates on my nerves

rechoncho ADJ plump, chubby, roly-poly

recibidor -ora MF receiver; M reception room

recibimiento M reception

recibir VT (premio) to receive, to get; (visitas) to receive, to welcome; (una noticia trágica) to take; — **noticias de** to hear from; —**se** to graduate; —**se de médico** to graduate from medical school

recibo M receipt; **de** — acceptable; **al** — **de** upon receipt of; **acusar** — to acknowledge receipt; **acuse de** — acknowledgment of receipt

reciclaje M recycling

reciclar VI/VT to recycle

recidiva F relapse

recién ADV recently; — **casado** newlywed; — **comprado** brand-new; — **llegado** newly arrived; — **nacido** newborn; — **me entero** it's news to me

reciente ADJ recent

recinto M enclosure

recio ADJ strong, rugged

recipiente M container

recíproco ADJ reciprocal

recitación F recitation

recital M recital

recitar VT to recite, to speak

reclamación F (protesta) protest; (demanda) claim

reclamante MF claimant

reclamar VT (protestar) to protest; (demandar) to claim; VI (aves) to call

reclamo M (reclamación) claim; (queja) complaint; (voz de animal) call, cry; (dispositivo) bird call; (señuelo) decoy

reclinar VT to lean; —**se** to recline

recluir[19] VT to confine; —**se** to be a recluse

recluso -sa MF (preso) inmate; (ermitaño) recluse

recluta F recruitment; MF (voluntario) recruit; (forzoso) conscript

reclutamiento M (voluntario) recruitment; (forzoso) conscription

reclutar VT (voluntariamente) to recruit; (por la fuerza) to draft, to conscript

recobrar VI to recover, to recuperate; VT to recover, to regain

recodo M bend, turn

recoger[45] VT (el cabello) to gather; (un cuarto) to tidy up; (citas en un texto) to collect; (la mesa) to clear; (polvo) to sweep up; (a un desamparado) to shelter; (los frutos del campo) to glean; —**se** (retirarse) to retire, to withdraw; (acumularse) to gather

recogida F (del cabello) gathering; (de un cuarto) tidying up; (de la mesa) clearing; (de un desamparado) sheltering

recogido ADJ (apartado) secluded; (tranquilo) peaceful, quiet

recogimiento M (aislamiento) seclusion; (meditación) meditation

recolección F (de frutos, datos) collecting, gathering; (de carga) pickup; (cosecha) harvest

recolectar VT to gather, to forage

recomendable ADJ advisable

recomendación F recommendation

recomendar[1] VT to recommend

recomienda, recomiende *ver* recomendar

recompensa F recompense, reward

recompensar VT to recompense, to reward

reconcentrar VI to concentrate intensely; —**se** to concentrate, to become absorbed in thought

reconciliación F reconciliation

reconciliar VT to reconcile

recóndito ADJ remote

reconfortante ADJ heartwarming, comforting

reconfortar VT to comfort

reconocer[35] VT (identificar) to recognize; (admitir) to admit, to acknowledge; (explorar) to reconnoiter

reconocible ADJ recognizable

reconocimiento M (identificación) recognition; (admisión, agradecimiento)

acknowledgment; (exploración) scouting; —
de habla speech recognition; — **de voz**
voice recognition; — **visual** visual
recognition; **hacer un** — to reconnoiter
reconozca, reconozco *ver* reconocer
reconsiderar VT to reconsider
reconstrucción F reconstruction
reconstruir[19] VT to reconstruct, to rebuild
reconstruya, reconstruye,
reconstruyendo, reconstruyera,
reconstruyese *ver* reconstruir
recopilación F collection, compilation
recopilar VT to compile
récord M record
recordar[5] VT (acordarse) to remember, to
recollect, to recall; (hacer acordar) to remind
recordatorio M reminder
recorrer VT (andar una distancia) to cover;
(examinar) to go over, to look over
recorrido M (ruta) run, route; (distancia)
distance
recortado ADJ jagged
recortar VT (pelo, hilos, presupuesto) to trim;
(uñas, periódicos) to clip; (una película) to
shorten; —**se** to be outlined
recorte M (de pelos, hilos) trimming; (de uñas,
periódicos) clipping; (de sueldo, de gastos)
cut; (de recursos) cutback; (sobrante)
trimming; — **salarial** pay cut
recostar[5] VT (sobre) to lay; (contra) to lean; —**se**
to recline
recoveco M (en un camino) turn; (rincón)
cranny
recreación F recreation
recrear VT to entertain; —**se** to amuse oneself
recreativo ADJ recreational; **actividades**
recreativas leisure activities; **sala**
recreativa game room
recreo M (recreación) recreation, relaxation;
(tiempo de descanso) recess; (lugar de juego)
playground
recriminar VT to recriminate
recrudecer[35] VI to flare up
recrudecimiento M flareup
recta F (de una pista) straight; (en béisbol)
fastball; — **final** final stretch
rectangular ADJ rectangular
rectángulo M rectangle
rectificar[30] VT to rectify
rectitud F uprightness, righteousness
recto ADJ (no curvo) straight; (honrado) upright,
righteous; (estricto) strict; **todo** — straight
ahead; M rectum
rector -ora MF university president, chancellor
recua F herd
recubrir[74] VT to cover; — **con pintura** to coat
with paint
recuento M account; — **sanguíneo** blood
count

recuerda, recuerde *ver* recordar
recuerdo M (acción de recordar, cosa recordada)
memory, recollection; (objeto que hace
recordar) souvenir, token; —**s** regards; **dale**
—**s a tu hermana** say hi to your sister
recular VI (retroceder) to move backward;
(retroceder en un coche) to back up;
(retroceder ante un desafío) to back down
recuperación F (salarial, de salud) recovery; (de
datos, documentos guardados) retrieval; (de
objetos, datos, documentos perdidos)
recovery
recuperar VT (una cosa perdida) to recover;
(datos, documentos guardados) to retrieve;
(tiempo perdido) to make up for; (dinero
perdido) to recoup; —**se** to recuperate
recurrente ADJ MF (que reclama) complainant;
ADJ (repetitivo) recurring, recurrent
recurrir VT to appeal; — **a** to resort to, to have
recourse to
recurso M (acción de recurrir) recourse;
(reclamación) appeal; —**s** resources; —**s**
humanos HR [human resources]; —**s**
naturales natural resources
recusar VT (a una persona) to reject; (a un juez)
to challenge
red F (para pescar, de tenis) net; (malla tejida)
mesh; (de conexiones, para computadora)
network; (para engañar) snare; (internet)
World Wide Web, Internet; — **[de área]**
local local area network
redacción F (ensayo) composition; (acción de
redactar) drafting; (en un periódico) editorial
department
redactar VT (un ensayo) to draft; (trabajo
escolar) to compose
redactor -ora MF editor
redada F (de peces) catch, haul; (policial) raid
redar VT to throw a net
redecilla F hairnet
redención F redemption
redil M sheepfold, sheep pen; **volver al** — to
come back into the fold
redimir VT (a un pecador) to redeem; (a un
esclavo) to set free
rédito M (de ahorros) interest; (de acciones)
yield
redituar[76] VT to yield
redoblar VT (esfuerzos) to double; VI/VT (un
tambor) to roll
redoble M drumroll
redoma F flask
redonda F whole note; **a la** — all around
redondear VT (una figura) to make round; (una
cifra) to round up
redondel M ring
redondez F roundness
redondo ADJ round; **en** — all around; **caer** — to
collapse; **salir** — to turn out perfect

reducción F reduction, cutback; **— de sueldo** cut in salary; **hacer — de personal** to cut back on personnel

reducidor -ora MF *Am* fence

reducir[38] VT (una cantidad) to reduce; (un hueso) to set; (actividades) to curtail, to cut down on; (costos) to cut; (personal) to downsize, to cut back on; **—se a** to boil down to

reduje, redujera, redujese *ver* reducir

redundante ADJ redundant

reduzca, reduzco *ver* reducir

reedificar[30] VT to rebuild

reelección F reelection

reelegir[14] VT reelect

reembolsar VT to reimburse, to refund

reembolso M reimbursement, refund

reemplazable ADJ replaceable

reemplazar[47] VT to replace

reemplazo M replacement, substitute

reencarnación F reincarnation

reescribir[74] VT to rewrite

reestructuración F restructuring

reexpedir[9] VT to forward

referencia F reference

referéndum M referendum

referente LOC ADV **— a** relative to

referir[8] VT (narrar) to narrate; **—se a** to refer to

refiera, refiere *ver* referir

refinación F refinement

refinado ADJ refined, genteel

refinamiento M refinement

refinanciar VI/VT to refinance

refinar VT to refine

refinería F refinery

refiriendo, refiriera, refiriese *ver* referir

reflector M (en una bicicleta) reflector; (en deportes) floodlight; (militar, policial) searchlight

reflejar VT (luz) to reflect; (imagen) to mirror; **—se** to be reflected

reflejo M (luz) reflection; (movimiento) reflex; **—s** frosting; ADJ reflex

reflexión F reflection

reflexionar VI to reflect; **— sobre** to think over

reflexivo ADJ (gramatical) reflexive; (pensativo) thoughtful

reflujo M (de agua) ebb; (gástrico) reflux

reforma F (política) reform; (religiosa) reformation

reformador -ora MF reformer

reformar VT (un gobierno, a un delincuente) to reform; (ropa) to make alterations in; **—se** to mend one's ways

reformatorio M reformatory

reformista MF reformer

reforzado ADJ reinforced; M reinforcement

reforzar[49] VT (una construcción) to reinforce; (las defensas) to beef up; (un argumento) to bolster, to buttress

refracción F refraction

refractario ADJ refractory

refrán M proverb, saying

refrenar VT (un caballo) to rein in; (emociones) to restrain, to check

refrendar VT (una sentencia) to uphold; (un documento) to countersign, to endorse

refrendario -ria MF endorser

refrendo M endorsement

refrescante ADJ refreshing

refrescar[30] VT to refresh (también pantalla de computadora); (el tiempo) to get cool; **—se** to cool off

refresco M (bebida) soft drink; (comida ligera) refreshment

refriega F fray, scuffle

refrigeración F refrigeration

refrigerador ADJ refrigerating; M refrigerator

refrigerante ADJ cooling; M coolant

refrigerar VT to cool, to refrigerate

refrigerio M refreshment

refrito ADJ (comida) refried; M (obra) rerun

refuerzo M (acción de reforzar) reinforcement; (de tela) backing; (de una vacuna) booster

refugiado -da MF refugee

refugiar VT to shelter; **—se** to take shelter

refugio M refuge, shelter; **— antiaéreo** bomb shelter; **— fiscal** tax shelter

refulgente ADJ resplendent

refundir VT to recast

refunfuñar VI to grumble, to mutter

refunfuño M grumbling, muttering

refunfuñón -ona ADJ grouchy, grumpy; MF grouch

refutar VT to refute

regadera F watering can

regadío M (tierra irrigada) irrigated land; (riego) irrigation

regalar VT (dar como presente) to give as a gift; (vender barato, donar) to give away; (agasajar) to regale

regaliz M licorice

regalo M (presente) present, gift; (para los sentidos) treat, delight

regañar VI (un perro) to snarl; VT (a un niño) to scold, to go off on; (constantemente) to nag; LOC ADV **a regañadientes** reluctantly

regaño M scolding, reprimand

regañón -ona ADJ nagging, scolding; MF scold

regar[41] VT (campos) to irrigate; (flores) to water

regate M dribble

regatear VI (precios) to haggle, to bargain; (fútbol) to dribble

regateo M bargaining

regazo M lap

regeneración F regeneration; **— audible** audible feedback

regente MF, **regenta** F regent; F regent's wife; ADJ ruling

reggae M reggae

régimen M (gobierno) regime; (dieta) diet; — **de vida** lifestyle

regimiento M regiment

regio ADJ (propio del rey) regal; (excelente) swell

región F region

regional ADJ regional

regir[14] VT to govern (también en sintaxis); VI to be in force; —**se por** to be guided by

registrador -ora MF (empleado) recorder, registrar; M — **de vuelo** flight recorder

registrar VT (examinar) to search; (dejar constancia) to record, to register; (inscribir) to log; — **al desnudo** to strip-search

registro M (de la voz, lingüístico) register; (de nacimientos) record, register; (del equipaje) search; (de un órgano) stop; (en la computadora) log; — **al desnudo** strip search

regla F (norma) rule; (utensilio para medir) ruler; (menstruación) period; **en** — in order; **por** — **general** as a general rule

reglamentación F (acción de reglamentar) regulation; (conjunto de reglas) regulations

reglamento M regulations; —**s y disposiciones administrativas** rules and regulations

regocijar VT to gladden; —**se** to rejoice

regocijo M joy, rejoicing

regodearse VI (en la desgracia propia) to wallow; (en la desgracia ajena) to gloat

regodeo M (en la desgracia propia) wallowing; (en la desgracia ajena) gloating

regordete ADJ plump

regresar VI to return

regreso M return; **estar de** — to be back

reguero M trail; **correr como un** — **de pólvora** to spread like wildfire

regulación F (acción de regular) regulation; (de una máquina) adjustment

regulador M regulator, governor, throttle; — **de voltaje** dimmer

regular VT (reglamentar) to regulate; (ajustar una máquina) to adjust; ADJ regular; **una paliza** — quite a beating; ADV so-so

regularidad F regularity

regularizar[47] VT (reglamentar) to regulate; (formalizar) to formalize; —**se** to become regular

regurgitar VI/VT to regurgitate

rehabilitación F rehabilitation

rehabilitador ADJ remedial

rehabilitar VT to rehabilitate

rehacer[54, 74] VT to remake; —**se** to recover

rehén MF hostage

rehuir[19] VT (a una persona) to shun; (responsabilidades) to shirk

rehusar[26] VT to refuse; —**se a** to refuse to

reimpresión F reprint

reina F queen

reinado M reign

reinante ADJ (política, opinión) prevailing; (monarca) ruling

reinar VI to reign

reincidencia F (episodio) relapse; (cualidad) recidivism

reincidir VI to relapse

reiniciar VT to reboot, to reset

reino M (territorio de un rey) kingdom, realm; (período de reinado) reign; (división biológica) kingdom; (ámbito) realm

reinserción F reinsertion; — **laboral** reemployment

reinstaurar VT to reinstate

reintegrar VT to rebate; —**se a** to return to

reintegro M rebate

reinvertir VI/VT to reinvest, to roll over

reír[10] VI to laugh; —**se de** to laugh at

reiterar VT to reiterate

reivindicación F (demanda) demand; (rehabilitación) vindication; (responsabilidad) responsibility; **la** — **del atentado** the responsibility for the act

reivindicar[30] VT (vengar) to vindicate; (responsabilizarse) to take responsibility, to claim

reja F (enrejado) grate, grating; (pieza de arado) plowshare; **entre** —**s** behind bars

rejilla F (para equipaje) luggage rack; (de coche) grille

rejuvenecer[35] VT to rejuvenate; VI to become rejuvenated

relación F (conocido) relation, connection; (trato) relationship, involvement; (relato) account, report; (lista) list; **relaciones** (conocidos) connections; (trato) dealings; **relaciones públicas** public relations; **con** — **a** in relation to

relacionado ADJ related, germane

relacionar VT to relate, to connect; —**se con** to relate to

relajación F relaxation

relajamiento M relaxation

relajante ADJ (actividad) relaxing; (droga) sedative; M — **muscular** muscle relaxant

relajar VT to relax; —**se** (abandonarse moralmente) to become lax; (tranquilizarse) to chill [out], to relax

relajo M (aflojamiento) relaxation; (desorden) mess

relamerse VI to lick one's lips

relámpago M lightning

relampaguear VI (el cielo) to lightning; (los ojos, cosa reluciente) to flash

relampagueo M flash of lightning

relatar VT to relate, to recount

relatividad F relativity

relativo ADJ relative; — **a** relative to

relato M (informe) account; (cuento) story, tale
relé M relay
relegar[40] VT to relegate
relevancia F importance
relevante ADJ important
relevar VT (a un trabajador, guardia) to relieve
relevista MF (atletismo) relay runner; (béisbol) reliever; — **de cierre** (béisbol) closer
relevo M (soldado) relief; **carrera de —s** relay race
relicario M reliquary, locket
relieve M relief; **de —** (mapa) relief; (persona) prominent; **poner de —** to emphasize; **letras en —** raised letters
religión F religion
religioso -sa ADJ religious; M monk; F nun
relinchar VI to neigh
relincho M neigh
reliquia F relic
rellenado M filling
rellenar VT (un vaso) to refill, to replenish; (un tanque de gasolina) to fill, to fill up; (un formulario) to fill out; (un hueco) to fill in; (una almohada) to stuff
relleno ADJ (un pimiento) stuffed; (la cara) full, round; (la figura, el cuerpo) plump; M (de comida) stuffing, dressing; (de un colchón) padding
reloj M (de pared) clock; (de muñeca, bolsillo) watch; (de horno) timer; — **de pulsera** wristwatch; — **de sol** sundial; — **despertador** alarm clock; **contra —** against the clock; **como un —** regularly, like clockwork
relojería F (tienda) watch shop; (actividad) clock-making
relojero -ra MF watchmaker
reluciente ADJ shining
relucir[39] VI to shine; **sacar a —** to bring up
relumbrar VI to glare
relumbre M glare
REM M REM
remachar VT (una victoria, un clavo) to clinch; (un remache) to rivet
remache M (acción de remachar) riveting; (clavo) clinching; (tachuela, clavija) rivet
remanente M remainder
remar VI/VT to row, to paddle
remarcado VT mark-up
rematador -ora MF auctioneer
rematar VT (acabar) to finish; (matar) to finish off; (perfeccionar) to give the finishing touches to; (subastar) to auction; VI (patear un balón) to take a shot
remate M (de una obra) finishing touch; (tiro) shot; (subasta) auction; (tenis) smash; — **de un chiste** punch line; **loco de —** stark raving mad
remedador -ora MF mimic

remedar VT to mimic, to ape, to mock
remediar VT to remedy
remedio M remedy, cure; **sin —** unavoidable; **no tiene —** it can't be helped; **no tengo más —** I can't help it; **el — es peor que la enfermedad** the remedy is worse than the disease
remedo M mockery
remendar[1] VT (ropa) to mend, to patch; (calcetines) to darn; (zapatos) to repair
remendón -ona MF cobbler
remero -ra MF rower
remesa F (de mercancías) shipment; (de dinero) remittance
remiendo M (de ropa) patch; (de zapatos) repair
remilgado ADJ fussy, prim
remilgo M fussiness, primness
reminiscencia F reminiscence
remisión F remission
remitente MF sender
remitir VT (enviar) to remit; (dirigir a otra parte de un texto) to refer; — **se** (ceder) to yield; **a las pruebas me remito** the evidence speaks for itself
remo M (pala) oar, paddle; (deporte) rowing
remodelación F (de una casa) remodeling; (de una ciudad) redevelopment, renewal; (de una organización) reorganization
remodelar VI/VT to remodel
remojar VT to soak
remojo M soaking; **poner en —** to soak
remojón M soaking
remolacha F beet
remolcador M tugboat
remolcar[30] VT to tow
remolino M (de viento) whirlwind; (de agua) whirlpool, eddy; (de pelo) cowlick; (juguete) pinwheel; — **de gente** throng, crowd
remolón -ona ADJ dallying; MF dallier
remolonear VI to dally
remolque M (acción de remolcar) tow; (vehículo remolcado) towed vehicle; (vehículo que remolca) tow truck; (caravana de camión) trailer; **llevar a —** to tow
remontada F (deporte) comeback
remontar VT (una cometa) to fly; (una pendiente, un río) to go up; — **se** to rise; **el globo se remonta** the balloon goes up; **el coche se remonta a los años 20** the car dates from the '20s; **para comprenderlo, debemos remontarnos a su juventud** in order to understand him, we must go back to his youth
remorder[6] VT to gnaw at
remordimiento M remorse
remoto ADJ remote, distant; **no tiene la más remota idea** he doesn't have the slightest idea
remover[6] VT (un cargo, un obstáculo) to

remove; (un asunto problemático) to stir up
remuneración F remuneration, compensation
remunerar VT remunerate, compensate
remunerado ADJ gainful
renacentista ADJ Renaissance
renacer³⁵ VI to be reborn
renacimiento M (resurgimiento) revival; (período histórico) Renaissance
renacuajo M (cría de rana) tadpole; (hombre esmirriado) shrimp
renal ADJ renal
rencilla F quarrel
rencor M rancor; **guardar** — to bear a grudge
rencoroso ADJ resentful
rendición F surrender
rendido ADJ exhausted
rendija F crack
rendimiento M (lo rendido) yield, output; (productividad) performance; — **previo** past performance
rendir⁹ VT (someter) to subdue; (producir) to yield; (fatigar) to fatigue; — **homenaje** to pay homage; — **cuentas a** to answer to; VI (obtener buenos resultados) to perform well; —**se** (darse por vencido) to surrender, to give in; (fatigarse) to become fatigued
renegado -da MF renegade
renegar⁴¹ VT (negar) to deny insistently; (repudiar) to renounce; — **de** to gripe about
renegociar VI/VT to renegotiate
renglón M linc; **a** — **seguido** immediately following
rengo ADJ lame
renguear VI to limp
renguera F limp
reno M reindeer
renombrado ADJ renowned
renombre M renown; **de** — of note
renovable ADJ renewable
renovación F renewal; — **urbana** urban renewal
renovador -ora ADJ (artista) innovating; (baño) refreshing; MF innovator
renovar⁵ VT (un edificio) to renovate; (ataques, temores) to renew
renquear VT to limp
renta F (de una persona) income; (de un gobierno) revenue; (alquiler) rent; — **anual** annuity; —**s internas** internal revenue; **vivir de la** — to live on the interest
rentabilidad F profitability; **cuentas y depósitos de alta** — high-return accounts and deposits
rentable ADJ (negocio, inversión) profitable; (idea) viable
renuencia F reluctance
renuente ADJ reluctant, loath; **ser** — **a** to be loath to
renueva, renueve *ver* renovar

renuevo M sprout
renuncia F (dimisión) resignation; (a un derecho) waiver; (a una herencia) renunciation
renunciar VI — **a** (un cargo) to resign; (la ciudadanía) to renounce; (un derecho) to relinquish, to waive
reñido ADJ contested
reñir¹¹ VI (discutir) to quarrel, to bicker, to argue; (pelear) to fight, to scuffle; (rezongar) to scold
reo -a MF defendant, accused
reojo M **mirar de** — to look out of the corner of one's eye
reorganización F reorganization
reorganizar⁴⁷ VT to reorganize, to regroup
repaginar VT to repaginate
repantigarse⁴⁰ VI to lounge
reparación F (compensación) reparation, redress; (arreglo) repair
reparador -ra ADJ refreshing; M serviceman; F service woman
reparar VT (arreglar) to repair; (compensar) to redress; — **en** to notice
reparo M **no tener** —**s en** to have no qualms about; **sin** —**s** freely; **hacer** —**s** to object
repartición F distribution
repartir VT (tierras, un botín) to distribute; (volantes) to hand out; (periódicos) to deliver; (naipes) to deal; (días libres) to space out
reparto M (de tierras) distribution; (de periódicos) delivery; (de naipes) dealing; (ruta de entrega) route; (lista de actores) cast; — **proporcional** apportionment
repasar VT (una lección) to review, to go over again; (en la memoria) to retrace; (leer por encima) to skim
repaso M review
repelente ADJ repellent
repeler VT to repel, to repulse
repente M **de** — suddenly
repentinamente ADV suddenly
repentino ADJ sudden
repercusión F repercussion
repercutir VI to have repercussions
repertorio M repertoire
repetición F (reiteración) repetition; (en tenis) let
repetido ADJ repeated; **repetidas veces** repeatedly
repetir⁹ VI/VT (reiterar) to repeat; VI (eructar) to belch; (tomar una segunda ración) to have seconds; — **como loro** to parrot; —**se** to recur
repicar³⁰ VI/VT to ring
repique M ringing, ring
repiquetear VI/VT to ring
repiqueteo M ringing
repisa F shelf

repita, repitiendo, repitiera, repitiese, repito *ver* repetir

replegar[41] VT to fold; **—se** to retreat

repleto ADJ replete

réplica F (contestación) reply, comeback; (copia) replica; (temblor secundario) aftershock

replicación F replication

replicar[30] VI/VT (responder) to reply, to rejoin; (reproducirse) to replicate

repliegue M (pliegue marcado) crease; (retirada) retreat

repollo M cabbage

reponer[56, 74] VT (reemplazar) to replace; (restituir) to restore; (replicar) to reply; (una obra de teatro) to revive; (una película) to show again; **—se** to recover one's health

reportaje M feature story

reportar VT (beneficios) to yield; VI (en una organización) to answer to; **—se enfermo** to call in sick

reportero -ra MF reporter

reposado ADJ quiet, calm

reposar VI to repose, to rest; **dejar—** to let steep; M SG **reposacabezas** headrest; M SG **reposapiés** footrest

reposición F (reemplazo) replacement; (de una obra de teatro) revival

reposo M (descanso) repose, rest; (sosiego) calm

repostería F (establecimiento) pastry shop; (actividad) baking

repostero -ra MF pastry cook

reprender VT to reprimand, to scold, to rebuke

reprensión F rebuke

represa F (dique) dam; (reservorio de agua) reservoir

represalia F reprisal

represar VT to dam

representación F (interpretación) representation; (delegación) delegation; (de un papel) portrayal; (de una obra de teatro) performance

representante MF (legislativo) representative; (comercial) agent

representar VT (una imagen) to represent, to depict; (una obra de teatro) to perform; (un personaje) to portray; **tiene treinta años, pero no los representa** he's thirty years old, but he doesn't look it; **tu presencia representa mucho para mí** your presence means a lot to me

representativo ADJ representative

represión F (psicológica) repression; (política) repression, suppression, crackdown

represivo ADJ repressive

reprimenda F reprimand, rebuke

reprimido ADJ repressed, pent-up

reprimir VT (impulsos) to repress; (una tendencia) to check; (enemigos políticos) to suppress, to crack down on; (una rebelión) to quell

reprobación F reproof

reprobar[5] VT to reprove; VI/VT (no aprobar un examen) to flunk, to fail

reprochar VT to reproach, to rebuke

reproche M reproach, rebuke

reproducción F reproduction

reproducir[38] VI/VT to reproduce; **—se** to reproduce, to breed

reproductor -ora ADJ breeding; **aparato —** VCR; MF breeding animal

reproduje, reprodujera, reprodujese, reproduzca, reproduzco *ver* reproducir

reptar VI to crawl

reptil M reptile

república F republic

republicano -na ADJ & MF republican; (del Partido Republicano) Republican

repudiar VT (a la sociedad) to repudiate; (a un hijo) to disown; (una herencia) to renounce

repuesto M spare part; **de —** spare

repugnancia F repugnance, disgust, revulsion

repugnante ADJ repugnant, disgusting, loathsome

repugnar VI to be repugnant; VT to disgust, to cloy

repulir VT to polish up

repulsa F rebuff, repulse

repulsar VT to repulse

repulsivo ADJ repulsive, creepy

repuntar VI to rally

reputación F reputation

reputado ADJ reputable

requemar VT to burn

requerimiento M request

requerir[8] VT to require

requesón M cottage cheese

requiebros M PL advances

requisa F requisition

requisar VT (interceptar, incautar) to commandeer, to requisition; (registrar) to search

requisito M requirement, requisite

res F animal; **— lanar** sheep; **— vacuna** cow

resabio M (dejillo) aftertaste; (vicio) bad habit

resaca F (de mar) undertow; (malestar físico) hangover

resaltar VI (sobresalir) to stand out; (poner de relieve) to highlight

resarcir[33] VT to compensate for

resbaladizo ADJ slippery, slick

resbalar VI (deslizar) to slip; (ser/estar resbaladizo) to be slippery; **—se** to slip

resbalón M slip; **darse un —** to slip

resbaloso ADJ (que resbala) slippery; *Méx fam* (inmoral) sleazy

rescatar VT (a un secuestrado) to ransom; (a una persona en peligro) to rescue

rescate M (para un secuestrado) ransom; (de una

persona en peligro) rescue
rescindir VT to rescind
rescoldo M embers
resecar[30] VT to dry; —**se** to dry out
reseco ADJ dried-up, parched
resentido ADJ resentful
resentimiento M resentment, grudge;
    guardar — to hold a grudge, to have hard
    feelings
resentirse[8] VI to hurt, to suffer; — **de** to resent
reseña F book review
reseñar VT to review
reserva F (de provisiones, de oro, de jugadores,
    del ejército) reserve; (de localidades, de hotel,
    de indios) reservation; (de animales)
    preserve; **sin —s** without reservations;
    tener —s to have reservations
reservación F *Am* reservation
reservado ADJ (distante) aloof; (discreto)
    reserved
reservar VT to reserve; **me reservo mi
    opinión** I'll spare you my opinion
resfriado M common cold; **estoy —** I've got a
    cold
resfriarse VI to catch cold
resfrío M cold, head cold
resguardar VT to shelter; —**se de** to seek
    shelter from
resguardo M (abrigo) shelter; (comprobante)
    deposit slip
residencia F residence
residencial ADJ (para vivir) residential; (en las
    afueras) suburban
residente ADJ & MF resident
residir VI to reside
residuo M residue
resignación F resignation
resignarse VI to resign oneself
resina F resin
resistencia F (fuerza opuesta) resistance; (de la
    calefacción) element; (aguante) endurance,
    stamina
resistente ADJ resistant, tough
resistir VT (una tentación) to resist; (un ataque)
    to withstand; —**se a un arresto** to resist
    arrest; VI to resist, to hold [up]
resollar[5] VI (por enfermedad) to wheeze;
    (después de un esfuerzo) to pant; (por alivio)
    to sigh
resolución F (acción de resolver) resolution;
    (ánimo) determination, resolve; — **óptica**
    optical resolution
resolver[6, 74] VT (decidir) to decide; (solucionar)
    to solve; —**se a** to resolve to
resonancia F resonance
resonar[5] VI (sonidos) to resound, to boom; (una
    polémica) to resonate
resoplar VI (con enfado) to huff and puff; (un
    caballo) to snort

resoplido M (con enojo) puff; (de caballo) snort
resorte M spring
respaldar VT to back, to stand behind
respaldo M (parte de una silla) back; (apoyo)
    support, backing; — **automático** automatic
    backup; — **de archivos** backup; — **global**
    global backup
respectivo ADJ respective
respecto LOC ADV — **a/de** with respect to,
    concerning; **a ese** — on that score; **con** — **a**
    with regard to, regarding, vis-à-vis
respetable ADJ respectable
respetar VT to respect
respeto M respect, regard; **con todo** — with all
    due respect; **faltar el/al** — to slight, to
    disregard
respetuoso ADJ respectful
respingado M upturned
respingar[40] VI (dar respingos) to buck;
    (asustarse) to shy away
respingo M (salto) buck; (susto) start
respiración F respiration, breathing; — **boca a
    boca** mouth-to-mouth resuscitation
respirar VI/VT (inhalar y exhalar) to breathe;
    (sentir alivio) to breathe easy; **dejar** — to
    give a breather
respiratorio ADJ respiratory
respiro M (acto de respirar) breathing;
    (descanso) respite; **dame un** — I need a
    break
resplandecer[35] VI (brillar) to glare; (de
    felicidad) to glow
resplandeciente ADJ resplendent, radiant
resplandor M brilliance, radiance
responder VI (reaccionar) to respond; VT
    (contestar) to answer; (corresponder) to
    correspond
respondón ADJ saucy
responsabilidad F (obligación de aceptar
    consecuencias) responsibility; (obligación de
    informar) accountability
responsabilizar VT to hold liable, to hold
    responsible
responsable ADJ (que debe aceptar las
    consecuencias) responsible; (obligado
    legalmente) liable; (que tiene que informar)
    accountable
respuesta F response, answer
resquebrajadura F crack
resquebrajar VI to crack
resquicio M (rendija) crack; (laguna legal)
    loophole
resta F subtraction
restablecer[35] VT (un servicio) to reestablish;
    (una costumbre) to revive; —**se** to recover
restador -ora MF receiver
restante ADJ remaining
restañar VT to stanch/staunch
restar VT (sustraer) to subtract; (quitar) to take

away from; (quedar) to remain; —
importancia a to make light of
restauración F restoration
restaurante M restaurant
restaurar VT (el gobierno) to restore; (muebles)
to refurbish
restitución F restitution
restituir[19] VT to pay back, to give back
resto M (lo demás) rest; (sobrante) remainder;
(tenis) return of service; **—s** (de un edificio)
remains; (de una comida) leftovers; **echar el**
— to go all out
restorán M restaurant
restregar[41] VT to scrub, to scour
restricción F restriction
restringir[46] VT to restrict, to constrain
resucitación F resuscitation, revival
resucitar VT to resuscitate, to revive
resuello M (por enfermedad) wheeze; (por
fatiga) panting
resuelto ADJ (de carácter decidido) resolute,
strong-willed; (de actitud decidida) resolved
resuelto, resuelva, resuelve ver resolver
resulta LOC ADV **de —s** as a result
resultado M (de una operación matemática)
result; (de un suceso) outcome; (de un
partido) score; **— final** (fútbol) final score;
—s científicos findings; **—s electorales**
returns; **como —** as a result; **dar buen —** to
pan out; **dar por —** to result in
resultante ADJ resulting, consequent
resultar VI to result; **— de** to result from;
resulta que it turns out that; **resultó ser**
un idiota he turned out to be an idiot, he
proved to be an idiot
resumen M summary, abstract; **en —** in sum, in
brief
resumir VT to summarize, to sum up; **—se a** to
be condensed to, to boil down to
resurgimiento M revival
resurgir[46] VI to arise again
resurrección F resurrection
retablo M altarpiece
retaguardia F rear guard
retal M remnant
retama F broom
retar VT to challenge
retardar VI/VT to retard
retardo M lag
retazo M remnant
retén M (aparato) retainer; (de vigilancia)
checkpoint
retención F retention; **— de líquido** fluid
retention; **— impositiva** tax withholding
retendrá, retendría ver retener
retener[58] VT (una pelota, la atención) to hold;
(salarios, fondos) to garnish, to withhold
retenga, retengo ver retener
retina F retina

retintín M (en los oídos) ringing; (de cascabeles)
jingle
retirada F (de tropas) retreat, withdrawal; (de
un diplomático, producto) recall
retirar VT (apartar) to move away; (dinero) to
withdraw; (algo dicho) to take back,
withdraw; (un producto) to recall; **—se** (para
dormir, de un empleo, de la carrera militar)
to retire; (un ejército) to retreat, to pull back
retiro M (refugio) retreat; (jubilación)
retirement; (de fondos) withdrawal; **— de**
deuda debt retirement
reto M challenge
retocar[30] VT to retouch, to touch up
retomar VT to take up again
retoñar VI to sprout
retoño M sprout, shoot, bud
retoque M retouching
retorcer[34] VT (una toalla mojada) to wring out;
(la muñeca) to wrench, to twist; **—se** (de
dolor) to writhe; (de inquietud) to squirm
retorcido ADJ (persona) devious; (rama) gnarled
retorcimiento M (de dolor) writhing; (de
inquietud) squirming
retórica F rhetoric
retornar VT to return
retorno M (de un viajero) return (también en un
teclado); (de una costumbre, moda) revival;
— de línea automático word wrap
retozar[47] VI (en juegos infantiles) to frolic, to
romp; (en juegos eróticos) to cavort
retozo M frolic, romp
retractarse VI to take back one's words
retraer[59] VT (las garras) to retract; **—se** to
withdraw
retraído ADJ shy
retraimiento M shyness
retrasado ADJ (falto de desarrollo) backward;
(deficiente mental) retarded
retrasar VT (atrasar) to delay; (un reloj) to set
back; **—se** to fall behind
retraso M delay, lag
retratar VT (describir) to portray; (pintar un
retrato) to paint a portrait
retrato M (pintura) portrait; (descripción)
portrayal
retreta F retreat
retrete M lavatory
retribución F (acción de retribuir)
remuneration; (pago) salary
retro ADJ retro
retroactivo ADJ retroactive
retroalimentación F feedback
retroceder VI (recular) to step back; (por miedo)
to recoil, to shrink back; (en un coche) to back
up; (al mecanografiar) to backspace; (dar
marcha atrás) to backtrack; (tropas) to retreat,
to fall back; (una inundación) to recede
retroceso M (pérdida) step back; (de un arma de

fuego) recoil; (económico) recession; (en un teclado) backspace
retrogradismo M backwardness
retrógrado ADJ backward
retroiluminación F backlighting
retroiluminado ADJ backlit
retroproyector M overhead projector
retrovirus M retrovirus
retrucar[30] VT to counter
retruécano M play on words
retumbar VI to rumble, to roll
retumbo M rumble
retuve, retuviera, retuviese ver retener
reubicar[30] VT to relocate
reuma M rheumatism
reumatismo M rheumatism
reumatoide ADJ rheumatoid
reunificación F reunification
reunión F (de negocios) meeting; (informal) get-together; (de ex-alumnos) reunion
reunir[27] VT (juntar) to gather; (convocar) to reunite, to bring together; (coleccionar) to collect; (juntar coraje) to muster; (juntar dinero) to raise; —**se** (formal) to meet; (informal) to get together; (un gentío) to gather
revancha F (venganza) revenge; (en deportes) return game
revelación F revelation
revelado M film development
revelador ADJ revealing
revelar VT (un secreto) to reveal; (película) to develop; (un escándalo) to expose; (información) to disclose; —**se** to show oneself
revendedor-ora MF (de mercadería) middleman; (de entradas) scalper
revender VT (vender de nuevo) to resell; (entradas) to scalp
reventar[1] VI/VT (estallar) to burst, to bust; (morir) to die; (fastidiar) to annoy
reventón M (acción de reventar) bursting; (de un neumático) blowout
reverberar VI to reverberate
reverdecer[35] VI (ponerse verde de nuevo) to become green again; (renovarse) to gain new strength
reverencia F (adoración) reverence; (gesto) bow
reverenciar VT to revere
reverendo-da ADJ & MF reverend
reverente ADJ reverent
reverso M reverse
revertir[8] VI to revert; — **en beneficio de** to be of benefit to
revés M (lado opuesto) reverse; (en tenis) backhand; (contratiempo) setback, downturn; **al** — (con lo de adelante hacia atrás) backwards; (con lo de arriba hacia abajo) upside down; (con lo de adentro hacia

afuera) inside out; **dar vuelta al** — to turn inside out
revestimiento M overlay; (de piso) flooring; (de pared exterior) siding; (de pared interior) paneling
revestir[9] VT (un camino) to surface; (una pared) to cover; (conllevar) to be marked by
revisar VT (examinar) to review, to go over; (un coche) to service
revisión F (de un libro) review; (de una película vieja) revival; (médica, mecánica) checkup
revisor-ora MF (en un tren, autobús) conductor; (de un texto) proofreader
revista F (inspección) inspection; (de tropas) muster; (publicación) magazine, journal, periodical; (espectáculo) revival; — **de historietas** comic book; — **electrónica** e-zine; **pasar** — to pass in review
revistar VT to inspect
revitalizar VT to revitalize
revivir VI/VT to revive
revocación F (de un derecho, de un fallo) revocation; (de una ley) repeal
revocar[30] VT (un fallo) to reverse; (una ley) to repeal; (una pared) to plaster
revolcar[31] VT (derribar) to knock over; —**se** (cerdos) to wallow; (niños) to roll around
revolear VT to roll
revolotear VI to flutter, to flit
revoltijo M (de cosas) jumble; (de pelo) muss
revoltoso-sa ADJ unruly, disorderly; MF troublemaker
revolución F (cambio radical) revolution; (giro) revolution, turn; **revoluciones por minuto** revolutions per minute
revolucionario-ria ADJ revolutionary, earthshaking; MF revolutionary
revolver[6,74] VT (remover) to stir up; (registrar) to rummage in; (desordenar) to mess up; (huevos) to scramble; (ensalada) to toss; **eso me revuelve el estómago** that makes my stomach turn; —**se en la cama** to toss and turn in bed
revólver M revolver, pistol
revuelo M stir, commotion
revuelta F revolt
revuelto ADJ (el mar) rough; (el ánimo) restless; (el pelo) disheveled; **huevos** —**s** scrambled eggs
rey M king; **los** —**es Magos** the Wise Men
reyerta F melee, squabble
rezagarse[40] VI to straggle behind, to lag behind
rezar[47] VI/VT (a Dios) to pray; (un letrero) to say
rezo M prayer
rezongar[40] VI/VT (murmurar) to grumble; (quejarse) to gripe
rezongón-ona ADJ grumpy; MF grouch
rezumar VT to ooze
ría, ríe ver reír

riachuelo M brook
riada F flash flood
ribazo M steep bank
ribera F shore, bank; (de río) riverbank
ribereño ADJ on the bank
ribete M (de uniforme) trimming; (de alfombra) binding; (de ropa) piping; (de mosaico) border; **tener —s de** to have hints of
ribetear VT (un uniforme) to trim; (una alfombra) to bind; (un diseño) to border
ricacho ADJ very rich
rico ADJ (persona) rich, wealthy, affluent; (suelo) rich; (adorno) exquisite; (manjar) delicious; (niño) cute
ridiculizar⁴⁷ VT to ridicule, to deride
ridículo ADJ (sin sentido) ridiculous; (absurdo, risible) ludicrous; **hacer el —** to act the fool; **poner en —** to ridicule; **ponerse en —** to make a spectacle of oneself
riego M irrigation
riel M rail
rienda F rein; **dar — suelta** to give a free hand
riendo, riera, rieron, riese ver reír
riesgo M risk; **— ocupacional** occupational hazard/risk; **en —** at risk; **correr un —** to run a risk
rifa F raffle
rifar VT to raffle
rifirrafe M free-for-all
rifle M rifle
rigidez F rigidity
rígido ADJ rigid
rigor M (exactitud) rigor; (dureza) harshness; **en — in** reality; **de —** indispensable
riguroso ADJ (estricto) rigorous; (duro) harsh
rima F rhyme
rimar VI/VT to rhyme
rimbombante ADJ grandiose
rímel M mascara
rin M rim
rincón M (ángulo) corner; (lugar retirado) nook, alcove
rinconera F (estantería) corner cupboard; (mesa) corner table
rinda, rinde, rindiendo, rindiera, rindiese ver rendir
ring M boxing ring
ringlera F row
rinoceronte M rhinoceros
rinoplastia F rhinoplasty, *fam* nose job
rinovirus M rhinovirus
riña F (discusión) quarrel; (pelea) scrap, fight, spat
riñón M (órgano) kidney; (región lumbar) lower back
río M river; **— abajo** downstream
rió ver reír
ripio M rubble
riqueza F wealth; **—s** riches

risa F (carcajada) laugh; (acción, sonido de reír) laughter; **reventar/desternillarse de — to** burst with laughter; **morirse de — to** die laughing; **¡qué —!** what a joke!
risco M crag, bluff
risible ADJ laughable
risita F (burlona) snicker; (ahogada) chuckle
risotada F guffaw, gale of laughter
ristra F string
risueño ADJ (sonriente) smiling; (alegre) cheerful
rítmico ADJ rhythmical
ritmo M rhythm; **— cardíaco** heart rate; **— de vida** pace of life
rito M rite
ritual ADJ & M ritual
rival ADJ & MF rival
rivalidad F rivalry; **— entre hemanos** sibling rivalry
rivalizar⁴⁷ VI to rival; **— con** to compete with
rizado ADJ curly; M curling
rizar⁴⁷ VT (pelo) to curl, to crimp; (agua) to ripple
rizo M (en el pelo) curl, ringlet; (en el agua) ripple, ruffle; (pirueta de avión) loop
robar VT (a una persona) to rob; (un objeto, dinero) to steal; **—se una base** to steal a base
roble M oak tree
robledal M oak grove
robo M (violento) robbery; (furtivo) theft; **— a mano armada** armed robbery, holdup; **— con allanamiento** burglary; **— de base** base steal; **— de identidad** identity theft
robot M robot
robótica F robotics
robusto ADJ (fuerte) robust; (grueso) stout, stocky; (sólido) sturdy
roca F rock
roce M (de una bala) graze; (de dos superficies) rub, rubbing; (con la ley, la policía) brush
rociada F (acción de rociar) sprinkling, spraying; (de insultos) volley
rociar²⁸ VI/VT (con agua) to spray, to sprinkle; (con jugo, aliño) to baste
rocín M nag
rocío M (del alba) dew; (en aerosol) spray, mist
rock M rock
rocoso ADJ rocky
rodada F (superficial) track; (profunda) rut
rodadura F rolling
rodaja F flat round slice
rodaje M (de un coche) running; (de una película) shoot
rodante ADJ rolling
rodar⁵ VI (girar) to roll; (caer) to tumble down; (vagar) to roam; (filmar) to shoot
rodear VT (cercar) to surround; (cubrir) to wrap around; (evitar) to go around
rodeo M (desvío) detour; (modo de expresarse)

circumlocution; (espectáculo) rodeo
rodilla F knee; **de —s** on one's knees; **hincarse de —s** to kneel down
rodillo M (para pintar) roller; (para cocinar) rolling pin; (para caminos) road roller
rododendro M rhododendron
roedor M rodent
roer[73] VI/VT to gnaw
rogar[42] VT to pray, to beg, to beseech; **hacerse [del]** — to play hard to get; **se ruega no molestar** please do not disturb
rojez F redness
rojizo ADJ reddish
rojo ADJ & M red; **al — vivo** red-hot
rol M role
roletazo M ground ball; **lo sacaron con un —** he grounded out
rollizo ADJ plump; M log
rollo M (de papel, de película, de grasa) roll; (de árbol) log; (de cuerda) reel; (de tela) bolt; (discurso aburrido) long story; (mentira) lie; (lío) mess, hassle; (relación amorosa) affair; (manuscrito) scroll; (de alambre) coil; **dar el — to hassle
ROM M ROM
romance ADJ Romance; M (lengua románica) Romance language; (español) Spanish language; (relación amorosa) romance; (composición métrica) ballad; **en buen —** in plain language
románico ADJ (arte) Romanesque; (lengua) Romance
romano -na ADJ & MF Roman
romanticismo M (corriente literaria) romanticism; (sentimentalismo) romance
romántico -ca ADJ & MF romantic
rombo M diamond
romería F pilgrimage
romero -ra MF (persona) pilgrim; M rosemary
romo ADJ (sin punta) blunt; (sin filo) dull
romper[74] VI/VT (un jarrón) to break; VT (relaciones) to sever; **— a** to start to; **— con** to break up with; **— el alba** to dawn; **— filas** to break ranks; **— un contrato** to break a contract; **rompió las aguas / la fuente** her water broke; **de rompe y rasga** coarse; M SG **rompecabezas** jigsaw puzzle; M SG **rompehuelgas** strikebreaker; M SG **rompeolas** breakwater
rompible ADJ breakable
rompientes M PL surf
rompimiento M (con el pasado) break; (de una promesa) breach
rompope M *Méx* eggnog
ron M rum
roncar[30] VI to snore
roncha F (de sarampión) spot; (de mosquito) bite
ronco ADJ hoarse, raspy
ronda F (de policía) patrol, beat; (de niños)

circle; (de bebidas, de negociaciones, de golf) round
rondar VT (patrullar) to patrol; (acercarse) to hang around; (cantar serenatas) to serenade; **rondaba los cuarenta** she was around forty years old
ronquera F hoarseness
ronquido M snore
ronronear VI to purr
ronroneo M purr
ronzal M halter
roña F (enfermedad de plantas) scab; (sarna) mange; MF (tacaño) skinflint
roñoso ADJ (planta) scabby; (animal) mangy; (persona) stingy
ropa F clothing, clothes; **— blanca** linens; **— vieja** stew made from leftover meat
ropaje M apparel
ropería F checkroom
ropero M (armario) wardrobe; (cuarto) closet
roque M castle
rorro M baby
rosa F (flor) rose; (marca) blemish; **— de los vientos** mariner's compass; ADJ INV (rosado) rose-colored, pink; (homosexual) *fam* gay
rosado ADJ (saludable) rosy; (de color de rosa) rose-colored, pink; M rosé wine
rosal M rosebush
rosario M rosary
rosbif M roast beef
rosca F (de tornillo) screw; (pan) ring-shaped roll; **pasarse de —** to go off the deep end
roséola F roseola
rostro M (cara) face; (morro) nerve
rotación F rotation
rotar VI/VT to rotate
rotativo ADJ (movimiento) rotary; (cultivos) rotating; M newspaper
rotatorio ADJ rotary
roto ADJ (averiado) broken; (cansado) exhausted; (ropa, voz) ragged
roto *ver* romper
rotor M rotor
rótula F kneecap
rotular VT to label
rótulo M (título) title; (etiqueta) label
rotundo ADJ resounding; **una negativa rotunda** a categorical denial
rotura F (de un aparato) break; (de un órgano, tubo) rupture; **— de servicio** (tenis) service break
roturar VT to plow
round M (en boxeo) round
rozadura F chafing
rozamiento M friction
rozar[47] VT (herir levemente) to graze; (arañar) to scrape; (irritar) to rub, to chafe; (limpiar un terreno) to clear; **—se con alguien** to have dealings with someone; **rozaba en los**

cuarenta she was almost forty years old
Ruanda F Rwanda
ruandés -esa ADJ & MF Rwandan
rubéola/rubeola F rubella
rubí M (piedra preciosa) ruby; (en un reloj) jewel
rubicundo ADJ (permanente) ruddy; (temporal) flush
rubio -a ADJ & MF blond
rubor M (de la piel) blush, flush; (de las mejillas) bloom, glow
ruborizarse[47] VI to blush
rúbrica F (trazo) flourish; (título) title
rucio ADJ gray
rudeza F rudeness, coarseness
rudo ADJ rude, coarse; **— golpe** hard blow
rueca F spinning wheel
rueda F (de coche) wheel; (de personas) circle; (rodaja) slice; **— de prensa** news conference; **ir sobre —s** to be smooth sailing
ruedo M (de un circo) ring; (de vestido) hem
ruego M (plegaria) prayer; (petición) plea, entreaty
rufián M (matón) ruffian; (proxeneta) pimp
rugby M rugby
rugido M roar
rugir[46] VI (animal) to roar; (estómago) to growl
rugoso ADJ rough
ruibarbo M rhubarb
ruido M noise; **— de fondo** background noise; **mucho — y pocas nueces** much ado about nothing
ruidoso ADJ noisy, loud
ruin ADJ (persona, cosa) vile; (animal) puny
ruina F (destrucción) destruction; (edificio derruido, estado de pobreza) ruin; (persona) wreck; (perjuicio) downfall; **en —s** in ruins
ruindad F (actitud) vileness; (acto) vile act
ruinoso ADJ ruinous
ruiseñor M nightingale
rulero M RP roller, curler
ruleta F roulette
rulo M roller, curler
Rumania F Romania, Rumania
rumano -na ADJ & MF Romanian, Rumanian
rumba F rumba
rumbear VI (dirigirse a) to head in a certain direction; (bailar) to dance the rumba
rumbo M course, route; **— a** toward
rumiar VI (meditar, comer el rumen) to ruminate; (reflexionar) to ruminate, to mull over, to brood over
rumor M rumor
runrún M (rumor) rumor; (sonido sordo) humming
ruptura F (de relaciones) break; (de órganos internos) rupture
rural ADJ rural
Rusia F Russia
ruso -sa ADJ & MF (persona) Russian; M (lengua)
Russian
rústico ADJ (rural) rustic, rural; (tosco) coarse; **en rústica** paperback
ruta F (itinerario) route; (carretera) highway; (en informática) path
rutina F routine

Ss

sábado M Saturday
sábalo M shad
sábana F bed sheet
sabana F savannah
sabañón M chilblain
saber[71] VI/VT to know; (tener sabor) to taste; **— nadar** to know how to swim; **supo la verdad** he found out the truth; **las vacaciones me han sabido a poco** my vacation was too short; **— a ciencia cierta** to know for sure; **— de biología** to know all about biology; **a —** namely; **hacer —** to let know; **para que sepas** for your information; **sabérselas todas** to know the ropes; **vaya a —** who knows? **no sabe un comino** he doesn't know squat; **— a** to taste like; **sabe bien** it tastes good; M knowledge, learning; **a mi leal — y entender** as far as I know; M SG **sabelotodo** know-it-all
sabiduría F wisdom
sabiendas LOC ADV **a —** knowingly
sabiondo -da ADJ & MF wise guy; know-it-all
sabio -bia ADJ wise, sage; MF (estudioso) scholar; (sabedor) sage, wise person
sable M saber
sabor M taste, flavor
saborear VT to savor, to relish
sabotaje M sabotage
sabotear VT to sabotage
sabrá, sabría ver saber
sabroso ADJ (comida) savory, tasty; (cuento) juicy
sabueso M (perro) bloodhound; (detective) sleuth
sacador -ora MF (en deportes) server
sacar[30] VT (cosas de la maleta, a pasear) to take out; (manchas, dinero del banco) to get out; (los zapatos) to take off; (malas notas, carnet de conducir) to get; (una copia) to make; (una foto) to take; (una conclusión) to draw; (la lengua, la cabeza por la ventana) to stick out; (una pelota de tenis) to serve; (una asignatura escolar) Esp to pass; **— ampollas** to blister; **— brillo** to polish up; **— provecho [de]** to benefit [from]; **— a bailar** to ask to dance; **— a colación** to broach; **— a luz** to divulge; **—**

de un apuro to bail out; **me saca de quicio** he gets my goat, he gets on my nerves; — **el cuerpo** to dodge; — **el mejor partido de** to make the best of; —**le el jugo a algo** to make the most of; — **en limpio** to deduce; —**se el sombrero** *Am* to take off one's hat; ¡**sáquese de allí!** *Am* get out of there! — **punta** to sharpen; — **a alguien** (béisbol) to get someone out; M SG **sacabocados** punch; M SG **sacacorchos** corkscrew; M SG **sacamuelas** quack dentist; M SG **sacapuntas** pencil sharpener

sacarina F saccharine

sacarosa F sucrose

sacerdocio M priesthood

sacerdote M priest

saciar VT to satiate; —**se** to be satiated

saco M (bolsa) sack; (chaqueta) blazer, sport coat; (aparato de boxeo) punching bag; (parte de órgano interno) sac; — **de dormir** sleeping bag; — **de noche** overnight bag; **echar en** — **roto** to waste one's effort

sacramento M sacrament

sacrificar[30] VT (en un rito religioso) to sacrifice; (una mascota) to put to sleep

sacrificio M sacrifice (también en béisbol)

sacrilegio M sacrilege

sacrílego ADJ sacrilegious

sacristán M sexton

sacro M sacrum

sacudida F (sacudón) shake, jolt; (de terremoto) tremor; (de la cabeza) toss; (eléctrica) shock

sacudir VT (sarandear) to shake; (las alfombras) to beat; (el polvo) to dust; **ir sacudiéndose** to rattle along, to jolt along; —**se de alguien** to get rid of someone

sádico ADJ sadistic

sadismo M sadism

sadomasoquismo M sadomasochism

saeta F arrow

safari M safari

sagaz ADJ shrewd, astute

sagrado ADJ sacred, holy; **Sagradas Escrituras** Holy Scripture

sahumar VT to perfume with incense

sahumerio M burning of incense

sainete M one-act farce; **esa familia es un** — that family is a complete mess

sal F (mineral) salt; (gracia) wit; — **de Epsom** Epsom salt; — **gorda** cooking salt; — **yodada** iodized salt; — **de mesa** table salt; **dar** — to spice up; — **y pimienta** (condimentos) salt and pepper; (gracia) life, spark

sal *ver* salir

sala F (de estar) parlor, living room; (grande) hall, large room; — **de justicia** courtroom; — **de clase** classroom; — **de chat** chat room; — **de cuidados intensivos** intensive

care unit; — **de espera** waiting room; — **de directorio** boardroom; — **de lectura** reading room; — **de operaciones** operating room; — **de recuperación** recovery room

salado ADJ (con sal) salty, savory; (gracioso) witty; *Am* (caro) expensive; M (acción) salting

salamandra F salamander

salar VT to salt; —**se** to become salty

salarial ADJ salary, wage

salario M pay, wages; — **base** base pay; — **bruto** gross pay; — **de subsistencia** living wage; — **mínimo** minimum wage

salchicha F sausage

saldar VT to settle

saldo M (resultado final) balance; (venta especial) sale; —**s** (restos) remnants; — **pendiente** balance due

saldrá, saldría *ver* salir

salegar[40] VT to give salt to; M salt lick

salero M (dispensador) salt cellar, salt shaker; (gracia) charm

saleroso ADJ charming

salga, salgo *ver* salir

salida F (partida) departure; (puerta) exit, way out; (comienzo de una carrera) start; (militar) sally; (eléctrica, de computadora) output; (de una crisis) way out; **este artículo tiene mucha** — this article sells well; **dar la** — to start a race; — **del sol** sunrise; — **de emergencia** emergency exit; — **en falso** false start

saliente ADJ (roca) salient, projecting; (gobierno) outgoing; M salient, projection, overhang

salina F salt mine

salino ADJ saline

salir[57] VI (del interior al exterior, para divertirse) to go out; (de un país) to depart, to leave; (del trabajo) to quit; (de un programa de computadora) to exit, to quit; (manchas de tinta) to come out; (un anillo del dedo) to come off; (el sol) to rise; (una publicación) to appear; (flores) to sprout; — **a bolsa** to go public; — **del armario** *Esp* to come out; — **del clóset** *Am* to come out; **trabajando no se puede** — **de pobre** you can't work your way out of poverty; **salió a su madre** she takes after her mother; — **a la luz** to surface; — **adelante** to overcome difficulties; — **bien** to turn out well; — **con** to date; — **ganando** to come out ahead; — **mal** to go wrong; ¿**a cuánto sale?** how much is it? **no me sale ser amable con él** I can't bring myself to be nice to him; —**se** (gotear) to leak; (rebosar) to overflow; (proyectarse) to stick out

salitre F saltpeter

saliva F saliva

salmón M salmon

salmonela F salmonella
salmuera F brine
salobre ADJ salty
salomonense ADJ & MF Solomon Islander
salón M (de estar) living room, parlor; (de conferencias) hall; — **de belleza** beauty salon; — **de clase** classroom; — **de exposición y ventas** showroom; — **de exhibición** exhibition hall; — **de té** tearoom
salpicadero M dashboard
salpicadura F spatter, splash, splatter
salpicar[30] VI/VT (humedecer) to sprinkle, to spatter, to splash; (adornar) to punctuate; (dispersar) to intersperse
salpicón M meat salad
salpimentar[1] VT to salt and pepper
salsa F (blanca) sauce; (picante) salsa; **en su —** in her element; — **tártara** tartar sauce; — **de soya** soy sauce; — **de tomate** ketchup
saltar VI/VT (brincar) to jump, to leap; (una cerca) to jump over, to vault; (un renglón) to skip; (una ley) to ignore; VI (los fusibles) to trip; — **a la vista** to be obvious; — **sobre** to pounce on; **se le saltaron los ojos** his eyes bugged out; **se le saltó un botón** one of his buttons popped off; **se me saltaban las lágrimas** it brought tears to my eyes; M SG **saltamontes** grasshopper
salteador -ora MF bandit
saltear VT to stir-fry
salto M jump, leap; — **alto** high jump; — **con esquí** ski jump; — **con pértiga** pole vault; — **de agua** waterfall; — **de cama** dressing gown; — **de línea** return; — **de línea forzado** hard return; — **de línea suave** soft return; — **de longitud** broad jump; — **de página** page break; — **de página forzado** forced page break, hard page break; — **de página suave/automático** soft page break; — **del ángel** swan dive; — **mortal** somersault; — **triple** triple jump; **a — de mata** from hand to mouth; **dar un —** (saltar) to jump; (el corazón) to skip a beat
saltón ADJ (que salta) jumping; (que resalta) bulging; M grasshopper
salubridad F sanitation
salud F health; — **mental** mental health; — **pública** public health; **curarse en —** to take precautions; INTERJ cheers!
saludable ADJ healthy, healthful
saludar VT (decir hola) to greet; (dar la bienvenida) to salute, to hail; (en el ejército) to salute; (hacer un gesto amistoso con la mano) to wave
saludo M (hola) greeting, salutation; (gesto) wave; (militar) salute; **retirar el — a alguien** to stop speaking to someone; —**s** best wishes, regards

salva F salvo
salvación F salvation
salvado M (harina) bran; (béisbol) save
salvador -ora MF savior; ADJ saving
salvadoreño -ña ADJ & MF Salvador[i]an
salvaguarda F safeguard
salvaguardar VT to safeguard
salvajada F (acción) savage act; (comentario) savage remark
salvaje ADJ (feroz) savage; (no domesticado) wild; MF savage
salvajismo M savagery
salvamento M (de gente) rescue; (de bienes, propiedades) salvage; (béisbol) save
salvar VT (la vida, el alma) to save; (de un peligro) to rescue; (propiedad) to salvage; (un obstáculo) to clear; (un camino difícil) to negotiate; — **el pellejo** to save one's skin; **el puente salva el río** the bridge spans the river; —**se** to pull through; —**se por poco** to have a narrow escape; **sálvese quien pueda** every man for himself; M SG **salvapantallas** screen saver; M SG **salvavidas** (aparato) life preserver, life jacket; MF (persona) lifeguard
salvia F sage
salvo ADJ safe; **a —** safe; M —**conducto** safe-conduct; PREP save, except; — **en caso de desastre** barring a disaster
Samoa F Samoa
samoano -na ADJ & MF Samoan
sanar VI/VT to heal; M **sanalotodo** cure-all
sanatorio M (para convalecientes) sanatorium; (para enfermos) hospital
sanción F sanction
sancionar VT to sanction
sandalia F sandal
sandez F (acción) stupidity, foolishness; (dicho) foolish remark
sandía F watermelon
saneamiento M sanitation
sanear VT to drain
sangrar VI/VT to bleed; VT (un árbol) to tap; (un párrafo) to indent
sangre F blood; — **fría** coolness under pressure; **a — fría** in cold blood; **hacerse mala —** to get upset; **eso lo llevo en la —** that's in my blood; **de — caliente** warm-blooded; — **azul** blue blood; **sudar —** to sweat bullets; **de pura —** thoroughbred; **chupar la — a alguien** to be a parasite on someone
sangría F (bebida) wine punch; (acción de sangrar) bleeding; (espacio tipográfico) indentation; (pérdida) drain
sangriento ADJ (manchado de sangre, que provoca pérdida de sangre) bloody; (sanguinario) bloodthirsty
sanguijuela F leech
sanguinario ADJ bloody, vicious
sanguíneo ADJ blood; **grupo —** blood group

sanidad F public health
sanitario -ria ADJ sanitary; M —s bathroom fittings; MF public health worker
sanmarinense ADJ & MF San Marinese
sanmarinés -esa ADJ & MF San Marinese
sano ADJ (persona) healthy; (juicio) sound; (dieta) healthful; (vaso) unbroken; — **y salvo** safe and sound; **en su — juicio** of sound mind
sánscrito M Sanskrit
sanseacabó INTERJ **te quedas y** — you're staying and that's that
santalucense ADJ & MF St. Lucian
santiamén LOC ADV **en un** — in a jiffy, lickety-split
santidad F sanctity, holiness
santificar[30] VT to sanctify
santiguarse[25] VI to cross oneself
santo -ta ADJ saintly, holy; **esperar todo el** — **día** to wait the whole blessed day; MF saint; **día del** — saint's day; **quedarse para vestir** —**s** to be a spinster; **¿a** — **de qué?** for what reason? **¡por todos los** —**s!** my goodness!
santotomense ADJ & MF São Tomean
santuario M sanctuary
santurrón -ona ADJ & MF goody-goody
saña F fury
sañudo ADJ furious
sapo M toad (también hombre feo); **echar** —**s y culebras** to swear, to curse; **sentirse como un** — **de otro pozo** to feel like a fish out of water
saque M (tenis) service, serve; — **de inicio** (fútbol) kickoff; — **de banda** throw-in; — **de esquina** corner kick; — **de meta** goal kick; — **de puerta** goal kick; — **inicial** kick-off; — **ganador** ace; — **y volea** (tenis) serve and volley
saquear VT to sack, to plunder, to pillage
saqueo M sacking, plundering, pillaging
sarampión M measles; — **alemán** rubella
sarape M *Méx* serape
sarcasmo M sarcasm
sarcástico ADJ sarcastic
sarcófago M sarcophagus
sarcoma M sarcoma
sardina F sardine
sardo -da ADJ & MF Sardinian
sardónico ADJ sardonic
sargento -ta MF sergeant; F battle-ax[e]
sarmentoso ADJ gnarled
sarmiento M vine
sarna F mange
sarnoso ADJ mangy
sarpullido M rash
sarro M tartar, plaque
sarta F string; **una** — **de mentiras** a pack of lies; **una** — **de idiotas** a bunch of idiots

sartén F frying pan, skillet
sastre -tra MF tailor
sastrería F tailor shop
satánico ADJ satanic
satélite M satellite; — **artificial** man-made satellite
satén M satin
sátira F satire
satírico ADJ satirical
satirizar[47] VT to satirize
satisfacción F satisfaction
satisfacer[54, 74] VT (un deseo) to satisfy; (una deuda) to pay; —**se** to be satisfied
satisfactorio ADJ (aceptable) satisfactory; (exitoso) successful
satisfaga, satisfago, satisfará, satisfaría *ver* satisfacer
satisfecho ADJ contented, satisfied
satisfecho, satisfice, satisficiera, satisficiese *ver* satisfacer
saturar VT (una solución) to saturate; (un mercado) to glut; (líneas de teléfono) to overload
sauce M willow; — **llorón** weeping willow
saudí, saudita ADJ & MF Saudi Arabian
savia F sap
saxofón M saxophone
sazón F season; **a la** — at that time; **en** — ripe
sazonar VT (condimentar) to season, to flavor; (madurar) to ripen
scooter M scooter
scout MF scout
se PRON PERS — **coronó a sí mismo** he crowned himself; — **lavó la cara** he washed his face; — **besaron** they kissed each other; — **habla español** Spanish is spoken; — **lo puede combatir** it can be fought
sé *ver* saber
sea, seas *ver* ser
sebo M tallow, fat
seborrea F seborrhea
secador M hair dryer
secadora F clothes dryer
secante ADJ drying
secar[30] VT (la ropa) to dry; (las manos) to dry off; —**se** (planta) to dry up; (río) to run dry; (madera) to season
sección F (militar) platoon; (de un almacén) department; (un texto) section
seccionar VT to section
seco ADJ (ropa) dry; (río) dried-up; (planta) withered; (respuesta) curt, brief; **en** — on dry land; **parar en** — to stop short; **quedar** — to fall dead; **estar** — to be broke; **lavar en** — to dry-clean; **a secas** plain
secreción F secretion
secretar VT to secrete
secretaría F secretariat
secretariado M (profesión) secretarial

profession; (secretaría) secretariat; (conjunto de secretarias) secretarial pool

secretario -ria MF secretary; **— general** secretary general

secretear VI to whisper

secreto ADJ (oculto) secret; (policía) undercover; M (cosa oculta) secret; (condición de oculto) secrecy; **— a voces** open secret; **en —** in secret; **— bancario** account holder confidentiality

secta F sect

sector M sector

sectorial ADJ sectorial

secuaz M henchman

secuela F consequence; **—s** aftermath

secuencia F (de acontecimientos) sequence; (de datos) string

secuenciar VT to sequence

secuestrador -ora MF kidnapper

secuestrar VT (a una persona) to kidnap, to abduct; (una propiedad) to seize; (un avión) to hijack

secuestro M (de una persona) kidnapping; (de propiedad) seizure; (de un avión) hijacking

secular ADJ secular

secundar VT (apoyar) to second; (imitar) to imitate; (seguir) to follow suit

secundaria F secondary school

secundario ADJ secondary

sed F thirst; **tener —** to be thirsty

seda F silk; **como una —** (suave) soft as silk; (afable) sweet-tempered

sedación F sedation

sedán M sedan

sedante ADJ & M sedative

sedar VT to sedate

sedativo ADJ & M sedative

sede F (gubernamental) seat; (religiosa) see; **— central** headquarters

sedentario ADJ sedentary

sedería F (conjunto de artículos de seda) silk goods; (tienda de sedas) silk shop

sedero -ra MF (que vende) silk dealer; (que fabrica) silk weaver; ADJ **industria sedera** silk industry

sedición F sedition

sediento ADJ thirsty; **estar — de** to thirst for

sedimento M sediment

sedoso ADJ silken, silky

seducción F seduction

seducir[38] VT (corromper) to seduce; (atraer) to entice; (persuadir con argucias) to lure

seductivo ADJ alluring

seductor -ora ADJ alluring; M seducer; F seductress

sefardí ADJ Sephardic; MF Sephardi; M (variedad del español) Sephardi

sefardita ADJ & MF Sephardi

segador -ora MF (persona) mower, reaper; F (máquina) mower, reaper

segar[41] VT (hierba) to mow; (mies) to reap

seglar ADJ secular; M layman; F laywoman

segmento M segment

segregar[40] VT (separar) to segregate; (producir secreciones) to secrete

seguido ADJ in a row; **dos horas seguidas** two hours in a row; ADV straight through; **trabajaron —** they worked continuously

seguidor -ora MF follower

seguimiento M (persecución) pursuit; (atención continuada) follow-up

seguir[12] VT (camino, instrucciones) to follow; (estudios) to pursue; (progreso de un avión) to track; **sigue trabajando** he keeps on working, he continues to work; **sigue allí** he is still there; **de lo anterior se sigue que** from the preceding it follows that; **— los pasos de** to follow in the footsteps of; **—le la corriente a alguien** to play along with someone; **— el tren** to keep up; **— el hilo de** to keep track of; **— la pista de** to trail

según PREP according to; **— se mire** depending on how you see it; **— pasa el tiempo** as time goes by; **— tus instrucciones** per your instructions; CONJ as; **— se informa** reportedly; **lo haré — me digas** I will do it as you tell me to

segundero M second hand

segundo -da ADJ & ADV second; MF second in command; **— tiempo** (fútbol) second half; **— servicio** (tenis) second serve; **segunda base** (posición en béisbol) second base; M (jugador) second baseman; **segunda hipoteca** second mortgage; **segunda intención** ulterior motive; **de segunda mano** secondhand, preowned; **de segunda** second-rate

segundón -ona MF (hijo) second-born child; (persona mediocre) also-ran

seguramente ADV certainly, surely; **lenta pero —** slowly but surely

seguridad F (contra el delito) security; (contra accidentes) safety; **— en sí mismo** self-confidence; **— social** social security

seguro ADJ (a prueba de delincuentes) secure; (que no ofrece o siente duda) sure, certain; (libre de peligro) safe; (firme) stable; **es — que** it is certain that; **su — servidor** yours truly; **— de sí mismo** self-assured; M (contrato contra riesgos) insurance; (dispositivo) safety device, restraint; **— contra accidentes** accident insurance; **— contra daños a terceros** liability insurance; **— contra incendios** fire insurance; **— contra inundaciones** flood insurance; **— contra todo riesgo** comprehensive insurance; **— de discapacidad** disability insurance; **— de**

vida life insurance; — **de vida a término** term life insurance; — **de vida permanente** whole life insurance; — **médico** health insurance; **en** — in safety; **sobre** — without risk

seis NUM six

selección F selection, choice; — **de texto** highlighting; — **natural** natural selection; — **nacional** national team

seleccionado M — **nacional** national team

seleccionar VT to select, to choose

selectivo ADJ selective

selecto ADJ select, choice

sellar VT (poner sello) to stamp; (precintar) to seal

sello M (de correo) stamp; (de documento oficial) seal; (instrumento) seal, stamp; (de discos) label; — **de goma** rubber stamp; — **fiscal** revenue stamp

selva F (templada o fría) forest; (tropical) jungle; — **virgen** virgin forest

semáforo M traffic light

semana F week; **entre** — during the week

semanal ADJ weekly

semanario M weekly publication

semántica F semantics

semblante M countenance

semblanza F biographical sketch

sembrado M sown ground

sembradora F planting machine

sembrar[1] VT (plantar) to sow, to plant; (esparcir) to scatter; (minas) to lay; (pánico, alegría) to spread

semejante ADJ similar, like; — **afirmación** such a statement; **un tipo** — such a guy; M fellow human being

semejanza F resemblance, similarity; **a** — **de** in the manner of

semejar VT to resemble

semen M semen, sperm

semental ADJ stud; M stud, stallion

semestral ADJ biannual

semestre M semester

semianual ADJ biannual

semicírculo M semicircle

semiconductor M semiconductor

semifinal ADJ & F semifinal

semilla F seed

semillero M (seedbed); — **de vicios** hotbed of vice

seminario M (religioso) seminary; (universitario) seminar

semítico ADJ Semitic

senado M senate

senador -ora MF senator

sencillez F simplicity; **con** — simply

sencillo ADJ (no complicado, humilde) simple; (fácil) easy, simple; (sin adornos) plain; (no afectado) straightforward; M (béisbol) single

senda F (construida) path, pathway; (natural) track, trail

sendero M (construido) path, pathway; (natural) track, trail

sendos ADJ **tenían** — **sombreros** each one had a hat

Senegal M Senegal

senegalés -esa ADJ & MF Senegalese

senil ADJ senile

senilidad F senility

seno M (pecho) breast; (hueco) sinus; (útero) womb; (en matemática) sine; — **de la familia** bosom of the family

sensación F (física) sensation; (mental) feeling, impression; **tengo la** — **de que** I have the feeling that; **fue la** — **de la fiesta** she was the life of the party

sensacional ADJ sensational

sensatez F common sense

sensato ADJ sensible, level-headed

sensibilidad F (modo de pensar) sensibility; (percepción) sensitiveness

sensibilizar[47] VT to sensitize

sensible ADJ (que siente) sensitive; (notable) perceptible; **tengo el brazo muy** — **por el accidente** my arm is very tender because of the accident; **Juana es muy** — **en estas ocasiones** Juana is very emotional on these occasions

sensiblería F sentimentality

sensiblero ADJ sentimental, mushy

sensitivo ADJ sensitive

sensor M sensor

sensorial ADJ sensory

sensual ADJ (carnal) sensual; (de los sentidos) sensuous

sensualidad F sensuality

sentada F (acto de sentarse) sitting; (protesta) sit-in; **de una** — at one sitting

sentado ADJ **dar por** — to take for granted

sentar[1] VT to seat; — **bien** to agree with; **me sentó muy mal lo que dijo** what he said did not sit well with me; **este peinado te sienta** this hairdo becomes you; **no te sienta ese traje** that suit does not fit you; — **precedente** to set a precedent; —**se** to sit down

sentencia F (dicho) maxim; (fallo) ruling; (condena) sentence; (indemnización) award

sentenciar VT (condenar) to sentence; (fallar) to rule

sentido ADJ heartfelt; M (facultad) sense; (significado) meaning; (dirección) way; — **común** common sense; — **de la vista** sense of sight; — **del gusto** sense of taste; — **del humor** sense of humor; — **del oído** sense of hearing; — **del olfato** sense of smell; — **del tacto** sense of touch; **aguzar el** — to prick up one's ears; **de un solo** — one-way; **de dos**

—s two-way; **dejar sin —** to render unconscious; **en cierto —** in a sense; **perder el —** to faint; **quedar —** to have one's feelings hurt; **sin —** meaningless; **tener —** to make sense

sentimental ADJ sentimental

sentimentalismo M sentimentality

sentimiento M feeling, sentiment

sentir[8] VT (percibir) to feel; (oír) to hear; (lamentar) to regret; **—se** to feel; **—se capaz de** to feel up to; **—se de los pies** to have pains in the feet

seña F (gesto) sign; (rasgo) trait; (marca) mark; **—s** name and address; **por más —s** as an additional proof; **—s de vida** life signs; **hablar por —s** to use sign language; **hacer —s** to signal

señal F (de tráfico, de violencia, de vida, de la cruz) sign; (de violencia) mark; (de radio) signal; (pago anticipado) deposit; **en — de** in token of

señalar VT (marcar, señalar) to mark; (mostrar, mencionar) to point out; (fijar) to fix; **—se** to distinguish oneself

señor M (título) Mr.; (forma de tratamiento) sir; (dueño) *lit* master, lord; **el Señor** the Lord; **un gran —** a great man

señora F (dama) lady; (forma de tratamiento) madam, ma'am; (título) Mrs., Ms.; (esposa) wife

señorear VI to dominate

señoría F lordship; **su —** Your Honor

señorial ADJ lordly

señorío M (dominio) dominion; (dignidad) lordship

señorita F miss; **toda una —** quite a young lady

señorito M (joven) master; (dandi) dandy

señuelo M decoy, lure

sepa, sepamos *ver* saber

separación F separation

separado ADJ (apartado) separate; (estado civil) separated; **por —** separately

separar VT (apartar) to separate; (clasificar) to sort out; (despedir de un cargo) to remove; **—se** to separate, to part company

separata F offprint, reprint

septentrional ADJ northern

septicemia F blood poisoning

septiembre, setiembre M September

séptimo ADJ & M seventh

sepulcro M tomb

sepultar VT to bury, to inter

sepultura F (acción) burial; (lugar) grave, tomb; **dar —** to bury

sepulturero -ra MF gravedigger

sequedad F dryness

sequía F drought

séquito M retinue, entourage

ser[65] VI to be; **— de Valencia** to be from Valencia; **— de madera** to be made of wood; **a no — que** unless; **así es** that's right; **érase una vez** once upon a time; **es decir** that is to say; **es de esperar** it is to be expected; **es más** what's more; **la boda es hoy** the wedding takes place today; **son las nueve** it is nine o'clock; **somos cuatro** there are four of us; V AUX to be; **fue elegido presidente** he was elected president; M (entidad viviente) being; (esencia) essence; (existencia) existence; **un — humano** a human being

serbio -bia ADJ Serbian; MF (persona) Serb, Serbian; M (lengua) Serbian

serenar VI to quiet; **—se** (el alma) to become serene, to calm down; (el tiempo) to clear up

serenata F serenade; **dar —** to serenade

serenidad F serenity, peace of mind

sereno ADJ (mar, alma) serene; (cielo) clear; **al —** in the night air; M night watchman

serie F series; **— de instrucciones** (en un programa de computadora) macro; **en —** serial; **— ofensiva** offensive series

seriedad F seriousness, earnestness

serio ADJ (problema) serious; (persona) earnest, serious; **en —** seriously

sermón M (prédica) sermon; (reprimenda) lecture

sermonear VI/VT (predicar) to preach; (reprender) to lecture

serpentear VI to wind, to meander

serpiente F snake

serrado ADJ serrated

serranía F mountainous region

serrano -na M mountain man; F mountain woman; ADJ **zona serrana** mountain region

serrín M sawdust

serrucho M handsaw

servicial ADJ helpful

servicio M (también en tenis) service; (sirvientes) servants; (para un comensal) place setting; (aseo) restroom, facilities; **— a la habitación** room service; **— de ayuda al usuario** helpdesk; **— de contestador** answering service; **— de entrega** delivery service; **— directo** ace; **— militar** military service; **a su —** at your service; **de — pesado** heavy-duty; **estar en —** to be in commission; **poner en —** to commission, to put into service

servidor -ora MF (persona) servant; **un —** yours truly; **su seguro —** yours truly; M (ordenador) server; **— remoto** remote server

servidumbre F servitude

servil ADJ (personalidad) servile; (trabajo) menial

servilleta F napkin

servir[9] VI to serve; **— de** to serve as; **— para** to be used for; **para —le** at your service; **no — para nada** to be of no use; **¿en qué le**

puedo —? how can I help you? **—se de** to make use of; **sírvase usted hacerlo** please do it

sésamo M sesame; **¡ábrete —!** open sesame!

sesenta NUM sixty

sesgado ADJ biased

sesgar[40] VT (una tela) to cut on the bias; (una opinión) to slant; (las estadísticas) to skew

sesgo M (en la tela) bias; (de los ojos, de orientación) slant; **al —** obliquely

sesión F (reunión, período) session; (de fotografía) sitting; (de una película) showing; **— de ejercicio** workout

seso M brain; **de poco —** foolish; **devanarse los —s** to rack one's brain

sestear VI to take a nap

sesudo ADJ (persona) brainy; (explicación) intelligent; (testarudo) *Méx* stubborn

set M set

seta F mushroom

setenta NUM seventy

seto M hedge

sétter M setter

seudónimo M pseudonym, pen name

severidad F severity, harshness

severo ADJ severe, stern, harsh

sevillano -na ADJ & MF Sevillian; F PL Sevillian dances

sexar VT to sex

sexismo M sexism

sexista MF sexist

sexo M (género, acto) sex; (órganos) genitals; **el bello —** the fair sex; **— seguro** safe sex

sexto ADV, ADJ & M sixth

sexual ADJ sexual

sexualidad F sexuality

sexy ADJ sexy

Seychelles F PL Seychelles

SFA [Sistema de frenos antibloqueo] M ABS

shock M shock

short, shorts M shorts

si CONJ if; **yo voy — tú vas** I'm going if you're going; **no sé — viene o no** I don't know whether she's coming or not; **¡— ya te lo dije!** but I already told you! **— bien** although; **por — acaso** just in case; **— Dios quiere** God willing; **— no me equivoco** unless I'm mistaken

sí ADV yes; *fam* yeah; **¿—?** really? **— que fui** I did go; **creo que —** I think so; M consent; **me dio el —** she said yes; PRON himself, herself, itself, oneself, themselves; **de por —** in itself; **estar sobre —** to be on the alert; **volver en — to** come to; **pagado de —** self-satisfied; **estar fuera de —** to be beside oneself; **hablar para —** to talk to oneself; **dio todo de —** she gave her all; **cada cual para —** every man for himself

sicario M hitman

sicomoro M sycamore

SIDA [síndrome de inmunodeficiencia adquirida] M AIDS

siderurgia F steel industry

sidra F cider

siega F (de la hierba) mowing; (de las mieses) reaping

siembra F (acción de sembrar) sowing; (época) sowing time

siempre ADV always; **— nos has apoyado** you've always been very supportive of us; **desde —** since forever; **para/por —** forever; **por — jamás** forevermore; **— que** (en cualquier momento) whenever; (con tal que) provided that; **— y cuando** provided that; **como —** as usual; **hoy no eres el mismo de —** you're not yourself today

sien F temple

sienta, siente *ver* sentar, sentir

sierpe F *lit* serpent

sierra F (herramienta) saw; (cordillera) small mountain range; **— de cadena** chainsaw

siesta F siesta, afternoon nap; **dormir la —** to take an afternoon nap

siete NUM seven

sífilis F syphilis

sifón M (para líquidos) siphon; (tubo) trap

siga, sigamos *ver* seguir

sigilo M stealth

sigla F acronym

siglo M century

signatario -ria MF signer

significación F (sentido) meaning; (importancia) significance

significado M meaning, sense

significar[30] VT to mean, to signify

significativo ADJ significant, meaningful

signo M sign; **— de admiración** exclamation point; **— de igual** equal sign; **— de interrogación** question mark; **— de más** plus sign; **— de menos** minus sign; **— de multiplicación** multiplication sign; **—s vitales** vital signs

sigo, siguiendo *ver* seguir

siguiente ADJ following; **al día —** the next day

siguiera, siguiese *ver* seguir

sílaba F syllable

silbar VI (soplar aire) to whistle; (rechiflar) to hiss

silbato M whistle (también en fútbol)

silbido M whistle

silenciador M (de arma) silencer; (de coche) muffler

silenciar VT to silence

silencio M silence, quiet; **guardar —** to keep quiet

silenciosamente ADV quietly

silencioso ADJ silent, quiet

silicio M silicon

silla F chair; (de montar) saddle; **— de ruedas** wheelchair; **— eléctrica** electric chair; **— plegadiza** folding chair
sillín M saddle, seat
sillón M (mueble) armchair
silo M silo
silogismo M syllogism
silueta F silhouette
siluro M catfish
silvestre ADJ wild
silvicultura F forestry
sima F chasm
simbiosis F symbiosis
simbólico ADJ symbolic
simbolismo M symbolism
simbolizar[47] VT to symbolize
símbolo M symbol; **— de status** status symbol; **— sexual** sex symbol
simetría F symmetry
simétrico ADJ symmetrical
simiente F seed
símil M simile
similar ADJ similar
similitud F resemblance, similarity
simio M ape
simpatía F friendliness; **no le tengo mucha —** I don't like him much
simpático ADJ (amistoso) nice, friendly, congenial; (sistema nervioso) sympathetic
simpatizante ADJ supporting, sympathizing; MF supporter, sympathizer
simpatizar[47] VI (con alguien) to like; (con una idea) to be sympathetic toward
simple ADJ (no complicado) simple; (mero) mere; (tonto) simpleminded
simplemente ADV simply, merely
simpleza F (sencillez) simplicity; (estupidez) stupidity
simplicidad F simplicity
simplificar[30] VT to simplify
simplista ADJ (intepretación) simplistic; (explicación) glib, simplistic
simplón -ona ADJ simpleminded; MF simpleton
simposio M symposium
simulación F simulation
simulacro M **— de batalla** mock battle; **— de incendio** fire drill
simulador -ora MF simulator; M **— de vuelo** flight simulator
simular VT to simulate, to feign
simultanear VI perform simultaneously
simultáneo ADJ simultaneous
sin PREP without; **— aliento** out of breath; **— amueblar** unfurnished; **— azúcar** sugar-free; **— comentarios** no comment; **— compromiso** without obligation; **— condiciones** unconditionally, with no strings attached; **— culpa** no-fault; **— declarar** unreported; **— derecho**
nonvoting; **— duda** without doubt, undoubtedly; **— embargo** nevertheless; **— escrúpulos** unscrupulous; **— excepciones** across the board; **— falta** without fail; **— garantía** unsecured; **— intereses** interest-free; **— lujos** no-frills; **— marcar** unmarked; **— peligro** safely; **— percances** safely; **— problemas** trouble-free; **— receta** over-the-counter; **— restricciones** open-ended; **— riesgo** risk-free; **— seguro médico** uninsured; **— sentido** meaningless
sinagoga F synagogue
sincerarse VI to clear the air, to come clean
sinceridad F sincerity
sincero ADJ (personalidad) sincere; (opinión) candid; (agradecimiento) heartfelt, wholehearted
sincrónico ADJ (proceso) synchronous; (enfoque lingüístico) synchronic
sincronización F timing
sincronizar[47] VT to synchronize
sindical ADJ (relativo al síndico) trustee; (relativo al sindicato) union; **dirigente —** union leader
sindicar[30] VT to unionize, to syndicate
sindicato M (de trabajadores) syndicate, trade union, labor union; (de bancos) syndicate
síndico -ca MF receiver, trustee
síndrome M syndrome; **— de abstinencia** withdrawal symptoms; **— de choque tóxico** toxic shock syndrome; **— de Down** Down's syndrome; **— de muerte infantil súbita** crib death, sudden infant death syndrome
sinergia F synergy
sinfín M **un — de cosas** a lot of things
sinfonía F symphony
Singapur M Singapore
singapurense ADJ & MF Singaporean
singular ADJ (número) singular; (excepcional) unique
siniestro ADJ sinister; M disaster
sinnúmero M myriad
sino CONJ but; **no vino — que llamó** she didn't come but instead called; **no tengo dos — tres** I have not two but three; **no es — madera** it's only wood
sinónimo ADJ synonymous; M synonym
sinopsis F synopsis
sinrazón F injustice
sinsabor M trouble
sinsonte M mockingbird
sintamos *ver* sentir
sintaxis F syntax
síntesis F synthesis; **— de habla** speech synthesis; **— de habla** voice synthesis
sintético ADJ (producto) synthetic; (fibras) man-made
sintetizador M synthesizer
sintetizar[47] VT to synthesize

sintiendo, sintiera, sintiese ver sentir
síntoma M symptom
sintonía F tuning; **en —** on the same wavelength
sintonizador M tuner
sintonizar[47] VT (una emisora) to tune in; (un sintonizador) to fine-tune; **los dos sintonizan bien** the two are on the same wavelength
sinuoso ADJ (camino) sinuous, winding; (comportamiento) devious
sinusitis F sinusitis
sinvergüenza MF creep
siquiera ADV at least; **dame — unos días** give me a few days at least; **ni —** not even
sirena F (ninfa, bocina) siren; (mitad mujer, mitad pez) mermaid
Siria F Syria
sirio -ria ADJ & MF Syrian
sirve, sirviendo, sirviera, sirviese ver servir
sirviente MF, **sirvienta** F servant
sisar VT to pilfer, to swipe
sisear VI to hiss
siseo M hiss, hissing
sísmico ADJ seismic
sistema M system; **— binario** binary system; **— de asistencia de salud** health care system; **— de cifrado** encryption system; **— de reconocimiento óptico de caracteres** optical character recognition; **— experto** expert system; **— inmune** immune system; **— mundial de posicionamiento** global positioning system; **— nervioso central** central nervous system; **— operativo** operating system; **— solar** solar system
sistemático ADJ systematic
sistematizar[47] VI/VT to systematize
sistémico ADJ systemic
sistólico ADJ systolic
sitial M **— de honor** seat of honor
sitiar VT to besiege
sitio M (espacio vacío) room; (ubicación) place, site; (asedio) siege; **no hay —** there's no room; **esto no está en su —** this is out of place; **— web** website; **poner — a** to lay siege to; **poner a alguien en su —** to put someone in his place
sito ADJ situated
situación F (circunstancia) situation; (legal, financiera, social) status
situado ADJ situated; **estar —** to be located
situar[26] VT to locate, to place; **—se** to be located
sketch M sketch, skit
slalom M slalom
smog M smog
smoking M dinner jacket
so PREP **— pena de** under penalty of; **— pretexto de** under the pretext of; INTERJ whoa; ADV **— tonto** you stupid idiot!

sobaco M armpit
sobar VT (la masa) to knead; (a una persona) to fondle; (un traje) to wear out
soberanía F sovereignty
soberano -na ADJ & MF sovereign
soberbia F pride, haughtiness
soberbio ADJ (orgulloso) proud, haughty; (magnífico) magnificent
sobornar VT to bribe
soborno M (acción) bribery; (mordida) bribe, fam payola
sobra F surplus; **—s** leftovers, leavings; **de — sabes** you know full well; **está de —** it is superfluous; **las piezas de —** spare parts
sobrado ADJ more than enough
sobrante ADJ leftover, remaining; surplus
sobrar VI (dinero, libros) to be left over, to remain; (personas) to be in the way
sobre PREP (encima de) above, over; (en contacto con) on, upon; (acerca de) about; **un préstamo — su coche** a loan on his car; **— todo** above all, especially; **— las 9:30** at about 9:30; **marchar — Madrid** to march toward Madrid; M (para cartas) envelope; (de sopa) packet; **— manila** manila envelope; **irse al —** to hit the sack
sobreactuar[26] VI to ham it up
sobrealimentador M supercharger
sobrecalificado ADJ overqualified
sobrecarga F overload; **— de voltaje** power surge; **— sensorial** sensory overload
sobrecargar[40] VT to overload
sobrecogedor ADJ awesome
sobrecoger[45] VI/VT to awe; **—se** to be in awe; **—se de pánico** to be panic-stricken
sobrecogimiento M awe
sobrecompensar VI to overcompensate
sobrecorrección F overcorrection
sobredosis F overdose
sobreendeudado N debt-ridden
sobreentenderse[2] VI to be understood
sobreentendido ADJ understood; M assumption
sobreestimar VT to overestimate
sobreexcitado ADJ overexcited, wired
sobreexcitar VT to overexcite
sobreextendido ADJ overextended
sobregirar VT to overdraw
sobregiro M overdraft
sobrehumano ADJ superhuman
sobrellevar VT to bear, to endure
sobremanera ADV beyond measure
sobremesa F after-dinner conversation
sobrenadar VI to float
sobrenatural ADJ supernatural
sobrenombre M nickname
sobrepasar VT to exceed
sobrepeso M overweight
sobreponerse[56, 74] VT to superimpose; VI **— a**

(valer más que) to outweigh; (recuperarse) to get over

sobreproteger[45] VT to overprotect, to smother

sobrepujar VT to surpass

sobresaliente ADJ outstanding; MF understudy

sobresalir[57] VI (ser notable) to stand out; (estar en un plano más saliente) to project, to jut out; (ser excelente) to excel

sobresaltar VT to startle, frighten; **—se** to be startled, to start

sobresalto M start, scare

sobrestante M foreman

sobresueldo M extra pay

sobretasa F surtax

sobretodo M overcoat

sobrevenir[61] VI to happen unexpectedly

sobrevivencia F survival

sobreviviente MF survivor; ADJ surviving

sobrevivir VI/VT to survive

sobriedad F sobriety

sobrino -na M nephew; F niece; **— nieto** great-nephew; **sobrina nieta** great-niece

sobrio ADJ sober

socarrar VT to singe

socarrón ADJ sarcastic

socarronería F sarcasm

socavar VT (excavar por debajo) to dig under; (debilitar) to undermine, to undercut

socavón M sinkhole; shaft, tunnel

sociable ADJ sociable, gregarious

social ADJ social

socialismo M socialism

socialista ADJ & MF socialist

socializar[47] VT to socialize

sociedad F (grupo humano) society; (firma) company, partnership; **— anónima** corporation; **— de consumo** consumer society; **alta —** high society

socio -cia MF (de una firma) partner; (de un club) member; **— minoritario** minority partner; **— principal** senior partner; **— comercial** trading partner

socioeconómico ADJ socioeconomic

sociología F sociology

sociópata MF sociopath

socorrer VT to help

socorro INTERJ & M help; **acudir al — de** to go to the rescue of; **pedir —** to cry out for help

soda F soda

sodio M sodium

sodomía F sodomy

soez ADJ vulgar

sofá M sofa, couch; **—-cama** sleeper, sofa bed

sofisma M fallacy

sofisticado ADJ sophisticated

sofocante ADJ suffocating, oppressive

sofocar[30] VI/VT (ahogar) to suffocate; (una rebelión) to quash, to quell, to suppress; (un incendio) to put out

sofoco M suffocation

softball M softball

software M software; **— de fuente abierta** open source software

soga F rope; **estar con la — al cuello** to have a rope around one's neck

sois ver ser

soja F (planta) soy; (semilla) soybean

sojuzgar[40] VT to subjugate, to subdue

sol M sun; **de — a —** from sunrise to sunset; **hace —** it is sunny; **tomar el —** to sunbathe; **ella es un —** she's a gem; **arrimarse al — que más calienta** to know which side one's bread is buttered on

solamente ADV only, solely

solana F sunny place

solapa F lapel

solapado ADJ underhanded

solar M (terreno) lot; (casa ancestral) manor; ADJ solar

solaz M lit recreation

soldado -da MF soldier; **— raso** private; **— de línea** regular soldier

soldador M soldering iron

soldadura F (acción de adherir con estaño) soldering; (resultado) solder; (acción de adherir sin estaño) welding; (resultado) weld; **— autógena** arc welding

soldar[5] VI/VT (con estaño) to solder; (sin estaño) to weld; **—se** to mend

soleado ADJ sunny

solear VT to put in the sun; **—se** to sun oneself

soledad F solitude, loneliness

solemne ADJ solemn; **— disparate** downright foolishness

solemnidad F solemnity

solenoide M solenoid

soler[6, 73] VI **suelo levantarme a las siete** I usually get up at seven; **solía acostarme tarde** I used to go to bed late; **no suele importarle** he usually doesn't mind

solferino ADJ reddish-purple

solicitante MF applicant

solicitar VT (permiso) to request; (un puesto, una beca) to apply for

solícito ADJ solicitous

solicitud F (para beca, puesto) application; (de información, permiso) request; **— de préstamo** loan application; **a — de** at the request of

solidaridad F solidarity

solidario ADJ supportive, sympathetic

solidez F solidity

solidificar[30] VT to solidify

sólido ADJ (materia) solid; (mueble) sturdy; (argumento) strong; M solid

solista MF soloist

solitario -ria ADJ solitary; MF (persona) recluse; M (juego de cartas, brillante) solitaire; F

tapeworm
sollozar[47] VI to sob
sollozo M sob
solo ADJ (desamparado) lonely, lonesome; (no acompañado) alone; **tengo un — coche** I have only one car; **a solas** alone; **habla solo** he talks to himself; **ni una sola palabra** not a single word; ADV just, only; **— quiero saber** I just/only want to know; M solo
solomillo M sirloin
solsticio M solstice
soltar[5] VT (a un prisionero) to let go, to release; (el vientre) to loosen; (una carcajada) to let out; (bombas) to drop; (un disparate) to say; **— amarras** to cast off; **— el hervor** to come to a boil; **— tacos** to swear; **—se** to loosen up; **—se el pelo** to kick up one's heels
soltero -ra ADJ single, unmarried; M bachelor; F unmarried woman
solterón -ona M old bachelor; F *pey* spinster
soltura F ease; **hablar con —** to speak fluently
soluble ADJ soluble
solución F solution; **— salina** saline solution
solucionar VT to solve
solventar VT to settle
solvente ADJ & M solvent
somalí ADJ & MF Somalian
Somalia F Somalia
sombra F (de una figura) shadow; (protección del sol) shade; (para ojos) eye shadow; **hacer —** to overshadow; **dar —** to shade; **no fiarse ni de su propia —** to be scared of one's own shadow; **a la —** in the shade; **sin — de duda** without a shadow of a doubt
sombreado ADJ (protegido del sol) shady; (oscuro) shadowy
sombrear VT to shade
sombrerería F millinery
sombrerero -ra MF milliner
sombrero M hat; **— de copa** top hat; **— hongo** derby
sombrilla F parasol
sombrío ADJ (oscuro) dark; (triste) somber, gloomy
somero ADJ (agua) shallow; (discusión) superficial
someter VT (proponer algo) to submit; (poner bajo dominio) to subject; **—se a** to undergo
sometimiento M (propuesta) submission; (dominio) subjection
somnífero M sleeping pill
somnolencia F drowsiness, sleepiness
somnoliento ADJ drowsy
somos *ver* ser
son M sound; LOC ADV **al — de** to the sound of; **venimos en — de paz** we come in peace
son *ver* ser
sonaja F rattle
sonajero M rattle

sonámbulo -la MF sleepwalker
sonar[5] VI (hacer un sonido) to sound; (mencionarse) to be mentioned; (ser familiar) to sound familiar; **— a** to sound like; VT (bocina) to sound; (tambor) to beat; (campana, timbre) to ring; **—se la nariz / los mocos** to blow one's nose; **suena que** it is rumored that; M sonar
sonda F (de médico) catheter; (cohete) probe; **— de alimentación** feeding tube; **tirar una —** to sound
sondear VT (medir la oportunidad) to sound, to fathom; (investigar la opinión) to sound out
sondeo M survey
soneto M sonnet
sonido M sound
sonoridad F (de la voz) sonority; (de un instrumento) tone; (de un sonido lingüístico) voicing
sonoro ADJ sonorous
sonreír[10] VI to smile
sonriente ADJ smiling
sonrisa F smile
sonrojarse VI to blush
sonrojo M blush, flush
sonrosado ADJ rosy
sonsacar[30] VT to extract
soñador -ora MF dreamer
soñar[5] VI/VT to dream; **— con** to dream of; **— despierto** to daydream; **— que** to dream that; **ni — fam** fat chance
soñoliento ADJ sleepy
sopa F (líquido) soup; (pan mojado) sop; **estar hecho una —** to be sopping wet; **— crema** cream soup
sopapo M smack
sopera F soup tureen
sopesar VT to weigh
sopetón LOC ADV **de —** all of a sudden
soplador -ora MF blower
soplar VI/VT (el viento) to blow; (la sopa) to blow on; (en un examen) to whisper the answers
soplete M blowtorch
soplo M breath, puff; **en un —** in a jiffy; **— cardíaco** heart murmur
soplón -ona MF informer, snitch, stool pigeon
sopor M lethargy
soportar VT (un peso) to support, to bear; (una molestia, a una persona) to stand, to bear; (un programa de computadora) to support
soporte M (de un peso, de un programa) support; (de una bicicleta) kickstand; **— técnico** technical support
soprano M (voz) soprano; F (cantante) soprano
sorber VI/VT to sip; **—se los mocos** to sniffle
sorbete M sherbet
sorbo M sip; **de un —** in one gulp
sordera F deafness
sórdido ADJ sordid, tawdry, sleazy

sordina F mute

sordo -da ADJ (persona) deaf; (dolor) dull; (sonido) dull, muffled; **hacer oídos —s** to turn a deaf ear; MF deaf person; **hacerse el — to** pretend not to hear

sordomudo -da ADJ deaf and dumb; MF deaf-mute

sorna F irony

sorprendente ADJ surprising, startling

sorprendentemente ADV surprisingly

sorprender VT to surprise; **—se** to be surprised

sorpresa F surprise; **— de cumpleaños** party favor; **para mi —** to my surprise; **pillar por — to** catch by surprise

sortear VT (elegir al azar) to draw lots, to raffle; (esquivar) to dodge

sorteo M drawing, raffle

sortija F (anillo) ring; (de pelo) ringlet

sortilegio M spell, charm

SOS M SOS

sosa F soda

sosegado ADJ composed, sedate

sosegar[41] VT to calm, to quiet; **—se** to quiet down, to compose oneself

sosiego M quiet, calm

soslayo LOC ADV **de —** oblique, slanting; **mirar de —** to look out of the corner of one's eye

soso ADJ (comida) tasteless, insipid; (persona) dull

sospecha F suspicion

sospechar VT to suspect

sospechoso -sa ADJ suspicious; MF suspect

sostén M (apoyo, sustento) support, prop; (persona que sostiene) supporter, provider; (prenda) brassiere; **— de la familia** breadwinner

sostendrá, sostendría ver sostener

sostener[58] VT (una nota musical) to hold, to sustain; (una familia) to support; (un peso) to support, to hold; (una opinión) to claim, to uphold

sostenga, sostengo ver sostener

sostenible ADJ sustainable

sostenido ADJ sustained; M sharp

sostiene, sostienes, sostuve, sostuviera, sostuviese ver sostener

sota F jack, knave

sótano M cellar, basement

soto M thicket

soy ver ser

soya F (semilla) soybean; (planta) soy

squash M squash

Sr. M Mr.

Sra. F (casada) Mrs.; (sin indicación de estado civil) Ms.

S.R.C. [se ruega contestar] LOC RSVP

status M status

stop M stop sign

strip-tease M striptease

striptisero -ra MF stripper

su ADJ POS (de él) his; (de ella) her; (de usted, ustedes) your; (de ellos, ellas) their

suave ADJ (pelo, piel) soft; (tiempo, droga) mild; (brisa, persona, animal) gentle; (coñac) smooth; **hablan —** they speak gently

suavemente ADV lightly, gently

suavidad F (de pelo, piel) softness; (de coñac) smoothness; (de tiempo, droga) mildness; (de brisa, persona, animal) gentleness

suavizante M fabric softener

suavizar[47] VT to soften

suazi ADJ & MF Swazi

Suazilandia F Swaziland

subalterno -na ADJ & MF subordinate

subarrendar VI/VT to sublet

subasta F auction

subastador -ora MF auctioneer

subastar VT to sell at auction, to auction

subcomité M subcommittee

subconsciente ADJ subconscious

subcontratar VT to subcontract, to contract out, to farm out

subdesarrollado ADJ underdeveloped

súbdito -ta MF subject

subdividir VT subdivide

subdivisión F subdivision

subempleado ADJ underemployed

subestimar VT to underestimate

subgerente MF assistant manager

subida F (de precios, de río) rise; (de montaña) climb; (de drogas) high; (cuesta) slope; **—s y bajadas** ups and downs

subido ADJ (color) bright; **— de tono** risqué

subíndice M subscript

subir VI (los precios) to rise, to go up; (la marea) to surge; (a un tren) to board; (a un autobús, coche) to get into; VT (algo del sótano) to bring up; (una montaña) to climb; (precios) to raise; **— a la red** to upload; **—se** to ride up; **el vino se me sube a la cabeza** wine goes to my head; M **subibaja** seesaw

súbitamente ADV suddenly

súbito ADJ sudden

subjetividad F subjectivity

subjetivo ADJ subjective

subjuntivo ADJ & M subjunctive

sublevación F revolt

sublevar VT (instigar) to incite to rebellion; (indignar) to infuriate; **—se** to revolt

sublime ADJ sublime

submarino ADJ underwater; M submarine

suboficial M noncommissioned officer

subordinado -da ADJ & MF subordinate

subordinar VT to subordinate

subproducto M by-product

subproletariado M underclass

subrayado ADJ underlined; M underscore, underlining

subrayar VT (con una línea) to underline, to underscore; (enfatizar) to emphasize, to underscore

subrepticio ADJ surreptitious

subrutina F subroutine

subsanar VT (una deficiencia) to remedy; (un error) to correct

subsecretario -ia MF undersecretary; **— de justicia** solicitor general

subsidiar VT to subsidize

subsidiario ADJ subsidiary

subsidio M subsidy

subsiguiente ADJ subsequent

subsistencia F survival

subsistir VI to subsist, to survive

subteniente MF second lieutenant

subterfugio M subterfuge

subterráneo ADJ subterranean, underground; M subway

subtítulo M (de un capítulo, película) subtitle; (pie de foto) caption

subtotal M subtotal

suburbano -na ADJ of shantytowns; MF shantytown resident

suburbio M shantytown

subvaluar[26] VT to underestimate

subvención F subsidy

subvencionar VT to subsidize

subversivo ADJ subversive

subyacente ADJ underlying

subyacer[37] VI to underlie

subyugar[40] VT (dominar) to subjugate; (hechizar) to charm

succión F suction

sucedáneo -a ADJ & MF substitute

suceder VI to happen, to occur; **— al trono** to succeed to the throne; VT to succeed

sucesión F (herencia, secuencia) succession; (heredero) descendant

sucesivo ADJ successive; **en lo —** in the future

suceso M (evento) event, occurrence; (incidente) incident

sucesor -ora MF successor

suciedad F (porquería) dirt, filth; (cualidad de sucio) filthiness

sucinto ADJ concise

sucio ADJ (baño, ropa) dirty, filthy; (trabajo, chiste) dirty; (conciencia) guilty; **blanco —** off-white; **este traje es —** this suit gets dirty easily

sucumbir VI to succumb

sucursal F branch, subsidiary

sudadera F sweatshirt

sudado ADJ sweaty

Sudáfrica F South Africa

sudafricano -na ADJ & MF South African

Sudamérica F South America

sudamericano -na ADJ & MF South American

Sudán M Sudan

sudanés -esa ADJ & MF Sudanese

sudar VT to sweat; **— la gota gorda** to sweat blood

sudeste ADJ southeast, southeastern; M southeast

sudoeste ADJ southwest, southwestern; M southwest

sudor M sweat

sudoración F sweating

sudoroso ADJ sweaty

Suecia F Sweden

sueco -ca ADJ Swedish; M (lengua) Swedish; MF Swede; **hacerse el —** to pretend not to understand

suegro -a M father-in-law; F mother-in-law

suela F (de zapato) sole; (pez) flounder

suela, suele ver soler

sueldo M salary

suelo M (tierra) soil, ground; (piso) floor; **arrastrar por el —** to drag; **por los —s** at rock-bottom

suelta, suelte ver soltar

suelto ADJ (no atado) loose, unattached; (flojo) loose; (libre) free; M loose change

suena, suene ver sonar

sueña, sueñe ver soñar

sueño M (acto de dormir) sleep; (acto de soñar) dream; (ganas de dormir) sleepiness; **en —s** dreaming; **conciliar el —** to get to sleep; **tener —** to be sleepy; **ni en —[s]** never; **perder el —** to lose sleep; **— húmedo** wet dream; **— profundo** sound sleep; **estar en el séptimo —** to be deeply asleep

suero M serum; **— de leche** buttermilk; **— fisiológico** saline solution

suerte F (destino) fate; (fortuna) luck; (clase) kind; **de —** in luck; **dejar a su —** to leave to his own devices; **echar —s** to cast lots; **mala —** (desgracia) bad luck; (lo siento) too bad; **tener —** to be lucky; **tentar a la —** to court danger; **tocarle algo en —** a alguien to be one's lot

suertudo -da ADJ lucky; MF lucky devil

suéter M sweater

suficiencia F adequacy; **¡tiene una —!** she's so arrogant!

suficiente ADJ (adecuado) sufficient, adequate; (arrogante) smug; M (calificación mínima) lowest passing grade; PRON enough; **ser —** to be enough; **tiempo más que —** ample time

sufijo M suffix

sufragar[40] VT to defray; **— los gastos** to meet the expenses

sufragio M suffrage

sufrido ADJ (madre) long-suffering; (tela) durable

sufrimiento M suffering

sufrir VI/VT (pasar apremios) to suffer; VT (soportar) to stand; (una lesión) to sustain;

(un cambio) to undergo; (una pena) to grieve; **— de** to suffer from; **— de los pies** to have foot pains

sugerencia F suggestion

sugerir[8] VT to suggest

sugestión F suggestion

sugiere, sugirió, sugiriendo, sugiriera, sugiriese *ver* sugerir

suicida MF suicide [victim]

suicidarse VI to commit suicide

suicidio M suicide

suite F suite

Suiza F Switzerland

suizo -za ADJ & MF Swiss; M sweet roll

sujeción LOC ADV **con — a** subject to

sujetar VT (fijar) to attach; (unir) to hold; (someter) to subdue, to hold down; **—se** to hold on; M SG **sujetalibros** bookend; M SG **sujetapapeles** paper clip

sujeto ADJ held by; **— a** subject to; M (de oración, de experimento) subject; (individuo) individual

sulfato M sulfate

sulfurarse VI to hit the roof

sulfúrico ADJ sulfuric

sulfuro M sulfide

suma F (resultado aritmético) sum; (operación aritmética) addition; (cantidad) amount, sum; **en —** in sum

sumadora F adding machine

sumamente ADV extremely

sumar VT to add, to add up; **—se a** to join

sumario M brief; ADJ summary

sumergible ADJ waterproof

sumergir[46] VT to submerge, to dip; **—se** to dive; **—se en** to immerse oneself in

sumidero M (socavón) sinkhole; (desagüe) drain

suministrar VT to furnish, to supply with

suministro M provision, supply; **— de energía** power supply; **—s** supplies, provisions

sumir VT to immerse

sumisión F submission

sumiso ADJ submissive

súmmum M ultimate, acme; **el — de la moda** the cat's meow

sumo ADJ utmost, paramount; **a lo —** at the most

suntuoso ADJ sumptuous, luxurious

supe, supiera, supiese *ver* saber

súper ADJ & ADV super; F (gasolina) high-octane gasoline; M (supermercado) supermarket

superabundancia F overabundance, glut

superación F (de expectativas) surpassing; (de límites) exceeding; (de un récord) breaking; (de una dificultad) overcoming

superar VT (las expectativas) to surpass; (un límite) to exceed; (una dificultad) to overcome, to surmount; (una prueba) to pass; (a un rival) to outdo; **—se** to improve oneself

superávit M surplus

supercomputadora F supercomputer

superdirecta F overdrive

superdotado ADJ gifted

superego M superego

superestrella F superstar

superficial ADJ (conocimiento, herida, persona) superficial; (persona) shallow

superficialidad F shallowness

superficie F (parte exterior) surface; (de una figura geométrica) area

superfluo ADJ superfluous

superíndice M superscript

superintendente MF superintendent

superior ADJ (mejor) superior; (más alto) higher; (más grande, intenso) greater; MF superior

superioridad F superiority

superlativo ADJ & M superlative

supermercado M supermarket

superordenador M supercomputer

superponer[56, 74] VT to superimpose

superpotencia F superpower

superproducción F overproduction

supersónico ADJ supersonic

superstición F superstition

supersticioso ADJ superstitious

supervisar VT to supervise

supervisión F supervision

supervisor -ora MF supervisor

supervivencia F survival; **la — del más apto** the survival of the fittest

superviviente ADJ surviving; MF survivor

superyó M superego

supino ADJ supine

suplantar VT to supplant

suplementar VT to supplement

suplementario ADJ supplemental

suplemento M supplement

suplente ADJ & MF substitute

súplica F entreaty, plea

suplicar[30] VT to plead, to beseech

suplicio M ordeal

suplir VT (sustituir) to substitute for; (compensar) to make up for

supondrá, supondría *ver* suponer

suponer[56, 74] VT (dar por sentado) to suppose, to presume, to surmise; (implicar) to involve; **es de — que ya esté preparado** presumably he's already prepared

suponga, supongo *ver* suponer

suposición F supposition, surmise

supositorio M suppository

supremacía F supremacy

supremo ADJ supreme

supresión F (de una idea) suppression; (de una palabra) deletion

suprimir VT (una idea) to suppress; (la

esclavitud) to abolish; (una palabra) to delete
supuestamente ADV supposedly, allegedly
supuesto ADJ (hipotético) supposed; (alegado)
alleged, ostensible; **dar por** — to assume;
por — of course; M supposition, assumption
supuesto ver suponer
supuración F discharge
supurante ADJ festering, running
supurar VI to fester, to discharge
supuse, supusiera, supusiese ver suponer
sur ADJ & M south; **hacia el** — southward;
rumbo al — southward
surcar³⁰ VT to plow
surco M (en la tierra) furrow; (en un camino) rut;
(en un disco) groove; (en el rostro) wrinkle
surcoreano -na ADJ & MF South Korean
sureño -ña ADJ southern; MF southerner
sureste ADJ southeast, southeastern; M
southeast
surfear VI/VT to surf (también en el internet)
surfing M surfing; **hacer** — to surf
surgimiento M rise
surgir⁴⁶ VI (situación) to arise; (manantial) to
rise; (problema) to emerge, to crop up
Surinam M Surinam, Suriname
surinamés -esa ADJ & MF Surinamer
surmenage M burnout
suroeste ADJ southwest, southwestern; M
southwest
surrealismo M surrealism
surrealista ADJ surreal, surrealistic; MF
surrealist
surtido M stock, assortment; ADJ assorted
surtidor M (bomba) pump; (chorro, pieza de
carburador) jet
surtir VT to provide; — **efecto** to produce the
desired effect; — **un pedido** to fill an order
susceptible ADJ susceptible
suscitar VT to stir up
suscribir⁷⁴ VT (una opinión) to subscribe to, to
endorse; (un seguro) to underwrite; —**se a** to
subscribe to
suscripción F subscription
suscriptor -ora MF (de un revista) subscriber;
(en el mercado de acciones) underwriter
susodicho ADJ above-mentioned
suspender VT (colgar) to suspend, to hang;
(interrumpir) to suspend, to stop; (cancelar)
to cancel; (castigar) to suspend; VI/VT (no
aprobar) to fail, to flunk
suspense M suspense
suspensión F suspension
suspenso ADJ hanging; **quedarse** — to freeze;
M (en un examen) failure; (en una película)
suspense; **en** — in suspense
suspensorio M jock [strap]
suspicaz ADJ suspicious
suspirar VT to sigh; — **por** to yearn for
suspiro M sigh

sustancia F substance; — **peligrosa** hazardous
substance
sustancial ADJ substantial
sustancioso ADJ substantial
sustantivo M noun; ADJ substantive
sustentable ADJ sustainable
sustentar VT to sustain
sustento M (alimento) sustenance; (apoyo)
support; **ganarse el** — to earn a living
sustitución F substitution; — **protésica de la
cadera** hip replacement
sustituible ADJ replaceable
sustituir¹⁹ VI/VT to substitute for, to replace;
Juan sustituyó a María John substituted
for Mary; **sustituí la leche por agua** I
replaced the milk with water
sustituto -ta MF substitute
**sustituya, sustituye, sustituyendo,
sustituyera, sustituyese** ver sustituir
susto M scare, fright
sustracción F subtraction
sustraer⁵⁹ VT to take away; —**se a** to avoid
susurrar VI/VT (una persona, el viento) to
whisper; (agua) to murmur, to ripple; (hojas)
to rustle
susurro M (de una persona, del viento) whisper;
(del agua) murmur; (de las hojas) rustle
sutil ADJ subtle
sutileza F (delicadeza) subtlety; (fineza excesiva)
nicety, quibble
sutilizar⁴⁷ VT to quibble over
sutura F suture
suyo ADJ & PRON POS (de él) his; (de ella) her; (de
usted, de ustedes) your; (de ellos, de ellas)
their; PRON (de él) his; (de ella) hers; (de
usted, de ustedes) yours; (de ellos, de ellas)
theirs; **salirse con la suya** to get one's own
way; **hacer de las suyas** to be up to one's
tricks; **los** —**s** his/her/your/their family
swing M swing

Tt

tabaco M tobacco
tábano M horsefly
tabaquismo M smoking
taberna F tavern, saloon
tabernero -ra MF bartender
tabicar³⁰ VT to partition
tabique M partition
tabla F (madera) board, plank; (teatro) stage;
(pliegue) pleat; (gráfica) table, chart; — **de
surf** surfboard; — **de planchar** ironing
board; —**s** (escenario) stage; —**s de la ley** the
tables of the law; —**s de multiplicar**

multiplication tables; — **periódica** periodic table; — **de contenidos** table of contents; — **de cortar** cutting board; **hacer —s** to tie

tablado M stage

tablero M (para juegos de mesa) board; (de instrumentos) panel, instrument panel; (de coche) dashboard; (pizarra) blackboard; (para noticias) bulletin board; — **de mando** control panel

tableta F (de aspirina) tablet; (de chocolate) bar

tablilla F (de arcilla) tablet; (de cama) slat; (para fracturas) splint

tabloide M tabloid

tablón M plank

tabú M taboo

tabulador M tab

tabular VT (en una tabla, planilla) to tabulate, to chart; (en la computadora) to tab

taburete M stool, footstool

TAC [tomografía axial computarizada] F CAT scan

tacañería F stinginess, tightness

tacaño -ña ADJ stingy, miserly; MF miser, penny-pincher

tacha F (mancha visible) blemish; (al honor) blot

tachado M strikethrough

tachar VT (borrar) to cross out, to delete; (acusar) to accuse of

tachón M crossing out

tachonar VT to stud

tachuela F tack, thumbtack

tácito ADJ tacit

taciturno ADJ taciturn

taco M (de artillería) wad; (palo de billar) billiard cue; (comida ligera) snack; (palabrota) swear word; (comida) *Méx* taco; **—s** (en el zapato) cleats; **soltar —s** *Esp* to swear

tacómetro M tachometer

tacón M heel

taconear VI to click one's heels

taconeo M clicking

táctica F tactic

táctil ADJ tactile

tacto M (acción de tocar) touch; (sentido) sense of touch; (diplomacia) tact; **con mucho —** gently

TAE [tasa anual equivalente] F APR

tahúr -ura MF gambler

tailandés -esa ADJ & MF Thai, Thailander

Tailandia F Thailand

taimado ADJ sly, devious

Taiwán M Taiwan

taiwanés -esa ADJ & MF Taiwanese

tajada F (de pan, jamón) slice; (de carne) slab; **sacar —** to take one's cut

tajante ADJ (inequívoco) unequivocal; (cortante) sharp

tajar VT to slice

tajear VI/VT to slash

tajo M (corte) slash, hack; (cañón) gorge; (separación) gap

tal ADJ such; — **cual** just so; — **vez** perhaps; **un — García** a certain García; **a — grado** to such an extent; **de — palo — astilla** a chip off the old block; **en — caso** in such a case; CONJ — **como** like, just as; **con — [de] que** provided that; ADV **¿qué —?** how is it going? PRON **y —** and so on; **como si —** as if nothing had happened

taladrar VT to bore, to drill

taladro M drill

talante M temperament

talar VT (un árbol) to chop down; (un bosque) to lumber

talco M talcum

talento M talent

talentoso ADJ talented, gifted

talismán M charm

talla F (altura) height; (moral, intelectual) stature; (de ropa) size; (de madera) carving

tallado M carving

tallar VT (piedra) to carve; (madera) to whittle, to carve; (naipes) to deal

tallarín M noodle

talle M (cintura) waist, waistline; **tiene buen —** she has a good figure; **corto de —** short-waisted

taller M (para trabajo manual, enseñanza artística, congresos) workshop; (de artista plástico) studio; (de mecánico) garage, shop

tallo M stalk, stem

talón M (de pie, calcetín) heel; (de cheque) stub; — **de Aquiles** Achilles' heel; **girar sobre los talones** to turn on one's heels; **pisarle los talones a alguien** to be hot on someone's heels

talonario M checkbook

talonear VI to walk briskly

tamal M tamale

tamaño M size; **de — mediano** medium-sized; **de — natural** life-sized; ADJ such a big, so big a; **tamaña injusticia** such a big injustice

tambalearse VI (un borracho) to stagger; (un boxeador) to reel; (un viejo) to dodder; (un objeto) to wobble

tambaleo M stagger

también ADV also, too, as well; **este — me gusta** I like this one too, I like this one as well, I also like this one

tambor M (instrumento musical, pieza de máquina) drum; (músico) drummer; (cilindro) cylinder; **a — batiente** with fanfare

tamborilear VI to drum, to tap

tamborilero -ra MF drummer

tamiz M sieve

tamizar[47] VT to sift

tampoco CONJ either; **no lo hizo —** he did not

do it either; **ni yo** — me either/neither
tampón M tampon
tan ADV **es** — **rica** she is so rich; — **alto como
Juan** as tall as Juan; — **pronto como** as soon
as; **es** — **idiota** he's such an idiot; **vecinos** —
simpáticos such nice neighbors
tanda F (de personas) group; (de galletas) batch;
(de ejercicios) set
tándem M tandem
tanga F thong
tangente ADJ & F tangent; **salirse por la** —
(irse de tema) to go off on a tangent; (evadir)
to beat around the bush
tangerina F tangerine
tangible ADJ tangible
tango M tango
tanque M tank
tantán M African drum
tantear VT (calcular) to estimate roughly;
(averiguar) to sound out, to feel out;
(apuntar) to score; (palpar) to grope
tanteo M (cálculo) estimate; (número de tantos)
score; **al** — approximately
tanto ADJ, PRON, & ADV **lloró** — **que se le
enrojecieron los ojos** he cried so much his
eyes got red; **yo tengo** — **como tú** I have as
much as you do; **me quiere** — he loves me
so; **no te quiero** — I don't love you that
much; **a cada** —**s pasos** every so many
steps; **cuarenta y** —**s** forty-odd; **a** — **el kilo**
at so much per kilo; **el** — **por ciento** at such
and such a percentage; **estar al** — to be in the
know; **no es para** — it's not such a big deal;
— **da** it's all the same; — **como** as much as; —
en la ciudad como en el campo both in
the city and in the country; **entre/mientras**
— meanwhile; **mantenerse al** — to stay
informed; **otros** —**s** just so many more; **por
lo** — therefore; **a las tantas** until late at
night; M (en los deportes) point
Tanzania F Tanzania
tanzano -na ADJ & MF Tanzanian
tañer[15] VT *lit* (una guitarra) to play; VI (una
campana) to ring, to toll
tañido M (de guitarra) twang; (de campanas) toll
tapa F (de botella) cap; (de libro) cover; (de
coche) hood; (de olla, bote) lid, top; *Esp*
(comida) bar snack
tapadera F (de recipiente) lid; (de un fraude)
cover
tapado ADJ stuffy
tapar VT (una olla) to cover; (una salida) to
block; (un caño) to plug up, to stop up;
(encubrir) to cover up for; M SG **tapacubos**
hubcap; M SG **tapajuntas** flashing; M SG
taparrabos loincloth
tapete M runner
tapia F garden wall
tapiar VT to board up

tapicería F (para paredes) tapestry; (para
muebles) upholstery; (tienda de textiles de
decoración) tapestry shop; (arte) tapestry
making; (tienda de textiles para muebles)
upholstery shop
tapioca F tapioca
tapir M tapir
tapiz M (para pared) tapestry, wall hanging;
(para muebles) upholstery
tapizar[47] VT to upholster
tapón M (de botella) stopper; (de lavabo) plug;
(de corcho) cork; (en baloncesto) block; — **de
oído** earplug; **tapones** (en el zapato de
fútbol) cleats
taponar VT (baloncesto) to block
taponazo M pop of a cork
taquigrafía F shorthand
taquígrafo -fa MF stenographer
taquilla F ticket office, box office
tarambana MF dork, knucklehead
tarántula F tarantula
tararear VI/VT to hum
tarareo M hum, humming
tarascada F (mordedura) snap, bite; (réplica)
rude answer
tardanza F lateness
tardar VI to take time; **¿cuánto tarda el
trámite de divorcio?** how long does it take
to get divorced? —**se** to take a long time; **tu
padre se tarda** your father is taking a long
time; **a más** — at the latest
tarde F (después del almuerzo) afternoon; (hacia
el anochecer) evening; **buenas** —**s** good
afternoon; ADV late; **ya es** — it is late; — **o
temprano** sooner o later; **más** — later on;
llegar — to be late
tardío ADJ late
tardo ADJ *lit* slow
tarea F (trabajo) task, chore; (escolar) homework
tarifa F (impuesto) tariff; (lista de precios) list of
prices; (de transporte) fare; (precio
estipulado) rate
tarima F platform
tarjeta F card (también dispositivo de
computadora); — **amarilla** yellow card; —
bancaria bank card; — **comercial** business
card; — **de circuito integrado** smart card;
— **de sonido** sound card; — **gráfica**
graphics card; — **inteligente** smart card; —
postal postcard; — **de cobro automático /
— de débito** debit card; — **de crédito** credit
card; — **de Navidad** Christmas card; — **roja**
red card; **marcar** — to punch in
tarro M jar
tarta F tart, pie
tartajear VI to stutter
tartamudear VI to stutter, to stammer
tartamudeo M stammer, stutter
tartamudez F stuttering

tartamudo -da MF stutterer, stammerer; ADJ stuttering, stammering
tártaro M tartar
tartera F round baking pan
tarugo M (trozo de madera) piece of wood; (tonto) blockhead
tasa F (índice) rate; (impuesto) tax; — **de desempleo** unemployment rate; — **de interés** interest rate; — **de mortalidad** death rate; — **de natalidad** birth rate; — **de ocupación** occupancy rate; — **de paro** unemployment rate; — **prima** prime rate
tasación F valuation, appraisal
tasajo M jerky
tasar VT to appraise, to assess
tatarabuelo -la M great-great-grandfather; F great-great-grandmother
tataranieto -ta M great-great-grandson; F great-great-granddaughter
tatuaje M tattoo
tatuar[26] VT to tattoo
tauromaquia F bullfighting
taxi M taxi, taxicab
taxidermia F taxidermy
taxista MF taxi driver, cab driver
taxonomía F taxonomy
Tayikistán M Tajikistan
tayiko -ka ADJ & MF Tajik
taza F (de té, café) cup; (del inodoro) bowl
tazón M (para beber) mug; (para comer) bowl
té M (bebida) tea; (fiesta) tea party
te PRON PERS you; **yo** — **amo** I love you; — **digo mañana** I'll tell you tomorrow; **no** — **mires en el espejo** don't look at yourself in the mirror
teatral ADJ theatrical
teatro M theater; — **de títeres** puppet show; **no hagas** — don't make such a production
techado M (techo) roof; (acción de techar) roofing
techar VT to roof
techo M (exterior) roof; (interior) ceiling; — **de cristal** glass ceiling
techumbre F roof
tecla F key; — **de alt** alt key; — **de alternativa gráfica** alt gr key; — **de borrado** delete key; — **de cambio** shift key; — **de comando** command key; — **de control** control key; — **de escape** escape key; — **de fin** end key; — **de función** function key; — **de mayúsculas** shift key; — **de ordenación** sort key; — **de reinicio** reset key; — **de retorno** return key; — **de retroceso** backspace key, return key; — **de tabulación** tab key; — **fin** end key; **dar uno en la** — to hit the nail on the head
teclado M keyboard; — **numérico** keypad
teclear VT (pulsar las teclas) to key in, to type; (hacer ruido) to click

tecleo M keying in, clicking
técnica F (método) technique; (tecnología) technology
técnico -ca ADJ technical; MF (en mecánica) technician; (de fútbol) coach
tecnología F technology; — **de punta** cutting-edge technology
tecnológico ADJ technological
tectónica F tectonics
tedio M boredom
tedioso ADJ tedious
tee M tee
teja F (de cerámica) tile; (de madera u otros materiales) shingle
tejado M roof
tejar M tile factory; VT to cover with tiles
tejedor -ora MF weaver
tejer VI/VT (cesta, tela) to weave; (suéter) to knit; M **tejemaneje** (fraude) hanky-panky; (actividad) goings-on
tejido M (tela) textile, fabric; (de células) tissue; (acción de hilar) weaving; (acción y efecto de tejer) knitting
tejo M disk
tejón M badger
tela F (paño) cloth, fabric; (lienzo para pintar) canvas; (de araña) web; (dinero) money; — **adhesiva** adhesive tape; — **de cebolla** onion skin; **en** — hardbound; **poner en** — **de juicio** to call into question
telar M loom
telaraña F cobweb, spider's web
tele F TV
telebobo -ba MF couch potato
telecomunicación F telecommunication
teleconferencia F teleconference
teledifusión F telecast
teledirección F remote guidance
teleférico M cable car
telefonazo M buzz, ring
telefonear VI/VT to telephone, to phone
telefónico ADJ **llamada telefónica** telephone call
telefonista MF telephone operator
teléfono M (aparato) telephone, phone; (número) telephone number
telegrafiar[28] VI/VT to telegraph, to wire
telegráfico ADJ telegraphic
telégrafo M telegraph
telegrama M telegram
telemarketing M telemarketing
telemercadeo M telemarketing
telémetro M range finder
telenovela F soap opera
teleobjetivo M zoom lens
telepatía F telepathy
telescopio M telescope
telespectador -ora MF viewer
telesquí M ski lift

teletipo M Teletype™

teletrabajo M telecommuting

televidente MF television viewer

televisar VT to televise

televisión F television; — **de alta definición** high-definition television

televisivo ADJ (apto para la televisión) televisable; (relativo a la televisión) television

televisor M television set; — **a/en color** color television

telón M theater curtain; — **de acero** iron curtain

tema M (de una obra literaria, musical) theme; (de conversación) topic, subject; (de un CD) song, track

temario M agenda

temático ADJ thematic

temblar[1] VI (la mano, la tierra) to tremble; (la voz) to shake, to quaver; (de frío) to shiver; (de miedo) to shudder; (la luz) to flicker

temblequear VI to dodder

temblón ADJ trembling

temblor M (acción de temblar) trembling; (de tierra) tremor; (de una llama) flicker; (de la voz) quaver; (de frío) shiver; (de miedo) shudder; — **de tierra** earthquake

tembloroso ADJ (mano) shaky; (llama) flickering; (voz) quavering; (de miedo) shuddering; (de frío) shivering

temer VI/VT to fear, to be afraid [of]; — **por** to fear for; **mucho me temo que** I fear that

temerario ADJ rash, reckless

temeridad F temerity, recklessness

temeroso ADJ fearful

temible ADJ dreadful, dread

temor M fear

témpano M (bloque de hielo) block of ice; (persona fría) cold fish

temperamento M temperament, disposition

temperancia F temperance

temperatura F temperature

tempestad F tempest, storm; **una — en un vaso de agua** a tempest in a teapot

tempestuoso ADJ tempestuous, stormy

templado ADJ (clima) moderate, temperate; (ánimo) serene; (actitud) moderate

templanza F temperance

templar VT (moderar, dar fuerza) to temper; (calentar) to warm up; (una guitarra) to tune

temple M (dureza) temper; (coraje) mettle; **de mal —** in a bad mood

templo M temple

temporada F season (también de fútbol); — **baja** off-season; — **de caza** hunting season

temporal ADJ (relativo al tiempo) temporal; (secular) worldly; (no permanente) temporary; M storm; **capear el —** to weather the storm

tempranero -ra ADJ early rising; MF early riser

temprano ADJ & ADV early

tenacidad F tenacity

tenaz ADJ tenacious

tenazas F PL (de cangrejo) pincers; (de mecánico) pliers; (de dentista) forceps; (para hielo) tongs

tendedero M clothesline

tendencia F tendency; (orientación) orientation; (de la moda) trend; **de — mayoritaria** mainstream; — **a la baja** downturn; — **al alza** upturn, upward trend

tender[2] VT (un mantel) to spread out; (la ropa) to hang out; (la mano) to extend; (un cable) to lay; (una trampa) to set; VI — **a** to tend to; —**se** to stretch out

tendero -ra MF (de una tienda) storekeeper; (de una tienda de comestibles) grocer

tendido M (de cables) laying; (de ropa mojada) hanging out; (conjunto de cables) cables

tendinitis F tendonitis

tendón M tendon, sinew; — **de Aquiles** Achilles' tendon

tendrá, tendría ver tener

tenebroso ADJ (oscuro) dark; (sombrío) gloomy

tenedor -ora M table fork; MF holder, payee; — **de libros** bookkeeper

teneduría F — **de libros** bookkeeping

tener[58] VT to have; **tiene el pelo castaño** she has brown hair, her hair is brown; — **en cuenta** to bear in mind; — **en mucho** to esteem highly; — **por** to consider; — **que** to have to; — **ganas** to feel like; **tengo escrita la carta** I have the letter written; — **éxito** to be successful; — **miedo** to be afraid; — **sueño** to be sleepy; — **frío** to be cold; — **hambre** to be hungry; **tiene cinco años** she is five years old; —**se** to stand straight; **no — más remedio** to have no other choice; — **que ver con** to have to do with

tenería F tannery

tenga, tengo ver tener

tenia F tapeworm

teniente MF lieutenant

tenis M (juego) tennis; M PL (zapatos) sneakers, tennis shoes

tenista MF tennis player

tenor M (voz, estilo) tenor; (tono) tone, tenor; ADJ **saxofón —** tenor saxophone

tensión F tension

tenso ADJ (nervioso) tense; (extendido) taut

tentación F temptation

tentáculo M tentacle

tentador ADJ tempting

tentar[1] VT to tempt; — **a la suerte** to court danger; — **por todos los medios** to try everything

tentativa F attempt, try

tentativo ADJ tentative

tentempié M snack

tenue ADJ (tela) delicate; (luz) tenuous, dim, faint; (sonido) feeble

tenuidad F faintness, softness

teñir[11] VT (de color) to dye; (de emoción) to tinge

teología F theology

teológico ADJ theological

teólogo -ga MF theologian

teoría F theory; **en —** in theory

teórico ADJ theoretical

tepe M sod

tequila M tequila

terabyte M terabyte

terapeuta MF therapist

terapéutico ADJ therapeutic

terapia F (médica) therapy; (psicológica, marital) counseling; **— de electroshock** shock therapy; **— electroconvulsiva** shock therapy; **— hormonal** hormone therapy; **— ocupacional** occupational therapy

tercero ADJ third; **tercera base** third base; **tercera persona** third person; **tercera edad** old age; **tercer mundo** third world; M (en un contrato) third party; (en béisbol) third baseman

terciar VI/VT to arbitrate

tercio M third

terciopelo M velvet

terco ADJ obstinate, stubborn

tergiversación F distortion, misrepresentation

tergiversar VT (palabras) to distort; (datos) to skew

termal ADJ thermal

térmico ADJ heat, thermal

terminación F (de un proyecto) termination, completion; (de una palabra, cuento) ending; (de un piso) finish

terminal ADJ terminal; MF (de aeropuerto, de omnibus) terminal; M (de computadora, eléctrica) terminal

terminante ADJ (negativa) flat; (prohibición) absolute

terminar VI/VT (completar) to finish, to conclude; VI (tener como final) to end; **— por** to end up; **no termino de entender** I still can't understand; **terminó con las ratas** he got rid of the rats; **sin —** unfinished

término M (final) end; (período de tiempo) period; (límite) boundary; (palabra) term; **— medio** medium; **a —** (trabajo) with a deadline; (embarazo) full-term; **en primer —** first of all; **en —s generales** in general terms; **en último —** as a last resort; **estar en buenos —s** to be on good terms; **por — medio** on average; **poner —** to end

terminología F terminology

termita F termite

termo M thermos

termodinámico ADJ thermodynamic

termómetro M thermometer

termonuclear ADJ thermonuclear

termostato M thermostat

ternero -ra MF (animal) calf; F (carne) veal

terneza F tenderness

terno M three-piece suit

ternura F tenderness

terquedad F obstinacy, stubbornness

terraplén M embankment

terrateniente MF landholder

terraza F (terreno) terrace; (de casa) veranda; (delante de un bar) deck; (azotea) flat roof

terremoto M earthquake

terrenal ADJ earthly

terreno M (campo) piece of land, tract of land; (lote) lot; (formación geológica) terrain; (campo científico) field; **— de juego parejo** level playing field; **ganarle — a alguien** to gain on someone; **perder —** to lose ground; **tantear el —** to put out feelers; **todo —** with four-wheel drive

terrestre ADJ terrestrial, earthly

terrible ADJ terrible, awful

terrier M terrier

territorio M territory

terrón M (de tierra) clod; (de azúcar) lump

terror M terror, dread

terrorismo M terrorism

terrorista ADJ & MF terrorist

terso ADJ (liso) smooth; (pulido) polished

tersura F smoothness

tertulia F social gathering

tesis F thesis; **— doctoral** dissertation

tesón M determination

tesonero ADJ determined

tesorería F treasury

tesorero -ra MF treasurer

tesoro M (riqueza) treasure; (tesorería) treasury

test M test

testaferro M straw man

testamentaria F (gestiones) execution; (bienes) estate

testamento M testament, will

testarudez F stubbornness

testarudo ADJ stubborn, headstrong

testículo M testicle

testificar[30] VI to testify

testigo MF witness; **— de cargo** witness for the prosecution; **— ocular** eyewitness; M proof

testimoniar VI to give testimony

testimonio M testimony, proof, evidence; **levantar falso —** to bear false witness; **en — de su amor** as a testament to his love

testosterona F testosterone

teta F (de animal) teat; (de mujer) *vulg* tit, jug

tétanos M SG tetanus, lockjaw

tetera F teapot, teakettle

tetilla F nipple

tetina F nipple

tetraciclina F tetracycline

tetraplégico -ca ADJ & MF quadriplegic
tétrico ADJ gloomy
teutónico ADJ Teutonic
textear VT to text
textil ADJ & M textile
texto M (algo escrito) text; (libro escolar) textbook; — **listo para cámara** camera-ready copy
textual ADJ verbatim
textura F texture
tez F complexion
ti PRON PERS you; **para** — for you; **te lo doy a** — I give it to you
tía F (pariente) aunt; (prostituta) *pey* hooker; *fam* (mujer) woman, chick; — **abuela** great-aunt
tibieza F (poco fervor, afecto) lukewarmness; (calor) warmth
tibio ADJ (ni caliente ni frío) tepid, lukewarm; (templado) warm
tiburón M shark
tic M twitch, tic
tictac M **hacer** — to tick
tiempo M (cronológico) time; (climático) weather; (gramatical) tense; (de un partido de cuatro tiempos) quarter; (de un partido de dos tiempos) half; — **compartido** timeshare; — **completo** full-time; — **de descuento** extra time; — **extra** overtime; — **libre** leisure hours, free time; — **parcial** part-time; — **pretérito** past tense; — **real** real time; — **suplementario** (fútbol americano) overtime; (fútbol) extra time; — **y medio** time and a half; **a** — on time; **al mismo** — at the same time; **antes de** — ahead of time; **a su** — in due course; **a un** — at the same time; **con** — in advance; **de medio** — half-time; **en aquel** — back then; **en mis** —**s** in my day; **hace buen** — the weather is nice; **hace mucho** — a long time ago; **mal** — rough weather; **motor de dos** —**s** two-stroke motor; **perder el** — to goof off, to waste time; **tener** — **de sobra** to have time to spare; **todo el** — all the time; **tomar el** — to clock
tienda F (de venta) store; (de campaña) tent; — **minorista** retail store; — **virtual** online store
tienda, tiende *ver* tender
tiene, tienes *ver* tener
tientas LOC ADV **a** — blindly; **andar a** — to feel one's way
tiento M care; **coger el** — to get the hang of something
tierno ADJ (fácil de cortar) tender; (joven) young; (cariñoso) affectionate
tierra F (planeta) earth; (superficie) land; (país) country; (suelo) soil; — **adentro** inland; —**s altas** highlands; —**s bajas** lowlands; — **batida** clay; — **de cultivo** farmland; — **de**

nadie no-man's-land; — **firme** mainland; —**s raras** rare earths; **bajo** — underground; **caer a** — to fall to the ground; **dar en** — con alguien to overthrow someone; **echar por** — to knock down; **por** — overland
tieso ADJ (articulación) stiff; (persona) erect; **quedarse** — *fam* to kick the bucket
tiesto M flowerpot
tiesura F stiffness
tifoideo -a ADJ & F typhoid
tifón M typhoon
tifus M (causado por salmonella) typhoid fever; (causado por rickettsia) typhus
tigre M tiger
tijera[s] F SG/PL (instrumento para cortar) scissors; (patada de fútbol) scissor kick
tijereta F scissor kick
tijeretada F snip
tijeretazo M snip
tijeretear VT to snip
tildar VT to brand
tilde F (en la ñ) tilde; (en las vocales) accent [mark]
tilín M *fam* ding-a-ling
timador M confidence man
timbrar VT to stamp
timbrazo M ring
timbre M (aparato) buzzer, doorbell; (cualidad de la voz) timbre; (sello) stamp; (impuesto) stamp tax; (insignia heráldica) crest
timidez F timidity, shyness
tímido ADJ timid, shy, bashful
timo M confidence game, scam; — **en pirámide** Ponzi scheme
timón M helm, rudder
timonear VT to steer
timonel M pilot
timorato ADJ timorous, faint-hearted
tímpano M eardrum
tina F (bañera) tub; (de tintorero) vat
tinaja F large earthen jar
tinglado M (armazón) shed; (plataforma) platform
tinieblas F PL darkness; **en** — in the dark
tinitus M tinnitus
tino M (buen juicio) good judgment; (puntería) marksmanship
tinta F ink; **medias** —**s** wishy-washiness
tinte M (sustancia) dye, stain; (matiz) tint
tintero M inkwell; **eso se me quedó en el** — I never got to that
tintín M clink
tintinear VI to tinkle, to clink
tintineo M tinkle, tinkling
tinto ADJ red
tintorería F dry cleaner
tintorero -ra MF dry cleaner
tintura F (en medicina) tincture; (tinte) dye, tint
tiñoso ADJ scabby

tío -a M (hermano de la madre o el padre) uncle; — **abuelo** great-uncle; (tipo) guy; F (hermana de la madre o el padre) aunt; (tipa) woman, gal; (prostituta) *pey* whore

tíovivo M merry-go-round

tipear, tipiar VI/VT to type

típico ADJ typical

tiple M treble

tipo -pa M (especie, imprenta) type; (tío) *fam* guy, dude; *Am* rate of interest; — **de cambio** rate of exchange; — **de interés** interest rate; — **de letra** typeface, font; — **de letra por omisión** base font; **un buen** — (hombre guapo) a good-looking fellow; (buena persona) a regular guy; **tiene buen** — he's good looking; F (tía) *pey* woman, broad

tipografía F printing

tipología F typology

tira F (de papel, tocino, tela) strip; (de cuero, zapato) strap; — **cómica** comic strip

tirada F (de una pelota) throw; (de una publicación) issue, print run; (distancia) stretch; **de una** — all at once

tirador -ora MF (persona que dispara) shooter; M (tirachinas) slingshot; (pomo de la puerta) knob

tiranía F tyranny

tiránico ADJ tyrannical

tirano -na ADJ tyrannical; MF tyrant

tirante ADJ (cable) taut; (relaciones) strained; M (de caballería) trace; (de vestido) strap; (apoyo) brace, strut; —**s** suspenders

tirantez F tension, strain

tirar VT (pelota) to throw, to toss, to pitch; (derechos, dinero) to throw away; (una bala) to shoot; (una moneda) to flip, to toss; (dados) to cast; (una cuerda) to pull, to tug; VI/VT (en baloncesto) to shoot; VI — **a puerta** to shoot at goal; —**se** (echarse) to lie down; (en fútbol) to fake a foul; — **al suelo** to throw down; — **a** to tend toward; — **abajo** to knock over; — **de** to tug at; — **la cadena** to flush; — **la casa por la ventana** to live it up; — **la chancleta** to kick up one's heels; —**se pedos** to fart; —**se solo** to go it alone; **tirárselas de** to pretend to be; **no me tira la política** I'm not attracted to politics; **el coche tira a un lado** the car pulls to one side; **ir tirando** to get along; **trabajar con él es un constante tira y afloja** working with him is a roller-coaster; M **tirabuzón** (sacacorchos) corkscrew; (espiral) coil; M SG **tirachinas** slingshot

tiritar VI (de frío) to shiver; (de miedo) to shudder

tiro M (lanzamiento) throw; (disparo) shot; (deporte) shooting; (de cocaína) hit; (de dados) roll; (de caballos) team; (de chimenea) draft; (fútbol) shot; — **al arco** archery; — **al**

blanco target practice; — **de esquina** corner kick; — **de penalidad** penalty kick; — **en suspensión** jump shot; — **libre** (baloncesto) free throw; (fútbol) free kick; **errar el** — to miss the mark; **matar a** —**s** to gun down; **ni a** —**s** absolutely not; **pegarle un** — **a alguien** to shoot someone; **me salió el** — **por la culata** the plan backfired on me

tiroides ADJ & M thyroid

tirón M (tironeo) jerk, tug, pull; (atracción fuerte, lesión de un músculo) pull; **de un** — all at once; **un** — **de orejas** a slap on the wrist

tironear VI/VT to jerk, to tug at

tirotear VI to shoot; —**se** to exchange shots

tiroteo M (tiros) shooting, gunfire; (entre bandos) shootout

tirria F dislike; **tenerle** — **a una persona** to have a strong dislike for someone

tisana F herbal tea

tísico ADJ consumptive

tisis F consumption

titánico ADJ titanic

titanio M titanium

títere M (marioneta) puppet; (persona) puppet, dupe; —**s** puppet show; **no dejar** — **con cabeza** to leave no one standing

titilación F flicker

titilar VI to flicker, to twinkle

titileo M twinkle

titubear VI (vacilar) to hesitate, to waver; (oscilar) to totter, to dodder

titubeo M hesitation

titular VT to entitle; —**se** to graduate; ADJ permanent; M (de periódico) headline; MF (de cargo) incumbent

titularidad F tenure

título M (de una obra, persona, liga) title; (derecho) claim, legal right; (universitario) degree, diploma; — **de propiedad** title deed; —**s de crédito** credits; **a** — **de** by way of

tiza F chalk

tiznado ADJ sooty

tiznar VT to smear with soot

tizne M soot

tizón M (leña) burning log; (parásito) smut

TNT M TNT

toalla F towel; **tirar la** — to throw in the towel

toallero M towel rack

tobillo M ankle

tobogán M slide

tocado M headdress; ADJ touched

tocador M (mueble) dressing table, vanity table; (habitación) *lit* boudoir

tocante a PREP concerning

tocar[30] VT (con los dedos) to touch; (un instrumento musical) to play; (una campana) to ring; (un timbre) to buzz; (a la puerta) to knock; (la bocina) to honk, to blast; (una alarma) to sound; (mencionar) to touch upon; — **en** to stop over in; —**le a uno** to be one's turn; — **fondo** to hit bottom; — **la pelota** (béisbol) bunt; M SG **tocadiscos** record player

tocayo -ya MF namesake

tocino M bacon

tocón M stump

todavía ADV still, as yet, yet; — **está aquí** she's still here; ¿— **no has comido?** have you not eaten yet? — **no ha llegado** she still has not arrived, as yet she has not arrived; **me dio — más** she gave me even more

todo ADJ all; (cada uno) every, each; — **hombre** every man; —**s los días** every day; **a — correr** at top speed; **a toda costa** at all costs; **a toda marcha** in high gear; **a toda vela** under full sail; **a toda velocidad** at full speed; **a — volumen** at full blast; **de — corazón** wholeheartedly; **de —s modos** still, anyway, all the same; **del —** entirely; **en — caso** in any case, at any rate, in any event; **es — un personaje** he's quite a character; **por — lados** everywhere; — **el día** all day; — **el tiempo** all the time; — **el mundo** everyone; **todas las noches** nightly; **toda la noche** all through the night; **toda clase de** all sorts of; **en/por todas partes** everywhere, far and wide; **con toda el alma** from the bottom of one's heart; **con toda sinceridad** in all earnestness; PRON **de una vez por todas** once and for all; — **se vale** anything goes; —**s** everybody; —**s juntos** all together; ADV — **derecho** straight ahead; — **lo contrario** quite the opposite; — **recto** straight ahead; — **sucio** all dirty; — **o nada** all or nothing; **ante —** first of all; **así y —** in spite of that; **con —** in spite of that; **del —** completely; **sobre —** especially; M whole; —**poderoso** almighty; **el — es más que la suma de las partes** the whole is more than the sum of its parts

toga F (de catedrático) gown; (de juez) robe

Togo M Togo

togolés -esa ADJ & MF Togolese

toldería F Indian village

toldo M awning, canopy

tolerancia F tolerance

tolerante ADJ tolerant, broad-minded

tolerar VT to tolerate; **no lo puedo —** I can't stand it

tolete M oarlock

toma F (de una ciudad) taking; (cinematográfica) take; (de juramento) administration; (de teléfono) jack; — **de agua** faucet; — **de corriente** electric outlet; — **de poder** takeover; — **y daca** give-and-take

tomar VT (una pastilla) to take; (un juramento) to administer; (un vestido) to take in; (a un empleado) to hire; (una bebida) to drink; — **a pecho** to take to heart; — **asiento** to take a seat; — **desprevenido** to take by surprise; — **el sol** to sunbathe; —**lo a mal** to take the wrong way; — **el pelo a** to make fun of, to kid, to pull someone's leg; — **medidas** to take action; — **posesión** to take possession; — **una decisión** to make a decision; —**le las medidas a alguien** to measure someone for clothes; —**se de la mano** to hold hands; —**se la molestia** to bother to

tomate M tomato

tomillo M thyme

tomo M volume

tomografía F scan; — **axial computarizada** CAT scan; — **cerebral** brain scan

ton LOC ADV **sin — ni son** for no reason

tonada F tune

tonel M (barril) barrel; (persona) *pey* fatso

tonelada F ton

tóner M toner

Tonga F Tonga

tongano -na ADJ & MF Tongan

tongo M setup

tonicidad F tone; — **muscular** muscle tone

tónico -ca ADJ & M tonic; F (tono) tone; (agua) tonic [water]

tono M (al hablar) tone; (musical) pitch; (intervalo musical) step; — **de ocupado** busy signal; — **menor** minor key; — **muscular** muscle tone; **a —** on key; **bajar el —** to lower the volume; **darse —** to put on airs; **de buen —** in good taste; **fuera de —** out of place; **subido de —** risqué

tontear VI to fool around

tontería F (cualidad de tonto) stupidity; (hecho o dicho tonto) foolishness, nonsense

tonto -ta ADJ (ingenuo) foolish; (de poca inteligencia) stupid, dumb; **a tontas y a locas** haphazardly; MF (persona ingenua) fool; (persona de poca inteligencia) *fam* dummy, blockhead, dimwit; — **de capirote** dunce; **hacer[se] el —** to play the fool

topacio M topaz

topar VT to stop; —**se con** to bump into

tope M (de precios) ceiling, cap; (de tren) bumper; (de puerta) doorstop; **a —** a lot; **hasta el —** to the maximum; **estar hasta el —** to be completely full

topetazo M butt

tópico M (lugar común) cliché; (tema) topic; ADJ topical

topless ADJ topless

topo M mole (también espía)

toque M (con la mano) touch; (de campana) ringing; (de tambor) beat; (de trompeta) blare; (de pintura) dab; — **de queda** curfew;

— **de pelota** (béisbol) bunt; **dar los últimos —s** to put the finishing touches; **dar —s** to dab; **un — femenino** a woman's touch

toquetear VI/VT (mercancías) to finger; (por placer sexual) *vulg* to grope, to feel up/off

toqueteo M feel

tórax M thorax

torbellino M whirlwind

torcedura F twist, sprain, strain

torcer[34] VT (el cuello) to twist; (una articulación) to sprain, to strain; (tergiversar) to distort; **—le el pescuezo a alguien** to wring someone's neck; VI (un río) to bend

torcido ADJ crooked, bent

tordo M thrush

torear VT (lidiar) to fight a bull; (provocar) to provoke

torero -ra MF bullfighter

tormenta F storm; **— de arena** sandstorm; **— eléctrica** electrical storm

tormento M torment

tormentoso ADJ stormy

tornadizo ADJ changeable

tornado M tornado, twister

tornar VI (regresar) to return; VT (cambiar) to turn; **— a hacer algo** to do something again

tornasolado ADJ iridescent

tornear VT to turn on a lathe

torneo M tournament

tornillo M screw; **— de banco** vise; **faltarle a uno un —** to have a screw loose

torniquete M (eje giratorio) turnstile; (contra hemorragia) tourniquet

torno M (para levantar cosas pesadas) hoist, winch; (para cerámica) lathe, pottery wheel; **en — [a]** around

toro M bull; **coger/agarrar el — por los cuernos** to take the bull by the horns

toronja F grapefruit

torpe ADJ (poco habilidoso) clumsy, awkward; (lento) slow, sluggish

torpedear VT to torpedo

torpedero -ra MF (en béisbol) shortstop; M (barco) torpedo boat; (avión) torpedo plane

torpedo M torpedo

torpeza F (falta de habilidad) clumsiness; (lentitud) slowness, sluggishness

torpor M torpor

torrar VT to roast

torre F (de castillo) tower; (de buque de guerra) turret; (en ajedrez) castle; **— de control** control tower; **— de marfil** ivory tower; **— de perforación** oil derrick; **— de vigilancia** watchtower

torrencial ADJ torrential

torrente M torrent; **— de lágrimas** flood of tears; **— sanguíneo** bloodstream

torreón M large tower

torreta F turret

tórrido ADJ torrid

torsión F torsion

torso M torso

torta F (postre) cake; (bofetada) slap

tortícolis F kink

tortilla F (de huevo) omelet; (de harina) *Méx* tortilla; **se dio vuelta la —** the tables have turned

tortillera F *ofensivo* dyke

tórtola F turtledove

tortuga F tortoise, turtle; **— marina** sea turtle; **a paso de —** at a snail's pace

tortuoso ADJ (camino) tortuous; (carácter) devious

tortura F torture

torturante ADJ torturous

torturar VT to torture

torvo ADJ fierce

tos F cough; **— ferina** whooping cough

tosco ADJ coarse, crude

toser VI to cough

tosquedad F coarseness, crudeness

tostada F toast

tostado ADJ (pan) toasted; (café) roasted; M (acción de tostar pan) toasting; (color, bronceado) tan; (acción de tostar café) roasting

tostador -ora MF toaster

tostar[5] VT (pan) to toast; (piel) to tan; (café) to roast

total ADJ & M total; **en —** all together; **—, a mí no me importa** anyway, I don't care

totalidad F **la — del dinero** all the money; **en su —** as a whole

totalitario ADJ totalitarian

totalmente ADV totally, perfectly

tour M tour

tóxico ADJ toxic

toxina F toxin

traba F (estorbo) hindrance; (de caballo) hobble

trabajador -ora ADJ (esforzado) hardworking; (proletario) working; MF worker

trabajar VI/VT to work; **— un taxi** to drive a taxi; VI (una tienda) to be open; **— duro** to work hard; **— horas extras** to work overtime

trabajo M (actividad) work; (acción de trabajar) working; (empleo) job; (informe académico) paper; **— manual** manual labor; **da mucho —** it's a lot of work; **sin —** unemployed

trabajoso ADJ laborious

trabar VT (una puerta) to jam; (un caballo) to hobble; (a un boxeador) to clinch; (una salsa) to thicken; (negociaciones) to impede; **— amistad con alguien** to strike up a friendship with someone; **— batalla** to join battle; **— conversación** to strike up a conversation; M SG **trabalenguas** tongue

twister
tracción F traction
tractocamión M tractor-trailer
tractor M tractor
tradición F tradition
tradicional ADJ traditional
traducción F translation
traducir[38] VI/VT to translate
traductor -ora MF translator
traduje, tradujera, tradujese, traduzca, traduzco ver traducir
traer[59] VT (venir con) to bring; (llevar puesto) to have on; (contener) to feature; — **a colación** to bring up; — **a mal a alguien** to mistreat someone; **este niño se las trae** this child is something else; **¿qué te traes entre manos?** what are you up to? —**se secretos** to have secrets
tráfago M bustle
traficante MF dealer
traficar[30] VI to traffic, to trade
tráfico M traffic
tragar[40] VI/VT (ingerir) to swallow; (comer) *fam* to stuff one's face; (consumir gasolina) to guzzle; (aguantar) to stand; (hacer desaparecer) to engulf; —**se algo** to swallow [accidentally]; **no me lo trago** I don't buy that; M **tragaluz** skylight; M/F SG **tragamonedas/tragaperras** slot machine
tragedia F tragedy
trágico ADJ tragic
trago M (lo tragado) swallow; (bebida alcohólica) shot, slug; **a —s** (beber) in sips; (poco a poco) little by little; **echar/tomar un —** to take a drink; **pasar un mal —** to suffer a difficulty
traición F (política) treason; (personal) betrayal; (acto desleal) treachery; **a —** by treachery
traicionar VT to double-cross
traicionero ADJ treacherous
traidor -ora ADJ treacherous; MF (político) traitor; (personal) betrayer
traiga, traigo ver traer
trailer M trailer
traílla F leash
traje M (conjunto) suit; (de fiesta) gown; — **de baño** swimsuit
traje, trajera, trajese ver traer
trajeado ADJ **bien —** well-dressed
trajín M hustle and bustle
trajinar VI to rush around
trama F (argumento) plot; (intriga) scheme; (conjunto de hilos) woof
tramador -ora MF plotter
tramar VT (con hilos) to weave; (intrigar) to plot, to scheme
tramitación F processing
tramitar VT to take steps to obtain
trámite M procedure, paperwork
tramo M (de carretera) stretch; (de puente) span;

(de hielo) patch; (de escalera) flight
tramoyista MF stagehand
trampa F (de caza) trap, snare; (engaño) trick; — **de arena** (golf) sand trap; **hacer —** to cheat, to trick; **tender una —** to set a trap
trampear VI to cheat
trampilla F trapdoor
trampolín M (de piscina) springboard; (de circo) trampoline
tramposo -sa ADJ deceitful; MF cheat
tranca F crossbar
trance M (momento difícil) pass, difficult moment; (estado mental) trance; **el último —** the last moment of life; **a todo —** at any cost
tranco M stride; **a —s** hurriedly; **en dos —s** in a jiffy
tranquera F wooden fence
tranquilidad F tranquillity, calm, quiet
tranquilizante M tranquilizer
tranquilizar[47] VT to quiet, to calm down; —**se** to calm down, to wind down
tranquilo ADJ (silencioso) quiet, peaceful; (apacible) calm, cool; (despreocupado) calm, at ease; (no excitable) sedate, laid-back; (sin olas) smooth, tranquil
transacción F transaction; — **comercial** business transaction; **transacciones** trading; **transacciones a precio de mercado** arm's-length transactions
transar VI to compromise
transatlántico ADJ transatlantic; M transatlantic liner
transbordar VI to transfer
transbordo M transfer
transcribir[74] VT to transcribe
transcripción F transcript
transcultural ADJ cross-cultural
transcurrir VI to elapse
transcurso M passing, passage; **en el — de un año** in the course of a year
transeúnte MF passerby, transient
transexual ADJ & MF transsexual
transferencia F transfer; — **electrónica** wire transfer
transferible ADJ transferable
transferir[8] VT to transfer (también en computadora)
transformación F transformation
transformador M transformer
transformar VT to transform
transfusión F transfusion; **dar una — de sangre** to give a transfusion
transgénico ADV genetically modified
transgredir[73] VT to transgress
transgresión F transgression
transgresor -ora MF lawbreaker
transición F transition
transigir[46] VI to compromise

transistor M transistor
transitable ADJ passable
transitar VI/VT to travel
transitivo ADJ transitive
tránsito M (acción de viajar) transit, passage; (tráfico) traffic; **de/en** — in transit
transitorio ADJ transitory
transmisible ADJ communicable
transmisión F transmission; — **automática** automatic transmission; — **por la web** webcast
transmisor M transmitter; ADJ transmitting
transmitir VI/VT (enviar) to transmit; (una enfermedad) to communicate; (por radio o televisión) to broadcast; — **por la web** to webcast
transnacional ADJ transnational
transparencia F (visual) transparency; (institucional) openness
transparente ADJ transparent
transpiración F perspiration, sweating
transpirar VI/VT to transpire, to perspire
transportación F transportation, transport
transportar VT (mercancías, gente) to transport; (mercancías) to ship, to haul
transporte M (acción) transport, transportation; (vehículo de transporte) transport [vessel]; — **de locura** fit of madness; — **público** mass transit
transportista MF teamster, trucker
transversal ADJ transverse; F transversal
transverso ADJ transverse
tranvía M (transporte urbano) streetcar, trolley; (tren de cercanías) local train
trapacería F racket
trapacero -ra MF racketeer
trapeador M mop
trapear VI/VT Am to mop
trapecio M trapeze
trapezoide ADJ & M trapezoid
trapiche M sugar mill
trapisonda F trick
trapo M rag; —**s** fam duds; **a todo** — at full speed; **tratar a alguien como un** — to treat someone like dirt; —**s sucios** dirty laundry
tráquea F trachea, windpipe
traqueotomía F tracheotomy
traquetear VI (hacer sonido) to rattle, to clatter; (llevar a todos lados) to drag from place to place
traqueteo M rattle, clatter
tras PREP (temporal) after; (espacial) after, behind, in back of; **correr** — to run after; **día** — **día** day after day; **una vez** — **otra** time after time
trascendencia F (concepto filosófico) transcendence; (importancia) importance
trascendental ADJ (que sobrepasa la realidad) transcendental; (importante) important

trascendente ADJ (que sobrepasa la realidad) transcendental; (importante) important
trascender VT (sobrepasar) to transcend; VI (surgir) to emerge; (extender) to extend
trasegar[41] VT (vino) to pour from one container to another; (objetos) to move around; (papeles) to shuffle
trasero ADJ (punto, asiento) rear, back; (pata) hind; M (de persona) fam rear, rear end, bottom
traslación F transfer
trasladar VT (a un empleado) to transfer; (una reunión) to postpone; —**se** to travel
traslado M transfer
traslapo M overlap
trasnochar VI to stay up late
traspapelar VT to mislay, to misplace; —**se** to become mislaid
traspasar VT (pasar por) to transfix; (ir más allá de) to go beyond; (pasar un límite) to transgress, to cross over; (una propiedad) to transfer
traspaso M transfer
traspié M stumble, slip; **dar un** — to stumble
trasplantar VT to transplant
trasplante M transplant
trasponer[56, 74] VT to transpose
trasquilar VT (una oveja) to shear; (a una persona) to fleece
trastabillar VI to stumble
trastazo M bump
traste M (de guitarra) fret, stop; (trasero) buttocks; **dar al** — **con** to destroy; **irse al** — to go down the drain
trasto M piece of junk; —**s** stuff
trastocar[30] VT to disrupt
trastornar VT (alterar psíquicamente) to disturb; (alterar el funcionamiento) to disrupt; —**se** to go crazy
trastorno M (molestia) trouble; (patología) disorder; — **bipolar** bipolar disorder; — **de Asperger** Asperger's syndrome; — **de déficit de atención** attention deficit disorder; — **de la alimentación** eating disorder; — **de la personalidad** personality disorder; — **de personalidad múltiple** multiple personality disorder; — **del sueño** sleep disorder
trasudar VI/VT to perspire
trata F trade; — **de blancas** white slave trade
tratable ADJ (curable) treatable; (amistoso) approachable
tratado M (acuerdo) treaty; (libro) treatise
tratamiento M (acción de tratar) treatment; (fórmula de cortesía) form of address; — **de canal** root canal; — **de convalecencia** aftercare; — **de residuos** waste treatment; — **de textos** Esp word processing; — **postoperatorio** aftercare

tratante MF dealer, trader

tratar VT (una enfermedad, a un paciente, un asunto) to treat; VI (intentar) to try; — **como** to treat like; — **con** to have dealings with; — **de** to try to, to attempt; — **sobre** to be about; **lo trató de imbécil** she called him an idiot; —**le a uno de** to address someone as; — **en** to deal in; —**se con** to have to do with; —**se de** to be a question of, to be about

trato M (acuerdo) treatment; (acción de tratar) dealings; (convenio) deal; (comercio) trade; (modales) manners; ¡— **hecho!** it's a deal! **tener buen —** to have good manners; **cerrar un —** to strike a bargain

trauma M trauma

traumático ADJ traumatic

traumatismo M trauma

través LOC ADV **a/al — de** through, across; **a — de las declaraciones** throughout the declarations; **de —** across; **mirar de —** to look askance [at]

travesaño M crossbar (también en fútbol)

travesía F crossing, sea voyage, passage

travestí, travesti MF cross-dresser, transvestite

travestido -da MF transvestite

travesura F mischief, prank; —**s** naughtiness; **hacer —s** to play pranks

traviesa F railway tie

travieso ADJ mischievous, naughty

trayecto M course, route

trayectoria F (de proyectil) trajectory, path; (profesional) career, track record

trayendo ver traer

traza F (huella) trace; (aspecto) appearance; **tiene —s de no acabar nunca** it looks as if it will never end

trazado M (de ciudad) layout; (de edificio) blueprint; (de un plan) outline

trazador M — **gráfico** plotter

trazar[47] VT (un dibujo) to trace, to sketch; (un plan) to outline; (un edificio) to blueprint; — **el curso** to plot a course

trazo M stroke

trébol M clover

trece NUM thirteen

trecho M stretch; **a —s** at intervals; **de — en —** at intervals

tregua F (de guerra) truce; (descanso) lull, respite

treinta NUM thirty (también en tenis)

treintañero -ra MF thirtysomething

tremendo ADJ (extraordinario) tremendous; (terrible) terrible

trementina F turpentine

tremolar VI (bandera) to flutter; (voz) to trill

trémolo M quaver

trémulo ADJ tremulous, trembling

tren M train; — **de aterrizaje** landing gear; —

de carga / de mercancías freight train; — **de cercanías** local train; — **de vida** lifestyle; — **expreso** express train; **a todo —** at top speed; **perder el —** to miss the boat; **seguir el —** to keep up

trenza F braid

trenzar[47] VT to braid

trepador -ora ADJ (planta) climbing; (ciclista) climber; MF social climber; F climbing plant

trepar VI to climb

trepidar VI to tremble

tres NUM three

trescientos NUM three hundred

treta F trick, wile

triaje M triage

triangular ADJ triangular

triángulo M triangle; — **recto** right triangle

tribu F tribe

tribulación F tribulation

tribuna F (de orador) rostrum; (para el público) grandstand

tribunal M (sala del juez) court, courtroom; (cuerpo de jueces) panel of judges

tributable ADJ taxable

tributar VT to pay tribute with; VI to pay taxes

tributario ADJ & M tributary

tributo M (pago obligatorio) tribute; (impuesto) tax

triceps M triceps

triciclo M tricycle

tridimensional ADJ three-dimensional

trifulca F fight

trigo M wheat

trigueño ADJ (tez) swarthy; (pelo) dark-blond

trillado ADJ trite

trilladora F threshing machine

trillar VT to thresh

trillizo -za ADJ & MF triplet

trilogía F trilogy

trimestral ADJ quarterly

trimestre M quarter

trinar VI to trill; **está que trina** she is furious

trinchante M carving knife

trinchar VT to carve

trinche M pitchfork

trinchera F (fosa) trench; (gabardina) trench coat

trinchero M carving table

trineo M sleigh, sled

trinitense ADJ & MF Trinidadian

trino M trill

trinquete M ratchet

trío M trio

tripas F PL guts; **hacer de — corazón** to pluck up one's courage

triple ADJ triple; M (también en béisbol) triple; (baloncesto) three-point basket

triplicar[30] VT to triple, to treble

trípode M tripod

triptongo M triphthong
tripulación F crew
tripulante MF crew member
tripular VT to man
triquiñuela F caper
triquitraque M firecracker
triscar[30] VI to frisk
triste ADJ sad, sorrowful
tristeza F sadness, sorrow
tristón ADJ glum
tritón M newt
trituradora F (para desechos) garbage disposal unit; (para papel) paper shredder
triturar VI/VT (documentos) to shred; (granos) to grind
triunfador -ora MF winner; ADJ triumphant
triunfal ADJ triumphal
triunfante ADJ triumphant
triunfar VT to triumph
triunfo M triumph
trivial ADJ trivial, commonplace, trite
trizas F PL **hacer —** to tear into shreds
trocar[31] VT (transformar) to change into; (cambiar una cosa por otra) to exchange
trocear VT to divide into pieces
trocha F trail
trofeo M trophy
troje M granary
trola F whopper
trole M trolley
trolebús M trolley bus
tromba F waterspout; **salir en —** to storm out
trombón M trombone
trombosis F thrombosis; **— coronaria** coronary thrombosis
trompa F (de elefante) trunk; (instrumento musical) horn; **— de Eustaquio** eustachian tube; **— de Falopio** fallopian tube
trompada F blow with the fist
trompeta F trumpet
trompetazo M trumpet blast
trompetear VI to trumpet
trompo M spinning top
tronada F thunderstorm
tronar[5] VI to thunder
tronchar VT to chop off
tronco M (de árbol) trunk, log; (del cuerpo) trunk, torso; **— del encéfalo** brain stem; **dormir como un —** to sleep like a log
tronera F (de buque) gun port; (de mesa de billar) pocket
trono M throne (también wáter)
tropa F (en el ejército) troop; (oficiales) rank and file; **—s de asalto** storm troops; **—s de choque** shock troops
tropel LOC ADV **en —** in droves
tropezar[48] VI to stumble, to trip; **—[se] con alguien** to run into someone; **— con algo** to come across something

tropezón M stumble, trip; **salir a tropezones** to stumble out; **darse un —** to stumble
tropical ADJ tropical
trópico M tropic
tropiezo M stumble
troquel M die
trotar VI to trot, to jog
trote M trot; **al —** at a trot; **no estoy para estos —s** I'm too old for this
troza F log
trozar[47] VT to cut up
trozo M (de roca, madera, torta) piece; (de un texto) section; (de carbón) lump; (de carne) slab
trucha F trout
truco M clever trick
truculento ADJ gruesome
trueno M thunder
trueque M (intercambio) exchange; (transacción sin dinero) bartering
truhán -ana MF scoundrel
truja F cigarette
trust M trust
tu ADJ POS your
tú PRON PERS you
tuba F tuba
tuberculosis F tuberculosis
tubería F (tubo) pipe; (conjunto de tubos) piping
tubo M (cilindro hueco) tube; (de agua, órgano) pipe; (digestivo) tract; **— de ensayo** test tube; **— de escape** tailpipe; **— digestivo** gastrointestinal tract
tubular ADJ tubular
tuerca F nut
tuerto ADJ one-eyed
tuétano M marrow; **hasta los —s** through and through
tufillo M whiff
tufo M (humo) fumes; (hedor) stench
tugurio M hovel; **—s** slums
tulipán M tulip
tullido -da ADJ crippled; MF pey cripple
tullir VT to cripple; **—se** to become crippled
tumba F (panteón) tomb; (sepultura) grave; **soy una —** my lips are sealed
tumbar VT to knock down, to flatten; **—se** to lie down, to stretch out
tumbo M tumble, somersault; **dar —s** (persona) to stagger; (coche) to bump along
tumor M tumor; **— cerebral** brain tumor; **— maligno** malignancy
tumorectomía F lumpectomy
tumulto M (alboroto) tumult, uproar; (muchedumbre) mob
tumultuoso ADJ tumultuous
tuna F (fruta) prickly pear; Esp (grupo de cantantes) minstrel group
tunante -ta MF scamp
tunda F thrashing

túnel M tunnel
tunesino -na ADJ & MF Tunisian
Túnez M Tunisia
tungsteno M tungsten
túnica F tunic; — **de laboratorio** lab gown
tupido ADJ dense, compact
tupir VT (hacer tupido) to compact; (cubrir) to cover; —**se** to stuff oneself
turba F (muchedumbre) mob; (carbón fósil) peat
turbación F confusion
turbamulta F throng
turbante M turban
turbar VT to disturb; —**se** to become disturbed
turbina F turbine
turbio ADJ (pasado, secreto) dark; (agua, materia) murky
turbocompresor M turbocharger
turborreactor M turbojet
turbulencia F turbulence
turbulento ADJ turbulent
turco -ca ADJ Turkish; MF Turk; M (lengua) Turkish
turcomano -na ADJ & MF Turkmen
turismo M (actividad) tourism; (conjunto de turistas) tourists; **hacer** — to go sightseeing
turista MF tourist
turístico ADJ (relativo al turismo) tourist; **atracción turística** tourist attraction; **clase turística** coach class
Turkmenistán M Turkmenistan
turnarse VI to take turns
turno M (vuelta) turn; (de trabajo) shift; (en béisbol) at bat
turquesa F turquoise
Turquía F Turkey
turrón M nougat
tutear VT to address as "tú"
tutela F guardianship
tutelar VT to have charge of
tutor -ora MF (de un menor) guardian; M (de planta) prop
tutorial M tutorial
Tuvalu M Tuvalu
tuvaluano -na ADJ & MF Tuvaluan
tuve, tuviera, tuviese ver tener
tuyo ADJ & PRON POS your, yours; **el amigo** — your friend; **esto es** — this is yours
twccd M tweed

Uu

u CONJ or
ubicación F location
ubicar[30] VT (situar) to locate; (identificar) to place; —**se** to be located

ubicuo ADJ ubiquitous
ubre F udder
UCP [unidad central de proceso] F CPU
Ucrania F Ukraine
ucraniano -na ADJ & MF Ukrainian
UE [Unión Europea] F EU
ufanarse VI to glory [in], to be proud [of]
ufano ADJ proud
Uganda F Uganda
ugandés -esa ADJ & MF Ugandan
ujier M bailiff
úlcera F (lesión superficial) sore; (en el estómago) ulcer; (en la boca) canker, canker sore
ulcerar VI to ulcerate
ulceroso ADJ ulcerous
ulterior ADJ ulterior
últimamente ADV of late
ultimar VT to finalize
ultimátum M ultimatum
último ADJ (palabra, capítulo) last, final; (destino) ultimate; (más reciente) latest; **estar en las últimas** to be on one's last legs; **la última palabra** the last word; **en los —s tiempos** lately; **en última instancia** ultimately; **a última hora** at the last moment; **por** — finally
ultrajante ADJ outrageous
ultrajar VT to outrage
ultraje M outrage, indignity
ultraligero M ultralight
ultramar LOC ADV **de** — overseas
ultramoderno ADJ ultramodern
ultrasonido M ultrasound
ultratumba LOC ADV **de** — from beyond the grave
ultravioleta ADJ & M ultraviolet
ulular VI (viento) to howl; (búho) to hoot
ululato M (viento) howling; (búho) hooting
umbral M threshold, doorstep; — **de rentabilidad** breakeven point
umbrío ADJ shady
un, uno, una ART INDEF a, an; **un hombre** a man; **un actor** an actor; **una mujer** a woman; **una manzana** an apple; NUM one; **de a** — one at a time; **es la una** it is one o'clock; PRON one; **uno por uno** one by one; —**s** some; **unos cuantos** some; **uno tiene que cuidarse** you've got to take care of yourself; **yo tengo uno** I have one; **uno tras otro** one after the other; **uno más** (tenis) let; **uno al lado del otro** side by side; **los unos a los otros / el uno al otro** one another / each other
unánime ADJ unanimous
unanimidad F unanimity
uncir[33] VT (a un buey) to yoke; (a un carro) to hitch
ungüento M ointment, salve

único ADJ (solo) only; **una única vez** a single time; (extraordinario) unique; **eres —** you're one of a kind

unidad F (indivisibilidad) unity; (ejemplar) unit; (fracción militar) unit, outfit; (de computadora) drive; **— central de proceso/procesamiento** central processing unit; **— de cuidado coronario** coronary care unit; **— de cuidados intensivos** intensive care unit; **— de disco duro** hard disk drive; **— de disquete** diskette drive; **— monetaria** currency unit

unido ADJ united; **una familia unida** a close-knit family

unificar[30] VT to unify

uniformar VT (estandarizar) to standardize; (dar uniformes) to furnish with uniforms

uniforme ADJ & M uniform

uniformidad F uniformity

unilateral ADJ unilateral

unión F (acción de unir, cosas unidas) union; (lugar en que se unen dos cosas) junction; (indivisibilidad) unity

unir VT (una nación) to unite; (dos construcciones) to join; (cinta magnética, genes) to splice; (caños) to couple; VI/VT (con lazos) to bind

unisex ADJ INV unisex

unísono ADJ unison; **al —** in unison

unitario ADJ (partidario de la unidad) unitarian; (que tiene unidad) unitary

universal ADJ universal

universidad F (de enseñanza e investigación) university; (de enseñanza) college

universitario -ria ADJ university; (relativo a los deportes) collegiate; MF college student

universo M universe

untar VT (la piel con crema) to oil; (el pan con mantequilla) to spread on; (la cara con pintura) to smear; **—le la mano a alguien** to grease someone's palm

untuoso ADJ (graso) oily; (zalamero) slick, unctuous

uña F (de dedo) fingernail; (de gato) claw; **— encarnada** hangnail; **como — y carne** thick as thieves; **con —s y dientes** tooth and nail

uñero M hangnail

uranio M uranium

urbanidad F refinement, polish

urbanismo M (modo de vida) urbanism; (planificación) city planning

urbanización F development

urbanizar[47] VT to build up

urbano ADJ (relativo a la ciudad) urban; (refinado) suave; **autobús —** city bus

urbe F metropolis

urdimbre F warp

urdir VT (una tela) to weave; (una historia) to concoct; (un plan) to devise, to work out

uretra F urethra

urgencia F (prisa) urgency; (crisis médica) emergency; **con —** urgently; **—s** emergency room

urgente ADJ urgent, pressing

urgir[46] VT to urge; VI to be urgent

úrico ADJ uric

urinario ADJ urinary; M urinal

URL M URL

urna F (para cenizas) urn; (electoral) ballot box; **acudir a las —s** to go to the polls

urólogo -ga MF urologist

urraca F (ave) magpie; (persona acaparadora) packrat

urticaria F hives

Uruguay M Uruguay

uruguayo -ya ADJ & MF Uruguayan

usado ADJ (utilizado) used; (desgastado) worn

usar VT (emplear) to use; (ponerse) to wear; **—se** to be in use; **sin —** unused

USB M USB

uso M (empleo) use; (costumbre) usage, custom; **al — de la época** according to the custom of the time

usted PRON PERS you; **—es** you, you all, y'all

usual ADJ usual

usuario -ria MF (de un servicio) user; (en una biblioteca) borrower

usufructo M enjoyment

usufructuar[26] VT to enjoy the use of

usura F usury

usurero -ra MF usurer, loan shark

usurpar VT to encroach upon, to usurp

utensilio M utensil

uterino ADJ uterine

útero M uterus, womb

útil ADJ useful, helpful; M PL **—es** utensils

utilidad F usefulness, utility

utilitario ADJ utilitarian

utilización F use, utilization

utilizar[47] VT (emplear) to utilize; (explotar) to use

utopía F utopia

uva F grape

úvula F uvula

uvular ADJ uvular

Uzbekistán M Uzbekistan

uzbeko -ka ADJ & MF Uzbek

Vv

va, vamos *ver* ir

vaca F cow; **— marina** sea cow

vacación F vacation; **de vacaciones** on

vacation
vacante ADJ vacant; F vacancy, opening
vaciar[28] VT (una botella) to empty; (una naranja) to hollow out; (una estatua) to cast; (una computadora) to dump
vacilación F hesitation
vacilante ADJ (dudoso) vacillating, hesitating; (tembloroso) shaky
vacilar VI to vacillate, to hesitate, to waver; — [con] *fam* to make fun [of]
vacío ADJ (envase) empty; (casa) vacant; (comentarios) idle; (expresión) blank; M (condición) emptiness; (lugar) void; (espacio sin aire) vacuum; **envasado al —** vacuum-packed; **hacer el —** to give the cold shoulder
vacuna F (inoculación) vaccine; (enfermedad) cowpox
vacunación F vaccination
vacunar VI/VT to vaccinate
vacuno ADJ bovine
vadear VT to ford
vado M ford, crossing
vagabundear VI to wander idly
vagabundo -da ADJ vagabond, vagrant; MF (pordiosero) tramp, bum; (trabajador errante) drifter, transient; (en la playa) beachcomber
vagancia F vagrancy
vagar[40] VI to wander, to roam
vagina F vagina
vaginal ADJ vaginal
vaginitis F vaginitis
vago -ga ADJ (idea) vague; (silueta) shadowy; (impresión) faint, vague; (persona) lazy; MF vagrant, tramp
vagón M railway car; — **restaurante** dining car
vaguedad F faintness
vahído M dizzy spell
vaho M steam
vaina F (de una espada) sheath; (de legumbres) pod, shell; (molestia) nuisance; (cosa mal recordada) thing
vainilla F vanilla
vaivén M swaying, swinging; **vaivenes** ups and downs
vajilla F tableware, dishes; — **de barro** earthenware; — **de porcelana** chinaware
vale M voucher; INTERJ oh well, OK
valedero ADJ valid
valenciano -na ADJ & MF Valencian
valentía F courage, valor, bravery
valentón -ona ADJ cocky; MF cocky person
valer[60] VT (tener un determinado valor) to be worth; VI (ser válido) to be valid; (estar permitido) to be allowed; (ser de utilidad) to be useful; — **la pena** to be worthwhile; — **más que** to outweigh; **—se de** to avail oneself of; **—se por sí mismo** to be

self-sufficient; **¿cuánto vale?** how much is it? **hacer — los derechos** to assert one's rights; **hacerse —** to stand up for oneself; **le valió una paliza** that earned him a beating; **más vale solo que mal acompañado** better alone than in poor company; **no hay pero que valga** no buts about it; **más vale tarde que nunca** better late than never; **no vale ni un comino** it's not worth a hoot; **no vale** that's not fair; **¡vale!** OK! **¡válgame Dios!** gracious! **todo vale** anything goes
valeroso ADJ valorous, brave
valga, valgo *ver* valer
valía F worth
validez F validity
válido ADJ (entrada, cupón) valid; (cheque) good; (argumento) solid
valiente ADJ valiant, brave, courageous
valija F (para viajes) valise, suitcase; (para el correo) pouch
valioso ADJ valuable
valla F (en un jardín) fence; (en carreras) hurdle
vallar VT to fence
valle M valley, vale
valor M (precio) value, worth; (valentía) valor, mettle; — **contable** book value; **—es** securities; **—es en cartera** holdings; — **nominal** face value, par value; **—es respaldados por hipoteca** mortgage-backed securities; **armarse de —** to muster up one's courage
valoración F valuation
valorar VT (apreciar) to value; (determinar el valor) to appraise; (aumentar el valor) to make more valuable
valorizar[47] VT to make more valuable; **—se** to become more valuable
vals M waltz
valsar VI to waltz
valuación F valuation, appraisal
valuar[26] VT to appraise
valva F valve
válvula F valve; — **reguladora de aceleración** throttle
vampiresa F vamp
vampiro M vampire
vanagloria F boastfulness
vanagloriarse VI to boast
vanaglorioso ADJ boastful
vándalo -la MF vandal
vanguardia F vanguard; **a la —** at the forefront
vanidad F vanity, conceit
vanidoso ADJ vain
vano ADJ vain; **en —** in vain
Vanuatu M Vanuatu
vanuatuense ADJ & MF Vanuatuan
vapor M (de agua) vapor, steam; (buque) steamship; **—es** fumes; **cocer al —** to steam; **echar —** to give off steam

vapulear VT to thrash
vapuleo M thrashing
vaquería F cowshed
vaqueriza F cowshed
vaquero -ra M cowboy; **—s** blue jeans; F cowgirl; ADJ **botas vaqueras** cowboy boots
vaqueta F cowhide
vaquilla F heifer
vara F (rama) stick; (palo) rod
varadero M dry dock
varar VT to beach, to strand; VI to run aground
varear VT to whip with a stick
variable ADJ variable, changeable; F variable
variación F variation
variado ADJ varied
variante F variant
variar[28] VI/VT to vary
varicela F chicken pox
várices, varices F PL varicose veins
varicoso ADJ varicose
variedad F variety, assortment
varilla F (palo delgado) small rod; (para azotar) switch; (de paraguas) rib
vario ADJ varied; **—s** various, several
variopinto ADJ variegated
varita F wand
varón M male [person]
varonil ADJ (masculino) manly; (hombruno) mannish
vasco -ca ADJ & MF Basque; M (lengua) Basque
vascuence ADJ Basque; M (lengua) Basque
vascular ADJ vascular
vasectomía F vasectomy
vaselina F Vaseline™
vasija F vessel
vaso M (de vidrio) glass; (de papel, plástico) cup; (corto y grueso) tumbler; (sanguíneo) vessel; **— de precipitado** beaker
vástago M (de planta) shoot, sprout; (de persona) offspring; (de motor) rod
vasto ADJ vast
vataje M wattage
vaticinar VT to foretell
vaticinio M prediction
vatio M watt
vaya, vayamos, ve ver ir
vea, veamos ver ver
vecindad F (cercanía) vicinity; (barrio) neighborhood
vecindario M neighborhood
vecino -na MF (cercano, contiguo) neighbor; (residente de una zona) resident; ADJ neighboring
vector M vector
vedar VT to prohibit
vega F fertile plain
vegan ADJ & MF vegan
vegetación F vegetation
vegetal ADJ vegetable; M vegetable, plant

vegetar VI to vegetate
vegetariano -na ADJ & MF vegetarian
vehemencia F vehemence
vehemente ADJ vehement
vehículo M vehicle
veía, veíamos ver ver
veinte NUM twenty
veintena F (aproximadamente) group of [about] twenty; (exactamente) score
veinticinco NUM twenty-five
veintiuno NUM twenty-one; M (juego de naipes) blackjack
vejancón -ona M codger; F old woman
vejar VT to humiliate
vejestorio -ria M codger; F old woman
vejete M codger
vejez F old age
vejiga F (órgano) bladder; (ampolla) blister
vela F (período de vigilancia) vigil, watch; (de cera) candle; (de un navío) sail; **a toda —** under full sail; **en —** without sleep; **hacerse a la —** to set sail
velada F (noche) evening; (fiesta) evening party
velador M nightstand
velar VI (no dormir) to keep vigil, to stay awake; (cubrir con velo) to veil; (exponer a la luz una película fotográfica) to expose; **— por** to look after
velatorio M wake
veleidoso ADJ fickle
velero M sailboat; ADJ swift-sailing
veleta F weathervane; MF fickle person
vello M (del cuerpo) body hair; (de frutas) fuzz
vellón M fleece
velloso ADJ fuzzy
velludo ADJ hairy
velo M veil; **— del paladar** soft palate
velocidad F velocity, speed; **— de transferencia** transfer rate; **a toda —** at full speed
velocímetro M speedometer
velorio M wake
veloz ADJ swift, fast
ven ver venir
vena F (vaso sanguíneo, veta) vein; (estado de ánimo) mood; (de locura) streak; **estar en —** to be in the mood, to be inspired
venado M (animal) deer; (macho) stag; (carne) venison
vencedor -ora ADJ winning; MF winner, victor
vencer[32] VT (a un enemigo) to conquer, to vanquish; (a un equipo) to defeat, to beat; (obstáculos) to overcome; (en valor, inteligencia) to surpass; VI **—se** (un plazo) to expire; (un colchón) to cave in
vencido ADJ (derrotado) defeated; (a pagar) due, overdue, past due; **darse por —** to give up, to surrender
vencimiento M (de una deuda) maturity; (de un

contrato) expiration

venda F (para una herida) bandage; (sobre los ojos) blindfold

vendaje M bandage; — **quirúrgico** surgical dressing

vendar VT (una herida) to bandage; (los ojos) to blindfold

vendaval M gale

vendedor -ora MF vendor, seller, salesperson; — **mayorista** wholesaler

vender VI/VT (comercializar) to sell; (traicionar) to betray; —**se a** to go over to; **se vende** for sale

vendetta F vendetta

vendible ADJ marketable

vendimia F vintage

vendrá, vendría ver venir

veneciana F venetian blind

veneno M (sustancia dañina) poison; (ponzoña de víbora) venom

venenoso ADJ (planta) poisonous; (víbora) venomous

venerable ADJ venerable

veneración F veneration, reverence

venerar VT (a una persona) to venerate, to revere; (a Dios) to worship

venéreo ADJ venereal

venezolano -na ADJ & MF Venezuelan

Venezuela F Venezuela

venga, vengamos ver venir

vengador -ora ADJ avenging; MF avenger

venganza F vengeance, revenge, payback

vengar[40] VT to avenge; —**se de** to retaliate for, to avenge, to take revenge

vengativo ADJ vindictive, vengeful

venida F coming

venidero ADJ forthcoming

venir[61] VI to come; — **a colación** to come up [in conversation]; — **al caso / a cuento** to be relevant; — **bien** to be convenient; —**le a uno bien** to be suitable to someone; —**se** *fam* to come [sexually]; —**se abajo** to collapse; **¿a qué viene eso?** what is the point of that? **el año que viene** next year; **lo mejor está por** — the best is yet to come; **no me vengas con excusas** no excuses; **venga lo que venga** come what may

venta F sale; — **al por mayor** wholesale; — **al por menor** retail; — **de liquidación** fire sale; **en** — for sale; **poner a la** — to put up for sale

ventaja F (también en tenis) advantage; (en una carrera) head start; — **al resto** ad out; — **al saque** ad in; — **al servicio** ad in

ventajoso ADJ advantageous

ventana F window (también digital); **tirar por la** — to throw out the window

ventanal M large window

ventanilla F [de coche, avión] window; (de la nariz) nostril

ventarrón M gale, high wind

ventear VI to sniff the wind

ventilación F (aireado) ventilation; (hueco para el aire) vent

ventilado ADJ airy

ventilador M (abertura) ventilator; (aparato) electrical fan

ventilar VT to ventilate, to air out; (una cuestión) to air

ventisca F blizzard

ventisquero M (lugar ventoso) place prone to blizzards; (lugar nevado) snowfield

ventolera F gust of wind; **darle a uno la** — **de** to take a notion to

ventosear VI to break wind

ventoso ADJ windy, breezy

ventrículo M ventricle

venturoso ADJ fortunate; **futuro** — bright future

veo ver ver

ver[72, 74] VI/VT (un paisaje) to see; (televisión, espectáculos) to watch; (un programa de computadora) to view; **a** — let's see; **eso aún está por** —**se** that is still to be seen; **no lo puedo** — I can't stand him; **no veo la hora de terminar** I'm dying / I can't wait to finish; **no tener nada que** — **con** not to have anything to do with; **te veo preocupado** you look worried; **a mi modo de** — in my opinion; —**se obligado a** to be obliged to; **vérselas con algo** to confront something; **vérselas negras** to have a hard time

vera LOC ADV **a la** — beside

veracidad F truthfulness

veranear VI to spend the summer

veraneo M summer vacation

veraniego ADJ summer

verano M summer

veras LOC ADV **de** — really; **¿de** —? oh really? oh yeah?

veraz ADJ truthful

verbal ADJ verbal

verbena F carnival

verbo M verb

verborrágico ADJ long-winded

verboso ADJ verbose, wordy

verdad F truth; **¿**—? really? — **a medias** half-truth; **de** — indeed; **una pistola de** — a real pistol; **faltar a la** — to fib

verdaderamente ADV really, truly

verdadero ADJ true, real

verde ADJ green (también inmaduro, sin experiencia, ecologista); (chiste) off-color; — **oliva** olive-green; **ponerse** — to stuff oneself; M green; **poner** — **a alguien** to run someone down

verdear VI/VT to turn green

verdín M scum
verdor M greenness
verdoso ADJ greenish
verdugo M executioner, hangman
verdugón M welt
verdulero -ra MF vegetable vendor
verdura F (hortaliza) vegetable; (verdor) *lit* verdure; **—s** produce
vereda F (en el campo) path; (para peatones) *Am* sidewalk; **entrar en —** to toe the line
veredicto M verdict
verga F (percha para vela) yard; (pene) *vulg* dick
vergonzoso ADJ (que da vergüenza) shameful, disgraceful; (que siente vergüenza) sheepish, bashful
vergüenza F (humillación) shame; (incomodidad) embarrassment; (escándalo) disgrace; **tener —** to be ashamed; **tener — ajena** to cringe; **es una —** it's a shame; **me dan — mis dientes** I'm embarrassed about my teeth; **me da — decírtelo** I'm embarrassed to tell you
vericueto M twists and turns
verídico ADJ truthful, true
verificación F verification, cross-check
verificar[30] VT to verify, to check; **—se** to take place
verja F grate
vermú M vermouth
vernáculo ADJ & M vernacular
verruga F wart; **— genital** genital wart
versado ADJ versed
versalillas F PL small caps
versalitas F PL small caps
versar VI **— sobre** to deal [with], to treat
versátil ADJ versatile
versículo M Bible verse
versión F (de un texto) version; (traducción) translation; (de una canción) rendition; **— beta** beta version; **— impresa** printout; **— original** original [of a film]
verso M line [of poetry]; **— libre** free verse; **— suelto/blanco** blank verse
versus PREP versus
vértebra F vertebra
vertebrado ADJ & M vertebrate
vertebral ADJ spinal
vertedero M dump, landfill
verter[2] VT (echar líquido) to pour; (vaciar) to pour out; (derramar) to spill; **— en** to empty into; **—se** to spill
vertical ADJ (en ángulo recto) vertical; (erguido) upright; (empinado) sheer
vertido M (acción) dumping; (lo vertido) waste; **— de petróleo** oil spill
vertiente F (pendiente) slope; (cuenca) watershed; ADJ flowing
vertiginoso ADJ dizzy, giddy
vértigo M (falta de equilibrio) vertigo; (frenesí)

hectic pace
vertigoso ADJ dizzy, giddy
vesícula F gall bladder
vestíbulo M (de un edificio) vestibule, lobby; (de una casa) hallway
vestido M dress; **— de noche** evening gown; **— de novia** bridal dress
vestidura F attire
vestigio M vestige, trace, remnant
vestimenta F attire, dress; (estrafalaria) getup
vestir[9] VT to dress, to clothe; **—se** to get dressed; **—se de gala** to dress up
vestuario M (ropa) wardrobe; (en el teatro) costumes; (lugar para vestirse) changing room
veta F (de minerales) vein, seam; (de madera) grain; (de humor) strain
vetar VT to veto
veteado ADJ veined
veterano -na ADJ & MF veteran
veterinario -ria MF veterinarian; ADJ veterinary; F veterinary medicine
veto M veto
vetusto ADJ ancient
vez F time; **a la —** at the same time; **a su —** in turn; **a veces** sometimes; **cada — más** more and more; **cada — que** whenever; **de — en cuando** from time to time; **de una —** (por entero) all at once; (por fin) one and for all; **de una — por todas** once and for all; **en — de** instead of, in lieu of; **por primera —** for the first time; **otra —** again; **una — [que]** once; **una — tras otra** over and over; **una y otra —** over and over again; **raras veces** seldom; **hacer las veces de** to take the place of
vía F (camino) road; (de ferrocarril) track; (medio de acceso) avenue; **— de transmisión local** local bus; **— Láctea** Milky Way; **— navegable** waterway; **— respiratoria** airway; **—s urinarias** urinary tract; **por — de** by means of; **en —s de** in the process of; PREP vía
viabilidad F viability
viable ADJ viable
viaducto M tunnel
viajante MF traveler; **— de comercio** ; M traveling salesman; F saleswoman
viajar VI (por tierra, aire) to travel, to journey; (por mar) to voyage; (con drogas) to trip
viaje M (por tierra, aire) trip, journey; (por mar) voyage; (en coche, caballo) ride; (por efecto de las drogas) trip; **— de ida y vuelta** round trip; **buen —** have a nice trip; **de —** out of town
viajero -ra MF traveler
viandante MF passerby
viático M (de viaje) per diem; (religioso) last rites
víbora F viper; **— de cascabel** rattlesnake

vibración F (de una cuerda) vibration; (de la lengua) trill
vibrador M vibrator
vibrante ADJ vibrating
vibrar VI/VT to vibrate
vicegobernador -ora MF lieutenant governor
vicepresidente MF, **vicepresidenta** F vice president
vicerrector -ora MF provost
viceversa ADV vice versa
viciado ADJ (aire) stale; (costumbre) stuffy; (corrupto) foul
viciar VT (estropear) to foul; (corromper) to corrupt
vicio M (mala costumbre) vice, bad habit; **de —** unjustifiably; **quitarse el — de** to wean oneself of
vicioso ADJ (persona) dissolute; (gasto) unjustifiable; (gramática) faulty
vicisitud F vicissitude
víctima F (de un crimen) victim; (en un accidente) casualty, victim
victimizar[47] VT to victimize
victoria F victory
victorioso ADJ victorious
vid F vine, grapevine
vida F life; **— media** half-life; **— mía** sweetheart; **— nocturna** nightlife; **— sentimental** love life; **así es la —** that's life; **de toda la —** lifelong; **de — o muerte** life-and-death; **en la — voy a hacer eso** I would never do that; **esto es —** this is the life; **ganarse la —** to earn a living; **mujer de mala —** *fam* hooker; **sin —** lifeless
vidente MF seer; ADJ seeing
vídeo, video M (aparato) VCR; (técnica) video; (cinta) videocassette
videocámara F camcorder
videocasete F videocassette
videoclip M videoclip
videoconferencia F videoconference
videoconsola F video console
videojuego M video game
vidriado M glaze; ADJ glazed
vidriar VT to glaze
vidriera F show window
vidriero -ra MF glazier, glassmaker
vidrio M (sustancia) glass; (en una ventana) pane; **pagar los —s rotos** to be left holding the bag
vidrioso ADJ glassy
vieira F scallop
viejo -ja ADJ old; (chiste) stale; M (anciano) old man; (padre) father; **— amigo** longtime friend; **— verde** dirty old man; **los —s** the old folks; F (anciana) old woman; (madre) mother
viento M wind; **hace —** it is windy; **a los cuatro —s** in all directions

vientre M (abdomen) abdomen; (barriga) belly; (útero) womb
viernes M Friday
Vietnam M Vietnam
vietnamita ADJ & MF INV Vietnamese
viga F (de madera) beam, rafter; (de metal) girder
vigencia F **entrar en —** to go into effect; **estar en —** to be in force
vigente ADJ effective, in force
vigésimo NUM twentieth
vigía F lookout, reef; MF lookout
vigilancia F (cuidado) vigilance; (en una tienda) surveillance
vigilante ADJ vigilant; M watchman; F watchwoman
vigilar VI/VT to keep watch [over]; VT to keep an eye on; (policía) to stake out
vigilia F vigil, watch
vigor M vigor; **en —** in force; **entrar en —** to become effective
vigorizar[47] VT to invigorate
vigoroso ADJ vigorous
VIH [virus de inmunodeficiencia humana] M HIV
vil ADJ vile, base, low
vileza F villainy, baseness
vilipendiar VT to revile
villa F (aldea) village; (casa) country house
villancico M Christmas carol
villanía F villainy
villano -na ADJ villainous; MF villain
vilo LOC ADV **en —** (en el aire) suspended; (en ascuas) in suspense
vinagre M vinegar
vinculación F connection
vincular VT to link (también para páginas web); **—se** to link up
vínculo M link, tie; (en la web) link
vindicar[30] VT to vindicate
vine, viniendo, viniera, viniese *ver* venir
vinilo M vinyl
vino M wine; **— blanco** white wine; **— espumoso** sparkling wine; **— rosado** rosé wine; **— tinto** red wine
viña F vineyard
viñatero -ra MF winegrower
viñedo M vineyard
viola F viola
violación F (de la ley) violation, infringement; (sexual) rape
violado ADJ & M violet
violar VT (una ley) to violate, to break; (una mujer) to rape, to ravish; (una promesa) to breach; (una cerradura) to pick; (derechos) to infringe upon; (mandamientos) to trespass against
violencia F violence; **— doméstica** domestic violence

violentar VT (a una persona) to manhandle; (una casa) to break into; **—se** to get mortified

violento ADJ (deporte, tratamiento) violent, rough; (marido) abusive; (entrada) forcible; (ataque) vicious

violeta ADJ & M violet

violín M (para música clásica) violin; (para música folclórica) fiddle

violinista MF violinist

violonchelo M cello

VIP M VIP

virada F veer

viraje M swerve

viral ADJ viral

virar VI/VT (vehículo) to swerve, to veer; VI (barco) to tack

virgen ADJ & MF virgin; ADJ (cassette) blank; (selva) undisturbed

virginal ADJ virginal

viril ADJ virile, manly

virilidad F virility, manliness

virología F virology

virreinato M viceroyalty

virrey M viceroy

virtual ADJ virtual

virtud F (moral) virtue; (práctica) asset

virtuosismo M virtuosity

virtuoso -sa ADJ (moral) virtuous; ADJ & MF (artístico) virtuoso

viruela F smallpox

virulento ADJ virulent

virus M virus (también de computadoras); **— de inmunodeficiencia humana** human immunodeficiency virus

viruta F wood shaving

visa F visa

visado M visa

visar VT to endorse

visceral ADJ visceral

viscoso ADJ viscous

visera F visor

visibilidad F visibility

visible ADJ visible

visigodo -da ADJ Visigothic; MF Visigoth

visillo M window shade

visión F (capacidad de ver, lo visto) vision; (persona fea) sight; **— en túnel** tunnel vision

visionario -ria ADJ & MF visionary

visita F (acción de visitar) visit; (persona) visitor, caller; (a un edificio) tour; (en una página web) hit; **— de médico** house call

visitación F visitation

visitador -ora MF visitor, caller; (inspector) inspector; (vendedor de medicamentos) pharmaceutical sales representative

visitante MF caller, visitor; ADJ visiting (también en fútbol)

visitar VT (a un amigo, país) to visit; (a un paciente) to make a house call

vislumbrar VT to make out

viso M slip

visón M mink

víspera LOC ADV **en —s de** on the eve of

vista F (panorama) view, vista; (visión) eyesight; **a la —** in sight; **— cansada** eye strain; **a primera —** at first sight; **a simple —** with the naked eye; **bajar la —** to lower one's eyes; **conocer de —** to know by sight; **con —s** with a view to; **en —de** considering; **hacer la — gorda** to look the other way; **¡hasta la —!** good-bye; **perder de —** to lose sight of; **tener a la —** to have before one's eyes; **tener — a** to look out on

vistazo M glance, glimpse, look; **dar/echar un — a** to glance over

visto ADJ **bien —** well thought of; **mal —** looked down upon; **— que** whereas; M **— bueno** approval; **dar el —bueno** to approve

visto ver ver

vistoso ADJ showy

visual ADJ visual

visualizador M display

visualizar[47] VT (en la imaginación) to visualize; (en pantalla) to display

vital ADJ vital; **fuerzas —es** life force

vitalicio ADJ life, for life; M lifetime pension

vitalidad F vitality

vitamina F vitamin

viticultor -ora MF winegrower

vítor M cheer

vitorear VI/VT to cheer

vitral M stained-glass window

vitrina F (ventana) shop window; (armario) showcase

vituperación F vituperation

vituperar VT to revile

vituperio M vituperation

viudo -da M widower; F widow; **viuda negra** black widow spider

vivacidad F vivacity

vivaracho ADJ vivacious

vivaz ADJ vivacious, lively

víveres M PL provisions

vivero M nursery

viveza F (vivacidad) liveliness; (inteligencia) cleverness

vívido ADJ vivid

vivienda F (casa) dwelling; (alojamiento) housing; **— unifamiliar** single-family home

viviente ADJ living

vivir VI/VT to live; **vive una vida normal** he leads a normal life; **vivieron felices y comieron perdices** they lived happily ever after; **¡viva!** hurrah! **¡viva el rey!** long live the king!

vivisección F vivisection

vivo ADJ (viviente) alive, living; (ágil) lively;

(vistoso, intenso) vivid; (listo) clever; **en —**
before a live audience; **en — y en directo**
live; **de viva voz** by word of mouth

vocablo M word

vocabulario M vocabulary

vocación F (profesional) vocation, calling;
(religioso) call

vocal ADJ (de la voz) vocal; (no consonántico)
vowel; F vowel; MF member

vocálico ADJ vocalic

vocear VI/VT (gritar) to cry out; (anunciar) to
page

vocerío M clamor

vocero -ra MF spokesperson

vociferante ADJ vociferous

vociferar VI to clamor

vodevil M vaudeville

vodka M vodka

volado ADJ (drogado) high; (escrito arriba)
superscript

volador ADJ flying

volante ADJ flying; M (en un vestido) ruffle, frill;
(en un coche) steering wheel; (en un motor)
flywheel; (folleto) leaflet, handbill

volar⁵ VI/VT to fly; **— por su cuenta** to fly solo;
ir volando to hurry; VT (un puente) to blow
up; VI (hojas) to blow; **—se** (hacer explosión)
to blow up; (enojarse) to lose one's temper;
(irse volando) to fly away; (drogarse) *fam* to
get stoned

volátil ADJ volatile

volcada F **hacer una —** (baloncesto) to dunk
the ball

volcán M volcano

volcánico ADJ volcanic

volcar³¹ VT (voltear) to tip over, to knock over;
(derramar) to spill; (vaciar) to empty; VI to
roll over; **—se** (un coche) to tip over, to
overturn; (en baloncesto) to dunk

volea F (en vóleibol) volley; (en béisbol) fly ball;
(en tenis) volley

volear VI/VT to volley

voleibol, vóleibol M volleyball

volición F volition

volqueta F *Am* dump truck

volquete M dump truck

voltaje M voltage

voltear VT (una lámpara) to knock over, to turn
over; (la cara) to turn away

voltereta F somersault, tumble; **dar una —** to
somersault; **dar —s** to tumble

voltio M volt

voluble ADJ (malhumorado) moody; (mercado
de valores) volatile

volumen M volume

voluminoso ADJ voluminous, bulky

voluntad F will; **a —** at will; **buena —** good
will, willingness; **mala —** ill will; **por su
propia —** of his own volition

voluntario -ria ADJ voluntary; MF volunteer

voluntarioso ADJ (bien dispuesto) willing;
(testarudo) willful

voluptuoso ADJ voluptuous

voluta F scroll; **—s de humo** spirals of smoke

volver⁶, ⁷⁴ VI (regresar al punto de partida) to
return, to come back; (ir de nuevo) to return,
to go back, to go again; **— a comer** to eat
again; **— del revés** to turn inside out; **— en
sí** to regain consciousness; **—se** (regresar) to
go back; (ponerse) to become; **—se contra** to
turn against; **—se atrás** to turn back; **—se
hacia** to go toward; **—se loco** to go crazy; VT
(la cara) to turn away; (la página) to turn; **—
las espaldas** to turn one's back

vomitar VI/VT to vomit, to throw up

vómito M vomit

voraz ADJ voracious, ravenous

vórtice M vortex

vos PRON *fam RP, Am Central* you

vosotros -as PRON PERS *Esp* you, you guys; (sur
de EEUU) you all, y'all

votación F voting

votante MF voter

votar VI (emitir el voto) to vote; VT (elegir) to
vote for; (aprobar) to vote into law; **— a/por**
to vote for; **— a favor** to vote in favor; **— en
contra** to vote against; **— es un deber
importante** voting is an important duty

voto M (opinión) vote; (promesa) vow; **— de
confianza** vote of confidence

voy *ver* ir

voz F (sonido, aptitud, voto) voice; (en un
diccionario) headword; **a — en cuello** at the
top of one's lungs; **alzar la —** to raise one's
voice; **correr la —** to be rumored; **en — alta**
aloud; **en — baja** quietly, softly; **a voces**
shouting; **dar voces** to shout

vozarrón M loud voice

vudú M voodoo

vuela, vuele *ver* volar

vuelco M **dar un —** to overturn, to turn over;
todo daría un — everything would change
radically; **me dio un — el corazón** my
heart skipped a beat

vuelo M (en avión) flight; (de una falda) flare; **al
— on** the fly; **de alto —** prestigious;
levantar/alzar el — to fly away

vuelta F (movimiento circular) turn; (regreso,
devolución) return; (carrera ciclista) tour; (en
una pista) lap; (curva) twist; (de un collar)
loop; (en deportes) round; (dinero) change; **—
de tuerca** unforeseen event; **a la — de la
esquina** around the corner; **a — de correo**
by return mail; **dar —** to turn upside down;
dar — al revés to turn inside out; **dar — a
una página / una llave** to turn a page / a
key; **dar —s** to spin; **dar —s en la cama** to
toss and turn; **dar — a algo** to turn

something upside down; **dar la —** to turn around; **dar una —** to take a walk, to take a spin; **darse —** to roll over; **estar de —** (de regreso) to be back; (desencantado) to be jaded; **me da —s la cabeza** my head is spinning; **no tiene — de hoja** there are no two ways about it
vuelto M *Am* change
vuelto, vuelva, vuelve *ver* volver
vuestro ADJ POS *Esp* **— hermano** your brother; **un amigo —** a friend of yours; PRON **el —** yours
vulgar ADJ (común) ordinary; (tosco) vulgar
vulgaridad F vulgarity
vulgo M common people
vulnerable ADJ vulnerable
vulva F vulva

Ww

wafle M waffle
waflera F waffle iron
wáter M toilet
web F web, Internet, World Wide Web
whisky M whisk[e]y; **— escocés** scotch
wifi [fidelidad inalámbrica] F Wi-Fi™
windsurf M windsurfing
wok M wok

Xx

xenofobia F xenophobia
xilofón, xilófono M xylophone

Yy

y CONJ and
ya ADV (desde antes) already; (ahora) now; (pronto) soon; **¡—!** enough! **— era hora** it was about time; **¡— lo creo!** I should say so! **— no** no longer; **— que** since; **— sea que** whether; **— te arreglo** I'll fix you; **— verás** mark my words; **— voy** I am coming
yacer[37] VI to lie
yacimiento M (de minerales) deposit; (de petróleo) field
yanqui ADJ & MF *pey* American

yapa F freebie
yarda F yard (también en fútbol americano)
yate M yacht
yegua F mare
yelmo M helmet
yema F (de huevo) egg yolk; (de una planta) bud, shoot; **— de huevo** egg yolk; **— del dedo** fingertip
Yemen M Yemen
yemení ADJ & MF Yemeni
yen M yen
yendo *ver* ir
yerba *ver* hierba
yermo ADJ (estéril) barren; (desolado) bleak, stark
yerno M son-in-law
yesca F tinder
yeso M (mineral) gypsum; (en construcción, medicina) plaster [of Paris]; (escayola) cast
Yibuti M Djibouti
yibutiano -na ADJ & MF Djiboutian
yo PRON PERS I; M (ego) ego
yodo M iodine
yoduro M iodide
yoga M yoga
yogur M yogurt
yo-yo M yo-yo
yuan M yuan
yuca F (ornamental) yucca; (comestible) manioc
yudo M judo
yugo M yoke
Yugoslavia F Yugoslavia
yugoslavo -va ADJ & MF Yugoslavian
yugular ADJ & F jugular
yunque M anvil
yunta F yoke
yuppie MF yuppie
yuxtaponer[56, 74] VT juxtapose

Zz

zacate M grass (también en tenis)
zafar VT to release; **—se** (soltarse) to slip off; (no cumplir) to cop out; **—se de un aprieto** to squirm out of a difficulty
zafio ADJ boorish
zafiro M sapphire
zafra F [sugar] harvest
zaga LOC ADV **a la —** behind; F **ir a la —** to be behind; **quedar a la —** to fall behind
zaguán M vestibule, hall
zaino ADJ chestnut-colored
zalamería F (tacto) smoothness; (lisonja) flattery
zalamero -ra MF flatterer; ADJ (empalagoso)

smooth, unctuous; (lisonjero) flattering
Zambia F Zambia
zambiano -na ADJ & MF Zambian
zambo ADJ knock-kneed
zambullida F dive, plunge
zambullir[16] VT to plunge, to dip; —**se** to dive, to plunge
zanahoria F carrot
zanca F leg of a wading bird
zancada F stride; **dar —s** to stride
zancadilla F intentional tripping; **hacer una —** to trip
zanco M stilt
zancudo ADJ long-legged, lanky; M *Am* mosquito
zángano M drone (también holgazán)
zangolotear VI/VT to jiggle
zangoloteo M jiggle
zanja F ditch, trench
zanjar VT to settle
zapapico M pickax[e]
zapata F brake shoe
zapatear VI to tap the feet in dancing
zapateo M tapping with the feet in dance
zapatería F shoe store
zapatero -ra MF (fabricante) shoemaker; (vendedor) shoe dealer; (remendón) cobbler
zapatilla F (pantufla) slipper; (de vestir) pump; —**s** sneakers
zapato M shoe; —**s con tacos** (fútbol americano) cleats; —**s con tapones** (fútbol) cleats; —**s del mismo par** matching shoes
zar M czar
zarandear VT to jiggle; —**se** to flop around
zarandeo M jiggle
zarcillo M (arete) earring; (de planta) tendril
zarigüeya F opossum
zarpa F claw
zarpar VI to sail, to set sail
zarpazo M blow with a claw; **dar —s** to claw
zarza F bramble, briar
zarzamora F blackberry
zepelín M blimp, zeppelin
zigoto M zygote
zigzag M zigzag
zigzaguear VI to zigzag, to weave one's way
Zimbabue M Zimbabwe
zimbabuo -bua ADJ & MF Zimbabwean
zirconio M zirconium
zócalo M baseboard; *Méx* main square
zodíaco M zodiac
zombi M zombie
zona F (área) zone; (culebrilla) shingles; **— de anotación/ensayo** (fútbol americano) end zone; **— de calentamiento** (béisbol) bullpen; **— de strike** (béisbol) strike zone; **— gris** gray area; **— tampón** buffer zone
zonificación F zoning
zonzo ADJ silly, foolish

zoo M zoo
zoología F zoology
zoológico ADJ zoological; M zoo
zoom M (de cámara fotográfica) zoom lens; (de computadora) zoom
zopenco -ca MF dolt, numbskull
zorrillo M skunk
zorro -a MF (animal) fox; F (hembra) vixen; (prostituta) *pey* prostitute; ADJ (astuto) foxy, cunning; (promiscuo) loose
zorzal M thrush
zozobra F anxiety, worry
zozobrar VI to founder
zueco M clog
zumbar VI (hacer sonidos los insectos) to buzz, to drone, to hum; (hacer ruido las máquinas) to whir, to whiz; (tintinear los oídos) to ring; (dar golpe) to sock
zumbido M (sonido de insectos) buzz, drone, hum; (sonido de máquina) whir, whiz; (sonido en los oídos) ring
zumo M fruit juice
zurcido M (remiendo) darn; (acción de remendar) darning
zurcir[33] VT to darn
zurdo -da ADJ left-handed, southpaw; MF *fam* southpaw
zuro M corncob
zurra F whipping
zurrar VT to whip, to thrash
zurullo M turd
zutano -na M so-and-so, what's-his-name; F so-and-so, what's-her-name

Inglés–Español · English–Spanish

Lista de abreviaturas / List of Abbreviations

adj	adjetivo	adjective
adv	adverbio, adverbial	adverb, adverbial
Am	América	America
art	artículo	article
Carib	Caribe	Caribbean
conj	conjunción	conjunction
def	definido	definite
dem	demostrativo	demonstrative
f	femenino	feminine
fam	familiar	familiar
indef	indefinido	indefinite
interj	interjección	interjection
interr	interrogativo	interrogative
inv	invariable	invariable
lit	literario	literary
loc	locución	locution
m	masculino	masculine
Mex	México	Mexico
n	sustantivo	noun
num	numeral	numeral
pej, pey	peyorativo	pejorative
pl	plural	plural
poss	posesivo	possessive
prep	preposición, preposicional	preposition, prepositional
pron	pronombre	pronoun
rel	relativo	relative
RP	Río de la Plata	River Plate
sg	singular	singular
Sp	España, español	Spain, Spanish
v aux	verbo auxiliar	auxiliary verb
vi	verbo intransitivo	intransitive verb
vt	verbo transitivo	transitive verb
vulg	vulgar	vulgar

Pronunciación inglesa

I. VOCALES

Símbolo fonético	Ortografía inglesa	Explicación
[i]	see, pea	como la *i* en hilo
[ɪ]	bit	el sonido más aproximado es la *i* en *virtud*, pero la [ɪ] inglesa es más abierta, tirando a *e*
[e]	late, they	equivale aproximadamente a *ei*
[ɛ]	set	semejante a la *e* de *perro*, pero más abierta
[ɝ]	work, bird	como la *u* de *cud* (ver abajo) pero articulada simultáneamente con una *r*
[æ]	sat	sonido intermedio entre *e* y *a*
[ɑ]	hot	como la vocal de *pan*
[ɔ]	saw, laud	sonido intermedio entre *a* y *o*
[o]	low, mode	equivale aproximadamente a *ou*
[ʊ]	book, pull	como la *u* de *turrón*, pero más abierta
[u]	June, moon	como la *u* de *uno*
[ʌ]	cud	una *e* muy relajada
[ə]	<u>a</u>dept	una *e* muy relajada y átona
[ɚ]	teach<u>er</u>	una *e* átona relajada articulada simultáneamente con una *r*

II. DIPTONGOS

Símbolo fonético	Ortografía inglesa	Explicación
[aɪ]	pie, aisle	como *ai* en *aire*
[aʊ]	now, foul	como *au* en *causa*
[ɔɪ]	boy	como *oy* en *hoy*
[ju]	use	como *iu* en *ciudad*

III. CONSONANTES

Símbolo fonético	Ortografía inglesa	Explicación
[b]	bat	semejante a la *b* española
[d]	day	semejante a la *d* española, pero articulada en los alvéolos y con más tensión
[f]	fun, photo	como la *f* española

[g]	go	como la *g* de *goma*, pero con más tensión
[h]	hat	muy suave como la *j* de los dialectos caribeños del español
[j]	year	como la *i* del diptongo de *hielo*
[k]	cat, kill	como la *c* de *carro*, pero seguida de aspiración en posición inicial de sílaba (sobre todo tónica)
[l]	let	como la *l* de *lado*
[ł]	ball	como la *l* final catalana
[m]	much	como la *m* española
[n]	no	como la *n* española
[p]	pea	como la *p* española, pero seguida de aspiración en posición inicial de sílaba (sobre todo tónica)
[r]	red	no tiene equivalente en español; se pronuncia con la punta de la lengua enrollada hacia arriba, sin tocar el paladar
[s]	sea	como la *s* hispanoamericana (no la castellana)
[t]	tea	como la *t* española pero articulada en los alvéolos y seguida de aspiración en posición inicial de sílaba (sobre todo tónica)
[v]	very	se articula con los dientes incisivos superiores colocados en el labio inferior
[w]	weed	equivale a la *u* del diptongo de *fui*
[z]	zero, rose	como la *s* de *mismo* cuando se sonoriza, pero aun más sonora
[ɒ]	latter, ladder	como la *r* de *para*
[θ]	thin	como la *z* del español castellano en *zagal*
[ð]	this	como la *d* de *cada*
[ʃ]	sheet, machine, notation	una *s* muy palatal como en francés *chapeau* o italiano *lasciare*
[ʒ]	measure, beige	como la *ll* argentina en *valle*, cuando es sonora
[tʃ]	church	como la *ch* de *charla*
[dʒ]	judge	como la *y* de *inyectar*
[ņ]	eaten, button	representa la *n* silábica, articulada sin la vocal anterior
[ŋ]	ring	como la *n* española en *mango* y *banco*
[ļ]	rental	representa la *l* silábica, articulada como la *l* final catalana
[hw]	where	combinación de los sonidos [h] y [w] arriba descritos

Notas sobre gramática inglesa

El sustantivo

Género. En la gramática inglesa el género solo desempeña un papel importante en el sistema pronominal, p. ej. **he runs** 'él corre', **she runs** 'ella corre', **I see him** 'lo veo', **I see her** 'la veo'. En los sustantivos que designan a personas, se emplean varios métodos para distinguir entre los sexos, v. gr. el agregado de un sufijo, como en **actor** 'actor', **actress** 'actriz', el agregado de una palabra, como en **baby boy** 'niño', **baby girl** 'niña', **she-bear** 'osa', **male nurse** 'enfermero', o el uso de palabras completamente distintas, como en **uncle** 'tío', **aunt** 'tía'.

Número. Generalmente se forma el plural añadiendo **-s** al singular: **paper, papers** 'papel, papeles', **book, books** 'libro, libros', **chief, chiefs** 'jefe, jefes'.

Los sustantivos que terminan en **-ss, -x, -sh, -z** y **-o** añaden **-es** para formar el plural: **kiss, kisses** 'beso, besos', **box, boxes** 'caja, cajas', **dish, dishes** 'plato, platos', **buzz, buzzes** 'zumbido, zumbidos', **hero, heroes** 'héroe, héroes' (excepción: **piano, pianos**). Esto vale también para **-ch** cuando se pronuncia [č], como en **arch, arches** 'arco, arcos', pero no cuando se pronuncia [k], como en **monarch, monarchs** 'monarca, monarcas'.

Los sustantivos que terminan en **-fe**, y ciertos sustantivos que terminan en **-f**, cambian estas letras en **v** y añaden **-es** en el plural: **leaf, leaves** 'hoja, hojas', **life, lives** 'vida, vidas', **wife, wives** 'esposa, esposas', **knife, knives** 'cuchillo, cuchillos' (pero **reef, reefs** 'arrecife, arrecifes').

Para formar el plural de los sustantivos terminados en **-y** precedida de consonante se cambia la **-y** en **-ies: fly, flies** 'mosca, moscas', **family, families** 'familia, familias'. En cambio, los sustantivos terminados en **-y** precedida de vocal forman el plural añadiendo **-s** al singular: **day, days** 'día, días'.

Ciertos sustantivos forman el plural de una manera irregular: **man, men** 'hombre, hombres', **woman, women** 'mujer, mujeres', **mouse, mice** 'ratón, ratones', **louse, lice** 'piojo, piojos', **goose, geese** 'ganso, gansos', **tooth, teeth** 'diente, dientes', **foot, feet** 'pie, pies', **ox, oxen** 'buey, bueyes'.

Ciertos sustantivos que terminan en **-is** forman el plural cambiando la **i** de la terminación en **e: axis, axes** 'eje, ejes', **crisis, crises** 'crisis' (sg., pl.).

El adjetivo

El adjetivo inglés es invariable en cuanto a género y número. Normalmente se coloca delante del sustantivo: **an interesting woman** 'una mujer interesante', **a large man** 'un hombre grande', **beautiful birds** 'aves hermosas'.

Los comparativos y superlativos. Aunque no hay una regla general, por lo común los adjetivos monosílabos, los adjetivos acentuados en la última sílaba y algunos bisílabos comunes forman el comparativo de aumento y el superlativo añadiendo **-er** y **-est** (como **tall**). Los demás adjetivos van precedidos de **more** (para el comparativo) y **most** (para el superlativo) (como **careful**). Nótese que (1) si la palabra termina en -**e** muda, se añaden -**r** y -**st** en vez de -**er** y -**est** (ver **wise**), (2) los adjetivos terminados en -**y** cambian esta letra en **i** (ver **happy**), (3) los adjetivos terminados en consonante (menos **r**) precedida de vocal doblan la consonante (ver **fat**):

Positivo	Comparativo	Superlativo
tall alto	**taller** más alto	**the tallest** el más alto
careful cuidadoso	**more careful** más cuidadoso	**the most careful** el más cuidadoso
wise sabio	**wiser** más sabio	**the wisest** el más sabio
happy feliz	**happier** más feliz	**the happiest** el más feliz
fat gordo	**fatter** más gordo	**the fattest** el más gordo

Los adjetivos siguientes forman el comparativo y el superlativo de una manera irregular:

good	**better**	**best**
bad, ill	**worse**	**worst**
much	**more**	**most**

El adverbio

Muchos adverbios se forman añadiendo -**ly** al adjetivo: **courteous** 'cortés', **courteously** 'cortésmente', **bold** 'atrevido', **boldly** 'atrevidamente'. Existen las irregularidades ortográficas siguientes en la formación de los adverbios que terminan en -**ly**: (1) los adjetivos terminados en -**ble** cambian la -**e** en -**y**: **possible, possibly,** (2) los terminados en -**ic** añaden -**ally: poetic, poetically,** (3) los terminados en -**ll** añaden solo -**y: full, fully,** (4) los terminados en -**ue** pierden la -**e** final: **true, truly,** (5) los terminados en -**y** cambian la -**y** en **i: happy, happily.**

La mayor parte de los adverbios forman el comparativo y el superlativo con los adverbios **more** 'más' y **most** 'el/la más'. Asimismo los adverbios monosílabos añaden -**er** y -**est:**

Positivo	Comparativo	Superlativo
boldly	**more boldly**	**most boldly**
generously	**more generously**	**most generously**
soon	**sooner**	**soonest**
early	**earlier**	**earliest**
late	**later**	**latest**
fast	**faster**	**fastest**

Los adverbios siguientes forman el comparativo y el superlativo de una manera irregular:

well	better	best
badly	worse	worst
little	less	least
far	farther, further	farthest, furthest

Sufijos comunes del inglés

-dom   a partir de bases nominales, forma sustantivos con los sentidos de dominio, jurisdicción, estado, condición: **kingdom** 'reino' (**king** 'rey'), **martyrdom** 'martirio' (**martyr** 'mártir'), **freedom** 'libertad' (**free** 'libre')

-ee   a partir de verbos, forma sustantivos indicando a la persona que recibe una acción: **addressee** 'destinatario' (**to address** 'dirigir'), **employee** 'empleado' (**to employ** 'emplear').

-eer   a partir de bases diversas, forma sustantivos que denotan oficio u ocupación: **auctioneer** 'subastador' (**to auction** 'subastar'), **puppeteer** 'titiritero' (**puppet** 'títere')

-en   *a.*   forma adjetivos que denotan la sustancia de que está hecha una cosa: **golden** 'dorado' (**gold** 'oro'), **wooden** 'de madera' (**wood** 'madera')
   b.   forma verbos a partir de adjetivos: **to whiten** 'blanquear' (**white** 'blanco'), **to darken** 'oscurecer' (**dark** 'oscuro')

-er   *a.*   forma sustantivos a partir de verbos para indicar agente: **player** 'jugador' (**to play** 'jugar'), **speaker** 'hablante' (**to speak** 'hablar'), **baker** 'panadero' (**to bake** 'hornear')
   b.   forma sustantivos a partir de sustantivos para denominar al residente de un lugar: **New Yorker** 'neoyorquino' (**New York** 'Nueva York'), **islander** 'isleño' (**island** 'isla')

-ess   se usa para formar el género femenino de ciertos sustantivos: **princess** 'princesa' (**prince** 'príncipe'), **countess** 'condesa' (**count** 'conde')

-fold   indica el número de veces que se repite algo: **twofold** 'dos veces' (**two** 'dos'), **hundredfold** 'cien veces' (**hundred** 'cien')

-ful   *a.*   forma adjetivos a partir de sustantivos para indicar la presencia de una cualidad: **hopeful** 'esperanzado' (**hope** 'esperanza'), **careful** 'cuidadoso' (**care** 'cuidado'), **willful** 'voluntarioso' (**will** 'voluntad')
   b.   forma adjetivos a partir de verbos para indicar tendencia: **forgetful** 'olvidadizo' (**to forget** 'olvidar')

c. forma sustantivos a partir de sustantivos indicando la capacidad:
handful 'puñado' (**hand** 'mano'), **spoonful** 'cucharada' (**spoon** 'cuchara')

-hood forma abstractos a partir de sustantivos concretos: **motherhood** 'maternidad' (**mother** 'madre'), **childhood** 'niñez' (**child** 'niño'), **likelihood** 'probabilidad' (**likely** 'probable')

-ing a. forma adjetivos a partir de verbos: **running water** 'agua corriente' (**to run** 'correr'), **drinking water** 'agua potable' (**to drink** 'beber'), **waiting room** 'sala de espera' (**to wait** 'esperar'), **washing machine** 'máquina lavadora' (**to wash** 'lavar')

b. se usa para formar sustantivos que expresan la acción de un verbo: **understanding** 'entendimiento' (**to understand** 'entender'), **supplying** 'abastecimiento' (**to supply** 'abastecer')

c. se usa para formar sustantivos que denominan una cosa que desempeña una acción: **clothing** 'ropa' (**to clothe** 'vestir'), **covering** 'cobertura' (**to cover** 'cubrir')

-ish forma adjetivos a partir de sustantivos indicando semejanza o atenuación: **boyish** 'como un niño' (**boy** 'niño'), **womanish** 'como mujer, mujeril' (**woman** 'mujer'), **whitish** 'blancuzco' (**white** 'blanco')

-less se agrega a sustantivos para indicar falta de algo: **childless** 'sin hijos' (**child** 'hijo'), **penniless** 'sin dinero' (**penny** 'centavo'), **endless** 'interminable, sin fin' (**end** 'fin')

-like se añade a sustantivos para indicar semejanza: **lifelike** 'que parece vivo' (**life** 'vida'), **childlike** 'infantil' (**child** 'niño'), **tigerlike** 'como un tigre' (**tiger** 'tigre')

-ly a. se añade a adjetivos para formar adverbios: **slowly** 'lentamente' (**slow** 'lento'), **happily** 'felizmente' (**feliz** 'happy')

b. deriva adjetivos a partir de sustantivos indicando una cualidad: **motherly** 'maternal' (**mother** 'madre'), **gentlemanly** 'caballeroso' (**gentleman** 'caballero'), **friendly** 'amistoso' (**friend** 'amigo')

c. deriva adjetivos o adverbios de tiempo a partir de sustantivos: **daily** 'diario', 'diariamente' (**day** 'día'), **weekly** 'semanal', 'semanalmente' (**week** 'semana')

-ness forma nombres de cualidades a partir de adjetivos: **goodness** 'bondad' (**good** 'bueno'), **darkness** 'oscuridad' (**dark** 'oscuro'), **foolishness** 'tontería' (**fool** 'tonto')

-ship		se emplea para derivar sustantivos a partir de sustantivos y verbos para denotar
	a.	cualidades abstractas: **friendship** 'amistad' (**friend** 'amigo')
	b.	arte o destreza: **horsemanship** 'equitación' (**horseman** 'jinete')
	c.	dignidad, oficio, cargo o título: **professorship** 'cátedra' (**professor** 'catedrático'), **lordship** 'señoría' (**lord** 'señor')
	d.	la duración de una acción: **courtship** 'cortejo' (**to court** 'cortejar')

-some   se añade a verbos para formar adjetivos que expresan tendencia excesiva: **tiresome** 'aburrido' (**to tire** 'aburrir'), **quarrelsome** 'pendenciero' (**to quarrel** 'discutir')

-th   es el sufijo que forma números ordinales a partir de los cardinales: **fifth** 'quinto' (**five** 'cinco'), **tenth** 'décimo' (**ten** 'diez')

-ward   se añade a sustantivos y adverbios para indicar movimiento hacia un lugar: **homeward** 'hacia casa' (**home** 'casa'), **downward** 'hacia abajo' (**down** 'abajo')

-wise,   se añaden a sustantivos para indicar dirección o posición: **edgewise** 'de
-ways   lado' (**edge** 'borde'), **lengthwise** 'a lo largo' (**length** 'largo'), **sideways** 'de lado' (**side** 'lado')

-y	*a.*	es un sufijo diminutivo: **doggy** 'perrito' (**dog** 'perro'), **Johnny** 'Juanito' (**John** 'Juan')
	b.	se añade a sustantivos para formar adjetivos que indican abundancia: **rocky** 'rocoso' (**rock** 'roca'), **rainy** 'lluvioso' (**rain** 'lluvia'), **hairy** 'peludo' (**hair** 'pelo'), **angry** 'enojado' (**anger** 'enojo')
	c.	se añade a sustantivos para formar adjetivos que expresan semejanza: **rosy** 'rosado' (**rose** 'rosa')

Verbos irregulares de la lengua inglesa

Se denominan verbos irregulares los que no forman el pretérito o el participio pasivo con la adición de **-d** o **-ed** al presente. Obsérvese que en ciertos verbos (aquí señalados con asterisco) coexiste la forma regular al lado de la irregular. Las formas poco usadas aparecen entre paréntesis.

Presente	*Pretérito*	*Participio pasivo*
*abide	(abode)	abided
am, is, are	was, were	been
arise	arose	arisen
*awake	awoke	awoken

Presente	*Pretérito*	*Participio pasivo*
bear	bore	borne
beat	beat	beaten
become	became	become
befall	befell	befallen
beget	begat	begotten
begin	began	begun
behold	beheld	beheld
bend	bent	bent
*beseech	(besought)	(besought)
beset	beset	beset
bet	bet	bet
bid 'ofrecer'	bid	bid
bid 'mandar'	bade	bidden
bind	bound	bound
bite	bit	bitten, bit
bleed	bled	bled
blow	blew	blown
break	broke	broken
breed	bred	bred
bring	brought	brought
build	built	built
*burn	burnt	burnt
burst	burst	burst
buy	bought	bought
cast	cast	cast
catch	caught	caught
choose	chose	chosen
cling	clung	clung
*clothe	(clad)	(clad)
come	came	come
cost	cost	cost
creep	crept	crept
cut	cut	cut
deal	dealt	dealt
dig	dug	dug
*dive	dove	dived
do	did	done
draw	drew	drawn
*dream	dreamt	dreamt
drink	drank	drunk
drive	drove	driven
*dwell	dwelt	dwelt
eat	ate	eaten
fall	fell	fallen

Verbos irregulares

Presente	Pretérito	Participio pasivo
feed	fed	fed
feel	felt	felt
fight	fought	fought
find	found	found
*fit	fit	fit
flee	fled	fled
fling	flung	flung
fly	flew	flown
forbear	(forbore)	(forborne)
forbid	forbade	forbidden
foresee	foresaw	foreseen
foretell	foretold	foretold
forget	forgot	forgotten
forgive	forgave	forgiven
forsake	forsook	forsaken
freeze	froze	frozen
get	got	got, gotten
give	gave	given
go	went	gone
grind	ground	ground
grow	grew	grown
hang[1]	hung	hung
have, has	had	had
hear	heard	heard
*hew	hewed	hewn
hide	hid	hidden, hid
hit	hit	hit
hold	held	held
hurt	hurt	hurt
keep	kept	kept
*kneel	knelt	knelt
*knit	knit	knit
know	knew	known
lay	laid	laid
lead	led	led
*lean	(leant)	(leant)
*leap	leapt	leapt
*learn	(learnt)	(learnt)
leave	left	left
lend	lent	lent
let	let	let

1. Es regular cuando significa 'ahorcar'.

Presente	Pretérito	Participio pasivo
lie[2]	lay	lain
*light	lit	lit
lose	lost	lost
make	made	made
mean	meant	meant
meet	met	met
mistake	mistook	mistaken
*mow	mowed	mown
pay	paid	paid
*plead	pled	pled
put	put	put
quit	quit	quit
read [rɪd]	read [rɛd]	read [rɛd]
rend	rent	rent
*rid	rid	rid
ride	rode	ridden
ring	rang	rung
rise	rose	risen
run	ran	run
*saw	sawed	sawn
say	said	said
see	saw	seen
seek	sought	sought
sell	sold	sold
send	sent	sent
set	set	set
*sew	sewed	sewn
shake	shook	shaken
*shave	shaved	shaven
*shear	sheared	shorn
shed	shed	shed
shine[3]	shone	shone
shoe	shod	shod
shoot	shot	shot
*show	showed	shown
shrink	shrank (shrunk)	shrunk (shrunken)
shut	shut	shut
sing	sang	sung
sink	sank	sunk
sit	sat	sat
slay	slew	slain

2. Es regular cuando significa 'mentir'.
3. Suele ser regular cuando es transitivo, en el sentido 'pulir, dar brillo'.

Verbos irregulares

Presente	Pretérito	Participio pasivo
sleep	slept	slept
slide	slid	slid
sling	slung	slung
slink	slunk	slunk
slit	slit	slit
*smell	(smelt)	(smelt)
smite	smote	smitten
*sow	sowed	sown
speak	spoke	spoken
*speed	sped	sped
*spell	(spelt)	(spelt)
spend	spent	spent
*spill	(spilt)	(spilt)
spin	spun	spun
spit	spat, spit	spat, spit
split	split	split
*spoil	(spoilt)	(spoilt)
spread	spread	spread
spring	sprang, sprung	sprung
stand	stood	stood
*stave	(stove)	(stove)
steal	stole	stolen
stick	stuck	stuck
sting	stung	stung
stink	stank	stunk
*strew	strewed	strewn
stride	strode	stridden
strike	struck	struck, stricken
string	strung	strung
*strive	strove	striven
swear	swore	sworn
*sweat	sweat	sweat
sweep	swept	swept
*swell	swelled	swollen
swim	swam	swum
swing	swung	swung
take	took	taken
teach	taught	taught
tear	tore	torn
tell	told	told
think	thought	thought
throw	threw	thrown
thrust	thrust	thrust
tread	trod	trodden

Presente	Pretérito	Participio pasivo
understand	understood	understood
undertake	undertook	undertaken
undo	undid	undone
uphold	upheld	upheld
upset	upset	upset
*wake	woke	woken
wear	wore	worn
weave	wove	woven
*wed	wed	wed
weep	wept	wept
*wet	wet	wet
win	won	won
wind	wound	wound
withdraw	withdrew	withdrawn
withhold	withheld	withheld
withstand	withstood	withstood
wring	wrung	wrung
write	wrote	written

Aa

a [ə, e] INDEF ART un *m*, una *f*; **what — fool!** ¡qué tonto! **such — fool** tan tonto; **I'm — teacher / Catholic** soy maestro / católico

AA [Alcoholics Anonymous] [éé] N AA *f*

aback [əbǽk] ADV **to be taken —** estar desconcertado

abandon [əbǽndən] VT abandonar; N **with wild —** desenfrenadamente

abandonment [əbǽndənmənt] N abandono *m*, desamparo *m*

abashed [əbǽʃt] ADJ humillado, avergonzado

abate [əbét] VI/VT (trend, payments) disminuir, mitigar[se]; (storm) calmarse, atenuarse

abbey [ǽbi] N abadía *f*

abbot [ǽbət] N abad *m*

abbreviate [əbríviet] VT abreviar

abbreviation [əbriviéʃən] N (act of abbreviating) abreviación *f*; (short form) abreviatura *f*

abdicate [ǽbdIket] VI/VT abdicar

abdomen [ǽbdəmən] N abdomen *m*, vientre *m*

abdominal [æbdámənl] ADJ abdominal; **— distension** distensión abdominal *f*

abduct [æbdΛkt] VT secuestrar, raptar

abduction [æbdΛkʃən] N secuestro *m*, rapto *m*

aberration [æbəréʃən] N anomalía *f*, aberración *f*

abet [əbét] VT instigar

abeyance [əbéəns] ADV LOC **in —** pendiente, en suspenso

abhor [əbhɔ́r] VT aborrecer

abhorrence [əbhɔ́rəns] N aborrecimiento *m*

abhorrent [əbhɔ́rənt] ADJ aborrecible

abide [əbáId] VT (tolerate) soportar; VI (dwell) morar, permanecer; **to — by** acatar, atenerse a

ability [əbílIDi] N (skill) habilidad *f*; (aptitude) capacidad *f*

abject [ǽbdʒékt] ADJ abyecto; **in — poverty** en extrema miseria

ablaze [əbléz] ADV en llamas

able [ébəl] ADJ hábil, capaz; **—-bodied** de cuerpo sano; **to be — to** (be capable of) poder; (have an acquired skill) saber

abnegate [ǽbnIget] VT renunciar

abnormal [æbnɔ́rməl] ADJ anormal

aboard [əbɔ́rd] ADV a bordo; **all —!** (train) ¡viajeros al tren! (ship) ¡pasajeros a bordo! **to go —** embarcarse, abordar

abode [əbód] N morada *f*

abode [əbód] *see* abide

abolish [əbálIʃ] VT abolir, suprimir

abolition [æbəlíʃən] N abolición *f*

abominable [əbámənəbəl] ADJ abominable

abomination [əbamənéʃən] N (action, thing) abominación *f*; (condition, vice) horror *m*

aboriginal [æbəríʤənəl] ADJ aborigen

aborigine [æbəríʤəni] N aborigen *mf*; **Australian —** aborigen australiano -na *mf*

abort [əbɔ́rt] VT (fetus) abortar; VI/VT (mission) suspender; (software) interrumpir; N (software) interrupción *f*

abortion [əbɔ́rʃən] N aborto *m*

abortionist [əbɔ́rʃənIst] N abortador -ora *mf*, abortero -ra *mf*

abortive [əbɔ́rDIv] ADJ frustrado

abound [əbáUnd] VI abundar; **to — with** abundar en

about [əbáUt] PREP (concerning) acerca de, tocante a; (near, surrounding) alrededor de, por; **to be — one's business** atender a su negocio; ADV más o menos, alrededor de; **at — ten o'clock** a eso de las diez, sobre las diez; **to be — to do something** estar por / para hacer algo, estar a punto de hacer algo; **I'm all — transparency** insisto en la transparencia

above [əbΛv] PREP **you could see the towers — the buildings** se veían las torres sobre los edificios; **everyone — five years of age** todos los de más de cinco años; **he's — me in the company** es mi superior en la compañía; **to be — suspicion** estar libre de toda sospecha; **I thought you were — such things** no pensaba que te rebajarías a eso; ADV **the apartment —** el apartamento de arriba; **books of fifty pages and —** libros de cincuenta páginas y más; **the remark quoted —** la observación anteriormente citada; **— all** sobre todo; **—-mentioned** susodicho, ya mencionado

abrasion [əbréʒən] N abrasión *f*

abrasive [əbrésIv] ADJ (material) abrasivo; (person, tone) irritante

abreast [əbrést] ADV al lado; **to keep —** mantenerse al corriente; **four —** de cuatro en fondo

abridge [əbríʤ] VT abreviar

abroad [əbrɔ́d] ADV en el extranjero; **to go —** ir al extranjero

abrupt [əbrΛpt] ADJ abrupto

ABS [antilock braking system] [ébíés] N SFA *m*

abscess [ǽbsɛs] N absceso *m*

abscond [æbskánd] VI fugarse

absence [ǽbsəns] N (nonpresence) ausencia *f*; (lack) falta *f*; **in the — of** a falta de

absent [ǽbsənt] ADJ ausente; **—-minded** distraído, despistado; **to be — from school** faltar a la escuela

absentee [æbsəntí] N ausente *mf*; **— landlord** propietario -ria ausente *mf*

absenteeism [æbsəntíIzəm] N ausentismo *m*

absolute [ǽbsəlút] ADJ (ruler, certainty)

absoluto; (prohibition) terminante
absolutely [æbsəlútli] ADV absolutamente; —
not en absoluto; INTERJ —! ¡sí, señor! ¡claro!
absolve [æbzálv] VT absolver
absorb [əbzɔ́rb] VT (liquid) absorber; (shock)
amortiguar; (people, information) asimilar;
he is —ed in his work está absorto en su
trabajo
absorption [əbzɔ́rpʃən] N absorción f
abstain [æbstén] VI abstenerse; — **from**
abstenerse de
abstention [æbsténʃən] N abstención f
abstinence [æbstənəns] N abstinencia f
abstract [æbstrækt] ADJ abstracto; N (summary)
resumen m, extracto m; **in the** — en
abstracto
abstraction [æbstrækʃən] N abstracción f
absurd [əbsɝ́d] ADJ absurdo, disparatado
absurdity [əbsɝ́DIDi] N (quality) absurdo m;
(action) disparate m
abundance [əbʌ́ndəns] N abundancia f
abundant [əbʌ́ndənt] ADJ abundante
abuse¹ [əbjús] N (of privileges) abuso m; (of
authority) abuso m, desmán m; (physical)
maltrato m; (verbal) injuria f
abuse² [əbjúz] VT (privileges) abusar de;
(physically) maltratar; (verbally) injuriar
abusive [əbjúsɪv] ADJ (physically) violento;
(verbally) injurioso
abysmal [əbízməł] ADJ abismal; — **results**
resultados desastrosos m pl
abyss [əbís] N abismo m
A/C [air conditioning] [ésí] N aire
acondicionado m
academic [ækədémɪk] ADJ (university)
académico; (school) escolar; N profesor -ora
universitario -ria mf
academy [əkǽDəmi] N academia f
accede [æksíd] VI acceder; — **to** acceder a
accelerate [ækséləret] VI/VT acelerar
acceleration [ækseləréʃən] N aceleración f
accelerator [ækséləreDɚ] N acelerador m
accent¹ [æksɛnt] N (pronunciation) acento m;
(written) tilde f, acento escrito/ortográfico m
accent² [æksént] VT (syllable) acentuar
accentuate [ækséntʃuet] VT (differences, facts,
syllables) acentuar, recalcar; (beauty) realzar
accept [æksépt] VT aceptar
acceptable [ækséptəbəł] ADJ aceptable
acceptance [ækséptəns] N (action) aceptación f;
(approval) aprobación f
access [ækses] N acceso m; — **code** código de
acceso m; — **provider** proveedor -ora de
acceso mf; — **denied** acceso denegado m; VT
acceder a
accessibility [æksesəbílIDi] N accesibilidad f
accessible [æksésəbəł] ADJ accesible
accessory [æksésəri] ADJ accesorio; N (to
clothes, to gadgets) accesorio m; (to a crime)

cómplice mf; — **slot** ranura para accesorios f
accident [æksIDənt] N accidente m; (mishap)
percance m; — **insurance** seguro contra
accidentes m; **by** — por casualidad
accidental [æksIdéntł] ADJ (injury) accidental;
(discovery, meeting) casual, fortuito
acclaim [əklém] VT aclamar; N aclamación f,
ovación f
acclamation [ækləméʃən] N aclamación f
acclimate [ǽkləmet] VI/VT (to physical
conditions) aclimatar[se]; (to an ambience)
acostumbrar[se]
accolade [ǽkəled] N elogio m
accommodate [əkámədet] VT (adjust) tener en
cuenta; (lodge) hospedar, alojar; (contain)
tener capacidad para; VI **to** — **oneself**
adaptarse
accommodation [əkɑmədéʃən] N (adjustment)
acomodación f, adaptación f; —**s** (lodging)
alojamiento m; (facilities) comodidades f pl
accompaniment [əkʌ́mpənImənt] N
acompañamiento m
accompanist [əkʌ́mpənIst] N acompañante mf
accompany [əkʌ́mpəni] VI/VT acompañar
accomplice [əkʌ́mplIs] N cómplice mf
accomplish [əkʌ́mplIʃ] VT (objective) lograr;
(mission) completar
accomplished [əkʌ́mplIʃt] ADJ (actor, athlete)
consumado; (musician) talentoso
accomplishment [əkʌ́mplIʃmənt] N
(achievement) logro m; (skill) habilidad f;
(completion) realización f
accord [əkɔ́rd] N acuerdo m, convenio m; **of
one's own** — voluntariamente; VT otorgar,
conceder
accordance [əkɔ́rdn̩s] ADV LOC **in** — **with** de
acuerdo con, de conformidad con
according to [əkɔ́rDIŋ] ADV LOC según
accordingly [əkɔ́rDIŋli] ADV (therefore) por
consiguiente; (correspondingly) como
corresponde
accordion [əkɔ́rDiən] N acordeón m
accost [əkɔ́st] VT abordar
account [əkáunt] N (bill) cuenta f; (story) relato
m, relación f; — **manager** administrador
-ora de cuentas mf; —**s payable** cuentas por/
a pagar f pl; —**s receivable** cuentas por/a
cobrar f pl; **to open [close] an** — abrir
[cerrar] una cuenta; **on** — **of** a causa de,
debido a; **on my** — por mí; **on one's own** —
por cuenta propia; **on no** — de ninguna
manera; **of no** — de ningún valor; **to take
into** — tener en cuenta; VI **to** — **for** dar
cuenta de; **how do you** — **for that?** ¿cómo
se explica eso?
accountability [əkauntəbílIDi] N
responsabilidad f
accountable [əkáuntəbəł] ADJ responsable
accountant [əkáuntn̩t] N Am contador -ra mf; Sp

contable *mf*

accounting [əkáʊntɪŋ] N contabilidad *f*; — **firm** empresa de contadores públicos *f*; — **period** ejercicio contable *m*

accredit [əkrédɪt] VT acreditar

acculturate [əkʌ́ltʃəret] VI/VT aculturar[se]

accumulate [əkjúmjəlet] VI/VT acumular[se]

accumulation [əkjumjəléʃən] N acumulación *f*

accuracy [ǽkjə·əsi] N (of measure, instrument) precisión *f*, exactitud *f*; (of a translation) fidelidad *f*

accurate [ǽkjə·ɪt] ADJ (measure, instrument) preciso, exacto; (translation) fiel

accursed [əkɜ́·sɪd] ADJ maldito

accusation [ækjuzéʃən] N acusación *f*

accuse [əkjúz] VT acusar

accused [əkjúzd] ADJ acusado; N acusado -da *mf*, reo -a *mf*, procesado -da *mf*

accuser [əkjúzə·] N acusador -ra *mf*

accustom [əkʌ́stəm] VT acostumbrar, habituar; **to — oneself** acostumbrarse, habituarse; **to be —ed to** tener la costumbre de, estar acostumbrado a

AC/DC [alternating current / direct current] [ésidísi] ADJ (electricity) alterna y continua; (sexuality) bisexual

ace [es] N (cards, athlete, aviator) as *m*; (tennis) saque ganador *m*, servicio directo *m*; VT (a test) sacarse la máxima nota en

acetaminophen [əsɛDəmínəfən] N acetaminofén *m*

acetone [ǽsəton] N acetona *f*

ache [ek] N dolor *m*; **—s and pains** achaques *m pl*; VT doler; **my stomach —s** me duele el estómago

achieve [ətʃív] VT (a goal) conseguir, lograr; (a level) alcanzar

achievement [ətʃívmənt] N (attainment) consecución *f*; (success) logro *m*, realización *f*

Achilles tendon [əkɪliz téndən] N tendón de Aquiles *m*

aching [ékɪŋ] ADJ doliente, dolorido

achy [éki] ADJ dolorido

acid [ǽsɪd] ADJ ácido; N ácido *m*; (hallucinogen) LSD *m*; — **rain** lluvia ácida *f*; — **test** prueba de fuego *f*

acidic [əsíDɪk] ADJ ácido

acidity [əsíDɪDi] N acidez *f*

acknowledge [æknálɪdʒ] VT (merits) reconocer; (faults) admitir, reconocer; (help) agradecer; **to — receipt** acusar recibo

acknowledgment [æknálɪdʒmənt] N (of merits) reconocimiento *m*; (of merits, faults) reconocimiento *m*, admisión *f*; (gratefulness) agradecimiento *m*; — **of receipt** acuse de recibo *m*

acme [ǽkmi] N súmmum *m*

acne [ǽkni] N acné *m*

acorn [ékɔrn] N bellota *f*

acoustics [əkústɪks] N acústica *f*

acquaint [əkwént] VT informar, familiarizar; **to — oneself with** informarse de, familiarizarse con; **to be —ed with** (a person, city, country) conocer; (a piece of news) estar enterado de

acquaintance [əkwéntn̩s] N (with facts) conocimiento *m*; (a person) conocido -a *mf*

acquiesce [ækwiés] VT asentir, condescender; (unwillingly) consentir

acquiescence [ækwiésəns] N asentimiento *m*, consentimiento *m*, condescendencia *f*

acquire [əkwáɪr] VT (knowledge, skill, purchase) adquirir; (fortune, information) obtener; (disease) contraer

acquisition [ækwəzíʃən] N (knowledge, skill, purchase) adquisición *f*; (fortune, information) obtención *f*

acquisitive [əkwízɪDɪv] ADJ codicioso

acquit [əkwít] VT absolver

acquittal [əkwídl̩] N absolución *f*

acre [ékə·] N acre [0.405 hectares] *m*

acrid [ǽkrɪd] ADJ acre

acrimony [ǽkrəmoni] N acritud *f*

acrobat [ǽkrəbæt] N acróbata *mf*

acrobatic [ækrəbǽDɪk] ADJ acrobático; N **—s** acrobacia *f*

acronym [ǽkrənɪm] N acrónimo *m*, sigla *f*

acrophobia [ækrəfóbiə] N acrofobia *f*

across [əkrɔ́s] PREP **to lay one stick — the other** poner dos palos cruzados; **there's a bridge — that river** hay un puente sobre ese río; **he came — his old love letters** encontró sus viejas cartas de amor; **the library is — the street** la biblioteca está al otro lado de la calle; — **the board** de manera uniforme, sin excepciones; ADV **cut the boards —** corta los tablones a lo ancho; **five hundred miles —** de quinientas millas de ancho; **the meaning doesn't come —** el significado no se entiende

acrylic [əkrílɪk] ADJ & N acrílico *m*

act [ækt] N (deed, part of play) acto *m*; (part of show) número *m*; (law) ley *f*, decreto *m*; — **of God** caso de fuerza mayor *m*; VI (behave) actuar, comportarse; (take measures) obrar; (play a part, chemical process) actuar; (represent) representar; (function) funcionar; **to — up** (child) portarse mal; (car) funcionar mal; **to — out** (event) representar; (feelings) exteriorizar

acting [ǽktɪŋ] N actuación *f*; (in a drama) representación *f*; ADJ (interim) interino; (substitute) suplente

action [ǽkʃən] N (practical measure, plot of a play) acción *f*; (deed) acto *m*; (functioning) funcionamiento *m*; **to take —** tomar medidas

actionable [ǽkʃənəbəl] ADJ accionable, procesable

activate [ǽktɪvet] VT activar
active [ǽktɪv] ADJ activo
activism [ǽktɪvɪzəm] N activismo *m*
activist [ǽktɪvɪst] N activista *mf*
activity [æktívɪDi] N actividad *f*
actor [ǽktɚ] N actor *m*
actress [ǽktrɪs] N actriz *f*
actual [ǽktʃuəł] ADJ verdadero, real
actually [ǽktʃuəli] ADV en realidad,
    efectivamente
actuary [ǽktʃuɛri] N actuario -ria *mf*
acuity [əkjúɪDi] N agudeza *f*
acumen [ǽkjəmən] N perspicacia *f*, agudeza *f*
acupuncture [ǽkjupʌŋktʃɚ] N acupuntura *f*
acupuncturist [ǽkjupʌ́ŋktʃɚɪst] N acupuntor
    -ora *mf*
acute [əkjút] ADJ (pain, illness) agudo;
    (observation) perspicaz, penetrante
AD [édí] ADV d.C.
ad [æd] N anuncio publicitario *m*; — **in** (tennis)
    ventaja al saque *f*, ventaja al servicio *f*; — **out**
    (tennis) ventaja al resto *f*; — **lib** ADJ
    improvisado; ADV improvisando; **to** — **lib** VI
    improvisar
adamant [ǽDəmənt] ADJ inflexible, firme
Adam's apple [ǽDəmz ǽpəł] N nuez de Adán *f*
adapt [ədǽpt] VT adaptar; VI **to** — **to** adaptar[se]
    a, acomodar[se] a
adaptation [æDæptéʃən] N adaptación *f*
adapter [ədǽptɚ] N adaptador *m*
add [æd] VT añadir, agregar; (find sum) sumar;
    —**ed cost** costo adicional *m*; **to** — **to**
    aumentar; **to** — **up** (find sum) sumar; (make
    sense) cuadrar; N —**on** accesorio *m*
addict [ǽDɪkt] N adicto -ta *mf*
addicted [ədíktɪd] ADJ adicto
addiction [ədíkʃən] N adicción *f*
addition [ədíʃən] N (of numbers) suma *f*; (to a
    collection, staff) adición *f*, adquisición *f*; (to a
    building) anexo *m*; **in** — **[to]** además [de]
additional [ədíʃənəł] ADJ adicional
additive [ǽDɪtɪv] N aditivo *m*
address¹ [ədrés] N (street) dirección *f*, domicilio
    m; (speech) discurso *m*; — **book** libreta de
    direcciones *f*; **form of** — tratamiento *m*
address² [ədrés] VT (write the address) dirigir;
    (speak to) dirigirse a; (deal with) ocuparse de
addressee [ædrɛsí] N destinatario -ria *mf*
adduce [ədús] VT aducir
adept [ədépt] ADJ hábil
adequacy [ǽDɪkwəsi] N suficiencia *f*
adequate [ǽDɪkwɪt] ADJ (sufficient) suficiente;
    (acceptable) aceptable
adhere [ædhír] VI adherirse; **to** — **to** adherirse a
adherence [ædhírəns] N adhesión *f*
adhesion [ædhíʒən] N (thing or tissue that
    adheres) adherencia *f*; (act of sticking
    together) adhesión *f*
adhesive [ædhísɪv] ADJ adhesivo; — **tape** cinta

adhesiva *f*
adjacent [ədʒésənt] ADJ adyacente
adjective [ǽdʒɪktɪv] ADJ & N adjetivo *m*
adjoin [ədʒɔ́ɪn] VT lindar con, colindar con;
    —**ing** colindante; VI estar contiguo a
adjourn [ədʒɚ́n] VT **to** — **the meeting** levantar
    la sesión; **meeting** —**ed** se levanta la sesión
adjournment [ədʒɚ́nmənt] N levantamiento de
    la sesión *m*
adjudge [ədʒʌ́dʒ] VT (declare) declarar; (deem)
    calificar
adjudicate [ədʒúDɪket] VI arbitrar; VT declarar
adjunct [ǽdʒʌŋkt] ADJ adjunto; N agregado -da
    mf
adjust [ədʒʌ́st] VT (fix) ajustar, graduar; (adapt a
    machine) regular; —**ed net income** ingreso
    neto ajustado *m*; VI ajustarse, adaptarse
adjustable [ədʒʌ́stəbəł] ADJ ajustable; —**-rate
    mortgage** hipoteca con tasa de interés
    ajustable *f*
adjustment [ədʒʌ́stmənt] N ajuste *m*; (to a
    machine) regulación *f*
administer [ædmínɪstɚ] VT (a business)
    administrar, gestionar; (a punishment)
    aplicar; (an oath) tomar[le]
administration [ædmɪnɪstréʃən] N
    administración *f*; (period in power) gestión *f*;
    (of punishment) aplicación *f*; (of an oath)
    toma *f*
administrative [ædmínɪstreDɪv] ADJ
    administrativo
administrator [ædmínɪstreDɚ] N
    administrador -ra *mf*; (civil) intendente *mf*
admirable [ǽdmɚəbəł] ADJ admirable
admiral [ǽdmɚəł] N almirante *m*
admiration [ædmɚéʃən] N admiración *f*
admire [ædmáɪr] VT admirar
admirer [ædmáɪrɚ] N admirador -ora *mf*;
    (suitor) pretendiente *mf*
admissible [ædmísəbəł] ADJ admisible
admission [ædmíʃən] N (acceptance) admisión
    f; (access, ticket price) entrada *f*; (confession)
    confesión *f*
admit [ædmít] VT (allow entry) admitir; (to a
    hospital) internar; (acknowledge) reconocer,
    admitir
admittance [ædmítn̩s] N entrada *f*; **no** —
    prohibida la entrada
admonish [ædmánɪʃ] VT amonestar
admonition [ædməníʃən] N (warning)
    advertencia *f*; (reproof) amonestación *f*
adobe [ədóbi] N (mud) adobe *m*; (house) casa de
    adobe *f*
adolescence [ædlésəns] N adolescencia *f*
adolescent [ædlésənt] ADJ & N adolescente *mf*
adopt [ədápt] VT (child, custom) adoptar;
    (suggestion) aprobar
adoption [ədápʃən] N (of a child, custom)
    adopción *f*; (of a suggestion) aprobación *f*

adoptive [ədáptɪv] ADJ adoptivo
adorable [ədórəbəł] ADJ adorable, precioso
adoration [æDəréʃən] N adoración f
adore [ədór] VT adorar; **I — playing tennis** me
 encanta jugar al tenis
adorn [ədórn] VT adornar, ornar
adornment [ədórnmənt] N adorno m
adrenal [ədrínł] ADJ suprarrenal
adrenaline [ədrénəlɪn] N adrenalina f
adrift [ədríft] ADJ & ADV a la deriva
adult [ədáłt] ADJ & N adulto -ta mf
adulterate [ədáłtəret] VT adulterar
adulterer [ədáłtərə] N adúltero -ra mf
adultery [ədáłtəri] N adulterio m
advance [ædvǽns] VI (move forward) avanzar;
 (make progress) avanzar, progresar; (bring
 forward) adelantar; VT (promote) promover;
 (propose) proponer; (pay beforehand)
 adelantar, anticipar; N (movement) avance m;
 (progress) adelanto m; (loan) adelanto m,
 anticipo m; **—s** (sexual) requiebros m pl; **in —**
 por adelantado, con anticipación
advanced [ædvǽnst] ADJ (idea, stage) avanzado;
 (country) adelantado
advancement [ædvǽnsmənt] N (movement)
 avance m; (rank) ascenso m; (knowledge)
 progreso m
advantage [ædvǽntɪʤ] N ventaja f (also tennis);
 it would be to your — te convendría; **to
 take — of** aprovecharse de
advantageous [ædvæntéʤəs] ADJ ventajoso,
 provechoso
advent [ǽdvɛnt] N advenimiento m
adventure [ædvɛ́ntʃə] N aventura f
adventurer [ædvɛ́ntʃərə] N aventurero -ra mf
adventuresome [ædvɛ́ntʃəsəm] ADJ atrevido,
 osado
adventurous [ædvɛ́ntʃəəs] ADJ (seeking
 adventure) aventurero, intrépido; (daring)
 atrevido, audaz
adverb [ǽdvəb] N adverbio m
adversary [ǽdvəseri] N adversario -ria mf
adverse [ǽdvə́s] ADJ adverso
adversity [ædvə́sɪDi] N adversidad f
advertise [ǽdvətaɪz] VT anunciar, hacer
 publicidad/propaganda para; VI hacer
 propaganda/publicidad; **to — for a cook**
 poner un anuncio buscando cocinero
advertisement [ædvətáɪzmənt] N anuncio
 publicitario m, aviso m
advertiser [ǽdvətaɪzə] N anunciante mf
advertising [ǽdvətaɪzɪŋ] N publicidad f; **—
 agency** agencia de publicidad f; **—
 campaign** campaña publicitaria f; **— agent**
 agente publicitario -ria mf
advice [ædváɪs] N consejo m; (expert)
 asesoramiento m
advisable [ædváɪzəbəł] ADJ aconsejable,
 recomendable

advise [ædváɪz] VI/VT (counsel) aconsejar,
 advertir; VT (inform) avisar, informar;
 (expertly) asesorar
adviser, advisor [ædváɪzə] N consejero -ra mf,
 asesor -ora mf
advocacy [ǽdvəkəsi] N defensa f
advocate[1] [ǽdvəkɪt] N (promoter) partidario -ria
 mf; (defender) defensor -ora mf, intercesor
 -ora mf; (lawyer) abogado -da mf
advocate[2] [ǽdvəket] VT abogar por, defender
aerial [ériəł] ADJ aéreo; N antena f
aerobic [eróbɪk] ADJ (exercise) aeróbico;
 (air-breathing) aerobio; N **—s** aeróbic m
aerodynamic [ɛrodaɪnǽmɪk] ADJ
 aerodinámico; N **—s** aerodinámica f
aeronautics [ɛrənóDɪks] N aeronáutica f
aerosol [érəsał] N aerosol m
aerospace [érospes] N espacio aéreo m; ADJ
 aeroespacial
aesthetic [ɛsθɛ́DɪK] ADJ estético; N **—s** estética f
affable [ǽfəbəł] ADJ afable
affair [əfér] N (social) acontecimiento social m;
 (business) asunto m, negocio m; (love)
 aventura amorosa f, affaire m
affect [əfɛ́kt] VT (have effect on) afectar; (move)
 conmover; (feign) fingir
affectation [æfɛktéʃən] N afectación f,
 melindre m
affected [əfɛ́ktɪd] ADJ (moved) afectado,
 conmovido; (feigned) fingido, artificioso,
 melindroso
affection [əfɛ́kʃən] N afecto m, cariño m
affectionate [əfɛ́kʃənɪt] ADJ afectuoso, cariñoso
affidavit [æfɪdévɪt] N declaración jurada f
affiliate[1] [əfíliet] VT afiliar; VI afiliarse, asociarse
affiliate[2] [əfíliɪt] N filial f
affiliation [əfɪliéʃən] N (relation) afiliación f;
 (membership) filiación f; **political —**
 filiación política f
affinity [əfínɪDi] N afinidad f
affirm [əfə́m] VT afirmar
affirmation [æfəméʃən] N afirmación f
affirmative [əfə́məDɪV] ADJ afirmativo; **—
 action** discriminación positiva f; N **reply in
 the —** dar una respuesta afirmativa
affix[1] [ǽfɪks] VT fijar; **to — one's signature**
 poner su firma, firmar
affix[2] [ǽfɪks] N afijo m
afflict [əflíkt] VT aquejar; **to be —ed with**
 padecer de, sufrir de
affliction [əflíkʃən] N (misery) aflicción f;
 (ailment) achaque m, mal m
affluent [ǽfluənt] ADJ (society) opulento;
 (person) rico
afford [əfɔ́rd] VT **I cannot — a car** no me
 alcanza el dinero para un coche; **he cannot
 — to waste time** no puede darse el lujo de
 perder tiempo; **I cannot — the risk** no me
 puedo permitir ese riesgo; **we will — you**

every opportunity se te darán todas las oportunidades

affordable [əfɔ́rDəbəł] ADJ asequible

affront [əfránt] N afrenta f

Afghan, Afghani [ǽfgæn/æfgǽni] ADJ & N afgano -na mf

Afghanistan [æfgǽnɪstæn] N Afganistán m

afire [əfáɪr] ADJ & ADV en llamas

afloat [əflót] ADJ & ADV flotando, a flote

afraid [əfréd] ADJ asustado; **to be — [of]** temer, tener miedo [a]

afresh [əfréʃ] ADV de nuevo, desde el principio

Africa [ǽfrɪkə] N África f

African [ǽfrɪkən] ADJ & N africano -na mf

African American [ǽfrɪkənəmérɪkən] ADJ & N afroamericano -na mf

after [ǽftɚ] PREP (temporal) después de, tras; (spatial) detrás de; **— all** después de todo; ADV después; CONJ después [de] que

afterbirth [ǽftɚbɝθ] N placenta f

aftercare [ǽftɚker] N (post-illness) tratamiento de convalecencia m; (postoperative) tratamiento post-operatorio m

after-hours [ǽftɚ áurz] ADV después de horas hábiles

afterlife [ǽftɚlaɪf] N el más allá m

aftermarket [ǽftɚmarkɪt] ADJ de mercado secundario; N (for merchandise) mercado secundario m; (for stocks) mercado extrabursátil m

aftermath [ǽftɚmæθ] N secuelas f pl

afternoon [ǽftɚnún] N tarde f; INTERJ **good** —! ¡buenas tardes!

aftershave [ǽftɚʃev] N loción para después del afeitado f

aftershock [ǽftɚʃak] N réplica f

aftertaste [ǽftɚtest] N (in the mouth) dejo m; (bad memory) resabio m

aftertax profit [ǽftɚtækspráfɪt] N ganancia neta f

afterthought [ǽftɚθɔt] N **it was just an —** se nos ocurrió después

afterward, afterwards [ǽftɚwɚd[z]] ADV después, posteriormente

again [əgén] ADV otra vez, de nuevo; **— and —** repetidas veces; **to fall —** volver a caerse

against [əgénst] PREP contra; **— the grain** a contrapelo; **— all odds** a pesar de todo

age [edʒ] N (of a person) edad f; (era) era f, época f; **— of consent** edad de consentimiento sexual f; **— discrimination** discriminación por edad f; **— limit** límite de edad m; **old —** vejez f; **of —** mayor de edad; **to come of —** llegar a la mayoría de edad; **under —** menor de edad; VI/VT envejecer

aged[1] [edʒd] ADJ (wine) añejo; **— forty** de cuarenta años

aged[2] [édʒɪd] ADJ anciano

ageless [édʒlɪs] ADJ (everlasting) eterno; (not

showing age) siempre joven; (classic) clásico

agency [édʒənsi] N agencia f; **through the — of** por mediación de

agenda [ədʒéndə] N orden del día m, agenda f

agent [édʒənt] N agente mf; (commercial) representante mf, gestor -ora mf; (legal) apoderado -da mf

aggrandize [əgrǽndaɪz] VT engrandecer

aggravate [ǽgrəvet] VT (worsen) exacerbar, agravar; (annoy) irritar, exasperar, exacerbar

aggregate [ǽgrɪgɪt] N conjunto m; (rock) agregado m; ADJ total, global

aggression [əgréʃən] N (attack) agresión f; (propensity to violence) agresividad f

aggressive [əgrésɪv] ADJ (violent) agresivo; (dynamic) emprendedor

aggressiveness [əgrésɪvnɪs] N agresividad f

aggressor [əgrésɚ] N agresor -ra mf

aghast [əgǽst] ADJ horrorizado

agile [ǽdʒəł] ADJ ágil

agility [ədʒílɪDi] N agilidad f

aging [édʒɪŋ] N (of a person) envejecimiento m; (of wine) maduración f

agitate [ǽdʒɪtet] VT (shake) agitar; (perturb) turbar; (campaign) alborotar

agitation [ædʒɪtéʃən] N agitación f

agitator [ǽdʒɪteDɚ] N agitador -ra mf

agnostic [ægnástɪk] ADJ & N agnóstico -ca mf

ago [əgó] ADV **many years —** hace muchos años; **long —** hace mucho tiempo

agog [əgág] ADJ planchado, boquiabierto

agonize [ǽgənaɪz] VI sufrir angustiosamente; **to — over** atormentarse por

agony [ǽgəni] N (pain) dolor m, tormento m; (anguish) angustia f

agoraphobia [ægəəfóbiə] N agorafobia f

agrarian [əgrériən] ADJ agrario

agree [əgrí] VI (be in agreement) estar de acuerdo; (in grammar, mathematics) concordar; (color, food) sentarle bien; **to — upon** acordar, convenir, pactar; **they —d to meet the next day** quedaron en reunirse al día siguiente, acordaron reunirse al día siguiente; **the two sides —d to a truce** los dos bandos pactaron una tregua

agreeable [əgríəbəł] ADJ (nice) agradable; (willing) conforme

agreement [əgrímənt] N (concord, document) acuerdo m, concertación f, convenio m; (grammatical) concordancia f; **to be in —** estar de acuerdo; **to come to an —** ponerse de acuerdo, pactar

agricultural [ægrɪkʌ́ltʃɚəł] ADJ (related to crops) agrícola; (related to crops and cattle) agropecuario

agriculture [ǽgrɪkʌltʃɚ] N agricultura f

aground [əgráund] ADV **to run —** encallar, varar

ahead [əhéd] ADV delante; **— of time**

adelantado, con antelación; **to go** — ir
adelante, adelantarse; **to get** — prosperar;
our team is — nuestro equipo va primero;
the years — los años venideros
aid [ed] N (help) asistencia f; (assistant) ayudante
mf; VT ayudar; **to** — **and abet** instigar
aide [ed] N (high-ranking) asesor -ora mf;
(low-ranking) ayudante mf
**AIDS [acquired immune deficiency
syndrome]** [edz] N SIDA m
ail [eł] VI/VT **what** —**s you?** ¿qué tienes? ¿qué te
aflige? **he's** —**ing** está enfermo
aileron [élərɑn] N alerón m
ailing [élɪŋ] ADJ (person) achacoso, enfermizo;
(economy) debilitado
ailment [éłmənt] N achaque m, dolencia f
aim [em] N (with a weapon) puntería f;
(objective) objetivo m; VT (a weapon) apuntar;
(a question, blow) dirigir; **to** — **to please**
tratar de agradar
aimless [émlɪs] ADJ (purposeless) sin propósito;
(directionless) sin rumbo
air [ɛr] N aire m; —**bag** airbag m, bolsa de aire f;
—**brake** freno neumático m; **to** —
condition poner aire condicionado; —
conditioner acondicionador de aire m; —
conditioning aire acondicionado m,
climatización f; —**craft** aeronave f; —**craft
carrier** portaaviones m sg; —**field**
aeródromo m; — **force** fuerza aérea f;
—**head** cabeza de chorlito mf; —**lift** puente
aéreo m; —**line** línea aérea f, areolínea f; —
mail correo aéreo m; —**plane** avión m; —
piracy piratería aérea f; —**port** aeropuerto
m; — **power** fuerza aérea f; — **pressure**
presión de aire f; — **raid** ataque aéreo m; —
rifle escopeta de aire comprimido f; —**ship**
dirigible m; — **strike** bombardeo aéreo m;
—**strip** pista de aterrizaje f; —**-to-** —
aire-aire; — **traffic control** control del
tráfico aéreo m; —**way** conducto de aire m,
vía respiratoria f; **up in the** — en el aire,
incierto; **in the open** — al aire libre; **to be
on the** — estar en el aire, emitirse; **to put on**
—**s** presumir, darse ínfulas; **to vanish into
thin** — evaporarse; VT (an opinion)
manifestar; **to** —**lift** aerotransportar; **to** —
out orear, ventilar; ADJ aéreo; —**borne**
(troops) aerotransportado; (particles)
transportado por el aire; — **conditioned** con
aire acondicionado, climatizado; —**tight**
hermético
aisle [aɪł] N pasillo m; (of a church) nave lateral f
ajar [ədʒár] ADJ entornado, entreabierto
aka [ékéé] ADV (also called) también conocido
como; (in police usage) alias
akin [əkín] ADJ (related) emparentado; (similar)
semejante
à la mode [ɑlɑmód] ADV con helado

alarm [əlárm] N (warning) alarma f; (worry)
inquietud f; — **clock** despertador m; **to
sound an** — tocar a rebato; VT (worry)
alarmar; (frighten) asustar
alarming [əlármɪŋ] ADJ alarmante
Albania [ælbéniə] N Albania f
Albanian [ælbéniən] ADJ & N albanés -esa mf
albatross [ǽłbətrɑs] N albatros m
albinism [ǽłbɪnɪzəm] N albinismo m
albino [ǽłbáɪno] N albino -na mf
album [ǽłbəm] N álbum m
alcohol [ǽłkəhɔł] N alcohol m
alcoholic [ǽłkəhɔ́łɪk] ADJ & N alcohólico -ca mf
alcoholism [ǽłkəhɔłɪzəm] N alcoholismo m
alcove [ǽłkov] N rincón m
ale [eł] N cerveza inglesa f
alert [əlɜ́t] ADJ (vigilant) alerta; (awake)
despierto; **to be** — (on guard) estar alerta;
(lively) ser despierto; N alerta f; VT alertar,
avisar
alfalfa [ælfǽłfɔ] N alfalfa f
algae [ǽłdʒi] N algas f pl
algebra [ǽłdʒəbrə] N álgebra f
Algeria [ældʒíriə] N Argelia f
Algerian [ældʒíriən] ADJ & N argelino -na mf
algorithm [ǽłgərɪðəm] N algoritmo m
alias [éliəs] N alias m sg
alibi [ǽłəbaɪ] N coartada f
alien [éliən] N (visitor from space) extraterrestre
mf; (foreigner) extranjero -ra mf; ADJ ajeno
alienate [éliənet] VT (people) alienar, alejar;
(property) enajenar
alight [əláɪt] VI (rider) apearse; (bird, insect)
posarse
align [əláɪn] VI/VT alinear[se]
alignment [əláɪnmənt] N alineación f
alike [əláɪk] ADJ parecido, igual; **to be** —
parecerse, ser iguales; ADV del mismo modo
alimentary [ælɪméntəri] ADJ alimenticio; —
canal canal alimentario m
alimony [ǽłəmoni] N pensión alimenticia f
alive [əláɪv] ADJ (living) vivo; — **with** lleno de;
the symphony came — **under his
direction** la sinfonía cobró vida bajo su
dirección
alkali [ǽłkəlaɪ] N álcali m
alkaline [ǽłkəlɪn] ADJ alcalino
all [ɔl] ADJ todo; — **the time** todo el tiempo; N
todo m; **to give one's** — dar todo de sí; PRON
todo; **is that** —? ¿eso es todo? — **or nothing**
todo o nada; ADV completamente, todo; — **at
once** (uninterrupted) de una vez; (sudden) de
repente; —**-inclusive** con todo incluido; —
time high máximo histórico m; — **told** en
conjunto; **he's** — **dirty** está todo sucio; **it is**
— **over** se acabó; **not at** — de ninguna
manera; **nothing at** — nada en absoluto;
once [and] for — de una vez por todas;
she's — **right** está bien; INTERJ — **right**

bueno

allay [əlé] VT (fear, doubt) calmar, disipar; (anger) aplacar

allegation [ælɪgéʃən] N acusación f

allege [əléʤ] VT (state) afirmar; (claim) alegar

alleged [əléʤd] ADJ (event) supuesto; (perpetrator) presunto

allegedly [əléʤɪdli] ADV supuestamente, presuntamente

allegiance [əlíʤəns] N lealtad f, fidelidad f; **to pledge — to the flag** jurar la bandera

allegory [ǽlɪgɔri] N alegoría f

allergen [ǽlə·ʤɪn] N alergeno/alérgeno m

allergic [əlɚʤɪk] ADJ alérgico

allergist [ǽlə·ʤɪst] N alergólogo -ga mf

allergy [ǽlə·ʤi] N alergia f

alleviate [əlíviet] VT (suffering) aliviar; (hunger) paliar

alley [ǽli] N callejón m; (tennis) pasillo de dobles m; **right up her —** ideal para ella

alliance [əláɪəns] N alianza f

allied [əláɪd, ǽlaɪd] ADJ aliado

alligator [ǽlɪgeɾə·] N caimán m; Am lagarto m

alliterate [əlíɾəret] VI hacer aliteración

allocate [ǽləket] VT asignar

allot [əlát] VT asignar

allotment [əlátmənt] N asignación f, cuota f

allow [əláu] VI/VT (permit) permitir; (make possible) posibilitar; (admit) admitir; **to — for** tener en cuenta

allowable [əláuəbəl] ADJ admisible, permisible

allowance [əláuəns] N (regular payment) asignación f, pensión f; (monthly payment) mensualidad f; (for a child) paga f, mesada f; (payment for a particular purpose) pago m; (food) ración f; **to make — for** tener en cuenta

alloy[1] [ǽlɔɪ] N aleación f

alloy[2] [əlɔ́ɪ] VT alear

allude [əlúd] VI aludir; **to — to** aludir a

allure [əlúr] VI/VT seducir, atraer; N atractivo m

alluring [əlúrɪŋ] ADJ seductivo, atractivo

allusion [əlúʒən] N alusión f

ally[1] [ǽlaɪ] N aliado -da mf

ally[2] [əláɪ] VT **to — oneself with** aliarse con

almanac [ɔ́lmənæk] N almanaque m

almighty [ɔlmáɪɾi] ADJ todopoderoso

almond [ɔ́mənd] N almendra f; **— tree** almendro m

almost [ɔ́lmost] ADV casi; **I — fell down** por poco me caigo

alms [ɔmz] N limosna f

aloe vera [ǽlovírə] N áloe m

alone [əlón] ADJ solo; **— among his contemporaries** único entre sus contemporáneos; ADV solo, solamente; **she — knew that** solo ella sabía eso; **all — a** solas; **to leave —** no tocar, dejar en paz

along [əlɔ́ŋ] PREP **he was walking — the**

street andaba por la calle; **all — the coast** a lo largo de toda la costa; **— with** junto con; **all —** desde el principio; **to carry — with oneself** llevar consigo; **to go — with** acceder a, conformarse con; **to get — with** llevarse bien con

alongside [əlɔ́ŋsáɪd] PREP al lado de; **— the boat** al lado del bote; ADV al lado, al costado; **the dog ran —** el perro corría al costado

aloof [əlúf] ADJ reservado, esquivo; ADV apartado

aloud [əláud] ADV en voz alta

alphabet [ǽlfəbɛt] N alfabeto m, abecedario m

alphanumeric [ælfənumérɪk] ADJ alfanumérico

alpine [ǽlpaɪn] ADJ alpino

already [ɔlrédi] ADV ya

also [ɔ́lso] ADV también, además; **—-ran** (horse, candidate) caballo/candidato vencido m

alt [ælt] see alternate[1]

altar [ɔ́ltə·] N altar m; **—piece** retablo m

alter [ɔ́ltə·] VI/VT (change) alterar; (neuter) capar, castrar

alteration [ɔltəréʃən] N (change) alteración f, cambio m; **—s** arreglos m pl, reformas f pl

altercation [ɔltə·kéʃən] N altercado m

alternate[1] [ɔ́ltə·nɪt] ADJ alternativo, alterno; **— route** ruta alternativa f; **— spelling** ortografía alterna f; **he visits us on — Mondays** nos visita un lunes sí y otro no; **alt key** tecla de alt f; **alt gr key** tecla de alternativa gráfica f; N suplente mf

alternate[2] [ɔ́ltə·net] VI/VT alternar

alternation [ɔltə·néʃən] N alternancia f

alternative [ɔltɚnəɾɪv] ADJ alternativo; **— minimum tax** contribución alternativa mínima f; N alternativa f

alternator [ɔ́ltə·neɾə·] N alternador m

although [ɔlðó] CONJ aunque, si bien

altimeter [æltímɪɾə·] N altímetro m

altitude [ǽltɪtud] N altura f, altitud f; **— sickness** mal de altura m

alto [ǽlto] N contralto mf; ADJ alto

altogether [ɔltəgéðə·] ADV (completely) completamente; (all included) en total

altruism [ǽltruɪzəm] N altruismo m

aluminum [əlúmənəm] N aluminio m; **— foil** papel de aluminio m

always [ɔ́lwez] ADV siempre

Alzheimer's disease [ɔ́ltshaɪmə·z dɪzíz] N enfermedad de Alzheimer f

a.m. [éém] ADV de la mañana

am [æm] see be

amalgamate [əmǽlgəmet] VI/VT (metals) amalgamar[se]; (companies) fusionar[se]

amass [əmǽs] VT acumular, amasar

amateur [ǽmət(ʃ)ə·] ADJ amateur; N amateur mf; aficionado -da mf

amaze [əméz] VT maravillar, asombrar

amazement [əmézmənt] N asombro m

amazing [əmézɪŋ] ADJ asombroso, increíble
Amazon [ǽməzɑn] N (region) Amazonia f;
(river) Amazonas m sg
ambassador [æmbǽsəDɚ] N embajador -ora mf
amber [ǽmbɚ] N ámbar m; ADJ (quality)
ambarino; (material) de ámbar; (color) [de]
color ámbar
ambidextrous [æmbɪdékstrəs] ADJ ambidiestro
ambience, ambiance [ǽmbiəns] N ambiente m
ambient [ǽmbiənt] ADJ ambiental; —
temperature temperatura ambiente f
ambiguity [æmbɪgjúɪDi] N ambigüedad f
ambiguous [æmbɪ́gjuəs] ADJ ambiguo
ambition [æmbɪ́ʃən] N ambición f, aspiración f
ambitious [æmbɪ́ʃəs] ADJ ambicioso
ambivalent [æmbívələnt] ADJ ambivalente
amble [ǽmbəł] VI deambular
ambulance [ǽmbjələns] N ambulancia f
ambulatory [ǽmbjələtɔri] ADJ ambulatorio
ambush [ǽmbuʃ] N emboscada f, celada f; **to lie
in** — tender una emboscada; VT emboscar
ameliorate [əmíliəret] VI/VT mejorar
amen [ámén] INTERJ amén
amenable [əménəbəł] ADJ bien dispuesto
amend [əménd] VT enmendar; **to make—s [for]**
compensar [por]
amendment [əméndmənt] N enmienda f
amenities [əménɪDiz] N PL comodidades f pl
America [əmérɪkə] N América f
American [əmérɪkən] ADJ & N (continental)
americano -na mf; (USA) americano -na mf,
norteamericano -na mf, estadounidense mf
amethyst [ǽməθɪst] N amatista f
amiable [émiəbəł] ADJ amable
amicable [ǽmɪkəbəł] ADJ amistoso, amigable
amid [əmíd] PREP en medio de, entre
amino acid [əmínoǽsɪd] N aminoácido m
amiss [əmís] ADV **something is** — algo anda
mal
ammonia [əmónjə] N amoníaco m
ammunition [æmjəníʃən] N munición f
amnesia [æmníʒə] N amnesia f
amnesty [ǽmnɪsti] N amnistía f
amniocentesis [æmniosɪntísɪs] N
amniocentesis f
amniotic [æmniáDɪk] ADJ amniótico; — **fluid**
líquido amniótico m
amoeba [əmíbə] N ameba f
among [əmʌ́ŋ] PREP entre
amoral [emɔ́rəł] ADJ amoral
amorous [ǽmərəs] ADJ (sexually aroused)
excitado; (in love) enamorado
amorphous [əmɔ́rfəs] ADJ amorfo
amortization [æməɚDizéʃən] N amortización f
amortize [ǽməɚtaɪz] VT amortizar
amount [əmáunt] N (of a substance) cantidad f,
(of money) suma f, importe m; — **due**
cantidad debida f, monto debido m; — **paid**
cantidad pagada f, monto pagado m; —

payable cantidad a pagar f; VI (add up to)
ascender [a]; **that—s to stealing** eso
equivale a robar
ampere [ǽmpír] N amperio m
amphetamine [æmféDəmin] N anfetamina f
amphibian [æmfíbiən] N anfibio m
amphibious [æmfíbiəs] ADJ anfibio
amphitheater [ǽmfəθiəDɚ] N anfiteatro m
ampicillin [æmpɪsílɪn] N ampicilina f
ample [ǽmpəł] ADJ (in quantity) suficiente; (in
size) amplio
amplifier [ǽmpləfaɪɚ] N amplificador m
amplify [ǽmpləfaɪ] VT (an explanation) ampliar;
(a sound) amplificar
amplitude [ǽmplɪtud] N amplitud f
amputate [ǽmpjətet] VT amputar
amuck, amok [əmʌ́k] ADV **to run** — (kill
people) perpetrar un ataque homicida; (go
crazy) volverse loco
amulet [ǽmjəlɪt] N amuleto m
amuse [əmjúz] VT (make laugh) divertir; (help
pass time) entretener; **to — oneself**
divertirse, entretenerse
amusement [əmjúzmənt] N diversión f,
entretenimiento m
amusing [əmjúzɪŋ] ADJ (entertaining) divertido;
(funny) gracioso, chistoso
amygdala [əmígdələ] N amígdala f
an [ən, æn] INDEF ART un m, una f
anabolic [ænəbálɪk] ADJ anabólico; — **steroid**
esteroide anabólico m
anachronism [ənǽkrənɪzəm] N anacronismo m
anaerobic [ænəróbɪk] ADJ anaerobio
anal [énł] ADJ anal; (neurotic) rígido, neurótico
analgesic [ænldʒízɪk] N & ADJ analgésico m
analogical [ænəládʒɪkəł] ADJ analógico
analogous [ənǽləgəs] ADJ análogo
analogue, analog [ǽnələg] ADJ analógico; —
device dispositivo analógico m
analogy [ənǽləʤi] N analogía f
analysis [ənǽlɪsɪs] N análisis m
analyst [ǽnəlɪst] N analista mf
analytic, analytical [ænəlíDɪk[əł]] ADJ
(approach) analítico; (person) analítico,
analista
analyze [ǽnəlaɪz] VT analizar
anarchist [ǽnɚkɪst] N anarquista mf
anarchy [ǽnɚki] N anarquía f
anathema [ənǽθəmə] N anatema m
anatomical [ænətámɪkəł] ADJ anatómico
anatomy [ənǽDəmi] N anatomía f
ancestor [ǽnsɛstɚ] N antepasado -da mf,
ascendiente mf
ancestral [ænséstrəł] ADJ ancestral, de los
antepasados; — **home** casa solariega f
ancestry [ǽnsɛstri] N linaje m, ascendencia f,
abolengo m
anchor [ǽŋkɚ] N ancla f; —**man** presentador m;
—**woman** presentadora f; **to drop** — anclar,

echar anclas; VT (a boat) anclar; (an argument) basar; VI echar anclas, fondear

anchovy [ǽntʃovi] N anchoa f

ancient [énʃənt] ADJ antiguo; *pej* vetusto

and [ænd] CONJ y; (before i, hi) e; — **so forth** etcétera, y así sucesivamente

Andalusia [ændəlúʒə] N Andalucía f

Andalusian [ændəlúʒən] ADJ & N andaluz -za *mf*

Andes [ǽndiz] N Andes *m pl*

Andorra [ændɔ́rə] N Andorra f

Andorran [ændɔ́rən] ADJ & N andorrano -na *mf*

androgynous [ændrádʒənəs] ADJ andrógino

anecdote [ǽnɪkdot] N anécdota f

anemia [ənímiə] N anemia f

anemic [əním ɪk] ADJ anémico

anesthesia [ænɪsθíʒə] N anestesia f

anesthesiologist [ænəsθiziálədʒɪst] N anestesiólogo -ga *mf*, anestesista *mf*

anesthesiology [ænɪsθiziálədʒi] N anestesiología f

anesthetic [ænɪsθɛ́DIk] ADJ anestésico; N (substance) anestesia f

anesthetize [ənɛ́sθətaɪz] VT anestesiar

aneurysm [ǽnjərɪzəm] N aneurisma *m*

anew [ənú] ADV de nuevo, otra vez

angel [éndʒəł] N ángel *m*

angelic [ændʒélɪk] ADJ angélico, angelical

anger [ǽŋgɚ] N enojo *m*, enfado *m*; VT enojar, enfadar

angina pectoris [ændʒáɪnəpéktɚɪs] N angina de pecho f

angiocardiography [ændʒiokɑrDiágrəfi] N angiocardiografía f

angiogram [ǽndʒiogræm] N angiograma *m*

angioplasty [ǽndʒiəplæsti] N angioplastia f; — **balloon** balón de angioplastia *m*

angle [ǽŋgəł] N (geometrical) ángulo *m*; (point of view) punto de vista *m*, perspectiva f; VI pescar

Anglo-Saxon [ǽŋglosǽksən] ADJ & N anglosajón -ona *mf*

Angola [æŋgólə] N Angola f

Angolan [æŋgólən] ADJ & N angolano -na *mf*, angoleño -ña *mf*

angry [ǽŋgri] ADJ enojado, enfadado

angst [áŋkst] N angustia f

anguish [ǽŋgwɪʃ] N angustia f, ansia f, congoja f

angular [ǽŋgjələ] ADJ angular; (face) anguloso

animal [ǽnəməł] ADJ & N animal *m*; — **rights** derechos de los animales *m pl*

animate[1] [ǽnəmɪt] ADJ animado

animate[2] [ǽnəmet] VT (enliven) animar; (encourage) alentar; —**d cartoon** dibujo animado *m*

animation [ænəméʃən] N animación f

animosity [ænəmásɪDi] N animosidad f, ojeriza f, encono *m*

anise [ǽnɪs] N anís *m*

ankle [ǽŋkəł] N tobillo *m*

annals [ǽnḷz] N anales *m pl*

annex[1] [ǽnɛks] N anexo *m*

annex[2] [ənéks] VT anexar

annexation [ænɛkséʃən] N anexión f

annihilate [ənáɪəlet] VT aniquilar

anniversary [ænəvɚ́səri] N aniversario *m*

annotate [ǽnətet] VT anotar

annotation [ænətéʃən] N (action, result) anotación f; (result) nota f

announce [ənáʊns] VT (make known) anunciar, dar a conocer; (declare) anunciar

announcement [ənáʊnsmənt] N (of an engagement, birth, candidacy) anuncio *m*; (of a conference or competition) convocatoria f

announcer [ənáʊnsɚ] N anunciador -ra *mf*; (on radio) locutor -ora *mf*

annoy [ənɔ́ɪ] VI/VT fastidiar, contrariar

annoyance [ənɔ́ɪəns] N fastidio *m*, contrariedad f

annual [ǽnjuəł] ADJ anual; N (book) anuario *m*; (plant) planta anual f

annuity [ənjúɪDi] N anualidad f, renta anual f

annul [ənʌ́ł] VT anular

annulment [ənʌ́łmənt] N anulación f

anomalous [ənámələs] ADJ anómalo

anomaly [ənáməli] N anomalía f

anonymous [ənánəməs] ADJ anónimo

anorak [ǽnəræk] N anorak *m*

anorexia [ænəréksiə] N anorexia f

anorexic [ænəréksɪk] ADJ anoréxico

another [ənʌ́ðɚ] ADJ otro; — **day** otro día; PRON otro; **I want** — quiero otro; **one** — el uno al otro, los unos a los otros

answer [ǽnsɚ] N (to a question) respuesta f, contestación f; (to a problem) solución f; VI contestar, responder; **to** — **for** ser responsable de/por; VT contestar

answering [ǽnsɚɪŋ] ADJ — **machine** contestador automático *m*; — **service** servicio telefónico contratado *m*, servicio de contestador *m*

ant [ænt] N hormiga f; —**eater** oso hormiguero *m*; —**hill** hormiguero *m*

antacid [æntǽsɪd] N & ADJ antiácido *m*

antagonism [æntǽgənɪzəm] N antagonismo *m*

antagonist [æntǽgənɪst] N antagonista *mf*

antagonize [æntǽgənaɪz] VT antagonizar

antarctic [æntárktɪk] ADJ antártico

Antarctica [æntárktɪkə] N Antártida f

antecedent [æntəsídṇt] ADJ & N antecedente *m*

antelope [ǽntəlop] N antílope *m*

antenna [ænténə] N antena f

anterior [æntíriɚ] ADJ anterior

anthem [ǽnθəm] N himno *m*

anthology [ænθálədʒi] N antología f

anthracite [ǽnθrəsaɪt] N antracita f

anthrax [ǽnθræks] N ántrax *m*

anthropologist [ænθrəpálədʒɪst] N antropólogo -ga *mf*

anthropology [ænθrəpáləʤi] N antropología f
anthropomorphize [ænθrəpəmórfaɪz] VI/VT antropomorfizar
antiabortion [æntiəbórʃən] ADJ antiaborto *inv*
antiaircraft [æntiérkræft] ADJ antiaéreo
antiallergic [æntiəlɟ́-ʤɪk] ADJ antialérgico
antibacterial [æntibæktíriəł] ADJ antibacteriano
antiballistic [æntibəlístɪk] ADJ antibalístico
antibiotic [æntɪbaɪáDɪk] N & ADJ antibiótico *m*
antibody [æntɪbaDi] N anticuerpo *m*
anticancer [æntikǽnsə-] ADJ anticanceroso f
anticipate [æntísəpet] VI/VT (foresee) prever; (jump the gun) anticiparse [a]
anticipation [æntɪsəpéʃən] N previsión f; **with great** — con gran expectación
anticlimactic [æntikləmǽktɪk] ADJ decepcionante
anticoagulant [æntikoǽgjələnt] ADJ & N anticoagulante *m*
anticonvulsant [æntikənváłsənt] ADJ & N anticonvulsivo *m*
antics [æntɪks] N payasadas f pl, monerías f pl, monadas f pl
antidepressant [æntidɪprésənt] ADJ & N antidepresivo *m*
antidiarrheal [æntidaɪəríəł] ADJ & N antidiarreico *m*
antidiuretic [æntidaɪəréDɪk] ADJ & N antidiurético *m*
antidote [ǽntɪdot] N antídoto *m*
antifreeze [ǽntɪfriz] N anticongelante *m*
antigen [ǽntɪʤən] N antígeno *m*
anti-glare [æntiglér] ADJ antirreflejante
Antigua and Barbuda [æntígəəndbɑrbúDə] N Antigua y Barbuda f
Antiguan [æntígən] ADJ & N antiguano -ana *mf*
antihistamine [æntihístəmin] N & ADJ antihistamínico *m*
anti-inflammatory [æntiɪnflǽmətɔri] ADJ & N antiinflamatorio *m*
antilock [ǽntilɑk] ADJ antibloqueo; — **brakes** frenos antibloqueo *mpl*
antimony [ǽntəmoni] N antimonio *m*
antioxidant [æntiáksɪDənt] N antioxidante *m*
antipathy [æntípəθi] N antipatía f
antiperspirant [æntipɟ́-spə-ənt] N antitranspirante *m*
antipsychotic [æntisaɪkáDɪk] ADJ & N antipsicótico *m*
antiquated [ǽntɪkweDɪd] ADJ (custom) anticuado; (word) desusado
antique [æntík] ADJ antiguo; N antigüedad f
antiquity [æntíkwɪDi] N antigüedad f
anti-Semitism [æntisémɪtɪzəm] N antisemitismo *m*
antiseptic [æntɪséptɪk] ADJ & N antiséptico *m*
antisocial [æntisóʃəł] ADJ antisocial
antispasmodic [æntispæzmáDɪk] ADJ & N

antiespasmódico *m*
antithesis [æntíθəsɪs] N antítesis f
antitoxin [æntitáksɪn] N antitoxina f
antitrust [æntitrást] ADJ antimonopolio, antitrust
antiviral [æntiváɪrəł] ADJ & N antiviral *m*
antivirus [æntivaɪrəs] ADJ antivirus
antler [æntlə-] N asta f, cuerno *m*
antonym [æntənɪm] N antónimo *m*
antsy [æntsi] ADJ (impatient) impaciente; (anxious) ansioso
anus [énəs] N ano *m*
anvil [ænvəł] N yunque *m*
anxiety [æŋzáɪɪDi] N ansiedad f, angustia f
anxious [ǽŋkʃəs] ADJ (worried) ansioso, preocupado; (desirous) ansioso, deseoso
any [éni] ADJ & PRON cualquier[a], cualesquier[a], alguno; — **woman** cualquier mujer, una mujer cualquiera; — **houses** unas casas cualesquiera; *lit* cualesquiera casas; **in** — **case** en todo caso; **do you have** — **money?** ¿tienes dinero? **I don't have** — no tengo; **do you like** — **of these?** ¿te gusta alguno de estos?
anybody [énibaDi] PRON alguien, cualquiera; — **could do that** cualquiera podría hacer eso; **is** — **here?** ¿hay alguien aquí? **he does not know** — no conoce a nadie
anyhow [énihaU] ADV de todos modos, en todo caso
anymore [énimór] ADV **he doesn't work** — ya no trabaja, no trabaja más
anyone [éniwan] PRON alguien, cualquiera; — **could do that** cualquiera podría hacer eso; **is** — **here?** ¿hay alguien aquí? **he does not know** — no conoce a nadie
anyplace [éniples] ADV en cualquier parte/lugar; **you can buy it** — se puede comprar en cualquier lugar; **he's not going** — no va a ninguna parte
anything [éniθɪŋ] PRON cualquier cosa, algo; — **is fine** cualquier cosa me viene bien; — **you wish** todo lo que quieras; **do you have** — **for a cough?** ¿tienes algo para la tos? **I don't know** — no sé nada
anytime [énitaɪm] ADV en cualquier momento
anyway [éniwe] ADV de todos modos, de cualquier manera, en todo caso
anywhere [énihwɛr] ADV en cualquier parte / lugar; **you can buy it** — se puede comprar en cualquier lugar; **he's not going** — no va a ninguna parte
aorta [eórDə] N aorta f
apart [əpárt] ADV **they are three miles** — están a tres millas de distancia; **they kept him** — **from the group** lo apartaron del grupo; **each factor viewed** — cada factor visto por separado; **to take** — desarmar, desmontar; **to tear** — despedazar, hacer

pedazos; **to tell** — distinguir

apartment [əpártmənt] N apartamento *m*; *Sp* piso *m*

apathetic [æpəθéDɪk] ADJ apático

apathy [ǽpəθi] N apatía *f*, abulia *f*

ape [ep] N simio *m*; VT remedar

aperture [ǽpəˑtʃəˑ] N abertura *f*; (of a pipe) luz *f*

apex [épɛks] N (of tongue) ápice *m*; (of a mountain) cumbre *f*

aphasia [əféʒə] N afasia *f*

aphrodisiac [æfrədíziæk] N afrodisíaco *m*

apiece [əpís] ADV cada uno

apnea [ǽpniə] N apnea *f*

apocalypse [əpákəlɪps] N apocalipsis *mf*

apogee [ǽpədʒi] N apogeo *m*

apologetic [əpɑlədʒéDɪk] ADJ lleno de disculpas

apologize [əpálədʒaɪz] VI disculparse

apology [əpálədʒi] N (expression of regret) disculpa[s] *f* [*pl*]; (justification) apología *f*

apoplexy [ǽpəplɛksi] N apoplejía *f*

apostle [əpásəl] N apóstol *m*

apostrophe [əpástrəfi] N (punctuation) apóstrofo *m*; (invocation) apóstrofe *m*

app [æp] N (computer software) aplicación *f*

appall [əpál] VT horrorizar

appalling [əpálɪŋ] ADJ horroroso

apparatus [æpəráɛDəs] N (single) aparato *m*; (group) maquinaria *f*

apparel [əpǽrəl] N indumentaria *f*, ropa *f*; (fine) ropaje *m*

apparent [əpǽrənt] ADJ (visible) visible; (clear) obvio, evidente; (seeming) aparente

apparition [æpəríʃən] N aparición *f*, fantasma *m*

appeal [əpíl] N (legal) apelación *f*, recurso *m*; (request) llamamiento *m*, llamado *m*; (attraction) atractivo *m*; VT apelar, recurrir [contra]; VI **to — to** atraer

appear [əpír] VI (show up) aparecer[se]; (seem) parecer, aparentar; (be published) salir; (come before a judge) comparecer

appearance [əpírəns] N (looks) apariencia *f*, traza *f*, estampa *f*; (act of appearing) aparición *f*; (coming before a judge) comparecencia *f*

appease [əpíz] VT aplacar, apaciguar

appeasement [əpízmənt] N aplacamiento *m*, apaciguamiento *m*

appellate [əpélɪt] N — **court** tribunal de apelaciones *m*

append [əpénd] VT adjuntar

appendage [əpéndɪdʒ] N apéndice *m*

appendectomy [æpɪndéktəmi] N apendicectomía *f*

appendicitis [əpɛndəsáɪdɪs] N apendicitis *f*

appendix [əpéndɪks] N apéndice *m*

appetite [ǽpɪtaɪt] N apetito *m*

appetizer [ǽpɪtaɪzəˑ] N aperitivo *m*

appetizing [ǽpɪtaɪzɪŋ] ADJ apetecible, apetitoso

applaud [əplɔ́d] VI/VT aplaudir

applause [əplɔ́z] N aplauso[s] *m* [*pl*]

apple [ǽpəl] N manzana *f*; — **grove** manzanar *m*; — **of my eye** niña de mis ojos *f*; —**sauce** compota de manzana *f*; — **tree** manzano *m*; **Adam's** — nuez de Adán *f*

appliance [əpláɪəns] N aparato *m*; (electric) aparato electrodoméstico *m*, electrodoméstico *m*

applicable [ǽplɪkəbəl] ADJ aplicable

applicant [ǽplɪkənt] N aspirante *mf*, solicitante *mf*

application [æplɪkéʃən] N (act of applying, computer software) aplicación *f*; (form) solicitud *f*, formulario *f*

applicator [ǽplɪkeDəˑ] N aplicador *m*

apply [əpláɪ] VT aplicar; **to — for** solicitar, pedir; **are you —ing for the scholarship?** ¿te presentas para la beca? ¿estás solicitando la beca? **to — oneself** aplicarse, dedicarse

appoint [əpɔ́ɪnt] VT (designate) nombrar, designar; (furnish) amueblar, equipar; **a well —ed house** una casa bien amueblada

appointee [əpɔɪntí] N persona nombrada *f*

appointment [əpɔ́ɪntmənt] N (designation) nombramiento *m*, designación *f*; (engagement) cita *f*; **doctor's** — cita/hora con el médico *f*; —**s** mobiliario *m* *sg*, accesorios *m* *pl*

apportion [əpɔ́rʃən] VT repartir proporcionalmente

apportionment [əpɔ́rʃənmənt] N reparto proporcional *m*

appraisal [əprézəl] N (of a property) tasación *f*, valuación *f*; (of a situation) evaluación *f*

appraise [əpréz] VT (a property) avaluar, valorar, tasar; (a situation) evaluar

appreciable [əpríʃəbəl] ADJ apreciable

appreciate [əpríʃiet] VT (value) apreciar, estimar; (recognize) darse cuenta, percibir; (thank) agradecer; **to — in value** apreciarse

appreciation [əpriʃiéʃən] N (esteem) aprecio *m*; (thanks) agradecimiento *m*; (monetary value) apreciación *f*, alza *f*

apprehend [æprɪhénd] VT (arrest) aprehender; (understand) comprender

apprehension [æprɪhénʃən] N (arrest) aprehensión *f*; (worry) aprensión *f*

apprehensive [æprɪhénsɪv] ADJ aprensivo

apprentice [əpréntɪs] N aprendiz -iza *mf*; VT poner de aprendiz

apprenticeship [əpréntɪsʃɪp] N aprendizaje *m*

apprise [əpráɪz] VT informar

approach [əprótʃ] N (act of approaching) aproximación *f*; (method) enfoque *m*, acercamiento *m*; (means of access) acceso *m*, entrada *f*; — **shot** golpe de aproximación *m*; VI (go nearer) acercarse, aproximarse; (in golf) aprochar; VT (a problem) abordar, enfocar; **to — someone about a problem** plantearle a alguien un problema

approachable [əprótʃəbəɫ] ADJ tratable
approbation [æprəbéʃən] N aprobación f
appropriate[1] [əprópriit] ADJ apropiado, adecuado
appropriate[2] [əprópriet] VT apropiarse; (funds) asignar
appropriation [əpropriéʃən] N (act of seizing) apropiación f; (assignment of funds) asignación f; (assigned funds) partida f
approval [əprúvəɫ] N aprobación f; **on** — a prueba
approve [əprúv] VI/VT aprobar
approximate[1] [əpráksəmɪt] ADJ aproximado
approximate[2] [əpráksəmet] VT aproximarse a
approximately [əpráksəmɪtli] ADV aproximadamente
APR [annual percentage rate] [épiár] N TAE f
apricot [æprɪkɑt] N albaricoque m; Am damasco m; Mex chabacano m
April [éprəɫ] N abril m
apron [éprən] N (for a cook) delantal m; (for a workman) mandil m
apropos [æprəpó] ADV a propósito; ADJ oportuno, pertinente; — **of** a propósito de
apt [æpt] ADJ (prone, able) capaz; (suited) pertinente; **is he — to be at home?** ¿estará en casa?
aptitude [æptɪtud] N aptitud f, capacidad f
aquamarine [ɑkwəmərín] N aguamarina f
aquarium [əkwériəm] N (tank) acuario m, pecera f; (building) acuario m
aquatic [əkwáDɪk] ADJ acuático
aqueduct [ækwɪdʌkt] N acueducto m
Arab [ǽrəb] ADJ & N árabe mf
Arabic [ǽrəbɪk] ADJ árabe, arábigo; N (language) árabe m
arable [ǽrəbəɫ] ADJ cultivable
Aragonese [ærəgəníz] ADJ & N aragonés -esa mf
arbiter [árbɪDəʳ] N árbitro -ra mf
arbitrariness [árbɪtrɛrɪnɪs] N arbitrariedad f
arbitrary [árbɪtrɛri] ADJ arbitrario; — **action** arbitrariedad f
arbitrate [árbɪtret] VI/VT (mediate) arbitrar [en], terciar [en]; (submit to mediation) someter al arbitraje
arbitration [ɑrbɪtréʃən] N arbitraje m
arbitrator [árbɪtreDəʳ] N árbitro -tra mf
arbor [árbəʳ] N pérgola f, glorieta f
arboreal [ɑrbóriəɫ] ADJ arbóreo
arc [ɑrk] N arco m
arcade [ɑrkéd] N (series of arcs) arcada f; (shops) galería f; (video game center) sala de juegos electrónicos f
arcane [ɑrkén] ADJ arcano
arch [ɑrtʃ] N arco m; (curved roof) bóveda f; — **way** arcada f; VI/VT arquear[se]
archaeological [ɑrkiəláʤɪkəɫ] ADJ arqueológico
archaeology, archeology [ɑrkiáləʤi] N

arqueología f
archaic [ɑrkéɪk] ADJ arcaico
archaism [árkeɪzəm] N arcaísmo m
archbishop [ɑrtʃbíʃəp] N arzobispo m
archenemy [ártʃénəmi] N archienemigo -ga mf
archer [ártʃəʳ] N arquero -ra mf
archery [ártʃəri] N tiro al arco m
archetype [árkɪtaɪp] N arquetipo m
archipelago [ɑrkəpéləgo] N archipiélago m
architect [árkɪtɛkt] N arquitecto -ta mf; (creator) artífice mf
architectural [ɑrkɪtéktʃəʳɫ] ADJ arquitectónico
architecture [árkɪtɛktʃəʳ] N arquitectura f
archive [árkaɪv] N archivo m
arctic [árktɪk] ADJ ártico
ardent [árdɪ̩nt] ADJ ardiente
ardor [árDəʳ] N ardor m, fervor m
arduous [árʤuəs] ADJ arduo
are [ɑr] see be
area [ériə] N (space) área f; (region) zona f; (of a geometric figure) superficie f, área f
arena [ərínə] N (for sports) estadio m; (in a circus) pista f
Argentina [ɑrʤəntínə] N Argentina f
Argentinian [ɑrʤəntíniən] ADJ & N argentino -na mf
argon [árgɑn] N argón m
argue [árgju] VT (reason) argüir, argumentar; VI (bicker) discutir, reñir
argument [árgjəmənt] N (reason) argumento m; (altercation) disputa f, discusión f
arid [ǽrɪd] ADJ árido
arise [əráɪz] VI (get up) levantarse; (appear) surgir; (result) provenir, resultar
arisen [ərízən] see arise
aristocracy [ærɪstákrəsi] N aristocracia f
aristocrat [ərístəkræt] N aristócrata mf
aristocratic [ərɪstəkrǽDɪk] ADJ aristocrático
arithmetic[1] [əríθmətɪk] N aritmética f
arithmetic[2] [ærɪθmédɪk] ADJ aritmético
ark [ɑrk] N arca f; **Noah's** — arca de Noé f
arm [ɑrm] N brazo m; —**chair** sillón m, butaca f; —**pit** sobaco m, axila f; —**rest** (in a car) apoyabrazos m sg; (on a sofa) brazo m; — **in** — del brazo; **at** —**'s length** a distancia; —**'s-length transactions** transacciones a precio de mercado f pl; **with open** —**s** con los brazos abiertos; —**s** armas f pl; VT armar; —**ed forces** fuerzas armadas f pl; —**ed robbery** robo a mano armada m
armada [ɑrmáDə] N armada f, flota f
armament [árməmənt] N armamento m
Armenia [ɑrmíniə] N Armenia f
Armenian [ɑrmíniən] ADJ & N armenio -nia mf
armful [ármfuɫ] N brazada f
armistice [ármɪstɪs] N armisticio m
armoire [ɑrmwár] N armario m
armor [árməʳ] N (of a knight) armadura f; (on a vehicle) blindaje m; (on insects) coraza f; VT (a

car) blindar; (a tank) acorazar
armored [ármə-d] ADJ (van) blindado; (tank)
acorazado
armory [ármərɪ] N armería f
army [ármi] N ejército m; (multitude)
muchedumbre f
aroma [ərómə] N aroma m
aromatic [ærəmǽdɪk] ADJ aromático
arose [əróz] see arise
around [əráund] ADV **there were books all** —
había libros por todos lados; **there is a
supermarket** — **here** hay un
supermercado por aquí; **it was the only
farm for miles** — era la única granja en
millas a la redonda; **the tree is forty
centimeters** — el árbol tiene cuarenta
centímetros de circunferencia; **I'll show you**
— te enseño el lugar; **the wheels turned** —
las ruedas giraban; **turn** — date la vuelta;
she finally came — al final la convencimos;
he hasn't been — no ha estado por aquí; —
five o'clock a eso de las cinco; PREP **a
ribbon** — **her wrist** una cinta alrededor de
su muñeca; **tie a string** — **your finger**
átate un hilo al dedo; **stay** — **the house**
quédate cerca de la casa; **we drove** — **the
block** dimos vuelta a la manzana; **he
wandered** — **the park** deambuló por el
parque; **the church** — **the corner** la iglesia
a la vuelta de la esquina; **a town with
mountains** — it un pueblo rodeado de
montañas; **motion** — **its axis** movimiento
en torno a su eje; — **-the-clock** veinticuatro
horas al día; **we walked** — **town** dimos una
vuelta por el pueblo
arouse [əráuz] VI despertar; VT (suspicion)
despertar; (sexual response) excitar
arraign [ərén] VT hacer comparecer ante un juez
arrange [əréndʒ] VT arreglar
arrangement [əréndʒmənt] N (array) arreglo m;
(placement) disposición f; (agreement)
acuerdo m; **to make** —**s [for]** hacer arreglos
[para]
array [əré] N (arrangement) abanico m, selección
f; (placement of troops) orden m, formación f;
(attire) gala f; (in software) vector m; VT
(troops) formar; (attire) ataviar
arrears [ərírz] ADV LOC **in** — atrasado; N atrasos
m pl
arrest [ərést] N arresto m, detención f; VI/VT
arrestar, detener
arrhythmia [əríðmiə] N arritmia f
arrival [əráɪvəł] N llegada f; lit arribo m; **the
new** —**s** los recién llegados
arrive [əráɪv] VI llegar; lit arribar
arrogance [ǽrəgəns] N arrogancia f
arrogant [ǽrəgənt] ADJ arrogante
arrow [ǽro] N flecha f; lit saeta f; —**head** punta
de flecha f

arsenal [ársənļ] N arsenal m
arsenic [ársənɪk] N arsénico m
arson [ársən] N incendio doloso m
art [art] N arte m [sg] f [pl]; (works) obras f pl;
(skill) destreza f; **fine** —**s** bellas artes f pl;
master of —**s** maestría en humanidades f; —
deco art déco m
arterial [artíriəł] ADJ arterial
arteriosclerosis [artiriosklərósɪs] N
arteriosclerosis f
artery [árdərɪ] N arteria f
artful [ártfəł] ADJ (aesthetic) artístico; (deceitful)
artero, astuto
arthritis [arθráɪdɪs] N artritis f
arthroscopic [arθrəskápɪk] ADJ artroscópico
arthroscopy [árθrəskapi] N artroscopia f
artichoke [árdɪtʃok] N alcachofa f
article [árdɪkəł] N artículo m; — **of clothing**
prenda de vestir f
articulate[1] [artíkjəlɪt] ADJ (clear) claro;
(eloquent) elocuente; **he's very** — se expresa
muy bien
articulate[2] [artíkjəlet] VI/VT (pronounce, join)
articular; (express) enunciar
articulation [artɪkjəléʃən] N articulación f
artifact [árdəfækt] N artefacto m, ingenio m
artifice [árdəfɪs] N artificio m
artificial [árdəfíʃəł] ADJ artificial; (affected)
afectado; — **insemination** inseminación
artificial f; — **intelligence** inteligencia
artificial f
artillery [artíləri] N artillería f
artisan [árdɪzən] N artesano -na mf, artífice mf
artist [árdɪst] N (painter, sculptor) artista mf;
(performer) intérprete mf
artistic [artístɪk] ADJ artístico
Aruba [ərúbə] N Aruba f
as [æz] CONJ — **for me** en lo que a mí respecta; —
if como sí; — **is** en la condición en que está;
— **it were** por decirlo así; — **of** a partir de; —
per según; — **the illness worsened** a
medida que empeoraba la enfermedad; — **yet**
hasta ahora, todavía; **the same** — lo mismo
que; **it broke** — **I was using it** se rompió
cuando lo usaba; **she knitted** — **we talked**
tejía mientras conversábamos; **he played** —
never before jugó como nunca; PREP — **a
child, I always felt loved** de niño, siempre
me sentí querido; — **a teacher, I must be
tough** como maestro, tengo que ser estricto;
ADV tan, tanto; — **large** — tan grande como;
— **long** — **you wish** todo el tiempo que
quieras; — **much** — tanto como; — **well**
también; **it's not** — **important** no es tan
importante
ASAP [as soon as possible] [ésæp] ADV lo
antes posible
asbestos [æzbéstəs] N asbesto m, amianto m
ascend [əsénd] VI ascender; —**ing order** orden

ascendente *m*

ascent [əsént] N ascenso *m*

ascertain [æsɚtén] VT averiguar, establecer

ascetic [əsɛ́DIk] ADJ ascético; N asceta *mf*

ascorbic [əskɔ́rbIk] ADJ ascórbico

ascribe [əskráIb] VT atribuir, imputar

aseptic [əsɛ́ptIk] ADJ aséptico

asexual [esékʃuəł] ADJ asexual

ash [æʃ] N (residue, remains) ceniza *f*; (species of tree) fresno *m*; —**tray** cenicero *m*; — **Wednesday** miércoles de ceniza *m*

ashamed [əʃémd] ADJ avergonzado; **to be** — tener vergüenza, avergonzarse

ashen [ǽʃən] ADJ ceniciento

ashore [əʃɔ́r] ADV (movement) a tierra; (location) en tierra; **to go** — desembarcar

Asia [éʒə] N Asia *f*

Asian [éʒən] ADJ & N asiático -ca *mf*

Asiatic [eʒiǽDIk] ADJ — **flu** gripe asiática *f*

aside [əsáId] ADV **all kidding** — bromas aparte; **his father took him** — su padre lo llamó aparte; **he threw his coat** — tiró su saco a un lado; PREP — **from** aparte de, además de; N (theater) aparte *m*

asinine [ǽsənaIn] ADJ necio

ask [æsk] VT (inquire) preguntar; (request) pedir; **to** — **a question** hacer una pregunta; **to** — **about** preguntar por; **to** — **for** pedir; **to** — **for someone** pedir para hablar con alguien; **to** — **a woman's hand in marriage** pedir la mano de una mujer; **to** — **out** invitar a salir; **what's your** —**ing price?** ¿cuánto pides? **you** —**ed for it** te lo has buscado

askance [əskǽns] ADV **to look** — (obliquely) mirar de soslayo/través/reojo; (suspiciously) mirar con recelo

askew [əskjú] ADJ ladeado, torcido

asleep [əslíp] ADJ dormido; **to fall** — dormirse; **my arm is** — se me ha dormido/entumecido el brazo

asparagus [əspǽrəgəs] N espárrago *m*

aspartame [ǽspɚtem] N aspartamo *m*

aspect [ǽspɛkt] N aspecto *m*

aspen [ǽspIn] N álamo temblón *m*

Asperger's disorder [ǽspɚgɚzdIsɔ́rDɚ] N trastorno de Asperger *m*

asphalt [ǽsfɑłt] N asfalto *m*

asphyxia [æsfíksiə] N asfixia *f*

aspiration [æspɚéʃən] N aspiración *f*

aspire [əspáIr] VI aspirar

aspirin [ǽsprIn] N aspirina *f*

ass [æs] N (animal) asno *m*, burro *m*, borrico *m*; (fool) *fam, pej* borrico -ca *mf*, idiota *mf*; (body part) *vulg* culo *m*; —**hole** *vulg* hijo de puta *m*; **to bust one's** — *vulg* romperse el culo

assail [əséł] VT (physically) asaltar, atacar; (verbally) atacar

assailant [əsélənt] N atacante *mf*, agresor -ora *mf*

assassin [əsǽsIn] N asesino -na *mf*

assassinate [əsǽsənet] VT asesinar

assassination [əsæsənéʃən] N asesinato *m*

assault [əsɑ́łt] N asalto *m*, agresión *f*; — **rifle** rifle de asalto *m*; — **and battery** agresión con lesiones *f*; VT asaltar, agredir; (sexually) violar

assay[1] [æsé] VT (situation) examinar, analizar; (metal) ensayar

assay[2] [ǽse] N ensayo *m*

assemble [əsémbəł] VI/VT (call together) reunir[se], congregar[se]; VT (put together) armar, montar

assembly [əsémbli] N (meeting) asamblea *f*, reunión *f*; (putting together) montaje *m*, armado *m*; — **language** lenguaje ensamblador *m*; — **line** cadena de producción *f*, línea de montaje *f*

assent [əsént] N asentimiento *m*; VI asentir

assert [əsɝt] VT (declare) aseverar, afirmar; **to** — **one's rights** hacer valer los derechos de uno; **to** — **oneself** obrar con firmeza

assertion [əsɝ́ʃən] N (declaration) aseveración *f*, afirmación *f*, aserto *m*; **an** — **of ownership** una afirmación de los derechos de propiedad

assess [əsés] VT (evaluate for tax purposes) tasar; (impose tax) gravar, imponer; (measure performance) evaluar

assessment [əsésmənt] N (estimate) avalúo *m*, tasación *f*; (tax) imposición *f*, gravamen *m*; (testing) evaluación *f*

asset [ǽset] N (useful thing) ventaja *f*; (useful quality) virtud *f*; —**s** activo *m*, bienes *m pl*; (on balance sheet) haber *m*, activo *m*; **personal** —**s** bienes muebles *m pl*; **real** —**s** bienes inmuebles *m pl*

assiduous [əsídʒuəs] ADJ (constant) asiduo; (industrious) diligente

assign [əsáIn] VT (allot) asignar; (appoint, designate) designar; (transfer property) ceder

assignment [əsáInmənt] N (act of assigning) asignación *f*; (task) encargo *m*, encomienda *f*; (mission) misión *f*; (transfer of property) cesión [de bienes] *f*; (homework) tarea *f*; (lesson) lección *f*

assimilate [əsíməlet] VI/VT asimilar[se]

assist [əsíst] VI/VT ayudar, asistir; N (in sports) asistencia *f*

assistance [əsístəns] N ayuda *f*, asistencia *f*

assistant [əsístənt] N ayudante *mf*, asistente -ta *mf*; ADJ auxiliar; — **manager** subgerente *mf*

assistantship [əsístəntʃIp] N ayudantía *f*

associate[1] [əsóʃiit] ADJ asociado; N (acquaintance) compañero -ra *mf*; (co-worker) colega *mf*; (employee) empleado -da *mf*

associate[2] [əsóʃiet] VI/VT asociar[se]; **to be** —**d with** asociarse con

association [əsosiéʃən] N asociación *f*

assonance [ǽsənəns] N asonancia f
assorted [əsɔ́rDɪd] ADJ variado, surtido
assortment [əsɔ́rtmənt] N (act of assorting)
clasificación f; (selection of wares) surtido m;
(selection of tools, etc.) colección f
assume [əsúm] VT (responsibility, role) asumir;
(right) arrogarse; (suppose) dar por sentado,
suponer; —**d name** alias m
assumption [əsʌ́mpʃən] N (premise) suposición
f, supuesto m; (unstated belief)
sobreentendido m; (seizure) toma f;
(acceptance of duties) asunción f
assurance [əʃúrəns] N (promise) promesa f,
palabra f; (reassurance) palabras de apoyo f pl;
(certainty) certeza f; (confidence) confianza f
assure [əʃúr] VT (give confidence) asegurar;
(encourage) infundir confianza
assuredly [əʃúrɪdli] ADV seguramente, sin duda
asterisk [ǽstərɪsk] N asterisco m
asteroid [ǽstərɔɪd] N asteroide m
asthma [ǽzmə] N asma m
asthmatic [æzmǽDɪk] ADJ asmático
astigmatism [əstígmətɪzəm] N astigmatismo m
astonish [əstánɪʃ] VT asombrar, pasmar
astonishing [əstánɪʃɪŋ] ADJ asombroso,
pasmoso
astonishment [əstánɪʃmənt] M asombro m,
pasmo m
astound [əstáund] VT pasmar, asombrar
astraddle [əstrǽdl] ADV a horcajadas
astray [əstré] ADV **to go** — perderse, extraviarse;
to lead — (seduce) llevar por mal camino,
seducir; (perplex) confundir
astride [əstráɪd] ADV a horcajadas
astringent [əstrínʤənt] ADJ & N astringente m
astrology [əstráləʤi] N astrología f
astronaut [ǽstrənɔt] M astronauta mf
astronautics [æstrənɔ́Dɪks] N astronáutica f
astronomer [əstránəmə] N astrónomo -ma mf
astronomic [æstrənámɪk] ADJ astronómico
astronomical [æstrənámɪkəl] ADJ astronómico
astronomy [əstránəmi] N astronomía f
astrophysics [æstrofízɪks] N astrofísica f
Asturian [æstúrɪən] ADJ & N asturiano -na mf
Asturias [æstúrɪəs] N Asturias f sg
astute [əstút] ADJ astuto, sagaz
asylum [əsáɪləm] N asilo m
asymmetric, asymmetrical [esɪmétrɪk[əl]]
ADJ; asimétrico
asymptomatic [esɪmptəmǽDɪk] ADJ
asintomático
at [æt] PREP — **the end of the story** al final de
la historia; — **five o'clock** a las cinco; —
high altitude a grandes alturas; — **last** por
fin, al fin; — **once** enseguida; — **the table** a/
en la mesa; — **five dollars a kilo** a cinco
dólares el kilo; — **Easter** en Pascua; — **home**
en casa; — **war** en guerra; **wait** — **the door**
espera en la puerta; **he is** — **peace with**

himself está en paz consigo mismo; **the
children are** — **play** los niños están
jugando; **look** — **that** mira eso; **amazed** —
pasmado por; **he laughed** — **me** se rió de mí
ate [et] *see* eat
atheism [éθiɪzəm] N ateísmo m
atheist [éθiɪst] N ateo -a mf
athlete [ǽθlit] N deportista mf; (track and field)
atleta mf; —**'s foot** pie de atleta m
athletic [æθléDɪk] ADJ deportivo; (concerning
track and field; well-built) atlético
athletics [æθléDɪks] N deporte m; (track and
field) atletismo m
Atlantic [ætlǽntɪk] ADJ atlántico; — **Ocean**
Océano Atlántico m
atlas [ǽtləs] N atlas m
ATM [automatic teller machine] [étiém] N
cajero automático m
atmosphere [ǽtməsfir] N (air) atmósfera f;
(mood) ambiente m
atmospheric [ætməsfírɪk] ADJ atmosférico
atom [ǽDəm] N átomo m; — **bomb** bomba
atómica f
atomic [ətámɪk] ADJ atómico; — **age** era
atómica f; — **energy** energía atómica f; —
number número atómico m; — **weight**
peso atómico m
atomize [ǽDəmaɪz] VT atomizar
atomizer [ǽDəmaɪzə] N atomizador m
atone [ətón] VI **to** — **for** expiar, purgar
atonement [ətónmənt] N expiación f,
purgación f
atop [ətáp] PREP encima de
atrium [étrɪəm] N (of office building, hotel)
vestíbulo m, patio central m; (of church)
atrio m
atrocious [ətróʃəs] ADJ atroz
atrocity [ətrásɪDi] N atrocidad f, barbaridad f
atrophy [ǽtrəfi] N atrofia f; VI/VT atrofiar[se]
attach [ətǽtʃ] VI/VT (pipe, cable) unir[se], juntar;
(paper) sujetar; (wages) retener; (significance)
atribuir; (an electronic file) adjuntar; **to be**
—**ed to someone** estar apegado a alguien
attaché [ætəʃé] N agregado -da mf
attachment [ətǽtʃmənt] N (act of attaching)
unión f; (pipe, cable) conexión f; (of wages)
retención f; (significance) atribución f; (to an
e-mail) adjunto m; (affection) apego m, cariño
m; (accessory) accesorio m
attack [ətǽk] N ataque m, acometida f; VI/VT
atacar, acometer
attain [ətén] VT (rank) alcanzar; (ambition)
lograr m, realizar f; VI (age) llegar a
attainment [əténmənt] N (rank) alcance m;
(ambition) logro m, realización f
attempt [ətémpt] N tentativa f, intento m;
(murder) atentado m; VT tratar [de], intentar
attend [əténd] VT (meeting) asistir a, acudir a; VI
to — **to** (a sick person) atender, cuidar; (a

speaker) prestar atención; **—ing physician** médico -ca tratante *mf*

attendance [əténdəns] N asistencia *f*

attendant [əténdənt] N (at a gas station) encargado -da *mf*; (servant) sirviente -ta *mf*; ADJ concomitante

attention [əténʃən] N atención *f*; (courtesy) atenciones *f pl*; — **deficit disorder** trastorno de déficit de atención *m*; **to pay —** prestar atención; **to pay — to** atender a; **to call —** llamar la atención; INTERJ **—!** ¡firmes!

attentive [əténtɪv] ADJ (focused) atento; (courteous) cortés

attenuate [əténjuet] VT atenuar

attest [ətést] VT (bear witness to) atestiguar; (manifest) demostrar; VI certificar, dar fe, atestar

attic [ǽDɪk] N desván *m*, altillo *m*

attire [ətáɪr] N atavío *m*, vestidura *f*; VT ataviar

attitude [ǽDɪtud] N (mental) actitud *f*; (physical) postura *f*; (insolence) insolencia *f*, descaro *m*

attorney [ətɝ́ni] N abogado -da *mf*, mandatario -ria *mf*; — **General** Ministro -tra de Justicia *mf*

attract [ətrǽkt] VT atraer; **to — attention** llamar la atención

attraction [ətrǽkʃən] N (act, power) atracción *f*; (charm) atractivo *m*; (of customers) captación *f*

attractive [ətrǽktɪv] ADJ atractivo; (beautiful) atractivo, agraciado

attractiveness [ətrǽktɪvnɪs] N atractivo *m*

attribute[1] [ǽtrəbjut] N atributo *m*

attribute[2] [ətríbjut] VT atribuir

attribution [ætrəbjúʃən] N atribución *f*

attrition [ətríʃən] N (wearing out) desgaste *m*; (casualties) bajas *f pl*; **war of —** guerra de agotamiento *f*

atypical [etípɪkəl] ADJ atípico

auburn [ɔ́bɚn] N & ADJ castaño rojizo *m*

auction [ɔ́kʃən] N subasta *f*, remate *m*; — **house** casa de subastas *f*; VI/VT subastar, rematar

auctioneer [ɔkʃənír] N subastador -ra *mf*, rematador -ra *mf*

audacious [ɔdéʃəs] ADJ audaz, atrevido

audacity [ɔdǽsɪDi] N audacia *f*, desfachatez *f*, atrevimiento *m*

audible [ɔ́Dəbəl] ADJ audible; — **feedback** regeneración audible *f*

audience [ɔ́Diəns] N público *m*, auditorio *m*; (TV, radio) audiencia *f*

audio [ɔ́Dio] ADJ de audio; — **book** audiolibro *m*; — **frequency** audiofrecuencia *f*; **—visual** audiovisual; **—visuals** audiovisuales *m pl*; N audio *m*

audiology [ɔDiáləʤi] N audiología *f*

audit [ɔ́Dɪt] VI/VT (class) asistir de oyente; (accounts) auditar; N auditoría *f*; — **cycle** ciclo de auditoría *m*

auditing [ɔ́Dɪtɪŋ] N auditoría *f*

audition [ɔdíʃən] N audición *f*; VI dar una audición [para]

auditor [ɔ́DɪDɚ] N (of accounts) auditor -ora *mf*, contralor -ora *mf*; (of a class) oyente *mf*

auditorium [ɔDɪtɔ́riəm] N auditorio *m*, paraninfo *m*

auditory [ɔ́DɪtɔrI] ADJ auditivo

augment [ɔgmént] VT incrementar, aumentar

August [ɔ́gəst] N agosto *m*

aunt [ænt] N tía *f*

aura [ɔ́rə] N aura *f*

aurora [ərɔ́rə] N aurora *f*; — **borealis** aurora boreal *f*

auspices [ɔ́spɪsɪz] N auspicios *m pl*

auspicious [ɔspíʃəs] ADJ propicio

austere [ɔstír] ADJ austero

austerity [ɔstérɪDi] N austeridad *f*

Australia [ɔstréljə] N Australia *f*

Australian [ɔstréljən] ADJ & N australiano -na *mf*

Austria [ɔ́striə] N Austria *f*

Austrian [ɔ́striən] ADJ & N austríaco -ca *mf*

authentic [əθéntɪk] ADJ auténtico

authenticate [əθéntɪket] VT autenticar

authentication [əθɛntɪkéʃən] N legalización *f*

authenticity [əθɛntísɪDi] N autenticidad *f*

author [ɔ́θɚ] N (professional) escritor -ra *mf*; (creator) autor -ora *mf*

authoritarian [əθɔrɪtériən] ADJ autoritario

authoritative [əθɔ́rɪteDɪv] ADJ (official) autorizado; (dictatorial) autoritario

authority [əθɔ́rɪDi] N autoridad *f*; (permission) autorización *f*; **to have on good —** saber de buena fuente; **it's not within your —** no está dentro de tus facultades

authorization [ɔθɚɪzéʃən] N autorización *f*

authorize [ɔ́θəraɪz] VT autorizar, habilitar

autism [ɔ́tɪzəm] N autismo *m*

autistic [ɔtístɪk] ADJ autista

auto [ɔ́Do] *see* automobile, automatic

autobiography [ɔDobaiágrəfi] N autobiografía *f*

autocrat [ɔ́Dəkræt] N autócrata *mf*

autograph [ɔ́Dəgræf] N autógrafo *m*

autoimmune [ɔDoɪmjún] ADJ autoinmune

automated [ɔ́DəmeDɪd] ADJ automatizado

automatic [ɔDəmǽDɪk] ADJ automático; (response) maquinal; — **backup** (copy) copia de respaldo automático *f*; (process) respaldo automático *m*; — **pilot** piloto automático *m*; — **transmission** transmisión automática *f*

automation [ɔDəméʃən] N automatización *f*

automobile [ɔ́Dəməbił] N automóvil *m*

automotive [ɔDəmóDɪv] ADJ (sport) automovilístico; (industry) automotor, automotriz

autonomic [ɔDənámɪk] ADJ autonómico

autonomous [ɔtánəməs] ADJ autónomo

autonomy [ɔtánəmi] N autonomía *f*

autopilot [ɔ́Dopaɪlət] N piloto automático *m*
autopsy [ɔ́tɑpsi] N autopsia *f*
autumn [ɔ́Dəm] N otoño *m*
autumnal [ɔtʌ́mnəl] ADJ otoñal
auxiliary [ɔgzíləri] ADJ & N auxiliar *mf*
avail [əvél] VI/VT servir; **to — oneself of**
 aprovecharse de; N utilidad *f*; **of no —** de
 ninguna utilidad; **to no —** en vano
availability [əveləbílɪDi] N (of a person, taxicab,
 funds) disponibilidad *f*; (of merchandise)
 existencias *f pl*
available [əvéləbəl] ADJ disponible, asequible
avalanche [ǽvəlæntʃ] N avalancha *f*, alud *m*
avarice [ǽvərɪs] N avaricia *f*
avaricious [ævəríʃəs] ADJ avaro, avariento
avatar [ǽvətɑr] N avatar *m*
avenge [əvéndʒ] VT vengar
avenger [əvéndʒɚ] N vengador -ra *mf*
avenue [ǽvənu] N avenida *f*; (means of access)
 vía *f*
aver [əvɚ́] VT afirmar
average [ǽvrɪdʒ] N promedio *m*; **on —** de
 promedio; ADJ medio, mediano; **just —**
 (person) del montón; (thing) nada del otro
 mundo; VT promediar; **he —s 20 miles an
 hour** hace un promedio de 20 millas por
 hora
averse [əvɚ́s] ADJ reacio; **he's not — to a glass
 of wine** no se opone a una copa de vino
aversion [əvɚ́ʒən] N aversión *f*
avert [əvɚ́t] VT (eyes) desviar, apartar; (danger)
 evitar
aviation [eviéʃən] N aviación *f*
aviator [évieDɚ] N aviador -ra *mf*
avid [ǽvɪd] ADJ ávido
avocado [ævəkáDo] N aguacate *m*; *Am* palta *f*
avocation [ævəkéʃən] N pasatiempo *m*
avoid [əvɔ́ɪd] VI/VT (stay away from) evitar;
 (dodge) esquivar
avow [əváʊ] VT confesar
avowal [əváʊəl] N confesión *f*
avuncular [əvʌ́ŋkjələ] ADJ propio de un tío; **—
 attitude** actitud paternal y amistosa
await [əwét] VT aguardar
awake [əwék] ADJ despierto; VI/VT despertar[se]
awaken [əwékən] VI/VT despertar[se]
award [əwɔ́rd] N premio *m*, galardón *m*;
 (judicial) adjudicación *f*; VT otorgar, adjudicar
aware [əwér] ADJ consciente, enterado; **I'm — of
 that** eso me consta
awareness [əwérnɪs] N conciencia *f*
away [əwé] ADV **far —** lejos; **— from his
 family** lejos de su familia; **she looked —**
 apartó la vista; **she's —** no está; **he's been
 painting — all day** se ha pasado todo el día
 pintando; **right —** ahora mismo, ahorita;
 ten miles — a diez millas de distancia; **to
 give —** regalar; **to go —** irse; **to take —**
 quitar; **to blow —** (destroy) [hacer] volar;

(astonish) dejar atónito
awe [ɔ] N sobrecogimiento *m*; **to be in —**
 sobrecogerse; VT sobrecoger
awesome [ɔ́səm] ADJ (awe-inspiring)
 sobrecogedor; (impressive) fabuloso
awestruck [ɔ́strʌk] ADJ pasmado
awful [ɔ́fəl] ADJ terrible, horroroso; ADV
 espantoso
awhile [əhwáɪl] ADV un rato
awkward [ɔ́kwəd] ADJ (clumsy) torpe,
 desmañado; (embarrassing) embarazoso;
 (unwieldy) incómodo
awl [ɔl] N punzón *m*
awning [ɔ́nɪŋ] N toldo *m*
awoke [əwók] *see* wake
awoken [əwókn̩] *see* wake
awry [ərái] ADJ (clothes) mal puesto; (hat)
 ladeado; **my plans went —** mis planes
 fracasaron rotundamente
ax, axe [æks] N hacha *f*; VT eliminar
axis [ǽksɪs] N eje *m*
axle [ǽksəl] N eje *m*
Azerbaijan [æzəbaɪdʒán] N Azerbaiyán *m*
Azerbaijani, Azerbaijanian [æzəbaɪdʒáni[ən]]
 ADJ & N azerbaijano -na *mf*, azerbaiyano -na
 mf
Aztec [ǽztɛk] ADJ & N azteca *mf*
azure [ǽʒə] ADJ [azul] celeste; N azul celeste *m*

Bb

babble [bǽbəl] N (baby talk) balbuceo *m*;
 (chatter) parloteo *m*; (murmur) murmullo *m*;
 VI (to talk like a baby) balbucear; (to chatter)
 parlotear; (to murmur) murmurar
baboon [bæbún] N babuino *m*
baby [bébi] N bebé *mf*; **who's the — in your
 family?** ¿quién es el menor/benjamín en tu
 familia? **— blue** celeste *m*; **— boomer**
 persona nacida entre 1946 y 1965 *f*; **—
 carriage** cochecito de bebé *m*; **— food**
 comida para bebés *f*; **— girl** nena *f*; **— sister**
 hermanita *f*; **— sitter** niñera *f*; **— talk** habla
 infantil *f*; **— tooth** diente de leche *m*; **to —sit**
 cuidar niños; **she had a —** dio a luz; VT
 mimar
baccalaureate [bækəlɔ́riət] N bachillerato *m*
bachelor [bǽtʃələ] N soltero *m*; **—'s degree**
 licenciatura *f*; **— of Arts** (degree) licenciatura
 en filosofía y letras *f*; (person) licenciado -da
 en filosofía y letras *mf*
bacillus [bəsíləs] N bacilo *m*
back [bæk] N (human body part) espalda *f*;
 (animal body part) lomo *m*; (opposite side)
 dorso *m*; (of chair) respaldo *m*, espaldar *m*;

—**ache** dolor de espalda *m*; —**bone** columna vertebral *f*, espinazo *m*; —**pack** mochila *f*; **behind one's** — a espaldas de uno; **he has no** —**bone** no tiene carácter; **in** — **of** detrás de, tras; **in the** — **of the house** atrás de la casa; **to fall on one's** — caer de espaldas; **to turn one's** — volver las espaldas; ADJ — **charges** cargos atrasados *m pl*; — **door** puerta trasera *f*; — **issues** números atrasados *m pl*; — **order** pedido pendiente *m*; — **taxes** impuestos atrasados *m pl*; **on the** — **burner** en suspenso; —-**and-forth movement** movimiento de vaivén *m*; VT respaldar, apoyar; VI dar marcha atrás; **to** — **down** echarse [para] atrás, recular; **to** — **up** (in a car) dar marcha atrás; (a file) hacer una copia de seguridad de; ADV (look) atrás / para atrás; (fall) de espaldas; **to** — **off** echarse atrás; — **and forth** de aquí para allá; **he ran** — **to the house** volvió corriendo a la casa; **he's** — **from work** está de vuelta del trabajo

backbite [bǽkbaɪt] VI/VT difamar

back date [bǽk det] VT antedatar

backer [bǽkɚ] N (financial) fiador -ra *mf*; (political) partidario -ria *mf*

backfire [bǽkfaɪr] VI (automobile) petardear, hacer detonaciones; (plan) ser contraproducente; N petardeo *m*

backgammon [bǽkgæmən] N backgammon *m*

background [bǽkgraʊnd] N (of a picture) fondo *m*; (experience) antecedentes *m pl*; (software) — **application** aplicación de fondo *f*; — **noise** ruido de fondo *m*; **I have a** — **in computers** tengo conocimientos de informática; **I know what goes on in the** — sé lo que pasa entre bastidores; **a humble** — orígenes humildes *m pl*

backhand [bǽkhænd] N revés *m*

backing [bǽkɪŋ] N (support) respaldo *m*, apoyo *m*; (guarantee) garantía *f*; (fabric) refuerzo *m*

backlash [bǽklæʃ] N reacción violenta *f*

backlighting [bǽklaɪDɪŋ] N retroiluminación *f*

backlit [bǽklɪt] ADJ retroiluminado

backlog [bǽklɑg] N atraso *m*

backpack [bǽklɑg] N mochila *f*; VI viajar con mochila

backseat [bǽksít] N asiento trasero *m*

backslash [bǽkslæʃ] N barra invertida *f*

backslide [bǽkslaɪd] VI volver a las andadas, reincidir

backspace [bǽkspes] N (action) retroceso *m*; (key) tecla de retroceso *f*; VI apretar la tecla de retroceso

backspin [bǽkspɪn] N efecto *m*, cortado *m*

backstage [bǽkstédʒ] ADV entre bastidores

backtrack [bǽktræk] VI retroceder, dar marcha atrás

backup [bǽkʌp] N (support) respaldo *m*; (copy) copia de seguridad *f*

backward [bǽkwɚd] ADV hacia atrás, para atrás; — **search** búsqueda hacia atrás *f*; **to go** — recular; ADJ (underdeveloped) atrasado; (reactionary) retrógrado

backwardness [bǽkwɚdnɪs] N (underdevelopment) atraso *m*; (conservatism) retrogradismo *m*; (timidity) timidez *f*

backyard [bǽkjárd] N patio trasero *m*

bacon [békən] N tocino *m*, Sp beicon *m*

bacteria [bæktíriə] N bacteria[s] *f* [*pl*]

bacterial [bæktíriəł] ADJ bacteriano

bacteriology [bæktiriáłədʒi] N bacteriología *f*

bad [bæd] ADJ malo; (man) perverso; (teeth) feo; (drug) dañoso; (flood) grave; (fruit) podrido; (very good) *vulg* de puta madre; — **blood** enemistad *f*; — **check** cheque sin fondos *m*; — **debt** deuda incobrable *f*; — **faith** mala fe *f*; **to go from** — **to worse** ir de mal en peor; **he has a** — **heart** está enfermo del corazón; **to look** — tener mal aspecto; *fam* quedar mal; ADV mal; **not** — no está nada mal; **too** — ¡qué pena! VT **to** —**mouth** difamar [a]

bade [bed] *see* bid

badge [bædʒ] N insignia *f*, chapa *f*

badger [bǽdʒɚ] N tejón *m*; VT acosar

badly [bǽdli] ADV (do) mal; (want) mucho; (hurt) gravemente

baffle [bǽfəł] VT (confuse) confundir; (frustrate) desconcertar; N deflector *m*

bag [bæg] N bolsa *f*, bolso *m*; (suitcase) maleta *f*; (under eyes) ojera *f*; — **lady** vagabunda *f*; —**pipe** gaita *f*; VT (groceries) empacar, embolsar; (prey) cazar

baggage [bǽgɪdʒ] N (suitcases) equipaje *m*; (impediments) bagaje *m*; — **car** vagón de equipajes *m*; — **check** contraseña de equipajes *f*; — **claim** recogida de equipaje *f*; — **tag** etiqueta *f*; — **inspection** revisión de equipaje *f*

baggy [bǽgi] ADJ flojo, holgado

Bahamas [bəháməz] N Bahamas *f pl*

Bahamian [bəhémiən] ADJ & N bahameño -ña *mf*

Bahrain [barén] N Bahréin *m*

Bahraini [baréni] ADJ & N bahreiní *mf*

bail [beł] N fianza *f*; —**out** rescate financiero *m*; **to let out on** — poner en libertad bajo fianza; VT pagar la fianza; **to** — **someone out** pagarle la fianza a alguien; **to** — **someone out of a predicament** sacar a alguien de un apuro; **to** — **out water** achicar, vaciar; VI **to** — **out** (of a plane) tirarse con paracaídas de un avión; (of a situation) abandonar

bailiff [bélɪf] N ujier *mf*

bait [bet] N cebo *m*; VT (prepare hook) cebar; (attract customers) seducir; (harass) acosar; — **and switch advertising** publicidad de cebo y anzuelo *f*

bake [bek] VI/VT (in an oven) hornear; (in the sun) calcinar, abrasar; **I'm baking in this heat** me estoy asando, me muero de calor
baker [békɚ] N panadero -ra *mf*; **—'s dozen** la docena del fraile *f*
bakery [békəri] N panadería *f*
baking [békɪŋ] N (act of baking) horneado *m*; (activity) repostería *f*; — **powder** polvo de hornear *m*; — **soda** bicarbonato de sodio *m*
balance [bǽləns] N (instrument) balanza *f*; (equilibrium) equilibrio *m*; (debit, credit) saldo *m*, balance *m*; — **due** saldo pendiente *m*; — **sheet** balance *m*; — **of payments** balanza de pagos *f*; — **of trade** balanza comercial *f*; **to lose one's** — perder el equilibrio; VT equilibrar, hacer equilibrio con; **to** — **the risks with the benefits** sopesar los riesgos y los beneficios; VI (accounts) cuadrar; **—ed budget** presupuesto equilibrado *m*; **to** — **a budget** equilibrar un presupuesto
balanced [bǽlənst] ADJ equilibrado
balancing [bǽlənsɪŋ] N equilibrado *m*
balcony [bǽɫkəni] N balcón *m*; (in a theater) palco *m*, entresuelo *m*
bald [bɔɫd] ADJ (person) calvo, pelón; (mountain) pelón; (tire) liso; — **eagle** águila americana de cabeza blanca *f*; **—headed** calvo; — **spot** calva *f*; **he went** — se quedó calvo
baldness [bɔ́ɫdnɪs] N calvicie *f*
bale [beɫ] N paca *f*, fardo *m*; VT empacar, enfardar
balk [bɔk] VI oponerse, rehusarse a
ball [bɔɫ] N (tennis, baseball, golf) pelota *f*, bola *f*; (baseball, opposite of strike) bola *f*; (basketball, football, soccer) balón *m*; (billiards) bola *f*; (of string, thread) ovillo *m*; (cannon) bala [de cañón] *f*; (dance) baile *m*; — **and chain** grillete *m*; — **bearing** cojinete de bolas *m*; — **game** juego de pelota *m*; (baseball) partido de béisbol *m*; **—park estimate** cifra aproximada *f*; **—s** (testicles) *vulg* pelotas *f pl*, *vulg* huevos *m pl*; *Sp vulg* cojones *m pl*; VT (string) ovillar; (have sex with) *Sp vulg* follar; *Am vulg* coger, culear
ballad [bǽləd] N balada *f*; (historical) romance *m*
ballast [bǽləst] N lastre *m*; (railroad) balasto *m*; VT lastrar
ballerina [bælərínə] N bailarina de ballet *f*
ballet [bælé] N ballet *m*
ballistic [bəlístɪk] ADJ balístico; — **missile** misil balístico *m*; N **—s** balística *f*
balloon [bəlún] N globo *m*; — **mortgage** hipoteca con pago final mayor *f*; VI (travel in a balloon) pasear en globo; VI/VT (grow) inflar[se]
ballot [bǽlət] N (system of voting) votación *f*; (paper) papeleta *f*; *Mex* boleta *f*; — **box** urna *f*
balm [bɑm] N bálsamo *m*
balmy [bámi] ADJ templado

baloney [bəlóni] N pamplinas *f pl*, paparruchas *f pl*
balsa [bɔ́ɫsə] N (wood) madera balsa *f*; (raft) balsa *f*
balsam [bɔ́ɫsəm] N (resin) bálsamo *m*; (tree) especie de abeto *m*
bamboo [bæmbú] N bambú *m*
ban [bæn] N prohibición *f*; (church) excomunión *f*; VT prohibir
banal [bénl] ADJ banal
banana [bənǽnə] N plátano *m*, banana *f*; — **grove** platanar *m*; — **split** banana split *m*; — **tree** plátano *m*, banano *m*
band [bænd] N (group) banda *f*, pandilla *f*; (group of musicians) banda *f*, conjunto *m*; (cloth) banda *f*; (ribbon) cinta *f*; (leather) tira *f*; **to join the —wagon** subirse al carro/tren; **—width** amplitud de banda *f*; VI/VT **to — together** unirse, juntarse
bandage [bǽndɪdʒ] N venda *f*, vendaje *m*; VT vendar
Band-aid® [bǽnded] N Curita® *f*, parche *m*
bandit [bǽndɪt] N bandido -da *mf*, bandolero -ra *mf*, salteador -ora *mf*
bang [bæŋ] N (blow) golpe *m*, golpazo *m*; (sound) estampido *m*, estallido *m*; **—s** fleco *m*, flequillo *m*; **I get a — out of seeing my grandkids** me emociona ver a mis nietos; VI/VT (hit) golpear; (make noise) hacer estrépito; (screw) *Sp vulg* follar; *Am vulg* coger, culear
Bangladesh [bæŋglədéʃ] N Bangladesh *m*
Bangladeshi [bæŋglədéʃi] ADJ & N bangladeshí *mf*, bangladesí *mf*, bengalés -esa
banish [bǽnɪʃ] VT desterrar
banishment [bǽnɪʃmənt] N destierro *m*, proscripción *f*
banister [bǽnɪstɚ] N barandal *m*, pasamano[s] *m*, balaustrada *f*
banjo [bǽndʒo] N banjo *m*
bank [bæŋk] N (financial institution) banco *m*; (in gambling) banca *f*; (of a body of water) orilla *f*, ribera *f*, margen *m*; (slope) escarpa *f*; — **card** tarjeta bancaria *f*; — **account** cuenta bancaria *f*; — **check** cheque de caja *m*; — **failure** quiebra bancaria *f*; **—note** billete *m*; — **statement** estado de cuenta *m*; — **vault** cámara *f*; ADJ bancario, de banco; VT (money) depositar en un banco; VI (snow, sand) amontonar; (airplane) ladear; **to — on** contar con; **to —roll** financiar
banker [bǽŋkɚ] N (bank owner) banquero -ra *mf*; (bank employee) bancario -ria *mf*
banking [bǽŋkɪŋ] N (activity) actividad bancaria *f*; (industry) banca *f*; ADJ bancario, de banco
bankrupt [bǽŋkrʌpt] ADJ en bancarrota, en quiebra; VT arruinar, quebrar
bankruptcy [bǽŋkrʌptsi] N bancarrota *f*, quiebra *f*; — **law** estatuto de quiebras *m*; —

proceedings juicio por quiebra *m*; **to go into** — declararse en quiebra

banner [bǽnə-] N estandarte *m*, pendón *m*; ADJ sobresaliente

banquet [bǽŋkwɪt] N banquete *m*, gala *f*

baptism [bǽptɪzəm] N (sacrament) bautismo *m*; (action) bautizo *m*

baptize [bǽptaɪz] VT bautizar

bar [bɑr] N (of iron, sand, soap, of a tavern) barra *f*; (of chocolate) barra *f*, tableta *f*; (vertical rod) barrote *m*; (obstacle) barrera *f*, obstáculo *m*; (in music) compás *m*; (saloon) bar *m*; —**bell** barra para pesas *f*; —**code** código de barras *m*; —**code reader** lector de código de barras *m*; — **graph** gráfica de barras *f*; —**keeper/tender** tabernero -ra *mf*, cantinero -ra *mf*; —**room** bar *m*; —**room brawl** pelea de borrachos *f*; **behind** —**s** tras las rejas; **to be admitted to the** — recibirse de abogado; VT (door, exit) atrancar; (access) impedir; (from membership) excluir; — **none** sin excepción; —**ring a disaster** salvo en caso de desastre

barb [bɑrb] N púa *f*; —**ed wire** alambre de púas *m*; *Sp* alambre de espino *m*

Barbadian [bɑrbéɪdiən] ADJ & N barbadense *mf*

Barbados [bɑrbéɪdos] N Barbados *m*

barbarian [bɑrbériən] ADJ & N bárbaro -ra *mf*

barbaric [bɑrbǽrɪk] ADJ bárbaro

barbarous [bɑ́rbə-əs] ADJ bárbaro

barbecue [bɑ́rbɪkju] N (meat dish) barbacoa *f*, asado *m*, parrillada *f*; — **sauce** adobo de barbacoa *m*; VI/VT asar con adobo

barber [bɑ́rbə-] N peluquero *m*, barbero *m*; —**shop** peluquería *f*, barbería *f*

barbiturate [bɑrbítʃə-ɪt] N barbitúrico *m*

bard [bɑrd] N bardo *m*

bare [bɛr] ADJ (legs, walls) desnudo; (pantry) vacío; —**back** a pelo; —-**bones** básico; —**faced** descarado; —**foot** descalzo; **the** — **necessities** lo imprescindible; —**headed** con la cabeza descubierta; —**legged** con las piernas desnudas; — **majority** escasa mayoría *f*; **to lay** — poner al descubierto; **with his** — **hands** con las propias manos

barely [bérli] ADV apenas

bargain [bɑ́rgɪn] N (agreement) trato *m*; (inexpensive purchase) ganga *f*, ocasión *f*; — **basement** sección de ofertas *f*; **into the** — por añadidura; **to strike a** — cerrar un trato; VI (haggle) regatear; (expect) contar con

bargaining [bɑ́rgənɪŋ] N (haggling) regateo *m*; (negotiation) negociación *f*; —**ing position** posición de negociación *f*

barge [bɑrdʒ] N barcaza *f*; VI **to** — **into a room** irrumpir en un cuarto

baritone [bǽrɪton] N & ADJ barítono *m*

barium [bériəm] N bario *m*

bark [bɑrk] N (of a dog) ladrido *m*; (on a tree)

corteza *f*; VI/VT ladrar

harley [bɑ́rli] N cebada *f*

barn [bɑrn] N (for animals) establo *m*; (for grain) granero *m*; — **owl** lechuza *f*; —**yard** corral *m*

barnacle [bɑ́rnəkəł] N percebe *m*

barometer [bərɑ́mɪDə-] N barómetro *m*

baron [bǽrən] N barón *m*

baroque [bərók] ADJ & N barroco *m*

barracks [bǽrəks] N cuartel *m*

barracuda [bærəkúDə] N barracuda *f*

barrage [bərɑ́ʒ] N (of artillery fire) barrera de fuego *f*; (of questions) lluvia *f*, aluvión *m*

barrel [bǽrəł] N barril *m*, tonel *m*; (gun) cañón *m*, caño *m*; **he's a** — **of laughs** es un payaso; **he is scraping the bottom of the** — está desesperado; VI **to** — **along** ir disparado

barren [bǽrən] ADJ (land) árido, yermo; (female) estéril

barrette [bərét] N broche *m*

barricade [bærɪkéd] N barricada *f*; VT cerrar con barricadas; VI atrincherarse

barrier [bǽriə-] N barrera *f*; — **reef** barrera de coral *f*

barrio [bário] N barrio hispano *m*

barter [bɑ́rDə-] VI hacer trueque; VT trocar; N trueque *m*

bartering [bɑ́rDə-ɪŋ] N trueque *m*

basal cell carcinoma [bésəłsɛłkɑrsɪnómə] N carcinoma de célula basal *m*

basalt [bésɔłt] N basalto *m*

base [bes] N base *f*; —**ball** béisbol *m*; —**ball player** beisbolista *m*, pelotero -ra *mf*; —**board** zócalo *m*; ADJ bajo, vil; (metal) de baja ley; — **font** tipo de letra por omisión *m*; —**line** línea de fondo *f*; — **on balls** base por bolas *f*; — **pay** salario base *m*; —**s loaded** bases llenas *f pl*; — **steal** robo de base *m*; VI/VT basar, fundamentar; **to be** —**d on** fundamentarse en; **the general is** —**d in Berlin** el general está estacionado en Berlín

baseless [béslɪs] ADJ sin fundamento

basement [bésmənt] N sótano *m*

baseness [bésnɪs] N bajeza *f*, vileza *f*

bash [bǽʃ] VT golpear; N (party) fiesta *f*

bashful [bǽʃfəł] ADJ tímido, vergonzoso

bashfulness [bǽʃfəłnɪs] N timidez *f*

basic [bésɪk] ADJ básico

basin [bésɪn] N (bowl) palangana *f*, jofaina *f*; (of a fountain) pilón *m*; (geographical formation) cuenca *f*; (pond) estanque *m*

basis [bésɪs] N fundamento *m*, base *f*; **on the** — **of** en base a, con base en; **on a regular** — regularmente

bask [bǽsk] VI (in the sun) asolearse; (in praise) deleitarse

basket [bǽskɪt] N canasta *f*, cesta *f*, cesto *m*; (in basketball) canasta *f*; —**ball** (game) baloncesto *m*, básquetbol *m*, básquet *m*; (ball) balón de baloncesto *m*; — **case** (crazy person)

chiflado -da *mf*; (helpless person) caso
perdido *m*; **to make a —** (in basketball)
encestar
basketful [bǽskɪtfʌł] N (contents of a basket)
canasto *m*; (large amount) montón *m*
basketry [bǽskɪtri] N cestería *f*
Basque [bæsk] ADJ & N (person) vasco -ca *mf*;
(language) vascuence *m*, vasco *m*, euskera *m*
bass[1] [bes] N (voice, bass guitar) bajo *m*; (double
bass) contrabajo *m*; — **clef** clave de fa *f*; —
drum bombo *m*; — **horn** tuba *f*
bass[2] [bæs] (marine fish) lubina *f*; (freshwater
fish) perca *f*
bassist [bésɪst] N bajista *mf*
bassoon [bæsún] N fagot *m*
bastard [bǽstə˞d] N & ADJ (illegitimate) bastardo
-da *mf*; N (mean person) *offensive* hijo de puta
m, cabrón *m*
baste [best] VT (fabric) hilvanar; (meat) rociar
bat [bæt] N (baseball, cricket) bate *m*; (animal)
murciélago *m*; VT golpear; **he is at —** está al
bate; **it was his first at-** — fue su primer
turno; VI (baseball) batear; **not to — an eye**
no pestañear
batch [bætʃ] N (of cookies) hornada *f*; (of cement,
files) tanda *f*; (of data) colección *f*
bath [bæθ] N baño *m*; —**robe** bata [de baño] *f*; *Sp*
albornoz *m*; —**room** (in a house) baño *m*,
cuarto de baño *m*; (public) *Sp* aseo *m*; *Am*
servicio *m*, baño *m*; —**tub** bañera *f*
bathe [beð] VI/VT bañar[se]; **bathing suit** traje
de baño *m*
bather [béðə˞] N bañista *mf*
baton [bətán] N batuta *f*
battalion [bətǽljən] N batallón *m*
batter [bǽɾə˞] N (in baking) pasta *f*, masa *f*; (in
baseball) bateador -ora *mf*; —**'s box** caja de
bateo *f*; VT golpear
battery [bǽɾəri] N (of car, artillery, in baseball)
batería *f*; (of electronic devices) pila *f*; (of
tests) serie *f*; (assault) asalto *m*
batting [bǽɾɪŋ] N bateo *m*; — **average**
porcentaje de bateo *m*
battle [bǽɾl] N batalla *f*; —**-ax[e]** (weapon)
hacha de guerra *f*; (woman) *pej* sargenta *f*; —
cry grito de guerra *m*; —**field** campo de
batalla *m*; —**ship** acorazado *m*; VI batallar; **to
— cancer** luchar contra el cáncer
bawl [bɔł] VI berrear; **to — somebody out**
echarle la bronca a uno
bay [be] N (body of water) bahía *f*; (howl) aullido
m; — **leaf** hoja de laurel *f*; — **window**
ventana saliente *f*; **to hold at —** tener a raya;
ADJ bayo; VI aullar
bayonet [beənét] N bayoneta *f*
bazaar [bəzár] N (market place) bazar *m*;
(benefit) kermés *f*
bazooka [bəzúka] N bazuca *f*
be [bi] VI ser, estar; **I am from Uruguay** soy de

Uruguay; **there were four of us** éramos
cuatro; **he is a doctor** es médico; **it's her** es
ella; **sugar is sweet** el azúcar es dulce;
London is in England Londres está en
Inglaterra; **this water is cold** esta agua está
fría; **the windows were open** las ventanas
estaban abiertas; **there is a problem** hay un
problema; **to — cold/warm/hungry/
right / in a hurry** tener frío/calor/hambre/
razón/prisa; **to be cold/hot/windy** hacer
frío/calor/viento
beach [bitʃ] N playa *f*; —**comber** vagabundo -da
mf; —**head** cabeza de playa *f*; VT varar,
encallar
beacon [bíkən] N faro *m*
bead [bid] N (of glass) cuenta *f*; (of sweat) gota *f*,
perla *f*; **to get a — on somebody** apuntarle
a alguien; VT (string) enhebrar/ensartar
cuentas; (decorate) adornar con cuentas
beagle [bígəl] N beagle *m*
beak [bik] N pico *m*
beaker [bíkə˞] N vaso de precipitados *m*
beam [bim] N (of light) rayo *m*, haz *m*; (of a
building) viga *f*; (of a ship) manga *f*; (of a
scale) brazo *m*; **broad in the —** ancho de
caderas; VI/VT (light, radio) emitir; (smile)
estar radiante
bean [bin] N judía *f*, habichuela *f*; *Sp* alubia *f*; *Am*
frijol *m*, *Am* poroto *m*; **Lima —** haba *f*;
—**stalk** tallo de habas / frijol *m*; **Jack and
the —stalk** Juanito y las habichuelas; **I
don't know —s about that** no sé ni papa /
ni jota de eso
bear [ber] N oso *m*; — **hug** abrazo fuerte *m*; —
market mercado bajista *m*; VT (hold up,
tolerate) soportar, aguantar; (suffer)
sobrellevar; (have a child) dar a luz; (produce
young) parir; (produce fruit) producir; **to —
down** (mash) apretar; (push) pujar; **to — a
grudge** guardar rencor; **to — in mind** tener
en cuenta; **to — oneself with dignity**
portarse con dignidad; **to — out** confirmar;
to — testimony dar testimonio; **to —
interest** devengar interés; **to — gifts** traer
regalos; **to — a resemblance** parecerse; **to
— the cost of something** asumir el costo
de algo; **it doesn't — repeating** no merece
repetirse
bearable [bérəbəl] ADJ llevadero, soportable
beard [bird] N (on a man) barba *f*; (of wheat)
aristas *f pl*
bearded [bírdɪd] ADJ barbado, barbudo
bearer [bérə˞] N portador -ora *mf*
bearing [bérɪŋ] N porte *m*; **to lose one's —s**
perder el rumbo, desorientarse; **it has no —
on our situation** no tiene relación con
nuestra situación
bearish [bérɪʃ] ADJ (of bears) osuno; (of stock
market) bajista

beast [bist] N bestia f

beat [bit] VT (wings, eggs) batir; (a person) golpear; (a drum) tocar; (an opponent) vencer; (tempo) marcar; VI (heart) latir; (drum) sonar; **to — around the bush** andarse por las ramas; **to — off** (repulse) rechazar; (masturbate) vulg hacerse una paja; **to — up** dar una paliza; **—s me!** ¡ni idea! N (blow) golpe m; (drum) toque m; (heart) latido m; (tempo) compás m; (policeman's territory) ronda f; ADJ cansado

beaten [bítn̩] ADJ (mixed) batido; (defeated) vencido; **— path** camino trillado m

beaten [bítn̩] see beat

beater [bíDɚ] N batidor m

beating [bíDɪŋ] N (whipping) paliza f; (pulsation) latido m

beau [bo] N pretendiente m

beautiful [bjúDəfəł] ADJ hermoso; **— people** jet set m

beautify [bjúDəfaɪ] VT embellecer, hermosear

beauty [bjúDi] N belleza f, hermosura f; (woman) beldad f; **— contest/pageant** concurso/ certamen de belleza m; **— parlor** salón de belleza m

beaver [bívɚ] N (animal) castor m; (vagina) vulg chichi m, conejo m

became [bikém] see become

because [bɪkɔ́z] CONJ porque; **— of** por, a causa de, debido a

beckon [békən] VT llamar por señas

become [bɪkÁm] VT (turn into) convertirse en; **the water became ice** el agua se convirtió en hielo; **he became a doctor** llegó a ser médico; (suit) sentar bien; **that suit —s you** ese traje te luce bien; VI (change emotional or physical condition) ponerse; **she became ill** se puso enferma; (undergo a drastic change) volverse; **he became crazy** se volvió loco; **to — angry** enojarse; **to — frightened** asustarse; **to — old** envejecer; **what has — of him?** ¿qué ha sido de él?

becoming [bɪkÁmɪŋ] ADJ (appropriate) propio; **that dress is — to you** te sienta bien ese vestido

bed [bɛd] N (furniture) cama f; lit lecho m; (of a river) cauce m; (of the sea) fondo m; (in a garden) cuadro m; **—bug** chinche mf; **—clothes** ropa de cama f; **—pan** cuña f, chata f; **—ridden** postrado en cama; **—rest** reposo m; **—rock** lecho de roca m; **—room** alcoba f, dormitorio m; Mex recámara f; **at the —side** al lado de la cama; **—side table** mesita de noche f; **—side manner** manera de tratar a los pacientes f; **—sore** llaga f; **—spread** colcha f; **—spring** resorte del colchón m; **—time** hora de dormir f; **—wetting** enuresis nocturna f; **to go to —** acostarse; **to put to —** acostar

bedding [bɛ́Dɪŋ] N ropa de cama f

bee [bi] N (insect) abeja f; (social gathering) tertulia f; **to have a — in one's bonnet** tener una idea metida en la cabeza; **—hive** colmena f; **— sting** picadura de abeja f

beech [bitʃ] N haya f; **—nut** hayuco m

beef [bif] N (meat) carne de vaca/res f; (complaint) queja f; **— jerky** cecina f; **—steak** bistec m; VI quejarse; **to — up** reforzar

been [bɪn] see be

beep [bip] N pitazo m; VI/VT (alarm) sonar; (horn) tocar

beeper [bípɚ] N buscapersonas m sg

beer [bir] N cerveza f

beet [bit] N remolacha f

beetle [bídl̩] N escarabajo m

befall [bɪfɔ́ł] VT acontecerle a

befallen [bɪfɔ́lən] see befall

befell [bɪfɛ́ł] see befall

befit [bɪfít] VT convenir

before [bɪfɔ́r] ADV (temporal) antes, con anterioridad; (spatial) delante; PREP (temporal) antes de; (spatial) delante de; lit ante; CONJ antes [de] que, antes de; **— beginning** antes de que comiences, antes de comenzar; **—-tax earnings** ganancias pre-impositivas f pl

beforehand [bɪfɔ́rhænd] ADV de antemano, con anterioridad

befriend [bɪfrénd] VT hacerse amigo de

beg [bɛg] VI (ask for alms) mendigar, pedir limosna; VI/VT (implore) rogar; **to — for mercy** pedir misericordia; **she —ged me to do it** me rogó que lo hiciera; **to — the question** dar por sentado lo mismo que se arguye

began [bɪgǽn] see begin

begat [bɪgǽt] see beget

beget [bɪgét] VT engendrar

beggar [bégɚ] N mendigo -ga mf

begin [bɪgín] VI/VT comenzar, empezar; **the ten dollars won't — to cover the expense** los diez dólares ni siquiera cubren los gastos

beginner [bɪgínɚ] N principiante mf

beginning [bɪgínɪŋ] N principio m; (temporal only) comienzo m; **— with** comenzando con/ por; **at the —** al/por el principio

begotten [bɪgátn̩] see beget

begrudge [bɪgrÁdʒ] VT aceptar de mala gana

begun [bɪgÁn] see begin

behalf [bɪhǽf] PREP LOC **on — of** (in place of) por, en nombre de, de parte de; (in favor of) a favor de

behave [bɪhév] VI portarse, comportarse; **— yourself!** ¡pórtate bien!

behavior [bɪhévjɚ] N comportamiento m, conducta f

behavioral [bɪhévjərəł] ADJ conductual, relativo

a la conducta / al comportamiento
behead [bɪhéd] VT decapitar, descabezar
beheld [bɪhéłd] *see* behold
behind [bɪháɪnd] ADV detrás; (in payments, schedule) atrasado; **he fell — his competitors** quedó a la zaga de sus competidores; **an hour —** una hora de retraso; **from —** desde atrás; **to fall —** atrasarse; **to leave something —** dejar atrás algo; PREP detrás de, tras; **we're all — you** todos te apoyamos; **who's — this evil plot?** ¿quién está detrás de este plan macabro? — **one's back** a espaldas de uno; N trasero *m*
behold [bɪhółd] VT contemplar; — **the future king!** ¡he aquí el futuro rey!
behoove [bɪhúv] VI **it behooves [one]** le corresponde [a uno]
beige [beʒ] ADJ & N beige *m*
being [bíɪŋ] N ser *m*; **for the time —** por ahora
Belarus [belərús] N Bielorrusia *f*
belated [bɪléɒɪd] ADJ atrasado, tardío
belch [bɛłtʃ] VI eructar, repetir; N eructo *m*
belfry [bɛ́łfri] N campanario *m*
Belgian [bɛ́łdʒən] ADJ & N belga *mf*
Belgium [bɛ́łdʒəm] N Bélgica *f*
belief [bɪlíf] N creencia *f*; (strong opinion) convicción *f*
believable [bɪlívəbəł] ADJ creíble
believe [bɪlív] VI/VT creer
believer [bɪlívɚ] N creyente *mf*; (proponent) partidario -ria *mf*
belittle [bɪlídl] VT (a person) menospreciar, disminuir; (a situation) minimizar
belittling [bɪlídlɪŋ] N menosprecio *m*, disminución *f*
Belize [bəlíz] N Belice *m*
Belizean [bəlíziən] ADJ & N beliceño -ña *mf*
bell [bɛł] N campana *f*; (small) campanilla *f*; **—boy/hop** botones *m sg*; **— curve** curva de campana *f*; **—flower** campanilla *f*, campánula *f*; **— jar** campana de cristal *f*; **— pepper** pimiento *m*, morrón *m*; **— tower** campanario *m*; **with all the —s and whistles** con todos los accesorios
bellicose [bɛ́lɪkos] ADJ belicoso
belligerent [bəlídʒɚənt] ADJ & N beligerante *mf*
bellow [bɛ́lo] VI/VT bramar, berrear; N bramido *m*; **—s** fuelle *m*
belly [bɛ́li] N barriga *f*, vientre *m*, panza *f*; **—ache** dolor de barriga *m*; **— button** ombligo *m*; **— dance** danza del vientre *f*; **— laugh** carcajada *f*
belong [bɪlɔ́ŋ] VI (ownership) pertenecer; **this car —s to me** este coche me pertenece; (correspondence) corresponder; **this key —s to this door** esta llave corresponde a esta puerta; (placement) ir; **this —s on the shelf** esto va en el estante
belongings [bɪlɔ́ŋɪŋz] N pertenencias *f pl*

beloved [bɪlávɪd] ADJ querido; N amado -da *mf*
below [bɪló] ADV abajo; **five — [zero]** cinco bajo cero; PREP bajo, debajo de, abajo de
belt [bɛłt] N (for the waist) cinturón *m*, cinto *m*; (for a machine) correa *f*; (region) zona *f*; — **line** cintura *f*; VT pegar; **to — out a song** cantar una canción a voz en cuello
bemoan [bɪmón] VT lamentarse de, quejarse de
bench [bɛntʃ] N banco *m*; (without a back) banqueta *f*; (in sports) banco *m*, banquillo *m*; (in court) estrado *m*; **—mark** (upper limit) cota *f*; (parameter) punto de referencia *m*; — **price** precio de referencia *m*; **opinion of the —** opinión del tribunal *f*
bend [bɛnd] VI/VT (make curved) doblar[se]; (force) someter; **to — over** inclinarse; **to — over backward** desvivirse; **to — the rules** hacer una excepción; N (road) curva *f*, recodo *m*; **—s** enfermedad de los buzos *f*
bending [bɛ́ndɪŋ] N doblado *m*
beneath [bɪníθ] ADV abajo; PREP debajo de, bajo; (in rank) inferior a; — **contempt** totalmente despreciable; **that's — me** no es digno de mí
benediction [bɛnɪdíkʃən] N bendición *f*
benefactor [bɛ́nəfæktɚ] N benefactor -ora *mf*; *lit* bienhechor -ora *mf*
beneficent [bənéfɪsənt] ADJ benéfico
beneficial [bɛnəfíʃəł] ADJ beneficioso
beneficiary [bɛnəfíʃiɛri] N beneficiario -ria *mf*
benefit [bɛ́nəfɪt] N beneficio *m*, provecho *m*; — **performance** función de beneficencia *f*; VI/VT beneficiar[se], sacar provecho
benevolence [bənévələns] N benevolencia *f*
benevolent [bənévələnt] ADJ benévolo
benign [bɪnáɪn] ADJ benigno
Benin [benín] N Benín *m*
Beninese [beniníz] ADJ & N beninés -esa *mf*
bent [bɛnt] N inclinación *f*; **to be — on** estar resuelto a
bent [bɛnt] *see* bend
benzine [bénzin] N bencina *f*
bequeath [bɪkwíð] VT legar, heredar
bequest [bɪkwést] N legado *m*
berate [bɪrét] VT reprender
bereaved [bɪrívd] ADJ de luto
beret [bəré] N boina *f*
berry [bɛ́ri] N baya *f*
berserk [bɚrzɚ́k] ADJ fuera de sí; **he went —** se puso hecho una fiera, se enfureció
berth [bɚθ] N litera *f*; **to give a wide — to** mantener una distancia prudencial de
beseech [bɪsítʃ] VT suplicar, rogar
beset [bɪsét] VT (attack) acosar; (surround) rodear
beside [bɪsáɪd] PREP al lado de; **sit down — me** siéntate a mi lado; **to be — oneself** estar fuera de sí; **that is — the point** eso no viene al caso; ADV al lado
besides [bɪsáɪdz] ADV además; **they have a**

table but not much — tienen una mesa pero poca cosa más; PREP además de, aparte de

besiege [bisídʒ] VT (lay siege) sitiar, cercar; (importune) importunar, asediar

best [best] ADJ mejor; **—-case scenario** la mejor situación; — **man** padrino de boda m; — **seller** bestseller m; **she's the** — ella es la mejor; ADV mejor; **at** — a lo más, en el mejor de los casos; N **the** — **is still to come** lo mejor está por venir; **to do one's** — hacer lo mejor posible; **to get the** — **of a person** ganarle a una persona; **to make the** — **of** sacar el mejor partido de; VT vencer

bestial [béstʃəł] ADJ bestial

bestow [bistó] VT conferir; **to** — **gifts upon** dar regalos a

bet [bɛt] N apuesta f; VI/VT apostar; **to** — **on** apostar por

beta [béDə] N — **blocker** betabloqueador m, betabloqueante m; — **test** prueba beta f; — **version** versión beta f

betray [bitré] VT (a person) traicionar; (a secret) revelar; (a feeling) traslucir, delatar; **to** — **one's ignorance** hacer patente su ignorancia

betrayal [bitréəl] N traición f

betrayer [bitréə·] N traidor -ra mf

betrothal [bitróðəł] N esponsales f pl

better [béDə·] ADJ mejor; — **half** media naranja f; **the** — **part of a year** la mayor parte de un año; ADV mejor; **he lives** — **than a mile away** vive a más de una milla; **so much the** — tanto mejor; **—-off** en mejor posición económica; **to be** — **off** estar mejor así; **to change for the** — cambiar para bien; **to get** — mejorar[se], aliviarse; VT mejorar; **to** — **oneself** mejorarse, mejorar de situación; N **the** — **of the two** el/la mejor de los dos

better, bettor [béDə·] N apostador -ra mf

between [bitwín] PREP entre; ADV en medio

bevel [bévəł] N bisel m; VT biselar

beverage [bévridʒ] N bebida f

bevy [bévi] N (of birds, people) bandada f; (of deer) manada f

beware [biwér] VI cuidarse [de]; — **of the dog** cuidado con el perro

bewilder [biwíłdə·] VT dejar perplejo, aturdir; **to be —ed** estar perplejo

bewilderment [biwíłdə·mənt] N perplejidad f, aturdimiento m

bewitch [biwítʃ] VT hechizar, embrujar

beyond [bijánd] ADV más allá; PREP más allá de; — **my reach** fuera de mi alcance; N **the great** — el más allá

Bhutan [butǽn] N Bután m

Bhutanese [butn̩íz] ADJ & N butanés -esa mf

biannual [baɪǽnjuəł] ADJ bianual, semestral, semianual

bias [báɪəs] N (prejudice) prejuicio m; (in fabric) sesgo m; ADJ sesgado, oblicuo; VT predisponer; **—ed** parcial

bib [bib] N babero m; (of an apron) pechera f

Bible [báɪbəł] N Biblia f

biblical [bíblɪkəł] ADJ bíblico

bibliography [bɪbliágrəfi] N bibliografía f

bicarbonate [baɪkárbənɪt] N bicarbonato m

bicep, biceps [báɪsɛp[s]] N bíceps m sg

bicker [bíkə·] VI reñir

bicuspid [baɪkáspɪd] ADJ bicúspide

bicycle [báɪsɪkəł] N bicicleta f; VI andar en bicicleta

bid [bɪd] N (in an auction, contest) licitación f, puja f; (in card games) apuesta f; (attempt) tentativa f; VI/VT (offer) pujar; (command) mandar; (invite) rogar; (enter a bid in cards) apostar; **to** — **good-bye** despedirse; **to** — **up** pujar el precio

bidden [bídn̩] see bid

bidding [bídɪŋ] N (in auction) puja f; **at someone's** — por orden de alguien; **to do someone's** — cumplir con los deseos de alguien

bide [baɪd] VI/VT **to** — **one's time** esperar una oportunidad

biennium [baɪéniəm] N bienio m

bifurcate [báɪfə·ket] VI/VT bifurcar[se]

big [bɪg] ADJ grande; — **Bang Theory** Teoría del Big Bang f; — **brother** hermano mayor m; — **bucks** mucha plata f; — **business** el gran capital m; — **deal** asunto importante m; — **deal!** ¡no es para tanto! — **Dipper** Osa Mayor f; — **enchilada** fam mandamás m, fam pez gordo m; **—-headed** cabezón, cabezudo; **—-hearted** magnánimo; — **house** fam gayola f; — **kahuna** fam mandamás m, fam pez gordo m; — **name** personalidad prominente f; — **picture** panorama general m; — **shot** fam pez gordo m; — **sister** hermana mayor f; **—-ticket** caro; **—-wig** fam pez gordo m; — **with child** embarazada; **jazz was** — **in the 1920s** el jazz era popular en los años veinte; **she's a** — **deal** es una persona importante; ADV **she wants to go** —**time** se muere por ir; **to talk** — jactarse, fanfarronear; Am lucirse; **to go over** — tener éxito; **to be** — **on** ser entusiasta de

bigamy [bígəmi] N bigamia f

bigot [bígət] N intolerante mf

bigotry [bígətri] N intolerancia f

bike [baɪk] N (bicycle) bici f; (motorcycle) moto f

biker [báɪkə·] N (bicyclist) ciclista mf; (motorcyclist) motociclista mf

bikini [bikíni] N bikini m

bilateral [baɪlǽDə·əł] ADJ bilateral

bile [baɪł] N (secretion) bilis f; (ill temper) mal genio m; — **duct** conducto biliar m

bilingual [baɪlíŋgwəł] ADJ & N bilingüe *mf*
bilingualism [baɪlíŋgwəlɪzəm] N bilingüismo *m*
bill [bɪł] N (statement) factura *f*; (in a restaurant) cuenta *f*; (poster) cartel *m*; (bank note) billete *m*; (for movies, theater) programa *m*; (of a bird) pico *m*; (legislative) proyecto de ley *m*; —**board** cartelera *f*; —**fold** cartera *f*, billetera *f*; — **of exchange** letra de cambio *f*; — **of lading** conocimiento de embarque *m*; — **of rights** declaración de derechos *f*; — **of sale** escritura de venta *f*; VT cobrar, mandar la factura a
billable [bíləbəł] ADJ facturable
billiards [bíljɚdz] N billar *m*
billing [bílɪŋ] N (theater) orden de importancia en espectáculos *m*; (business) facturación *f*; — **cycle** ciclo de facturación *m*
billion [bíljən] NUM mil millones *m pl*
billow [bílo] N (of smoke) nube *f*; (of water) ola *f*; VI ondular, hacer olas
bimbo [bímbo] N gachí *f*; *pej* putilla *f*, *pej* putón *m*
bimonthly [baɪmánθli] ADV bimestral
bin [bɪn] N (for clothes, food) cajón *m*, recipiente *m*; (on an airplane) portaequipajes *m sg*; (for coal) carbonera *f*; (for grain) granero *m*
binary [báɪnɛri] ADJ binario; — **star** estrella binaria *f*
bind [baɪnd] VI/VT (unite) unir; (connect) ligar; (tie) atar; (put a cover on a book) encuadernar; (press tightly) apretar; (oblige by contract) obligar
binding [báɪndɪŋ] N (of a book) encuadernación *f*; (on a rug) ribete *m*; ADJ obligatorio
binge [bɪndʒ] N (alcoholic) juerga *f*, parranda *f*; (food) comilona *f*; VI (on alcohol) emborracharse; (on food) atiborrarse
bingo [bíŋgo] N bingo *m*
binoculars [bənɑ́kjəlɚz] N gemelos *m pl*, prismáticos *m pl*
binomial [baɪnómiəł] N binomio *m*; ADJ binomial
biochemistry [baɪokémɪstri] N bioquímica *f*
biodegradable [baɪodɪgrédəbəł] ADJ biodegradable
bioengineering [baɪoɛndʒəníɾɪŋ] N bioingeniería *f*
biofeedback [baɪofídbæk] N biofeedback *m*, retroalimentación biológica *f*
biography [baɪágrəfi] N biografía *f*
biological [baɪəláʤɪkəł] ADJ biológico
biologist [baɪáləʤɪst] N biólogo -ga *mf*
biology [baɪáləʤi] N biología *f*
biopsy [báɪɑpsi] N biopsia *f*
biorhythm [báɪoɾɪðəm] N biorritmo *m*
biotechnology [baɪotɛknáləʤi] N biotecnología *f*
bipartisan [baɪpárdɪzən] ADJ bipartidista
bipolar [baɪpólɚ] ADJ bipolar; — **disorder** trastorno bipolar *m*

birch [bɚtʃ] N abedul *m*
bird [bɚd] N ave *f*; (small) pájaro *m*; — **of prey** ave de rapiña *f*; — **seed** alpiste *m*; **odd** — persona peculiar *f*
birth [bɚθ] N (act of being born) nacimiento *m*; (act of giving birth) parto *m*; (lineage) linaje *m*; (origin) origen *m*; — **canal** canal de parto *m*; — **certificate** certificado de nacimiento *m*, fe/acta de nacimiento *f*; — **control** (policy) control de la natalidad *m*; (devices) anticonceptivos *m pl*; —**day** cumpleaños *m sg*; **in his / her** —**day suit** como Dios lo/la trajo al mundo; —**mark** antojo *m*, marca de nacimiento *f*; —**place** lugar de nacimiento *m*; —**rate** natalidad *f*, tasa de natalidad *f*; —**right** derechos de nacimiento *m pl*; (of oldest child) primogenitura *f*; **to give** — dar a luz, parir, alumbrar; **by** — de nacimiento
biscuit [bískɪt] N panecillo *m*
bisect [báɪsɛkt] VT bisecar
bisexual [baɪsékʃuəł] ADJ bisexual
bishop [bíʃəp] N obispo *m*; (in chess) alfil *m*
bison [báɪsən] N bisonte *m*, búfalo *m*
bit [bɪt] N (small piece) pedacito *m*, trocito *m*; (some) poquito *m*; (of a bridle) bocado *m*, freno *m*; (of a drill) broca *f*, barrena *f*; (computer) bit *m*; **I don't care a** — no me importa en absoluto
bit [bɪt] *see* bite
bitch [bɪtʃ] N (dog) perra *f*; (woman) *offensive* hija de puta *f*, cabrona *f*; (situation) plomazo *m*, *Sp vulg* coñazo *m*; VI quejarse
bite [baɪt] VI/VT morder; (be duped) dejarse engañar; (insect, fish, snake) picar; **to** — **off** arrancar de un mordisco; N (act, wound) mordedura *f*, dentellada *f*; (morsel, small meal) bocado *m*, bocadito *m*; (of an insect) picadura *f*, roncha *f*
bitten [bɪtn̩] *see* bite
bitter [bíɾɚ] ADJ (taste) amargo; (cold) glacial; (enemy) acérrimo; (person) resentido; —**sweet** dulceamargo, agridulce; **to fight to the** — **end** luchar hasta morir; N —**s** cerveza amarga *f*
bitterness [bíɾɚnɪs] N (taste) amargor *m*; (feelings) amargura *f*; (anger) rencor *m*, resentimiento *m*
biweekly [baɪwíkli] ADV (every two weeks) quincenal; (twice a week) bisemanal
bizarre [bɪzár] ADJ (event) extraño; (appearance) estrafalario
blab [blæb] VI parlotear; VT descubrir el pastel
black [blæk] ADJ (color, ethnicity) negro; (night) oscuro; —**-and-blue** lleno de moretones, amoratado; N negro -a *mf*; — **bean** frijol negro *m*; —**berry** zarzamora *f*, mora *f*; —**bird** mirlo *m*; —**board** pizarrón *m*, pizarra *f*; — **death** peste negra *f*; — **eye** ojo amoratado/morado *m*; —**head** espinilla *f*; —

hole agujero negro *m*; **—jack** (weapon) cachiporra*f*; (card game) black-jack *m*, veintiuno *m*; **—list** lista negra*f*; **— magic** magia negra*f*; **—mail** chantaje *m*; **— mark** mancha*f*; **— market** mercado negro *m*; **—out** apagón *m*; **— pepper** pimienta negra *f*; **— pudding** morcilla*f*; **— sheep** oveja negra*f*; **—smith** herrero *m*; **—smith's shop** herrería*f*, forja*f*; **—top** asfalto *m*; **— widow spider** viuda negra*f*; **to put down in — and white** poner por escrito; VI **to — out** (faint) desmayarse, perder el conocimiento; VT **to —mail** chantajear

blacken [blǽkən] VT ennegrecer, negrear; VI (sky) oscurecerse

blackness [blǽknɪs] N negrura*f*

bladder [blǽDɚ] N vejiga*f*

blade [bled] N (of a knife) hoja*f*; (of grass) brizna *f*; (of an oar) pala*f*, paleta*f*; (of a propeller) aspa*f*

blame [blem] VT culpar, echar la culpa a, achacar la culpa a; **to be to —** tener la culpa; N (responsibility) culpa*f*; (reproof) reproche *m*

blameless [blémlɪs] ADJ intachable

blanch [blæntʃ] VI palidecer; VT (whiten) blanquear; (scald) escaldar

bland [blænd] ADJ insulso

blank [blæŋk] ADJ (not written on) en blanco; (not recorded on) virgen; (unadorned, expressionless) vacío; (confused) desconcertado; **— cartridge** cartucho de fogueo *m*; **— check** cheque en blanco *m*; **— verse** verso blanco *m*; N (place to be filled in on a form) espacio [en blanco] *m*; (gap) vacío *m*; VI **to — out** quedarse en blanco

blanket [blǽŋkɪt] N manta*f*, frazada*f*; *Am* cobija *f*; ADJ global; VT cubrir

blare [blɛr] VI hacer un ruido estruendoso; N estruendo *m*; (of a trumpet) toque *m*

blaspheme [blæsfím] VI/VT blasfemar [contra]

blasphemy [blǽsfəmi] N blasfemia*f*

blast [blæst] N (of wind) ráfaga*f*; (of criticism) lluvia*f*; (of a trumpet) trompetazo *m*; (explosive charge) carga*f*; (explosion) explosión*f*; **— furnace** alto horno *m*; **—off** despegue *m*; **we had a —** lo pasamos bomba; **at full —** a todo volumen; VI/VT (blow a horn) pitar, tocar; (shatter) volar; (criticize) criticar duramente; (blow hard) azotar; **to — off** despegar

blatant [blétṇt] ADJ descarado

blaze [blez] N (flame) llamarada*f*; (fire) incendio *m*; (glow) resplandor *m*; (mark) señal*f*; **— of anger** arranque de ira *m*; VI (burn) arder; (shine) resplandecer; **to — a trail** marcar una senda

blazer [bléz ɚ] N blazer *m*, saco *m*

bleach [blitʃ] VI/VT (intentional) blanquear[se]; (accidental) desteñir[se]; N blanqueador *m*; *Sp* lejía*f*

bleachers [blitʃɚz] N gradas*f pl*

bleak [blik] ADJ (terrain) yermo, desolado; (winter) crudo; (wind) helado; (future) negro

bleary [blíri] ADJ nublado

bleat [blit] N balido *m*; VI balar

bled [blɛd] *see* bleed

bleed [blid] VI (lose blood) sangrar; (run, as in colors) correrse, desteñir[se]; **my heart —s for the poor** los pobres me dan lástima; VT (let blood) desangrar; (extort) extorsionar; (clean brakes) purgar

blemish [blémɪʃ] N mancha*f*, tacha*f*; VT manchar

blend [blɛnd] VI/VT (tea, paint) mezclar, entremezclar; (sea and sky) fundirse; (voices) armonizar; N mezcla*f*

blender [bléndɚ] N licuadora*f*

bless [blɛs] VT bendecir; INTERJ **— you!** ¡salud! ¡Jesús!

blessed[1] [blésɪd] ADJ (beatified) beato; (happy) bienaventurado, feliz; **— event** feliz acontecimiento *m*; **the whole — day** todo el santo día; **not a — drop of rain** ni una bendita gota de agua

blessed[2] [blɛst] ADJ **— with** dotado de

blessing [blésɪŋ] N bendición*f*; **to say the —** dar gracias

blew [blu] *see* blow

blight [blaɪt] N (plant disease) quemadura*f*, añublo *m*; (scourge) lacra*f*; VT (cause to wither) marchitar; (ruin) arruinar

blimp [blɪmp] N zepelín *m*

blind [blaɪnd] ADJ ciego; **— alley** callejón sin salida *m*; **— date** cita a ciegas*f*; **—fold** venda para los ojos*f*; **to —fold** vendar los ojos a; **— man's bluff** juego de la gallina ciega *m*; **— spot** ángulo muerto *m*; **to fly —** volar a ciegas; **to go —** quedarse ciego; N (shade) persiana*f*; (hunter's hiding place) escondite *m*; VT (make blind) cegar; (darken) oscurecer

blinder [bláɪndɚ] N anteojera*f*

blindly [bláɪndli] ADV a ciegas

blindness [bláɪndnɪs] N ceguera*f*

blink [blɪŋk] VI/VT (move eyelids) pestañear, parpadear; (go on and off, as of a light) parpadear; (ignore) pasar por alto; (flee a challenge) rajarse; N parpadeo *m*, pestañeo *m*; **on the —** averiado

blinker [blíŋkɚ] N intermitente *m*

blinking [blíŋkɪŋ] N parpadeo *m*

blip [blɪp] N (on radar) punto *m*; (moment) bache *m*

bliss [blɪs] N dicha*f*, felicidad absoluta*f*

blister [blístɚ] N ampolla*f*; (small) vejiga*f*; VT sacar ampollas; VI ampollarse

blitz [blɪts] N ataque relámpago *m*

blizzard [blízɚd] N ventisca*f*

bloat [blot] VI hinchar[se], abotagar[se]

bloated [blóʊɪd] ADJ hinchado, inflado
blob [blɑb] N pedazo de algo sin forma *m*
block [blɑk] N (piece of stone, cement) bloque *m*; (piece of wood) trozo de madera *m*; (toy) cubo *m*; (in sports) bloqueo *m*; (in basketball) tapón *m*; (length from one street to the next) cuadra *f*; (square block) manzana *f*; (obstacle) obstáculo *m*; (group of tickets) sección *f*; **—buster** éxito de taquilla *m*; **—head** tarugo -ga *mf*, alcornoque *m*; VT (obstruct, also in sports) bloquear, tapar; (in basketball) taponar; (stop a pass) parar; **to — out** (an essay) esbozar, bosquejar; (the sun) ocultar
blockade [blɑkéd] N bloqueo *m*; VT bloquear
blockage [blɑkɪdʒ] N obstrucción *f*
blocking [blɑkɪŋ] N bloqueo *m*
blog [blɑg] N blog *m*; VI bloguear; **—ging** blogueo *m*
blogger [blɑgɚ] N bloguero -ra *mf*
blond [blɑnd] ADJ & N rubio -a *mf*
blood [blʌd] N sangre *f*; **—bank** banco de sangre *m*; **—bath** carnicería *f*, baño de sangre *m*; **— count** recuento sanguíneo *m*; **— group** grupo sanguíneo *m*; **—hound** sabueso *m*; **— plasma** plasma sanguíneo *m*; **— poisoning** septicemia *f*; **— pressure** presión arterial *f*; **— relative** pariente consanguíneo *mf*; **—shed** derramamiento de sangre *m*; **—shot** inyectado de sangre; **—thirsty** sanguinario, sangriento; **— type** grupo sanguíneo *m*; **— vessel** vaso sanguíneo *m*; **in cold — a** sangre fría
bloody [blʌdi] ADJ (violent) sangriento; (smeared) ensangrentado
bloom [blum] N (flower) flor *f*; (flowering) floración *f*; (youthfulness) lozanía *f*; (flush) rubor *m*; **in —** en flor; VI florecer
blooming [blúmɪŋ] ADJ (flowering) floreciente; (thriving) lozano
blooper [blúpɚ] N perla *f*
blossom [blásəm] N (flower) flor *f*; VI florecer
blot [blɑt] N (on paper) mancha *f*, borrón *m*; (on honor) tacha *f*; VI/VT manchar[se], emborronar[se]; **to — out** (obscure) borrar, tachar
blotch [blɑtʃ] VT borronear, manchar, cubrir con manchas; N mancha *f*, borrón *m*
blouse [blaʊs] N blusa *f*
blow [blo] VI (wind) soplar; (leaf) volar; (siren) sonar; (horse) resoplar; VT (play a horn) sonar; **to — a fuse** quemar un fusible; **to — away** (amaze) dejar atónito; (carry away on the wind) llevarse el viento; **to — down** tirar abajo; **to —-dry** secar con secador; **to — off** (ignore) ignorar; **to — one's nose** sonarse las narices / la nariz; **to — on the soup** soplar la sopa; **to — one's brains out** levantarse la tapa de los sesos; **to — out** reventar[se]; **to — over** (knock down) derribar; (dissipate)

disiparse; **to — up** (a balloon) inflar, hinchar; (a bridge) volar; **this party —s** esta fiesta es pésima; N (stroke, shock) golpe *m*; (wind) tempestad *f*; (breath) soplo *m*; **— job** *vulg* mamada *f*; **—out** (tire failure) reventón *m*; (party) fiestón *m*; **—pipe** cerbatana *f*; **—torch** soplete *m*; **—up** (fight) pelea *f*, riña *f*; (photo) ampliación *f*; **to come to —s** irse a las manos
blower [blóɚ] N (artisan) soplador *m*; (machine) aventadora *f*
blown [blon] *see* blow
blue [blu] ADJ azul; (sad) triste, melancólico; (from cold) amoratado; N azul *m*; **—bell** campanilla *f*; **—berry** arándano *m*; **—bird** pájaro azul *m*; **—blood** sangre azul *f*; **— book** lista de precios de mercado *f*; **—-chip** de primera línea; **—-collar** de clase obrera; **—jay** arrendajo *m*; **— jeans** vaqueros *m pl*; **—print** (of a building) cianotipo *m*; (of a project) plan *m*, trazado *m*; **—-ribbon** distinguido; **— whale** ballena azul *f*; **light —** [azul] celeste *m*; **the —s** (sadness) melancolía *f*, murria *f*; (genre of music) blues *m pl*; VI ponerse azul, azulear; VT azular, teñir de azul; **to —print** trazar
bluff [blʌf] N (cliff) acantilado *m*, risco *m*; (false boast) bluff *m*; (in poker) farol *m*; VT hacer un bluff; **to call a —** poner en evidencia
bluffer [blʌfɚ] N bluff *m*
bluing [blúɪŋ] N añil *m*
bluish [blúɪʃ] ADJ azulado
blunder [blʌndɚ] N disparate *m*, patochada *f*; VI meter la pata; **to — upon/into** tropezar con
blunt [blʌnt] ADJ (not sharp) romo; (rounded) contundente; (frank) directo, franco; VT despuntar
blur [blɚ] VT (to obscure) emborronar, desvanecer; (to make vision blurry) nublar; VI empañarse, nublarse; N [indistinct sight] mancha *f*; **it's a — in my mind** sólo tengo un recuerdo vago de eso
blurred [blɚd] ADJ borroso
blurry [blɚi] ADJ borroso
blurt [blɚt] VT **to — [out]** espetar
blush [blʌʃ] VI sonrojarse, ponerse colorado, ruborizarse; N (act of blushing) sonrojo *m*; (effect of blushing) rubor *m*; **at first — a** primera vista
bluster [blʌstɚ] VI (blow hard) soplar fuerte, rugir; (boast) fanfarronear; N (sound of wind) ventarrón *m*; (attitude) fanfarronería *f*
blustering [blʌstɚɪŋ] ADJ fanfarrón, jactancioso; **— wind** ventarrón *m*
BM [bowel movement] [bíém] N defecación *f*
boa constrictor [bóəkənstríktɚ] N boa *f*
boar [bɔr] N jabalí *m*
board [bɔrd] N (wood) tabla *f*, listón *m*; (for a game) tablero *m*; (meals) pensión *f*; (for

bulletins) cartelera *f*; — **of directors** junta directiva *f*; —**ing school** pensionado *m*, internado *m*; —**inghouse** pensión *f*; — **of trustees** patronato *m*; —**room** sala de directorio *f*; **on** — a bordo; **to go by the** — irse por la borda; vi (lodge) alojarse; **to** — **up** tapiar, cerrar con tablas; vt (boat, plane, train) abordar; (provide lodging) alojar

boarder [bórɖɚ] N pensionista *mf*

boast [bost] N alarde *m*; vi jactarse, vanagloriarse, blasonar; vt **the town** —**s two new schools** el pueblo ostenta dos escuelas nuevas

boastful [bóstfəł] ADJ jactancioso, vanaglorioso

boastfulness [bóstfəłnɪs] N jactancia *f*, vanagloria *f*

boat [bot] N (any water vessel) embarcación *f*; (open and small) bote *m*, lancha *f*; (closed, larger) barco *m*; —**house** cobertizo para botes *m*; —**man** barquero *m*, botero *m*

boating [bóɖɪŋ] N navegación *f*; **to go** — navegar

bob [bɑb] N (horsetail) cola cortada *f*; (of the head) sacudida *f*; (haircut) melena corta *f*; (of a pendulum) pesa *f*, plomada *f*; —**tail** rabón *m*; vi sacudirse; (a ship) cabecear; vt **to** — **one's hair** cortarse el pelo en melena

bobbin [bábɪn] N carrete *m*, bobina *f*

bobcat [bábkæt] N lince rojo *m*

bode [bod] vi **that doesn't** — **well** eso no augura nada bueno

bodice [bádɪs] N corpiño *m*

bodily [bádḷi] ADJ corporal; — **harm** daño físico *m*

body [báɖi] N (of a person, animal, wine, fabric) cuerpo *m*; (torso) tronco *m*; (corpse) cuerpo *m*, cadáver *m*; (of a text, army, etc.) parte principal *f*; (of water) masa *f*; (of a car) carrocería *f*; (of an airplane) fuselaje *m*; — **armor** armadura corporal *f*, armadura de cuerpo *f*; — **bag** bolsa para cadáveres *f*; —-**building** culturismo *m*; — **count** número de muertos *m*; —**guard** guardaespaldas *m sg*; — **language** lenguaje corporal *m*; — **temperature** temperatura *f*; — **shop** taller de carrocería *m*; vt **to** —**search** cachear

bog [bɑg] N pantano *m*; vi hundir[se]; **to get** —**ged down** atascarse

bogey [bógi] N (golf) bogey *m*

bogeyman [búgimæn] N coco *m*; *RP* cuco *m*

bogus [bógəs] ADJ falso, fraudulento; — **company** compañía fantasma *f*

Bohemian [bohímiən] ADJ & N bohemio -a *mf*

boil [bɔɪł] vi/vt (water) hervir; (eggs) cocer; (ocean) bullir; (angry person) echar chispas; **to** — **down to** reducirse a; **to** — **over** derramarse; N (inflammation) forúnculo *m*, divieso *m*; (act of boiling) hervor *m*; —**ing point** punto de ebullición *m*; **to come to a**

— soltar/romper el hervor

boiler [bɔ́ɪlɚ] N caldera *f*

boisterous [bɔ́ɪstɚəs] ADJ bullicioso

bold [boɫd] ADJ (not fearful) atrevido, osado; (unconventional) audaz; (visually striking) llamativo; —-**faced** descarado; —**face type** negrita *f*, negrilla *m*

boldness [bóɫdnɪs] N (courage) atrevimiento *m*, osadía *f*; (unconventional attitude) audacia *f*

Bolivia [bəlíviə] N Bolivia *f*

Bolivian [bəlíviən] ADJ & N boliviano -na *mf*

bolster [bóɫstɚ] N cojín cilíndrico *m*; vt reforzar; **to** — **someone's courage** alentar a alguien

bolt [boɫt] N (door lock) pestillo *m*, cerrojo *m*; (crossbar) aldaba *f*; (pin) perno *m*, tornillo grande *m*; (of cloth) rollo *m*; **it came as a** — **from the blue** cayó como bomba; vt (fasten) atornillar; (lock door) cerrar con tranca, atrancar; (devour) engullir; (break with) romper con; vi echarse a correr

bomb [bɑm] N bomba *f*; —**shell** bomba *f*; — **shelter** refugio antiaéreo *m*; vt (attack with bombs) bombardear; vi (fail) fracasar

bombard [bɑmbárd] vt bombardear

bombardier [bɑmbɚdír] N bombardero -ra *mf*

bombardment [bɑmbárdmənt] N bombardeo *m*

bombastic [bɑmbǽstɪk] ADJ grandilocuente, ampuloso

bomber [bámɚ] N bombardero *m*, avión de bombardeo *m*

bombing [bámɪŋ] N (from airplanes) bombardeo *m*; (terrorist) atentado *m*

bona fide [bónəfaɪd] ADJ genuino; — **offer** oferta seria *f*

bonbon [bánbɑn] N caramelo *m*; (chocolate) bombón *m*

bond [bɑnd] N (tie) lazo *m*; (fetter) cadenas *f pl*; (financial instrument) bono *m*, obligación *f*; (adhesion) adherencia *f*; (chemical) enlace *m*; vi/vt (stick to) adherirse; (connect) establecer vínculos

bondage [bándɪʤ] N (slavery) servidumbre *f*, esclavitud *f*; (sexual practice) prácticas sadomasoquistas *f pl*

bonded [bándɪd] ADJ afianzado

bonding [bándɪŋ] N (mother-child) lazos afectivos *m pl*; (male) compenetración *f*

bondsman [bándzmən] N fiador *m*

bone [bon] N hueso *m*; (of fish) espina *f*; — **china** porcelana fina *f*; — **graft** injerto óseo *m*; —**head** estúpido -da *mf*; — **marrow** médula ósea *f*; —**yard** cementerio *m*; — **of contention** manzana de la discordia *f*; **to make no** —**s about it** no andarse con rodeos; vt deshuesar; (fish) quitar las espinas; **to** — **up on something** estudiar algo; (have intercourse) *Sp vulg* follar; *Am vulg* coger,

culear
bonfire [bánfaɪr] N hoguera f, fogata f
bonnet [bánɪt] N gorro m
bonus [bónəs] N (extra salary) gratificación f,
prima f; (at Christmas) aguinaldo m
bony [bóni] ADJ (with large bones) huesudo;
(made of bones) óseo
boo [bu] VI/VT abuchear, rechiflar; INTERJ ¡bu! N
rechifla f, abucheo m
boob [bub] N fam teta f; Am fam chiche m; Mex
fam chichi f; RP fam lola f; — **tube** fam caja
boba f
boo-boo [búbu] N (minor injury) lastimadura f;
Sp fam pupa f; Am nana f; **to make a** — meter
la pata
booby [búbi] N (fool) bobo -a mf; (bird) bobo m;
— **hatch** fam loquería f; — **prize** premio
al peor competidor m; — **trap** trampa
explosiva f
booger [búgɚ] N moco [seco] m
book [bʊk] N libro m; —**binding**
encuadernación f; —**case** estante m,
estantería f, biblioteca f; —**end** sujetalibros m
sg; —**keeper** tenedor -ra de libros mf; Sp
contable mf; —**keeping** teneduría de libros f,
contabilidad f; —**mark** marcador de libros
m; —**mobile** biblioteca móvil f; — **review**
reseña f; —**seller** librero -ra mf; —**shelf**
estante m; —**store** librería f; — **value** valor
contable m; **by the** — siguiendo las reglas;
on the —**s** registrado en los libros; **to keep**
—**s** llevar los libros; VT (reserve) reservar;
(hire) contratar; (record charges against)
fichar
bookish [búkɪʃ] ADJ (person) estudioso;
(allusion) libresco
booklet [búklɪt] N cartilla f
boom [bum] VI (resound) resonar; (prosper)
prosperar; N (noise) explosión f; (increase)
auge m
boon [bun] N (blessing) bendición f; (favor)
favor m
boondocks [búndɑks] ADV LOC [out] in the —
fam en los quintos infiernos, en el quinto pino
boondoggle [búndɑgəl] N despilfarro m
boor [bur] N patán -ana m
boorish [búrɪʃ] ADJ grosero, zafio
boost [bust] VT (to shove) empujar [desde abajo o
detrás]; (to promote) estimular, impulsar; N
(shove) empujón [desde abajo] m; (aid)
estímulo m, impulso m; — **in prices** alza de
precios f
booster [bústɚ] N (person) animador -ra mf;
(rocket) acelerador m; (electronic device)
amplificador m; (vaccination) refuerzo m
boot [but] N (shoe) bota f; (trunk of a car) cajuela
f; (clamp for cars) cepo m; —**black**
limpiabotas m sg; — **disk** disco de iniciación
m; —**legger** contrabandista de licores m;

—**licker** vulg lameculos mf; —**able diskette**
disquete de iniciación f; **to give the** — poner
de patitas en la calle; **to** — por añadidura; VT
dar una patada a; **to** — **[out]** echar a patadas;
to — **up** (a computer) iniciar
booth [buθ] N (telephone) cabina f; (sales) puesto
m; (ticket) taquilla f
booty [búbi] N (loot) botín m; (buttocks)
trasero m
booze [buz] N fam bebercio m, bebida alcohólica f
borax [bóræks] N bórax m
border [bórdɚ] N (line between countries)
frontera f; (edge, brink) borde m; (bed of
flowers) ariete m; (design) ribete m; —
control control fronterizo m; — **patrol**
officer carabinero -ra mf; ADJ —**line** (on a
border) fronterizo; (not up to standards)
dudoso; VI/VT (make a design) ribetear; **to** —
on colindar con; **it** —**s on madness** raya en
la locura
bordering [bórdɚɪŋ] ADJ limítrofe
bore [bɔr] N (hole) agujero m; (of a gun, cylinder)
calibre m; (uninteresting person) aburrido -da
mf, pesado -da mf; (uninteresting thing) lata f;
VT (make a hole) taladrar, horadar; (fail to
interest) aburrir
bore [bɔr] see bear
bored [bɔrd] ADJ aburrido; **I'm** — estoy aburrido
boredom [bórdəm] N aburrimiento m, tedio m
boric acid [bórɪk ǽsɪd] N ácido bórico m
boring [bórɪŋ] ADJ aburrido; **he's** — es aburrido
born [bɔrn] ADJ nacido; **he's a** — **dancer** es un
bailarín nato; **she's a** — **liar** es una
mentirosa de nacimiento; **to be** — nacer
borne [bɔrn] see bear
boron [bórɑn] N boro m
borrow [báro] VT pedir prestado; **I** —**ed money**
from Fred le pedí dinero prestado a Fred;
may I — **your car?** ¿me prestas tu coche? **I**
—**ed these books from the library** saqué
estos libros de la biblioteca
borrower [bároɚ] N (of money) prestatario -ria
mf; (of library books) usuario -ria mf
Bosnia and Herzegovina
[bázniənhɜ·tsəgəvínə] N Bosnia-Herzegovina f
Bosnian [bázniən] ADJ & N bosnio -nia mf
bosom [búzəm] N pecho m, seno m; **in the** — **of**
the family en el seno de la familia; —
buddy amigo íntimo m
boss [bɔs] N jefe -fa mf; (on a plantation) mayoral
m, capataz m; (political) dirigente m; (mafia)
capo m; VT **to** — **around** mandonear
bossy [bósi] ADJ mandón
botanical [bətǽnɪkəl] ADJ botánico
botany [bátni] N botánica f
botch [bátʃ] VT chapucear, estropear; N
chapucería f, chapuza f
both [boθ] ADJ & PRON ambos, los dos
bother [báðɚ] VT molestar, fastidiar; VI

molestarse, tomarse la molestia; N molestia *f*
bothersome [báðɚsəm] ADJ (activity) molesto, enojoso; (person) enfadoso, molesto
botox [bótɑks] N bótox *m*
Botswana [bɑtswánə] N Botsuana *f*
bottle [bádl̩] N botella *f*; (for medicine, perfume) frasco *m*; **—neck** atascadero *m*, embotellamiento *m*; **— top** chapa de botella *f*; VT embotellar; **to — up** atascar, embotellar
bottom [bádəm] N (of a hole) fondo *m*; (of a pile, page, bed) pie *m*; (lower part) base *f*, parte de abajo *f*; (buttocks) trasero *m*; **to be at the — of the class** ser el último de la clase; **to hit — tocar fondo; who is at the — of all this?** ¿quién está detrás de todo esto? ADJ de abajo; **— line** (business) balance final *m*; (essential element) lo esencial; VI **to — out** tocar fondo
bottomless [bádəmlɪs] ADJ sin fondo; **— supply** recursos ilimitados *m pl*; **— accusation** acusación infundada *f*; **he's a — pit** es un barril sin fondo
botulism [bátʃəlɪzəm] N botulismo *m*
boudoir [búdwɑr] N tocador *m*
bough [baU] N rama *f*
bought [bɔt] *see* buy
bouillon [búljɑn] N caldo *m*
boulder [bóɫdɚ] N peña *f*, pedrusco *m*
boulevard [búləvɑrd] N bulevar *m*
bounce [baUns] N (of a ball) bote *m*, rebote *m*; (vitality) vitalidad *f*; VT echar, botar; **to — a check** rebotar un cheque; VI rebotar; **to — back** recuperarse
bouncer [baUnsɚ] N gorila *m*
bound [baUnd] N (jump) salto *m*; **—s** límite *m*, confín *m*; ADJ (tied up) atado; (confined) confinado; (obliged) obligado; (as a book) encuadernado; **to be — for** ir rumbo a; **to be — up in one's work** estar absorto en su trabajo; **it is — to happen** es seguro que pasará; **I am — to do it** estoy resuelto a hacerlo; VI (jump) saltar; (be contiguous) lindar
bound [baUnd] *see* bind
boundary [báUndri] N (of a country, city) límite *m*, término *m*; (of a property) linde *mf*, lindero *m*
boundless [báUndlɪs] ADJ ilimitado, sin límites
bountiful [báUntəfəɫ] ADJ abundante
bounty [báUnti] N (abundance) abundancia *f*; (reward) recompensa *f*
bouquet [buké] N (of flowers, large) ramo *m*; (of flowers, small) ramillete *m*; (of wine) aroma *m*, bouquet *m*
bourgeois [burʒwá] ADJ & N burgués -sa *mf*
bourgeoisie [burʒwazí] N burguesía *f*
bout [baUt] N (sports) encuentro *m*; **a — of flu** una gripe
boutique [butík] N boutique *f*
bovine [bóvaIn] ADJ vacuno

bow[1] [baU] N (gesture) reverencia *f*; (prow) proa *f*; VI (bend at the waist) hacer una reverencia; (yield) someterse; **to — out** retirarse; VT inclinar
bow[2] [bo] N (for arrows, violin) arco *m*; (curve) curva *f*; (decoration) moño *m*; **—knot** lazada *f*; **—-string** cuerda de arco *f*; ADJ **—-legged** patizambo; VI/VT (bend) arquear[se]; (play a violin with a bow) tocar con arco
bowel [báUəɫ] N **—s** intestinos *m pl*; **—s of the earth** entrañas de la tierra *f pl*; **— movement** evacuación del vientre *f*
bower [báUɚ] N enramada *f*
bowl [boɫ] N (container) bol *m*, tazón *m*; (dish) plato hondo *m*; (depression) cuenco *m*; (of a toilet) taza *f*; (of a pipe) cazoleta *f*; VT **to — over** apabullar, deslumbrar
bowling [bólɪŋ] N boliche *m*, bowling *m*; **let's go** — vamos al boliche; **— alley** boliche *m*, bolera *f*
box [bɑks] N caja *f*; (for jewelry) estuche *m*; (in the theater) palco de teatro *m*; (for the jury) tribuna *f*; (on a page) cuadro *m*; (in soccer) área de penales *f*; **— car** vagón de carga *m*; **— office** taquilla *f*; **— seat** asiento de palco *m*; VT (put in a box) meter en una caja; (hit) abofetear; (engage in sport) boxear
boxer [báksɚ] N (fighter) boxeador -ra *mf*, pugilista *mf*; (breed of dog) bóxer *m*; **— shorts** calzoncillo[s] *m*
boxing [báksɪŋ] N boxeo *m*, pugilato *m*; **— glove** guante de boxeo *m*; **— ring** ring *m*, cuadrilátero *m*
boy [bɔI] N (baby) niño *m*; (young man) muchacho *m*, chico *m*; **— scout** boy scout *m*; **—friend** novio *m*
boycott [bɔIkɑt] VT boicotear; N boicoteo *m*, boicot *m*
boyhood [bɔIhUd] N niñez *f*, juventud *f*
boyish [bɔIIʃ] ADJ de muchacho
brace [bres] N (in construction) tirante *m*; (pair) par *m*; (printed character) corchete *m*; (of a carpenter) berbiquí *m*; **—s** (for teeth) aparato ortodóntico *m*; (for a leg) aparato ortopédico *m*; VT (against a shock) agarrarse; (support) asegurar
bracelet [bréslɪt] N brazalete *m*, pulsera *f*
bracket [brǽkɪt] N (support) soporte *m*, sostén *m*; (typographic sign) paréntesis recto *m*, corchete *m*; (division) banda *f*; VT (fix with brackets) fijar con soportes; (write in brackets) colocar entre paréntesis rectos; (associate) agrupar
brag [brǽg] VI jactarse [de], hacer alarde [de]
braggart [brǽgɚt] ADJ & N fanfarrón -na *mf*
braid [bred] N trenza *f*; VT trenzar
brain [bren] N cerebro *m*; (food) seso *m*; **she blew out his —s** le levantó la tapa de los sesos; **he's short on —s** es corto de

inteligencia; **he is the —s in this operation** él es el cerebro en esta operación; **to rack one's —s** devanarse los sesos, romperse la cabeza; — **death** muerte cerebral *f*; — **drain** fuga de cerebros *f*; — **scan** tomografía cerebral *f*; — **trust** grupo de expertos *m*; — **stem** tronco del encéfalo *m*; —**storming** lluvia de ideas *f*; — **tumor** tumor cerebral *m*; VT **to — someone** romperle la crisma a alguien; **to —wash** lavarle el cerebro a; ADJ —**-dead** clínicamente muerto, en estado vegetativo

brainy [bréni] ADJ sesudo

brake [brek] N freno *m*; — **drum** tambor del freno *m*; — **fluid** líquido para frenos *m*; —**man** guardafrenos *m sg*; — **shoe** zapata *f*; **to apply the —s** frenar; VI/VT frenar

bramble [brémbəł] N zarza *f*

bran [bræn] N salvado *m*; (for birds) afrecho *m*

branch [bræntʃ] N (of a plant, of a family) rama *f*; (of a train track) ramal *m*; (of antlers) brazo *m*; (of a science) ramo *m*; (of a business) sucursal *f*; (of the armed forces) arma *f*; (in a computer program) bifurcación *f*; (of a river) tributario *m*; VI/VT ramificar[se]

brand [brænd] N (make, mark) marca *f*; (of humor, etc.) tipo *m*; (mark of disgrace) estigma *m*; — **awareness** conciencia de marca *f*; — **loyalty** lealtad de marca *f*; — **name** marca *f*; ADJ —**-new** flamante, recién comprado; VT (burn) herrar, marcar; (stigmatize) estigmatizar; **to — as** tildar de, tachar de

brandish [brǽndɪʃ] VT blandir, esgrimir

brandy [brǽndi] N (fine) brandy *m*; (cheap) aguardiente *m*

brash [bræʃ] ADJ (impudent) descarado; (impetuous) impetuoso

brass [bræs] N (metal) latón *m*; (attitude) descaro *m*; (high-ranking officers) la plana mayor; — **instrument** instrumento de metal *m*; **to get down to — tacks** ir al grano; ADJ de latón

brassiere [brəzír] N sostén *m*

brat [bræt] N mocoso -sa *mf*

bravado [brəvádo] N alarde *m*

brave [brev] ADJ valiente, gallardo; N guerrero indio *m*; VT desafiar

bravery [brévəri] N valentía *f*, gallardía *f*

brawl [brɔł] N reyerta *f*, riña *f*, pelotera *f*; VI reñir

bray [bre] N rebuzno *m*; VI rebuznar

brazen [brézən] ADJ (impudent) descarado; (made of brass) de latón

brazier [bréʒɚ] N brasero *m*

Brazil [brəzíł] N Brasil *m*

Brazilian [brəzíljən] ADJ & N brasileño -ña *mf*, brasilero -ra *mf*

breach [britʃ] N (opening) brecha *f*; (infraction) infracción *f*; (severance) ruptura *f*; — **of**

— **contract** incumplimiento de contrato *m*; — **of faith** abuso de confianza *m*; VT (make an opening) abrir una brecha en; (violate a law) violar, infringir

bread [bred] N pan *m*; —**basket** panera *f*; — **box** panera *f*; —**winner** sostén de la familia *m*; ADJ —**-and-butter** básico; VT empanar

breadth [bredθ] N anchura *f*, ancho *m*; (size) extensión *f*; (perspective) amplitud *f*

break [brek] VI (fracture) romperse; (pause) parar; VT (a record) batir; (a code) descifrar; (a law) violar; (news) dar, divulgar; (a bone) fracturar; (a horse) domar, desbravar; (a habit) quitar[se]; (a contract, promise) romper; (one's spirit) quebrar, doblegar; (one's heart) desgarrar; (cause to go bankrupt) arruinar; **to — a ten-dollar bill** conseguir cambio para un billete de diez dólares; **to — away** escaparse; **to — down** (a person) descomponerse; (a car) averiarse; (resistance) vencer; (continuity) interrumpir; **to — even** quedar a mano; **to — into** violentar; **to — loose** liberarse; **to — out** (war) estallar; (one's face) brotarse; (from prison) escaparse; **to — up** (into pieces) quebrarse; (a relationship) romper con; N (weather) cambio *m*; (from work) descanso *m*; (with tradition) quiebre *m*, rompimiento *m*; (of a bone) fractura *f*; (from prison) fuga *f*; (opportunity) oportunidad *f*; —**-in** hurto con escalo *m*; —**down** (analysis) análisis *m*; (automotive) avería *f*; (nervous) colapso *m*; —**down of charges** desglose de cargos *m*; —**even point** umbral de rentabilidad *m*; — **point** (in tennis) bola de break *f*, bola de ruptura *f*; —**through** adelanto *m*; (military) penetración *f*; —**water** rompeolas *m sg*; **give me a —!** ¡déjame en paz! **lucky —** golpe de suerte *m*

breakable [brékəbəł] ADJ quebradizo, rompible

breaker [brékɚ] N rompiente *f*

breakfast [brékfəst] N desayuno *m*; VI desayunar

breast [brest] N (of a woman) seno *m*, pecho *m*; *fam* teta *f*; (of a bird) pechuga *f*; —**bone** esternón *m*; — **cancer** cáncer de mama *m*; —**-feeding** lactancia materna *f*; —**stroke** (estilo de natación) pecho *m*; VI/VT **to —-feed** amamantar, dar de mamar

breath [breθ] N aliento *m*; *lit* hálito *m*; (current of air) soplo *m*; **in the same —** al mismo tiempo; **out of —** sin aliento; **to catch one's —** recobrar el aliento; **to hold one's —** aguantar la respiración; **to take a —** inhalar; **to take a deep —** respirar hondo; **under one's —** entre dientes, por lo bajo; ADJ —**taking** impresionante

breathe [brið] VI/VT respirar; **to — in** inspirar, aspirar; **to — into** infundir; **to — out** exhalar, espirar; **he did not — a word** no dijo palabra

breathing [bríðɪŋ] N respiración f

breathless [bréθlɪs] ADJ sin aliento

breathlessness [bréθlɪsnɪs] N falta de aire f

bred [brɛd] see breed

breed [brid] VT (mate) criar; (bring up) educar; (give rise to) engendrar; VI reproducirse, multiplicarse; N (species) raza f; (type) clase f

breeder [brídɚ] N (person who breeds) criador -ora mf; (animal used for breeding) [animal] reproductor m

breeding [brídɪŋ] N (of animals) cría f; (of people) educación f, modales m pl

breeze [briz] N brisa f

breezy [brízi] ADJ (windy) ventoso; (jaunty) ameno

brevity [brévɪDi] N brevedad f

brew [bru] VT (coffee) hacer; (mischief) fomentar, tramar; (beer) fabricar; VI (storm) armarse una tormenta; **let the tea —** deja reposar el té; N (mixture) mezcla f; (beer) cerveza f

brewery [brúəri] N cervecera f, fábrica de cerveza f

briar [bráɪɚ] N zarza f

bribe [braɪb] N soborno m, cohecho m; Mex mordida f; VT sobornar

bribery [bráɪbəri] N soborno m

brick [brɪk] N ladrillo m; **—bat** (piece of brick) pedazo de ladrillo m; (insult) insulto m; **—layer** albañil m; **—laying** albañilería f; VT (adorn with bricks) revestir de ladrillo; (pave with bricks) enladrillar

bridal [bráɪdl̩] ADJ nupcial; **— dress** vestido de novia m

bride [braɪd] N novia f; **—groom** novio m; **—smaid** dama de honor f

bridge [brɪʤ] N puente m; (of the nose) caballete m; (card game) bridge m; VT (a river) tender un puente sobre; (a gap) llenar, salvar

bridle [bráɪdl̩] N (harness) brida f; (restraint) freno m; VT (put on a bridle) poner una brida; (restrain) frenar; VI (be insulted) ofenderse

brief [brif] ADJ (short) breve, escueto; (concise) conciso, escueto; (curt) seco; N sumario m, resumen m; (report) expediente m; **—case** portafolio[s] m sg, maletín m; **—s** calzoncillos m pl; **in —** en suma; VT informar

briefing [brífɪŋ] N reunión para dar instrucciones f

brigade [brɪgéd] N brigada f

bright [braɪt] ADJ (shining) brillante; (full of light) iluminado; (smart) inteligente; (promising) venturoso, prometedor; (radiant) radiante; (colorful) subido

brighten [bráɪtn̩] VT (a room) iluminar; VI **to — up** (person) animar[se]; (sky) despejarse

brightness [bráɪtnɪs] N (light) claridad f; (cheerfulness) viveza f; (intelligence)

inteligencia f

brilliance [bríljəns] N (of hair, of a historical period) brillantez f; (of intellect) genio m

brilliant [bríljənt] ADJ (shining) brillante; (intelligent) genial; (splendid) espléndido; N brillante m, diamante m

brim [brɪm] N borde m; (of a hat) ala f; **to fill to the —** llenar hasta el borde; **to be filled to the —** estar de bote en bote; VI **to — over** rebosar; **to be —ming with** estar rebosante de

brine [braɪn] N salmuera f

bring [brɪŋ] VT traer; (cause) ocasionar, causar; **to — about** producir, ocasionar; **to — down** (kill) bajar; (depress) deprimir; **to — forth** (give birth) dar a luz; (produce) producir; **to — to a stop** parar; **to — a session to a close** clausurar una sesión; **to — together** reunir, juntar; **to — oneself to do something** poder hacer algo; **to — a good price** redituar una buena ganancia; **to — up** (raise children) criar, educar; (mention) mencionar

brink [brɪŋk] N borde m; **on the — of** al borde de

brisk [brɪsk] ADJ (walk) rápido; (weather) fresco; (trading) activo

bristle [brɪsl̩] N cerda f; VI erizar[se]; **to — with** estar erizado de

bristly [brísli] ADJ (with bristles) erizado, cerdoso; (irascible) irascible

Britain [brítn̩] N Gran Bretaña f

British [brítɪʃ] ADJ británico

brittle [brídl̩] ADJ quebradizo, frágil

brittleness [brídlnɪs] N fragilidad f

broach [brotʃ] VT sacar a colación

broad [brɔd] ADJ (wide) ancho; (vast) vasto; (ample) amplio; **—band** banda ancha f; **—cast** emisión f; (on TV) transmisión por televisión f; **—cast station** emisora f; **— hint** insinuación clara f; **— jump** salto de longitud m; **—-minded** tolerante; **—side** andanada f; **— spectrum antibiotic** antibiótico de amplio espectro m; **in — daylight** en pleno día; N pej tipa f; VT **to —cast** (communicate electronically) transmitir, emitir, radiar

broadcasting [brɔ́dkæstɪŋ] N (radio) radiodifusión f; (TV) transmisión por televisión f

brocade [brokéd] N brocado m

broccoli [brákəli] N brócoli m, brécol m

brochure [broʃʊ́r] N folleto m

broil [brɔɪl] VI/VT asar[se] [a la parrilla]

broiler [brɔ́ɪlɚ] N (oven) parrilla f; (chicken) pollo [para asar] m

broke [brok] ADJ **to be —** estar limpio, estar pelado; **to go —** irse a la quiebra

broke [brok] see break

broken [brókən] ADJ (fragmented) roto, quebrado; (tamed) domado; (not functioning) descompuesto; (not continuous) interrumpido; —-**down** averiado, descompuesto; — **English** inglés chapurrado/chapurreado m; —**hearted** deshecho, con el corazón destrozado

broken [brókən] *see* break

broker [brókə-] N (intermediary) agente mf; (stock salesperson) corredor -ora de bolsa mf

brokerage [brókə-ɪdʒ] N correduría f

bromide [brómaɪd] N bromuro m

bromine [brómin] N bromo m

bronchial [bráŋkiəł] ADJ bronquial; — **tube** bronquio m

bronchitis [braŋkáɪdɪs] N bronquitis f

bronco [bráŋko] N caballo no domado m

bronze [branz] N bronce m; VT broncear

brooch [brutʃ] N broche m, prendedor m

brood [brud] N pollada f, nidada f; VI/VT empollar; **to** — **over** rumiar

brook [brʊk] N riachuelo m, cañada f; VT tolerar

broom [brum] N (tool) escoba f; (plant) retama f; —**stick** palo de escoba m

broth [brɔθ] N caldo m

brothel [bráθəł] N burdel m

brother [bráðə-] N hermano m; —-**in-law** cuñado m; **oh** —**!** ¡caray!

brotherhood [bráðə-hʊd] N hermandad f

brotherly [bráðə-li] ADJ fraternal

brought [brɔt] *see* bring

brow [braʊ] N (eyebrow) ceja f; (ridge of eye) arco superciliar m; (forehead) frente f

brown [braʊn] ADJ (skin) moreno; (eyes, shoes, clothes) café, marrón; (hair) castaño; (dun) pardo; (tanned) bronceado; — **bear** oso pardo m; —-**noser** vulg lameculos mf sg, adulón -ona mf; — **rice** arroz integral m; — **sugar** azúcar moreno -na mf; VI/VT (food) dorar[se]; N (color) café m, castaño m, moreno m, pardo m; VI **to** —-**nose** vulg lamer culos

brownie [bráʊni] N bizcocho de chocolate m; — **points** méritos m pl

browse [braʊz] VT (a book) hojear; VI (grass) pacer, pastar; (Internet) navegar

browser [bráʊzə-] N navegador m

browsing [bráʊzɪŋ] N navegación f

bruise [bruz] N (on skin) moretón m, cardenal m, contusión f; (on fruit) magulladura f, cardenal m; VI/VT magullar[se], machucar[se]

brunch [brʌntʃ] N brunch m, desayuno tardío m

Brunei [brunáɪ] N Brunéi m

Bruneian [brunáɪən] ADJ & N bruneano -na mf

brunette, brunet [brunét] ADJ & N moreno -na mf, morocho -cha mf; Cuba trigueño -ña mf

brunt [brʌnt] N impacto m

brush [brʌʃ] N (for teeth, clothes) cepillo m; (for paint, shaving) brocha f; (artist's) pincel m; (vegetation) maleza f; (contact) roce m; —-**off**

despedida brusca f; —**wood** (dead) broza f; (live) maleza f; VT (clean with a brush) cepillar; (touch lightly) rozar; **to** — **aside** echar a un lado; **to** — **up on** repasar; **to** — **off** (clean) quitar con cepillo; (reject) despedir bruscamente a alguien

brusque [brʌsk] ADJ brusco

Brussels sprouts [brásəłspraʊts] N coles de Bruselas f pl, repollitos de Bruselas m pl

brutal [brúdl] ADJ brutal

brutality [brutǽlɪDi] N brutalidad f

brute [brut] N (animal) bestia f; (person) bruto -ta mf; ADJ bruto

bubble [bábəł] N burbuja f; (in soap) pompa f; (in boiling water) borbollón m; (illusion) encanto m; — **bath** baño de burbujas m; —**gum** chicle de globo m; —-**jet printer** impresora de burbuja f; VI (make bubbles) borbotar, borbollar; (boil) bullir, hervir; **to** — **over with joy** rebosar de alegría

bubonic plague [bubánɪkplég] N plaga bubónica f

buck [bʌk] N (deer) gamo m; (male of other animals) macho m; (leap of horse) respingo m; — **private** soldado raso m; —**shot** posta f, perdigón m; —**skin** gamuza f; —**wheat** trigo sarraceno m; **to pass the** — echarle el muerto a uno; ADJ —**toothed** de dientes salidos; VI (horse) respingar, corcovear; **to** — **a trend** oponerse; **to** — **up** cobrar ánimo

bucket [bákɪt] N cubo m, balde m; (of a loader) cuchara f; — **seat** asiento delantero individual m

buckle [bákəł] N (clasp) hebilla f; (kink in a board) torcedura f; VT (to clasp) abrocharse; (to bend) torcerse, pandearse; **to** — **down** esforzarse; **to** — **up** abrocharse

bud [bʌd] N botón m, retoño m; VI (make buds) echar retoños

Buddhism [búdɪzəm] N budismo m

Buddhist [búdɪst] ADJ & N budista mf

buddy [bádi] N camarada mf

budge [bʌdʒ] VI moverse

budget [bádʒɪt] N presupuesto m; VT (money) presupuestar; (time, personal resources) administrar; — **cycle** ciclo presupuestario m; — **deficit** déficit presupuestario m

budgetary [bádʒɪtɛri] ADJ presupuestario

budgeting [bádʒɪdɪŋ] N presupuestación f

buff [bʌf] N (leather) gamuza f; (tan color) color beige m; (wheel for polishing) pulidor m; (devotee) aficionado m; **in the** — en cueros; ADJ (beige) de color beige; (muscular) musculoso; VT pulir

buffalo [báfəlo] N bisonte m, búfalo m; — **wings** alitas f pl

buffer [báfə-] N (in a computer) memoria intermedia f; (shock absorber) amortiguador m; (polishing device) pulidor -ra mf; — **zone**

zona tampón f
buffet[1] [bʌ́fɪt] N (blow) golpe m, puñetazo m;
(shock) azote m; VT (hit) golpear; (hit
repeatedly) azotar
buffet[2] [bəfé] N (cabinet) aparador m; (meal)
buffet m
buffoon [bəfún] N payaso -a mf, bufón -ona mf
bug [bʌg] N bicho m; (disease-causing) microbio
m, virus m; (for eavesdropping) micrófono
oculto m; (in a computer program) fallo m,
bicho m; VT (bother) molestar; (install
microphones) colocar micrófonos ocultos;
his eyes —ged out se le saltaron los ojos
buggy [bʌ́gi] N (cart) calesa f; (baby carriage)
cochecillo m
bugle [bjúgəɫ] N clarín m; VI tocar el clarín
build [bɪɫd] VT (construct) construir, edificar;
(manufacture) fabricar; **to — into**
incorporar; **to — up** (make stronger)
fortalecer; (accumulate) acumular; (enhance)
desarrollar; (urbanize) urbanizar; N **—-up** (of
military forces) concentración f; (of
substance) acumulación f; (of anticipation)
aumento m; N (of human body) complexión f
builder [bɪ́ldə-] N contratista mf, constructor
-ora mf
building [bɪ́ldɪŋ] N (thing built) edificio m; (act
of building) construcción f, edificación f;
(unit in a housing complex) bloque m; **—
block** (solid mass) bloque [de construcción]
m; (toy) cubo m; (essential element) elemento
fundamental m
built [bɪɫt] ADJ **—-in** (furniture appliance)
empotrado; (feature) incorporado; **—-in
part** parte integrante f; **—-to-order** hecho a
pedido; **—-up** urbanizado
built [bɪɫt] see build
bulb [bʌɫb] N (plant) bulbo m; (light) bombilla f;
Am foco m
bulbous [bʌ́ɫbəs] ADJ bulboso
Bulgaria [bʌɫgériə] N Bulgaria f
Bulgarian [bʌɫgériən] ADJ & N búlgaro -ra mf
bulge [bʌɫdʒ] N bulto m, protuberancia f; VI
abultar, hincharse
bulgy [bʌ́ɫdʒi] ADJ abultado
bulimia [bjulímiə] N bulimia f
bulk [bʌɫk] N (mass) cantidad f, volumen m;
(greater part) mayor parte f; **— storage**
almacenamiento masivo m; **in —** a granel; VI
to — up echar músculos
bulky [bʌ́ɫki] ADJ voluminoso
bull [bʊɫ] N toro m; **—dog** buldog m; **—dozer**
bulldozer m; **—fight** corrida de toros f;
—fighter torero m; **—fighting**
tauromaquia f; **—frog** rana grande f; **—
market** mercado alcista m; **—pen** (baseball)
zona de calentamiento f; **—shit** disparates m
pl, mentiras f pl; **that's —shit** y una polla
[como una olla]; **—'s eye** diana f; **to hit the**

—'s-eye dar en el blanco; ADJ **—headed**
terco, obstinado
bullet [bʊ́lɪt] N bala f; ADJ **—proof** antibalas inv,
antibalístico
bulletin [bʊ́lɪtn̩] N boletín m; **— board** tablero
m, cartelera f
bullion [bʊ́ljən] N oro en lingotes m
bully [bʊ́li] N matón -ona mf, bravucón -ona mf;
VT intimidar
bulwark [bʊ́ɫwə-k] N baluarte m
bum [bʌm] N (lazy person) holgazán -ana mf;
(hobo) vagabundo -da mf; (sports fan)
fanático -ca mf; ADJ (accusation) falso; (knee)
vulg jodido; VI **to — around** holgazanear; VT
to — something from someone
gorronearle algo a alguien
bumblebee [bʌ́mbəɫbi] N abejorro m, abejón m
bummer [bʌ́mə-] N vulg cagada f
bump [bʌmp] VT chocar; **to — along** ir dando
tumbos; **to — off** despachar; **to — into**
toparse con; N (blow) choque m, trastazo m;
(lump) protuberancia f; (lump on a person)
chichón m
bumper [bʌ́mpə-] N parachoques m sg, tope m;
— car coche de choque m, autito chocador m;
— crop cosecha abundante f; **—-to-—
traffic** caravana de autos f; **— sticker**
autoadhesivo m
bumpy [bʌ́mpi] ADJ bacheado, lleno de baches
bun [bʌn] N (bread) bollo m; (in hair) moño m;
—s fam nalgas f pl
bunch [bʌntʃ] N (of things) manojo m; (of
people) montón m, grupo m; (of grapes,
bananas) racimo m; (of flowers) ramillete m;
VI/VT juntar[se], agrupar[se]
bundle [bʌ́ndl] N (of things) paquete m, fardo m,
envoltorio m; (of clothes) lío m, atado m; (of
belongings) hato m, petate m; (of firewood)
haz m; VT (tie together) liar, atar; **to — up**
abrigarse; **to — off** despachar
bungalow [bʌ́ŋgəlo] N bungaló m
bungee jumping [bʌ́ndʒidʒʌ́mpɪŋ] N bungee m,
puénting m
bungle [bʌ́ŋgəɫ] VT estropear; VI chapucear
bunion [bʌ́njən] N juanete m
bunk [bʌŋk] N (place to sleep) litera f; (nonsense)
tonterías f pl; **— bed** litera f; VI dormir en una
litera
bunker [bʌ́ŋkə-] N búnker m
bunny [bʌ́ni] N conejito m
bunt [bʌnt] N (baseball) toque de pelota m; VT
tocar la pelota
buoy [búi] N boya f; VI boyar; **to — up** mantener
a flote, animar
buoyant [bɔ́iənt] ADJ (floating) boyante,
flotante; (optimistic) optimista
burden [bɝ́dn̩] N (load) carga f; (responsibility)
peso m; **— of proof** peso de la prueba m; VT
(heavily) recargar; (oppressively) agobiar

burdensome [bɜ́dn̩səm] ADJ agobiante, gravoso

bureau [bjúro] N (government department) oficina f, agencia f; (chest of drawers) cómoda f

bureaucracy [bjʊrákrəsi] N burocracia f

bureaucrat [bjúrəkræt] N burócrata mf

burglar [bɜ́glɚ] N ladrón -ona mf; — **alarm** alarma antirrobo f; — **proof** a prueba de robos

burglary [bɜ́glɚi] N robo con allanamiento m

burial [bériəl] N entierro m, enterramiento m; — **ground** enterramiento m; — **place** lugar de sepultura m

Burkina Faso [bəkínəfáso] N Burkina Faso m

burlap [bɜ́læp] N arpillera f

burlesque [bəlésk] ADJ burlesco; N espectáculo de variedades m

burly [bɜ́li] ADJ corpulento

Burma [bɜ́mə] N Birmania f

Burmese [bəmíz] ADJ & N birmano -na mf

burn [bɜn] VI/VT quemar[se], abrasar[se]; (a house) incendiar[se]; (a CD) quemar; (food) quemar[se], requemar[se]; **he got —ed in the transaction** lo estafaron en el negocio; **the bulb is still —ing** la bombilla sigue prendida; **the iodine —ed his skin** el yodo le quemó la piel; VI (with heat, passion) arder, abrasar; **my skin —s** me arde la piel; **he's —ing with desire** arde en deseos; **to — down** incendiarse; **to — off** (fog) disiparse; **to — out** (bulb) fundirse; (worker) agotarse; **to — up** quemarse completamente; N quemadura f; —**out** surmenage m

burner [bɜ́nɚ] N (person or thing that burns something) quemador -ra mf; (on stove) hornilla f; **Bunsen —** mechero Bunsen m

burning [bɜ́nɪŋ] ADJ (desire) ardiente, abrasador; (question) urgente; N (caused by acid) ardor m; (caused by fire) quemadura f

burnish [bɜ́nɪʃ] VT bruñir

burnt [bɜrnt] see burn

burp [bɜp] N eructo m; VI eructar, repetir

burr, bur [bɜ] N abrojo m

burrow [bɜ́o] N madriguera f; VI (dig) hacer madrigueras; (live) vivir en una madriguera

bursitis [bəsáɪdɪs] N bursitis f

burst [bɜst] VI reventar[se]; **to — into a room** irrumpir en un cuarto; **to — into tears** romper en llanto; **to — out** salir disparado; **to — with laughter** estallar/reventar de risa; N (of activity) explosión f; (of laughter) carcajada f; (of machine-gun fire) ráfaga f; (of speed) aceleración f

Burundi [bʊrúndi] N Burundi m

Burundian [bʊrúndiən] ADJ & N burundés -esa mf

bury [béri] VT (body, treasure) enterrar; (body) sepultar; **to be buried in thought** estar absorto/meditabundo

bus [bʌs] N autobús m, ómnibus m; Mex camión m; RP colectivo m; Chile micro m; Cuba guagua f; (in a computer) bus m; VT transportar en autobús

bush [bʊʃ] N (plant) arbusto m, mata f; (region) matorral m; **to beat around the —** andarse por las ramas

bushed [bʊʃt] ADJ fatigado

bushel [bʊ́ʃəl] N fanega f

bushing [bʊ́ʃɪŋ] N buje m, cojinete m

bushy [bʊ́ʃi] ADJ (whiskers) espeso; (plants) poblado de arbustos

business [bíznɪs] N (trade, store) negocio m; (occupation) ocupación f; (commercial activity) comercio m; — **acumen** buen sentido para los negocios m; — **agreement** convenio comercial m; — **card** tarjeta comercial f; — **day** día hábil m; — **group** grupo empresarial m; — **hours** horas hábiles f pl, horario de atención al público m; — **is booming** el negocio florece; —**like** (efficient) eficiente; (cold) impersonal; —**man** hombre de negocios m, negociante m; — **suit** traje m; — **transaction** negocio m, transacción comercial f; —**woman** mujer de negocios f, negociante f; **I'm tired of the whole —** este asunto me tiene harto; **I mean —** hablo en serio; **to do — with** comerciar con; **he has no — doing it** no tiene derecho a hacerlo; **it's none of your —** no es asunto tuyo; **mind your own —** no te metas en lo que no te importa

bust [bʌst] N (statue, body part) busto m; VI/VT (burst, hit, break) reventar; (force into bankruptcy) hacer quebrar; (lower in rank) degradar

bustle [bʌ́səl] N (noise) bullicio m; (movement) ajetreo m, tráfago m; VI (move busily) ajetrear[se]; (be crowded) bullir

busy [bízi] ADJ ocupado, atareado; (overdecorated) recargado; —**body** entrometido -da mf; — **signal** señal de ocupado f; VI **to — oneself** ocuparse

but [bʌt] CONJ (on the contrary) pero; (excepting) sino; PREP menos; **any day — today** cualquier día menos hoy; **he's nothing — trouble** sólo da problemas; ADV — **for you** si no fuera por ti

butane [bjúten] N butano m

butch [bʊtʃ] ADJ (of a woman) marimacha, camionera; (of a man) machote

butcher [bʊ́tʃɚ] N carnicero -ra mf; —**'s shop** carnicería f; VT (cattle) matar; (people) masacrar; (performance) estropear

butchery [bʊ́tʃəri] N carnicería f

butler [bʌ́tlɚ] N mayordomo m

butt [bʌt] N (of body) fam culo m; (of a rifle) culata f; (of a cigarette) colilla f; (blow with head) topetazo m, cabezada f, cabezazo m; **the**

— **of ridicule** el blanco de las burlas; VT
embestir, topar; **to — in** entrometerse; **to —
into a conversation** meter baza; *Am* meter
la cuchara
butter [bʌ́Də] N mantequilla *f*; —**cup** botón de
oro *m*; — **dish** mantequera *f*; —**fingers**
manos de mantequilla *mf sg*; —**milk** suero de
leche *m*; —**scotch** dulce de azúcar y
mantequilla *m*; VT (bread) untar con
mantequilla; (a cakepan) enmantecar
butterfly [bʌ́Də-flaɪ] N mariposa *f*; — **stroke**
estilo mariposa *m*
buttery [bʌ́Də-i] ADJ mantecoso
buttocks [bʌ́Dəks] N nalgas *f pl*, asentaderas *f pl*,
cachas *f pl*
button [bʌ́tn̩] N botón *m*; —**hole** ojal *m*; VI/VT
abotonar[se]; VI **to** —**hole** hacer ojales; VT **to**
—**hole someone** detener a alguien
buttress [bʌ́trɪs] N apoyo *m*, sostén *m*; (of a
building) contrafuerte *m*; VT apoyar, reforzar
buxom [bʌ́ksəm] ADJ (full-bosomed) pechugona;
(fat and cheerful) frescachona, jamona
buy [baɪ] VT comprar; **to — on credit** comprar a
crédito; **to — in installments** comprar a
plazos; **to — off** sobornar; **to — out** comprar
la parte de; **to — up** acaparar; **I don't — that**
no me lo trago; N (purchase) compra *f*;
(bargain) ganga *f*
buyer [báɪə] N comprador -ra *mf*
buying [báɪɪŋ] N — **frenzy** frenesí de compras
m; — **habits** hábitos de compras *m pl*
buzz [bʌz] N zumbido *m*; (feeling of intoxication)
borrachera *f*; (phone call) telefonazo *m*;
—**word** palabra de moda *f*; — **saw** sierra
circular *f*; VI (insect, ears) zumbar; (group)
murmurar; VT hacer zumbar; **to — the bell**
tocar el timbre; **to give someone a** —
pegarle/echarle un telefonazo a alguien; **to —
off** largarse; — **off!** ¡no jodas!
buzzard [bʌ́zəd] N buitre *m*
buzzer [bʌ́zə] N timbre *m*, chicharra *f*
by [baɪ] PREP por; — **and** — a la larga; — **chance**
por casualidad; — **dint of** a fuerza de; — **far**
con mucho; — **night** de noche; — **the way** a
propósito; — **the liter** por litro; — **this
time tomorrow** mañana a esta hora; — **two
o'clock** para las dos; **we drove** — **the
church** pasamos por la iglesia; **a 4** — **3
room** un cuarto de 4 por 3; **multiply 2** — **2**
multiplica 2 por 2; **we live** — **the church**
vivimos al lado de la iglesia; **she had a son**
— **him** tuvo un hijo con él; **piece** — **piece**
pedazo a/por pedazo; ADV **the factory is
close** — la fábrica está cerca; **the bus drove**
— pasó el autobús
bye-bye [báɪbáɪ] INTERJ ¡adiós! ¡chaucito!
bygones [báɪɡɔnz] N **let** — **be** — lo pasado
pisado
bylaw [báɪlɔ] N estatuto *m*

by-line [báɪlaɪn] N pie de autor *m*
bypass [báɪpæs] VT evitar; N desvío *m*; —
operation bypass *m*
by-product [báɪprɑDəkt] N subproducto *m*;
(chemical) derivado *m*
bystander [báɪstændə] N persona presente *f*
byte [baɪt] N byte *m*, octeto *m*

Cc

cab [kæb] N (of a truck) cabina *f*; (taxi) taxi *m*; —
driver taxista *mf*
cabaret [kæbəré] N cabaret *m*
cabbage [kǽbɪʤ] N col *f*, repollo *m*, berza *f*
cabin [kǽbɪn] N (hut) cabaña *f*; (in an airplane)
cabina *f*; (in a ship) camarote *m*
cabinet [kǽbnɪt] N (for dishes) armario *m*; (for
medicines) botiquín *m*; (for display) vitrina *f*;
(of ministers) gabinete *m*; —**level
appointment** nombramiento ministerial *m*;
—**maker** ebanista *mf*
cable [kébəl] N cable *m*; (on ships) amarra *f*;
(telegram) telegrama *m*; — **car** funicular *m*,
teleférico *m*; — **television** televisión por
cable *f*, cablevisión *f*; VI/VT telegrafiar
caboose [kəbús] N furgón de cola *m*
cache [kæʃ] N (of weapons) alijo *m*; (in a
computer) caché *m*; — **memory** memoria de
caché *f*
cachet [kæʃé] N caché *m*
cackle [kǽkəl] VI (hen) cacarear; (people)
parlotear; N (hen) cacareo *m*; (people)
parloteo *m*
cacophony [kəkɑ́fəni] N cacofonía *f*
cactus [kǽktəs] N cacto *m*, cactus *m*
cad [kæd] N *pej* canalla *mf*
cadaver [kədǽvə] N cadáver *m*
caddie [kǽDi] N caddy *m*, caddie *m*
cadence [kédn̩s] N cadencia *f*
cadet [kədét] N cadete *mf*
cadmium [kǽdmiəm] N cadmio *m*
café [kæfé] N (coffee only) café *m*; (coffee and
food) cafetería *f*
cafeteria [kæfɪtíriə] N cafetería *f*
caffeine [kæfín] N cafeína *f*
cage [keʤ] N jaula *f*; VT enjaular
cahoots [kəhúts] ADV LOC **in** — arreglados
cajole [kəʤól] VI/VT engatusar, persuadir con
halagos
cake [kek] N pastel *m*, torta *f*; (sponge) bizcocho
m; (soap) pastilla *f*; **a piece of** — pan comido;
to take the — ser el colmo; VI/VT
apelmazar[se]
calamine [kǽləmaɪn] N calamina *f*
calamity [kəlǽmɪDi] N calamidad *f*

calcium [kǽlsiəm] N calcio *m*
calculate [kǽlkjəlet] VI/VT calcular; **his actions were —d to fool us** con sus acciones trataba de engañarnos
calculating [kǽlkjəleDɪŋ] ADJ calculador
calculation [kælkjəléʃən] N cálculo *m*
calculator [kǽlkjəleDɚ] calculadora *f*
calculus [kǽlkjələs] N cálculo *m*
calendar [kǽlɪndɚ] N calendario *m*; **— year** año civil *m*
calf [kæf] N (of leg) pantorrilla *f*, canilla *f*; (animal) ternero -ra *mf*, becerro -rra *mf*; **— skin** piel de becerro *f*
caliber [kǽləbɚ] N calibre *m*
calibrate [kǽləbret] VT calibrar, graduar
calico [kǽlɪko] N calicó *m*
caliper [kǽləpɚ] N (on brakes) calibrador *m*; (for measuring) calibre *m*
call [kɔl] VT (summon, by telephone, a name, a strike) llamar; (cry out) gritar; (a meeting) convocar; **she —ed me a liar** me llamó mentiroso; **— me back** llámame tú, devuélveme la llamada; VI/VT (birds) reclamar; **to — roll** pasar lista; VI (call out) gritar; **to — a meeting to order** abrir la sesión; **to — at a port** hacer escala en un puerto; **to — for** pedir; **to — off** cancelar; **to — on** (visit) visitar; (depend on) acudir a; **to — together** convocar; **to — up** llamar por teléfono; N (by telephone) llamada *f*; (summons) llamamiento *m*, llamado *m*; (to the ministry) vocación *f*; (for conference papers) convocatoria *f*; (device for calling birds) reclamo *m*; **— girl** prostituta de cita *f*; **to be on —** estar de guardia; **there's no — for panic** no hay motivo de alarma; **it's your —** tú decides; **within —** al alcance de la voz
caller [kɔ́lɚ] N visita *f*, visitante *mf*; (by telephone) persona que llama *f*; **— ID** identificador de llamadas *m*
calligraphy [kəlígrəfi] N caligrafía *f*
calling [kɔ́lɪŋ] N vocación *f*
callous [kǽləs] ADJ (having calluses) calloso; (insensitive) insensible
callus [kǽləs] N callo *m*
calm [kam] ADJ tranquilo, reposado, calmo; N calma *f*, tranquilidad *f*, sosiego *m*; VT calmar, tranquilizar, sosegar; **to — down** calmar[se]
calmness [kámnɪs] N calma *f*, tranquilidad *f*
calorie [kǽləri] N caloría *f*
calumny [kǽləmni] N calumnia *f*
cam [kæm] N leva *f*
Cambodia [kæmbóDiə] N Camboya *f*
Cambodian [kæmbóDiən] ADJ & N camboyano -na *mf*
camcorder [kǽmkɔrDɚ] N videocámara *f*
came [kem] *see* come
camel [kǽməl] N camello *m*

cameo [kǽmio] N camafeo *m*; **— appearance** actuación especial *f*
camera [kǽmrə] N cámara *f*, cámara fotográfica *f*; **—man** cámara *m*, camarógrafo *m*; **—-ready copy** texto listo para cámara *f*; **—woman** cámara *f*, camarógrafa *f*
Cameroon [kæmərún] N Camerún *m*
Cameroonian [kæmərúniən] ADJ & N camerunés -esa *mf*
camouflage [kǽməflɑʒ] N camuflaje *m*; VT camuflar
camp [kæmp] N (campsite) campamento *m*; (faction) bando *m*; **—fire** fogata *f*, hoguera *f*; **—ground** campamento *m*, cámping *m*; **—site** campamento *m*; VI/VT acampar
campaign [kæmpén] N campaña *f*; VI hacer campaña
camper [kǽmpɚ] N acampante *mf*, campista *mf*
camphor [kǽmfɚ] N alcanfor *m*
camping [kǽmpɪŋ] N cámping *m*, acampada *f*; **let's go —** vamos de camping / de acampada
campus [kǽmpəs] N campus *m*
can [kæn] N lata *f*, bote *m*; **— of worms** caja de Pandora *f*; **— opener** abrelatas *m sg*; VT enlatar; V AUX **— you come tomorrow?** ¿puedes venir mañana? **— you see me?** ¿me ves? **I — ride a bicycle** sé andar en bicicleta; **a —-do attitude** un espíritu emprendedor
Canada [kǽnəDə] N Canadá *m*
Canadian [kənédiən] ADJ & N canadiense *mf*
canal [kənǽl] N canal *m*
canary [kənéri] N canario *m*; **Canary Islands** Islas Canarias *f pl*
Canary Islands [kənériáɪlənz] N Islas Canarias *f pl*
cancel [kǽnsəl] VT cancelar; (a stamp) matasellar; (an order) anular
cancellation [kænsəléʃən] N (of a flight, performance) cancelación *f*; (of an order) anulación *f*
cancer [kǽnsɚ] N cáncer *m*; **— patient** canceroso -sa *mf*; ADJ **—-causing** cancerígeno
cancerous [kǽnsɚəs] ADJ canceroso
candelabrum, candelabra [kændəlábrəm -brə] N candelabro *m*
candid [kǽndɪd] ADJ franco, sincero
candidacy [kǽndɪDəsi] N candidatura *f*
candidate [kǽndɪDɪt] N (for office) candidato -ta *mf*; (for a job) aspirante *mf*, postulante *mf*
candle [kǽndl] N vela *f*, candela *f*; (on the altar) cirio *m*; **—stick** candelero *m*
candor [kǽndɚ] N franqueza *f*
candy [kǽndi] N dulce *m*, caramelo *m*, confite *m*; (with chocolate) bombón *m*; **— store** bombonería *f*; VT confitar, acaramelar; (nuts) garapiñar; VI (syrup) cristalizarse
cane [ken] N (sugar) caña *f*; (walking) bastón *m*; **— chair** silla de mimbre *f*

canine [kénaɪn] ADJ canino, perruno; N (dog) can m, perro m; (tooth) canino m
canister [kǽnɪstə-] N lata f
canker [kæŋkə-] N úlcera f
cannery [kǽnəri] N fábrica de conservas f
cannibal [kǽnəbəl] N caníbal m
cannon [kǽnən] N cañón m; — **fodder** carne de cañón f
canny [kǽni] ADJ sagaz, astuto
canoe [kənú] N canoa f
canon [kǽnən] N (rule, melody, body of works) canon m; (priest) canónigo m
canopy [kǽnəpi] N (of a bed) dosel m; (of a building) toldo m
cantaloupe [kǽntḷop] N melón m
canteen [kæntín] N (snack bar) cantina f; (container) cantimplora f
canvas [kǽnvəs] N (fabric) lona f; (for painting) lienzo m
canvass [kǽnvəs] VI/VT (poll) encuestar; (solicit votes) solicitar votos en; (solicit sales) buscar pedidos comerciales en; N solicitud f
canyon [kǽnjən] N cañón m
cap [kæp] N (head covering without visor) gorro m; (head covering with visor) gorra f; (of a bottle) tapa f; (of a pen) capucha f, contera f; (limit) tope m; (for capgun) fulminante m, pistón m; VT (to cover, put a cap on) tapar; (to complete) rematar; (to limit) limitar
capability [kepəbílɪDi] N capacidad f
capable [képəbəl] ADJ capaz
capacious [kəpéʃəs] ADJ amplio
capacity [kəpǽsɪDi] N capacidad f
cape [kep] N (clothing) capa f; (promontory) cabo m
caper [képə-] N (skipping) cabriola f; (prank) treta f, triquiñuela f; (crime) delito m; (food) alcaparra f; VI retozar
Cape Verde [kepvə́-d] N Cabo Verde m
Cape Verdean [kepvə́-Diən] ADJ & N caboverdiano -na mf
capillary [kǽpəlɛri] N & ADJ [vaso] capilar m
capital [kǽpɪdḷ] N (city) capital f; (wealth) capital m; (of a column) capitel m; (letter) mayúscula f; **to make — of** sacar partido de, aprovecharse de; ADJ (city) capital; (financial) de capital; — **gains** ganancias en bienes de capital f pl; — **investment** inversión de capital f; — **punishment** pena de muerte f
capitalism [kǽpɪdḷɪzəm] N capitalismo m
capitalist [kǽpɪdḷɪst] N capitalista mf
capitalistic [kǽpɪdḷístɪk] ADJ capitalista
capitalization [kæpɪdḷɪzéʃən] N capitalización f
capitalize [kǽpɪdḷaɪz] VT (finance) capitalizar; (write) escribir con mayúscula; **to — on** sacar provecho de
capitol [kǽpɪdḷ] N capitolio m
capitulate [kəpítʃəlet] VI capitular
cappuccino [kæpətʃíno] N capuchino m

caprice [kəprís] N capricho m
capricious [kəpríʃəs] ADJ caprichoso
capsize [kǽpsaɪz] VI/VT volcar[se]
capsule [kǽpsəl] N cápsula f
captain [kǽptɪn] N capitán m; VT capitanear
caption [kǽpʃən] N (with illustration) pie m; (subtitle) subtítulo m
captivate [kǽptəvet] VT cautivar
captive [kǽptɪv] ADJ & N cautivo -va mf; — **animals** animales en cautiverio m pl
captivity [kæptívɪDi] N cautiverio m
captor [kǽptə-] N captor -ra mf
capture [kǽptʃə-] VT (apprehend, record data) capturar; (give expression to) plasmar; (attract) cautivar; (conquer) tomar; N captura f
car [kar] N (automobile) coche m, automóvil m; Am carro m, auto m; (railroad) vagón m, coche m; (elevator) cabina f; Am elevador m; — **bomb** coche bomba m; —**fare** pasaje m; —**jacking** secuestro de vehículo m; —**load** carga de un coche f; —**port** cochera f; — **wash** túnel de lavado m; ADJ —**sick** mareado; **to get —sick** marearse en el coche
caramel [kǽrəməl] N caramelo m
carat [kǽrət] N quilate m
caravan [kǽrəvæn] N caravana f
carbohydrate [karbəháɪdret] N carbohidrato m, hidrato de carbono m
carbon [kárbən] N carbono m; — **copy** copia en papel carbón f; — **dioxide** dióxido de carbono m; — **monoxide** monóxido de carbono m; — **paper** papel carbón m
carburetor [kárbəreDə-] N carburador m
carcass [kárkəs] N (of an animal) cuerpo muerto m; (of a ship) casco m
carcinogen [karsínədʒən] N cancerígeno m, carcinógeno m
carcinoma [karsənómə] N carcinoma m
card [kard] N (piece of stiff paper) tarjeta f; (for games) naipe m, carta f; (for boxing events) programa m; (for textiles) carda f; (witty person) gracioso -sa mf; (in a computer) tarjeta f, placa f; —**board** (thick) cartón m; (thin) cartulina f; — **reader** lector de tarjetas m; — **sharp** fullero -ra mf; **pack of —s** baraja f; **to play —s** jugar a la baraja, jugar a los naipes; **he's holding all the —s** tiene todas las ventajas; VT (comb) cardar; (ask for identification) pedir identificación
cardiac [kárDiæk] ADJ cardiaco, cardíaco
cardinal [kárdnəl] ADJ (number, main) cardinal; (colored red) rojo, bermellón; N (bishop, bird) cardenal m
cardioangiogram [karDioǽndʒiəgræm] N cardioangiograma m
cardiogram [kárDiogræm] N cardiograma m
cardiologist [karDiálədʒɪst] N cardiólogo -ga mf
cardiology [karDiálədʒi] N cardiología f

cardiopulmonary [kɑrdiopÚɫmənɛri] ADJ cardiopulmonar; — **bypass** puente cardiopulmonar *m*

cardiovascular [kɑrdiováskjələ-] ADJ cardiovascular

care [kɛr] N (worry) preocupación *f*; (attention) cuidado *m*, atención *f*, tiento *m*; (extreme attention) esmero *m*, primor *m*; —**giver** cuidador -ra de enfermos *mf*; —**taker** (of a house) casero -ra *mf*; **to be under the** — **of** estar al cuidado de; **to take** — **of** cuidar de, atender; ADJ —**free** despreocupado; VI (be concerned) importarle a uno; **to** — **about** interesarle a uno, importarle a uno; **to** — **for** (look after) cuidar de; (love) tenerle cariño a; **to** — **to** tener ganas de; **I couldn't** — **less** me importa un rábano; **what does he** —? ¿a él qué le importa? **would you** — **for a drink?** ¿te puedo ofrecer algo?

careen [kərín] VI ladearse a toda velocidad

career [kərír] N carrera *f*, trayectoria *f*

careful [kérfəɫ] ADJ (cautious) cuidadoso, cauteloso; (painstaking) esmerado; **to be** — tener cuidado

carefully [kérfəli] ADV (safely) con cuidado; (painstakingly) esmeradamente

carefulness [kérfəɫnɪs] N cuidado *m*

careless [kérlɪs] ADJ descuidado

caress [kərés] N caricia *f*; VT acariciar

cargo [kárgo] N cargamento *m*

Caribbean [kærəbíən] N Caribe *m*; ADJ caribeño

caricature [kérɪkətʃə-] N caricatura *f*; VT caricaturizar

caries [kériz] N caries *f*

carnage [kárnɪdʒ] N carnicería *f*

carnal [kárnl] ADJ carnal

carnation [karnéʃən] N (flower) clavel *m*; (color) rosado *m*

carnival [kárnəvəɫ] N carnaval *m*; (traveling) feria *f*

carnivorous [karnívə-əs] ADJ carnívoro, carnicero

carol [kérəɫ] N villancico *m*; VI cantar villancicos

carom [kérəm] N carambola *f*; VI rebotar

carotid artery [kərádɪdárDəri] N [arteria] carótida *f*

carouse [kəráuz] VI andar de parranda

carp [karp] N carpa *f*; VI (complain) quejarse

carpenter [kárpəntə-] N carpintero -ra *mf*

carpentry [kárpəntri] N carpintería *f*

carpet [kárpɪt] N alfombra *f*; —**bagger** político -ca oportunista *mf*; VT alfombrar

carriage [kérɪdʒ] N (wheeled vehicle) carruaje *m*, coche *m*; (posture) porte *m*

carrier [kériə-] N (one who carries) portador -ra *mf*; (postal worker) cartero -ra *mf*; (transport company) mensajería *f*

carrion [kériən] N carroña *f*

carrot [kérət] N zanahoria *f*

carry [kéri] VT llevar; **do you** — **Italian wine?** ¿venden vino italiano? **the bill carried** se aprobó el proyecto de ley; **you** — **yourself well** te comportas bien; **he can't** — **a tune** no puede seguir una tonada; **this suitcase will** — **a lot** esta maleta es espaciosa; **to** — **away** llevarse; **he got carried away** se le fue la mano; **to** — **on** continuar; **to** — **out** (complete) llevar a cabo, ejecutar; (take out) sacar; N —**-on** maleta de mano *f*

cart [kart] N (also golf) carro *m*; VT acarrear

cartilage [kárdl̩ɪdʒ] N cartílago *m*

carton [kártn̩] N caja de cartón *f*

cartoon [kartún] N (drawing) caricatura *f*; (strip) tira cómica *f*; (film) dibujo animado *m*

cartoonist [kartúnɪst] N caricaturista *mf*

cartridge [kártrɪdʒ] N cartucho *m*; — **belt** cartuchera *f*, canana *f*

carve [karv] VI/VT (a piece of wood) tallar; (a turkey) trinchar; **to** — **out a career** labrarse una carrera

carving [kárvɪŋ] N (action) tallado *m*; (figure) talla *f*; — **knife** trinchante *m*

cascade [kæskéd] N cascada *f*

case [kes] N caso *m*; (box) caja *f*; (of a pillow) funda *f*; — **history** historia clínica *f*; **in** — **[that]** en caso de [que]; **in** — **it rains** por si llueve; **in any** — en todo caso; **just in** — por si acaso; **get off my** —! ¡déjame en paz! —**-sensitive** sensible a la diferencia entre mayúsculas y minúsculas

cash [kæʃ] N efectivo *m*; — **advance** anticipo en efectivo *m*; — **and carry** al contado y sin entrega a domicilio; — **flow** corriente en efectivo *f*; — **on delivery** entrega contra reembolso *f*; — **payment** pago en efectivo *m*; — **register** caja registradora *f*; **to pay** — pagar al contado; VT cobrar

cashew [kéʃu] N marañón *m*, castaña de cajú *f*, *Sp* anacardo *m*

cashier [kæʃír] N cajero -ra *mf*; —**'s check** cheque de caja *m*

casino [kəsíno] N casino *m*

cask [kæsk] N tonel grande *m*

casket [késkɪt] N ataúd *m*

casserole [késərol] N (container) cazuela *f*; (food) guiso *m*

cassette [kəsét] N cassette *mf*, casete *mf*

cast [kæst] VT (throw) tirar, echar; (form an object) moldear, vaciar; (give out dramatic roles) repartir papeles; **to** — **a ballot** votar; **to** — **about** buscar; **to** — **a glance** echar un vistazo; **to** — **aside** desechar; **to** — **doubt** poner en duda; **to** — **light on** aclarar; **to** — **lots** echar suertes; **to** — **off** (a ship) soltar amarras; (something rejected) deshacerse de; **to** — **out** exiliar; **to be** — **down** estar abatido; N (form) molde *m*; (in theater) reparto *m*, elenco *m*; (for broken bones) yeso;

to put in a — enyesar; — **iron** hierro
fundido *m*
castanet [kǽstənɛt] N castañuela*f*
caste [kæst] N casta*f*
castigate [kǽstɪget] VT (criticize) criticar,
reprender; (punish) castigar
Castile [kæstíł] N Castilla*f*
Castilian [kæstíljən] N & ADJ castellano -na *mf*;
— **speaker** castellanohablante *mf*; ADJ —
speaking castellanohablante
casting [kǽstɪŋ] N (throwing) tiro *m*; (piece of
metal) pieza fundida*f*; (selection of actors)
cásting *m*
castle [kǽsəł] N castillo *m*; (chess piece) torre*f*,
roque *m*
castor oil [kǽstəɔɪł] N aceite de ricino *m*
castrate [kǽstret] VT castrar; (animals) capar
casual [kǽʒuəł] ADJ (informal) informal;
(offhand) al pasar
casualty [kǽʒuəłti] N (of war) baja*f*; (in an
accident) víctima*f*
cat [kæt] N (domestic) gato -ta *mf*; (others) felino
m; —**'s meow** súmmum *m*; —**fish** siluro *m*;
—**house** burdel *m*
Catalan [kǽdļæn] ADJ & N catalán -ana *mf*;
(language) catalán *m*
catalog, catalogue [kǽdļɔg] N catálogo *m*; VT
catalogar
Catalonia [kædļóniə] N Cataluña*f*
Catalonian [kædļóniən] ADJ catalán
catalyst [kǽdļɪst] N catalizador *m*
cataract [kǽDərækt] N catarata*f*
catastrophe [kətǽstrəfi] N catástrofe*f*
catatonia [kædətóniə] N catatonia*f*
catch [kætʃ] VT (a criminal, ball) atrapar; *Sp*,
Cuba coger; (a fish) pescar, capturar;
(someone in an act) pillar; (a bus) agarrar;
(what someone said) comprender, agarrar; **to**
— **a glimpse of** vislumbrar; **to** — **cold**
resfriarse; **to** — **fire** prenderse fuego; **to** —
on (understand) caer en cuenta; (become
popular) ponerse de moda; **to** — **oneself**
contenerse; **to** — **one's eye** llamarle a uno la
atención; **to** — **sight of** avistar; **to** —
unawares sorprender; **to** — **up** (with a
person) alcanzar; (on work) ponerse al día,
actualizarse, VI (get entangled) enredarse;
(snap into place) agarrar; N (act of catching
prey, quantity caught) captura*f*, redada*f*,
pesca*f*; (prey) presa*f*; (device) pestillo *m*; (act
of catching a ball) atrapada*f*; —**phrase**
eslogan *m*; — **twenty-two** paradoja*f*; **he is**
a good — es un buen partido; **to play** —
jugar a la pelota; **what's the** —? ¿cuál es la
treta?
catcher [kǽtʃ] N (baseball) receptor -ora *mf*
catching [kǽtʃɪŋ] ADJ contagioso
catchy [kǽtʃi] ADJ pegadizo
catechism [kǽDɪkɪzəm] N catecismo *m*

category [kǽDɪgɔri] N categoría*f*
cater [kéDə] VI/VT abastecer de alimentos
[banquetes, fiestas, etc.]; **to** — **to** atender a
caterpillar [kǽDəpɪlə] N (insect) oruga*f*;
(tractor) tractor oruga *m*, caterpillar *m*
cathedral [kəθídrəł] N catedral*f*
catheter [kǽθIDə] N catéter *m*, sonda*f*
catheterization [kæθəDə-ɪzéʃən] N
cateterización*f*
catheterize [kǽθəDə-aɪz] VT cateterizar
cathode [kǽθod] N cátodo *m*; — **rays** rayos
catódicos *m pl*
Catholic [kǽθlɪk] N & ADJ católico -ca *mf*
Catholicism [kəθálɪsɪzəm] N catolicismo *m*
CAT [computerized axial tomography]
scan [kǽtskæn] N TAC*f*
catsup [kǽtʃəp] N cátsup *m*, ketchup *m*, salsa de
tomate*f*
cattle [kǽdļ] N ganado [vacuno] *m*; —**breeding**
ganadería*f*; —**man** ganadero *m*; — **rustler**
cuatrero *m*; — **rustling** abigeato *m*
catty [kǽdi] ADJ malicioso
caught [kɔt] *see* catch
cauliflower [kɔ́lɪflauə] N coliflor*f*
cause [kɔz] N causa*f*, causante*f*; — **for**
celebration motivo de celebración *m*; **the**
democratic — la causa democrática*f*;
without — sin motivo; VT (make happen)
causar, ocasionar; (motivate) motivar; **to** —
to flee hacer huir; **the heat** —**d her to**
faint el calor la hizo desmayar
caustic [kɔ́stɪk] ADJ cáustico
cauterize [kɔ́DəraIz] VT cauterizar
caution [kɔ́ʃən] N (prudence) cautela*f*, recato *m*;
(warning) advertencia*f*; —! ¡cuidado!
¡atención! VT advertir; **to** — **against**
desaconsejar
cautious [kɔ́ʃəs] ADJ cauto, cauteloso, precavido
cava [kávə] N (wine) cava*f*
cavalier [kævəlír] N caballero *m*, galán *m*; ADJ
(disdainful) desdeñoso; (overly casual)
displicente
cavalry [kǽvəłri] N caballería*f*
cave [kev] N cueva*f*, caverna*f*; —**man** hombre
de las cavernas *m*; VI **to** — **in** (yield) ceder;
(collapse) derrumbarse, desplomarse
cavern [kǽvən] N caverna*f*, gruta*f*
cavity [kǽvɪDi] N cavidad*f*; (in a tooth) caries*f*;
(nasal) fosa*f*
cavort [kəvɔ́rt] VI cabriolar, retozar
caw [kɔ] N graznido *m*; VI graznar
CD [compact disc] [sídí] N CD *m*, disco
compacto *m*; — **player** reproductor de discos
compactos *m*; —-**ROM** CD-ROM *m*
cease [sis] VI cesar; VT interrumpir; N —-**fire**
alto el fuego *m*; *Am* cese el fuego *m*
ceaseless [sísłɪs] ADJ incesante
cedar [síDə] N cedro *m*
cede [sid] VT ceder

ceiling [síliŋ] N techo *m*, cielo raso *m*; (cap) tope *m*; (sky) altura máxima *f*
celebrate [séləbret] VI/VT celebrar, festejar
celebrated [séləbreDɪd] ADJ célebre
celebration [sɛləbréʃən] N (action) celebración *f*, festejo *m*; (festivities) fiesta *f*
celebratory [səlébrətori] ADJ festivo
celebrity [səlébrɪDi] N celebridad *f*
celery [séləri] N apio *m*
celestial [səléstʃəł] ADJ celeste; (heavenly) celestial; — **body** astro *m*
celibate [séləbɪt] ADJ célibe
cell [sɛł] N (room) celda *f*; (structural) célula *f*; — **biology** citología *f*
cellar [sélɚ] N sótano *m*; (for wine) bodega *f*, cava *f*
cello [tʃélo] N violonchelo *m*
cellophane [séləfen] N celofán *m*
cellular [séljəlɚ] ADJ celular; — **phone** celular *m*; *Sp* móvil *m*
cellulite [séljəlaɪt] N celulitis *f*
celluloid [séljəlɔɪd] N celuloide *m*
cellulose [séljəlos] N celulosa *f*
cement [sɪmént] N cemento *m*; (glue) adhesivo *m*; — **mixer** hormigonera *f*; VI/VT cementar
cemetery [sémɪteri] N cementerio *m*
censor [sénsɚ] N censor -ora *mf*; VT censurar
censorship [sénsɚʃɪp] N censura *f*
censure [sénʃɚ] N censura *f*; VT censurar
census [sénsəs] N censo *m*; **to take a** — censar
cent [sent] N centavo *m*, céntimo *m*
centennial [sɛnténiəł] ADJ & N centenario *m*
center [séntɚ] N centro *m*; (in basketball) centro *m*, *Am* pivot *m*; — **forward** (soccer) ariete *mf*; — **of gravity** centro de gravedad *m*; VI/VT centrar[se]
centigrade [séntɪgred] ADJ centígrado
centimeter [séntəmiDɚ] N centímetro *m*
centipede [séntəpid] N ciempiés *m*
central [séntrəł] ADJ central; (downtown) céntrico; N central de teléfonos *f*; — **heating** calefacción central *f*; — **nervous system** sistema nervioso central *m*; — **processing unit** unidad central de proceso/procesamiento *f*
Central [séntrəł] ADJ — **African Republic** República Centroafricana *f*; — **America** Centroamérica *f*; — **American** centroamericano
centralize [séntrəlaɪz] VI/VT centralizar[se]; **to be/become —d** centralizarse
centrifugal [sɛntrífəgəł] ADJ centrífugo
centripetal [sɛntrípɪdl̩] ADJ centrípeto
century [séntʃəri] N siglo *m*
CEO [chief executive officer] [síío] N *Am* director -ora general *mf*, *Sp* consejero -ra, delegado -da *mf*
ceramic [səræmɪk] ADJ cerámico; N —**s** cerámica *f*

cereal [síriəł] N (breakfast food) cereal *m*; (the grain itself) grano *m*; ADJ cereal
cerebral [səríbrəł] ADJ cerebral; — **concussion** conmoción cerebral *f*; — **cortex** corteza cerebral *f*; — **embolism** embolia cerebral *f*; — **hemorrhage** hemorragia cerebral *f*; — **palsy** parálisis cerebral *f*
ceremonial [sɛrəmóniəł] ADJ & N ceremonial *m*
ceremonious [sɛrəmóniəs] ADJ ceremonioso
ceremony [sérəmoni] N ceremonia *f*
certain [sɚ́tn̩] ADJ seguro; — **people** determinadas personas *f pl*; — **rules are inviolable** ciertas/determinadas reglas son inviolables; **death and taxes are** — lo único seguro son los impuestos y la muerte; **he's** — **to come** seguro que viene; **it is** — **that it rained** seguro que llovió
certainly [sɚ́tn̩li] ADV seguramente, sin duda; **she** — **gets her way** no cabe duda de que se sale con la suya; INTERJ ¡cómo no!
certainty [sɚ́tn̩ti] N certeza *f*, certidumbre *f*
certificate [sɚtífɪkɪt] N certificado *m*; — **of baptism** fe de bautismo *f*; — **of deposit** certificado de depósito *m*
certification [sɚDəfɪkéʃən] N certificación *f*
certify [sɚ́Dəfaɪ] VT certificar; **certified check** cheque certificado *m*; **certified mail** correo certificado *m*; **certified public accountant** contador -ora público -ca *mf*
cervical [sɚ́vɪkəł] ADJ cervical
cervix [sɚ́vɪks] N (neck) verviz *f*; (uterine) cérvix *m*, cuello uterino *m*
cesarean section [sɪzériənsékʃən] N cesárea *f*
cessation [sɛséʃən] N cese *m*
cesspool [séspuł] N pozo séptico *m*, fosa séptica *f*
Chad [tʃæd] N Chad *m*
Chadian [tʃǽDiən] ADJ & N chadiano -na *mf*
chafe [tʃef] VI/VT rozar[se]; N rozadura *f*
chaff [tʃæf] N ahechaduras *f pl*
chagrin [ʃəgrín] N mortificación *f*; VT mortificar
chain [tʃen] N cadena *f*; — **reaction** reacción en cadena *f*; — **saw** sierra *f*; — **smoker** persona que fuma como una chimenea *f*; — **store** tienda de cadena *f*; VI/VT encadenar[se]
chair [tʃɛr] N silla *f*; (academic) cátedra *f*; (of a meeting) presidente -ta *mf*; (of a department) jefe -fa *mf*; —**man** presidente *m*, director *m*, jefe *m*; —**manship** dirección *f*; —**person** presidente -ta *mf*, jefe -fa *mf*; —**woman** presidenta *f*, jefa *f*
chalk [tʃɔk] N (substance) caliza *f*; (piece) tiza *f*; —**board** pizarrón *m*, pizarra *f*, tablero *m*; VT marcar con tiza; **to** — **up** (attribute) atribuir; (score) marcar
chalky [tʃɔ́ki] ADJ de/con/como tiza
challenge [tʃǽlɪndʒ] N desafío *m*, reto *m*; (of a jury) recusación *f*; VT (defy) desafiar, retar; (take exception) cuestionar, disputar; (recuse) recusar; **to be vertically —d** ser muy bajito

chamber [tʃémbɚ] N (legislative) cámara f; (in a palace) aposento m; (of a cannon) recámara f; —**maid** camarera f, mucama f; — **music** música de cámara f; — **of commerce** cámara de comercio f; — **pot** orinal m; —**s** (of a judge) despacho m

chameleon [kəmíljən] N camaleón m

chamois [ʃǽmi] N gamuza f

champagne [ʃæmpén] N champán m, champaña mf

champion [tʃǽmpiən] N campeón -ona mf; (of a cause) defensor -ora mf, paladín m; VT defender

championship [tʃǽmpiənʃɪp] N campeonato m

chance [tʃæns] N (opportunity) oportunidad f; (probability) probabilidad f; (unpredictable element) casualidad f, azar m; **by** — por casualidad; **game of** — juego de azar m; **to take a** — correr riesgo, arriesgarse; ADJ casual; VI arriesgarse; **we** —**d to meet him at the bar** nos encontramos con él en el bar por casualidad

chancellor [tʃǽnsəlɚ] N (chief minister) canciller m; (of a university) rector -ora de universidad mf

chandelier [ʃændəlír] N araña de luces f

change [tʃendʒ] VT cambiar; **to** — **clothes** cambiarse de ropa; **to** — **into** transformar[se] en; **to** — **trains** cambiar de tren; N cambio m; (money returned) vuelta f; Am vuelto m; (fresh clothes) muda de ropa f; — **of heart** cambio de opinión m; — **over** (tennis) cambio de lado m; —-**up** (baseball) cambio m, cambio de velocidad m

changeable [tʃéndʒəbəl] ADJ (variable) cambiante, variable; (fickle) inconstante, tornadizo; — **silk** seda tornasolada f

channel [tʃǽnl] N canal m; (bed of stream) cauce m; VT canalizar, encauzar

chant [tʃænt] N (plain song) canto llano m; (hymn) cántico m; (repeated slogan) cantinela f; VI/VT (sing) cantar; (repeat a slogan) corear

chaos [kéas] N caos m

chaotic [keáDɪk] ADJ caótico

chap [tʃæp] VI/VT cuartear[se], agrietar[se]; —**ped lips** labios agrietados m pl; —**stick**® crema para los labios f; N (fellow) tipo m

chaparral [ʃæpərǽl] N chaparral m

chapel [tʃǽpəl] N capilla f

chaperon, chaperone [ʃǽpəron] N chaperón -ona f; VI ir de chaperón -ona

chaplain [tʃǽplɪn] N capellán m

chapter [tʃǽptɚ] N capítulo m

char [tʃɑr] VI/VT (reduce to ashes) carbonizar[se]; (scorch) chamuscar[se]

character [kǽrɪktɚ] N carácter m; (of a novel) personaje m; — **actor** actor de carácter m; **Chinese** —**s** caracteres chinos m pl; **he's quite a** — es todo un personaje; **that's out**

of — **for him** eso no es característico de él

characteristic [kærɪktərístɪk] ADJ característico; N característica f; (genetic) carácter m

characterization [kærɪktɚ-ɪzéʃən] N caracterización f

characterize [kǽrɪktəraɪz] VT (describe) caracterizar; (attribute) calificar

charade [ʃəréd] N farsa f; —**s** charada f

charcoal [tʃárkoɫ] N carbón de leña m; — **drawing** dibujo al carbón m

charge [tʃɑrdʒ] VT (demand money) cobrar; (load) cargar; (buy on credit) cargar a cuenta; (attack) embestir; (in basketball) cargar; **to** — **off a loss** restar una pérdida; **to** — **someone with a task** encargarle a alguien una tarea; **to** — **with murder** acusar de homicidio; N (mission) misión f, encargo m; (accusation) cargo m, acusación f; (charge in account) cargo m, débito m; (explosives, electricity) carga f; (attack) embestida f; — **account** cuenta de crédito f; — **card** tarjeta de crédito f; **there will be a** — **for delivery** se cobra entrega a domicilio; **to be in** — **of** estar a cargo de; **under my** — a mi cargo

charger [tʃárdʒɚ] N (for a battery) cargador m; (horse) corcel m

chariot [tʃǽriət] N carro de guerra m

charisma [kərízmə] N carisma m

charitable [tʃǽrɪDəbəl] ADJ caritativo

charity [tʃǽrɪDi] N (virtue, aid to the poor) caridad f; (institution) institución benéfica f, institución de beneficencia f; **to give to** — dar dinero a las instituciones benéficas; **to live on** — vivir de la caridad

charlatan [ʃárlətən] N charlatán -ana mf

charm [tʃɑrm] N (attractiveness) encanto m, saleroso m; (trinket) dije m; (spell) sortilegio m, hechizo m; (amulet) talismán m, amuleto m; VT (delight) encantar; (influence) hechizar, subyugar

charming [tʃármɪŋ] ADJ encantador, saleroso; Sp majo

chart [tʃart] N (table) tabla f; (graph) gráfica f; (marine map) carta f; (of musical hits) lista de éxitos f; VT (in a table) tabular; (in a graph) graficar; (a region) cartografiar; **to** — **a course** trazar una ruta

charter [tʃárDɚ] N (of a city) fuero m; (of an organization) estatuto m; (document granting rights) constitución f, carta f; (hire) flete m; — **flight** [vuelo] chárter m; — **member** socio -cia fundador -ora mf; VT (a corporation) aprobar los estatutos; (a flight) fletar

chase [tʃes] VT (hunt) cazar; (follow rapidly) perseguir; **to** — **after** correr tras; **to** — **away** ahuyentar; N caza f, persecución f

chasm [kǽzəm] N sima f

chassis [tʃǽsi] N chasis m, bastidor m

chaste [tʃest] ADJ casto, honesto
chastise [tʃǽstaɪz] VT (punish) castigar; (criticize) criticar
chastisement [tʃæstáɪzmənt] N (punishment) castigo *m*; (criticism) crítica *f*
chastity [tʃǽstɪDi] N castidad *f*, honestidad *f*
chat [tʃæt] N charla *f*; *Mex* plática *f*; — **room** sala de chat *f*; VI charlar; *Mex* platicar; VI chatear
chattel [tʃǽdl] N (movable property) bien mueble *m*; (slave) esclavo -va *mf*
chatter [tʃǽDɚ] VI (jabber) cotorrear, parlotear; VT (click rapidly) castañetear; N (of speech) cotorreo *m*, parloteo *m*; (of teeth) castañeteo *m*; —**box** charlatán -ana *mf*, cotorra *f*
chauffeur [ʃofɚ] N chófer *m*
chauvinism [ʃóvənɪzəm] N (nationalist) chovinismo *m*; (sexist) machismo *m*
cheap [tʃip] ADJ (economical) barato; (stingy) avaro; **life is** — **there** la vida no vale nada allí; **talk is** — hablar no cuesta nada; **to feel** — sentirse despreciable; N — **shot** golpe bajo *m*; —**skate** tacaño -ña *mf*
cheapen [tʃípən] VI/VT (lower in price) abaratar[se]; VT (lower in esteem) desvalorizar
cheapness [tʃípnɪs] N (low price) baratura *f*; (stinginess) avaricia *f*
cheat [tʃit] N tramposo -sa *mf*, fullero -ra *mf*; VT engañar; **to** — **at cards** hacer trampa en/a las cartas, trampear; **to** — **on a test** copiar; **to** — **on one's spouse** engañar a la pareja de uno
check [tʃɛk] VT (stop) refrenar; (restrain) reprimir; (leave luggage) facturar; (leave a coat) dejar; (verify) comprobar, verificar; *Am* chequear; *Mex* checar; (in chess) dar jaque; **to** — **against** cotejar con; **to** — **into a hotel** registrarse; **to** — **into something** averiguar algo; **to** — **off** puntear; **to** — **out a book** sacar [prestado] un libro; **to** — **up on** controlar; **that** —**s out** lo hemos comprobado; N (bank) cheque *m*; (means of restraint) control *m*; (ticket) ficha *f*; (mark) marca *f*; (in a restaurant) cuenta *f*; (in fabric) cuadro *m*; (checked fabric) tela a cuadros *f*; (examination) comprobación *f*; (in chess) jaque *m*; —**book** chequera *f*, talonario *m*; —**ing account** cuenta corriente *f*; — **kiting** giro de cheques sin fondos *m*; —**list** lista de control *f*; —**mate** jaque mate *m*; —**out counter** caja *f*; —**point** control *m*, retén *m*; —**room** guardarropa *m*; — **stub** talón *m*; —**up** examen físico *m*
checker [tʃɛkɚ] N (on a fabric) cuadro *m*; (on a checkerboard) casilla *f*; (game piece) ficha *f*; (cashier) cajero -ra *mf*; (person who checks) verificador -ora *mf*; —**board** tablero *m*; —**ed cloth** tela a cuadros *f*; —**ed past** pasado oscuro *m*; —**s** juego de damas *m*; VT cuadricular

cheek [tʃik] N (on face) mejilla *f*; *Am* cachete *m*; (impudence) descaro *m*; (of buttocks) nalga *f*; —**bone** pómulo *m*
cheer [tʃir] N (shout) viva *m*, vítor *m*; (applause) aplausos *m pl*; (encouragement) ánimo *m*; (joy) alegría *f*; —**leader** animador -ora *mf*; *Am* porrista *mf*; INTERJ —**s!** ¡salud! VI/VT vitorear; **to** — **on** dar ánimo; **to** — **up** animar[se]
cheerful [tʃírfəł] ADJ (person) risueño, alegre; (room) alegre
cheerfulness [tʃírfəłnɪs] N alegría *f*
cheerless [tʃírlɪs] ADJ triste, sombrío
cheese [tʃiz] N queso *m*; —**burger** hamburguesa con queso *f*; —**cake** tarta de queso *f*
cheesy [tʃízi] ADJ (of cheese) de queso; (cheap) barato; (uncool) *Sp* hortera
cheetah [tʃíDə] N guepardo *m*
chef [ʃef] N chef *mf*
chemical [kémɪkəł] ADJ químico; — **engineering** ingeniería química *f*; — **warfare** guerra química *f*; N producto químico *m*
chemist [kémɪst] N químico -ca *f*
chemistry [kémɪstri] N química *f*
chemotheraphy [kimoθérəpi] N quimioterapia *f*
cherish [tʃérɪʃ] VT apreciar; **I** — **the memory of him** tengo muy buenos recuerdos de él
cherry [tʃéri] N cereza *f*; — **tree** cerezo *m*
chess [tʃes] N ajedrez *m*; —**board** tablero de ajedrez *m*
chest [tʃest] N (body part) pecho *m*; (box) arca *f*; — **of drawers** cómoda *f*
chestnut [tʃésnʌt] N castaña *f*; — **tree** castaño *m*; ADJ castaño; (horse) zaino
chew [tʃu] VT (food) masticar; (nonfood) mascar; —**ing gum** goma de mascar *f*; *Am* chicle *m*; **to** — **a hole** hacer un agujero a mordiscones; **to** — **out** reprender; **to** — **over** meditar sobre; **to** — **up** romper a mordiscones; N mascada *f*, bocado *m*
chewy [tʃúi] ADJ correoso
chic [ʃik] ADJ & N chic *m*
chick [tʃɪk] N (young chicken) pollito *m*; (young bird) pichón *m*; (young woman) *fam* chavala *f*, tía *f*; —**pea** garbanzo *m*
chicken [tʃíkɪn] N gallina *f*; (flesh) pollo *m*; — **coop** gallinero *m*; —**-hearted** cobarde; — **pox** varicela *f*
chicory [tʃíkəri] N achicoria *f*
chide [tʃaɪd] VT regañar
chief [tʃif] N jefe *m*; (of a tribe) cacique *m*; — **of staff** (military) jefe del estado mayor *m*; (of a division) secretario -ria general *mf*; ADJ principal; — **justice** presidente de la Suprema Corte de los Estados Unidos *m*
chieftain [tʃíftən] N cacique *m*
chiffon [ʃɪfán] N chifón *m*
chigger [tʃígɚ] N nigua *f*

chilblain [tʃíblen] N sabañón *m*
child [tʃaɪld] N (young person) niño -ña *mf*;
(offspring) hijo -ja *mf*; **—birth** parto *m*,
alumbramiento *m*; **—like** infantil, aniñado;
—proof a prueba de niños; **—'s play** cosa de
niños *f*; **to be with** — estar embarazada; ADJ
of —bearing age en edad de procrear
childhood [tʃáɪldhʊd] N niñez *f*, infancia *f*
childish [tʃáɪldɪʃ] ADJ infantil, pueril
childless [tʃáɪldlɪs] ADJ sin hijos
Chile [tʃíli] N Chile *m*
Chilean [tʃílian] ADJ & N chileno -na *mf*
chili, chile [tʃíli] N (pepper) chile *m*, ají *m*; (meat
dish) chile con carne *m*
chill [tʃɪł] N (coldness) frío *m*; (fear, cold with
shivering) escalofrío *m*; **it had a —ing
effect on the group** le cayó al grupo como
un baldazo de agua fría; VI/VT enfriar[se]; **to
— out** tranquilizarse, relajarse
chilly [tʃíli] ADJ frío
chime [tʃaɪm] N (sound) repique *m*; (instrument)
carillón *m*, carrillón *m*; VI repicar; VT tañer;
to — in intervenir [en una conversación]
chimney [tʃímni] N chimenea *f*
chimpanzee [tʃɪmpænzí] N chimpancé *m*
chin [tʃɪn] N barbilla *f*, mentón *m*
china [tʃáɪnə] N (material) porcelana *f*, china *f*;
(dishes) vajilla de porcelana *f*, china *f*;
—ware vajilla de porcelana *f*
China [tʃáɪnə] N China *f*
Chinese [tʃaɪníz] ADJ chino; N (inhabitant of
China) chino -na *mf*; (language) chino *m*
chink [tʃɪŋk] N grieta *f*
chip [tʃɪp] N (of wood) astilla *f*; (in glass)
desportilladura *f*; (in gambling) ficha *f*; (in
computers) chip *m*; **he's a — off the old
block** de tal palo, tal astilla; **he has a — on
his shoulder** guarda resentimientos; VI/VT
(wood) astillar[se]; (glass, plaster)
desportillarse, desconchar[se]; (paint)
descascarar[se]; (in golf) chipear; **to — in**
contribuir; **to — a tooth** romperse un diente
chipmunk [tʃípmʌŋk] N ardilla listada *f*
chiropractic [kaɪrəpræktɪk] ADJ quiropráctico;
N quiropráctica *f*
chiropractor [káɪrəpræktɚ] N quiropráctico -ca
mf
chirp [tʃɝp] N pío *m*, gorjeo *m*; VI/VT piar,
gorjear
chisel [tʃízəł] N escoplo *m*; (for stone) cincel *m*;
(for wood) formón *m*; VT cincelar; (swindle)
estafar
chiseler [tʃízlɚ] N estafador -ra *mf*
chit-chat [tʃíttʃæt] N palique *m*; VI charlar
chivalrous [ʃívəłrəs] ADJ (of knights)
caballeresco; (courteous to women)
caballeroso
chivalry [ʃívəłri] N caballerosidad *f*
chloride [klóraɪd] N cloruro *m*

chlorine [klórin] N cloro *m*
chloroform [klórəfɔrm] N cloroformo *m*
chlorophyl, chlorophyll [klórəfɪł] N clorofila *f*
chocolate [tʃáklɪt] N chocolate *m*; (bar)
chocolatina *f*; **— pot** chocolatera *f*
choice [tʃɔɪs] N (act of selecting, thing selected)
selección *f*; (alternative) opción *f*; **to have no
other** — no tener más remedio; ADJ selecto
choir [kwaɪr] N coro *m*
choke [tʃok] VI/VT (suffocate) ahogar[se];
(strangle) estrangular[se]; (on food)
atragantarse, atorarse; (obstruct) tapar[se]; VI
(in sports) bloquearse; **I'm all —d up** estoy
muy conmovido; **to — back/down**
contener; N (act of choking on something)
atragantamiento *m*; (act of choking someone)
estrangulación *f*; (device in cars) obturador *m*;
(in sports) bloqueo *m*
cholera [kálə̇ə] N cólera *m*
choleric [kálə̇ɪk] ADJ colérico
cholesterol [kəléstə̇ɔł] N colesterol *m*
choose [tʃuz] VI/VT elegir, seleccionar, escoger;
to — to optar por
choosy [tʃúzi] ADJ quisquilloso
chop [tʃap] VI/VT cortar; **to — down** talar; **to —
off** mochar, tronchar; **to — up** picar; N (act
of chopping) golpe *m*; (cut of meat) chuleta *f*;
—s morro *m*; **—stick** palillo *m*
choppy [tʃápi] ADJ picado, agitado
choral [kʰʌ́rəł] ADJ coral
chord [kɔrd] N (mathematical) cuerda *f*;
(musical) acorde *m*; **it struck a — with me**
me conmovió
chore [tʃɔr] N tarea *f*, faena *f*, quehacer *m*; **it's
such a** — es un trabajo horrible
choreography [kɔriágrəfi] N coreografía *f*
chorus [kɔ́rəs] N coro *m*
chose [tʃoz] *see* choose
chosen [tʃózən] ADJ **my — profession** la
profesión de mi preferencia; **the — one** el
elegido, la elegida
chosen [tʃózən] *see* choose
christen [krísən] VT bautizar
Christendom [krísəndəm] N cristianismo *m*
christening [krísənɪŋ] N bautizo *m*, bautismo *m*
Christian [krístʃən] ADJ & N cristiano -na *mf*; **—
name** nombre de pila *m*
Christianity [krɪstʃiǽnɪdi] N cristianismo *m*
Christmas [krísməs] N Navidad *f*, Pascua de
Navidad *f*; **— card** tarjeta de Navidad *f*; **—
Eve** Nochebuena *f*; **— gift** regalo de Navidad
m; **— tree** árbol de Navidad *m*; ADJ navideño
chrome [krom] N cromo *m*; ADJ cromado
chromium [krómiəm] N cromo *m*
chromosome [króməsom] N cromosoma *m*
chronic [kránɪk] ADJ crónico
chronicle [kránɪkəł] N crónica *f*; VT registrar
chronicler [kránɪklɚ] N cronista *mf*
chronological [kranládʒɪkəł] ADJ cronológico

chronology [krənáɫədʒi] N cronología f
chronometer [krənámɪDɚ] N cronómetro m
chrysalis [krísəlɪs] N crisálida f
chrysanthemum [krɪsǽnθəməm] N crisantemo m
chubby [tʃʌ́bi] ADJ rechoncho, gordito
chuck [tʃʌk] N (cut of meat) paletilla f; VT (to throw) lanzar; (to discard) tirar, botar
chuckle [tʃʌ́kəɫ] N risita f; VI reírse levemente
chum [tʃʌm] N compinche mf
chunk [tʃʌŋk] N trozo m, pedazo m; **a — of cash** un montón de plata
church [tʃɚtʃ] N iglesia f; **—man** clérigo m
churn [tʃɚn] N mantequera f; VI/VT (make butter) batir; (agitate) agitar, revolver
CIA [Central Intelligence Agency] [síáɪé] N CIA f
cicada [sɪkéDə] N chicharra f
cider [sáɪDɚ] N (alcoholic) sidra f; (non-alcoholic) Am jugo de manzana m; Sp zumo de manzana m
cigar [sɪgár] N puro m, habano m; **— store** tabaquería f; **close, but no —** bien, pero te quedaste corto
cigarette [sɪgərét] N cigarrillo m; Sp pitillo m; Am cigarro m; **— case** cigarrera f; Sp pitillera f; **— holder** boquilla f; **— lighter** encendedor m
cinch [sɪntʃ] N (for a saddle) cincha f; (something easy) pan comido m; (favorite) favorito -ta mf; VT cinchar
cinder [síndɚ] N ceniza f, rescoldo m
cinema [sínəmə] N cine m
cinematography [sɪnəmətágrəfi] N cinematografía f
cinnamon [sínəmən] N canela f; **— tree** canelo f
cipher [sáɪfɚ] N cifra f, guarismo m; VI/VT cifrar[se]
circle [sɚkəɫ] N círculo m; (literary) ámbito m, círculo m; VT (draw a circle) encerrar en un círculo; VI (go around) dar una vuelta
circuit [sɚkɪt] N circuito m; **— board** circuito impreso m; **— breaker** cortacircuitos m sg
circuitry [sɚkɪtri] N circuitería f
circular [sɚkjələ] ADJ circular; **— saw** sierra circular f; N circular f
circulate [sɚkjələt] VI circular; VT (distribute) poner en circulación
circulation [sɚkjəléʃən] N circulación f
circulatory [sɚkjələtɔri] ADJ circulatorio; **— system** aparato circulatorio m
circumcise [sɚkəmsaɪz] VT circuncidar
circumference [səkʌ́mfɚəns] N circunferencia f
circumlocution [sɚkəmlokjúʃən] N circunlocución f, rodeo m
circumscribe [sɚkəmskráɪb] VT circunscribir
circumspect [sɚkəmspɛkt] ADJ circunspecto
circumstance [sɚkəmstæns] N circunstancia f; **—s** condiciones financieras f pl

circumstantial [sɚkəmstǽnʃəɫ] ADJ circunstancial; **— evidence** pruebas circunstanciales f pl
circumvent [sɚkəmvɛ́nt] VT evitar, obviar
circus [sɚkəs] N circo m
cirrhosis [sɪrósɪs] N cirrosis f
cirrus [síɾəs] N cirro m
cistern [sístɚn] N cisterna f, aljibe m
citadel [síDədɛɫ] N ciudadela f
citation [saɪtéʃən] N (summons) citación f; (quote, quotation) cita f; (commendation for bravery) mención f
cite [saɪt] VT (quote, summon) citar; (comment on) mencionar
citizen [síDɪzən] N (of a nation) ciudadano -na mf; (of a city or region) habitante mf
citizenship [síDɪzənʃɪp] N ciudadanía f
citrus [sítrəs] ADJ & N cítrico m
city [síDi] N ciudad f; **— council** concejo m; **— hall** ayuntamiento m, alcaldía f; **— planning** urbanismo m; ADJ municipal, urbano
civic [sívɪk] ADJ cívico; N **—s** educación cívica f
civil [sívəɫ] ADJ (civilian) civil; (polite) cortés; **— disobedience** desobediencia civil f; **— engineer** ingeniero -ra civil mf; **— rights** derechos civiles m pl; **— service** administración pública f; **— war** guerra civil f
civilian [sɪvíljən] ADJ & N civil mf
civility [sɪvílɪDi] N civilidad f, cortesía f
civilization [sɪvəlɪzéʃən] N civilización f
civilize [sívəlaɪz] VT civilizar
clad [klæd] ADJ vestido
claim [klem] VT (demand) reclamar, reivindicar; (assert) sostener, pretender; **to — to be** pretender ser; **to — responsibility** atribuirse la responsabilidad; **to — a mine** denunciar una mina; N (demand) reclamación f, reclamo m; (assertion) afirmación f; (right) derecho m, título m; (on insurance) demanda f, denuncia f
claimant [klémənt] N demandante mf, reclamante mf; (to the throne) pretendiente mf
clairvoyant [klɛrvɔ́ɪənt] ADJ & N clarividente mf
clam [klæm] N almeja f; VI **to — up** callarse
clamber [klǽmbɚ] VI/VT (climb with effort) trepar con dificultad; (climb on all fours) subir gateando
clammy [klǽmi] ADJ frío y húmedo
clamor [klǽmɚ] N clamor m, vocerío m; VI clamar, vociferar
clamorous [klǽməəs] ADJ clamoroso
clamp [klæmp] N (support) grapa f; (vice) tornillo m; (wrap-around) abrazadera f; (medical) pinza f; VT sujetar; **to — down on** reprimir
clan [klæn] N clan m
clandestine [klændéstɪn] ADJ clandestino

clang [klæŋ] VI sonar; N sonido metálico *m*
clap [klæp] N (tap) palmada *f*; (blow) golpe seco
m; (gonorrhea) gonorrea *f*; — **of thunder**
trueno *m*; VT (on the back) palmear; (in
approval) aplaudir; (a book) cerrar de golpe
clapper [klǽpə-] N badajo *m*
clarification [klærəfɪkéʃən] N aclaración *f*
clarify [klǽrəfaɪ] VT aclarar, clarificar
clarinet [klærənét] N clarinete *m*
clarity [klǽrɪɒi] N claridad *f*
clash [klæʃ] N (noise) estruendo metálico *m*;
(collision) choque *m*; (conflict) conflicto *m*,
enfrentamiento *m*; VI/VT (collide) chocar;
(oppose, fight) enfrentarse a; (not go with) no
combinar, no pegar
clasp [klæsp] N (fastener) broche *m*, cierre *m*;
(grip) apretón *m*; VT (fasten) abrochar; (grip)
apretar; (embrace) abrazar, prender
class [klæs] N clase *f*; (graduation class)
promoción *f*, graduación *f*; **in a — by itself**
único; —**mate** compañero -ra de clase *mf*,
condiscípulo -la *mf*; —**room** salón de clase *m*,
aula *f*; — **struggle** lucha de clases *f*; VI/VT
clasificar[se]
classic [klǽsɪk] ADJ & N clásico -ca *mf*
classical [klǽsɪkəl] ADJ clásico
classicism [klǽsɪsɪzəm] N clasicismo *m*
classification [klæsəfɪkéʃən] N clasificación *f*
classify [klǽsəfaɪ] VT clasificar; **classified ad**
anuncio clasificado *m*
classy [klǽsi] ADJ elegante
clatter [klǽɒə-] N (noise) estrépito *m*;
(movement) traqueteo *m*; VI (make noise)
causar estrépito; (move) traquetear
clause [klɔz] N cláusula *f*
claustrophobia [klɔstrəfóbiə] N claustrofobia *f*
claustrophobic [klɔstrəfóbɪk] ADJ
claustrofóbico
clavicle [klǽvɪkəl] N clavícula *f*
claw [klɔ] N (of a bear) garra *f*, zarpa *f*; (of a cat)
uña *f*; (of a crab) pinza *f*; (of a hammer) orejas
f pl; VI/VT arañar; **they —ed their way**
through se abrieron paso con las uñas
clay [kle] N arcilla *f*; (for ceramics) greda *f*; (in
tennis) tierra batida *f*
clean [klin] ADJ limpio; (free from impurities,
not ornate) puro; (honorable) decente; —-
cut (person) acicalado; (concept) bien
definido; — **joke** broma inocente *f*; —-
shaven afeitado; **he has a — record** no
tiene antecedentes; **you'd better come —**
deberías confesar; VI/VT limpiar; **he —ed me**
out me limpió, me desvalijó; **to — up** (a
room) limpiar, asear; (a document) pasar en
limpio; (get rich) forrarse; N —**up** limpieza *f*
cleaner [klínə-] N limpiador -ra *mf*; —**s**
tintorería *f*
cleanliness [klénlɪnɪs] N limpieza *f*; (personal)
aseo *m*

cleanse [klɛnz] VT limpiar
cleanser [klénzə-] N limpiador *m*
clear [klir] ADJ claro; (skin, conscience) limpio;
(sky) despejado; (path) libre; —-**cut** (clearly
defined) bien definido; (obvious) claro; —-
headed lúcido; — **profit** ganancia neta *f*; **to**
keep — of someone evitar a alguien; **to**
pass — through pasar de lado a lado; N **to**
be in the — estar libre de culpa; VT (the
mind, confusion, voice) aclarar[se]; (a road,
one's reputation, computer screen) limpiar;
(of criminal charges) absolver; (of suspicion)
eximir; (liquid) clarificar; (a legislative bill,
plan) aprobar, obtener autorización para;
(land for farming) desmontar; (a hurdle)
salvar; (a net gain) sacar; **to — the air**
sincerarse; **to — the table** levantar la mesa;
to — up (a mystery) aclarar[se]; (the sky)
despejar[se]
clearance [klírəns] N (space) espacio libre *m*;
(vertical) margen de altura *m*; (permission)
autorización *f*; — **sale** liquidación *f*
clearing [klírɪŋ] N (terrain) claro *m*; (of checks)
compensación *f*; — **house** banco de
compensación *m*
cleats [klits] N (projection) tacos *m pl*, tapones *m*
pl; (shoes) zapatos con tacos *m pl*
cleavage [klívɪʤ] N (cut) hendidura *f*; (in dress)
escote *m*
cleave [kliv] VT hender[se]; **to — to** adherirse a
cleaver [klívə-] N cuchilla *f*
clef [klɛf] N clave *f*
cleft [klɛft] N hendidura *f*; ADJ hendido, partido;
— **lip** labio leporino *m*; — **palate** paladar
hendido *m*
clemency [klémənsi] N clemencia *f*
clench [klɛntʃ] VT agarrar, asir; (teeth, fist)
apretar
clergy [klɚ́ʤi] N clero *m*, clerecía *f*; —**man**
clérigo *m*, pastor *m*; —**woman** pastora *f*
clerical [klérɪkəl] ADJ (of the clergy) clerical,
eclesiástico; (of office personnel) de oficina;
— **error** error de copia *m*; — **work** trabajo
de escritorio *m*
clerk [klɚk] N (sales) dependiente -ta *mf*; (office)
empleado -da de oficina *mf*; (court)
escribiente *mf*, actuario -ria *mf*; VI trabajar
como actuario -ria
clever [klévə-] ADJ (ingenious) ingenioso; (smart)
listo, vivo; (dexterous) habilidoso
cleverness [klévə-nɪs] N (ingenuity) ingenio *m*;
(intelligence) inteligencia *f*, viveza *f*;
(dexterity) habilidad *f*
cliché [kliʃé] N cliché *m*, muletilla *f*; *Sp* tópico *m*
click [klɪk] N (sound) clic *m*, chasquido *m*; (sound
of heels) taconeo *m*; (on a computer) clic *m*,
pulsación *f*; VI chascar; (on a computer) hacer
clic, oprimir, pulsar; (heels) taconear; VT
chascar, chasquear; — **and drag** pulsar y

arrastrar
clickable image [klíkəbəłímɪʤ] N imagen en donde se puede pulsar *f*
client [kláɪənt] N (of professional or store) cliente -ta *mf*; (of social service) beneficiario -ria *mf*
clientele [klaɪəntéɫ] N clientela *f*
cliff [klɪf] N precipicio *m*, despeñadero *m*; (by the sea) acantilado *m*
climate [kláɪmɪt] N clima *m*
climatic [klaɪmǽDɪk] ADJ climático
climax [kláɪmæks] N clímax *m*, punto culminante *m*; VI culminar, alcanzar el clímax
climb [klaɪm] N (ascent) subida *f*; (in alpinism) escalada *f*; VI/VT (ascend) subir; (ascend with effort) trepar[se] [a], encaramar[se] [a]; VT (a mountain, wall) escalar; **to — down** bajar
climber [kláɪmə] N (in alpinism) escalador -ora *mf*; (plant) trepadora *f*
clinch [klɪntʃ] VT (resolve) rematar; (hammer down) remachar; (hug, in boxing) trabar; (secure) sujetar; (finalize) cerrar; N (nail) remache *m*; (embrace) abrazo *m*; (in boxing) clinch *m*
cling [klɪŋ] VI (to stick to) pegarse; (to hold onto) aferrarse
clinic [klínɪk] N clínica *f*; (workshop) taller *m*
clinical [klínɪkəɫ] ADJ clínico; **— trial** ensayo clínico *m*
clink [klɪŋk] N tintín *m*; VI tintinear
clip [klɪp] VT (cut) cortar; (trim) recortar; (shear) esquilar; (shorten) acortar; (hit) tocar; (fasten) abrochar; (attach paper) sujetar con un clip; N (fastener) gancho *m*; (for paper) clip *m*; (of cartridge) cargador *m*; (brooch) broche *m*; **—board** portapapeles *m sg*
clipper [klípə] N (shearer) esquilador -ra *mf*; **—s** (scissors) tijeras *f pl*; (hair trimmer) maquinilla *f*
clipping [klípɪŋ] N recorte *m*
clique [klɪk] N (political) camarilla *f*; (in school) pandilla *f*
clitoris [klíDə-ɪs] N clítoris *m*
cloak [klok] N capa *f*; (military) capote *m*; **—room** guardarropa *m*; VT (put a cloak on) vestirse con una capa; (hide) encubrir
clock [klɑk] N reloj *m*; **—-making** relojería *f*; **— radio** radio reloj *f*; **—work** maquinaria de reloj *f*; **like —work** con precisión, sin falta; VT **you swim and I'll — you** tú nadas y yo te tomo el tiempo; **the police —ed him at 90 mph** la policía lo pescó haciendo noventa millas por hora
clockwise [klákwaɪz] ADV en el sentido de las manecillas de reloj
clod [klɑd] N (piece of dirt) terrón *m*, pelotón *m*; (dolt) tonto -ta *mf*, necio -cia *mf*
clog [klɑg] VI/VT obstruir[se], tapar[se]; N (shoe)

zueco *m*; **— dance** baile zapateado *m*
cloister [klɔ́ɪstə] N claustro *m*; (monastery) monasterio *m*; VT enclaustrar
clone [klon] N clon *m*; VT clonar
cloning [klónɪŋ] N clonaje *m*, clonación *f*
close[1] [kloz] VI/VT cerrar[se]; VT (a hole) tapar; **to — an account** cerrar una cuenta; **to — a meeting** levantar una sesión; **to — down a store** clausurar una tienda; **to — in upon** (oppress) oprimir; (approach) cercar a uno; **to — out** liquidar; N fin *m*; (act of closing) cierre *m*; **at the —** al cierre
close[2] [klos] ADJ (near) cercano; (dense) tupido; (intimate) íntimo, entrañable; **— attention** mucha atención *f*; **— by** cercano, *Am* aquí nomás; **—-fought** reñido; **—-knit** muy unido; **— translation** traducción fiel *f*; **at — range** de cerca; **that was a — call** nos salvamos por poco; N **—up** primer plano *m*; ADV cerca
closed [klozd] ADJ cerrado; **— circuit** circuito cerrado *m*; **—-minded** cerrado; **—-mindedness** cerrazón *f*
closely [klósli] ADV (examine) de cerca; (resemble) mucho; (study) detenidamente; (work) estrechamente
closeness [klósnɪs] N (of location) cercanía *f*; (of friendship) intimidad *f*; (correctness) fidelidad *f*
closer [klózə] N (baseball) relevista de cierre *mf*, cerrador -ora *mf*
closet [klázɪt] N ropero *m*, armario *m*; VI enclaustrarse; ADJ a escondidas
closure [klóʒə] N (conclusion) cierre *m*; (sense of completeness) clausura *f*
clot [klɑt] VI/VT coagular[se]; N coágulo *m*, cuajarón *m*
cloth [klɔθ] N tela *f*, tejido *m*; (wool) paño *m*; ADJ de tela; **— bound** encuadernado en tela; **man of the —** clérigo *m*
clothe [kloð] VT vestir; N **—s** ropa *f*; **—sline** tendedero *m*; **—spin** pinza *f*
clothier [klóðjə] N comerciante en ropa o paño *mf*
clothing [klóðɪŋ] N ropa *f*
clotting [kláDɪŋ] N coagulación *f*
cloud [klaʊd] N nube *f*; **—burst** chaparrón *m*, aguacero *m*; VT nublar, anublar; (make indistinct, place under suspicion) enturbiar; **to — up** nublarse, anublarse; **to be on — nine** estar en el séptimo cielo; **under a —** bajo sospecha
cloudiness [kláʊDɪnɪs] N nebulosidad *f*, nubosidad *f*
cloudless [kláʊDlɪs] ADJ despejado
cloudy [kláʊDi] ADJ nublado; *Sp* nuboso; (gloomy) sombrío
clout [klaʊt] N influencia *f*
clove [klov] N clavo *m*; **— of garlic** diente

de ajo *m*

cloven [klóvən] ADJ hendido; —-**hoofed** patihendido

clover [klóvə-] N trébol *m*; —**leaf** trébol *m*; **to be in** — vivir en el lujo

clown [klaʊn] N payaso *m*; VI payasear, bufonear

cloy [klɔɪ] VI/VT (to satiate) hastiar; (to be too sweet for) repugnar

club [klʌb] N (society, nightclub) club *m*; (stick) porra *f*, garrote *m*; (suit of cards) basto *m*; —**foot** pie zambo *m*; —**house** casa de club *f*; VT aporrear

cluck [klʌk] VI cloquear; N cloqueo *m*

clue [klu] N pista *f*, indicio *m*; **to have no** — no tener ni noción

clueless [klúlɪs] ADJ (absent-minded) despistado; (uninformed) en ayunas

clump [klʌmp] N (of bushes) matorral *m*; (of trees) arboleda *f*; VI/VT apiñar[se]

clumsiness [klʌ́mzɪnɪs] N torpeza *f*

clumsy [klʌ́mzi] ADJ torpe, desmañado, chambón; *Sp* patoso

clung [klʌŋ] *see* cling

clunker [klʌ́ŋkə-] N cacharro *m*

cluster [klʌ́stə-] N grupo *m*; (of grapes) racimo *m*; VI/VT agrupar[se], arracimar[se]

clutch [klʌtʃ] N (in a car) embrague *m*; — **pedal** pedal del embrague *m*; **to step on the** — pisar el embrague; —**es** garras *f pl*; VT (seize) asir; (hold) apretar

clutter [klʌ́də-] N desparramo *m*, desorden *m*, confusión *f*; VT **books** —**ed her desk** tenía libros desparramados por todo el escritorio

coach [kotʃ] N (carriage) coche *m*, carruaje *m*, carroza *f*; (bus) autobús *m*; (in sports) entrenador -ra *mf*; (in soccer) técnico -ca *mf*, director -ora técnico -ca *mf*; (in air travel) clase turista *f*; (tutor) profesor -ra particular *mf*; —**man** cochero *m*; VI/VT entrenar

coagulant [koǽgjələnt] ADJ & N coagulante *m*

coagulate [koǽgjəlet] VI/VT coagular[se]

coagulation [koæɡjəléʃən] N coagulación *f*

coal [kol] N carbón *m*; — **bin** carbonera *f*; — **tar** alquitrán *m*

coalition [koəlíʃən] N coalición *f*

coarse [kɔrs] ADJ (fabric) burdo, basto; (sand) grueso; (manners, language) grosero, tosco, rudo

coarseness [kɔ́rsnɪs] N (fabric) bastedad *f*; (language, manners) tosquedad *f*, rudeza *f*; (of a joke) chocarrería *f*

coast [kost] N costa *f*; — **Guard** Guardia Costera *f*; —**line** costa *f*; ADJ & ADV —**-to-** — de costa a costa; VI (on a sled) deslizar[se]; (in a car, on a bike) tirarse por una bajada; **he** —**ed through medical school** la Facultad de Medicina le resultó muy fácil

coastal [kóstl̩] ADJ costero

coat [kot] N abrigo *m*; (of paint) capa *f*, mano *f*;

(on animals) pelaje *m*; — **of arms** escudo de armas *m*, blasón *m*; — **rack** percha *f*, perchero *m*; —**tail** faldón *m*; VT cubrir; (with paint) recubrir, dar una mano a; (with grease) engrasar; (with soap) enjabonar; (with sugar) bañar

coax [koks] VT persuadir con halagos, engatusar

coaxial cable [koǽksiəłkébəł] N cable coaxial *m*

cob [kab] N mazorca *f*, panoja *f*; —**web** telaraña *f*

cobalt [kóbɔłt] N cobalto *m*

cobbler [káblə-] N (person who repairs shoes) zapatero -ra *mf*, remendón -ona *mf*; (dessert) budín de bizcocho y fruta *m*

cobblestone [kábəłston] N adoquín *m*

cobra [kóbrə] N cobra *f*

cocaine [kokén] N cocaína *f*

coccyx [káksɪks] N cóccix *m*

cock [kak] N (rooster) gallo *m*; (male bird) macho de ave de corral *m*; (faucet) llave *f*; (gun part) martillo *m*; (penis) *vulg* polla *f*, pija *f*; —**fight** riña de gallos *f*; —**pit** (for cockfights) gallera *f*; (in an airplane) cabina *f*; —**scomb** cresta de gallo *f*; ADJ —**sure** gallito; VT (a gun) amartillar; (one's head) ladear

cock-a-doodle-doo [kákədudl̩dú] INTERJ quiquiriquí

cockatoo [kákətu] N cacatúa *f*

cocker spaniel [kákə-spǽnjəł] N cócker *m*

cockroach [kákrotʃ] N cucaracha *f*

cocktail [kákteł] N cóctel *m*; — **party** cóctel *m*

cocky [káki] ADJ gallito, valentón

cocoa [kóko] N (powder) cacao *m*; (drink) chocolate *m*

coconut [kókənʌt] N coco *m*

cocoon [kəkún] N capullo *m*

cod [kad] N *Sp* abadejo *m*; *Am* bacalao *m*; —-**liver oil** aceite de hígado de bacalao *m*

coddle [kádl̩] VT mimar

code [kod] N código *m*; — **switching** alternancia de códigos *f*; VT codificar

codeine [kódin] N codeína *f*

codger [kádʒə-] N vejete *m*, vejancón *m*

codify [kádəfaɪ] VT codificar

coding [kódɪŋ] N codificación *f*

coed [kóɛd] ADJ mixto; N alumna universitaria *f*

coefficient [koəfíʃənt] N coeficiente *m*

coerce [koɔ́s] VT forzar, obligar

coercion [koɔ́ʒən] N coacción *f*

coexist [koɪgzíst] VI coexistir, convivir

coexistence [koɪgzístəns] N coexistencia *f*, convivencia *f*

coffee [kófi] N café *m*; (with a little milk) cortado *m*; — **bean** grano de café *m*; — **break** descanso para tomar el café *m*; — **bush** cafeto *m*; — **maker** máquina de café *f*, cafetera *f*; —**pot** cafetera *f*; — **shop** (for coffee) café *m*; (for coffee and light meals) cafetería *f*; — **table** mesa baja *f*

coffer [kófə-] N cofre *m*

coffin [kɔ́fɪn] N ataúd *m*, féretro *m*
cog [kɑg] N diente *m*; **—wheel** rueda dentada *f*
cogent [kóʤənt] ADJ convincente
cognac [kónjæk] N coñac *m*
cognate [kágnet] ADJ & N cognado *m*
cognitive [kágnɪDɪv] ADJ cognitivo
cohabitate [kohǽbɪtet] VI cohabitar, convivir
cohabitation [kohæbɪtéʃən] N cohabitación *f*, convivencia *f*
coherent [kohírənt] ADJ coherente; (sticking together) cohesivo
cohesion [kohíʒən] N cohesión *f*
coiffure [kwɑfjúr] N peinado *m*
coil [kɔɪł] VI/VT arrollar[se], enrollar[se]; (snake) enroscar[se]; N (roll) rollo *m*; (spiral) tirabuzón *m*; (electric) bobina *f*; **— spring** muelle en espiral *m*
coin [kɔɪn] N moneda *f*; ADJ **—-operated** de monedas; VT acuñar (also words)
coinage [kɔ́ɪnɪʤ] N acuñación *f* (also of words)
coincide [koɪnsáɪd] VI coincidir
coincidence [koínsɪDəns] N coincidencia *f*, casualidad *f*
coitus [kóɪDəs] N coito *m*
coke [kok] N (coal) cok *m*, coque *m*; (cocaine) *fam* coca *f*
cola [kólə] N gaseosa *f*
colander [káləndɚ] N colador *m*
cold [kołd] ADJ frío; **— cream** cold cream *m*; **— cuts** fiambres *m pl*; **— fish** *fam* témpano *m*; **— snap** ola de frío *f*; **— sore** herpes *m sg*; **— war** guerra fría *f*; **to be —** tener frío; **to be out —** quedar seco; **it is — today** hace frío hoy; **he gave me the — shoulder** me hizo el vacío; **he quit — turkey** dejó de un día para otro; **he got — feet** se acobardó; N frío *m*; (illness) resfrío *m*, resfriado *m*, catarro *m*; **to catch a —** resfriarse
coldness [kółdnɪs] N frialdad *f*
colic [kálɪk] N cólico *m*
colicky [kálɪki] ADJ que sufre de cólico
coliseum [kɑlɪsíəm] N coliseo *m*
collaborate [kəlǽbəret] VI colaborar
collaboration [kəlæbəréʃən] N colaboración *f*
collaborator [kəlǽbəreDɚ] N colaborador -ora *mf*
collage [kəláʒ] N collage *m*
collagen [káləʤən] N colágeno *m*
collapse [kəlǽps] VI (fold into sections) plegarse; (cave in) hundirse, derrumbarse; (fail) fracasar; (faint) desmayarse; (empty of air, decline in value) colapsar[se]; N (falling in) derrumbe *m*, derrumbamiento *m*, desplome *m*; (breakdown) colapso *m*
collar [kálɚ] N (for restraining dogs, necklace) collar *m*; (of a shirt) cuello *m*; **—bone** clavícula *f*; VT acollarar; (grab by the neck) agarrar por el cuello; **I was —ed by the boss** el jefe me agarró de charla

collate [kólet] VT (put in order) colacionar; (compare) cotejar
collateral [kəlǽDɚəł] ADJ (on the side) colateral; (auxiliary) subsidiario; N garantía subsidiaria *f*; **— damage** daño colateral *m*
colleague [kálig] N colega *mf*
collect [kəlékt] VT (gather) recoger; (build a collection) coleccionar; (receive taxes) recaudar; VI/VT (receive payment) cobrar, percibir; (assemble) reunir[se]; (accumulate) acumular[se]; **to — oneself** calmarse; N **— call** llamada de cobro revertido *f*, llamada por/a cobrar *f*; **— on delivery** pago contra reembolso *m*
collection [kəlékʃən] N (set of collectibles, clothes) colección *f*; (for charity) colecta *f*; (of taxes) recaudación *f*, cobranza *f*, cobro *m*; (of data, fruit) recolección *f*; (of texts) recopilación *f*; (of water) captación *f*
collective [kəléktɪv] ADJ colectivo; **— bargaining** convenio colectivo *m*; N colectivo *m*, colectividad *f*
collector [kəléktɚ] N (of taxes) recaudador -ora *mf*; (of collectibles) coleccionista *mf*; (of other things) colector -ora *mf*
college [kálɪʤ] N (institution) universidad *f*; (university division) facultad *f*; (association) colegio *m*; **let's give it the old — try** esforcémonos al máximo
collegial [kəlíʤəł] ADJ cooperador
collegiate [kəlíʤɪt] ADJ universitario
collide [kəláɪd] VI/VT chocar
collie [káli] N collie *m*
collision [kəlíʒən] N colisión *f*, choque *m*
colloid [kálɔɪd] N coloide *m*
colloquial [kəlókwiəł] ADJ coloquial; **— expression** frase familiar *f*
colloquium [kəlókwiəm] N coloquio *m*, jornada *f*
collusion [kəlúʒən] N confabulación *f*
cologne [kəlón] N colonia *f*
Colombia [kəlámbiə] N Colombia *f*
Colombian [kəlámbiən] ADJ & N colombiano -na *mf*
colon[1] [kólən] N (punctuation) dos puntos *m pl*; (bowels) colon *m*
colon[2] [kəlón] (currency of El Salvador and Costa Rica) colón *m*
colonel [kɝ́nł] N coronel *m*
colonial [kəlóniəł] ADJ colonial
colonist [kálənɪst] N (settler) colono *m*; (colonizer) colonizador -ra *mf*
colonization [kɑlənɪzéʃən] N colonización *f*
colonize [kálənaɪz] VT colonizar
colonoscopy [kolənáskəpi] N colonoscopia *f*
colony [káləni] N colonia *f*
color [kálɚ] N color *m*; (colorfulness) colorido *m*; **— blindness** ceguera cromática *f*; **— monitor** monitor [a] color *m*; **— scanner** escáner color *m*; **the —s** la bandera; **he**

showed his true —s se mostró tal cual era; **persons of —** gente de color f; **a — TV** un televisor en/a color; ADJ **—-blind** daltónico; **—fast** de colores firmes; VT (give color) colorear; (make colorful) dar colorido; (influence) influir; (blush) ruborizarse

colorectal cancer [kolərɛ́ktlkǽnsɚ] N cáncer de colon m

colored [kʌ́lɚd] ADJ coloreado; (biased) sesgado

colorful [kʌ́ləfəl] ADJ (full of color) colorido; (animals, plants) pintado; (eccentric) pintoresco

coloring [kʌ́lɚɪŋ] N (tone) colorido m; (action) coloración f; (substance) colorante m

colorless [kʌ́lɚlɪs] ADJ (without color) incoloro; (bleached) descolorido

colossal [kəlásəl] ADJ colosal

colostomy [kəlástəmi] N colostomía f

colt [kolt] N potro m

column [káləm] N columna f

columnist [káləmnɪst] N columnista mf

coma [kómə] N coma m

comatose [kómətos] ADJ comatoso

comb [kom] N (for hair) peine m; (of a rooster) cresta f; (for wool) carda f; (for horses) almohaza f; (of honey) panal m; VT (hair) peinar; (wool) cardar; (search an area) peinar, batir; **to — one's hair** peinarse

combat¹ [kámbæt] N combate m

combat² [kəmbǽt] VI/VT combatir

combatant [kəmbǽtn̩t] ADJ & N combatiente mf

combative [kəmbǽDɪv] ADJ combativo

combination [kɑmbənéʃən] N combinación f; — **lock** cerradura de combinación f

combine¹ [kəmbáɪn] VI/VT combinar[se]

combine² [kámbaɪn] N cosechadora f

combo [kámbo] N combo m

combustible [kəmbʌ́stəbəl] ADJ & N combustible m

combustion [kəmbʌ́stʃən] N combustión f

come [kʌm] VI (arrive) venir; (have an orgasm) fam venirse; Sp fam correrse; **an idea came to me** se me ocurrió una idea; **Christmas is coming** llega la Navidad; **milk —s from cows** la leche se saca de las vacas; **no harm will — to you** no te va a pasar nada; **the dress —s to her knees** el vestido le llega a las rodillas; **to — about** suceder; **to — across** (find) encontrar; (make an impression) parecer; **to — along** (accompany) acompañar; (appear) surgir; **how's your paper coming along?** ¿cómo va tu trabajo? **to — again** volver, volver a venir; **to — back** volver; **to make a —back** resurgir; (in sports) recuperarse; **to — down with a cold** cogerse un resfriado; **to — downstairs** bajar; **to — from** ser de; **to — in** entrar; **to — out** (of a place) salir; (reveal one's homosexuality) Am salir del clóset, Sp

salir del armario; **to — over** venir para acá; **to — to** volver en sí; **to — together** (meet) juntarse, unirse; (reach agreement) ponerse de acuerdo; **to — up** subir; **your name came up** tu nombre vino a colación; **to — up short** quedarse corto; N (semen) vulg leche f; **—back** (reply) réplica f; (in sports) remontada f, recuperación f

comedian [kəmíDiən] N cómico -ca mf, comediante mf

comedy [káməDi] N (genre) comedia f; (profession) humorismo m

comet [kámɪt] N cometa m

comfort [kʌ́mfɚt] VT reconfortar; N (feeling of ease) comodidad f, confort m, holgura f; (solace) consuelo m

comfortable [kʌ́mfɚDəbəl] ADJ cómodo, confortable; — **life** vida holgada/ desahogada f

comforter [kʌ́mfɚDɚ] N edredón m

comic [kámɪk] ADJ cómico, chistoso, gracioso; — **book** revista de historietas f, cómic m; —**s** tiras cómicas f pl, historietas f pl; — **strip** tira cómica f

comical [kámɪkəl] ADJ cómico, gracioso

coming [kʌ́mɪŋ] N venida f; — **of Christ** advenimiento de Cristo m; — **from** proveniente de, originario de; —**s and goings** idas y venidas f pl; ADJ que viene, próximo

comma [kámə] N coma f

command [kəmǽnd] VT (order) mandar; (have authority over) comandar; **to — respect** inspirar respeto, imponerse; N (order) mandato m, orden f; (post) comandancia f; (dominance) dominio m; (on a computer) comando m; — **key** tecla de comando f; **he has a good — of English** domina bien el inglés; **to be in — of** estar al mando de; **to be under the — of** estar al mando de; **at your — a sus órdenes**

commandeer [kɑməndír] VT apoderarse de; (for the military) requisar

commander [kəmǽndɚ] N (leader) jefe -fa mf; (army officer) comandante mf; (navy officer) capitán -ana de fragata mf; — **in chief** comandante en jefe mf

commandment [kəmǽndmənt] N mandamiento m

commemorate [kəmɛ́məret] VT conmemorar

commemoration [kəmɛməréʃən] N conmemoración f

commence [kəmɛ́ns] VI/VT comenzar, principiar

commencement [kəmɛ́nsmənt] N (beginning) comienzo m; (graduation) graduación f, colación f

commend [kəmɛ́nd] VT (praise) alabar; (entrust) encomendar

commendation [kɑməndéʃən] N (praise) alabanza *f*; (mention) mención de honor *f*

commensurate [kəménsə-ɪt] ADJ proporcional, acorde

comment [kámɛnt] N comentario *m*; **no** — sin comentarios; VI/VT comentar

commentary [káməntɛri] N comentario *m*

commentator [kámənteɒ-] N (person who comments) comentador -ra *mf*; (talking head) comentarista *mf*

commerce [kámə-s] N comercio *m*

commercial [kəmə́-ʃəł] ADJ comercial; N (on radio or television) anuncio *m*

commercialize [kəmə́-ʃəlaɪz] VT comercializar

commiserate [kəmízəret] VI/VT compadecerse de

commiseration [kəmɪzəréʃən] N conmiseración *f*

commissary [kámɪsɛri] N economato *m*

commission [kəmíʃən] N (act, committee, payment) comisión *f*; (of a broker) corretaje *m*; (charge) encargo *m*; (mission) misión *f*; (title) nombramiento *m*; **to be in** — estar en servicio; **to be out of** — estar fuera de servicio; **to put out of** — (object) inutilizar; (person) retirar de servicio; VT (authorize) comisionar; (order) encargar; (appoint) nombrar; (get ready) poner en servicio; **—ed officer** oficial *m*

commissioner [kəmíʃənə-] N comisario -ria *mf*

commit [kəmít] VT (perpetrate) cometer; (entrust) encargar; (direct) destinar; **to — an error** cometer un error; **to — a foul** cometer/hacer falta; **to — oneself to** comprometerse a/con; **to — to an asylum** internar; **to — to memory** aprender de memoria

commitment [kəmítmənt] N compromiso *m*

committed [kəmíɒɪd] ADJ (to a cause) comprometido

committee [kəmíɒi] N comité *m*, comisión *f*

commode [kəmód] N wáter *m*, inodoro *m*

commodity [kəmáɒiti] N (product) mercancía *f*, artículo *m*, producto *m*; (raw material) materia prima *f*

common [kámən] ADJ (shared, frequent) común; (general) general; (vulgar) ordinario; (unremarkable) simple; **— cold** resfriado *m*; **— denominator** denominador común *m*; **— law** derecho consuetudinario *m*; **— sense** sentido común *m*, sensatez *f*; **— soldier** soldado raso *m*; **— stock** acciones ordinarias *f pl*; **—wealth** (state) estado *m*; (republic) república *f*; ADJ **—place** trivial; N **—s** (land) ejido *m*

commotion [kəmóʃən] N conmoción *f*, revuelo *m*

communal [kəmjúnḷ] ADJ comunitario

commune[1] [kəmjún] VI (communicate)

comunicarse, departir; (take communion) comulgar

commune[2] [kámjun] N comuna *f*

communicable [kəmjúnɪkəbł] ADJ comunicable; (disease) transmisible

communicate [kəmjúnɪket] VI/VT comunicar[se]; (disease) transmitir[se]

communication [kəmjunɪkéʃən] N comunicación *f*

communicative [kəmjúnɪkəDIv] ADJ comunicativo

communion [kəmjúnjən] N comunión *f*

communiqué [kəmjunɪké] N comunicado *m*

communism [kámjənɪzəm] N comunismo *m*

communist [kámjənɪst] N & ADJ comunista *mf*

community [kəmjúnɪDi] N comunidad *f*, colectividad *f*; **— spirit** espíritu comunitario *m*

commute [kəmjút] VT (reduce a sentence) conmutar; VI viajar diariamente al trabajo

commuter [kəmjúɒ-] N persona que viaja diariamente al trabajo *f*

Comoros [káməroz] N Comoras *f pl*

compact[1] [kámpækt, kəmpǽkt] ADJ compacto; (dense) tupido, apretado; (concise) conciso; (make denser) tupir

compact[2] [kámpækt] N (agreement) pacto *m*; (case for powder) polvera *f*; **— disk** disco compacto *m*; VT compactar

compactness [kɑmpǽktnɪs] N densidad *f*; (conciseness) concisión *f*

companion [kəmpǽnjən] N (comrade, partner) compañero -ra *mf*; (caregiver) acompañante *mf*

companionship [kəmpǽnjənʃɪp] N compañía *f*

company [kámpəni] N compañía *f*; **to keep — with** codearse con, frecuentar

comparable [kámpə-əbł] ADJ comparable

comparative [kəmpǽrəDIv] ADJ comparativo

compare [kəmpér] VI/VT comparar[se]; **beyond** — incomparable, sin parangón

comparison [kəmpǽrɪsən] N comparación *f*; **in — with** comparado con

compartment [kəmpártmənt] N compartimiento *m*

compass [kámpəs] N (for drawing) compás *m*; (for directions) brújula *f*

compassion [kəmpǽʃən] N compasión *f*

compassionate [kəmpǽʃənɪt] ADJ compasivo

compatibility [kəmpæɒəbílɪDi] N compatibilidad *f*

compatible [kəmpǽɒəbł] ADJ compatible (also of computers)

compatriot [kəmpétriət] N compatriota *mf*

compel [kəmpéł] VT (force) obligar; (demand) exigir

compelling [kəmpélɪŋ] ADJ (argument) convincente; (story) emocionante

compensate [kámpənset] VT (make up for)

compensar, resarcir; (pay) remunerar
compensation [kɑmpənséʃən] N (making up
for) compensación f; (remuneration)
remuneración f
compete [kəmpít] VI/VT competir
competence [kámpɪɒəns] N competencia f
competent [kámpɪɒənt] ADJ competente
competition [kɑmpɪtíʃən] N competencia f;
(sports match) competición f, contienda f
competitive [kəmpéɒɪɒɪv] ADJ competitivo; —
examination Sp oposición f; Am concurso
m; — **sports** deportes de competición m pl
competitiveness [kəmpéɒɪtɪvnɪs] N
competitividad f
competitor [kəmpéɒɪɒə] N (business)
competidor -ora mf; (sports) atleta mf
compilation [kɑmpɪléʃən] N recopilación f
compile [kəmpáɪł] VT recopilar, compilar
compiler [kəmpáɪlə] N compilador m; —
language lenguaje compilador m
complacency [kəmplésənsi] N confianza
infundada f
complacent [kəmplésənt] ADJ confiado
complain [kəmplén] VI quejarse
complainant [kəmplénənt] ADJ & N recurrente
mf
complaint [kəmplént] N queja f; (official)
reclamo m; (civil charge) demanda f;
(ailment) dolencia f
complement[1] [kámpləmənt] N complemento
m; (of staff) dotación f
complement[2] [kámpləmɛnt] VT complementar
complementary [kampləméntri] ADJ
complementario
complete [kəmplít] ADJ completo, pleno; **a —
stranger** un perfecto desconocido; VT
completar; **to — a pass** completar un pase
completion [kəmplíʃən] N finalización f,
terminación f; **she brought the project to
—** completó el proyecto
complex[1] [kəmplɛ́ks] ADJ complejo
complex[2] [kámplɛks] N complejo m
complexion [kəmplɛ́kʃən] N (skin) cutis m;
(color) tez f; (perspective) cariz m
complexity [kəmplɛ́ksɪɒi] N complejidad f
compliance [kəmpláɪəns] N (obedience)
conformidad f, acatamiento m; (polite
reverence) pleitesía f; **in — with** en
conformidad con
complicate [kámplɪket] VT complicar
complicated [kámplɪkeɒɪd] ADJ complicado
complication [kamplɪkéʃən] N complicación f
complicity [kəmplísɪɒi] N complicidad f
compliment [kámpləmənt] N cumplido, halago
m; (on looks) piropo m; (from a suitor)
galantería f; **to pay someone a —** hacerle un
cumplido a alguien; **to send one's —s** enviar
saludos; VI/VT elogiar, halagar
comply [kəmpláɪ] VI obedecer; **to — with**

cumplir con, acatar
component [kəmpónənt] ADJ & N componente m
compose [kəmpóz] VI/VT componer; **to —
oneself** sosegarse
composed [kəmpózd] ADJ sosegado; **to be — of**
estar compuesto de, componerse de, constar
de
composer [kəmpózə] N compositor -ra mf
composite [kəmpázɪt] ADJ compuesto; N
amalgama f
composition [kampəzíʃən] N (make-up, musical
piece) composición f; (aggregate material)
compuesto m; (school essay) composición f,
redacción f
composure [kəmpóʒə] N compostura f
compound[1] [kámpaʊnd] ADJ & N compuesto m;
— **fracture** fractura expuesta f; — **interest**
interés compuesto m
compound[2] [kampáʊnd] VT (combine)
combinar; (worsen) empeorar
comprehend [kamprɪhénd] VT comprender
comprehensible [kamprɪhénsəbəł] ADJ
comprensible
comprehension [kamprɪhénʃən] N
comprensión f
comprehensive [kamprɪhénsɪv] ADJ
exhaustivo; — **insurance** seguro contra
todo riesgo m
compress[1] [kamprés] VT comprimir; **—ed disk**
disco comprimido m; **—ed file** archivo
comprimido m
compress[2] [kámprɛs] N compresa f
compression [kampréʃən] N compresión f
comprise [kampráɪz] VT comprender, incluir;
to be —d of comprender, incluir
compromise [kámprəmaɪz] N (arrangement)
arreglo por concesiones mutuas m,
compromiso m; (intermediate thing) cruce m,
término medio m; VI/VT (make agreement)
transigir; Am transar; (jeopardize)
comprometer
comptroller [kəntrólə] N controlador -ra mf;
Am contralor -ora mf
compulsion [kəmpʌ́łʃən] N (impulse)
compulsión f, coacción f; (coercion) coerción f
compulsive [kəmpʌ́łsɪv] ADJ compulsivo
compulsory [kəmpʌ́łsəri] ADJ obligatorio,
obligado
computation [kampjʊtéʃən] N cómputo m,
cálculo m
compute [kəmpjút] VI/VT computar, calcular
computer [kəmpjúɒə] N Am computadora f; Sp
ordenador m; — **engineer** ingeniero -ra en
computación mf, ingeniero -ra informático
-ca mf; — **graphics** gráficos por
computadora/ordenador m pl; — **literacy**
(process) alfabetización digital f; (result)
alfabetismo digital m; — **science** informática
f; — **virus** virus de computadora/

ordenador *m*
computerization [kəmpjuʊʒɪzéʃən] N *Sp*
ordenación *f*, *Am* computarización *f*
computerize [kəmpjúʊərɪz] VI/VT
informatizar, computarizar
computing [kəmpjúʊɪŋ] N informática *f*; ADJ
informático
comrade [kámræd] N camarada *mf*
concave [kánkev] ADJ cóncavo
conceal [kənsíⱡ] VT encubrir, ocultar, disimular
concealment [kənsíⱡmənt] N encubrimiento *m*,
disimulo *m*
concede [kənsíd] VI/VT (recognize) conceder,
reconocer; (allow) conceder
conceit [kənsít] N (vanity) vanidad *f*; (literary
device) concepto *m*
conceited [kənsíʊɪd] ADJ engreído, presumido
conceivable [kənsívəbəⱡ] ADJ imaginable,
concebible
conceive [kənsív] VI/VT concebir; (a plan)
concebir, idear
concentrate [kánsəntret] VI/VT concentrar[se]
concentration [kansəntréʃən] N concentración
f; — **camp** campo de concentración *m*
concept [kánsɛpt] N concepto *m*
conception [kənsépʃən] N concepción *f*
conceptual [kənséptʃuəⱡ] ADJ conceptual
concern [kənsɝn] VT (be of interest) concernir,
atañer; (worry) preocupar; **to — oneself
with** ocuparse de; **to whom it may —** a
quien corresponda; N (interest) interés *m*;
(matter) asunto *m*; (worry) preocupación *f*;
(company) compañía *f*; **to be of no —** no
tener consecuencia
concerned [kənsɝnd] ADJ (involved)
involucrado; (anxious) preocupado; **as far as
I am —** en lo que a mí respecta; **to be —
about** preocuparse por
concerning [kənsɝnɪŋ] PREP tocante a,
respecto a
concert¹ [kánsɝt] N concierto *m*
concert² [kənsɝt] VT concertar
concession [kənséʃən] N concesión *f*
conciliate [kənsíliet] VI/VT (make compatible)
conciliar; (appease) aplacar
conciliation [kənsɪliéʃən] N conciliación *f*
concise [kənsáɪs] ADJ conciso, sucinto
conciseness [kənsáɪsnɪs] N concisión *f*
conclude [kənklúd] VI/VT concluir
conclusion [kənklúʒən] N conclusión *f*
conclusive [kənklúsɪv] ADJ concluyente
concoct [kənkákt] VT (contrive) fabricar, urdir;
(prepare by cooking) preparar
concoction [kənkákʃən] N mejunje *m*
concord [kánkɔrd] N (peace) concordia *f*;
(agreement) convenio *m*, acuerdo *m*
concrete¹ [kankrít] ADJ concreto
concrete² [kánkrit] N hormigón *m*; (made of
concrete) de hormigón

concubine [káŋkjəbaɪn] N concubina *f*
concur [kənkɝ] VI estar de acuerdo
concussion [kənkʌ́ʃən] N (brain injury)
conmoción cerebral *f*; (shock) concusión *f*
condemn [kəndém] VT condenar; (acquire
public ownership) expropiar; (declare unsafe)
declarar ruinoso
condemnation [kandɛmnéʃən] N condenación
f, condena *f*
condensation [kandɛnséʃən] N condensación *f*;
(of a book) compendio *m*
condense [kəndéns] VI/VT condensar[se]
condescend [kandəsénd] VI condescender a
condescension [kandəsénʃən] N
condescendencia *f*
condiment [kándəmənt] N condimento *m*,
aliño *m*
condition [kəndíʃən] N condición *f*; **he's got a
heart —** sufre del corazón, tiene una
afección cardíaca; **he's in good physical —**
está en buen estado físico; **the patient is in
critical —** el paciente está en estado crítico;
on — that a condición de que; VT (restrict on
a condition, establish a conditioned response)
condicionar; (accustom oneself)
acostumbrarse
conditional [kəndíʃən�î] ADJ & N condicional *m*
conditioning [kəndíʃənɪŋ] N condicionamiento
m
condolences [kəndólənsɪz] N pésame *m*,
condolencias *f*; **to express one's —** dar las
condolencias
condom [kándəm] N condón *m*, preservativo *m*
condominium [kandəmíniəm] N condominio
m
condone [kəndón] VT tolerar
conducive [kəndúsɪv] ADJ conducente
conduct¹ [kándʌkt] N conducta *f*,
comportamiento *m*
conduct² [kəndʌ́kt] VI/VT (behave) conducirse,
comportarse; (carry out) llevar a cabo;
(direct, lead) dirigir; (serve as channel for)
conducir
conduction [kəndʌ́kʃən] N conducción *f*
conductor [kəndʌ́ktɚ] N (substance that
conducts) conductor *m*; (of an orchestra)
director -ora *mf*; (of a train) revisor -ora *mf*
conduit [kánduɪt] N conducto *m*
cone [kon] N cono *m*; (container) cucurucho *m*
confection [kənfékʃən] N (of clothes) confección
f; (of candy) confitura *f*
confectionery [kənfékʃənɛri] N confitería *f*;
(shop) dulcería *f*; (candies) dulces *m pl*
confederacy [kənféɖ əsi] N confederación *f*
confederate¹ [kənféɖ əɪt] ADJ & N confederado
-da *mf*
confederate² [kənféɖəret] VI/VT confederar[se]
confederation [kənfeɖəréʃən] N confederación *f*
confer [kənfɝ] VT (grant) conferir, atribuir;

(consult) consultar; (negotiate) conferenciar
conference [kánfə-əns] N (consultation)
consulta *f*; (professional meeting) congreso
m; (legislative) asamblea general *f*; (sports
league) liga *f*; — **call** llamada en conferencia *f*
confess [kənfés] VI/VT confesar[se]
confession [kənféʃən] N confesión *f*
confessional [kənféʃənl] N confesionario *m*
confessor [kənfésə-] N confesor *m*
confidant [kánfɪdɑnt] N confidente *mf*
confide [kənfáɪd] VI/VT (entrust) confiar; VI (tell
secrets to) hacer confidencias a
confidence [kánfɪDəns] N confianza *f*;
(certainty) seguridad *f*; (secret
communication) confidencia *f*; — **game** timo
m; — **man** timador *m*, embaucador *m*; **in** —
en confianza
confident [kánfɪDənt] ADJ seguro; **he's a** —
person tiene mucha confianza
confidential [kɑnfɪdénʃəł] ADJ confidencial;
(secretary, etc.) de confianza
configuration [kənfɪgjəréʃən] N configuración *f*
(also for computers)
configure [kənfígjə-] VT configurar
confine[1] [kənfáɪn] VT confinar, recluir; **to** —
oneself to limitarse a
confine[2] [kánfaɪn] N confín *m*
confinement [kənfáɪnmənt] N confinamiento *m*
confirm [kənfɝ́m] VT confirmar
confirmation [kɑnfə-méʃən] N confirmación *f*
confiscate [kánfɪkɪet] VT confiscar
confiscation [kɑnfɪskéʃən] N confiscación *f*
conflagration [kɑnfləgréʃən] N incendio *m*
conflict[1] [kánflɪkt] N conflicto *m*, contienda *f*; —
of interest conflicto de intereses *m*
conflict[2] [kənflíkt] VI oponerse
confluence [kánfluəns] N confluencia *f*
conform [kənfɔ́rm] VI/VT conformar[se]
conformity [kənfɔ́rmɪDi] N (agreement)
conformidad *f*; (passive acquiescence)
conformismo *m*
confound [kənfáund] VT (bewilder)
desconcertar; (confuse) confundir; — **it!** *fam*
¡caramba!
confront [kənfrʌ́nt] VT (set face to face, fight)
confrontar; (face up to) enfrentarse a
confrontation [kɑnfrəntéʃən] N confrontación
f, enfrentamiento *m*
confuse [kənfjúz] VT confundir
confused [kənfjúzd] ADJ (person) confundido;
(situation) confuso; **to become** —
confundirse
confusing [kənfjúzɪŋ] ADJ confuso
confusion [kənfjúʒən] N confusión *f*
congeal [kəndʒíł] VI/VT cuajar[se]
congenial [kəndʒínjəł] ADJ agradable, simpático
congenital [kəndʒénɪdļ] ADJ congénito
congestion [kəndʒéstʃən] N congestión *f*
congestive heart failure [kəndʒɛstɪv hárt feljə-]

ADJ insuficiencia cardíaca congestiva *f*
conglomeration [kənglɑməréʃən] N (unit)
conglomeración *f*; (mass) conglomerado *m*
Congo [káŋgo] N Congo *m*
Congolese [kaŋgəlíz] ADJ & N congoleño -ña *mf*
congratulate [kəngrǽtʃələt] VT felicitar
congratulation [kəngrǽtʃəléʃən] N felicitación
f, parabién *m*; —**s!** ¡enhorabuena! ¡albricias!
congregate [káŋgrɪget] VI/VT congregar[se]
congregation [kaŋgrɪgéʃən] N (worshipers)
fieles *m pl*, feligreses *m pl*; (act of
congregating, committee of cardinals)
congregación *f*
congress [káŋgrɪs] N (professional) congreso *m*;
(political) asamblea legislativa *f*; (US)
congreso *m*; —**man** (US) congresista *m*;
—**woman** (US) congresista *f*
congressional [kəngréʃənl] ADJ congresual
congruence [kəngrúəns] N congruencia *f*
conifer [kánəfə-] N conífera *f*
conjecture [kəndʒéktʃə-] N conjetura *f*; VI/VT
conjeturar
conjugal [kándʒəgəł] ADJ conyugal
conjugate [kándʒəget] VI/VT conjugar[se]
conjugation [kandʒəgéʃən] N conjugación *f*
conjunction [kəndʒʌ́ŋkʃən] N conjunción *f*
conjunctivitis [kəndʒʌŋktəváɪDɪs] N
conjuntivitis *f*
conjure [kándʒə-] VT invocar; **to** — **up** evocar; VI
hacer hechizos
connect [kənékt] VI/VT conectar[se], enlazar[se];
(buildings, callers) comunicar[se]; (concepts)
relacionar[se]; (pipes) acoplar[se]; —**ing rod**
biela *f*
connection [kənékʃən] N (act of connecting)
conexión *f*, vinculación *f*; (of telephone)
comunicación *f*, enganche *m*; (of concepts)
relación *f*; (of pipes) acople *m*; (affinity)
afinidad *f*; (supplier) contacto *m*; —**s**
contactos *m pl*, enchufe *m*
connectivity [kanektívɪDi] N conectividad *f*
connive [kənáɪv] VI conspirar
connoisseur [kanəsúr] N conocedor -ora *f*
connotation [kanətéʃən] N connotación *f*
conquer [káŋkə-] VT (win) conquistar;
(overcome) vencer
conqueror [káŋkərə-] N conquistador -ora *mf*;
(one who overcomes) vencedor -ora *mf*
conquest [káŋkwɛst] N conquista *f*
conscience [kánʃəns] N conciencia *f*
conscientious [kanʃiéntʃəs] ADJ concienzudo
conscious [kánʃəs] ADJ consciente
consciousness [kánʃəsnɪs] N conciencia *f*; **to
lose** — perder el conocimiento
conscript[1] [kənskrípt] VT reclutar
conscript[2] [kánskrɪpt] N recluta *mf*
conscription [kənskrípʃən] N reclutamiento *m*
consecrate [kánsɪkret] VT consagrar
consecration [kansɪkréʃən] N consagración *f*

consecutive [kənsékjədɪv] ADJ consecutivo
consensus [kənsénsəs] N consenso *m*
consent [kənsént] N consentimiento *m*; VI consentir
consequence [kánsɪkwɛns] N consecuencia *f*; (negative) secuela *f*
consequent [kánsɪkwənt] ADJ consiguiente, resultante; N (in mathematics) consecuente *m*; (in logic) consiguiente *m*
consequently [kánsɪkwəntli] ADV por consiguiente, en consecuencia
conservation [kɑnsɚvéʃən] N conservación *f*, preservación *f*
conservatism [kənsɚ́vətɪzəm] N conservadurismo *m*
conservative [kənsɚ́vədɪv] ADJ & N conservador -ora *mf*
conservatory [kənsɚ́vətɔri] N conservatorio *m*
conserve[1] [kənsɚ́v] VT conservar, preservar
conserve[2] [kánsɚv] N confitura *m*
consider [kənsídɚ] VT considerar
considerable [kənsídɚəbəl] ADJ considerable
considerate [kənsídɚɪt] ADJ considerado
consideration [kənsɪdəréʃən] N consideración *f*; (respect) miramiento *m*; (payment) remuneración *f*
considering [kənsídɚɪŋ] PREP en vista de, teniendo en cuenta; **she cooks well,** — para ser ella, cocina bien
consign [kənsáɪn] VT consignar
consignee [kɑnsaɪní] N consignatario -ria *mf*
consignment [kənsáɪnmənt] N consignación *f*; **on** — a/en consignación
consist [kənsíst] VI consistir [en]
consistency [kənsístənsi] N (adherence to principles) coherencia *f*, consecuencia *f*; (density) consistencia *f*
consistent [kənsístənt] ADJ (adherent to principles) consecuente, coherente; (cohering) consistente
consolation [kɑnsəléʃən] N consuelo *m*, consolación *f*
console[1] [kənsóɫ] VT consolar
console[2] [kánsoɫ] N consola *f*
consolidate [kənsálɪdet] VI/VT consolidar[se]
consolidation [kənsɑlɪdéʃən] N consolidación *f*
consonant [kánsənənt] N consonante *f*; ADJ consonante, conforme
consort[1] [kənsɔ́rt] VI **to** — **with** asociarse con
consort[2] [kánsɔrt] N consorte *mf*
consortium [kənsɔ́rʃiəm] N consorcio *m*
conspicuous [kənspíkjuəs] ADJ evidente
conspiracy [kənspírəsi] N conspiración *f*, conjura *f*
conspirator [kənspírədɚ] N conspirador -ora *mf*, conjurado -da *mf*
conspire [kənspáɪr] VI conspirar, conjurar
constable [kánstəbəl] N oficial de policía *mf*; (keeper of fortress) condestable *m*

constancy [kánstənsi] N constancia *f*
constant [kánstənt] ADJ & N constante *f*
constellation [kɑnstəléʃən] N constelación *f*
consternation [kɑnstɚnéʃən] N consternación *f*
constipate [kánstəpet] VT estreñir
constipated [kánstəpedɪd] ADJ estreñido
constipation [kɑnstəpéʃən] N estreñimiento *m*
constituent [kənstítʃuənt] ADJ componente, constitutivo; N (component) componente *m*; (voter) votante *mf*; (part of a sentence) constituyente *m*
constitute [kánstɪtut] VT constituir
constitution [kɑnstɪtúʃən] N constitución *f*
constitutional [kɑnstɪtúʃənḷ] ADJ constitucional; N caminata *f*
constrain [kənstrén] VT constreñir, restringir
constraint [kənstrént] N constreñimiento *m*
constrict [kənstríkt] VT constreñir
constriction [kənstríkʃən] N (action) constricción *f*; (place) estrechamiento *m*
construct[1] [kənstrʌ́kt] VT construir
construct[2] [kánstrʌkt] N invención *f*
construction [kənstrʌ́kʃən] N construcción *f*; — **company** constructora *f*
constructive [kənstrʌ́ktɪv] ADJ constructivo
construe [kənstrú] VT interpretar
consul [kánsəl] N cónsul *mf*
consulate [kánsəlɪt] N consulado *m*
consult [kənsʌ́ɫt] VI/VT consultar; VI (serve as a consultant) asesorar
consultant [kənsʌ́ɫtənt] N asesor -ora *mf*
consultation [kɑnsəɫtéʃən] N consulta *f*
consultative [kənsʌ́ɫtədɪv] ADJ consultivo
consulting [kənsʌ́ɫtɪŋ] N asesoramiento *m*, consultoría *f*; ADJ consultor; — **firm** firma consultora *f*
consumable [kənsúməbəɫ] ADJ — **goods** bienes consumibles *m pl*
consume [kənsúm] VI/VT consumir
consumer [kənsúmɚ] N consumidor -ora *mf*; — **confidence index** índice de confianza del consumidor *m*; — **credit** crédito al consumidor *m*; — **protection** protección al consumidor *f*
consumerism [kənsúmərɪzəm] N consumismo *m*
consuming [kənsúmɪŋ] ADJ (need) imperioso; (drive) abrasador
consummate[1] [kánsəmet] VT consumar
consummate[2] [kánsəmɪt] ADJ consumado
consumption [kənsʌ́mpʃən] N (using up) consumo *m*; (wasting of the body) consunción *f*; (tuberculosis) tisis *f*
consumptive [kənsʌ́mptɪv] ADJ tísico
contact [kántækt] N contacto *m*; — **lens** lente de contacto *mf*; VI/VT (touch) tocar; (communicate with) contactar
contagion [kəntédʒən] N (spread) contagio *m*; (disease spread) enfermedad contagiosa *f*

contagious [kəntédʒəs] ADJ contagioso
contain [kəntén] VI/VT contener
container [kənténə-] N recipiente *m*; (on a ship) contenedor *m*; **—ship** buque portacontenedores *m*
containerize [kənténəraɪz] VT contenedorizar
containment [kənténmənt] N contención *f*
contaminate [kəntǽmənet] VT contaminar
contamination [kəntæmənéʃən] N contaminación *f*
contemplate [kántəmplet] VT (observe) contemplar; (consider) considerar
contemplation [kantəmpléʃən] N (observation) contemplación *f*; (consideration) consideración *f*
contemporary [kəntémpəɾeri] ADJ contemporáneo
contempt [kəntémpt] N desprecio *m*, menosprecio *m*; **— of court** desacato al tribunal *m*
contemptible [kəntémptəbəl] ADJ despreciable, rastrero
contemptuous [kəntémptʃuəs] ADJ desdeñoso
contend [kənténd] VI (struggle) contender, lidiar; (argue) disputar; VT afirmar
content¹ [kəntént] ADJ (happy) contento; (resigned) conforme; N **to one's heart's —** a discreción
content², contents [kántɛnt[s]] N contenido *m*
contented [kəntɛ́ntɪd] ADJ contento, satisfecho
contention [kənténʃən] N (opinion) opinión *f*; **in —** (disputed) en discusión; (still eligible) con posibilidades
contentious [kənténʃəs] ADJ conflictivo
contentment [kəntɛ́ntmənt] N contento *m*
contest¹ [kántɛst] N (competition) concurso *m*, certamen *m*; (struggle) contienda *f*
contest² [kəntɛst] VT (compete) contender; (dispute) disputar; (challenge) impugnar
contestant [kəntɛstənt] N concursante *mf*, participante *mf*
context [kántɛkst] N contexto *m*
contiguous [kəntígjuəs] ADJ contiguo, pegado
continent [kántənənt] N (landmass) continente *m*; ADJ (sexually abstinent) continente; (of bodily functions) capaz de controlar los esfínteres
continental [kantnɛ́ntl] ADJ continental
contingency [kəntíndʒənsi] N contingencia *f*; **— fund** fondo de contingencia *m*; **— planning** planificación para contingencias *f*
contingent [kəntíndʒənt] ADJ & N contingente *m*
continual [kəntínjuəl] ADJ continuo
continuance [kəntínjuəns] N continuación *f*; (delay) aplazamiento *m*
continuation [kəntɪnjuéʃən] N continuación *f*
continue [kəntínju] VI/VT continuar
continuing [kəntínjuɪŋ] ADJ continuado; **— education** educación para adultos *f*

continuity [kantɪnúɪDi] N continuidad *f*
continuous [kəntínjuəs] ADJ (uninterrupted in time) continuo; (uninterrupted in space) ininterrumpido
contortion [kəntɔ́rʃən] N contorsión *f*
contour [kántur] N contorno *m*
contra account [kántrə əkaʊnt] N cuenta de contrapartida *f*
contraband [kántrəbænd] N contrabando *m*
contraception [kantrəsépʃən] N anticoncepción *f*
contraceptive [kantrəséptɪv] ADJ & N anticonceptivo *m*
contract¹ [kántrækt] N contrato *m*; **— killer** asesino -na a sueldo *mf*; **by —** por contrato
contract² [kəntrækt] VI/VT contraer[se]; (assign by contract) contratar; **to — out** subcontratar
contraction [kəntrækʃən] N contracción *f*; (in childbirth) contracción *f*, pujo *m*
contractor [kántræktə-] N contratista *mf*
contractual agreement [kəntræktʃuələgrímənt] N acuerdo contractual *m*
contradict [kantrədíkt] VI/VT contradecir
contradiction [kantrədíkʃən] N contradicción *f*
contradictory [kantrədíktəri] ADJ contradictorio
contraption [kəntræpʃən] N chisme *m*, coso *m*
contrary [kántreri] ADJ contrario, opuesto; (obstinate) testarudo; N lo contrario; **on the —** al contrario
contrast¹ [kántræst] N contraste *m*
contrast² [kəntræst] VI/VT contrastar
contravene [kantrəvín] VT contravenir
contribute [kəntríbjut] VI contribuir; (to a newspaper) colaborar; VT contribuir con, aportar
contribution [kantrəbjúʃən] N (donation, article) contribución *f*; (scientific) aporte *m*, aportación *f*
contributor [kəntríbjəDə-] N colaborador -ra *mf*
contrite [kəntráɪt] ADJ contrito
contrivance [kəntráɪvəns] N artefacto *m*
contrive [kəntráɪv] VI/VT ingeniar; **he —d to get their money** se las ingenió para sacarles el dinero
contrived [kəntráɪvd] ADJ artificioso
control [kəntróɫ] VI/VT controlar; N control *m*; (of a machine) mando *m*; **who's in —?** ¿quién manda? **under —** bajo control; **— freak** mandón -ona *mf*; **— key** tecla de control/mando *f*; **— panel** panel de control *m*; **— tower** torre de control *f*
controller [kəntróɫə-] N (comptroller) controlador -ora *mf*; Am contralor *m*; (device) regulador *m*
controversial [kantrəvɜ́-ʃəɫ] ADJ controvertido
controversy [kántrəvɜ-si] N controversia *f*, polémica *f*
contusion [kəntúʒən] N contusión *f*,

magulladura *f*
conundrum [kənÁndrəm] N (riddle) adivinanza *f*, acertijo *m*; (mystery) enigma *m*
convalesce [kɑnvəlés] VI convalecer
convalescence [kɑnvəlésəns] N convalecencia *f*
convalescent [kɑnvəlésənt] ADJ & N convaleciente *mf*
convection [kənvékʃən] N convección *f*
convene [kənvín] VT convocar; VI reunirse
convenience [kənvínjəns] N (practicality) conveniencia *f*; (appliance) comodidad *f*; — **store** autoservicio *m*; **at your** — cuando le venga bien
convenient [kənvínjənt] ADJ conveniente, oportuno; (at hand) accesible
convent [kánvɛnt] N convento *m*
convention [kənvénʃən] N (political assembly) convención *f*; (professional assembly) congreso *m*; (pact) convenio *m*; (international agreement, acceptable usage) convención *f*
conventional [kənvénʃənl̩] ADJ (not original) convencional; (traditional) clásico; — **loan** préstamo convencional *m*
conventioneer [kənvɛnʃənír] N congresista *mf*
converge [kənvɝ́ʤ] VI converger
convergence [kənvɝ́ʤəns] N convergencia *f*
conversant [kənvɝ́sənt] ADJ — **with** versado en
conversation [kɑnvɚséʃən] N conversación *f*; — **piece** tema de conversación *m*
converse [kənvɝ́s] VI conversar
conversion [kənvɝ́ʒən] N conversión *f*
convert[1] [kənvɝ́t] VI/VT convertir[se]
convert[2] [kánvɝt] N converso -sa *mf*
converter [kənvɝ́Dɚ] N convertidor *m*
convertible [kənvɝ́Dəbəl] ADJ convertible; (car) descapotable; — **assets** activo convertible *m*; N (car) descapotable *m*
convex [kánvɛks] ADJ convexo
convey [kənvé] VT (carry) llevar; (transfer) transferir; (transmit) transmitir; (communicate) comunicar
conveyance [kənvéəns] N (vehicle) vehículo *m*; (transfer of property) transferencia *f*; (document) escritura de traspaso *f*
conveyer, conveyor [kənvéɚ] N transmisor -ora *mf*; — **belt** cinta transportadora *f*
convict[1] [kánvɪkt] N convicto -ta *mf*
convict[2] [kənvíkt] VI/VT declarar culpable
conviction [kənvíkʃən] N (belief) convicción *f*, convencimiento *m*; (act of convicting) declaración de culpabilidad *f*; (on one's record) condena *f*
convince [kənvíns] VT convencer
convincing [kənvínsɪŋ] ADJ convincente, contundente
convocation [kɑnvəkéʃən] N (act) convocación *f*; (group of people) asamblea *f*
convoke [kənvók] VT convocar
convoluted [kɑnvəlúDɪd] ADJ retorcido

convoy [kánvɔɪ] N convoy *m*; VT convoyar
convulse [kənvÁls] VI/VT convulsionar[se]
convulsion [kənvÁlʃən] N convulsión *f*
coo [ku] VI arrullar; N arrullo *m*
cook [kʊk] N cocinero -ra *mf*; —**book** libro de cocina *m*; VT cocinar, guisar; **to** — **the books** falsificar los libros de contabilidad; **to** — **up a plan** urdir un plan; **her** —**ing is outstanding** cocina muy bien; **now we're** —**ing!** ahora sí
cookery [kúkəri] N cocina *f*
cookie [kúki] N (sweet food) galletita dulce *f*; (computer record) archivo cookie *m*
cool [kuł] ADJ (not hot) fresco; (indifferent) frío, indiferente; (calm) tranquilo; (good) excelente; *Carib* chévere; *RP* macanudo; *Sp* guay; *Sp vulg* cojonudo; **that's not** — eso no se hace; —**ing-off period** tregua *f*; N (cold) fresco *m*; (composure) tranquilidad *f*; VT (make cooler) enfriar; (air condition) refrigerar; **to** — **off** (get cold) enfriarse; (get cooler) refrescar[se]; (calm down) calmarse
coolant [kúlənt] N refrigerante *m*
cooler [kúlɚ] N (room) cámara frigorífica *f*; (container) nevera portátil *f*
coolness [kúłnɪs] N (cold weather) fresco *m*, frescor *m*; (indifference) frialdad *f*, indiferencia *f*
coon [kun] N (raccoon) mapache *m*; **a** —**'s age** una eternidad
co-op [kóɑp] N cooperativa *f*
coop [kup] N jaula *f*; (for chickens) gallinero *m*; VT enjaular; **to** — **up** encerrar
cooperate [kóɑpəret] VI cooperar
cooperation [koɑpəréʃən] N cooperación *f*
cooperative [kóɑpəəDIv] ADJ (helpful) cooperativo; (relative to a cooperative) cooperativista; N cooperativa *f*
coordinate[1] [koɔ́rdṇɪt] ADJ coordinado; N coordenada *f*; —**s** (clothes) conjunto *m*
coordinate[2] [koɔ́rdṇet] VI/VT coordinar
coordinating [koɔ́rdṇeDIŋ] ADJ coordinador
coordination [koɔrdṇéʃən] N coordinación *f*
coordinator [koɔ́rdṇeDɚ] N coordinador -ora *mf*
cop [kɑp] N *fam* poli *mf*, polizonte *m*; VI **to** — **out** zafarse
copayment [kópemənt] N copago *m*
cope [kop] VI **to** — **with** arreglárselas con; **I cannot** — **with this** no puedo con esto
copious [kópiəs] ADJ copioso
copper [kápɚ] N cobre *m*; (cop) *fam* poli *mf*; ADJ de cobre
copulate [kápjəlet] VI copular
copulation [kɑpjəléʃən] N copulación *f*
copy [kápi] N (reproduction) copia *f*; (specimen, example) ejemplar *m*; (news story) texto *m*; —**cat** copión -ona *mf*; — **machine** copiadora *f*; — **protection** protección contra copias *f*; —**right** copyright *m*, derechos de autor *m pl*;

this material is —righted reservados todos los derechos; VT copiar; **to —right** registrar los derechos

coquette [kokét] N coqueta *f*

coral [kɔ́rəł] N coral *m*; ADJ (related to coral) coralino; (made of coral) de coral; — **reef** arrecife de coral *m*

cord [kɔrd] N (thread) cuerda *f*; (for shoes) cordón *m*; (firewood measure) medida de leña *f*; —**s** pantalones de pana *m pl*

cordial [kɔ́rdʒəł] ADJ cordial; N licor *m*

cordless [kɔ́rdlɪs] ADJ inalámbrico

corduroy [kɔ́rDərɔɪ] N pana *f*; —**s** pantalones de pana *m pl*

core [kor] N (of fruit) corazón *m*; (of a problem) meollo *m*; (of a magnet, reactor) núcleo *m*; — **business** negocio principal *m*; — **inflation** inflación básica *f*; VT despepitar

cork [kɔrk] N (woody material) corcho *m*; (stopper, buoy) tapón *m*; —**screw** sacacorchos *m sg*, tirabuzón *m*; — **tree** alcornoque *m*; VT tapar con un corcho

corn [kɔrn] N (plant) maíz *m*; (painful growth) callo *m*; —**bread** pan de maíz *m*; —**cob** mazorca *f*; *Sp* zuro *m*; — **on the cob** choclo *m*; *Mex* elote *m*; —**ed beef** corned beef *m*; —**field** maizal *m*; *Mex* milpa *f*; —**flakes** copos de maíz *m pl*; —**meal** harina de maíz *f*; —**starch** Maicena™ *f*

corner [kɔ́rnə] N (angle) ángulo *m*; (of a space) rincón *m*; (of two streets) esquina *f*; —**back** (football) esquinero *m*; — **kick** (soccer) saque/tiro de esquina *m*, córner *m*; —**stone** piedra angular *f*; — **table** mesa rinconera *f*; VT (trap) arrinconar, acorralar; (monopolize) monopolizar; VI doblar, *Sp* girar; — **the market** acaparar el mercado

cornered [kɔ́rnəd] ADJ (animal) acorralado; (person) arrinconado

cornet [kɔrnét] N corneta *f*

cornice [kɔ́rnɪs] N cornisa *f*

corny [kɔ́rni] ADJ sensiblero; (joke) viejo

corollary [kɔ́rəlɛri] N corolario *m*

coronary [kɔ́rənɛri] ADJ coronario; — **bypass** puente cardiopulmonar *m*; — **care unit** unidad de cuidado coronario *f*; — **failure** insuficiencia coronaria *f*; — **thrombosis** trombosis coronaria *f*

coronation [kɔrənéʃən] N coronación *f*

coroner [kɔ́rənə] N médico -ca forense *mf*

corporal [kɔ́rpəəł] ADJ corporal; N (rank) cabo *m*

corporate [kɔ́rpəɪt] ADJ corporativo; — **backing** patrocinio empresarial *m*; — **officers** ejecutivos -vas de empresa *mf pl*

corporation [kɔrpəréʃən] N sociedad anónima *f*

corps [kor] N cuerpo *m*

corpse [kɔrps] N cadáver *m*

corpulent [kɔ́rpjələnt] ADJ corpulento

corpus [kɔ́rpəs] N corpus *m*

corpuscle [kɔ́rpʌsəł] N corpúsculo *m*; (of blood) glóbulo *m*

corral [kərǽł] N corral *m*; VT acorralar

correct [kərékt] VT corregir; ADJ correcto; **that is** — es cierto

correction [kərékʃən] N corrección *f*; (for glasses) graduación *f*

correctness [kəréktnɪs] N corrección *f*

corrector [kəréktə] N corrector -ora *mf*

correlate[1] [kɔ́rəlet] VI/VT correlacionar

correlate[2] [kɔ́rəlɪt] N correlato *m*

correlation [kɔrəléʃən] N correlación *f*

correspond [kɔrɪspánd] VI (be in agreement) corresponder, responder; (exchange letters) cartearse, escribirse

correspondence [kɔrɪspándəns] N correspondencia *f*

correspondent [kɔrɪspándənt] ADJ correspondiente; N (writer of letters) correspondiente *mf*; (news gatherer) corresponsal *mf*, enviado -da *mf*

corresponding [kɔrɪspándɪŋ] ADJ correspondiente; (secretary) encargado de la correspondencia

corridor [kɔ́rɪdɔr] N corredor *m*, pasillo *m*

corroborate [kərábəret] VT corroborar

corrode [kəród] VI/VT corroer[se]

corrosion [kəróʒən] N corrosión *f*

corrupt [kərápt] ADJ (dishonest) corrupto; (rotten) corrompido; **to become** — corromperse; VT corromper, viciar; —**ed file** archivo corrupto *m*

corruption [kərápʃən] N corrupción *f*

corset [kɔ́rsɪt] N corsé *m*

cortex [kɔ́rtɛks] N córtex *m*, corteza cerebral *f*

corticosteriod [kɔrDɪkostérɔɪd] N corticoesteroide *m*

cortisone [kɔ́rDɪzon] N cortisona *f*

cosigner [kósaɪnə] N cosignatario -ria *mf*

cosmetic [kazmɛ́Dɪk] ADJ & N cosmético *m*; — **surgery** cirugía estética *f*

cosmic [kázmɪk] ADJ cósmico

cosmology [kazmálədʒi] N cosmología *f*

cosmonaut [kázmənɔt] N cosmonauta *mf*

cosmopolitan [kazməpálɪtn̩] ADJ cosmopolita

cosmos [kázmos] N cosmos *m*

cost [kɔst] N costo *m*; *Sp* coste *m*; —**s** (in court) costas *f pl*; **at** — al coste/costo; **at all** —**s** a toda costa; — **of living** costo/coste de vida *m*; **to sell at** — vender al costo / al coste; VT costar; **how much does this** —? ¿cuánto vale/cuesta esto? ADJ —**-benefit analysis** análisis costo-beneficio *m*; — **effective** económico

costar [kóstar] N coprotagonista *mf*, oponente *mf*

Costa Rica [kóstəríkə] N Costa Rica *f*

Costa Rican [kóstəríkən] ADJ & N costarricense *mf*, costarriqueño -ña *mf*

costly [kɔ́stli] ADJ costoso, caro
costume [kástum] N (style of clothing)
  vestimenta f; (in the theater) vestuario m;
  (disguise) disfraz m; — **jewelry** bisutería f
cot [kɑt] N catre m
cottage [kɑ́dɪʤ] N (small house) casita f;
  (vacation house) cabaña f, chalé m; — **cheese**
  requesón m
cotter pin [kɑ́də-pɪn] N chaveta f
cotton [kɑ́tn̩] N algodón m; — **candy** algodón de
  azúcar m; — **gin** desmontadora de algodón f;
  —**seed** semilla de algodón f; —**wood** álamo
  [de Virginia] m
couch [kaʊtʃ] N sofá m; (psychiatrist's) diván m;
  — **potato** telebobo -ba mf; VT expresar
cougar [kúgə-] N puma f
cough [kɔf] VI toser; **to** — **up** (spit) expectorar;
  (hand over) soltar, largar; N tos f; — **drop**
  pastilla para la tos f; — **syrup** jarabe para la
  tos m
could [kʊd] V AUX I — **do it if I wanted** podría
  hacerlo si quisiera; — **you arrive early?**
  ¿podrías llegar temprano? — **I leave early?**
  ¿puedo salir temprano? **you** — **be right**
  quizá tengas razón
council [káʊnsəł] N (religious) concilio m;
  (advisory) consejo m, junta f; (provincial)
  diputación f; (municipal) concejo m; —**man**
  concejal m; —**woman** concejal f, concejala f
councilor [káʊnsələ-] N concejal mf
counsel [káʊnsəł] N (advice) consejo m; (lawyer)
  abogado -da mf; VI/VT (give advice) aconsejar
counseling [káʊnsəlɪŋ] N (academic)
  asesoramiento m, orientación f;
  (psychological, marriage) terapia f
counselor [káʊnsələ-] N consejero -ra mf;
  (lawyer) abogado -da mf
count [kaʊnt] VI/VT contar; **to** — **in** incluir; **to** —
  on contar con; **to** — **oneself lucky**
  considerarse dichoso; **to** — **out** excluir; N
  (reckoning) cuenta f; (charge) cargo m;
  (noble) conde m; (in baseball) conteo m;
  —**down** cuenta regresiva f
countenance [káʊntn̩əns] N (expression)
  semblante m; (face) cara f; VT (tolerate)
  tolerar; (approve) aprobar
counter [káʊntə-] N (in a kitchen) Sp encimera f;
  Am mostrador m; (in a store) mostrador m; (in
  a bar) barra f; (in board games) tablero m;
  (counting device) contador m; **over the** — sin
  receta; ADJ contrario, opuesto; ADV — **to**
  contra; **to run** — **to** ser contrario a; VT (an
  argument) retrucar (a blow), devolver; VI/VT
  (reply) replicar
counteract [kaʊntə-ǽkt] VT contrarrestar
counterattack [káʊntə-ətæk] N contraataque m;
  VI/VT contraatacar
counterbalance[1] [kaʊntə-bǽləns] VI/VT
  contrapesar

counterbalance[2] [káʊntə-bæləns] N
  contrapeso m
counterclockwise [kaʊntə-klákwaɪz] ADV en el
  sentido opuesto al de las manecillas del reloj
counterculture [káʊntə-kʌltʃə-] N contracultura
  f
counterespionage [kaʊntə-éspiənɑʒ] N
  contraespionaje m
counterexample [káʊntə-ɪgzæmpəł] N
  contraejemplo m
counterfeit [káʊntə-fɪt] N falsificación f; ADJ
  falso; — **money** moneda falsa f; VT falsificar
countermand[1] [kaʊntə-mǽnd] VT
  contramandar
countermand[2] [káʊntə-mænd] N contraorden f
countermeasure [káʊntə-mɛʒə-] N
  contramedida f
counteroffer [káʊntə-ɔfə-] N contraoferta f
counterpart [káʊntə-part] N homólogo -ga mf
counterproductive [kaʊntə-prədáktɪv] ADJ
  contraproducente
counterrevolution [kaʊntə-revəlúʃən] N
  contrarrevolución f
countersign [káʊntə-saɪn] N contraseña f; VT
  refrendar
countess [káʊntɪs] N condesa f
countless [káʊntlɪs] ADJ incontables,
  innumerables
country [kántri] N (nation) país m; (territory)
  territorio m; (homeland) patria f; (rural area)
  campo m; ADJ (of the countryside) rural;
  (uncouth) rústico; — **club** club campestre m;
  — **code** código de país m; —**man**
  compatriota m; — **music** música country f;
  — **of origin** país de origen m; —**side** (rural
  area) campo m; (scenery) paisaje m;
  —**woman** compatriota f
county [káʊnti] N condado m; — **fair** feria [de
  ganado] f; — **seat** capital de condado f
coup [ku] N (success) golpe maestro m; (putsch)
  golpe de estado m; — **d'état** golpe de
  estado m
coupe [kup] N cupé m
couple [kápəł] N (of times, of forces, of people)
  par m; (romantic) pareja f; VI/VT (pair up)
  formar parejas; VT (connect) acoplar; VI
  (copulate) copular
couplet [káplɪt] N pareado m
coupling [káplɪŋ] N (mechanical action)
  acoplamiento m, enganche m; (device) acople
  m, enganche m; (mating) cópula f
coupon [kjúpɑn] N cupón m
courage [kɝ́ɪʤ] N valentía f, valor m, coraje m
courageous [kəréʤəs] ADJ valiente
courier [kúriə-] N mensajero -ra mf
course [kɔrs] N (of a river, of study, of a disease)
  curso m; (of a road, route) trayecto m; (of a
  ship, plane) derrotero m; (progression of
  time) marcha f; (dish) plato m; — **of action**

línea de conducta f, proceder m; **in the — of a year** en el transcurso de un año; **in due —** a la larga; INTERJ **of —** claro, por supuesto, naturalmente; VI correr, fluir

court [kɔrt] N (courtyard) patio m; (atrium) patio interior m; (in sports) cancha f, pista f; (in a city) plazuela f, plazoleta f; (lower tribunal) juzgado m; (higher tribunal) tribunal m; (session) audiencia f; (royal residence, retinue) corte f; **—-martial** consejo de guerra m; **— of law** tribunal de justicia m; **— order** orden judicial f; **— reporter** estenotipista mf; **— room** tribunal m; **—yard** patio m; **to settle out of —** llegar a un arreglo extrajudicial; **to pay — to** cortejar; VT cortejar, galantear; **to — danger** tentar a la suerte; **to —-martial** someter a consejo de guerra; VI estar de novios

courteous [kɝ̄Diəs] ADJ cortés

courtesy [kɝ̄Disi] N (attitude) cortesía f; (act) fineza f, atención f

courtier [kɔ́rDiɚ] N (member of the court) cortesano -na mf; (sycophant) adulador -ora mf

courtship [kɔ́rtʃɪp] N cortejo m

cousin [kʌ́zən] N primo -ma mf; **first —** primo -ma hermano -na mf

cove [kov] N ensenada f

covenant [kʌ́vənənt] N pacto m; (religious) alianza f

cover [kʌ́vɚ] VI/VT cubrir, recubrir; (with lid, screen) tapar; (replace) sustituir; (include, deal with) comprender; (traverse) recorrer; (sing) hacer una versión; **—ed losses** pérdidas cubiertas f pl; **to — one's ass** cuidarse la retaguardia; **to — up** (wrap up) tapar bien; (hide) ocultar; N (lid) tapa f; (book) cubierta f, tapa f; (blanket) manta f; (for appliances, furniture) funda f; (front for activity) tapadera f, pantalla f; (shelter) resguardo m, abrigo m; **—all** mono m; **— charge** entrada f; **— girl** modelo de portada f; **— letter** carta con anexos f, carta de remisión f; **—-up** encubrimiento m; **to send under separate —** enviar por separado; **to take —** resguardarse; **under —** de incógnito; **under — of dark** bajo el manto de la noche

coverage [kʌ́vɚɪdʒ] N cobertura f; **— level** nivel de cobertura m

covert [kóvɝ̄t] ADJ encubierto

covet [kʌ́vɪt] VT (desire wrongfully) codiciar; (want) ansiar

covetous [kʌ́vɪDəs] ADJ codicioso

cow [kaʊ] N (bovine female) vaca f; (female of other animals) hembra f; **—bell** cencerro m, esquila f; **—boy** vaquero m; **—hide** cuero de vaca m, vaqueta f; **—lick** remolino m; **—pox** vacuna f; **—shed** vaquería f, vaqueriza f; **to have a —** tener una pataleta; VT intimidar

coward [káʊɚd] N cobarde mf

cowardice [káʊɚDɪs] N cobardía f

cowardly [káʊɚdli] ADJ cobarde

cower [káʊɚ] VI achicarse

cowl [kaʊł] N capucha f

coy [kɔɪ] ADJ (coquettish) remilgado; (evasive) esquivo

coyote [kaɪóDi, káɪot] N coyote m

cozy [kózi] ADJ (warm) acogedor; (beneficial) conveniente; VI **to — up to** adular

CPA [certified public accountant] [sípíé] N contador -ora público -ca con licencia mf

CPI [consumer price index] [sípíáɪ] N índice de precios al consumidor m

CPR [cardiopulmonary resuscitation] [sípíár] N reanimación cardiopulmonar f

CPU [central processing unit] [sípíjú] N UCP f

crab [kræb] N cangrejo m; (mechanism) carro corredizo m; (grouch) cascarrabias mf sg; **— apple** manzana silvestre f; **—s** (parasites) ladillas f pl; VI (fish) pescar cangrejos; (complain) quejarse

crack [kræk] VI (single fissure) rajarse; (multiple fissures) resquebrajarse, agrietarse; (psychological breakdown) sufrir un ataque de nervios; (of voice) quebrarse; VT (knuckles) hacer un chasquido con, chascar, chasquear; (nuts) cascar; (jokes) contar; (a prisoner) quebrar; (a case) resolver; (a code) descifrar; (a door) entreabrir; **to — down on** reprimir; **that —s me up** eso me hace desternillar de risa; N (fissure) rajadura f, grieta f, resquebrajadura f; (sound) chasquido m; (joke) pulla f, chanza f; (of the butt) vulg raja f; **— cocaine** crack m; **—down** represión f; **—house** fumadero m; **—pot** excéntrico -ca mf; **at the — of dawn** al romper el alba; **I'd like a — at the championship** me gustaría poder participar en el campeonato

cracked [krækt] ADJ rajado, quebrado; (crazy) chiflado; **it's not all it's — up to be** no es para tanto

cracker [krǽkɚ] N galleta f

crackle [krǽkəł] N (of paper) crujido m; (of fire) crepitación f; VI crujir, crepitar

cradle [krédł] N cuna f

craft [kræft] N (skill) destreza f; (cunning) astucia f; (occupation) arte m, oficio m; (boat) embarcación f; **—sman** artesano m; **—swoman** artesana f; VT fabricar

crafty [krǽfti] ADJ astuto, taimado

crag [kræg] N risco m, peñasco m, peñón m

craggy [krǽgi] ADJ peñascoso

cram [kræm] VT (pack in) embutir; VI (study intensely) memorizar; Sp empollar; **the bar was —med with people** el bar estaba atestado

cramp [kræmp] N (spasm) calambre m; (staple) grapa f; VI/VT (to suffer a spasm)

acalambrar[se]; VT (to staple) engrapar;
you're —ing my style me estorbas
cranberry [krǽnbɛri] N arándano rojo *m*
crane [kren] N (bird) grulla *f*; (machine) grúa *f*;
VT **to — one's neck** estirar el cuello
cranium [kréniəm] N cráneo *m*
crank [kræŋk] N (mechanism) manivela *f*;
(grouch) cascarrabias *mf sg*; (overzealous
advocate) fanático -ca *mf*; —**case** cárter
superior del aceite *m*; —**shaft** cigüeñal *m*;
VI/VT arrancar con manivela
cranky [krǽŋki] ADJ (irritable) irritable;
(eccentric) excéntrico
cranny [krǽni] N (crevice) rendija *f*; (corner)
recoveco *m*
crap [kræp] N (excrement) *vulg* mierda *f*;
(nonsense) estupideces *f pl*; **to take a —** *vulg*
cagar; —**s** dados *m pl*; VI *vulg* cagar
crappy [krǽpi] ADJ *vulg* de porquería
crash [kræʃ] VI (collide) estrellarse; (market)
quebrar; (stay overnight with someone)
quedarse a dormir; (hang up, as with a
computer) bloquearse, caerse; (sleep) dormir;
VT **to — a party** colarse en una fiesta; N
(noise) estallido *m*; (collision) choque *m*;
(financial collapse) quiebra *f*, colapso *m*;
(computer failure) bloqueo *m*, caída *f*; —
landing aterrizaje forzoso *m*
crass [kræs] ADJ craso
crate [kret] N cajón *m*, guacal *m*; VT poner en
cajones
crater [kréDɚ] N cráter *m*
cravat [krəvǽt] N corbata *f*
crave [krev] VT anhelar; **I — chocolate** me
muero por un chocolate
craving [krévɪŋ] N antojo *m*
crawl [krɔł] VI (on hands and knees) gatear; (on
the belly) arrastrarse, reptar; (proceed
slowly) avanzar a paso de tortuga; **to be
—ing with** hormiguear de; N (swimming
stroke) crol *m*; **traffic is going at a —** el
tráfico va a paso de tortuga
crayon [kréɑn] N lápiz de color *m*, Crayola™ *f*
craze [krez] N (fad) moda pasajera *f*; VI/VT
enloquecer[se]
craziness [krézɪnɪs] N locura *f*, chifladura *f*
crazy [krézi] ADJ & N loco -ca *mf*; **I'm — about
you** estoy loco por ti; **that's —!** ¡qué locura!
to go — volverse loco, enloquecerse
creak [krik] N (of wooden floor) crujido *m*; (of a
hinge) rechinamiento *m*; VI (a wooden floor)
crujir; (a hinge) rechinar
cream [krim] N (milk product) crema *f*; *Sp* nata *f*;
(medicament) crema *f*; — **cheese** queso de
untar *m*, queso crema *m*; — **of tomato soup**
sopa crema de tomate *f*; **the — of the crop** la
flor y nata; VT (decream) desnatar; (butter,
sugar) batir; (vegetables) preparar con salsa
blanca; (defeat) aplastar

creamy [krími] ADJ cremoso
crease [kris] N (in trousers) raya *f*, repliegue *m*;
(wrinkle) arruga *f*; VT (trousers) planchar la
raya; (wrinkle) arrugar
create [kriét] VI/VT crear
creation [kriéʃən] N creación *f*
creationism [kriéʃənɪzəm] N creacionismo *m*
creative [kriéDɪv] ADJ creativo
creativity [kriətívɪDi] N creatividad *f*
creator [kriéDɚ] N creador -ra *mf*
creature [krítʃɚ] N (being) ser *m*; (animal)
animal *m*; **a — of your imagination** un
producto de tu imaginación
credence [krídn̩s] N crédito *m*
credentials [krɪdéntʃəłz] N credenciales *f pl*
credibility [krɛdɪbílɪDi] N credibilidad *f*
credible [krédəbəł] ADJ creíble
credit [krédɪt] N crédito *m*; (commendation)
reconocimiento *m*; — **approval** aprobación
de crédito *f*; — **card** tarjeta de crédito *f*; —
counseling asesoramiento de crédito *m*; —
line línea de crédito *f*; — **history** historial de
crédito *m*; — **rating** calificación crediticia *f*;
— **report** informe de crédito *m*; —**s** créditos
m pl; — **underwriters** aseguradores de
crédito *m pl*; — **union** banco cooperativo *m*;
on — a crédito; **to give — to** (believe) dar
crédito; (ascribe) acreditar; ADJ —**worthy**
solvente; VT (believe) creer; (enter as credit)
acreditar; (attribute) atribuir; — **an account**
abonar/acreditar a una cuenta
creditor [krédɪDɚ] N acreedor -ora *mf*
credulous [krédʒələs] ADJ crédulo
creed [krid] N credo *m*
creek [krik] N arroyo *m*, quebrada *f*
creep [krip] VI (crawl on belly) arrastrarse;
(crawl on all fours) gatear; (grow upward)
trepar; (go slowly) andar a paso de tortuga; **to
— up on** acercarse furtivamente a; N
(obnoxious person) *pej* persona repulsiva *f*,
sinvergüenza *mf*; **that gives me the —s** eso
me da asco; *Sp* eso me da grima
creeper [krípɚ] N enredadera *f*, planta
trepadora *f*
creepy [krípi] ADJ repulsivo
cremate [krímet] VT cremar
Creole [kríoł] ADJ & N criollo -lla *mf*
creosote [kríosot] N creosota *f*
crepe [krep] N (fabric) crespón *m*; (band of
fabric) crespón negro *m*
crept [krɛpt] *see* creep
crescent [krésənt] N media luna *f*; ADJ creciente
crest [krɛst] N (of a wave, rooster) cresta *f*; (of
feathers) penacho *m*, copete *m*; (of mountain)
cima *f*, cumbre *f*; (of heraldic arms) timbre *m*;
—**fallen** alicaído, cabizbajo; VI **the river
—ed at two meters above flood level** el
río creció hasta dos metros por encima de lo
normal

crevice [krévɪs] N grieta *f*

crew [kru] N (for ships, etc.) tripulación *f*; (of workers) cuadrilla *f*; — **member** tripulante *mf*

crib [krɪb] N (bed) cuna *f*; (manger) pesebre *m*; (bin for grain) granero *m*; (cheat notes) hoja para copiar *f*; — **death** síndrome de muerte súbita infantil *m*; VI copiar

cricket [kríkɪt] N (insect) grillo *m*; (game) críquet *m*

crime [kraɪm] N (illegal act) delito *m*; (act of violence against people) crimen *m*; (criminal activity) delincuencia *f*, criminalidad *f*

criminal [krímənəł] ADJ & N delincuente *mf*, malhechor -ora *mf*; (perpetrator of violent crimes) criminal *mf*; — **record** antecedentes delictivos *m pl*

crimp [krɪmp] VT rizar; N rizo *m*

crimson [krímzən] ADJ & N carmesí *m*, carmín *m*

cringe [krɪnʤ] VI **it makes me** — me da vergüenza ajena

cripple [krípəł] N *offensive* tullido -da *mf*; (in the legs) *pey* cojo -ja *mf*; (in the arms) *offensive* manco -ca *mf*; VT tullir

crisis [kráɪsɪs] N crisis *f*

crisp [krɪsp] ADJ (apple, bacon) crocante, crujiente; (weather) fresco y despejado; (hair) crespo; VI/VT volver crujiente

crispy [kríspi] ADJ crocante, crujiente

criterion [kraɪtíriən] N criterio *m*

critic [krídɪk] N crítico -ca *mf*

critical [krídɪkəł] ADJ crítico; — **stage** punto culminante *m*

criticism [krídɪsɪzəm] N crítica *f*

criticize [krídɪsaɪz] VT criticar

croak [krok] VI (make the sound of a frog) croar; (make the sound of a crow) graznar; (die) *fam* espichar; N (sound made by frogs) canto de rana *m*; (sound made by crows) graznido *m*

Croatia [kroéʃə] N Croacia *f*

Croatian [kroéʃən] ADJ & N croata *mf*

crochet [kroʃé] N ganchillo *m*, croché *m*, crochet *m*; — **hook** aguja de croché *f*; VI hacer ganchillo, hacer croché

crock [krɑk] N (pot) vasija *f*; (lies) pamplinas *f pl*

crockery [krákəri] N loza *f*

crocodile [krákədaɪł] N cocodrilo *m*

croissant [krəsánt] N cruasán *m*, croissant *m*

crony [króni] N compinche *mf*, compadre *m*, comadre *f*

cronyism [króniɪzəm] N amiguismo *m*

crook [krʊk] N (criminal) delincuente *mf*; (curve) curva *f*; (hook) gancho *m*; (staff) cayado *m*

crooked [krúkɪd] ADJ (bent) torcido; *Am* chueco; (dishonest) deshonesto

crop [krɑp] N (harvest) cosecha *f*; (group of contemporaries) promoción *f*; (of a bird) buche *m*; (horse whip) fusta *f*; — **rotation** rotación de cultivos *f*; VT (graze) pastar,

pacer; (trim) recortar; **to** — **up** surgir

croquet [kroké] N cróquet *m*

cross [krɔs] N (symbol) cruz *f*; (street intersection) cruce *m*; (soccer) pase cruzado *m*; (act of mixing) cruzamiento *m*; (in boxing) cruzado *m*; — **bar** (soccer) travesaño *m*, larguero *m*; (in gymnastics) barra *f*; (in high jump) listón *m*; (of a door) tranca *f*; — **-check** verificación *f*; — **court shot** golpe cruzado *m*; — **-dresser** travesti *mf*, travestí *mf*; — **-fertilization** fecundación cruzada *f*; — **piece** cruceta *f*; — **-reference** referencia cruzada *f*; — **road** encrucijada *f*; — **section** corte transversal *m*; — **walk** cruce peatonal *m*, cebra *f*; — **word puzzle** crucigrama *m*; **to bear one's** — cargar la cruz; VI/VT (intersect, form a cross, breed, meet) cruzar[se]; (make sign of the cross) santiguarse; **to** — **-check** verificar; **to** — **-dress** transvestir[se]; VT (betray) traicionar; (move to other side) cruzar; **to** — **examine** interrogar; **to** — **out** tachar; **to** — **over** (change allegiance) cambiar de bando; (go to the other side) traspasar; **to** — **-reference** hacer una referencia cruzada; **you've** — **ed the line** te pasaste de la raya; ADJ (transverse) transversal; (angry) enojado; — **-country** a campo traviesa; — **-cultural** transcultural; — **-eyed** bizco; **to be** — **-eyed** bizquear

crossing [krɔ́sɪŋ] N (street or railroad intersection, pedestrian path) cruce *m*; (hybridization, act of mixing) cruzamiento *m*; (of ocean) travesía *f*; (of a border) paso *m*; (of a river) vado *m*

crotch [krɑtʃ] N entrepierna *f*

crotchety [krátʃɪdi] ADJ cascarrabias *inv*

crouch [kraʊtʃ] VI (stoop) agacharse; (prepare to spring) agazaparse

croup [krup] N tos *f*, croup *m*

crow [kro] N (bird) cuervo *m*; (sound of rooster) canto del gallo *m*; — **bar** alzaprima *f*; — **'s-foot** pata de gallo *f*; **to eat** — comerse sus propias palabras; VI cantar; (gloat, brag) jactarse

crowd [kraʊd] N (group of people) muchedumbre *f*, gentío *m*, aglomeración *f*; (at a performance) público *m*; (clique) pandilla *f*; VI (push forward) agolparse; VI/VT (gather in large numbers) apiñar[se], amontonar[se], aglomerar[se]; (gather in a confined space) hacinar[se]

crowded [kráʊdɪd] ADJ **it is** — **in here** hay demasiada gente aquí; **the restaurant is** — el restaurante está lleno

crown [kraʊn] N corona *f*; (of head) coronilla *f*, crisma *f*; (of a hat) copa *f*; — **jewels** joyas de la corona *f pl*; VT coronar; (hit on head) dar un coscorrón

crucial [krúʃəł] ADJ (element) fundamental;

(moment) crucial
crucible [krúsəbəl] N crisol *m*
crucifix [krúsəfɪks] N crucifijo *m*
crucify [krúsəfaɪ] VT crucificar
crud [krʌd] N (filth) mugre *f*; (worthless thing, sickness, despicable person) *fam* porquería *f*
crude [krud] ADJ (vulgar, unpolished) basto, tosco; — **oil** petróleo crudo *m*
cruel [krúəl] ADJ cruel
cruelty [krúəlti] N crueldad *f*
cruise [kruz] VI (take a cruise) tomar un crucero; (patrol) patrullar; (seek sexual partners) salir a buscar plan; — **control** control de crucero *m*; **cruising speed** velocidad de crucero *f*; N crucero *m*; — **missile** misil crucero *m*
cruiser [krúzɚ] N crucero *m*
crumb [krʌm] N (small) miga *f*, migaja *f*; (large) mendrugo *m*; VT (break into crumbs) desmigajar; (remove crumbs) sacar las migas
crumble [krʌ́mbəl] VI/VT (bread) desmigajar[se]; (clods of dirt) desmenuzar[se]; (house) desmoronar[se]
crummy [krʌ́mi] ADJ (place) *fam* de mala muerte; (object) *fam* de porquería; (show) flojo
crumple [krʌ́mpəl] VI/VT (crush) arrugar[se]; VI (collapse) aplastarse
crunch [krʌntʃ] VI/VT (eat noisily) mascar; N (sound) crujido *m*; (shortage) crisis *f*; —**es** abdominales *m pl*
crunchy [krʌ́ntʃi] ADJ crocante, crujiente
crusade [kruséd] N cruzada *f*; VI (engage in a campaign) hacer una campaña
crusader [kruséDɚ] N cruzado -da *mf*; **a — for human rights** un paladín de los derechos humanos
crush [krʌʃ] VI/VT aplastar, machacar; (stone) demoler; N (act of crushing) aplastamiento *m*; (crowd) tumulto *m*; (infatuation) enamoramiento *m*; —**ing victory** victoria contundente *f*
crust [krʌst] N (of bread, earth) corteza *f*; (of bread) costra *f*; (of pie) tapa *f*
crusty [krʌ́sti] ADJ (with a crust) costroso; (grouchy) irascible
crutch [krʌtʃ] N muleta *f*
cry [kraɪ] N (shout) grito *m*; (weeping) llanto *m*; (call of a bird) reclamo *m*; —**baby** llorón -ona *mf*; **a far — from** muy distante de, muy lejos de; VI (shout) gritar; (weep) llorar; **to — over spilt milk** hacer como la lechera; **to — for attention** reclamar atención; **to — for help** pedir socorro; **to — out** vocear
cryogenic [kraɪədʒénɪk] ADJ criogénico
crystal [krístl̩] N cristal *m*; — **ball** bola de cristal *f*; — **clear** cristalino
crystalline [krístlɪn] ADJ cristalino
crystallize [krístl̩aɪz] VI/VT cristalizar[se]
cub [kʌb] N (lion) cachorro *m*; (bear) osezno *m*;

(whale) ballenato *m*; (wolf) lobato *m*, lobezno *m*; — **reporter** reportero -ra novato -ta *mf*
Cuba [kjúbə] N Cuba *f*
Cuban [kjúbən] ADJ & N cubano -na *mf*
cubbyhole [kʌ́bihol] N casilla *f*
cube [kjúb] N cubo *m*; — **root** raíz cúbica *f*; VT (cut) cortar en cubos; (raise to the third power) elevar al cubo
cubic [kjúbɪk] ADJ cúbico
cubicle [kjúbɪkəl] N cubículo *m*
cubism [kjúbɪzəm] N cubismo *m*
cuckold [kʌ́kəld] N cornudo *m*, cabrón *m*; VT poner los cuernos a
cuckoo [kúku] N cuclillo *m*, cuco *m*; — **clock** reloj de cucú *m*; ADJ & N chiflado -da *mf*; INTERJ cucú
cucumber [kjúkʌmbɚ] N pepino *m*
cud [kʌd] N **to chew the —** rumiar
cuddle [kʌ́dl̩] VI/VT hacer[se] mimos; N mimo *m*
cuddly [kʌ́dli] ADJ mimoso
cudgel [kʌ́dʒəl] N porra *f*; VT aporrear
cue [kju] N (in theater) pie *m*; (psychological stimulus) estímulo *m*; — **ball** bola blanca *f*; — **stick** taco de billar *m*; VT dar pie, dar la señal
cuff [kʌf] N (of sleeve, glove) puño *m*; (of pants) bajo *m*; (blow) bofetada *f*; **hand—s** esposas *f pl*; VT (in making pants) hacer los bajos; (put on handcuffs) esposar; (hit) abofetear
cuisine [kwɪzín] N cocina *f*
cul-de-sac [kʌ́ldəsæk] N callejón sin salida *m*
culinary [kjúlənɛri, kʌ́lənɛri] ADJ culinario
cull [kʌl] VT (choose) seleccionar, entresacar; (collect) recoger
culminate [kʌ́lmənet] VI/VT culminar
culmination [kʌlmənéʃən] N culminación *f*
culprit [kʌ́lprɪt] N culpable *mf*
cult [kʌlt] N (sect) secta religiosa *f*; (worship) culto *m*
cultivable [kʌ́ltəvəbəl] ADJ cultivable
cultivate [kʌ́ltəvet] VT cultivar
cultivated [kʌ́ltəveDɪd] ADJ (land) cultivado; (plant) de cultivo; (person) culto
cultivation [kʌltəvéʃən] N (tillage) cultivo *m*; (education) cultura *f*
cultivator [kʌ́ltəveDɚ] N (person) cultivador -ora *mf*; (implement) cultivadora *f*
cultural [kʌ́ltʃəəl] ADJ cultural
culture [kʌ́ltʃɚ] N cultura *f*; (microorganisms) cultivo *m*; — **shock** choque cultural *m*; VT (microorganisms) cultivar
cultured [kʌ́ltʃəd] ADJ (person) culto; (pearl) cultivado, de cultivo
cumbersome [kʌ́mbɚsəm] ADJ (bulky) voluminoso; (unwieldy) incómodo
cumulative [kjúmjələDɪv] ADJ acumulativo
cumulus [kjúmjələs] N cúmulo *m*
cunnilingus [kʌnɪlíŋgəs] N cunilinguo *m*
cunning [kʌ́nɪŋ] ADJ (sly) astuto, zorro; N astucia *f*, maña *f*

cunt [kʌnt] N *Sp vulg* coño *m*; *Mex vulg* chocho *m*; *RP vulg* concha *f*

cup [kʌp] N (with handle) taza *f*, pocillo *m*; (without handle) vaso *m*; (measure) taza *f*; (trophy, brassiere part) copa *f*; **—board** armario *m*, aparador *m*

cur [kɜ˞] N (dog) perro *m*; (villain) *pej* villano -na *mf*

curable [kjúrəbəł] ADJ curable

curator [kjúreDɚ] N conservador -ora *mf*

curb [kɜ˞b] N (of a street) *Sp* bordillo *m*; *Mex* borde *m*; *RP* cordón *m*; (of a well) brocal *m*; (restraint) freno *m*, restricción *f*; VT (emotions) refrenar; (spending) limitar

curd [kɜ˞d] N cuajada *f*; VI/VT cuajar[se], coagular[se]

curdle [kɜ˞dl̩] VI/VT cuajar[se], coagular[se]; **my blood —d** se me heló la sangre

cure [kjur] N (healing, preserving meat) cura *f*, curación *f*; (method) tratamiento *m*; VI/VT curar[se]; **—-all** sanalotodo *m*

curfew [kɜ˞fju] N toque de queda *m*, queda *f*

curio [kjúrio] N curiosidad *f*

curiosity [kjʊriásɪDi] N curiosidad *f*

curious [kjúriəs] ADJ curioso

curl [kɜ˞ł] VI/VT (form ringlets) rizar[se], ensortijar[se]; (coil) enroscar[se]; (smoke) alzarse en espirales; **to — up** ovillar[se]; N (of hair) rizo *m*, bucle *m*; (of smoke) espiral *f*

curler [kɜ˞lɚ] N *Sp* rulo *m*; *Mex* tubo *m*; *RP* rulero *m*

curly [kɜ˞li] ADJ rizado

currant [kɜ˞ənt] N (fruit) grosella *f*; (tree) grosellero *m*

currency [kɜ˞ənsi] N (money) moneda *f*, divisa *f*; (acceptance) aceptación *f*; **— exchange** mercado de divisas *m*; **— unit** unidad monetaria *f*

current [kɜ˞ənt] ADJ (commonly used) corriente; (prevalent) actual; **the — issue of a magazine** el último número de una revista; **— year** año en curso *m*; N (of river, electricity, air) corriente *f*

currently [kɜ˞əntli] ADV actualmente

curriculum [kəríkjələm] N plan de estudios *m*, currículo *m*

curry [kɜ˞ri] N curry *m*

curse [kɜ˞s] N (ill wish) maldición *f*; (swear word) palabrota *f*; VI/VT (wish ill) maldecir; (swear) decir palabrotas

cursive [kɜ˞sɪv] ADJ cursivo; N cursiva *f*

cursor [kɜ˞sɚ] N cursor *m*

curt [kɜ˞t] ADJ (abrupt) seco, brusco; (brief) breve

curtail [kɚtéł] VT restringir, cercenar

curtain [kɜ˞tn̩] N cortina *f*; (theater) telón *m*; VT ponerle cortinas a

curvature [kɜ˞vətʃʊr] N curvatura *f*; (of the spine) desviación *f*

curve [kɜ˞v] N (also in baseball) curva *f*; **he**

threw me a — me agarró desprevenido; VI/VT encorvar[se]; (road) torcer[se], desviar[se]

curved [kɜ˞vd] ADJ curvo

cushion [kúʃən] N (pad) almohadilla *f*; (emergency resources, pad of air) colchón *m*; (pillow) almohadón *m*; (decorative pillow) cojín *m*; VT (put pads) poner almohadones; (soften a blow) amortiguar

cuspid [kʌ́spɪd] N colmillo *m*

cuss [kʌs] VI decir palabrotas; N **—word** *fam* palabrota *f*; **strange old —** *fam* bicho raro *m*

custard [kʌ́stɚd] N flan *m*, natilla[s] *f sg or pl*

custodian [kʌstóDiən] N (caretaker) cuidador -ora *mf*; (guardian) custodio -dia *mf*

custody [kʌ́stədi] N custodia *f*; **to take into —** detener

custom [kʌ́stəm] N costumbre *f*, uso *m*; **—s** (government department) aduana *f*; (taxes) derechos de aduana *m pl*; **—[s]house** aduana *f*; ADJ **—-built** construido por encargo; **—-made** hecho a medida

customary [kʌ́stəmɛri] ADJ acostumbrado

customer [kʌ́stəmɚ] N cliente -ta *mf*; **— base** clientela *f*; **— care** atención al cliente *f*; **— rights** derechos del cliente *m pl*; ADJ **—-oriented** orientado al cliente

customize [kʌ́stəmaɪz] VT adaptar por encargo

cut [kʌt] VI/VT cortar; (shorten) acortar; (harvest) talar; (lower) rebajar; **—!** ¡corte[n]! **to — a deal** llegar a un arreglo; **to — across** (take a shortcut) cortar por; (transcend) trascender; **to — and paste** cortar y pegar; **to — back** reducir; **to — class** faltar a clase; **to — costs** reducir costos; **to — down on** reducir; **to — in** (interrupt) interrumpir; (in traffic) atravesarse; **to — prices** bajar los precios; **may I — in?** ¿me permite? **to — off** (interrupt) interrumpir; (intercept) interceptar; **to — out** omitir; **to be — out for** estar hecho para; **to — up** (divide) trozar; (misbehave) portarse mal; N corte *m*; (in salary) recorte *m*, reducción *f*; (of prices) rebaja *f*; (of a suit) hechura *f*, corte *m*; (insult) desaire *f*; **—back** recorte *m*; **— glass** cristal labrado *m*; **—off date** fecha límite *f*; ADJ **—-and-dried** predeterminado; **—-rate** de rebajas; **—throat** despiadado

cutaneous [kjuténiəs] ADJ cutáneo

cute [kjut] ADJ mono, rico; **to act —** ser afectado, ser melindroso

cuticle [kjúDɪkəł] N cutícula *f*

cutlery [kʌ́tləri] N (knives, knife store) cuchillería *f*; (eating utensils) cubiertos *m pl*

cutlet [kʌ́tlɪt] N filete *m*

cutter [kʌ́Dɚ] N (person) cortador -ora *mf*; (device) cortadora *f*; (sleigh) trineo *m*; **Coast Guard —** guardacostas *m sg*

cutting [kʌ́Dɪŋ] ADJ (sharp) cortante; (cold) penetrante; (sarcastic) mordaz, sarcástico; **—**

board tabla de cortar *f*; — **edge** filo *m*; —-
edge technology tecnología de punta *f*; N
(action) cortado *m*
CV [curriculum vitae] [sívî] N currículo *m*,
currículum vitae *m*
cyanide [sáɪənaɪd] N cianuro *m*
cybercafe [saɪbə-kafé] N cibercafé *m*
cybernetics [saɪbə-néDɪks] N cibernética *f*
cyberpunk [sáɪbə-pʌnk] N ciberpunk *m*
cyberspace [sáɪbə-spes] N ciberespacio *m*
cyborg [sáɪbɔrg] N cyborg *m*
cycle [sáɪkəl] N ciclo *m*
cyclical [síklɪkəl] ADJ cíclico
cyclone [sáɪklon] N ciclón *m*
cyclotron [sáɪklətran] N ciclotrón *m*
cylinder [sílɪndə-] N cilindro *m*; (of a gun)
tambor *m*; — **head** culata *f*
cylindrical [sɪlíndrɪkəl] ADJ cilíndrico
cymbal [símbəl] N címbalo *m*, platillo *m*
cynic [sínɪk] N cínico -ca *mf*
cynical [sínɪkəl] ADJ cínico
cynicism [sínɪsɪzəm] N cinismo *m*
cypress [sáɪprɪs] N ciprés *m*
Cypriot, Cypriote [sípriət] ADJ & N chipriota *mf*
Cyprus [sáɪprəs] N Chipre *m*
cyst [sɪst] N quiste *m*
cystic [sístɪk] ADJ cístico; — **fibrosis** fibrosis
cística *f*
cytology [saɪtáládʒi] N citología *f*
czar [zɑr] N zar *m*
Czech [tʃɛk] ADJ & N checo -ca *mf*; — **Republic**
República Checa *f*

Dd

dab [dæb] VT (pat) dar toques; (apply) aplicar con
golpecitos; N toque *m*
dabble [dæbəl] VI (splash) chapotear; (be
interested superficially) ser aficionado a
dachshund [dáksənd] N perro salchicha *m*
dad [dæd] N papá *m*
daddy [dæDi] N papaíto *m*, papito *m*, papacito *m*
daffodil [dæfədɪł] N narciso *m*
dagger [dægə-] N daga *f*, puñal *m*
dahlia [dǽljə] N dalia *f*
daily [déli] ADJ diario; — **planner** agenda *f*; —
wage jornal *m*, salario *m*; N (newspaper)
diario *m*
dainty [dénti] ADJ (delicate) delicado, exquisito;
(finicky) remilgado
dairy [déri] N (milk) lechería *f*; (cheese) quesería
f; ADJ (industry) lechero; (product) lácteo; N
producto lácteo *m*
daisy [dézi] N margarita *f*; **to be pushing up
daisies** *fam* estar criando malvas
dale [deł] N valle *m*

dally [dǽli] VI (flirt) coquetear; (risk danger)
jugar con fuego; (waste time) remolonear
dam [dæm] N presa *f*, represa *f*; VT represar
damage [dǽmɪdʒ] N daño *m*, destrozo *m*; —
control control de daños *m*; —**s** daños y
perjuicios *m pl*; **to pay** —**s** indemnizar *m*;
VI/VT dañar[se]
damaging [dǽmɪdʒɪŋ] ADJ perjudicial
dame [dem] N (noblewoman) dama *f*; (woman)
pej tipa *f*
damn [dæm] VT condenar; **it's not worth a** —
no vale un comino; INTERJ *vulg* ¡maldito sea!
damnation [dæmnéʃən] N condenación *f*,
perdición *f*
damned [dæmd] ADJ condenado
damp [dæmp] ADJ húmedo; N humedad *f*; VT
(wet) humedecer; (deaden) amortiguar;
(extinguish) apagar
dampen [dǽmpən] VT (wet) humedecer;
(deaden) amortiguar; (depress) deprimir
dampness [dǽmpnɪs] N humedad *f*
damsel [dǽmzəl] N damisela *f*
dance [dæns] N (act of dancing, party, activity)
baile *m*; (artistic activity, animal courtship
movements) danza *f*; — **music** música
bailable *f*; VI/VT (at a party) bailar; (in ballet,
of animals) danzar; **she** —**d her way to
stardom** llegó al estrellato bailando
dancer [dǽnsə-] N bailarín -ina *mf*, danzante *mf*
dancercise [dǽnsə-saɪz] N baile aeróbico *m*
dandelion [dǽndlaɪən] N diente de león *m*
dandruff [dǽndrəf] N caspa *f*
dandy [dǽndi] N dandi *m*, señorito *m*; ADJ
estupendo
Dane [den] N danés -esa *mf*
danger [dénḍʒə-] N peligro *m*
dangerous [dénḍʒə-əs] ADJ peligroso
dangle [dǽŋgəl] VI/VT (hang) colgar; (sway)
bambolear[se]; **her legs were dangling off
the bench** sus piernas pendían del banco
Danish [dénɪʃ] ADJ danés; N bollo dulce *m*
dapple, dappled [dǽpəl[d]] ADJ pinto, moteado
dare [dɛr] VI/VT (be brave) atreverse [a], osar;
(challenge) desafiar; **how** — **you?** ¿cómo te
atreves? N desafío *m*; —**devil** temerario -ria
mf
daring [dérɪŋ] N atrevimiento *m*, osadía *f*; ADJ
atrevido, osado, arriesgado
dark [dɑrk] ADJ (in color) oscuro; (of hair)
moreno, morocho, trigueño; (gloomy)
sombrío, tenebroso; (evil, ignorant) oscuro;
(shameful) turbio; — **Ages** [Alta] Edad Media
f; —**room** cuarto oscuro *m*; —-**skinned**
moreno; N oscuridad *f*; **after** — después de
que oscurece
darken [dárkən] VI/VT oscurecer
darkness [dárknɪs] N (complete) oscuridad *f*,
tinieblas *f pl*; (partial) penumbra *f*
darling [dárlɪŋ] ADJ & N amado -da *mf*, querido

-da *mf*; **my** — vida mía, amor mío

darn [dɑrn] VT zurcir, remendar; **—ing needle** aguja de zurcir *f*; N zurcido *m*; **it is not worth a** — no vale un comino; INTERJ ¡caramba! ¡caracoles!

dart [dɑrt] N (missile) dardo *m*; (tuck) pinza *f*; (swift movement) movimiento rápido *m*; **—board** diana *f*; **to play —s** jugar a los dardos; VI disparar; **to** — **out** salir disparado

dash [dæʃ] VI/VT (of waves, porcelain) estrellar[se]; VT (plans) frustrar; VI (hopes) desplomarse; **to** — **by** pasar corriendo; **to** — **off/out** salir disparado; **to** — **off a letter** escribir de prisa una carta; N (line) raya *f*; (run) corrida *f*; (race) carrera *f*; (small amount) pizca *f*; (splash) salpicadura *f*; **the one hundred-meter** — la carrera de los cien metros llanos/planos; **—board** tablero *m*, salpicadero *m*

data [déɒə, dǽɒə] N datos *m pl*; **—base** base de datos *f*; **—bank** banco de datos *m*; — **encryption** cifrado de datos *m*; — **file** archivo de datos *m*; — **input** entrada de datos *f*; — **management** gestión de datos *f*; — **processing** procesamiento de datos *m*, fichero de datos *m*; — **recovery** recuperación de datos *f*; — **storage** almacenamiento de datos *m*

date [det] N (time) fecha *f*; (appointment) cita *f*; (person) acompañante *mf*; (fruit) dátil *m*; — **due** fecha de vencimiento *f*; **out of** — anticuado; **to** — hasta ahora; **up to** — al día; VI (be dated) estar fechado; (go out socially) salir; VT (write the date) fechar; (show to be old-fashioned) delatar la edad; (go out socially) salir con; **to** — **from** datar de, remontarse a

dated [déɒɪd] ADJ (having a date) fechado; (old-fashioned) anticuado

daub [dɔb] VT (smear) embarrar, embadurnar; (apply unskillfully) pintarrajear

daughter [dɔ́ɒɚ] N hija *f*; — **-in-law** nuera *f*

daunt [dɔnt] VT (intimidate) intimidar; (dishearten) desanimar

dauntless [dɔ́ntlɪs] ADJ intrépido

davenport [dǽvənpɔrt] N sofá grande *m*

dawn [dɔn] N alba *f*, amanecer *m*, aurora *f*; **the** — **of civilization** los albores de la civilización; VI amanecer, aclarar; **it just —ed on me that** caí en [la] cuenta de que

day [de] N día *m*; — **after tomorrow** pasado mañana *m*; — **before yesterday** anteayer *m*; **—break** amanecer *m*; **at —break** al amanecer; **—care** guardería *f*; **—dream** fantasía *f*; — **laborer** jornalero -ra *mf*; **—light** luz del día *f*; **—light saving time** adelanto de la hora en verano *m*; **—time** día *m*; **—time activity** actividad diurna *f*; **—-to-** — día a día; **by** — de día; **by the** — por día;

eight-hour — jornada de ocho horas *f*; **in my** — en mis tiempos; **in the old —s** antaño; **make my** — dame el gusto; **New Year's** — Año Nuevo *m*; ADJ diurno; VI **to —dream** soñar despierto

daze [dez] VT aturdir; N **to be in a** — estar aturdido

dazzle [dǽzəl] VI/VT deslumbrar

deacidify [diəsídɪfaɪ] VT neutralizar la acidez

deacon [díkən] N diácono *m*

deactivate [diǽktɪvet] VI/VT desactivar

deactivation [diæktɪvéʃən] N desactivación *f*

dead [dɛd] ADJ muerto; **he's a** — **duck** está muerto; — **-end job** puesto sin perspectivas *m*; — **sure** completamente seguro; — **tired** muerto de cansancio; N — **air** aire viciado *m*; **—beat** moroso -sa *mf*; **—bolt** pestillo *m*; — **end** callejón sin salida *m*; — **letter** letra muerta *f*; **—line** fecha límite *f*; — **link** enlace muerto *m*; **—lock** punto muerto *m*; **—pan** de palo; — **ringer** fiel retrato *m*; **—wood** (person) persona inútil *f*; (thing) cosa inútil *f*; **the** — los muertos; **in the** — **of the night** en el silencio de la noche; **in the** — **of winter** en pleno invierno; VI **to —lock** trancarse

deaden [dédn̩] VT amortiguar

deadly [dédli] ADJ (enemy) mortal; (poison) letal; (weapon) mortífero; ADV mortalmente; — **dull** sumamente aburrido

deaf [dɛf] ADJ sordo; — **-mute** ADJ & N sordomudo -da *mf*

deafen [défən] VT (make deaf) ensordecer; (deaden) amortiguar

deafening [défənɪŋ] ADJ ensordecedor, atronador

deafness [défnɪs] N sordera *f*

deal [dil] VT (cards) dar, repartir; (drugs) vender; (a blow) dar, asestar; **to** — **in** comerciar en; **biology —s with the study of life** la biología se ocupa del estudio de la vida; **I have to** — **with all kinds of people** tengo que vérmelas con todo tipo de gente; N (business transaction) trato *m*, negocio *m*; (shady transaction) componenda *f*; (act of dealing cards) reparto *m*; **a great** — **of** una gran cantidad de; **it's a** — ¡trato hecho! **I got a raw** — me clavaron

dealer [dílɚ] N (in cars, antiques) comerciante *mf*; (in drugs, arms) traficante *mf*; (of cards) el/la que reparte *mf*

dealership [dílɚʃɪp] N concesionario *m*

dealings [dílɪŋz] N trato *m*, relaciones *f pl*; (business) negocios *m pl*

dealt [dɛlt] *see* deal

dean [din] N (of university, professional group) decano -na *mf*; (in church) deán *m*

dear [dir] ADJ (beloved) querido; (expensive) caro; (cherished) apreciado; — **Sir/Madam**

Estimado señor / Estimada señora; **my —est wish** mi deseo más ferviente; N **he's such a —!** ¡es un amor! **my —** querido mío m / querida mía f; ADV caro; **that cost me —** eso me costó caro; **— me!** ¡Dios mío! **oh —!** ¡Dios mío!

dearth [dɜ·θ] N escasez f

death [dɛθ] N muerte f; **—bed** lecho de muerte m; **— benefits** beneficios por fallecimiento m; **— certificate** partida de defunción f; **— penalty** pena de muerte f; **— rate** tasa de mortalidad f; **— row** pabellón de los condenados a muerte m; **he's on — row** está condenado a muerte; **— squad** escuadrón de la muerte m; **— toll** mortandad f; **—trap** trampa mortal f; **— wish** instinto suicida m; **to put to —** ejecutar; **we have discussed this to —** hemos discutido esto hasta el hartazgo; **I'm sick to — of this job** estoy harto de este trabajo

debacle [dɪbákəl] N debacle f

debase [dɪbés] VT degradar, envilecer

debatable [dɪbéɒəbəl] ADJ discutible

debate [dɪbét] N debate m; VI/VT (discuss) debatir, discutir; (weigh a decision) considerar

debilitate [dɪbílɪtet] VT debilitar

debilitating [dɪbílɪteɒɪŋ] ADJ debilitante

debit [débɪt] N débito m, adeudo m; (column in an account) debe m; (total sum owed) pasivo m; **— card** tarjeta de débito f; VT adeudar; **to — an account** adeudar una cuenta

debriefing [dɪbrífɪŋ] N informe m

debris [dəbrí] N (ruins) escombros m pl; (detritus) detritus m [pl]

debt [dɛt] N deuda f; **— relief** alivio de la deuda m; **bad —** cuenta incobrable f; **to get into —** endeudarse; ADJ **—-ridden** sobreendeudado

debtor [déɒə·] N deudor -ora mf

debug [dibʌ́g] VT depurar

debugger [dibʌ́gə·] N depurador m

debugging [dibʌ́gɪŋ] N depuración f

debunk [dibʌ́ŋk] VT (ideas, beliefs) desacreditar; (myths) desmitificar

debut [debjú] N (of a play or film) estreno m; (in society) presentación en sociedad f; **to make a —** (an actor) debutar; (in society) presentarse en sociedad; VI/VT (a film) estrenar[se]; (a product) lanzar[se] al mercado

decade [déked] N década f, decenio m

decadence [dékəɒəns] N decadencia f

decadent [dékəɒənt] ADJ decadente

decaffeinated [dɪkǽfɪneɒɪd] ADJ descafeinado

decal [díkæl] N calcomanía f, autoadhesivo m

decalcification [dikælsɪfɪkéʃən] N descalcificación f

decanter [dɪkǽntə·] N garrafa f

decapitate [dɪkǽpɪtet] VT decapitar

decathlon [dɪkǽθlɑn] N decatlón m

decay [dɪké] VI/VT (biological matter) descomponer[se]; (teeth) cariar[se]; VI (health) deteriorarse; (radioactive matter) desintegrarse; N (moral) decadencia f; (biological) descomposición f; (nuclear) desintegración f; (tooth) caries f

decayed [dɪkéd] ADJ (flesh) putrefacto; (tooth) cariado

decease [dɪsís] N muerte f, fallecimiento m; VI morir, fallecer

deceased [dɪsíst] ADJ & N difunto -ta mf

deceit [dɪsít] N engaño m, trampa f

deceitful [dɪsítfəl] ADJ tramposo, engañoso

deceive [dɪsív] VI/VT engañar

decelerate [diséləret] VI desacelerar

December [dɪsémbə·] N diciembre m

decency [dísənsi] N decencia f

decent [dísənt] ADJ decente

decentralization [disɛntrəlɪzéʃən] N descentralización f

deception [dɪsépʃən] N engaño m

deceptive [dɪséptɪv] ADJ engañoso; **— practice** práctica comercial desleal f

decibel [désəbəl] N decibelio m

decide [dɪsáɪd] VT (make a decision) decidir; (award victory) fallar; **what —d you to come?** ¿qué te motivó a venir?

decided [dɪsáɪDɪd] ADJ (resolute) decidido; (clear) claro

deciduous [dɪsídʒuəs] ADJ deciduo, caduco; **— tooth** diente de la primera dentición m

decimal [désəməl] ADJ decimal

decimate [désəmet] VT diezmar

decipher [dɪsáɪfə·] VT descifrar

decision [dɪsíʒən] N decisión f; (in court) fallo m

decisive [dɪsáɪsɪv] ADJ decisivo

deck [dɛk] N (of a boat) cubierta f; (of a house) terraza f; (of playing cards) baraja f; **hit the —!** ¡cuerpo a tierra! VT (knock down) tumbar; (decorate) decorar; **to — oneself out** emperifollarse

declaration [dɛkləréʃən] N declaración f, pronunciamiento m

declare [dɪklér] VI/VT declarar, afirmar

decline [dɪkláɪn] N (deterioration) decadencia f; (slope) declive m; (reduction in prices) baja f; VI/VT declinar; (an offer) rechazar; **to — to do something** negarse a hacer algo

decode [dikód] VT descodificar

decompose [dikəmpóz] VI/VT descomponer[se]

decompress [dikəmprés] VT descomprimir

decongest [dikəndʒést] VT descongestionar

decongestant [dikəndʒéstənt] N descongestionante m

decontaminate [dikəntǽmɪnet] VT descontaminar

decontamination [dikəntæmɪnéʃən] N descontaminación f

decorate [dékəret] VT decorar; (award medals)

condecorar

decoration [dɛkəréʃən] N (embellishment) adorno *m*; (interior decorating) decoración *f*; (medal of honor) condecoración *f*

decorative [dékə-əDIv] ADJ decorativo

decorous [dékə-əs] ADJ decoroso

decorum [dɪkɔ́rəm] N decoro *m*

decoy [díkɔɪ] N (artifact) señuelo *m*, reclamo *m*; (live animal or person) cimbel *m*; VT atraer con señuelo/cimbel

decrease[1] [díkris] N disminución *f*, merma *f*

decrease[2] [dɪkrís] VI/VT disminuir, mermar

decree [dɪkrí] N decreto *m*; VI/VT decretar

decrepit [dɪkrépɪt] ADJ decrépito

decrepitude [dɪkrépɪtud] N decrepitud *f*

decry [dɪkráɪ] VT condenar

decrypt [dikrípt] VT descifrar

decryption [dikrípʃən] N descifrado *m*, descodificación *f*

dedicate [déDɪket] VI/VT dedicar[se]; VT (a highway) inaugurar

dedication [dɛDɪkéʃən] N (act of dedicating) dedicación *f*; (in a book) dedicatoria *f*; (of a highway, etc.) inauguración *f*

deduce [dɪdús] VT deducir

deduct [dɪdʌ́kt] VT deducir

deductible [dɪdʌ́ktəbəl] ADJ deducible, desgravable; N deducible *m*

deduction [dɪdʌ́kʃən] N deducción *f*

deed [did] N (action) acción *f*; (exploit) hazaña *f*; (certificate of ownership) escritura *f*

deem [dim] VT considerar

deep [dip] ADJ (extending down) hondo, profundo; (dark) oscuro; (of a voice) grave; — **in debt** cargado de deudas; — **in thought** absorto; —**-sea** de altura; **he's got — pockets** es un ricachón; **he went off the — end with his hobby** se le fue la mano con el pasatiempo; **she went — into the woods** se adentró en el bosque; **ten meters —** de diez metros de profundidad; N — **freeze** congelador *m*; **the —** el piélago, el abismo; ADV **to dive —** bucear en las profundidades; VT **to —-six** hacer desaparecer

deepen [dípən] VI/VT ahondar, profundizar

deer [dir] N ciervo *m*, venado *m*; —**skin** gamuza *f*

deface [dɪfés] VT (disfigure) desfigurar; (smear with paint) pintarrajear; (mutilate) mutilar

defame [dɪfém] VT difamar

default [dɪfɔ́lt] N (negligence) negligencia *f*; (failure to pay) incumplimiento *m*; (failure to appear in court) rebeldía *f*; (computer setting) opción por defecto *f*; **in —** en mora; **by —** por defecto, por omisión; (in sports) por abandono de los contrincantes; VI (on a loan) incumplir, no pagar; (in a sports match) no comparecer

defeat [dɪfít] VT vencer, derrotar; N derrota *f*

defecate [défɪket] VI defecar, evacuar

defect[1] [dífɛkt] N defecto *m*

defect[2] [dɪfɛ́kt] VI desertar

defection [dɪfékʃən] N defección *f*

defective [dɪféktɪv] ADJ defectuoso

defend [dɪfénd] VI/VT defender

defendant [dɪféndənt] N (criminal) acusado -da *mf*, reo -a *mf*; (civil) demandado -da *mf*

defender [dɪféndə-] N defensor -ora *mf*; (sports) defensa *mf*

defense [dɪféns] N defensa *f*

defenseless [dɪfénslɪs] ADJ indefenso

defensible [dɪfénsəbəl] ADJ defendible

defensive [dɪfénsɪv] ADJ defensivo; — **medicine** medicina defensiva *f*; N **on the —** a la defensiva

defer [dɪfɚ́] VT (a meeting) diferir, posponer; (a payment) prorrogar; (an appointment) dilatar; (from military service) eximir; **to — to another's opinion** remitirse a la opinión de otro

deference [défə-əns] N deferencia *f*

deferral [dɪfɚ́əl] N aplazamiento *m*

defiance [dɪfáɪəns] N (challenge) desafío *m*; (resistance to authority) rebeldía *f*; **in — of** en abierta oposición a

defiant [dɪfáɪənt] ADJ desafiante

defibrillate [diffbrəlet] VT desfibrilar

defibrillation [difɪbrɪléʃən] N desfibrilación *f*

defibrillator [difíbrɪleDə-] N desfibrilador *m*

deficiency [dɪfíʃənsi] N deficiencia *f*

deficient [dɪfíʃənt] ADJ deficiente

deficit [défɪsɪt] N déficit *m*; — **spending** gastos deficitarios *m pl*

defile [dɪfáɪl] VT (violate) mancillar; (desecrate) profanar; (to make dirty) ensuciar

define [dɪfáɪn] VI/VT definir

defining [dɪfáɪnɪŋ] ADJ decisivo

definite [défənɪt] ADJ (clearly defined) definido, determinado; (certain) seguro; **she was — in her demands** ella fue terminante es sus exigencias; — **article** artículo definido *m*

definitely [défənɪtli] ADV sin duda, definitivamente

definition [dɛfəníʃən] N definición *f*

definitive [dɪfínɪDɪv] ADJ (final) definitivo; (authoritative) de mayor autoridad

deflate [dɪflét] VI/VT desinflar[se]

deflation [dɪfléʃən] N deflación *f*

deflect [dɪflékt] VI/VT desviar[se]

deforestation [difɔrɪstéʃən] N deforestación *f*

deform [dɪfɔ́rm] VI/VT deformar[se]

deformed [dɪfɔ́rmd] ADJ deforme

deformity [dɪfɔ́rmɪDi] N (body part) deformidad *f*; (act or result of deforming) deformación *f*

defraud [dɪfrɔ́d] VT defraudar

defray [dɪfré] VT sufragar, costear

defrost [dɪfrɔ́st] VI/VT descongelar[se]

deft [dɛft] ADJ diestro, habilidoso

defunct [dɪfʌ́ŋkt] ADJ caduco; **the Whig party**

is now — el partido de los whigs se disolvió
defuse [difjúz] VT (bomb) desactivar; (situation) distender
defy [dɪfáɪ] VT (challenge) desafiar; (resist) resistir
degenerate[1] [dɪdʒénəɪt] ADJ & N degenerado -da *mf*
degenerate[2] [dɪdʒénəret] VI degenerar[se]
degenerative [dɪdʒénəətɪv] ADJ degenerativo; — **joint disease** artrosis *f*, enfermedad degenerativa articular *f*
degradation [dɛgrədéʃən] N degradación *f*
degrade [dɪgréd] VI/VT degradar[se]
degree [dɪgrí] N (stage) grado *m*; (academic) título *m*; **by —s** gradualmente; **to a —** hasta cierto punto; **to get a —** graduarse
dehumanize [dihjúmənaɪz] VI/VT deshumanizar
dehumidifier [dihjumíDɪfaɪə] N deshumidificador *m*
dehydrate [dihaɪdret] VI/VT deshidratar[se]
deign [den] VI dignarse
deity [díɪDi] N deidad *f*
déjà vu [deʒavú] N deja vu *m*
dejected [dɪdʒéktɪd] ADJ abatido, desconsolado
dejection [dɪdʒékʃən] N abatimiento *m*, desconsuelo *m*
delay [dɪlé] N demora *f*, retraso *m*; VT demorar, retrasar; VI demorar, retrasarse
delectable [dɪléktəbəł] ADJ delicioso; N delicia *f*
delegate[1] [délɪgɪt] N delegado -da *mf*
delegate[2] [délɪget] VT delegar
delegation [dɛlɪgéʃən] N delegación *f*, representación *f*
delete [dɪlít] VT (omit) suprimir; (cross out) tachar; — **key** tecla de borrado *f*
deleterious [dɛlɪtíriəs] ADJ nocivo
deletion [dɪlíʃən] N supresión *f*
deliberate[1] [dɪlíbəɪt] ADJ (intentional) deliberado; (careful) cuidadoso
deliberate[2] [dɪlíbəret] VI/VT deliberar
deliberately [dɪlíbəɪtli] ADV a propósito, deliberadamente
deliberation [dɪlɪbəréʃən] N deliberación *f*
delicacy [délɪkəsi] N (fineness, precision, sensitivity) delicadeza *f*; (food) manjar *m*, delicatessen *f pl*, golleria *f*; (breakability) fragilidad *f*
delicate [délɪkɪt] ADJ delicado, tenue; (breakable) frágil; (acute) fino
delicatessen [dɛlɪkətésən] N (store) tienda de fiambres *f*, charcuteria *f*; RP rotisería *f*; (foods) delicatessen *f pl*
delicious [dɪlíʃəs] ADJ delicioso, rico
delight [dɪláɪt] N (pleasure) deleite *m*, regalo *m*; (source of pleasure) delicia *f*; VI/VT deleitar[se]
delighted [dɪláɪDɪd] ADJ encantado; **to be — to** alegrarse de; **I'm — to meet you** me alegro de conocerla; **I'd be — to dance with you**

me encantaría bailar contigo
delightful [dɪláɪtfəł] ADJ encantador
delimit [dɪlímɪt] VT delimitar
delineate [dɪlíniet] VT delinear
delinquent [dɪlíŋkwənt] ADJ & N (debtor) moroso -sa *mf*; (wrongdoer) delincuente *mf*; (juvenile) delincuente juvenil *mf*
delirious [dɪlíriəs] ADJ (hysterical) delirante; (happy) contentísimo; **to be** — delirar
delirium [dɪlíriəm] N delirio *m*
deliver [dɪlívə] VT (hand over) entregar; (hand out) repartir; (liberate) liberar; (pronounce a speech) pronunciar; (administer a blow) dar; (have a baby) dar a luz; (assist a birth) atender en un parto; **to — the goods** cumplir con lo prometido
deliverance [dɪlívəəns] N liberación *f*
delivery [dɪlívəri] N (handing out) entrega *f*, expedición *f*; (things to be delivered) pedido *m*; (birth) parto *m*; (speaking) ejecución *f*, expresión oral *f*; **on** — a la entrega; — **service** servicio de entrega *m*; — **truck** camión de reparto *m*; **to take** — aceptar entrega
dell [dɛł] N hondonada *f*
deltoids [dɛłtɔɪdz] N deltoides *m sg*
delude [dɪlúd] VT engañar
deluge [déljudʒ] N diluvio *m*; VT abrumar
delusion [dɪlúʒən] N (act of deluding, state of being deluded) engaño *m*; —**s of grandeur** delirios de grandeza *m pl*
deluxe [dɪláks] ADJ de lujo
demagogue, demagog [déməgag] N demagogo -ga *mf*
demand [dɪmǽnd] VT (ask for) exigir; (require) requerir, exigir; N exigencia *f*, reivindicación *f*; **on** — por demanda
demanding [dɪmǽndɪŋ] ADJ exigente
demarcate [dɪmárket] VT demarcar
demean [dɪmín] VT menospreciar
demeanor [dɪmínə] N conducta *f*, comportamiento *m*
demented [dɪméntɪd] ADJ demente
dementia [dɪménʃə] N demencia *f*
demijohn [démidʒan] N damajuana *f*
demise [dɪmáɪz] N fallecimiento *m*, desaparición *f*
demo [démo] N demostración *f*
demobilize [dimóbəlaɪz] VT desmovilizar
democracy [dɪmákrəsi] N democracia *f*
democrat [déməkræt] N demócrata *mf*
democratic [dɛməkrǽDɪk] ADJ democrático
democratization [dɪmakrəDɪzéʃən] N democratización *f*
demographics [dɛməgrǽfɪks] N demografía *f*
demolish [dɪmálɪʃ] VT demoler, derrumbar
demon [dímən] N demonio *m*
demonstrate [démənstret] VT (prove) demostrar; (show a product) hacer una

demostración; VI manifestar

demonstration [dɛmənstréʃən] N (proof, exhibition) demostración f; (protest) manifestación f, concentración f

demonstrative [dɪmánstrəDɪv] ADJ demostrativo

demonstrator [démənstreDə-] N manifestante mf

demoralize [dɪmɔ́rəlaɪz] VT desmoralizar

demote [dɪmót] VT degradar, bajar de categoría

den [dɛn] N (of an animal) guarida f; (room in a house) cuarto de estar m; (cave) cueva f; — **of iniquity** antro de perdición m

dengue fever [déŋgi fívə-] N dengue m

denial [dɪnáɪəl] N (assertion that an allegation is false) desmentido m; (refusal to approve) denegación f, negativa f; (refusal to recognize) negación f; **he is in** — no lo quiere aceptar

denigrate [dénɪgret] VT denigrar

denim [dénɪm] N tela de vaquero f

Denmark [dénmɑrk] N Dinamarca f

denomination [dɪnɑmənéʃən] N (name, monetary value) denominación f; (sect) secta religiosa f

denominator [dɪnámɪneDə-] N denominador m

denotation [dinotéʃən] N denotación f

denote [dɪnót] VT denotar

denounce [dɪnáUns] VT denunciar

dense [dɛns] ADJ (compacted) denso, tupido, cerrado; (stupid) fam burro, duro de entendederas

density [dénsɪDi] N densidad f

dent [dɛnt] N abolladura f; **to make a** — **in a task** hacer mella en una tarea; VI/VT abollar[se]

dental [déntl] ADJ dental; — **care** cuidado dental m; — **floss** hilo dental m; — **hygienist** higienista dental mf; — **implant** implante dental m; — **plaque** placa dental f; — **school** facultad de odontología f

dentifrice [déntəfrɪs] N dentífrico m, pasta dental f

dentist [déntɪst] N dentista mf

dentistry [déntɪstri] N odontología f

dentures [déntʃə-z] N dientes postizos m pl

denunciation [dɪnʌnsiéʃən] N denuncia f, acusación f

deny [dɪnáɪ] VT (state that something is false) negar, desmentir; (refuse to approve) rechazar; **to** — **oneself** abstenerse

deodorant [dióDə-ənt] N desodorante m

deodorize [dióDəraɪz] VT desodorizar

deoxidize [diáksɪdaɪz] VT desoxidar

depart [dɪpárt] VI (leave) salir, partir; (deviate) desviarse, apartarse; (die) fallecer, dejar de existir

departed [dɪpárDɪd] ADJ & N difunto -ta mf

department [dɪpártmənt] N (of company,

school, country) departamento m; (of government) ministerio m; (of a store) sección f; (of knowledge, expertise) especialidad f; — **head** jefe -fa de departamento mf; — **store** gran almacén m

departure [dɪpártʃə-] N (scheduled) salida f; (not scheduled) partida f; (deviation) desviación f

depend [dɪpénd] VI depender; **to** — **on** (rely on) contar con; (be conditioned by) depender de; —**ing on the number of guests** dependiendo de la cantidad de invitados

dependable [dɪpéndəbəl] ADJ confiable, fiable

dependence [dɪpéndəns] N dependencia f

dependency [dɪpéndənsi] N dependencia f

dependent [dɪpéndənt] ADJ dependiente; **success is** — **on perseverance** el éxito depende de la perseverancia; N familiar a cargo mf

depict [dɪpíkt] VT (verbally) describir; (visually) representar

depilate [dépəlet] VT depilar[se]

depilatory [dɪpílətɔri] ADJ & N depilatorio m

deplane [diplén] VI desembarcar

deplete [dɪplít] VT agotar

depletion [dɪplíʃən] N agotamiento m

deplorable [dɪplɔ́rəbəl] ADJ deplorable

deplore [dɪplɔ́r] VT deplorar

deploy [dɪplɔ́ɪ] VT desplegar

deport [dɪpɔ́rt] VT deportar; VI comportarse

deportment [dɪpɔ́rtmənt] N comportamiento m, conducta f

depose [dɪpóz] VT (overthrow) deponer, derrocar; (testify) declarar; (take testimony) tomar declaración

deposit [dɪpázɪt] VT (add to an account) depositar; Sp ingresar; (place) colocar; N (amount added to an account) depósito m; Sp ingreso m; (of a mineral) yacimiento m; (earnest money) señal f, anticipo m; — **slip** hoja de depósito f

deposition [depəzíʃən] N (removal from office) deposición f; (testimony) declaración f

depositor [dɪpázɪDə-] N depositante mf

depot [dípo] N (of trains) estación f; (of buses) terminal mf; (for storage) almacén m, depósito m; (for military training) cuartel m

depraved [dɪprévd] ADJ depravado

deprecate [déprɪket] VT despreciar

depreciate [dɪpríʃiet] VT (currency) depreciar[se]; (goods) desvalorizar[se], amortizar[se]

depreciation [dɪpriʃiéʃən] N (of currency) depreciación f; (of goods) amortización f

depress [dɪprés] VT deprimir

depressed [dɪprést] ADJ deprimido

depressing [dɪprésɪŋ] ADJ deprimente

depression [dɪpréʃən] N depresión f

deprive [dɪpráɪv] VT privar

depth [dɛpθ] N (of hole, feeling) profundidad f,

hondura f; (of the voice) gravedad f; **in the
—s** en las profundidades; **in —** a fondo;
what is the — of that bookshelf? ¿cuánto
miden estos estantes de fondo? **he has sunk
to such —s** ha caído muy bajo; **in the — of
the night** bien entrada la noche; **in the —
of winter** en lo más crudo del invierno
deputation [dɛpjətéʃən] N delegación f
deputy [dépjəDi] N (elected official) diputado -da
mf; (substitute) suplente mf
derail [diréɫ] VI/VT descarrilar[se]
deranged [dɪréndʒd] ADJ trastornado, demente
derby [dɝbi] N (hat) sombrero hongo m; (race)
derby m
deregulate [dirégjəlet] VT desregular
derelict [dérəlıkt] ADJ (deserted) abandonado;
(negligent) negligente; N (ship) buque
abandonado m; (person) vagabundo -da mf
dereliction [dɛrəlíkʃən] N — **of duties**
abandono de funciones m
deride [dɪráId] VT escarnecer, ridiculizar
derision [dɪríʒən] N escarnio m
derivation [dɛrəvéʃən] N derivación f
derivative [dɪrívəDIv] ADJ & N derivado m
derive [dɪráIv] VI/VT derivar[se]; **to — pleasure
from** disfrutar de
dermabrasion [dɝməbreʒən] N abrasión
cutánea f, dermabrasión f
dermatologist [dɝmətáləʤIst] N dermatólogo
-ga mf
dermatology [dɝmətáləʤi] N dermatología f
derogatory [dɪrágətɔri] ADJ despectivo
derrick [dérık] N torre de perforación f
descend [dɪsénd] VI/VT descender; **—ing sort**
clasificación descendiente f; **to — upon** caer
sobre
descendant [dɪséndənt] ADJ & N descendiente
mf
descent [dɪsént] N (act of descending, decline)
descenso m; (slope) bajada f; (lineage)
descendencia f
describe [dɪskráIb] VT describir
description [dɪskrípʃən] N descripción f,
caracterización f; **of all —s** de todas clases
descriptive [dɪskríptIv] ADJ descriptivo
desecrate [désıkret] VT profanar
desecration [dɛsıkréʃən] N profanación f
desegregate [diségrıget] VI/VT eliminar la
segregación racial
deselect [disılékt] VT anular [una selección
previa]
desensitize [disénsıtaIz] VT insensibilizar
desert[1] [dézɝt] ADJ (barren, empty) desierto; (of
the desert) desértico; N desierto m
desert[2] [dɪzɝt] VI/VT (a person, place)
abandonar; (military service) desertar
deserter [dɪzɝDɝ] N desertor -ora mf
desertion [dɪzɝʃən] N (of a person or place)
abandono m; (from the military) deserción f

deserve [dɪzɝv] VT merecer
deserving [dɪzɝvIŋ] ADJ merecedor
desiccate [désıket] VI/VT desecar[se]
design [dɪzáIn] VI/VT (prepare a sketch of)
diseñar, trazar; (plan) planear, idear; N
(model, pattern) diseño m; (sketch) esbozo m;
he has —s on her le ha echado el ojo
designate [dézɪgnet] VT designar, denominar;
—d hitter bateador -ora designado -da mf
designation [dɛzɪgnéʃən] N denominación f,
designación f
designer [dɪzáInɝ] N diseñador -ora mf; **—
drugs** drogas de diseño f pl
desirability [dɪzaIrəbílıDi] N deseabilidad f,
conveniencia f
desirable [dɪzáIrəbəɫ] ADJ deseable
desire [dɪzáIr] VT desear; **I — your
cooperation** requiero tu cooperación; N
deseo m
desirous [dɪzáIrəs] ADJ deseoso
desist [dɪsíst] VI desistir
desk [dɛsk] N escritorio m; (school) pupitre m;
—top computer Am computadora de
escritorio f, Sp ordenador de sobremesa m;
—top publishing edición de sobremesa f,
autoedición f
desolate[1] [désəlıt] ADJ (barren) desolado
desolate[2] [désəlet] VT desolar, asolar
desolation [dɛsəléʃən] N desolación f,
asolamiento m
despair [dɪspér] N desesperanza f; VI
desesperarse, perder la esperanza
despairing [dɪspérIŋ] ADJ de desesperación
desperate [déspɝIt] ADJ desesperado
desperately [déspɝItli] ADV desesperadamente;
— ill gravemente enfermo; **he's — looking
for funds** está desesperado buscando
financiación
desperation [dɛspɝéʃən] N desesperación f
despicable [dɪspíkəbəɫ] ADJ despreciable,
deleznable
despise [dɪspáIz] VT despreciar, menospreciar
despite [dɪspáIt] N despecho m; PREP a pesar de
despoil [dɪspóIɫ] VT despojar
despondency [dɪspándənsi] N abatimiento m,
desaliento m
despondent [dɪspándənt] ADJ abatido,
desalentado
despot [déspət] N déspota mf
despotic [dɪspáDık] ADJ despótico
despotism [déspətIzəm] N despotismo m
dessert [dɪzɝt] N postre m
destabilize [distébəlaIz] VT desestabilizar
destination [dɛstənéʃən] N destino m
destine [déstIn] VT destinar; **she's —d for
greatness** promete grandes cosas
destiny [déstəni] N destino m
destitute [déstItut] ADJ menesteroso, indigente;
— of falto de, desprovisto de

destroy [dɪstrɔ́ɪ] VT (demolish) destruir,
deshacer; (kill an animal) sacrificar; (ruin a
reputation) arruinar
destroyer [dɪstrɔ́ɪə˞] N (person who destroys)
destructor -ora *mf*; (ship) destructor *m*
destructible [dɪstrʌ́ktəbəł] ADJ destructible
destruction [dɪstrʌ́kʃən] N (act of demolishing)
destrucción *f*; (act of killing) matanza *f*; (act of
ruining a reputation) ruina *f*
destructive [dɪstrʌ́ktɪv] ADJ destructivo,
destructor
detach [dɪtǽtʃ] VT separar, desprender; (troops)
destacar
detachment [dɪtǽtʃmənt] N (physical)
separación *f*; (emotional) desapego *m*; (of
troops) destacamento *m*; (of the retina)
desprendimiento *m*
detail[1] [díteł] N detalle *m*, pormenor *m*;
(military) destacamento *m*; **to go into** —
detallar, pormenorizar
detail[2] [dɪtéł] VT detallar, pormenorizar; (assign
duties) destacar
detain [dɪtén] VT detener
detect [dɪtékt] VT detectar
detection [dɪtékʃən] N detección *f*
detective [dɪtéktɪv] N detective *mf*; — **novel**
novela policial *f*
detector [dɪtéktə˞] N detector *m*
detention [dɪténʃən] N (in jail) detención *f*; (in
school) castigo *m*
deter [dɪtɝ́] VT (dissuade) disuadir; (prevent)
prevenir
detergent [dɪtɝ́dʒənt] N detergente *m*
deteriorate [dɪtíriəret] VI deteriorar[se]
deterioration [dɪtiriəréʃən] N deterioro *m*
determination [dɪtɝmənéʃən] N (act of
determining) determinación *f*; (resolution)
resolución *f*; (persistence) tesón *m*,
perseverancia *f*
determine [dɪtɝ́mɪn] VT determinar; **to** — **to
do something** decidirse a hacer algo
determined [dɪtɝ́mɪnd] ADJ (resolute) decidido,
resuelto; (persistent) tesonero
determiner [dɪtɝ́mɪnə˞] N (grammatical)
determinante *m*
determining [dɪtɝ́mɪnɪŋ] ADJ determinante
detest [dɪtést] VT detestar, abominar de
detestable [dɪtéstəbəł] ADJ detestable
dethrone [diθrón] VT destronar
detonate [détṇet] VI/VT detonar
detonation [détṇéʃən] N detonación *f*
detour [dítur] N desvío *m*; VI/VT desviar[se]
detoxification [ditaksəfɪkéʃən] N
destoxificación *f*
detract [dɪtrǽkt] VT distraer; VI **to** — **from**
disminuir
detrimental [dɛtrəméntḷ] ADJ perjudicial
deuce [dus] N (in tennis) deuce *m*, cuarenta
iguales

devaluation [divæljuéʃən] N devaluación *f*
devastate [dévəstet] VT devastar, asolar
devastating [dévəsteDɪŋ] ADJ devastador
develop [dɪvéləp] VI/VT (mature, elaborate)
desarrollar[se]; (build houses on) construir,
edificar; (treat film) revelar; **she** —**ed an
allergy** le vino una alergia; —**ing country**
país en desarrollo *m*
developer [dɪvéləpə˞] N (of computer programs)
desarrollador -ora *mf*; (of real estate)
promotor -ora *mf*; **a late** — persona de
maduración tardía *f*
development [dɪvéləpmənt] N (evolution)
desarrollo *m*; (buildings) urbanización *f*,
colonia *f*; (of a photograph) revelado *m*
developmental [dɪvɛləpméntḷ] ADJ relativo al
desarrollo
deviate [díviet] VI/VT desviar[se]
deviation [diviéʃən] N desviación *f*
device [dɪváɪs] N (gadget) dispositivo *m*; (literary
convention) recurso *m*; (emblem) divisa *f*;
they left me to my own —**s** me dejaron
que me las arreglara sola
devil [dévəł] N diablo *m*; **lucky** —! ¡suertudo!
what the — **are you saying?** ¿qué diablos
dices? —**'s advocate** abogado del diablo *m*
devilish [dévəlɪʃ] ADJ (evil) diabólico; (extreme)
endiablado, endemoniado
deviltry [dévəłtri] N (mischief) diablura *f*;
(witchcraft) brujería *f*
devious [díviəs] ADJ (roundabout) sinuoso,
tortuoso; (crafty) taimado, retorcido
devise [dɪváɪz] VT idear, urdir
devoid [dɪvɔ́ɪd] ADJ — **of** falto de, desprovisto de
devolution [dɛvəlúʃən] N devolución *f*
devote [dɪvót] VT dedicar; (consecrate) consagrar
devoted [dɪvóDɪd] ADJ (friend) leal; (parent)
dedicado; (worshiper) devoto
devotion [dɪvóʃən] N devoción *f*
devour [dɪváur] VT devorar
devout [dɪváut] ADJ devoto
dew [du] N rocío *m*; —**drop** gota de rocío *f*;
—**point** punto de condensación *m*
dexterity [dɛkstériDi] N destreza *f*
dextrose [dékstros] N dextrosa *f*
diabetes [daɪəbíDiz] N diabetes *f*
diabolic [daɪəbúlɪk] ADJ diabólico
diacritic [daɪəkríDɪk] ADJ & N diacrítico *m*
diagnose [daɪəgnós] VT diagnosticar
diagnosis [daɪəgnósɪs] N diagnóstico *m*,
diagnosis *f*
diagnostic [daɪəgnástɪk] ADJ diagnóstico
diagonal [daɪǽgənḷ] ADJ & N diagonal *f*
diagram [dáɪəgræm] N diagrama *m*
dial [dáɪəł] N (of a watch, clock) esfera *f*; (of
radio) dial *m*; — **tone** *Sp* señal de marcar *f*;
Am tono de discar *m*; VI/VT (a telephone
number) *Sp* marcar; *Am* discar
dialect [dáɪəlɛkt] N dialecto *m*

dialectic [daɪəléktɪk] ADJ dialéctico; N dialéctica *f*
dialectology [daɪəlɛktálədʒi] N dialectología *f*
dialogue, dialog [dáɪəlɑg] N diálogo *m*; VI
  dialogar
dialysis [daɪǽlɪsɪs] N diálisis *f*
diameter [daɪǽmɪDə-] N diámetro *m*
diamond [dáɪəmənd] N (stone) diamante *m*;
  (shape) rombo *m*
diaper [dáɪpə-] N pañal *m*; VT poner pañales
diaphragm [dáɪəfræm] N diafragma *m*
diarrhea [daɪəríə] N diarrea *f*
diary [dáɪəri] N diario *m*
diastolic [daɪəstálɪk] ADJ diastólico
diatribe [dáɪətraɪb] N diatriba *f*
dice [daɪs] N PL dados *m pl*; VT cortar en cubos;
  no —! (impossibility) no hay forma, *Am* ¡ni
  modo! (refusal) de ninguna manera
dichotomy [daɪkáDəmi] N dicotomía *f*
dick [dɪk] N (penis) *vulg* polla *f*, pija *f*, verga *f*,
  rabo *m*; (detective) sabueso -sa *mf*; **—head**
  offensive capullo *m*; VI **to — somebody**
  around fastidiar a alguien
dicker [díkə-] VI regatear
dictate [díktet] VI/VT dictar; N dictado *m*,
  precepto *m*
dictation [dɪktéʃən] N dictado *m*; **to take —**
  escribir al dictado
dictator [díkteDə-] N dictador -ora *mf*
dictatorship [dɪktéDə-ʃɪp] N dictadura *f*
diction [díkʃən] N dicción *f*
dictionary [díkʃənɛri] N diccionario *m*
did [dɪd] *see* do
didactic [daɪdǽktɪk] ADJ didáctico
die [daɪ] VI morir[se]; **to — down/away**
  disminuir; **to — off** irse muriendo; **to — out**
  morirse, extinguirse; **my car —d** se me
  murió el coche; N (game piece) dado *m*;
  (press) molde *m*; (stamp) cuño *m*, troquel *m*;
  —hard intransigente *mf*
diesel [dízəł] N diesel *m*; **— engine** motor
  diesel *m*
diet [dáɪɪt] N (food) dieta *f*; (controlled intake of
  food) dieta *f*, régimen *m*; **to be/go on a —**
  estar a dieta/régimen; **to put on a —** poner a
  dieta; VI estar a dieta, hacer dieta
dietary [dáɪɪtɛri] ADJ dietético
dietitian [daɪɪtíʃən] N dietista *mf*
differ [dífə-] VI diferir; **to — with** disentir, no
  estar de acuerdo con; **to — from** ser
  diferente de
difference [dífə-əns] N diferencia *f*; **it makes**
  no — no importa, da igual
different [dífə-ənt] ADJ diferente, distinto
differential [dɪfərénʃəł] ADJ & N (difference, car
  part) diferencial *m*; **— equation** diferencial *f*
differentiate [dɪfərénʃiet] VI/VT diferenciar[se],
  distinguir[se]
differentiation [dɪfərɛnʃiéʃən] N diferenciación *f*
differently [dífə-əntli] ADV de manera

diferente; **they act —** no se comportan igual
difficult [dífɪkəłt] ADJ difícil
difficulty [dífɪkʌlti] N dificultad *f*; **with —** con
  dificultad, difícilmente
diffident [dífɪDənt] ADJ tímido
diffuse[1] [dɪfjúz] VI/VT difundir
diffuse[2] [dɪfjús] ADJ difuso
diffusion [dɪfjúʒən] N difusión *f*
dig [dɪg] VI/VT cavar; (by machine) excavar;
  (superficially) escarbar; **to — in the files**
  escarbar en los archivos; **to — under**
  socavar; **to — up** desenterrar; **he dug his**
  heels into the ground clavó los talones en
  el suelo; **I — your new shoes** están muy
  buenos tus zapatos nuevos; N (archaeological
  site) excavación *f*; (sarcastic remark) pulla *f*; **a**
  — in the ribs un codazo
digest[1] [dɪdʒést] VI/VT digerir
digest[2] [dáɪdʒest] N (summary) compendio *m*;
  (legal) digesto *m*
digestible [dɪdʒéstəbəł] ADJ digerible, digestible
digestion [dɪdʒéstʃən] N digestión *f*
digestive [dɪdʒéstɪv] ADJ digestivo
digit [dídʒɪt] N dígito *m*
digital [dídʒɪdl̩] ADJ digital; **— camera** cámara
  digital *f*; **— computer** *Am* computadora
  digital *f*, *Sp* ordenador digital *m*; **—**
  photography fotografía digital *f*
digitalize [dídʒɪdlaɪz] VT digitalizar
digitize [dídʒɪtaɪz] VT digitalizar
dignified [dígnəfaɪd] ADJ digno
dignitary [dígnɪteri] N dignatario -ria *mf*
dignity [dígnɪDi] N dignidad *f*
digress [dɪgrés] VI divagar
digression [dɪgréʃən] N digresión *f*
dike [daɪk] N dique *m*
dilapidated [dɪlǽpɪdeDɪd] ADJ (machine)
  destartalado; (furniture) desvencijado;
  (house) derruido, venido abajo
dilate [dáɪlet] VI/VT dilatar[se]
dilation [daɪléʃən] N dilatación *f*
dilemma [dɪlémə] N dilema *m*
dilettante [dílɪtant] N diletante *mf*
diligence [dílədʒəns] N diligencia *f*
diligent [dílədʒənt] ADJ diligente, hacendoso
dill [dɪł] N eneldo *m*; **— pickle** pepinillo en
  vinagre con eneldo *m*
dilute [dɪlút] VI/VT diluir[se]; ADJ diluido
dim [dɪm] ADJ (light) tenue; (outline) difuso;
  (room) oscuro, en penumbras; (person) *fam*
  de pocas luces; **—wit** *fam* tonto, bobo; VI/VT
  (make less bright) atenuar; VT (switch to low
  beam) bajar
dime [daɪm] N moneda de diez centavos *f*;
  unskilled workers are a — a dozen
  sobran los obreros no cualificados
dimension [dɪménʃən] N dimensión *f*
diminish [dɪmínɪʃ] VI/VT disminuir, menguar;
  the law of —ing returns la ley de los

rendimientos decrecientes
diminution [dɪmənúʃən] N disminución f, mengua f
diminutive [dɪmínjətɪv] ADJ diminuto; N diminutivo m
dimmer [dímə-] N regulador de voltaje m
dimness [dímnɪs] N oscuridad f, penumbra f
dimple [dímpəł] N hoyuelo m; VT formar hoyuelos
din [dɪn] N estruendo m, estrépito m
dine [daɪn] VI cenar; **to — out** cenar afuera
diner [dáɪnə-] N (restaurant) cafetería f; (on a train) coche comedor m; (person) comensal mf
ding-a-ling [díŋəlɪŋ] N (silly person) ganso -sa mf; (eccentric person) excéntrico -ca mf; (sound) tilín m
dingy [díndʒi] ADJ deslucido
dining [dáɪnɪŋ] ADJ **— car** coche comedor m; **— room** comedor m
dinner [dínə-] N (main meal) comida f; (at midday) almuerzo m; (in the evening) cena f; **— jacket** smoking m; **—time** hora de la comida f
dinosaur [dáɪnəsɔr] N dinosaurio m
dint [dɪnt] ADV LOC **by — of** a fuerza de
dip [dɪp] VT (make wet) mojar; (scoop) sacar; (immerse) sumergir; (immerse in insecticide) bañar; (immerse in sauce, coffee) pringar, mojar; VI (sun) hundirse; (stocks) bajar; (road) hacer una bajada; (airplane) descender súbitamente; N (act of wetting) mojada f; (portion of ice-cream) bola f, cucharada f; (sauce) mojo m; (reduction in sales) disminución f; (low place in a road) declive m; (low place in the land) hondonada f; (swim) baño m; (airplane maneuver) descenso rápido m; (irritating person) pej pesado -da mf
diphtheria [dɪpθíriə] N difteria f
diphthong [dífθɔŋ] N diptongo m
diploma [dɪplómə] N diploma m
diplomacy [dɪplóməsi] N diplomacia f
diplomat [dípləmæt] N diplomático -ca mf
diplomatic [dɪpləmǽDɪk] ADJ diplomático
dipper [dípə-] N cucharón m, cazo m
dire [daɪr] ADJ terrible, espantoso; **— need** necesidad acuciante f; **— predictions** predicciones funestas f pl; **— situation** situación extrema f
direct [dɪrékt] ADJ directo; **— current** corriente continua f; **— object** complemento directo m; **— quotation** cita textual f; ADV directo, directamente; VI/VT dirigir; **he —ed me to leave** me mandó irme
direction [dɪrékʃən] N dirección f; **—s** indicaciones f pl; **I'm thinking in that —** me inclino por eso
directive [dɪréktɪv] ADJ directivo; N directiva f
director [dɪréktə-] N (theater, movies) director

-ra mf; (film, TV) realizador -ora mf
directory [dɪréktəri] N directorio m
dirigible [dərídʒəbəł] ADJ & N dirigible m
dirt [dɝt] N (filth) suciedad f; (foul substance) mugre f; (vile person) offensive mierda f; (earth) tierra f; **—bag** offensive porquería f; **I've got some — on him** le conozco los trapos sucios; ADJ **— cheap** baratísimo; **— poor** pobrísimo
dirty [dɝDi] ADJ sucio, mugriento; **— joke** chiste verde m; **— look** mirada asesina f; **— money** dinero sucio m; **— shame** pena horrible f; **— trick** trampa f; **— word** palabrota f; Sp taco m; **— work** trabajo sucio m; VI/VT ensuciar; ADV **to talk —** decir cosas obscenas
disability [dɪsəbílɪDi] N incapacidad f, discapacidad f, minusvalía f; **— insurance** seguro de discapacidad m
disable [dɪsébəł] VT (person) incapacitar; (device) desactivar
disabled [dɪsébəłd] ADJ discapacitado, minusválido
disabuse [dɪsəbjúz] VT desengañar
disadvantage [dɪsɪdvǽntɪdʒ] N desventaja f; **to be at a —** estar en desventaja
disadvantaged [dɪsɪdvǽntɪdʒd] ADJ carenciado
disagree [dɪsəgrí] VI (differ in opinion) disentir, no estar de acuerdo; (differ) diferir; **pizza —s with me** no me cae bien la pizza
disagreeable [dɪsəgríəbəł] ADJ desagradable
disagreement [dɪsəgrímənt] N (lack of agreement, argument) desacuerdo m; (discrepancy) discrepancia f
disallow [dɪsəláu] VT desaprobar; (in sports) anular
disappear [dɪsəpír] VI desaparecer
disappearance [dɪsəpírəns] N desaparición f
disappoint [dɪsəpɔ́ɪnt] VI/VT decepcionar, desilusionar; **to be —ed** estar desilusionado
disappointing [dɪsəpɔ́ɪntɪŋ] ADJ decepcionante
disappointment [dɪsəpɔ́ɪntmənt] N decepción f, desilusión f
disapproval [dɪsəprúvəł] N desaprobación f
disapprove [dɪsəprúv] VI/VT desaprobar
disarm [dɪsárm] VI/VT desarmar[se]
disarmament [dɪsárməmənt] N desarme m
disarray [dɪsəré] VT desordenar; N confusión f, desorden m; **in —** en desorden
disaster [dɪzǽstə-] N desastre m
disastrous [dɪzǽstrəs] ADJ desastroso
disavow [dɪsəváu] VT negar
disband [dɪsbǽnd] VT disolver; VI desbandarse
disbelief [dɪsbɪlíf] N incredulidad f
disbelieve [dɪsbɪlív] VI/VT descreer de
disburse [dɪsbɝs] VT desembolsar
disbursement [dɪsbɝsmənt] N desembolso m
discard[1] [dɪskárd] VT (a card) descartar; (garbage) desechar
discard[2] [dískard] N (card) descarte m; (garbage)

desecho *m*

discern [dɪsɚn] VT (distinguish mentally) discernir; (perceive) percibir

discernment [dɪsɚnmənt] N discernimiento *m*

discharge[1] [dɪstʃárdʒ] VI/VT (battery, load, firearm) descargar[se]; (obligation) cumplir; (prisoner) poner en libertad, soltar; (odor) despedir; (soldier) dar de baja; (patient) dar de alta; (a debt) pagar; (pus) supurar

discharge[2] [dístʃardʒ] N (of a battery, load, firearm) descarga *f*; (of an obligation) cumplimiento *m*; (of a prisoner) puesta en libertad *f*; (of an odor) emisión *f*; (of a soldier) baja *f*; (of a patient) alta *f*; (of a debt) pago *m*; (of oil) pérdida *f*; (of pus) supuración *f*; (uterine, vaginal) flujo *m*; (from a job) despido *m*

disciple [dɪsáɪpəl] N discípulo -la *mf*

discipline [dísəplɪn] N disciplina *f*; VT disciplinar

disclaimer [dɪsklémɚ] N descargo de responsabilidad *m*

disclose [dɪsklóz] VT revelar

disco [dísko] N discoteca *f*

discolor [dɪskálɚ] VI/VT decolorar[se]

discomfort [dɪskámfɚt] N malestar *m*

disconcert [dɪskənsɚt] VT desconcertar

disconnect [dɪskənékt] VI/VT desconectar; N desconexión *f*

disconnected [dɪskənéktɪd] ADJ (broken) desconectado; (incoherent) inconexo

disconsolate [dɪskánsəlɪt] ADJ desconsolado

discontent [dɪskəntént] N descontento *m*

discontinue [dɪskəntínju] VT suspender, interrumpir

discontinuous [dɪskəntínjuəs] ADJ discontinuo

discord [dískɔrd] N (lack of concord) discordia *f*, desavenencia *f*; (dissonance) disonancia *f*, discordancia *f*

discotheque [dískotɛk] N discoteca *f*

discount [dískaʊnt] VT (deduct from a charge, take into account in advance) descontar; (sell at a reduced price) rebajar; (disregard) ignorar; N descuento *m*; **at a** — con descuento, con rebaja

discourage [dɪskɚɪdʒ] VT desanimar, desalentar; **to — from** disuadir de

discouragement [dɪskɚɪdʒmənt] N desánimo *m*, desaliento *m*

discourse[1] [dískɔrs] N (conversation, talk) discurso *m*; (treatise) disertación *f*

discourse[2] [dɪskɔrs] VI (talk) discurrir; (treat a subject) disertar

discourteous [dɪskɚɾiəs] ADJ descortés

discourtesy [dɪskɚɾɪsi] N descortesía *f*

discover [dɪskávɚ] VT descubrir

discoverer [dɪskávərɚ] N descubridor -ora *mf*

discovery [dɪskávəri] N descubrimiento *m*

discredit [dɪskrédɪt] VT (injure the reputation

of) desacreditar; (give no credence to) no creer; N descrédito *m*

discreet [dɪskrít] ADJ discreto

discrepancy [dɪskrépənsi] N discrepancia *f*

discrete [dɪskrít] ADJ (separate) separado; (en matemáticas) discreto

discretion [dɪskréʃən] N discreción *f*; **at your own** — a discreción; **at the judge's** — al arbitrio del juez

discretionary [dɪskréʃnɛri] ADJ discrecional; — **income** ingresos discrecionales *m pl*

discriminate [dɪskrímənet] VI/VT distinguir; **to — against** discriminar a

discrimination [dɪskrɪmɪnéʃən] N discriminación *f*

discuss [dɪskás] VT discutir

discussion [dɪskáʃən] N discusión *f*

disdain [dɪsdén] N desdén *m*, desprecio *m*; VT (treat with contempt) desdeñar; (think unworthy of a response) no dignarse a

disdainful [dɪsdénfəl] ADJ desdeñoso

disease [dɪzíz] N enfermedad *f*

diseased [dɪzízd] ADJ enfermo

disembark [dɪsɪmbárk] VI/VT desembarcar

disenfranchise [dɪsɪnfrǽntʃaɪz] VT (politician) proscribir; (minorities) privar de derechos, desheredar

disengage [dɪsɪngédʒ] VI/VT (a clutch) soltar[se]; (from a situation) distanciar[se]

disentangle [dɪsɪntǽŋgəl] VI/VT desenredar[se], desenmarañar[se]

disfavor [dɪsfévɚ] VT mirar con malos ojos; N **to fall into** — (a person) caer en desgracia; (a fashion) caer en desuso

disfigure [dɪsfígjɚ] VT desfigurar

disgrace [dɪsgrés] N (dishonor) deshonra *f*; (shame) vergüenza *f*; **to fall into** — caer en desgracia; VT deshonrar

disgraceful [dɪsgrésfəl] ADJ vergonzoso

disgruntled [dɪsgrántld] ADJ descontento, resentido

disguise [dɪsgáɪz] VT disfrazar[se]; N disfraz *m*

disgust [dɪsgást] VT (repel) asquear, repugnar; (displease) disgustar; N asco *m*, repugnancia *f*

disgusted [dɪsgástɪd] ADJ asqueado, repugnado

disgusting [dɪsgástɪŋ] ADJ asqueroso, repugnante

dish [dɪʃ] N (plate, food, quantity) plato *m*; (serving container) fuente *f*; (attractive person) *fam* bombón *m*; —**es** vajilla *f*; —**cloth/towel** paño de cocina *m*, repasador *m*; —**washer** lavaplatos *m sg*, lavavajillas *m sg*; —**water** agua de fregar *f*; VI/VT (serve food) servir; **to — out** repartir

dishearten [dɪshártn̩] VT desanimar, descorazonar, desalentar

disheartening [dɪshártnɪŋ] ADJ descorazonador, desalentador

dishevel [dɪʃévəl] VT desgreñar

disheveled [dɪʃévəɫd] ADJ (hair) desgreñado, revuelto; (clothes) desaliñado
dishonest [dɪsánɪst] ADJ deshonesto
dishonesty [dɪsánɪsti] N deshonestidad *f*
dishonor [dɪsánɚ] N deshonra *f*; VT deshonrar; (a check) no pagar
dishonorable [dɪsánɚəbəɫ] ADJ deshonroso
disillusion [dɪsɪlúʒən] N desilusión *f*, desencanto *m*; VT desilusionar, desencantar
disinfect [dɪsɪnfékt] VT desinfectar
disinfectant [dɪsɪnféktənt] N desinfectante *m*
disinfection [dɪsɪnfékʃən] N desinfección *f*
disinfestation [dɪsɪnfɛstéʃən] N desinfestación *f*
disinformation [dɪsɪnfɚméʃən] N desinformación *f*
disinherit [dɪsɪnhérɪt] VT desheredar
disintegrate [dɪsíntɪgret] VI/VT desintegrar[se]
disintegration [dɪsɪntɪgréʃən] N desintegración *f*
disinterested [dɪsíntrɪstɪd] ADJ desinteresado
disjointed [dɪsʤɔ́ɪntɪd] ADJ desarticulado
disk, disc [dɪsk] N disco *m*; (game piece) tejo *m*; (in a computer) disco *m*, disquete *m*; — **brake** freno de disco *m*; — **capacity** capacidad de almacenamiento de disco *f*; — **drive** disquetera *f*; — **jockey** pinchadiscos *mf sg*
diskette [dɪskét] N disquete *m*; — **drive** unidad de disquete *f*
dislike [dɪsláɪk] N aversión *f*, tirria *f*; VT **I — parties** no me gustan las fiestas
dislocate [dɪslóket] VT dislocar, descoyuntar
dislocation [dɪslokéʃən] N dislocación *f*, luxación *f*
dislodge [dɪsláʤ] VT (force out) desatascar; (displace) desprender
disloyal [dɪslɔ́ɪəɫ] ADJ desleal
dismal [dízməɫ] ADJ pésimo; **a — failure** un fracaso rotundo
dismantle [dɪsmǽntl] VT (a factory) desmantelar; (a car, watch) desmontar
dismay [dɪsmé] VT (disappoint) consternar; (daunt) desalentar; (alarm) alarmar; N (disappointment) consternación *f*; (loss of courage) desaliento *m*; (alarm) alarma *f*
dismember [dɪsmémbɚ] VT desmembrar
dismiss [dɪsmís] VT (fire a private employee) despedir; (fire a public employee) destituir, cesar; (reject a possibility) desechar, descartar; (discharge from military service) dar de baja; (reject a claim) desestimar; (ignore a person) ningunear; **class —ed!** ¡pueden retirarse!
dismissal [dɪsmísəɫ] N (firing) destitución *f*, despido *m*; (of a possibility) rechazo *m*; (from military service) baja *f*; (of a claim) desestimación *f*; (of a person) ninguneo *m*
dismount [dɪsmáʊnt] VI (get off a horse) desmontarse, apearse; (take apart) desarmar; N bajada *f*

disobedience [dɪsəbíDiəns] N desobediencia *f*
disobedient [dɪsəbíDiənt] ADJ desobediente
disobey [dɪsəbé] VI/VT desobedecer
disorder [dɪsɔ́rDɚ] N (confusion) desorden *m*; (public disturbance) desorden público *m*; (illness) trastorno *m*, desarreglo *m*
disorderly [dɪsɔ́rDɚli] ADJ (untidy) desordenado; (unruly) revoltoso; — **conduct** alteración del orden público *f*
disorganization [dɪsɔrgənɪzéʃən] N desorganización *f*
disorganized [dɪsɔ́rgənaɪzd] ADJ desorganizado
disown [dɪsón] VT repudiar
disparage [dɪspǽrɪʤ] VT denigrar
disparate [díspɚɪt] ADJ dispar
dispassionate [dɪspǽʃənɪt] ADJ desapasionado
dispatch [dɪspǽtʃ] VT despachar; N (sending off) envío *m*; (putting to death) ejecución *f*; (news story, official communication) despacho *m*; (promptness) prontitud *f*
dispel [dɪspéɫ] VT disipar
dispensable [dɪspénsəbəɫ] ADJ prescindible
dispensary [dɪspénsəri] N dispensario *m*
dispensation [dɪspɛnséʃən] N (relaxation of law) dispensa *f*; (act of handing out) dispensación *f*
dispense [dɪspɛ́ns] VT (goods) dispensar; (justice) administrar; **to — from an obligation** eximir de una obligación; **to — with** prescindir de
dispersal [dɪspɚ́səɫ] N dispersión *f*
disperse [dɪspɚ́s] VI/VT dispersar[se]; ADJ disperso
dispersed [dɪspɚ́st] ADJ disperso
displace [dɪsplés] VT (evict) desalojar; (take up space, remove from office) desplazar; **—d person** (domestic) desplazado -da *mf*; (foreign) expatriado -da *mf*
displacement [dɪsplésmənt] N (of refugees, of a ship) desplazamiento *m*; (of an engine) cilindrada *f*
display [dɪsplé] VT (exhibit) exhibir, exponer; (unfold) desplegar; (flaunt) ostentar; (show on a computer screen) visualizar; N (of wares, etc.) exhibición *f*, despliegue *m*; (advertisement) cartel *m*; (flaunting) ostentación *f*; (computer screen) pantalla *f*, visualizador *m*, display *m*
displease [dɪsplíz] VT contrariar, desagradar, descontentar; VI molestar
displeasure [dɪspléʒɚ] N disgusto *m*, desagrado *m*
disposable [dɪspózəbəɫ] ADJ — **income** ingresos disponibles *m pl*
disposal [dɪspózəɫ] N (arrangement) disposición *f*; (elimination) eliminación *f*
dispose [dɪspóz] VT (give inclination) predisponer; (set in order, make ready) disponer; **to — of** descartar, eliminar

disposition [dɪspəzíʃən] N (attitude) temperamento *m*; (inclination) inclinación *f*; tendencia *f*; (arrangement, disposal) disposición *f*

dispossess [dɪspəzés] VT desposeer

disproportionate [dɪsprəpórʃənɪt] ADJ desproporcionado

disprove [dɪsprúv] VT refutar

dispute [dɪspjút] N disputa *f*; VT discutir, impugnar

disqualify [dɪskwáləfaɪ] VT (deprive of rights) inhabilitar; (exclude from a sport event) descalificar

disregard [dɪsrɪgárd] VT hacer caso omiso de, ignorar; N (neglect) descuido *m*; (disrespect) falta de respeto *f*

disrepair [dɪsrɪpér] N mal estado *m*; **in —** deteriorado

disreputable [dɪsrépjəDəbəł] ADJ (of bad reputation) de mala reputación; (shabby) de mala muerte

disrespect [dɪsrɪspékt] N desacato *m*, falta de respeto *f*; VT faltar el respeto

disrespectful [dɪsrɪspéktfəł] ADJ irrespetuoso

disrobe [dɪsrób] VI/VT desvestir[se]

disrupt [dɪsrʌ́pt] VT (cause disorder) trastornar, trastocar; (interrupt) interrumpir

dissatisfied [dɪssǽDɪsfaɪd] ADJ insatisfecho, disconforme

dissatisfy [dɪssǽDɪsfaɪ] VT no satisfacer

dissect [daɪsékt] VT (cut apart) disecar; (analyze argument) analizar minuciosamente

dissemble [dɪsémbəł] VI/VT (hide) disimular; (feign) fingir

disseminate [dɪsémənet] VT (spread out) diseminar, propagar; (publicize) divulgar

dissemination [dɪsɛmənéʃən] N (spreading out) diseminación *f*; (publicizing) divulgación *f*

dissension [dɪsénʃən] N disensión *f*, disenso *m*

dissent [dɪsént] VI disentir; N disenso *m*

dissertation [dɪsɚtéʃən] N (formal discourse) disertación *f*; (doctoral treatise) tesis de doctorado *f*

dissident [dísɪDənt] N disidente *mf*

dissimilar [dɪssímələ˞] ADJ diferente

dissimulation [dɪsɪmjəléʃən] N disimulo *m*

dissipate [dísəpet] VI/VT disipar[se]

dissipation [dɪsəpéʃən] N disipación *f*

dissolute [dísəlut] ADJ disoluto, vicioso

dissolution [dɪsəlúʃən] N disolución *f*

dissolve [dɪzáłv] VI/VT disolver[se]

dissuade [dɪswéd] VT disuadir

distance [dístəns] N distancia *f*, recorrido *m*; **— learning** educación a distancia *f*; **in the —** a lo lejos, en la lejanía; VT distanciarse de, distanciar

distant [dístənt] ADJ (far away, aloof) distante; (remote) lejano, remoto; **to be — from** distar de

distaste [dɪstést] N aversión *f*

distasteful [dɪstéstfəł] ADJ desagradable

distemper [dɪstémpə˞] N moquillo *m*

distend [dɪsténd] VI/VT distender[se]

distill [dɪstíł] VI/VT destilar[se]

distillation [dɪstəléʃən] N destilación *f*

distillery [dɪstíləri] N destilería *f*

distinct [dɪstíŋkt] ADJ (different) distinto; (clear) bien delineado, neto

distinction [dɪstíŋkʃən] N (honor) distinción *f*; (differentiation) distinción *f*, diferenciación *f*; **he passed with —** aprobó con sobresaliente

distinctive [dɪstíŋktɪv] ADJ distintivo

distinguish [dɪstíŋgwɪʃ] VI/VT distinguir

distinguished [dɪstíŋgwɪʃt] ADJ distinguido

distinguishing [dɪstíŋgwɪʃɪŋ] ADJ distintivo

distort [dɪstórt] VT (an object) deformar; (reports, sound) distorsionar

distortion [dɪstórʃən] N (object) deformación *f*; (image, sound) distorsión *f*; (of a statement) tergiversación *f*

distract [dɪstrǽkt] VT distraer, entretener

distracted [dɪstrǽktɪd] ADJ distraído, disperso

distraction [dɪstrǽkʃən] N distracción *f*; **to drive to —** volver loco

distraught [dɪstrót] ADJ angustiado

distress [dɪstrés] N (anxiety) angustia *f*; (pain) dolor *m*, congoja *f*; **to be in —** (a person) estar en apuros; (a ship, plane) estar en peligro; VT (cause anxiety) angustiar, atribular; (cause pain) acongojar, afligir

distressing [dɪstrésɪŋ] ADJ inquietante

distribute [dɪstríbjut] VT distribuir, repartir

distribution [dɪstrəbjúʃən] N distribución *f*, reparto *m*

distributor [dɪstríbjəDə˞] N distribuidor *m*

district [dístrɪkt] N distrito *m*, comarca *f*; **— attorney** fiscal de distrito *mf*

District of Columbia [dístrɪktəvkəlʌ́mbiə] N Distrito de Columbia *m*

distrust [dɪstrʌ́st] N desconfianza *f*; VT desconfiar de

distrustful [dɪstrʌ́stfəł] ADJ desconfiado

disturb [dɪstɝ́b] VI/VT (interrupt, interfere, perplex) perturbar; (trouble) turbar, perturbar, trastornar; (mess up) desarreglar; **do not —** se ruega no molestar

disturbance [dɪstɝ́bəns] N disturbio *m*; (weather) perturbación *f*

disuse [dɪsjús] N desuso *m*; **to fall into —** caer en desuso

ditch [dɪtʃ] N (trench) zanja *f*; (roadside) cuneta *f*; (for irrigation) acequia *f*; VT (make ditches) abrir zanjas; (get rid of) deshacerse de; (crash-land an airplane on water) hacer un amarizaje

dither [díðə˞] VI (hesitate) titubear; N **it threw her into a —** se puso muy nerviosa

ditsy [dítsi] ADJ atolondrado, cabeza de chorlito

ditto [dído] PRON & ADV ídem

diuretic [daɪərɛ́DIk] ADJ & N diurético *m*

diurnal [daɪɜ́·nl] ADJ diurno

divan [dɪvǽn] N diván *m*, canapé *m*

dive [daɪv] VI (into water) zambullirse, chapuzar, *Am* tirarse un clavado; (into an activity) zambullirse; (with scuba equipment) bucear; (airplane) bajar en picado -da; (submarine) sumergirse; N (of a person) zambullida *f*, chapuz *m*; (of an airplane) picado -da *mf*; (cheap bar) antro *m*

diver [dáɪvɚ] N saltador -ora *mf*; (high-dive) clavadista *mf*; (scuba) buzo *mf*

diverge [dɪvɜ́·dʒ] VI (branch off, differ in opinion) divergir; VI/VT (deviate) desviar

divergence [dɪvɜ́·dʒəns] N (separation, difference in opinion) divergencia *f*; (deviation) desviación *f*

diverse [dɪvɜ́·s] ADJ (of various kinds) diverso; (different) diferente

diversify [dɪvɜ́·səfaɪ] VI/VT diversificar[se]

diversion [dɪvɜ́·ʒən] N (entertainment) entretenimiento *m*; (distraction) distracción *f*; (military) diversión *f*; (turning aside) desvío *m*, desviación *f*

diversity [dɪvɜ́·sIDi] N diversidad *f*

divert [dɪvɜ́·t] VI/VT (turn aside) desviar, distraer; (distract) entretener

diverticulitis [dɪvɚtɪkjəláɪDɪs] N diverticulitis *f*

divest [dɪvɛ́st] VT (strip) despojar; (get rid of) deshacerse de

divide [dɪváɪd] VI/VT dividir[se]; (classify) clasificar[se]; N línea divisoria *f*

dividend [dívɪdɛnd] N dividendo *m*

divine [dɪváɪn] ADJ divino; VI/VT adivinar

divinity [dɪvínɪDi] N (godhead, state or quality of being divine) divinidad *f*; (theology) teología *f*

division [dɪvíʒən] N división *f*

divorce [dɪvɔ́rs] N divorcio *m*; VI/VT divorciar[se]

divot [dívət] N (golf) chuleta *f*

divulge [dɪvʌ́ldʒ] VT divulgar, publicar

dizziness [dízInɪs] N mareo *m*

dizzy [dízi] ADJ (person) mareado; (height) vertigoso; (speed) vertiginoso; — **spell** vahido *m*

DJ [**disc jockey**] [dídʒe] N pinchadiscos *mf sg*

Djibouti [dʒɪbúti] N Yibuti *m*

Djiboutian [jɪbúDiən] ADJ & N yibutiano -na *mf*

DNA [**deoxyribonucleic acid**] [díéné] N ADN *m*

do [du] VI/VT hacer; **to — away with** eliminar; **to — one's hair** arreglarse el pelo; **to — the dishes** lavar los platos; **to — drugs** tomar drogas; **to — in** matar; **to — time** cumplir una condena; **to — well** prosperar; **to — without** prescindir de; **we were —ing 100 kph** íbamos a cien kph; **to have nothing to — with** no tener nada que ver con; **that will — basta; that won't —** eso no sirve; **I'm**

—ing well estoy bien; **I did him last night** *fam* me lo tiré anoche; **this will have to —** habrá que conformarse con esto; **—- it-yourself** hágalo usted mismo; V AUX **I feel as you —** pienso igual que tú; **how — you —?** ¿cómo estás? **— you hear me?** ¿me oyes? **yes, I —** sí; **— come again** vuelve por favor; N (hairstyle) peinado *m*; (party) fiesta *f*

DOA [**dead on arrival**] [díóé] ADJ muerto -ta antes de ingresar al hospital

docile [dásəl] ADJ dócil

dock [dɑk] N (pier) muelle *m*; (for landing) desembarcadero *m*, atracadero *m*; (water between piers) dique *m*, dársena *f*; **— worker** trabajador -ora portuario -ria *mf*; **dry —** dique seco *m*; VI/VT (a boat) atracar; (a space ship) acoplar[se]; (wages) descontar

doctor [dáktɚ] N (physician) médico -ca *mf*; (PhD, scholar) doctor -ora *mf*; (expert) especialista *mf*; VT (treat) atender; (cure) curar; (restore) restaurar; (counterfeit) alterar; **I —ed up this recipe** le hice unos retoques a esta receta

doctorate [dáktɚɪt] N doctorado *m*

doctrine [dáktrɪn] N doctrina *f*

document[1] [dákjəmənt] N documento *m*

document[2] [dákjəmɛnt] VT documentar

documentary [dakjəmɛ́ntəri] N documental *m*

documentation [dakjəmɪntéʃən] N documentación *f*

dodder [dádɚ] VI (stumble along) tambalearse, titubear; (shake) temblequear

dodge [dadʒ] VT esquivar, sortear; VI (be evasive) dar rodeos; (move sideways) apartarse, echarse a un lado; N evasiva *f*

doe [do] N cierva *f*; (female of various animals) hembra *f*

dog [dɔg] N perro *m*, perra *f*; **—catcher** perrero -ra *mf*; **— collar** collar de perro *m*; **—fight** (dogs) pelea de perros *f*; (aircraft) combate aéreo *m*; (people) reyerta *f*; **—house** casilla de perro *f*; *Sp* caseta *f*; **to be in the —house** haber caído en desgracia, estar en capilla; **— paddle** natación estilo perrito *m*; **—sled** trineo para perros *m*; **— tag** placa de identificación *f*; **—wood** cornejo *m*; **to go to the —s** venirse abajo; ADJ **—-eared** sobado, muy gastado; **—gone** maldito; VT (follow) seguir la pista de; (harass) hostigar; **to —- paddle** nadar estilo perrito

doggy [dɔ́gi] N perrito -ta *mf*; **— bag** bolsa para las sobras *f*

dogma [dɔ́gmə] N dogma *m*

dogmatic [dɔgmǽDɪk] ADJ dogmático

doily [dɔ́ɪli] N mantelito *m*

doings [dúɪŋz] N actividades *f pl*

dole [doɬ] N (alms) limosna *f*; **to be on the —** estar cobrando el seguro de desempleo/paro; **to — out** repartir

doleful [dólfəł] ADJ apesadumbrado, triste
doll [dał] N (toy) muñeco -ca *mf*; (attractive female) muñeca *f*; —**house** casa de muñecas *f*; VI **to get** —**ed up** emperifollarse, empaquetarse
dollar [dálə⸱] N dólar *m*; — **diplomacy** diplomacia del dólar *f*; — **sign** signo del dólar *m*
dolly [dáli] N (doll) muñeca *f*; (cart) carretilla *f*
dolphin [dółfɪn] N (mammal) delfín *m*; (fish) dorado *m*
dolt [dołt] N zopenco -ca *mf*
domain [domén] N dominio *m*
dome [dom] N (roof) cúpula *f*, domo *m*; (head) coco *m*, pelada *f*
domestic [dəméstɪk] ADJ (appliance, pet, chore) doméstico; (devoted to homemaking) hogareño; (home-loving) casero; (of a country) interno, nacional; — **violence** violencia doméstica *f*; N doméstico -ca *mf*
domesticate [dəméstɪket] VI/VT (animals) domesticar; (plants) aclimatar
domicile [dáməsaɪł] N domicilio *m*
dominant [dámənənt] ADJ dominante
dominate [dámənet] VI/VT dominar; VI señorear
domination [damənéʃən] N (act of dominating) dominación *f*; (rule) dominio *m*
domineer [damənír] VI/VT dominar, mandonear
domineering [damənírɪŋ] ADJ tiránico, mandón
Dominica [dəmínɪkə] N Dominica *f*
Dominican [dəmínɪkən] ADJ & N (of Dominica) dominiqués -esa *mf*; (of the Dominican Republic) dominicano -na *mf*
Dominican Republic [dəmínɪkənrɪpábłɪk] N República Dominicana *f*
dominion [dəmínjən] N dominio *m*, señorío *m*
domino [dáməno] N (game, costume) dominó *m*; (piece) ficha *f*
don [dɑn] N (title, form of address, mafia boss) don *m*; (lecturer) profesor -ora universitario -ria *mf*; VT ponerse, vestirse
donate [dónet] VI/VT donar
donation [donéʃən] N donación *f*
done [dʌn] *see* do
done [dʌn] ADJ terminado, acabado; **when you are** — cuando termines; **to be all** — **in** estar muerto de cansancio; **the meat is well** — está bien asada la carne; **that sort of thing just isn't** — eso no se hace
donkey [dáŋki] N burro *m*, asno *m*, borrico *m*
donor [dónə⸱] N donante *mf*, donador -ora *mf*
doodad [dúdæd] N (trinket) chuchería *f*; (device) chisme *m*, coso *m*
doohickey [dúhɪki] N chisme *m*, coso *m*
doom [dum] N perdición *f*; —**sday** día del juicio final *m*; VT condenar; **to be** —**ed to failure**

estar condenado al fracaso
door [dɔr] N puerta *f*; —**bell** timbre *m*; —**keeper** portero -ra *mf*; —**knob** pomo *m*; —**man** portero *m*; —**mat** felpudo *m*; —**step** umbral *m*; —**way** puerta *f*, portal *m*; **I showed him the** — lo eché; ADJ —**-to**-— de puerta a puerta
dopamine [dópəmin] N dopamina *f*
dope [dop] N (narcotic) droga *f*; (stimulant) estimulante *m*; (information) chismes *m pl*; (moron) *fam* zopenco; VT dopar; **to** — **oneself up** medicarse en exceso
dork [dɔrk] N *fam* idiota *mf*, tarambana *mf*
dorky [dɔ́rki] ADJ **that's a** — **dress** *fam* pareces una tonta con ese vestido
dormant [dɔ́rmənt] ADJ latente
dormitory [dɔ́rmɪtɔri] N residencia estudiantil *f*
DOS [**Disk Operating System**] [dɑs] N DOS *m*
dose [dos] N dosis *f*; VT dosificar
dossier [dɔ́sie] N expediente *m*
dot [dɑt] N punto *m*; (on a tie) pinta *f*; —**-com** punto com; —**-matrix printer** impresora de matriz de puntos *f*; —**ted eighth note** corchea con puntillo *f*; **on the** — en punto; VT marcar con puntos
dotage [dótɪdʒ] N chochez *f*, chochera *f*; **to be in one's** — chochear, estar chocho
dote [dot] VI **to** — **on** estar chocho con
double [dʌ́bəł] ADJ doble; — **agent** doble agente *mf*; —**-barreled** de doble caño; — **bass** contrabajo *m*; — **bed** cama doble *f*; —**-blind test** prueba de doble incógnita *f*; — **bind** dilema *m*; — **boiler** baño de María *m*; —**-breasted** cruzado; — **chin** papada *f*; — **cross** traición *f*; — **click** doble pulsación *f*; — **dealing** duplicidad *f*; — **entry** entrada por partida doble *f*; — **fault** doble falta *f*; — **indemnity** doble indemnización *f*; — **play** doble matanza *f*; — **sided** de dos caras; — **shift** turno doble *m*; — **standard** trato discriminatorio *m*; — **vision** doble visión *f*; **to do a** — **take** quedar atónito; ADV **to sleep** — dormir de a dos; N (in baseball) doble *m*, doblete *m*; (in tennis) —**s** dobles *m pl*, juego de dobles *m*; VI/VT duplicar[se]; (an effort) redoblar[se]; (fold, be twice as old, challenge a bid) doblar[se]; **to** — **up** (bend over) doblarse; (crowd) amontonarse; **to** —**-check** verificar; **to** —**-click** pulsar dos veces; **to** —**-cross** traicionar; **to** —**-date** salir dos parejas juntas; **to** —**-talk** salirse con evasivas; **this sofa** —**s as a bed** este sofá sirve también de cama
doubt [daʊt] VI/VT dudar; (not trust) desconfiar; N duda *f*; **beyond a** — indudablemente; **in** — en duda; **no** —! ¡sin duda!
doubtful [dáʊtfəł] ADJ dudoso
doubtless [dáʊtlɪs] ADV (certainly) sin duda; (probably) probablemente

douche [duʃ] N ducha vaginal *f*; **—bag** *offensive* porquería *f*

dough [do] N pasta *f*, masa *f*; (money) pasta *f*, mosca *f*; **—nut** rosquilla *f*; *Mex* dona *f*; *Sp* donut *m*

douse [daʊs] VI/VT empapar; (a flame) apagar [con agua]

dove [dʌv] N paloma *f*

dove [dov] *see* dive

dowdy [dáʊDi] ADJ (article of clothing) pasado de moda; (person) sin gracia

dowel [dáʊəl] N clavija *f*

down [daʊn] ADV abajo; **— and dirty** sucio; **— and out** tirado; **to be — with** estar de acuerdo con; **to come — with a cold** caer con gripe, *Sp* cogerse un resfriado; **to fall —** caerse; **to get — to work** aplicarse al trabajo; **to go/come —** bajar; **to lie —** acostarse, echarse; **to put someone —** denigrar a alguien; **to turn — the volume** bajar el volumen; **to water — a drink** rebajar una bebida con agua; **to write —** anotar; **two blocks —** dos calles más abajo; **slow —**! ¡anda más despacio! **the wind died —** amainó el viento; **one — and two to go** hicimos uno y nos quedan dos por hacer; **prices are —** han bajado los precios; **the system is —** se cayó el sistema; **they're — on me** están mal conmigo; PREP **— the street** calle abajo; ADJ (depressed) abatido; N (turn for the worse) revés *m*; (feathers) plumón *m*; VT (knock, shoot) derribar; (drink quickly) despachar de un solo trago; (defeat) vencer; (football play) oportunidad *f*

downcast [dáʊnkæst] ADJ abatido, cabizbajo

downfall [dáʊnfɔl] N ruina *f*

downgrade [dáʊngred] N declive *m*, pendiente *f*; VT quitarle importancia a

downhill[1] [dáʊnhíl] ADV cuesta abajo; **his health is going —** su salud se deteriora

downhill[2] [dáʊnhíl] ADJ **a — slope** una pendiente; N bajada contra-reloj *f*

download [dáʊnlod] VT descargar; N descarga *f*

down payment [dáʊnpémənt] N entrega inicial *f*, entrada *f*

downplay [dáʊnple] VT quitar la importancia a

downpour [dáʊnpɔr] N aguacero *m*

downright [dáʊnraɪt] ADJ absoluto; **— foolishness** reverenda tontería *f*; **he was — angry** echaba chispas

downshift [dáʊnʃɪft] VI rebajar [el cambio]

downside [dáʊnsaɪd] N inconveniente *m*

downsize [dáʊnsaɪz] VI (personnel) hacer reducción; VT (an object or organization) reducir el tamaño de; (one's lifestyle) simplificar *f*; **he got —d** perdió el trabajo cuando hicieron reducción de personal

downstairs[1] [dáʊnstɛrz] ADV abajo; (in the apartment one floor lower) en el piso de abajo

downstairs[2] [dáʊnstɛrz] ADJ de abajo; N planta baja *f*

downstream [dáʊnstrím] ADV río abajo

downtime [dáʊntaɪm] N (of a machine) tiempo de inactividad *m*; (of a person) horas de ocio *f* pl

down-to-earth [dáʊntəśθ] ADJ sensato, práctico

downtown [dáʊntáʊn] ADV (toward) al centro; (in) en el centro; ADJ del centro, céntrico; N centro *m*

downturn [dáʊntɜn] N tendencia a la baja *f*

down under [dáʊnʌ́ndə] ADV en/a Australia

downward [dáʊnwəd] ADJ descendente; **— mobility** descenso social *m*; **—s** hacia abajo

downwind [dáʊnwínd] ADV en la dirección del viento

downy [dáʊni] ADJ sedoso, suave

dowry [dáʊri] N dote *f*

doze [doz] VI dormitar; N siesta *f*

dozen [dʌ́zən] N docena *f*

drab [dræb] ADJ triste; N pardo *m*

draft [dræft] N (of air) corriente *f*; (drink) trago *m*; (bank) giro *m*; (outline) esbozo *m*; (military) conscripción *f*, quinta *f*; (of a ship) calado *m*; **— beer** cerveza de barril *f*; **— horse** caballo de tiro *m*; **—sman** dibujante *m*; VT (to sketch) esbozar; (to compose) redactar; (to select for military service) conscribir

drag [dræg] VI/VT (haul slowly) arrastrar[se]; (search a body of water) dragar; **don't — me into this** no me metas en esto; **to —- and-drop/release** arrastrar y soltar; **to — on and on** eternizarse; **to — out** estirar; N (dredge) draga *f*; (boring person) pesado -da *mf*; (hassle) lata *f*; (counterforce) resistencia *f*; (on a cigarette) pitada *f*; **— race** carrera de dragsters *f*; **— strip** pista de dragsters *f*; **in — vestido de mujer**

dragon [drǽgən] N dragón *m*; **—fly** libélula *f*

drain [dren] N (channel) desagüe *m*, sumidero *m*; (depletion of resources) sangría *f*, fuga *f*; **—pipe** desaguadero *m*, desagüe *m*; **to go down the —** irse por la borda; VI/VT (empty a sink) desagotar[se], desaguar[se]; (exhaust) agotar[se]; VT (wetlands) drenar, sanear; VI (a battery) descargarse

drainage [drénɪdʒ] N (act of draining) desagüe *m*, drenaje *m*; (system for draining) drenaje *m*; **— pipe** tubo de desagüe *m*

drake [drek] N pato [macho] *m*

drama [drámə] N drama *m*

dramatic [drəmǽDɪk] ADJ dramático

dramatically [drəmǽDɪkli] ADV (changing) de forma fundamental, fundamentalmente; (presenting) de manera dramática/teatral

dramatist [drámətɪst] N dramaturgo -ga *mf*

dramatize [drámətaɪz] VI/VT dramatizar

drank [dræŋk] *see* drink
drape [drep] VI (hang in folds) colgar, drapear;
  VT (cover) cubrir; N cortina *f*
drapery [drépəri] N cortinado *m*, colgadura *f*
drastic [dræstɪk] ADJ drástico
draw [drɔ] VT (a picture) dibujar; (lines, shapes)
  trazar; (a cart) tirar de; (a curtain) correr;
  (cards, blood, water, conclusion, strength)
  sacar; (a crowd) atraer; (comparison,
  distinction) hacer; (a sword) desenvainar; VI
  (of a boat) tener calado; (of a fireplace) tirar;
  (in sports, have the same score) empatar;
  (receive money) cobrar; (withdraw money)
  retirar, sacar; **to — aside** apartar[se]; **to —
  away** separar[se]; **to — a breath** aspirar,
  tomar aliento; **to — a blank** quedarse en
  blanco; **to — in** involucrar; **to — lots/
  straws** echar a la suerte, sortear; **to — near**
  acercarse; **to — off** irse, retirarse; **to — on**
  (be based on) basarse en; (have recourse to)
  recurrir a; **to — out** (remove) sacar;
  (prolong) alargar, prolongar; **to — up**
  (approach) acercar[se]; (write) redactar;
  (shrink) encoger; N (in sports, tie game)
  empate *m*; (lot) número sorteado *m*;
  (attraction) atracción *f*; **—back**
  inconveniente *m*; **—bridge** puente
  levadizo *m*
drawer [drɔɚ] N cajón *m*; (small) gaveta *f*; **—s**
  calzones *m pl*
drawing [drɔ́ɪŋ] N (picture) dibujo *m*; (raffle)
  sorteo *m*; **— room** sala [de recibo] *f*
drawn [drɔn] ADJ demacrado; **—-out**
  interminable
drawn [drɔn] *see* draw
dread [drɛd] N pavor *m*, terror *m*, espanto *m*; VT
  I — going to the dentist me aterra ir al
  dentista
dreadful [drédfəl] ADJ horrendo, espantoso,
  temible
dream [drim] N sueño *m* (also aspiration);
  (reverie) ensueño *m*, ensoñación *f*; (fancy)
  ilusión *f*; **—land** tierra del ensueño *f*; **—
  team** equipo de estrellas *m*; **— world** mundo
  de ensueño *m*; VI/VT soñar; **to — of** soñar
  con; **I wouldn't — of stealing** no se me
  ocurriría robar; **to — that** soñar que; **to —
  up** imaginar; ADJ **a — holiday** unas
  vacaciones perfectas
dreamer [drímɚ] N (impractical person)
  soñador -ora *mf*; (visionary) visionario -ria *mf*
dreamt [drɛmt] *see* dream
dreary [dríri] ADJ sombrío, deprimente
dredge [drɛdʒ] N draga *f*; VT (a river) dragar;
  (facts) desenterrar, sacar a luz
dregs [drɛgz] N heces *f pl*, poso *m*; **— of society**
  escoria de la sociedad *f*
drench [drɛntʃ] VT empapar, calar; **—ed in
  blood** bañado en sangre

dress [drɛs] N (article of clothing for women)
  vestido *m*; (attire) ropa *f*; (formal) traje de
  etiqueta *m*, ropa de etiqueta *f*; (costume)
  vestimenta *f*; **—maker** modista *mf*; **—
  rehearsal** ensayo general *m*; **— shirt**
  camisa para traje *f*; **what's the — code?**
  ¿cómo hay que ir vestido? VI/VT vestir; VT
  (store window) arreglar; (slaughtered
  animals) limpiar; (salad) aderezar; (hides)
  adobar; (a wound) vendar; **to — down**
  (scold) regañar; (wear casual clothes) ponerse
  ropa informal; **to — up** (wear fine clothes)
  vestirse de gala; (make more appealing)
  embellecer
dresser [drésɚ] N cómoda *f*; **she is a good —** se
  viste con elegancia
dressing [drésɪŋ] N (act, result) vestir *m*; (for
  salad) aderezo *m*; (for fowl) relleno *m*; (for
  wounds) gasa *f*, vendaje *m*; **—-down** regaño
  m; **— gown** bata *f*; **— room** (in a theater)
  camerino *m*; (in a store) probador *m*; **— table**
  tocador *m*
drew [dru] *see* draw
dribble [drífbəl] VI (trickle) gotear; (drool)
  babear; VT (a ball) driblar, regatear; (liquid)
  rociar; N (trickle) goteo *m*; (small quantity)
  chorrito *m*; (of a ball) drible *m*, regate *m*
dried [draɪd] ADJ seco; **— fig** higo paso/seco *m*;
  —-up (without water) seco; (wizened)
  arrugado
drift [drɪft] N (direction) deriva *f*; (current)
  corriente *f*; (meaning) sentido *m*, tenor *m*;
  (pile) montón *m*, acumulación *f*; **—wood**
  madera flotante *f*; **do you get my —?** ¿me
  captas la onda? VI (float) flotar; (be adrift) ir a
  la deriva; (wander) errar; **he —ed off** se
  durmió; VI/VT (deviate) desviar[se];
  (accumulate) amontonar[se], acumular[se]
drifter [dríftɚ] N (wanderer) vagabundo -da *mf*;
  (of a worker) itinerante *mf*
drill [drɪɫ] N (tool) taladro *m*; (dental) fresa *f*;
  (training) ejercicios *m pl*; (procedure)
  procedimiento *m*; (rehearsal) simulacro *m*;
  (cloth) dril *m*; VI/VT (make a hole) taladrar,
  perforar, barrenar; (train) entrenar[se],
  adiestrar[se]; VI (train) hacer ejercicios;
  (practice) practicar; VT hacer practicar
drink [drɪŋk] VI/VT (person) beber; (animal)
  abrevar; (absorb, take in) absorber; **to — up**
  apurar el trago; **to — to someone's health**
  brindar por alguien; N bebida *f* (also
  alcoholic); (a measure of beverage) trago *m*
drinkable [dríŋkəbəl] ADJ potable
drinking [dríŋkɪŋ] ADJ **— water** agua potable *f*;
  he has a — problem tiene problemas con el
  alcohol
drip [drɪp] N goteo *m*; (a bore) plasta *mf*; VI
  gotear
drive [draɪv] VI/VT (a car) conducir, manejar; (an

animal) arrear; VI (go in a vehicle) ir en coche; VT (move forth) impulsar, impeler; (convey) llevar [en coche]; (force) forzar; (a nail) clavar; (a ball) tirar, golpear; **to — a hard bargain** regatear mucho; **to — away** ahuyentar; **to — someone mad** volver loco a alguien; **what are you driving at?** ¿qué quieres decir con eso? N (ride) paseo [en coche] *m*; (of an animal) arreo *m*; (urge) impulso *m*; (of a computer) unidad *f*; (military offensive) ofensiva *f*; (road) carretera *f*; (driveway) camino *m*; (campaign) campaña *f*; (energy) empuje *m*; (propulsion system) propulsión *f*; (of a ball) tiro *m*; (in tennis and golf) drive *m*; **—-by shooting** tiroteo desde un coche *m*; **—-in** drive-in *m*, establecimiento en que el cliente es atendido en el coche *m*; **—-in movie theater** autocine *m*; **—way** camino de entrada *m*, entrada de coches *f*; **front wheel—** tracción delantera *f*

drivel [drívəl] N (saliva) baba *f*; (idiocy) tontería *f*; VI babearse

driveling [drívəliŋ] ADJ baboso; **he's a — idiot** es un oligofrénico

driven [drívən] *see* drive

driver [dráivɚ] N (chauffeur) chofer *mf*, conductor -ra *mf*; (of animals) arriero -ra *mf*; (golf club) driver *m*; (in a computer) controlador *m*

driving [dráiviŋ] ADJ **— force** impulso *m*; **— rain** lluvia torrencial *f*; **— school** autoescuela *f*

drizzle [drízəl] VI lloviznar; N llovizna *f*

drone [dron] N (male bee, idler) zángano *m*; (remote-controlled vehicle) vehículo teledirigido *f*; (drudge) esclavo *m*; (sound) zumbido *m*; VI/VT (make a sound) zumbar; (talk) hablar monótonamente

drool [druł] N baba *f*; VI babearse

droop [drup] VI (sag) colgarse; (flag) languidecer; (wither) marchitarse; **his shoulders —** tiene los hombros caídos; **—ing ears** orejas gachas *f pl*

drop [drɑp] N (liquid quantity) gota *f*; (descent) caída *f*; (incline) declive *m*; (in value) baja *f*; (in prices) caída *f*; (lozenge) pastilla *f*; (of mail, etc.) buzón *m*, punto de recolección *m*; (of supplies) lanzamiento *m*; **—out** (student) desertor -ora escolar *mf*; (marginalized person) marginado -da *mf*; **— shot** dejada de volea *f*; VI caer; (let fall) dejar caer, descargar; (in golf) dropar; **to — a line** mandar unas líneas; **to — from sight** desaparecer; **to — in** caer de sorpresa; **to — out** (sports) retirarse; (school) abandonar; **why don't you — by?** ¿por qué no pasas por aquí? VI/VT (a course) abandonar; (a curtain) bajar; ADJ **—-dead beautiful** hermosísima

dropper [drɑpɚ] N gotero *m*

drought [draʊt] N sequía *f*

drove [drov] N tropel *m*

drove [drov] *see* drive

drown [draʊn] VI/VT ahogar[se]

drowning [dráʊniŋ] N ahogamiento *m*

drowse [draʊz] VI (be half-asleep) dormitar; (feel drowsy) estar amodorrado

drowsiness [dráʊzinis] N modorra *f*, somnolencia *f*

drowsy [dráʊzi] ADJ amodorrado, somnoliento; **to become —** amodorrarse

drudge [drʌʤ] N esclavo del trabajo *m*, fregona *f*; VI trabajar como un esclavo

drug [drʌg] N (chemical substance, narcotic) droga *f*; (medicine) medicamento *m*; **—ged** drogado, endrogado; **— abuse** abuso de drogas *m*; **— addict** drogadicto -ta *mf*; **—store** (drugs) farmacia *f*; (non-drug items) droguería *f*; perfumería *f*; **— trafficker** narcotraficante *mf*; VT (stupefy with drugs) drogar; (mix with a drug) adulterar con droga

druggist [drʌgist] N farmacéutico -ca *mf*, droguero -ra *mf*

drum [drʌm] N (musical instrument) tambor *m*; (of ear) tímpano *m*; (receptacle for storing liquids) barril *m*; **—head** parche *m*; **—stick** (music) palillo de tambor *m*; (fowl) pata *f*; VI (play a drum) tocar el tambor; (beat rhythmically) tamborilear; **to — out** expulsar; **to — up** fomentar; **I'm trying to — this idea into his head** le estoy repitiendo esta idea con insistencia

drummer [drʌmɚ] N (classical) tambor *m*; (folk) tamborilero -ra *mf*; (rock & roll) baterista *mf*

drunk [drʌŋk] ADJ & N borracho -cha *mf*; *fam* mamado -da *mf*; **to get —** emborracharse

drunk [drʌŋk] *see* drink

drunkard [drʌŋkɚd] N borracho -cha *mf*, borrachín -ina *mf*

drunken [drʌŋkən] ADJ borracho, embriagado

drunkenness [drʌŋkənnis] N borrachera *f*, embriaguez *f*

dry [drai] ADJ seco; (sober) sobrio; (topic, book) árido, aburrido; **— land** tierra firme *f*; **— cleaner** (business) tintorería *f*; (owner of business) tintorero -ra *mf*; **— cleaning** limpieza en seco *f*; **— county** condado seco *m*; **— wit** humor agudo *m*; **— goods** géneros *m pl*; **— measure** medida para áridos *f*; **— run** prueba *f*; **— ice** hielo seco *m*; **— dock** dique seco *m*, varadero *m*; VI/VT (wet clothes) secar[se]; (leather) resecar[se]; **to — up** secarse, resecarse; **to — out** desintoxicar[se]

dryer [dráiɚ] N (hair) secador *m*; (clothes) secadora *f*

dryness [dráinis] N (skin) sequedad *f*; (land, lecture) aridez *f*

dual [dúəl] ADJ (function) doble; (ownership) compartido

dub [dʌb] VT (translate a film) doblar; (give a nickname) apodar

dubious [dúbiəs] ADJ dudoso

duchess [dátʃis] N duquesa *f*

duck [dʌk] N (bird) pato *m*; (downward dodge) agachada *f*; VI/VT (plunge under water) hundir[se]; (bend down) agachar[se]; VT (avoid) esquivar

duckling [dáklɪŋ] N patito *m*

duct [dʌkt] N conducto *m*; — **tape** cinta aislante *f*

ductile [dáktl] ADJ dúctil

dud [dʌd] N (disappointing thing) chasco *m*; (useless person) inútil *m*; (unexploded bomb) bomba que no estalla *f*; —**s** (clothes) ropa *f*, *fam* trapos *m pl*; (belongings) pertenencias *f pl*

dude [dud] N (dandy) chulo *m*; (fellow) tipo *m*

due [du] ADJ (payable) pagadero; (immediately owed) vencido; (fitting, rightful) debido; (adequate) suficiente; — **date** fecha de vencimiento *f*; — **diligence** diligencia debida *f*; **in** — **time/course** a su debido tiempo; **the train is** — **at two o'clock** se supone que el tren llega a las dos; ADV — **east** hacia el este; N (punishment) merecido *m*; **give Mary her** —; **she's honest** tienes que reconocer que María es honrada; —**s** cuotas *f pl*

duel [dúəl] N duelo *m*; VI/VT batirse en/a duelo [con alguien]

duet [duét] N (played) dúo *m*; (sung) dueto *m*

dug [dʌg] *see* dig

dugout [dágaʊt] N (canoe) piragua *f*; (underground refuge) trinchera *f*

DUI [**driving under the influence**] [díjúáɪ] N delito de conducir en estado de ebriedad *m*

duke [duk] N duque *m*; **to put up one's** —**s** levantar los puños; VT **to** — **it out** arreglarlo con los puños

dukedom [dúkdəm] N ducado *m*

dull [dʌl] ADJ (lackluster) opaco; (listless, muted) apagado; (boring) aburrido, soso, desanimado; (blunt) romo, desafilado; (sluggish, stupid) lento; (pain) sordo; VI/VT (a knife) desafilar[se]; (color) opacar[se]; (sound, impact) amortiguar[se]; (pain) aliviar[se]; (senses) embotar[se], entorpecer[se]

duly [dúli] ADV debidamente

dumb [dʌm] ADJ (mute) mudo; (dull) tonto; —**bell** (handweight) mancuerna *f*; (stupid person) bobo -ba *mf*; —**founded** patitieso, atónito; VT **to** — **down** simplificar demasiado

dumbness [dámnɪs] N (muteness) mudez *f*; (foolishness) estupidez *f*

dummy [dámi] N (figure) muñeco *m*; (fool) tonto -ta *mf*; *offensive* pendejo -ja *mf*; (front) hombre de paja *m*; ADJ (fake) falso; **a** — **president** un títere

dump [dʌmp] VT (unload) descargar; (empty)

botar; (transfer computer data) vaciar; (dismiss) echar, despedir; (discard waste) tirar la basura, descargar desechos; (flood a market) hacer dumping; (abandon) plantar; **to** — **on** (criticize) criticar; (unload problems) descargarse; N (place for waste) vertedero *m*, basural *m*, basurero *m*; (of weapons) depósito *m*; (act of discarding) vertido *m*; (act or effect of defecating) *vulg* cagada *f*; —**truck** camión volteador *m*, volquete *m*, *Am* volqueta *f*; **to be in the** —**s** estar deprimido, estar depre; **to take a** — *vulg* cagar

dumping [dámpɪŋ] N vertido *m*

dunce [dʌns] N burro -rra *mf*, tonto -ta de capirote *mf*

dune [dun] N duna *f*, médano *m*

dung [dʌŋ] N boñiga *f*, bosta *f*; —**hill** estercolero *m*

dungeon [dándʒən] N mazmorra *f*

dunk [dʌŋk] VT (a donut) remojar; (a basketball) volcar, enterrar; (a person) sumergir

duodenum [duədínəm] N duodeno *m*

dupe [dup] N (gullible person) ingenuo -nua *mf*, inocente *mf*; *Sp* primo -ma *mf*; (manipulated person) títere *m*; VT embaucar

duplex [dúpleks] N & ADJ dúplex *m*

duplicate¹ [dúplɪkɪt] ADJ & N duplicado *m*; **in** — por duplicado

duplicate² [dúplɪket] VT duplicar[se]

duplicity [duplísɪDi] N duplicidad *f*

durability [dʊrəbílɪDi] N durabilidad *f*

durable [dúrəbəl] ADJ (long-lasting) duradero; (serviceable) sufrido

duration [dʊréʃən] N duración *f*

duress [dʊrés] N coacción *f*

during [dúrɪŋ] PREP durante

dusk [dʌsk] N atardecer *m*, anochecer *m*; **at** — al atardecer

dusky [dáski] ADJ (dark) oscuro; (gloomy) sombrío

dust [dʌst] N polvo *m*; —**pan** pala *f*; **to bite the** — (die) *fam* espichar; (lose) morder el polvo de la derrota; **cloud of** — polvareda *f*; VI/VT (remove dust) quitar/sacudir el polvo [a]; VT (sprinkle with powder) espolvorear; VI (become dusty) empolvarse; **to** — **off** desempolvar

duster [dástɚ] N plumero *m*

dusty [dásti] ADJ polvoriento

Dutch [dʌtʃ] ADJ & N holandés -esa *mf*; (language) holandés *m*; **to go** — pagar a escote

Dutchman [dátʃmən] N holandés *m*

duty [dúDi] N deber *m*, obligación *f*; (tax on imports) derechos aduaneros *m pl*; (any tax) impuesto *m*; **to be on** — estar de guardia; **to be off** — no estar de guardia; ADJ —**-free** libre de impuestos

DVD [**digital versatile disc**] [dívidí] N DVD *m*

dwarf [dwɔrf] ADJ & N enano -na *mf*; VT hacer parecer pequeño

dwarfism [dwɔ́rfɪzəm] N enanismo *m*

dwell [dwɛl] VI morar, habitar; **to — on a subject** dilatarse en un asunto

dweller [dwélə-] N habitante *mf*, morador -ora *mf*

dwelling [dwélɪŋ] N vivienda *f*, domicilio *m*

dwelt [dwɛlt] *see* dwell

DWI [driving while intoxicated] [dídʌ́bəljuáɪ] N delito de conducir en estado de ebriedad *m*

dwindle [dwíndl̩] VI/VT menguar, mermar

dye [daɪ] N tinte *m*, tintura *f*; VT teñir

dying [dáɪɪŋ] ADJ moribundo

dyke [daɪk] N *offensive* tortillera *f*

dynamic [daɪnǽmɪk] ADJ dinámico; N dinámica *f*

dynamite [dáɪnəmaɪt] N dinamita *f*; VT dinamitar; ADJ fabuloso

dynamo [dáɪnəmo] N dínamo *m*

dynasty [dáɪnəsti] N dinastía *f*

dysentery [dísənteri] N disentería *f*

dysfunction [dɪsfʌ́ŋkʃən] N disfunción *f*

dyslexia [dɪsléksiə] N dislexia *f*

Ee

each [itʃ] ADJ cada; **— person** cada persona; PRON cada uno; **— receives a prize** cada uno recibe un premio; **they looked at — other** se miraron el uno al otro

eager [ígə-] ADJ (enthusiastic) ansioso; (avid) ávido

eagerness [ígə-nɪs] N (enthusiasm) ansia *f*, afán *m*; (strong desire) avidez *f*

eagle [ígəl] N águila *f*; **— -eye** ojo de lince *m*

eaglet [íglɪt] N aguilucho *m*

ear [ir] N (outer organ) oreja *f*; (inner organ, sense of hearing, musical aptitude) oído *m*; (of corn) mazorca *f*; *Am* elote *m*; **—ache** dolor de oídos *m*; **—drops** gotas para los oídos *f pl*; **—drum** tímpano *m*; **—lobe** lóbulo de la oreja *m*; **— muff** orejera *f*; **—phone** audífono *m*, auricular *m*; **—plug** tapón del oído *m*; **—ring** pendiente *m*, zarcillo *m*, arete *m*; **by —** de oído; **within—shot** al alcance del oído; **he has the — of the governor** el gobernador le presta mucha atención; VT **to —mark** asignar

earful [írfʊl] N **I got an —** (scolding) me echó un rapapolvo; (gossip) me dio la lata

early [ɝ́li] ADJ temprano; **— detection** diagnóstico precoz *m*; **— man** hombre primitivo *m*; **— retirement** jubilación anticipada *f*; **— riser/bird** madrugador -ora

mf, mañanero -ra *mf*; **the — bird gets the worm** al que madruga, Dios lo ayuda

earn [ɝn] VI/VT (money, admiration, etc.) ganar; (salary) cobrar, ganar; (interest) devengar; **—ed run** carrera limpia *f*; **—ed run average** promedio de carreras limpias permitidas *m*; **to — a living** ganarse la vida

earnest [ɝ́nɪst] ADJ (sincere) serio, formal; (grave) grave; **in —** en serio; **— money** señal *f*; *Mex* enganche *m*

earnestness [ɝ́nɪstnɪs] N (sincerity) seriedad *f*, formalidad *f*; (gravity) gravedad *f*; **in all —** con toda sinceridad

earnings [ɝ́nɪŋz] N (of a person) ingresos *m pl*; (of a business) ganancias *f pl*

earth [ɝθ] N tierra *f*; **—mover** excavadora *f*; **—quake** terremoto *m*, temblor de tierra *m*; **—worm** lombriz *f*; **the —** la Tierra; ADJ **—shaking** revolucionario

earthen [ɝ́θən] ADJ (wall) de tierra; (pot) de barro; **—ware** vajilla de barro *f*, cerámica *f*

earthly [ɝ́θli] ADJ terrenal; **— possessions** bienes terrenales *m pl*; **to be of no — use** no servir para nada

earthy [ɝ́θi] ADJ natural; (person) campechano; (sense of humor, joke) basto; **— smell** olor a tierra *m*

ease [iz] N (facility) facilidad *f*; (unaffectedness) soltura *f*, desparpajo *m*; (comfort) comodidad *f*; (lack of worry) tranquilidad *f*; (fullness of a garment) holgura *f*; **at —** (military) en descanso; (comfortable) tranquilo, a gusto; **a life of —** una vida desahogada; **ill at —** incómodo; VT (make easier) facilitar; VI/VT (relieve pain) aliviar[se]; (release from tension) aflojar[se]; (relieve anxiety) tranquilizar[se]; **to — up** aflojar

easel [ízəl] N caballete *m*

east [ist] N este *m*, oriente *m*; ADJ del este, oriental; ADV **— of here** al este [de aquí]; **to go —** ir al / hacia el este; **back —** en el este

Easter [ístə-] N Pascua *f*; **— egg** huevo de Pascua *m*; **— Sunday** Domingo de Pascua *m*

eastern [ístə-n] ADJ oriental, del este

eastward [ístwə-d] ADV & ADJ hacia el este

easy [ízi] ADJ (simple) fácil, sencillo; (compliant) fácil; (comfortable) cómodo; (informal) desenvuelto; (unworried) tranquilo; **— chair** poltrona *f*; **— -going** calmoso; **— terms** facilidades de pago *f pl*; **— does it** despacio; **take it —** cálmate; **he's on — street** vive en la abundancia; **within — reach** al alcance de la mano; ADV **go — on me** sea bueno

eat [it] VI/VT comer[se]; VT (costs) absorber; **to — away** corroer, comer; **to — breakfast** desayunar[se]; **to — dinner** (midday) comer; (evening) cenar; **to — lunch** comer, almorzar; **to — one's heart out** morirse de envidia; **to — one's words** tragarse las

palabras; **to — supper** cenar; **to — up**
comerse todo; **what's —ing you?** ¿qué
bicho te picó?

eaten [ítn̩] *see* eat

eating [íDIŋ] N (act) comer *m*; (food) comida *f*; —
disorder trastorno de la alimentación *m*; —
utensils cubiertos *m pl*; — **apples**
manzanas para comer *f pl*

eaves [ivz] N PL alero *m*; **to —drop** escuchar
furtivamente

e-banking [íbæŋkIŋ] N banca electrónica *f*

ebb [ɛb] N (flowing back) reflujo *m*; (decay)
decadencia *f*; — **tide** reflujo *m*; **to be at a**
low — estar en un punto bajo; VI (tide) bajar;
(energy) decaer

ebony [ébəni] N ébano *m*

e-book [íbʊk] N libro electrónico *m*

e-business [íbIznIs] N comercio electrónico *m*

eccentric [ɛkséntrIk] ADJ & N excéntrico -ca *mf*

ecclesiastic [IkliziǽstIk] ADJ & N eclesiástico *m*

echelon [éʃəlɑn] N (military formation) escalón
m; (rank) nivel *m*, estrato *m*

echo [éko] N eco *m*; VI hacer eco; **the gym —ed**
with laughter el gimnasio resonó de risas;
VT repetir

echocardiogram [ɛkokárDiəgræm] N
ecocardiograma *m*

eclectic [IkléktIk] ADJ ecléctico

eclipse [Iklíps] N eclipse *m*; VT eclipsar

eco-friendly [ikofréndli] ADJ ecológico

ecological [ikəládʒIkəl] ADJ ecológico

ecology [Ikálədʒi] N ecología *f*

e-commerce [íkámə·s] N comercio electrónico *m*

economic [ɛkənámIk] ADJ económico; N **—s**
economía *f*

economical [ɛkənámIkəl] ADJ económico

economist [Ikánəmist] N economista *mf*

economize [IkánəmaIz] VI economizar

economy [Ikánəmi] N economía *f* (also thrift);
ADJ — **car** coche económico *m*; — **class** clase
turista *f*

ecosystem [íkosIstəm] N ecosistema *m*

ecstasy [ékstəsi] N éxtasis *m* (also drug)

Ecuador [ékwədɔr] N Ecuador *m*

Ecuadorian [ɛkwədɔ́riən] ADJ & N ecuatoriano
-na *mf*

ecumenical [ɛkjəménIkəl] ADJ ecuménico

eczema [égzəmə] N eccema *m*

eddy [éDi] N remolino *m*; VI arremolinarse

edge [ɛdʒ] N borde *m*, canto *m*; (of a knife) filo *m*;
(of a block) arista *f*; **to be on** — estar
nervioso; **her voice has an — to it** tiene la
voz penetrante; **a competitive** — una
ventaja sobre la competencia; VT (make an
edge) hacerle el borde; (sharpen) afilar;
(move sideways) meterse de costado; **to —**
out ganar por un pelito; **to — up**
aproximarse; ADV **—wise** de costado

edgy [édʒi] ADJ nervioso

edible [éDəbəl] ADJ & N comestible *m*

edict [íDIkt] N edicto *m*, bando *m*

edifice [éDəfIs] N edificio *m*

edify [éDəfaI] VT edificar

edit [éDIt] VT (revise, correct) corregir; (serve as
editor) editar; (revise a film) montar; **to —**
out eliminar; N corrección *f*

edition [Idíʃən] N edición *f*

editor [éDItə·] N (director of a publication)
redactor -ora *mf*; (compiler, radio or film
worker) editor -ora *mf*; (proofreader)
corrector -ora *mf*

editorial [ɛDItɔ́riəl] ADJ editorial; N editorial *f*

editorialize [ɛDItɔ́riəlaIz] VI editorializar

educate [édʒəkét] VT educar

education [ɛdʒəkéʃən] N educación *f*, enseñanza
f; (academic subject) pedagogía *f*; **school of**
— escuela normal *f*

educational [ɛdʒəkéʃənl̩] ADJ educativo

educator [édʒəkeDə·] N educador -ora *mf*

EEG [electroencephalogram] [íídʒí] N
electroencefalograma *m*

eel [il] N anguila *f*

eerie [íri] ADJ misterioso

effect [Ifékt] N efecto *m*; **to go into** — entrar en
vigencia, ponerse en operación; **in —**
vigente, operativo; **I wrote a letter to that**
— escribí una carta en ese sentido; **personal**
—s efectos personales *m pl*; VT efectuar

effective [IféktIv] ADJ efectivo, eficaz; (a law)
vigente; — **date** fecha de vigencia *f*

effectively [IféktIvli] ADV (well) eficazmente; (in
fact) de hecho, en efecto

effectiveness [IféktIvnIs] N efectividad *f*,
eficacia *f*

effectual [Iféktʃuəl] ADJ eficaz

effeminate [IfémənIt] ADJ afeminado

efficacy [éfIkəsi] N eficacia *f*

efficiency [IfíʃənsI] N eficiencia *f*; —
apartment estudio *m*

efficient [Ifíʃənt] ADJ eficiente; (motor)
económico

effigy [éfədʒi] N efigie *f*; **to burn in** — quemar
en efigie

effort [éfə·t] N (exertion) esfuerzo *m*; (work of
art) obra *f*; (campaign) campaña *f*

effrontery [Ifrántəri] N descaro *m*

effusive [IfjúsIv] ADJ efusivo

egg [ɛg] N huevo *m*; (female gamete) óvulo *m*;
(fellow) tipo *m*; **—beater** batidor de huevos
m; **—head** empollón -na *mf*; **—nog** rompopo
m, rompope *m*, ponche de huevo *m*; **—plant**
berenjena *f*; **—shell** cáscara de huevo *f*; —
white clara de huevo *f*; — **yolk** yema de
huevo *f*; **to have — on one's face** estar
avergonzado, quedar mal; **to lay an** — (of a
hen) poner un huevo; (fail) fracasar; **to walk**
on —shells ir pisando huevos; ADJ **—-**
shaped ovoide; VT **to — on** incitar

ego [ígo] N (self) yo *m*, ego *m*; (vanity) ego *m*; (self-esteem) amor propio *m*; **winning the prize was an — trip for him** ganar el premio le aceitó el ego
egocentric [igoséntrɪk] ADJ egocéntrico
egotism [ígətɪzəm] N egotismo *m*
Egypt [ídʒɪpt] N Egipto *m*
Egyptian [ɪdʒípʃən] ADJ & N egipcio -cia *mf*
eight [et] NUM ocho; — **hundred** ochocientos
eighteen [ettín] NUM dieciocho
eighth [etθ] ADJ, N & ADV octavo *m*; — **note** corchea *f*
eighty [éɖi] NUM ochenta
either [íðɚ] ADJ & PRON — **will do** cualquiera de los dos está bien; **choose — suit** elige uno de los dos trajes; **choose —** elige uno [u otro] de los dos; **there were flowers on — side of the road** había flores a ambos lados de la carretera; ADV **if you don't, I won't —** si tú no lo haces, yo tampoco; **I'll go — by bus or by car** voy [o] en autobús o en auto
ejaculate [ɪdʒǽkjəlet] VI/VT eyacular; (exclaim) exclamar
eject [ɪdʒékt] VT (throw out) echar, expulsar; VI/VT (throw from a plane) eyectar[se]
ejection [ɪdʒékʃən] N expulsión *f*
EKG [electrocardiogam] [íkédʒí] N electrocardiograma *m*
elaborate[1] [ɪlǽbəɪt] ADJ (ornate) elaborado; (detailed) detallado
elaborate[2] [ɪlǽbəret] VI/VT (create) elaborar; (develop) desarrollar
elapse [ɪlǽps] VI transcurrir, pasar
elastic [ɪlǽstɪk] ADJ elástico; N elástico *m*; (rubber band) goma elástica *f*
elasticity [ɪlæstísɪɖi] N elasticidad *f*
elated [ɪléɖɪd] ADJ eufórico
elbow [éɫbo] N codo *m*; VI/VT codear, dar codazos; **to — one's way through** abrirse paso a codazos
elder [éɫdɚ] ADJ (older) mayor; N (older person) mayor *mf*; (old person) anciano -na *mf*; (in a church) miembro del consejo de una iglesia *m*; **our —s** nuestros mayores *m pl*
elderly [éɫdɚli] ADJ anciano
e-learning [ílɚnɪŋ] N educación en línea *f*
elect [ɪlékt] ADJ (elected) electo; (chosen by God) elegido; VI/VT elegir
election [ɪlékʃən] N elección *f*
elector [ɪléktɚ] N elector -ora *mf*
electoral [ɪléktɚəɫ] ADJ electoral
electric [ɪléktrɪk] ADJ eléctrico; (exciting) electrizante; (excited) electrizado; — **chair** silla eléctrica *f*; — **eel** anguila eléctrica *f*; — **eye** célula fotoeléctrica *f*; — **meter** contador eléctrico *m*; — **storm** tormenta eléctrica *f*
electrical [ɪléktrɪkəɫ] ADJ eléctrico; — **engineer** ingeniero -ra electricista *mf*; — **engineering** ingeniería eléctrica *f*; — **tape** cinta aislante *f*

electrician [ɪlɛktríʃən] N electricista *mf*
electricity [ɪlɛktrísɪɖi] N electricidad *f*
electrify [ɪléktrəfaɪ] VT (apply electricity) electrificar; (thrill) electrizar
electrocardiogram [ɪlɛktrokárɖɪəgræm] N electrocardiograma *m*
electrocute [ɪléktrəkjut] VT electrocutar
electrode [ɪléktrod] N electrodo *m*
electroencephalogram [ɪlɛktroɛnséfələgræm] N electroencefalograma *m*
electrolysis [ɪlɛktrálɪsɪs] N electrólisis *f*
electromagnet [ɪlɛktromǽgnɪt] N electroimán *m*
electromagnetic [ɪlɛktromægnéɖɪk] ADJ electromagnético
electron [ɪléktrɑn] N electrón *m*; — **microscope** microscopio electrónico *m*
electronic [ɪlɛktránɪk] ADJ electrónico; — **banking** banca electrónica *f*; — **mail** correo electrónico *m*; —**s** electrónica *f*; — **signature** firma electrónica *f*
elegance [élɪgəns] N elegancia *f*, gallardía *f*
elegant [élɪgənt] ADJ elegante, gallardo; (gift) de lujo
element [éləmənt] N elemento *m*; (component part) componente *m*, pieza *f*; (for heating) resistencia *f*; **the —s** los elementos
elemental [ɛləméntl] ADJ elemental; — **forces** fuerzas de la naturaleza *f pl*
elementary [ɛləméntri] ADJ elemental; — **school** escuela primaria *f*
elephant [éləfənt] N elefante -ta *mf*
elevate [éləvet] VT elevar
elevation [ɛləvéʃən] N (action of elevating, elevated place) elevación *f*; (altitude) altura *f*
elevator [éləveɖɚ] N ascensor *m*; Am elevador *m*; (for grain) elevador *m*
eleven [ɪlévən] NUM once
elf [ɛlf] N elfo *m*; (mischievous person) pillo -lla *mf*
elicit [ɪlísɪt] VT provocar; **to — admiration** despertar admiración
eligibility [ɛlɪdʒəbílɪɖi] N elegibilidad *f*
eligible [élɪdʒəbəɫ] ADJ elegible; **an — bachelor** un buen partido; **you are — for a scholarship** tienes derecho a solicitar una beca
eliminate [ɪlímənet] VT eliminar
elimination [ɪlɪmənéʃən] N eliminación *f*
elite [ɪlít] N elite *f*, élite *f*
elitist [ɪlíɖɪst] ADJ & N elitista *mf*
elk [ɛlk] N alce *m*
elliptical [ɪlíptɪkəɫ] ADJ elíptico
elm [ɛlm] N olmo *m*
elongate [ɪlɔ́ŋget] VI/VT alargar[se]
elope [ɪlóp] VI fugarse para casarse a escondidas
eloquence [éləkwəns] N elocuencia *f*
eloquent [éləkwənt] ADJ elocuente
El Salvador [ɛɫsǽɫvədɔr] N El Salvador *m*

else [ɛɫs] ADJ & ADV **who — was there?** ¿quién más estaba? **someone —'s son** el hijo de otro; **somebody —** [algún] otro; **or —** si no; **leave town or —** vete del pueblo o sufre las consecuencias / o verás lo que es bueno; **nobody —** nadie más; **nothing —** nada más; **how —?** ¿de qué otra forma? ADV **—where** (location) en otra parte / en otro lado; (movement) a otra parte / a otro sitio

elucidate [Ilúsɪdet] VI/VT elucidar, dilucidar, esclarecer

elucidation [IlusɪdéʃƏn] N elucidación f, dilucidación f

elude [Ilúd] VT eludir

elusive [Ilúsɪv] ADJ (slippery) escurridizo; (evasive) esquivo; (difficult to understand) difícil de entender

emaciated [IméʃieDɪd] ADJ escuálido, descarnado

e-mail [ímeɫ] N correo electrónico m; — **address** dirección de correo electrónico f

emanate [émƏnet] VI/VT emanar

emanation [emƏnéʃƏn] N emanación f

emancipate [Imǽnsɘpet] VT emancipar

emancipation [ImænsƏpéʃƏn] N emancipación f

emasculate [Imǽskjɘlet] VT castrar; (remove testicles) castrar, emascular

embalm [Imbám] VT (the body of a deceased person) preparar; (a mummy) embalsamar

embalming [ImbámIŋ] N preparación del cuerpo f

embankment [ImbǽŋkmƏnt] N terraplén m

embargo [Imbárgo] N embargo m; VT imponer un embargo a/contra

embark [Imbárk] VI/VT embarcar[se]

embarrass [ImbǽrƏs] VT (cause shame) hacerle pasar vergüenza a; (cause discomfit, financial difficulties) poner en aprietos; **—ed** avergonzado, en aprietos; **I'm —ed about my teeth** me dan vergüenza mis dientes; **I'm —ed to tell you** me da vergüenza decírtelo

embarrassing [ImbǽrƏsIŋ] ADJ (shameful) vergonzoso, penoso; (hindering) embarazoso

embarrassment [ImbǽrƏsmƏnt] N (shame) vergüenza f, bochorno m, pena f; (act of embarrassing) vergüenza f; (financial difficulty) aprieto m; **he's an — to the company** hace quedar mal a la compañía; **we have an — of riches** nadamos en la abundancia

embassy [émbƏsi] N embajada f

embattled [Imbǽdɫd] ADJ hostigado, agobiado

embed [Imbéd] VT incrustar

embedded [ImbéDɪd] ADJ incrustado

embellish [ImbélIʃ] VT adornar, ornamentar

ember [émbɚ] N ascua f, brasa f

embezzle [Imbézɘɫ] VT desfalcar, malversar

embezzlement [ImbézɘɫmƏnt] N desfalco m,

peculado m, malversación f

embitter [ImbíDɚ] VT amargar

emblem [émblƏm] N emblema m, divisa f

embody [Imbádi] VT (personify) personificar; (to provide with a body) encarnar

embolism [émbƏlIzƏm] N embolia f

embrace [Imbrés] VI/VT (hug, adopt) abrazar[se]; (include) abarcar; N abrazo m

embroider [ImbrɔIDɚ] VI/VT bordar, recamar

embroidery [ImbrɔIDƏri] N bordado m

embroil [ImbrɔIɫ] VT (involve in a conflict) meter en un lío; (throw into confusion) embrollar

embryo [émbrio] N embrión m

embryonic [embriánɪk] ADJ embriónico, embrionario

emerald [émƏɘɫd] N esmeralda f

emerge [Imɝ́dʒ] VI (come into view) emerger; (arise, as a question, problem) surgir

emergency [Imɝ́dʒƏnsi] N emergencia f; — **brake** freno de emergencia m; — **exit** salida de emergencia f; — **room** urgencias f pl

emergent [Imɝ́dʒƏnt] ADJ emergente

emerging [Imɝ́dʒIŋ] ADJ emergente

emigrant [émIgrƏnt] ADJ & N emigrante mf

emigrate [émIgret] VI emigrar

emigration [emIgréʃƏn] N emigración f

eminence [émƏnƏns] N eminencia f

eminent [émƏnƏnt] ADJ eminente

emissary [émIseri] N emisario -ria mf

emission [ImíʃƏn] N emisión f

emit [Imít] VT (light, sound) emitir; (smells) despedir; (sparks) echar

emoticon [ImóDIkɑn] N emoticón m, emoticono m

emotion [ImóʃƏn] N emoción f

emotional [ImóʃƏnɫ] ADJ (of the emotions) emocional; (arousing or expressing emotions) emotivo; (easily moved) sensible

empathy [émpƏθi] N empatía f

emperor [émpƏrɚ] N emperador m; — **penguin** pingüino emperador m

emphasis [émfƏsɪs] N énfasis m, hincapié m

emphasize [émfƏsaɪz] VT enfatizar, hacer hincapié en, subrayar

emphatic [ImfǽDɪk] ADJ enfático

emphysema [emfɪsímƏ] N enfisema m

empire [émpaɪr] N imperio m

empirical [empírɪkɫ] ADJ empírico

employ [ImplɔI] VT emplear; (hire) emplear, ocupar; N empleo m; **to be in someone's —** trabajar a las órdenes de alguien

employee [ImplɔIí] N empleado -da mf

employer [ImplɔIɚ] N patrón -na mf; **—s'** patronal

employment [ImplɔImƏnt] N empleo m; (occupation) ocupación f; — **bureau** agencia de empleo f; — **opportunities** oportunidades laborales f pl; **place of —**

lugar de trabajo *m*

empower [ɪmpáʊɚ] VT (authorize) autorizar; (give strength) potenciar

empress [émprɪs] N emperatriz *f*

emptiness [émptɪnɪs] N vacío *m*

empty [émpti] ADJ (devoid of content) vacío; (devoid of activity) desocupado; —**-handed** con las manos vacías; VI/VT vaciar[se], volcar[se]; (flow into) desembocar; N **to run on** — (of a car, person) quedarse sin combustible

emulate [émjəlet] VT emular (also computer term)

enable [ɪnébəɫ] VT permitir

enact [ɪnǽkt] VT (a law) promulgar; (a role) desempeñar

enamel [ɪnǽməɫ] N esmalte *m*; VT esmaltar

enamor [ɪnǽmɚ] VT enamorar; **to be —ed of** estar enamorado de

encamp [ɪnkǽmp] VI acampar

encephalitis [ɪnsɛfəláɪdɪs] N encefalitis *f*

enchant [ɪntʃǽnt] VT (bewitch) hechizar; (delight) encantar

enchanting [ɪntʃǽntɪŋ] ADJ encantador

enchantment [ɪntʃǽntmənt] N encantamiento *m*, encanto *m*, hechicería *f*

encircle [ɪnsɚkəɫ] VT cercar, ceñir

enclave [ánklev] N enclave *m*

enclose [ɪnklóz] VT (confine someone or something) encerrar; (fence in) cercar; (put in the same envelope) adjuntar, anexar

enclosure [ɪnklóʒɚ] N (wall or fence) cerca *f*; (enclosed area) cercado *m*, recinto *m*; (enclosed document) documento adjunto *m*; (act of enclosing) encierro *m*

encode [ɪŋkód] VT codificar

encoding [ɪŋkódɪŋ] N codificación *f*

encompass [ɪnkámpəs] VT (include) abarcar, englobar; (surround) circundar

encore [ánkɔr] N bis *m*; INTERJ ¡otra!

encounter [ɪnkáʊntɚ] VI/VT encontrar[se]; **they —ed the enemy army** se enfrentaron con el ejército enemigo; N (meeting, athletic event) encuentro *m*; (battle) enfrentamiento *m*

encourage [ɪnkɚɪdʒ] VT (inspire with confidence) alentar, animar; (promote) fomentar, estimular

encouragement [ɪnkɚɪdʒmənt] N (inspiration) aliento *m*, ánimo *m*; (promotion) estímulo *m*, fomento *m*

encouraging [ɪŋkɚədʒɪŋ] ADJ alentador

encroach [ɪnkrótʃ] VT **to — upon** (liberties) cercenar; (territory) usurpar; (time) quitar

encrypt [ɪnkrípt] VT codificar, cifrar

encryption [ɪŋkrípʃən] N cifrado *m*

encumber [ɪnkámbɚ] VT (block) impedir; (burden) agobiar; (charge an account) gravar

encumbrance [ɪŋkámbrəns] N gravamen *m*

encyclopedia [ɪnsaɪkləpídiə] N enciclopedia *f*

end [ɛnd] N (temporal) fin *m*, término *m*; (limit, boundary) final *m*, extremo *m*; (tip) cabo *m*; (aim) fin *m*; (in football) exterior *m*; — **key** tecla [de] fin *f*; —**-of-life care** cuidado terminal *m*; — **table** mesa pequeña *f*; — **zone** zona de ensayo *f*, zona de anotación *f*; **at the** — **of the movie** al final de la película; **the north** — **of town** el barrio norte; **no** — **of things** un sinfín de cosas; **at the** — **of the day** al fin y al cabo; **on** — de punta; **for days on** — día tras día; **to put an** — **to** poner fin a; VI/VT terminar; (a street) morir; **he —ed his life** puso fin a su vida; **a prayer —s the class** la clase termina con una oración; **a war to** — **all wars** una guerra que supera a todas las anteriores; ADV — **to** — uno tras otro

endanger [ɪndéndʒɚ] VT poner en peligro; —**ed species** especie en peligro de extinción *f*

endear [ɪndír] VI **to** — **oneself** congraciarse; **his humor —ed him to her** se ganó la simpatía de ella gracias a su humor

endearing [ɪndírɪŋ] ADJ entrañable

endeavor [ɪndévɚ] VT (try) tratar de, intentar, procurar; VI (strive) esforzarse por; N esfuerzo *m*

endemic [ɪndémɪk] ADJ endémico

ending [éndɪŋ] N final *m*; (of a story) desenlace *m*; (derivational, inflectional) terminación *f*; (inflectional) desinencia *f*

endless [éndlɪs] ADJ (having no end) interminable; (continuous) sin fin; (infinite) eterno

endocrine [éndəkrɪn] ADJ endocrino

endocrinology [ɛndəkrɪnálədʒi] N endocrinología *f*

endoderm [éndodɚm] N endodermo *m*

endorphin [ɪndórfɪn] N endorfina *f*

endorse [ɪndórs] VT (sign a check) endosar; (support) respaldar; (authorize a document) refrendar, visar

endorsement [ɪndórsmənt] N (signature) endoso *m*; (backing) respaldo *m*; (authorization) refrendo *m*

endorser [ɪndórsɚ] N (check signer) endosante *mf*; (supporter) partidario -ria *mf*; (authorizer) refrendario -ria *mf*

endow [ɪndáʊ] VT (grant funds) hacer un legado; (furnish powers) dotar

endowment [ɪndáʊmənt] N (funds granted) legado *m*, dotación *f*; (power) dote *f*; — **annuity** anualidad dotal *f*; — **fund** fondo de un legado *m*

endurance [ɪndúrəns] N (stamina) resistencia *f*; (ability to bear pain) aguante *m*

endure [ɪndúr, ɪndjúr] VT (undergo) sobrellevar, soportar, pasar; VI (live on) durar; (bear up) aguantar

enema [énəmə] N enema *m*, lavativa *f*

enemy [ɛ́nəmi] N enemigo -ga *mf*
energetic [ɛnəʤɛ́DIk] ADJ enérgico
energy [ɛ́nəʤi] N energía *f*; — **policy** política energética *f*
enervate [ɛ́nəvet] VT enervar, debilitar
enforce [ɪnfɔ́rs] VT hacer cumplir
enforcement [ɪnfɔ́rsmənt] N **the sheriff is responsible for the — of the law** el alguacil es responsable de hacer cumplir la ley
engage [ɪngéʤ] VT (hire) contratar; (attract) captar, atraer; (interlock) engranar; **to — the brake** poner el freno; **to — someone in conversation** trabar conversación con alguien; **to — in battle** trabar batalla; **to be —d in something** estar ocupado en algo; **to be —d to be married** estar comprometido [para casarse], estar prometido
engaged [ɪngéʤd] ADJ comprometido
engagement [ɪngéʤmənt] N (commitment) compromiso *m*; (betrothal) compromiso *m*, noviazgo *m*; (employment) empleo *m*; (battle) batalla *f*; (gear interlocking) engranaje *m*
engender [ɪnʤéndə] VT engendrar
engine [ɛ́nʤin] N (machine) máquina *f*; (in a vehicle) motor *m*; (locomotive) locomotora *f*; — **block** bloque del motor *m*
engineer [ɛnʤənír] N ingeniero -ra *mf*; (of locomotive) maquinista *mf*; VT (create) idear; (plot) maquinar
engineering [ɛnʤənírɪŋ] N ingeniería *f*
English [ɪ́nglɪʃ] ADJ inglés; N (spin) efecto *m*; **the —** los ingleses; **—man, —woman** inglés -esa *mf*
engrave [ɪngrév] VI/VT grabar
engraver [ɪngrévə] N grabador -ora *mf*
engraving [ɪngrévɪŋ] N grabado *m*
engross [ɪngrós] VT absorber
engrossed [ɪngróst] ADJ absorto
engulf [ɪngʌ́lf] VT (swallow) tragar; (overwhelm) abrumar
enhance [ɪnhǽns] VT (intensify) realzar; (improve) mejorar
enigma [ɪnígmə] N enigma *m*
enjoin [ɪnʤɔ́in] VT instar; **to — from** prohibir
enjoy [ɪnʤɔ́i] VI/VT (take pleasure) disfrutar [de], gozar [de]; (benefit from) gozar [de]; —**!** ¡que lo disfrutes! **to — oneself** divertirse; **to — the use of** usufructuar
enjoyable [ɪnʤɔ́iəbəl] ADJ (pleasant) agradable, gozoso; (fun) ameno
enjoyment [ɪnʤɔ́imənt] N (act of enjoying) goce *m*, disfrute *m*; (right of use) usufructo *m*; (pleasure) placer *m*, gozo *m*
enlarge [ɪnlárʤ] VI/VT agrandar[se]; VT (blow up a photo) ampliar; VI **to — upon** explayarse sobre, extenderse sobre
enlargement [ɪnlárʤmənt] N (photo, building) ampliación *f*; (act of enlarging) agrandamiento *m*; (temporary swelling)

dilatación *f*
enlighten [ɪnláitṇ] VT (morally) iluminar; (intellectually) explicar, ilustrar
enlightenment [ɪnláitṇmənt] N (moral) iluminación *f*; (intellectual) explicación *f*; **the — la Ilustración**
enlist [ɪnlíst] VI/VT (for the army) alistar[se]; (for a campaign) conseguir el apoyo de
enlistment [ɪnlístmənt] N alistamiento *m*
enliven [ɪnláivən] VT animar, avivar
enmity [ɛ́nmiDi] N enemistad *f*
ennoble [ɪnnóbəl] VT ennoblecer
enormous [ɪnɔ́rməs] ADJ enorme, descomunal
enough [ɪnʌ́f] ADJ suficiente; ADV **he's tall —** tiene altura suficiente; N lo suficiente; **we have — to live comfortably** tenemos lo suficiente como para vivir cómodamente; **that is —** con eso basta; **more than —** bastante; INTERJ ¡basta!
enrage [ɪnréʤ] VT enfurecer
enrapture [ɪnrǽptʃə] VT embelesar
enrich [ɪnrítʃ] VT enriquecer
enrichment [ɪnrítʃmənt] N enriquecimiento *m*
enroll [ɪnróɫ] VI/VT matricular[se], inscribir[se]
enrollment [ɪnróɫmənt] N matrícula *f*, inscripción *f*; **what is your —?** ¿cuántos alumnos tienes matriculados?
ensemble [ɑnsámbəl] N conjunto *m*
ensign [ɛ́nsɪn] N (naval rank) alférez de fragata *mf*; (flag) enseña *f*; (badge) insignia *f*
enslave [ɪnslév] VT esclavizar
ensnare [ɪnsnér] VT atrapar, coger en una trampa
ensue [ɪnsú] VI (follow) ocurrir después, suceder; (result from) resultar; **the ensuing events** los sucesos subsiguientes
ensure [ɪnʃúr] VT asegurar
entail [ɪntél] VT implicar, conllevar
entangle [ɪntǽŋgəl] VT enredar
enter [ɛ́ntə] VT (go in) entrar en/a; (join) ingresar en/a; (write) escribir; (put data in a computer) dar entrada a; (put data in account books) asentar; (start negotiations) iniciar; VI/VT (register for a competition) inscribir[se]; VI salir / entrar a escena; **to — into** (make an agreement) concertar; (form part of) figurar en
enterprise [ɛ́ntəpraiz] N empresa *f*
enterprising [ɛ́ntəpraizɪŋ] ADJ emprendedor
entertain [ɛntətén] VI/VT (amuse) divertir, recrear; (host) invitar; **we — a lot** tenemos invitados muy a menudo; (consider) contemplar; (harbor) abrigar
entertainer [ɛntəténə] N artista *mf*
entertaining [ɛntéténɪŋ] ADJ (fun) divertido; (serving as pastime) entretenido; (pleasant) ameno
entertainment [ɛntəténmənt] N (source of fun) diversión *f*; (pastime) entretenimiento *m*; (of

guests) agasajo *m*
enthrall [ɪnθrɔ́l] vt (captivate) cautivar,
hechizar; (make a slave of) esclavizar
enthusiasm [ɪnθúziæzəm] N entusiasmo *m*
enthusiast [ɪnθúziɪst] N entusiasta *mf*
enthusiastic [ɪnθuziǽstɪk] ADJ entusiasta; **I'm**
very — about the trip estoy muy
entusiasmado con el viaje
entice [ɪntáɪs] vi/vt (attract) atraer; (lure)
tentar; (seduce) seducir
entire [ɪntáɪr] ADJ (unbroken) entero; (complete)
completo; **the — crew** toda la tripulación, la
tripulación entera
entirety [ɪntáɪrɪDi] N totalidad *f*
entitle [ɪntáɪdl] vt (give a title) titular, intitular;
(give a right) dar derecho
entitlement [ɪntáɪdlmənt] N derecho *m*
entity [ɛ́ntɪDi] N (institution) entidad *f*; (being)
ente *m*, ser *m*
entomology [ɛntəmáləʤi] N entomología *f*
entourage [ántʊraʤ] N séquito *m*, cortejo *m*
entrails [ɛ́ntrelz] N entrañas *f pl*
entrance[1] [ɛ́ntrəns] N (act, point of entering)
entrada *f*; (permission to enter) ingreso *m*; —
examination examen de ingreso *m*
entrance[2] [ɪntrǽns] vt embelesar
entrant [ɛ́ntrənt] N participante *mf*; —**s in the**
law profession abogados recién recibidos *m*
pl
entrap [ɪntrǽp] vt (ensnare) coger con una
trampa; (deceive) embaucar
entreaty [ɪntríDi] N súplica *f*, ruego *m*
entrench [ɪntréntʃ] vi (establish) afianzar[se];
(dig trenches) atrincherar; **a deeply —ed**
habit un hábito muy arraigado
entrepreneur [antrəprənúr] N empresario -ria
mf
entrepreneurship [antrəprənúrʃɪp] N espíritu
emprendedor *m*
entropy [ɛ́ntrəpi] N entropía *f*
entrust [ɪntrʌ́st] vt confiar, encomendar
entry [ɛ́ntri] N (act, point of entry) entrada *f*;
(permission to enter) ingreso *m*; (record)
anotación *f*; (contestant) participante *mf*;
(dictionary definition) entrada *f*, artículo *m*;
(computer) entrada *f*; (in bookkeeping)
asiento *m*; **double — accounting**
contabilidad por partida doble *f*; ADJ —-**level**
que no requiere experiencia
enumerate [ɪnúməret] vt enumerar
enunciate [ɪnʌ́nsiet] vi/vt (pronounce)
articular; (state a theory) enunciar;
(proclaim) proclamar
envelop [ɪnvéləp] vt envolver
envelope [ɛ́nvəlop] N sobre *m*
enviable [ɛ́nviəbəl] ADJ envidiable
envious [ɛ́nviəs] ADJ envidioso
environment [ɪnváɪə-nmənt] N ambiente *m*,
medio ambiente *m*; (biological) medio

ambiente *m*, ecología *f*; (in computers)
entorno *m*; ADJ ambiental; (biological)
medioambiental, ecológico
environmental [ɪnvaɪə-nméntl] ADJ ambiental;
(biological) medioambiental, ecológico; —
impact study estudio del impacto
ambiental *m*
environmentalist [ɪnvaɪə-néntlɪst] N
ecologista *mf*
envisage [ɪnvízɪʤ] vt anticipar, prever
envision [ɪnvíʒən] vt imaginar
envoy [ánvɔɪ] N enviado -da *mf*
envy [ɛ́nvi] N envidia *f*; vi/vt envidiar
enzyme [ɛ́nzaɪm] N enzima *f*
ephemeral [ɪfémə-əl] ADJ efímero
epic [ɛ́pɪk] ADJ épico; N (poem) epopeya *f*; (genrc)
épica *f*
epicenter [ɛ́pɪsentə-] N epicentro *m*
epidemic [ɛpɪdémɪk] ADJ epidémico; N
epidemia *f*
epidermis [ɛpɪdə́-mɪs] N epidermis *f*
epiglottis [ɛpɪglaDɪs] N epiglotis *f*
epilepsy [ɛ́pələpsi] N epilepsia *f*
epileptic [ɛpəléptɪk] ADJ epiléptico
epilogue, epilog [ɛ́pələɡ] N epílogo *m*
epiphany [ɪpíʃəni] N epifanía *f*
episode [ɛ́pɪsod] N episodio *m*
episodic [ɛpɪsáDɪk] ADJ (sporadic) episódico;
(serial) en episodios
epitaph [ɛ́pɪtæf] N epitafio *m*
epitome [ɪpíDəmi] N epítome *m*
epoch [ɛ́pək] N época *f*; —-**making**
trascendental
Epsom salt [ɛ́psəmsɔ́lt] N sal de Epsom *f*
equal [íkwəl] ADJ igual; — **rights** igualdad de
derechos *f*; **an — contest** una competición
pareja; **to be — to a task** ser capaz de
cumplir una tarea; N igual *m*; — **sign** signo
de igual *m*; vt igualar
equality [ɪkwálɪDi] N igualdad *f*
equalize [íkwəlaɪz] vt igualar; (electronically)
ecualizar
equalizer [íkwəlaɪzə-] N (in soccer) gol del
empate *m*
equally [íkwəli] ADV igualmente
equate [ɪkwét] vt equiparar
equation [ɪkwéʒən] N ecuación *f*
equator [ɪkwéDə-] N ecuador *m*
Equatorial Guinea [ɛkwətɔ́riəlɡíni] N Guinea
Ecuatorial *f*
equidistant [ikwɪdístənt] ADJ equidistante
equilibrium [ikwəlíbriəm] N equilibrio *m*
equine [íkwaɪn] ADJ & N equino *m*
equinox [íkwənʊks] N equinoccio *m*
equip [ɪkwíp] vt equipar
equipment [ɪkwípmənt] N (supplies) equipo *m*;
(act of equipping) equipamiento *m*
equitable [ɛ́kwɪDəbəl] ADJ equitativo, justo
equity [ɛ́kwɪDi] N equidad *f*, valor libre de

hipoteca de una propiedad *m*; **equities**
acciones *f pl*
equivalent [ɪkwívələnt] ADJ & N equivalente *m*
equivocal [ɪkwívəkəł] ADJ equívoco
era [írə] N era *f*
eradicate [ɪrǽDɪket] VT (extirpate) erradicar;
(pull up by roots) arrancar
eradication [ɪrǽDɪkéʃən] N erradicación *f*
erase [ɪrés] VI/VT borrar[se]
eraser [ɪrésɚ] N (pencil) goma de borrar *f*;
(blackboard) borrador *m*
erasure [ɪréʃɚ] N (act of erasing) borrado *m*;
(smudge) borrón *m*
erect [ɪrékt] ADJ (of an organ) erecto; (of the
body) erguido; VT erigir
erectile [ɪréktaɪł] ADJ eréctil
erection [ɪrékʃən] N erección *f*
ergonomic [ɝɡənámɪk] ADJ ergonómico
ergonomics [ɝɡənámɪks] N ergonomía *f*
Eritrea [ɛrɪtríə] N Eritrea *f*
Eritrean [ɛrɪtríən] ADJ & N eritreo -a *mf*
ermine [ɝ́mɪn] N armiño *m*
erode [ɪród] VI/VT erosionar[se]
erogenous [ɪrádʒənəs] ADJ erógeno
erosion [ɪróʒən] N erosión *f*
erotic [ɪráDɪk] ADJ erótico
eroticism [ɪráDɪsɪzəm] N erotismo *m*
err [ɛr] VI errar
errand [érənd] N mandado *m*, recado *m*; — **boy**
mandadero *m*
errant [érənt] ADJ errante
erratic [ɪrǽDɪk] ADJ (unpredictable) irregular,
errático; (eccentric) excéntrico; (wandering)
errante
erroneous [ɪróniəs] ADJ erróneo, errado
error [érɚ] N (also in baseball) error *m*; **to be
in** — estar errado; — **message** mensaje de
error *m*
erudite [érjədaɪt] ADJ erudito
erudition [ɛrjədíʃən] N erudición *f*
erupt [ɪrʌ́pt] VI (volcano) hacer erupción; (angry
person) estallar; (pimples) salir
eruption [ɪrʌ́pʃən] N erupción *f*
escalate [éskəlet] VI (prices) aumentar;
(violence) intensificarse, aumentar
escalator [éskəleDɚ] N escalera mecánica *f*
escapade [éskəped] N (adventure) aventura *f*;
(prank) travesura *f*
escape [ɪskép] N (of gas) escape *m*; (from reality)
escape *m*, evasión *f*; (of prisoners) fuga *f*,
evasión *f*; (means of escaping) escapatoria *f*;
— **key** tecla de escape *f*; VI escapar[se],
evadirse; VT (elude) eludir; **his name** —**s me**
no me acuerdo de su nombre
escort[1] [éskɔrt] N (people who accompany)
escolta *mf*; (male companion) acompañante
m; (paid female companion) señorita de
compañía *f*
escort[2] [ɪskɔ́rt] VT (protect) escoltar;

(accompany) acompañar
escrow [éskro] N — **account** cuenta de depósito
en garantía *f*; ADV LOC **in** — en custodia
escudo [ɪskúdo] N escudo *m*
Eskimo [éskəmo] N esquimal *mf*
esophagus [ɪsáfəɡəs] N esófago *m*
esoteric [ɛsətérɪk] ADJ esotérico
especial [ɪspéʃəl] ADJ especial
especially [ɪspéʃəli] ADV (above all)
especialmente; (mainly) sobre todo; **he's** —
tired today hoy está más cansado que de
costumbre
espionage [éspiənaʒ] N espionaje *m*
esplanade [ésplənad] N explanada *f*
espouse [ɪspáʊz] VT defender, abrazar
essay[1] [ése] N ensayo *m*
essay[2] [esé] VT ensayar
essence [ésəns] N esencia *f*; **time is of the** — el
tiempo apremia
essential [ɪsénʃəl] ADJ esencial
establish [ɪstǽblɪʃ] VT (cause to be accepted,
prove the validity of) establecer; (found)
fundar
establishment [ɪstǽblɪʃmənt] N (action or fact)
establecimiento *m*, conformación *f*;
(authority) establishment *m*; (of a custom,
system) implantación *f*; (of a regime)
instauración *f*
estate [ɪstét] N (piece of land) hacienda *f*;
(possessions) bienes *m pl*; (property)
propiedades *f pl*; (of a deceased person)
testamentaria *f*; — **tax** impuesto de
sucesión *m*
esteem [ɪstím] VT (regard highly) estimar;
(consider) considerar; N estima *f*
estimate[1] [éstəmet] VT estimar, evaluar; VI
hacer una estimación
estimate[2] [éstəmɪt] N (calculation) estimación *f*;
(approximate charge) presupuesto *m*
estimation [estəméʃən] N (opinion) juicio *m*;
(esteem) estima *f*; (estimate) estimación *f*; **in
my** — a mi juicio
Estonia [ɛstóniə] N Estonia *f*
Estonian [ɛstóniən] ADJ & N estonio -nia *mf*
estrange [ɪstréndʒ] VT (alienate) enajenar; **to
become** —**d** separarse
estrogen [éstrədʒən] N estrógeno *m*
estuary [éstʃuɛri] N estuario *m*
et cetera, etc. [ɛtsétrə] ADV etcétera, etc.
etch [ɛtʃ] VI/VT (engrave) grabar; (outline)
perfilar[se]
etching [étʃɪŋ] N grabado *m*
eternal [ɪtɝ́nl] ADJ eterno
eternity [ɪtɝ́nɪDi] N eternidad *f*
ethanol [éθənał] N etanol *m*
ether [íθɚ] N éter *m*
ethernet [íθɚnɛt] N ethernet *m*
ethical [éθɪkəł] ADJ ético
ethics [éθɪks] N ética *f*

Ethiopia [iθiópiə] N Etiopía f
Ethiopian [iθiópiən] ADJ & N etíope mf
ethnic [éθnɪk] ADJ étnico; (dances, clothes)
tradicional; — **Chinese** de ascendencia
china; — **cleansing** limpieza étnica f
ethnicity [εθnísɪDi] N etnicidad f; (group) grupo
étnico m
ethnography [εθnágrəfi] N etnografía f
ethnology [εθnálədʒi] N etnología f
ethyl alcohol [éθəlǽɫkəhɑɫ] N alcohol etílico m
etiquette [éDɪkɪt] N etiqueta f
etymology [εDəmálədʒi] N etimología f
EU [European Union] [íjú] N UE f
eucalyptus [jukəlíptəs] N eucalipto m
eulogy [júlədʒi] N (praise) elogio m; (at a funeral)
panegírico m
eunuch [júnək] N eunuco m
euphemism [júfəmɪzəm] N eufemismo m
euphoria [jufɔ́riə] N euforia f
euro [júro] N euro m
Europe [júrəp] N Europa f
European [jurəpíən] ADJ & N europeo -a mf; —
Union Unión Europea f; — **Union budget**
presupuesto comunitario m
Eustachian tube [justéʃən] N trompa de
Eustaquio f
euthanasia [juθəné ʒə] N eutanasia f
evacuate [ɪvǽkjuet] VI/VT (remove due to
danger, defecate) evacuar; (empty a building)
desalojar
evade [ɪvéd] VT (taxes, responsibilities) evadir,
burlar; (questions) eludir
evaluate [ɪvǽljuet] VT (assess) evaluar;
(appraise) avaluar, tasar
evaluation [ɪvæljuéʃən] N evaluación f
evangelical [ivændʒélɪkəɫ] ADJ evangélico
evaporate [ɪvǽpəret] VI/VT evaporar[se]; VI
(vanish) esfumarse
evaporation [ɪvæpəréʃən] N evaporación f
evasion [ɪvéʒən] N (escape) evasión f;
(subterfuge) evasiva f
evasive [ɪvésɪv] ADJ evasivo
eve [iv] N (day before) víspera f; (evening)
atardecer m; **on the — of** en vísperas de
even [ívən] ADJ (flat) plano, llano; (smooth) liso;
(parallel) paralelo; (without fluctuation)
parejo; (equal) igual; (divisible by two) par;
(placid) tranquilo; —**handed** imparcial; —-
tempered apacible; **an — dozen** una
docena exacta; **to be — with someone** estar
a mano con alguien; **to get — with**
someone desquitarse de alguien; ADV (still,
yet) aun; (for extreme case) hasta, inclusive,
incluso; — **if/though** aun cuando; — **my**
mother went hasta mi madre fue; — **so** aun
así; **it's — more expensive** es aun más caro;
not — ni siquiera; VI/VT (make a surface
even) nivelar[se]; (make accounts even)
emparejar

evening [ívnɪŋ] N tarde f; (dusk) atardecer m; —
gown vestido de fiesta m, vestido de noche
m; — **party** velada f; — **star** lucero de la
tarde m; **good** —! ¡buenas noches!
event [ɪvént] N (happening) hecho m, evento m;
(of importance) acontecimiento m, suceso m;
in any — en todo caso; **in the** — **of** en caso
de
eventful [ɪvéntfəɫ] ADJ agitado, movido
eventual [ɪvéntʃuəɫ] ADJ (later) posterior; (final)
final
eventuality [ɪventʃuǽlɪDi] N eventualidad f
eventually [ɪvéntʃuəli] ADV a la larga
ever [évɚ] ADV alguna vez; —**more** para
siempre; — **since** desde entonces; **have you**
— **studied French?** ¿alguna vez has
estudiado francés? **how did you** — **do this?**
¿cómo pudiste hacer esto? **for** — **and** — por/
para siempre jamás; **hardly** — casi nunca; **if**
— si alguna vez; **more than** — más que
nunca; **the best friend I** — **had** el mejor
amigo que he tenido jamás; **for** —**more**
para/por siempre jamás; ADJ —**green** [planta]
perenne f; —**lasting** eterno
every [évri] ADJ (each) cada; — **child is**
different cada niño es diferente; (all)
todo[s]; — **once in a while** de vez en
cuando; — **other day** cada dos días, un día sí
y otro no; —**where** (location) por/en todas
partes; (direction) a todas partes; **we go** —
Friday vamos todos los viernes; PRON
—**body** todos -das mf pl, todo el mundo m; —
day todos los días; —**one** todos -das mf pl,
todo el mundo m; —**thing** todo; **you are**
—**thing to me** eres todo para mí; ADJ —**day**
(of clothes) de diario, de todos los días; (of
occurrences) cotidiano
evict [ɪvíkt] VT desalojar
evidence [évɪDəns] N evidencia f; (data in court)
prueba f; **to be in** — ser evidente; VI/VT
evidenciar[se], demostrar[se]
evident [évɪDənt] ADJ evidente
evil [ívəɫ] ADJ (wicked) malo, malvado; (harmful)
maligno; N (force of nature) mal m; (human
wickedness) maldad f; —**doer** malhechor
-ora mf; — **eye** mal de ojo m; **the lesser of**
two —**s** el mal menor
evocation [evəkéʃən] N evocación f
evoke [ɪvók] VT (call up) evocar; (elicit) provocar
evolution [evəlúʃən] N evolución f
evolutionary [evəlúʃənεri] ADJ evolutivo
evolve [ɪváɫv] VI/VT desarrollar[se]; VI
evolucionar
ewe [ju] N oveja f
ex [εks] N ex mf
exacerbate [ɪgzǽsɚbet] VI/VT exacerbar
exact [ɪgzǽkt] ADJ exacto; VT exigir
exacting [ɪgzǽktɪŋ] ADJ exigente
exactly [ɪgzǽktli] ADV exactamente,

precisamente; **he's not — a genius** no es un genio ni mucho menos / no es ningún genio que digamos; **they arrived — at three** llegaron exactamente a las tres

exaggerate [ɪgzǽdʒəret] VT exagerar

exalt [ɪgzɔ́lt] VT exaltar

exam [ɪgzǽm] N examen *m*

examination [ɪgzæmənéʃən] N examen *m* (also medical)

examine [ɪgzǽmɪn] VT (inspect) examinar; (analyze) analizar

example [ɪgzǽmpəł] N ejemplo *m*

exasperate [ɪgzǽspəret] VT exasperar

excavate [ékskəvet] VT excavar

excavator [ékskəveDɚ] N (person) excavador -ora *mf*; (machine) excavadora *f*

exceed [ɪksíd] VT (go beyond) exceder, rebasar; (be superior to) superar, sobrepasar

exceeding [ɪksíDɪŋ] N superación *f*

exceedingly [ɪksíDɪŋli] ADV sumamente, extremadamente

excel [ɪksél] VI sobresalir, lucirse, descollar

excellence [éksələns] N excelencia *f*

excellent [éksələnt] ADJ excelente

except [ɪksépt] PREP excepto, menos; **all the students — Pam** todos los estudiantes menos Pam; CONJ excepto, salvo; **the cars are identical — that one is older** los coches son idénticos salvo que uno es más viejo; **we would go to the beach, — for the inclement weather** iríamos a la playa si no fuera por el mal tiempo; VT exceptuar

excepting [ɪkséptɪŋ] PREP exceptuando

exception [ɪksépʃən] N excepción *f*; **with the — of** con/a excepción de; **to take — (object)** objetar; (resent) ofenderse

exceptional [ɪksépʃənl] ADJ (unusual) excepcional; (gifted) superdotado; (handicapped) con necesidades especiales

excerpt[1] [éksɚpt] N fragmento *m*

excerpt[2] [éksɚpt, ɪksɚ́pt] VT seleccionar fragmentos

excess [ékses] N exceso *m*, hartazgo *m*; — **baggage** exceso de equipaje *m*; — **profits tax** impuesto sobre ganancias excesivas *m*; — **weight** exceso de peso *m*; **in — of twenty pounds** más de veinte libras; **to drink to —** beber en exceso

excessive [ɪksésɪv] ADJ excesivo, desmedido

exchange [ɪkstʃéndʒ] VT (replace with something similar) cambiar; (give mutually) intercambiar; (trade political prisoners, books, CDs) canjear; (barter) permutar; **to — greetings** saludarse; N (replacement) cambio *m*; (interchange) intercambio *m*; (barter) permuta *f*; (of prisoners, books) canje *m*; (for stock trading) bolsa *f*; (for commodity trading) lonja *f*; (telephone) central de teléfonos *f*; — **student** estudiante de

intercambio *mf*; **rate of —** tipo de cambio *m*, tasa de cambio *f*

excise [éksaɪz] N impuesto sobre bienes de consumo *m*

excite [ɪksáɪt] VT (agitate, arouse) excitar, alborotar; (enthuse) entusiasmar

excited [ɪksáɪDɪd] ADJ (agitated, aroused) excitado; (enthusiastic) entusiasmado, ilusionado; **to get — (aroused)** excitarse; (enthused) entusiasmarse

excitement [ɪksáɪtmənt] N (arousal) excitación *f*; (enthusiasm) entusiasmo *m*

exciting [ɪksáɪDɪŋ] ADJ (stimulating) excitante; (thrilling) emocionante, apasionante

exclaim [ɪksklém] VI exclamar

exclamation [ɛkskləméʃən] N exclamación *f*; — **point** signo de admiración *m*

exclude [ɪksklúd] VT excluir

exclusion [ɪksklúʒən] N exclusión *f*

exclusive [ɪksklúsɪv] ADJ exclusivo; — **of** sin incluir

excommunicate [ɛkskəmjúnɪket] VT excomulgar

excrement [ékskrəmənt] N excremento *m*

excrescence [ɪkskrésəns] N excrecencia *f*

excrete [ɪkskrít] VI/VT excretar

excretion [ɪkskríʃən] N excreción *f*

excruciating [ɪkskrúʃieDɪŋ] ADJ insoportable, atroz

excursion [ɪkskɚ́ʒən] N excursión *f*

excusable [ɪkskjúzəbəł] ADJ excusable, disculpable

excuse[1] [ɪkskjúz] VT (release from a duty, seek exemption) excusar, eximir; (forgive) disculpar, perdonar; — **me!** (forgive me) disculpe; (let me pass) con permiso; (excuse me?) ¿cómo? ¿perdón? *Mex* ¿mande?

excuse[2] [ɪkskjús] N excusa *f*, disculpa *f*; **it's a poor — for a car** no merece llamarse un coche

executable [ɛgzəkjúDəbəł] ADJ ejecutable

execute [éksɪkjut] VT ejecutar (also computer term); (by firing squad) fusilar

execution [ɛksɪkjúʃən] N ejecución *f*; (by firing squad) fusilamiento *m*; — **wall** paredón *m*

executioner [ɛksɪkjúʃənɚ] N verdugo *mf*

executive [ɪgzékjəDɪv] ADJ ejecutivo; N (person) ejecutivo -va *mf*; (branch of government) poder ejecutivo *m*

executor [ɪgzékjəDɚ] N albacea *mf*

exemplary [ɪgzémpləri] ADJ ejemplar

exemplify [ɪgzémpləfaɪ] VT ejemplificar

exempt [ɪgzémpt] VT eximir, dispensar; ADJ exento, libre

exemption [ɪgzémpʃən] N exención *f*, franquicia *f*

exercise [éksɚsaɪz] N ejercicio *m*; —**s** ceremonia *f*; VT ejercer; VI hacer ejercicio; — **electrocardiogram** prueba de esfuerzo

máximo *f*; **to be —d about something**
estar disgustado por algo
exert [ɪgzɔ́t] vт ejercer; **to — oneself**
esforzarse, empeñarse
exertion [ɪgzɔ́ʃən] N (use of powers, faculties)
ejercicio *m*; (vigorous action) esfuerzo *m*,
empeño *m*
exfoliation [ɪksfoliéʃən] N exfoliación *f*
exhale [ɛkshéł] vт exhalar; vɪ espirar
exhaust [ɪgzɔ́st] vт agotar, desmadejar; (a
topic) tratar exhaustivamente; N (from a car)
escape *m*
exhausted [ɪgzɔ́stɪd] ADJ rendido, agotado
exhausting [ɪgzɔ́stɪŋ] ADJ agotador
exhaustion [ɪgzɔ́stʃən] N (act or process of
exhausting) agotamiento *m*; (weakness,
tiredness) fatiga *f*
exhaustive [ɪgzɔ́stɪv] ADJ exhaustivo
exhibit [ɪgzíbɪt] vɪ/vт (manifest) exhibir; (put
on view) exponer; N exposición *f*
exhibition [ɛksəbíʃən] N (manifestation, show
of skills) exhibición *f*; (public display of
objects) exposición *f*
exhibitionism [ɛksɪbíʃənɪzəm] N
exhibicionismo *m*
exhilarated [ɪgzíləreDɪd] ADJ exultante
exhort [ɪgzɔ́rt] vт exhortar
exhumation [ɛgzjuméʃən] N exhumación *f*
exile [égzaɪł] N exilio *m*, destierro *m*; (person
exiled) exiliado -da *mf*, desterrado -da *mf*; vт
exiliar
exist [ɪgzíst] vɪ existir
existence [ɪgzístəns] N existencia *f*
existential [ɛgzɪsténʃəł] ADJ existencial
existing [ɪgzístɪŋ] ADJ existente
exit [égzɪt] N salida *f*; vɪ/vт salir [de]; (theater)
hacer mutis; **— interview** entrevista de
salida *f*; **— strategy** estrategia de salida *f*; vɪ
salir; **he —ed the building** salió del edificio
exodus [éksədəs] N éxodo *m*
exonerate [ɪgzánəret] vт exonerar
exorbitant [ɪgzɔ́rbɪDənt] ADJ exorbitante
exorcise [éksɔrsaɪz] vт exorcisar
exorcism [éksɔrsɪzəm] N exorcismo *m*
exotic [ɪgzáDɪk] ADJ exótico
expand [ɪkspǽnd] vɪ/vт expandir[se],
ampliar[se]; (an equation, an idea)
desarrollar[se]; (through heat) dilatar[se];
—ed memory memoria expandida *f*
expanse [ɪkspǽns] N extensión *f*
expansion [ɪkspǽnʃən] N expansión *f*; (of an
equation, of an idea) desarrollo *m*; (through
heat) dilatación *f*; **— slot** ranura para
accesorios *f*
expansive [ɪkspǽnsɪv] ADJ expansivo
expatriate[1] [ɛkspétriet] vɪ/vт expatriar[se]
expatriate[2] [ɛkspétriɪt] N expatriado -da *mf*
expect [ɪkspékt] vт esperar; **we — guests**
esperamos visita[s]; **I — you to be on time**

cuento con que vengas puntualmente; **I'm
—ed to work fifty hours a week** tengo
que trabajar cincuenta horas por semana; **I —
you're tired** estarás cansado; **she's —ing**
está embarazada/encinta
expectation [ɛkspɛktéʃən] N (anticipation)
expectación *f*; (expected thing) expectativa *f*;
he has great —s tiene grandes expectativas
expectorant [ɪkspéktəənt] ADJ & N expectorante
m
expectorate [ɪkspéktəret] vɪ/vт expectorar
expedient [ɪkspíDiənt] ADJ conveniente,
expeditivo
expedite [ékspɪdaɪt] vт (facilitate) agilizar; (deal
with promptly) despachar
expedition [ɛkspɪdíʃən] N expedición *f*
expeditionary [ɛkspɪdíʃənɛri] ADJ
expedicionario
expel [ɪkspéł] vт (discharge) expeler; (throw out)
expulsar
expend [ɪkspénd] vт gastar, agotar
expenditure [ɪkspéndɪtʃə] N gasto *m*
expense [ɪkspéns] N gasto *m*; **— account** cuenta
de gastos *f*; **they had fun at my —** se
divirtieron a mi costa
expensive [ɪkspénsɪv] ADJ caro
experience [ɪkspíriəns] N experiencia *f*; vт
experimentar; **—d** experimentado
experiment [ɪkspérəmənt] N experimento *m*; vɪ
experimentar
experimental [ɪkspɛrəméntḷ] ADJ experimental
experimentation [ɪkspɛrɪməntéʃən] N
experimentación *f*
expert [ékspɔt] N experto -ta *mf*; ADJ experto,
idóneo, perito; **— system** sistema experto *m*
expertise [ɛkspə-tíz] N pericia *f*
expiration [ɛkspəréʃən] N (of a contract)
vencimiento *m*, caducidad *f*; (breathing out)
espiración *f*
expire [ɪkspáɪr] vɪ (die, terminate) expirar;
(breathe out) espirar; (lapse) vencer, caducar
explain [ɪksplén] vт explicar; **he tried to —
away his absence** trató de justificar su
ausencia
explainable [ɪksplénəbəł] ADJ explicable
explanation [ɛksplənéʃən] N explicación *f*
explanatory [ɪksplǽnətɔri] ADJ explicativo
expletive [éksplɪDɪv] N palabrota *f*
explicable [ɪksplíkəbəł] ADJ explicable
explicit [ɪksplísɪt] ADJ explícito
explode [ɪksplód] vɪ/vт estallar, hacer
explosión, explotar; vт (a theory) hacer
añicos; vɪ (population) dispararse
exploit[1] [éksplɔɪt] N hazaña *f*, proeza *f*
exploit[2] [ɪksplɔ́ɪt] vт explotar
exploitation [ɛksplɔɪtéʃən] N explotación *f*
exploration [ɛkspləréʃən] N exploración *f*
exploratory [ɪksplɔ́rətɔri] ADJ exploratorio
explore [ɪksplɔ́r] vɪ/vт explorar; (a topic) bucear

explorer [ɪksplɔ́rɚ] N explorador -ora *mf*
explosion [ɪksplóʒən] N explosión *f*, estallido *m*
explosive [ɪksplósɪv] ADJ & N explosivo *m*
exponent [ɪkspónənt] N exponente *m*
export[1] [ɪkspɔ́rt] VI/VT exportar
export[2] [ékspɔrt] N exportación *f*
exportation [ɛkspɔrtéʃən] N exportación *f*
exporter [ɪkspɔ́rɖɚ] N exportador -ora *mf*
exporting [ɪkspɔ́rɖɪŋ] N exportación *f*; — **firm** empresa exportadora *f*
expose [ɪkspóz] VT (to lay open to danger, exhibit, subject to light) exponer; (to make known) revelar; (to unmask) desenmascarar
exposition [ɛkspəzíʃən] N exposición *f*
exposure [ɪkspóʒɚ] N (to danger, to light, act of exposing) exposición *f*; (disclosure) revelación *f*; **to die of** — morir de frío
expound [ɪkspáʊnd] VI/VT exponer, explicar
express [ɪksprés] VT expresar; (send by mail) enviar por correo expreso; (squeeze out) exprimir; ADJ (clearly indicated) expreso; — **delivery** envío rápido *m*; — **train** tren expreso *m*; ADV por expreso; N (train) expreso *m*
expression [ɪkspréʃən] N expresión *f*
expressive [ɪksprésɪv] ADJ expresivo
expressiveness [ɪksprésɪvnɪs] N expresividad *f*
expropriate [ɛksprópriet] VT expropiar
expulsion [ɪkspʌ́lʃən] N expulsión *f*
exquisite [ɛkskwízɪt] ADJ exquisito, primoroso; (pain) penetrante
extant [ékstənt] ADJ existente
extemporaneous [ɪkstɛmpəréniəs] ADJ improvisado
extend [ɪksténd] VI/VT extender[se]; (a street) ampliar[se]; **he —ed his hand to her** le tendió la mano
extended [ɪksténdɪd] ADJ (extensive) extenso; (prolonged) prolongado; (folded out) extendido; — **coverage** cobertura extendida *f*; — **care facility** centro de atención médica prolongada *m*
extension [ɪksténʃən] N extensión *f* (also phone line); (of a deadline) prórroga *f*; (addition) anexo *m*, ampliación *f*; — **cord** extensión *f*
extensive [ɪksténsɪv] ADJ extenso; (agriculture) extensivo
extent [ɪkstént] N extensión *f*; **to a great** — en alto grado; **to such an — that** a tal grado que; **to the — that you are able** en la medida en que seas capaz; **to a certain** — hasta cierto punto
extenuate [ɪksténjuet] VT atenuar
exterior [ɪkstíriɚ] ADJ & N exterior *m*
exterminate [ɪkstɝ́mənet] VT exterminar
extermination [ɪkstɝmənéʃən] N exterminio *m*, exterminación *f*
external [ɪkstɝ́nl] ADJ externo; (concerned with foreign countries) exterior

extinct [ɪkstíŋkt] ADJ extinto
extinguish [ɪkstíŋgwɪʃ] VT apagar, extinguir
extol [ɪkstól] VT ensalzar, enaltecer
extort [ɪkstɔ́rt] VT extorsionar
extortion [ɪkstɔ́rʃən] N extorsión *f*
extra [ékstrə] ADJ de más, adicional; **make some — cakes** haz unos pasteles de más / adicionales / extras; N extra *m* (including newspaper, actor); ADV extra; extrasensorial; (soccer) — **time** tiempo suplementario *m*, tiempo de descuento *m*; ADJ —**marital** extramarital; —**ordinary** extraordinario; —**sensory** extrasensorial
extract[1] [ékstrækt] N (something extracted) extracto *m*; (passage from a book) fragmento *m*
extract[2] [ɪkstrǽkt] VT extraer; (a secret) sonsacar
extraction [ɪkstrǽkʃən] N extracción *f*
extradite [ékstrədaɪt] VT extraditar
extradition [ɛkstrədíʃən] N extradición *f*
extraneous [ɪkstréniəs] ADJ superfluo
extrapolate [ɪkstrǽpəlet] VI/VT extrapolar
extravagance [ɪkstrǽvəgəns] N (unnecessary expense) despilfarro *m*, derroche *m*; (excess) exceso *m*; (oddity) extravagancia *f*
extravagant [ɪkstrǽvəgənt] ADJ (shopper) gastador, derrochador; (price) exorbitante; (praise, demand) excesivo
extreme [ɪkstrím] ADJ & N extremo *m*; **to go to —s** exagerar, llegar a extremos; **to the** — extremadamente, sumamente
extremely [ɪkstrímli] ADV extremadamente, sumamente; **it's — cold** hace un frío que pela; **she's — intelligent** es inteligentísima
extremity [ɪkstrémɪdi] N extremidad *f*
extricate [ékstrɪket] VT sacar; VI **to — oneself from** conseguir salir de
extrovert [ékstrəvɝt] N extrovertido -da *mf*
extroverted [ékstrəvɝdɪd] ADJ extrovertido
exuberant [ɪgzúbɚənt] ADJ exuberante
exude [ɪgzúd] VI/VT (liquid) exudar; (cheerfulness, confidence) emanar
exult [ɪgzʌ́lt] VI exultar
eye [aɪ] N ojo *m* (also of hurricane, needle, tools); (look) mirada *f*; —**ball** globo ocular *m*; —**brow** ceja *f*; — **chart** cartilla de examen de vista *f*; — **contact** contacto visual *m*; —**dropper** cuentagotas *m sg*; — **drops** colirio *m*, gotas oftálmicas *f pl*; —**glass** (of a telescope, microscope) ocular *m*; —**glasses** anteojos *m pl*, lentes *m pl*; — **injury** lesión ocular *f*; —**lash** pestaña *f*; —**lid** párpado *m*; —**liner** delineador *m*; — -**opener** revelación *f*; —**piece** ocular *m*; —**sight** vista *f*; —**sore** monstruosidad *f*; — **shadow** sombra para ojos *f*; — **socket** órbita *f*; — **strain** vista cansada *f*; —**tooth** colmillo *m*; —**witness** testigo ocular *mf*; **my —s are bad** tengo mala vista; **in the twinkling of an** — en un

abrir y cerrar de ojos; **her dress caught his
— su** vestido le llamó la atención; **to keep an
— on** cuidar, vigilar; **to see — to —** estar de
acuerdo; **in the —s of the law** ante la ley; **to
give someone the —** hacerle ojito a
alguien; **to have —s for someone** estar
prendado de alguien; **to keep one's — open**
tener cuidado; VT mirar

eyeful [áɪfʊɫ] N **we got an —** vimos más que
suficiente

e-zine [ízin] N revista electrónica f

Ff

fable [fébəɫ] N fábula f

fabric [fǽbrɪk] N tela f, tejido m; (wool) paño m;
(of society) estructura f; **— softener**
suavizante m

fabricate [fǽbrɪket] VT (goods) fabricar; (a story)
inventar

fabulous [fǽbjələs] ADJ fabuloso

facade [fəsád] N fachada f

face [fes] N (of head, coin, cube, facial
expression) cara f; (of a building) frente m; (of
a watch) esfera f; (of the Earth) faz f; **—cloth**
toalla para la cara f, **—lift** lifting m; **— value**
valor nominal m; **about —!** ¡media vuelta!
left —! ¡a la izquierda! **on the — of it**
aparentemente; **she put on a brave —** se
comportó con entereza; **to make —s** hacer
muecas; **to lose —** quedar mal; **to save —**
quedar bien; **to show one's —** aparecerse;
ADJ **—-to-—** cara a cara; ADV **in the — of**
ante, frente a; VT (stand opposite to) encarar;
(meet defiantly) enfrentar, enfrentarse con,
afrontar; (look forward) mirar a/hacia; (to
have the front toward) dar a/hacia; (to put on
facing) ribetear; **to — down** intimidar; **to —
the music** dar la cara; **to — with marble**
revestir de mármol

faceless [féslɪs] ADJ (anonymous) anónimo;
(without a face) sin cara

facet [fǽsɪt] N faceta f

facetious [fəsíʃəs] ADJ gracioso

facial [féʃəɫ] ADJ facial; N limpieza de cutis f

facilitate [fəsílɪtet] VT facilitar

facility [fəsílɪDi] N (skill) facilidad f; **facilities**
(of a building) instalaciones f pl; (restroom)
aseo m, servicio m

fact [fækt] N hecho m; **hard —s** datos concretos
m pl; **is that a —!** ¡no me digas! **as a matter
of —** de hecho; **in —** de hecho; **it's a — of
life** así son las cosas

faction [fǽkʃən] N facción f

factor [fǽktɚ] N factor m; VT descomponer en

factores; VI **to — in** tener en cuenta

factory [tǽktəri] N fábrica f

factual [fǽktʃuəɫ] ADJ (of facts) fáctico; (based on
facts) objetivo; **— error** error de hecho m

faculty [fǽkəɫti] N (ability) facultad f; (in a
college) profesorado m, cuerpo docente m,
claustro m

fad [fæd] N moda pasajera f

fade [fed] VI/VT (cloth) decolorar[se],
desteñir[se]; (color) deslavar[se]; VI (strength)
disminuir; (lights) apagarse; (feelings, colors)
desvanecerse

fag [fæg] N offensive marica m, maricón m

faggot [fǽgət] N (male homosexual) offensive
marica m, maricón m; (bundle) haz m

fail [feɫ] VI (faculties, organs, machinery,
structure) fallar; (experiment, plan) fracasar,
frustrarse; (health) decaer; (business)
quebrar, hacer bancarrota; VI/VT (exam,
student) suspender, reprobar; **he —ed to
remember their anniversary** no se
acordó de su aniversario; **don't — to come**
no dejes de venir; **without —** sin falta

failure [féljɚ] N (of a plan, a person) fracaso m;
(of organs) insuficiencia f; (of faculties)
deterioro m; (of machinery) falla f, Sp fallo m
(of business), quiebra f, bancarrota f; (in an
exam) suspenso m; (to keep a promise, to
reach a goal) incumplimiento m; **her — to
respond puzzled me** su falta de respuesta
me confundió

faint [fent] ADJ (sound) débil; (light) tenue;
(image) vago; **to feel —** sentirse mareado;
—-hearted timorato, cobarde; N desmayo
m, desfallecimiento m; VI desmayarse,
desfallecer

faintness [féntnɪs] N (of sound) debilidad f; (of
light) tenuidad f; (of an image) vaguedad f

fair [fɛr] ADJ (just) justo; (by the rules) limpio;
(large) considerable; (of weather) bueno; (of
sky) despejado; (of wind) propicio; (of
complexion) blanco; **— market price** precio
justo en el mercado m; **— play** juego limpio
m; **— chance of success** buena probabilidad
de éxito f; **the — sex** el sexo bello; **that's
not —!** ¡no vale! ¡no es justo! ADV **to play —**
jugar limpio; N feria f; **—ground** real de la
feria m; **—way** calle f, fairway m

fairly [férli] ADV (justly) justamente;
(moderately) medianamente; **— difficult**
bastante difícil

fairness [férnɪs] N (justice) justicia f; (whiteness)
blancura f

fairy [féri] N hada f; (male homosexual) offensive
maricón m; **— godmother** hada madrina f;
—land país de las hadas m; **— tale** cuento de
hadas m

faith [feθ] N fe f; (fidelity) fidelidad f; **— healing**
curanderismo m; **in good —** de buena fe; **to**

have — **in someone** tener confianza en alguien; **to keep** — cumplir con la palabra

faithful [féθfəł] ADJ fiel

faithfulness [féθfəłnɪs] N fidelidad *f*

faithless [féθlɪs] ADJ (disloyal) desleal, falso; (lacking in faith, fidelity) infiel

fake [fek] N (object) objeto falso *m*; (person who fakes) farsante *mf*; ADJ falso; — **pearls** perlas de fantasía *f pl*; N (in sports) amague *m*, finta *f*; VT (render false, counterfeit) falsificar; **to** — **a foul** tirarse; VI/VT (feign) fingir

falcon [fǽłkən] N halcón *m*

Falkland Islands [fɔ́kləndáɪləndz] N Islas Malvinas *f pl*

fall [fɔ́ł] VI (drop) caer[se]; (slope downward) bajar; (be assigned to) tocar a, recaer sobre; **to** — **asleep** dormirse; **to** — **back** retroceder; **to** — **back on** recurrir a; **to** — **behind** atrasarse, retrasarse; **to** — **down** (drop) caerse; (fail) fallar; **to** — **in with** asociarse con; **to** — **in love** enamorarse; **to** — **off** disminuir; **to** — **out with** reñir con; **to** — **through** quedar en la nada; **he** —**s for blondes** se enamora de las rubias; **you** — **for it** te dejas engañar; N (drop) caída *f*; (of a terrain) declive *m*; (season) otoño *m*; — **guy** cabeza de turco *mf*; —**ing out** desavenencia *f*, pique *m*; —**ing star** estrella fugaz *f*; —**s** catarata *f*, salto de agua *m*

fallacious [fələ́ʃəs] ADJ falaz

fallacy [fǽləsi] N (false notion) falacia *f*; (false argument) sofisma *m*

fallen [fɔ́lən] *see* fall

fallible [fǽləbəł] ADJ falible

Fallopian tubes [fəlópiəntúbz] ADJ trompas de Falopio *f pl*

fallout [fɔ́laʊt] N (particle-settling) precipitación radiactiva *f*; (consequences) repercusiones *f pl*

fallow [fǽlo] ADJ baldío, en barbecho; N barbecho *m*; VT dejar en barbecho

false [fɔ́łs] ADJ falso; **to bear** — **witness** jurar en falso; — **advertising** publicidad engañosa *f*; — **alarm** falsa alarma *f*; — **arrest** detención ilegal *f*; — **pretense** estafa *f*; — **start** salida en falso *f*; — **step** paso en falso *m*; — **teeth** dentadura postiza *f*

falsehood [fɔ́łshʊd] N falsedad *f*, mentira *f*

falseness [fɔ́łsnɪs] N falsedad *f*

falsify [fɔ́łsəfaɪ] VT falsificar, falsear

falter [fɔ́łtɚ] VI (hesitate) vacilar, entrecortarse; (stutter) titubear

fame [fem] N fama *f*

famed [femd] ADJ afamado

familiar [fəmíljɚ] ADJ (generally known) familiar, conocido; (informal) familiar; (too friendly) confianzudo; (closely personal) íntimo; **to be** — **with a subject** conocer bien un tema

familiarity [fəmɪljǽrɪɒi] N familiaridad *f*

family [fǽmli] N familia *f*; — **doctor** médico general *m*; — **jewels** *vulg* cojones *m pl*; — **man** hombre de familia *m*; — **name** apellido *m*; — **planning** planificación familiar *f*; — **practice** medicina familiar *f*; — **room** cuarto de estar *m*; — **tree** árbol genealógico *m*; — **values** valores tradicionales *m pl*

famine [fǽmɪn] N (lack of food) hambruna *f*, hambre *f*; (scarcity) escasez *f*

famished [fǽmɪʃt] ADJ hambriento, muerto de hambre; **to be** — morirse de hambre

famous [féməs] ADJ famoso

fan [fæn] N (handheld) abanico *m*; (electrical) ventilador *m*; (for cleaning grain) aventadora *f*; (of sports) aficionado -da *mf*, hincha *mf*; (of a person) admirador -ora *mf*; — **belt** correa del ventilador *f*; — **mail** correo de admiradores *m*; VT (blow air) abanicar; (enliven) avivar; **to** — **out** abrirse en abanico

fanatic [fənǽDɪk] ADJ & N fanático -ca *mf*

fanaticism [fənǽDɪsɪzəm] N fanatismo *m*

fanciful [fǽnsɪfəł] ADJ (whimsical) caprichoso; (imaginary) imaginario; (given to fantasy) fantasioso

fancy [fǽnsi] N fantasía *f*; (whim) capricho *m*; **to strike one's** — gustarle a alguien; **to take a** — **to** aficionarse a; **he took a** — **to his teacher** se enamoró de su maestra; ADJ (luxurious) de lujo; (elaborate) elaborado; (strange) estrafalario; — **free** despreocupado; — **work** bordado fino *m*; VT imaginar[se]; **he fancies himself an artist** se cree artista; **just** — **the idea!** ¡figúrate!

fanfare [fǽnfɛr] N fanfarria *f*; **with great** — con bombo y platillo

fang [fæŋ] N colmillo *m*

fantasize [fǽntəsaɪz] VI fantasear

fantastic [fæntǽstɪk] ADJ fantástico

fantasy [fǽntəsi] N fantasía *f*

FAQ [frequently asked questions] [fæk] N preguntas frecuentes *f pl*

far [fɑr] ADV lejos; — **and away** sin duda; — **and wide** por todas partes; — **away/off** lejos, lejano; — **be it from me to complain** no es mi intención quejarme; — **more money** mucho más dinero; — **off we could see land** a lo lejos divisábamos tierra; **as** — **as I know** que yo sepa; **as** — **as I'm concerned** en lo que a mí respecta; **by** — con mucho; **how** — **do I need to walk?** ¿cuánto tengo que caminar? **how** — **is the church?** ¿a cuánto queda la iglesia? **so** — hasta ahora; **we talked** — **into the night** hablamos hasta entrada la noche; **we traveled as** — **as Chicago** viajamos hasta Chicago; ADJ lejano; —**fetched** (implausible) inverosímil, peregrino; (forced) traído por los cabellos; —**flung** remoto; —**off** distante; —**out** radical, poco convencional; —

reaching de gran alcance; **—sighted** (with defective vision) présbita, hipermétrope; (seeing the future) con visión de futuro; **the — corner** la esquina de más allá; **it is a — cry from what you said** dista mucho de lo que dijiste

farce [fɑrs] N farsa f

fare [fɛr] N (ticket) billete m; (ticket price) pasaje m; (price of transport) tarifa f; (food) comida f; (taxi patron) pasajero -ra mf; **—well** despedida f; **to bid —well to** despedirse de; **—well!** ¡adiós! VI **I —d well in the course** me fue bien en el curso

farm [fɑrm] N (large) hacienda f; (small) granja f; **—hand** labrador -ora mf, peón m; **—house** alquería f, caserío m; **—land** tierra de cultivo f; **— produce** productos agrícolas m pl; **—yard** (enclosed) corral m; (open) patio m; VI/VT cultivar; **to — out** (lease) dar en arriendo; (distribute) repartir; (subcontract) subcontratar

farmer [fɑrmɚ] N agricultor -ora mf; (small) granjero -ra mf; (large) hacendado -da mf

farming [fɑrmɪŋ] N agricultura f; ADJ agrícola mf

fart [fɑrt] N vulg pedo m; **old —** fam, pej viejo pesado m; VI vulg tirar[se] pedos; **to — around** vulg rascarse el culo

farther [fɑrðɚ] ADV más lejos; **it's an even — distance** es una distancia mayor todavía; **the concept was extended —** el concepto se extendió más; **— on** más adelante; ADJ más lejano

farthest [fɑrðɪst] ADJ el más lejano; ADV lo más lejos

fascinate [fǽsənet] VI/VT fascinar, alucinar

fascinating [fǽsəneDɪŋ] ADJ fascinante

fascination [fæsənéʃən] N fascinación f

fascism [fǽʃɪzəm] N fascismo m

fascist [fǽʃɪst] N fascista mf

fashion [fǽʃən] N (style) moda f; (way) manera f, modo m; **— plate** figurín m; **after a —** más o menos; **to be in —** estar de moda; VT hacer; (with metal) forjar; (with putty) moldear; (character) formar

fashionable [fǽʃənəbəl] ADJ de moda

fast [fæst] ADJ (quick) rápido, veloz; (ahead, of a watch) adelantado; (firm, permanent) firme; (closed) atrancado; (loyal) fiel; (dissolute) disipado; **—ball** recta f; **— break** contraataque m; **— food** comida rápida f; **life in the — lane** vida loca f; **— money** dinero mal habido m; **— woman** mujer ligera de cascos f; ADV (quickly) rápido, rápidamente; (firmly) firmemente; **— asleep** profundamente dormido; N ayuno m; VI ayunar; VI/VT **to —-forward** avanzar

fasten [fǽsən] VT (with buckles, buttons, hooks) abrochar[se], prender; (with ribbon, thread) atar; (door) atrancar

fastener [fǽsənɚ] N cierre m

fastidious [fæstíDɪəS] ADJ (hard to please) maniático; (painstaking) minucioso

fasting [fǽstɪŋ] N ayuno m

fat [fæt] ADJ gordo; **— cat** pez gordo m; **— cell** célula adiposa f; **— chance** ¡ni soñar! **—head** idiota mf; **— job** trabajo lucrativo m; **— profits** pingües ganancias f pl; **to get —** engordar; N (oily substance) grasa f; (animal tissue) gordura f, sebo m; **the — of the land** la abundancia de la tierra

fatal [fédl] ADJ letal

fatality [fətælɪDi] N víctima fatal f; **— rate** índice de mortalidad m

fate [fet] N (lot) destino m, fatalidad f, hado m; (outcome) suerte f; VT destinar

father [fɑ́ðɚ] N padre m; **— figure** figura paterna f; **—-in-law** suegro m; **—land** patria f; VT engenderar

fatherhood [fɑ́ðɚhʊd] N paternidad f

fatherly [fɑ́ðɚli] ADV paternal

fathom [fǽðəm] N braza f; VT (measure) sondear; (understand) comprender

fatigue [fətíg] N fatiga f; **—s** ropa de faena f; VI/VT fatigar[se], rendir[se]

fatness [fǽtnɪs] N gordura f

fatso [fǽtso] N pej gordinflón m, tonel m

fatten [fǽtn̩] VT engordar, cebar

fatty [fǽDi] ADJ adiposo, graso; **— acids** ácidos grasos m pl; N (insult for fat people) pej gordo -da mf

faucet [fɔ́sɪt] N grifo m, llave f

fault [fɔlt] N (defect, misdeed) falta f; (responsibility) culpa f; (geological) falla f; **—finder** criticón -ona mf; **no-—** sin culpa; **careful to a —** demasiado cuidadoso; **to be at —** ser culpable; **to find — with** criticar a

faultless [fɔ́ltlɪs] ADJ perfecto

faulty [fɔ́lti] ADJ defectuoso; (grammar) vicioso

fauna [fɔ́nə] N fauna f

faux pas [fopɑ́] N gaffe f, metedura de pata f

favor [févɚ] N (kind act, goodwill) favor m, gracia f; (popularity) popularidad f; (party gift) sorpresa f; VT (give help, show preference) favorecer; (foster) propiciar; (approve of) estar a favor de; **they are —ed to win** son los favoritos; **she —s her mother** se parece a su madre; **he's out of —** ha caído en desgracia

favorable [févɚəbəl] ADJ favorable

favorite [févɚɪt] ADJ & N preferido -da mf, favorito -ta mf, predilecto -ta mf

favoritism [févɚɪtɪzəm] N favoritismo m

fawn [fɔn] N cervatillo m; VI **to — over** adular

fax [fæks] N fax m, facsímil m; VT faxear, enviar por fax

FBI [Federal Bureau of Investigation] [éfbíáí] N FBI m

fear [fır] N miedo *m*, temor *m*; — **of God** temor de Dios *m*; VI/VT (be afraid of) temer, tenerle miedo a; (suspect) temerse; **to — for** temer por

fearful [fírfəl] ADJ (causing fear) terrible, espantoso; (showing fear) temeroso, miedoso, medroso

fearless [fírlıs] ADJ intrépido

fearlessness [fírlısnıs] N intrepidez *f*

feasible [fízəbəl] ADJ factible

feast [fist] N (party, religious celebration) fiesta *f*; (abundant meal) festín *m*, banquete *m*; VI **to — on** darse un festín de; **to — one's eyes on** deleitarse la vista con

feat [fit] N (heroic act) hazaña *f*; (achievement) logro *m*

feather [féðɚ] N pluma *f*; **a — in one's cap** un triunfo personal; —**weight** peso pluma *m*; **birds of a — flock together** Dios los cría y ellos se juntan; VI/VT (grow feathers, cover with feathers) emplumar; (change blade angle) poner horizontal

feature [fítʃɚ] N (characteristic) aspecto *m*, característica *f*; (newspaper article) reportaje *m*; (facial) facción *f*, fisonomía *f*, rasgo *m*; — **article** artículo principal *m*; — **film** largometraje *m*; VT (give prominence to) destacar; (depict) mostrar; **this film —s John Smith** esta película cuenta con la actuación de John Smith; — **that!** ¡imagínate! VI figurar

February [fébjuɛri] N febrero *m*

fecal [fíkəl] ADJ fecal

feces [físiz] N PL heces *f pl*

fed [fɛd] *see* feed

federal [fédɚəl] ADJ federal

federation [fɛdɚéʃən] N federación *f*

fee [fi] N (professional) honorarios *m pl*; (artist) cachet *m*; (admission) derecho de admisión *m*; —**s** (university) matrícula *f*

feeble [fíbəl] ADJ (person) débil, endeble; (sound, light) tenue; —-**minded** (retarded) *pej* retrasado; (stupid) tonto

feed [fid] VI/VT (supply with food, materials) alimentar[se]; (prompt lines) apuntar; (broadcast) transmitir; **he —s sugar cubes to his horse** le da terrones de azúcar a su caballo; **I fed him a lie** le dije una mentira; **to be fed up** estar harto, estar hasta la coronilla; VI **to — into** desembocar en; N (fodder) pienso *m*, cebo *m*; (transmission) transmisión *f*; —**back** (electronic, mechanical) retroalimentación *f*; (critical) respuesta *f*, reacción *f*

feeding [fíDıŋ] N alimentación *f*; —**ing frenzy** (of the press) escándalo periodístico *m*; (of sharks, etc.) carnicería *f*; — **tube** sonda de alimentación *f*

feel [fil] VI/VT (perceive, experience) sentir[se]; (examine with the hands) palpar, manosear; (suffer) sufrir; (have an opinion) creer; VI (grope, check out) tantear; (seem) parecer; **to — one's way** tantear el camino, andar a tientas; **I — for you** te compadezco; **to — up/off** toquetear, manosear; **it —s soft** está suave al tacto; **I — like a coffee** tengo ganas de tomar un café; **to — up to something** sentirse capaz de algo; N (feeling) sensación *f*; (sense) tacto *m*; (ability) don *m*; (groping) manoseo *m*, toqueteo *m*

feeler [fílɚ] N (of insects) antena *f*; (of snails) cuerno *m*; (person who feels) persona emotiva *f*; **to put out —s** tantear el terreno

feeling [fílıŋ] N (sense of touch) tacto *m*; (instance of physical perception) sensación *f*; (emotion) sentimiento *m*; (opinion) opinión *f*; (compassion) compasión *f*; **a — of sadness** un sentimiento de tristeza; **with —** con sentimiento; **to hurt someone's —s** herirle los sentimientos a alguien; ADJ sensible

feign [fen] VI/VT fingir, simular, aparentar

feisty [fáısti] ADJ (aggressive) pugnaz, belicoso; (energetic) vivaz

feline [fílaın] ADJ felino

fell [fɛl] VT (an animal) derribar; (a tree) talar; N (pelt) piel de animal *f*; **in one — swoop** de un golpe

fell [fɛl] *see* fall

fellatio [fəléʃio] N felación *f*

fellow [félo] N (member) miembro *m*; (scholar) becario -ria *mf*; (man or boy) tipo *m*; — **citizen** conciudadano -na *mf*; — **man** prójimo *m*; — **student** compañero -ra de clase *mf*

fellowship [féloʃıp] N (friendly relations) amistad *f*; (community of interest) confraternidad *f*; (scholarship) beca *f*

felony [féləni] N delito grave *m*

felt [fɛlt] N fieltro *m*; ADJ de fieltro

felt [fɛlt] *see* feel

female [fímel] N (animal) hembra *f*; (person) mujer *f*; ADJ (animal, fastener) hembra; (person) femenino

feminine [fémənın] ADJ femenino

femininity [fémənínıti] N feminidad *f*

feminism [fémənızəm] N feminismo *m*

feminist [fémınıst] ADJ & N feminista *mf*

femur [fímɚ] N fémur *m*

fence [fɛns] N (barrier) cerca *f*, cerco *m*, valla *f*; (person who deals in stolen goods) *Am* reducidor -ora *mf*, *Sp* perista *mf*; (store for stolen goods) tienda de artículos robados *f*; **to be sitting on the —** estar indeciso; VT (enclose) cercar, vallar; **to — in** cercar; **to — off** dividir con una cerca; VI (sport) practicar esgrima

fencing [fénsıŋ] N (dealing in stolen goods) tráfico en artículos robados *m*; (barrier) cerca *f*; (construction of barrier) cerco *m*; (sport) esgrima *f*

fender [fɛ́ndɚ] N guardabarro[s] *m sg*, guardafango *m*; — **bender** choquecito *m*

ferment[1] [fɜ́ment] N fermento *m*

ferment[2] [fɚmént] VI/VT fermentar[se]

fermentation [fɜmɛntéʃən] N fermentación *f*

fern [fɜn] N helecho *m*

ferocious [fərófəs] ADJ feroz, fiero

ferocity [fərásɪDi] N ferocidad *f*, fiereza *f*

ferret [fɛ́rɪt] N hurón *m*; VI **to — out** hurgar

Ferris wheel [fɛ́rɪshwił] N rueda gigante *f*

ferry [fɛ́ri] N ferry *m*, transbordador *m*; — **boat** ferry *m*; VT transportar de una orilla a otra; VI viajar en ferry

fertile [fɜ́dl̩] ADJ fértil, fecundo

fertility [fɚtílɪDi] N fertilidad *f*

fertilization [fɜdl̩ɪzéʃən] N fertilización *f*, fecundación *f*

fertilize [fɜ́dl̩aɪz] VT fertilizar; (female, egg) fecundar; (land) abonar

fertilizer [fɜ́dl̩aɪzɚ] N fertilizante *m*, abono *m*

fervent [fɜ́vənt] ADJ ferviente

fervor [fɜ́vɚ] N fervor *m*

fester [fɛ́stɚ] VI (form pus) supurar; (rankle) enconarse

festival [fɛ́stəvəł] N festival *m*

festive [fɛ́stɪv] ADJ festivo

festivity [fɛstívɪDi] N festividad *f*

fetal [fídl̩] ADJ fetal; — **position** posición fetal *f*; — **monitoring** monitorización fetal *f*

fetch [fɛtʃ] VT *Sp* ir a por; *Am* ir a buscar; **the ring —ed a fancy price** nos dieron una buena suma por el anillo; VI/VT (dog) buscar

fetching [fɛ́tʃɪŋ] ADJ atractivo

fetish [fɛ́Dɪʃ] N fetiche *m*

fetter [fɛ́Dɚ] N grillete *m*; VT engrillar

fetus [fíDəs] N feto *m*

feud [fjud] N enemistad hereditaria *f*; VI pelear

feudal [fjúdl̩] ADJ feudal

fever [fívɚ] N fiebre *f*, calentura *f*; — **blister** herpes febril *m*; — **pitch** punto álgido *m*

feverish [fívɚɪʃ] ADJ (related to fever) febril; (having a fever) afiebrado, destemplado

few [fju] ADJ & PRON pocos; —**er than expected** menos de los que se esperaba; **a —** unos pocos, algunos; **the —** una minoría

fiancé [fiɑnsé] N novio *m*, prometido *m*; —**e** novia *f*, prometida *f*

fiasco [fiǽsko] N fiasco *m*

fib [fɪb] N mentirilla *f*; VI decir mentirillas

fiber [fáɪbɚ] N (textile) fibra *f*; (animal, vegetable) hebra *f*; —**optic** de fibra óptica; —**glass** fibra de vidrio *f*

fibrous [fáɪbrəs] ADJ fibroso

fickle [fíkəł] ADJ veleidoso, mudable

fiction [fíkʃən] N ficción *f*

fictional [fíkʃən̩l] ADJ novelesco

fictitious [fɪktíʃəs] ADJ ficticio

fiddle [fídl̩] N violín *m*; VI (play the violin) tocar el violín; **to — around** perder el tiempo; **to — with** juguetear con; **they like to — with the computer** siempre juguetean con la computadora

fidelity [fɪdélɪDi] N fidelidad *f*; **high —** alta fidelidad *f*

fidget [fídʒɪt] VI estar inquieto; **stop —ing!** ¡deja de moverte!

fiduciary [fɪdúʃiɛri] ADJ & N fiduciario -ria *mf*

field [fíłd] N (land, computers, heraldry, optics) campo *m*; (in sports) campo *m*; *Am* cancha *f*; (of oil) yacimiento *m*; (group of competitors) participantes *mf pl*; (of knowledge) campo *m*, terreno *m*; — **artillery** artillería de campaña *f*; — **day** (day for outdoor activity) día de campo *m*; (for military maneuvers) día de maniobras *m*; (unrestrained enjoyment) festín *m*; — **glasses** binoculares *m pl*; — **goal** gol de campo *m*; — **mouse** ratón de campo *m*; — **trip** (in school) paseo escolar *m*; (in science) viaje de estudio *m*; —**work** trabajo de campo *m*; VT (a baseball) atrapar, fildear; (questions) contestar

fielding [fíłdɪŋ] N (of questions) contestación *f*; (of baseballs) fildeo *m*

fiend [find] N (devil) demonio *m*, diablo *m*; (fanatic) fanático -ca *mf*

fierce [fɪrs] ADJ (animals) feroz, fiero; (illness) espantoso; (storms, etc.) furioso, espantoso; (competition, debate) intenso, encarnizado; (look) torvo

fierceness [fɪrsnɪs] N ferocidad *f*, bravura *f*

fiery [fáɪəri] ADJ (passionate) fogoso; (hot, causing burning sensation) ardiente

fife [faɪf] N pífano *m*

fifteen [fɪftín] NUM quince

fifth [fɪfθ] ADJ & N quinto *m*; (measure of liquor) tres cuartos de un litro *m pl*

fifty [fífti] NUM cincuenta; ADV **to go —-—** ir a medias; ADJ **a —-— chance** un cincuenta por ciento de probabilidades

fig [fɪg] N higo *m*; — **leaf** hoja de higuera *f*; — **tree** higuera *f*; **it's not worth a —** no vale ni un pepino/pito

fight [faɪt] N (combat) lucha *f*, combate *m*; **the — against AIDS** la lucha contra el SIDA; (argument) pelea *f*, riña *f*; VI/VT (combat) luchar [con], pelear [con]; VI (argue) pelear, reñir; **to — a duel** batirse a duelo; **to — back** (to hold back) contener; (resist) resistir; **to — it out** arreglarlo a los golpes; **to — off** rechazar; **to — one's way through** abrirse camino a la fuerza

fighter [fáɪDɚ] N (boxer) boxeador -ora *mf*; (someone who fights) luchador -ora *mf*; (dog, cock) animal de pelea/riña *m*; — **airplane** avión caza *m*

fighting [fáɪDɪŋ] N (fight) lucha *f*; ADJ

combativo; — **chance** posibilidad remota *f*;
— **words** palabras incendiarias *f pl*
figurative [fígjə-əDIV] ADJ (art) figurativo;
(language) figurado
figure [fígjə-] N (number, amount) cifra *f*; (form,
bodily shape, representation, dance move,
syllogism) figura *f*; (character) personaje *m*;
—**head** figurón de proa *m*; — **of speech**
figura retórica *f*; —**s** (written symbols)
números *m pl*; — **skating** patinaje artístico
m; **to cut a poor** — dar una mala impresión;
VI (appear) figurar; VI/VT (think)
imaginar[se], figurar[se]; **to — in** tener en
cuenta; **to — on** contar con; **to — out** (solve)
resolver; (calculate) calcular; **it —s!** no me
extraña, era de esperar; VT calcular
Fijian [fídʒiən] N fijiano -na *mf*
Fiji Islands [fídʒiáiləndz] N Islas Fiji *f pl*
filament [fíləmənt] N filamento *m*
file [faɪɫ] N (documents) archivo *m*; (for
computers) archivo *m*, fichero *m*; (official
report) expediente *m*, legajo *m*; (line) fila *f*;
(tool) lima *f*; — **compression** compresión
de archivos *f*; — **format** formato de archivo/
fichero *m*; —**name** nombre de archivo *m*; —
server servidor *m*; **on**— archivado; **filing
cabinet** fichero *m*, archivador *m*; VT (papers)
archivar; (news story) entregar; (tax return,
claim, etc.) presentar; **to — a suit** entablar
una demanda, querellarse; VI (for a job)
presentarse; (walk in a line) desfilar; VI/VT
(smooth) limar
filial [fíliəɫ] ADJ filial
filiation [fɪliéʃən] N filiación *f*
filibuster [fíləbʌstə-] VI/VT practicar
obstrucción parlamentaria; N filibusterismo
m, obstrucción *f*
filigree [fílɪgri] N filigrana *f*
fill [fɪɫ] VI/VT (glass, container) llenar[se]; (a hole,
a pastry, land) rellenar; **the smell —ed the
room** la habitación se llenó del olor; **the
airline —ed the position** la compañía
aérea llenó el cargo; **the new employee
—ed the vacancy** el nuevo empleado ocupó
el cargo vacante; VT (a tooth) empastar;
(prescription, order) despachar; (a need)
satisfacer; VI (sails) hinchar; **to — out** llenar;
to — in (inform) informar; (fill out a form)
llenar; (replace) sustituir; **to — up** llenarse
hasta el tope
fillet[1] [fɪlé] N filete *m*; VT filetear
fillet[2] [fílɪt] N cinta *f*
filling [fílɪŋ] N (act) rellenado *m*; (filler) relleno
m; (of a tooth) empaste *m*; — **station**
estación de servicio *f*, gasolinera *f*
filly [fíli] N potranca *f*
film [fɪɫm] N (video) película *f*, filme *m*;
(celluloid) película *f*, cinta *f*; (thin coating)
película *f*; — **industry** industria

cinematográfica *f*; —**maker** cineasta *mf*;
VI/VT filmar, cinematografiar
filming [fílmɪŋ] N filmación *f*
filter [fíltə-] N filtro *m*; VI/VT filtrar[se]
filtering [fíltə-ɪŋ] N filtración *f*
filth [fɪlθ] N (dirt, despicable person) mugre *f*,
suciedad *f*; (moral impurity) porquería *f*;
(vulgar material) obscenidades *f pl*
filthiness [fílθɪnɪs] N suciedad *f*
filthy [fílθi] ADJ (dirty) cochino, mugriento;
(vile) puerco, cochino; *Sp* guarro; (obscene)
obsceno; — **rich** riquísimo
filtration [fɪltréʃən] N filtración *f*
fin [fɪn] N aleta *f*
final [fáɪnɫ] ADJ (result, conclusion) final; (last)
último; (conclusive) definitivo; — **score**
resultado final *m*; — **stretch** recta final *f*; N
(in sports) final *f*; (exam) examen final *m*
finalist [fáɪnɫɪst] N finalista *mf*
finalize [fáɪnɫaɪz] VT completar, ultimar
finally [fáɪnɫi] ADV (at last) finalmente, por fin;
(lastly) finalmente, por último
finance [fáɪnæns] N finanza *f*; —**s** finanzas *f pl*;
VI/VT (to fund) financiar; (to purchase on
credit) comprar financiado
financial [fɪnǽnʃəɫ] ADJ financiero; —
disclosure divulgación financiera *f*
financier [fɪnænsír] N financiero -ra *mf*
financing [fáɪnænsɪŋ] N financiamiento *m*; *Am*
financiación *f*
find [faɪnd] VT hallar, encontrar; (discover)
descubrir; (determine innocence or guilt)
declarar; VI (determine officially) fallar; **to —
fault with** criticar a, censurar a; **to — out**
(discover) descubrir; (verify) averiguar; N
hallazgo *m*
finding [fáɪndɪŋ] N fallo *m*; —**s** resultados *m pl*
fine [faɪn] ADJ (wine, sand, hair, precious metal)
fino; (thread) delgado; (cloth) delicado;
(artist, athlete) consumado; (manners)
refinado; (good-looking person) atractivo,
guapo; (weather) bueno; (distinction) sutil; —
arts bellas artes *f pl*; — **print** letra pequeña *f*,
letra chica *f*; **I'm** — estoy bien; **to feel** —
sentirse muy bien de salud; **to have a** —
time pasarlo bien; N multa *f*; VT multar; **to
—-tune** (a receiver) sintonizar; (an engine)
ajustar; (a plan) afinar
finery [fáɪnəri] N galas *f pl*
finesse [fɪnés] N (subtlety) sutileza *f*; (tact)
diplomacia *f*; VI usar artimañas; VT conseguir
por artimañas
finger [fíŋgə-] N dedo *m*; — **food** canapé *m*,
aperitivo *m*; —**nail** uña *f*; —**print** huella
dactilar/digital *f*; —**tip** punta del dedo *f*; **at
one's —tips** al alcance de la mano; **little** —
dedo meñique *m*; **middle** — dedo del
corazón *m*; **to give someone the** — hacerle
un gesto obsceno a alguien; **I'll keep my —s**

crossed cruzo los dedos; **to wrap someone around one's** — meterse a alguien en el bolsillo; **I can't put my** — **on it** no sabría decir lo que es; VT (play a guitar) tañer; (squeal on) delatar

finicky [fínɪki] ADJ melindroso, dengoso

finish [fínɪʃ] VI/VT (end) terminar[se], finalizar[se]; VT (polish) pulir; (varnish) barnizar; (kill) liquidar; **to** — **off** acabar con, rematar; **to** — **up** terminar; N (ending) final m; (decisive end) fin m; (polish, treatment) acabado m; (varnish) barniz m; (coat of paint) última mano f; — **line** meta f; **with a rough** — sin pulir

finished [fínɪʃt] ADJ (doomed) acabado; (polished) pulido

finite [fáɪnaɪt] ADJ finito

Finland [fínlənd] N finlandia f

Finn [fɪn] N finlandés -esa mf, finés -esa mf

Finnish [fínɪʃ] ADJ finlandés, finés

fir [fɝ] N abeto m

fire [faɪr] N (flame) fuego m; (conflagration) incendio m; (passion) ardor m; (for cigarettes, hearths) lumbre f; — **alarm** alarma contra incendios f; —**cracker** triquitraque m; — **drill** simulacro de incendio m; — **department** cuerpo de bomberos m; — **engine** coche de bomberos m, autobomba f; — **escape** escalera de incendios f; — **extinguisher** extinguidor [de incendios] m, extintor m; — **fighter** bombero -ra mf; —**fly** luciérnaga f; — **hydrant** boca de incendio f; — **insurance** seguro contra incendios m; —**man** (who extinguishes) bombero m; (who stokes) fogonero m; —**place** hogar m, chimenea f; —**proof** ininflamable, a prueba de incendio; — **sale** venta de liquidación f; —**side** hogar m; — **station** estación de bomberos f; — **trap** edificio sin medios de escape en caso de incendio m; —**wall** cortafuegos m sg; —**wood** leña f; —**works** fuegos artificiales m pl; **when he finds out, there will be** —**works** cuando se entere, se va a armar la gorda; **to be on** — estar quemándose; **to catch** — incendiarse, prenderse fuego; **to set** — **to** prender fuego a, incendiar; **under** — bajo fuego; **to play with** — jugar con fuego; **firing pin** percutor m; **firing squad** pelotón de fusilamiento m; VT (pottery) cocer; (an employee) despedir; (a projectile) lanzar; **to** —**proof** hacer incombustible, ignifugar; VI/VT (a gun) disparar; VI **to** — **up** entusiasmar; **to** — **off** (gun) disparar; (letter) despachar

firm [fɝm] ADJ (solid, unwavering) firme; (fixed) fijo; (not fluctuating, as prices) estable; VI/VT **to** — **up** (finalize) concretar; (harden) endurecer; N firma f; —**ware** programas almacenados en circuitos integrados m pl

firmly [fɝmli] ADV con firmeza, firmemente

firmness [fɝmnɪs] N firmeza f

first [fɝst] ADJ primero; — **aid** primeros auxilios m pl; — **base** primera base f, inicial f; — **baseman** primera base mf, inicialista mf; **to get to** — **base** comenzar con éxito; —**born** primogénito -ta mf; — **chapter** capítulo primero m, primer capítulo m; — **class** primera clase f; —-**class** de primera clase; — **cousin** primo hermano; —-**degree** (burn) de primer grado; (murder) en primer grado; — **floor** (ground floor) planta baja f; **for the** — **time** por primera vez; — **half** primer tiempo m; —**hand** de primera mano; — **lady** primera dama f; — **name** nombre de pila m; — **person** primera persona f; —-**rate** de primera clase; ADV (before anything else) primero; **I'd die** — antes la muerte; **at** — al principio; — **off** al principio; N (first in series) primero -ra mf; (low gear) primera f

fiscal [fískəl] ADJ fiscal; — **period** año fiscal m

fish [fɪʃ] N (in water) pez m; (out of water) pescado m; — **farm** piscifactoría f; —**hook** anzuelo m; — **market** pescadería f; — **story** patraña f; **like a** — **out of water** como sapo de otro pozo; **neither** — **nor fowl** ni chicha ni limonada; **I have other** — **to fry** tengo otras cosas mejores que hacer; VI/VT pescar; **to** — **out** sacar, rebuscar; **to** — **for compliments** buscar cumplidos; **to** —**tail** colear

fisherman [fíʃɚmən] N pescador m

fishery [fíʃəri] N (for breeding) piscifactoría f; (for fishing) pesquería f; (industry) industria pesquera f

fishing [fíʃɪŋ] N pesca f; — **pole/rod** caña de pescar f; — **tackle** aparejos de pescar m pl; **to go** — ir de pesca

fishy [fíʃi] ADJ (of smell, taste) a pescado; (suspicious) sospechoso

fissure [fíʃɚ] N fisura f

fist [fɪst] N puño m; —**fight** pelea a puñetazos f

fistula [fístʃələ] N fístula f

fit [fɪt] ADJ (suited) apto; (healthy) en buen estado físico; **are you** — **for driving?** ¿estás en condiciones de manejar? ADV **he didn't see** — **to greet her** no se dignó a saludarla; N (process of fitting) prueba f; (mechanical union) encaje m; (attack of a disease) ataque m; (sudden outburst) rapto m; (of anger, coughing) acceso m; **to throw a** — tener una pataleta; **by** —**s and starts** a trompicones; **that suit is a good** — ese traje le queda bien; VT (be suitable for) adecuarse a; (be in agreement with) cuadrar con, ajustarse a; (measure for clothes) tomarle las medidas a; (make suitable) capacitar, preparar; **to** — **in with** acomodarse a; **I tried to** — **you in** traté de incluirte; VI (conform to contours of a person) quedarle bien a alguien; (conform to the contours of a mechanism) encajar

fitness [fítnɪs] N (suitability) aptitud *f*; (health) buen estado físico *m*

fitting [fídɪŋ] ADJ apropiado; N ajuste *m*; (trying on) prueba *f*

five [faɪv] NUM cinco; — **hundred** quinientos

fix [fɪks] VT (repair, arrange) arreglar; (place permanently, determine) fijar; (prepare food) preparar; **to — up** arreglar, aviar; **to get an animal —ed** castrar a un animal; **I was —ing to call** estaba a punto de llamar; **I'll — you!** ¡ya te arreglo! N (predicament) apuro *m*, aprieto *m*; (temporary repair) arreglo provisorio *m*; (narcotic injection) chute *m*; **to get a — on** localizar

fixed [fɪkst] ADJ (stationary) fijo; (arranged in advance) arreglado; — **term** a plazo fijo; —- **rate mortgage** hipoteca de tasa fija *f*

fixture [fíkstʃɚ] N (bath, kitchen component) instalaciones *f pl*; **she's a permanent — in this office** está siempre en la oficina

fizzle [fízəl] VI (fail) fracasar; **to — [out]** (make a noise) apagarse chisporroteando; (interest) esfumarse

flabby [flǽbi] ADJ flácido/fláccido

flaccid [flǽsɪd] ADJ flácido/fláccido

flag [flæg] N (also in golf) bandera *f*; —**pole** mástil *m*; —**staff** mástil *m*; —**stone** losa *f*, baldosa *f*; VT (adorn with flags) embanderar; (mark with flags) marcar con banderas; (for attention) marcar, identificar; **to — [down]** hacer parar; VI (diminish) menguar

flagrant [flégrənt] ADV flagrante

flair [fler] N (aptitude) aptitud *f*, facilidad *f*; (style) estilo *m*

flak [flæk] N (antiartillery fire) fuego antiaéreo *m*; (criticism) crítica *f*

flake [flek] N (snow) copo *m*; (small thin piece) escama *f*; (eccentric person) chiflado -da *mf*; VI descascararse

flamboyant [flæmbóɪənt] ADJ (clothes) llamativo; (behavior) extravagante

flame [flem] N llama *f*; — **thrower** lanzallamas *m sg*; **old —** viejo amor *m*; VI llamear, flamear, encenderse

flaming [flémɪŋ] ADJ (emitting flames) llameante; (like a flame) flamígero; (ardent) ardiente; — **red** rojo encendido

flammable [flǽməbəl] ADJ inflamable

flank [flæŋk] N (of a bastion or army) flanco *m*; (of an animal) ijar *m*; VT flanquear

flannel [flǽnl] N franela *f*, lanilla *f*

flap [flæp] VI (wings) aletear; (flag) flamear; VT (wings) batir; (arms) sacudir; N (of a jacket, pocket) cartera *f*; (of a saddle, table) hoja *f*; (of an airplane) alerón *m*; (action of flapping) aleteo *m*

flare [fler] VI (burn unsteadily) llamear; (become

wider) ensancharse; **to — up** (fire) avivarse; (activity, illness) recrudecer; VT (a skirt) levantar; (a flame) avivar; (a pipe) abocinar; (signal by flare) señalar con bengala; N (flaring light, burst of flame) llamarada *f*; (signal light) bengala *f*; (sudden emotional outburst) arranque *m*; (outward curvature) vuelo *m*; —**up** recrudecimiento *m*

flash [flæʃ] N (of light) destello *m*, ráfaga *f*; (of explosion) fogonazo *m*; (news, camera, vision, computer memory) flash *m*; —**back** flashback *m*, escena retrospectiva *f*; —**bulb** flash *m*; — **flood** riada *f*; —**light** linterna *f*; — **of hope** rayo de esperanza *m*; — **of lightning** relampagueo *m*, rayo *m*; **in a —** en un instante; VI/VT (shine) destellar [sobre]; (expose oneself) exhibir[se]; VI (gleam) relucir, fulgurar, relampaguear; (appear) aparecer; VT (display) ostentar; **to — by** pasar como un relámpago

flashing [flǽʃɪŋ] ADJ destellante

flashy [flǽʃi] ADJ (colorful) llamativo; (ostentatious) ostentoso; (tasteless) chillón, de mal gusto

flask [flæsk] N (glass container) frasco *m*; (in a laboratory) matraz *m*, redoma *f*; (for alcoholic beverages) petaca *f*

flat [flæt] ADJ (surface) plano; (land) llano; (skin) liso; (spatial orientation) horizontal, acostado; (city) arrasado, aplastado; (shoes, nose) chato; (tire) desinflado, pinchado; (color) apagado; (beer, tonic water) sin gas; (mood) soso; (paint) mate; (denial) terminante; (photo) sin contraste; (pitch) demasiado grave; (musical note) bemol; —**footed** con pie plano; — **rate** tarifa fija *f*; — **tax** impuesto de tasa única *m*; **trading was —** hubo poco movimiento bursátil; **to be — broke** estar completamente pelado; **to fall —** (of a body) caer de plano/redondo; (of a joke) caer mal; (of a plan) fracasar; N (shoe) zapato sin tacón *m*; (flat tire) desinflado *m*, pinchadura *f*, pinchazo *m*; (wooden box) caja para plantas *f*; (musical note) bemol *m*; —**iron** plancha *f*; ADV —**-out** (directly) absolutamente; (at full speed) a toda velocidad; **in two minutes** — en dos minutos exactos

flatten [flǽtn] VI/VT (make flat) achatar[se], aplanar[se]; VT (knock down) tumbar, voltear; (raze) arrasar

flatter [flǽDɚ] VI/VT (manipulate) lisonjear, adular; (praise) halagar; **this picture —s you** esta foto te favorece; **I was —ed by his attentions** me halagaron sus atenciones

flatterer [flǽDərɚ] N lisonjero -ra *mf*, adulador -ora *mf*

flattering [flǽDɚɪŋ] ADJ (comment) lisonjero, halagüeño; (person) adulón

flattery [flǽɒɔri] N lisonja f, adulación f, halago m

flatulence [flǽtʃələns] N flatulencia f

flaunt [flɔnt] VI/VT ostentar, lucir[se]

flavor [flévɚ] N (taste, quality) sabor m; (flavoring) condimento m; VT sazonar

flavorless [flévɚlɪs] ADJ insípido

flaw [flɔ] N (in character, in construction) defecto m; (in an argument) falla f

flawless [flɔ́lɪs] ADJ (logic) impecable; (behavior) intachable, irreprochable; (appearance) perfecto

flax [flæks] N lino m

flea [fli] N pulga f; — **collar** collar antipulgas m; — **market** Sp rastro m; Am mercado de [las] pulgas m

fled [flɛd] see flee

flee [fli] VI huir; VT huir de

fleece [flis] N vellón m; VT (shear) trasquilar, esquilar; (defraud) estafar; (in card games) pelar, desplumar

fleet [flit] N (of boats, buses) flota f; (of cars) parque m; ADJ veloz

fleeting [flídɪŋ] ADJ fugaz, efímero, pasajero

flemish [flémɪʃ] ADJ & N flamenco -ca mf

flesh [flɛʃ] N carne f; (of a fruit) pulpa f; — **and blood** carne y hueso; **of my own — and blood** de mi propia sangre; **in the —** en persona; VI/VT **to — out** (a character) dar cuerpo a; (an argument) desarrollar

fleshy [fléʃi] ADJ (succulent) carnoso; (fat) metido en carnes

flew [flu] see fly

flexibility [flɛksəbílɪɒi] N flexibilidad f

flexible [fléksəbəł] ADJ flexible

flicker [flíkɚ] VI (stars) titilar; (candle) parpadear; N (of light) parpadeo m, titilación f; (of hope) rayo m

flier [fláɪɚ] N (one who flies) volador -ora mf; (aviator) aviador -ora mf; (leaflet) volante m

flight [flaɪt] N (act of flying, trip) vuelo m; (trajectory) trayectoria f; (flock of birds) bandada f; (group of military aircraft) escuadrilla f; (escape) fuga f, huida f; — **attendant** auxiliar de vuelo mf; — **plan** plan de vuelo m; — **school** escuela de aviación f; — **recorder** caja negra f; — **simulator** simulador de vuelo m, registrador de vuelo m; **a — of fancy** una fantasía; — **of stairs** tramo de escalera m; **to put to —** poner en fuga; **to take —** darse a la fuga

flimsy [flímzi] ADJ (structure, argument) endeble; (excuse) flojo, pobre

flinch [flɪntʃ] VI pestañear

fling [flɪŋ] VT arrojar, lanzar; **she flung herself at the attacker** se le tiró arriba al atacante; **he flung himself into his work** se dedicó de lleno a su trabajo; **he flung**

open the door abrió la puerta de golpe; N (act of flinging) lanzamiento m; (sexual affair) aventura f

flint [flɪnt] N pedernal m

flip [flɪp] VT (a coin) tirar; (a switch on) levantar; (a switch off) bajar; (a pancake) dar vuelta; VI (go head over heels) dar una voltereta; (get excited, go crazy) volverse loco; **to — through** hojear; —**-flop** (reversal of opinion) giro de 180 grados m; (backward somersault) voltereta para atrás f; (slipper) chancleta f; — **side** la otra cara de la moneda

flippant [flípənt] ADJ (frivolous) frívolo, displicente; (impudent) impertinente

flipper [flípɚ] N aleta f

flirt [flɝt] VI coquetear; N coqueto -ta mf

flirtation [flɝtéʃən] N coquetería f, coqueteo m

flit [flɪt] VI revolotear; **a smile — s across her face** una sonrisa le cruza la cara

float [flot] VI (rest on water, air, fluctuate freely) flotar; (in soup) sobrenadar; (drift) errar, ir a la deriva; **she —ed down the stairs** se deslizó por la escalera; VT (set afloat) poner a flote; (start a company, scheme) lanzar; (issue shares) emitir; (let fluctuate) dejar flotar; (try out an idea) proponer; N (thing that floats) flotador m; (on a line) corcho m, boya f; (in a parade) carro alegórico m, carroza f; (with soda) gaseosa con helado f

flock [flɑk] N (birds, children) bandada f; (sheep) rebaño m; (worshipers) grey f; (people) muchedumbre f; VI acudir en masa, afluir; **to — around someone** rodear a alguien; **to — together** andar juntos

flog [flɑg] VT azotar

flood [flʌd] N inundación f; (of tides) creciente f; —**gate** (of a dam) compuerta f; (of a canal lock) esclusa f; — **insurance** seguro contra inundaciones m; —**light** reflector m; — **of tears** torrente de lágrimas m; **the — el** Diluvio Universal; VI/VT inundar[se], anegar[se]; (car) ahogar[se], emborrachar[se]

floor [flɔr] N (surface of a room, vehicle) suelo m, piso m; (story) piso m; (of sea) fondo m; (for dancing) pista f; (minimum level) mínimo m; **to have the —** tener la palabra; VT (knock down) tumbar, derribar; (stun, surprise) asombrar; — **it!** ¡acelera! Sp ¡mete caña!

flooring [flɔ́rɪŋ] N revestimiento m

flop [flɑp] VI (flail) zarandearse; (fish) dar coletazos; (drop) dejarse caer; (fail) fracasar; **to — down** dejarse caer, desplomarse; **to — over** voltear[se] flojamente; N (failure) fracaso m; (sound) ruido sordo m

floppy [flápi] ADJ caído; — **disk** disquete m, floppy m

flora [flɔ́rə] N flora f

florist [flɔ́rɪst] N florista mf; —**'s shop** florería f

floss [flɔs] N (silk fibers) seda floja f; (for

embroidery) hilo de seda *m*; (dental) hilo dental *m*; VI/VT pasar hilo dental [por]

flounder [fláʊndɚ] VI (in mud, etc.) andar/ moverse con dificultades; (for an answer) quedarse sin saber qué decir, perder pie; N platija *f*

flour [flaʊr] N harina *f*

flourish [flɜ́ɪʃ] VI (prosper) florecer, prosperar; VT (brandish) blandir; N (ornament, florid language, brandishing) floreo *m*; (of music) floritura *f*; (of a signature) rúbrica *f*; **in full** — en plena eclosión

flow [flo] VI (run) fluir, correr; (issue forth) surgir, brotar; (come and go) circular; (fall loosely) caer; (abound) abundar; (rise) crecer; **to — into** desembocar en, afluir a; N (of liquid) flujo *m*; (of electricity) corriente *f*; (of traffic, blood, air) circulación *f*; **—chart** diagrama de flujo *m*, organigrama *m*; **— of words** torrente de palabras *m*

flower [fláʊɚ] N flor *f*; (paragon) flor y nata *f*; **in** — en flor; **— bed** *Mex, Sp* arriate *m*; *RP* cantero *m*; **—pot** maceta *f*, tiesto *m*; **— vase** florero *m*; VI florecer

flowery [fláʊɚi] ADJ (of a garden, language) florido; (of a pattern) floreado; (of a fragrance) floral

flowing [flóɪŋ] ADJ (liquid) fluyente; (clothing) suelto

flown [flon] *see* fly

flu [flu] N gripe *f*, *Am* gripa *f*

fluctuate [flʌ́ktʃuet] VI fluctuar

fluctuation [flʌktʃuéʃən] N fluctuación *f*

fluency [flúənsi] N fluidez *f*

fluent [flúənt] ADJ fluido; **he is — in French** habla francés con fluidez/soltura

fluff [flʌf] VT mullir; (blunder) pifiar; N pelusa *f*; (blunder) pifia *f*; **this book is pure —** este libro es insustancial

fluffy [flʌ́fi] ADJ (airy) mullido; (covered with fluff) peludo

fluid [flúɪd] ADJ & N fluido *m*, líquido *m*; **— ounce** onza líquida [29.42 mililiters] *f*; **— retention** retención de líquido *f*

fluke [fluk] N (of whale) aleta *f*; (chance) chiripa *f*; **by a —** por chiripa

flung [flʌŋ] *see* fling

flunk [flʌŋk] VI/VT *Am* reprobar, *Sp* suspender; VI **to — out** *Am* salir reprobado, *Sp* salir suspendido

flunky [flʌ́ŋki] N (lackey, servant) lacayo *m*; (yes-man) adulón *m*

fluorescent [flʊrésənt] ADJ fluorescente; **— light** tubo fluorescente *m*

fluoride [flɔ́raɪd] N (chemical) fluoruro *m*; (dental aid) flúor *m*

fluorine [flɔ́rin] N flúor *m*

flurry [flɜ́ɪ] N (of snow) nevisca *f*; (of activity) frenesí *m*

flush [flʌʃ] N (rosy glow, heat) rubor *m*; (of anger) arranque *m*; (of youth, color) resplandor *m*; (of embarrassment) sonrojo *m*; (in poker) color *m*; **did you hear the — of the toilet?** ¿oíste el sonido de la cisterna? ADJ (well supplied, rich) forrado; (ruddy, reddish) rubicundo; (full) rebosante; **— with** a[l] ras de; **— against** pegado a; VI/VT (make or turn red) sonrojar[se], ruborizar[se]; (activate toilet) tirar la cadena; (rinse) baldear

fluster [flʌ́stɚ] VI/VT agitar[se], poner[se] nervioso

flute [flut] N (musical instrument) flauta *f*; (of a column) estría *f*; VT estriar

flutter [flʌ́dɚ] VI (wings) aletear; (butterfly) revolotear; (flag) tremolar; (heart) palpitar; VT (agitate) agitar; N (of wings) aleteo *m*; (of excitement) agitación *f*; (of a fly) tremolar *m*; (of the heart) palpitación *f*

flux [flʌks] N flujo *m*; **a state of —** un estado de cambio continuo

fly [flaɪ] VI (through air) volar; (from danger) huir; (flag) ondear; (kite) remontar; VT (aircraft) pilotar; (air cargo) transportar en avión; **to — away** volarse; **to — into a rage** montar en cólera; **to — off the handle** perder los estribos; **to — open [shut]** abrirse [cerrarse] de un golpe; **to — out of a room** salir disparado de un cuarto; **that idea won't —** esa idea no va a ser aceptada; **he flew the coop** se escapó; N (insect) mosca *f*; (over a zipper) bragueta *f*; **— ball** (in baseball) volea *f*, bombo *m*, elevado *m*, palomita *f*; **—catcher** papamoscas *m sg*; **—swatter** matamoscas *m sg*; **—wheel** volante *m*; **on the —** al vuelo

flying [fláɪŋ] ADJ (passing through the air) volador; (fluttering) ondeante; **with — colors** con distinción; **— saucer** platillo volador *m*; N **I hate —** no me gusta viajar en avión

foam [fom] N (suds, padding) espuma *f*; **— rubber** goma espuma *f*; VI hacer espuma; **to — at the mouth** echar espuma por la boca

focus [fókəs] N foco *m*; VI/VT (bring into or be in focus) enfocar[se]; (concentrate) centrarse; **to — on** fijarse en

fodder [fádɚ] N forraje *m*

foe [fo] N enemigo -ga *mf*

fog [fɑg] N niebla *f*; **to be in a —** estar confundido; **—horn** sirena de niebla *f*; VI/VT (confuse) ofuscar; (spray with insecticide) fumigar; (become faded) velar[se]; **to — up** (window) empañar[se]; (one's sight) nublar[se]; **the airport was —ged in** el aeropuerto estaba cerrado por niebla

foggy [fági] ADJ (weather) brumoso, nebuloso; (window) empañado; (confused) confuso; (blurred, as a photograph) borroso

foil [fɔɪł] N (any metal) hoja de metal *f*; (aluminum) papel de aluminio *m*; (on mirrors) azogue *m*; (rapier) florete *m*; (thing contrasted) contraste *m*; VT frustrar

fold [fołd] VI/VT (sheets) doblar[se]; (paper, folding chairs) plegar[se]; (wings, flag) replegar[se]; (in cards) abandonar; (close a business) cerrar[se]; (end a performance) bajar de cartel; **to — one's arms** cruzarse de brazos; N (pleat, hollow) pliegue *m*; (crease) doblez *m*; (enclosure) redil *m*, aprisco *m*; (sheep) rebaño *m*; (congregation) grey *f*; **to rejoin the —** volver al redil; **three—** tres veces

folder [fółdɚ] N (file) carpeta *f*; (instrument for folding) plegadera *f*

folding [fółdɪŋ] ADJ plegadizo, plegable; **— chair** silla plegadiza *f*; **— screen** biombo *m*; N doblado *m*

foliage [fóliɪʤ] N follaje *m*, fronda *f*, ramaje *m*

folic acid [fólɪkǽsɪd] N ácido fólico *m*

folio [fólio] N (page) folio *m*; (book) libro en folio *m*

folk [fok] N (people) gente *f*; (nation) pueblo *m*; ADJ popular; **— dance** baile folclórico/ folklórico *m*; **—lore** folclore/folklore *m*; (traditional stories) leyendas tradicionales *f* *pl*; **— medicine** medicina tradicional *f*; **— music** música folclórica/folklórica *fi* **song** canción tradicional *f*; **— tale** cuento folclórico/folklórico *m*; **old —s** los viejos; **—s** (relatives) parientes *m pl*; *fam* (parents) padres *m pl*, viejos *m pl*

folkloric [foklórɪk] ADJ folclórico/folklórico

follicle [fálɪkəł] N folículo *m*

folliculitis [fəlɪkjəláɪdɪs] N foliculitis *f*

follow [fálo] VI/VT seguir; VI (be a consequence) seguirse; (come next) ira continuación; **to — suit** seguir el ejemplo, secundar; **to — through** llevar a cabo; **to — up [on]** (pursue) obtener más detalles [sobre]; (develop) desarrollar; N **—through** (in sports) acompañamiento *m*, continuación *f*; **—-up** seguimiento *m*

follower [fáloɚ] N seguidor -ora *mf*

following [fáloɪŋ] N seguidores -oras *mf pl*; **the —** lo siguiente; ADJ siguiente

foment [fomént] VT fomentar

fond [fɑnd] ADJ **I'm — of cats** soy amigo de los gatos, me encantan los gatos; **I'm — of Chinese food** me gusta la comida china; **I'm — of John** le tengo cariño a Juan; **— hopes** ilusión *f*; **to become — of** encariñarse de

fondle [fándḷ] VI/VT (touch affectionately) acariciar; (grope) manosear, sobar

fondness [fándnɪs] N (affection) cariño *m*, afecto *m*; (liking or weakness) afición *f*

font [fɑnt] N (of water) pila *f*; (of characters) tipo de letra *m*

food [fud] N comida *f*, alimento *m*; **— chain** cadena alimenticia *f*; **— poisoning** intoxicación por alimentos *f*; **— stamps** cupones para alimentos *m pl*; **—stuff** producto alimenticio *m*; **— for thought** algo para reflexionar

fool [fuł] N (foolish person) tonto -ta *mf*, bobo -ba *mf*, necio -cia *mf*; (jester) bufón *m*; **—proof** (plan) infalible, a prueba de fallos; (device) a prueba de tontos; **to make a — of** hacer quedar como un tonto; **to play the —** hacer el tonto; **I'm a card-playing —** soy loco por los naipes; VI bromear; **to — around** tontear; VT engañar

foolish [fúlɪʃ] ADJ tonto, necio

foolishness [fúlɪʃnɪs] N tontería *f*, bobería *f*, sandez *f*

foot [fʊt] N pie *m*; (of an animal) pata *f*; **—- and-mouth disease** fiebre aftosa *f*; **—ball** (American) fútbol americano *m*; (soccer) fútbol *m*; (ball) balón [de fútbol] *m*, pelota [de fútbol] *f*; **— fault** falta de pie *f*; **—hill** pie de la montaña *m*; **—hold** punto de apoyo *m*; **—lights** candilejas *f pl*; **—man** lacayo *m*; **—note** nota al pie de página *f*, llamada *f*; **—path** senda *f*; **—print** huella *f*, pisada *f*; **—race** carrera a pie *f*; **— soldier** soldado de infantería *m*; **—step** pisada *f*, paso *m*; **print** huella *f*, pisada *fi* **stool** taburete *m*; **—wear** calzado *m*; **—work** (in sports) juego de piernas *m*; **to follow in the —steps of** seguir los pasos de; **he has a —hold in the computer business** ha logrado establecerse en el negocio de la informática; **it'll take some pretty fancy —work to get out of this** va a ser difícil zafarse de esto; **on —** a pie; **to put one's — in it** meter la pata; VT **to — it** andar a pie; VT **to — the bill** pagar la cuenta

footing [fúdɪŋ] N (basis) base *f*; (foothold) punto de apoyo *m*; **to be on a friendly — with** tener relaciones amistosas con; **to lose one's — perder pie**

for [fɔr] PREP para, por; **this gift is — John** este regalo es para John; **we're headed — the beach** vamos para la playa; **this is a device — sorting letters** este es un aparato para clasificar cartas; **they gave me enough food — three people** me dieron comida [como] para tres personas; **she's studying — the bar** está estudiando para el examen de abogacía; **the party is planned — Saturday** la fiesta está organizada para el sábado; **he has a good eye — talent** tiene buen ojo para descubrir talento; **he works — IBM** trabaja para IBM; **smoking is bad — your health** fumar es perjudicial para la salud; **he's mature — his age** es maduro para su edad; **I've come — the money** he venido por el dinero; **she asked — you** preguntó por ti; **I walk to work — the exercise** voy al trabajo andando por el ejercicio; **we went to Spain — a month** fuimos a España por un mes; **she did it — the first time** lo hizo por primera vez; **my wife signed — me** mi esposa firmó por mí; **mothers feel love — their children** las madres sienten amor por sus hijos; **they fired him — arriving late** lo echaron por llegar tarde; **run — your life!** ¡corre por tu vida! **she took me — a fool** me tomó por tonto; **thanks — the help** gracias por la ayuda; **I paid ten dollars — the book** pagué diez dólares por el libro; **I'm — gun control** estoy por el control de armas; **— all her intelligence** a pesar de su inteligencia; **that's not — you to decide** a ti no te toca decidir esto; **as — him** en cuanto a él; **it's time — me to go** es hora de que me vaya; **to know — a fact** saber a ciencia cierta; CONJ porque, pues; **I wish to eat, — I'm hungry** quiero comer, pues tengo hambre

forage [fɔ́rɪʤ] N (feed) forraje m; (searching) recolección f; VI (gather food) forrajear; VT (feed) dar forraje a; (collect) recolectar

foray [fɔ́re] N incursión f, correría f; VI (explore) incursionar; (maraud) saquear

forbade [fɔrbéd] see forbid

forbear [fɔrbér] VT abstenerse de; VI contenerse

forbid [fəbíd] VT prohibir

forbidden [fəbídn̩] ADJ prohibido

forbidden [fɔrbídn̩] see forbid

forbidding [fəbídɪŋ] ADJ (strict) severo; (daunting) imponente

force [fɔrs] N fuerza f; **— out** (baseball) out forzado m; **in —** (effective) en vigor, vigente; (in large numbers) en masa; **armed —s** fuerzas armadas f pl; VT (oblige, compel) obligar; (rape, break open) forzar; **she —d a laugh** soltó una risa forzada; **to — upon** imponer; **to — one's way** abrirse paso a la fuerza; **to — out** (from a place) echar a la fuerza; (in baseball) forzar out

forced [fɔrst] ADJ forzado, obligado; (of a landing) forzoso; **— page break** salto de página forzado m

forceful [fɔ́rsfəl] ADJ (of personality) fuerte; (of arguments) convincente, contundente; (of behavior) enérgico

forceps [fɔ́rsəps] N (in obstetrics) fórceps m; (in dentistry) tenazas f pl, gatillo m

forcible [fɔ́rsəbəl] ADJ (done by force) forzoso; (effective) convincente; **— entry** allanamiento de morada m

ford [fɔrd] N vado m; VT vadear

fore [fɔr] ADJ delantero; (of a ship) de proa; N **to come to the —** ponerse en evidencia; INTERJ (in golf) ¡cuidado!

forearm [fɔ́rɑrm] N antebrazo m

forebear [fɔ́rbɛr] N antepasado -da mf

forebode [fɔrbód] VT (foretell) presagiar; (have a presentiment) presentir

foreboding [fɔrbódɪŋ] N (omen) presagio m; (presentiment) presentimiento m

forecast [fɔ́rkæst] N pronóstico m; VI/VT pronosticar

foreclose [fɔrklóz] VI ejecutar una hipoteca

foreclosure [fɔrklóʒɚ] N ejecución f

forefather [fɔ́rfɑðɚ] N antepasado m

forefront [fɔ́rfrʌnt] ADV LOC **at the —** a la cabeza, a la vanguardia

forego, forgo [fɔrgó] VT abstenerse de

foregone [fɔ́rgɔn] ADJ **it's a — conclusion** eso es de cajón

foreground [fɔ́rgraʊnd] N primer plano m

forehand [fɔ́rhænd] N (in tennis) derecha f, golpe de derecha m

forehead [fɔ́rɪd] N frente f

foreign [fɔ́rɪn] ADJ (from another country) extranjero; (not local) foráneo; (alien) ajeno; **— affairs** relaciones exteriores f pl; **— aid** ayuda exterior f; **— body** cuerpo extraño m; **—-born** nacido en el extranjero; **— currency** divisa f; **— debt** deuda exterior f; **— exchange** cambio de divisas m; **— exchange system** sistema cambiario m; **— matter** materia extraña f; **— policy** política exterior f; **— trade** comercio exterior m

foreigner [fɔ́rənɚ] N extranjero -ra mf

foreman [fɔ́rmən] N (in a factory) capataz m, sobrestante m; (of a jury) presidente m

foremost [fɔ́rmost] ADJ principal, preeminente

forensic [fərénzɪk] ADJ forense

forerunner [fɔ́rrʌnɚ] N (precursor) precursor -ora mf; (omen) presagio m; (harbinger) mensajero -ra mf

foresaw [fɔrsɔ́] see foresee

foresee [fɔrsí] VT prever, prevenir

foreseeable [fɔrsíəbəl] ADJ previsible

foreseen [fɔrsín] see foresee

foresight [fɔ́rsaɪt] N previsión f

foreskin [fɔ́rskɪn] N prepucio m

forest [fɔ́rɪst] N (temperate) bosque m; (tropical) selva f; **— fire** incendio forestal m; **— ranger** guardabosque[s] m sg

forestall [fɔrstɔ́l] VT bloquear

forester [fɔ́rɪstɚ] N (forest ranger) guardabosque[s] m sg

forestry [fɔ́rɪstri] N silvicultura f; **— division** división forestal f

foretell [fɔrtél] VT predecir, vaticinar

foretold [fɔrtóld] see foretell

forever [fɔrévɚ] ADV para siempre; **I'm — having to pick up after him** siempre tengo que estar juntando sus cosas; **we can't go on like this —** no podemos seguir así por toda la vida

foreword [fɔ́rwɚd] N prólogo m
forfeit [fɔ́rfɪt] VT perder; N (fine) multa f; (loss) pérdida f
forfeiture [fɔ́rfɪtʃɚ] N confiscación f, pérdida f
forgave [fɔrgév] see forgive
forge [fɔrdʒ] N fragua f, forja f; VT (plans) fraguar; (metal, agreement) forjar, fraguar; VI/VT (signature, legal document) falsificar; **to — ahead** abrirse paso
forgery [fɔ́rdʒəri] N falsificación f
forget [fɚgét] VI/VT olvidar, olvidarse de; **I forgot my keys** se me olvidaron las llaves; **to — oneself** meter la pata; N **—-me-not** nomeolvides mf
forgetful [fɚgétfəl] ADJ olvidadizo; **— of** negligente de
forgetfulness [fɚgétfəlnɪs] N falta de memoria f
forgive [fɚgív] VI/VT perdonar; (a debt) perdonar, disculpar
forgiven [fɚgívən] see forgive
forgiveness [fɚgívnɪs] N perdón m
forgiving [fɚgívɪŋ] ADJ clemente
forgo [fɔrgó] see forego
forgot [fɔrgát] see forget
forgotten [fɔrgátn̩] see forget
fork [fɔrk] N (for eating) tenedor m; (for hay) horca f, trinche m; (for tuning) diapasón m; (in a road) bifurcación f; **—lift** montacargas de horquilla m sg; VI bifurcarse; **to — over** soltar
forlorn [fɔrlɔ́rn] ADJ desamparado, abandonado
form [fɔrm] N forma f; (type) modalidad f; (physical condition) condiciones físicas f pl; (document to be filled in) formulario m; VI/VT formar[se]
formal [fɔ́rməl] ADJ formal; **— attire** ropa de etiqueta f; **— dance** baile de etiqueta m
formaldehyde [fɔrmǽldɪhaɪd] N formaldehído m
formality [fɔrmǽlɪDi] N (conventionality) formalidad f; (rigidity) formalismo m; (legal step) trámite m
format [fɔ́rmæt] N formato m; VT formatear
formation [fɔrméʃən] N formación f
formative [fɔ́rməDɪv] ADJ formativo
formatting [fɔ́rmæDɪŋ] N formateo m
former [fɔ́rmɚ] ADJ **the — capital** la antigua capital; **my — husband** mi ex-marido; **the — president** el ex-presidente; **in — times** antiguamente; PRON aquel [aquella, etc.], ese [esa, etc.]
formerly [fɔ́rmɚli] ADV antes, anteriormente
formidable [fɔ́rmɪDəbəl] ADJ formidable
formula [fɔ́rmjələ] N fórmula f, formulación f; (for babies) preparado para biberón m
formulate [fɔ́rmjəlet] VT formular
formulation [fɔrmjəléʃən] N formulación f
fornicate [fɔ́rnɪket] VI fornicar
forsake [fɔrsék] VT abandonar, desamparar

forsaken [fɔrsékən] see forsake
forsook [fɔrsúk] see forsake
fort [fɔrt] N fuerte m, fortaleza f; **to hold [down] the —** quedar de guardián
forth [fɔrθ] ADV (time) en adelante; (space) hacia adelante; **to go —** irse; **and so —** etcétera, y así sucesivamente
forthcoming [fɔrθkámɪŋ] ADJ (approaching) venidero, próximo; (available) disponible; (frank, friendly) abierto; (soon to be published) de próxima aparición
forthright [fɔ́rθraɪt] ADJ directo
forthwith [fɔrθwíθ] ADV en seguida, al punto
fortification [fɔrDəfɪkéʃən] N fortificación f
fortify [fɔ́rDəfaɪ] VT (building, body) fortificar; (food) enriquecer; (hair, mind) fortalecer; (argument) reforzar
fortitude [fɔ́rDɪtud] N fortaleza f, entereza f
fortress [fɔ́rtrɪs] N fortaleza f
fortuitous [fɔrtúɪDəs] ADJ (coincidental) fortuito; (lucky) afortunado
fortunate [fɔ́rtʃənɪt] ADJ afortunado
fortunately [fɔ́rtʃənɪtli] ADV afortunadamente
fortune [fɔ́rtʃən] N fortuna f; **— teller** adivino -na mf; **it cost me a —** me costó un dineral; **to tell someone's —** decirle la buenaventura a alguien
forty [fɔ́rDi] NUM cuarenta; **— love** (in tennis) quince a nada
forum [fɔ́rəm] N foro m
forward [fɔ́rwɚd] ADJ (toward the front) hacia adelante; (leading, in the front) delantero; (pushy) descarado; ADV adelante, en adelante; **to bring —** presentar; VT reexpedir; N (in sports) delantero -ra mf; (in basketball) alero -ra mf
fossil [fásəl] N fósil m; (old fogey) carcamal m, carca mf; **— fuel** combustible fósil m
foster [fɔ́stɚ] VT (promote) fomentar, promover; (bring up) criar; **— family** familia de acogida f
fought [fɔt] see fight
foul [faʊl] ADJ (dirty, illicit) sucio; (disgusting) asqueroso; (of a smell) fétido; (of weather) inclemente; (of winds) adverso; (morally offensive) vil; (of air) viciado; **—mouthed** mal hablado; **the police suspect — play** la policía sospecha que fue un crimen; N (in sports) falta f, faul m; **—-up** desastre m; VT (make dirty) ensuciar; (pollute) viciar; (tarnish) manchar; VI cometer una falta; **to — up** estropear
found [faʊnd] VT (establish) fundar; (build) cimentar
found [faʊnd] see find
foundation [faʊndéʃən] N (establishment, institution) fundación f; (of a building) cimiento m; (of an argument) fundamento m; (cosmetic) base f

founder [fáUndəʳ] N (establisher) fundador -ora *mf*; (smith) fundidor -ora *mf*; VI (sink) zozobrar, irse a pique; (fail) fracasar

foundry [fáUndri] N fundición *f*

fountain [fáUntn̩] N fuente *f*; — **pen** pluma fuente *f*

four [fɔr] NUM cuatro; — **hundred** cuatrocientos; —**score** ochenta; N —-**eyes** *fam* cuatro ojos *mf sg*; —-**letter word** palabrota *f*; —**some** grupo de cuatro *m*

fourteen [fɔrtín] NUM catorce

fourth [fɔrθ] ADJ cuarto; N cuarta parte *f*; **the Fourth of July** el cuatro de julio

fowl [faUɫ] N (domestic) ave de corral *m*; (wild) ave *m*

fox [faks] N zorro *m*, zorra *f*; (crafty person) persona astuta *f*; (attractive person) guapetón -ona *mf*; —**hole** madriguera *f*; (military) trinchera *f*

foxy [fáksi] ADJ (crafty) zorro; (attractive) sexy

foyer [fɔ́Iəʳ] N vestíbulo *m*

fraction [frǽkʃən] N fracción *f*, quebrado *m*

fracture [frǽktʃəʳ] N fractura *f*; VI/VT fracturar[se]

fragile [frǽdʒəɫ] ADJ frágil

fragment[1] [frǽgmənt] N fragmento *m*

fragment[2] [frægmént] VI/VT fragmentar[se]

fragmentation [frægməntéʃən] N fragmentación *f*

fragrance [frégrəns] N fragancia *f*

fragrant [frégrənt] ADJ fragante

frail [freɫ] ADJ frágil, débil

frailty [frélti] N fragilidad *f*, debilidad *f*

frame [frem] N (of a building, airplane, furniture) armazón *m*; (of eyeglasses) montura *f*, armadura *f*; (of a car) chasis *m*; (of a person's body) estatura *f*; (of a picture, door) marco *m*; (for embroidery) bastidor *m*; (on a strip of film) imagen *f*; — **of mind** disposición *f*; —**work** (of a house, structure) armazón *m*; (of reference) marco *m*, esquema *m*; VT (a document) forjar; (a question, plan) formular; (a picture) enmarcar; (a person) tenderle una trampa

franc [fræŋk] N franco *m*

France [fræns] N Francia *f*

franchise [frǽntʃaIz] N (license) concesión *f*, franquicia *f*; (voting privilege) derecho al voto *m*; VT conceder en franquicia, dar la concesión para

frank [fræŋk] ADJ franco, abierto; VT franquear; N salchicha alemana *f*

frankfurter [frǽŋkfɜʳDəʳ] N salchicha alemana *f*

frankness [frǽŋknIs] N franqueza *f*

frantic [frǽntIk] ADJ (wild) frenético; (desperate) desesperado

fraternal [frətɜ́ʳnɫ] ADJ fraternal, fraterno

fraternity [frətɜ́ʳnIDi] N (relationship) fraternidad *f*, confraternidad *f*; (student association) asociación estudiantil *f*

fraternize [frǽDəʳnaIz] VI confraternizar, fraternizar

fraud [frɔd] N (deceit) fraude *m*; (impostor) farsante *mf*, impostor -ora *mf*

fraudulent [frɔ́dʒələnt] ADJ (of a business, etc.) fraudulento; (of a person) engañoso

fray [fre] N (fight) reyerta *f*, riña *f*; (harsh debate) refriega *f*; VI/VT (rub, wear out) desgastar[se], deshilachar[se]; (strain) crispar[se]

freak [frik] N (anomaly) anomalía *f*; (monster) monstruo *m*, anormal *mf*; (enthusiast) fanático -ca *mf*; (pervert) pervertido -da *mf*; ADJ (unusual) insólito; VI chiflar, flipar; **to — out** chiflar[se], flipar[se]

freakish [fríkIʃ] ADJ insólito

freckle [frékəɫ] N peca *f*; VI/VT cubrir[se] de pecas

freckled [frékəɫd] ADJ pecoso

free [fri] ADJ (having liberty, unrestricted, loose, uncombined chemically, independent) libre; (unobstructed, unoccupied) libre, despejado; (without charge) gratis, gratuito; (generous) generoso; (unstinted) sin límites, descontrolado; (frank) franco, abierto; — **and clear** libre de gravámenes; — **and easy** despreocupado; — **delivery** entrega gratuita *f*; — **enterprise** empresa libre *f*; — **fall** caída libre *f*; —-**for-all** rifirrafe *m*; — **kick** tiro libre *m*; —**lance** freelance *m*; — **lunch/ride** algo gratis *m*; — **market** mercado libre *m*; — **radical** radical libre *m*; — **speech** libertad de expresión *f*; — **spirit** espíritu fuerte *m*; —**style** estilo libre *m*, crol *m*; —**thinker** libre pensador -ora *mf*; — **throw** tiro libre *m*; — **trade** libre comercio *m*; — **verse** verso libre *m*; —**way** autopista *f*, autovía *f*; — **will** libre albedrío *m*; **to give someone a — hand** dar rienda suelta a alguien; **to set — **poner en libertad; **sugar-** sin azúcar; ADV libremente; — **lance** por cuenta propia; **for — **gratis; VT (liberate) liberar; (deliver, rid) librar; (untie a knot) desenredar; (drain) desatascar; **to —load** gorronear; **to — up** (time) dejar libre

freebie [fríbi] N yapa *f*

freedom [frídəm] N libertad *f*; — **of speech** libertad de expresión *f*; **we all want — from fear** todos queremos vivir libres de miedo; **I want — from having to go to work every day** no quiero tener que ir a trabajar todos los días

freeze [friz] VI/VT (food, water) congelar[se]; (accounts) bloquear[se], congelar[se]; **to —-dry** liofilizar; **he froze to death** murió congelado; **my computer froze up** se me colgó la computadora / el ordenador; VI (of temperature) helar; N (action or state of being frozen) congelación *f*; (cold snap) helada *f*

freezer [fríʳzəʳ] N congelador *m*

freezing [frízɪŋ] ADJ helado; — **cold** frío glacial
m; — **point** punto de congelación m
freight [fret] N (load) carga f; (charge) flete m,
porte m; — **train** tren de carga m, tren de
mercancías m
freighter [frédɚ] N buque de carga m
French [frentʃ] ADJ francés; — **dressing** salsa
francesa f; — **fries** Am papas fritas f pl; Sp
patatas fritas f pl; — **horn** corno francés m; —
kiss beso francés m; —**man** francés m;
—**woman** francesa f; N (language) francés;
the — los franceses
frenzy [frénzi] N frenesí m; **he worked**
himself into a — se puso histérico
frequency [fríkwənsi] N frecuencia f
frequent [fríkwənt] ADJ frecuente; VT frecuentar
frequently [fríkwəntli] ADV con frecuencia, a
menudo; — **asked questions** preguntas
frecuentes f pl
fresh [frɛʃ] ADJ (pure, cool, not stale, not frozen,
not tired) fresco; (new) nuevo; (bold)
impertinente, atrevido; (healthy) lozano; —
paint pintura fresca f; — **water** agua dulce f;
ADV — **out of school** recién salido de la
escuela; **we're** — **out of ideas** se nos
acabaron las ideas
freshen [fréʃən] VI/VT refrescar[se]; **to** — **up**
arreglarse, lavarse
freshman [fréʃmən] N (student) estudiante de
primer año mf; (novice) novato -ta mf
freshness [fréʃnɪs] N (of food, of temperature)
frescor m, frescura f; (of skin, flowers, youth)
lozanía f; (of an idea) originalidad f;
(impudence) descaro m
fret [fret] VI/VT (worry) preocupar[se]; (irritate)
irritar[se]; N traste m
fretful [frétfəl] ADJ ansioso, inquieto
friar [fráɪɚ] N fraile m
friction [fríkʃən] N fricción f, rozamiento m
Friday [fráɪDe] N viernes m
fried [fraɪd] ADJ frito
friend [frend] N amigo -ga mf
friendliness [fréndlɪnɪs] N afabilidad f,
simpatía f
friendly [fréndli] ADJ amistoso, simpático,
amigable; — **advice** consejo de amigo m;
user- — fácil de usar
friendship [fréndʃɪp] N amistad f
frigate [frígɪt] N fragata f
fright [fraɪt] N (fear) espanto m, susto m;
(grotesque thing or person) espantajo m,
esperpento m; **to take** — asustarse
frighten [fráɪtn] VI/VT espantar[se], asustar[se];
to — **away** ahuyentar, espantar
frightened [fráɪtn̩d] ADJ asustado, espantado;
to get — espantarse
frightful [fráɪtfəl] ADJ espantoso, pavoroso; **we**
had a — **time** lo pasamos horrible; **he's a** —
flatterer es un adulón espantoso

frigid [frídʒɪd] ADJ (of weather) gélido; (of sexual
response) frígida; (of personal relations) frío
frigidity [frɪdʒídɪDi] N frigidez f
frill [frɪl] N (trimming) volante m; (something
superfluous) adorno m; **no-** —**s** sin lujos
fringe [frɪndʒ] N (of a rug) fleco m, orla f; (of a
city) periferia f; (of a political party) extremo
m; (of society) margen m; — **benefits**
prestaciones f pl, complementos m pl; VT
orlar, poner un fleco
Frisbee® [frízbi] N disco volador m
frisk [frɪsk] VI/VT (frolic) retozar, triscar;
(search) cachear
frisky [fríski] ADJ retozón
fritter [frídɚ] VI/VT desmenuzar[se]; VI irse
gastando de poco a poco; **to** — **away**
malgastar; N buñuelo m, churro m
frivolity [frɪválɪDi] N frivolidad f
frivolous [frívələs] ADJ frívolo
fro [fro] ADV **to and** — de aquí para allá
frock [frak] N (dress) vestido m; (habit) hábito m
frog [frag] N (animal) rana f; (fastener) alamar m;
(of a hoof) ranilla f; (French person) pej
franchute -ta mf; **to have a** — **in one's**
throat tener gallos en la garganta; —**man**
hombre rana m
frolic [frálɪk] N retozo m; VI retozar
from [fram, frəm] PREP desde, de, por; — **here**
to there desde aquí hasta allá; — **two to**
four de las dos a las cuatro; — **what I can**
tell por lo que yo veo; **four hours** — **now**
de aquí a cuatro horas, dentro de cuatro
horas; **different** — **the other one** diferente
del otro; **to come** — **Minnesota** ser de
Minesota; **death** — **starvation** muerte por
inanición f
front [frʌnt] N frente m; (cover for illegal
activity) pantalla f; —**runner** favorito -ta
mf; —**wheel drive** tracción delantera f; **in**
— **of** en frente de, delante de; ADJ delantero;
VI/VT (face) dar a; (cover up) servir de pantalla
frontal [frʌntl] ADJ frontal
frontier [frʌntír] N frontera f; ADJ fronterizo; —
spirit espíritu pionero m; — **town** pueblo
fronterizo m
frost [frost] N helada f, escarcha f; VI/VT helar,
escarchar; VT (a cake) bañar; (glass) esmerilar;
(hair) hacer rayitos/reflejos; —**bite** necrosis
por congelación f
frosting [fróstɪŋ] N (of a cake) baño m; (for glass)
esmerilado m; (of hair) rayos m pl, reflejos m
pl
frosty [frósti] ADJ (cold, unfriendly) helado;
(covered with frost) escarchado
froth [froθ] N espuma f; VI echar espuma; VT
batir
frown [fraʊn] VI fruncir el ceño; **to** — **on**
desaprobar; N ceño m
froze [froz] see freeze

frozen [frózən] ADJ congelado

frozen [frózən] *see* freeze

fructose [frúktos] N fructosa *f*

frugal [frúgəł] ADJ (economical) económico, ahorrativo; (meager) frugal

fruit [frut] N (food) fruta *f*; (plant part, product of labor) fruto *m*; (male homosexual) *offensive* maricón *m*; **—cake** (food) torta de frutas secas *f*; (crazy person) *fam* chiflado -da *mf*

fruitful [frútfəł] ADJ fructífero

fruitless [frútlɪs] ADJ infructuoso

frumpy [frʌ́mpi] ADJ matrona

frustrate [frʌ́stret] VT frustrar; **to get —d** frustrar[se]

frustration [frʌstréʃən] N frustración *f*

fry [fraɪ] VI/VT (cook, also execute by electrocution) freír[se]; **—ing pan** sartén *f*; N (fried potato) papa/patata frita *f*; (gathering with fried food) fiesta con comida frita *f*; (young fish) alevín *m*; **small —** gente menuda *f*

fuck [fʌk] VI/VT (have intercourse) *Sp vulg* follar; *Am vulg* coger, culear; (treat harshly) *vulg* joder; INTERJ **to — around** (be idle) *vulg* rascarse las bolas; (be promiscuous) *vulg* coger/follar con todo el mundo; **to — up** *vulg* cagar, joder; **to be —ed up** (mentally ill, in trouble) *vulg* estar jodido; (under the influence) estar colocado; (confused) estar confundido; N (sexual act) *fam* polvo *m*; **—up** *offensive* pendejo -ja *mf*; **he's a good —** *vulg* folla/coge muy bien; **what the — do you want?** *vulg* ¿qué carajo quieres? ¿qué demonios quieres? **—!** *vulg* ¡mierda! ¡coño! **— off!** *vulg* ¡vete a la mierda! **— you!** *vulg* ¡vete a la mierda!

fucker [fʌ́kɚ] N (person who fucks) *vulg* follador -ora *mf*; (annoying person) *offensive* hijo -ja de puta *mf*

fucking [fʌ́kɪŋ] ADJ *vulg* jodido, de mierda, *Mex* pinche; **the whole — day** *fam* todo el maldito día

fudge [fʌʤ] N turrón blando de chocolate *m*; VI (cheat) hacer trampa; (avoid an issue) dar rodeos

fuel [fjúəł] N (combustible) combustible *m*, carburante *m*; (topic) tema *m*; **— injection** inyección *f*; **— oil** fuel *m*; VT (a vehicle) llenar el tanque, cargar de combustible; (fire, debate) avivar

fugitive [fjúʤɪdɪv] ADJ (fleeing) fugitivo; (transitory) fugaz; N fugitivo -va *mf*, prófugo -ga *mf*

fulfill [fułfíł] VT (promise, order) cumplir; (need) satisfacer; **she doesn't feel —ed** no se siente realizada

fulfillment [fułfíłmənt] N (of a promise, order) cumplimiento *m*; (of a need) satisfacción *f*; (of a person) realización *f*; (of a dream)

culminación *f*

full [fuł] ADJ (completely filled) lleno; (complete) completo; (a dress) amplio; (a person's figure) relleno; (sated) harto; **—-blooded** de raza; **—-blown** (of disease) declarado; (complete) auténtico; **—-bodied** con cuerpo; **—-fledged** verdadero; **—-grown** adulto; **— house** full *m*; **—-length** (movie) de largometraje; (mirror) de cuerpo entero; **— moon** luna llena *f*; **— name** nombre completo *m*; **—-scale** (model) de tamaño natural; (war) total; (investigation) exhaustivo; **—-service** de servicio completo; **—-size** (bed) de matrimonio; (model) de tamaño natural; **—-term** a término; **— time** tiempo completo *m*, de tiempo completo; **to pay in —** pagar el total de la deuda; ADV **you know — well** sabes perfectamente; **it hit him — in the chest** le pegó en pleno pecho

fully [fúli] ADV (entirely) completamente, plenamente; (at least) al menos

fumble [fʌ́mbəł] N pérdida de balón *f*; VI (search for) buscar a tientas; (move clumsily) andar a tientas; (blunder) meter la pata; (football) perder el balón; **he —d his way into the living room** entró a tientas a la sala

fume [fjum] VI (be angry) rabiar; (emit vapors, smoke) emitir humo; N **—s** gases *m pl*, vapores *m pl*, tufo *m*

fumigate [fjúmɪget] VT fumigar

fun [fʌn] N diversión *f*; **for —** por gusto; **to make — of** burlarse de; **to have —** divertirse; ADJ divertido

function [fʌ́ŋkʃən] N función *f*; **— key** tecla de función *f*; VI (work) funcionar; (serve) oficiar

functional [fʌ́ŋkʃənl] ADJ funcional

fund [fʌnd] N (of money) fondo *m*; (of knowledge) acervo *m*; **—-raising** recaudación de fondos *f*; VT financiar

fundamental [fʌndəméntl] ADJ fundamental; N fundamento *m*

fundamentalism [fʌndəméntlɪzəm] N fundamentalismo *m*

fundamentally [fʌndəméntli] ADV fundamentalmente

funding [fʌ́ndɪŋ] N financiamiento *m*, financiación *f*

funeral [fjúnəˌəł] N funeral *m*, entierro *m*, exequias *f pl*; **— director** director -ora de pompas fúnebres *mf*; **— home** casa de pompas fúnebres *f*, funeraria *f*; **— service** funeral *m*; **it's your —** te estás cavando tu propia tumba; ADJ (march, procession) fúnebre; (pyre) funerario; (expenses) de entierro

funereal [fjuníriəł] ADJ lúgubre

fungible [fʌ́nʤɪbəł] ADJ fungible

fungicide [fʌ́nʤɪsaɪd] N fungicida *m*

fungus [fʌ́ŋgəs] N hongo *m*

funky [fʌ́ŋki] ADJ (of music) funky; (strange) estrafalario, raro; (smelly) hediondo

funnel [fʌ́nl̩] N (for liquids) embudo *m*; (in a chimney) humero *m*; VT canalizar, encauzar

funny [fʌ́ni] ADJ (amusing) cómico, chistoso, gracioso; (strange) raro; — **farm** *fam* loquero *m*, loquería *f*; **that's not** — eso no tiene gracia; **don't get** — **with me** no te pases de listo; N **funnies** historietas *f pl*, tiras cómicas *f pl*; ADV raro

fur [fɝ] N (hair) pelo *m*; (coat) pelaje *m*; (hide) piel *f*; — **store** peletería *f*; VT forrar de piel

furious [fjúriəs] ADJ (person) furioso, sañudo, rabioso; (fight, storm) feroz; (activity) febril

furlough [fɝlo] N licencia *f*, permiso *m*; VT dar licencia

furnace [fɝnɪs] N (for heating) caldera *f*; (in industry) horno *m*

furnish [fɝnɪʃ] VT (put in furniture) amueblar; (equip) equipar; (provide) proporcionar, suministrar, facilitar

furniture [fɝnɪtʃɚ] N muebles *m pl*, mobiliario *m*; — **store** mueblería *f*

furrow [fɝo] N surco *m*; VT (soil) arar; (face) fruncir

furry [fɝi] ADJ peludo

further [fɝðɚ] ADV **we want to go** — queremos ir más lejos; **I refuse to discuss this** — me niego a seguir discutiendo esto; (additionally) [lo que] es más; ADJ (more distant) más lejano; (additional) adicional; VT (promote) promover; ADV —**more** además

furthest [fɝðɪst] ADJ [el] más lejano, [el] más remoto; ADV más lejos

furtive [fɝDɪv] ADJ (stealthy) furtivo; (shifty) sospechoso

fury [fjúri] N furia *f*, furor *m*, saña *f*

fuse [fjuz] N (in an explosive) mecha *f*; (in a circuit) fusible *m*; **he has a short** — tiene pocas pulgas; **he blew a** — estalló; VT (to join) fusionar; VI/VT (to merge) fusionar[se]; (to blend metals) fundir[se]

fuselage [fjúsəlɑʒ] N fuselaje *m*

fusion [fjúʒən] N fusión *f*

fuss [fʌs] N (bustle) alboroto *m*, bulla *f*; (uproar) escándalo *m*; (argument) discusión *f*; VI (worry about trifles) preocuparse por naderías; (complain) quejarse

fussiness [fʌ́sinɪs] N remilgo *m*, ñoñería *f*

fussy [fʌ́si] ADJ (particular) quisquilloso, remilgado; (whiny) quejica, cargoso

futile [fjúdl̩] ADJ inútil

futility [fjutílɪDi] N inutilidad *f*

future [fjútʃɚ] N futuro *m*, porvenir *m*; —**s** futuros *m pl*; ADJ futuro

fuzz [fʌz] N (fluff) pelusa *f*; (fine hair) vello fino *m*; (on the lip) bozo *m*

fuzzy [fʌ́zi] ADJ (fluffy) cubierto de pelusa; (hairy) velloso; (blurred) borroso; (muddled) confuso

FYI [**for your information**] [éfwáiái] ADV para su información

Gg

gab [gæb] VI parlotear, charlar; N parloteo *m*, charla *f*; **gift of** — labia *f*, facundia *f*

gable [gébl̩] N hastial *m*; — **roof** tejado de dos aguas *m*; — **window** buhardilla *f*

Gabon, Gabun [gəbón] N Gabón *m*

Gabonese [gæbəníz] ADJ & N gabonés -esa *mf*

gad [gæd] VI **to** — **about** callejear

gadget [gǽdʒɪt] N coso *m*, chisme *m*

gaffe [gæf] N gaffe *f*, metedura de pata *f*

gag [gæg] VT (stop up mouth, silence) amordazar; (cause to choke) dar arcadas; VI tener arcadas; N (thing stuffed into mouth) mordaza *f*; (joke) gag *m*, burla *f*; — **order** orden de supresión de la libertad de expresión *f*

gaiety [géiDi] N alegría *f*; **gaieties** festejos *m pl*

gain [gen] VT ganar; VI **to** — **on** irse acercando a; VI/VT (watch) adelantar; N (profit, act of gaining) ganancia *f*; (in weight) aumento *m*

gainful [génfl̩] ADJ remunerado

gait [get] N marcha *f*, paso *m*

galaxy [gǽləksi] N galaxia *f*

gale [gel] N ventarrón *m*, vendaval *m*; —**force winds** vientos huracanados *m pl*; — **of laughter** risotada *f*

Galicia [gəlíʃə] N Galicia *f*

Galician [gəlíʃən] ADJ & N gallego -ga *mf*

gall [gɔl] N (bile, bitterness) hiel *f*; (impudence) morro *m*; (of a plant) agalla *f*; — **bladder** vesícula [biliar] *f*; —**nut** agalla *f*; —**stone** cálculo biliar *m*; VT (irritate) irritar

gallant[1] [gǽlənt] ADJ (brave) valiente; (attentive to women) galante

gallant[2] [gəlánt] N galán *m*

gallantry [gǽləntri] N (courage) valentía *f*, bizarría *f*; (chivalrous attention) galantería *f*

gallery [gǽləri] N (art, shopping) galería *f*; (theater) paraíso *m*, gallinero *m*; (golf) público *m*

galley [gǽli] N (kitchen) cocina *f*; (boat) galera *f*; — **proof** galerada *f*

gallium [gǽliəm] N galio *m*

gallon [gǽlən] N galón [3.7853 liters] *m*

gallop [gǽləp] VI galopar; N galope *m*

gallows [gǽloz] N horca *f*, cadalso *m*

galore [gəlór] ADV en abundancia

galoshes [gəlɑ́ʃɪz] N chanclos *m pl*

galvanize [gǽlvənaɪz] VT (metals) galvanizar; (a crowd) electrizar

Gambia [gǽmbiə] N Gambia *f*

Gambian [gǽmbiən] ADJ & N gambiano -na *mf*
gamble [gǽmbəɫ] VI jugar; VT jugarse; **I'll — my whole fortune on this venture** voy a jugarme todo en este negocio; **to — away** perder en el juego; N (risk) riesgo *m*; (bet) apuesta *f*
gambler [gǽmblɚ] N apostador -ora *mf*, tahúr *m*
gambling [gǽmblɪŋ] N juego [de apuestas] *m*
game [gem] N juego *m*; (match of chess, etc.) partida *f*; (sports match) partido *m*; (wild animals and their meat) caza *f*; **— console** consola de juegos *f*; **— plan** (deporte) plan de juego *m*; (negocios) estrategia *f*; **— point** punto de juego *m*; **— room** sala recreativa *f*; **— show** programa concurso *m*; **to be fair —** ser blanco legítimo; ADJ **I'm — for some tennis** me apunto para jugar al tenis; **he has a — knee** tiene la rodilla lisiada
gamut [gǽmət] N gama *f*
gander [gǽndɚ] N ganso [macho] *m*; **to take a — at** echarle un vistazo a
gang [gæŋ] N (of youths, thieves, etc.) pandilla *f*, gavilla *f*, banda *f*; (group of friends) grupo *m*; **—plank** pasarela *f*; **—way** (passage way) pasillo *m*; (on a ship) pasamano *m*; **—way!** ¡abran cancha! VI **to — up on** conspirar contra, conspirar en masa
gangrene [gǽŋgrin] N gangrena *f*; VI/VT gangrenar[se]
gangster [gǽŋstɚ] N gángster *m*, maleante *m*
gap [gæp] N (breach) brecha *f*, hueco *m*; (of memory) laguna *f*; (of time) intervalo *m*; **she has a — between her teeth** tiene los dientes separados; VT espaciar [correctamente]
gape [gep] VI mirar boquiabierto
garage [gəráʒ] N (for parking) garaje *m*; (for repairing) taller mecánico *m*; **— sale** venta de garaje *f*; VT estacionar en un garaje
garb [garb] N vestimenta *f*, atavío *m*; VT vestir, ataviar
garbage [gárbɪʤ] N basura *f*; **— can** bote de basura *m*; **— disposal unit** trituradora *f*; **—man** basurero *m*; **— truck** camión de la basura *m*; **what a load of —!** ¡qué montón de mentiras!
garden [gárdn̩] N jardín *m*; **— of Eden** jardín del Edén *m*; VI cultivar un jardín
gardener [gárdnɚ] N jardinero -ra *mf*
gargle [gárgəɫ] VI hacer gárgaras; VT hacer gárgaras con; N (liquid) gargarismo *m*; (sound) gárgara *f*
garland [gárlənd] N guirnalda *f*
garlic [gárlɪk] N ajo *m*
garment [gármənt] N prenda *f*
garner [gárnɚ] VT cosechar
garnet [gárnɪt] N granate *m*
garnish [gárnɪʃ] VT (decorate) decorar; (decorate food) aderezar, guarnecer; (withhold wages) retener; N (decoration) adorno *m*,

decoración *f*
garret [gǽrɪt] N desván *m*, buhardilla *f*
garrison [gǽrɪsən] N guarnición *f*; VT guarnecer
garrulous [gǽrələs] ADJ locuaz, gárrulo
garter [gárDɚ] N liga *f*; **— belt** liguero *m*, portaligas *m sg*; **— snake** culebra de jaretas *f*; VT sujetar con ligas
gas [gæs] N (vapor) gas *m*; (fuel) gasolina *f*; (flatulence) gases *m pl*; **— chamber** cámara de gas *f*; **— mask** máscara de gas *f*; **— pedal** acelerador *m*; **— station** gasolinera *f*; **to step on the —** acelerar; **we had a —** lo pasamos bomba; VT asfixiar con gas, matar en la cámara de gas; **to — up** llenar el tanque
gaseous [gǽʃəs] ADJ gaseoso
gash [gæʃ] N tajo *m*; VT hacer un tajo en
gasket [gǽskɪt] N junta [de culata] *f*
gasoline [gǽsəlin] N gasolina *f*, nafta *f*
gasp [gæsp] N (cry) grito sofocado *m*; (pant) jadeo *m*, boqueada *f*; VI (cry out) dar un grito sofocado; (in surprise) quedar boquiabierto; (for breath) jadear, boquear
gastric [gǽstrɪk] ADJ gástrico; **— ulcer** úlcera gástrica *f*
gastritis [gæstráɪDɪs] N gastritis *f*
gastroenteritis [gæstroɛntəráɪDɪs] N gastroenteritis *f*
gastrointestinal [gæstroɪntéstɪnl̩] ADJ gastrointestinal; **— tract** tubo digestivo *m*
gastronomy [gæstránəmi] N gastronomía *f*
gate [get] N (to a garden) portón *m*; (to a city) puerta *f*; (at an airport) puerta de embarque *f*; **—way** (entrance, access) puerta [de entrada] *f*; (in computers) portal *m*
gather [gǽðɚ] VT (bring together) reunir, allegar; (pick) recolectar; (deduce) deducir, colegir; (sew) fruncir; VI (come together) reunirse; (collect) juntarse; (contract into folds) fruncirse; **to — dust** juntar polvo/ tierra; **to — speed** acelerar; N frunce *m*
gathering [gǽðɚɪŋ] N (meeting) asamblea *f*; (social) tertulia *f*; (assemblage of people) concurrencia *f*, reunión *f*; (act of gathering fruit, etc.) recolección *f*
gaudy [gɔ́di] ADJ (of bright color) chillón; (ostentatious) llamativo
gauge [geʤ] VT (measure) medir; (estimate) estimar; (calibrate) calibrar; N (measurement standard) medida *f*; (caliber) calibre *m*; (measuring device) medidor *m*; (track width) entrevía *f*
gaunt [gɔnt] ADJ demacrado
gauntlet [gɔ́ntlɪt] N (glove) guante *m*; (mailed glove) guantelete *m*; **to throw down the —** retar, desafiar; **to run the —** sufrir acosos
gauze [gɔz] N gasa *f*
gave [gev] *see* give
gavel [gǽvəɫ] N martillo *m*
gawk [gɔk] VT mirar boquiabierto

gawky [gɔ́ki] ADJ torpe, desgarbado

gay [ge] ADJ (happy) alegre, festivo; (homosexual) gay, homosexual; N *fam* gay *m*, homosexual *m*

gaze [gez] VI mirar fijamente, contemplar; N mirada fija *f*

gazelle [gəzέł] N gacela *f*

gazette [gəzét] N gaceta *f*

gear [gir] N (equipment) equipo *m*; (cog) rueda dentada *f*; (assembly of cogs) engranaje *m*; (transmission speed) marcha *f*, cambio *m*; (personal property) pertenencias *f pl*; —**box** caja de cambios *f*; —**shift lever** palanca de cambios *f*; **to be in** — estar engranado; **to change** —**s** cambiar de marcha, poner el cambio; **to put into** — engranar; **to put out of** — desengranar; VI **to** — **up** prepararse

gearing [gírɪŋ] N engranaje *m*

gecko [gέko] N geco *m*

geek [gik] N persona que tiene exagerada pasión por la informática *f*

Geiger counter [gáɪgə-káʊntə-] N contador Geiger *m*

gel [ʤεł] VI/VT cuajar[se]

gelatin [ʤέlətn̩] N gelatina *f*

gem [ʤεm] N (precious stone) gema *f*; (valuable person) joya *f*; —**stone** piedra preciosa *f*

gender [ʤέndə-] N género *m*; — **discrimination** discriminación de género *f*; — **gap** diferencias entre los sexos *f pl*; —- **specific** propio de un solo sexo

gene [ʤin] N gen *m*; — **marker** marcador genético *m*; N — **pool** conjunto de genes de una población *m*; — **splicing** empalme genético *m*; — **therapy** terapia genética *f*

genealogy [ʤiniálədʒi] N genealogía *f*

general [ʤέnə-əł] ADJ & N general *mf*; **in** — por lo general; — **practitioner** médico -ca general *mf*

generality [ʤεnərǽlɪɒi] N generalidad *f*

generalization [ʤεnə-əlɪzéʃən] N generalización *f*

generalize [ʤέnə-əlaɪz] VI/VT generalizar

generally [ʤέnə-əli] ADV generalmente

generate [ʤέnəret] VT generar

generation [ʤεnəréʃən] N generación *f*; — **gap** brecha generacional *f*, abismo generacional *m*

generator [ʤέnəreɒə-] N generador *m*

generic [ʤənέrɪk] ADJ genérico; — **brand** marca genérica *f*

generosity [ʤεnərásɪɒi] N generosidad *f*, largueza *f*

generous [ʤέnə-əs] ADJ generoso

genetic [ʤənέɒɪk] ADJ genético; — **code** código genético *m*; — **engineering** ingeniería genética *f*; — **fingerprinting** identificación genética *f*; — **marker** marcador genético *m*; N —**s** genética *f*

genetically [ʤənέɒɪkli] ADV — **modified** transgénico

genial [ʤínjəł] ADJ afable, de buen genio

genital [ʤέnɪdl̩] ADJ genital; — **herpes** herpes genital *m*; — **wart** verruga genital *f*; N —**s** genitales *m pl*, sexo *m*

genius [ʤínjəs] N genio *m*

genocide [ʤέnəsaɪd] N genocidio *m*

genome [ʤínom] N genoma *m*

genre [ʒánrə] N género *m*

genteel [ʤεntíł] ADJ refinado

gentile [ʤέntaɪł] ADJ & N gentil *mf*

gentle [ʤέntl̩] ADJ (kindly) amable; (mild, slow, gradual) suave; (tame) manso

gentleman [ʤέntl̩mən] N caballero *m*

gentlemanly [ʤέntl̩mənli] ADJ caballeroso

gentleness [ʤέntl̩nɪs] N (kindness) amabilidad *f*; (mildness) suavidad *f*; (tameness) mansedumbre *f*

gently [ʤέntli] ADV (smoothly) suavemente; (tactfully) con mucho tacto

genuine [ʤέnjuɪn] ADJ genuino

genus [ʤínəs] N género *m*

geocentric [ʤiosέntrɪk] ADJ geocéntrico

geographical [ʤiəgrǽfɪkəł] ADJ geográfico

geography [ʤiágrəfi] N geografía *f*

geological [ʤiəládʒɪkəł] ADJ geológico

geology [ʤiálədʒi] N geología *f*

geometric [ʤiəmέtrɪk] ADJ geométrico

geometry [ʤiámɪtri] N geometría *f*

geophysics [ʤiofízɪks] N geofísica *f*

geopolitical [ʤiopəlíɒɪkəł] ADJ geopolítico

Georgia [ʤɔ́rʤə] N Georgia *f*

Georgian [ʤɔ́rʤən] ADJ & N georgiano -na *mf*

geostationary [ʤiostéʃɒnεri] ADJ geoestacionario

geothermal [ʤioθɝ́məł] ADJ geotérmico

geranium [ʤəréniəm] N geranio *m*

geriatric [ʤεriǽtrɪk] ADJ geriátrico; N —**s** geriatría *f*

germ [ʤɝm] N (microorganism) microbio *m*, germen *m*; (bud, embryo, rudiment) germen *m*; — **warfare** guerra biológica *f*

German [ʤɝ́mən] ADJ & N alemán -na *mf*; — **measles** rubeola, rubéola *f*; — **shepherd** pastor alemán *m*

germane [ʤɝmén] ADJ pertinente, relacionado

Germanic [ʤɝ-mǽnɪk] ADJ germánico -ca

Germany [ʤɝ́məni] N Alemania *f*

germinate [ʤɝ́mənet] VI germinar; VT hacer germinar

gerund [ʤέrənd] N gerundio *m*

gestate [ʤέstet] VI/VT gestar[se]

gestation [ʤεstéʃən] N gestación *f*

gesticulate [ʤεstíkjəlet] VI gesticular

gesture [ʤέstʃə-] N gesto *m*, ademán *m*; (token) muestra *f*; VI gesticular

gesundheit [gəzúnthaɪt] INTERJ (after a sneeze) ¡salud! *Sp* ¡Jesús!

get [gεt] VT (receive, earn) recibir; (obtain)

obtener; (reach by phone) comunicarse con; (hear, understand) entender; (seize) agarrar; *Sp* coger; (prevail) conseguir, lograr; (affect) afectar; (catch disease) pescar; *Sp* coger; **to — across** comunicar; **to — ahead** prosperar; **to — along [with]** llevarse bien [con]; **to — angry** enojarse; **to — around** (skirt) esquivar, evitar; (go out) salir mucho; **to — away** escapar[se]; **to — away with** quedar impune; **to — back** (return) volver; (recover something) recuperar; **to — back at** vengarse de; **to be —ting on in years** ponerse viejo; **to — by** (go past) pasar; (survive) ir tirando; **to — dark** oscurecer; **to — down** (lower oneself) bajar; (depress) deprimir; (swallow) tragar; **to — down to business / brass tacks** ir al grano; **to — going** ponerse en marcha; **to — in** (enter) entrar; (arrive) llegar; (a vehicle) subir a; **to — it** captar, entender; **to — married** casarse; **to — nowhere** no llegar a ningún lado; **to — off** (dismount, get down) bajar; (not receive punishment) salir impune; (leave work) salir; **to — off on** enloquecerse por; **to — off someone's back** dejar de fastidiar; **to — old** envejecer; **to — on** montarse a; **to — out** (take out) sacar; (exit) salir; **to — over** (recuperate) recuperarse, sobreponerse a; (forgive) olvidar; **to — ready** preparar[se]; **to — rich** enriquecerse; **to — rid of** deshacerse de; **to — sick** enfermarse; **to — somewhere** tener resultado; **to — through** (survive an ordeal) sobrevivir; (reach by phone, be understood) comunicarse; (complete) lograr terminar; **to — to someone** afectar a alguien; **to — together** reunirse; **to — up** (arise) levantarse; (prepare) montar; **I got him to do it** conseguí/logré que lo hiciera; **I have got to do it** tengo que hacerlo; **we got our house painted** nos pintaron la casa; **he got a year in jail** le dieron un año de cárcel; **we — to stay up late in summer** en el verano nos dejan quedarnos despiertos hasta tarde; **that —s my goat** eso me fastidia; N **—away** (escape) escape *m*; (vacation) escapada *f*; **—-together** reunión *f*; **—up** disfraz *m*, atuendo *m*; **from the —-go** desde el principio
geyser [gáizɚ] N géiser *m*
Ghana [gánə] N Ghana *f*
Ghanaian [gániən] ADJ & N ghanés -esa *mf*
ghastly [gǽstli] ADJ (horrible) horrendo, espantoso; (cadaverous) cadavérico
ghetto [gɛ́Do] N gueto *m*
ghost [gost] N fantasma *m*; **— town** pueblo fantasma *m*; **—writer** colaborador -ora anónimo -ma *mf*; **not a — of a chance** ni la menor posibilidad
ghostly [góstli] ADJ fantasmagórico

ghoul [guɫ] N fantasma *m*
giant [dʒáiənt] N & ADJ gigante -ta *mf*
gibberish [dʒíbɚiʃ] N jerigonza *f*
gibbon [gíbən] N gibón *m*
Gibraltar [dʒɪbrɔ́ɫtɚ] N Gibraltar *m*
Gibraltarian [dʒɪbrɔɫtériən] ADJ & N gibraltareño -ña *mf*
giddy [gíDi] ADJ (dizzy) mareado; (of heights) vertigoso; (of speed) vertiginoso
gift [gɪft] N (thing given, act of giving) regalo *m*, presente *m*; (special ability) don *m*; **— certificate** vale por un regalo *m*; **— tax** impuesto sobre las donaciones *m*; **—-wrap** envolver para regalo; VT regalar
gifted [gíftɪd] ADJ (artist) talentoso; (child) superdotado
gigabyte [gígəbait] N gigabyte *m*
gigahertz [gígəhɚts] N gigahercio *m*
gigantic [dʒaigǽntɪk] ADJ gigantesco, gigante
giggle [gígəɫ] VI reír tontamente; N risita tonta *f*
gild [gɪɫd] VT dorar
gill [gɪɫ] N agalla *f*
gilt [gɪɫt] ADJ & N dorado *m*
gimmick [gímɪk] N treta *f*, estratagema *f*
gin [dʒɪn] N (liquor) ginebra *f*; **— rummy** gin rummy *m*
ginger [dʒíndʒɚ] N jengibre *m*; **— ale** ginger ale *m*; **—bread** pan de jengibre *m*
gingham [gíŋəm] N guingán *m*
gingivitis [dʒɪndʒəváidis] N gingivitis *f*
giraffe [dʒərǽf] N jirafa *f*
gird [gɚd] VT ceñir; **to — oneself** prepararse
girder [gɚ́Dɚ] N viga *f*
girdle [gɚ́dl̩] N faja *f*; VT rodear
girl [gɚɫ] N (female child) niña *f*; (young female) muchacha *f*, joven *f*, chica *f*; (servant) muchacha *f*, chacha *f*; **—friend** novia *f*
girlhood [gɚ́ɫhud] N niñez *f*
girlish [gɚ́ɫɪʃ] ADJ de niña
girth [gɚθ] N (of things) circunferencia *f*; (of persons) contorno *m*; (of horses) cincha *f*; VT cinchar
gist [dʒɪst] N esencia *f*, lo esencial
GI [gastrointestinal] tract [dʒíái] N tubo digestivo *m*
give [gɪv] VT dar; (a gift) regalar; (a party) organizar; (a name) poner; (a donation) donar; **I don't — a hoot** me importa un comino; VI dar; (yield) ceder; (break) romperse; **to — away** (a gift) regalar, donar; (the bride) entregar; (a secret) revelar; **to — back** devolver; **to — in** (acknowledge defeat) rendirse; **to — off** emitir, despedir, desprender; **to — out** (announce) anunciar; (distribute) repartir; (become exhausted) rendirse; (run out) acabarse; **to — over** entregar; **to — up** (surrender) darse por vencido; (stop) dejar [de]; **we'll work on this two years, — or take a month** vamos

a trabajar en esto dos años, un mes más, un mes menos; N elasticidad *f*; — **and take** toma y daca *m*

given [gívən] ADJ (stated, fixed) dado; (bestowed) regalado; — **name** nombre de pila *m*; — **that she's not here** dado que ella no está; — **to** propenso a; N premisa *f*

given [gívən] *see* give

giver [gívɚ] N dador -ora *mf*, donador -ora *mf*

gizmo [gízmo] N coso *m*, chisme *m*

glacial [gléʃəł] ADJ glacial

glacier [gléʃɚ] N glaciar *m*

glad [glæd] ADJ contento; **I'm — to see you** me alegro de verte; **I'd be — to help** sería un placer ayudarte

gladden [glædn̩] VT alegrar, regocijar, alborozar

gladiator [glædɪeɗɚ] N gladiador *m*

glamorous [glæmɚəs] ADJ glamoroso, encantador

glamour [glæmɚ] N (charm) glamour *f*, encanto *m*; (excitement) atractivo *m*

glance [glæns] VI echar un vistazo; **to — off** rebotar con efecto; N (look) vistazo *m*; (bounce) rebote oblicuo *m*

gland [glænd] N glándula *f*

glandular [glændʒələ] ADJ glandular

glare [glɛr] N (bright light) relumbre *m*; (stare) mirada furiosa *f*; VI (shine) relumbrar; (stare fiercely) lanzar una mirada hostil

glaring [glérɪŋ] ADJ (blinding) deslumbrante; (obvious) evidente; (hostile) hostil

glass [glæs] N (substance) vidrio *m*; (window pane) vidrio *m*, cristal *m*; (tumbler) vaso [de vidrio] *m*; (mirror) espejo *m*; (glassware) cristalería *f*; (magnifier) lupa *f*; —**blowing** soplado de vidrio *m*; — **ceiling** techo de cristal *m*; — **cutter** cortavidrio *m*; —**es** anteojos *m pl*, lentes *m pl*, gafas *f pl*; — **eye** ojo de vidrio *m*; —**maker** vidriero -ra *mf*; —**ware** cristalería *f*

glassy [glǽsi] ADJ vidrioso

glaucoma [glɔkómə] N glaucoma *m*

glaze [glez] VT (windows) poner vidrios a; (ceramics) vidriar; (food) glasear; (wood) barnizar; VI vidriarse; N (pottery) vidriado *m*, barniz *m*; (food) glaseado *m*

glazier [gléʒɚ] N vidriero -ra *mf*

gleam [glim] N reflejo *m*, brillo *m*; **a — of hope** un rayo de esperanza; VI brillar, relucir

glean [glin] VT (grain) espigar; (information) extraer, deducir

glee [gli] N regocijo *m*, júbilo *m*; — **club** coro *m*

glib [glɪb] ADJ (fluent) de mucha labia; (superficial) simplista, superficial

glide [glaɪd] VI (slide) deslizarse; (fly) planear; N (sliding movement) deslizamiento *m*; (flight) planeo *m*

glider [gláɪɗɚ] N planeador *m*

glimmer [glímɚ] N luz trémula *f*; **a — of hope** un destello de esperanza; **the — of an idea** el atisbo de una idea; VI guiñar, emitir una luz trémula

glimpse [glɪmps] N (look) ojeada *f*, vistazo *m*; (hint) atisbo *m*; VT ojear

glint [glɪnt] N destello *m*; VI destellar

glisten [glísən] VI brillar, relucir

glitch [glɪtʃ] N fallo *m*, problema técnico *m*

glitter [glíɗɚ] VI destellar; N (light) destello *m*; (showiness) brillo *m*; (sparkling powder) brillantina *f*

gloat [glot] VI regodearse; N regodeo *m*

glob [glɑb] N pegote *m*

global [glóbəł] ADJ global, mundial; — **backup** respaldo global *m*; — **positioning system** sistema mundial de posicionamiento *m*; — **warming** calentamiento global *m*

globalization [globəlɪzéʃən] N globalización *f*

globe [glob] N globo *m*; (map of the Earth) globo terráqueo *m*

globule [glábjuł] N glóbulo *m*

globulin [glábjəlɪn] N globulina *f*

gloom [glum] N (darkness) oscuridad *f*; (melancholy) melancolía *f*, tristeza *f*

gloomy [glúmi] ADJ (dark, depressing) sombrío, lúgubre, tenebroso; (melancholic) melancólico, deprimido

glorify [glɔ́rəfaɪ] VT glorificar

glorious [glɔ́riəs] ADJ (wonderful) magnífico, excelente; (related to glory) glorioso

glory [glɔ́ri] N gloria *f*; VI **to — in** regocijarse con

gloss [glɔs] N (shine, cosmetic) brillo *m*; (marginal note) glosa *f*; (in a dictionary) acepción *f*; VT (polish) lustrar, dar brillo a; (explain) glosar; **to — over** disfrazar, encubrir

glossary [glɔ́səri] N glosario *m*

glossy [glɔ́si] ADJ lustroso; (paper) glaseado

glottal [glɑdl̩] ADJ (cancer) glótico; (phonetic) glotal

glottis [glɑ́ɗɪs] N glotis *f*

glove [glʌv] N guante *m*; (baseball) guante *m*, manopla *f*; — **compartment** guantera *f*

glow [glo] N incandescencia *f*; (of cheeks) rubor *m*; (of emotion) calor *m*; VI resplandecer; (of metal) estar al rojo vivo; (of cheeks) ruborizarse; **to — with health** estar rebosante de salud; —**worm** luciérnaga *f*

glowing [glóɪŋ] ADJ (with light) incandescente; (colors) vivo; (with health) rebosante; (report) favorable

glucose [glúkos] N glucosa *f*

glue [glu] N cola *f*, pegamento *m*; VT (put glue on) engomar; (stick together) pegar; (stick wood together) encolar; **she's —d to the television** está pegada al televisor

glum [glʌm] ADJ tristón

glut [glʌt] VI/VT (with food) hartar[se]; VT (with products) saturar; N superabundancia *f*

gluten [glútn̩] N gluten *m*
glutton [glátn̩] N glotón -ona *mf*
gluttonous [glátn̩əs] ADJ glotón
gluttony [glátn̩i] N glotonería *f*, gula *f*
glycerin [glísə·ɪn] N glicerina *f*
gnarled [nɑrld] ADJ (knotty) nudoso, sarmentoso; (twisted) retorcido
gnash [næʃ] VI/VT rechinar
gnat [næt] N jején *m*
gnaw [nɔ] VI/VT (bite, corrode) roer; (torment) remorder; **to — a hole** hacer un agujero a mordiscos
GNP [gross national product] [ʤiénpí] N PNB *m*
gnu [nu] N ñu *m*
go [go] VI (move) ir; (function) andar, marchar; **—ing price** precio vigente *m*; **to — against** oponerse a; **to — ahead** seguir adelante; **to — all out** dar todo de sí; **to — along** conformarse; **to — around** (circumvent) dar la vuelta a; (circulate) circular; (be sufficient) alcanzar; **to — around with** andar con; **to — away** irse; **to — back** volver; **to — back on one's word** faltar a la palabra; **to — beyond** traspasar; **to — by** (pass) pasar; (be guided by) guiarse por; **to — by another name** usar otro nombre; **to — crazy** enloquecerse; **to — down** (descend) bajar; (fall) caer, estrellarse; (lose) perder; (be accepted) gustar; **to — down on** practicar sexo oral a; **to — for it** atreverse; **— for it!** ¡adelante! ¡atrévete! **to — in with** participar; **to — it alone** tirarse solo; **to — off** (explode) estallar; (happen) suceder; (leave) irse; **to — off on** regañar; **to — on** (happen) pasar; (continue) seguir; **to — out** (extinguish) apagarse; (socialize) salir; **to — over** (review) repasar, revisar; (read) leer; (cross) cruzar; **to — through** (suffer) sufrir; (examine) examinar; (be approved) ser aprobado; (spend) gastar; **to — through with** llevar a cabo; **to — to sleep** dormirse; **to — under** (go bankrupt) quebrar; (sink) hundirse; **to — up** (building) levantarse; (prices) subir; **pizza to —** pizza para llevar; **to let —** soltar[se]; **the car went for a good price** el coche se vendió a un buen precio; **he's smart, as dogs —** para ser perro, es inteligente; **that old couch has got to —** hay que deshacerse de ese sofá viejo; **cows — "moo"** las vacas hacen "mu"; **they — straight for the pizza** se van derechito a la pizza; **she's —ing to buy a house** va a comprar una casa; **anything —es** todo vale; **what I say —es** lo que yo digo, vale; **don't — to any trouble** no te molestes; **— figure!** ¡vaya a saber uno! **I've got to — [to the bathroom]** tengo que ir [al baño]; N (energy) energía *f*; (attempt) intento *m*; —-

ahead visto bueno *m*; —-**between** intermediario -ria *mf*; —-**cart** kart *m*; **in one** — de una vez; **on the** — a las corridas; **at the first** — de primera; **they made a — of it** tuvieron éxito; **it's a** — ¡trato hecho! **from the word** — desde el vamos
goad [god] N aguijada *f*; VT aguijonear
goal [goł] N (objective) meta *f*; (score) gol *m*; — **area** área de penales *f*; —**keeper** portero -ra *mf*, arquero -ra *mf*; — **kick** saque de meta *m*, saque de puerta *m*; — **line** línea de meta *f*; — **post** palo *m*, poste *m*
goalie [góli] N guardameta *mf*
goat [got] N cabra *f*; —**herd** cabrero -ra *mf*; **he gets my —** me saca de quicio
goatee [gotí] N perilla *f*
gobble [gábəł] VI/VT (devour) engullir; VI (turkey) gluglutear; **to — up** engullir
gobbledygook [gábəłdigʊk] N jerigonza *f*
gobbler [gáblə·] N pavo *m*
goblet [gáblɪt] N copa *f*
goblin [gáblɪn] N duende *m*
god, God [gɑd] N dios *m*, Dios *m*; — **bless you!** (blessing) ¡que Dios te bendiga! (after a sneeze) ¡salud! ¡Jesús! —**child** ahijado -da *mf*; —**damned** *vulg* maldito; —**father** padrino *m*; —**forsaken** de mala muerte; —-**given** divino; —**mother** madrina *f*; —**send** bendición *f*; — **willing** si Dios quiere; **by —** por Dios; **my —!** ¡Dios mío!
goddess [gádɪs] N diosa *f*
godless [gádlɪs] ADJ impío
godly [gádli] ADJ piadoso
goggles [gágəłz] N gafas protectoras *f pl*, antiparras *f pl*
going [góɪŋ] ADJ que marcha bien; —**s-on** tejemanejes *m pl*
goiter [góɪdə·] N bocio *m*
gold [gołd] N oro *m*; — **bullion** oro en lingotes *m*; — **digger** mujer cazafortunas *f*; —**finch** jilguero *m*; —**fish** pez dorado *m*; — **medal** medalla de oro *f*; —**smith** orfebre *m*; **a heart of** — un corazón de oro
golden [gółdən] ADJ (made of gold) de oro, áureo; (of gold color) dorado; — **eagle** águila dorada *f*; — **parachute** paracaídas dorado *m sg*; — **retriever** golden retriever *m*; — **rule** regla de oro *f*
golf [gɑłf] N golf *m*; — **bag** bolsa de golf *f*; — **ball** pelota de golf *f*; — **cart** coche/cochecito de golf *m*; — **club** (stick) palo de golf *m*; (place) club de golf *m*; — **course** campo de golf *m*
gonad [gónæd] N gónada *f*
gondola [gándələ] N (boat, basket under a balloon) góndola *f*; (cable car) cabina *f*
gone [gɔn] ADJ **my computer is** — desapareció mi computadora; **the candy is all** — se acabaron los dulces

gone [gɔn] *see* go
gong [gɑŋ] N batintín *m*, gong *m*
gonorrhea [ɡɑnɔríə] N gonorrea *f*
good [gʊd] ADJ bueno; (valid) válido; — **faith**
buena fe *f*; —-**for-nothing** inútil,
zanguango; — **for two burritos** vale por
dos burritos; —-**looking** guapo, apuesto; —-
natured apacible, bonachón, de buen genio;
—**will** buena voluntad *f*; **for** — para siempre;
a — **hour** una hora larga; **a** — **many**
muchos; **to have a** — **time** divertirse; **to**
make — cumplir; **to smell** — oler bien; N
(moral act, benefit) bien *m*; **for your own** —
por tu propio bien; INTERJ ¡bien! —
afternoon buenas tardes; —**bye** adiós; —
day buenos días; — **evening** buenas noches;
— **morning** buenos días; — **night** buenas
noches; N —**s** mercancías *f pl*; —**s and**
services bienes y servicios *m pl*; **to deliver**
the —**s** cumplir lo prometido
goodly [gúdli] ADJ (considerable) considerable;
(of fine appearance) de buen aspecto
goodness [gúdnɪs] N bondad *f*; (of food) calidad
f; INTERJ ¡Dios mío!
goody [gʊDi] N golosina *f*; —-— santurrón -ona
mf; INTERJ ¡qué bien!
goof [guf] VI pifiar; **to** — **off** perder el tiempo; **to**
— **up** pifiarla; N pifia *f*
goofy [gúfi] ADJ (person) bobalicón; (idea) tonto
goose [gus] N (bird, fool) ganso -sa *mf*; —**berry**
(berry) grosella espinosa *f*; (bush) grosellero
m; —**bumps** carne de gallina *f*; — **egg** cero
m; VT **to** — **someone** sorprender a alguien
tocándole entre las nalgas
GOP [Grand Old Party] [ʤíópí] N Partido
Republicano *m*
gopher [gófɚ] N ardilla de tierra *f*
gore [gɔr] N sangre derramada *f*; VT cornear
gorge [gɔrʤ] N (body part) garganta *f*; (ravine)
garganta *f*, tajo *m*; VI **to** — **one's self [on]**
atracarse [de], darse un atracón [de]
gorgeous [gɔ́rʤəs] ADJ (woman, outfit)
precioso; (weather) espléndido
gorilla [gərílə] N gorila *mf*; (thug) matón *m*
gory [gɔ́ri] ADJ (of a battle) sangriento; (of a
surface) ensangrentado
gospel [gáspəl] N evangelio *m*; (music) gospel *m*;
— **truth** pura verdad *f*
gossip [gásəp] N (rumor) chismorreo *m*,
murmuración *f*, habladurías *f pl*; (person)
chismoso -sa *mf*; (woman) comadre *f*; **a piece**
of — un chisme *m*; VI chismear, murmurar
gossipy [gásəpi] ADJ chismoso, lenguaraz
got [gɑt] *see* get
Gothic [gáθɪk] ADJ gótico; N (language) gótico *m*,
godo *m*; (style) estilo gótico *m*
gotten [gɑtn̩] *see* get
gouge [gaʊʤ] N gubia *f*; VT (scoop) sacar con
gubia; (overcharge) cobrar de más; **to** —

someone's eyes out arrancarle los ojos a
alguien
gourd [gɔrd] N calabaza *f*
gourmet [gɔrmé] N & ADJ gourmet *mf*; —
cheese queso fino *m*
gout [gaʊt] N gota *f*
govern [gávɚn] VI/VT gobernar, regir; VT (in
grammar) regir
governability [gʌvɚnəbílɪDi] N gobernabilidad *f*
governess [gávɚnɪs] N institutriz *f*
governing [gávɚnɪŋ] N gobernación *f*; —
principle principio rector *m*
government [gávɚnmənt] N gobierno *m*; (in
grammar) rección *f*; — **agency** agencia
gubernamental *f*; —-**backed** respaldado por
el gobierno
governmental [gʌvɚnméntl] ADJ
gubernamental, gubernativo
governor [gávɚnɚ] N (leader) gobernador -ora
mf; (of an engine) regulador *m*
gown [gaʊn] N (woman's dress) vestido *m*; (for
sleeping) camisón *m*; (in hospital) bata *f*; (for
graduation) toga *f*
grab [græb] VT agarrar, prender; **how does**
that idea — **you?** ¿qué te parece esa idea? VI
to — **at** tratar de agarrar; N agarrón *m*; **up**
for —**s** a la rebatiña
grace [gres] N gracia *f*; (of movement) garbo *m*;
(of expression) donaire *m*; **to say** — dar la
oración; **to be in the good** —**s of someone**
gozar del favor de alguien, disfrutar de la
gracia de alguien; VT (adorn) adornar;
(honor) honrar, agraciar
graceful [grésfəl] ADJ (of movement) grácil,
garboso; (of behavior) donoso
gracefulness [grésfəlnɪs] N gracia *f*, donaire *m*
gracious [gréʃəs] ADJ (kind) gentil, cortés;
(elegant) elegante; (merciful) misericordioso;
—! ¡válgame Dios!
graciousness [gréʃəsnɪs] N gentileza *f*
gradation [gredéʃən] N gradación *f*
grade [gred] N (rank) grado *m*; (category) calidad
f; (year in school) año *m*, curso *m*; (marks)
nota *f*, calificación *f*; (slope) declive *m*; **to**
make the — alcanzar el nivel deseado; —
point average promedio de notas *m*; VT
(classify) clasificar; (assign grades) calificar,
corregir; (level) nivelar
gradual [grǽʤuəl] ADJ gradual
graduate[1] [grǽʤuɪt] N (advanced student)
estudiante de posgrado *mf*; (degree-holder)
graduado -da *mf*, egresado -da *mf*; ADJ
de posgrado; — **school** programa de
posgrado *m*
graduate[2] [grǽʤuet] VI graduarse, titularse; VT
(confer a degree) dar un diploma a; (mark a
scale) graduar
graduation [grǽʤuéʃən] N graduación *f*
graffiti [grəfíDi] N grafiti *m*, pintada *f*

graft [græft] N (of plant, tissue) injerto *m*; (corruption) concusión *f*, corrupción *f*; VI/VT injertar[se]

grain [gren] N (cereal, seed) grano *m*, mies *f*; (photographic texture) grano *m*; (of gold) pepita *f*; (of wood, meat, stone) veta *f*; (texture) textura *f*; (small amount) pizca *f*; **against the** — a/al redopelo, a contrapelo

gram [græm] N gramo *m*

grammar [grǽmɚ] N gramática *f*

grammatical [grǝmǽDɪkǝɫ] ADJ gramatical

granary [grénɚi] N granero *m*, troje *m*

grand [grænd] ADJ (splendid) grandioso, espléndido; (lofty) elevado; (impressive) impresionante; **—child** nieto -ta *mf*; **—children** nietos *m pl*; **—daughter** nieta *f*; **—father** abuelo *m*; **—fathered** eximido por la cláusula del abuelo; **— jury** jurado de acusación *m*; **—mother** abuela *f*; **—ma** abuelita *f*; **—pa** abuelito *m*; **—parent** abuelo *m*; **—parents** abuelos *m pl*; **— piano** piano de cola *m*; **—son** nieto *m*; **—stand** tribuna *f*; **a — old man** un gran señor; **the — total** el total

grandeur [grǽndʒɚ] N grandiosidad *f*

grandiose [grǽndios] ADJ (complex) complejo; (of speech) grandilocuente, rimbombante; (imposing) grandioso

granite [grǽnɪt] N granito *m*

grant [grænt] VT (give) conceder, otorgar, dispensar; (accept) admitir; (transfer) ceder; **to take for —ed** (an assumption) dar por sentado; (a person) no valorar; N (something granted) concesión *f*; (act of granting) concesión *f*, otorgamiento *m*; (subsidy, e.g., for scientists) subvención *f*

granular [grǽnjǝlɚ] ADJ granuloso

granulate [grǽnjǝlet] VI/VT granular[se]

grape [grep] N uva *f*; **—fruit** pomelo *m*, toronja *f*; **—vine** vid *f*; (ornamental) parra *f*; **I heard it through the —vine** me lo contó un pajarito

graph [græf] N (curve) gráfica *f*; **— paper** papel cuadriculado *m*; VT grafiar

graphic [grǽfɪk] ADJ gráfico; **— design** diseño gráfico *m*; N gráfico *m*; **—s** gráfica *f*; **—s card** tarjeta gráfica *f*

graphite [grǽfaɪt] N grafito *m*

grapple [grǽpǝɫ] VI/VT (hold) aferrar; (struggle) luchar, lidiar

grasp [græsp] VT (seize) agarrar, asir, aferrar; (understand) comprender; VI **to — at/for** tratar de agarrar; N (hold) agarre *m*, asidero *m*; (comprehension) comprensión *f*; **within one's —** al alcance; **to have a good — of a subject** dominar una materia

grass [græs] N (plant) hierba *f*; (lawn) césped *m*; (pasture) pasto *m*; (in tennis) césped *m*, hierba *f*; (marijuana) marihuana *f*, maría *f*;

—hopper saltamontes *m sg*, saltón *m*; **—land** pradera *f*, pastizal *m*; **— roots** las bases *f pl*

grassy [grǽsi] ADJ herboso

grate [gret] N (of a fireplace) parrilla *f*; (partition, guard) reja *f*, verja *f*; VT (install a grate) enrejar; (mince) rallar; (rub teeth together) crujir, rechinar; VI **to — on** rechinar

grateful [grétfǝɫ] ADJ agradecido

grater [gréDɚ] N rallador *m*

gratification [grǽDǝfɪkéʃǝn] N gratificación *f*

gratify [grǽDǝfaɪ] VT complacer, gratificar

grating [gréDɪŋ] N reja *f*, enrejado *m*, rejilla *f*; ADJ (discordant) rechinante; (irritating) irritante

gratitude [grǽDɪtud] N gratitud *f*

gratuitous [grǝtúɪDǝs] ADJ gratuito

gratuity [grǝtúɪDi] N propina *f*

grave [grev] ADJ grave; N fosa *f*, sepultura *f*; **—digger** sepulturero *m*; **—stone** lápida *f*; **—yard** cementerio *m*; **—yard shift** turno de la noche *m*; **to have one foot in the —** *fam* estar por reventar

gravel [grǽvǝɫ] N grava *f*; VT cubrir con grava

gravitation [grævɪtéʃǝn] N gravitación *f*

gravitational [grævɪtéʃǝnɫ] ADJ gravitatorio

gravity [grǽvɪDi] N gravedad *f* (also seriousness)

gravy [grévi] N jugo de carne *m*; **the rest is —** el resto es fácil

gray [gre] ADJ gris; (hair) canoso; (horse) rucio; **— area** zona gris *f*; **—-haired** cano, canoso; **— matter** materia gris *f*, N gris *m*; VI/VT agrisar; (hair) encanecer

grayish [gréɪʃ] ADJ grisáceo

graze [grez] VI/VT (feed) pacer, pastar, apacentar; (brush) rozar; N roce *m*

grease [gris] N grasa *f*; VT engrasar; **to — someone's palm** untarle la mano a alguien, engrasar a alguien

greasy [grísi, grízi] ADJ (covered with grease) grasiento; (impregnated with grease) grasoso; (hair) graso

great [gret] ADJ (large, numerous) grande; (good, excellent, considerable) gran; **—-aunt** tía abuela *f*; **—-grandchild** bisnieto -ta *mf*; **—-grandfather** bisabuelo *m*; **—-grandmother** bisabuela *f*; **—-grandchild** tataranieto -ta *mf*; **a — tree blocked the path** un árbol grande bloqueaba el camino; **she's a — friend** es una gran amiga; **a — while** un largo rato; **she's — at tennis** juega muy bien al tenis; **a — deal of** mucho; ADV muy bien, excelente; **she did —** le fue muy bien; N **the —s** los/las grandes *mf*; **they occur in —er numbers** son más numerosos; **he's the —est** es el mejor; INTERJ ¡qué bien!

greatly [grétli] ADV **it's — improved** lo han mejorado mucho / está mucho mejor; **we're**

— **interested** estamos muy interesados

greatness [grétnɪs] N grandeza f

Greece [gris] N Grecia f

greed [grid] N codicia f

greedy [grídi] ADJ (covetous) codicioso; (voracious) voraz; (eager) ávido

Greek [grik] ADJ & N griego -ga mf; **that's — to me** para mí es chino

green [grin] ADJ (green in color, verdant, unripe, inexperienced, nauseated, environmentally conscious) verde; **—back** dólar m; **— bean** Sp judía verde f; Mex ejote m; RP chaucha f; Carib habichuela; **— card** tarjeta verde f; **—horn** novato -ta mf; **—house** invernadero m; **—house effect** efecto invernadero m; **— light** luz verde f; **— pepper** pimiento verde m; N (color) verde m; (lawn) césped m; (pasture) prado m; (in golf) green m; (commons) ejido m; **—s** verduras de hoja verde f pl

greenish [gríniʃ] ADJ verdoso

greenness [grínnɪs] N verdor m

greet [grit] VT (say hello) saludar; (welcome) dar la bienvenida; (receive) recibir

greeting [grídɪŋ] N saludo m; **— card** tarjeta de felicitación f; **—s!** ¡saludos!

gregarious [grɪgériəs] ADJ (person) sociable; (animal) gregario

gremlin [grémlɪn] N duende m

Grenada [grənéɖə] N Granada f

grenade [grənéd] N granada f

Grenadian [grənéɖiən] ADJ & N granadino -na mf

grew [gru] see grow

greyhound [gréhaʊnd] N galgo m

griddle [grídl] N plancha f

gridlock [grídlɑk] N paralización f; VI paralizarse

grief [grif] N congoja f, pesar m, pesadumbre f; **to come to —** sufrir una desgracia; **to give someone —** meterse con alguien, jorobar a alguien; **good —!** ¡caramba! ADJ **—-stricken** acongojado, desconsolado

grievance [grívəns] N (complaint) queja f; (cause for complaint) motivo de queja m

grieve [griv] N estar de duelo; **to — for/over** llorar, lamentar [la muerte de alguien]; **he's grieving over the loss of his dog** lamenta la muerte de su perro; VT **that —s me** eso me apena

grieved [grivd] ADJ apenado

grievous [grívəs] ADJ (painful) doloroso, penoso; (atrocious) grave, atroz; (sorrowful) dolido

grill [grɪl] N (metal grid, restaurant fixture) parrilla f; (food) parrillada f; VI/VT asar a la parrilla; (interrogate) interrogar

grille [grɪl] N parrilla f

grim [grɪm] ADJ (news, situation) desalentador;

(war) cruento; (joke) macabro

grimace [grímɪs] N mueca f, mohín m; VI hacer muecas

grime [graɪm] N mugre f, suciedad f

grimy [gráɪmi] ADJ mugriento, sucio; **to make —** percudir; **to get —** percudirse

grin [grɪn] VI sonreír; N sonrisa f; **wipe that — off your face** deja de reírte

grind [graɪnd] VI/VT (mill finely) moler; (mill coarsely) triturar; (make shiny) pulir; (rub harshly) rechinar; (study hard) estudiar mucho; Sp empollar; **to — to a halt** pararse con un chirrido; N (drudgery) trabajo pesado m; (overzealous student) empollón -ona mf; **—stone** muela f; **the daily —** la lucha diaria; **to keep one's nose to the —stone** matarse trabajando/estudiando

grinder [gráɪndə] N (for coffee, pepper) molinillo m; (for meat) picadora f; (for sharpening tools) afilador m

grip [grɪp] N (hold) agarre m; (control) control m; (handle) mango m; (on a baseball bat, golf club) agarre m, empuñadura f; **he had a firm — on the tool** tenía bien agarrada la herramienta; **get a — on yourself** contrólate, cálmate; VT (seize) agarrar, asir; (take hold, interest) atrapar

gripe [graɪp] VI quejarse, rezongar, renegar; N queja f

grisly [grízli] ADJ cruento, espantoso

gristle [grísəl] N cartílago m

grit [grɪt] N (sand) arena f; (pluck) firmeza f, fam cojones m pl; **—s** sémola de maíz f; VT **to — one's teeth** apretar los dientes

gritty [grídi] ADJ (sandy) arenoso; (plucky) resuelto, fam cojonudo

grizzly [grízli] ADJ (grayish) grisáceo; **— bear** oso pardo m

groan [gron] N quejido m, gemido m; VI quejarse, gemir; (creak) crujir

grocer [grósə] N tendero -ra mf; Mex abarrotero -ra mf; Carib bodeguero -ra mf; RP almacenero -ra mf

grocery [grósəri] N tienda de comestibles f; Mex tienda de abarrotes f; Carib bodega f; RP almacén m; **groceries** comestibles m pl

groin [grɔɪn] N ingle f

groom [grum] N (in a wedding) novio m; (in a stable) mozo de cuadra m, caballerizo m; VT (a horse) almohazar; (prepare for a position) preparar; **to — oneself** arreglarse; **well- —ed** bien arreglado

groove [gruv] N (narrow cut) estría f, ranura f; (on a record, road) surco m; (routine) rutina f; VT estriar, acanalar

grope [grop] VI (feel one's way) andar a tientas; (search) buscar a tientas; VT manosear, toquetear; N manoseo m, toqueteo m

gross [gros] ADJ (before deductions) bruto;

(flagrant) flagrante; (indecent) grosero; (overall) general; (disgusting) asqueroso; — **domestic product** producto interno bruto *m*; — **income** ingreso bruto *m*; — **pay** salario bruto *m*; N gruesa *f*; VT recaudar en bruto; **to — out** dar asco, asquear

grotesque [grotésk] ADJ grotesco

grotto [grádo] N gruta *f*

grouch [grautʃ] N cascarrabias *mf sg*, refunfuñón -ona *mf*, rezongón -ona *mf*; VI refunfuñar

grouchy [gráutʃi] ADJ cascarrabias, refunfuñón

ground [graʊnd] N (land, electrical cable) tierra *f*; (soil) suelo *m*; (basis) fundamento *m*; — **ball** (in baseball) roletazo *m*; — **floor** planta baja *f*; —**hog** marmota *f*; —**s** (reason) motivo *m*; (dregs) borra *f*, poso *m*; (tract of land) terreno *m*; **to gain/lose** — ganar/perder terreno; **to stand one's** — ponerse firme; **from the — up** de piso a techo; VT (a wire) conectar a tierra; (a ship) hacer encallar; (punish) poner en penitencia; **the 747 was —ed** se prohibió volar en el 747

ground [graʊnd] *see* grind

groundless [gráʊndlɪs] ADJ infundado

group [grup] N grupo *m*; — **discount** descuento por grupo *m*; — **therapy** terapia de grupo *f*; VI/VT agrupar[se]

grouper [grúpɚ] N mero *m*

groupie [grúpi] N admiradora *f*

grouping [grúpɪŋ] N agrupamiento *m*

grove [grov] N arboleda *f*, plantío *m*; **orange** — naranjal *m*

grovel [grávəl] VI arrastrarse, humillarse

grow [gro] VI (naturally increase in size) crecer; (increase) aumentar, acrecentarse; (expand) desarrollarse; VT (crops) cultivar; (beard) dejarse crecer; **to — old** envejecer; **to — up** madurar; **Thai food —s on you** la comida tailandesa acaba gustándote

growing [gróɪŋ] N cultivo *m*; — **pains** (physical symptom) dolores del crecimiento *m pl*; (troubles) dificultades iniciales *f pl*; **he's a — boy** es un muchacho en crecimiento

growl [graʊl] VI gruñir; (of thunder) retumbar; (of stomach) rugir; N gruñido *m*

grown [gron] ADJ adulto; — **man** hombre hecho y derecho *m*; N —**-up** adulto *m*; ADJ —-up para adultos

grown [gron] *see* grow

growth [groθ] N (increase in size) crecimiento *m*; (increase in number) aumento *m*, acrecentamiento *m*; (tumor) bulto *m*; (expansion) desarrollo *m*; — **hormone** hormona del crecimiento *f*; **a — industry** una industria en expansión

grudge [grʌdʒ] N resentimiento *m*

grueling [grúlɪŋ] ADJ arduo

gruesome [grúsəm] ADJ cruento, truculento

gruff [grʌf] ADJ (manner) bronco; (voice) ronco

grumble [grámbəl] VI/VT refunfuñar, rezongar; N refunfuño *m*, gruñido *m*

grumpy [grámpi] ADJ refunfuñón, gruñón, rezongón

grunt [grʌnt] VI/VT gruñir; N gruñido *m*

guarantee [gærəntí] N (promise, pledge) garantía *f*; (guaranty) fianza *f*; VT (promise, pledge) garantizar; (warrant) dar fianza, avalar; —**d loan** préstamo garantizado *m*

guarantor [gǽrəntɔr] N fiador -ora *mf*

guaranty [gǽrənti] N (guarantee) garantía *f*; (thing taken as security) fianza *f*; (guarantor) fiador -ora *mf*

guard [gɑrd] VT custodiar; (watch over) vigilar; (protect) proteger; VI **to — against** guardarse de; N (person that guards) guardia *mf*, guarda *mf*; (of a machine) dispositivo protector *m*; **to be on** — estar alerta / estar en guardia; — **dog** perro guardián *m*; —**rail** baranda *f*, pasamano *m*

guardian [gárdiən] N guardián -ana *mf*; (legal) tutor -ora *mf*; — **angel** ángel de la guarda *m*

guardianship [gárdiənʃɪp] N tutela *f*

Guatemala [gwɑdəmálə] N Guatemala *f*

Guatemalan [gwɑdəmálən] ADJ & N guatemalteco -ca *mf*

guava [gwávə] N guayaba *f*

guerrilla [gərílə] N — **army** guerrilla *f*

guess [gɛs] VT (hazard, conjecture) adivinar; (suppose) suponer; N (conjecture) conjetura *f*; (supposition) suposición *f*; **I'll give you three —es** te doy tres oportunidades para adivinar

guest [gɛst] N (to a party, function) invitado -da *mf*; (at a restaurant) cliente *mf*; (overnight) huésped *mf*

guffaw [gəfɔ́] N carcajada *f*, risotada *f*

guidance [gáɪdn̩s] N (act of guiding) dirección *f*; (counsel) orientación *f*; (in a missile) teledirección *f*

guide [gaɪd] VT (serve as a guide) guiar; (direct the course of) dirigir; (counsel) orientar; —**d missile** misil guiado *m*; N (person) guía *mf*; (publication, mechanism) guía *f*; —**book** guía *f*; — **dog** perro guía *m*; —**lines** directivas *f pl*, pautas *f pl*, directrices *f pl*

guild [gɪld] N gremio *m*, corporación *f*

guile [gaɪl] N astucia *f*

guilt [gɪlt] N culpa *f*; — **trip** manipulación por acusaciones falsas *f*

guiltless [gíltlɪs] ADJ inocente

guilty [gílti] ADJ culpable; **we find the defendant not** — hallamos al acusado inocente

Guinea [gíni] N Guinea *f*; — **pig** conejillo de Indias *m*; —**-Bissau** Guinea-Bissau *f*

Guinean [gíniən] ADJ & N guineano -na *mf*

guise [gaɪz] ADV LOC **under the — of** so/bajo pretexto de; **in the — of** a manera de

guitar [gɪtár] N guitarra *f*
gulf [gʌlf] N (body of water) golfo *m*, (abyss, gap) abismo *m*; — **Stream** Corriente del Golfo *f*
gull [gʌl] N (bird) gaviota *f*; (dupe) crédulo -la *mf*; *Sp* primo -ma *mf*
gullet [gʌlɪt] N gaznate *m*
gullible [gʌləbəɬ] ADJ crédulo, ingenuo
gully [gʌli] N barranco *m*, barranca *f*; (gutter) alcantarilla *f*
gulp [gʌlp] VT tragar saliva; N trago *m*
gum [gʌm] N goma *f*; (for chewing) chicle *m*; —**s** encías *f pl*; VT **to — up** (ruin) jorobar; (stick) pegotear
gumption [gʌmpʃən] N (initiative) iniciativa *f*, arranque *m*; (courage) agallas *f pl*
gun [gʌn] N (firearm) arma de fuego *f*; (revolver) revólver *m*; (rifle) rifle *m*; (shotgun) escopeta *f*; (cannon) cañón *m*; (for painting, nailing) pistola *f*; VT (an engine) acelerar; —**boat** cañonero *m*; —**fire** tiroteo *m*; —**man** pistolero *m*; —**powder** pólvora *f*; —**shot** disparo *m*; —**shot wound** herida de bala *f*; **at —point** a mano armada; **to stick to one's —s** mantenerse firme; **don't jump the —** no te precipites; **to be under the —** estar bajo mucha presión; VT **to — down** matar a tiros; **to — for** andar a la caza de
gung-ho [gʌŋhó] ADJ fanático, entusiasta
gunner [gʌnɚ] N (shooting artillery) artillero -ra *mf*; (shooting a machine gun) ametrallador -ora *mf*
gurgle [gɝgəɬ] VI (water) borbotar; (baby) gorjear; N (of water) borboteo *m*; (of a baby) gorjeo *m*
gush [gʌʃ] VI (liquids) chorrear, brotar; (talk effusively) hablar con efusividad
gust [gʌst] N ráfaga *f*; — **of wind** racha/ráfaga de viento *f*, ventolera *f*; VI soplar en ráfagas
gusto [gʌsto] N (pleasure) placer *m*; (enthusiasm) entusiasmo *m*
gut [gʌt] N tripa *f*; (belly) barriga *f*; — **feeling** corazonada *f*; —**s** (intestines) entrañas *f pl*; (courage) *fam* cojones *m pl*; VT (eviscerate) destripar; (destroy the insides of) destrozar el interior de; (strip) desarmar
gutsy [gʌtsi] ADJ *fam* cojonudo
gutter [gʌdɚ] N (in the street) alcantarilla *f*; (on the roof) canaleta *f*, desagüe *m*; (squalor) miseria *f*
guy [gaɪ] N (man) tipo *m*; *Sp* tío *m*; **you —s** ustedes; *Sp* vosotros/vosotras; — **wire** cable *m*
Guyana [gaɪánə] N Guyana *f*
Guyanese [gaɪəníz] ADJ & N guyanés -esa *mf*
gym [dʒɪm] N gimnasio *m*
gymnasium [dʒɪmnéziəm] N gimnasio *m*
gymnastics [dʒɪmnǽstɪks] N gimnasia *f*
gynecologist [gaɪnəká4ədʒɪst] N ginecólogo -ga *mf*

gynecology [gaɪnəkáɬədʒi] N ginecología *f*
gyp [dʒɪp] VT estafar, timar; N estafa *f*, timo *m*
gypsum [dʒɪpsəm] N yeso *m*
gypsy [dʒɪpsi] N & ADJ gitano -na *mf*
gyrate [dʒáɪret] VI girar
gyroscope [dʒáɪrəskop] N giroscopio *m*

Hh

habit [hǽbɪt] N (custom) hábito *m*, costumbre *f*; (clerical dress) hábito *m*; (vice) vicio *m*; —**forming** adictivo
habitat [hǽbɪtæt] N hábitat *m*
habitual [həbítʃuəɬ] ADJ habitual
hack [hæk] N (cut) tajo *m*, machetazo *m*; (cough) tos seca *f*; (horse for hire) caballo de alquiler *m*; (nag) jamelgo *m*; (writer) escritor -ora mercenario -ria *mf*; —**saw** sierra para metales *f*; VI/VT tajar, cortar a machetazos; VI toser con tos seca
hacker [hǽkɚ] N pirata informático -ca *mf*
had [hæd] *see* have
hag [hæg] N (witch) bruja *f*; (ugly old woman) vieja fea *f*
haggard [hǽgɚd] ADJ demacrado
haggle [hǽgəɬ] VI regatear
hail [heɬ] N (precipitation) granizo *m*; (greeting) saludo *m*; (shout) llamada *f*; — **Mary** Ave María *f*; —**storm** granizada *f*; VI (precipitate) granizar; VT (greet) saludar; (call out) llamar; (acclaim) aclamar; **to — from** ser oriundo de
hair [hɛr] N pelo *m*; (of the head only) cabello *m*; (of the body only) vello *m*; (on plants) pelusa *f*; —**brush** cepillo para el cabello *m*; —**cut** corte de pelo *m*; **to get a —cut** cortarse el pelo; —**do** peinado *m*; —**dresser** peluquero -ra *mf*, peinador -ora *mf*; — **follicle** folículo capilar *m*; —**line** nacimiento del pelo *f*; —**line fracture** fractura fina *f*; —**piece** postizo *m*; —**pin** horquilla *f*; —**raising** horripilante, espeluznante; —**spray** fijador *m*
hairless [hɛrlɪs] ADJ (deprived of hair) pelado; (growing no hair) lampiño
hairy [hɛri] ADJ (including head) peludo; (body only) velludo
Haiti [héɖi] N Haití *m*
Haitian [héʃən] ADJ & N haitiano -na *mf*
hake [hek] N merluza *f*
half [hæf] N mitad *f*; — **an apple** media manzana *f*; ADJ medio; —**-baked** (not fully cooked) a medio cocer; (not fully developed) mal concebido; —**-breed** mestizo -za *mf*; — **brother** medio hermano *m*; —**-cocked** mal preparado; **he went off —-cocked** actuó

precipitadamente; —-**cooked** a medio cocer; —-**dozen** media docena *f*; —**hearted** desganado; —-**hour** media hora *f*; —-**life** vida media *f*; —-**moon** media luna *f*; — **note** blanca *f*; —-**open** entreabierto, entornado; — **past one** la una y media; —**time** medio tiempo *m*, descanso *m*; —-**truth** verdad a medias *f*; — **volley** media volea *f*; —**way** a medio camino; —**way house** casa de rehabilitación *f*; —**way measures** medidas parciales *f pl*; —**way point** punto medio *m*; —-**wit** *pej* imbécil *mf*, papamoscas *mf*; **at** —-**mast** a media asta; **to do something** —**way** hacer algo a medias; **to go halves** ir a medias

halibut [hǽləbət] N hipogloso *m*

halitosis [hælɪtósɪs] N halitosis *f*

hall [hɔl] N (corridor) corredor *m*, pasillo *m*; (large room) salón *m*, sala *f*; (building) edificio *m*; —**mark** distintivo *m*; —**way** (corridor) corredor *m*, pasillo *m*; (entrance) zaguán *m*, vestíbulo *m*

Halloween [hæləwín] N víspera del día de Todos los Santos *f*, noche de brujas *f*

hallucinate [həlúsənet] VI alucinar

hallucination [həlusənéʃən] N alucinación *f*

hallucinogen [həlúsənədʒən] N alucinógeno *m*

halo [hélo] N halo *m*, aureola *f*

halogen [hǽlədʒən] ADJ halógeno

halt [hɔlt] N **to come to a** — detenerse; VI/VT parar, detener[se]; —! ¡alto!

halter [hɔ́ltɚ] N cabestro *m*

halting [hɔ́ltɪŋ] ADJ vacilante

halve [hæv] VT partir por la mitad

ham [hæm] N (meat) jamón *m*; (attention getter) payaso *m*; —**string** (human) ligamento de la corva *m*; (horse) tendón del jarrete *m*; **to** — **it up** sobreactuar, exagerar

hamburger [hǽmbɚgɚ] N (meat) carne picada de vaca/res *f*; (sandwich, patty) hamburguesa *f*

hamlet [hǽmlɪt] N aldea *f*, poblado *m*, caserío *m*

hammer [hǽmɚ] N martillo *m*; VI/VT martillar, amartillar; **to** — **out** (an agreement) forjar; (differences) negociar

hammock [hǽmək] N hamaca *f*

hamper [hǽmpɚ] N canasto *m*, cesto *m*; VT impedir, embarazar

hamster [hǽmstɚ] N hámster *m*

hand [hænd] N mano *f*; (of a clock) aguja *f*, manecilla *f*; (farm helper) peón *m*; —**bag** (purse) bolsa *f*, cartera *f*; (valise) maletín *m*; —**ball** (American game) pelota *f*, frontón *m*; (European game) balonmano *m*; (in soccer) mano *f*; —**bill** volante *m*; —**cuffs** esposas *f pl*; — **grenade** granada de mano *f*, bomba de piña *f*; —**gun** revólver *m*; — **in** — [cogidos] de la mano; —**kerchief** pañuelo *m*; —**out** (notes) repartido *m*, ejemplario *m*; (alms)

limosna *f*; —**saw** serrucho *m*; —**shake** apretón de manos *m*; —**stand** pino *m*, paro de manos *m*; —**work** trabajo manual *m*; —**writing** letra *f*; **at** — (within reach) al alcance; (about to happen) cerca; **in** — (under control) bajo control; (available) disponible, en mano; **on** — disponible, a mano; **on the other** — en cambio, por otra parte; **to have one's** —**s full** estar ocupadísimo; ADJ —**held** de mano; —**made** hecho a mano; —-**picked** cuidadosamente seleccionado; —**s-on** práctico; VT entregar, dar; **to** —**cuff** esposar; **to** — **down** (a thing) pasar; (a judgment) pronunciar; **to** — **in** entregar; **to** — **over** entregar

handful [hǽndfʊl] N manojo *m*, puñado *m*

handicap [hǽndikæp] N (physical disability) impedimento *m*, minusvalía *f*; (mental disability) retardo *m*; (disadvantage) desventaja *f*; (in golf) hándicap *m*; — **race** carrera de hándicap *f*; VT (hinder) perjudicar, handicapar; (injure) lisiar; **physically** —**ped** minusválido físico

handiwork [hǽndiwɚk] N labor *f*

handle [hǽndl̩] N (straight) mango *m*; (curved) asa *f*; (of a drawer) manija *f*; (of a knife) empuñadura *f*, puño *m*; —**bar** manubrio *m*; VT (manage) manejar; (touch) manipular, tocar; (deal in) comerciar en; **the car** —**s easily** el coche tiene buena maniobrabilidad

handling [hǽndlɪŋ] N (dealing) manejo *m*; (touching) manipulación *f*; (charge) porte *m*; (of a car) maniobrabilidad *f*; — **charges** cargos de tramitación *m pl*

handsome [hǽnsəm] ADJ guapo, bien parecido; **a** — **sum** una suma considerable

handy [hǽndi] ADJ (near) a [la] mano; (practical) práctico; (skillful) hábil, diestro; N —**man** hombre habilidoso *m*

hang [hæŋ] VI/VT colgar, suspender; VT (door) colocar; (one's head) inclinar; (a condemned person) ahorcar; VI pender; — **in there!** ¡ánimo! **to** — **around** quedarse por ahí, rondar; **to** — **on** (hold tight) agarrarse bien; (persevere) aguantar; (wait) esperar; **to** — **out** (be outside) estar fuera; (socialize with) andar [con]; **to** — **over** sobresalir; **to** — **paper on a wall** empapelar una pared; **to** — **up** colgar; **sentenced to** — condenado a la horca; N caída *f*; — **glider** ala delta *f*; —**man** verdugo *m*; —**nail** padrastro *m*, uña encarnada *f*, uñero *m*; —**out** sitio frecuentado *m*; —**over** resaca *f*; —-**up** complejo *m*; **to get the** — **of something** agarrarle la onda a algo

hangar [hǽŋɚ] N hangar *m*

hanger [hǽŋɚ] N colgadero *m*; (for clothes) percha *f*

hanging [hǽŋɪŋ] N muerte en la horca *f*; —**s**

colgaduras *f pl*, tapiz *m*; ADJ colgante

hanky-panky [hǽŋkipǽŋki] N (deceit) tejemaneje *m*; (illicit sexual activity) aventuras *f pl*

haphazard [hæphǽzəd] ADV a la buena de Dios; ADJ irregular

happen [hǽpən] VI suceder, pasar, acontecer; **I — to know** da la casualidad de que sé; **to — to pass by** acertar a pasar; **to — upon** encontrarse con, toparse con

happening [hǽpənɪŋ] N acontecimiento *m*, suceso *m*

happily [hǽpɪli] ADV (in a state of happiness) felizmente; (luckily) afortunadamente; **they lived — ever after** vivieron felices y comieron perdices

happiness [hǽpɪnɪs] N felicidad *f*, dicha *f*

happy [hǽpi] ADJ (satisfied) feliz, dichoso; (pleased) contento; (lucky) afortunado; — **ending** final feliz *m*; **to be — to** hacer algo de buena gana

harangue [hərǽŋ] N arenga *f*; VT arengar

harass [hərǽs] VT acosar, hostigar

harassment [hərǽsmənt] N acoso *m*, hostigamiento *m*

harbor [hárbə-] N (for ships) puerto *m*; (refuge) refugio *m*; — **authority** autoridad portuaria; VT (refugees, criminals, suspicions) albergar; (hopes) abrigar

hard [hɑrd] ADJ (firm) duro; (erect) tieso; (difficult) difícil; (arduous) arduo; **to play —ball** ser despiadado; —**-boiled egg** huevo duro *m*; — **cash** dinero contante y sonante *m*; — **coal** antracita *f*; — **copy** copia en papel *f*, copia impresa *f*; — **core** núcleo resistente *m*; —**-core** (pornography) duro; (politics) radical; — **disk** disco duro *m*; — **disk drive** unidad de disco duro *f*; — **feelings** resentimiento *m*; — **hat** casco *m*; —**headed** testarudo; —**hearted** duro de corazón; — **liquor** bebida alcohólica fuerte *f*; — **luck** mala suerte *f*; — **of hearing** medio sordo; —**-on** erección *f*; **he had a —-on** la tenía dura; — **page break** salto de página forzado *m*; — **palate** paladar óseo *m*; —**-pressed** en aprietos; — **return** salto de línea forzado *m*; —**ware** (metal articles) ferretería *f*; (computer) hardware *m*; —**ware store** ferretería *f*; —**wood** madera noble *f*; — **water** agua dura *f*; — **winter** invierno crudo *m*; —**-wired** programado; —**-working** trabajador; ADV (fall, push) con fuerza; (work) duro, con ahinco

harden [hárdn̩] VI/VT (make or become hard) endurecer[se]; (make or become experienced) curtir[se]

hardening [hárdn̩ɪŋ] N endurecimiento *m*

hardly [hárdli] ADV (scarcely) apenas, difícilmente; (at all) en absoluto; — **anyone**

casi nadie; — **surprising** nada sorprendente

hardness [hárdnɪs] N dureza *f*

hardship [hárdʃɪp] N penuria *f*, penalidad *f*

hardy [hárɒi] ADJ robusto

hare [hɛr] N liebre *f*; —**brained** descabellado; —**lip** labio leporino *m*; —**lipped** con labio leporino, labihendido

harem [hérəm] N harén *m*

harm [hɑrm] N daño *m*, mal *m*, perjuicio *m*; VT (object) dañar; (person) hacer daño; (chances) perjudicar

harmful [hármfəł] ADJ perjudicial, dañino, nocivo

harmless [hármlɪs] ADJ inocuo, inofensivo

harmonic [hɑrmánɪk] ADJ & N armónico *m*

harmonious [hɑrmóniəs] ADJ armonioso

harmonize [hármənaɪz] VI/VT armonizar

harmony [hárməni] N armonía *f*

harness [hárnɪs] N arnés *m*, jaez *m*, guarnición *f*; VT (put on a harness) enjaezar; (utilize) aprovechar

harp [hɑrp] N arpa *f*; VI (play the harp) tocar el arpa; (insist) machacar; **to — on** insistir sobre

harpoon [hɑrpún] N arpón *m*; VT arponear

harpsichord [hárpsɪkɔrd] N clavicémbalo *m*

harrowing [hǽroɪŋ] ADJ angustioso; — **adventure** aventura espeluznante *f*

harry [hǽri] VT acosar, hostigar

harsh [hɑrʃ] ADJ (words) duro; (surface) áspero; (character, discipline) severo, férreo; (winter) crudo, riguroso

harshness [hárʃnɪs] N (of words) dureza *f*; (of a surface) aspereza *f*; (of character, discipline) severidad *f*; (of a winter) rigor *m*

harvest [hárvɪst] N cosecha *f*; (of sugar) zafra *f*; VT cosechar

has [hæz] *see* have

hash [hæʃ] N guisado *m*, picadillo *m*

hashish [hæʃíʃ] N hachís *m*

hassle [hǽsəł] N rollo *m*, lío *m*; VT jorobar

haste [hest] N prisa *f*; **in —** de prisa; **to make —** darse prisa, apresurarse; *Am* apurarse

hasten [hésən] VI apresurarse; *Am* apurarse; VT acelerar, adelantar

hasty [hésti] ADJ apresurado, precipitado, presuroso; *Am* apurado; **to be —** precipitarse, apresurarse

hat [hæt] N sombrero *m*

hatch [hætʃ] VI/VT (chicks) empollar; (plot, scheme) fraguar, maquinar; N (chicks) nidada *f*; (opening) escotilla *f*; — **way** escotilla *f*

hatchet [hǽtʃɪt] N hacha *f*; — **job** crítica feroz *f*; — **man** sicario *m*; **to bury the —** hacer las paces

hate [het] N odio *m*; VI/VT odiar; **I — to admit it** me molesta admitirlo; **I — eating leftovers** detesto comer restos

hateful [hétfəł] ADJ odioso, aborrecible

hatred [hétrɪd] N odio *m*

haughtiness [hɔ́ɒɪnɪs] N altivez f, altanería f, soberbia f

haughty [hɔ́ɒi] ADJ altivo, altanero, soberbio

haul [hɔł] VT (transport) transportar; (drag) arrastrar; (pull) jalar [de], tirar [de]; N (quantity transported) carga f; (tug) tirón m; (catch of fish) redada f; (stolen goods) botín m; **long** — distancia larga f

haunch [hɔntʃ] N anca f

haunt [hɔnt] VI/VT (frequent) frecuentar, rondar; (enchant) embrujar; **that idea —s me** me obsesiona esa idea; **—ed house** casa embrujada f; N (of animals, criminals) guarida f; (of people socializing) sitio frecuentado m

have [hæv] V AUX haber; VT tener; **to — to** tener que; **to — a baby** dar a luz; **to — a look at** echar una mirada a; **to — a suit made** mandarse hacer un traje; **— him come later** dile que venga más tarde; **what did she — on?** ¿qué tenía puesto? **we've been had** nos estafaron

haven [hévən] N abrigo m, refugio m

havoc [hævək] N estrago m; **to wreak** — hacer estragos

hawk [hɔk] N gavilán m; VT pregonar

hay [he] N heno m; **— fever** alergia al polen f; **— loft** henil m; **—seed** paleto -ta mf; **—stack** almiar m; **to look for a needle in a —stack** buscar una aguja en un pajar

hazard [hǽzəd] N (chance) azar m; (danger) peligro m; VT arriesgar, aventurar

hazardous [hǽzə-Dəs] ADJ peligroso; — **substance** sustancia peligrosa f

haze [hez] N neblina f, calina f; VT atormentar [como parte de un rito de iniciación]

hazel [hézəl] N avellano m; **—nut** avellana f; ADJ de avellano

hazy [hézi] ADJ (weather) brumoso; (idea) confuso, vago

HDL [high density lipoprotein] [étʃdíél] N LAD f

he [hi] PRON él; —-**goat** macho cabrío m; — **who** el que, quien

head [hɛd] N (of body) cabeza f; (of bed) cabecera f; (chief) jefe -fa mf; **—ache** dolor de cabeza m; — **coach** entrenador -ora en jefe mf; — **cold** resfrío m; **—count** recuento de personas m; **—dress** tocado m, adorno para la cabeza m; **—gear** (hat) sombrero m; (helmet) casco m; (for a horse) cabezada f; **—hunter** cazatalentos mf sg; **—land** cabo m, promontorio m; **—light** faro delantero m; **—line** titular m; **—long** (head first) de cabeza; (hastily) precipitadamente; **— of hair** cabellera f; **— of state** mandatario -ria mf; **—phone** audífono m, auricular m; **—quarters** (military) cuartel general m; (police) jefatura f; (corporation) oficina

central f; **—rest** reposacabezas m sg; **—set** auriculares m pl; **—s or tails** cara o cruz; **I can't make —s or tails of it** esto no tiene ni pies ni cabeza; **— start** ventaja f; **—stone** lápida f; **—strong** testarudo; **—way** avance m; **—word** voz f; **to make —way** avanzar, progresar; **it went to his** — se le fue a la cabeza; **to be out of one's** — desvariar; **to come to a** — (a crisis) precipitarse; (an abscess) supurar; **to keep one's** — mantener la calma; VT (lead) encabezar; (steer) dirigir; (in soccer) cabecear; VI dirigirse; **to — up** liderar; **to — off** atajar; ADV —-**on** de frente, frontal

header [hɛ́Də-] N (in soccer) cabezazo m, pase de cabeza m; (in text) cabecera f, encabezado m

heading [hɛ́Dɪŋ] N encabezamiento m

heal [hił] VT curar; VI (get well) sanar, curarse; (form a scar) cicatrizarse

health [hɛłθ] N salud f; **— care** asistencia médica f; **— care system** sistema de asistencia de salud m; **— care provider** profesional de la salud mf; **— food** comida macrobiótica f; **— insurance** seguro de salud m

healthful [hɛ́łθfəł] ADJ saludable, sano

healthy [hɛ́łθi] ADJ sano, saludable

heap [hip] N montón m, pila f; VT amontonar, apilar; VI **to — up** amontonarse

hear [hir] VI/VT (perceive) oír; VT (listen) escuchar; **to — about/of someone/ something** oír hablar de alguien/algo; **to — from someone** tener noticias de alguien; **I won't — of your leaving** no quiero saber de que te vayas

heard [hɝd] see hear

hearer [hírə-] N oyente mf

hearing [hírɪŋ] N (sense) oído m; (trial) audiencia f; **within** — al alcance del oído; — **aid** audífono m; ADJ —-**impaired** sordo

hearsay [hírse] N testimonio de oídas m; **by** — de oídas

hearse [hɝs] N coche fúnebre m, carroza f

heart [hart] N (organ) corazón m; (spirit) ánimo m; **—ache** angustia f; **— attack** ataque cardíaco m; **—beat** latido m; **I would do it in a —beat** lo haría sin pestañear; **—burn** acidez de estómago f; **— disease** enfermedad coronaria f; **— murmur** soplo cardíaco m; **at —** en realidad, en el fondo; **from the bottom of one's** — de corazón, con toda el alma; **to learn by** — aprender de memoria; **to take** — cobrar ánimo; **to take to** — tomar a pecho; ADJ —**broken** inconsolable; **—felt** sincero, sentido; **my —felt sympathy** mi más sentido pésame; —-**warming** reconfortante

hearten [hártn̩] VT animar

hearth [harθ] N hogar m

heartless [hártlɪs] ADJ despiadado, desalmado

hearty [hárɒi] ADJ (cordial) cordial; (strong) fuerte; — **appetite** apetito saludable *m*; **a — laugh** una risa desbordante; — **meal** una comida abundante

heat [hit] N (warmth) calor *m*; (passion) ardor *m*; (estrus) celo *m*; (source of heat) calefacción *f*; (preliminary race) eliminatoria *f*; — **exchange** equilibrio térmico *m*; —**stroke** insolación *f*; VI/VT calentar[se]; **to — up** acalorarse

heater [hírɒ] N calentador *m*

heating [hírɒɪŋ] N calefacción *f*; — **pad** almohadilla eléctrica *f*

heave [hiv] VT (raise) levantar; (throw) arrojar, lanzar; (sigh) exhalar; (pull) jalar; VI (pant) jadear; (vomit) hacer arcadas; N (throw) lanzamiento *m*; (pull) tirón *m*

heaven [hévən] N cielo *m*

heavenly [hévənli] ADJ celestial; — **bodies** cuerpos celestes *m pl*; **it was** — estuvo divino

heavily [hévəli] ADV (fall) pesadamente; (drink) mucho; **he's breathing** — está jadeando; **he's** — **indebted** está muy endeudado / tiene muchas deudas

heaviness [hévɪnɪs] N pesadez *f*

heavy [hévi] ADJ (weighty) pesado; (thick) grueso, pesado; (dense) denso; (oppressive) opresivo; — **artillery** artillería pesada *f*; — **breathing** jadeos *m pl*; —-**duty** de servicio pesado; —-**handed** severo, autoritario; **with a — heart** abatido; — **rain** lluvia fuerte *f*; — **schedule** agenda cargada *f*; —**weight** peso pesado *m*; N villano -na *mf*

Hebrew [híbru] N & ADJ hebreo -a *mf*; (language) hebreo *m*

heck [hɛk] INTERJ ¡caramba! **what the — are you doing?** ¿qué demonios haces? **that was a — of a good game** fue un partidazo

hectare [héktɛr] N hectárea *f*

hectic [héktɪk] ADJ febril, agitado

hedge [hɛdʒ] N (row of bushes) seto *m*; (precaution) precaución *f*; — **fund** fondo especulativo *m*; —**hog** erizo *m*; VI/VT (a bet) cubrir[se]; VT (a question) evadir

hedonism [hídnɪzəm] N hedonismo *m*

heebie-jeebies [híbidʒíbiz] N **it gives me the** — me pone los pelos de punta

heed [hid] VT atender; N atención *f*, cuidado *m*; **to pay — to** prestar atención a

heel [hił] N (of foot or sock) talón *m*; (of shoe) tacón *m*; **to kick up one's** —**s** tirar la chancleta, soltarse el pelo; VT poner tacón a; VI/VT seguir de cerca

hegemony [hɪdʒém(ə)ni] N hegemonía *f*

heifer [héfɚ] N novilla *f*, vaquilla *f*

height [haɪt] N (of a building, mountain) altura *f*; (of a person) estatura *f*; (utmost point) colmo *m*

heighten [háɪtn̩] VI/VT (increase) aumentar[se]; (intensify) realzar

Heimlich maneuver [háɪmlɪkmənúvɚ] N maniobra de Heimlich *f*

heinous [hénəs] ADJ aborrecible

heir [ɛr] N heredero -ra *mf*; — **apparent** presunto heredero *m*, presunta heredera *f*; —**s and assigns** herederos y cesionarios *m pl*

heiress [ɛ́rɪs] N heredera *f*

held [hɛłd] *see* hold

helicopter [hélɪkɑptɚ] N helicóptero *m*

helium [híliəm] N helio *m*

helix [hílɪks] N hélice *f*

hell [hɛł] N infierno *m*; —-**raiser** camorrista *mf*

hello [hɛló] INTERJ ¡hola! (on the telephone) hola; *Sp* diga; *Mex* bueno

helm [hɛłm] N timón *m*

helmet [hɛ́łmɪt] N (for bikes, etc.) casco *m*; (armor) yelmo *m*

help [hɛłp] N (aid) ayuda *f*; (rescue) auxilio *m*; (remedy) remedio *m*; (employee) empleado -da *mf*; — **desk** servicio de ayuda al usuario *m*; INTERJ ¡auxilio! ¡socorro! VI/VT (aid) ayudar, asistir; (rescue) auxiliar, socorrer; — **yourself** sírvete; **he cannot — it** no puede evitarlo; **he cannot — but come** no puede menos que venir; **may I — you?** ¿en qué le puedo servir?

helper [hɛ́łpɚ] N ayudante *mf*, asistente *mf*

helpful [hɛ́łpfəl] ADJ (useful) útil; (willing to help) servicial

helping [hɛ́łpɪŋ] N porción *f*

helpless [hɛ́łplɪs] ADJ desamparado, desvalido

helplessness [hɛ́łplɪsnɪs] N desamparo *m*, desvalimiento *m*

hem [hɛm] N dobladillo *m*, *Am* ruedo *m*; VT hacer dobladillos en, orillar; **to — in** arrinconar; **to — and haw** vacilar

hematoma [himətómə] N hematoma *m*

hemisphere [hémɪsfɪr] N hemisferio *m*

hemlock [hémlɑk] N cicuta *f*

hemoglobin [híməglobɪn] N hemoglobina *f*

hemophilia [himəfíliə] N hemofilia *f*

hemorrhage [hémərɪdʒ] N hemorragia *f*

hemorrhoids [hémərɔɪdz] N hemorroides *f pl*

hemp [hɛmp] N cáñamo *m*

hen [hɛn] N (chicken) gallina *f*; (female bird) ave hembra *f*; ADJ —**pecked** dominado por su mujer

hence [hɛns] ADV de ahí; —**forth** de aquí en adelante, de hoy en adelante; **a week —** de aquí a una semana

hepatitis [hɛpətáɪdɪs] N hepatitis *f*

her [hɚ] PRON **I see** — la veo; **I talk to —** le hablo [a ella]; **I went with —** fui con ella; POSS ADJ **this is — dog** este es su perro, este es el perro de ella

herald [hérəłd] N heraldo *m*; VT anunciar, proclamar

herb [ɚb] N hierba *f*

herbal [ɜ́ːbəł] ADJ de hierbas; — **tea** tisana f
herbicide [hɜ́ːbɪsaɪd] N herbicida m
herbivore [hɜ́ːbəvɔr] N herbívoro m
herbivorous [hɜˈbívərəs] ADJ herbívoro
herd [hɜːd] N (of animals) manada f; (of goats) hato m; (of sheep) rebaño m; (of horses, donkeys) recua f; **the common** — el populacho, la chusma; —**sman** pastor m; VT arrear; VI ir en manada
here [hir] ADV aquí, acá; — **it is** aquí está; —**after** en adelante; **the** —**after** el más allá; —**by** (in writing) por la presente; **I** —**by pronounce you husband and wife** los declaro marido y mujer; —**in** en el presente; —**'s to you!** ¡a tu salud! —**tofore** hasta ahora; —**with** (hereby) por la presente; (attached) adjunto; **come** —! ¡ven acá! **the** — **and now** el presente; **that is neither** — **nor there** eso no viene al caso
hereditary [hərédɪtɛri] ADJ hereditario
heredity [hərédɪti] N herencia f
heresy [hérɪsi] N herejía f
heretic [hérɪtɪk] N hereje mf
heritage [hérɪtɪdʒ] N herencia f, patrimonio m
hermaphrodite [həˈmǽfrədaɪt] N hermafrodita mf
hermetic [hɜˈmédɪk] ADJ hermético
hermit [hɜ́ːmɪt] N ermitaño -ña mf; — **crab** ermitaño m
hernia [hɜ́ːniə] N hernia f; —**ted** herniado; —**ted disk** hernia de disco f
hero [híro] N (brave man) héroe m; (main character) protagonista mf
heroic [hɪróɪk] ADJ heroico
heroin [héroɪn] N heroína f
heroine [héroɪn] N heroína f
heroism [héroɪzəm] N heroísmo m
heron [hérən] N garza f
herpes [hɜ́ːpiz] N herpes m
herring [hérɪŋ] N arenque m
hers [hɜːz] PRON **this book is** — este libro es suyo / de ella; **these things are** — estas cosas son suyas; — **is bigger** el suyo / la suya es más grande; **a friend of** — un amigo suyo / de ella
herself [hɜˈsɛ́łf] PRON ella misma; **she's not** — **today** hoy no es la misma de siempre; **she was sitting by** — estaba sentada sola; **she** — **did it** lo hizo sola, lo hizo ella misma; **she talks to** — ella habla para sí, habla consigo misma; **she looked at** — **in the mirror** se miró en el espejo; **she bought** — **a house** se compró una casa
hesitant [hézɪtənt] ADJ vacilante
hesitate [hézɪtet] VI (pause) vacilar; (stutter) titubear; (doubt) dudar
hesitating [hézɪteDɪŋ] ADJ vacilante
hesitation [hɛzɪtéʃən] N (pause) vacilación f; (stammer) titubeo m; (doubt) duda f

heterogeneous [hɛDəˈədʒíniəs] ADJ heterogéneo
heterosexual [hɛDərosékʃuəł] ADJ heterosexual
hexagon [héksəgɑn] N hexágono m
hey [he] INTERJ ¡oiga!
heyday [héde] N auge m
hi [haɪ] INTERJ hola; **say** — **to your sister for me** dale recuerdos a tu hermana de mi parte
hiatus [haɪéDəs] N hiato m
hibernate [háɪbəˌnet] VI hibernar
hiccup, hiccough [híkʌp] N hipo m; VI hipar, tener hipo
hick [hɪk] N & ADJ paleto -ta mf
hickory [híkəri] N nogal americano m
hid, hidden [hɪd, hídn̩] see hide
hidden [hídn̩] ADJ (out of sight) oculto; (illegal) clandestino; — **agenda** intereses ocultos m pl
hide [haɪd] VI/VT ocultar[se], esconder[se]; — **and seek** escondite m, escondidas f pl; —**out** escondite m; N cuero m, piel f, pellejo m
hideous [hídiəs] ADJ horrendo, espantoso
hierarchy [háɪərɑrki] N jerarquía f
hieroglyphic [haɪrəglífɪk] ADJ & N jeroglífico m
high [haɪ] ADJ alto; (intoxicated) ebrio; (on drugs) volado; — **altitude sickness** enfermedad de altura f; — **and dry** (ship) en seco; (person) colgado; — **blood pressure** hipertensión f; —**brow** culto; —**class** de clase; — **contrast** alto contraste m; — **definition television** televisión de alta definición f; — **density** alta densidad f; —**er-up** superior; —**er education** educación superior f; — **explosive** explosivo de alta potencia m; — **fever** fiebre elevada f; — **fidelity** alta fidelidad f; — **finance** altas finanzas f pl; —**-grade** de calidad superior; —**-handed** arbitrario; — **jump** salto alto m; —**lands** tierras altas f pl; —**-level** de alto nivel; —**light** lo más destacado; —**lighting** (on a computer) selección de texto f; —**lights** (in hair) claritos m pl, mechas f pl; —**-minded** idealista; —**-octane gasoline** súper m; —**-pitched** agudo; — **point** culminación f; —**-powered** de alta potencia; —**-pressure** estresante, intenso; —**-priced** caro; —**-quality** de alta calidad; —**-return** de alta rentabilidad; —**-rise** de muchos pisos; —**-risk** de alto riesgo; —**-risk behavior** conducta de alto riesgo f; —**-risk patient** paciente con alto riesgo mf; — **school** escuela secundaria f, colegio m; Sp instituto m; — **seas** alta mar f; —**-sounding** altisonante; —**-speed** de alta velocidad; — **spirits** buen ánimo m; —**-strung** nervioso; —**-tech** alta tecnología f; — **temperature** temperatura máxima f; — **tide** pleamar f; —**way** carretera f, ruta f; — **wind** ventarrón m; **in** — **gear** a toda marcha; **two feet** — dos pies de altura; **it is** — **time that** ya era hora de que; **to look**

— **and low** buscar por todas partes; N flash
m, subida*f*; VT **to —light** (emphasize)
destacar, resaltar
highly [háili] ADV — **amusing** sumamente
divertido; — **paid** muy bien pagado; —
qualified altamente cualificado; **he spoke**
— **of her** habló muy bien de ella
highness [háinis] N alteza*f*
hijack [háiʤæk] VT secuestrar [un vehículo]
hike [haik] N caminata*f*; **take a —**! ¡ve a freír
espárragos! VI salir a caminar
hilarious [hilériəs] ADJ graciosísimo, para
morirse de risa
hill [hił] N (elevated area) colina*f*, cerro *m*; (pile)
montón *m*; —**billy** paleto -ta *mf*; —**side**
ladera*f*; —**top** cumbre*f*, cima*f*
hillock [hílək] N otero *m*
hilly [híli] ADJ accidentado
hilt [hiłt] N empuñadura*f*; **to the** — al máximo
him [him] PRON **I see** — lo veo; *Sp* le veo; **I talk
to** — le hablo; **I went with** — fui con él
himself [himséłf] PRON él mismo; **he** — **wrote
the letter** él mismo escribió la carta; **he's
not** — **today** hoy no es el mismo de siempre;
he was sitting by — estaba sentado solo;
he talks to — él habla para sí, habla consigo
mismo; **he looked at** — **in the mirror** se
miró en el espejo; **he bought** — **a house** se
compró una casa
hind [haind] ADJ trasero; —**most** último; **in**
—**sight** a posteriori; N cierva*f*
hinder [híndɚ] VT impedir, entorpecer, estorbar
Hindi [híndi] N hindi *m*
hindrance [híndrəns] N obstáculo *m*,
impedimento *m*, traba*f*
Hindu [híndu] ADJ & N hindú *mf*
hinge [hinʤ] N gozne *m*, quicio *m*; VT engoznar,
poner goznes; VI **to** — **on** depender de
hint [hint] N (clue) indirecta*f*, pista*f*; (trace) dejo
m; **to take the** — darse por enterado; VT
insinuar
hip [hip] N cadera*f*; — **replacement**
(operation) sustitución protésica de la cadera
f; (prosthesis) prótesis de cadera*f*
Hippocratic oath [hipəkrǽɒikóθ] N juramento
hipocrático *m*
hippopotamus [hipəpápəməs] N hipopótamo *m*
hire [hair] VT (engage for work) contratar; VI/VT
(rent) alquilar[se]; — **and fire** contratar y
despedir; **to** — **out** dar en alquiler, alquilar;
N (engagement) contratación*f*; (employee)
nuevo -va empleado -da *mf*; (rent) alquiler *m*
his [hiz] POSS ADJ **this is** — **dog** este es su
perro / el perro de él; PRON **these things
are** — estas cosas son suyas; — **is right here**
el suyo / la suya está aquí; **a friend of** — un
amigo suyo / una amiga suya
Hispanic [hispǽnik] ADJ hispánico, hispano; N
hispano -na *mf*

hiss [his] VI sisear; (to boo) silbar; N siseo *m*
histamine [hístəmin] N histamina*f*
historian [históriən] N historiador -ra *mf*
historic [histórik] ADJ histórico
historical [histórikəł] ADJ histórico
history [hístəri] N historia*f*
histrionics [histriániks] N histrionismo *m*
hit [hit] VT (a target) dar en; (a car) chocar con; (a
key) pulsar, tocar; (a baseball) batear; **to** — **a
homerun** batear un jonrón, pegar un
cuadrangular; **to** — **it off** llevarse bien desde
el principio; **to** — **the mark** acertar, dar en
el blanco; **to** — **upon an idea** dar con una
idea; **to** — **on a person** tratar de ligar con
alguien; N (blow) golpe *m*; (success) éxito *m*;
(dose) dosis*f*; **that was a** — **with me** me
encantó; —**man** sicario *m*; —**s** (on a website)
visitas*f pl*; ADJ —-**and-run** que se da a la fuga
después de atropellar a alguien; —-**or-miss**
al azar
hitch [hitʃ] VT atar, amarrar; (pants) levantar;
(yoke) uncir, enganchar; **to get** —**ed** casarse;
to —**hike** *Sp* hacer autostop; *Am* hacer dedo;
N (knot) nudo *m*; (difficulty) dificultad*f*;
(period) período *m*
hither [híðɚ] ADV acá; — **and thither** acá y
allá; —**to** hasta ahora
HIV [**human immunodeficiency virus**]
[étʃáiví] N VIH *m*
hive [haiv] N (shelter for bees) colmena*f*; (colony
of bees) enjambre *m*; —**s** urticaria*f*
HMO [**health maintenance organization**]
[étʃémó] N organización de mantenimiento de
salud*f*
hoard [hord] N reserva*f*; VI/VT acaparar
hoarse [hors] ADJ ronco; (like alcoholics)
aguardentoso
hoarseness [hórsnis] N ronquera*f*
hoax [hoks] N engaño *m*
hobble [hábəł] VI (limp) cojear; VT (tie to impede
walking) manear; (hinder) trabar; N cojera*f*;
(rope) traba*f*, manea*f*
hobby [hábi] N hobby *m*
hobo [hóbo] N vagabundo *m*
hockey [háki] N hockey *m*
hodgepodge [háʤpaʤ] N mezcolanza*f*,
batiburrillo *m*
hoe [ho] N azada*f*, azadón *m*; VI/VT limpiar con
azadón
hog [hag] N puerco *m*, cerdo *m*, marrano *m*; *Am*
chancho *m*; —**wash** pamplinas*f pl*; **to live
high on the** — vivir en la abundancia; VT
acaparar, adueñarse de
hoist [hoist] VT izar; N torno *m*, guinche *m*
hokey [hóki] ADJ sensiblero
hold [hołd] VT (bear) llevar, sujetar; (contain)
contener; (detain) detener; (decide legally,
sustain a note) sostener; (opine) opinar; **to** —
back detener; **to** — **down** sujetar; **to** —

forth perorar; **to — hands** tomarse de la mano; **to — in place** sujetar; **to — a meeting** celebrar una reunión; **to — someone responsible** hacerle a uno responsable; **to — someone to his word** obligar a uno a cumplir con su palabra; **to — oneself erect** ponerse derecho; **to — one's own** defenderse; **to — one's tongue** callarse, morderse la lengua; — **the pickles on that burger!** una hamburguesa sin pepinillos, por favor; VI (remain fast) aguantar, resistir; (occupy a position) ocupar; (be valid) ser válido; **to — off** mantener[se] a distancia; **to — off doing something** abstenerse de hacer algo; **to — liable** responsabilizar; **to — on** (not let go) agarrar[se], sujetar[se]; (stop) esperar; (persist) persistir; **to — out** aguantar; **to — still** quedarse/estarse quieto; **to — tight** agarrarse; **to — to one's promise** cumplir con la palabra; **to — up** (raise) alzar; (detain) detener; (rob) atracar, asaltar; (persevere) aguantar; **how much does it — ?** ¿Qué capacidad tiene? N (grip) agarro *m*; (thing to grasp) asidero *m*; (dominion) dominio *m*; (wrestling move) llave *f*; (in music) calderón *m*; (of a ship) bodega *f*; —**up** golpe *m*, atraco *m*; **to get — of** agarrar; **to take — of** *Sp* coger, agarrar; **to have a good — on something** agarrarse bien de algo

holder [hółdɚ] N (person) tenedor -ora *mf*, poseedor -ora *mf*; (device) receptáculo *m*

holding [hółdɪŋ] N propiedad *f*; — **company** holding *m*; —**s** (financial) valores en cartera *m pl*; (of a library) fondos *m pl*

hole [hoł] N agujero *m*; (in a wall) boquete *m*; (of an animal) madriguera *f*; (in the ground, in golf) hoyo *m*; **to be in a** — hallarse/estar en un apuro/aprieto; —**in-one** hoyo en uno *m*

holiday [hálɪde] N día de fiesta *m*; —**s** vacaciones *f pl*

holiness [hólɪnɪs] N santidad *f*

holistic [holístɪk] ADJ holístico

Holland [hálənd] N Holanda *f*

hollow [hálo] ADJ (empty) hueco; (concave) cóncavo; (sunken) hundido; (insincere) falso; N (cavity) hueco *m*, concavidad *f*; (valley) hondonada *f*, hondo *m*; VT **to — out** ahuecar, vaciar

holly [háli] N acebo *m*

holocaust [háləkɔst] N holocausto *m*

holster [hółstɚ] N pistolera *f*, funda de pistola *f*

holy [hóli] ADJ santo, sagrado; — **Bible** Santa Biblia *f*; — **cow/Moses/mackerel!** ¡que increíble! *Sp* ¡jobar! — **Ghost** Espíritu Santo *m*; — **Spirit** Espíritu Santo *m*; — **war** guerra santa *f*; — **water** agua bendita *f*

homage [hámɪʤ] N homenaje *m*; **to pay —** rendir homenaje, honrar

home [hom] N casa *f*, hogar *m*; (for old people, orphans) asilo *m*, hogar *m*; —**boy** amigo del barrio *m*; — **economics** economía doméstica *f*; — **delivery** entrega a domicilio *f*; — **equity loan** préstamo garantizado por el valor residual de la vivienda *m*; — **game** partido en casa *m*; —**land** patria *f*; —**less** sin techo; — **office** (headquarters) oficina central *f*; (at home) oficina en el hogar *f*; —**owner** propietario -ria de vivienda *mf*; —**owners' association** asociación de propietarios de vivienda *f*; — **page** página de inicio *f*; — **plate** goma *f*, plato *m*; — **rule** autonomía *f*; — **run** jonrón *m*, cuadrangular *m*; **at** — en casa; **to be** —**sick** echar de menos / extrañar [a la familia]; —**sickness** morriña *f*, añoranza *f*; — **stretch** último trecho *m*; —**work** tarea domiciliaria *f*, deber *m*; ADJ doméstico; ADV (direction) a casa; (location) en casa; **to strike** — dar en el blanco; ADJ —**made** casero

homely [hómli] ADJ (ugly) feo; (familiar) familiar, doméstico

homeopathic [homiopǽθɪk] ADJ homeopático

homeopathy [homiápəθi] N homeopatía *f*

homestead [hómstɛd] N heredad *f*, casa de la familia *f*

homeward [hómwɚd] ADV a casa; — **bound** camino a casa

homicide [hámɪsaɪd] N homicidio *m*

homogeneous [homəʤínəs] ADJ homogéneo

homogenize [həmáʤənaɪz] VT homogeneizar

homonym [hámənɪm] N homónimo *m*

homophobia [homəfóbiə] N homofobia *f*

homophobic [homəfóbɪk] ADJ homofóbico

homosexual [homosékʃuəl] ADJ & N homosexual *mf*

Honduran [handúrən] ADJ & N hondureño -ña *mf*

Honduras [handúrəs] N Honduras *f*

hone [hon] VT afilar; **to — one's skills** desarrollar las destrezas; N piedra de afilar *f*

honest [ánɪst] ADJ honrado, honesto; **I'll be — with you** voy a ser franco contigo; —! ¡de veras!

honesty [ánɪsti] N (integrity) honradez *f*, honestidad *f*; (sincerity) franqueza *f*

honey [háni] N (sweet substance) miel *f*; (endearment) querido -da *mf*; —**bee** abeja *f*; —**comb** panal *m*; —**suckle** madreselva *f*

honeymoon [hánimun] N luna de miel *f*; VI pasar la luna de miel

honk [haŋk] N (of a car) bocinazo *m*, pitazo *m*; (of a goose) graznido *m*; VI/VT (car) tocar la bocina; VI (goose) graznar

honor [ánɚ] N (respect, privilege) honor *m*; (good reputation) honra *f*; **with —s** con honores; **your —** su señoría; VT (revere) honrar; (accept invitation, check) aceptar; **to**

— **a promise** cumplir [con] una promesa

honorable [ánǝǝbǝł] ADJ honorable

honorary [ánǝreri] ADJ honorario

hood [hʊd] N (of a coat) capucha *f*, caperuza *f*; (of a car) capó *m*; *Am* tapa *f*; VT encapuchar

hoodlum [húdlǝm] N maleante *mf*, gamberro -rra *mf*

hoof [hʊf] N casco *m*, pezuña *f*; VI **to — it** ir andando

hook [hʊk] N (for lifting) gancho *m*, garfio *m*; (for fishing) anzuelo *m*; — **and eye** alamar *m*, macho y hembra *m*; **by — or by crook** por las buenas o por las malas; —**up** conexión *f*, enganche *m*; VT (snag) enganchar; (a dress) abrochar; **to — up** conectar, enganchar

hooked [hʊkt] ADJ (shaped like a hook) ganchudo; (addicted) enganchado

hooker [húkǝ] N prostituta *f*; *pej* tía *f*, puta *f*

hooky [húki] N **to play** — hacer novillos

hooligan [húlɪgǝn] N *Sp* gamberro -rra *mf*, *Am* patotero -ra *mf*

hoop [hup] N (also in basketball) aro *m*

hoot [hut] VI/VT (of owl) ulular; (in derision) abuchear; N (of an owl) ululato *m*; (cry of derision) abucheo *m*; **I don't give a** — no me importa un comino; **it's a** — es para morirse de risa

hop [hɑp] VI saltar, brincar; **to — on** subirse a montar; N (short jump) saltito *m*, brinco *m*; (dance) bailongo *m*; —**s** lúpulo *m*

hope [hop] N esperanza *f*; VI/VT esperar; **to — for** esperar; **to — against —** esperar lo imposible

hopeful [hópfǝł] ADJ (having hopes) esperanzado; (giving hopes) esperanzador, alentador

hopefully [hópfǝli] ADV — **she'll come** ojalá [que] venga

hopeless [hóplɪs] ADJ (without hope) desesperanzado; (with no solution) irremediable; (unattainable) inalcanzable; — **cause** causa perdida *f*; **it is** — no tiene remedio; **the new secretary is — with numbers** el nuevo secretario es un desastre con los números

hopelessness [hóplɪsnɪs] N desesperanza *f*

horde [hɔrd] N (of people) horda *f*; (of animals) plaga *f*

horizon [hǝráɪzǝn] N horizonte *m*

horizontal [hɔrɪzántł] ADJ horizontal

hormone [hɔ́rmon] N hormona *f*; — **therapy** terapia hormonal *f*

horn [hɔrn] N (of an animal, substance) cuerno *m*, asta *f*; (of an automobile) bocina *f*, claxon *m*; (musical) corno *m*, trompa *f*; — **of plenty** cuerno de la abundancia *m*; **to toot one's own** — darse autobombo; VI **to — in** entrometerse

hornet [hɔ́rnɪt] N avispón *m*; —**'s nest**

avispero *m*

horny [hɔ́rni] ADJ (with hard skin) calloso; (sexually excited) *Sp fam* cachondo; *Am fam* caliente

horoscope [hɔ́rǝskop] N horóscopo *m*

horrendous [hɔréndǝs] ADJ horrendo

horrible [hɔ́rǝbǝł] ADJ horrible

horrid [hɔ́rɪd] ADJ horrendo

horrify [hɔ́rǝfaɪ] VT horrorizar

horror [hɔ́rǝ] N horror *m*

hors d'oeuvre [ɔrdɹ́v] N entremés *m*

horse [hɔrs] N caballo *m*; —**back** lomo de caballo *m*; **to ride —back** montar a caballo, cabalgar; —**fly** tábano *m*; —**laugh** carcajada *f*; —**play** payasadas *f pl*; —**power** caballo de fuerza *m*; — **race** carrera de caballos *f*; —**radish** rábano picante *m*; — **sense** sentido común *m*; —**shoe** herradura *f*; **hold your** —**s!** ¡para el carro! VI **to — around** payasear

horticulture [hɔ́rdɪkʌłtʃǝ] N horticultura *f*

hose [hoz] N (for legs) medias *f pl*; (for liquids) manguera *f*, manga *f*

hosiery [hóʒǝri] N (stockings) medias *f pl*; (shop for stockings) calcetería *f*

hospice [háspɪs] N (inn) hospicio *m*; (hospital) hospital para enfermos terminales *m*

hospitable [haspídǝbǝł] ADJ hospitalario, acogedor

hospital [háspɪdł] N hospital *m*

hospitality [haspɪtǽliɾi] N hospitalidad *f*

hospitalize [háspɪdlaɪz] VT internar

host [host] N (also computer) anfitrión *m*; (in a home or hotel, for a parasite) huésped *m*; (on television) presentador -ora *mf*; (army) hueste *f*; (multitude) multitud *f*, cúmulo *m*; (wafer) hostia *f*

hostage [hástɪdʒ] N rehén *mf*

hostel [hástl] N hostal *m*

hostelry [hástlri] N hostería *f*

hostess [hóstɪs] N anfitriona *f*

hostile [hástl] ADJ hostil; — **takeover** compra hostil *f*

hostility [hastíliɾi] N hostilidad *f*

hot [hɑt] ADJ (at high temperature) caliente; (sweltering) caluroso; (spicy) picante; (sexy) bueno; (sexually aroused) *Sp* cachondo; *Am* caliente; (stolen) robado; (recent) de último momento; (popular) popular; — **and heavy** apasionado, apasionadamente; —**bed** semillero *m*; — **dog** perro caliente *m*; —**headed** impetuoso, exaltado; —**house** invernadero *m*; — **potato** patata caliente *f*; — **seat** situación embarazosa *f*; —**shot** estrella *f*; — **tub** jacuzzi *m*; **it is — today** hace calor hoy; — **under the collar** enojado; VT **to — -wire** hacerle un puente a

hotel [hotéł] N hotel *m*; —**keeper** hotelero -ra *mf*

hound [haʊnd] N perro de caza *m*, sabueso *m*; VT acosar, perseguir

hour [aʊr] N hora *f*; — **hand** horario *m*; **his finest** — su mejor momento *m*

hourly [áʊrli] ADV (on the hour) cada hora; (by the hour) por horas; — **wages** salario por hora *m*

house[1] [haʊs] N (residence) casa *f*; (legislature) cámara legislativa *f*; — **arrest** detención domiciliaria *f*; —**boat** casa flotante *f*; —**cleaning** limpieza de la casa *f*; —**hold** casa *f*, familia *f*; —**keeper** (in a house) ama de llaves *f*; (in a home) encargado -da de limpieza *mf*; —**keeping** mantenimiento del hogar *m*; —**top** techo *m*, tejado *m*; —**wife** ama de casa *f*; —**work** trabajo de casa *m*, quehaceres domésticos *m pl*; **in-** — interno; **on the** — la casa paga; **to keep** — cuidar la casa; —**hold expenses** gastos del hogar *m pl*; —**-to-** — puerta a puerta

house[2] [haʊz] VI/VT alojar

housing [háʊzɪŋ] N (place to live) vivienda *f*; (protective covering) caja *f*

hovel [hávəł] N (hut) choza *f*, cabaña *f*, tugurio *m*; (open shed) cobertizo *m*

hover [hávə‑] VI (bird) cernerse; (hang in air) estar suspendido; (linger) rondar; —**craft** aerodeslizador *m*

how [haʊ] ADV cómo; — **about your mom?** ¿y tu mamá? — **beautiful!** ¡qué hermoso! — **come?** ¿por qué? — **early [late, soon]?** ¿cuándo? ¿a qué hora? — **far is it?** ¿a qué distancia está? ¿cuánto dista de aquí? — **long?** ¿cuánto tiempo? — **many?** ¿cuántos? — **much is it?** ¿cuánto vale? — **old are you?** ¿cuántos años tienes? **no matter** — **much it rains** por mucho que llueva; **he knows** — **difficult it is** él sabe lo difícil que es

however [haʊévə‑] CONJ sin embargo, no obstante; ADV — **you want it** como quieras; — **difficult it may be** por muy difícil que sea; — **much it rains** por mucho que llueva

howl [haʊł] VI aullar; (wind) ulular; (with laughter) reír a carcajadas; N aullido *m*, alarido *m*

HQ [headquarters] [étʃkjú] N oficina central *f*, sede central *f*

HR [human resources] [étʃár] N recursos humanos *m pl*

HTML [HyperText Markup Language] [étʃtiémét] N HTML *m*

hub [hʌb] N (center of wheel) cubo *m*; (center of activity) núcleo *m*; —**cap** tapacubos *m sg*

hubbub [hábʌb] N alboroto *m*, barullo *m*

huckster [hákstə‑] N (peddler) vendedor ambulante *m*; (promoter) mercachifle *m*

huddle [hádḷ] VI/VT (form a group) apiñar[se]; (curl up) acurrucar[se]; (consult)

conferenciar; N tropel *m*; (group meeting for consultation) reunión *f*; **to be in a** — estar agrupados; **to get in a** — agruparse

hue [hju] N matiz *m*

huff [hʌf] N **to get into a** — enojarse; VI **to** — **and puff** resoplar

hug [hʌg] VI/VT abrazar[se]; **to** — **the coast** costear; N abrazo *m*

huge [hjudʒ] ADJ enorme, fiero

hull [hʌł] N (of a ship, airplane) casco *m*; (of beans, peas) vaina *f*; (of fruits, nuts) cáscara *f*; VT (beans, peas) desvainar; (nuts) cascar

hum [hʌm] VI/VT (person) tararear; (insect, machine) zumbar; (place of activity) hervir; **to** — **to sleep** arrullar; N (of voice) tarareo *m*; (of insect, machine) zumbido *m*

human [hjúmən] ADJ & N humano *m*; — **being** ser humano *m*; — **immunodeficiency virus** virus de inmunodeficiencia humana *m*

humane [hjumén] ADJ humano, humanitario

humanism [hjúmənɪzəm] N humanismo *m*

humanitarian [hjumænɪtériən] ADJ humanitario

humanity [hjumǽnɪDi] N humanidad *f*; **humanities** humanidades *f pl*

humble [hámbəł] ADJ humilde; VT humillar

humid [hjúmɪd] ADJ húmedo

humidify [hjumíDəfaɪ] VT humidificar

humidity [hjumíDɪDi] N humedad *f*

humiliate [hjumíliet] VT humillar, vejar

humiliation [hjumɪliéʃən] N humillación *f*

humility [hjumílɪDi] N humildad *f*

hummingbird [hámɪŋbɚd] N colibrí *m*

humor [hjúmə‑] N humor *m*, humorismo *m*; **out of** — de mal humor, malhumorado; VT complacer a

humorous [hjúmə‑əs] ADJ gracioso, chistoso

hump [hʌmp] N joroba *f*, giba *f*, corcova *f*; **we're over the** — ya pasamos lo peor; —**back** jorobado -da *mf*; —**back whale** ballena jorobada *f*, yubarta *f*; VI/VT (have sex with) *Sp vulg* follar; *Am* coger, culear

hunch [hʌntʃ] N presentimiento *m*, corazonada *f*; —**back** (person) jorobado -da *mf*; (hump) corcova *f*; VI encorvar

hundred [hándrɪd] NUM cien[to]; **a** — **people** cien personas; **a** — **and fifty people** ciento cincuenta personas; N cien/ciento *m*; —**s** centenares *m pl*, cientos *m pl*

hundredth [hándrɪdθ] ADJ centésimo

hung [hʌŋ] *see* hang 'ahorcar'

Hungarian [hʌŋgériən] ADJ & N húngaro -ra *mf*

Hungary [háŋgəri] N Hungría *f*

hunger [háŋgə‑] N hambre *f*; VI pasar hambre; **to** — **for** ansiar, anhelar

hungry [háŋgri] ADJ hambriento; **to be** — tener hambre; **to go** — pasar hambre

hunk [hʌŋk] N pedazo *m*, cacho *m*; **he's a real** — es un cacho de hombre, es un papacito

hunt [hʌnt] VI/VT (seek prey) cazar; **to — down** dar caza a; **to — for** buscar; N (activity of hunting) caza *f*; (instance of hunting) cacería *f*; (search) búsqueda *f*

hunter [hʌ́ntɚ] N (who captures game) cazador -ora *mf*; (seeker) buscador -ora *mf*; (dog) perro de caza *m*

hunting [hʌ́ntɪŋ] N caza *f*; **— knife** cuchillo de caza *m*

huntsman [hʌ́ntsmən] N cazador *m*

hurdle [hɝ́dl̩] N (impediment) obstáculo *m*; (in races) valla *f*; VT saltar

hurl [hɝł] VI/VT arrojar, lanzar, precipitar

hurrah [hərá] INTERJ ¡hurra!

hurricane [hɝ́ɪken] N huracán *m*

hurried [hɝ́id] ADJ apresurado; *Am* apurado

hurry [hɝ́i] VI darse prisa, apresurarse; *Am* apurarse; **to — in [out]** entrar [salir] de prisa; **to — up** apresurar[se], dar[se] prisa; *Am* apurar[se]; VT apresurar; *Am* apurar; N prisa *f*; *Am* apuro *m*; **to be in a —** tener prisa; *Am* estar apurado

hurt [hɝt] VI/VT (to injure) lastimar[se], hacer[se] daño; (damage) dañar[se]; (harm) perjudicar[se]; **to — someone's feelings** lastimar/herir a alguien; VI (suffer pain) doler; **my tooth —s** me duele la muela / el diente; N (damage) daño *m*; (wound) herida *f*, lastimadura *f*; ADJ (physically) lastimado, herido; (emotionally) herido; **to get —** lastimarse

hurtful [hɝ́tfəł] ADJ hiriente

husband [hʌ́zbənd] N marido *m*, esposo *m*; VT administrar

hush [hʌʃ] VI/VT aquietar[se], callar[se]; —! ¡chitón! ¡silencio! **to — up a scandal** encubrir un escándalo; N silencio *m*; **he gave her — money** compró su silencio

husk [hʌsk] N (shell) cáscara *f*; (pod) vaina *f*; (of corn) *Am* chala *f*, *Sp* farfolla *f*; VT (corn) quitar la chala/farfolla a; (beans, peas) desvainar

husky [hʌ́ski] ADJ (build) ronco; (strong) recio; N (breed of dog) husky *m*, perro esquimal *m*

hustle [hʌ́səł] VI (work energetically) afanarse; (swindle) estafar; VT (hurry along) empujar; N (bustle) ajetreo *m*; (scheme) timo *m*; **— and bustle** ajetreo *m*, trajín *m*

hut [hʌt] N choza *f*, cabaña *f*

hyacinth [háɪəsɪnθ] N jacinto *m*

hybrid [háɪbrɪd] ADJ híbrido

hybridization [haɪbrɪdɪzéʃən] N hibridación *f*

hydrate [háɪdret] N hidrato *m*; VI/VT hidratar[se]

hydraulic [haɪdrɔ́lɪk] ADJ hidráulico

hydrocarbon [háɪdrəkɑrbən] N hidrocarburo *m*

hydroelectric [haɪdroɪléktrɪk] ADJ hidroeléctrico

hydrogen [háɪdrədʒən] N hidrógeno *m*; **— bomb** bomba de hidrógeno *f*; **— peroxide** peróxido de hidrógeno *m*, agua oxigenada *f*

hydrophobia [haɪdrəfóbiə] N hidrofobia *f*

hydroplane [háɪdrəplen] N hidroavión *m*

hyena [haɪínə] N hiena *f*

hygiene [háɪdʒin] N higiene *f*

hygienic [haɪdʒénɪk] ADJ higiénico

hygienist [haɪdʒínɪst] N higienista *mf*

hymen [háɪmən] N himen *m*

hymn [hɪm] N himno *m*

hype [haɪp] N exageración *f*; VT promocionar [exageradamente]

hyper [háɪpɚ] ADJ hiperactivo

hyperactive [haɪpɚǽktɪv] ADJ hiperactivo

hyperbaric chamber [haɪpɚbǽrɪk tʃémbɚ] N cámara hiperbárica *f*

hyperdocument [haɪpɚdákjəmənt] N hiperdocumento *m*

hyperlink [háɪpɚlɪŋk] N hiperenlace *m*, hipervínculo *m*

hypermedia [haɪpɚmídiə] N hipermedia *m*

hypersensitive [haɪpɚsénsɪdɪv] ADJ hipersensible

hypertension [haɪpɚténʃən] N hipertensión *f*, presión arterial alta *f*

hyperventilate [haɪpɚvéntl̩et] VI hiperventilar

hyphen [háɪfən] N guión *m*

hypnosis [hɪpnósɪs] N hipnosis *f*

hypnotherapy [hɪpnoθérəpi] N hipnoterapia *f*

hypnotize [hípnətaɪz] VT hipnotizar

hypoallergenic [haɪpoælɚdʒénɪk] ADJ hipoalérgico

hypochondriac [haɪpokándriæk] N hipocondríaco *mf*, hipocondriaco *mf*

hypocrisy [hɪpákrɪsi] N hipocresía *f*

hypocrite [hípəkrɪt] N hipócrita *mf*

hypocritical [hɪpəkrídɪkəł] ADJ hipócrita, doblado

hypodermic needle [haɪpədɝ́mɪk nídl̩] N aguja hipodérmica *f*

hypoglycemia [haɪpoglaɪsímiə] N hipoglucemia *f*

hypothesis [haɪpáθɪsɪs] N hipótesis *f*

hypothyroidism [haɪpoθáɪrɔɪdɪzəm] N hipotiroidismo *m*

hysterectomy [hɪstəréktəmi] N histerectomía *f*

hysterical [hɪstérɪkəł] ADJ (out of control) histérico; (funny) desternillante

Ii

I [aɪ] PRON yo

I-beam [áɪbim] N viga doble *f*

Iberian [aɪbíriən] ADJ ibérico

Ibero-American [aɪbiroəmérɪkən] ADJ iberoamericano -na

ibuprofen [aɪbjuprófɪn] N ibuprofeno *m*

ice [aɪs] N hielo *m*; — **age** periodo glaciar *m*; —**berg** iceberg *m*; —**box** nevera *f*; refrigerador *m*; — **cream** helado *m*; — **cream cone** cucurucho de helado *m*; — - **cream parlor** heladería *f*; — **hockey** hockey sobre hielo *m*; — **skates** patines de cuchilla *m pl*; — **water** agua helada *f*; **to break the** — romper el hielo; **on** — en suspenso; VI/VT (freeze) helar[se]; (cover with ice) cubrir[se] de hielo; VT (cover with icing) bañar; (insure a deal) cerrar; **to** —-**skate** patinar sobre hielo; —**d tea** té helado *m*

Iceland [áɪslənd] N Islandia *f*

Icelander [áɪsləndɚ] N islandés -esa *mf*

Icelandic [aɪslǽndɪk] ADJ islandés

icicle [áɪsɪkəl] N carámbano *m*

icing [áɪsɪŋ] N (frosting) baño *m*; (formation of ice) formación de hielo *f*

icon [áɪkɑn] N icono *m*, ícono *m* (also computer term)

ICU [**intensive care unit**] [áɪsíjú] N unidad de cuidados intensivos *f*

icy [áisi] ADJ helado

ID [**identification card**] [áɪdí] N tarjeta de identidad *m*

idea [aɪdíə] N idea *f*

ideal [aɪdíəł] N ideal *m*; ADJ ideal, idóneo

idealism [aɪdíəlɪzəm] N idealismo *m*

idealist [aɪdíəlɪst] N idealista *mf*

idealistic [aɪdiəlístɪł] ADJ idealista

identical [aɪdéntɪkəł] ADJ idéntico; — **twins** gemelos *m pl*, gemelas *f pl*

identification [aɪdentəfɪkéʃən] N identificación *f*; — **card** tarjeta de identidad *m*, cédula de identidad *f*

identify [aɪdéntəfaɪ] VI/VT identificar[se]

identity [aɪdéntɪDi] N identidad *f*; — **theft** robo de identidad *m*

ideological [aɪdiəládʒɪkəł] ADJ ideológico

ideology [aɪdiáládʒi] N ideología *f*

idiocy [ídiəsi] N idiotez *f*

idiom [ídiəm] N modismo *m*

idiosyncrasy [ɪdiosínkrəsi] N idiosincrasia *f*

idiot [ídiət] N idiota *mf*, gilipollas *mf sg*

idiotic [ɪdiádɪk] ADJ idiota

idle [áɪdl] ADJ (not active) ocioso; (lazy) perezoso, holgazán; (of a machine, worker) parado; (of an engine) en ralentí; (meaningless) vacío; VI (person) holgazanear; (motor) girar en vacío; VT (cause to be idle) dejar parado/desocupado

idleness [áɪdlnɪs] N (inactivity) ociosidad *f*, ocio *m*, holganza *f*; (sloth) pereza *f*

idler [áɪdlɚ] N holgazán -ana *mf*, zanguango -ga *mf*

idol [áɪdl̩] N ídolo *m*

idolatry [aɪdáłətri] N idolatría *f*

idolize [áɪdl̩aɪz] VT idolatrar

idyll [áɪdl̩] N idilio *m*

if [ɪf] CONJ si; — **I were you** en tu lugar / yo que

tú; — **only I had known** de haber sabido / ojalá hubiera sabido; **he's tall,** — **a bit stooped** es alto, aunque un poco encorvado; N —**s** condiciones *f pl*; **no** —**s, ands, or buts** no hay pero que valga

igloo [íglu] N iglú *m*

ignite [ɪgnáɪt] VI/VT encender[se], prender fuego [a]

ignition [ɪgníʃən] N ignición *f*, encendido *m*; — **switch** llave de contacto *f*

ignoble [ɪgnóbəł] ADJ innoble

ignorance [ígnərəns] N ignorancia *f*

ignorant [ígnərənt] ADJ ignorante

ignore [ɪgnór] VT ignorar

ilk [ɪłk] N ralea *f*, calaña *f*

ill [ɪł] ADJ enfermo, malo; — **fortune** mala suerte *f*; — **nature** mal genio *m*, mala índole *f*; — **repute** mala fama *f*; — **will** mala voluntad *f*; N (sickness) enfermedad *f*; (calamity) calamidad *f*; ADJ —-**advised** imprudente; — **at ease** incómodo; —-**bred** maleducado; —-**fated** fatídico, funesto, desastrado; —-**gotten** mal adquirido; —- **humored** malhumorado; —-**mannered** maleducado, grosero; —-**natured** de mal genio; ADV **we can** — **afford to stop now** no podemos darnos el lujo de detenernos ahora

illegal [ɪlígəł] ADJ ilegal

illegitimate [ɪlɪdʒídəmɪt] ADJ ilegítimo

illicit [ɪlísɪt] ADJ ilícito

illiteracy [ɪlíDərəsi] N analfabetismo *m*

illiterate [ɪlíDərɪt] ADJ & N analfabeto -ta *mf*

illness [íłnɪs] N enfermedad *f*

illuminate [ɪlúmənət] VI/VT iluminar[se]

illumination [ɪlumənéʃən] N iluminación *f*

illusion [ɪlúʒən] N ilusión *f*

illusory [ɪlúzəri] ADJ ilusorio

illustrate [íləstret] VI/VT ilustrar

illustration [ɪləstréʃən] N ilustración *f*, estampa *f*

illustrator [íləstreDɚ] N ilustrador -ra *mf*, dibujante *mf*

illustrious [ɪlÁstriəs] ADJ ilustre, eximio

image [ímɪdʒ] N imagen *f*

imagery [ímɪdʒri] N conjunto de imágenes *m*

imaginary [ɪmǽdʒəneri] ADJ imaginario, fabuloso

imagination [ɪmædʒənéʃən] N imaginación *f*, fantasía *f*

imaginative [ɪmǽdʒənəDIV] ADJ imaginativo, fantasioso

imagine [ɪmǽdʒɪn] VI/VT imaginar[se]; — **that!** ¡figúrate!

imbalance [ɪmbǽləns] N desequilibrio *m*

imbecile [ímbəsəł] N imbécil *mf*

imbibe [ɪmbáɪb] VI/VT beber

imbue [ɪmbjú] VT imbuir, infundir

IMF [**International Monetary Fund**] [áɪéméf] N FMI *m*

imitate [ímɪtet] VT imitar
imitation [ɪmɪtéʃən] N imitación f; — **leather**
imitación de cuero f
imitator [ímɪteDɚ] N imitador -ora mf
immaculate [ɪmǽkjəlɪt] ADJ inmaculado
immaterial [ɪmətíriəł] ADJ inmaterial; **it is —
to me** me es indiferente
immature [ɪmətʃúr] ADJ inmaduro
immediate [ɪmídiɪt] ADJ inmediato
immediately [ɪmídiɪtli] ADV inmediatamente,
enseguida
immense [ɪméns] ADJ inmenso
immensity [ɪménsɪDi] N inmensidad f
immerse [ɪmɚ́s] VT (submerge) sumergir;
(absorb) sumir
immersed [ɪmɚ́st] ADJ inmerso
immigrant [ímɪɡrənt] ADJ & N inmigrante mf
immigrate [ímɪɡret] VI inmigrar
immigration [ɪmɪɡréʃən] N inmigración f
imminent [ímənənt] ADJ inminente
immobile [ɪmóbəł] ADJ inmóvil
immobilize [ɪmóbəlaɪz] VT inmovilizar
immodest [ɪmádɪst] ADJ inmodesto
immodesty [ɪmádɪsti] N inmodestia f
immoral [ɪmɔ́rəł] ADJ inmoral
immorality [ɪmɔrǽlɪDi] N inmoralidad f
immortal [ɪmɔ́rdl̩] ADJ & N inmortal mf
immortality [ɪmɔrtǽlɪDi] N inmortalidad f
immovable [ɪmúvəbəł] ADJ inamovible
immune [ɪmjún] ADJ inmune; — **system**
sistema inmune m
immunity [ɪmjúnɪDi] N inmunidad f
immunodeficiency [ɪmjənodɪfíʃənsi] N
inmunodeficiencia f
immutable [ɪmjúDəbəł] ADJ inmutable
impact [ímpækt] N impacto m; VI/VT repercutir
[sobre]; —**ed molar** muela impactada f
impair [ɪmpér] VT dañar, deteriorar,
menoscabar; —**ed** con las facultades
disminuidas
impairment [ɪmpérmənt] N daño m, deterioro
m, menoscabo m
impala [ɪmpálə] N impala m
impale [ɪmpéł] VT empalar
impart [ɪmpárt] VT (bestow knowledge)
impartir; (reveal) revelar
impartial [ɪmpárʃəł] ADJ imparcial
impartiality [ɪmpɑrʃiǽlɪDi] N imparcialidad f
impasse [ímpæs] N impasse m
impassioned [ɪmpǽʃənd] ADJ apasionado
impassive [ɪmpǽsɪv] ADJ impasible
impatience [ɪmpéʃəns] N impaciencia f
impatient [ɪmpéʃənt] ADJ impaciente
impeach [ɪmpítʃ] VT acusar formalmente; **to —
a person's honor** poner en tela de juicio el
honor de uno
impeachment [ɪmpítʃmənt] N impeachment m
impede [ɪmpíd] VT obstaculizar, estorbar, trabar
impediment [ɪmpéDəmənt] N impedimento m,

obstáculo m; (of speech) defecto m
impel [ɪmpéł] VT impeler
impending [ɪmpéndɪŋ] ADJ inminente
impenetrable [ɪmpénɪtrəbəł] ADJ impenetrable
imperative [ɪmpérəDɪv] ADJ (like a command)
imperativo; (necessary) imperioso; N
(command, grammatical mood) imperativo
m; (obligation) obligación f
imperceptible [ɪmpɚséptəbəł] ADJ
imperceptible
imperfect [ɪmpɚ́fɪkt] ADJ & N imperfecto m
imperial [ɪmpíriəł] ADJ imperial
imperialism [ɪmpíriəlɪzəm] N imperialismo m
imperil [ɪmpérəł] VT poner en peligro
imperious [ɪmpíriəs] ADJ imperioso
impersonal [ɪmpɚ́sən̩l] ADJ impersonal
impersonate [ɪmpɚ́sənet] VT (assume traits of)
hacerse pasar por; (mimic) imitar
impersonator [ɪmpɚ́səneDɚ] N imitador -ora
mf
impertinence [ɪmpɚ́tn̩əns] N impertinencia f
impertinent [ɪmpɚ́tn̩ənt] ADJ impertinente
impervious [ɪmpɚ́viəs] ADJ impermeable; (to
reason) refractario
impetigo [ɪmpɪtáɪɡo] N impétigo m
impetuous [ɪmpétʃuəs] ADJ impetuoso
impetus [ímpəDəs] N ímpetu m, empuje m
impious [ímpiəs] ADJ impío
implacable [ɪmplǽkəbəł] ADJ implacable
implant[1] [ɪmplǽnt] VT implantar
implant[2] [ímplænt] N implante m
implantation [ɪmplæntéʃən] N implantación f
implement[1] [ímpləmənt] N implemento m,
utensilio m
implement[2] [ímpləment] VT implementar,
instrumentar
implementation [ɪmpləmɪntéʃən] N
implementación f
implicate [ímplɪket] VT implicar, involucrar
implication [ɪmplɪkéʃən] N implicación f; **by —**
implícitamente
implicit [ɪmplísɪt] ADJ implícito
implore [ɪmplɔ́r] VI/VT implorar
imply [ɪmplái] VT dar a entender
impolite [ɪmpəláit] ADJ descortés
import[1] [ɪmpárt] VT (bring in) importar
import[2] [ímpɔrt] N (act of importing, thing
imported) importación f; (significance)
significado m; —**export company**
compañía de importación y exportación f
importance [ɪmpɔ́rtn̩s] N importancia f,
relevancia f
important [ɪmpɔ́rtn̩t] ADJ importante,
relevante
impose [ɪmpóz] VT imponer; **to —** [**upon**]
abusar [de]
imposing [ɪmpózɪŋ] ADJ imponente,
impresionante
imposition [ɪmpəzíʃən] N (act of imposing,

burden) imposición *f*; (abuse) abuso *m*
impossibility [ɪmpɑsəbílɪDi] N imposibilidad *f*
impossible [ɪmpásəbəl] ADJ (not possible)
imposible; (unbearable) insoportable; **to
make** — imposibilitar
impostor [ɪmpástə˞] N impostor -ora *mf*
impotence [ímpətəns] N impotencia *f*
impotent [ímpətənt] ADJ impotente
impoverish [ɪmpávə˞ɪʃ] VT empobrecer
impregnate [ɪmprégnet] VT (cause to be
permeated) impregnar; (make pregnant)
fecundar, preñar
impress [ɪmprés] VT (make a mark by pressing)
estampar; VI/VT (affect deeply) impresionar
impression [ɪmpréʃən] N impresión *f*; (feeling)
impresión *f*, sensación *f*
impressive [ɪmprésɪv] ADJ impresionante
imprint[1] [ímprɪnt] N (indentation) impresión *f*,
marca *f*; (printer's mark) pie de imprenta *m*
imprint[2] [ɪmprínt] VT (impress on) imprimir;
(fix firmly in mind) grabar
imprison [ɪmprízən] VT (in jail) encarcelar;
(anywhere) apresar
imprisonment [ɪmprízənmənt] N
encarcelamiento *m*
improbable [ɪmprábəbəl] ADJ improbable
impromptu [ɪmprámptu] ADJ improvisado; **he
gave the speech** — improvisó el discurso; N
impromptu *m*
improper [ɪmprápə˞] ADJ indecoroso,
inconveniente
improve [ɪmprúv] VI/VT mejorar[se]; **to —
upon** mejorar
improvement [ɪmprúvmənt] N (of a plan)
mejora *f*; (in health) mejoría *f*
improvisation [ɪmprɑvɪzéʃən] N improvisación *f*
improvise [ímprəvaɪz] VI/VT improvisar
imprudent [ɪmprúdn̩t] ADJ imprudente,
desatinado
impudence [ímpjədəns] N impertinencia *f*,
descaro *m*, desparpajo *m*
impudent [ímpjədənt] ADJ impertinente,
descarado
impulse [ímpʌls] N impulso *m*; **to act on** —
obrar impulsivamente
impulsive [ɪmpʌ́lsɪv] ADJ impulsivo
impunity [ɪmpjúnɪDi] N impunidad *f*
impure [ɪmpjúr] ADJ impuro
impurity [ɪmpjúrɪDi] N impureza *f*
in [ɪn] PREP en; (in tennis) buena, dentro; —
London en Londres; — **haste** de prisa; —
the morning por/en la mañana; — **writing**
por escrito; **she was walking** — **the street**
andaba por la calle; **to arrive** — **London**
llegar a Londres; **the books** — **the box** los
libros de la caja; **at two** — **the morning** a
las dos de la mañana; **dressed** — **white**
vestido de blanco; **the tallest** — **his class** el
más alto de su clase; **to come** — **a week**

venir dentro de una semana; ADV adentro,
dentro; **is she** — **or out?** ¿está adentro o
afuera? **to be all** — estar rendido; **to be** —
with someone estar bien con alguien; **to
come** — entrar; **to have it** — **for someone**
tenerle ojeriza a una persona; **to put** —
meter; **the doctor is** — el doctor está; **hats
are** — los sombreros están de moda; —**field**
cuadro interior *m*; N —**patient** paciente
internado -da *mf*; —**patient care**
internación *f*; —**seam** entrepierna *f*; —**step**
empeine *m*; ADJ **the** — **place to eat** el
restaurante de moda; **an** — **joke** una broma
para un grupo selecto
inability [ɪnəbílɪDi] N inhabilidad *f*,
incapacidad *f*
inaccessible [ɪnæksésəbəl] ADJ inaccesible,
inasequible
inaccurate [ɪnǽkjə˞ɪt] ADJ (not precise)
inexacto, impreciso; (wrong) incorrecto
inactive [ɪnǽktɪv] ADJ inactivo
inactivity [ɪnæktívɪDi] N inactividad *f*
inadequate [ɪnǽDɪkwɪt] ADJ (insufficient)
insuficiente; (unacceptable) inaceptable
inadmissible [ɪnədmísəbəl] ADJ inadmisible
inadvertent [ɪnədvɝ́tn̩t] ADJ (unintentional)
involuntario; (careless) descuidado,
negligente
inadvisable [ɪnədváɪzəbəl] ADJ desaconsejable
inane [ɪnén] ADJ necio
inanimate [ɪnǽnəmɪt] ADJ inanimado
inasmuch as [ɪnəzmʌ́tʃæz] CONJ puesto que
inattentive [ɪnəténtɪv] ADJ desatento
inaudible [ɪnɔ́Dəbəl] ADJ inaudible
inaugurate [ɪnɔ́gjəret] VT (initiate) inaugurar;
(induct into office) investir de un cargo
inauguration [ɪnɔgjəréʃən] N (initiation)
inauguración *f*; (induction) investidura *f*
inboard [ínbɔrd] ADJ dentro del casco
inborn [ɪnbɔ́rn] ADJ innato
Inca [íŋkə] ADJ & N inca *mf*
incandescence [ɪŋkændésəns] N
incandescencia *f*
incandescent [ɪnkændésənt] ADJ incandescente
incantation [ɪnkæntéʃən] N conjuro *m*
incapable [ɪnképəbəl] ADJ incapaz
incapacitate [ɪnkəpǽsɪtet] VT incapacitar
incarcerate [ɪnkársəret] VT encarcelar
incarnation [ɪnkɑrnéʃən] N encarnación *f*
incendiary [ɪnséndieri] ADJ & N incendiario -ria
mf; — **bomb** bomba incendiaria *f*
incense[1] [ínsɛns] N incienso *m*
incense[2] [ɪnsɛns] VT encolerizar
incentive [ɪnséntɪv] N incentivo *m*, acicate *m*
inception [ɪnsépʃən] N comienzo *m*
incessant [ɪnsésənt] ADJ incesante
incest [ínsɛst] N incesto *m*
incestuous [ɪnséstʃuəs] ADJ incestuoso
inch [ɪntʃ] N pulgada [2.54 centímetros] *f*; **to be**

within an — of estar a un punto de; VI
   avanzar poco a poco
incidence [ínsɪdəns] N incidencia f
incident [ínsɪdənt] N incidente m, lance m;
   (crime, accident) suceso m
incidental [ɪnsɪdéntl] ADJ (happening in
   accordance with) accesorio; — **music** música
   incidental f; N —**s** gastos menores m pl
incidentally [ɪnsɪdéntl̩i] ADV a propósito
incinerate [ɪnsínəret] VT incinerar
incipient [ɪnsípiənt] ADJ incipiente, naciente
incision [ɪnsíʒən] N incisión f
incisive [ɪnsáɪsɪv] ADJ incisivo
incisor [ɪnsáɪzɚ] N (tooth) incisivo m
incite [ɪnsáɪt] VT incitar
inclement [ɪnklémənt] ADJ inclemente
inclination [ɪnklənéʃən] N (slope) inclinación f;
   (tendency) afición f, inclinación f
incline¹ [ɪnkláɪn] VI/VT inclinar[se]
incline² [ínklaɪn] N declive m, pendiente f
include [ɪnklúd] VT incluir
including [ɪŋklúdɪŋ] ADJ **it costs a thousand
   dollars, not — air travel** cuesta mil
   dólares, sin incluir el vuelo; **that whole
   week, — Saturday** toda esa semana,
   incluyendo el sábado / el sábado inclusive; —
   you, there are four of us incluyéndote a ti,
   somos cuatro
inclusion [ɪŋklúʒən] N (acceptance) inclusión f;
   (addition) incorporación f
inclusive [ɪnklúsɪv] ADJ inclusivo; **from
   Monday to Friday** — de lunes a viernes
   inclusive
incoherent [ɪnkohírənt] ADJ incoherente
income [ínkʌm] N Sp renta f; Am ingreso m; —
   tax Sp impuesto sobre la renta m; Am
   impuesto sobre ingresos m; — **tax return**
   declaración de impuestos sobre la renta / los
   ingresos f
incoming [ínkʌmɪŋ] ADJ entrante
incomparable [ɪnkámpəəbəl] ADJ
   incomparable, sin parangón
incompatible [ɪnkəmpǽDəbəl] ADJ
   incompatible
incompetent [ɪnkámpɪtənt] ADJ incompetente
incomplete [ɪnkəmplít] ADJ incompleto
incomprehensible [ɪnkɑmprɪhénsəbəl] ADJ
   incomprensible
inconceivable [ɪnkənsívəbəl] ADJ inconcebible
inconclusive [ɪnkənklúsɪv] ADJ no concluyente
inconsiderate [ɪnkənsíDəɪt] ADJ
   desconsiderado
inconsistency [ɪnkənsístənsi] N (condition)
   inconsecuencia f; (instance) incoherencia f
inconsistent [ɪnkənsístənt] ADJ inconsecuente
inconspicuous [ɪnkənspíkjuəs] ADJ poco
   llamativo; **to be** — pasar inadvertido
inconstancy [ɪnkánstənsi] N inconstancia f
inconstant [ɪnkánstənt] ADJ inconstante

incontinent [ɪnkántənənt] ADJ incontinente
incontrovertible [ɪnkɑntrəvɝ́Dəbəl] ADJ
   incontrovertible
inconvenience [ɪnkənvínjəns] N (state of being
   inconvenient) inconveniencia f; (thing that is
   inconvenient) molestia f, inconveniente m;
   VT incomodar, molestar
inconvenient [ɪnkənvínjənt] ADJ (bothersome)
   incómodo; (untimely) inoportuno
incorporate [ɪnkɔ́rpəret] VI/VT (include)
   incorporar[se]; (form a corporation)
   constituir[se] en sociedad
incorporation [ɪnkɔrpəréʃən] N (inclusion)
   incorporación f; (integration) integración f
incorrect [ɪnkərékt] ADJ incorrecto
incorrigible [ɪnkɔ́rɪdʒəbəl] ADJ incorregible
increase¹ [ɪnkrís] VI/VT aumentar[se],
   incrementar[se]
increase² [ínkris] N aumento m, incremento m
increasingly [ɪnkrísɪŋli] ADV cada vez más
incredible [ɪnkréDəbəl] ADJ increíble
incredulous [ɪnkréʤələs] ADJ incrédulo
increment [ínkrəmənt] N incremento m
incriminate [ɪnkrímənet] VT incriminar
incubator [íŋkjəbeDɚ] N incubadora f
inculcate [ɪnkʌ́lket] VT inculcar
incumbent [ɪnkʌ́mbənt] ADJ **a duty — upon
   me** un deber que me incumbe; N titular m
incur [ɪnkɝ́] VT (an expense) incurrir en; (a debt)
   contraer
incurable [ɪŋkjúrəbəl] ADJ incurable
indebted [ɪndéDɪd] ADJ endeudado, en deuda
indebtedness [ɪndéDɪdnɪs] N endeudamiento
   m, adeudo m
indecency [ɪndísənsi] N indecencia f
indecent [ɪndísənt] ADJ indecente; — **exposure**
   delito de exhibicionismo m
indecision [ɪndɪsíʒən] N indecisión f
indeed [ɪndíd] ADV de verdad; INTERJ
   (ironically) ¡no me digas! (sincerely) ¡tienes
   razón! ¡efectivamente!
indefensible [ɪndɪfénsəbəl] ADJ indefendible
indefinite [ɪndéfənɪt] ADJ indefinido
indelible [ɪndéləbəl] ADJ indeleble
indelicate [ɪndélɪkɪt] ADJ (tactless) indelicado;
   (offensive) indecoroso
indemnify [ɪndémnəfaɪ] VT indemnizar
indemnity [ɪndémnɪDi] N indemnización f
indent [ɪndént] VI/VT sangrar
indentation [ɪndentéʃən] N (notch) muesca f;
   (blank space) sangría f
independence [ɪndɪpéndəns] N independencia f
independent [ɪndɪpéndənt] ADJ independiente,
   autónomo
indestructible [ɪndɪstrʌ́ktəbəl] ADJ
   indestructible
indeterminate [ɪndɪtɝ́mənɪt] ADJ
   indeterminado
index [índɛks] N índice m; — **card** ficha f; —

finger índice *m*; VT (incorporate into an index) poner en el índice; (make the index) poner/hacer un índice; (adjust wages) indexar
indexing [índɛksɪŋ] N indexación *f*
India [índiə] N India *f*
Indian [índiən] ADJ & N indio -a *mf*; — **Ocean** Océano Indico *m*
indicate [índɪket] VT indicar
indication [ɪndɪkéʃən] N indicación *f*
indicative [ɪndíkəDɪv] ADJ & N indicativo *m*
indicator [índɪkeDə-] N indicador *m*
indict [ɪndáɪt] VT acusar
indictment [ɪndáɪtmənt] N acusación *f*
indifference [ɪndífrəns] N indiferencia *f*
indifferent [ɪndífrənt] ADJ indiferente
indigenous [ɪndídʒənəs] ADJ (person) indígena; (plant, animal) autóctono
indigent [índɪdʒənt] ADJ & N indigente *mf*
indigestion [ɪndɪdʒéstʃən] N indigestión *f*
indignant [ɪndígnənt] ADJ indignado
indignation [ɪndɪgnéʃən] N indignación *f*
indignity [ɪndígnɪDi] N ultraje *m*, afrenta *f*
indigo [índɪgo] N índigo *m*, añil *m*; — **blue** azul añil *m*
indirect [ɪndɪrékt] ADJ indirecto; — **object** complemento/objeto indirecto *m*
indiscreet [ɪndɪskrít] ADJ indiscreto
indiscretion [ɪndɪskréʃən] N indiscreción *f*
indispensable [ɪndɪspénsəbəl] ADJ indispensable, imprescindible
indispose [ɪndɪspóz] VT indisponer
indisposed [ɪndɪspózd] ADJ indispuesto; **to become** — indisponerse
indistinct [ɪndɪstíŋkt] ADJ indistinto
individual [ɪndəvídʒuəl] ADJ individual; N individuo *m*, persona *f*; *pej* sujeto *m*, individuo *m*
individualism [ɪndəvídʒuəlɪzəm] N individualismo *m*
individualist [ɪndəvídʒuəlɪst] N individualista *mf*
individuality [ɪndəvɪdʒuǽlɪDi] N individualidad *f*
indivisible [ɪndəvízəbəl] ADJ indivisible
indoctrinate [ɪndáktrɪnet] VT adoctrinar
indolence [índələns] N indolencia *f*, desidia *f*
indolent [índələnt] ADJ indolente, haragán
indomitable [ɪndámɪDəbəl] ADJ indomable
Indonesia [ɪndənízə] N Indonesia *f*
Indonesian [ɪndənízən] ADJ & N indonesio -sia *mf*
indoor [índɔr] ADJ interior
indoors [ɪndɔ́rz] ADV dentro; **to go** — entrar, ir para adentro
induce [ɪndús] VT inducir
inducement [ɪndúsmənt] N aliciente *m*, incentivo *m*
induct [ɪndʌ́kt] VT (initiate) admitir, iniciar; (draft) reclutar

induction [ɪndʌ́kʃən] N (philosophical, electrical) inducción *f*; (into an organization) admisión *f*, iniciación *f*
indulge [ɪndʌ́ldʒ] VT mimar, consentir; VI **to** — **in** darse a, entregarse a; **to** — **oneself [in]** darse el gusto [de]
indulgence [ɪndʌ́ldʒəns] N (act or state of indulging, religious) indulgencia *f*; (thing indulged in) exceso *m*, lujo *m*
indulgent [ɪndʌ́ldʒənt] ADJ indulgente; (toward a child) complaciente
industrial [ɪndʌ́striəl] ADJ industrial
industrialist [ɪndʌ́striəlɪst] N industrial *mf*
industrialization [ɪndʌstriəlɪzéʃən] N industrialización *f*
industrious [ɪndʌ́striəs] ADJ (student) aplicado, diligente; (worker) industrioso
industry [índəstri] N (manufacturing) industria *f*; (hard work) diligencia *f*; — **standards** normas industriales *f pl*
inebriated [ɪníbrieDɪd] ADJ ebrio
inedible [ɪnéDəbəl] ADJ incomestible, incomible
ineffable [ɪnéfəbəl] ADJ inefable
ineffective [ɪnɪféktɪv] ADJ ineficaz, ineficiente
ineffectual [ɪnɪféktʃuəl] ADJ ineficaz
inefficient [ɪnɪfíʃənt] ADJ ineficiente
ineligible [ɪnélɪdʒəbəl] ADJ inelegible
inept [ɪnépt] ADJ inepto
inequality [ɪnɪkwálɪDi] N desigualdad *f*
inert [ɪnɚ́t] ADJ inerte
inertia [ɪnɚ́ʃə] N inercia *f*
inescapable [ɪnɪsképəbəl] ADJ inevitable, ineludible
inestimable [ɪnéstəməbəl] ADJ inestimable
inevitable [ɪnévɪDəbəl] ADJ inevitable
inexcusable [ɪnɪkskjúzəbəl] ADJ inexcusable
inexhaustible [ɪnɪgzóstəbəl] ADJ inagotable
inexorable [ɪnéksə-əbəl] ADJ inexorable
inexpensive [ɪnɪkspénsɪv] ADJ económico, barato
inexperienced [ɪnɪkspíriənst] ADJ no experimentado, inexperto
inexplicable [ɪnɪksplíkəbəl] ADJ inexplicable
infallible [ɪnfǽləbəl] ADJ infalible
infamous [ínfəməs] ADJ infame, de mala fama
infamy [ínfəmi] N infamia *f*
infancy [ínfənsi] N primera infancia *f*
infant [ínfənt] N bebé *mf*
infantile [ínfəntaɪl] ADJ infantil
infantry [ínfəntri] N infantería *f*; —**man** infante *m*
infatuated [ɪnfǽtʃueDɪd] ADJ enamorado
infect [ɪnfékt] VT (cause disease) infectar; (spread a mood) contagiar
infection [ɪnfékʃən] N infección *f*
infectious [ɪnfékʃəs] ADJ (disease) infeccioso, contagioso; (mood) contagioso
infer [ɪnfɚ́] VT inferir, deducir
inference [ínfə-əns] N inferencia *f*, deducción *f*

inferior [ɪnfíriɚ] ADJ inferior
inferiority [ɪnfiriɔ́rɪDi] N inferioridad *f*; —
  complex complejo de inferioridad *m*
infernal [ɪnfɜ́ːnl̩] ADJ infernal
inferno [ɪnfɜ́ːno] N (fire) incendio *m*; (hot place)
  infierno *m*
infertility [ɪnfɚtílɪDi] N infertilidad *f*
infest [ɪnfést] VT infestar, plagar
infestation [ɪnfestéʃən] N infestación *f*
infiltrate [ɪnfíltret] VI/VT infiltrar[se]; **to — an
  organization** infiltrarse en una
  organización
infinite [ínfənɪt] ADJ & N infinito *m*
infinitive [ɪnfínɪDɪv] ADJ & N infinitivo *m*
infinity [ɪnfínɪDi] N (large number) infinidad *f*;
  (space) infinito *m*
infirm [ɪnfɜ́ːm] ADJ enfermizo, achacoso
infirmary [ɪnfɜ́ːməri] N enfermería *f*
infirmity [ɪnfɜ́ːmɪDi] N enfermedad *f*, achaque *m*
inflame [ɪnflém] VT (with infection)
  inflamar[se]; (with passion) enardecer[se];
  (with fire) encender[se]
inflammation [ɪnfləméʃən] N inflamación *f*
inflate [ɪnflét] VI/VT (fill with air) inflar[se],
  hinchar[se]; (exaggerate) exagerar
inflation [ɪnfléʃən] N (rise in prices) inflación *f*;
  (introduction of air) inflado *m*
inflexible [ɪnfléksəbəl] ADJ inflexible
inflict [ɪnflíkt] VT (impose on) infligir; **to — a
  blow** asestar un golpe
influence [ínfluəns] N influencia *f*, influjo *m*; VT
  influir en/sobre, incidir en; — **peddling**
  tráfico de influencias *m*
influential [ɪnfluénʃəl] ADJ influyente
influenza [ɪnfluénzə] N gripe *f*
influx [ínflʌks] N (of fluid, goods) entrada *f*; (of
  people) afluencia *f*
infomercial [ínfomɚʃəl] N infomercial *m*,
  publirreportaje *m*
inform [ɪnfɔ́rm] VI/VT (give knowledge)
  informar[se]; VT (inspire) inspirar; **to —
  against/on** delatar a, denunciar a
informal [ɪnfɔ́rməl] ADJ informal
informant [ɪnfɔ́rmənt] N informante *mf*
information [ɪnfɚméʃən] N (news, data, details,
  act of informing) información *f*; (details)
  informes *m pl*; — **superhighway** autopista
  de la información *f*
informative [ɪnfɔ́rməDɪv] ADJ informativo
informer [ɪnfɔ́rmɚ] N informante *mf*, delator
  -ora *mf, pej* soplón -ona *mf*
infotainment [ɪnfoténmənt] N entretenimiento
  informativo *m*
infraction [ɪnfrǽkʃən] N infracción *f*
infrared [ɪnfrəréd] ADJ & N infrarrojo *m*
infrastructure [ínfrəstrʌktʃɚ] N
  infraestructura *f*
infringe [ɪnfríndʒ] VT infringir; VI **to — upon**
  violar

infringement [ɪnfríndʒmənt] N infracción *f*,
  violación *f*
infuriate [ɪnfjúriet] VT enfurecer, sublevar
infuse [ɪnfjúz] VT infundir
ingenious [ɪndʒínjəs] ADJ ingenioso
ingenuity [ɪndʒənúɪDi] N ingenio *m*, inventiva *f*
ingenuous [ɪndʒénjuəs] ADJ ingenuo *f*
ingenuousness [ɪndʒénjuəsnɪs] N ingenuidad *f*
ingest [ɪndʒést] VI/VT ingerir
ingrate [íngret] N ingrato -ta *mf*
ingratitude [ɪngrǽDɪtud] N ingratitud *f*
ingredient [ɪngríDiənt] N ingrediente *m*
ingrown [íngron] ADJ encarnado
inhabit [ɪnhǽbɪt] VT habitar
inhabitant [ɪnhǽbɪtənt] N habitante *mf*
inhale [ɪnhél] VI/VT inhalar, aspirar
inherent [ɪnhérənt] ADJ inherente
inherit [ɪnhérɪt] VI/VT heredar
inheritance [ɪnhérɪDəns] N herencia *f*; — **tax**
  impuesto a la herencia *m*
inherited [ɪnhérɪDɪd] ADJ patrimonial
inhibit [ɪnhíbɪt] VT inhibir, cohibir
inhibiting [ɪnhíbɪDɪŋ] ADJ inhibidor
inhibition [ɪnɪbíʃən] N inhibición *f*, cohibición *f*
inhibitor [ɪnhíbɪDɚ] N inhibidor *m*
inhospitable [ɪnhɑspíDəbəl] ADJ (person)
  inhospitalario; (place) inhóspito
inhuman [ɪnhjúmən] ADJ inhumano
inimitable [ɪnímɪDəbəl] ADJ inimitable
initial [ɪníʃəl] ADJ & N inicial *f*; VT firmar las
  iniciales
initialize [ɪníʃəlaɪz] VT inicializar
initially [ɪníʃəli] ADV al comienzo, inicialmente
initiate [ɪníʃiet] VT iniciar
initiative [ɪníʃəDɪv] N iniciativa *f*
inject [ɪndʒékt] VI/VT inyectar[se], pinchar[se]
injection [ɪndʒékʃən] N inyección *f*
injunction [ɪndʒʌ́ŋkʃən] N mandato judicial *m*,
  orden judicial *f*
injure [índʒɚ] VI/VT herir[se]; (sports)
  lesionar[se]
injurious [ɪndʒúriəs] ADJ (harmful) perjudicial;
  (defamatory) injurioso
injury [índʒəri] N herida *f*, lesión *f*; — **time**
  (soccer) descuento *m*
injustice [ɪndʒʌ́stɪs] N injusticia *f*
ink [ɪŋk] N tinta *f*; VT (mark with ink) entintar;
  (sign) firmar; — **cartridge** cartucho de tinta
  m; —**-jet printer** impresora de inyección de
  tinta *f*; —**pad** almohadilla *f*; —**well** tintero *m*
inkling [íŋklɪŋ] N idea *f*
inlaid [ínled] ADJ incrustado; — **work**
  incrustación *f*
inland [ínlənd] ADJ interior; ADV tierra adentro
inlay¹ [ɪnlé] VT incrustar
inlay² [ínle] N incrustación *f*
inmate [ínmet] N (in a prison) preso -sa *mf*,
  recluso -sa *mf*; (in an asylum) internado -da
  mf; (in a hospital) paciente *mf*

inn [ɪn] N posada f, fonda f; **—keeper** posadero -ra mf, fondista mf
innate [ɪnét] ADJ innato
inner [ínə-] ADJ (inside) interior; (intimate) íntimo; **— city** zona céntrica empobrecida f; **— ear** oído interno m; **—most** más recóndito; **— tube** cámara f
inning [ínɪŋ] N entrada f
innocence [ínəsəns] N (absence of guilt) inocencia f; (naiveté) candidez f, candor m
innocent [ínəsənt] ADJ & N inocente mf
innocuous [ɪnákjuəs] ADJ innocuo, inocuo
innovate [ínəvet] VI innovar
innovating [ínəveDɪŋ] ADJ innovador, renovador
innovation [ɪnəvéʃən] N innovación f
innovative [ínəveDɪV] ADJ innovador
innovator [ínəveDə-] N innovador -ora mf
innuendo [ɪnjuéndo] N insinuación f
innumerable [ɪnúmə-əbəl] ADJ innumerables
inoculate [ɪnákjəlet] VI/VT inocular[se]
inoffensive [ɪnəfénsɪv] ADJ inofensivo
inoperable [ɪnápə-əbəl] ADJ inoperable
inopportune [ɪnapə-tún] ADJ inoportuno
inordinate [ɪnɔ́rdṇɪt] ADJ desmesurado
inorganic [ɪnɔrgǽnɪk] ADJ inorgánico; **— chemistry** química inorgánica f
input [ínpʊt] N (electric, computer) entrada f; (opinion) opinión f; VT ingresar/entrar datos
inquire [ɪŋkwáɪr] VI/VT inquirir, preguntar; **to — about/after** preguntar por; **to — into** indagar, investigar
inquiry [íŋkwəri] N (scientific) investigación f; (police) pesquisa f; **we made inquiries about hotels** hicimos averiguaciones acerca de hoteles
inquisition [ɪŋkwɪzíʃən] N inquisición f
inquisitive [ɪnkwízɪDɪV] ADJ (curious) inquisitivo, curioso; (asking many questions) preguntón
insane [ɪnsén] ADJ demente, loco; **— asylum** manicomio m
insanity [ɪnsǽnɪDi] N locura f, demencia f
insatiable [ɪnséʃəbəl] ADJ insaciable
inscribe [ɪnskráɪb] VT (mark) inscribir; (engrave) grabar; (dedicate) dedicar
inscription [ɪnskrípʃən] N (marks, engraving) inscripción f; (dedication) dedicatoria f
inscrutable [ɪnskrúDəbəl] ADJ inescrutable
insect [ínsɛkt] N insecto m
insecticide [ɪnsɛ́ktɪsaɪd] N insecticida m
insectivorous [ɪnsɛktívə-əs] ADJ insectívoro
insecure [ɪnsɪkjúr] ADJ inseguro
insecurity [ɪnsɪkjúrɪDi] N inseguridad f
insemination [ɪnsɛmɪnéʃən] N inseminación f
insensible [ɪnsénsəbəl] ADJ insensible
insensitive [ɪnsénsɪDɪV] ADJ insensible
inseparable [ɪnsépə-əbəl] ADJ inseparable
insert¹ [ɪnsɨt] VT insertar, introducir; (into a

text) intercalar
insert² [ínsɨt] N encarte m
insertion [ɪnsɨ́ʃən] N inserción f; (into a text) intercalación f
inside¹ [ɪnsáɪd] PREP dentro de; ADV dentro, adentro
inside² [ínsaɪd] N interior m; **— job** delito cometido por un empleado m; **—s** entrañas f pl; **— track** pista interior f; **to turn — out** volver del revés; **he passed me on the —** me pasó por la derecha; ADJ (interior) interior
insider [ɪnsáɪDə-] N privilegiado -da mf; **— trading** abuso de información privilegiada m
insidious [ɪnsíDiəs] ADJ insidioso
insight [ínsaɪt] N (intuition) perspicacia f; (discernment) discernimiento m
insignia [ɪnsígniə] N insignia f
insignificant [ɪnsɪgnífɪkənt] ADJ insignificante, menudo, nimio
insincere [ɪnsɪnsír] ADJ insincero
insinuate [ɪnsínjuet] VT insinuar
insinuation [ɪnsɪnjuéʃən] N insinuación f
insipid [ɪnsípɪd] ADJ insípido, soso
insist [ɪnsíst] VI/VT insistir; **to — on** insistir en
insistence [ɪnsístəns] N insistencia f
insistent [ɪnsístənt] ADJ insistente
insole [ínsoł] N plantilla f
insolence [ínsələns] N insolencia f
insolent [ínsələnt] ADJ insolente, atrevido
insoluble [ɪnsáljəbəl] ADJ insoluble
insolvent [ɪnsáłvənt] ADJ insolvente
insomnia [ɪnsámniə] N insomnio m
inspect [ɪnspékt] VT inspeccionar; **to — the troops** pasar revista a la tropa, revistar a la tropa
inspection [ɪnspékʃən] N inspección f; (of troops) revista f
inspector [ɪnspéktə-] N inspector -ora mf
inspiration [ɪnspəréʃən] N inspiración f
inspire [ɪnspáɪr] VI/VT inspirar
instability [ɪnstəbílɪDi] N inestabilidad f
install [ɪnstół] VT instalar; N **— program** programa instalador m
installation [ɪnstəléʃən] N instalación f
installment [ɪnstółmənt] N (payment of debt) cuota f; (of a book) entrega f, fascículo m; **to pay in —s** pagar a plazos
instance [ínstəns] N ejemplo m; **for —** por ejemplo; **court of first —** tribunal de primera instancia m
instant [ínstənt] N instante m; **this —** ahora mismo; ADJ inmediato; **— coffee** café instantáneo m; **— messaging** mensajería instantánea f
instantaneous [ɪnstənténiəs] ADJ instantáneo
instead [ɪnstéd] ADV **— of** en lugar de, en vez de; **she didn't want a desk, so she ordered a chair —** no quería un escritorio, así que pidió

una silla en su lugar
instigate [ínstɪget] VT instigar
instigator [ínstɪgeɒɚ] N (of a crime) instigador
-ora *mf*; (of an event) causante *mf*
instill [ɪnstíl] VT inculcar
instinct [ínstɪŋkt] N instinto *m*
instinctive [ɪnstíŋktɪv] ADJ instintivo
institute [ínstɪtut] N instituto *m*; VT instituir
institution [ɪnstɪtúʃən] N institución *f*
institutional [ɪnstɪtúʃənəl] ADJ institucional
instruct [ɪnstrʌ́kt] VT (teach) instruir;
(command, advise) dar instrucciones;
(command) mandar
instruction [ɪnstrʌ́kʃən] N instrucción *f*; —**s**
(orders) órdenes *f pl*; (information)
instrucciones *f pl*, indicaciones *f pl*
instructive [ɪnstrʌ́ktɪv] ADJ instructivo
instructor [ɪnstrʌ́ktɚ] N (of skills) instructor
-ora *mf*; (of knowledge) profesor -ora *mf*
instrument [ínstrəmənt] N instrumento *m*; —
panel salpicadero *m*, tablero *m*
instrumental [ɪnstrəméntl] ADJ instrumental;
to be — in ser fundamental para
insubordinate [ɪnsəbórdnɪt] ADJ insubordinado
insufferable [ɪnsʌ́fəəbəl] ADJ insufrible
insufficiency [ɪnsəfíʃənsi] N insuficiencia *f*
insufficient [ɪnsəfíʃənt] ADJ insuficiente
insulate [ínsəlet] VT aislar
insulation [ɪnsəléʃən] N aislamiento *m*
insulator [ínsəleɒɚ] N (material) aislante *m*;
(device) aislador *m*
insulin [ínsəlɪn] N insulina *f*; — **shock** choque
insulínico *m*
insult[1] [ɪnsʌ́lt] VT insultar, injuriar
insult[2] [ínsʌlt] N insulto *m*, injuria *f*
insulting [ɪnsʌ́ltɪŋ] ADJ insultante, injurioso
insuperable [ɪnsúpəəbəl] ADJ insuperable
insurable [ɪnʃúrəbəl] ADJ asegurable
insurance [ɪnʃúrəns] N seguro *m*; — **agent**
agente de seguros *mf*; — **company** compañía
de seguros *f*; — **policy** póliza de seguro *f*
insure [ɪnʃúr] VI/VT asegurar[se]
insurgent [ɪnsɚ́dʒənt] N alzado -da *mf*
insurmountable [ɪnsəmáuntəbəl] ADJ
insuperable
insurrection [ɪnsərékʃən] N insurrección *f*
intact [ɪntǽkt] ADJ intacto
intangible [ɪntǽndʒəbəl] ADJ intangible
integer [íntɪdʒɚ] N (número) entero *m*
integral [íntɪgrəl] ADJ (complete) integral;
(forming part of) integrante; — **calculus**
cálculo integral *m*; N integral *f*
integrate [íntɪgret] VT integrar; VI integrarse a
integration [ɪntɪgréʃən] N integración *f*
integrity [ɪntégrɪDi] N integridad *f*
intellect [íntlɛkt] N intelecto *m*
intellectual [ɪntlɛ́ktʃuəl] ADJ & N intelectual *mf*
intelligence [ɪntélɪdʒəns] N inteligencia *f* (also
secret information); — **quotient** coeficiente

intelectual / de inteligencia *m*
intelligent [ɪntélɪdʒənt] ADJ inteligente
intelligible [ɪntélɪdʒəbəl] ADJ inteligible
intend [ɪnténd] VT pensar; **to — to do**
something pensar hacer algo; **a book —ed**
for children un libro destinado/dirigido a
los niños
intense [ɪnténs] ADJ intenso
intensify [ɪnténsɪfaɪ] VI/VT intensificar[se]
intensity [ɪnténsɪDi] N intensidad *f*
intensive [ɪnténsɪv] ADJ intensivo; — **care unit**
sala de cuidados intensivos *f*
intent [ɪntént] N intención *f*, propósito *m*; **to/**
for all —s and purposes en la práctica; ADJ
atento; — **on** resuelto a
intention [ɪnténʃən] N intención *f*
intentional [ɪnténʃənəl] ADJ intencional; —
base on balls base por bolas intencional *f*
intentionally [ɪnténʃənəli] ADV a propósito
inter [ɪntɚ́] VT sepultar
interact [ɪntɚǽkt] VI interactuar
interaction [ɪntɚǽkʃən] N interacción *f*
interactive [ɪntɚǽktɪv] ADJ interactivo
intercede [ɪntɚsíd] VI interceder
intercept [ɪntɚsépt] VT interceptar
interception [ɪntɚsépʃən] N interceptación *f*
intercession [ɪntɚséʃən] N intercesión *f*
interchange[1] [íntɚtʃendʒ] N cambio *m*; (on
road) enlace *m*; Sp intercambiador *m*
interchange[2] [ɪntɚtʃéndʒ] VI/VT cambiar,
intercambiar
intercourse [íntɚkɔrs] N (sexual) relación
sexual *f*; (social) comunicación *f*, trato *m*
interest [íntrɪst] N interés *m*; (financial) interés
m, rédito *m*; (share in a business)
participación *f*; —**-bearing** que devenga
intereses; —**-free** libre de intereses, sin
intereses; — **rate** tasa de interés *f*; **mining**
—**s** los negocios mineros; VT interesar; **may I**
— **you in a cookie?** ¿te puedo ofrecer una
galleta?
interested [íntrɪstɪd] ADJ interesado; — **party**
parte interesada *f*; **to be/become — in**
interesarse en/por
interesting [íntrɪstɪŋ] ADJ interesante
interface [íntɚfes] N interface *mf*, interfaz *f*
interfere [ɪntɚfír] VI interferir; (meddle)
entrometerse; **to — with** interferir en
interference [ɪntɚfírəns] N interferencia *f*,
injerencia *f*
interferon [ɪntɚfíran] N interferón *m*
interim [íntɚɪm] N ínterin *m*; ADJ (person)
interino; (decision) provisional
interior [ɪntíriɚ] ADJ & N interior *m*; —
decoration decoración de interiores *f*; —
design diseño de interiores *m*
interjection [ɪntɚdʒékʃən] N interjección *f*,
exclamación *f*
interlace [ɪntɚlés] VI/VT entrelazar[se]

interlinear [ɪntərlínɪə-] ADJ interlineal
interlock [ɪntə-lák] VI/VT (gears) engranar[se]; (branches, etc.) entrelazar[se]; N interlock m
interlocking [ɪntə-lákɪŋ] ADJ (gears) engranado; (branches) entrelazado
interlude [íntə-lud] N (interval) intervalo m; (musical) interludio m; (theatrical) entremés m
intermediary [ɪntə-mídɪɛri] ADJ intermediario
intermediate [ɪntə-mídɪɪt] ADJ intermedio
interment [ɪntɔ́-mənt] N entierro m
interminable [ɪntɔ́-mənəbəł] ADJ interminable
intermingle [ɪntə-míŋgəł] VI/VT entremezclar[se]
intermission [ɪntə-míʃən] N entreacto m, intervalo m
intermittent [ɪntə-mítn̩t] ADJ intermitente
intern [íntɔ-n] VT internar, confinar; N (prisoner, doctor) interno -na mf
internal [ɪntɔ́-n̩l] ADJ interno, interior; —-**combustion engine** motor de combustión interna m; — **hard disk** disco duro interno m; — **revenue** rentas internas f pl; — **Revenue Service** Hacienda f
internalize [ɪntɔ́-nəlaɪz] VT interiorizar, internalizar
international [ɪntə-nǽʃən̩l] ADJ internacional; — **law** derecho internacional m
Internet [íntə-nɛt] N internet m, red f, web f; — **access** acceso a internet m; — **access provider** proveedor de acceso a internet m; — **banking** banca por internet f; — **community** comunidad internauta f; — **user** internauta mf
internist [íntɔ́-nɪst] N internista mf
internship [íntɔ-nʃɪp] N (medical) internado m; (student) práctica f
interpersonal [ɪntə-pɔ́-sən̩l] ADJ interpersonal
interpose [ɪntə-póz] VI/VT interponer[se]
interpret [ɪntɔ́-prɪt] VI/VT interpretar
interpretation [ɪntɔ-prɪtéʃən] N interpretación f
interpreter [ɪntɔ́-prɪtə-] N intérprete mf
interracial [ɪntə-réʃəł] ADJ interracial
interrelated [ɪntə-rɪlédɪd] ADJ interrelacionado
interrogate [ɪntérəget] VI/VT interrogar
interrogation [ɪntɛrəgéʃən] N interrogación f, interrogatorio m
interrogative [ɪntɛrágədɪv] ADJ interrogativo; N palabra/oración interrogativa f
interrupt [ɪntərápt] VI/VT interrumpir
interruption [ɪntərápʃən] N interrupción f
intersect [ɪntə-sékt] VI/VT (math) intersecar[se]; (road) cruzar[se]
intersection [íntə-sɛkʃən] N (math) intersección f; (street) cruce m, intersección f
intersperse [ɪntə-spɔ́-s] VT (scatter) esparcir; (intermingle) entremezclar, entreverar; (spice up) salpicar
interstate [íntə-stet] ADJ interestatal; —

highway autopista interestatal f
interstellar [ɪntə-stéłə-] ADJ interestelar
interstice [ɪntɔ́-stɪs] N intersticio m
intertwine [ɪntə-twáɪn] VI/VT entrelazar[se]
interval [íntə-vəł] N intervalo m
intervene [ɪntə-vín] VI intervenir; (mediate) interponerse, mediar
intervening [ɪntə-vínɪŋ] ADJ interventor
intervention [ɪntə-vénʃən] N intervención f; (mediation) mediación f
interview [íntə-vju] N entrevista f; (for entertainment) Sp interviú f; VT entrevistar; VI entrevistarse
intestinal [ɪntéstən̩l] ADJ intestinal; — **flora** flora intestinal f; — **obstruction** obstrucción intestinal f
intestine [ɪntéstɪn] ADJ & N intestino m; **small** — intestino delgado m; **large** — intestino grueso m
intimacy [íntəməsi] N intimidad f
intimate[1] [íntəmɪt] ADJ íntimo, entrañable; (knowledge) profundo
intimate[2] [íntəmet] VT insinuar, dar a entender
intimation [ɪntəméʃən] N insinuación f
intimidate [ɪntímɪdet] VT intimidar, acobardar
into [íntu] PREP **she came** — **the room** entró en/a la habitación; **he put it** — **the box** lo metió en la caja; **he translated it** — **German** lo tradujo al alemán; **he ran** — **a tree** chocó contra un árbol; **it fell** — **oblivion** cayó en el olvido; **he went** — **medicine** entró a medicina; **I'm really** — **pop music** me ha dado por la música pop
intolerable [ɪntálə-əbəł] ADJ intolerable
intolerance [ɪntálə-əns] N intolerancia f
intolerant [ɪntálə-ənt] ADJ intolerante
intonation [ɪntənéʃən] N entonación f
intoxicate [ɪntáksɪket] VI/VT embriagar (also exhilarate); (poison) intoxicar
intoxication [ɪntaksɪkéʃən] N (drunkenness) embriaguez f; (poisoning) intoxicación f
intransigent [ɪntrǽnzɪdʒənt] ADJ intransigente
intransitive [ɪntrǽnzɪdɪv] ADJ intransitivo
intrauterine device [ɪntrəjúpə-ɪndváɪs] N dispositivo intrauterino m
intravenous [ɪntrəvínəs] ADJ intravenoso; — **feeding** alimentación intravenosa f
intrepid [ɪntrépɪd] ADJ intrépido
intricate [íntrɪkɪt] ADJ intrincado
intrigue[1] [ɪntríg] VI/VT intrigar
intrigue[2] [íntrig] N intriga f
intrinsic [ɪntrínzɪk] ADJ intrínseco
introduce [ɪntrədús] VT (put in, bring) introducir; (make acquainted) presentar
introduction [ɪntrədákʃən] N (of a book) introducción f; (of a custom or system) introducción f, implantación f; (to a person) presentación f
introspection [ɪntrəspékʃən] N introspección f

introvert [íntrəvɜ⋅t] N introvertido -da *mf*
introverted [íntrəvɜ⋅DId] ADJ introvertido
intrude [Intrúd] VI/VT interrumpir; (penetrate, of rock) penetrar
intruder [Intrúdɚ] N intruso -sa *mf*
intrusion [Intrúʒən] N (interruption) interrupción *f*; (penetration) intrusión *f*
intrusive [Intrúsɪv] ADJ (rock) intrusivo; (people) entrometido
intubation [Intjubéʃən] N intubación *f*
intuition [Intuíʃən] N intuición *f*
intuitive [IntúɪDIv] ADJ intuitivo
inundate [ínəndet] VT inundar
invade [Invéd] VI/VT invadir
invader [InvéDɚ] N invasor -ora *mf*
invalid[1] [ínvəlɪd] ADJ & N (infirm) inválido -da *mf*
invalid[2] [Invǽlɪd] ADJ (not valid) nulo
invaluable [Invǽljuəbəɫ] ADJ invalorable, inestimable
invariable [Invériəbəɫ] ADJ invariable
invariably [Invériəbli] ADV siempre
invasion [Invéʒən] N invasión *f*
invasive [Invésɪv] ADJ invasivo
invent [Invént] VT inventar
invention [Invénʃən] N (act of inventing, thing invented) invención *f*, invento *m*; (falsehood) invención *f*
inventive [Invéntɪv] ADJ inventivo
inventor [Invéntɚ] N inventor -ora *mf*
inventory [ínvəntɔri] N inventario *m*; VT inventariar
inverse [Invɜ́⋅s] ADJ & N inverso *m*
inversion [Invɜ́⋅ʒən] N inversión *f*
invert [Invɜ́⋅t] VT invertir
invest [Invést] VI/VT (money) invertir; (a rank upon someone) investir
investigate [Invéstɪget] VI/VT investigar, indagar
investigation [Invɛstɪgéʃən] N investigación *f*
investigator [InvéstɪgeDɚ] N investigador -ora *mf*
investment [Invéstmənt] N (of money) inversión *f*; (of rank) investidura *f*; — **broker** corredor -ora de bolsa *mf*
investor [Invéstɚ] N inversionista *mf*, inversor -ora *mf*
invigorate [Invígəret] VT vigorizar
invincible [Invínsəbəɫ] ADJ invencible
invisible [Invízəbəɫ] ADJ invisible
invitation [Invɪtéʃən] N invitación *f*
invite[1] [Inváɪt] VI/VT invitar; **to — trouble** buscarse problemas
invite[2] [ínvaɪt] N *fam* invitación *f*
inviting [InváɪDɪŋ] ADJ atractivo, seductor
in vitro fertilization [Invítrofɚdlɪzéʃən] N fertilización in vitro *f*
invocation [Invəkéʃən] N invocación *f*
invoice [ínvɔɪs] N factura *f*; VT facturar

invoke [Invók] VT invocar
involuntary [Inválənteri] ADJ involuntario
involve [Inváɫv] VT (take, last) suponer; **how much time will this —?** ¿cuánto tiempo supone esto?; (consist of, entail) consistir en, involucrar; **what does your work —?** ¿en qué consiste tu trabajo?; (be in question) ser cuestión de; **national security is —d!** ¡es una cuestión de seguridad nacional!; (implicate) implicar; **they tried to — her** trataron de implicarla; (wrapped up in) estar metido; **he's very —d in the family business** está muy metido en el negocio familiar; (have a liaison) enredarse; **she got —d with a married man** se enredó con un hombre casado
involved [Inváɫvd] ADJ complicado, enrevesado
involvement [Inváɫvmənt] N (in a crime) implicación *f*; (in a project) participación *f*; (with a person) relación *f*
inward [ínwɚd] ADV hacia dentro; ADJ interior
iodide [áɪədaɪd] N yoduro *m*
iodine [áɪədaɪn] N yodo *m*
ion [áɪɑn] N ión *m*
ionize [áɪənaɪz] VT ionizar
ipecac syrup [ípɪkæksírəp] N jarabe de ipecacuana *m*
IPO [initial public offering] [áɪpíó] N oferta pública inicial *f*
IQ [intelligence quotient] [áɪkjú] N coeficiente de inteligencia *m*
Iran [Irán] N Irán *m*
Iranian [Iréniən] ADJ & N iraní *mf*
Iraq [Irǽk] N Irak *m*
Iraqi [Irǽki] ADJ & N iraquí *mf*
irascible [Irǽsəbəɫ] ADJ irascible
irate [aɪrét] ADJ airado
ire [aɪr] N ira *f*
Ireland [áɪrlənd] N Irlanda *f*
iridescent [Irɪdésənt] ADJ iridiscente, tornasolado
iridium [IríDiəm] N iridio *m*
iris [áɪrɪs] N (part of eye) iris *m*; (plant, flower) lirio *m*; (rainbow) arco iris *m*
Irish [áɪrɪʃ] ADJ irlandés; N (language) irlandés *m*; **the —** los irlandeses
irk [ɜ⋅k] VT fastidiar; **—ed** fastidiado
irksome [ɜ́⋅ksəm] ADJ engorroso, molesto
iron [áɪɚn] N (element, golf club) hierro *m*; (appliance) plancha *f*; **in —s** en grilletes; — **deficiency anemia** anemia por deficiencia de hierro *f*; **—work** herrajes *m pl*; **—works** fundición *f*; ADJ férreo, de hierro; VI/VT planchar; **to — out a difficulty** allanar una dificultad
ironic [aɪránɪk] ADJ irónico
ironing [áɪɚnɪŋ] N planchado *m*
irony [áɪrəni] N ironía *f*; (mockery) ironía *f*, sorna *f*

irradiate [ɪréɒiet] VT irradiar
irrational [ɪrǽʃənl] ADJ irracional
irrefutable [ɪrɪfjúɒəbəł] ADJ irrefutable
irregular [ɪrégjələ˞] ADJ irregular
irregularity [ɪrɛgjəlǽrɪɒi] N irregularidad *f*
irrelevant [ɪrélɒvənt] ADJ no pertinente; **your age is** — tu edad no viene al caso
irreparable [ɪrépɒ˞əbəł] ADJ irreparable
irreplaceable [ɪrɪplésəbəł] ADJ irreemplazable
irreproachable [ɪrɪprótʃəbəł] ADJ irreprochable
irresistible [ɪrɪzístəbəł] ADJ irresistible
irresponsibility [ɪrɪspɑnsəbílɪɒi] N irresponsabilidad *f*
irresponsible [ɪrɪspánsəbəł] ADJ irresponsable
irretrievable [ɪrɪtrívəbəł] ADJ irrecuperable
irreverent [ɪrévɒ˞ənt] ADJ irreverente
irreversible [ɪrɪv-ɔ˞səbəł] ADJ irreversible
irrevocable [ɪrévəkəbəł] ADJ irrevocable
irrigate [írɪget] VI/VT (a garden) irrigar, regar; (the eyes) irrigar
irrigation [ɪrɪgéʃən] N riego *m*, irrigación *f*; — **ditch** acequia *f*
irritable [írɪɒəbəł] ADJ irritable, colérico
irritate [írɪtet] VT irritar
irritating [írɪteɒɪŋ] ADJ irritante
irritation [ɪrɪtéʃən] N irritación *f*
IRS [Internal Revenue Service] [áɪárés] N Hacienda *f*
is [ɪz] *see* be
Islam [ízlɑm] N islamismo *m*, islam *m*
Islamic [ɪzlámɪk] ADJ islámico
island [áɪlənd] N isla *f*
islander [áɪləndə˞] N isleño -ña *mf*
isle [aɪł] N isla *f*
isobar [áɪsəbɑr] N isobara *f*
isolate [áɪsəlet] VT aislar
isolation [aɪsəléʃən] N aislamiento *m*, marginación *f*
isolationism [aɪsəléʃənɪzəm] N aislacionismo *m*
isometric [aɪsəmétrɪk] ADJ isométrico
isotope [áɪsətop] N isótopo *m*, isotopo *m*
Israel [ízriəł] N Israel *m*
Israeli [ɪzréli] ADJ & N israelí *mf*
issue [íʃu] N (of printed matter) tirada *f*; (of stock, bonds) emisión *f*; (copy of a magazine) número *m*, entrega *f*; (of a fluid) flujo *m*; (problem) problema *m*, tema *m*; (progeny) descendencia *f*; **he's got —s** es muy acomplejado; **to take — with** discrepar de; VT (written material) publicar; (a decree) promulgar; (a permit, document) expedir; (shares) emitir; (to flow) brotar; (to come out of) salir de; (to descend from) descender de
isthmus [ísməs] N istmo *m*
it [ɪt] PRON — **all started yesterday** todo empezó ayer; — **is necessary** es necesario; — **is raining** llueve, está lloviendo; — **is said that** se dice que; — **is two o'clock** son las dos; — **was broken** estaba roto; **who is**

—? ¿quién es? **if — weren't five o'clock** si no fueran las cinco; **I saw** — lo/la vi; **he talked about** — habló de eso; **what time is** —? ¿qué hora es? **how is — going?** ¿qué tal? **I don't get** — no entiendo; **you're** —! ¡tú la quedas! / ¡tú la traes!
IT [information technology] [áɪtí] N informática *f*
Italian [ɪtǽljən] ADJ & N italiano -na *mf*
italic [ɪtǽlɪk] ADJ itálico; N **—s** letra bastardilla/ cursiva *f*
italicize [ɪtǽlɪsaɪz] VT poner en bastardilla/ cursiva
Italy [ɪdḷi] N Italia *f*
itch [ɪtʃ] VI/VT picar; **to be —ing to** tener ganas de; N (sensation) comezón *f*, picazón *f*; (longing) ansia *f*
itching [ítʃɪŋ] N comezón *f*, picazón *f*
itchy [ítʃi] ADJ que pica; **it feels** — me pica
item [áɪɒəm] N (piece of news) artículo *m*; (topic of gossip) tema de conversación *m*; (unit) ítem *m*; (couple) pareja *f*
itemize [áɪɒəmaɪz] VT (list) enumerar; (break down) desglosar; **—d invoice** factura detallada *f*
itinerant [aɪtínɒ˞ənt] ADJ itinerante, ambulante
itinerary [aɪtínɒ˞eri] N (schedule) itinerario *m*; (guidebook) guía de viajeros *f*
its [ɪts] POSS ADJ su/sus, de él, de ella, de ello
itself [ɪtséłf] PRON **this story wrote** — esta historia se escribió sola; **the bike was standing by** — la bici estaba parada sola; **the dog bit** — el perro se mordió [a sí mismo]; **the fox found — a hole** la zorra se encontró una guarida
IUD [intrauterine device] [áɪjúdí] N DIU *m*
IV [intravenous] [áɪví] ADJ intravenoso
Ivorian [aɪvɔ́riən] ADJ & N marfileño -ña *mf*
ivory [áɪvri] N marfil *m*; — **tower** torre de marfil *f*
Ivory Coast [áɪvrikóst] N Costa de Marfil *f*
ivy [áɪvi] N hiedra *f*

Jj

jab [dʒæb] VI/VT (hit) golpear; (hit with elbow) codear; N (blow) golpe *m*; (blow with elbow) codazo *m*; (in boxing) jab *m*, puñetazo directo *m*
jabber [dʒǽbə˞] VI (unintelligibly) farfullar; (incessantly) charlotear; N (unintelligible) farfulla *f*; charloteo *m*
jack [dʒæk] N (tool) gato *m*; (card) sota *f*; (plug-in) hembra *f*, toma *f*; (flag) bandera de proa *f*; **—ass** asno *m*, burro *m* (also person);

—hammer martillo neumático *m*; **—knife** navaja *f*; **— of all trades** hombre orquesta *m*; **—pot** premio gordo *m*; **—rabbit** liebre americana *f*; **you don't know** — no sabes ni un comino; VI/VT **to — off** *vulg* hacer[se] una paja; VT **to — up** (a car) alzar con gato; (prices) subir

jackal [ʤǽkəł] N chacal *m*

jacket [ʤǽkɪt] N (clothing) chaqueta *f*; (of a book) forro *m*; (of a potato) piel *f*

jade [ʤed] N jade *m*

jaded [ʤédɪd] ADJ (disenchanted) de vuelta; (sated) hastiado

jagged [ʤǽgɪd] ADJ recortado, desigual

jaguar [ʤǽgwɑr] N jaguar *m*

jail [ʤeł] N cárcel *f*; **—break** fuga *f*; VT encarcelar

jailer [ʤélɚ] N carcelero -ra *mf*

jalopy [ʤəlápi] N cacharro *m*

jam [ʤæm] VT (stuff) embutir; (block) atestar; (immobilize) trabar; (make unworkable) obstruir, atascar, atorar; (stop radio signals) interferir; VI (become stuck or unworkable) atascarse; (crowd in) apiñarse; **to — on the brakes** frenar de golpe; **to — one's fingers** pillarse los dedos; N (jelly) mermelada *f*, dulce *m*; (difficult situation) aprieto *m*; (traffic) embotellamiento *m*; **— session** jam *m*

Jamaica [ʤəmékə] N Jamaica *f*

Jamaican [ʤəmékən] ADJ & N jamaicano -na *mf*, jamaiquino -na *mf*

janitor [ʤǽnɪDɚ] N conserje *m*

January [ʤǽnjuɛri] N enero *m*

Japan [ʤəpǽn] N Japón *m*

Japanese [ʤæpəníz] ADJ & N japonés -esa *mf*

jar [ʤɑr] VI/VT (shake) sacudir[se]; (clash) chocar; **to — one's nerves** ponerle a uno los nervios de punta; N (container) tarro *m*, frasco *m*, pote *m*; (large earthen container) tinaja *f*; (collision) choque *m*; (shake) sacudida *f*

jargon [ʤárgən] N jerga *f*

jasmine [ʤǽzmɪn] N jazmín *m*

jasper [ʤǽspɚ] N jaspe *m*

jaundice [ʤóndɪs] N ictericia *f*

jaundiced [ʤóndɪst] ADJ ictérico

jaunt [ʤɔnt] N excursión *f*; VI pasear

javelin [ʤǽvlɪn] N jabalina *f*

jaw [ʤɔ] N (of animal) quijada *f*; (of human) mandíbula *f*; (of mammals) fauces *f pl*; **—bone** mandíbula *f*, maxilar *m*

jay [ʤe] N arrendajo *m*

jazz [ʤæz] N jazz *m*; VI **to — up** animar

jealous [ʤéləs] ADJ (possessive) celoso; (envious) envidioso; (protective) protector

jealousy [ʤéləsi] N celos *m pl*

jeans [ʤinz] N jeans *m pl*, vaqueros *m pl*

jeer [ʤir] VI/VT (mock) mofarse [de], burlarse [de]; (boo) abuchear, befar; N (act of mockery)

mofa *f*, burla *f*; (boos) abucheo *m*, befa *f*

jelly [ʤéli] N jalea *f*; **—fish** medusa *f*

jeopardize [ʤépɚdaɪz] VT comprometer, poner en peligro

jeopardy [ʤépɚdi] ADV LOC **in** — en peligro

jerk [ʤɚk] N (quick pull) tirón *m*; (muscular contraction) espasmo *m*; (idiot) *pej* pelmazo *m*; VI/VT tironear; **to — around** manipular, *vulg* joder; **to — off** *vulg* hacerse una paja

jerky [ʤɚ́ki] ADJ espasmódico; N tasajo *m*

jersey [ʤɚ́zi] N jersey *m*

jest [ʤest] N broma *f*, chanza *f*; **in** — en broma; VI bromear

jester [ʤéstɚ] N bufón *m*

Jesuit [ʤézuɪt] N jesuita *m*

jet [ʤet] N (stream) chorro *m*; (spout) surtidor *m*; (stone) azabache *m*; — **[air]plane** avión a reacción *m*; — **engine** motor a reacción *m*; — **lag** jet lag *m*; **—liner** avión a reacción de pasajero *m*; — **propulsion** propulsión a chorro *f*; — **set** jet *m*, jet-set *m*; — **stream** (of air) corriente en chorro *f*; (of a jet) chorro *m*; ADJ **-black** negro como el azabache; VI (stream out) salir a chorros; (travel) volar en avión a reacción; VT (spew out) lanzar a chorros; (transport) transportar en avión a reacción

jettison [ʤéDɪsən] VT echar por la borda

Jew [ʤu] N judío -a *mf*

jewel [ʤúəł] N (ornament, prized person) joya *f*, alhaja *f*; (stone) gema *f*; (watch jewel) rubí *m*; **— box** joyero *m*

jeweler [ʤúəlɚ] N joyero -ra *mf*; **—'s shop** joyería *f*

jewelry [ʤúəłri] N joyas *f pl*, alhajas *f pl*; **— box** alhajero *m*; **— store** joyería *f*

Jewish [ʤúɪʃ] ADJ judío

jiffy [ʤífi] ADV LOC **in a** — en un santiamén

jig [ʤɪg] N (dance) giga *f*; **—saw** sierra de vaivén *f*; **—saw puzzle** rompecabezas *m sg*; VI (dance) bailotear

jiggle [ʤígəł] VI/VT zangolotear[se], zarandear[se]; N zangoloteo *m*, zarandeo *m*

jilt [ʤɪłt] VT dejar plantado

jingle [ʤíŋgəł] VI tintinear; VT agitar; N retintín *m*; (short song) jingle *m*

jinx [ʤɪŋks] N persona que trae mala suerte *f*; VT traer mala suerte

job [ʤab] N (task) tarea *f*; (position) trabajo *m*, empleo *m*; (theft) golpe *m*; **to be out of a** — estar sin trabajo; *Sp* estar en [el] paro; **by the** — a destajo; **to do a good** — hacer buen trabajo; VI trabajar a destajo; **on-the-** **training** capacitación en el lugar de trabajo *f*

jobber [ʤábɚ] N (day-worker) trabajador -ora a destajo *mf*; (wholesaler) vendedor -ora mayorista *mf*

jobless [ʤáblɪs] ADJ sin trabajo; *Sp* en paro

jock [ʤak] N deportista *mf*; **— [strap]**

suspensorio *m*

jockey [ʤáki] N jockey *m*; VI **to — for position** disputarse la posición

jocular [ʤákjələ˞] ADJ jocoso

jog [ʤag] VI (run) correr, trotar; VT (refresh) refrescar; N trote *m*; **to go for a —** salir a correr

jogging [ʤágɪŋ] N jogging *m*, footing *m*

john [ʤɑn] N (urinal) *fam* meadero *m*; (customer of a prostitute) *fam* putañero *m*

join [ʤɔɪn] VI/VT juntar[se]; (pipes) acoplar[se], unir[se]; (bones) articular[se]; (a club) asociarse [a]; (the navy, etc.) alistarse [en]

joint [ʤɔɪnt] N (point of contact) juntura *f*, junta *f*; (connection between bones) articulación *f*, coyuntura *f*; (nodule on a plant) nudo *m*; (marijuana cigarette) porro *m*; (dive, bar) antro *m*; **out of —** descoyuntado; ADJ (shared) común; **— account** cuenta conjunta *f*; **— action** acción colectiva *f*; **— custody** custodia compartida *f*; **— owner** copropietario -ria *mf*; **— session** sesión plena *f*; **— venture** joint venture *m*

jointly [ʤɔɪntli] ADV conjuntamente

joke [ʤok] N broma *f*, chiste *m*; VI bromear

joker [ʤókə˞] N (person who jokes) bromista *mf*, guasón -ona *mf*; (card) comodín *m*

jokingly [ʤókɪŋli] ADV en broma

jolly [ʤáli] ADJ jovial

jolt [ʤoɫt] N sacudida *f*; VT sacudir; **to — along** avanzar a los tumbos

Jordan [ʤɔ́rdn̩] N Jordania *f*

Jordanian [ʤɔrdéniən] ADJ & N jordano -na *mf*

jostle [ʤásəɫ] VI/VT codear[se], dar empujones [a]; N empujón *m*

jot [ʤɑt] VT **to — down** apuntar; N pizca *f*

journal [ʤ˞nl̩] N (diary) diario *m*; (periodical) revista *f*; (logbook) cuaderno de bitácora *m*

journalism [ʤ˞nəlɪzəm] N periodismo *m*

journalist [ʤ˞nəlɪst] N periodista *mf*

journalistic [ʤ˞nəlístɪk] ADJ periodístico

journey [ʤ˞ni] N viaje *m*; VI viajar

joust [ʤaʊst] N justa *f*

jowl [ʤáʊɫ] N carrillo *m*, moflete *m*

joy [ʤɔɪ] N (delight) alegría *f*, regocijo *m*, alborozo *m*; (source of delight) deleite *m*; **—ride** paseo en coche robado *m*; **—stick** joystick *m*, palanca de mando *f*

joyful [ʤɔ́ɪfəɫ] ADJ alborozado

joyous [ʤɔ́ɪəs] ADJ jubiloso, alegre

jubilant [ʤúbələnt] ADJ jubiloso

jubilee [ʤubəlí] N jubileo *m*

Judaism [ʤúdiɪzəm] N judaísmo *m*

judge [ʤʌʤ] N juez -eza *mf*; (in tennis) juez -eza de silla *mf*; **to be a good — of character** saber juzgar a la gente; VI/VT juzgar; (estimate) calcular

judgment [ʤʌʤmənt] N juicio *m*; (in court) fallo *m*; **— day** día del juicio final *m*

judicial [ʤudíʃəɫ] ADJ judicial

judicious [ʤudíʃəs] ADJ juicioso, sensato

judo [ʤúdo] N judo *m*, yudo *m*

jug [ʤʌg] N (pitcher) jarro *m*, jarra *f*; (storage jar) pote *m*; **—s** *vulg* tetas *f pl*

juggle [ʤʌ́gəɫ] VI/VT hacer juegos malabares [con], hacer malabarismo [con]; **to — the accounts** manipular las cuentas

juggler [ʤʌ́glə˞] N malabarista *mf*

jugular [ʤʌ́gjələ˞] N yugular *f*

juice [ʤus] N jugo *m*; (fruit only) *Sp* zumo *m*

juicer [ʤúsə˞] N exprimidor *m*

juicy [ʤúsi] ADJ jugoso; **a — story** un cuento sabroso

juke [ʤuk] N (in sports) amague *m*, finta *f*; **—box** juke-box *m*

July [ʤulái] N julio *m*

jumble [ʤʌ́mbəɫ] VI/VT revolver[se] *m*; N revoltijo *m*

jumbo [ʤʌ́mbo] ADJ jumbo, gigantesco; **— jet** jumbo *m*

jump [ʤʌmp] VI (spring) saltar; (increase, as temperature, prices) dar un salto; VT (capture in checkers) comer; (ride a horse over barrier) hacer saltar; (mug) asaltar; (cross a river, mountains, etc.) salvar; **to — at** abalanzarse sobre; **to — over** saltar; **to —-start** hacer un puente; **to — the track** descarrilarse; **to — to conclusions** hacer deducciones precipitadas; N salto *m*; (in prices) subida repentina *f*; **—rope** cuerda de saltar *f*; **— shot** tiro en suspensión *m*; **—suit** mono *m*

jumper [ʤʌ́mpə˞] N (person who jumps) saltador -ora *mf*; (dress) jumper *m*; *Sp* pichi *m*; **— cable** puente *m*

jumpy [ʤʌ́mpi] ADJ nervioso, asustadizo

junction [ʤʌ́ŋkʃən] N (act or state of joining) unión *f*; (joining of two rivers) confluencia *f*; (of two railways) empalme *m*, entronque *m*; (of roads) cruce *m*

juncture [ʤʌ́ŋktʃə˞] N (point where joined) juntura *f*; **at this —** en esta coyuntura

June [ʤun] N junio *m*

jungle [ʤʌ́ŋgəɫ] N selva *f*, jungla *f*; **the law of the —** la ley de la selva

junior [ʤúnjə˞] ADJ (younger) menor; (more recent) más nuevo, de menos antigüedad; **— college** institución para los dos primeros años de la licenciatura *f*; **John Smith Jr.** John Smith, hijo; N estudiante del tercer año *mf*

juniper [ʤúnəpə˞] N enebro *m*

junk [ʤʌŋk] N (useless articles) trastos viejos *m pl*; (metal) chatarra *f*; (Chinese boat) junco *m*; **— dealer** chatarrero -ra *mf*; **— food** comida basura *f*, porquerías *f pl*; **— mail** publicidad por correo *f*; **— e-mail** correo electrónico basura *m*; **—yard** chatarrería *f*; VT desechar, echar a la basura

junkie [ʤʌ́ŋki] N *fam* drogata *mf*, drogota *mf*
jurisdiction [ʤʊrɪsdíkʃən] N jurisdicción *f*
jurisprudence [ʤʊrɪsprúdn̩s] N jurisprudencia *f*
juror [ʤúrɚ] N miembro de un jurado *m*, jurado
   -da *mf*
jury [ʤúri] N jurado *m*; — **box** banco de jurado
   m; VT **to** —-**rig** chapucear
just [ʤʌst] ADJ justo; ADV (exactly) exactamente,
   precisamente; (only) solo; — **like that** Am
   así nomás; **he** — **left** acaba de salir; **she is** —
   a little girl no es más que una niña; **you'll**
   — **have to wait** tendrás que esperar; —
   barely apenas; **the meeting is** — **starting**
   la reunión apenas comienza; **that is** — **what**
   I wanted to talk to you about
   precisamente de eso te quería hablar
justice [ʤʌ́stɪs] N (fairness) justicia *f*; (judge)
   juez -eza *mf*; **to bring to** — enjuiciar; **the**
   painting doesn't do him — el retrato no le
   favorece
justification [ʤʌstəfɪkéʃən] N justificación *f*
justify [ʤʌ́stəfaɪ] VT justificar
jut [ʤʌt] VI sobresalir, proyectarse
juvenile [ʤúvənaɪł] ADJ juvenil; — **delinquent**
   delincuente juvenil *mf*
juxtapose [ʤʌ́kstəpoz] VT yuxtaponer

Kk

kangaroo [kæŋgərú] N canguro *m*
karat, carat [kérət] N quilate *m*
kayak [káɪæk] N kayak *m*
Kazak, Kazakh [kəzǽk] ADJ & N kazako -ka *mf*
Kazakhstan [kəzákstɑn] N Kazajstán *m*
keel [kił] N quilla *f*; VI/VT volcar[se]; **to** — **over**
   (ship) volcar[se]; (person) caer de cabeza,
   desplomarse
keen [kin] ADJ (edge) afilado; (perception) fino;
   (mind) agudo, penetrante
keenness [kínnɪs] N (of a blade) lo afilado; (of
   perception) fineza *f*; (of mind) agudeza *f*
keep [kip] VI (continue) seguir; (not spoil)
   aguantar; VT (retain) guardar; (maintain)
   mantener; (employ) tener; (look after) cuidar;
   to — **a diary** llevar un diario; **to** — **a secret**
   guardar un secreto; **to** — **at it** persistir; **to** —
   away mantener[se] alejado; **to** — **back** (stay
   away) tener a raya; (restrain) contener; **to** —
   bad company andar en mala compañía; **to**
   — **from** (prevent) impedir; (protect)
   proteger contra; **to** — **[on] talking** seguir
   hablando; **to** — **the door open** mantener la
   puerta abierta; **to** — **off the grass** no pisar el
   césped; **to** — **up** (perform as well) seguir el
   tren; (stay informed) mantenerse al tanto; **to**

— **one's hands off** no tocar; **to** — **someone**
   posted mantener al corriente a alguien; **to** —
   quiet estarse callado; **to** — **to the right**
   mantenerse a la derecha; **to** — **track of** (do
   accounts) llevar la cuenta de; (consider) no
   perder de vista; **to** — **watch** vigilar; **he** —**s a**
   maid tiene una criada; **she kept me on the**
   phone me [re]tuvo en el teléfono; N **for** —**s**
   (forever) para siempre; (for real) en serio;
   —**sake** recuerdo *m*
keeper [kípɚ] N (of people) guardián *m*; (of
   things) custodio *m*
keeping [kípɪŋ] N custodia *f*; **in** — **with** en
   armonía con
keg [kɛg] N barril *m*
Kegel exercises [kégəł ɛksɚsaɪzɪz] N ejercicios
   de Kegel *m pl*
kennel [kénl̩] N residencia de perros *f*
Kenya [kénjə] N Kenia *f*
Kenyan [kénjən] ADJ & N keniata *mf*
kept [kɛpt] *see* keep
kernel [kɝn̩l] N (seed) semilla *f*, grano *m*;
   (essence) meollo *m*
kerosene [kérəsin] N queroseno *m*
kestrel [késtrəł] N cernícalo *m*
ketchup [kétʃəp] N salsa de tomate *f*, cátsup *m*
kettle [kédl̩] N caldera *f*, hervidor *m*; (for tea)
   tetera *f*; —**drum** tímpano *m*, timbal *m*;
   that's another — **of fish** es harina de otro
   costal
key [ki] N (for locks) llave *f*; (secret, book of
   answers) clave *f*; (for winding) clavija *f*; (on
   keyboard) tecla *f*; (island) cayo *m*; (music)
   clave *f*; —**board** teclado *m*; —**hole** ojo de la
   cerradura *m*; — **indicator** indicador clave *m*;
   —**note** tónica *f*; —**note address** discurso de
   apertura *m*; —**pad** teclado numérico *m*;
   —**ring** llavero *m*; — **signature** armadura *f*;
   —**stone** piedra angular *f*; —**stroke**
   pulsación [de la tecla] *f*; —**word** palabra clave
   f; —**word search** búsqueda por palabra
   clave *f*; **to sing on** — cantar a tono; ADJ
   clave; VT (scratch) rayar; **to be** —**ed up** estar
   sobreexcitado
kg [kíləgræm] *see* kilogram
khaki [kǽki] N kaki *m*, caqui *m*
kick [kɪk] VI/VT (person) patear; (horse) dar coces
   [a], cocear; VI (gun) dar un culatazo,
   retroceder; **to** — **around** (discuss) discutir;
   (to mistreat) dar por la cabeza; **to** — **at** dar
   patadas; **to** — **out** echar a patadas; **to** —**start**
   arrancar; **to** — **the bucket** estirar la pata; **to**
   — **up a lot of dust** levantar una polvareda;
   to — **a habit** dejar un vicio; N (by a person)
   patada *f*, puntapié *m*; (by a soccer player)
   patada *f*; (of a horse) coz *f*; Am patada *f*; (of a
   gun) culatazo *m*; (in the air) pataleo *m*; **this**
   whisky has a — este whisky es fuerte; **I get**
   a — **out of swimming** me encanta nadar;

—back comisión ilegal *f*; *Mex* mordida *f*;
—off (football) saque de inicio *m*; (soccer) saque inicial *m*; **—stand** soporte *m*

kid [kɪd] N (young goat) cabrito *m*, chivo *m*; (leather) cabritilla *f*; (child) niño -ña *mf*; (young person) chico -ca *mf*; **— stuff** juego de niños *m*; VI bromear, embromar, tomar el pelo

kidnap [kídnæp] VT secuestrar, raptar

kidnapper [kídnæpɚ] N secuestrador -ora *mf*

kidnapping [kídnæpɪŋ] N secuestro *m*, rapto *m*

kidney [kídni] N riñón *m*; **— bean** judía *f*; **— failure** insuficiencia renal *f*; **— stone** cálculo renal *m*

kill [kɪł] VI/VT matar; (drink completely) terminar; (turn off) apagar; **that comedian —s me** ese cómico me mata de risa; N (animal killed) caza *f*; (slaughter) matanza *f*; **—joy** aguafiestas *mf sg*

killer [kílɚ] N asesino -na *mf*; **— bee** abeja asesina *f*; **— whale** orca *f*; **a — game** un partidazo

killing [kílɪŋ] N (slaughter) matanza *f*; (murder) asesinato *m*; (animal killed) caza *f*; **to make a — llenarse de oro

kilo [kílo] N kilo *m*, quilo *m*

kilobyte [kíləbaɪt] N kilobyte *m*

kilogram [kíləgræm] N kilogramo *m*

kilometer [kɪlámɪdɚ] N kilómetro *m*

kilowatt [kíləwɑt] N kilovatio *m*; **—-hour** kilovatio-hora *f*

kin [kɪn] N parentela *f*, parientes *m pl*; **—sman** pariente *m*; **—swoman** parienta *f*; **next of — deudos *m pl*

kind [kaɪnd] ADJ (benevolent) bondadoso, bueno; (words) amable; **to be — to animals** ser cariñoso con los animales; **—hearted** de buen corazón; **— of tired** algo cansado; N clase *f*, tipo *m*, género *m*; **to pay in — (without money) pagar en especie; (retaliate) pagar con la misma moneda

kindergarten [kíndɚgɑrtn̩] N jardín infantil / de niños *m*; *Sp* parvulario *m*

kindle [kíndl̩] VT (fire) prender; (interest) despertar, provocar; VI encenderse

kindling [kíndlɪŋ] N leña ligera *f*, astillas *f pl*

kindly [káɪndli] ADJ bondadoso, bueno; ADV (with kindness) amablemente; (please) por favor; **we thank you — le agradecemos mucho; **not to take — to criticism** no aceptar de buen grado las críticas

kindness [káɪndnɪs] N (state) bondad *f*, amabilidad *f*; (act) favor *m*

kindred [kíndrɪd] ADJ emparentado; **— spirits** espíritus afines *m pl*, almas gemelas *f pl*

kinesiology [kəniziáləʤi] N quinesiología *f*

kinesthesia [kɪnɪsθízə] N cinestesia *f*

king [kɪŋ] N rey *m* (also in chess, cards); (in checkers) dama *f*; **—fisher** martín pescador

m; **—pin** (in a mechanism) pivote central *m*; (in bowling) bolo central *m*; (person) figura central *f*; ADJ **—-sized** extra grande

kingdom [kíŋdəm] N reino *m*

kingly [kíŋli] ADJ real

kink [kɪŋk] N (bend) doblez *m*; (pain) tortícolis *f*

kinky [kɪŋki] ADJ crespo; (sex) pervertido, *Sp* morboso

kinship [kínʃɪp] N (family connection) parentesco *m*; (likeness) afinidad *f*

kiosk [kíɑsk] N quiosco *m*

Kiribati [kirəbáɾi] N Kiribati *m*

kiss [kɪs] VI/VT besar[se]; N beso *m*

kit [kɪt] N (of tools) caja *f*; (of first aid) botiquín *m*; (of sewing notions) costurero *m*

kitchen [kítʃɪn] N cocina *f*; **—ware** utensilios de cocina *m pl*

kite [kaɪt] N (toy) cometa *f*; (bird) milano *m*

kitten [kítn̩] N gatito *m*

kitty [kídi] N (young cat) gatito *m*, minino *m*; (petty cash) caja chica *f*, fondo *m*

kleptomania [klɛptəméniə] N cleptomanía *f*

kleptomaniac [klɛptəméniæk] N cleptómano -na *mf*

knack [næk] N buena mano *f*, maña *f*; **once you get the — una vez que le agarras la vuelta/onda

knapsack [næpsæk] N mochila *f*

knave [nev] N pícaro *m*; (in cards) sota *f*

knead [nid] VT amasar, sobar

knee [ni] N rodilla *f*; **—cap** rótula *f*; **—-deep** hasta las rodillas; **—-jerk liberal** liberal fanático *m*; **—-jerk reaction** reacción visceral *f*; VT dar un rodillazo

kneel [nił] VI arrodillarse

knell [nɛł] N doble *m*; VI doblar

knelt [nɛłt] *see* kneel

knew [nu] *see* know

knickknack [níknæk] N chuchería *f*, baratija *f*

knife [naɪf] N cuchillo *m*; (big) cuchilla *f*; (folding) navaja *f*; (for carving) trinchante *m*; VT acuchillar; **at —point** a punta de cuchillo

knight [naɪt] N caballero *m*; (in chess) caballo *m*; **— errant** caballero andante *m*; VT armar caballero

knighthood [náɪthʊd] N (all knights) caballería *f*; (title) orden de la caballería *f*

knit [nɪt] VI/VT tejer; **to — one's brow** fruncir el entrecejo / el ceño

knitting [nídɪŋ] N tejido *m*; **— needle** aguja de punto *f*

knob [nɑb] N (on a door) pomo *m*, perilla *f*, tirador *m*; (protuberance) protuberancia *f*

knock [nɑk] VI (hit) golpear; (precombust) golpetear; (call at the door) llamar, tocar; VT (criticize) criticar; **to — a hole in the wall** hacer un agujero en la pared a golpes; **to — down** derribar, echar abajo, tumbar; **to — off** (stop working) terminar; (reduce) rebajar;

(make fall) tirar; (kill) liquidar; — **it off!**
¡basta! **to — into** golpearse contra; **to — out**
noquear; **to — over** voltear, revolcar; **to —
up** *vulg* preñar; N (pounding) golpe *m*, toque
m; (criticism) crítica *f*; (in a motor) golpeteo
m; —**out** (boxing) nocaut *m*; (attractive
person) bomba *f*; ADJ —-**kneed** patizambo,
zambo
knocker [nákə-] N (handle on door) llamador *m*,
aldaba *f*; (breast) *vulg* teta *f*
knoll [noł] N morro *m*, loma *f*
knot [nɑt] N nudo *m* (also in wood, unit of
speed); (of people) grupo *m*; (swelling)
chichón *m*; VI/VT anudar[se]
knotty [náɒi] ADJ (full of knots) nudoso;
(difficult) dificultoso, enredado
know [no] VI/VT (to have knowledge of, to know
how to) saber; VT (to be acquainted with, have
sexual intercourse with) conocer; (to
recognize) reconocer; (distinguish)
distinguir; **to — how to swim** saber nadar;
to — of estar enterado de; N **to be in the —**
estar al tanto; —-**how** pericia *f*; —-**it-all**
sabelotodo *mf*
knowing [nóɪŋ] ADJ (complicitous) cómplice;
(astute) astuto
knowingly [nóɪŋli] ADV a sabiendas
knowledge [nálɪʤ] N (awareness) conocimiento
m; (information known) saber *m*,
conocimientos *m pl*; **not to my —** no que yo
sepa
known [non] ADJ **little —** poco conocido; **well
—** bien conocido; **he's — for his cooking** se
le conoce por su cocina; **the truth wasn't —
until last year** no se supo la verdad hasta el
año pasado
known [non] *see* know
knuckle [nákəł] N nudillo *m*; —**ball** bola de
nudillos *f*; —**head** tarambana *mf*; VI **to —
down** arremangarse, aplicarse con empeño;
to — under someterse
Korea [kɔríə] Corea *f*
Korean [kɔríən] ADJ & N coreano -na *mf*
kosher [kóʃə-] ADJ kosher
Kuwait [kuwét] N Kuwait *m*
Kuwaiti [kuwéɒi] ADJ & N kuwaití *mf*
Kyrgyzstan [kírgistɑn] N Kirguistán *m*

Ll

lab [læb] *see* laboratory
label [lébəł] N (sticker) etiqueta *f*, rótulo *m*;
(characterization) calificativo *m*; (brand)
marca *f*; (of recording companies) sello *m*; VT
etiquetar, rotular
labial [lébiəł] ADJ labial

labium [lébiəm] N labio *m*
labor [lébə-] N trabajo *m*, labor *f*; (body of
workers) mano de obra *f*; (working class) clase
obrera *f*; (uterine contractions) trabajo de
parto *m*; —-**intensive** que requiere mucha
mano de obra; — **pains** dolores de parto *m pl*;
— **union** sindicato *m*; **to be in —** estar de
parto; ADJ laboral; VI (work) trabajar;
(dedicate oneself) afanarse; **to — under a
disadvantage** sufrir una desventaja
laboratory [lǽbrətɔri] N laboratorio *m*
laborer [lébərə-] N jornalero -ra *mf*; (unskilled)
peón -ona *mf*
laborious [ləbóriəs] ADJ (industrious) laborioso;
(difficult) trabajoso
labrador [lǽbrədɔr] N (dog) labrador *m*
labyrinth [lǽbərɪnθ] N laberinto *m*
lace [les] N (cloth) encaje *m*; (cord) cordón *m*; VT
(to adorn with lace) bordar con encaje; (to
insert laces into) poner cordones a; (to spike)
echar alcohol; VI atarse
lack [læk] N falta *f*, carencia *f*; VI/VT carecer de,
faltarle a uno; **he —s courage** le falta
valentía; —**luster** mediocre
lackey [lǽki] N lacayo *m*
lacking [lǽkɪŋ] ADJ (deficient) deficiente; **good
bars are — in this town** faltan buenos
bares en este pueblo; — **in** falto de, carente de
laconic [ləkɑ́nɪk] ADJ lacónico
lacquer [lǽkə-] N laca *f*; VT lacar, laquear
lactation [læktéʃən] N lactancia *f*
lactic acid [lǽktɪkǽsɪd] N ácido láctico *m*
lactose [lǽktos] N lactosa *f*; — **intolerance**
intolerancia a la lactosa *f*
ladder [lǽdə-] N escalera *f*
laden [lédn̩] ADJ cargado
ladle [lédl̩] N cucharón *m*, cazo *m*; VT servir con
cucharón
lady [léɒi] N señora *f*, dama *f*; —**bug** mariquita *f*;
—**like** muy fina; —**love** amada *f*; **ladies'
room** *Sp* aseo de damas *m*, *Am* servicio de
damas *m*
lag [læg] VI (fall behind) quedarse atrás,
rezagarse; (flag) disminuir; N retardo *m*,
retraso *m*
lagoon [ləgún] N laguna *f*
laid [led] *see* lay
laid-back [ledbǽk] ADJ apacible, tranquilo
lain [len] *see* lie 'estar situado'
lair [lɛr] N guarida *f*
lake [lek] N lago *m*
lamb [læm] N cordero *m*; (yearling) borrego *m*
lame [lem] ADJ cojo; *Am* rengo; —**brained**
idiota; — **duck** funcionario -ria cesante *mf*;
— **excuse** pretexto tonto *m*; VT dejar cojo
lament [ləmént] N lamento *m*; VI lamentar[se];
VT llorar
lamentable [ləméntəbəł] ADJ lamentable
lamentation [læməntéʃən] N lamentación *f*,

lamento *m*
laminate [lǽmənet] VT laminar
lamp [læmp] N lámpara *f*; (on a street) farol *m*;
—**post** farol *m*; —**shade** pantalla *f*
LAN [**local area network**] [læn] N red [de área]
local *f*
lance [læns] N lanza *f*; (lancet) lanceta *f*; VT
lancear; (a wound) abrir con una lanceta
lancet [lǽnsɪt] N lanceta *f*
land [lænd] N tierra *f*; (lot) terreno *m*; (country)
país *m*, tierra *f*; —**fill** vertedero *m*; — **grant**
university universidad con terrenos
concedidos por el estado *f*; —**lady** casera *f*,
propietaria *f*; —**lord** casero *m*, propietario *m*;
—**mark** (marker) hito *m*, mojón *m*;
(historical) hito *m*; — **mine** mina *f*; —**owner**
hacendado -da *mf*; —**scape** (terrain) paisaje
m; (in printing) orientación horizontal *f*;
—**scape architecture** paisajismo *m*;
—**slide** (mass of land) derrumbe *m*,
desprendimiento *m*; (election) victoria
aplastante *f*; — **use** ordenamiento territorial
m; VI/VT (a ship) atracar; (an airplane)
aterrizar; **you'll** — **in jail** terminarás en la
cárcel; VT (a fish) *Sp* coger; *Am* pescar; (a job)
conseguir
landing [lǽndɪŋ] N (of a ship) desembarco *m*; (of
cargo) desembarque *m*; (of an airplane)
aterrizaje *m*; (place) desembarcadero *m*; (on
stairs) descansillo *m*; — **field** campo de
aterrizaje *m*; — **gear** tren de aterrizaje *m*; —
strip pista de aterrizaje *f*
lane [len] N (country road) sendero *m*; (road
division) carril *m*; (for ships) ruta *f*
language [lǽŋgwɪʤ] N lengua *f*, idioma *m*;
(faculty of speech, computer code) lenguaje *m*
languid [lǽŋgwɪd] ADJ lánguido
languish [lǽŋgwɪʃ] VI languidecer
languor [lǽŋgɚ] N languidez *f*
lanky [lǽŋki] ADJ larguirucho, zancudo
lanolin [lǽnəlɪn] N lanolina *f*
lantern [lǽntɚn] N farol *m*; (of a lighthouse)
faro *m*, linterna *f*
Laos [léɑs] N Laos *m*
Laotian [leóʃən] ADJ & N laosiano -na *mf*
lap [læp] N (part of body) regazo *m*; (part of a
race) vuelta *f*; —**dog** perro faldero *m*; —**top**
computer *Am* computadora portátil *f*, *Sp*
ordenador portátil *m*; **to live in the** — **of**
luxury vivir en la abundancia; VI/VT lamer
lapel [ləpél] N solapa *f*
lapidary [lǽpɪdɛri] ADJ & N lapidario -ria *mf*
lapse [læps] N (period of time) lapso *m*;
(linguistic error) lapsus *m*; (defect in
memory) fallo *m*; (fall) caída *f*; (termination)
caducidad *f*; VI (fall) caer; (decline) decaer;
(end) caducar, vencer
larceny [lárʂəni] N latrocinio *m*, hurto *m*
lard [lɑrd] N manteca *f*; VT enmantecar; (with

bacon) mechar
large [lɑrʤ] ADJ grande; —**-scale** a gran escala;
a — **company** una gran compañía / una
compañía grande; **at** — (not in jail) suelto,
libre; N tamaño grande *m*
largely [lárʤli] ADV (in the greatest number) en
su mayoría; (to the greatest degree) en gran
parte
lariat [lǽriət] N reata *f*
lark [lɑrk] N (bird) alondra *f*; (bit of fun)
diversión *f*; **to go on a** — ir de jarana
larva [lárvə] N larva *f*
laryngeal [lərínʤəl] ADJ laríngeo; — **angina**
angina laríngea *f*
laryngitis [lǽrənʤáɪdɪs] N laringitis *f*
larynx [lǽrɪŋks] N laringe *f*
lascivious [ləsíviəs] ADJ lascivo
laser [lézɚ] N láser *m*; — **beam** rayo láser *m*; —
printer impresora láser *f*
lash [læʃ] N (blow with a whip, tail, etc.) azote *m*,
latigazo *m*; (blow of waves) embate *m*; (part of
eye) pestaña *f*; VT (whip) azotar; (tie) amarrar;
to — **out at** fustigar
lasso [lǽso] N lazo *m*, reata *f*; VT lazar; *Am*
enlazar
last [læst] ADJ (in a series) último; (definitive)
final; —**-ditch** desesperado; — **minute** de
último momento; — **name** apellido *m*; —
night anoche; — **rites** extrema unción *f*,
viático *m*; — **straw** colmo *m*; — **word** última
palabra *f*; — **year** el año pasado; **next to the**
— penúltimo; ADV último; **to arrive** — ser el
último en llegar; **when** — **seen** cuando se lo
vio por última vez; **at** — finalmente; N el
último; (of a shoe) horma *f*; VI durar; (live on)
perdurar
lasting [lǽstɪŋ] ADJ duradero, perdurable
lastly [lǽstli] ADV por último
latch [lætʃ] N pestillo *m*, picaporte *m*, cierre *m*; VI
cerrar con el pestillo; **to** — **on** agarrarse de;
to — **onto** pegarse a
late [let] ADJ (tardy) tardío; (hour) avanzada;
(recent) reciente, último; (recently deceased)
finado; — **afternoon** atardecer *m*; —**comer**
rezagado -da *mf*; — **fee** recargo por mora *m*;
ADV tarde; — **in the night** a una hora
avanzada de la noche; — **into the night**
hasta cualquier hora de la noche; — **in the**
week a finales de la semana; **it is** — ya es
tarde; **of** — últimamente; **to be** — llegar
tarde; **to work** — trabajar hasta tarde; **the**
train was ten minutes — el tren llegó con
diez minutos de retraso
lately [létli] ADV últimamente
lateness [létnɪs] N tardanza *f*
latent [létṇt] ADJ latente
later [léDɚ] ADJ posterior; ADV más tarde, con
posterioridad; **see you** — hasta luego; — **on**
más tarde

lateral [lǽɒə-əł] ADJ lateral

latest [léDɪst] ADJ último; **the — fashion** la última moda; **the — news** las últimas novedades; N **at the —** a más tardar

latex [léteks] N látex *m*

lathe [leð] N torno *m*

lather [lǽðə-] N (foam) espuma *f*; (sweat) sudor *m*; **he got into a —** se puso histérico; VT enjabonar; VI hacer espuma

Latin [lǽtn̩] ADJ latino; **— America** América Latina *f*, Latinoamérica *f*; **— American** latinoamericano -na *mf*; N (language) latín *m*

latitude [lǽDɪtud] N latitud *f*; (freedom) flexibilidad *f*

latrine [lətrín] N letrina *f*

latter [lǽɒə-] ADJ último; **in the — days of the Roman Republic** en los últimos días de la República Romana; **toward the — part of the week** a finales de la semana; **the —** este *m*, esta *f*

lattice [lǽDɪs] N enrejado *m*, entramado *m*; (of a window) celosía *f*

Latvia [lǽtviə] N Letonia *f*

Latvian [lǽtviən] ADJ & N letón -ona *mf*

laud [lɔd] VT loar

laudable [lɔ́Dəbəl] ADJ laudable, loable

laugh [læf] VI reír[se]; **to — at** reírse de; **to — loudly** reírse a carcajadas; **to — up/in one's sleeve** reírse para sus adentros; **she —ed in his face** se rió en su cara; N risa *f*; **we did it for —s** lo hicimos por diversión

laughable [lǽfəbəł] ADJ risible

laughingstock [lǽfɪŋstɑk] N hazmerreír *m*

laughter [lǽftə-] N risa *f*

launch [lɔntʃ] VT (a boat) botar; (a rocket, new product) lanzar; (software) iniciar; **to — forth/out** lanzarse; N lancha *f*; (act of launching a boat) botadura *f*; (act of launching a rocket) lanzamiento *m*

launder [lɔ́ndə-] VI/VT (clothes) lavar; (money) blanquear, lavar; (wash and iron clothes) lavar y planchar

Laundromat™ [lɔ́ndrəmæt] N lavadero automático *m*

laundry [lɔ́ndri] N (business establishment) lavandería *f*, lavadero *m*; (room in house) cuarto de lavado *m*, lavadero *m*; (clothes to be washed) ropa sucia *f*; (washed clothes) ropa limpia *f*

laurel [lɔ́rəl] N laurel *m* (also honor); **to rest on one's —s** dormirse sobre los laureles

lava [lávə] N lava *f*

lavatory [lǽvətɔri] N (basin) lavabo *m*; (bathroom) baño *m*, retrete *m*

lavender [lǽvəndə-] N espliego *m*, lavanda *f*; ADJ lavanda

lavish [lǽvɪʃ] ADJ (generous) pródigo, espléndido; (abundant) abundante, copioso; VT prodigar; **to — praise upon** colmar de alabanzas a

law [lɔ] N ley *f*; (discipline) derecho *m*, jurisprudencia *f*; (police) policía *f*; **— and order** orden público *m*; **—breaker** infractor -ora *mf*, transgresor -ora *mf*; **—maker** legislador -ora *mf*; **— of diminishing returns** ley de [los] rendimientos decrecientes *f*; **— student** estudiante de derecho *mf*; **—suit** pleito *m*, litigio *m*; **to practice —** ejercer la abogacía; **to take the — into one's hands** hacer justicia por mano propia; ADJ **—-abiding** respetuoso de las leyes

lawful [lɔ́fəł] ADJ (in accordance with the law) legal; (allowed by law) lícito; (recognized by law) legítimo

lawless [lɔ́lɪs] ADJ (anarchic) anárquico; (illegal) ilegal

lawn [lɔn] N césped *m*, grama *f*; **— mower** cortadora de césped *f*

lawyer [lɔ́jə-] N abogado -da *mf*

lax [læks] ADJ laxo

laxative [lǽksəDɪv] ADJ & N laxante *m*, purgante *m*

laxity [lǽksɪDi] N flojedad *f*, laxitud *f*

lay [le] VT colocar; (eggs) poner; (a cable) tender; (to have sexual intercourse with) *fam* tirarse a; **to — aside** (abandon) dejar de lado; (save) guardar; **to — a wager** apostar; **to — bare** poner al descubierto; **to — bricks** poner ladrillos; **to — down arms** rendir las armas; **to — down the law** imponerse; **to — hold of** asir, agarrar; **to — into** atacar; **to — off a workman** despedir temporalmente a un obrero; **to — one's head on a pillow** recostar la cabeza sobre una almohada; **to — open** exponer; **to — out a plan** trazar un plan; **to — up** almacenar; **to be laid up** estar en cama; **to — waste to** asolar; N situación *f*, orientación *f*; **she's an easy —** *fam* es una mujer fácil; **—man** (nonexpert) lego *m*; (clergy) laico *m*; **—off** despido temporal de un empleado *m*; **—out** diseño/trazado de página *m*; ADJ lego, laico

lay [le] *see* lie 'estar situado'

layer [léə-] N capa *f*; (geological) estrato *m*; (hen) gallina ponedora *f*; **— cake** tarta de capas *f*

laziness [lézinɪs] N pereza *f*, holgazanería *f*, flojera *f*

lazy [lézi] ADJ perezoso, holgazán, flojo

LBO [leveraged buyout] [ɛ́lbíó] N compra apalancada *f*

LDL [low density lipoprotein] [ɛ́ldíɛ́l] N LBD *f*

lead[1] [lɛd] N (metal) plomo *m*; (graphite) mina *f*; **— poisoning** intoxicación con plomo *f*

lead[2] [lid] VT (guide) guiar; (guide a horse) llevar de la rienda; (induce, take) llevar, inducir; (be in charge, be first) encabezar, liderar; (direct) dirigir; (be superior to) estar a la cabeza de; **to**

— **a life of ease** llevar una vida fácil; **to** —
the way mostrar el camino; VI (provide
passage to, result in) llevar a; (be first) estar a
la cabeza; **to** — **astray** llevar por mal
camino; N (first position) delantera f, primer
lugar m; (clue) indicio m; (most important
role) papel principal m, liderazgo m; —**off**
comienzo; — **story** noticia principal f; **to**
take the — (in sports) ponerse por delante
en el marcador

leaden [lédṇ] ADJ (of lead) de plomo; (color)
plomizo; (oppressive, slow) pesado

leader [líɖɚ] N (in politics) líder mf, caudillo m;
(in a race) líder mf; (in music) director -ora
mf; (as a guide) guía mf

leadership [líɖɚʃɪp] N dirección f, liderazgo m

leading [líɖɪŋ] ADJ (most important) principal;
(arriving first) delantero; — **indicators**
indicadores anticipados m pl; — **man** actor
principal m

leaf [lif] N hoja f; VI echar hojas; **to** — **through a**
book hojear un libro

leafless [líflɪs] ADJ sin hojas, deshojado

leaflet [líflɪt] N (small leaf) folíolo m; (printed
matter) volante m; (folded printed matter)
pliego m

leafy [lífi] ADJ (with foliage) frondoso; (in the
form of leaves) de hoja

league [lig] N (alliance) liga f; (unit of distance)
legua f; VI/VT aliar[se]

leak [lik] N (in a roof) gotera f; (in a boat, bucket,
etc.) agujero m; (of information) filtración f;
(of gas, steam, electricity) escape m, fuga f; VI
(roof) gotear[se]; (boat) hacer agua; (gas)
salirse, escaparse; (information) filtrarse; VT
revelar información interna confidencial

leaky [líki] ADJ (roof) que tiene goteras; (boat)
que hace agua; (gas, electricity) que pierde

lean [lin] VI/VT (incline) inclinar[se]; (support)
apoyar[se], reclinar[se], recostar[se]; **to** — **on**
presionar; ADJ magro; — **year** mal año m

leap [lip] VI/VT saltar; **to** — **at a chance**
aprovechar una oportunidad; **to** — **to mind**
ocurrírsele a uno; N salto m; —**frog** pídola f;
— **year** año bisiesto m

leapt [lɛpt] see leap

learn [lɜn] VI/VT aprender; (find out) enterarse
de

learned [lɜ́nɪd] ADJ erudito, letrado

learner [lɜ́nɚ] N estudiante mf; (driver)
aprendiz -iza mf

learning [lɜ́nɪŋ] N (result) erudición f, saber m;
(process) aprendizaje m; — **disability**
problema de aprendizaje m

learnt [lɜnt] see learn

lease [lis] N (action) arrendamiento m; (contract)
contrato de arrendamiento m; (period)
período de arrendamiento m; **for** — se
arrienda; **to have a new** — **on life** nacer de

nuevo; VI/VT arrendar

leash [liʃ] N traílla f, correa f

least [list] ADJ **he doesn't have the** — **chance**
no tiene la más mínima posibilidad; **the** —
amount of money la menor cantidad de
dinero; — **common denominator** mínimo
común denominador m; ADV menos; **the** —
important el/la menos importante; **at** — al
menos, por lo menos; N **I received the** — **of**
anyone yo fui el que recibió menos de todos

leather [léðɚ] N cuero m; ADJ de cuero; — **strap**
correa f

leave [liv] VT (a person, thing) dejar; (a place)
salir de, irse de; VI salir, partir; **to** — **off**
(stop) parar de; (omit) omitir; **to** — **out**
omitir; **I have two books left** me quedan
dos libros; N permiso m; **to be on** — estar de
licencia; — **of absence** licencia f; **to take** —
of despedirse de

leaven [lévən] N levadura f; VT leudar

leavings [lívɪŋz] N (leftovers) sobras f pl; (refuse)
desperdicios m pl

Lebanese [lɛbəníz] ADJ & N libanés -esa mf

Lebanon [lébənən] N Líbano m

lecherous [létʃəəs] ADJ lujurioso

lecture [léktʃɚ] N (presentation) conferencia f,
disertación f; (sermon) sermón m;
(long-winded speech) perorata f; VI (present)
dar una conferencia, disertar; VT (scold)
sermonear

lecturer [léktʃərɚ] N conferenciante mf;
(academic rank) profesor -ora mf

led [lɛd] see lead

LED [**light-emitting diode**] [ɛ́lídí] N LED m

ledge [lɛʤ] N cornisa f

ledger [léʤɚ] N libro mayor m

leech [litʃ] N sanguijuela f

leer [lir] VT (sideways) mirar de soslayo;
(lecherously) mirar con lujuria; N (sideways)
mirada de soslayo f; (lecherous) mirada
lujuriosa f

leeway [líwe] N margen de maniobra m; (of a
ship) deriva f

left [lɛft] ADJ izquierdo; —-**click** presionar el
botón izquierdo del ratón; —-**handed** zurdo;
—-**handed compliment** alabanza irónica f;
—-**handed tool** herramienta para zurdos f;
— **justification** alineación a la izquierda f;
—-**wing** de izquierdas; N izquierda f; **at /**
on/to/toward the — a/hacia la izquierda;
to make a — doblar/girar a la izquierda

left [lɛft] see leave

leftist [léftɪst] N & ADJ izquierdista mf

leg [lɛg] N (human) pierna f; (animal, furniture)
pata f; (wading bird) zanca f; (of a journey)
etapa f; **to be on one's last** —**s** estar en las
últimas; **to pull someone's** — tomarle el
pelo a alguien; **to stretch one's** —**s** estirar
las piernas

legacy [légəsi] N legado *m*
legal [lígəł] ADJ (in accordance with the law) legal; (permitted by law) lícito; (recognized by law) legítimo; (having to do with the law) jurídico; — **age** mayoría de edad *f*; — **code** ordenamiento *m*; — **fees** honorarios del abogado *m pl*; — **holiday** día feriado *m*; — **procedure** procedimiento jurídico *m*; — **tender** moneda de curso legal *f*
legality [lɪgǽlɪɾi] N legalidad *f*
legalization [ligəlɪzéʃən] N legalización *f*
legalize [lígəlaɪz] VT legalizar
legation [lɪgéʃən] N legación *f*
legend [léʤənd] N leyenda *f* (also inscription); (of a map) clave *f*
legendary [léʤəndɛri] ADJ legendario
leggings [légɪŋz] N (ankle to knee) polainas *f pl*; (trousers) leggings *m pl*
legible [léʤəbəł] ADJ legible
legion [líʤən] N legión *f*
legionnaire [liʤənér] N legionario *m*; —'s **disease** enfermedad del legionario *f*, legionelosis *f*
legislate [léʤɪslet] VI/VT legislar
legislation [leʤɪsléʃən] N legislación *f*
legislative [léʤɪsleɪɪv] ADJ legislativo
legislator [léʤɪsleɪɚ] N legislador -ora *mf*
legislature [léʤɪsletʃɚ] N legislatura *f*
legitimacy [ləʤíɾəməsi] N legitimidad *f*
legitimate [lɪʤíɾəmɪt] ADJ legítimo
legitimize [ləʤíɾəmaɪz] VT legitimar
legume [légjum] N legumbre *f*
leisure [líʒɚ] N ocio *m*, holgura *f*; — **activities** actividades recreativas *f pl*; — **hours** horas de ocio *f pl*, tiempo libre *m*; **to be at** — estar desocupado; **do it at your** — hazlo cuando te convenga
leisurely [líʒɚli] ADJ lento, deliberado; ADV sin prisa
lemon [lémən] N limón *m*; ADJ de limón; — **tree** limonero *m*
lemonade [lɛmənéd] N limonada *f*
lend [lɛnd] VI/VT prestar; **to** — **a hand** dar una mano
lender [léndɚ] N (person who lends) prestador -ora *mf*; (professional) prestamista *mf*
length [lɛŋkθ] N (of an object, road) largo *m*, largura *f*, longitud *f*; (of a movie) duración *f*; (of a book) extensión *f*; **at** — (in detail) pormenorizadamente; (finally) finalmente; **by two** —**s** por dos cuerpos; **two meters in** — dos metros de largo; **to go to any** —**s** hacer lo imposible
lengthen [léŋkθən] VI/VT alargar[se]
lengthwise [léŋkθwaɪz] ADV & ADJ a lo largo
lengthy [léŋkθi] ADJ largo, prolongado
lenient [líniənt] ADJ indulgente
lens [lɛnz] N lente *m*; (of the eye) cristalino *m*
Lent [lɛnt] N Cuaresma *f*

lent [lɛnt] *see* lend
lentil [léntḷ] N lenteja *f*
Leon [león] N León *m*
Leonese [liəníz] ADJ leonés
leopard [lépɚd] N leopardo *m*
leprosy [léprəsi] N lepra *f*
lesbian [lézbiən] ADJ lesbiano; N lesbiana *f*
lesion [líʒən] N lesión *f*
Lesotho [ləsóto] N Lesoto *m*
less [lɛs] ADJ, ADV & PREP menos; **I have** — **than you do** tengo menos que tú; — **and** — cada vez menos
lessen [lésən] VI/VT disminuir, aminorar
lessening [lésənɪŋ] N disminución *f*
lesser [lésɚ] ADJ menor
lesson [lésən] N lección *f*
lest [lɛst] CONJ no sea que; — **you should think I'm teasing** para que no vayas a creer que estoy bromeando
let [lɛt] VT (permit) dejar, permitir; (rent) alquilar; — **him come** que venga; —'s **do it** hagámoslo; **to** — **be** dejar en paz; **to** — **down** (lower) bajar; (disappoint) decepcionar; **to** — **go** soltar; **to** — **in** dejar entrar; **to** — **know** hacer saber; **to** — **off** (not punish) dejar ir; (allow to get off) dejar bajar; **to** — **through** dejar pasar; **to** — **up** (permit to stand) dejar incorporarse; (cease) disminuir; N (in tennis) repetición *f*; —**down** desilusión *f*; —**up** tregua *f*
lethal [líθəł] ADJ letal
lethargic [ləθárʤɪk] ADJ aletargado, letárgico
lethargy [léθɚʤi] N letargo *m*; **to fall into a** — aletargarse
letter [léɾɚ] N (of alphabet) letra *f*; (missive) carta *f*; — **carrier** cartero -ra *mf*; —**head** membrete *m*; —**head paper** papel membretado *m*; —-**spacing** espacio entre caracteres *m*; —**s** letras *f pl*; **the** — **of the law** la letra de la ley *f*; **to the** — al pie de la letra; VT grabar
lettuce [léɾɪs] N lechuga *f*
leukemia [lukímiə] N leucemia *f*
levee [lévi] N dique *m*
level [lévəł] ADJ llano, plano; —-**headed** sensato; — **playing field** terreno de juego parejo *m*; — **with** a nivel de; **a** — **tablespoon** una cucharada al ras; N nivel *m* (also tool); **on the** — en serio; VT (make level) nivelar, igualar; (to demolish) arrasar, allanar; (to knock down a person) tumbar; (to aim criticism) dirigir; (to aim a gun) apuntar; **to** — **off** quedar paralelo al suelo; **to** — **with** hablar en serio con/a
lever [lévɚ] N palanca *f*
leverage [lévɚɪʤ] N (influence) palanca *f*; (physical, financial) apalancamiento *m*
levity [lévɪɾi] N ligereza *f*
levy [lévi] N (of taxes) recaudación *f*; (of troops)

leva f; VT (taxes) recaudar; (troops) reclutar,
hacer una leva de
lewd [lud] ADJ lascivo
lewdness [lúdnɪs] N lascivia f
lexical [lɛ́ksɪkəł] ADJ léxico
lexicography [lɛksɪkágrəfi] N lexicografía f
lexicon [lɛ́ksɪkan] N léxico m
liability [laɪəbílɪɒi] N (disadvantage) desventaja
f; (debit) pasivo m; (debts) deudas f pl;
(responsibility) responsabilidad legal f; —
insurance seguro contra daños a terceros m;
liabilities obligaciones f pl
liable [láɪəbəł] ADJ responsable; — **to** propenso
a; **she's — to get angry** es probable que se
enoje
liaison [liézan] N (connection) enlace m; (illicit
love affair) aventura f
liar [láɪ�] N mentiroso -sa mf, embustero -ra mf
libel [láɪbəł] N libelo m, difamación f; VT difamar
liberal [líbəðəł] ADJ & N liberal mf
liberalism [líbəðəlɪzəm] N liberalismo m
liberality [lɪbərǽlɪɒi] N (generosity) liberalidad
f; (tolerance) tolerancia f
liberalization [lɪbəðəlɪzéʃən] N liberalización f
liberalize [líbəðəlaɪz] VI/VT liberalizar[se]
liberate [líbəret] VT (give freedom to) libertar,
liberar; (release from obligation) librar; (give
off) desprender
liberation [lɪbəréʃən] N liberación f
liberator [líbəreDəð] N libertador -ora mf
Liberia [laɪbíriə] N Liberia f
Liberian [laɪbíriən] ADJ & N liberiano -na mf
libertine [líbəðtin] ADJ & N libertino -na mf,
calavera m
liberty [líbəðDɪ] N libertad f; **at —** autorizado
libidinous [lɪbídnəs] ADJ libidinoso
libido [lɪbíDo] N libido f
librarian [laɪbrériən] N bibliotecario -ria mf
library [láɪbrɛri] N biblioteca f
libretto [lɪbrɛ́Do] N libreto m
Libya [líbjə] N Libia f
Libyan [líbjən] ADJ & N libio -bia mf
license [láɪsəns] N (permission) permiso m;
(driver's permit, poetic freedom) licencia f; —
plate placa f, matrícula f; VT (issue license to)
otorgar una licencia; (give permission)
autorizar
licensing authority [láɪsənsɪŋ əθɔ́rɪɒi] N
autoridad para otorgar licencias f
licentious [laɪsɛ́nʃəs] ADJ licencioso
lick [lɪk] VT (touch with tongue) lamer (also
waves); (thrash) dar una paliza; (defeat)
derrotar; N lamida f, lengüetazo m; (blow)
golpe m; **not to do a — of work** no mover
un dedo
lickety-split [lɪkɪDisplít] ADV en un santiamén
licking [líkɪŋ] N paliza f
licorice [líkəðɪʃ] N regaliz m
lid [lɪd] N (of a container) tapadera f, tapa f; (of

eye) párpado m; (on prices) tope m
lie [laɪ] N (falsehood) mentira f, embuste m;
(orientation of an object) orientación f; —
detector detector de mentiras m; **to give
the — to** desmentir; VI mentir; **to — one's
way out of a situation** salirse de una
situación a mentiras; (be buried) yacer; (to be
on a flat surface) estar; (to be situated) estar
situado; (be horizontal) tumbarse, acostarse;
he's lying in bed está acostado en la cama;
to — back recostarse; **to — down** acostarse,
tumbarse; **to — in wait** acechar
Liechtenstein [líktənstaɪn] N Liechtenstein m
Liechtensteiner [líktənstaɪnə-] N
liechtensteiniano -na mf
lien [lin] N gravamen m, carga f
lieu [lu] ADV LOC **in — of** en vez de
lieutenant [luténənt] N teniente mf; — **colonel**
teniente coronel mf; — **governor**
vicegobernador -ora mf
life [laɪf] N vida f; — **-and-death** de vida o
muerte; **—boat** bote de salvamento m; —
cycle ciclo vital m; — **expectancy**
expectancy de vida f; **—guard** salvavidas mf
sg; — **imprisonment** prisión perpetua f; —
insurance seguro de vida m; — **jacket**
salvavidas m sg; — **of the party** alma de la
fiesta f; — **preserver** salvavidas m sg; — **raft**
balsa salvavidas f; — **savings** ahorros de toda
la vida m pl; **—span** duración de la vida f;
—style estilo de vida m; **—support
system** (in space) equipo de vida m; (in a
hospital) máquina corazón-pulmón f; **—time**
vida f; ADJ (relative to life) vital; (for duration
of life) vitalicio; ADJ **—like** natural, que
parece vivo; **—long** de toda la vida; **—-sized**
de tamaño natural
lifeless [láɪflɪs] ADJ (without living things) sin
vida; (dead) muerto, sin vida; (fainted)
desfallecido; (without liveliness) sin
animación
lifer [láɪfə-] N (prisoner) condenado -da a cadena
perpetua mf; (soldier) militar de carrera m
lift [lɪft] VT (hoist) levantar; (steal) robar;
(plagiarize) copiar; VI (disperse) disiparse; (go
up) elevarse; N (upward force) empuje m;
(feeling) mejoría de ánimo f; (device for
lifting) montacargas m sg; **to give someone
a —** llevar en coche; Mex dar un aventón;
—off despegue m
ligament [lígəmənt] N ligamento m
ligature [lígətʃə-] N ligadura f
light [laɪt] N (luminescence) luz f; (device) luz f,
lámpara f; (for traffic) semáforo m;
(perspective) perspectiva f; (for cigarettes)
fuego m; **—-emitting diode** diodo
electroiluminiscente m; **—house** faro m; **—-
year** año luz m; ADJ (well-lighted) claro; (of
little weight) ligero, leve; (of clothes) fresco;

Am liviano; — **blue** azul claro *m*; —-**headed** mareado; —**hearted** alegre; — **rain** lluvia fina *f*; —-**skinned** de tez blanca; — **touch** mano delicada *f*; —**weight** de peso ligero; **to make** — **of** restar importancia a; VI/VT (turn on, ignite) encender[se], prender[se]; (provide light, brighten) iluminar[se]; (land on) posarse en; **to** — **up** (cigarette) prender, encender; (face) iluminarse; **to** — **upon** caer sobre

lighten [láɪtn̩] VI/VT (make / become lighter) aligerar[se], alivianar[se]; (brighten) iluminar[se]; — **up!** ¡no tomes las cosas a la tremenda!

lighter [láɪdɚ] N encendedor *m*

lighting [láɪDɪŋ] N iluminación *f*; (in the street) alumbrado *m*

lightly [láɪtli] ADV (toast) ligeramente; (touch) levemente, suavemente; **I don't take your criticism** — no tomo tus críticas a la ligera

lightness [láɪtnɪs] N (little weight) ligereza *f*, levedad *f*; (brightness) claridad *f*

lightning [láɪtnɪŋ] N relámpago *m*; — **bug** luciérnaga *f*; — **rod** pararrayos *m sg*; **it happened at** — **speed** pasó como rayo; VI relampaguear

likable [láɪkəbəɫ] ADJ agradable, simpático

like [laɪk] ADV & PREP como; **to feel** — **going** tener ganas de ir; **to look** — **someone** parecerse a alguien; **it looks** — **rain** parece que va a llover; ADJ semejante, parecido; **in** — **manner** del mismo modo; —-**minded** del mismo parecer; N —**s** gustos *m pl*, preferencias *f pl*; VT gustarle a uno; **he** —**s dogs** le gustan los perros; **do whatever you** — haz lo que quieras; CONJ **he talked** — **he was crazy** hablaba como si estuviera loco; **she came** — **you predicted she would** vino, tal como tú pronosticaste; **I'm** —, **"you're crazy"** yo pensé/dije, "estás loco"; INTERJ **he was,** —, **way too old** era como que demasiado viejo

likelihood [láɪklihʊd] N probabilidad *f*; **in all** — **he came** lo más probable es que haya venido

likely [láɪkli] ADJ (probable) probable; (believable) creíble; (promising) prometedor; **John is** — **to win** es probable que gane Juan; ADV probablemente

liken [láɪkən] VT comparar

likeness [láɪknɪs] N (similarity) parecido *m*; (portrait) retrato *m*

likewise [láɪkwaɪz] ADV (the same thing) lo mismo; **we did** — hicimos lo mismo; (similarly) asimismo; (also) también

liking [láɪkɪŋ] N preferencia *f*, gusto *m*

lilac [láɪlək] N lila *f*; ADJ lila

lily [líli] N lirio *m*, azucena *f*; ADJ —-**white** (very white) blanquísimo; (pure) puro; (for whites only) exclusivamente para blancos

limb [lɪm] N (branch) rama *f*; (appendage) miembro *m*

limber [límbɚ] ADJ flexible; VT hacer flexible; VI **to** — **up** estirarse

lime [laɪm] N (mineral) cal *f*; (fruit, color) lima *f*; —**light** candilejas *f pl*; **in the** —**light** en el candelero; —**stone** piedra caliza *f*; — **tree** limero *m*

limit [límɪt] N límite *m*; **to the** — al máximo; VT limitar

limitation [lɪmɪtéʃən] N limitación *f*

limitless [límɪtlɪs] ADJ ilimitado

limousine [líməzin] N limusina *f*

limp [lɪmp] N cojera *f*, renguera *f*; VI cojear, renguear, renquear; ADJ (body) flácido; (plants) mustio

limpid [límpɪd] ADJ límpido

line [laɪn] N (bus route, telephone connection) línea *f*; (of words) renglón *m*, línea *f*; (row) raya *f*, hilera *f*; (cord) cuerda *f*; (persons waiting) cola *f*, fila *f*; (business) ramo *m*; (wrinkle) arruga *f*; (boundary) límite *m*; — **drive** (baseball) línea *f*; — **of credit** línea de crédito *f*; — **of scrimmage** línea de golpeo *f*; —**s** (in a play) parte *f*; —**sman** juez-eza de línea *mf*; —**up** hilera de personas *f*; (sports) alineación *f*; **drop me a** — escríbeme unas líneas; **out of** — irrespetuoso; **to get in** — hacer cola; VI/VT (border) alinear, bordear; (put in a lining) forrar; **to** — **up** alinear[se]; ADJ **off-** — fuera de línea; **on-** — en línea

lineage [líniɪdʒ] N linaje *m*, estirpe *f*

linear [líniɚ] ADJ lineal

lined [laɪnd] ADJ (with lines) rayado; (with a lining) forrado

linen [línɪn] N (fabric) lino *m*; (bedclothes) ropa blanca *f*

liner [láɪnɚ] N (ocean) transatlántico *m*; (air) avión comercial *m*; (eye) delineador *m*

linger [líŋgɚ] VI (stay) quedarse, demorarse; (persist) persistir; (saunter) rezagarse; (contemplate) detenerse; (delay death) aguantar

lingerie [lɑnʒəré] N lencería *f*

linguist [líŋgwɪst] N lingüista *mf*

linguistics [lɪŋgwístɪks] N lingüística *f*

liniment [línəmənt] N linimento *m*

lining [láɪnɪŋ] N forro *m*; **every cloud has a silver** — no hay mal que por bien no venga

link [lɪŋk] N (of a chain) eslabón *m*; (bond, tie) vínculo *m*; (rail, radio connection) enlace *m*; (computer) enlace *m*, vínculo *m*; VI/VT enlazar[se], conectar[se]; (on a computer) vincular

linnet [línɪt] N pardillo *m*

linoleum [lɪnóliəm] N linóleo *m*

linseed [línsid] N linaza *f*; — **oil** aceite de linaza *m*

lint [lɪnt] N pelusa *f*

lion [láɪən] N león *m*; —**'s share** la parte del león
lioness [láɪənɪs] N leona *f*
lip [lɪp] N labio *m*; (of a pitcher) borde *m*; —
balm crema para labios *f*; —**stick** lápiz de
labios *m*, carmín *m*; **don't give me no** —**!** no
me contestes; VI **to** —**read** leer los labios
liposuction [láɪposʌkʃən] N liposucción *f*
liqueur [lɪkɜ́] N licor *m*
liquid [líkwɪd] ADJ líquido; — **assets** activo
líquido *m*; — **measure** medida para líquidos
f; N líquido *m*
liquidate [líkwɪdet] VI/VT liquidar
liquidation [lɪkwɪdéʃən] N liquidación *f*
liquidity [lɪkwídɪDi] N liquidez *f*
liquor [líkɜ] N bebida espirituosa *f*
lira [lírə] N lira *f*
lisp [lɪsp] N ceceo *m*; VI cecear
list [lɪst] N (series of items) lista *f*; (of a ship)
escora *f*; — **price** precio de lista *m*; — **server**
servidor de lista *m*; VT (make a list) hacer una
lista de; VI (lean) escorar; **this chair** —**s for
two hundred dollars** esta silla está a
doscientos dólares
listen [lísən] VI/VT (hear) escuchar, oír; (heed)
escuchar, prestar atención; **to** — **in** (on radio)
sintonizar; (eavesdrop) escuchar a hurtadillas
listener [lísənɜ] N oyente *mf*; **radio** —
radioescucha *mf*, oyente *mf*
listing [lístɪŋ] N listado *m*
listless [lístlɪs] ADJ lánguido
lit [lɪt] ADJ (provided with light) iluminado;
(tipsy) alegre, alumbrado
lit [lɪt] *see* light
literacy [líDəəsi] N (action of making literate)
alfabetización *f*; (rate) alfabetismo *m*
literal [líDəəɫ] ADJ literal
literary [líDəreri] ADJ literario
literate [líDəɪt] ADJ (who can read and write)
alfabeto; (erudite) erudito, letrado; **he's
barely** — apenas sabe leer y escribir
literature [líDəətʃɜ] N literatura *f*; (handbills)
impresos *m pl*, folletos *m pl*; **the scientific**
— la literatura científica
lithium [líθiəm] N litio *m*; —**-ion battery**
batería de iones de litio *f*
Lithuania [lɪθuénɪə] N Lituania *f*
Lithuanian [lɪθuénɪən] ADJ & N lituano -na *mf*
litigant [líDɪgənt] N litigante *mf*
litigation [lɪDɪgéʃən] N litigio *m*, pleito *m*
litter [líDɜ] N (young animals) camada *f*, cría *f*;
(stretcher) camilla *f*; (straw) cama de paja para
animales *f*; (trash) basura *f*; (for cats) arena
higiénica *f*; VI/VT (dirty) ensuciar; (strew)
esparcir; VI (give birth) parir
little [líDɫ] ADJ (small) pequeño, chico; (not
much) poco; — **brother** hermano menor *m*,
hermanito *m*; — **finger** [dedo] meñique *m*; —
pig puerquito *m*; **a** — **coffee** un poco de café;
a — **while** un ratito, un poco; ADV & N poco;

— **by** — poco a poco
livable [lívəbəɫ] ADJ funcional
live[1] [lɪv] VI/VT vivir; **to** — **together** convivir;
to — **up to** cumplir; **to** — **it up** tirar la casa
por la ventana; **long** — **the king!** ¡viva el
rey! ADJ **all the** —**long day** todo el santo día
live[2] [laɪv] ADJ vivo; (ammunition) cargado; —
coal ascua encendida *f*; — **oak** roble de
Virginia *m*; —**stock** ganado *m*, ganadería *f*; —
wire (electric) cable cargado *m*; (person)
persona vivaz *f*; **before a** — **audience** en
vivo; —**-in** con cama; ADV en vivo y en
directo
livelihood [láɪvlihʊd] N sustento *m*
liveliness [láɪvlɪnɪs] N viveza *f*, animación *f*
lively [láɪvli] ADJ (party) animado; (person)
vivaz, avispado; ADV con animación
liver [lívɜ] N hígado *m*
livid [lívɪd] ADJ (pallid, bluish) lívido; (angry)
furibundo
living [lívɪŋ] N (life) vida *f*; — **expenses** gastos
de subsistencia *m pl*; — **room** sala *f*, living *m*;
— **together** cohabitación *f*; — **wage** salario
de subsistencia *m*; — **will** documento de
instrucciones previas *m*, documento de
voluntad anticipada *m*; **to earn/make a** —
ganarse la vida; **the** — los vivos; ADJ vivo,
viviente
lizard [lízɜd] N lagartija *f*
llama [lámə] N llama *f*
load [lod] N (supported mass) carga *f*; (weight)
peso *m*; (ship cargo) cargamento *m*; **no-**—
fund fondo sin comisión de entrada *m*; —**s of**
montones de; VI/VT cargar; **to** — **down**
colmar; **to** — **oneself down** agobiarse
loaf [lof] N hogaza de pan *f*, pan *m*; VI holgar,
holgazanear, haraganear
loafer [lófɜ] N (idler) holgazán -ana *mf*, haragán
-ana *mf*, gandul -la *mf*; (shoe) mocasín *m*
loan [lon] N préstamo *m*; (to a government)
empréstito *m*; — **application** solicitud de
préstamo *f*; — **guarantee** garantía de
préstamo *f*; — **officer** funcionario -ria de
préstamos *mf*; — **shark** usurero -ra *mf*; —
word préstamo *m*; VI/VT prestar
loath [loθ] ADJ renuente; **to be** — **to** ser
renuente a
loathe [loð] VT aborrecer
loathsome [lóðsəm] ADJ repugnante,
abominable
lob [lɑb] VT tirar por lo alto; N (tennis) globo *m*
lobby [lábi] N (vestibule) vestíbulo *m*; (special
interest) grupo de presión *m*, lobby *m*; VI/VT
(influence) presionar
lobbyist [lábiist] N representante de un grupo de
presión *mf*
lobe [lob] N lóbulo *m*
lobotomy [ləbáDəmi] N lobotomía *f*
lobster [lábstɜ] N langosta *f*

local [lókəł] ADJ local; **— bus** (computer) vía de transmisión local *f*; **— printer** impresora local *f*; **— train** tren de cercanías *m*

localize [lókəlaɪz] VT localizar

locate [lóket] VI/VT (establish in a place) situar, ubicar; (find) localizar; VI (settle) radicarse, establecerse

location [lokéʃən] N (position) ubicación *f*, emplazamiento *m*; (finding) localización *f*; **on — en** exteriores

lock [lɑk] N (door) cerradura *f*; (canal) esclusa *f*; (firearms, wrestling) llave *f*; (of hair) mecha *f*, mechón *m*; **—jaw** tétanos *m sg*; **—-out** cierre patronal *m*; **—smith** cerrajero -ra *mf*; **to have a — on the award** tener asegurado el premio; VI/VT cerrar con llave; (make immovable) trabar[se]; **to — in** encerrar; **to — out** dejar afuera; **to — up** (door) cerrar con llave; (animal) encerrar; (prisoner) encarcelar; (valuables) poner bajo llave

locker [lákɚ] N (for athletic equipment) casillero *m*; (for frozen food) cámara frigorífica *f*; **— room** vestuario *m*

locket [lákɪt] N relicario *m*, guardapelo *m*

locomotive [lokəmóDɪv] N locomotora *f*

locust [lókəst] N langosta *f*; **— tree** algarrobo *m*

lodge [laʤ] N (of fraternal organization) logia *f*; (cabin) cabaña *f*; (hotel) posada *f*, mesón *m*; VI/VT alojar[se], hospedar[se]; **to — a complaint** presentar una queja

lodger [láʤɚ] N inquilino -na *mf*

lodging [láʤɪŋ] N alojamiento *m*, hospedaje *m*, albergue *m*

loft [lɔft] N (attic) desván *m*; (for choir) coro *m*; (for hay) pajar *m*; VT tirar por lo alto

lofty [lɔ́fti] ADJ elevado, encumbrado

log [lɑg] N (wood) leño *m*, madero *m*, rollizo *m*; (ship record) cuaderno de bitácora *m*; (record of activity) diario *m*; (on a computer) registro *m*; **— cabin** cabaña de troncos *f*; VI/VT (cut trees) cortar; **—-in name** nombre de acceso *m*; VT (write down) anotar; **to — in** ingresar al sistema; **to — off/out** finalizar una sesión; VT registrar una acción

logarithm [lágərɪðəm] N logaritmo *m*

logic [láʤɪk] N lógica *f*; **— board** placa lógica *f*

logical [láʤɪkəł] ADJ lógico

logically [láʤɪkli] ADV lógicamente

logistics [ləʤístɪks] N logística *f*

loin [lɔɪn] N ijada *f*; (in animals) ijar *m*; (cut of meat) lomo *m*; **—s** entrañas *f pl*

loiter [lɔ́ɪDɚ] VI (idly) holgazanear; (with ill intent) merodear; **to — behind** rezagarse

loll [lɑł] VI arrellanarse

lollipop [lálipap] N *Sp* pirulí *m*; *Mex* paleta *f*; *RP* chupetín *m*

lone [lon] ADJ (solitary) solitario; (only) único

loneliness [lónlinɪs] N soledad *f*

lonely [lónli] ADJ solo

lonesome [lónsəm] ADJ solo

long [lɔŋ] ADJ largo; **a — way from home** lejos de casa; **to work — hours** trabajar muchas horas; **— distance** de larga distancia; **— division** división de más de una cifra *f*; **—hand** letra manuscrita *f*; **— johns** calzoncillos largos *m pl*; **— jump** salto largo *m*; **—-lasting** duradero, perdurable; **—-lived** (batteries) duradero; (people) longevo; **—-range** (missiles) de largo alcance; (plans) a largo plazo; **—shoreman** estibador *m*; **—-suffering** sufrido; **—-term** a largo plazo; **—-term care** atención médica a largo plazo *f*; **—time friend** viejo amigo; **— underwear** calzoncillo largo *m*; **—-winded** verborrágico, palabrero; **it's a — shot** es muy improbable; ADV mucho, mucho tiempo; **— ago** hace mucho tiempo; **— before** mucho antes; **— live . . . !** ¡viva . . . ! **all winter —** todo el invierno; **how — did he stay?** ¿cuánto tiempo se quedó? **not for —** no por mucho tiempo; **so —!** ¡hasta luego! **to be — in coming** tardar en venir; **three meters —** tres metros de largo; **will you be —?** ¿tardarás mucho? **the whole day —** todo el santo día; VI **to — for** anhelar

longer [lɔ́ŋgɚ] ADJ más largo; ADV más; **no —** ya no; **how much —?** ¿hasta cuándo?

longevity [lɑnʤévIDi] N longevidad *f*

longing [lɔ́ŋɪŋ] N anhelo *m*; ADJ anhelante

longitude [lánʤɪtud] N longitud *f*

look [lʊk] VI (see) mirar; (seem) parecer; **it —s good on you** te queda bien, te luce; **to — after** atender, cuidar; **to — alike** parecerse; **to — down on someone** despreciar a alguien; **to — for** (search for) buscar; (anticipate) esperar; **I — forward to it** lo espero con ansia, me da mucha ilusión; **to — into** investigar; **she —s her age** aparenta la edad que tiene; **to — out on** dar a, tener vista a; **to — out of** asomarse a; **— out!** ¡cuidado! **to — over** dar un vistazo a; **to — up** (upward) levantar la vista; (in a directory) buscar; **to — up to** admirar; N (gaze) mirada *f*; (examination) vistazo *m*; **—-alike** doble *mf*; **—out** (person) vigía *mf*, (place) mirador *m*, vigía *f*; **to be on the —out** estar alerta; **—s** aspecto *m*, pinta *f*; **good —s** belleza *f*

looking glass [lʊ́kɪŋglæs] N espejo *m*

loom [lum] N telar *m*; VI (appear indistinctly) dibujarse; (threaten) cernerse

loon [lún] N (bird) somorgujo *m*; (person) chiflado -da *mf*

loony [lúni] ADJ chiflado

loop [lup] N (for fastening) presilla *f*; (in a rope) lazo *m*; (of a flight) rizo *m*; (electric) circuito cerrado *m*; (computer programming, ice-skating) bucle *m*; **—hole** escapatoria *f*; **in the —** al corriente, al tanto de lo que pasa; VI (make a loop) hacer un lazo; (curve around) serpentear; (loop the loop) rizar el rizo; VT enlazar

loose [lus] ADJ (free) suelto; (not tight) flojo; (approximate) libre; (unfettered) desatado; (immoral) disoluto; (promiscuous) fácil; — **cannon** mono con una metralleta *m*; — **change** suelto *m*, cambio *m*; — **end** cabo suelto *m*; —-**fitting** holgado; —-**jointed** de articulaciones flexibles; —-**leaf** [de] hojas sueltas; **to let** — soltar; VT desatar, soltar

loosen [lúsən] VI/VT (untie) soltar[se], desatar; (make/become less tight/dense/strict) aflojar[se]

looseness [lúsnɪs] N (of skin) flojedad *f*; (of morals) relajamiento *m*; (of clothing) holgura *f*; (of soil) friabilidad *f*; (of translation) lo libre

loot [lut] N botín *m*; VI/VT saquear

lop [lɑp] VT (cut) cortar; (eliminate) eliminar; VI caer[se]; ADJ —**sided** (leaning to one side) ladeado; (unbalanced) desequilibrado; (listing) escorado

lope [lop] VI correr a pasos largos

loquacious [lokwéʃəs] ADJ locuaz

loquat [lókwɑt] N níspero *m*

lord [lɔrd] N señor *m*; (God) Señor *m*; (British title) lord *m*; —'**s Prayer** Padrenuestro *m*; **my** —! ¡Dios mío! VI **to** — **it over someone** tratarle a alguien con arrogancia

lordly [lɔ́rdli] ADJ (kingly) señorial; (haughty) altivo

lordship [lɔ́rdʃɪp] N (title) señoría *f*; (power) señorío *m*

lore [lɔr] N saber *m*

lose [luz] VI/VT perder; (a pursuer) dejar atrás; **to** — **sight of** perder de vista; **to** — **oneself in thought** ensimismarse

loser [lúzɚ] N perdedor -ora *mf*

loss [lɔs] N (destruction) pérdida *f*; (misplacement) pérdida *f*, extravío *m*; (sports) derrota *f*; **to be at a** — no saber qué hacer; **to sell at a** — vender con pérdida; —**es** bajas *f pl*

lost [lɔst] ADJ perdido; — **cause** caso perdido *m*; — **in thought** absorto; **to get** — perderse, extraviarse

lost [lɔst] *see* lose

lot [lɑt] N (parcel) lote *m*; (fate) suerte *f*, destino *m*; (piece of land) solar *m*, terreno *m*; **the** — todo; **a** — **of / **—**s of** mucho[s]; **a** — **of money** mucho dinero; **by** — al azar; **to draw** —**s** echar suertes; **to fall to one's** — caerle en suerte a uno; ADV **a** — **better** mucho mejor

lotion [lóʃən] N loción *f*

lottery [lɑ́ɾəri] N lotería *f*

loud [laʊd] ADJ (noisy) ruidoso; (strong) fuerte; (ostentatious) chillón; —**speaker** altavoz *m*, altoparlante *m*; —**mouth** bocazas *mf sg*; ADV fuerte, alto

Lou Gehrig's disease [lugérɪgz dɪziz] N enfermedad de Lou Gehrig *f*

lounge [laʊnʤ] VI repantigarse, arrellanarse; N (waiting room) sala de espera *f*; (room in bar) salón *m*; (divan) diván *m*; — **chair** diván *m*

louse [laʊs] N piojo *m*

lousy [láʊzi] ADJ (infested with lice) piojoso; (contemptible) despreciable; (poorly done) pésimo

lout [laʊt] N bruto *m*

lovable [lávəbɫ] ADJ adorable

love [lʌv] N (affection) amor *m*; (fondness) afición *f*; (in tennis) nada *f*; — **affair** aventura *f*, amorío *m*; — **at first sight** amor a primera vista *m*, flechazo *m*; — **life** vida sentimental *f*; — **seat** confidente *m*; **books were her great** — los libros fueron su gran pasión; **to be in** — estar enamorado; **to fall in** — **with** enamorarse de; **to make** — **to** hacerle el amor a; VI/VT amar, querer; **I** — **to eat apples** me encanta comer manzanas

loveliness [lávlinɪs] N (beauty) hermosura *f*; (charm) encanto *m*

lovely [lávli] ADJ (beautiful) hermoso; (charming) encantador; (pleasant) ameno

lover [lávɚ] N (sexually involved) amante *mf*; (in love) enamorado -da *mf*, amante *mf*; (interested in) aficionado -da *mf*

loving [lávɪŋ] ADJ cariñoso, afectuoso

low [lo] ADJ (not high) bajo; (base) vil; (humble) humilde; (downcast) abatido; (deep in pitch) grave; — **beam** luces cortas *f pl*; —**brow** poco culto; —-**budget** de bajo presupuesto; —-**cal** de bajas calorías; —-**cost** de bajo precio; —**down** verdad *f*; —-**end** de baja calidad; — **gear** primera marcha *f*; —-**grade** (inferior) inferior; (low) bajo; —-**income** de bajos ingresos; —-**key** tranquilo; —**land** tierra baja *f*; —-**level** de bajo nivel; —-**life** canalla *f*; — **quality** baja calidad *f*; —-**tech** sencillo; — **tide** bajamar *f*, marea baja *f*; **dress with a** — **neck** vestido escotado *m*; **to be** — **on something** estar escaso de algo; **to be in** — **spirits** estar abatido/desanimado; ADV bajo; **to buy** — comprar barato; N (sound of a cow) mugido *m*; VI mugir

lower [lóɚ] VI/VT bajar; (prices) rebajar; (flag, sail) arriar; ADJ más bajo, inferior; —**case** minúscula *f*; — **house** cámara de diputados *f*

lowliness [lólɪnɪs] N humildad *f*

lowly [lóli] ADJ humilde

loyal [lɔ́ɪəɫ] ADJ leal

loyalty [lɔ́ɪəɫti] N lealtad *f*

LSD [**lysergic acid diethylamide**] [éɫésdí] N LSD *m*

lubricant [lúbrɪkənt] ADJ & N lubricante *m*

lubricate [lúbrɪket] VI/VT lubricar

lucid [lúsɪd] ADJ lúcido

lucidity [lusídɪDi] N lucidez *f*

luck [lʌk] N suerte *f*; **in —** de suerte; **to be out of** — estar de mala suerte; VI **to — into** conseguir por un golpe de suerte; **to — out** tener suerte
luckily [lʌ́kəli] ADV afortunadamente
lucky [lʌ́ki] ADJ afortunado; **— charm** amuleto de la suerte *m*; **to be —** tener suerte
lucrative [lúkrəDIV] ADJ lucrativo
ludicrous [lúDIkrəs] ADJ ridículo
lug [lʌg] VT acarrear
luggage [lʌ́gɪʤ] N equipaje *m*; **— rack** rejilla *f*
lukewarm [lúkwɔ́rm] ADJ (not warm or cold) tibio; (indifferent) indiferente
lull [lʌl] VT (put to sleep) arrullar; VI/VT (soothe) calmar[se]; N (calm) calma *f*, tregua *f*; (sound) arrullo *m*
lullaby [lʌ́ləbaɪ] N canción de cuna *f*, nana *f*
lumbago [lʌmbégo] N lumbago *m*
lumbar [lʌ́mbɑr] ADJ lumbar
lumber [lʌ́mbɚ] N madera *f*; **—jack** leñador *m*; **—man** maderero *m*; **— mill** aserradero *m*; **—yard** almacén de maderas *m*; VI/VT (cut trees) talar; (move heavily) moverse pesadamente; (make a low noise) tronar
luminous [lúmənəs] ADJ luminoso
lump [lʌmp] N (in breast) bulto *m*; (in sauce) grumo *m*; (in throat) nudo *m*; (of coal) trozo *m*; (of food) plasta *f*; (on head) chichón *m*; (of sugar) terrón *m*; **to take one's —s** recibir palos; **— sum** pago global *m*; VT juntar; VI agrumarse
lumpectomy [lʌmpéktəmi] N tumorectomía *f*
lumpy [lʌ́mpi] ADJ grumoso
lunar [lúnɚ] ADJ lunar; **— eclipse** eclipse lunar *m*
lunatic [lúnətɪk] ADJ & N lunático -ca *mf*, loco -ca *mf*; **— fringe** extremistas *mf pl*
lunch [lʌntʃ] N comida *f*, almuerzo *m*; **—time** hora de comer/almorzar *f*; **out to —** (having lunch) almorzando; (crazy) en la luna; VI comer, almorzar
lung [lʌŋ] N pulmón *m*
lunge [lʌnʤ] N arremetida *f*; VI arremeter, abalanzarse; **to — at** arremeter contra, abalanzarse sobre
lupus [lúpəs] N lupus *m*
lurch [lɝtʃ] N tambaleo *m*; **to give a —** tambalearse; **to leave someone in the —** dejar a alguien en la estacada; VI tambalearse, dar barquinazos
lure [lʊr] N (thing that attracts) atractivo *m*, gancho *m*; (in hunting) señuelo *m*; (in fishing) cebo *m*; VT atraer, seducir
lurid [lúrɪd] ADJ (gruesome) sangriento; (shocking) escabroso
lurk [lɝk] VI (lie in wait) estar en acecho, acechar; (move furtively) moverse furtivamente
luscious [lʌ́ʃəs] ADJ (delicious) exquisito, delicioso; (sexy) voluptuoso

lust [lʌst] N (sexual desire) lujuria *f*, lascivia *f*; (craving) deseo *m*, ansia *f*; VI desear; **to — after** codiciar
luster [lʌ́stɚ] N lustre *m*, brillo *m*
lustful [lʌ́stfəl] ADJ lujurioso
lusty [lʌ́sti] ADJ (robust) robusto; (full of lust) lujurioso
Luxembourg [lʌ́ksəmbɚg] N Luxemburgo *m*
Luxembourger [lʌ́ksəmbɚgɚ] N luxemburgués -esa *mf*
Luxembourgian [lʌ̀ksəmbɚ́giən] ADJ luxemburgués
luxurious [lʌgʒúriəs] ADJ (characterized by luxury) lujoso; (luxuriant) exuberante
luxury [lʌ́gʒəri] N lujo *m*; **— tax** impuesto suntuario *m*; ADJ de lujo
lye [laɪ] N lejía *f*
lying [láɪɪŋ] ADJ mentiroso
Lyme disease [láɪm dɪziz] N enfermedad de Lyme *f*
lymph [lɪmf] N linfa *f*; **— node** nodo linfático *m*
lymphocyte [lɪ́mfəsaɪt] N linfocito *m*
lymphoma [lɪmfómə] N linfoma *m*
lynch [lɪntʃ] VT linchar
lynx [lɪŋks] N lince *m*
lyre [laɪr] N lira *f*
lyric [lírɪk] N poema lírico *m*; **— poetry** lírica *f*; **—s** letra *f*; ADJ lírico
lyrical [lírɪkəl] ADJ lírico
lyricism [lírɪsɪzəm] N lirismo *m*

Mm

ma'am [mæm] N señora *f*
Macao [məkáu] N Macao *m*
macaroni [mækəróni] N macarrones *m pl*
Macedonia [mæsɪdóniə] N Macedonia *f*
Macedonian [mæsɪdóniən] ADJ & N macedonio -nia *mf*
machine [məʃín] N máquina *f*; (of government) maquinaria *f*, aparato *m*; **— gun** (not portable) ametralladora *f*; (portable) metralleta *f*; **— language** lenguaje de máquina *m*, lenguaje máquina *m*; ADJ **—made** hecho a máquina; VT trabajar a máquina
machinery [məʃínəri] N maquinaria *f*
machinist [məʃínɪst] N maquinista *mf*, operario -ria *mf*
mackerel [mækɚəl] N caballa *f*
macro [mækro] N serie de instrucciones *f*
mad [mæd] ADJ (crazy) loco; (angry) rabioso, enojado; (hydrophobic) rabioso; **— cow disease** encefalopatía espongiforme bovina *f*, enfermedad de las vacas locas *f*; **—man**

loco *m*; **to be — about someone** estar loco por alguien; **to drive —** enloquecer, volver loco; **to get —** enojarse; **to go —** volverse loco, enloquecerse; **like —** como loco
Madagascan [mæDəgǽskən] ADJ & N malgache *mf*
Madagascar [mæDəgǽskɑr] N Madagascar *m*
madam [mǽDəm] N (title) señora *f*; (of a brothel) madama *f*
maddening [mǽdn̩ɪŋ] ADJ enloquecedor
made [med] ADJ **— -to-measure** hecho a la medida; **— -to-order** hecho por encargo; **— -up** (invented) inventado, falso; (wearing makeup) maquillado; **to be — of** ser de; **to have something —** mandar hacer algo; **I'm a — man** estoy hecho; **to have it —** estar hecho
made [med] *see* make
madness [mǽdnɪs] N (insanity) locura *f*; (anger) rabia *f*
Mafia [máfiə] N mafia *f*
mafioso [mɑfióso] N mafioso *m*
magazine [mǽgəzin] N (publication) revista *f*; (room for ammunition) polvorín *m*; (part of gun) cargador *m*
magic [mǽdʒɪk] N magia *f*; ADJ mágico; **— bullet** panacea *f*; **— wand** varita mágica *f*
magical [mǽdʒɪkəl] ADJ mágico
magician [mədʒíʃən] N (person adept at magic) mágico -ca *mf*; (person adept at finances) mago -ga *mf*
magistrate [mǽdʒɪstret] N magistrado -da *mf*
magma [mǽgmə] N magma *m*
magnanimous [mægnǽnəməs] ADJ magnánimo
magnate [mǽgnet] N magnate *m*
magnesia [mægnízə] N magnesia *f*
magnesium [mægníziəm] N magnesio *m*
magnet [mǽgnɪt] N imán *m*
magnetic [mægnéDɪk] ADJ magnético; **— pole** polo magnético *m*; **— resonance imaging** imagen por resonancia magnética *f*; **— tape** cinta magnetofónica *f*
magnetism [mǽgnɪtɪzəm] N magnetismo *m*
magnetize [mǽgnɪtaɪz] VT magnetizar, imantar
magnificence [mægnífɪsəns] N magnificencia *f*
magnificent [mægnífɪsənt] ADJ magnífico
magnify [mǽgnɪfaɪ] VT (to make larger) aumentar; (to make louder) amplificar; (to exaggerate) exagerar, magnificar
magnitude [mǽgnɪtud] N magnitud *f*
magnolia [mægnóljə] N (flower) magnolia *f*; (tree) magnolio *m*
magpie [mǽgpaɪ] N urraca *f* (also hoarder)
mahogany [məhágəni] N caoba *f*
maid [med] N criada *f*, sirvienta *f*; (in hotel) camarera *f*; **— of honor** dama de honor *f*
maiden [médn̩] N *lit* doncella *f*, virgen *f*; **— voyage** primer viaje *m*; **— name** nombre de soltera *m*

mail [meł] N correo *m*; (electronic) mensaje *m*; (of metal) malla *f*; **—bag** cartera *f*; **—box** buzón *m*; **—man** cartero *m*; **— order** pedido por correo *m*; **— order business** negocio de ventas por correo *m*; VT echar al correo; **—ing list** lista de correo *f*
maim [mem] VT mutilar
main [men] ADJ principal; **— office** oficina central *f*; N (pipe) cañería principal *f*; (sea) alta mar *f*; **—frame** *Sp* ordenador central *m*, *Am* computadora central *f*; **—land** continente *m*; **—spring** muelle real *m*; **—stream** tendencia mayoritaria *f*; **—stream engineering** ingeniería conforme a la corriente dominante *f*; **—stay** pilar *m*, puntal *m*; **— street** calle principal *f*
mainly [ménli] ADV principalmente, fundamentalmente
maintain [mentén] VT (repair, support) mantener; (assert) afirmar
maintenance [méntn̩əns] N (repairs) mantenimiento *m*; (monetary support) manutención *f*; **— cost** costo de mantenimiento *m*
maize [mez] N maíz *m*
majestic [mədʒéstɪk] ADJ majestuoso
majesty [mǽdʒɪsti] N majestad *f*; **Your —** Su Majestad
major [médʒɚ] ADJ (greater) mayor, más grande; (large) grande; **— key** mayor *m*; N (military rank) comandante *m*; (field of study) especialidad *f*, carrera *f*; **— league** liga mayor *f*; VI especializarse
majority [mədʒɔ́rɪDi] N (greater number) mayoría *f*; (age) mayoría de edad *f*; **— ownership** propiedad mayoritaria *f*; **the —** el grueso
make [mek] VT (do) hacer; (create) fabricar; (cause) causar; (earn) ganar; (a speech) pronunciar; **to — a clean breast of** sacarse del pecho; **to — a decision** tomar una decisión; **to — a living** ganarse la vida; **to — a train** llegar a tiempo para tomar un tren; **to — a turn** girar, doblar; **to — away with** fugarse con; **to — believe** hacer de cuenta que; **to — out** (see) vislumbrar, divisar; (read) descifrar; (kiss) *Sp* morrear; *Am* besuquearse; **to — possible** posibilitar; **to — too much of** exagerar; **to — up** (a story) inventar; (after a quarrel) hacer las paces; (a loss) recuperar; (one's face) maquillarse; (one's mind) decidirse; **to — up for** compensar; **two plus two —s four** dos y dos son cuatro; **what do you — of that?** ¿cómo interpretas eso? **I'll — it up to you** te voy a compensar por eso; **you'll — a good teacher** vas a ser un buen profesor; N (brand) marca *f*; **— -up** (composition)

composición *f*; (character) carácter *m*;
(cosmetics) maquillaje *m*; ADJ —**shift**
provisional
maker [mékɚ] N (creator) creador -ora *mf*,
hacedor -ora *mf*; (manufacturer) fabricante *m*
makings [mékɪŋz] N (potential) potencial *m*;
(ingredients) ingredientes *m pl*
maladjusted [mælədʒʌ́stɪd] ADJ inadaptado
malady [mǽlədi] N mal *m*
malaise [məléz] N malestar *m*
malaria [məlériə] N malaria *f*, paludismo *m*
Malawi [məláwi] N Malawi *m*
Malawian [məláwiən] ADJ & N malawiano -na
mf
Malaysia [məléʒə] N Malasia *f*
Malaysian [məléʒən] ADJ & N malasio -sia *mf*
malcontent [mǽlkəntɛnt] ADJ & N descontento
-ta *mf*
Maldives [mɔ́ldaɪvz] N Maldivas *f pl*
Maldivian [mɔ́ldíviən] ADJ & N maldivo -va *mf*
male [meł] ADJ (animal, plant) macho; (person)
varón; (trait) masculino; N (animal, plant)
macho *m*; (person) varón *m*
malevolent [məlévələnt] ADJ malévolo
malformation [mælfɔrméʃən] N malformación *f*
malfunction [mælfʌ́ŋkʃən] N funcionamiento
defectuoso *m*; VI funcionar mal
Mali [máli] N Malí *m*
Malian [máliən] ADJ & N malí *mf*
malice [mǽlɪs] N malicia *f*; **with —
aforethought** con premeditación y alevosía
malicious [məlíʃəs] ADJ malicioso
malign [məláɪn] VT calumniar, difamar
malignancy [məlígnənsi] N (quality)
malignidad *f*; (tumor) tumor maligno *m*
malignant [məlígnənt] ADJ maligno
mall [mɔł] N (closed street) paseo *m*; (enclosed
shopping area) galería *f*, centro comercial *m*
mallet [mǽlɪt] N mazo *m*
malnourished [mælnɚ́rɪʃt] ADJ desnutrido
malnutrition [mælnutríʃən] N desnutrición *f*
malpractice [mælpræktɪs] N negligencia *f*, mala
práctica *f*
malt [mɔłt] N malta *f*; —**ed milk** leche
malteada *f*
Malta [mɔ́łtə] N Malta *f*
Maltese [mɔłtíz] ADJ & N maltés -esa *mf*
mama, mamma [mámə] N mamá *f*; —**'s boy**
nene de mamá *m*
mammal [mǽməł] N mamífero *m*
mammary [mǽməri] ADJ mamario
mammography [mæmágrəfi] N mamografía *f*
mammoth [mǽməθ] ADJ enorme; N mamut *m*
man [mæn] N hombre *m*; (servant) criado *m*; (in
games) pieza *f*, ficha *f*; — **and wife** marido y
mujer; —**hunt** persecución *f*; —**kind**
humanidad *f*; —**of-war** (ship) buque de
guerra *m*; (jellyfish) medusa *f*; —**power** (for
work) mano de obra *f*; —**slaughter**

(accidental) homicidio culposo *m*, homicidio
involuntario *m*; (unpremeditated) homicidio
sin premeditación *m*; —**-to-— defense**
defensa al hombre *f*, defensa de asignación *f*,
defensa individual *f*; **every — for himself**
cada cual para sí; **to a —** unánimamente; ADJ
—**-eating** que come carne humana; —-
made (fiber) sintético; (lake) artificial;
INTERJ ¡hombre! VT (a fort) guarnecer; (a
ship) tripular; **to —handle** violentar
manage [mǽnɪdʒ] VT (succeed in) conseguir,
lograr; (direct) dirigir, administrar,
gestionar; (maneuver) manejar; VI **to —
without help** arreglárselas sin ayuda
manageable [mǽnɪdʒəbəł] ADJ manejable;
(hair) dócil
managed [mǽnɪdʒd] ADJ — **care** plan de salud
administrado *m*; — **funds** fondos
administrados *m pl*
management [mǽnɪdʒmənt] N (act of
managing) dirección *f*, gestión *f*; (persons
controlling a business) gerencia *f*, patronal *f*,
gestión *f*; (area of study) empresariales *f pl*
manager [mǽnɪdʒɚ] N (of a store) gerente -ta
mf; (of a company) director -ora *mf*
mandate [mǽndet] N mandato *m*; VT decretar
mandatory [mǽndətɔri] ADJ obligatorio
mandolin [mǽndəlɪn] N mandolina *f*
mane [men] N (of a lion) melena *f*; (of a horse)
crin *f*
maneuver [mənúvɚ] N maniobra *f*; VI/VT
maniobrar
manganese [mǽŋgəniz] N manganeso *m*
mange [mendʒ] N sarna *f*, roña *f*
manger [méndʒɚ] N pesebre *m*
mangle [mǽŋgəł] VT (mutilate) magullar,
mutilar; (ruin) estropear
mango [mǽŋgo] N mango *m*
mangrove [mǽŋgrov] N mangle *m*
mangy [méndʒi] ADJ sarnoso
manhood [mǽnhʊd] N virilidad *f*; (male
genitals) miembro viril *m*; (men collectively)
hombres *m pl*; (adult age) edad adulta *f*
mania [méniə] N manía *f*
maniac [méniæk] N maníaco -ca *mf*, maniaco -ca
mf
maniacal [mənáɪəkəł] ADJ maníaco
manic-depressive [mǽnɪkdɪprésɪv] ADJ
maniaco-depresivo
manicure [mǽnɪkjʊr] N manicura *f*; VT
manicurar
manifest [mǽnəfɛst] ADJ manifiesto; N (list of
cargo) manifiesto *m*, hoja de ruta *f*; VT (show)
manifestar, poner de manifiesto; (express)
declarar
manifestation [mænəfɛstéʃən] N
manifestación *f*
manifesto [mænɪfɛ́sto] N manifiesto *m*
manifold [mǽnəfołd] ADJ diverso; N (on a

motor) colector *m*

manila [mənílə] N abacá *m*; — **envelope** sobre manila *m*

manioc [mǽniak] N mandioca *f*, yuca *f*

manipulate [mənípjəlet] VT manipular

manipulation [mənɪpjəléʃən] N manipulación *f*

manlike [mǽnlaɪk] ADJ (manly) varonil; (mannish) hombruna; (resembling a human) de hombre

manliness [mǽnlinɪs] N virilidad *f*

manly [mǽnli] ADJ varonil, viril

manner [mǽnɚ] N (way) manera *f*, modo *m*, forma *f*; (type) tipo *m*; (outward bearing) aire *m*, ademán *m*, porte *m*; —s modales *m pl*, crianza *f*; **in the** — **of** a la manera de

mannerism [mǽnərɪzəm] N peculiaridad *f*

mannish [mǽnɪʃ] ADJ hombruno, varonil

manor [mǽnɚ] N feudo *m*, solar *m*; — **house** casa solariega *f*

mansion [mǽnʃən] N mansión *f*

mantel [mǽntl] N repisa de chimenea *f*

mantle [mǽntl] N manto *m*

mantra [mǽntrə] N mantra *f*

manual [mǽnjuəɫ] ADJ & N manual *m*; — **labor** trabajo manual *m*

manufacture [mǽnjəfǽktʃɚ] VT fabricar, manufacturar; (clothes, shoes) confeccionar; N fabricación *f*, manufactura *f*; (of clothes, shoes) confección *f*

manufacturer [mǽnjəfǽktʃərɚ] N fabricante *m*; —**'s suggested retail price** precio sugerido por el fabricante *m*

manufacturing [mǽnjəfǽktʃɚɪŋ] N fabricación *f*, manufactura *f*; ADJ fabril, manufacturero; — **empire** imperio industrial *m*

manure [mənúr] N estiércol *m*; VT estercolar, abonar

manuscript [mǽnjəskrɪpt] ADJ & N manuscrito *m*

many [méni] ADJ muchos; — **apples** muchas manzanas; — **came** vinieron muchos; — **a time** muchas veces; **a great** — muchísimos; **as** — **as** tantos como; **as** — **as five** hasta cinco; **how** —? ¿cuántos? **three books too** — tres libros de más; **too** — demasiados

map [mæp] N (geographical) mapa *m*; (of streets) plano *m*; VT trazar un mapa de; **to** — **out** planear

maple [mépəɫ] N *Sp* arce *m*; *Am* maple *m*; — **syrup** miel de arce/maple *f*

mar [mɑr] VT estropear

marathon [mǽrəθɑn] N maratón *mf*

marble [mɑ́rbəɫ] N mármol *m*; (toy) canica *f*, bola *f*; **to play** —**s** jugar a las canicas; ADJ de mármol, marmóreo

march [mɑrtʃ] N marcha *f*; VI marchar; (leave) marcharse; **to** — **in** entrar; **to** — **out** marcharse; VT hacer marchar

March [mɑrtʃ] N marzo *m*

mare [mɛr] N yegua *f*

margarine [mɑ́rdʒɚɪn] N margarina *f*

margin [mɑ́rdʒɪn] N margen *m*; — **of error** margen de error *m*; — **of safety** margen de seguridad *m*; **on** — comprado en cuenta de margen

marginal [mɑ́rdʒənl] ADJ marginal

marginalization [mɑrdʒənl̩ɪzéʃən] N marginación *f*

marginalize [mɑ́rdʒənl̩aɪz] VT marginar

marigold [mǽrɪgoɫd] N caléndula *f*, maravilla *f*

marijuana, marihuana [mærəwánə] N marihuana *f*, mariguana *f*

marinate [mǽrənet] VT marinar

marine [mərín] ADJ (of the sea) marino; (maritime) marítimo; — **corps** infantería de marina *f*; N soldado de infantería de marina *m*

marionette [mæriənét] N marioneta *f*

marital [mǽrɪdl̩] ADJ conyugal, matrimonial; — **status** estado civil *m*

maritime [mǽrɪtaɪm] ADJ marítimo

mark [mɑrk] N marca *f*, seña *f*; (token) señal *f*; (indication) seña *f*; (grade) nota *f*, calificación *f*; (former German currency) marco *m*; —**down** rebaja de precio *f*; —**sman** tirador *m*; **he's a good** —**sman** tiene muy buena puntería / muy buen tino; —**-up** (amount above wholesale price) margen de ganancia *m*; **the halfway** — el punto medio, la mitad; **to hit the** — dar en el blanco; **on your** —, **get set, go!** ¡en sus marcas, listos y ya! ¡en sus marcas, listos, fuera! **to make one's** — distinguirse; **to miss the** — errar el tiro; **easy** — blanco fácil *m*; VT (write on) marcar; (indicate) señalar; (observe) observar, notar; (grade) calificar; —**ed for greatness** destinado a la grandeza; — **my words!** ¡ya verás! **to** — **down prices** rebajar los precios; **to** — **off** acotar, deslindar; **to** — **up prices** subir los precios

marker [mɑ́rkɚ] N marcador *m*

market [mɑ́rkɪt] N mercado *m*; — **analysis** análisis de mercado *m*; —**place** mercado *m*; — **price** precio de mercado *m*; — **share** sector del mercado *m*; **I'm in the** — **for** estoy buscando; VT comercializar, mercadear

marketable [mɑ́rkɪɖəbəɫ] ADJ vendible

marketing [mɑ́rkɪɖɪŋ] N (field of study) mercadotecnia *f*, marketing *m*; (selling) comercialización *f*

marmalade [mɑ́rməled] N mermelada de naranja *f*

maroon [mərún] ADJ & N bordó/bordeaux *m*; VT abandonar

marquis [mɑrkí] N marqués *m*

marquise [mɑrkíz] N marquesa *f*

marriage [mǽrɪdʒ] N matrimonio *m*; (combination) combinación *f*; — **license** licencia de matrimonio *f*

marriageable [mǽrɪdʒəbəl] ADJ casadero
married [mǽrɪd] ADJ (united in marriage)
casado; (relation to marriage) conyugal; —
couple matrimonio *m*; **to get** — casarse
marrow [mǽro] N (in the bones) médula *f*;
(food) tuétano *m*; (essential part) meollo *m*
marry [mǽri] VT (to marry off) casar; (to get
married) casarse con; VI casarse
marsh [marʃ] N pantano *m*, ciénaga *f*
marshal [márʃəl] N (military) mariscal *m*;
(police chief) alguacil *m*; (of a parade) maestro
de ceremonia *m*; VT (facts, forces) reunir;
(troops) formar
Marshallese [marʃəlíz] ADJ & N marshalés -esa
mf
Marshall Islands [márʃəláɪləndz] N Islas
Marshall *f pl*
marshmallow [márʃmɛlo] N malvavisco *m*
marshy [márʃi] ADJ pantanoso, cenagoso
martial [márʃəl] ADJ marcial; — **arts** artes
marciales *f pl*; — **law** ley marcial *f*
martin [mártn̩] N avión *m*
martini [martíni] N martini *m*
martyr [márDɚ] N mártir *m*; VT martirizar
martyrdom [márDɚdəm] N martirio *m*
marvel [márvəl] N maravilla *f*; VI maravillarse
marvelous [márvələs] ADJ maravilloso
Marxism [márksɪzəm] N marxismo *m*
mascara [mæskǽrə] N rímel *m*
mascot [mǽskat] N mascota *f*
masculine [mǽskjəlɪn] ADJ masculino
mash [mæʃ] VT aplastar, pisar; —**ed potatoes**
puré de papas/patatas *m*; N (pulpy mass) puré
m; (food for livestock) afrecho *m*; (malt) malta
remojada *f*
mask [mæsk] N máscara *f*, careta *f*; VT
enmascarar; —**ed ball** baile de máscaras *m*
masochism [mǽsəkɪzəm] N masoquismo *m*
mason [mésən] N (builder) albañil *m*;
(Freemason) masón *m*
masonry [mésənri] N (bricklaying) albañilería *f*;
(fraternal order) masonería *f*
masquerade [mæskəréd] N mascarada *f*; VI **to**
— **as** hacerse pasar por
mass [mæs] N masa *f*; (in church) misa *f*; —
communication comunicación de masas *f*;
— **marketing** comercialización masiva *f*; —
media medios de comunicación [de masas] *m*
pl; — **production** fabricación en masa *f*; —
storage almacenamiento masivo *m*; —
transit transporte público *m*; —
unemployment desempleo/paro masivo *m*;
the —**es** las masas *f pl*; VI/VT juntar[se] en
masa; (troops) concentrar[se]
massacre [mǽsəkɚ] N masacre *m*; VT masacrar
massage [məsáʒ] N masaje *m*; — **parlor** salón
de masajes *m*; VT (give a massage) masajear;
(change data) manipular
masseur [məsɚ́] N masajista *m*

masseuse [məsús] N masajista *f*
massive [mǽsɪv] ADJ (severe) masivo; (solid)
macizo; (large) enorme
mast [mæst] N mástil *m*, árbol *m*
mastectomy [mæstéktəmi] N mastectomía *f*
master [mǽstɚ] N (person in control) amo -a *mf*,
señor -ora *mf*; (owner of slave or animal) amo
-a *mf*; (best representative, skilled laborer)
maestro *m*; (young boy) señorito *m*; (tape or
disk) original *m*; —**'s degree** maestría *f*; ADJ
(dominant) dominante; — **bedroom**
dormitorio principal *m*; — **key** llave maestra
f; — **mind** cerebro *m*; — **piece** obra maestra
f; VT dominar; **to** — **mind** planificar y dirigir
masterful [mǽstɚfəl] ADJ magistral
masterly [mǽstɚli] ADJ magistral
mastery [mǽstɚi] N dominio *m*
mastiff [mǽstɪf] N mastín *m*, alano *m*
masturbate [mǽstɚbet] VI/VT masturbar[se]
mat [mæt] N (floor covering) estera *f*; (for wiping
feet) felpudo *m*; (in gymnastics) colchoneta *f*;
(of hair) maraña *f*; VI enmarañarse
match [mætʃ] N (pair) pareja *f*; (chess game)
partida *f*; (tennis, golf game) partido *m*;
(boxing encounter) combate *m*; (device for
fire) fósforo *m*, cerilla *f*; —**ball** bola de
partido *f*; —**box** cajita de fósforos *f*; —**maker**
casamentero -ra *mf*; —**point** punto de
partido *m*; **he has no** — no tiene igual; **he is**
a good — es un buen partido; **the hat and**
coat are a good — el abrigo y el sombrero
hacen juego; VI/VT hacer juego [con]; VI (to
correspond) estar de acuerdo; **the colors**
don't — los colores no combinan; VT (equal)
igualar; (come to correspond) poner de
acuerdo; (form pairs) parear
matching [mǽtʃɪŋ] ADJ emparejados; — **colors**
colores que combinan *m pl*; — **pair** pareja *f*;
— **shoes** zapatos del mismo par *m pl*
matchless [mǽtʃlɪs] ADJ sin par
mate [met] N (one of a pair) pareja *f*; (friend)
compañero -ra *mf*; (on a ship) oficial *m*; (in
chess) mate *m*; VI/VT aparear[se]
material [mətíriəl] ADJ (made of matter)
material; (pertinent) pertinente; N
(substance) material *m*; (fabric) tejido *m*,
género *m*
materialism [mətíriəlɪzəm] N materialismo *m*
materialize [mətíriəlaɪz] VI/VT materializar[se],
plasmarse
maternal [mətɚ́nl̩] ADJ (motherly) maternal;
(on mother's side of family) materno
maternity [mətɚ́nɪDi] N maternidad *f*; — **leave**
licencia por maternidad *f*
math [mæθ] N matemática[s] *f* [*pl*]
mathematical [mæθəmǽDɪkəl] ADJ
matemático
mathematician [mæθəmətíʃən] N matemático
-ca *mf*

mathematics [mæθəmǽDɪks] N matemática[s]*f* [*pl*]

matinee [mætn̩é] N matiné*f*

mating [méDɪŋ] N (copulation) cópula*f*; (reproduction) reproducción*f*

matriarch [métriɑrk] N matriarca*f*

matriculate [mətríkjəlet] VI/VT matricular[se]

matriculation [mətrɪkjəléʃən] N matriculación *f*, matrícula*f*

matrilineal [mætrəlíniəɫ] ADJ matrilineal

matrimony [mǽtrəmoni] N matrimonio *m*

matrix [métrɪks] N matriz*f*

matron [métrən] N (married woman or widow) matrona*f*; (in a hospital) jefa de enfermeras*f*

matter [mǽDɚ] N (substance, pus) materia*f*; (affair) asunto *m*; (printed) impreso *m*; (reading) material de lectura *m*; **— for complaint** motivo de queja *m*; **a — of two minutes** cosa de dos minutos*f*; **as a — of fact** de hecho, precisamente; **it is of no —** no tiene importancia; **no — what you say** no importa lo que digas; **as a — of course** por rutina; **what is the —?** ¿qué pasa? VI importar; **it doesn't —** no importa

mattress [mǽtrɪs] N colchón *m*

maturation [mætʃəréʃən] N maduración*f*

mature [mətʃúr] ADJ maduro; **a — note** un pagaré vencido/pagadero *m*; **for — audiences** para adultos; VI/VT madurar[se]; (a savings bond) vencer[se]

maturing [mətʃúrɪŋ] N maduración*f*

maturity [mətúrɪDi] N madurez*f*; (of a debt) vencimiento *m*

maul [mɔɫ] VT atacar, herir gravemente

Mauritania [mɔrɪténiə] N Mauritania*f*

Mauritanian [mɔrɪténiən] ADJ & N mauritano -na *mf*

Mauritian [mɔríʃən] ADJ & N mauriciano -na *mf*

Mauritius [mɔríʃəs] N Mauricio *m*

maverick [mǽvɚɪk] N cimarrón *m*; (person) inconformista *mf*, cimarrón -ona *mf*

maxim [mǽksɪm] N máxima*f*, sentencia*f*

maximize [mǽksəmaɪz] VT maximizar

maximum [mǽksəməm] ADJ & N máximo *m*

may [me] V AUX **— I sit down?** ¿puedo sentarme? **— you have a merry Christmas** que pases una feliz Navidad; **it — be that** puede ser que; **it — rain** puede [ser] que llueva, tal vez llueva; **she — have been late** puede [ser] que haya llegado tarde; **be that as it —** sea como fuere

May [me] N mayo *m*; **— Day** primero de mayo *m*; **—pole** mayo *m*

Maya [máɪə] N & ADJ maya *mf*

Mayan [máɪən] N & ADJ maya *mf*

maybe [mébi] ADV quizá[s], tal vez

mayonnaise [méənez] N mayonesa*f*, mahonesa*f*

mayor [méɚ] N alcalde *m*

mayoralty [méɚəɫti] N alcaldía*f*

maze [mez] N laberinto *m*

MBA [master of business administration] [émbíé] N máster en administración de empresas *m*, maestría en administración de empresas*f*

MD [medicinae doctor] [émdí] N doctor -ora en medicina *mf*

me [mi] PRON **she sees —** me ve; **he talks to —** me habla; **he comes with —** viene conmigo; **he did it for —** lo hizo para mí

meadow [méDo] N pradera*f*, prado *m*; **—lark** alondra*f*

meager [mígɚ] ADJ escaso, exiguo

meal [miɫ] N (repast) comida*f*; (flour) harina*f*; **—time** hora de comer*f*

mean [min] ADJ (unkind) cruel; (petty) vil; (humble) humilde; (stingy) mezquino; (difficult) de mal genio; (middle) medio; **—-spirited** mezquino; **I make a — lasagna** me sale muy rica la lasagna; N (average) media*f*, promedio *m*; **—s** medios *m pl*; **the ends justify the —s** el fin justifica los medios; **a man of —s** un hombre adinerado; **by —s of** por medio de; **—s of transport** medios de transporte *m pl*; **—s test** prueba de ingresos*f*; **by all —s** (of course) por supuesto; (using all resources) por todos los medios; **by no —s** de ningún modo; VT (intend) querer, tener intenciones de; (signify) querer decir, significar; **he —s well** tiene buenas intenciones; **winning —s everything to them** lo que más les importa es ganar; **they are meant for each other** son el uno para el otro

meander [miǽndɚ] VI (be winding) serpentear; (to wander) vagar

meaning [mínɪŋ] N (sense) significado *m*, sentido *m*; (purpose) sentido *m*; ADJ **well-—** bien intencionado

meaningful [mínɪŋfəɫ] ADJ (result, event) significativo, trascendente; (sentence) coherente

meaningless [mínɪŋlɪs] ADJ sin sentido

meanness [mínnɪs] N (cruelty) crueldad*f*; (pettiness) mezquindad*f*

meant [mɛnt] *see* mean

meantime [míntaɪm] ADV LOC **in the —** mientras tanto

meanwhile [mínhwaɪɫ] ADV mientras tanto

measles [mízəɫz] N sarampión *m*

measurable [méʒɚəbəɫ] ADJ medible, mensurable

measure [méʒɚ] N (dimension) medida*f*; (criterion) criterio *m*; (in musical bar) compás *m*; (bill) proyecto de ley *m*; **beyond —** sobremanera; **—** medida de áridos*f*; **in large —** en gran parte; **—s** medidas*f pl*; VI/VT medir; **to — up** compararse con;

measuring tape cinta de medir *f*, metro *m*
measured [mέʒəd] ADJ (rhythmical)
acompasado; (moderate) moderado,
mesurado
measurement [mέʒəmənt] N (act of
measuring) medición *f*; (dimension) medida
f, dimensión *f*
meat [mit] N carne *f*; (essential point) meollo *m*;
—**ball** albóndiga *f*; —**loaf** pan/pastel de
carne *m*
meaty [mídi] ADJ (with meat) con mucha carne;
(substantial) sustancioso
mechanic [mɪkǽnɪk] ADJ & N mecánico *m*; N —**s**
mecánica *f*
mechanical [mɪkǽnɪkəl] ADJ mecánico
mechanism [mέkənɪzəm] N mecanismo *m*
medal [mέdl̩] N medalla *f*; VI ganar una medalla
meddle [mέdl̩] VI entrometerse, inmiscuirse
meddler [mέdlə] N entrometido -da *mf*
meddlesome [mέdl̩səm] ADJ entrometido
media [mídiə] N (communication) medios *m* pl,
media *m* pl, medios de comunicación masiva
m pl; (cables) cables del ordenador/ de la
computadora *m* pl
median [mídiən] ADJ mediano; N (middle value,
line) mediana *f*
mediate [mídiet] VI/VT mediar
mediation [midiéʃən] N mediación *f*
mediator [mídieDə] N mediador -ora *mf*
medical [mέdɪkəl] ADJ médico; — **chart** hoja
clínica *f*; — **exam** examen médico *m*; —
examiner médico -ca forense *mf*; —
history historia clínica *f*; — **record**
expediente médico *m*; — **school** facultad de
medicina *f*
medicate [mέdɪket] VT medicar
medication [mεdɪkéʃən] N medicación *f*
medicine [mέdɪsɪn] N (profession) medicina *f*;
(drug) medicamento *m*, fármaco *m*; — **ball**
balón medicinal *m*; — **cabinet** botiquín *m*; —
man curandero *m*
medieval [mɪdívəl] ADJ medieval
mediocre [midiókə] ADJ mediocre
mediocrity [midiákrɪDi] N mediocridad *f*
meditate [mέdɪtet] VI meditar
meditation [mεdɪtéʃən] N meditación *f*,
recogimiento *m*
Mediterranean [mεdɪtərénɪən] ADJ
mediterráneo
medium [mídiəm] N (substance, agency) medio
m; (person who contacts spirits) médium *mf*;
— **of exchange** medio de cambio *m*; ADJ
mediano; ADV término medio
medley [mέdli] N (music) popurrí *m*; (mixture)
mezcla *f*
meek [mik] ADJ manso
meekness [míknɪs] N mansedumbre *f*
meet [mit] VT (encounter) encontrarse con;
(make acquaintance) conocer; (face in

conflict) enfrentar; (satisfy) satisfacer; (pay)
pagar; **to — a deadline** cumplir el plazo; **to
— expenses** sufragar los gastos; **to —
halfway** partir la diferencia; **to — a train**
esperar un tren; **I will — you at the station**
nos encontramos/vemos en la estación; **have
you met my brother?** ¿conoces a mi
hermano? **we were met with disapproval**
se nos recibió con desaprobación; VI
(encounter) encontrarse; (make
acquaintance) conocerse; (have a meeting)
reunirse; (cross) cruzarse; **to — in battle**
trabar batalla; **to — with** (intentional)
reunirse con; (unintentional) tropezar con; N
encuentro deportivo *m*, competición *f*
meeting [mídɪŋ] N reunión *f*, junta *f*; (political)
mitin *m*; (crossing of roads) cruce *m*
megabyte [mέgəbaɪt] N megabyte *m*
megahertz [mέgəhɜtz] N megahertz *m*,
megahercio *m*
megalomania [mεgəloménɪə] N megalomanía *f*
megaphone [mέgəfon] N megáfono *m*, bocina *f*
melancholy [mέlənkɑli] N melancolía *f*; ADJ
melancólico
melanoma [mεlənómə] N melanoma *m*
meld [mεld] VT fusionar
melee [méle] N reyerta *f*, tumulto *m*
mellow [mέlo] ADJ (soft) dulce, suave; (gentle)
tranquilo; VI/VT suavizar[se]
melodic [məládɪk] ADJ melódico
melodious [məlódiəs] ADJ melodioso, melódico
melodrama [mέlodrɑmə] N melodrama *m*
melody [mέlədi] N melodía *f*
melon [mέlən] N melón *m*
melt [mεlt] VI/VT (liquefy) derretir[se]; (dissolve)
disolver[se]; —**ing pot** crisol *m*; N —**down**
(fusion) catástrofe por fusión nuclear
incontrolada *f*; (any developing disaster)
catástrofe *f*
member [mέmbə] N miembro *m* (also body
part)
membership [mέmbəʃɪp] N (number) número
de miembros/socios *m*; (state) calidad de
miembro/socio *f*
membrane [mέmbren] N membrana *f*
memento [məmέnto] N recuerdo *m*
memoir [mέmwɑr] N memoria *f*; —**s** memorias *f*
pl, autobiografía *f*
memorable [mέməəbəl] ADJ memorable
memorandum [mεmərǽndəm] N
memorándum *m*
memorial [məmɔ́riəl] N (monument)
monumento conmemorativo *m*; (petition)
memorial *m*; ADJ conmemorativo
memorize [mέməraɪz] VI/VT memorizar
memory [mέməri] N (faculty) memoria *f*;
(recollection) recuerdo *m*; — **cache** caché de
memoria *f*; — **map** mapa de memoria *m*
menace [ménɪs] N amenaza *f*; VI/VT amenazar

mend [mɛnd] VT remendar; **to — matters** enmendar la situación; **to — one's ways** enmendarse, reformarse; VI (sick person) mejorarse; (bones) soldarse; N remiendo *m*; **to be on the —** ir mejorando

menial [mínɪəł] ADJ (lowly) bajo; (job) servil; N criado -da *mf*

meningitis [mɛnɪndʒáɪDɪs] N meningitis *f*

menopause [mɛ́nəpɔz] N menopausia *f*

menstruate [mɛ́nstruet] VI menstruar

menstruation [mɛnstruéʃən] N menstruación *f*

mental [mɛ́ntl] ADJ mental; (insane) *fam* chiflado; **— health** salud mental *f*; **— illness** enfermedad mental *f*; **— retardation** retraso mental *m*

mentality [mɛntǽlɪDi] N mentalidad *f*

mention [mɛ́nʃən] VT mencionar; **don't — it** no hay de qué; N mención *f*

mentor [mɛ́ntɔr] N mentor -ora *mf*

menu [mɛ́nju] N (list of dishes) carta *f*, menú *m*; (computer) menú *m*; **— bar** (computer) barra de menú *f*

meow [mjaU] INTERJ miau

mercantile [mɝ́kəntił] ADJ mercantil

mercenary [mɝ́səneri] ADJ mercenario

merchandise¹ [mɝ́tʃəndaɪs] N mercancía *f*, mercadería *f*

merchandise² [mɝ́tʃəndaɪz] VT comercializar

merchandising [mɝ́tʃəndaɪzɪŋ] N mercadeo *m*, comercialización *f*

merchant [mɝ́tʃənt] N (trader) comerciante *m*, mercader *m*; ADJ mercante; **— marine** marina mercante *f*

merciful [mɝ́sɪfəł] ADJ misericordioso

merciless [mɝ́sɪlɪs] ADJ despiadado

mercury [mɝ́kjəri] N mercurio *m*; (on a mirror) azogue *m*

mercy [mɝ́si] N (compassion) misericordia *f*, clemencia *f*, piedad *f*; **to be at the — of** estar a merced de; **— killing** eutanasia *f*

mere [mir] ADJ mero, simple; **a — trifle** una nonada

merely [mírli] ADV (only) solo, solamente; (simply) simplemente

merge [mɝdʒ] VI/VT (forces) unir[se]; (colors) fundir[se]; (companies) fusionar[se]; (data files) fusionar; N fusión *f*

merger [mɝ́dʒɚ] N fusión *f*; **—s and acquisitions** fusiones y adquisiciones *f pl*

meridian [məríDiən] ADJ & N meridiano *m*

merit [mɛ́rɪt] N mérito *m*; **— pay** paga por mérito *f*; **— raise** aumento por mérito *m*; VT merecer

meritorious [mɛrɪtɔ́riəs] ADJ meritorio

mermaid [mɝ́med] N sirena *f*

merriment [mɛ́rɪmənt] N alegría *f*, algazara *f*

merry [mɛ́ri] ADJ alegre; **—-go-round** tiovivo *m*; **—maker** fiestero -ra *mf*, juerguista *mf*; **—making** fiesta *f*, juerga *f*; **to make —**

divertirse; INTERJ **— Christmas** Feliz Navidad *f*, Felices Pascuas

mesa [mésə] N mesa *f*

mesh [mɛʃ] N (of metal) malla *f*; (of fiber) red *f*; (of gears) engranaje *m*; VI engranar

mesmerize [mɛ́zməraɪz] VI/VT hipnotizar

mess [mɛs] N (state of confusion) desorden *m*, desarreglo *m*; (disorderly person) desordenado -da *mf*, mugriento -ta *mf*; (confused person) desastre *m*; (difficult situation) lío *m*, jaleo *m*; (food for soldiers) rancho *m*; (cafeteria) cantina *f*; **— hall** cantina *f*; **— of fish** plato de pescado *m*; **to make a — of** (a room) ensuciar, desordenar; (a project) estropear; VI/VT **to — around** (waste time) perder el tiempo; (philander) correr detrás de las mujeres; **to — up** (a room) alborotar, desordenar; (clothes, hair) desarreglar; (a project) estropear; (make a muddle of) *vulg* cagarla; **to — with** meterse con

message [mésɪdʒ] N mensaje *m*, recado *m*; **I get the —** ya caí en cuenta

messenger [mésəndʒɚ] N mensajero -ra *mf*

messy [mési] ADJ (chaotic) desordenado; (embarrassing) embarazoso

met [mɛt] *see* meet

metabolic [mɛDəbálɪk] ADJ metabólico

metabolism [mətǽbəlɪzəm] N metabolismo *m*

metal [mɛ́dl] N metal *m*; **— detector** detector de metales *m*; ADJ de metal, metálico

metallic [mətǽlɪk] ADJ metálico

metallurgy [mɛ́dlɚdʒi] N metalurgia *f*

metamorphosis [mɛDəmɔ́rfəsɪs] N metamorfosis *f*

metaphor [mɛ́Dəfɔr] N metáfora *f*

metaphysical [mɛDəfízɪkəł] ADJ metafísico

metaphysics [mɛDəfízɪks] N metafísica *f*

metastasis [mətǽstəsɪs] N metástasis *f*

metastasize [mətǽstəsaɪz] VI metastatizar

meteor [míDiɔr] N meteoro *m*; **— shower** lluvia de meteoritos *f*

meteorite [míDiəraɪt] N meteorito *m*

meteorological [miDiəɑládʒɪkəł] ADJ meteorológico

meteorology [miDiərálədʒi] N meteorología *f*

meter [míDɚ] N (unit of length) metro *m*; (measuring device) contador *m*, medidor *m*

methane [mɛ́θen] N metano *m*

method [mɛ́θəd] N método *m*

methodical [məθáDɪkəł] ADJ metódico

methodology [mɛθədálədʒi] N metodología *f*

meticulous [mətíkjələs] ADJ detallista

metric [mɛ́trɪk] ADJ métrico

metro [mɛ́tro] N metro *m*

metronome [mɛ́trənom] N metrónomo *m*

metropolis [mətrápəlɪs] N metrópoli *f*, urbe *f*

metropolitan [mɛtrəpálɪDən] ADJ metropolitano

mettle [médl] N temple *m*, valor *m*

mew [mju] N maullido *m*; VI maullar

Mexican [méksɪkən] ADJ & N mexicano -na *mf*

Mexico [méksɪko] N México *m*

mezzanine [mézənin] N entrepiso *m*, entresuelo *m*

mickey mouse [míkimáʊs] ADJ poco serio, informal

microbe [máɪkrob] N microbio *m*

microbiology [maɪkrobaɪáləʤi] N microbiología *f*

microcomputer [maɪkrokəmpjúDə·] N *Am* microcomputadora *f*; *Sp* microordenador *m*

microeconomics [maɪkroɛkənámɪks] N microeconomía *f*

microfiche [máɪkrofiʃ] N microficha *f*

microfilm [máɪkrofɪlm] N microfilme *m*

micromanage [maɪkrománɪʤ] VI/VT administrar con excesivo control

micron [máɪkrɑn] N micrón *m*, micrómetro *m*

Micronesia [maɪkroníʒə] N Micronesia *f*

Micronesian [maɪkrəníʒən] ADJ & N micronesio -sia *mf*

microorganism [maɪkroɔ́rgənɪzəm] N microorganismo *m*

microphone [máɪkrəfon] N micrófono *m*

microprocessor [maɪkroprásɛsə·] N microprocesador *m*

microscope [máɪkrəskop] N microscopio *m*

microscopic [maɪkrəskápɪk] ADJ microscópico

microsurgery [maɪkrosɚ́ʤəri] N microcirujía *f*

microwave [máɪkrowev] N microonda *f*; — **oven** [horno] microondas *m sg*

mid [mɪd] ADJ medio; —**air** en el aire; —**day** [del] mediodía *m*; —**field player** (soccer) centrocampista *m*; —**life** madurez *f*; —**life crisis** crisis de la edad madura *f*; —**night** [de] medianoche *f*; —**shipman** guardiamarina *m*; **in** —**stream** (of a river) en medio del río; (of a task) en plena actividad; —**summer** pleno verano *m*; —**term examination** examen a mitad del curso *m*; —**way** a medio camino, a mitad del camino; —**wife** partera *f*, comadre *f*

middle [mídl] ADJ (average) medio, mediano; (intermediate) intermedio; (central) central; —**-aged** de mediana edad; — **Ages** Edad Media *f*; — **class** clase media *f*, burguesía *f*; —**-class neighborhood** barrio de clase media; — **ear** oído medio *m*; — **finger** dedo mayor *m*, dedo del corazón *m*; —**man** intermediario *m*, revendedor *m*; — **management** administración intermedia *f*; — **name** segundo nombre *m*; —**-of-the-road** moderado; —**-sized** [de] tamaño mediano; N medio *m*; (waist) cintura *f*; **in the** — **of** en el medio de; **I'm in the** — **of something** estoy ocupado haciendo algo; **toward the** — **of the month** a mediados

del mes

midget [míʤɪt] N enano -na *mf*

MIDI [musical instrument digital interface] [mídi] N interfaz digital de instrumentos musicales *f*

midst [mɪdst] ADV LOC medio *m*, centro *m*; **in the** — **of** en medio de, entre; **in our** — entre nosotros

mien [min] N porte *m*

might [maɪt] V AUX **it** — **be that** podría ser que; **he said it** — **rain tomorrow** dijo que tal vez lloviera mañana; **she** — **have been late** puede ser que haya llegado tarde; N poder *m*, poderío *m*

mighty [máɪDi] ADJ (strong) poderoso, potente; (large) imponente; ADV muy

migraine [máɪgren] N migraña *f*, jaqueca *f*

migrant [máɪgrənt] ADJ migratorio, migrante; N trabajador -ora itinerante *mf*, bracero -ra *mf*

migrate [máɪgret] VI (also computers) migrar

migration [maɪgréʃən] N migración *f*

migratory [máɪgrətɔri] ADJ migratorio

mild [maɪld] ADJ (gentle) suave; (moderate) moderado; (not serious) leve

mildew [míldu] N moho *m*

mildness [máɪldnɪs] N (gentleness) suavidad *f*; (lack of gravity) levedad *f*

mile [maɪl] N milla *f*; —**stone** hito *m*

mileage [máɪlɪʤ] N (distance, odometer reading) millaje *m*, kilometraje *m*; **this car gets good** — este coche es económico; **what kind of** — **are you getting?** ¿cuántos kilómetros por litro hace tu coche?

milieu [mɪljú] N ambiente *m*

militance [mílɪtəns] N militancia *f*

militancy [mílɪtənsi] N militancia *f*

militant [mílɪtənt] ADJ & N (fanatic) militante *mf*; (combatant) combatiente *mf*

military [mílɪtɛri] ADJ militar; N **the** — (armed forces) el ejército; (military personnel) los militares

militia [məlíʃə] N milicia *f*

milk [mɪlk] N leche *f*; — **chocolate** chocolate con leche *m*; —**maid** lechera *f*; —**man** lechero *m*; — **shake** batido *m*; VT (exploit) exprimir; **he's** —**ing it for all it's worth** le está sacando todo el jugo

milky [mílki] ADJ (consistency) lechoso; (product) lácteo; — **Way** Vía Láctea *f*

mill [mɪl] N (building) molino *m*; (factory) fábrica *f*; (for sugar) trapiche *m*, ingenio *m*; (rotating tool) fresa *f*; (small grinder) molinillo *m*; —**stone** muela de molino *f*; **a** —**stone around your neck** una piedra al cuello; VT (grind grain) moler; (cut wood) aserrar; (cut grooves on coins) acordonar; (machine) fresar; **to** — **around** dar vueltas

millennium [məlíniəm] N milenio *m*

miller [mílə·] N (person who mills) molinero -ra

mf; (machine for milling) fresadora *f*; (moth) mariposa nocturna *f*

milligram [mílɪgræm] N miligramo *m*

milliliter [mílǝliDǝ-] N mililitro *m*

millimeter [mílǝmiDǝ-] N milímetro *m*

milliner [mílǝnǝ-] N sombrerero -ra *mf*

millinery [mílǝnɛri] N (shop) sombrerería *f*; (hats) sombreros de señora *m pl*

million [míljǝn] N millón *m*; **a — dollars** un millón de dólares

millionaire [mɪljǝnér] N millonario -ria *mf*

millionth [míljǝnθ] ADJ & N millonésimo *m*

mime [maɪm] N (actor) mimo *m*; (technique, performance) pantomima *f*; VI hacer la mímica

mimic [mímɪk] VT imitar, remedar; N mono -na *mf*, remedador -ora *mf*

mince [mɪns] VT picar, desmenuzar; **not to — words** no tener pelos en la lengua; **—meat** picadillo *m*; **I'm going to make —meat of you** te voy a hacer picadillo

mind [maɪnd] N (thinking process) mente *f*; (person of intellect) inteligencia *f*; (opinion) parecer *m*, opinión *f*; **— games** manipulación psicológica *f*; **— over matter** el espíritu sobre la materia; **—-set** actitud *f*, forma de pensar *f*; **to be out of one's —** estar loco; **to bear in —** tener en cuenta; **to change one's —** cambiar de parecer/opinión; **to give someone a piece of one's —** cantarle a alguien las cuarenta; **I have a — to** me dan ganas de; **to make up one's —** decidirse; **to my —** a mi modo de ver; **to speak one's — freely** hablar con toda franqueza; **what do you have in —?** ¿qué tienes en mente? **to call to —** recordar; **to keep one's — on one's work** concentrarse en el trabajo; ADJ **—-altering** alucinógeno; VT (take care of) cuidar; (pay attention to) atender a; (obey) obedecer; **I don't —** no tengo inconveniente en ello; **— what you say** cuidado con lo que dices; **to — one's own business** no meterse en lo ajeno

mindful [máɪndfǝl] ADJ atento

mine [maɪn] PRON **this book is —** este libro es mío; **these things are —** estas cosas son mías; **— is bigger** el mío / la mía es más grande; **a friend of —** un amigo mío / una amiga mía; N mina *f* (also explosive device); **—field** campo minado *m*; **— sweeper** dragaminas *m sg*, barreminas *m sg*; VT (plant explosives) minar; (dig out minerals) extraer; (exploit an area for minerals) explotar; VI (lay mines) sembrar minas; (dig a mine) cavar una mina; **to — for** extraer

miner [máɪnǝ-] N minero -ra *mf*

mineral [mínǝ-ǝl] ADJ & N mineral *m*; **— rights** derechos mineros *m pl*; **— water** agua mineral *f*

mingle [míŋgǝl] VI mezclarse; (sounds) confundirse; VT mezclar

miniature [míniǝtʃǝ-] N miniatura *f*; ADJ en miniatura

minicomputer [mɪnikǝmpjúDǝ-] N *Am* minicomputadora *f*; *Sp* miniordenador *m*

minimal [mínǝmǝl] ADJ mínimo

minimize [mínǝmaɪz] VT minimizar

minimum [mínǝmǝm] ADJ & N mínimo *m*; **— wage** salario mínimo *m*

mining [máɪnɪŋ] N (exploitation of mines) minería *f*; (act of mining) minado *m*; ADJ minero; **open —** minería a cielo abierto *f*

miniskirt [mínɪskɜ-t] N minifalda *f*

minister [mínɪstǝ-] N (official) ministro -tra *mf*; (pastor) pastor -ora *mf*, clérigo *m*; VI **to — to** atender a

ministerial [mɪnɪstíriǝl] ADJ ministerial

ministry [mínɪstri] N (government agency) ministerio *m*; (functions of pastor) clerecía *f*

minivan [mínivæn] N camioneta *f*

mink [mɪŋk] N visón *m*

minnow [míno] N pececillo *m*

minor [máɪnǝ-] ADJ (smaller) menor, más pequeño; (of secondary importance) menor; **— key** tono menor *m*; **— league** liga menor *f*; N (young person) menor de edad *mf*; (musical interval) tono menor *m*; (subfield) asignatura secundaria *f*; VI tener como segunda especialización

minority [mǝnóriDi] N (smaller part or group) minoría *f*; (state of being underage) minoridad *f*; (member of a minority) miembro de una minoría *m*; ADJ minoritario; **— partner** socio -cia minoritario -ria *mf*

mint [mɪnt] N (flavor) menta *f*, hierbabuena *f*; (candy) pastilla de menta *f*; (money) casa de la moneda *f*; VT acuñar

minus [máɪnǝs] PREP **seven — four** siete menos cuatro; **we came — my brother** vinimos sin mi hermano; N signo de menos *m*; ADJ negativo

minuscule [mínǝskjuł] ADJ minúsculo

minute[1] [mínɪt] N minuto *m*; **— hand** minutero *m*; **—s** actas *f pl*

minute[2] [maɪnút] ADJ (small) diminuto; (detailed) detallado, minucioso

miracle [mírǝkǝl] N milagro *m*

miraculous [mɪrǽkjǝlǝs] ADJ milagroso

mirage [mɪráʒ] N espejismo *m*

mire [maɪr] N (mud) cieno *m*, fango *m*; (muddy place) ciénaga *f*; VI/VT (bog down) atascar[se] en el fango; (be or get covered with mud) enlodar[se]

mirror [mírǝ-] N espejo *m*; (large) luna *f*; **— image** imagen especular *f*; VT reflejar

mirth [mɜ-θ] N risa *f*, hilaridad *f*

mirthful [mɜ-θfǝl] ADJ risueño

miry [máɪri] ADJ cenagoso, fangoso

misanthropy [mɪsǽnθrəpi] N misantropía f
misappropriation [mɪsəproprié∫ən] N
malversación f
misbehave [mɪsbɪhév] VI portarse mal
miscalculate [mɪskǽłkjəlet] VI/VT (in math)
calcular mal; (in situations) equivocarse
miscarriage [mískærɪʤ] N aborto espontáneo
m, malparto m; — **of justice** injusticia f
miscarry [mɪskǽri] VI (abort) abortar
espontáneamente; (fail) malograrse,
frustrarse
miscellaneous [mɪsəléniəs] ADJ diverso; (texts)
misceláneo; — **expenses** gastos varios mf
mischief [míst∫ɪf] N travesura f, diablura f,
picardía f; (serious prank) barrabasada f,
bellaquería f; **this will come to** — va a
suceder una desgracia
mischievous [míst∫əvəs] ADJ travieso, pícaro
misconception [mɪskənsép∫ən] N concepto
erróneo m
misconduct[1] [mɪskándʌkt] N (bad behavior)
mala conducta f; (malfeasance) mala
administración f
misconduct[2] [mɪskəndʌ́kt] VT administrar mal;
to — **oneself** portarse mal
miscue [mɪskjú] N pifia f; VI/VT pifiar
misdeed [mɪsdíd] N fechoría f
misdemeanor [mɪsdɪmínɚ] N delito menor m
miser [máɪzɚ] N avaro -ra mf, tacaño -ña mf
miserable [mízɚəbəł] ADJ infeliz, desdichado; **a**
— **day** un día asqueroso; **a** — **failure** un
fracaso rotundo
miserly [máɪzɚli] ADJ avariento, tacaño
misery [mízɚri] N (wretchedness) desgracia f;
(poverty) miseria f; (unhappiness)
infelicidad f
misfit [mísfɪt] N inadaptado -da mf
misfortune [mɪsfɔ́rt∫ən] N desgracia f, desdicha
f, desventura f
misgivings [mɪsgívɪŋz] N aprensión f, recelo m
misguided [mɪsgáɪdɪd] ADJ mal aconsejado,
poco feliz
mishap [míshæp] N contratiempo m, percance m
misinform [mɪsɪnfɔ́rm] VT desinformar, dar
información errónea
misjudge [mɪsʤʌ́ʤ] VT juzgar mal
mislay [mɪslé] VT (keys, etc.) extraviar, perder;
(a document) traspapelar; (lay wrong) colocar
mal
mislead [mɪslíd] VT (in the wrong direction)
guiar por mal camino; (into error) engañar,
confundir
misleading [mɪslídɪŋ] ADJ engañoso
mismanage [mɪsmǽnɪʤ] VT administrar mal
misogyny [mɪsáʤəni] N misoginia f
misplace [mɪsplés] VT (lose keys, etc.) extraviar;
(lose a document) traspapelar; (place wrong)
colocar mal; **she** — **d her trust** confió en la
persona equivocada

misprint [mísprɪnt] N errata f, error de
imprenta m
misrepresent [mɪsrɛprɪzént] VT distorsionar,
tergiversar
misrepresentation [mɪsrɛprɪzenté∫ən] N
distorsión f, tergiversación f
miss [mɪs] VI (fail to hit) errar; (misfire) fallar; VT
(fail to hit) errar, no acertar; (fail to be on
time for) perder; (fail to attend) faltar a; (feel
absence of) echar de menos; Am extrañar; **he
just** — **ed being killed** por poco se mata; N
(of a target) tiro errado m; (in a motor) falla f;
(from class) falta f; (young woman) señorita f;
— **Smith** la señorita Smith
misshapen [mɪ∫épən] ADJ deforme
missile [mísəł] N (projectile) proyectil m;
(guided weapon) misil m
missing [mísɪŋ] ADJ (not present) ausente; (lost)
perdido; — **link** eslabón perdido m; **one
book is** — falta un libro
mission [mí∫ən] N misión f; — **statement**
declaración de la misión f
missionary [mí∫ənɛri] ADJ & N misionero -ra mf;
— **position** posición del misionero f
misspell [mɪsspéł] VT (written) escribir mal;
(oral) deletrear mal
misstatement [mɪsstétmənt] N declaración
errónea/falsa f
misstep [místɛp] N paso en falso m
mist [mɪst] N (of water droplets) neblina f,
bruma f; (of perfume) rocío m; VI lloviznar;
VT rociar
mistake [mɪsték] N error m, equivocación f;
(orthographical) falta f; **to make a** —
equivocarse; VI/VT equivocar[se]; **I** — **my
sister for my mother** confundo a mi
hermana con mi madre
mistaken [mɪstékən] ADJ equivocado; **to be** —
estar equivocado, equivocarse; **unless I'm** —
si no me equivoco
mistaken [mɪstékən] see mistake
mister [místɚ] N señor m
mistletoe [mísəłto] N muérdago m
mistook [mɪstúk] see mistake
mistreat [mɪstrít] VT maltratar
mistreatment [mɪstrítmənt] N maltrato m
mistress [místrɪs] N (of a household) señora f;
(employing servants, animal owner) ama f;
(lover) amante f
mistrial [místraɪł] N proceso viciado de
nulidad m
mistrust [mɪstrást] N desconfianza f; VT
desconfiar de
mistrustful [mɪstrástfəł] ADJ desconfiado,
receloso
misty [místi] ADJ (foggy) neblinoso, brumoso;
(in tears) nublado; (blurry) empañado
misunderstand [mɪsʌndɚstǽnd] VT
comprender mal, malinterpretar

misunderstanding [mɪsʌndəˈstǽndɪŋ] N
(confusion) malentendido *m*; (failure to
understand) equivocación *f*, mala inteligencia
f; (argument) desavenencia *f*
misuse[1] [mɪsjús] N (of drugs) abuso *m*; (of a
word) mal uso *m*; (of funds) malversación *f*
misuse[2] [mɪsjúz] VT (drugs) abusar de; (a friend)
maltratar; (a word) emplear mal; (funds)
malversar
mite [maɪt] N ácaro *m*; ADV **a — greedy** un
poquito codicioso
mitigate [mítɪget] VT mitigar
mitochondria [maɪDoʊkándriə] N mitocondria *f*
mitten [mítn̩] N manopla *f*
mix [mɪks] VI/VT mezclar[se]; **to — up**
confundir; N mezcla *f*; (for baking) preparado
m; **—-up** (confusion) confusión *f*; (fight)
pelea *f*
mixed [mɪkst] ADJ mixto; **— bag** grupo
heterogéneo *m*; **— doubles** dobles mixtos *m*
pl; **— drink** cóctel *m*; **—-up** confundido
mixer [míksə] N (appliance) batidora *f*; (party)
fiesta *f*; (soda) refresco *m*; (sound technician)
mezclador -ora *mf*; (sound device)
mezcladora *f*
mixture [míkstʃə] N mezcla *f*
moan [mon] N quejido *m*, gemido *m*; VI gemir,
quejarse; VI/VT lamentar
moat [mot] N foso *m*
mob [mɑb] N (disorderly crowd) tumulto *m*,
turba *f*; (crowd) muchedumbre *f*, populacho
m; (mafia) mafia *f*; VT (attack) asaltar; (crowd)
atestar
mobile [móbəl] ADJ móvil; (personnel) que tiene
movilidad; **— home** casa prefabricada *f*; **—
Internet** internet móvil *m*; **— phone**
[teléfono] móvil *m*, [teléfono] celular *m*
mobility [mobílɪDi] N movilidad *f*
mobilization [mobəlɪzéʃən] N movilización *f*
mobilize [móbəlaɪz] VI/VT movilizar[se]
moccasin [mákəsɪn] N mocasín *m* (also snake)
mock [mɑk] VI (ridicule) burlar[se]; VT (imitate)
remedar; ADJ de práctica; **— battle**
simulacro de batalla *m*; N **—-up** maqueta *f*,
modelo *m*
mockery [mákəri] N (ridicule) burla *f*;
(imitation) remedo *m*; (travesty) farsa *f*
mockingbird [mákɪŋbɜd] N sinsonte *m*
mode [mod] N modo *m*; **— of delivery** modo de
entrega *m*; **— of payment** forma de pago *f*
model [mádl̩] N (guide) modelo *m*; (person)
modelo *mf*, maniquí *mf*; ADJ modelo,
ejemplar; **— school** escuela modelo *f*; VI/VT
modelar; (display clothes) lucir
modem [móDəm] N módem *m*
moderate[1] [máDə-ɪt] ADJ (not excessive)
moderado, mesurado; (person) comedido;
(weather) templado; (price) módico; N
moderado -da *mf*

moderate[2] [máDəret] VI/VT moderar[se] (also
preside at meetings)
moderation [mɑDəréʃən] N moderación *f*,
mesura *f*
modern [máDən] ADJ moderno; **— age**
modernidad *f*
modernism [máDə-nɪzəm] N modernismo *m*
modernity [mədɜ́-nɪDi] N modernismo *m*
modernization [mɑDə-nɪzéʃən] N
modernización *f*
modernize [máDə-naɪz] VI/VT modernizar[se],
innovar
modernness [máDə-nnɪs] N modernismo *m*
modest [máDɪst] ADJ (humble) modesto; (chaste)
recatado, honesto
modesty [máDɪsti] N (humility) modestia *f*;
(chastity) recato *m*, pudor *m*, honestidad *f*
modification [mɑDəfɪkéʃən] N modificación *f*
modify [máDəfaɪ] VT modificar
modulate [mádʒələt] VI/VT modular[se]
modulation [madʒəléʃən] N modulación *f*
module [mádʒul] N módulo *m*
mohair [móhɛr] N mohair *m*
moist [mɔɪst] ADJ húmedo
moisten [mɔ́ɪsən] VI/VT humedecer[se]
moisture [mɔ́ɪstʃə] N humedad *f*
moisturizer [mɔ́ɪstʃəráɪzə] N [crema] hidrante/
humectante *f*
molar [mólə] ADJ molar; N muela *f*, molar *m*
molasses [məlǽsɪz] N melaza *f*
mold [mold] N (form) molde *m*; (fungi) moho *m*;
(mettle) temple *m*; VT (shape) moldear,
plasmar; (adapt) amoldar; (fuse) fundir; VI/VT
(become moldy) enmohecer[se]
molder [móldə] VI/VT descomponerse; (paper)
enmohecerse
molding [móldɪŋ] N (adornment) moldura *f*;
(action of molding) moldeado *m*
Moldova [mɔldóvə] N Moldavia *f*
Moldovan [mɔldóvən] ADJ & N moldavo -va *mf*
moldy [móldi] ADJ mohoso
mole [mol] N (blemish) lunar *m*; (animal, spy)
topo *m*; (breakwater) rompeolas *m sg*
molecular [məlékjələ] ADJ molecular
molecule [málɪkjul̩] N molécula *f*
molest [məlést] VT abusar sexualmente de
mollify [máləfaɪ] VT apaciguar, aplacar
mollusk [máləsk] N molusco *m*
molt [molt] VI (birds) mudar la pluma; (snakes)
mudar la piel; N muda *f*
molten [móltn̩] ADJ fundido
molybdenum [məlíbdənəm] N molibdeno *m*
mom [mɑm] N mamá *f*; **— and pop store** tienda
familiar *f*
moment [mómənt] N momento *m*; **being a
parent has its —s** ser padre/madre tiene
sus momentos de recompensa
momentary [móməntəri] ADJ momentáneo
momentous [moméntəs] ADJ importante,

trascendental
momentum [mɔmɛ́ntəm] N (in physics) momento *m*; (in politics, sports) empuje *m*
mommy [mámi] N mami *f*
Monaco [mánəko] N Mónaco *m*
monarch [mánɑrk] N monarca *mf*
monarchical [mənárkɪkəł] ADJ monárquico
monarchist [mánə-kɪst] N monárquico -ca *mf*
monarchy [mánə-ki] N monarquía *f*
monastery [mánəstɛri] N monasterio *m*
Monday [mánde] N lunes *m*
Monegasque [mɑnɪgásk] ADJ & N monegasco -ca *mf*
monetary [mánɪtɛri] ADJ monetario
money [máni] N dinero *m*; —**-back guarantee** garantía de devolución de dinero *f*; — **belt** faltriquera en forma de cinturón *f*; — **changer** cambista *mf*; — **laundering** lavado de dinero *m*; — **machine** cajero automático *m*; — **market** mercado de valores *m*; — **market account** cuenta de mercado monetario *f*; — **order** giro postal *m*; **to get one's —'s worth** sacar jugo al dinero; ADJ —**-grubbing** codicioso; —**-making** lucrativo, rentable
moneyed [mánid] ADJ adinerado
Mongolia [mɑŋgóliə] N Mongolia *f*
Mongolian [mɑŋgóliən] ADJ & N mongol -ola *mf*
mongoloid [máŋgələɪd] ADJ mongoloide
mongoose [máŋgus] N mangosta *f*
mongrel [máŋgrəł] ADJ & N mestizo *m*
monitor [mánɪtə-] N monitor *m*; (in a school) celador -ora *mf*; — **lizard** varano *m*; VT monitorear
monitoring [mánɪtə-ɪŋ] N monitoreo *m*, monitorización *f*
monk [mʌŋk] N monje *m*, religioso *m*
monkey [máŋki] N mono *m*, mico *m*; — **bars** jaula de los monos *f*; — **business** (mischief) picardía *f*; (trickery) chanchullo *m*; — **wrench** llave inglesa *f*; **to have a — on one's back** estar adicto; VI **to — around** bobear, payasear; **to — with** bobear con
monogamy [mənágəmi] N monogamia *f*
monologue, monolog [mánəbg] N monólogo *m*
mononucleosis [mɑnonukliósɪs] N mononucleosis *f*
monopolize [mənápəlaɪz] VT monopolizar
monopoly [mənápəli] N monopolio *m*
monotonous [mənátṇəs] ADJ monótono
monotony [mənátṇi] N monotonía *f*
monsignor [mɑnsínjə-] N monseñor *m*
monster [mánstə-] N monstruo *m*; ADJ enorme, monstruo *inv*
monstrosity [mɑnstrásɪDi] N monstruosidad *f*
monstrous [mánstrəs] ADJ monstruoso
month [mʌnθ] N mes *m*
monthly [mánθli] ADJ mensual; — **installment** mensualidad *f*; N publicación

mensual *f*, mensuario *m*; ADV mensualmente
monument [mánjəmənt] N monumento *m*
monumental [mɑnjəmɛ́ntḷ] ADJ monumental
moo [mu] N mugido *m*; VI mugir
mooch [mutʃ] VI/VT gorronear; N pedigüeño -ña *mf*
mood [mud] N (emotional state) humor *m*, vena *f*, ánimo *m*; (grammatical category) modo *m*; **to be in a good —** estar de buen humor; **to be in the —** to tener ganas de
moody [múdi] ADJ (sullen) malhumorado; (changing) voluble
moon [mun] N luna *f*; —**beam** rayo de luna *m*; —**light** claro de la luna *m*, luz de la luna *f*; —**lighting** pluriempleo *m*; —**shine** bebida alcohólica destilada sin licencia *f*; **once in a blue —** de Pascuas a Ramos; VT *fam* mostrarle el culo [a alguien]
moor [mʊr] VI/VT amarrar; N páramo *m*
Moor [mʊr] N moro -ra *mf*
Moorish [múrɪʃ] ADJ morisco, moro
moose [mus] N alce *m*
moot [mut] ADJ **it became a — point** dejó de tener importancia
mop [mɑp] N (for floors) *Sp* fregona *f*, *Sp* mopa *f*; *Mex* trapeador *m*; (for dust) plumero *m*; (of hair) greña *f*; —**-up** (of an enemy) limpieza *f*; (of a task) remate *m*; VI/VT pasar la mopa [sobre]; *Am* trapear; **to — one's brow** enjugarse la frente; **to — up** (a spill) limpiar; (an enemy) acabar con; (a task) rematar
mope [mop] VI andar abatido
moped [móped] N ciclomotor *m*, scooter *m*
moral [mɔ́rəł] ADJ moral; N moraleja *f*; —**s** moral *f*
morale [mərǽł] N moral *f*
moralist [mɔ́rəlɪst] N moralista *mf*
morality [mɔrǽlɪDi] N moralidad *f*
moralize [mɔ́rəlaɪz] VI/VT moralizar
morbid [mɔ́rbɪd] ADJ mórbido, morboso
morbidity [mɔrbíDɪDi] N (predisposition to illness) morbilidad *f*; (producing illness) morbosidad *f*
more [mɔr] ADJ & ADV más; — **and** — cada vez más; — **or less** más o menos; **there is no —** no hay más; —**over** además
morgue [mɔrg] N depósito de cadáveres *m*, morgue *f*
moribund [mɔ́rəbʌnd] ADJ moribundo
morning [mɔ́rnɪŋ] N mañana *f*; — **glory** dondiego de día *m*; — **sickness** náuseas *f pl*; — **star** lucero del alba *m*; **good —!** ¡buenos días! **tomorrow —** mañana por la mañana; ADJ de la mañana, matutino
Moroccan [mərákən] ADJ & N marroquí *mf*
Morocco [məráko] N Marruecos *m*
moron [mɔ́rɑn] N imbécil *m*
morphine [mɔ́rfin] N morfina *f*
morsel [mɔ́rsəł] N bocado *m*

mortal [mɔ́rdl̩] ADJ & N mortal *mf*; — **sin** pecado mortal *m*

mortality [mɔrtǽlɪDi] N (rate) mortalidad *f*; (toll) mortandad *f*

mortar [mɔ́rDɚ] N (for pounding) mortero *m* (also ballistics); (for bricks) argamasa *f*, mezcla *f*; —**board** birrete *m*

mortgage [mɔ́rgɪʤ] N hipoteca *f*; VT hipotecar; ADJ hipotecario; —-**backed securities** valores respaldados por hipoteca *m pl*

mortgagor [mɔ́rgɪʤɚ] N deudor -ora hipotecario -ria *mf*

mortification [mɔ́rDəfɪkéʃən] N mortificación *f*

mortify [mɔ́rDəfaɪ] VI/VT mortificar[se]

mortuary [mɔ́rtʃuɛri] N mortuorio *m*

mosaic [mozéɪk] N mosaico *m*

Moslem [mázləm] ADJ & N musulmán -ana *mf*

mosque [mɔsk] N mezquita *f*

mosquito [məskíDo] N mosquito *m*; — **net** mosquitero *m*

moss [mɔs] N musgo *m*

mossy [mɔ́si] ADJ musgoso

most [most] ADJ — **children are good** la mayoría de los niños son buenos; — **people** la mayoría de la gente; **the** — **money** más dinero *m*; **the** — **votes** el mayor número de votos; **for the** — **part** generalmente; PRON **the** — **that I can do** lo más que puedo hacer; **we ate the** — comimos más que nadie; — **of the guests are here** ha llegado la mayoría de los invitados; ADV **the** — **ambitious** el más ambicioso; **a** — **pleasant day** un día de lo más agradable

mostly [móstli] ADV generalmente

motel [motέł] N motel *m*

moth [mɔθ] N (pest) polilla *f*; (nocturnal insect) mariposa nocturna *f*; —**ball** bolita de naftalina *f*; —-**eaten** apolillado

mother [mʌ́ðɚ] N madre *f*; —**board** placa madre *f*; — **country** madre patria *f*; —**fucker** *offensive* hijo de puta *m*; —-**in-law** suegra *f*; —-**of-pearl** madreperla *f*; — **tongue** lengua materna *f*; VT mimar a, cuidar de/a

motherhood [mʌ́ðɚhʊd] N maternidad *f*

motherly [mʌ́ðɚli] ADJ maternal

motif [motíf] N motivo *m*

motion [móʃən] N (movement) movimiento *m*; (signal) ademán *m*; (proposal) moción *f*; — **picture** película de cine *f*; —-**picture industry** industria cinematográfica *f*; — **sickness** mareo *m*; VI/VT hacer un ademán

motionless [móʃənlɪs] ADJ inmóvil

motivate [móDəvet] VT motivar

motivation [moDəvéʃən] N motivación *f*

motive [móDɪv] N motivo *m*; ADJ motriz

motley [mátli] ADJ abigarrado

motor [móDɚ] N motor *m*; —**bike** motocicleta pequeña *f*; —**boat** lancha a motor *f*; —**cycle**

motocicleta *f*; —**cyclist** motociclista *mf*; — **home** casa rodante *f*, caravana *f*; — **scooter** scooter *m*; — **vehicle** vehículo motorizado *m*; VI pasear en coche

motorist [móDɚɪst] N automovilista *mf*

motto [máDo] N lema *f*

mound [maʊnd] N montículo *m*; **burial** — túmulo *m*; — **of laundry** pila de ropa *f*

mount [maʊnt] VI/VT (get on) montar; VI (increase) subir; VT (assemble) armar; N (mountain) monte *m*; (getting on a horse) montar *f*; (animal for riding) montura *f*

mountain [maʊntn̩] N montaña *f*; — **bike** bicicleta de montaña *f*; — **climber** alpinista *mf*; — **climbing** alpinismo *m*, montañismo *m*; — **goat** cabra montés *f*; — **lion** puma *f*, gato montés *m*; — **range** (large) cordillera *f*; (small) sierra *f*; —**side** ladera [de una montaña] *f*; —**top** cumbre [de una montaña] *f*; ADJ (animal, person) montañés; (thing) de montaña

mountaineer [maʊntn̩ír] N alpinista *mf*

mountainous [maʊntn̩əs] ADJ montañoso

mourn [mɔrn] VI estar de duelo/luto; VT llorar; **to** — **for** llorar a

mourner [mɔ́rnɚ] N doliente *mf*

mournful [mɔ́rnfəł] ADJ lúgubre, triste

mourning [mɔ́rnɪŋ] N luto *m*, duelo *m*; **to be in** — estar de luto/duelo; ADJ de luto

mouse [maʊs] N ratón *m* (also computer); — **pad** alfombrilla [de ratón] *f*; — **port** puerto de ratón *m*; —**trap** ratonera *f*

mouth[1] [maʊθ] N boca *f*; (of a cave) abertura *f*; (of a river) desembocadura *f*; —**piece** (part of a trumpet) boquilla *f*; (spokesman) portavoz *mf*; —-**to-mouth resuscitation** respiración boca a boca *f*; —**wash** enjuague bucal *m*; ADJ -**watering** delicioso

mouth[2] [maʊð] VT articular silenciosamente una palabra; **to** — **off** contestar

mouthful [maʊθfʊł] N (of food) bocado *m*; (of liquid) bocanada *f*, buche *m*

movable [múvəbəł] ADJ movible, móvil

move [muv] VI (change position) mover[se] (also board games); (change residence) mudar[se] de casa, (sell) venderse; **to** — **away** (distance oneself) apartarse; (change residence) irse; **to** — **forward** avanzar; **to** — **on** seguir adelante; **to** — **out** mudarse de casa; VT (propose) proponer; (affect emotionally) conmover; N (act of changing position) movimiento *m*; (change of residence) mudanza *f*; (action toward a goal) paso *m*; (play, in games) jugada *f*; **get a** — **on there!** ¡date prisa! **he made the first** — dio el primer paso

movement [múvmənt] N (motion, part of a watch) movimiento *m*; (of troops) desplazamiento *m*; **to have a bowel** —

mover el vientre
mover [múvəʳ] N compañía de mudanzas *f*; —**s**
and shakers la plana mayor
movie [múvi] N película *f*, filme *m*; —**s** cine *m*;
—**making** cinematografía *f*
moving [múvɪŋ] ADJ (target) móvil; (car) en
    movimiento; (company) de mudanzas; (story)
    conmovedor; — **picture** película *f*; — **van**
    camión de mudanzas *m*
mow [mo] VT cortar; (harvest) segar
mower [móəʳ] N (for lawns) cortadora de
    céspedes *f*, cortacésped *m*; (farm implement)
    segadora *f*; (farmworker) segador -ora *mf*
mown [mon] *see* mow
Mozambican [mozæmbíkən] ADJ & N
    mozambiqueño -ña *mf*
Mozambique [mozæmbík] N Mozambique *m*
Mozarabic [mozǽrəbɪk] ADJ mozárabe
Mr. [místəʳ] N Sr. *m*
MRI [magnetic resonance imaging] [émáráɪ]
    N IRM *f*
Mrs. [mísɪz] N Sra. *f*
Ms. [mɪz] N Sra. *f*
much [mʌtʃ] ADJ & ADV mucho; — **the same**
    casi lo mismo; — **like the others** muy
    parecido a los demás; **as — as** tanto como;
    how — ? ¿cuánto? **too —** demasiado; **very —**
    muchísimo; **to make — of** dar mucha
    importancia a; — **as I'd like, I won't do it**
    aunque me gustaría, no lo voy a hacer; **that's**
    not — of a book ese libro no es gran cosa;
    she cried so — lloró tanto; **they need**
    water, — as they need sun necesitan agua,
    del mismo modo que necesitan sol
muck [mʌk] N (manure) estiércol *m*; (mire) cieno
    m, lodo *m*; (filth) porquería *f*; **to — up** *vulg*
    cagarla
mucous [mjúkəs] ADJ mucoso
mucus [mjúkəs] N mucosidad *f*
mud [mʌd] N lodo *m*, barro *m*; —**slinging**
    difamación *f*
muddle [mʌdl] VT (confuse) confundir; (make
    turbid) enturbiar; VI **to — along** ir tirando;
    to — through salir del paso; N (confusion)
    confusión *f*; (confused situation) embrollo *m*
muddy [mʌdi] ADJ (path) lodoso, barroso;
    (shoes) embarrado; (vague) confuso; VT
    (cover with mud) enlodar, embarrar; (make
    unclear) enturbiar
muff [mʌf] N manguito *m*; VT estropear
muffin [mʌfɪn] N mollete *m*
muffle [mʌfəl] VT amortiguar
muffler [mʌfləʳ] N (scarf) bufanda *f*; (exhaust
    device) silenciador *m*
mug [mʌg] N (ceramic) tazón *m*; (glass) jarra *f*;
    (face) jeta *f*; VT atracar
mugger [mʌɡəʳ] N asaltante *mf*; atracador -ora
    mf
muggy [mʌɡi] ADJ bochornoso

mulatto [muláDo] ADJ & N mulato -ta *mf*
mulberry [mʌlbɛri] N mora *f*; — **tree** moral *m*
mule [mjul] N mulo -la *mf* (also in drug
    trafficking)
mull [mʌl] VI/VT rumiar
multicultural [mʌltikʌltʃəʳəl] ADJ
    multicultural
multilateral [mʌltilǽDəʳəl] ADJ multilateral
multimedia [mʌltimíDiə] N & ADJ INV
    multimedia *m*
multiple [mʌltəpəl] N múltiplo *m*; ADJ múltiple;
    —**-choice** de opción múltiple; —
    personality disorder trastorno de
    personalidad múltiple *m*; — **sclerosis**
    esclerosis múltiple *f*
multiplication [mʌltəplɪkéʃən] N
    multiplicación *f*; — **sign** signo de
    multiplicación *m*; — **table** tabla de
    multiplicar *f*
multiplicity [mʌltəplísɪDi] N multiplicidad *f*
multiply [mʌltəplaɪ] VI/VT multiplicar[se]
multiscreen [mʌltiskrin] ADJ multipantalla
multitasking [mʌltitæskɪŋ] N multitarea *f*
multitude [mʌltitud] N multitud *f*
multiuser [mʌltijúzəʳ] N multiusuario -ria *mf*
multi-year [mʌltijír] ADJ multianual
mum [mʌm] ADJ callado; **to keep —** callarse la
    boca
mumble [mʌmbəl] VI/VT mascullar; N
    refunfuño *m*
mumbo jumbo [mʌmbodʒʌmbo] N jerigonza *f*
mummy [mʌmi] N momia *f*
mumps [mʌmps] N paperas *f pl*
munch [mʌntʃ] VT mascar
mundane [mʌndén] ADJ mundano
municipal [mjunísəpəl] ADJ municipal; —
    council concejo *m*
municipality [mjunɪsəpǽlɪDi] N municipio *m*,
    municipalidad *m*
munition [mjuníʃən] N munición *f*
mural [mjúrəl] ADJ & N mural *m*
murder [mɝDəʳ] N asesinato *m*, homicidio *m*; **to**
    get away with — salirse con la suya; **that**
    exam was — ese examen fue matador; VI/VT
    asesinar
murderer [mɝDərəʳ] N asesino *mf*, homicida *mf*
murderous [mɝDəəs] ADJ asesino, homicida
murky [mɝki] ADJ (of water, matter) turbio; (of
    sky) oscuro
murmur [mɝməʳ] N (noise) murmullo *m*,
    susurro *m*; (complaint) queja *f*; VI/VT (make
    noise) murmurar, susurrar; (complain)
    quejarse
muscle [mʌsəl] N músculo *m*; — **relaxant**
    relajante muscular *m*; — **strain** distensión
    muscular *f*; — **tone** tonicidad muscular *f*,
    tono muscular *m*
muscular [mʌskjələʳ] ADJ (relative to muscles)
    muscular; (endowed with muscles)

musculoso; — **dystrophy** distrofia muscular *f*

muse [mjuz] VI meditar; VT cavilar; N musa *f*

museum [mjuzíəm] N museo *m*

mushroom [mʌʃrum] N seta *f*, hongo *m*, champiñón *m*

mushy [mʌʃi] ADJ (soft) fofo; (sentimental) sensiblero

music [mjúzɪk] N música *f*; — **stand** atril *m*; — **video** *Am* video musical *m*; *Sp* vídeo musical *m*

musical [mjúzɪkəł] ADJ (pertaining to music) musical; (fond of music) aficionado a la música, melómano; — **comedy** comedia musical *f*

musician [mjuzíʃən] N músico -ca *mf*

muskrat [mʌskræt] N ratón almizclero *m*

Muslim [mʌzləm] ADJ & N musulmán -ana *mf*

muslin [mʌzlɪn] N muselina *f*

muss [mʌs] VT revolver, alborotar; N revoltijo *m*

mussel [mʌsəł] N mejillón *m*

must [mʌst] V AUX **you — arrive before nine** debes llegar antes de las nueve; **you really — eat at that restaurant** tienes que comer en ese restaurante; **you — be his son** debes [de] / has de ser su hijo; **they — have seen me** deben [de] haberme visto

mustache, moustache [mʌstæʃ] N bigote *m*; (large) mostacho *m*

mustard [mʌstəd] N mostaza *f*; — **gas** gas mostaza *m*

muster [mʌstə] VT (troops) formar; (courage) juntar, reunir; VI (assemble for inspection) formar; (come together) reunirse; **to — out** dar de baja; **to — up one's courage** juntar valor; N revista *f*; **to pass —** ser aceptable

musty [mʌsti] ADJ (stale smelling) con olor a encierro/humedad; (antiquated) anticuado

mutant [mjútn̩t] ADJ & N mutante *mf*

mutation [mjutéʃən] N mutación *f*

mute [mjut] ADJ mudo; N (mute person) mudo -da *mf*; (for musical instruments) sordina *f*

mutilate [mjúdl̩et] VT mutilar

mutiny [mjútn̩i] N motín *m*; VI amotinarse

mutter [mʌdə] VI/VT refunfuñar, musitar; N refunfuño *m*

mutton [mʌtn̩] N carne de cordero *f*

mutual [mjútʃuəł] ADJ mutuo; — **fund** fondo mutuo/mutual *m*

muzzle [mʌzəł] N (snout) hocico *m*; (mouthguard) bozal *m*; (gun opening) boca *f*; VT (a dog) abozalar, poner bozal a; (critics) amordazar, silenciar

my [maɪ] POSS ADJ mi; **these are — friends** estos son mis amigos; **oh —!** ¡Dios mío! — **foot!** ¡ni lo pienses!

Myanmar [mjɑnmár] N Myanmar *m*

myocardial infarction [maɪokárDiəł ɪnfárkʃən] N infarto del miocardio *m*

myopia [maɪópiə] N miopía *f*

myriad [míriəd] N miríada *f*, sinfín *m*; — **problems** un sinfín de problemas

myrtle [mɚdl̩] N mirto *m*, arrayán *m*

myself [maɪsɛ́łf] PRON **I — wrote the letters** yo mismo escribí las cartas; **I'm not — today** hoy no soy la misma de siempre; **I was sitting by —** estaba sentado solo; **I talk to —** hablo solo; **I looked at — in the mirror** me miré en el espejo; **I bought — a house** me compré una casa

mysterious [mɪstíriəs] ADJ misterioso

mystery [místəri] N misterio *m*

mystic [místɪk] ADJ & N místico -ca *mf*

mystical [místɪkəł] ADJ místico

myth [mɪθ] N mito *m*

mythic [míθɪk] ADJ mítico

mythical [míθɪkəł] ADJ mítico

mythological [mɪθəládʒɪkəł] ADJ mitológico

mythology [mɪθálədʒi] N mitología *f*

Nn

nab [næb] VT pescar; *Sp* coger

nag [næg] N (horse) jaca *f*, rocín *m*, penco *m*; (complainer) quejica *mf*; VI/VT regañar, criticar

nail [neł] N (for wood) clavo *m*; (of finger, toe) uña *f*; —-**biter** situación angustiante *f*; — **file** lima *f*; — **polish** esmalte para uñas *m*; **to hit the — on the head** dar en el clavo; VT (fasten) clavar; (nab) pescar; *Sp* coger

naive [naív] ADJ ingenuo, cándido, bonachón

naiveté [naivté] N ingenuidad *f*

naked [nékɪd] ADJ desnudo

nakedness [nékɪdnɪs] N desnudez *f*

name [nem] N nombre *m*; —-**brand** marca comercial *f*; —**plate** placa *f*; —**sake** tocayo *m*; —**tag** etiqueta de identificación *f*; — **of the game** lo esencial *m*; **to call someone —s** motejar a alguien; **to make a — for oneself** hacerse un nombre; **what is your —?** ¿cómo te llamas? VT nombrar; — **your price** haz una oferta

nameless [némlɪs] ADJ anónimo

namely [némli] ADV a saber, en concreto

Namibia [nəmíbiə] N Namibia *f*

Namibian [nəmíbiən] ADJ & N namibio -bia *mf*

nanny [næni] N niñera *f*

nanosecond [nænosɛkənd] N nanosegundo *m*

nanotechnology [nænotɛknálədʒi] N nanotecnología *f*

nap [næp] N (sleep) siesta *f*; (fibers) pelo *m*; **to take a —** echar/dormir una siesta; VI echar/dormir una siesta

napalm [népɑɫm] N napalm *m*
nape [nep] N nuca *f*
napkin [nǽpkɪn] N servilleta *f*
narcissism [nɑ́rsɪsɪzəm] N narcisismo *m*
narcissus [nɑrsísəs] N narciso *m*
narcolepsy [nɑ́rkələpsi] N narcolepsia *f*
narcotic [nɑrkɑ́dɪk] ADJ & N narcótico *m*,
   estupefaciente *m*
narcotrafficking [nɑrkotrǽfɪkɪŋ] N
   narcotráfico *m*
narrate [nǽret] VI/VT narrar
narration [nærésǝn] N narración *f*
narrative [nǽrǝdɪv] ADJ narrativo; N narrativa *f*
narrator [nǽredǝ-] N narrador -ora *mf*
narrow [nǽro] ADJ (of little width) estrecho,
   angosto; (limited in scope) limitado;
   (intolerant) intolerante; **to have a — escape**
   salvarse por poco; **— gauge** de vía angosta/
   estrecha; **—-minded** intolerante; N **—s**
   desfiladero *m*, estrecho *m*, angostura *f*; VI/VT
   angostar[se], estrechar[se]; **to — down**
   reducir
narrowness [nǽronɪs] N (quality of being
   narrow) estrechez *f*, angostura *f*
nasal [nézǝl] ADJ nasal
nastiness [nǽstɪnɪs] N (filth) suciedad *f*;
   (stinkiness) asquerosidad *f*; (rudeness,
   obscenity) grosería *f*
nasturtium [nǝstɨ̃-ʃǝm] N capuchina *f*
nasty [nǽsti] ADJ (mess) sucio; (smell)
   asqueroso; (comment) hiriente; (accident)
   feo; (word) grosero; (disposition) malo
natal [nédl̩] ADJ natal
nation [nésǝn] N nación *f*; ADJ **—wide** a escala
   nacional
national [nǽʃǝnl̩] ADJ nacional; **— park** parque
   nacional *m*; **— team** seleccionado nacional
   m; N ciudadano -na *mf*, nacional *mf*
nationalism [nǽʃǝnǝlɪzǝm] N nacionalismo *m*
nationalist [nǽʃǝnǝlɪst] N & ADJ nacionalista MF
nationality [nǽʃǝnǽlɪdi] N nacionalidad *f*;
   adjective of — gentilicio *m*
nationalize [nǽʃǝnǝlaɪz] VT nacionalizar
native [nédɪv] ADJ nativo; **— language** lengua
   nativa *f*; **— plants** flora nativa *f*; **my — Italy**
   mi Italia natal *f*; (innate) innato; N (person
   born in a place) natural *m*; (member of a tribal
   group) indígena *mf*, nativo -va *mf*; **he's a —
   of Italy** es oriundo de Italia
nativity [nǝtívɪdi] N nacimiento *m*; **— scene**
   pesebre *m*; **the —** la Natividad
NATO [North Atlantic Treaty Organization]
   [nédo] N OTAN *f*
natural [nǽtʃǝ-ǝl] ADJ natural; (inborn) innato;
   — childbirth parto natural *m*; **— gas** gas
   natural *m*; **— resources** recursos naturales
   m pl; **— selection** selección natural *f*; N
   (musical sign) becuadro *m*; **he is a — for
   that job** tiene aptitud natural para ese puesto

naturalist [nǽtʃǝ-ǝlɪst] N naturalista *mf*
naturalization [nǽtʃǝ-ǝlɪzésǝn] N
   naturalización *f*
naturalize [nǽtʃǝ-ǝlaɪz] VI/VT naturalizar[se]
naturally [nǽtʃǝ-ǝli] ADV (of course)
   naturalmente; **I have — curly hair** tengo
   rizos naturales
naturalness [nǽtʃǝ-ǝlnɪs] N naturalidad *f*
nature [nétʃǝ-] N naturaleza *f*; (disposition) genio
   m, natural *m*
naught [nɔt] N (zero) cero *m*; (nothing) nada *f*
naughtiness [nɔ́dɪnɪs] N travesuras *f pl*
naughty [nɔ́di] ADJ (child) travieso, pícaro,
   pillo; **— word** picardía *f*
Nauru [nɑúru] N Nauru *m*
Nauruan [nɑúrʊən] ADJ & N nauruano -na *mf*
nausea [nɔ́ziə] N náuseas *f pl*, mareo *m*
nauseate [nɔ́ziet] VT dar náuseas; **to be —d**
   tener náuseas
nauseating [nɔ́ziedɪŋ] ADJ nauseabundo,
   nauseoso
nauseous [nɔ́ʃəs] ADJ (feeling nausea) mareado,
   nauseoso; (causing nausea) nauseabundo,
   nauseoso
nautical [nɔ́dɪkǝl] ADJ náutico
naval [névǝl] ADJ naval; **— officer** oficial de
   marina *m*
Navarrese [nævǝríz] ADJ & N navarro -rra *mf*
nave [nev] N nave *f*
navel [névǝl] N ombligo *m*; **— orange** naranja
   de ombligo *f*
navigable [nǽvɪgǝbǝl] ADJ navegable
navigate [nǽvɪget] VI/VT navegar
navigation [nævɪgésǝn] N navegación *f*;
   (science) náutica *f*
navigator [nǽvɪgedǝ-] N navegante *mf*
navy [névi] N marina [de guerra] *f*, armada *f*; **—
   bean** judía blanca *f*; **— blue** azul marino *m*
nay [ne] N (refusal) no *m*; (negative vote) voto
   negativo *m*
Nazi [nɑ́tsi] N nazi *mf*
near [nir] ADV cerca; **— at hand** cerca, a la
   mano; **to come/go/draw —** acercarse; PREP
   cerca de; **— the end of the month** hacia
   fines del mes; **to be — death** estar a punto de
   morir; ADJ cercano, próximo; **— East**
   Cercano Oriente *m*, Oriente Próximo *m*;
   —sighted miope; **I had a — miss** por poco
   me sucede un accidente; VI/VT acercarse [a]
nearby [nírbáɪ] ADV cerca; ADJ cercano, próximo
nearly [nírli] ADV casi, cerca de; **I — did it** casi
   lo hago
nearness [nírnɪs] N cercanía *f*, proximidad *f*
neat [nit] ADJ (clean) limpio, pulcro; (ordered)
   ordenado; (cool) bueno
neatness [nítnɪs] N (cleanness) limpieza *f*,
   pulcritud *f*; (order) orden *m*
nebulous [nébjǝlǝs] ADJ nebuloso
nebulousness [nébjǝlǝsnɪs] N nubosidad *f*

necessary [nésɪseri] ADJ (needed) necesario; (involuntary) forzoso

necessitate [nəsésɪtet] VT requerir

necessity [nəsésɪDi] N necesidad *f*; **out of** — por necesidad

neck [nɛk] N (of a human) cuello *m*; (of an animal) pescuezo *m*; (of clothes) escote *m*; (throat) garganta *f*; — **and** — parejos; —**lace** collar *m*; —**line** escote *m*; — **of land** istmo *m*; —**tie** corbata *f*

necrology [nəkrálədʒi] N necrología *f*

necrosis [nəkrósɪs] N necrosis *f*

nectar [néktɚ] N néctar *m*

nectarine [nɛktərín] N nectarina *f*

need [nid] N (lack) necesidad *f*; (poverty) carencia *f*; **in** — en aprietos; **if** — **be** en caso de necesidad; VT necesitar, precisar; **you** — **to come at four** tienes que venir a las cuatro

needle [nídl̩] N aguja *f*; —**point** bordado *m*; —**work** (embroidery) bordado *m*; (sewing) costura *f*; VT pinchar

needless [nídlɪs] ADJ innecesario; — **to say** huelga decir

needy [nídi] ADJ necesitado, menesteroso

ne'er-do-well [nérduwɛl] N inútil *mf*

negate [nɪgét] VT negar

negation [nɪgéʃən] N negación *f*

negative [négəDɪv] ADJ negativo; **the search proved** — la búsqueda no dio resultado; N negativa *f*; (photographic) negativo *m*; **this plan has one** — este plan tiene una contra; INTERJ ¡negativo!

neglect [nɪglékt] VT (fail to heed) postergar; (fail to care for) descuidar; (fail to carry out) desatender; **you're** —**ing your friends** tienes abandonados a tus amigos; **to** — **to** olvidarse de; N negligencia *f*, descuido *m*

neglectful [nɪgléktfəl] ADJ negligente, descuidado

negligence [néglɪdʒəns] N negligencia *f*

negligent [néglɪdʒənt] ADJ negligente, descuidado

negligible [néglɪdʒəbəl] ADJ despreciable, minúsculo

negotiate [nɪgóʃiet] VI/VT (a contract) negociar, gestionar; (an obstacle) salvar

negotiating [nɪgóʃieDɪŋ] ADJ negociador

negotiation [nɪgoʃiéʃən] N negociación *f*, gestión *f*

negotiator [nɪgóʃieDɚ] N negociador -ora *mf*

Negro [nígro] ADJ & N negro -gra *mf*

neigh [ne] N relincho *m*; VI relinchar

neighbor [nébɚ] N (person who lives near) vecino -na *mf*; (fellow human) prójimo -ma *mf*; ADJ vecino; VI **to** — **with** lindar con

neighborhood [nébɚhʊd] N vecindario *m*, barrio *m*; **in the** — **of a hundred dollars** alrededor de cien dólares

neighboring [nébərɪŋ] ADJ vecino, colindante

neither [níðɚ] PRON ninguno de los dos, ni [el] uno ni [el] otro; — **of the two** ninguno de los dos; ADJ ninguno de los dos; — **one of us** ninguno de nosotros dos; CONJ ni; — **hot nor cold** ni caliente ni frío; — **will I** yo tampoco

nemesis [némɪsɪs] N némesis *f*

neologism [niálədʒɪzəm] N neologismo *m*

neon [nían] N neón *m*

neonatal [nionédl] ADJ neonatal

Nepal [nəpɔ́l] N Nepal *m*

Nepali [nəpóli] ADJ & N nepalés -esa *mf*, nepalí *mf*

nephew [néfju] N sobrino *m*

nephritis [nəfráɪDɪs] N nefritis *f*

nepotism [népətɪzəm] N nepotismo *m*

nerd [nɚd] N (technological adept) persona aficionada a las computadoras / los ordenadores *f*; (socially inept person) persona socialmente inepta *f*

nerve [nɚv] N (anatomy) nervio *m*; (courage) valor *m*; (impertinence) descaro *m*, morro *m*; — **cell** neurona *f*; — **gas** gas nervioso *m*; —- **[w]racking** angustiante; **he gets on my** —**s** me saca de quicio

nervous [nɚ́vəs] ADJ nervioso; — **breakdown** ataque de nervios *m*

nervousness [nɚ́vəsnɪs] N nerviosismo *m*

nest [nɛst] N nido *m*; (brood) nidada *f*; — **egg** ahorros *m pl*; — **of thieves** guarida de ladrones *f*; VI/VT anidar; (fit together) encajarse

nestle [nésəl] VI acurrucarse; VT apoyar, recostar

net [nɛt] N (fishing, network, tennis) red *f*; (in hair) redecilla *f*; —**work** red *f*; —**working** (social) relaciones profesionales *f pl*; (computer) diseño de redes y comunicaciones *m*; VT (catch a fish) pescar con red; (cover with a net) cubrir con una red; (catch a criminal) atrapar; (hit the tennis net) dar en la red; (make money after expenses) producir/ganar neto; ADJ neto; — **price** precio neto *m*; — **profit** ganancia neta *f*; — **assets** activo neto *m*; — **income** ingreso neto *m*; — **worth** patrimonio neto *m*

Netherlander [néðɚləndɚ] N holandés -esa *mf*

Netherlands [néðɚləndz] N Países Bajos *m pl*

nettle [nédl] N ortiga *f*

neural [núrəl] ADJ neural

neuralgia [nʊrǽldʒə] N neuralgia *f*

neurasthenia [nʊrəsθíniə] N neurastenia *f*

neurologist [nʊrálədʒɪst] N neurólogo -ga *mf*

neuron [núran] N neurona *f*

neurosis [nʊrósɪs] N neurosis *f*

neurosurgeon [nʊrosɚ́dʒən] N neurocirujano -na *mf*

neurosurgery [nʊrosɚ́dʒəri] N neurocirugía *f*

neurotic [nʊráDɪk] ADJ & N neurótico -ca *mf*

neurotransmitter [nʊrotrǽnzmɪDɚ] N neurotransmisor *m*

neuter [núDɚ] ADJ neutro; VT castrar

neutral [nútrəł] ADJ neutral, imparcial; (of colors) neutro; N punto muerto *m*
neutrality [nutrǽlɪDi] N neutralidad *f*
neutralize [nútrəlaɪz] VI/VT neutralizar[se]
neutron [nútrɑn] N neutrón *m*; — **bomb** bomba de neutrones *f*
never [névɚ] ADV nunca, jamás; — **mind** no te preocupes; **this will** — **do** esto no va a funcionar; —-**ending** interminable
nevertheless [nɛvɚðəlés] ADV & CONJ sin embargo, no obstante
new [nu] ADJ (not old) nuevo; (fresh) otro; **a** — **sheet of paper** otra hoja de papel; — **age** [**music**] [música] nueva era *f*; —**born baby** recién nacido -da *mf*; —**comer** recién llegado -da *mf*; —**fangled** moderno, recién inventado; —**found** nuevo; — **year** año nuevo *m*; — **Year's Eve** fin de año *m*; *Sp* nochevieja *f*
newly [núli] ADV recientemente; — **arrived** recién llegado; —**wed** recién casado
newness [núnɪs] N novedad *f*
news [nuz] N (item) noticias *f pl*; (latest gossip) novedades *f pl*; (newspaper) periódico *m*; **it is** — **to me** recién me entero; — **broadcast/ bulletin** noticiero *m*, noticiario *m*; —**cast** noticiero *m*, noticiario *m*, informativo *m*; — **clipping** recorte de diario *m*; —**letter** boletín informativo *m*; —**paper** periódico *m*, diario *m*; —**print** papel de periódico *m*; —**room** sala de redacción *f*; —**stand** quiosco *m*; **piece of** — noticia *f*; ADJ —**worthy** de interés periodístico
newt [nut] N tritón *m*
New Zealand [nuzílənd] N Nueva Zelanda *f*
New Zealander [nuzíləndɚ] N neozelandés -esa *mf*
next [nɛkst] ADJ (future) próximo, entrante; (following) siguiente; (contiguous) contiguo, de al lado; —-**door** de al lado; **who's** —? ¿quién sigue? ADV después, luego; — **best** segundo en calidad; **when** — **we meet** cuando nos volvamos a ver; PREP — **of kin** familiares *m pl*; — **to** junto a, al lado de
nibble [níbəł] VI/VT (bite) mordiscar, mordisquear; (eat) picotear; (of fish) picar; N (bite) mordisco *m*; (act of nibbling) mordisqueo *m*
Nicaragua [nɪkərágwə] N Nicaragua *f*
Nicaraguan [nɪkərágwən] ADJ & N nicaragüense *mf*
nice [naɪs] ADJ (kind) amable, simpático; (agreeable) *Am* lindo, *Sp* majo; **it's** — **and hot** está bien calentito
nicety [náɪsɪDi] N (subtlety) sutileza *f*; (detail) detalle *m*
niche [nɪtʃ] N (also environmental) nicho *m*; — **marketing** mercadeo de nicho *m*; **I've found my** — he encontrado mi lugar

nick [nɪk] N (chip) muesca *f*; (cut) corte *m*; **in the** — **of time** justo a tiempo; VT (chip) hacer muescas; (cut) cortar; —**name** apodo *m*, mote *m*, sobrenombre *m*; **to** —**name** apodar
nickel [níkəł] N (metal) níquel *m*; (coin) moneda de cinco centavos *f*; —-**plated** niquelado
nicotine [níkətin] N nicotina *f*
niece [nis] N sobrina *f*
Niger [náɪdʒɚ] N Níger *m*
Nigeria [naɪdʒíriə] N Nigeria *f*
Nigerian [naɪdʒíriən] ADJ & N nigeriano -na *mf*
Nigerien [naɪdʒírien] ADJ & N nigerino -na *mf*
niggardly [nígɚdli] ADJ mezquino
nigger [nígɚ] N *highly offensive* negro -gra de mierda *mf*
night [naɪt] N noche *f*; ADJ nocturno, de noche; —**club** club nocturno *m*; —**fall** anochecer *m*, atardecer *m*; —**gown** camisón *m*; —**life** vida nocturna *f*; *Sp* marcha *f*; —**light** lamparilla *f*; —**mare** pesadilla *f*; — **owl** trasnochador -ora *mf*; — **shift** turno de la noche *m*; —**stand** veladora *f*, mesilla de noche *f*; —**time** noche *f*; — **watchman** celador *m*
nightingale [náɪtŋgeł] N ruiseñor *m*
nightly [náɪtli] ADV todas las noches; ADJ nocturno
nihilism [náɪəlɪzəm] N nihilismo *m*
nil [nɪł] ADJ nulo
nimble [nímbəł] ADJ ágil
nincompoop [nínkəmpup] N *fam* tarambana *mf*, bobalicón -ona *mf*
nine [naɪn] NUM nueve; — **hundred** novecientos
nineteen [naɪntín] NUM diecinueve
ninety [náɪnti] NUM noventa
ninth [náɪnθ] ADJ & N noveno *m*
nip [nɪp] VT (pinch) pellizcar; (bite) mordiscar, mordisquear; (cause frostbite) helar; **to** — **in the bud** cortar de raíz; **to** — **off** despuntar; VI (drink in sips) dar sorbitos; N (pinch) pellizco *m*; (bite) mordisco *m*; (sip) traguito *m*, sorbito *m*; (cold) frío *m*; **it's going to be** — **and tuck** va a ser muy reñido
nipple [nípəł] N (on female breast) pezón *m*; (on male breast) tetilla *f*; (on bottle) tetina *f*
nitpick [nítpɪk] VI criticar detalles insignificantes
nitrate [náɪtret] N nitrato *m*
nitric acid [náɪtrɪkǽsɪd] N ácido nítrico *m*
nitrogen [náɪtrədʒən] N nitrógeno *m*
nitroglycerin [naɪtroglísɚɪn] N nitroglicerina *f*
nitty-gritty [níDigríDi] N **to get down to the** — ir al grano
no [no] ADV no; — **longer** ya no; — **man's land** tierra de nadie *f*; — **matter how much** por mucho que; — **one** ninguno, nadie; — **smoking** se prohíbe fumar; —**where** (location) en ninguna parte / ningún lado; (direction) a ninguna parte / ningún lado; **he**

was a —-show no se presentó; **a —-win
situation** una situación insoluble; **there is
— more** no hay más; ADJ ningun[o]; **I have
— friends** no tengo amigos; **it's a —-
brainer** la respuesta es obvia; **— friend of
mine will go hungry** ningún amigo mío
pasará hambre; **of — use** inútil; N (refusal)
no *m*; (negative vote) voto negativo *m*; ADJ —-
frills básico, sin lujos
nobility [nobílIDi] N nobleza *f*, hidalguía *f*
noble [nóbəl] ADJ & N noble *mf*; **—man**
hidalgo *m*
nobody [nóbaDi] PRON nadie, ninguno; N don
nadie, pelagatos *mf sg*
nocturnal [nɑktɨ̃·nl̩] ADJ nocturno
nod [nɑd] VI/VT (signal affirmation) asentir con
la cabeza; VI (doze) cabecear, dar cabezadas;
to — off dormirse; N (as signal) inclinación
de cabeza *f*, saludo con la cabeza *m*; (from
sleepiness) cabezada *f*
node [nod] N (of cells) nódulo *m*; (in plants) nudo
m; (in physics) nodo *m*
noise [nɔɪz] N ruido *m*; **— pollution**
contaminación sonora *f*; VI **it is being —d
about that** corre el rumor que
noiseless [nɔ́ɪzlɪs] ADJ silencioso
noisy [nɔ́ɪzi] ADJ ruidoso
nomad [nómæd] N nómada *mf*
nomenclature [nómɪnkletʃɚ] N nomenclatura *f*
nominal [námənl̩] ADJ nominal
nominate [námənet] VT nominar
nomination [nɑmənéʃən] N nominación *f*
nominee [nɑməní] N candidato -ta *mf*
nonchalant [nɑnʃəlánt] ADJ despreocupado
noncollectible [nɑnkəléktəbəl] ADJ incobrable
noncommercial [nɑnkəmɨ̃·ʃəl] ADJ no
comercial
noncommissioned officer [nɑnkəmíʃənd
ɔ́fɪsɚ] N suboficial *m*
nonconforming [nɑnkənfɔ́rmɪŋ] ADJ no
conforme
nonconformist [nɑnkənfɔ́rmɪst] ADJ & N
incomformista *mf*
none [nʌn] PRON ninguno; **I want — of that** no
me quiero meter en eso; **that is — of your
business** no es asunto tuyo; ADV **— too
soon** al último momento; **—theless** sin
embargo
nonentity [nɑnéntɪDi] N nulidad *f*
nonessential [nɑnɪsénʃəl] ADJ no esencial
nonexistent [nɑnɪgzístənt] ADJ inexistente
nonfiction [nɑnfíkʃən] N no ficción *f*
nongovernmental [nɑngʌvɚnméntl̩] ADJ no
gubernamental
nonnegotiable [nɑnnɪgóʃəbəl] ADJ no
negociable
nonpartisan [nɑnpárDɪzən] ADJ (neutral)
imparcial; (not affiliated) sin afiliación
política

nonperformance [nɑnpɚfɔ́rməns] N
incumplimiento *m*
nonproductive [nɑnprədʌ́ktɪv] ADJ
improductivo
nonprofit [nɑnpráfɪt] ADJ sin fines de lucro; N
organización sin fines de lucro *f*
nonrefundable [nɑnrɪfʌ́ndəbəl] ADJ no
reembolsable
nonresident [nɑnrézɪdənt] ADJ & N no residente
mf
nonsense [nánsɛns] N tonterías *f pl*, monsergas *f
pl*, estupideces *f pl*; **to talk —** decir
barbaridades/disparates
nonstop [nánstáp] ADJ sin escala, directo; ADV
sin parar
nontaxable [nɑntǽksəbəl] ADJ no tributable
nonvoting [nɑnvóDɪŋ] ADJ sin derecho a voto
noodle [núdl̩] N fideo *m*, tallarín *m*
nook [nʊk] N rincón *m*
noon [nun] N mediodía *m*; **— hour** mediodía *m*,
hora de comer; **—time** mediodía *m*
noose [nus] N soga *f*, lazo *m*; **with a — around
his neck** con la soga al cuello; VT (catch with
a rope) enlazar; (make a loop in) hacer un lazo
corredizo en
nope [nop] ADV no
nor [nɔr] CONJ ni; **we have neither eggs —
flour** no tenemos ni huevos ni harina
Nordic [nɔ́rDɪk] ADJ nórdico
norm [nɔrm] N norma *f*, normativa *f*
normal [nɔ́rməl] ADJ normal; (perpendicular)
normal; **to return to —** volver a la
normalidad; (perpendicular line) línea
perpendicular *f*
normalcy [nɔ́rməlsi] N normalidad *f*
normality [nɔrmǽlɪDi] N normalidad *f*
normalize [nɔ́rməlaɪz] VI/VT normalizar[se]
normally [nɔ́rməli] ADV (in a normal way) de
manera normal, con toda normalidad *f*;
(usually) normalmente
north [nɔrθ] N norte *m*; **—east** noreste, hacia el
noreste; **—west** noroeste *m*, hacia el
noroeste; ADJ (in the north) norte, norteño;
(from the north) del norte; **— America**
América del Norte *f*; **— American**
norteamericano -na *mf*; **—eastern** del
noreste; **— Korea** Corea del Norte *f*; **—
Korean** norcoreano -na; **— Pole** Polo Norte
m; **— wind** cierzo *m*, viento norte *m*; **the —
entrance** la entrada norte; ADV al norte,
hacia el norte
northern [nɔ́rðɚn] ADJ del norte; (from the
north) norteño; (in the north) septentrional;
— lights aurora boreal *f*
northerner [nɔ́rðɚnɚ] N norteño -ña *mf*
northward [nɔ́rθwɚd] ADV hacia el norte
Norway [nɔ́rwe] N Noruega *f*
Norwegian [nɔrwídʒən] ADJ & N noruego -ga *mf*
nose [noz] N nariz *f*; (of an airplane) morro *m*; (of

an animal) hocico *m*; (perspicacity) olfato *m*;
—**bleed** hemorragia nasal *f*; —**dive** caída en
picado *f*; — **job** rinoplastia *f*; **keep your** —
clean no te metas en líos; **on the** —
exactamente; **to pick one's** — hurgarse las
narices; VI/VT (move forward) entrar de
punta; (muzzle) hocicar; **to** — **around**
husmear
nostalgia [nɑstǽɫdʒə] N nostalgia *f*
nostalgic [nɑstǽɫdʒɪk] ADJ nostálgico
nostrils [nástrəlz] N narices *f pl*, ventanillas de la
nariz *f pl*
nosy, nosey [nózi] ADJ entrometido
not [nɑt] ADV no; **I'm** — **your friend** no soy tu
amigo; — **at all** (no way) de ningún modo;
(you're welcome) de nada; — **at all sure**
nada seguro; — **even a word** ni una palabra
notable [nódəbəɫ] ADJ notable, destacable
notably [nódəbli] ADV notablemente
notarize [nódəraɪz] VT notariar
notary [nódəri] N notario -ria *mf*; — **public**
notario -ria público -ca *mf*
notation [notéʃən] N (system of signs) notación
f; (act of writing) anotación *f*; (short note)
anotación *f*, apunte *m*
notch [nɑtʃ] N (nick) muesca *f*, mella *f*; (degree)
grado *m*; **a** — **above the rest** mejor que los
demás; VT hacer una muesca; **he** —**ed**
another win se anotó otra victoria
note [not] N (written) nota *f*, anotación *f*;
(musical) nota *f*; (touch) toque *m*; (financial)
pagaré *m*; (currency) billete *m*; —**book**
cuaderno *m*; (small) libreta *f*; —**s** apuntes *m*
pl; **of** — de renombre / de nota; **to take** — **of**
notar; ADJ —**worthy** notable; VT (notice)
notar; (write down) anotar, apuntar
noted [nódɪd] ADJ célebre
nothing [nʌ́θɪŋ] PRON nada; (score) cero, nada;
N (insignificant person) don nadie *m*;
(insignificant thing) nadería *f*; — **to it** no
tiene ciencia; ADV **it was** — **like that** no fue
así para nada; **we did it for** — (free) lo
hicimos gratis; (fruitlessly) lo hicimos en
balde
notice [nódɪs] N (information) aviso *m*;
(warning) advertencia *f*; (attention) atención
f; **a week's** — una semana de plazo; **to give**
— renunciar; **to take** — hacer caso; VT
(perceive) notar, advertir, percatarse [de];
(pay attention to) fijarse [en], reparar [en]
noticeable [nódɪsəbəɫ] ADJ perceptible,
apreciable
noticeably [nódɪsəbli] ADV notablemente
notification [nodəfɪkéʃən] N notificación *f*
notify [nódəfaɪ] VT notificar
notion [nóʃən] N noción *f*, idea *f*; (whim)
capricho *m*; —**s** mercería *f*
notorious [notóriəs] ADJ de mala fama; **he's a** —
liar tiene fama de mentiroso

nougat [núgət] N turrón *m*
noun [naʊn] N sustantivo *m*
nourish [nɝ́ɪʃ] VT (a person) nutrir, alimentar; (a
hope) abrigar
nourishing [nɝ́ɪʃɪŋ] ADJ nutritivo
nourishment [nɝ́ɪʃmənt] N (food) alimento *m*;
(act of nourishing) alimentación *f*
novel [návəɫ] N novela *f*; ADJ novedoso
novelist [návəlɪst] N novelista *mf*
novelty [návəɫti] N novedad *f*; **the** — **soon**
wore off se pasó la novedad; **novelties**
chucherías *f pl*
November [novémbɝ] N noviembre *m*
novice [návɪs] N novato -ta *mf*, pipiolo -la *mf*;
(religious) novicio -cia *mf*
novocaine [nóvəken] N novocaína *f*
now [naʊ] ADV ahora; — **and then** de vez en
cuando; — **that** ahora que; **he left just** —
salió hace poco, recién salió; —, —, **calm**
down! bueno, bueno, ¡cálmate!
nowadays [náʊədez] ADV hoy [en] día
noxious [nákʃəs] ADJ nocivo
nuance [núɑns] N matiz *m*
nuclear [núkliɝ] ADJ nuclear; — **energy**
energía nuclear *f*; — **family** familia nuclear
f; — **fission** fisión nuclear *f*; — **fusion**
fusión nuclear *f*; — **physics** física nuclear *f*;
— **weapon** arma nuclear *f*
nucleus [núkliəs] N núcleo *m*
nude [nud] ADJ & N desnudo *m*
nudge [nʌdʒ] VI/VT codear; N golpe suave con el
codo *m*
nugget [nʌ́gɪt] N (of gold) pepita *f*; (of chicken)
pedacito *m*; (of wisdom) perla *f*
nuisance [núsəns] N molestia *f*; Sp pesadez *f*;
(legal) perjuicio *m*; **you're such a** —!
¡qué pesado eres tú! — **tax** impuesto de
consumo *m*
nuke [nuk] N arma nuclear *f*; VT (bomb)
bombardear con armas nucleares; (cook)
calentar en microondas
null [nʌɫ] ADJ nulo; — **and void** nulo
nullify [nʌ́ləfaɪ] VT anular
numb [nʌm] ADJ entumecido; **to get** —
entumecerse; VT entumecer
number [nʌ́mbɝ] N número *m*; — **one** uno
mismo *m*; —**crunching** procesamiento de
datos numéricos complejos *m*; VI (total)
ascender a; **I** — **him among my friends** lo
cuento entre mis amigos; VT numerar
numberless [nʌ́mbɝlɪs] ADJ sin número
numbskull, numskull [nʌ́mskʌl] N zopenco
-ca *mf*
numeral [númərəɫ] N número *m*; ADJ numeral
numerical [numérɪkəɫ] ADJ numérico
numerous [númərəs] ADJ numeroso
nun [nʌn] N monja *f*, religiosa *f*
nuptial [nʌ́pʃəɫ] ADJ nupcial; N —**s** nupcias *f pl*
nurse [nɝs] N (for the sick) enfermero -ra *mf*;

(for children) niñera *f*; VT (give milk) amamantar, lactar; (tend to a sick person) cuidar; **to — a grudge** guardar rencor; **to — a cup of coffee** tomar una taza de café a sorbitos; **to — a cold** cuidarse durante un resfrío; VI (drink milk) mamar

nursery [nɜ́˞sri] N (children's room) cuarto para niños *m*; (day-care center) guardería *f*; (place for growing plants) almáciga *f*, vivero *m*, plantel *m*; **— rhyme** canción infantil *f*, ronda *f*; **— school** preescolar *m*; *Sp* parvulario *m*; *Am* jardín infantil *m*

nursing [nɜ́˞sɪŋ] N (profession) enfermería *f*; (care) cuidado *m*; **— home** (for old people) hogar de ancianos *m*; (for sick people) casa de salud *f*

nurture [nɜ́˞tʃə˞] VT (rear) criar; (feed) nutrir, alimentar; (encourage) fomentar; N (rearing) crianza *f*; (feeding) alimentación *f*

nut [nʌt] N (fruit) fruto seco *m*; (device) tuerca *f*; (person) excéntrico -ca *mf*; **—cracker** cascanueces *m sg*; **—meg** nuez moscada *f*; **—s** *vulg* cojones *m pl*; ADJ crazy; **—s and bolts** los fundamentos; **—shell** cáscara de fruto seco *f*; **in a —shell** en pocas palabras

nutrient [nútriənt] N nutriente *m*

nutrition [nutríʃən] N nutrición *f*, alimentación *f*

nutritious [nutríʃəs] ADJ nutritivo, alimenticio

nylon [náilɑn] N nilón *m*, nailon *m*

Oo

oak [ok] N roble *m*, encina *f*; **— grove** robledal *m*

oar [ɔr] N remo *m*; VI/VT remar, bogar; **—lock** tolete *m*

OAS [Organization of American States] [óéés] N OEA *f*

oasis [oésɪs] N oasis *m*

oat [ot] N avena *f*; **—meal** (flour) harina de avena *f*; (breakfast food) gachas de avena *f pl*; **—s** avena *f*

oath [oθ] N (pledge) juramento *m*; (curse) maldición *f*; (swear word) palabrota *f*, taco *m*; **to take an —** prestar juramento

obedience [obídiəns] N obediencia *f*

obedient [obídiənt] ADJ obediente

obese [obís] ADJ obeso

obesity [obísɪDi] N obesidad *f*

obey [obé] VI/VT obedecer

obituary [obítʃuɛri] N nota necrológica *f*, obituario *m*

object¹ [ábdʒɪkt] N objeto *m*; (of a verb) complemento *m*

object² [əbdʒékt] VI/VT objetar

objection [əbdʒékʃən] N objeción *f*

objectionable [əbdʒékʃənəbəɫ] ADJ objetable

objective [əbdʒéktɪv] ADJ objetivo; N objetivo *m*, finalidad *f*

objectivity [abdʒɛktívɪDi] N objetividad *f*

obligate [áblɪget] VT obligar

obligated [áblɪgeDɪd] ADJ obligado, comprometido

obligation [ablɪgéʃən] N obligación *f*; **under no — to buy** sin compromiso de compra

obligatory [əblígətɔri] ADJ obligatorio, obligado

oblige [əbláidʒ] VT (make obliged) obligar; VI/VT (do a favor for) complacer; VI (obey an order) obedecer; **much —d!** ¡muchas gracias! ¡muy agradecido!

obliging [əbláidʒɪŋ] ADJ complaciente; *Am* comedido

oblique [oblík] ADJ oblicuo

obliterate [əblíDəret] VT (blot out) tachar; (destroy) arrasar, destruir

oblivion [əblíviən] N olvido *m*

oblivious [əblíviəs] ADJ inconsciente; **— to the danger** ajeno al peligro

obnoxious [əbnákʃəs] ADJ (remark, behavior) ofensivo; (person) odioso

oboe [óbo] N oboe *m*

obscene [əbsín] ADJ obsceno; **his salary is —** lo que gana es escandaloso

obscenity [əbsénɪDi] N obscenidad *f*

obscure [əbskjúr] ADJ oscuro; VT oscurecer

obscurity [əbskjúrɪDi] N oscuridad *f*

obsequious [əbsíkwiəs] ADJ obsequioso

observance [əbzɜ́˞vəns] N observancia *f*

observant [əbzɜ́˞vənt] ADJ observador

observation [abzə˞véʃən] N observación *f*

observatory [əbzɜ́˞vətɔri] N observatorio *m*

observe [əbzɜ́˞v] VT observar; (holidays, rituals) guardar

observer [əbzɜ́˞və˞] N observador -ora *mf*; (of elections) interventor -ora *mf*

obsess [əbsés] VI/VT obsesionar[se]; **he's —ing over it** está obsesionado con eso

obsession [əbséʃən] N obsesión *f*

obsessive-compulsive [əbsésɪvkəmpʌ́ɫsɪv] ADJ obsesivo-compulsivo

obsolescence [absəlésəns] N desuso *m*

obsolete [absəlít] ADJ anticuado, desusado

obstacle [ábstəkəɫ] N obstáculo *m*

obstetrician [abstətríʃən] N obstetra *mf*

obstetrics [abstétrɪks] N obstetricia *f*

obstinacy [ábstənəsi] N obstinación *f*, terquedad *f*, porfía *f*

obstinate [ábstənɪt] ADJ obstinado, terco, recalcitrante; **to be —** obstinarse

obstruct [əbstrákt] VI/VT obstruir; (traffic) atascar, obstruir

obstruction [əbstrákʃən] N obstrucción *f*

obtain [əbtén] VT obtener, procurar; VI prevalecer

obtainable [əbténəbəɫ] ADJ conseguible

obviate [ábviet] VT obviar

obvious [ábviəs] ADJ obvio, evidente

obviously [ábviəsli] ADV & INTERJ evidentemente, obviamente

occasion [əkéʒən] N (moment) ocasión f; (chance) oportunidad f, ocasión f; (cause) motivo m; (event) acontecimiento m, ocasión f; VT ocasionar

occasional [əkéʒənḷ] ADJ ocasional

occasionally [əkéʒənḷi] ADV de vez en cuando, ocasionalmente

occidental [aksɪdéntḷ] ADJ & N occidental mf

occlusion [əklúʒən] N obstrucción f, oclusión f

occult [əkÁłt] ADJ oculto; N ocultismo m, ciencias ocultas f pl; VT ocultar

occupancy [ákjəpənsi] N ocupación f; — **rate** tasa de ocupación f

occupant [ákjəpənt] N ocupante mf

occupation [akjəpéʃən] N ocupación f

occupational [akjəpéʃənḷ] ADJ ocupacional; — **hazard/risk** riesgo ocupacional m; — **therapy** laborterapia f, terapia ocupacional f

occupy [ákjəpaɪ] VI/VT ocupar

occur [əkɚ] VI ocurrir, suceder; **it —red to me** se me ocurrió

occurrence [əkɚəns] N suceso m, acontecimiento m

ocean [óʃən] N océano m

oceanic [oʃiǽnɪk] ADJ oceánico

oceanography [oʃənágrəfi] N oceanografía f

ocelot [ásəlat] N ocelote m

o'clock [əklák] ADV **it is one** — es la una; **it is two** — son las dos

octagon [áktəgan] N octágono m, octógono m

octane [ákten] N octano m

octave [áktɪv] N octava f

October [aktóbɚ] N octubre m

octopus [áktəpəs] N pulpo m

oculist [ákjəlɪst] N oculista mf

OD [overdose] [ódí] N sobredosis f; VI tomar una sobredosis

odd [ad] ADJ (unusual) extraño; (not even) impar, non; —**ball** excéntrico -ca mf; — **change** suelto m, cambio m; — **job** trabajo ocasional m; — **shoe** zapato sin compañero m; ADV **thirty-** — treinta y tantos

oddity [ádɪti] N rareza f; (person) excéntrico -ca mf

odds [adz] N (probabilities) probabilidades f pl; — **and ends** cachivaches m pl; **the — are against me** llevo las de perder; **to be at —** estar en desacuerdo; ADJ —**-on favorite** favorito m

ode [od] N oda f

odious [ódiəs] ADJ odioso

odor [ódɚ] N olor m; (bad) hedor m

odorless [ódɚlɪs] ADJ inodoro

odorous [ódɚəs] ADJ oloroso

of [ʌv] PREP de; — **course** por supuesto, desde

luego; **a quarter — five** las cinco menos cuarto; **doctor — medicine** doctor -ora en medicina mf; **the smell — paint** el olor a pintura; **a friend — mine** un amigo mío

off [ɔf] ADV — **and on** de vez en cuando; — **the record** extraoficialmente; **ten cents —** rebaja de diez centavos f; **ten miles —** a diez millas de distancia; **to take a day —** tomarse un día libre; ADJ — **chance** posibilidad remota f; —**-color** verde; — **season** temporada baja f; — **year** de producción decreciente; **our deal is —** se canceló nuestro plan; **prices are —** los precios han caído; **you're — by a mile** estás equivocadísimo; **he's a little —** está tocadito; **with his hat —** sin el sombrero; **the electricity is —** está apagada la electricidad; **to be — to war** haberse ido a la guerra; **to be well —** tener mucho dinero; PREP — **course** fuera de curso; **he drove — the road** se salió de la carretera; **I bought it — a gypsy** se lo compré a un gitano; **he's — playing golf** se fue a jugar al golf; VT liquidar

off-duty [ɔfdúɖi] ADJ **to be —** no estar de turno

offend [əfɛ́nd] VI/VT (insult) ofender, afrentar; (affect disagreeably) desagradar

offender [əfɛ́ndɚ] N delincuente mf

offense[1] [əfɛ́ns] N (sin, insult) ofensa f; (misdemeanor) delito m; **no — was meant** no te lo tomes a mal

offense[2] [áfɛns] (in sports) ofensiva f

offensive [əfɛ́nsɪv] ADJ ofensivo; — **line** línea ofensiva f; — **series** serie ofensiva f, ataque m; N ofensiva f

offer [ɔ́fɚ] VT ofrecer; **to — to** ofrecerse a; N oferta f; **make an —** hacer una oferta

offering [ɔ́fɚɪŋ] N (thing given in worship) ofrenda f; (thing presented for sale) oferta f; (action of offering) ofrecimiento m

offhand [ɔ́fhǽnd] ADV **he remarked —** mencionó al descuido; ADJ **an — remark** un comentario descuidado

office [ɔ́fɪs] N (function) cargo m, función f; (place) oficina f, despacho m; (headquarters) oficinas f pl; — **boy** mandadero de oficina m; — **building** edificio para oficinas m; — **suite** (furniture) juego ofimático m; (rooms) suite f; (software) paquete de programas de productividad m; **through the —s of** por la intervención de

officer [ɔ́fɪsɚ] N (military) oficial m; (police) agente de policía mf; (of an organization) directivo -va mf

official [əfíʃəl] ADJ oficial; N funcionario -ria mf

officiate [əfíʃiet] VI oficiar; (in sports) arbitrar

officious [əfíʃəs] ADJ oficioso

off-key [ɔfkí] ADJ desafinado

off-limits [ɔflímɪts] ADJ vedado, de acceso

prohibido

off-line [ɔfláɪn] ADV fuera de línea

off-season [ɔfsizən] N temporada baja *f;* ADJ de temporada baja

offset[1] [ɔfsɛt] N offset *m*

offset[2] [ɔfsɛt, ɔfsét] VT compensar

offshore [ɔfʃɔ́r] ADJ & ADV cerca de la costa; — **account** cuenta en un paraíso fiscal *f;* — **drilling** explotación petrolífera en el fondo del mar *f*

offside [ɔfsáɪd] ADV fuera de juego

offspring [ɔfsprɪŋ] N prole *m*

offstage [ɔfstédʒ] ADV & ADJ entre bastidores, fuera de escena

off-the-record [ɔfθərékəd] ADJ oficioso

often [ɔfən] ADV a menudo; **how**—? ¿con qué frecuencia? ¿cada cuánto?

ogre [ógə] N ogro *m*

oh [o] INTERJ — **no!** ¡ay no! — **really?** ¿de veras? — **well** está bien, vale; — **yeah?** (not true) ¡qué va! (really?) ¿de veras?

ohm [om] N ohmio *m*

oil [ɔɪl] N (for cars, cooking) aceite *m;* (crude) petróleo *m;* —**can** alcuza *f,* aceitera *f;* —**cloth** hule *m,* tela de hule *f;* — **factory** aceitera *f;* — **field** campo petrolífero *m;* — **industry** industria petrolera *f;* — **lamp** quinqué *m;* — **painting** pintura al óleo *f,* óleo *m;* — **pan** cárter *m;* — **pipeline** oleoducto *m;* — **rig** plataforma petrolífera *f;* — **slick** mancha de petróleo *f;* — **spill** vertido de petróleo *m;* — **tanker** barco petrolero *m;* — **well** pozo de petróleo *m;* ADJ —-**bearing** petrolífero; —- **exporting** exportador de petróleo; —- **producing** petrolífero; VT (apply oil) aceitar; (bribe) untar

oily [ɔɪli] ADJ (food) aceitoso; (liquid) oleoso; (hair) graso; (person) untuoso

oink [ɔɪŋk] VI gruñir; N gruñido *m*

ointment [ɔɪntmənt] N ungüento *m*

OK/okay [oké] ADJ bueno; **he's an** — **guy** es un buen tipo; **his work is just** — su trabajo no es nada del otro mundo; ADV bien; **it's** — (fine) está bien; (adequate) es regular; N **to give one's** — dar el visto bueno; VT dar el visto bueno, aprobar; INTERJ bien, *Sp* vale

okra [ókrə] N quingombó *m*

old [old] ADJ viejo; (objects only) antiguo; (wine) añejo; — **age** vejez *f,* ancianidad *f;* —-**boy network** red favoritista entre hombres *f;* —- **fashioned** (unfashionable) pasado de moda; (antiquated) anticuado; (morally prudish) chapado a la antigua; — **fogey** carcamal *m,* carca *m;* — **hat** pasado de moda; — **maid** solterona *f;* —-**time** antiguo, viejo; —- **timer** (longtime member) miembro de la vieja guardia *m;* (oldster) viejo *m;* — **wives' tale** superstición *f;* — **world** viejo mundo *m;* **days of** — antaño; **how** — **are you?**

¿cuántos años tienes? — **man** (husband) marido *m;* (father) *fam* viejo *m;* **I'm not** — **enough to drive** soy muy joven para conducir; **to be an** — **hand at** ser ducho en

olden [oldn] ADJ **in** — **days** antaño

oldie [óldi] N viejo éxito *m*

oleander [óliændə] N adelfa *f*

olfactory [ɔlfǽktəri] ADJ olfatorio

olive [álɪv] N (tree) olivo *m;* (fruit) aceituna *f,* oliva *f;* — **branch** ramo de olivo *m;* — **grove** olivar *m;* — **oil** aceite de oliva *m;* — **wood** madera de olivo *m;* ADJ verde oliva

Olympiad [olímpiæd] N Olimpiada *f,* Olimpíada *f*

Olympic [olímpɪk] ADJ olímpico; — **Games** Olimpiadas *f pl,* Olimpíadas *f pl,* Juegos Olímpicos *m pl*

Oman [omán] N Omán *m*

Omani [ománi] ADJ & N omaní *mf*

omelet [ámlɪt] N tortilla francesa *f*

omen [ómən] N agüero *m,* presagio *m*

ominous [ámənəs] ADJ (threatening) amenazador; (like an omen) agorero

omission [omíʃən] N omisión *f*

omit [omít] VT omitir

omnipotence [amnípətəns] N omnipotencia *f*

omnipotent [amnípətənt] ADJ omnipotente

omniscience [amníʃəns] N omnisciencia *f*

omniscient [amníʃənt] ADJ omnisciente

omnivorous [amnívəəs] ADJ omnívoro

on [an] PREP en, sobre, encima de; — **the table** en / sobre / encima de la mesa; — **all sides** por todos lados; — **arriving** al llegar; — **board** a bordo; — **call** de guardia; — **credit** al fiado; — **drugs** drogado; — **horseback** a caballo; — **Monday** el lunes; — **purpose** a propósito; —-**screen** en la pantalla; — **the house** la casa paga; — **time** a tiempo; **a book** — **stamps** un libro sobre sellos; **do you have any cigarettes** — **you?** ¿tienes cigarros? **drunk** — **beer** borracho de cerveza; **to talk** — **the phone** hablar por teléfono; ADJ —**line** en línea; —**line banking** banca en línea *f;* —**line help** ayuda en línea *f;* ADV — **and** — dale que dale; **his hat is** — lleva puesto el sombrero; **the light is** — está encendida la luz; **there's a war** — estamos en guerra; **you're** — (broadcasting) estás en el aire; (acceptance) te acepto la propuesta

once [wʌns] ADV (in the past, a single time) una vez; (if ever) si alguna vez; — **and for all** una vez por todas, definitivamente; — **in a while** de vez en cuando; — **upon a time** érase una vez; **at** — de inmediato, enseguida; **just this** — sólo por esta vez; **cousin** — **removed** primo -ma segundo -da *mf;* CONJ una vez que, cuando; N una vez; —-**over** vistazo *m*

oncology [ankálədʒi] N oncología *f*

one [wʌn] NUM uno; — **book** un libro; — **hundred** cien; — **hundred and one** ciento uno; — **thousand** mil; —-**armed** manco; —-**armed bandit** tragaperras *mf sg*; —-**eyed** tuerto; — **John Smith** un tal John Smith; —-**man band** hombre orquesta *m*; —-**night stand** aventura sexual de una noche *f*, *Sp* flete *m*; — **on** — mano a mano; —-**sided fight** pelea desigual *f*; —-**upmanship** competitividad *f*; —-**way street** calle de sentido único *f*; **his** — **chance** su única oportunidad; **the** — **and only** el único; **this is** — **smart dog** es un perro muy listo; N & PRON uno *m*; — **at a time** de a uno; — **by** — uno por uno; **love** — **another** amaos los unos a los otros; **the** — **who** el/la que; **the green** — el verde; **this** — este/esta

oneself [wʌnsɛ́lf] PRON **to be** — ser uno mismo; **to sit by** — estar sentado solo; **to talk to** — hablar para sí; **to look at** — **in the mirror** mirarse en el espejo; **to buy** — **a house** comprarse una casa

ongoing [áŋgoɪŋ] ADJ continuo

onion [ʌ́njən] N cebolla *f*; — **patch** cebollar *m*

onlooker [ánlʊkɚ] N espectador -ora *mf*, mirón -ona *mf*

only [ónli] ADJ único; ADV solo, solamente; **I** — **just caught the train** por poco pierdo el tren; CONJ solo que, pero

onomatopoeia [ɑnəmɑɒəpíə] N onomatopeya *f*

onset [ánsɛt] N comienzo *m*

on-side kick [ónsaɪd kík] N patada lateral *f*

onto [ántu] PREP en, sobre, encima de; **she got** — **the plane late** subió tarde al avión; **he dropped it** — **the table** lo dejó caer en la mesa; **I'm** — **your plot** conozco tu plan

onward [ánwɚd] ADV hacia adelante

onyx [ániks] N ónix *m*

oops [ʊps] INTERJ ¡huy!

ooze [uz] VI/VT rezumar[se]; N cieno *m*

opal [ópəł] N ópalo *m*

opaque [opék] ADJ opaco

OPEC [Organization of Petroleum Exporting Countries] [ópɛk] N OPEP *f*

open [ópən] VI/VT abrir[se]; **to** — **into** comunicarse con; **to** — **one's way** abrirse paso; **to** — **onto** dar a; **to** — **up** abrirse; ADJ abierto; — **and shut** claro, evidente; — **code** código abierto *m*; — **door policy** política de acceso libre *f*; —-**ended** sin restricciones; —-**heart surgery** cirujía de corazón abierto *f*; —-**minded** de amplias miras; —-**mouthed** boquiabierto; — **question** cuestión discutible *f*; — **season** temporada de caza *f*; — **source software** software de fuente abierta *m*; — **to criticism** expuesto a la crítica; N (outdoors) aire libre *m*; (tournament) abierto *m*

opener [ópənɚ] N abridor *m*; (in sports) primer partido *m*; **for** —**s** para empezar

opening [ópənɪŋ] N (open space) abertura *f*; (act of making or becoming open, ceremony) apertura *f*; (beginning) comienzo *m*; (clearing) claro *m*; (vacancy) vacante *m*, apertura *f*; (pretext) oportunidad *f*; — **bid** oferta de apertura *f*; — **ceremony** ceremonia de apertura *f*; — **night** estreno *m*; **at the** — a/en la apertura

openness [ópənnɪs] N franqueza *f*, transparencia *f*, apertura *f*

opera [ápərə] N ópera *f*; — **glasses** gemelos *m pl*; — **house** ópera *f*

operable [ápəɒbəł] ADJ operable

operate [ápəret] VI (function) funcionar; (intervene surgically) operar; **to** — **on a person** operar a una persona; VT (run a machine) manejar; (administrate) dirigir; (make function) accionar

operating [ápəreDɪŋ] N — **costs** costos de operación *m pl*; — **room** sala de operaciones *f*, quirófano *m*; — **system** sistema operativo *m*

operation [ɑpəréʃən] N (surgical intervention, mission, math function) operación *f*; (function) funcionamiento *m*; (use of a machine) manejo *m*; **to be in** — (law) estar vigente; (machine) estar funcionando

operative [ápəɒDɪv] ADJ (law) vigente; (contract provision) pertinente; (word) clave, operativo; N (machine worker) operario -ria *mf*; (spy) agente *mf*

operator [ápəreDɚ] N (telephone, math) operador -ora *mf*; (machine) operario -ria *mf*; (stock) especulador -ora *mf*; **he's a smooth** — es un astuto

ophthalmologist [ɑfθəłmáɫədʒɪst] N oftalmólogo -ga *mf*

opiate [ópiət] N opiáceo *m*

opinion [əpínjən] N opinión *f*

opium [ópiəm] N opio *m*

opossum [əpásəm] N zarigüeya *f*

opponent [əpónənt] N opositor -ora *mf*, contrincante *mf*, adversario -ria *mf*, oponente *mf*

opportune [ɑpɚtún] ADJ oportuno

opportunistic [ɑpɚtunístɪk] ADJ oportunista, aprovechado

opportunity [ɑpɚtúnɪDi] N oportunidad *f*, ocasión *f*

oppose [əpóz] VI/VT oponer[se]

opposing [əpózɪŋ] ADJ opuesto, contrario; — **thumb** pulgar oponible *m*

opposite [ápəzɪt] ADJ (contrary) opuesto, contrario; — **to** frente a; PREP frente a, en frente de; N contrario *m*, opuesto *m*; ADV en frente

opposition [ɑpəzíʃən] N oposición *f*; **they met**

with little — encontraron poca resistencia
oppress [əprés] VT oprimir
oppression [əpréʃən] N opresión f
oppressive [əprésɪv] ADJ (regime) opresivo; (heat) bochornoso, sofocante
oppressor [əprésə-] N opresor -ora mf
optic [áptɪk] ADJ óptico; N —s óptica f
optical [áptɪkəl] ADJ óptico; — **character recognition** sistema de reconocimiento óptico de caracteres m; — **fiber** fibra óptica f; — **illusion** ilusión óptica f; — **resolution** resolución óptica f
optician [aptíʃən] N óptico -ca mf
optimal [áptəməl] ADJ óptimo
optimism [áptəmɪzəm] N optimismo m
optimist [áptəmɪst] N optimista mf
optimistic [aptəmístɪk] ADJ optimista
optimize [áptəmaɪz] VT optimizar
option [ápʃən] N opción f (also financial); (feature) extra m; **to leave one's —s open** no descartar posibilidades
optional [ápʃənl] ADJ opcional, optativo
optometrist [aptámɪtrɪst] N optometrista mf
optometry [aptámɪtri] N optometría f
opulence [ápjələns] N opulencia f
opulent [ápjələnt] ADJ opulento
or [ɔr] CONJ o; **seven — eight** siete u ocho
OR [operating room] [óár] N quirófano m, sala de operaciones f
oracle [ɔ́rəkəl] N oráculo m
oral [ɔ́rəl] ADJ oral; (hygiene) bucal
orange [ɔ́rɪndʒ] N naranja f; — **blossom** azahar m; — **grove** naranjal m; — **tree** naranjo m; ADJ & N anaranjado m
orangutan [əræŋətæn] N orangután m
orator [ɔ́rəDə-] N orador -ora mf
oratory [ɔ́rətɔri] N (skill in speaking) oratoria f; (place for prayer) oratorio m
orbit [ɔ́rbɪt] N órbita f; VI/VT orbitar
orbital [ɔ́rbɪdl] ADJ orbital
orbiter [ɔ́rbɪDə-] N orbitador m
orchard [ɔ́rtʃə-d] N huerto m; (large) huerta f
orchestra [ɔ́rkɪstrə] N orquesta f
orchestrate [ɔ́rkɪstret] VT orquestar
orchid [ɔ́rkɪd] N orquídea f
ordain [ɔrdén] VT (as minister) ordenar; (with an edict) decretar
ordeal [ɔrdíl] N suplicio m, tortura f; — **by fire** ordalía de fuego f
order [ɔ́rDə-] N (command) orden f, mandato m; (request, commission) pedido m; (sequence, obedience to law) orden m; **holy —s** órdenes sagradas f pl; **an apology is in** — corresponde una disculpa; **in — to** para; **in working** — en buen estado; **in — that** para que, a fin de que; **on** — encargado; **out of** — no funciona; **to put in** — ordenar; VI/VT (command, arrange) ordenar, mandar; (place an order) pedir

ordering [ɔ́rDə-ɪŋ] N (putting in order) ordenación f, ordenamiento m
orderly [ɔ́rDə-li] ADJ ordenado; N (military) ordenanza m; (hospital) camillero m
ordinal [ɔ́rdnəl] ADJ ordinal
ordinance [ɔ́rdnəns] N ordenanza f
ordinary [ɔ́rdņeri] ADJ común, corriente, ordinario; **do it the** — **way** hazlo de la forma habitual
ordination [ɔrdņéʃən] N ordenación f
ore [ɔr] N mineral m
oregano [ərégəno] N orégano m
organ [ɔ́rgən] N órgano m (also musical instrument)
organic [ɔrgǽnɪk] ADJ orgánico; — **chemistry** química orgánica f
organism [ɔ́rgənɪzəm] N organismo m
organist [ɔ́rgənɪst] N organista mf
organization [ɔrgənɪzéʃən] N organización f, planificación f
organizational [ɔrgənɪzéʃənl] ADJ organizativo; — **chart** organigrama m
organize [ɔ́rgənaɪz] VI/VT organizar[se]
organized [ɔ́rgənaɪzd] ADJ organizado
organizer [ɔ́rgənaɪzə-] N organizador -ora mf
organizing [ɔ́rgənaɪzɪŋ] ADJ organizativo
orgasm [ɔ́rgæzəm] N orgasmo m
orgy [ɔ́rdʒi] N orgía f
orient[1] [ɔ́riənt] N oriente m
orient[2] [ɔ́riənt] VT orientar
oriental [ɔriéntl] ADJ & N oriental mf
orientate [ɔ́rientet] VT orientar
orientation [ɔrientéʃən] N (guidance) orientación f; (tendency, leaning) tendencia f
orifice [ɔ́rəfɪs] N orificio m
origin [ɔ́rədʒɪn] N origen m, procedencia f; (of a river) naciente f, nacimiento m
original [ərídʒənl] ADJ original, originario; N original m
originality [ərɪdʒ ənǽlɪDi] N originalidad f
originate [ərídʒənet] VI/VT originar[se]
oriole [ɔ́riol] N oropéndola f
Orlon™ [ɔ́rlɑn] N orlón m
ornament[1] [ɔ́rnəmənt] N adorno m, ornamento m
ornament[2] [ɔ́rnəmɛnt] VT adornar, ornamentar
ornamental [ɔrnəmɛ́ntl] ADJ ornamental
ornamentation [ɔrnəmɪntéʃən] N ornamentación f
ornate [ɔrnét] ADJ adornado en exceso; — **style** estilo rebuscado m
ornithology [ɔrnəθɑ́lədʒi] N ornitología f
orphan [ɔ́rfən] ADJ & N huérfano -na mf; VT dejar huérfano a
orphanage [ɔ́rfənɪdʒ] N orfanato m, hospicio m
orthodontics [ɔrθədántɪks] N ortodoncia f
orthodox [ɔ́rθədɑks] ADJ ortodoxo
orthography [ɔrθágrəfi] N ortografía f
oscillate [ásəlet] VI oscilar; VT hacer oscilar

oscillation [asəléʃən] N oscilación f
osmosis [azmósɪs] N ósmosis f
osprey [áspre] N águila pescadora f
ossify [ásəfaɪ] vi osificarse
ostensible [asténsəbəł] ADJ supuesto
ostentation [astɪntéʃən] N ostentación f
ostentatious [astɪntéʃəs] ADJ ostentoso
osteoarthritis [astioɑrθráɪdɪs] N osteoartritis f
osteoporosis [astiopərósɪs] N osteoporosis f
ostracize [ástrəsaɪz] vt aislar
ostrich [ástrɪtʃ] N avestruz m
OTC [over-the-counter] [ótísí] ADJ extrabursátil
other [ʌ́ðɚ] ADJ, PRON, & N otro -tra mf; — **than Bob** salvo Bob; **every — day** cada dos días, un día sí y otro no; **—wise** de otro modo; **—worldly** fantástico
otter [ɑ́ðɚ] N nutria f
ouch [autʃ] INTERJ ¡ay!
ought [ɔt] v AUX **you — to sit down** deberías sentarte; **we — to get up early** deberíamos levantarnos más temprano
ounce [auns] N onza f
our [aur] POSS ADJ nuestro
ours [aurz] ADJ nuestro; **this book is —** este libro es nuestro; **these things are —** estas cosas son nuestras; PRON el nuestro / la nuestra; **— is bigger** el nuestro / la nuestra es más grande; **a friend of —** un amigo nuestro
ourselves [aursɛ́łvz] PRON **we made the cake —** nosotros mismos hicimos la torta; **we were sitting by —** estábamos sentados solos; **we look at — in the mirror** nos miramos en el espejo; **we bought — a house** nos compramos una casa
oust [aust] vt echar, expulsar
out [aut] ADV (outside) fuera; ADJ (turned off, extinguished) apagado; (tennis) fuera; (baseball) out; **—-of-date** pasado de moda, anticuado; N (way out) escape m; (baseball) out m; PREP **she ran — the door** salió corriendo por la puerta; **they locked me —** me dejaron fuera; **—-and-— criminal** criminal empedernido m; **—-and-— refusal** una negativa rotunda; **— of bounds** (golf) fuera de límites; **— of commission/ order** fuera de servicio; **— of fashion** pasado de moda; **— of fear** por miedo; **he's really — of it** está ido, está despistado; **— of joint** dislocado; **— of money** sin dinero; **— of print/stock** agotado; **— of touch with** desconectado de; **— of tune** desentonado; **— of work** desempleado; **— to lunch** fam chiflado; **made — of** hecho de; **miniskirts are on the way —** las minifaldas se están dejando de usar; **I had it — with him** me peleé con él; **you were — no estabas; before the week is —** antes de que termine la

semana; **the book is just —** acaba de publicarse el libro; **the secret is —** se ha divulgado el secreto; **we had some, but now we're —** teníamos, pero se nos acabó; **I'm — $10** perdí $10; INTERJ ¡fuera! vt (expel) expulsar; (expose) descubrir; vi **the truth will —** se descubrirá la verdad
outage [áudɪʤ] N apagón m
outbreak [áutbrek] N (of pimples) erupción f; (of war) comienzo m; (of disease) brote m
outburst [áutbɝst] N (emotional) arrebato m; (of tears) ataque m; (of violence) motín m, explosión f
outcast [áutkæst] ADJ & N marginado -da mf
outcome [áutkʌm] N resultado m, desenlace m
outcry [áutkraɪ] N clamor m, protesta f
outdated [autdéɪd] ADJ anticuado
outdo [autdú] vt superar
outdoor [áutdɔr] ADJ al aire libre; **— advertising** publicidad exterior f
outdoors [autdɔ́rz] ADV al aire libre, afuera
outer [áudɚ] ADJ exterior; **— ear** oído externo m; **— space** espacio exterior m
outfield [áutfiłd] N jardín m
outfielder [áutfiłdɚ] N jardinero -ra mf
outfit [áutfɪt] N (gear) equipo m; (clothes) conjunto m; (soldiers) unidad f; vi/vt equipar, habilitar
outfox [autfáks] vt ser más listo que
outgoing[1] [áutgoɪŋ] ADJ (leaving) saliente
outgoing[2] [autgóɪŋ] ADJ (extrovert) extrovertido
outgrow [autgró] vt **she will — her clothes** la ropa le quedará pequeña; **she will — her epilepsy** la epilepsia se le irá con la edad
outing [áudɪŋ] N excursión f, paseo m
outlandish [autlǽndɪʃ] ADJ estrafalario
outlast [autlǽst] vt (last longer than) durar más que; (live longer than) sobrevivir a
outlaw [áutlɔ] N bandido -da mf, forajido -da mf; vt prohibir
outlay[1] [áutle] N gasto m, desembolso m
outlay[2] [autlé] vt gastar, desembolsar
outlet [áutlɪt] N (exit) salida f; (stream) desagüe m, emisario m; (store) tienda f; (electric connection) toma de corriente f; **she needs an — for her talent** necesita canalizar su talento
outline [áutlaɪn] N (abstract) bosquejo m, esbozo m, trazado m; (boundary) contorno m; vt (summarize) bosquejar, esbozar; (draw) delinear; (plan) trazar
outlook [áutluk] N perspectiva f, panorama m
outlying [áutlaɪɪŋ] ADJ (marginal) periférico; (distant) remoto
outpatient [áutpeʃənt] N paciente ambulatorio -ria mf, paciente externo -na mf
output [áutput] N (production) rendimiento m; (computer information) salida f; **— device** dispositivo de salida m

outrage [áʊtredʒ] N (offense) ultraje *m*, agravio *m*, atropello *m*; (indignation) indignación *f*; VT (offend) ultrajar, agraviar; (enrage) indignar

outrageous [aʊtrédʒəs] ADJ (offensive) ultrajante; (exorbitant) exorbitante; (extravagant) extravagante

outreach[1] [áʊtritʃ] N extensión *f*

outreach[2] [aʊtrítʃ] VT exceder

outright[1] [aʊtráɪt] ADV completamente; **he bought it** — lo compró al contado; **he rejected it** — lo rechazó categóricamente

outright[2] [áʊtraɪt] ADJ — **denial** negativa rotunda *f*; — **lie** mentira descarada *f*

outset [áʊtset] N comienzo *m*, principio *m*

outshine [aʊtʃáɪn] VT eclipsar

outside[1] [aʊtsáɪd] ADV fuera, afuera; PREP fuera de

outside[2] [áʊtsaɪd] ADJ (external) exterior; (foreign) foráneo; N exterior *m*; — **chance** posibilidad remota *f*; — **interference** interferencia externa *f*; **in a week, at the** — en una semana, a lo sumo; **to close on the** — cerrar por fuera

outsider [aʊtsáɪdɚ] N forastero -ra *mf*

outskirts [áʊtskɚts] N alrededores *m pl*, afueras *f pl*

outsourcing [áʊtsɔrsɪŋ] N contratación externa *f*

outspoken [aʊtspókən] ADJ franco

outstanding [aʊtstǽndɪŋ] ADJ (excellent) sobresaliente, destacado; (pending) pendiente

outstretched [aʊtstrétʃt] ADJ extendido

outward [áʊtwɚd] ADJ exterior, externo; — **appearances** apariencias *f pl*; ADV hacia fuera; — **bound** que sale

outweigh [aʊtwé] VT (weigh more) pesar más que; (be more important) sobreponerse a, valer más que

outwit [aʊtwít] VT ser más listo que

oval [óvəl] ADJ oval, ovalado; N óvalo *m*

ovarian [ovériən] ADJ ovárico

ovary [óvəri] N ovario *m*

ovation [ovéʃən] N ovación *f*

oven [ʌ́vən] N horno *m*

over [óvɚ] PREP — **here** acá; — **in Japan** allá en Japón; — **many years** durante muchos años; — **the counter** (medicine) sin receta; (stocks) extrabursátil; — **the sea** al otro lado del mar; — **the hill** viejo; — **there** allá; **an umbrella** — **his head** un paraguas sobre la cabeza; **I heard it** — **the radio** lo oí por la radio; **he jumped** — **the fence** saltó por encima de la cerca; **he is** — **her in the hierarchy** él está por encima de ella en la jerarquía; **not** — **one year** no más de un año; **he hit him** — **the head with a rock** le golpeó en la cabeza con una piedra; **all** — **the city** por toda la ciudad; **I'm** — **it** (recovered)

me he recuperado; (no longer interested) ya no me interesa; ADV — **again** de nuevo, otra vez; — **against** en contraste con; — **and** — una y otra vez; —**generous** demasiado generoso; **do it** — hazlo de nuevo, hazlo otra vez; **the world** — por todo el mundo; **it is** — **with** se acabó; INTERJ — **and out** cambio y fuera

overachiever [ovɚətʃívɚ] N (bookish) empollón -ona *mf*; (successful) persona muy exitosa *f*

overactive [ovɚǽktɪv] ADJ hiperactivo, demasiado activo

overall [óvɚɔl] ADJ global, total; N —**s** mono *m*, overol *m*

overbearing [ovɚbérɪŋ] ADJ mandón -ona, dominante

overboard [óvɚbɔrd] ADV (into the water) al agua; **she went** — **on her project** se le fue la mano con su proyecto

overcast [óvɚkæst] ADJ nublado, encapotado; **to become** — nublarse, encapotarse

overcharge[1] [ovɚtʃárdʒ] VI/VT cobrar demasiado, cobrar de más

overcharge[2] [óvɚtʃɑrdʒ] N cobro excesivo *m*

overcoat [óvɚkot] N sobretodo *m*, gabán *m*

overcome [ovɚkʌ́m] VI/VT (to get the better of) superar; (to overwhelm) embargar; **to be** — **by weariness** estar agobiado

overcompensate [ovɚkámpɪnset] VI sobrecompensar

overcorrection [ovɚkərékʃən] N sobrecorrección *f*

overdose [óvɚdos] N sobredosis *f*; VI tomar una sobredosis

overdraft [óvɚdræft] N sobregiro *m*, descubierto *m*

overdraw [ovɚdrɔ́] VI/VT sobregirar[se]

overdrawn [ovɚdrɔ́n] ADJ en descubierto, sobregirado

overdrive [óvɚdraɪv] N superdirecta *f*

overdue [ovɚdú] ADJ (borrowed item) atrasado; (bill) vencido

overeat [ovɚít] VI comer en exceso

overestimate [ovɚéstɪmet] VT sobreestimar

overexcite [ovɚɪksáɪt] VT sobreexcitar

overextended [ovɚɪksténdɪd] ADJ sobreextendido

overflow[1] [ovɚfló] VI desbordar, rebosar

overflow[2] [óvɚflo] N desborde *m*

overgrown [ovɚgrón] ADJ cubierto, crecido; — **boy** muchacho demasiado crecido para su edad *m*

overhang[1] [ovɚhǽŋ] VI (jut) proyectarse; (hang over) estar suspendido

overhang[2] [óvɚhæŋ] N saliente *m*

overhaul[1] [óvɚhɔl] VT revisar

overhaul[2] [óvɚhɔl] N revisión *f*

overhead[1] [óvɚhɛd] N gastos generales *m pl*; ADJ elevado; — **projector** retroproyector *m*

overhead[2] [ovə-héd] ADV en lo alto
overhear [ovə-hír] VT oír por casualidad
overjoyed [ovə-ʤóɪd] ADJ rebosante de alegría
overkill [óvə-kɪł] N exageración f
overland [óvə-lænd] ADV & ADJ por tierra
overlap[1] [ovə-lǽp] VI/VT solapar[se], superponer[se]
overlap[2] [óvə-læp] N traslapo m
overlay[1] [ovə-lé] VT cubrir; (with gold, etc.) incrustar
overlay[2] [óvə-le] N cubierta f; (with metal, wood) revestimiento m, chapa f
overload[1] [ovə-lód] VT sobrecargar, recargar, saturar
overload[2] [óvə-lod] N sobrecarga f
overlook[1] [ovə-lúk] VT (fail to mention) pasar por alto, omitir; (pardon) perdonar; (look from above) mirar desde arriba; (afford a view of) dar a, tener vista a
overlook[2] [óvə-lʊk] N mirador m
overly [óvə-li] ADV excesivamente
overnight[1] [óvə-naɪt] ADJ — **delivery** entrega al otro día f; — **guest** invitado -da a dormir mf
overnight[2] [ovə-náɪt] ADV **he succeeded** — tuvo éxito de la noche a la mañana
overpass [óvə-pæs] N paso elevado m
overpower [ovə-páuə-] VT abrumar
overpowering [ovə-páuə-ɪŋ] ADJ abrumador
overpriced [ovə-práɪst] ADJ demasiado caro
overproduction [ovə-pɹədʌ́kʃən] N superproducción f
overqualified [ovə-kwáləfaɪd] ADJ sobrecalificado
overreach [ovə-rítʃ] VI **to** — **oneself** abarcar demasiado
overreact [ovə-riǽkt] VI reaccionar exageradamente
override [ovə-ráɪd] VT anular
overrule [ovə-rúł] VT anular
overrun[1] [ovə-rʌ́n] VT (overflow) desbordar; (exceed) exceder; (invade) infestar
overrun[2] [óvə-rʌn] N exceso de costos m
overseas [ovə-síz] ADV (beyond the sea) en ultramar; (abroad) en el extranjero
oversee [ovə-sí] VI (workers) dirigir, supervisar; (accounts) fiscalizar
overseer [óvə-sir] N capataz -za mf, supervisor -ora mf
overshadow [ovə-ʃǽdo] VT eclipsar, opacar
overshoe [óvə-ʃu] N chanclo m
oversight [óvə-saɪt] N (mistake) descuido m; (act of overseeing workers) supervisión f; (act of overseeing accounts) fiscalización f
overstep [ovə-stép] VT excederse en
overstrike [óvə-straɪk] VT imprimir un carácter directamente encima de otro
overt [ovə́t] ADJ evidente
overtake [ovə-ték] VT (pass someone) pasar, rebasar; (befall) abatirse sobre

overtax [ovə-tǽks] VT (tax too much) gravar excesivamente; (demand too much) exigir demasiado
overthrow[1] [ovə-θró] VT derrocar, derribar
overthrow[2] [óvə-θro] N derrocamiento m
overtime [óvə-taɪm] N (in a game) prórroga f, tiempo suplementario m; (at work) horas extras f pl; **to work** — hacer horas extras
overture [óvə-tʃə-] N (musical composition) obertura f; (initial move) propuesta f
overturn [ovə-tə́n] VI/VT volcar[se]; VT (a decision) anular; (a government) derrocar
overview [óvə-vju] N vista global f, panorama m
overweight[1] [ovə-wét] ADJ **he's** — pesa demasiado
overweight[2] [óvə-wet] N sobrepeso m
overwhelm [ovə-hwéłm] VT abrumar, agobiar
overwhelming [ovə-hwéłmɪŋ] ADJ (responsibility, task) abrumador, agobiante; (victory) arrollador
overwork[1] [ovə-wə́k] VI trabajar demasiado; VT hacer trabajar demasiado
overwork[2] [óvə-wə·k] N exceso de trabajo m
overwrite mode [óvə-raɪtmod] VT modo de reescritura m
ovulate [ávjəlet] VI ovular
ovulation [avjəléʃən] N ovulación f
owe [o] VI/VT deber; (a sum) adeudar, deber
owing [óɪŋ] ADJ debido; — **to** debido a
owl [auł] N lechuza f, búho m
own [on] ADJ & PRON propio; — **goal** autogol m, gol en contra m; **a house of his** — una casa suya; **to be on one's** — ser independiente; **to come into one's** — conseguir lo que uno se merece; **to hold one's** — mantenerse firme; VT poseer; **to** — **up [to]** confesar
owner [ónə-] N dueño -ña mf, propietario -ria mf; — **financing** financiamiento por el propietario m
ownership [ónə-ʃɪp] N propiedad f
ox [aks] N buey m
oxidation [aksɪdéʃən] N oxidación f
oxidize [áksɪdaɪz] VI/VT oxidar[se]
oxygen [áksɪʤən] N oxígeno m; — **tent** cámara de oxígeno f
oyster [ɔ́ɪstə-] N ostra f; (large) ostión m
ozone [ózon] N ozono m; — **layer** capa de ozono f

Pp

pace [pes] N paso m; —**maker** marcapasos m sg; VT (traverse) ir y venir por; (set the tempo) marcar al paso; (measure) medir a pasos
pacific [pəsífɪk] ADJ pacífico; — **Ocean** Océano

Pacífico *m*
pacification [pæsɪfɪkéʃən] N pacificación *f*
pacifier [pǽsəfaɪə-] N chupete *m*
pacifism [pǽsəfɪzəm] N pacifismo *m*
pacify [pǽsəfaɪ] VT (a country) pacificar; (a person) apaciguar
pack [pæk] N (of wolves) manada *f*; (of dogs) jauría *f*; (of cigarettes) cajilla *f*, cajetilla *f*; (of cloth) compresa *f*; (of cards) baraja *f*; (of cyclists) pelotón *m*; — **animal** acémila *f*, bestia de carga *f*; —**rat** rata urraca *f*; (person who saves everything) urraca *f*; **a** — **of lies** una sarta de mentiras *f*; VT empacar, empaquetar; (carry a gun) portar; (crowd) atestar; (load) cargar; **to** — **off** despachar; **to** — **one's bags** hacer las maletas
package [pǽkɪdʒ] N paquete *m* (also organized vacation); — **deal** (agreement) acuerdo global *m*; (tourism, travel) paquete turístico *m*; VT (gift) empaquetar; (food) envasar
packaging [pǽkɪdʒɪŋ] N embalaje *m*, empaque *m*
packer [pǽkə-] N empacador -ora *mf*, embalador -ora *mf*
packet [pǽkɪt] N paquete *m*
packing [pǽkɪŋ] N embalaje *m*
pact [pækt] N pacto *m*
pad [pæd] N (cushion) almohadilla *f* (also for ink); (block of paper) bloc *m*; (for aircraft) pista *f*; (for spacecraft) plataforma de lanzamiento *f*; VT (stuff with padding) acolchar; (add to dishonestly) rellenar
padding [pǽDɪŋ] N relleno *m*; (cotton) guata *f*; (of a speech) ripio *m*
paddle [pǽdl̩] N (for rowing) pala *f*, remo *m*; (for mixing, beating, ping-pong) paleta *f*; — **wheel** rueda de paleta *f*; VI (row) remar; VT hacer avanzar remando; (hit) dar una paletada
paddock [pǽDək] N (field) prado *m*; (enclosure at racetrack) paddock *m*
padlock [pǽdlɑk] N candado *m*; VT cerrar con candado
pagan [pégən] ADJ & N pagano -na *mf*
paganism [pégənɪzəm] N paganismo *m*
page [pedʒ] N (sheet) hoja *f*, página *f*; (boy servant) paje *m*; (hotel employee) botones *m sg*; — **break** salto de página *m*; VT (number pages) paginar; (call) llamar por altavoz; *Mex* vocear; **to** — **through** hojear
pageant [pǽdʒənt] N (parade) desfile *m*; (show) espectáculo *m*
pager [pédʒə-] N buscapersonas *m sg*
paid [ped] ADJ pagado; — **-up** liberado, totalmente pagado, pago
paid [ped] *see* pay
pail [pel] N balde *m*, cubeta *f*
pain [pen] N dolor *m*; (suffering) sufrimiento *m*; —**killer** analgésico *m*; **on** — **of** so pena de; **to take** —**s** esmerarse; **he's a** — es un

chinche; ADJ —**staking** esmerado; VT (physical) doler; (mental) apenar
painful [pénfəl] ADJ (hurting) doloroso; (distressing) penoso; (difficult) arduo
painless [pénlɪs] ADJ sin dolor, indoloro
paint [pent] N (substance) pintura *f*; (spotted horse) pinto *m*; —**brush** (for art) pincel *m*; (for a house) brocha *f*; VI/VT pintar; **to** — **the town red** irse de juerga
painter [péntə-] N pintor -ora *mf*
painting [péntɪŋ] N pintura *f*
pair [pɛr] N par *m*; (married couple) pareja *f*; **a** — **of scissors** unas tijeras, una tijera; VI/VT aparear[se], emparejar[se]; **to** — **off** aparearse
pajamas [pədʒáməz] N pijama/piyama *mf*
Pakistan [pǽkɪstæn] N Paquistán *m*
Pakistani [pækɪstǽni] ADJ & N paquistano -na *mf*
pal [pæl] N compañero -ra *mf*, compadre *m*, comadre *f*
palace [pǽlɪs] N palacio *m*
palate [pǽlɪt] N paladar *m*
palatial [pəléʃəl] ADJ suntuoso
Palau [pɑláu] N Paláu *m*
pale [pel] ADJ pálido, macilento; N **beyond the** — inaceptable; VI palidecer
paleness [pélnɪs] N palidez *f*
paleontology [peliəntálədʒi] N paleontología *f*
Palestine [pǽlɪstaɪn] N Palestina *f*
Palestinian [pæləstínɪən] ADJ palestino; N palestino -na *mf*
palette [pǽlɪt] N paleta *f*
palisade [pælɪséd] N empalizada *f*; —**s** acantilados *m pl*
pall [pɔl] VT (cover with a cloth) cubrir con un paño mortuorio; (satiate) hartar; VI (tire) cansar; N paño mortuorio *m*; —**bearer** portador del féretro *m*; **to cast a** — **on** empañar
palliative [pǽliəDɪv] N paliativo *m*
pallid [pǽlɪd] ADJ pálido
pallor [pǽlə-] N palidez *f*
palm [pɑm] N (part of hand) palma *f*; (tree) palmera *f*, palma *f*; — **Sunday** Domingo de Ramos *m*; —**top computer** *Am* computadora de mano *f*, *Sp* ordenador de mano *m*; VT (hide in palm) escamotear; **to** — **something off on someone** encajar algo a alguien
palpable [pǽlpəbəl] ADJ (perceptible) palpable; (tangible) tangible
palpitate [pǽlpɪtet] VI palpitar
palpitation [pælpɪtéʃən] N palpitación *f*
palsy [pɔ́lzi] N parálisis *f*
paltry [pɔ́ltri] ADJ miserable, despreciable
pamper [pǽmpə-] VT mimar, consentir
pamphlet [pǽmflɪt] N (informative) folleto *m*; (political) panfleto *m*
pan [pæn] N (for boiling) cazuela *f*, cacerola *f*,

cazo *m*; (for frying) sartén *f*; (for baking) molde *m*; —**handle** mango de sartén *m*; —**handler** pordiosero -ra *mf*; VT criticar duramente; VI **to — for gold** extraer oro; **to — out** dar buen resultado; **to —handle** mendigar, pordiosear

panacea [pǽnəsíə] N panacea *f*

Panama [pǽnəmɑ] N Panamá *f*

Panamanian [pǽnəméniən] ADJ & N panameño -ña *mf*

Pan-American [pǽnəmérɪkən] ADJ panamericano

pancake [pǽnkek] N panqueque *m*; **flat as a —** chato como una tabla

pancreas [pǽnkriəs] N páncreas *m*

panda [pǽndə] N panda *m*

pandemic [pændémɪk] ADJ pandémico *m*; N pandemia *f*

pander [pǽndɚ] VI consentir

panderer [pǽndərɚ] N proxeneta *mf*

pane [pen] N vidrio *m*, cristal *m*

panel [pǽnl̩] N (wall) revestimiento *m*; (group of experts) panel *m*; (of instruments) tablero *m*; VT revestir con paneles

paneling [pǽnl̩ɪŋ] N (wall) panel *m*

pang [pæŋ] N (sharp pain, hunger) punzada *f*; (anguish) remordimientos *m pl*

panic [pǽnɪk] ADJ & N pánico *m*; ADJ —-**stricken** sobrecogido de pánico

panorama [pænərǽmə] N panorama *m*

panoramic [pænərǽmɪk] ADJ panorámico

pansy [pǽnzi] N (flower) pensamiento *m*; (sissy) *offensive* marica *m*

pant [pænt] VI jadear

panther [pǽnθɚ] N pantera *f*

panties [pǽntiz] N *Sp* bragas *f pl*; *Mex* pantaletas *f pl*; *RP* bombacha *f*

pantomime [pǽntəmaɪm] N pantomima *f*

pantry [pǽntri] N despensa *f*, alacena *f*

pants [pænts] N pantalones *m pl*, pantalón *m*

pantyhose [pǽntihoz] N panty *m*

papa [pápə] N papá *m*

papacy [pépəsi] N papado *m*

papal [pépəl] ADJ papal

papaya [pəpáɪə] N papaya *f*; *Cuba* fruta bomba *f*

paper [pépɚ] N (material) papel *m*; (newspaper) periódico *m*; (assignment) trabajo *m*; (oral contribution) comunicación *f*; (written contribution) artículo *m*; —**back** libro en rústica *m*; — **clip** clip *m*, sujetapapeles *m sg*; — **cutter** guillotina *f*; — **feeder** alimentador de hojas *m*; — **money** papel moneda *m*; —**s** papeles *m pl*; — **shredder** trituradora *f*; —**weight** pisapapeles *m sg*; —**work** (forms) papeleo *m*; (procedures) trámites *m pl*; **on —** por escrito; VI/VT empapelar

paprika [pæpríkə] N pimentón *m*, páprika *f*

pap smear [pǽp smir] N citología *f*

Papua New Guinea [pǽpjuənugíni] N Papúa

Nueva Guinea *f*

Papua New Guinean [pǽpjuənugíniən] ADJ & N papú *mf*

par [pɑr] N (financial) paridad *f*; (in golf) par *m*; — **value** valor nominal *m*; **at —** a la par; **below —** bajo par; **to be on a — with** estar en pie de igualdad con; **to feel above —** sentirse mejor que lo normal; VT hacer el par

parachute [pǽrəʃut] N paracaídas *m sg*

parachuting [pǽrəʃuDɪŋ] N paracaidismo *m*

parachutist [pǽrəʃuDɪst] N paracaidista *mf*

parade [pəréd] N (procession) desfile *m*; (military review) parada *f*; — **ground** campo de maniobras *m*; VI desfilar; VT hacer ostentación de

paradigm [pǽrədaɪm] N paradigma *m*

paradise [pǽrədaɪs] N paraíso *m*

paradox [pǽrədɑks] N paradoja *f*

paradoxical [pærədáksɪkəl] ADJ paradójico

paraffin [pǽrəfɪn] N parafina *f*

paragraph [pǽrəgræf] N párrafo *m*; VT dividir en párrafos

Paraguay [pǽrəgwaɪ] N Paraguay *m*

Paraguayan [pærəgwáɪən] ADJ & N paraguayo -ya *mf*

parakeet [pǽrəkit] N perico *m*, periquito *m*

parallel [pǽrələl] ADJ & N paralelo *m*; (geometry) paralela *f*; — **port** puerto paralelo *m*; VT (run equidistant from) correr paralelo a; (compare) comparar

paralysis [pərǽləsɪs] N (of the body) parálisis *f*; (of a transportation system) paralización *f*

paralytic [pærəlíDɪk] ADJ paralítico -ca

paralyze [pǽrəlaɪz] VT paralizar

paramedic [pærəmédɪk] ADJ & N paramédico -ca *mf*

parameter [pərǽmɪDɚ] N parámetro *m*

paramilitary [pærəmílɪteri] ADJ & N paramilitar *mf*

paramount [pǽrəmaunt] ADJ supremo, sumo

paranoia [pærənɔ́ɪə] N paranoia *f*

paranoid [pǽrənɔɪd] ADJ & N paranoico -ca *mf*; — **delusion** delirio paranoico *m*

paranormal [pærənɔ́rməl] ADJ paranormal

paraphernalia [pærəfənéljə] N parafernalia *f*

paraphrase [pǽrətrez] N paráfrasis *f*; VI/VT parafrasear

paraplegic [pærəplídʒɪk] ADJ N parapléjico -ca *mf*

parapsychology [pærəsaɪkáləʤi] N parapsicología *f*

parasite [pǽrəsaɪt] N parásito *m*

parasitic [pærəsíDɪk] ADJ parasítico; — **disease** enfermedad parasitaria *f*

parasol [pǽrəsɔl] N parasol *m*, sombrilla *f*

paratroops [pǽrətrups] N tropas paracaidistas *f pl*

parcel [pársəl] N (package) paquete *m*; (lot) partida *f*; (land) parcela *f*; — **post** paquete postal *m*; VT (land) parcelar; **to — out** repartir

parch [partʃ] VT secar; **I'm —ed** estoy muerto de sed

parchment [pártʃmənt] N pergamino *m*

pardon [párdn] N perdón *m*, gracia *f*; (legal) indulto *m*; **I beg your —** perdone; VT perdonar, disculpar; (legally) indultar

pare [pɛr] VT mondar, pelar; **to — down expenditures** reducir gastos

parent [pérənt] N padre *m*, madre *f*; — **directory** directorio padre *m*; **—s** padres *m pl*

parental [pəréntl] ADJ parental; — **control** control paternal *m*

parenthesis [pərénθəsɪs] N paréntesis *m*

parenting [pérəntɪŋ] N — **guide** guía para padres *f*; — **skill** habilidad para educar a los hijos *f*; **good —** buena crianza de los hijos *f*

pariah [pəráɪə] N paria *mf*

parish [pérɪʃ] N parroquia *f*; — **priest** [cura] párroco *m*

parishioner [pəríʃənɚ] N feligrés -esa *mf*, parroquiano -na *mf*

parity [pérɪDi] N paridad *f*

park [park] N parque *m*; (for baseball) estadio de béisbol *m*; VI/VT estacionar, aparcar

parking [párkɪŋ] N estacionamiento *m*, aparcamiento *m*; — **lot** estacionamiento *m*, aparcamiento *m*; — **place** lugar de estacionamiento/aparcamiento *m*

Parkinson's disease [párkɪnsənzdɪziz] N enfermedad de Parkinson *f*

parlance [párləns] N habla *f*

parley [párli] N (peace negotiation) parlamento *m*; (discussion) discusión *f*; VI parlamentar

parliament [párləmənt] N parlamento *m*

parliamentary [parləméntri] ADJ parlamentario

parlor [párlɚ] N sala *f*, salón *m*; — **game** juego de salón *m*; **beauty —** salón de belleza *m*

parochial [pərókiəl] ADJ (of a parish) parroquial; (provincial) pueblerino

parody [pérədi] N parodia *f*; VT parodiar

parole [pəról] N libertad condicional *f*; VT poner en libertad condicional

parrot [pérət] N loro *m*, papagayo *m*; VT repetir como loro

parry [péri] VT (a blow) parar; (a remark) eludir; N parada *f*

parse [pars] VT analizar

parser [pársɚ] N analizador *m*

parsing [pársɪŋ] N análisis *m*

parsley [pársli] N perejil *m*

parsnip [pársnɪp] N chirivía *f*

parson [pársən] N pastor -ora *mf*

part [part] N (component) parte *f*; (role) papel *m*; (in hair) raya *f*; — **and parcel** parte esencial *f*; — **time** tiempo parcial *m*; **in foreign —s**

en el extranjero; **spare —s** piezas de repuesto *f pl*, repuestos *m pl*; ADJ **—-time** a tiempo parcial; VI/VT (cut into parts) partir[se]; (divide into parts) dividir[se]; (separate, leave) separar[se]; **to — company** separarse; **to — one's hair** hacerse la raya; **to — with** desprenderse de

partake [parték] VI **to — in** participar; **to — of** (share) compartir; (eat) comer

partial [párʃəl] ADJ parcial

participant [partísəpənt] ADJ & N participante *mf*, partícipe *mf*

participate [partísəpet] VI participar

participation [partɪsəpéʃən] N participación *f*

participle [párDɪsɪpəl] N participio *m*

particle [párDɪkəl] N partícula *f*; — **board** aglomerado *m*

particular [pɚtíkjəlɚ] ADJ particular; (fussy) quisquilloso; N **in —** en particular; **—s** particulares *m pl*

parting [párDɪŋ] N (farewell) despedida *f*; (separation) separación *f*; — **of the ways** encrucijada *f*

partisan [párDɪzən] N (supporter) partidario -ria *mf*, partidista *mf*; (guerrilla) partisano -na *mf*; ADJ (of supporters) partidario, partidista; (of guerrillas) de partisanos

partition [partíʃən] N (distribution) reparto *m*; (division) división *f*, partición *f*; (wall) tabique *m*, mampara *f*; VT (distribute) repartir; (divide) dividir; (divide with a wall) tabicar

partly [pártli] ADV en parte

partner [pártnɚ] N (in business) socio -cia *mf*; (in an activity) compañero -ra *mf*; (in dancing, sports, marriage) pareja *f*

partnership [pártnɚʃɪp] N (business) sociedad *f*; (relationship) asociación *f*

partridge [pártrɪʤ] N perdiz *f*

party [párDi] N (get-together) fiesta *f*; (political group) partido *m*; (group of people) partida *f*; (litigant) parte *f*; — **of four** mesa para cuatro *f*; — **animal** fiestero -ra *mf*, parrandero -ra *mf*; VI ir de juerga

pass [pæs] VI (to go by) pasar; **to — a kidney stone** expulsar un cálculo renal; **to — away** fallecer; **to — for** pasar por; **to — in review** pasar revista; **to — on** (die) fallecer; (approve) aceptar; (refuse) no querer; **to — out** desmayarse; **to — over** pasar por alto; **to — up an opportunity** dejar pasar una oportunidad; VT (a ball) pasar; (a law) aprobar; (an exam, test) aprobar; **to — judgment** juzgar; **to — oneself off as** hacerse pasar por; — **me the salt** pásame la sal, alcánzame la sal; N (road through mountains) paso *m*; (motion, permission) pase *m*; (for transportation) abono *m*; (over a surface) pasada *f*; (on an exam) aprobación *f*; (of a ball) pase *m*; **—key** llave maestra *f*;

—port pasaporte *m*; **—word** contraseña *f*, clave de seguridad *f*; **—word protected** protegido por contraseña; **he made a — at her** trató de ligar con ella

passable [pǽsəbəl] ADJ (penetrable) transitable; (mediocre) pasable

passage [pǽsɪʤ] N (fare, musical or textual phrase, alley) pasaje *m*; (passing of time) paso *m*, transcurso *m*; (hallway in a house) pasillo *m*; (secret pathway) pasadizo *m*; (crossing) travesía *f*; (approval of a bill) aprobación *f*; **—way** (corridor) corredor *m*, pasillo *m*; (alley) pasaje *m*

passenger [pǽsənʤɚ] N pasajero -ra *mf*

passerby [pǽsə-baɪ] N transeúnte *mf*, viandante *mf*

passing [pǽsɪŋ] N fallecimiento *m*; ADJ **each — day** cada día que pasa; **— grade** nota de aprobado *f*; **— fancy** capricho pasajero *m*; **— mention** mención al pasar *f*; **— shot** pasante *m*

passion [pǽʃən] N pasión *f*

passionate [pǽʃənɪt] ADJ apasionado

passive [pǽsɪv] ADJ pasivo; N pasiva *f*

past [pæst] ADJ pasado; **— due** en mora, vencido; **— participle** participio pasado *m*; **— perfect** pluscuamperfecto *m*; **— peformance** rendimiento previo *m*; **— precedents** precedentes anteriores *m pl*; **— tense** tiempo pretérito *m*; **the — president** el expresidente; PREP **— hope** más allá de toda esperanza; **— noon** después de mediodía; **the house — the store** la casa pasando la tienda; **we went — the tower** pasamos al lado de la torre; **half — two** las dos y media; **a woman — forty** una mujer de más de cuarenta años; ADV **for some time —** desde hace algún tiempo; **they drove —** pasaron en coche; N (time) pasado *m*; (tense) pretérito *m*

pasta [pástə] N pasta *f*

paste [pest] N (soft material, puree) pasta *f*; (glue) engrudo *m*; **—board** cartón *m*; VT pegar

pastel [pæstɫ́] ADJ & N pastel *m*

pasteurize [pǽstʃəraɪz] VT pasterizar/ pasteurizar

pastime [pǽstaɪm] N pasatiempo *m*

pastor [pǽstɚ] N pastor -ora *mf*

pastoral [pǽstə-əl] ADJ (literary) pastoril; (ecclesiastical) pastoral; N pastoral *f*; (literary work) égloga *f*

pastry [péstri] N (in general) pastelería *f*; (specific) pastel *m*; **— cook** pastelero -ra *mf*, repostero -ra *mf*; **— shop** pastelería *f*, repostería *f*

pasture [pǽstʃɚ] N (grassland) prado *m*; (grass) pasto *m*; (for horses) potrero *m*; VI/VT pastar, pacer, apacentar

pasty [pésti] ADJ pastoso

pat [pæt] ADJ banal; **down —** al dedillo; **to stand —** mantenerse firme; VI/VT dar palmaditas [a]; N palmadita *f*; N **— of butter** porción de mantequilla *f*

patch [pætʃ] N (piece of cloth to repair clothes) remiendo *m*, parche *m* (also for eye, computer); (spot or area, as of ice) tramo [con hielo] *m*; (plot) parcela *f*; VT (repair) remendar; **to — up a quarrel** hacer las paces

patent [pǽtnt] ADJ (evident) patente; (protected by patent) patentado; **— leather** charol *m*; N patente *f*; **— pending** patente en trámite; VT patentar

paternal [pətɚ́nl] ADJ (fatherly) paternal; (of the father's lineage) paterno

paternity [pətɚ́nɪDi] N paternidad *f*; **— test** prueba de paternidad *f*

path [pæθ] N (walkway) senda *f*, sendero *m*; (on a computer) ruta *f*; (of a projectile, storm) trayectoria *f*; **—way** senda *f*, sendero *m*

pathetic [pəθέDɪk] ADJ (moving) patético; (contemptible) lamentable

pathogen [pǽθəʤən] N patógeno *m*

pathology [pæθáləʤi] N patología *f*

pathos [péθɑs] N patetismo *m*

patience [péʃəns] N paciencia *f*

patient [péʃənt] ADJ & N paciente *mf*

patiently [péʃəntli] ADJ con paciencia

patriarch [pétriɑrk] N patriarca *m*

patriarchal [petriárkəl] ADJ patriarcal

patrimonial [pætrɪmóniəl] ADJ patrimonial

patrimony [pǽtrəmoni] N patrimonio *m*

patriot [pétriət] N patriota *mf*

patriotic [petriáDɪk] ADJ patriótico

patriotism [pétriətɪzəm] N patriotismo *m*

patrol [pətról] VI/VT patrullar, rondar; N patrulla *f*, ronda *f*; **— car** patrullero *m*; **—man** patrullero *m*

patron [pétrən] N (customer) cliente -ta *mf*; (benefactor) benefactor -ora *mf*, mecenas *mf*; (saint) patrono *m*

patronage [pétrənɪʤ] N (support of an artist) mecenazgo *m*; (clientele) clientela *f*; (political) clientelismo *m*; **we appreciate your —** agradecemos su preferencia

patronize [pétrənaɪz] VT (be condescending) tratar con condescendencia; (do business with) frecuentar

patter [pǽDɚ] VI (strike lightly) golpetear; (chatter) parlotear; N (small blows) golpeteo *m*; (chatter) parloteo *m*

pattern [pǽDɚn] N (for sewing) molde *m*; (for drawing) plantilla *f*; (of behavior) patrón *m*; VI/VT **to — something after** modelar algo a imitación de, basarse en el modelo de; **to — oneself after** seguir el ejemplo de

paucity [pósɪDi] N escasez *f*

paunch [pɔntʃ] N panza *f*, barriga *f*

pause [pɔz] N pausa f; VI (while talking) hacer pausa; (while moving) detenerse

pave [pev] VT (with asphalt) pavimentar; (with bricks) enladrillar; (with flagstones) enlosar; **to — the way for** preparar el camino para

pavement [pévmənt] N (roadway) calzada f; (of asphalt) pavimento m; (of bricks) enladrillado m; (of flagstones) enlosado m

pavilion [pəvíljən] N pabellón m

paw [pɔ] N pata f; (with claws) garra f; VT (touch with paw) tocar con la pata; (touch with claws) dar zarpazos; (grope) manosear

pawn [pɔn] N (object left in deposit) prenda f; (chess piece) peón m; (puppet) títere m; **—broker** prestamista mf; **—shop** casa de empeños f, monte de piedad m; **in —** en prenda; VT empeñar, dejar en prenda

pay [pe] VT (remit) pagar; VI (be profitable) ser provechoso, convenir; (be worthwhile) valer la pena; **to — attention** prestar atención, fijarse en; **to — back** (return) restituir; (retaliate) vengarse; **to — a compliment** hacer un cumplido; **to — homage** rendir homenaje; **to — one's respects** saludar; **to — off a debt** cancelar una deuda, amortizar una deuda; **to — out** desembolsar, pagar; **to — a visit** hacer una visita; **to — through the nose** pagar demasiado; **I will — for your meal** te pago la comida; N (payment) pago m; (wages) paga f, salario m; **—back** (payment) restitución f; (revenge) venganza f; **—check** cheque del sueldo m; **— cut** recorte salarial m; **—day** día de pago m; **— freeze** congelación salarial f; **—load** carga útil f; **—off** (pay) pago m; (reward) recompensa f; (bribe) soborno m; **— phone** teléfono público m; **— raise** aumento salarial / de sueldo m; **—roll** nómina f, planilla f; **— scale** escala salarial f; **to hit —dirt** encontrar una mina de oro

payable [péəbəl] ADJ pagadero

payee [peí] N tenedor -ora mf, beneficiario -ria mf

payment [pémənt] N pago m, abono m; **— in full** liquidación f; **car —s** cuotas del coche f pl

payola [peólə] N soborno m

PC [písí] N (personal computer) PC m; (political correctness) lo políticamente correcto; ADJ (politically correct) políticamente correcto

pea [pi] N guisante m; Am arveja f; **—nut** Sp cacahuete m; Mex cacahuate m; Am maní m; **—nut butter** Sp crema de cacahuete f; Mex crema de cacahuate f; Am manteca/mantequilla de maní f

peace [pis] N paz f; **— officer** oficial de policía m; **— of mind** serenidad f; **at —** en paz; **to keep the —** mantener el orden público; **to hold one's —** callar

peaceful [písfəl] ADJ pacífico, tranquilo

peach [pitʃ] N durazno m; Sp melocotón m; (nice thing or person) delicia f, monada f; **— tree** durazno m, duraznero m, Sp melocotonero m

peacock [píkɑk] N pavo real m, pavón m

peak [pik] N (of a mountain) pico m, cumbre f; (of production, of one's abilities) punto máximo m; (of one's career) punto culminante m; **— load** carga máxima f; **— season** temporada alta f; **— time** hora punta f

peal [piɫ] N (of bells) repique m; (of laughter) carcajada f; VI/VT repicar

pear [pɛr] N pera f; **— tree** peral m

pearl [pɝɫ] N perla f; **— necklace** collar de perlas m

pearly [pɝli] ADJ (color) nacarado, perlado; (with pearls) perlado; **the — gates** las puertas del cielo

peasant [pézənt] ADJ & N campesino -na mf

peat [pit] N turba f

pebble [pébəl] N guijarro m, piedrecilla f; (smooth) canto m

pecan [pɪkán] N pacana f

peccary [pékəri] N pecarí/pécari m

peck [pɛk] VI/VT (strike with beak) picar; (eat bit by bit) picotear; (kiss) dar un besito; **—ing order** jerarquía f; **to — a hole** agujerear a picotazos; N (quick stroke) picotazo m; (kiss) besito m; (measure) medida de áridos [9 litros] f; **you're in a — of trouble** estás metido en un lío

pectoral [péktəɫ] ADJ & N pectoral m

peculiar [pɪkjúljɚ] ADJ peculiar, particular

peculiarity [pɪkjuljæɪɾi] N peculiaridad f

pedagogical [pɛDəgádʒɪkəl] ADJ pedagógico

pedagogue [pɛDəgag] N pedagogo -ga mf

pedagogy [pɛDəgadʒi] N pedagogía f

pedal [pédl] N pedal m; VI/VT pedalear

pedant [pédn̩t] N pedante mf

pedantic [pədǽntɪk] ADJ pedante

peddle [pédl] VI/VT ir vendiendo de puerta en puerta; **to — gossip** repartir chismes

peddler [pédlɚ] N buhonero -ra mf, mercachifle m

pederast [péDəræst] N pederasta m

pederasty [péDəræsti] N pederastia f

pedestal [pédɪstl̩] N pedestal m

pedestrian [pədéstrɪən] N peatón -ona mf; ADJ pedestre

pediatrician [piDiətríʃən] N pediatra mf

pediatrics [piDiǽtrɪks] N pediatría f

pedigree [péDəgri] N (of persons) linaje m; (of animals) pedigrí m

pedophile [péDəfaɪl] N pedófilo -la mf

pedophilia [péDəfíliə] N pedofilia f

pee [pi] VI fam mear, hacer pipí; N fam pipí m

peek [pik] VI atisbar; N atisbo m

peel [piɫ] VI/VT (fruit, tree) pelar[se], descortezar[se]; (paint) descascarar[se]; **to**

keep one's eyes —ed mantener los ojos abiertos; N cáscara f
peeler [pílɚ] N pelador m
peep [pip] VI/VT (begin to appear) asomar[se]; VI (make sound of chicks) piar; **to — at** atisbar; N (look) atisbo m; (sound of chicks) pío m; **—hole** mirilla f; **— show** espectáculo de striptease m
peer [pir] N par m (also nobleman); **— group** grupo paritario m; VI (look attentively) escudriñar; (peep out) asomar
peerless [pírlɪs] ADJ incomparable, sin par
peeve [piv] VT irritar; **to get —d** ponerse de mal humor; N cosa que irrita f
peevish [pívɪʃ] ADJ malhumorado
peg [pɛg] N percha f; (on violin) clavija f; **to take a person down a —** bajarle los humos a alguien; VT (fix with pegs) clavar, clavetear; (set a price) fijar
pejorative [pɪʤɔ́rəDɪv] ADJ peyorativo, despectivo
pelican [pélɪkən] N pelícano m
pellet [pélɪt] N (ball) bola f, bolita f; (shot) perdigón m
pell-mell [pɛ́łmɛ́ł] ADJ confuso, tumultuoso; ADV a troche y moche
pelt [pɛłt] N piel f, pellejo m; VI/VT acribillar; **to — with stones** apedrear
pelvis [pélvɪs] N pelvis f
pen [pɛn] N (fountain) pluma f; (ballpoint) bolígrafo m; (for pigs) pocilga f; (for sheep) redil m; (for cows) corral m; **— holder** mango de pluma m, portaplumas m sg; **— name** seudónimo m; VT (write) escribir; (shut in) acorralar, encerrar; **— computer** Am bolígrafo-computadora portátil f, Sp bolígrafo-ordenador portátil m
penal [pínl] ADJ penal
penalize [pénəlaɪz] VT penar; (in sports) penalizar
penalty [pénlti] N (punishment) pena f, castigo m; (forfeiture) multa f; (in sports) penalidad f, infracción f; **— area** (in soccer) área de penales f; **— kick** (in soccer) tiro de penalidad f, penalti m; **— shootout** (in soccer) definición por penales f; **— stroke** (in golf) golpe de penalidad m
penance [pénəns] N penitencia f
pencil [pénsəl] N (writing instrument) lápiz m; (beam of light) haz m; **— sharpener** sacapuntas m sg
pendant [péndənt] ADJ pendiente
pendent [péndənt] N colgante m; ADJ pendiente
pending [péndɪŋ] ADJ pendiente; PREP **— his arrival** hasta que llegue, mientras no llegue
pendulum [pénʤələm] N péndulo m
penetrate [pénɪtret] VT penetrar
penetrating [pénɪtreDɪŋ] ADJ penetrante
penetration [pɛnɪtréʃən] N penetración f

penguin [péŋgwɪn] N pingüino m
penicillin [pɛnɪsílɪn] N penicilina f
peninsula [pənínsələ] N península f
penis [pínɪs] N pene m
penitent [pénɪtənt] ADJ & N penitente mf
penitentiary [pɛnɪténʃəri] N penitenciaría f, penal m
penmanship [pénmənʃɪp] N escritura f, caligrafía f
pennant [pénənt] N banderín m, gallardete m
penniless [pénɪlɪs] ADJ pobre, sin dinero
penny [péni] N centavo m; **—-pincher** tacaño-ña mf; **to cost a pretty —** costar un dineral
pension [pénʃən] N (paid to a worker) jubilación f; (paid to a worker's survivors) pensión f; **— fund** caja de jubilaciones f; VT jubilar, pensionar
pensioner [pénʃənɚ] N pensionista mf
pensive [pénsɪv] ADJ pensativo
pent [pɛnt] ADJ encerrado; **—-up** acumulado
pentagon [péntəgan] N pentágono m
penthouse [pénthaʊs] N penthouse m
penultimate [pɪnʌ́łtəmɪt] ADJ penúltimo
people [pípəl] N gente f; (national group) pueblo m; VT poblar
pep [pɛp] N energía f; VI **to — up** animar
pepper [pépɚ] N (black) pimienta f; (green) pimiento m; (plant, shaker) pimentero m; **—mint** menta f; VI **to — with bullets** acribillar a balazos
peptic ulcer [péptɪk ʌ́lsɚ] N úlcera péptica f
per [pɚ] PREP (for each) por; (according to) según; **— capita** per capita; **—cent** por ciento; **— diem** Am viático m, Sp dieta f
percale [pɚkéł] N percal m
perceive [pɚsív] VT percibir
percentage [pɚséntɪʤ] N porcentaje m
percentile [pɚséntaɪł] N percentil m
perceptible [pɚséptəbəł] ADJ perceptible
perception [pɚsépʃən] N percepción f
perceptive [pɚséptɪv] ADJ (pertaining to perception) perceptivo; (having keen perception) perspicaz
perch [pɚʧ] N (rod for birds) percha f; (type of fish) perca f; VT (alight) posarse; VI/VT (set) encaramar[se]
percolate [pɚ́kəlet] VI/VT filtrar[se]
percussion [pɚkʌ́ʃən] N percusión f
perdition [pɚdíʃən] N perdición f
perennial [pərénɪəł] ADJ perenne; **— plant** planta perenne f
perfect[1] [pɚ́fɪkt] ADJ perfecto; **a — stranger** un completo desconocido
perfect[2] [pɚfékt] VT perfeccionar
perfection [pɚfékʃən] N perfección f
perfectionist [pɚfékʃənɪst] N perfeccionista mf
perfectly [pɚ́fɪktli] ADV (completely) totalmente; (without error) a la perfección, perfectamente; **stand — still** no te muevas

perforate [pɚ́fəret] VI/VT perforar[se]; VT calar
perforation [pɚfəréʃən] N perforación f
perform [pəfɔ́rm] VT (a task) ejecutar, realizar; (a rite, ceremony) celebrar; (a contract) cumplir; (a play) representar; VI (give a performance) actuar; (play music) interpretar; (function) funcionar; (do well) rendir; **to — simultaneously** simultanear
performance [pɚfɔ́rməns] N (of a task) ejecución f; (of a ceremony) celebración f; (of a contract) cumplimiento m; (of a device) desempeño m, rendimiento m; (of a play) representación f; (of an actor) actuación f; (of music) interpretación f; — **review** evaluación del rendimiento f
performer [pɚfɔ́rmɚ] N (drama) artista mf, actor m, actriz f; (music) artista mf, intérprete mf
perfume¹ [pɚ́fjum] N perfume m
perfume² [pɚfjúm] VT perfumar
perfumery [pɚfjúməri] N (store) perfumería f; (collection) perfumes m pl
perhaps [pəhǽps] ADV tal vez, quizá[s], acaso
peril [pérəl] N peligro m
perilous [pérələs] ADJ peligroso
perimeter [pərímɪdɚ] N perímetro m
period [píriəd] N período m; (historical) época f; (punctuation) punto m; (menstruation) período m, regla f; **you can't go,** —! no puedes ir, y sanseacabó; **within a — of ten days** en el término de diez días
periodic [pɪriáɖɪk] ADJ periódico; — **table** tabla periódica f
periodical [pɪriáɖɪkəl] ADJ periódico; N revista f
peripheral [pərífɚəl] ADJ & N periférico m; — **vision** visión periférica f
periphery [pərífɚi] N periferia f
periscope [pérɪskop] N periscopio m
perish [périʃ] VI perecer
perishable [périʃəbəl] ADJ perecedero
peritonitis [pɛrɪtn̥áɪɖɪs] N peritonitis f
perjure [pɚ́ʤɚ] VI **to — oneself** perjurarse, jurar en falso
perjury [pɚ́ʤəri] N perjurio m
perks [pɚks] N beneficios adicionales m pl
permanence [pɚ́mənəns] N permanencia f
permanent [pɚ́mənənt] ADJ permanente; (of a position) titular
permeable [pɚ́miəbəl] ADJ permeable
permeate [pɚ́miet] VI/VT permear
permissible [pəmísəbəl] ADJ permisible, lícito
permission [pəmíʃən] N permiso m
permissive [pəmísɪv] ADJ permisivo
permit¹ [pəmít] VI/VT (allow) permitir; (make possible) posibilitar
permit² [pɚ́mɪt] N permiso m
permutation [pɚmjutéʃən] N permutación f
pernicious [pɚníʃəs] ADJ pernicioso
peroxide [pəráksaɪd] N peróxido m

perpendicular [pɚpɪndíkjələ] ADJ & N perpendicular f
perpetrate [pɚ́pɪtret] VT perpetrar
perpetual [pəpétʃuəl] ADJ perpetuo
perpetuate [pəpétʃuet] VT perpetuar
perplex [pəpléks] VT confundir, dejar perplejo; **—ed** perplejo
perplexity [pəpléksɪɖi] N perplejidad f
persecute [pɚ́sɪkjut] VT perseguir
persecution [pɚsɪkjúʃən] N persecución f
persecutor [pɚ́sɪkjuɖɚ] N perseguidor -ora mf
perseverance [pɚsəvírəns] N perseverancia f
persevere [pɚsəvír] VI perseverar, persistir
Persia [pɚ́ʒə] N Persia f
Persian [pɚ́ʒən] ADJ & N persa mf
persist [pəsíst] VI (continue, endure) persistir; (to be insistent) insistir
persistence [pəsístəns] N (endurance) persistencia f; (insistence) insistencia f
persistent [pəsístənt] ADJ (lasting) persistente; (insisting) insistente, machacón
person [pɚ́sən] N persona f
personable [pɚ́sənəbəl] ADJ agradable
personage [pɚ́sənɪʤ] N personaje m
personal [pɚ́sən̩] ADJ personal; — **computer** Sp ordenador personal m; Am computadora personal f; — **effects** efectos personales m pl; — **foul** falta personal f; — **identification number** número de identificación personal m; — **pronoun** pronombre personal m; — **property** bienes muebles m pl; **to make a — appearance** presentarse en persona
personality [pɚsənǽlɪɖi] N personalidad f; — **disorder** trastorno de la personalidad m
personally [pɚ́sənəli] ADV personalmente; **don't take it** — no lo tomes a pecho / a mal
personify [pɚsánəfaɪ] VT personificar
personnel [pɚsənɛ́l] N personal m
perspective [pəspɛ́ktɪv] N perspectiva f
perspicacious [pɚspɪkéʃəs] ADJ perspicaz
perspiration [pɚspəréʃən] N transpiración f
perspire [pəspáɪr] VI transpirar
persuade [pəswéd] VT persuadir, convencer
persuasion [pəswéʒən] N persuasión f; (belief) convicción f
persuasive [pəswésɪv] ADJ persuasivo, convincente
pert [pɚt] ADJ (insolent) insolente; (lively) vivaz
pertain [pətén] VI atañer, corresponder
pertinent [pɚ́tnənt] ADJ pertinente
perturb [pətɚ́b] VT perturbar
Peru [pərú] N Perú m
perusal [pərúzəl] N lectura f
peruse [pərúz] VT (read carefully) leer con cuidado; (read carelessly) hojear
Peruvian [pərúviən] ADJ & N peruano -na mf
pervade [pəvéd] VT difundirse por
perverse [pəvɚ́s] ADJ perverso
perversion [pəvɚ́ʒən] N perversión f

perversity [pɚvɚ́sɪDi] N perversidad *f*
pervert¹ [pɚvɚ́t] VT pervertir; (misconstrue) desvirtuar
pervert² [pɚ́vɚt] N pervertido -da *mf*
peso [péso] N peso *m*
pessimism [pésəmɪzəm] N pesimismo *m*
pessimist [pésəmɪst] N pesimista *mf*
pest [pɛst] N (insect, disease) peste *f*, plaga *f*; (person) pesado -da *mf*
pester [péstɚ] VT molestar
pesticide [péstɪsaɪd] N pesticida *m*
pestilence [péstələns] N pestilencia *f*
pet [pɛt] N (animal) mascota *f*; (favorite) favorito -ta *mf*, preferido -da *mf*; ADJ predilecto; — **name** apodo cariñoso *m*; VT (caress) acariciar; (pat) dar palmaditas a
petal [pédl] N pétalo *m*
petition [pətíʃən] N petición *f*, solicitud *f*; VI/VT peticionar, solicitar
petrify [pétrəfaɪ] VI/VT petrificar[se]
petroleum [pətróliəm] N petróleo *m*; — **products** productos petrolíferos *m pl*; — **jelly** vaselina *f*
petticoat [péDikot] N enaguas *f pl*
petty [péDi] ADJ (trivial) trivial; (mean) mezquino; — **cash** caja chica *f*; — **larceny** ratería *f*; — **officer** suboficial de marina *m*
petunia [pɪtúnjə] N petunia *f*
pew [pju] N banco *m* / banca *f* de iglesia
pewter [pjúDɚ] N peltre *m*
peyote [peóDi] N peyote *m*
phallus [fǽləs] N falo *m*
phantom [fǽntəm] N fantasma *f*
pharmaceutical [farməsúDɪkəł] ADJ farmacéutico; N producto farmacéutico *m*, fármaco *m*
pharmacist [fárməsɪst] N farmacéutico -ca *mf*
pharmacology [farməkáləʤi] N farmacología *f*
pharmacy [fárməsi] N farmacia *f*
pharynx [fǽrɪŋks] N faringe *f*
phase [fez] N fase *f*; VI **to — out** retirar por etapas; **to — in** incorporar paulatinamente
pheasant [fézənt] N faisán *m*
phenomenon [fɪnámənan] N fenómeno *m*
philanthropy [fɪlǽnθrəpi] N filantropía *f*
philharmonic [fɪlharmánɪk] ADJ filarmónico; N filarmónica *f*
Philippine [fɪ́ləpin] ADJ & N filipino -na *mf*
Philippines [fɪ́ləpinz] N filipinas *f pl*
philosopher [fɪlásəfɚ] N filósofo -fa *mf*
philosophical [fɪləsáfɪkəł] ADJ filosófico
philosophy [fɪlásəfi] N filosofía *f*
phishing [fíʃɪŋ] N phishing *m*
phlegm [flɛm] N flema *f*
phobia [fóbiə] N fobia *f*
phone [fon] N teléfono *m*; — **card** tarjeta telefónica *f*; VI/VT telefonear
phonetic [fənéDɪk] ADJ fonético
phonetics [fənéDɪks] N fonética *f*

phonograph [fónəgræf] N fonógrafo *m*
phonology [fənáləʤi] N fonología *f*
phony [fóni] ADJ falso
phosphate [fásfet] N fosfato *m*
phosphorus [fásfɚəs] N fósforo *m*
photo [fóDo] N foto *f*; — **finish** final muy reñido *m*
photocopier [fóDəkɑpiɚ] N fotocopiadora *f*
photocopy [fóDəkɑpi] N fotocopia *f*; VI/VT fotocopiar
photoelectric [foDoɪléktrɪk] ADJ fotoeléctrico
photogenic [foDəʤénɪk] ADJ fotogénico
photograph [fóDəgræf] N fotografía *f*; VT fotografiar
photographer [fətágrəfɚ] N fotógrafo -fa *mf*
photography [fətágrəfi] N fotografía *f*
photon [fótɑn] N fotón *m*
photosynthesis [foDosínθəsɪs] N fotosíntesis *f*
phrase [frez] N frase *f*; VI/VT expresar; (musical) frasear
phylum [fáiləm] N filo *m*
physical [fízɪkəł] ADJ físico; — **education** educación física *f*; — **geography** geografía física *f*; — **science** ciencia física *f*; — **therapy** fisioterapia *f*
physician [fɪzíʃən] N médico -ca *mf*; —'**s assistant** ayudante médico -ca sanitario -ria *mf*
physicist [fízɪsɪst] N físico ca *mf*
physics [fízɪks] N física *f*
physiological [fɪziəládʒɪkəł] ADJ fisiológico
physiology [fɪziáləʤi] N fisiología *f*
physique [fɪzík] N físico *m*
pianist [piænɪst] N pianista *mf*
piano [piǽno] N piano *m*; — **bench** banqueta de piano *f*; — **hammer** martinete *m*; — **player** pianista *mf*; — **stool** taburete de piano *m*
picaresque [pɪkərésk] ADJ picaresco
piccolo [píkələ] N flautín *m*, pícolo *m*
pick [pɪk] VT (choose) escoger, elegir; (gather flowers) juntar; (play a guitar) puntear; (clean teeth) mondarse; (eat with the bill) picotear; (provoke a fight) armar, entablar; VI picar; **to — at** picotear; **to — apart** criticar; **to — a lock** violar una cerradura con ganzúa; **to — on** meterse con; **to — out** (choose) escoger; (distinguish) distinguir; **to — pockets** ratear; **to — up** (gather) recoger; (lift) levantar; (learn) aprender; (order) ordenar; (improve) mejorar; (contact in hope of sex) ligar con; **to — up speed** acelerar la marcha; N (tool) pico *m*; (of a guitar) púa *f*; (act of selecting) selección *f*; (thing or person selected) elección *f*; (the best) lo selecto, lo mejor; —**ax[e]** zapapico *m*; —**lock** ganzúa *f*; —**pocket** ratero -ra *mf*, carterista *mf*; —**up** (taking on freight) recolección *f*; (improvement in business) recuperación *f*; (casual sexual acquaintance) ligue *m*, plan *m*;

(acceleration) aceleración *f*; **—up truck** camioneta *f*; ADJ **—-proof** a prueba de ladrones

picket [píkɪt] N piquete *m* (also union worker); **— fence** cerca de piquetes *f*; VT (fence) vallar; (block with workers) bloquear, *Am* piquetear

pickle [píkəɫ] N pepinillo en vinagre *m*, curtido *m*; **to be in a —** hallarse en un aprieto; VT encurtir, escabechar; **—d fish** pescado al/en escabeche *m*, pescado adobado *m*

picnic [píknɪk] N picnic *m*; **— area** merendero *m*; VI hacer un picnic

pictorial [pɪktóriəɫ] ADJ pictórico

picture [píktʃɚ] N (image) imagen *f*; (drawing) dibujo *m*; (photo) fotografía *f*; (situation) panorama *m*; (movie) película *f*; **— frame** marco *m*; **— gallery** galería de pinturas *f*; **— tube** tubo de imagen *m*; **she is the — of unhappiness** es la imagen de la infelicidad; VT (describe) describir; (imagine) imaginar

picturesque [pɪktʃərésk] ADJ pintoresco

pie [paɪ] N pastel *m*, tarta *f*; **— chart** diagrama de pastel *m*; **— graph** gráfica de pastel *f*; **— in the sky** castillos en el aire *m pl*; **it's as easy as —** es pan comido

piece [pis] N (of music, in a board game, of furniture) pieza *f*; (of wood, rock, pie) pedazo *m*, trozo *m*; **—meal** por partes; **— of advice** consejo *m*; **— of cake** pan comido *m*; **— of land** parcela *f*, terreno *m*; **— of one's mind** regaño *m*; **— of news** noticia *f*; **— of shit** *vulg* mierda *f*; **—work** trabajo a destajo *m*; **to go to —s** descomponerse; VI **to — together** (assemble) armar; (make sense of) atar cabos

pier [pir] N muelle *m*, embarcadero *m*; (breakwater) rompeolas *m sg*

pierce [pirs] VI/VT (make a hole in) agujerear, perforar; (penetrate) penetrar; (cause a sharp pain) punzar

piercing [pírsɪŋ] ADJ (glance, sound) penetrante; (pain) punzante; N perforación *f*

piety [páɪɪDi] N piedad *f*

pig [pɪg] N puerco *m*, cerdo *m*, cochino *m*; *Sp* guarro *m*; **—-headed** testarudo, cabezón; **—-iron** hierro en lingotes *m*; **— Latin** jerigonza *f*; **—pen** pocilga *f*; **—tail** coleta *f*

pigeon [píʤən] N paloma *f*; (young) pichón *m*; **—hole** casilla *f*; **— loft** palomar *m*; VT **to —hole** encasillar

piggy [pígi] N cerdito *m*; **—bank** alcancía *f*; *Sp* hucha *f*; ADV **—back** a hombros, a cuestas

pigment [pígmənt] N pigmento *m*

pike [paɪk] N (weapon) pica *f*; (fish) lucio *m*

pile [paɪɫ] N (ordered stack) pila *f*; (chaotic group) montón *m*, amontonamiento *m*; (surface of a carpet) pelo *m*; (post) pilote *m*; **— driver** martinete *m*; **—s** almorranas *f pl*; **—-up** accidente múltiple *m*; VI/VT apilar[se], amontonar[se]

pilfer [píɫfɚ] VI/VT ratear, sisar

pilferage [píɫfɚɪʤ] N ratería *f*

pilgrim [píɫgrəm] N peregrino -na *mf*, romero -ra *mf*

pilgrimage [píɫgrəmɪʤ] N peregrinación *f*, romería *f*

pill [pɪɫ] N píldora *f*, pastilla *f*; (naughty child) pesado -da *mf*

pillage [píliʤ] N pillaje *m*, saqueo *m*, rapiña *f*; VI/VT pillar, saquear

pillar [píɫɚ] N pilar *m*, columna *f*

pillow [pílo] N almohada *f*; **—case** funda *f*

pilot [páɪlət] N piloto *mf* (also test, light); (of a boat) timonel *m*, piloto *mf*; VT pilotar, comandar

pimp [pɪmp] N proxeneta *mf*, rufián *m*

pimple [pímpəɫ] N grano *m*, barro *m*

pin [pɪn] N (sewing implement) alfiler *m*; (ornament) prendedor *m*; (rod) pasador *m*, perno *m*; (bowling) bolo *m*; (electric) pata *f*, clavija *f*; **—cushion** alfiletero *m*; **—wheel** molinete *m*, remolino *m*; **to be on —s and needles** estar en ascuas; VT (affix with pins) prender; (in wrestling) inmovilizar; **to — someone down** (hold down) inmovilizar; (force to act) hacer que concrete detalles; **to — one's hopes on** poner sus esperanzas en; **to —point** localizar con precisión; **to — up** sujetar con alfileres

PIN [personal identification number] [pɪn] N PIN *m*

pincers [pínsɚz] N (of lobsters) pinzas *f pl*; (tool) tenazas *f pl*

pinch [pɪntʃ] VT (squeeze with fingers) pellizcar; (squeeze tightly, hamper) apretar; (steal) birlar; (arrest) prender; VI (be too tight) apretar; (economize) economizar; **—ed nerve** nervio pellizcado *m*, nervio pinzado *m*; N (act of pinching) pellizco *m*; (small amount) pizca *f*; (trying circumstances) aprieto *m*, apuro *m*; **— hitter** bateador -ora emergente *mf*; **— runner** corredor emergente *m*

pine [paɪn] N pino *m*; **—apple** piña *f*, ananá[s] *m*; **— cone** piña *f*; **— grove** pinar *m*; **— nut** piñón *m*; VI **to — away** languidecer; **to — for** anhelar, suspirar por

pingpong [píŋpɑŋ] N ping-pong *m*, tenis de mesa *m*

pinion [pínjən] N piñón *m*

pink [pɪŋk] N rosado *m*, rosa *m*; **—eye** conjuntivitis *f*; **— slip** notificación de despido *f*; **in the —** rebosante de salud; ADJ rosado, rosa

pinnacle [pínəkəɫ] N pináculo *m*

pint [paɪnt] N pinta *f*; ADJ **—-sized** diminuto

pinto bean [píntobin] N judía pinta *f*

pioneer [paɪənír] N pionero -ra *mf*; VI ser el primero en hacer algo; VT promover

pious [páɪəs] ADJ (religious) pío, piadoso; (hypocritical) beato

pipe [paɪp] N (for smoking) pipa f; (for water) tubo m, caño m; (of an organ) tubo m; (flute) caramillo m, flauta f; — **dream** ilusiones f pl; —**line** (for oil) oleoducto m; (for gas) gasoducto m; (for water) tubería f; **in the** —**line** en trámite; — **wrench** llave inglesa f; VT (convey water) conducir por cañerías; (make music) tocar la flauta; VI chillar; **to** — **down** callarse

piping [páɪpɪŋ] N (many pipes) cañería f, tubería f; (border on clothes) ribete m; (sound of pipes) sonido de la gaita/flauta m; ADJ — **hot** hirviendo

pipsqueak [pípskwik] N chisgarabís m, mequetrefe m

piracy [páɪrəsi] N piratería f

pirate [páɪrɪt] N pirata mf; VT piratear

piss [pɪs] VI/VT fam mear; **to** — **off** enfadar

pistol [pístl] N pistola f, revólver m; VT **to** — - **whip** dar culatazos

piston [pístn̩] N pistón m, émbolo m; — **ring** segmento de compresión m; — **rod** eje del pistón m

pit [pɪt] N (hole) hoyo m, pozo m; (in a garage, theater) foso m; (trap) trampa f; (seed) hueso m; (part of a racetrack) box m, paddock m; (part of the stomach) boca f; **fall** (trap) trampa f; (difficulty) dificultad f; **this is the** —**s** esto es lo peor; VI/VT (make holes) picarse; VT **to** — **against** oponer, enfrentar

pitch [pɪtʃ] VT (throw) tirar, lanzar; (try to sell) pregonar; **to** — **a tent** armar una tienda; VI (plane, ship) cabecear; **to** — **in** colaborar; N (throw) tiro m, lanzamiento m; (in music) tono m; (in printing) espaciado m; (slope) grado de inclinación m; (tar) brea f, pez f; — **dark** oscuro como boca del lobo; —**fork** horca f, horquilla f

pitcher [pítʃɚ] N (vessel) cántaro m, jarro m, jarra f; (in baseball) lanzador -ora mf; —**'s mound** montículo m

pith [pɪθ] N (in plants, feathers) médula f; (essence) meollo m

pithy [píθi] ADJ sustancial

pitiful [pídɪfəł] ADJ (deserving pity) lastimoso; (deserving contempt) despreciable

pitiless [pídɪlɪs] ADJ despiadado

pituitary [pɪtúɪteri] ADJ pituitario; — **gland** glándula pituitaria f

pity [pídi] N compasión f, lástima f; **what a** —! ¡qué lástima! VT compadecerse [de]

pivot [pívət] N pivote m; VI pivotar

pixel [píksəł] N píxel m

pizza [pítsə] N pizza f

placard [plǽkɚd] N cartel m

placate [pléket] VT apaciguar

place [ples] N (site) lugar m, sitio m; (position)

puesto m; **mat** mantel individual m; — **of birth** lugar de nacimiento m; — **of business** oficina f; — **of worship** templo m; — **setting** cubierto para una persona m; **in** — **of** en lugar de; **it is not my** — **to do it** no me corresponde a mí hacerlo; VT (put) colocar; (identify) situar, ubicar; **to** — **an order** hacer un pedido; **to** — **an ad** poner un anuncio; VI (in sports) clasificarse

placebo [pləsíbo] N placebo m

placement [plésmənt] N (in levels, categories) colocación f, posicionamiento m; (in space) emplazamiento m

placenta [pləséntə] N placenta f

placid [plǽsɪd] ADJ plácido

plagiarism [plédʒərɪzəm] N plagio m

plague [pleg] N plaga f, peste f; VT atormentar, apestar

plaid [plæd] N tela escocesa f

plain [plen] ADJ (without embellishment) sencillo, llano; (clear) claro; (downright, unadulterated) puro; (ordinary) común; (unattractive) poco atractivo; **in** — **sight** en plena vista; —**clothesman** policía en traje de civil m; —-**Jane** sencillo; ADV completamente; N llano m, llanura f

plaintiff [pléntɪf] N demandante mf, querellante mf

plan [plæn] N plan m; (drawing, sketch, map, outline) plano m; VI/VT planear, planificar; (diagram) hacer el plano de; —**ned parenthood** planificación familiar f

plane [plen] N (airplane) avión m; (surface) plano m; (tool) cepillo m; — **tree** plátano m; ADJ plano; — **geometry** geometría plana f; VI (glide, hover) planear; VT (smooth) cepillar, planear

planet [plǽnɪt] N planeta m

planetarium [plænɪtériəm] N planetario m

plank [plæŋk] N (board) tabla f, tablón m; (tenet) principio m, base f; VT entarimar

plankton [plǽŋktən] N plancton m

planning [plǽnɪŋ] N planeamiento m, planificación f

plant [plænt] N (vegetation) planta f; (industrial installation) fábrica f, planta f; (mole, spy) topo m; VT (plants) plantar; (ideas) sembrar; (a spy, evidence) colocar

plantain [plǽnten] N plátano m

plantation [plæntéʃən] N plantación f

plaque [plæk] N placa f; (on teeth) sarro m, placa f

plasma [plǽzmə] N plasma m, gas ionizado m

plaster [plǽstɚ] N (substance) yeso m; (preparation applied to body) emplasto m; — **of Paris** yeso m; VT (cover with plaster) revocar; (apply a preparation) emplastar; (cover with posters) cubrir, empapelar; (defeat) aplastar; **to** — **down one's hair** achatarse el pelo; **to get** —**ed** emborracharse

plastic [plǽstɪk] ADJ plástico; — **surgery** cirugía plástica/estética f

plate [plet] N (for food) plato m; (for collections) bandeja f; (metal) plancha f, lámina f; (license) placa f; — **glass** vidrio cilindrado m; — **tectonics** tectónica de placas f; VT (apply metal covering) chapar, enchapar; (apply armor) blindar

plateau [plætó] N meseta f, macizo m

platform [plǽtfɔrm] N plataforma f (also in politics, computers); (railway) andén m; (mobile) tarima f, tinglado m

platinum [plǽtṇəm] N platino m

platitude [plǽdɪtud] N lugar común m, perogrullada f

platter [plǽDɚ] N fuente f

plausible [plɔ́zəbəl] ADJ plausible

play [ple] VT (game) jugar; (an opponent) jugar contra; (an instrument) tocar; (a drama) representar; (a role) desempeñar; (bet on) apostar; **to — a joke** gastar una broma; **to — cards** jugar a los naipes; **to — havoc** hacer estragos; **to — tennis** jugar al tenis; **to — the fool** hacerse el tonto; VI (divert oneself, gamble) jugar; (kid) bromear; (make music) tocar; **to — along** seguir la corriente; **to — down** minimizar; **to be all —ed out** estar agotado; N (recreational activity, looseness) juego m; (instance of playing) jugada f; (theater work) obra de teatro f; — **on words** juego de palabras m; **—boy** playboy m; **—ground** recreo m, patio m; **—ing card** naipe m; **—mate** compañero -ra de juego mf; **—off [game]** [partido de] desempate m; **the —offs** las eliminatorias f pl; **—thing** juguete m

player [pléɚ] N (one who plays, gambler) jugador -ora mf; (musician) músico -ca mf; (influential person) persona influyente f; (womanizer) mujeriego m; (actor) actor m, actriz f; (participant) participante mf; — **piano** pianola f

playful [pléfəl] ADJ juguetón

playwright [pléraɪt] N dramaturgo -ga mf

plea [pli] N (entreaty) súplica f, ruego m; (allegation) alegato m; **to enter a — of guilty** declararse culpable

plead [plid] VI/VT (entreat) suplicar, rogar; (defend) abogar, defender; **to — guilty** declararse culpable

pleasant [plézənt] ADJ agradable, grato, placentero

pleasantry [plézəntri] N cortesía f

please [pliz] ADV por favor; VI/VT agradar, complacer; **as you —** como quieras; **to be —d to** tener el gusto de, tener gusto en; **to be —d with** estar satisfecho con

pleasing [plízɪŋ] ADJ agradable

pleasure [pléʒɚ] N placer m, gusto m, agrado m; — **trip** viaje de placer m

pleat [plit] N pliegue m, tabla f; (wide) tabla f; VT plisar; (wide) tablear

pled [plɛd] see plead

pledge [plɛdʒ] N (promise) promesa f; (security deposit) prenda f; (in a fraternity) miembro provisorio m; **as a — of** en prenda de; VI/VT (promise) prometer; VT (give as a deposit) empeñar; **to — one's word** dar la palabra; **to — to secrecy** exigir promesa de discreción

plenary [plénəri] ADJ & N plenario m

plentiful [pléntɪfəl] ADJ abundante, copioso

plenty [plénti] N abundancia f; — **of time** suficiente tiempo m; **that's —** con eso basta

pliable [pláɪəbəl] ADJ (flexible) flexible; (docile) dócil

pliant [plaɪənt] ADJ (flexible) flexible; (docile) dócil

pliers [pláɪɚz] N alicates m pl, tenazas f pl

plight [plaɪt] N aprieto m

plod [plɑd] VI (walk) caminar trabajosamente; (work) trabajar laboriosamente

plop [plɑp] VI hacer plaf; VT dejar caer; N plaf m

plot [plɑt] N (storyline) trama f, argumento m; (conspiracy) complot m, conspiración f; (land) parcela f, era f; (floor plan) plano m; VI/VT (plan secretly) tramar, conspirar, maquinar; VT (make a graph) hacer un gráfico; **to — a course** trazar un curso

plotter [plɑ́Dɚ] N (one who plots) conspirador -ora mf; (device) trazador de gráficos m

plover [plóvɚ] N chorlito m

plow [plaʊ] N arado m; **—share** reja de arado f; VI/VT arar; (uncultivated area) roturar; **to — through** abrirse paso

plowing [pláʊɪŋ] N labranza f

pluck [plʌk] VT (a feather, flower) arrancar; (bird) desplumar; (guitar) puntear, pulsar; **to — out/off** desprender; **to — up courage** animarse, cobrar ánimo; N (act of plucking) tirón m; (courage) valor m

plug [plʌg] N (stopper) tapón m; (horse) pej penco m; (electric) enchufe m; (advertisement) mención favorable f; (tobacco) rollo m; **—-in** (electrical) enchufe m; (computer accessory) plug-in m; VT (close) tapar; (advertise) hacer una mención favorable de; VI **to — along** no parar; **to — in** enchufar; **to — up** tapar

plum [plʌm] N (fruit) ciruela f; — **tree** ciruelo m; **that job is a real —** ese trabajo es estupendo

plumage [plúmɪdʒ] N plumaje m

plumb [plʌm] N (lead weight) plomada f; — **bob** plomada f; **to be out of —** no estar a plomo; ADJ (perpendicular) a plomo; ADV (in a vertical direction) a plomo; (completely) completamente; VT (measure depth) sondear; (test for verticality) aplomar; (examine) examinar

plumber [plʌ́mɚ] N plomero -ra mf; Sp

fontanero -ra *mf*

plumbing [plʌ́mɪŋ] N (work and trade) plomería *f*; *Sp* fontanería *f*; (system of pipes) cañerías *f pl*

plume [plum] N penacho *m*; VT adornar con plumas

plummet [plʌ́mɪt] VI precipitarse; N plomada *f*

plump [plʌmp] ADJ rechoncho, regordete, rollizo; VI/VT **to — down** dejar[se] caer

plunder [plʌ́ndɚ] N (act of plundering) pillaje *m*, saqueo *m*; (loot) botín *m*; VI/VT pillar, saquear

plunge [plʌndʒ] VI/VT (into water) zambullir[se], sumergir[se]; (into something solid) hundir[se]; VI (fall) precipitarse; (slope downward) bajar repentinamente; **to — headlong** echarse de cabeza; N zambullida *f*; (rush) salto *m*

plunger [plʌ́ndʒɚ] N (for a toilet) desatascador *m*; (of a pump) émbolo *m*

pluperfect [plupɚ́fɪkt] N pluscuamperfecto *m*

plural [plúrəl] ADJ & N plural *m*

plurality [plurǽlɪɾi] N pluralidad *f*

plus [plʌs] PREP más; N (advantage) ventaja *f*; **two — three** dos más tres *m*; **on the — side** en el lado positivo; **— sign** signo de más *m*

plush [plʌʃ] N felpa *f*; ADJ (fabric) afelpado; (hotel) lujoso

plutonium [plutóniəm] N plutonio *m*

ply [plaɪ] VT (use) manejar; (assail with questions) acosar; (navigate a body of water) surcar; VI (travel regularly) recorrer con regularidad; (work steadily) aplicarse; **to — a trade** ejercer un oficio; N (layer of cloth, rubber) capa *f*; (layer of plywood) chapa *f*; **—wood** madera compensada *f*, contrachapado *m*

pneumatic [numǽɾɪk] ADJ neumático

pneumonia [numónjə] N pulmonía *f*

poach [potʃ] VT (eggs) escalfar; VI/VT (game) cazar furtivamente

pocket [pákɪt] N (in clothes) bolsillo *m*; (vein of ore) filón *m*; (on a pool table) tronera *f*; (of air) bache *m*; (of poverty) bolsa *f*; **—book** cartera *f*, *Sp* bolso *m*; **— book** libro de bolsillo *m*; **—knife** navaja *f*; **— of resistance** foco de resistencia *m*; VT meterse en el bolsillo; (appropriate) embolsar; (knock in a billiard ball) meter en la tronera

pod [pad] N (seed vessel) vaina *f*; (herd of cetaceans) manada *f*

podiatrist [pədáɪətrɪst] N podólogo -ga *mf*

podiatry [pədáɪətri] N podiatría *f*

podium [pódiəm] N podio *m*

poem [póəm] N poema *m*, poesía *f*

poet [póɪt] N poeta *mf*

poetic [poéɾɪk] ADJ poético; **— justice** justicia divina *f*; N **—s** poética *f*

poetry [póɪtri] N poesía *f*

poignant [pɔ́ɪnjənt] ADJ conmovedor

poinsettia [pɔɪnséɾə] N flor de Pascua *f*

point [pɔɪnt] N (place) punto *m*; (score, in sports) punto *m*, anotación *f*; (sharp end) punta *f*; **— after touchdown** punto extra *m*; **— guard** (basketball) base *mf*, conductor -ora *mf*, guardia *mf*; **— of origin** punto de origen *m*; **— of view** punto de vista *m*; **it is not to the —** no viene al caso; **I don't see the —** no le veo el sentido; **on the —** of a punto de; ADV **—-blank** a quemarropa; VT (direct finger at) apuntar con, señalar con; (indicate) señalar; **to — at** (with finger) señalar; (with a gun) apuntar hacia; **to — out** señalar, indicar; **to — up** enfatizar

pointed [pɔ́ɪntɪd] ADJ (having a point) puntiagudo; (piercing) agudo; **— arch** arco ojival *m*

pointer [pɔ́ɪntɚ] N (stick) puntero *m*; (on a scale) indicador *m*; (dog) perro de muestra *m*; (advice) consejo *m*

pointless [pɔ́ɪntlɪs] ADJ inútil

poise [pɔɪz] N (balance, steadiness) equilibrio *m*; (dignified bearing) aplomo *m*; **to be —d to** estar listo para; VI/VT equilibrar[se]

poison [pɔ́ɪzən] N veneno *m*, ponzoña *f*; **— ivy** hiedra venenosa *f*; VT envenenar, emponzoñar

poisoning [pɔ́ɪzənɪŋ] N (accidental) intoxicación *f*; (intentional) envenenamiento *m*

poisonous [pɔ́ɪzənəs] ADJ venenoso, ponzoñoso

poke [pok] VT (jab) clavar, pinchar; (stir a fire) atizar; (thrust out, as one's head) asomar; **to — out an eye** sacar un ojo; VI **to — along** andar perezosamente; **to — around** husmear; **to — fun at** burlarse de; **to — into** meterse en; **to — out** (project) sobresalir; N pinchazo *m*

Poland [pólənd] N Polonia *f*

polar [pólɚ] ADJ polar; **— bear** oso polar *m*

polarity [pəlǽrɪɾi] N polaridad *f*

polarization [polɚɪzéʃən] N polarización *f*

polarize [pólɚaɪz] VI/VT polarizar[se]

pole [pol] N (long piece of wood, metal) poste *m*; (for a flag) asta *f*; (for vaulting) pértiga *f*, garrocha *f*; (earth's axis) polo *m*; (for skiing) bastón *m*; **— vault** salto con pértiga *m*

Pole [pol] N polaco -ca *mf*

polemic [pəlémɪk] ADJ polémico *m*; N polémica *f*

police [pəlís] N policía *f*; **— car** patrullero *m*; **— dog** perro policía *m*; **— force** cuerpo de policía *m*; **—man** policía *m*; **— officer** oficial de policía *mf*, *Am* carabinero -ra *mf*; **— operation** *Am* operativo policial *m*; **— report** parte policial *m*; **— state** estado policíaco *m*; **— station** comisaría de policía *f*; **—woman** policía *f*; VT patrullar

policy [pálɪsi] N (procedure) política *f*; (for insurance) póliza *f*

polio [pólio] N polio *f*

Polish [pólɪʃ] ADJ & N polaco -ca *mf*

polish [pálɪʃ] N (sheen) lustre *m*, refinamiento *m*; (refinement) urbanidad *f*, cultura *f*; (substance for furniture) cera *f*; (substance for shoes) betún *m*; VT (a speech) pulir; (a metal) sacar brillo; (a car) encerar; (shoes) lustrar, embetunar; **to — off** despachar; **to — up** (metal) sacar brillo; (speech) pulir

polite [pəláɪt] ADJ cortés

politeness [pəláɪtnɪs] N cortesía *f*

politic [pálɪtɪk] ADJ diplomático, político

political [pəlíDɪkəł] ADJ político; — **prisoner** preso -sa político -ca *mf*; — **science** ciencias políticas *f pl*

politically correct [pəlíDɪklikɔrékt] ADJ políticamente correcto

politician [pɑlɪtíʃən] N político -ca *mf*

politics [pálɪtɪks] N política *f*

polka [półkə] N polca *f*; — **dot** lunar *m*

poll [poł] N (survey) encuesta *f*; —**s** (elections) comicios *m pl*; (voting place) urna *f*; VT (survey) encuestar; (receive votes) obtener; (record vote of) registrar

pollen [pálən] N polen *m*

pollinate [pálənet] VT polinizar

pollute [pəlút] VI/VT contaminar

pollution [pəlúʃən] N contaminación *f*

polo [pólo] N polo *m*

polyester [pɑliéstɚ] N poliéster *m*

polygamy [pəlígəmi] N poligamia *f*

polyglot [páliglɑt] ADJ & N políglota *mf*

polygraph [páligræf] N polígrafo *m*

polymer [páləmɚ] N polímero *m*

polyp [pálɪp] N pólipo *m*

polyunsaturated [pɑliʌnsǽtʃəreDɪd] ADJ poliinsaturado

polyurethane [pɑlijúrəθen] N poliuretano *m*

pomegranate [pámɪgrænɪt] N granada *f*; — **tree** granado *m*

pomp [pɑmp] N pompa *f*, boato *m*, aparato *m*

pompous [pámpəs] ADJ pomposo, aparatoso

pond [pɑnd] N (natural) charca *f*; (artificial) estanque *m*; (for irrigation) balsa *f*

ponder [pándɚ] VI meditar; VT considerar

ponderous [pándɚəs] ADJ enorme

pontoon [pɑntún] N (on a bridge) pontón *m*; (on an airplane) flotador *m*

pony [póni] N póney *m*; —**tail** colita *f*, cola de caballo *f*; VI **to — up** soltar

Ponzi scheme [pánzi skím] N timo en pirámide *m pl*

poodle [púdl̩] N caniche *m*

pool [puł] N (puddle of water, blood, etc.) charco *m*; (swimming place) piscina *f*, *Mex* alberca *f*; (association of competitors) pool *m*; (game) pool *m*, billar *m*; (bets) pozo *m*; — **table** billar *m*; — **hall** billar *m*; VI acumularse; VT combinar fondos

poop [pup] N (part of ship) popa *f*; (excrement) *fam* caca *f*; VI *fam* hacer caca

poor [pʊr] ADJ (lacking money) pobre; (deficient) malo; **I'm a — cook** no sé cocinar; —**house** asilo para los pobres *m*; — **little thing** pobrecito -ta *mf*; N **the —** los pobres

pop [pɑp] VI (balloon) reventar, estallar; (eyes, cork) saltar; **to — in** entrar de paso; VT (make explode) hacer reventar; (take out cork) hacer saltar; (put) meter; (take, as pills) tomar; **to — a question** espetar una pregunta; **to — corn** hacer palomitas; N estallido *m*, detonación *f*; —**corn** palomitas *f pl*; — **music** música popular *f*; — **quiz** prueba sorpresa *f*; — **of a cork** taponazo *m*; —-**up menu** menú emergente *m*

pope [pop] N papa *m*

poplar [páplɚ] N álamo *m*, chopo *m*; — **grove** alameda *f*

poppy [pápi] N amapola *f*

popular [pápjəlɚ] ADJ popular; **he's very — with the ladies** tiene mucho éxito con las mujeres

popularity [pɑpjəlǽrɪDi] N popularidad *f*

populate [pápjəlet] VT poblar

population [pɑpjəléʃən] N población *f*

populous [pápjələs] ADJ populoso

porcelain [pórsəlɪn] N porcelana *f*

porch [pórtʃ] N porche *m*

porcupine [pórkjəpaɪn] N puercoespín *m*

pore [pɔr] N poro *m*; VI **to — over a book** estudiar detenidamente un libro

pork [pɔrk] N carne de cerdo *f*; — **chop** chuleta de cerdo *f*

porn [pɔrn] N porno *m*

pornography [pɔrnágrəfi] N pornografía *f*

porous [pórəs] ADJ poroso

porpoise [pórpəs] N marsopa *f*

port [pɔrt] N (harbor, computer) puerto *m*; (wine) oporto *m*; (left side of ship) babor *m*; — **city** ciudad portuaria *f*; —**hole** ojo de buey *m*; — **of entry** puerto de entrada *m*

portable [pórDəbəł] ADJ portátil

portal [pórdl̩] N portal *m* (also of Internet)

portent [pórtɛnt] N (omen) presagio *m*, agüero *m*; (marvel, prodigy) portento *m*

portentous [pɔrténtəs] ADJ (ominous) de mal agüero; (prodigious) portentoso

porter [pórDɚ] N mozo -za *mf*

portfolio [pɔrtfólio] N cartera *f*

portion [pórʃən] N porción *f*; VI **to — out** repartir

portly [pórtli] ADJ grueso

portrait [pórtrɪt] N (likeness) retrato *m*; (printing orientation) orientación vertical *f*

portray [pɔrtré] VT (draw, describe) retratar; (in a drama) representar

portrayal [pɔrtréəł] N (portrait) retrato *m*; (act of portraying) representación *f*, caracterización *f*

Portugal [pórtʃəgəł] N Portugal *m*

Portuguese [pórtʃəgiz] ADJ & N portugués -esa
mf

pose [poz] N (posture) pose f, postura f; (affected
attitude) afectación f; VI (sit as a model) posar;
(act affectedly) afectar una actitud; VT (to
make sit as model) hacer posar; (to present)
plantear; **to — as** hacerse pasar por

position [pəzíʃən] N (place) posición f; (job)
puesto m, colocación f; (political stance)
posicionamiento m; VI situar, colocar; **to —
oneself** posicionarse

positive [pázIDIv] ADJ positivo; — **proof** prueba
certera f; **I am —** estoy seguro

possess [pəzés] VT poseer

possessed [pəzést] ADJ (by a spirit) poseído; (by
an idea) obsesionado

possession [pəzéʃən] N posesión f; **to take —**
tomar posesión

possessive [pəzésIv] ADJ & N posesivo m

possessor [pəzésə·] N poseedor -ora f

possibility [pɑsəbílIDi] N posibilidad f

possible [pásəbəl] ADJ posible, eventual

post [post] N (pole) poste m; (position) puesto m;
(mail) correo m; —**card** tarjeta postal f;
—**haste** a la brevedad; —**man** cartero m;
—**mark** matasellos m; —**master** director de
correos m; — **office** oficina de correos f, casa
de correos f; —**office box** apartado postal
m; ADJ — **paid** porte pagado; VT (affix) fijar;
(announce) anunciar; (list) poner en lista;
(place) apostar, situar; (mail) echar al correo;
keep me —ed mantenme al tanto

postage [póstɪdʒ] N franqueo m; — **meter**
franqueadora f; — **stamp** Sp sello m; Am
estampilla f; Mex timbre m

postal [póstl] ADJ postal; **to go —** perpetrar un
ataque homicida, volverse loco

postdate [posdét] VT posfechar

poster [póstə·] N cartel m, póster m, afiche m; —
child modelo perfecto m

posterior [pastíriə·] ADJ posterior; N trasero m

posterity [pastérIDi] N posteridad f

postgraduate [postgrǽdʒuɪt] ADJ de posgrado;
N posgrado -da mf

posthumous [pástʃəməs] ADJ póstumo

postnasal [postnézəl] ADJ postnasal

postnatal [postnédl] ADJ posparto; — **care**
cuidado posparto m inv

postpartum [postpárɾəm] ADJ posparto m

postpone [postpón] VT posponer, aplazar

postponement [postpónmənt] N
aplazamiento m

postscript [póstskrɪpt] N posdata f

postulate[1] [pástʃəlet] VT postular

postulate[2] [pástʃəlɪt] N postulado m

posture [pástʃə·] N (carriage, attitude) postura f;
(affectation) afectación f; VI darse aires

postwar period [póstwár píriəd] N posguerra f

posy [pózi] N ramillete m

pot [pat] N (vessel) olla f, marmita f; (marijuana)
marihuana f; (hashish) fam chocolate m;
—**hole** bache m; ADJ —**-bellied** panzudo,
barrigón

potable [póDəbəl] ADJ potable

potassium [pətǽsiəm] N potasio m

potato [pətéDo] N Sp patata f; Am papa f; — **chip**
patata/papa frita [a la inglesa] f, chip m

potency [pótnsi] N potencia f

potent [pótnt] ADJ potente

potentate [pótntet] N potentado -da mf

potential [pəténʃəl] ADJ & N potencial m

potion [póʃən] N poción f

potter [páDə·] N alfarero -ra mf

pottery [páDəri] N (craft, shop) alfarería f;
(objects) cerámica f, objetos de alfarería m pl

pouch [pautʃ] N bolsa f; (for mail) valija f; (for
tobacco) petaca f

poultry [póltri] N aves de corral f pl

pounce [pauns] VI saltar; **to — upon/on**
abalanzarse sobre; **to — on an opportunity**
no dejar pasar una oportunidad; N salto m

pound [paund] N (unit of weight, British
currency) libra f; (place for stray dogs)
perrera f; VT (on a door) golpear; (seeds)
machacar; (a military target) bombardear; VI
(beat) latir con fuerza

pour [por] VT verter; VI (leave in masse) salir en
tropel; (rain) llover a cántaros; **to — out
one's feelings** desahogarse

pout [paut] VI hacer pucheros; N puchero m

poverty [pávə·Di] N pobreza f, penuria f; ADJ —-
stricken indigente

powder [páuDə·] N polvo m; (for the face) polvos
m pl; (for guns) pólvora f; — **compact**
polvera f; — **puff** borla f; **to take a —** poner
pies en polvorosa; VI/VT (use powder)
empolvar[se]; (pulverize) pulverizar[se]

power [páuə·] N (control, military might) poder
m, poderío m; (in physics, in math) potencia f;
(physical strength) fuerza f; (energy) energía
f; — **of attorney** poder m; — **plant** central
eléctrica f; —**-save mode** modo de ahorro de
energía m; — **steering** dirección asistida f; —
supply suministro de energía m; — **surge**
sobrecarga de voltaje f; **in —** oficialista;
legislative —s atribuciones legislativas f pl;
VI —**ed by gas** movido por gas; **to — down**
apagar; **to — on/up** encender

powerful [páuə·fəl] ADJ poderoso, potente

powerless [páuə·lɪs] ADJ impotente

PR [**public relations**] [piár] N relaciones
públicas f pl

practical [prǽktɪkəl] ADJ práctico; — **joke**
broma pesada f, chasco m; — **nurse**
enfermero -ra sin título mf

practically [prǽktɪkli] ADV prácticamente

practice [prǽktɪs] N (repeated exercise) práctica
f; (habit) costumbre f; (doctor's office)

consultorio *m*; (lawyer's office) bufete *m*; VI/VT practicar; VT (a profession) ejercer; **in** — en la práctica, prácticamente
practiced [prǽktɪst] ADJ experto, perito
practitioner [præktíʃənɚ] N practicante *mf*; **general** — médico -ca general *mf*
pragmatic [prægmǽDɪk] ADJ pragmático
prairie [préri] N pradera *f*, llanura *f*
praise [prez] N alabanza *f*, elogio *m*; VT alabar, elogiar; **—worthy** loable, encomiable
prance [præns] VI cabriolar, hacer cabriolas; N cabriola *f*
prank [præŋk] N travesura *f*, chasco *m*; **to play —s** hacer travesuras
prawn [prɔn] N langostino *m*; *Sp* gamba pequeña *f*
pray [pre] VI/VT (religious) rezar, orar; (beg) rogar, suplicar
prayer [prɛr] N (devout petition to God) oración *f*, rezo *m*; (entreaty) ruego *m*, súplica *f*
praying mantis [préɪŋmǽntɪs] N mantis religiosa *f*
preach [pritʃ] VI/VT predicar; (moralize) sermonear
preacher [prítʃɚ] N predicador -ora *mf*
preamble [príæmbəł] N preámbulo *m*
preapproved [priəprúvd] ADJ preaprobado
precancerous [prikǽnsɚəs] ADJ precanceroso
precarious [prɪkériəs] ADJ precario
precaution [prɪkɔ́ʃən] N precaución *f*
precautionary [prɪkɔ́ʃəneri] ADJ preventivo
precede [prɪsíd] VI/VT preceder
precedence [présɪDəns] N precedencia *f*, prioridad *f*
preceding [prɪsíDɪŋ] ADJ precedente, anterior
precept [prísɛpt] N precepto *m*
precinct [prísɪŋkt] N distrito *m*; (police station) comisaría *f*; **—s** límites *m pl*
precious [préʃəs] ADJ precioso; (overly refined) preciosista; — **little** muy poco; — **metal** metal precioso *m*; — **stone** piedra preciosa *f*
precipice [présəpɪs] N precipicio *m*, derrumbadero *m*
precipitate¹ [prɪsípɪtet] VI/VT precipitar[se]
precipitate² [prɪsípɪtɪt] ADJ & N precipitado *m*
precipitation [prɪsɪpɪtéʃən] N precipitación *f*
precipitous [prɪsípɪDəs] ADJ (steep) escarpado; (hasty) precipitado
precise [prɪsáɪs] ADJ preciso, exacto
precisely [prɪsáɪsli] ADV & INT precisamente, exactamente
precision [prɪsíʒən] N precisión *f*, exactitud *f*; (of expression) propiedad *f*
preclude [prɪklúd] VT excluir; **that doesn't — our considering your application** esto no obsta para que tengamos en cuenta su solicitud
precocious [prɪkóʃəs] ADJ precoz
precursor [prɪkɝ́sɚ] N precursor *m*

predator [préDətɚ] N depredador *m*
predatory [préDətɔri] ADJ (animal) depredador; (persona) rapaz
predecessor [préDɪsɛsɚ] N predecesor -ora *mf*, antecesor -ora *mf*
predestine [prɪdéstɪn] VT predestinar
predetermined [pridɪtɝ́mɪnd] ADJ predeterminado
predicament [prɪdíkəmənt] N aprieto *m*
predicate¹ [préDɪkɪt] ADJ & N predicado *m*
predicate² [préDɪket] VT basar
predict [prɪdíkt] VT predecir
prediction [prɪdíkʃən] N predicción *f*, vaticinio *m*
predilection [prɛdlékʃən] N predilección *f*
predispose [pridɪspóz] VI/VT predisponer
predisposition [pridɪspəzíʃən] N predisposición *f*
predominance [prɪdámənəns] N predominio *m*
predominant [prɪdámənənt] ADJ predominante
predominate [prɪdámənet] VI/VT predominar, preponderar
preeclampsia [priɪklǽmpsiə] N preeclampsia *f*
preexisting [priɪgzístɪŋ] ADJ preexistente
preface [préfɪs] N prefacio *m*, prólogo *m*; VT hacer una introducción; (a book) prologar
prefer [prɪfɝ́] VT preferir; **to — a claim** presentar una demanda
preferable [préfɚəbəł] ADJ preferible
preference [préfɚəns] N preferencia *f*
preferential [prefɚénʃəł] ADJ preferente
preferred [prɪfɝ́d] ADJ preferido; — **stocks** acciones preferentes *f pl*
prefix [prífɪks] N prefijo *m*; VT poner un prefijo
pregnancy [prégnənsi] N embarazo *m*; (of an animal) preñez *f*; — **test** prueba de embarazo *f*
pregnant [prégnənt] ADJ (person) embarazada, encinta; (animal) preñada; (full of meaning, rain) preñado, cargado
prehensile [prihénsəł] ADJ prensil
prehistoric [prihɪstɔ́rɪk] ADJ prehistórico
prejudge [priʤʌ́ʤ] VT prejuzgar
prejudice [préʤəDɪs] N (bias) prejuicio *m*; (harm) perjuicio *m*; VT (cause bias against) predisponer en contra; (harm) perjudicar
preliminary [prɪlímənɛri] ADJ & N preliminar *m*
prelude [prélud] N preludio *m*; VI/VT preludiar
premarital [primǽrɪdł] ADJ prematrimonial
premature [primətʃúr] ADJ prematuro; — **birth** parto prematuro *m*
premeditated [priméDɪteDɪd] ADJ premeditado
premenstrual [priménstruəł] ADJ premenstrual
premier [prɪmír] N primer ministro *m*; primera ministra *f*; ADJ principal
premiere [prɪmír] N estreno *m*, première *f*
premise [prémɪs] N premisa *f*; **—s** local *m*
premium [prímiəm] N (bonus) premio *m*;

(insurance) prima *f*; (surcharge) recargo *m*; **at a** — muy escaso; ADJ superior

premonition [prɛməníʃən] N premonición *f*

prenatal [prinédl̩] ADJ prenatal; — **care** atención prenatal *f*, cuidado prenatal *m*

prenuptial [prinʌ́pʃəl̩] ADJ prenupcial; — **agreement** capitulaciones matrimoniales *f pl*

preoccupy [priákjəpaɪ] VT absorber

preowned [prióndd] ADJ de segunda mano

prepacked [pripǽkt] ADJ preempacado

prepaid [pripéd] ADJ pagado de antemano; **to send** — enviar porte pagado

preparation [prɛpəréʃən] N (act of preparing) preparación *f*; (substance) preparado *m*; (for a trip) preparativos *m pl*

preparatory [prépəətɔri] ADJ preparatorio, preparativo

prepare [pripér] VI/VT preparar[sc]

preponderance [pripándəəns] N preponderancia *f*

preponderant [pripándəənt] ADJ preponderante

preposition [prɛpəzíʃən] N preposición *f*

preposterous [pripástəəs] ADJ absurdo

prerecorded [prirɪkɔ́rdɪd] ADJ pregrabado

prerequisite [prirékwəzɪt] N prerequisito *m*

prerogative [prɪrágəDɪv] N prerrogativa *f*

prescribe [prɪskráɪb] VT (order) prescribir; (medicine) recetar

prescription [prɪskrípʃən] N (order) prescripción *f*; (of medicine) receta *f*

presence [prézəns] N presencia *f*; — **of mind** aplomo *m*, presencia de ánimo *f*

present[1] [prézənt] N (time) presente *m*; (gift) regalo *m*, presente *m*; **at** — ahora; **for the** — por ahora; ADJ (at a place) presente; (at this time) actual; — **company excepted** con perdón de los presentes; — **participle** gerundio *m*; — **perfect** pretérito perfecto *m*; —**-day** actual

present[2] [prizént] VT presentar, entregar

presentable [prizéntəbl̩] ADJ presentable

presentation [prezəntéʃən] N (act of presenting) presentación *f*, entrega *f*; (speech) ponencia *f*; (exposition) planteamiento *m*

presentiment [prizéntəmənt] N presentimiento *m*

presently [prézəntli] ADV (soon) pronto; (now) actualmente

preservation [prezəvéʃən] N preservación *f*, conservación *f*

preservative [prizə́vəDɪv] N conservante *m*

preserve [prizə́v] VI/VT (protect) preservar; (keep food fresh) conservar; N (for game) coto *m*; (for animals) reserva *f*; —**s** mermelada *f*, dulce *m*

preset [prisét] ADJ preestablecido

preside [prizáɪd] VI presidir; **to** — **over a meeting** presidir una reunión

presidency [prézɪDənsi] N presidencia *f*

president [prézɪDənt] N presidente -ta *mf*

presidential [prezɪdénʃəl̩] ADJ presidencial

press [prɛs] VI/VT (bear down, squeeze) apretar, oprimir; (a computer key) oprimir, presionar; (iron) planchar; (force) presionar; (extract juice) prensar; (put under pressure) apremiar; **to** — **on** avanzar; **to** — **one's point** insistir en un argumento; **to** — **through** abrirse paso; N (newspapers) prensa *f*; (printing machine) imprenta *f*; (crowding) empuje *m*; — **conference** conferencia de prensa *f*; — **corps** cuerpo de prensa *m*; — **release** comunicado de prensa *m*

pressing [présɪŋ] ADJ apremiante, urgente

pressure [préʃə] N presión *f*; — **cooker** olla a presión *f*; — **gauge** manómetro *m*; — **group** grupo de presión *m*; VT apremiar, presionar

prestige [prestíʒ] N prestigio *m*

prestigious [prestíʤəs] ADJ prestigioso

presumably [prizúməbli] ADV — **he is already prepared** es de suponer que ya esté preparado

presume [prizúm] VI (be presumptuous) presumir; VT (suppose) suponer; (dare) atreverse a

presumption [prizʌ́mpʃən] N presunción *f*

presumptuous [prizʌ́mptʃuəs] ADJ presuntuoso, presumido

presuppose [prisəpóz] VT presuponer

pretax [pritǽks] ADJ antes de impuestos

preteen [pritín] ADJ & N preadolescente *mf*

pretend [priténd] VI/VT (make believe) hacer de cuenta que; (feign) fingir; VT (claim) pretender; **to** — **to the throne** pretender el trono

pretense [prítens] N (faked action or belief) engaño *m*; (false show) apariencia *f*; **under** — **of** so pretexto de

pretension [priténʃən] N pretensión *f*; (pretext) pretexto *m*

pretentious [priténʃəs] ADJ (full of pretension) pretencioso; (showy) ostentoso

pretext [prítɛkst] N pretexto *m*

pretrial [pritráɪl̩] ADJ anterior al juicio

pretty [príDi] ADJ bonito; (human only) *Sp* guapo; ADV bastante; — **well** bastante bien, francamente bien; VI/VT **to** — **up** embellecer

prevail [privél̩] VI (win) prevalecer; (be widespread, dominant) preponderar, imperar; **to** — **on/upon** persuadir

prevailing [privélɪŋ] ADJ (opinion) predominante; (feeling) reinante, imperante; — **winds** vientos predominantes

prevalent [prévələnt] ADJ prevaleciente, preponderante

prevent [privént] VT (keep from occurring) prevenir; VI/VT (impede) impedir

prevention [prɪvɛ́nʃən] N prevención f; (of a disease) prevención f, profilaxis f
preventive [prɪvɛ́ntɪv] ADJ preventivo, cautelar
preview [prívju] N preestreno m
previewing [prívjuwɪŋ] N previsualización f
previous [prívɪəs] ADJ previo, anterior
previously [prívɪəsli] ADV previamente, anteriormente
prey [pre] N (animal) presa f; VI **to — on** (animals) alimentarse de; (people) explotar; **it —s upon my mind** me tiene preocupado
price [praɪs] N precio m; **at any —** a toda costa; **— control** control de precios m; **— fixing** fijación de precios f; **— index** índice de precios m; **— tag** etiqueta de precio f; VT (set price) poner precio a; (ask price) averiguar el precio de
priceless [práɪslɪs] ADJ (without price) invalorable; (amusing) divertidísimo
pricey [práɪsi] ADJ caro
pricing [práɪsɪŋ] N fijación de precios f
prick [prɪk] N (puncture) pinchazo m; (sharp point) púa f; (penis) vulg pija f; (creep) offensive hijo de puta m; VI/VT pinchar, punzar; **to — up one's ears** parar las orejas
prickly [príkli] ADJ espinoso; **— heat** sarpullido causado por el calor m; **— pear** tuna f, nopal m
pride [praɪd] N orgullo m; (excessive) soberbia f; VI **to — oneself on** enorgullecerse de
priest [prist] N sacerdote m; (Catholic only) cura m
priesthood [prísthʊd] N sacerdocio m
prim [prɪm] ADJ remilgado
primarily [praɪmɛ́rɪli] ADV principalmente, más que nada
primary [práɪmɛri] N elección primaria f; ADJ primario; (main) fundamental, principal; **— care** atención primaria f; **— colors** colores primarios m pl; **— election** elección primaria f; **— school** escuela primaria f
primate [práɪmet] N primate m
prime [praɪm] ADJ (principal) fundamental; (of a number) primo; (select) de primera; **— minister** primer ministro m, primera ministra f; N (number) número primo m; **to be in one's —** estar en la flor de la edad, estar en la plenitud de la vida; **— rate** tasa prima f; VT preparar; (a pump) cebar
primer[1] [prímɚ] N (first book) manual elemental m
primer[2] [práɪmɚ] N (pump part) cebador m
primitive [prímɪdɪv] ADJ & N primitivo -va mf
prince [prɪns] N príncipe m
princely [prínsli] ADJ noble, principesco; **a — sum** una suma muy grande
princess [prínsɛs] N princesa f
principal [prínsəpəł] ADJ principal; N (money invested) capital m; (giver of power of

attorney) poderdante mf, mandante mf; (head of a school) director -ora mf
principle [prínsəpəł] N principio m
print [prɪnt] VI/VT imprimir; (write in block letters) escribir en letra de molde; **to — out** imprimir; N (type) letra de imprenta f; (of art) lámina f; (of photographs) copia f; (of finger) huella digital f; (on cloth) estampado m; **—out** versión impresa f; **in —** publicado, en venta; **out of —** agotado
printer [príntɚ] N (person) impresor -ora mf, gráfico -ca mf; (machine) impresora f; **— driver** controlador de impresora m; **— feeder** alimentador de impresora m
printing [príntɪŋ] N (art, trade) imprenta f; (process) impresión f, tipografía f; (block letters) letra de molde f, letra de imprenta f; **— press** imprenta f; **this book is in its second —** este libro está en su segunda tirada
prior [práɪɚ] ADJ previo; **— to** anterior a
priority [praɪɔ́rɪdi] N prioridad f; **having — prioritario
prism [prízəm] N prisma m
prison [prízən] N prisión f, cárcel f, presidio m
prisoner [prízənɚ] N (captive) prisionero -ra mf; (in jail) preso -sa mf, presidiario -ria mf; **— of war** prisionero -ra de guerra mf
pristine [prɪstín] ADJ (immaculate) puro; (perfect) perfecto
privacy [práɪvəsi] N privacidad f; **— statement** declaración sobre la privacidad f
private [práɪvɪt] ADJ (not public) privado; (individual) particular; **— enterprise** empresa privada f; **— eye** detective privado -da mf; **— parts** partes pudendas f pl; **— property** propiedad privada f; **—s** partes pudendas f pl; **— school** escuela privada f; **— sector** sector privado m; **a — citizen** un particular; **in —** en privado; N soldado raso m
privation [praɪvéʃən] N privación f
privatization [praɪvədɪzéʃən] N privatización f
privatize [práɪvətaɪz] VT privatizar
privilege [prívəlɪdʒ] N privilegio m
privileged [prívlɪdʒd] ADJ privilegiado
privy [prívi] ADJ **to be — to** estar enterado de; N retrete m
prize [praɪz] N (reward) premio m; (booty) botín m; **— fight** pelea de boxeo profesional f; **— fighter** boxeador -ora mf, pugilista mf; VT apreciar
pro [pro] N profesional mf
probability [prɑbəbílɪdi] N probabilidad f
probable [prɑ́bəbəł] ADJ probable
probate [próbet] N legalización de una validación testamentaria f
probation [probéʃən] N libertad condicional f
probationary [probéʃənɛri] ADJ probatorio; **— period** período de prueba m
probe [prob] VI/VT (explore with a probe)

sondear; (examine) examinar; N sonda f (also in space); (investigation) indagación f

problem [práblǝm] N problema m; **—s** problemática f

procedure [prǝsídʒǝ-] N procedimiento m; (legal) trámite m

proceed [prǝsíd] VI (originate) proceder; (continue) proseguir, continuar; **to — against** demandar a; **to — to** proceder a

proceeds [prósidz] N ganancia f, lo recaudado

proceedings [prǝsíDIŋz] N (events) acontecimientos m pl; (record of a conference) actas f pl, memoria f; (legal action) procedimiento m

process [práses] N proceso m; **in the — of** en vías de

processing [prásesiŋ] N (of applications) tramitación f; (of data, substances) procesamiento m; **— power** potencia procesadora f

procession [prǝséʃǝn] N procesión f

processor [prásesǝ-] N procesador m

pro-choice [protʃóis] ADJ pro-elección

proclaim [prǝklém] VT proclamar

proclamation [praklǝméʃǝn] N proclamación f, proclama f

procrastinate [prǝkrǽstǝnet] VI/VT dejar para último momento

procreate [prókriet] VI/VT procrear, engendrar

proctology [praktálǝdʒi] N proctología f

procure [prǝkjúr] VT procurar, obtener; VI ser proxeneta

prod [prad] VT aguijonear; **they —ded me into going / to go** insistieron en que fuera

prodigal [práDIgǝł] ADJ & N pródigo -ga mf

prodigious [prǝdídʒǝs] ADJ prodigioso

prodigy [práDǝdʒi] N prodigio m

produce¹ [pródus] N (vegetables) verduras f pl, hortalizas f pl

produce² [prǝdús] VI/VT producir; VT (present) presentar

producer [prǝdúsǝ-] N productor -ora mf; (of a movie) realizador -ora mf

product [práDǝkt] N producto m

production [prǝdÁkʃǝn] N producción f; (TV, radio) producción f, realización f; (exaggerated situation) teatro m

productive [prǝdÁktIv] ADJ productivo

productivity [praDǝktívIDi] N productividad f

profane [profén] ADJ profano; (vulgar) grosero; VT profanar

profanity [prǝfǽnIDi] N groserías f pl, palabrotas f pl

profess [prǝfés] VI (publicly accept, take vows) profesar; VT (state) afirmar; (claim) pretender

profession [prǝféʃǝn] N profesión f

professional [prǝféʃǝnł] ADJ & N profesional mf

professor [prǝfésǝ-] N profesor -ora universitario -ria mf; (full) catedrático -ca mf

proffer [práfǝ-] VT ofrecer; N oferta f

proficiency [prǝfíʃǝnsi] N competencia f

proficient [prǝfíʃǝnt] ADJ competente

profile [prófaił] N (contour) perfil m; **a high- — case** un caso muy sonado

profit [práfit] N (gain) ganancia f; **— and loss** ganancias y pérdidas f pl; **— margin** margen de ganancia m; **— sharing** participación en las ganancias de una empresa f; **at a —** con ganancia; **to turn a —** dar ganancia; **not for —** sin fines de lucro; VI salir ganando; **to — from** (benefit) aprovechar, sacar provecho de; (use to get an advantage) aprovecharse de; VT servir

profitability [prafiDǝbílIDi] N rentabilidad f

profitable [práfiDǝbǝł] ADJ (beneficial) provechoso; (lucrative) lucrativo, rentable

profound [prǝfáund] ADJ profundo

profundity [prǝfÁndIDi] N profundidad f

profuse [prǝfjús] ADJ profuso, pródigo

progesterone [prodʒéstǝron] N progesterona f

prognosis [pragnósis] N pronóstico m

program [prógrǽm] N programa m; VI/VT programar

programmable [progrǽmǝbǝł] ADJ programable

programmer [prógrǽmǝ-] N programador -ora mf

programming [prógrǽmiŋ] N programación f; **— language** lenguaje de programación m

progress¹ [prágres] N progreso m

progress² [prǝgrés] VI progresar

progression [prǝgréʃǝn] N progresión f

progressive [prǝgrésIv] ADJ (advancing) progresivo; ADJ & N (liberal) progresista mf, progresivo -va mf

prohibit [prohíbit] VT prohibir, vedar

prohibition [proǝbíʃǝn] N prohibición f

project¹ [prádʒekt] N proyecto m

project² [prǝdʒékt] VI/VT (plan) proyectar[se]; VI (jut out) sobresalir

projectile [prǝdʒéktaił] N proyectil m; ADJ arrojadizo

projection [prǝdʒékʃǝn] N (plan) proyección f; (jut) saliente f

projector [prǝdʒéktǝ-] N proyector m

proletariat [prolitériǝt] N proletariado m

pro-life [prólaif] ADJ antiaborto

proliferation [prǝlifǝréʃǝn] N proliferación f

prolific [prǝlifík] ADJ prolífico

prologue [prólɔg] N prólogo m

prolong [prǝlɔ́ŋ] VT prolongar

prolongation [prolɔŋgéʃǝn] N prolongación f

promenade [pramǝnéd] N paseo m; (dance) baile m; VI/VT pasear[se]

prominent [prámǝnǝnt] ADJ prominente

promiscuous [prǝmískjuǝs] ADJ promiscuo, liviano

promise [prámis] N promesa f; **he showed —**

prometía mucho; VI/VT prometer
promising [prámɪsɪŋ] ADJ prometedor
promissory [prámɪsɔri] ADJ promisorio; —
note pagaré *m*
promontory [práməntɔri] N promontorio *m*
promote [prəmót] VT (foster) promover,
fomentar; (advance in rank) ascender; (in
school) pasar de año, promover; (advertise)
promocionar
promoter [prəmóDɚ] N (fomenter) propulsor
-ora *mf*; (organizer) promotor -ora *mf*
promotion [prəmóʃən] N (act of promoting)
promoción *f*; (advance in rank) ascenso *m*
promotional [prəmóʃənl̩] ADJ promocional
prompt [prɑmpt] ADJ (quick) rápido; (punctual)
puntual; VT (cause) inducir; (in theater)
apuntar; **to give someone a** — apuntarle a
alguien
promptly [prámptli] ADV (soon) pronto;
(punctually) puntualmente
promulgate [prámətget] VT promulgar
prone [pron] ADJ (disposed) propenso, proclive;
(face down) boca abajo; (prostrate) postrado
prong [prɔŋ] N púa *f*, diente *m*
pronoun [prónaʊn] N pronombre *m*
pronounce [prənáʊns] VT (enunciate)
pronunciar; (declare) declarar
pronounced [prənáʊnst] ADJ pronunciado
pronouncement [prənáʊnsmənt] N
pronunciamiento *m*
pronunciation [prənʌnsiéʃən] N pronunciación
f
proof [pruf] N (evidence, test, trial printing)
prueba *f*; (of alcohol) graduación *f*, grado *m*;
— **of purchase** comprobante de compra *m*;
—**reader** corrector -ora de pruebas *mf*,
revisor -ora de pruebas *mf*; **fifty** —
veinticinco por ciento de graduación
alcohólica; **fire**— a prueba de incendios;
water— impermeable; **bullet**— a prueba de
balas
prop [prɑp] N (pole) puntal *m*; (in theater)
accesorio *m*; (propeller) hélice *f*; (support)
sostén *m*, apoyo *m*; (of a plant) tutor *m*; VT **to**
— **against** apoyar en, sostener en; **to** — **up**
apuntalar, sostener
propaganda [prɑpəgǽndə] N propaganda *f*
propagate [prápəget] VI/VT propagar[se]
propagation [prɑpəgéʃən] N propagación *f*
propane [própen] N propano *m*
propel [prəpéł] VT propulsar, impulsar
propeller [prəpélɚ] N hélice *f*
propensity [prəpénsɪDi] N propensión *f*
proper [prápɚ] ADJ (appropriate) apropiado;
(decorous) decoroso; (genuine) como Dios
manda; (correct) correcto; (in math,
grammar) propio; **to be** — **to** ser propio de
properly [prápɚli] ADV (appropriately)
apropiadamente; (correctly) correctamente;

(decorously) decorosamente
property [prápɚDi] N (characteristic) propiedad
f; (real estate) propiedad *f*, finca *f*; (assets)
bienes *m pl*; — **damage** daños materiales *m pl*
prophecy [práfɪsi] N profecía *f*
prophesy [práfɪsaɪ] VI/VT profetizar
prophet [práfɪt] N profeta -tisa *mf*
prophetic [prəfɛ́Dɪk] ADJ profético
propitious [prəpíʃəs] ADJ propicio
proponent [prəpónənt] N (person who
proposes) proponente *mf*; (adherent)
defensor -ora *mf*
proportion [prəpórʃən] N proporción *f*; **out of**
— desproporcionado; VT proporcionar; **well**
—**ed** bien proporcionado
proportional [prəpórʃənl̩] ADJ proporcional
proportionate [prəpórʃənɪt] ADJ proporcional
proposal [prəpózəł] N (suggestion) propuesta *f*;
(of marriage, dishonest) proposición *f*
propose [prəpóz] VI/VT (suggest) proponer; VI
(ask in marriage) declararse, hacer una
propuesta de matrimonio; **to** — **to do**
something proponerse hacer algo
proposition [prɑpəzíʃən] N proposición *f*; VT
hacer proposiciones deshonestas
proprietor [prəpráɪɪDɚ] N propietario -ria *mf*
propriety [prəpráɪɪDi] N decoro *m*
propulsion [prəpʌ́łʃən] N propulsión *f*
prorate [prorét] VT prorratear
prosaic [prozéɪk] ADJ prosaico
prose [proz] N prosa *f*
prosecute [prásɪkjut] VI/VT (take to court)
procesar, enjuiciar; VT (pursue) llevar
adelante
prosecution [prɑsɪkjúʃən] N (act of prosecuting)
procesamiento *m*; (officials who prosecute)
ministerio público *m*, fiscalía *f*
prosecutor [prásɪkjuDɚ] N fiscal *mf*
proselytize [prásəlɪtaɪz] VT convertir; VI buscar
ganar prosélitos
prospect [práspɛkt] N (outlook, possibility)
perspectiva *f*, expectativa *f*; (candidate)
candidato -ta *mf*; (possible client) posible
cliente -ta *mf*; VT prospectar; VI **to** — **for**
buscar
prospective [prəspɛ́ktɪv] ADJ posible, potencial
prospector [práspɛktɚ] N prospector -ora *mf*
prosper [práspɚ] VI prosperar
prosperity [prɑspérɪDi] N prosperidad *f*,
bonanza *f*
prosperous [práspərəs] ADJ próspero
prostate [prástet] N próstata *f*; — **gland**
próstata *f*
prosthesis [prɑsθísɪs] N prótesis *f*
prostitute [prástɪtut] N prostituto -ta *mf*; VT
prostituir
prostitution [prɑstɪtúʃən] N prostitución *f*
prostrate [prástret] VT postrar; ADJ (lying flat,
overcome) postrado; (lying face down) boca

abajo
protagonist [protǽgənɪst] N protagonista *mf*
protect [prətékt] VI/VT proteger, amparar
protection [prətékʃen] N protección *f*
protectionist [prətékʃənɪst] ADJ & N
proteccionista *mf*
protective [prətéktɪv] ADJ protector
protector [prətéktə-] N protector -ora *mf*
protectorate [prətéktərɪt] N protectorado *m*
protégé, protégée [próDəʒe] N protegido -da
mf
protein [prótin] N proteína *f*
protest[1] [prótest] N protesta *f*, reclamación *f*
protest[2] [prətést] VI/VT protestar, reclamar
Protestant [práDɪstənt] ADJ & N protestante *mf*
protestation [protestéʃən] N declaración *f*
protocol [próDəkɔł] N protocolo *m*
proton [prótɑn] N protón *m*
protoplasm [próDəplǽzəm] N protoplasma *m*
prototype [próDətaɪp] N prototipo *m*
protozoan [proDəzóən] N protozoario *m*
protract [protrǽkt] VT prolongar
protrude [protrúd] VI sobresalir, proyectarse
protuberance [prətúbərəns] N protuberancia *f*
proud [praʊd] ADJ orgulloso; (haughty)
soberbio; **to be — of** enorgullecerse de,
ufanarse de
prove [pruv] VT (demonstrate, verify) probar,
demostrar; VI resultar; **events have —d me
right** los hechos me han dado la razón
proverb [právɚb] N proverbio *m*, refrán *m*
provide [prəváɪd] VT (furnish) proveer,
proporcionar; (supply) abastecer, aportar;
(stipulate) estipular, prevenir; VI **to — for**
(support) mantener; (stipulate) estipular; **to
— with** proveer de, proporcionar; CONJ **—d
[that]** con tal [de] que, siempre que
providence [právɪDəns] N providencia *f*
provider [prəváɪDə-] N (supplier) proveedor -ora
mf; (breadwinner) sostén *m*
province [právɪns] N (area) provincia *f*;
(competence) competencia *f*
provincial [prəvínʃəł] ADJ (of a province)
provincial; (rustic) provinciano, pueblerino;
N provinciano -na *mf*
provision [prəvíʒən] N (act of providing, thing
provided) provisión *f*, suministro *m*,
prestación *f*; (precaution) medida *f*,
precaución *f*; (clause) estipulación *f*,
prevención *f*; **—s** provisiones *f pl*, víveres *m
pl*, bastimentos *m pl*, suministros *m*
provisional [prəvíʒənł] ADJ provisional
proviso [prəváɪzo] N condición *f*, estipulación *f*
provocation [pravəkéʃən] N provocación *f*
provoke [prəvók] VT provocar
provost [próvost] N vicerrector -ora *mf*
prow [praʊ] N proa *f*
prowess [práʊɪs] N valentía *f*
prowl [praʊł] VI/VT rondar en acecho

proximity [praksímɪDi] N proximidad *f*
proxy [práksi] N (person) apoderado -da *mf*;
(power of attorney) poder *m*; **by —** por poder
prude [prud] N mojigato -ta *mf*, gazmoño -ña *mf*
prudence [prúdns] N prudencia *f*
prudent [prúdnt] ADJ prudente
prudery [prúDəri] N mojigatería *f*, gazmoñería *f*
prudish [prúDɪʃ] ADJ mojigato, gazmoño
prune [prun] N ciruela pasa *f*; VI/VT podar
pry [praɪ] VT curiosear; **to — into** entrometerse;
to — open abrir por la fuerza; **to — a secret
out** extraer/arrancar un secreto
pseudonym [súdnɪm] N pseudónimo/
seudónimo *m*
psoriasis [səráɪəsɪs] N psoriasis/soriasis *f*
psych [saɪk] VT **to — out** intimidar
psicológicamente
psychedelic [saɪkɪdélɪk] ADJ psicodélico/
sicodélico
psychiatrist [saɪkáɪətrɪst] N psiquiatra/siquiatra
mf
psychiatry [saɪkáɪətri] N psiquiatría/siquiatría *f*
psychic [sáɪkɪk] ADJ psíquico/síquico; N médium
mf, psíquico -ca / síquico -ca *mf*
psychoanalysis [saɪkoǽnəlaɪz] N psicoanálisis/
sicoanálisis *m*
psychological [saɪkəládʒɪkəł] ADJ psicológico/
sicológico
psychologist [saɪkáləGɪst] N psicólogo -ga /
sicólogo -ga *mf*
psychology [saɪkáləGi] N psicología/sicología *f*
psychopath [sáɪkəpæθ] N psicópata/sicópata *mf*
psychosis [saɪkósɪs] N psicosis/sicosis *f*
psychosomatic [saɪkosəmǽDɪk] ADJ
psicosomático/sicosomático
psychotherapy [saɪkoθérəpi] N psicoterapia/
sicoterapia *f*
psychotic [saɪkáDɪk] ADJ psicótico/sicótico
puberty [pjúbɚDi] N pubertad *f*
pubic [pjúbɪk] ADJ púbico; **— hair** pelo púbico
m, *vulg* pendejo *m*
public [pábłɪk] ADJ público; **— domain** dominio
público *m*; **— health** salud pública *f*; **—
relations** relaciones públicas *f pl*; **— school**
escuela pública *f*; **— service** servicio público
m; **to go —** proceder a la venta pública de
acciones, salir a bolsa; N público *m*
publication [pʌblɪkéʃən] N publicación *f*
publicity [pʌblísɪDi] N publicidad *f*, propaganda
f; **— campaign** campaña publicitaria *f*
publicize [páblɪsaɪz] VT promocionar
publish [páblɪʃ] VI/VT publicar, editar; **—ing
house** [casa] editorial *f*
publisher [páblɪʃə-] N editor -ora *mf*
puck [pʌk] N puck *m*
pucker [pákə-] VI/VT fruncir[se]; N frunce *m*
pudding [púDɪŋ] N budín *m*, pudín *m*
puddle [pádł] N charco *m*
pudendum [pjudéndəm] N partes pudendas *f pl*

Puerto Rican [pɔrɒəríkən] ADJ & N puertorriqueño -ña *mf*
Puerto Rico [pɔrɒəríko] N Puerto Rico *m*
puff [pʌf] N (air) resoplido *m*, soplo *m*; (smoke) bocanada *f*; (on a cigarette) pitada *f*, chupada *f*; (of a sleeve) bullón *m*; — **pastry** masa de hojaldre *f*; VI (blow) resoplar; (breathe hard) jadear; (smoke a cigarette) echar bocanadas; **to** — **up** hincharse; **to** — **up with pride** henchirse de orgullo
pug [pʌg] N dogo *m*; — **nose** nariz chata *f*
puke [pjuk] VI/VT vomitar, lanzar; N vómito *m*
pull [pʊɫ] VI/VT (tug) tirar, jalar; (extract) arrancar, extraer; (stretch) estirar; (injure) desgarrar; **to** — **apart** destrozar; **to** — **down** (demolish) demoler; (earn) sacar; **to** — **for** hinchar por; **to** — **off** conseguir; **to** — **oneself together** calmarse; **to** — **over** parar; **to** — **up** parar; **to** — **through** salvarse; **to** — **strings** mover palancas; **to** — **out** (leave a place) salir; (back out) retirarse; **the train** — **ed into the station** el tren entró a la estación; N (act of pulling) tirón *m*; (force) fuerza *f*; (influence) influencia *f*; (injury) desgarro *m*; —-**down menu** menú abatible *m*
pullet [pʊ́lɪt] N polla *f*
pulley [pʊ́li] N polea *f*, carrucha *f*
pulmonary [pʌ́lmənɛri] ADJ pulmonar
pulp [pʌɫp] N (of paper, wood, fruit) pulpa *f*; (of grape, sugarcane, olive, etc.) bagazo *m*
pulpit [pʊ́ɫpɪt] N púlpito *m*
pulsar [pʌ́ɫsar] N púlsar *m*
pulsate [pʌ́ɫset] VI latir
pulse [pʌɫs] N pulso *m*; (single pulsation, act of pulsing) pulsación *f*
pulverize [pʌ́ɫvəraɪz] VT pulverizar[se]
puma [pjúmə] N puma *f*
pumice [pʌ́mɪs] N piedra pómez *f*
pump [pʌmp] N bomba *f*; (shoe) zapatilla *f*, zapato escotado *m*; (for gasoline) surtidor *m*; VI/VT bombear; (inflate) inflar; **to** — **someone for information** sonsacar [información] a alguien
pumpkin [pʌ́mpkɪn] N calabaza *f*
pun [pʌn] N juego de palabras *m*, retruécano *m*; VI hacer juegos de palabras
punch [pʌntʃ] N (blow) puñetazo *m*; (drink) ponche *m*; (drill) sacabocados *m sg*; (force) fuerza *f*, empuje *m*; — **bowl** ponchera *f*; — **line** remate de un chiste *m*; VI/VT (hit) dar un puñetazo; VT (drive cattle) arriar; (make a hole) agujerear; **to** — **in/out** marcar tarjeta
punctual [pʌ́ŋktʃuəɫ] ADJ puntual
punctuality [pʌ́ŋktʃuǽlɪ Di] N puntualidad *f*
punctuate [pʌ́ŋktʃuet] VI/VT puntuar; (interrupt) interrumpir; (accentuate) salpicar
punctuation [pʌ́ŋktʃuéʃən] N puntuación *f*
puncture [pʌ́ŋktʃɚ] VI/VT pinchar[se]; *Mex*

ponchar[se]; —**d tire** neumático pinchado *m*; N (action of perforating) perforación *f*; (hole) pinchazo *m*; — **wound** herida perforada *f*
pundit [pʌ́ndɪt] N experto -ta *mf*
pungent [pʌ́ndʒənt] ADJ (acrid) acre; (sarcastic) mordaz
punish [pʌ́nɪʃ] VT castigar, penar
punishment [pʌ́nɪʃmənt] N castigo *m*
punitive [pjúnɪ Dɪv] ADJ punitivo; — **damages** daños punitivos *m pl*
punk [pʌŋk] N (inexperienced boy) mocoso *m*; (hoodlum) gamberro *m*; (rock) punk *m*; (punker) punkero -ra *mf*
punt [pʌnt] N (kick) patada de despeje *f*; (boat) balsa *f*; VI/VT despejar; VI andar en balsa
punter [pʌ́ntɚ] N despejador *m*
puny [pjúni] ADJ endeble
pupil [pjúpəɫ] N (student) escolar *mf*; (part of eye) pupila *f*, niña *f*
puppet [pʌ́pɪt] N títere *m*, monigote *m*; — **show** teatro de títeres *m*
puppy [pʌ́pi] N cachorro *m*
purchase [pɚ́tʃəs] VI/VT comprar, adquirir; N compra *f*; (hold) asidero *m*; — **order** orden de compra *f*; — **price** precio de compra *m*
purchaser [pɚ́tʃəsɚ] N comprador *m*
purchasing [pɚ́tʃəsɪŋ] N compra *f*; — **agent** agente de compras *mf*; — **power** poder adquisitivo *m*
pure [pjʊr] ADJ puro; ADJ & N —**bred** purasangre *m*
puree [pjʊré] N puré *m*
purgative [pɚ́gə Dɪv] ADJ & N purgante *m*
purgatory [pɚ́gətɔri] N purgatorio *m*
purge [pɚdʒ] VI/VT purgar[se]; N purga *f*
purify [pjúrəfaɪ] VI/VT purificar[se], depurar[se]
purist [pjúrɪst] N purista *mf*
puritanical [pjʊrɪtǽnɪkəɫ] ADJ puritano
purity [pjúrɪ Di] N pureza *f*
purple [pɚ́pəɫ] N morado *m*, púrpura *f*; ADJ morado, púrpura
purport[1] [pɚ́pɔrt] N (meaning) significado *m*; (purpose) propósito *m*
purport[2] [pəpórt] VT pretender
purpose [pɚ́pəs] N propósito *m*, objetivo *m*; **on** — adrede, a propósito
purr [pɚ] N ronroneo *m* (also motors); VI ronronear
purse [pɚs] N bolso *m*, cartera *f*; VT **to** — **one's lips** fruncir los labios
pursuant [pəsúənt] ADV LOC — **to** conforme a, de acuerdo con
pursue [pəsú] VT (follow) perseguir; (strive) dedicarse a; (continue) continuar con; (practice a profession) ejercer
pursuer [pəsúɚ] N perseguidor -ora *mf*
pursuit [pəsút] N (chase) persecución *f*, seguimiento *m*, acoso *m*; (striving for) búsqueda *f*; (pastime) pasatiempo *m*;

(practice) ejercicio *m*; **in — of** (chasing) detrás de; (striving for) en busca de

pus [pʌs] N pus *m*

push [puʃ] VI/VT (shove) empujar; VT (pressure) presionar, promover; (sell drugs) camellear; **to — a button** apretar un botón; VI (in childbirth) pujar; **to — aside/away** apartar; **to — forward** abrirse paso, avanzar; **to — open** abrir de un empujón; **to — through** hacer pasar; N empujón *m*; (military) ofensiva *f*; **—-up** lagartija *f*; ADJ **—-button** de botones

pusher [púʃ~] N camello *mf*

pushy [púʃi] ADJ insistente

pussy [púsi] N (cat) minino *m*, gatito *m*; (female genitalia) *vulg* coño *m*; *Am vulg* concha *f*; **— willow** sauce *m*

put [put] VT poner, colocar; **to — a question** plantear una pregunta; **to — across** expresar; **to — away** guardar; **to — down** (write down) apuntar; (suppress) sofocar; (attribute) atribuir; (humiliate) humillar; (make a down payment) hacer un depósito; (a pet) sacrificar; **to — into** meter; **to — into words** expresar, decir; **to — in writing** poner por escrito; **to — off** (postpone) aplazar, posponer; (perturb) desagradar; (dissuade) disuadir; **to — on** ponerse; **to — on airs** darse tono; **to — on weight** engordar; **to — out** (extinguish) apagar, extinguir; (annoy) molestar; **to — the blame** echar la culpa; **to — to sea** echar al mar; **to — to sleep** sacrificar; **to — up** (construct) levantar; (lodge) alojar; **to — up for sale** poner a la venta; **to — up with** aguantar; **I felt —-upon** sentí que se habían aprovechado de mí; N **— option** opción de venta *f*; **—-down** insulto *m*

putrid [pjútrid] ADJ putrefacto

putt [pʌt] VI/VT potear; N pat

putter [pʌ́D~] VI entretenerse; N (golf) putter *m*

putty [pʌ́Di] N masilla *f*; VT rellenar con masilla

puzzle [pʌ́zəl] N (jigsaw) rompecabezas *m sg*; (riddle) acertijo *m*; (problem) enigma *m*; (crossword) crucigrama *m*; VT dejar perplejo, desconcertar; VI **to — out** desentrañar; **to — over** meditar sobre; **to be —d** estar perplejo

pygmy [pígmi] N pigmeo -a *mf*

pylon [páilɑn] N pilón *m*

pyramid [píromid] N pirámide *f*

pyromania [pairoméniə] N piromanía *f*

pyromaniac [pairoméniæk] N pirómano -na *mf*

pyrotechnics [pairətékniks] N pirotecnia *f*

python [páiθɑn] N pitón *mf*

Qq

Qatar [kətár] N Qatar *m*

Qatari [kətári] ADJ & N catarí *mf*

quack [kwæk] N (sound of duck) graznido *m*; (charlatan) matasanos *mf*, charlatán -ana *mf*; ADJ charlatán; VI graznar

quadrilateral [kwɑdrəlǽDə~əl] ADJ & N cuadrilátero *m*

quadriplegic [kwɑdrəplídʒik] ADJ & N tetraplégico -ca *mf*

quadruped [kwɑ́drəped] ADJ & N cuadrúpedo *m*

quadruplet [kwɑdrúplit] N cuatrillizo -za *mf*

quagmire [kwǽgmair] N (bog) cenagal *m*, atascadero *m*; (crisis) atolladero *m*, atascadero *m*

quail [kwel] N codorniz *f*

quaint [kwent] ADJ pintoresco

quake [kwek] N (instance of quaking) temblor *m*; (earthquake) terremoto *m*; VI temblar

qualification [kwɑləfikéʃən] N (for a race) clasificación *f*; (requirement) requisito *m*; **without —** sin reservas

qualify [kwáləfai] VT (characterize) calificar; (moderate) moderar; (provide with credentials) capacitar; VI (for a race) clasificarse; (for a position) estar capacitado

qualifying [kwáləfaiiŋ] ADJ calificativo

qualitative [kwáliteDiv] ADJ cualitativo

quality [kwáliDi] N (characteristic) cualidad *f*; (excellence) calidad *f*; **— control** control de calidad *m*

qualm [kwɔm] N escrúpulo *m*

quantify [kwántəfai] VT cuantificar

quantitative [kwántiteDiv] ADJ cuantitativo

quantity [kwántiDi] N cantidad *f*

quantum mechanics [kwántəmməkǽniks] N mecánica cuántica *f*

quarantine [kwɔ́rəntin] N cuarentena *f*; VT poner en cuarentena

quarrel [kwɔ́rəl] N riña *f*, rencilla *f*; VI reñir, pelear

quarrelsome [kwɔ́rəlsəm] ADJ pendenciero

quarry [kwɔ́ri] N (stone) cantera *f*; (game) presa *f*; VT explotar

quart [kwɔrt] N cuarto de galón [0.9463 litros] *m*

quarter [kwɔ́rDə~] N (one-fourth) cuarto *m*, cuarta parte *f*; (coin) moneda de 25 centavos *f*; (of a sporting match) tiempo *m*; (of a calendar or school year) trimestre *m*; (district) barrio *m*; **—back** mariscal de campo *m*; **—master general** intendente *mf*; **— note** negra *f*; **—s** alojamiento *m*; **from all —s** de todas partes; **to give no — to the enemy** no dar cuartel al enemigo; ADJ cuarto; VT (divide) cuartear, dividir en cuartos; (execute) descuartizar; (lodge troops) acuartelar, acantonar

quarterly [kwɔ́rDəli] ADV trimestralmente; ADJ trimestral; N publicación trimestral *f*

quartet [kwɔrtét] N cuarteto *m*

quartz [kwɔrts] N cuarzo *m*

quasar [kwézɑr] N cuásar *m*, quásar *m*

quash [kwɑʃ] VT (a rebellion) sofocar; (a decision) anular

quaver [kwévə] VI temblar; N temblor *m*; (in music) trémolo *m*

queasy [kwízi] ADJ nauseoso

queen [kwin] N reina *f*; (effeminate male homosexual) *offensive* loca *f*; *offensive* reinona *f*

queer [kwir] ADJ (strange) raro; (eccentric) excéntrico; (homosexual) *offensive* maricón; **to feel** — sentirse raro; N (homosexual) *offensive* marica *m*, maricón *m*; VT comprometer

quell [kwɛl] VT (suppress) reprimir, sofocar; (calm) calmar

quench [kwɛntʃ] VT (flames, thirst) apagar; (passions) aplacar, apagar

query [kwíri] N (question) pregunta *f*; (question mark) signo de interrogación *m*; (doubt) duda *f*; VT (ask) preguntar; (question) expresar dudas; (mark with a question mark) marcar con signo de interrogación

quest [kwɛst] N búsqueda *f*

question [kwéstʃən] N (thing asked) pregunta *f*; (issue) cuestión *f*; — **mark** signo de interrogación *m*; **beyond** — fuera de duda; **that is out of the** — ¡ni pensarlo! VT (ask) preguntar; (interrogate) interrogar; (call into doubt) dudar, cuestionar

questionable [kwéstʃənəbəl] ADJ (doubtful) cuestionable, discutible; (morally dubious) equívoco

questioner [kwéstʃənə] N interrogador -ora *mf*

questioning [kwéstʃənɪŋ] N interrogatorio *m*; ADJ (asking) interrogador; (doubting) cuestionador

questionnaire [kwɛstʃənér] N cuestionario *m*

queue [kju] N cola *f*, fila *f*; VT poner en la cola

quibble [kwíbəl] VI (split hairs) sutilizar; (evade) evadir; (argue) andar en dimes y diretes; N (hairsplitting) sutileza *f*; (evasion) evasiva *f*

quiche [kiʃ] N quiche *f*

quick [kwɪk] ADJ rápido, pronto; — -**tempered** irascible, geniudo; — -**witted** agudo; ADV rápido; N (flesh under nails) carne viva *f*; (the living) los vivos; **to cut to the** — herir en lo vivo; —**sand** arena movediza *f*; —**silver** mercurio *m*, azogue *m*

quicken [kwíkən] VI/VT (speed up) acelerar[se], aligerar[se]; (liven) avivar[se]

quickly [kwíkli] ADV rápido, deprisa, de prisa

quickness [kwíknɪs] N (speed) rapidez *f*; (of wit)

agudeza *f*

quiet [kwáɪɪt] ADJ (not noisy) silencioso; (not talking) callado; (restrained) tranquilo; (peaceful, still) reposado; **be** —! ¡silencio! ¡cállate! N (freedom from noise) silencio *m*; (tranquillity) tranquilidad *f*, sosiego *m*; VT (make quiet) acallar; (make tranquil) sosegar, tranquilizar, serenar; VI **to** — **down** calmarse

quietly [kwáɪtli] ADV (talk) en voz baja; (walk) silenciosamente; **they** — **went about buying up shares** fueron comprando acciones sin llamar la atención

quill [kwɪl] N (feather) pluma *f*; (hollow base of feather) cañón *m*; (spine on a porcupine) púa *f*

quilt [kwɪlt] N colcha de retazos *f*; VI/VT hacer una colcha de retazos

quinine [kwáɪnaɪn] N quinina *f*

quip [kwɪp] N ocurrencia *f*; VI decir ocurrencias

quirk [kwɝk] N excentricidad *f*

quit [kwɪt] VT (a competition) abandonar; (a place) irse de, salir de; (a job) dejar; (a computer program) salir; **to call it** —**s** abandonar; **to** — **smoking** dejar de fumar; VI (withdraw) abandonar; (stop) parar; (resign) renunciar

quite [kwaɪt] ADV (very) bastante; (entirely) del todo, enteramente; — **a person** una persona admirable *f*; — **a lot** bastante; **it's** — **the fashion** está muy de moda

quiver [kwívə] VI temblar; N (shake) temblor *m*; (sheath for arrows) carcaj *m*, aljaba *f*

quiz [kwɪz] N (test) prueba *f*; (show) concurso *m*; VI (give a quiz) examinar, poner una prueba; (interrogate) interrogar

quota [kwóDə] N cuota *f*

quotation [kwotéʃən] N cita *f*; (of a price) cotización *f*; — **marks** comillas *f pl*

quote [kwot] VI/VT (words) citar; (prices) cotizar; **to** — **from** citar a; N (of words) cita *f*; (of a price) cotización *f*; **in** —**s** entre comillas

quotient [kwóʃənt] N cociente *m*

Rr

R & D [research and development] [árn̩dí] N ID *mf*

rabbi [ræbaɪ] N rabino *m*

rabbit [ræbɪt] N conejo *m*

rabble [ræbəl] N chusma *f*, plebe *f*, gentuza *f*

rabid [ræbɪd] ADJ rabioso

rabies [rébiz] N rabia *f*

raccoon [rækún] N mapache *m*

race [res] N (lineage) raza *f*; (competition) carrera *f*; —**horse** caballo de carreras *m*; —**track** (for runners) pista *f*; (for horses) hipódromo *m*; VI (participate in competition) correr, competir en una carrera; (hurry) ir corriendo; (of heart) latir rápido; (of a motor) acelerar; VT (a horse) hacer correr; (an engine) acelerar; **I'll — you** te echo una carrera

racer [résɚ] N corredor -ora *mf*; (horse) caballo de carreras *m*

racial [réʃəł] ADJ racial

racism [résɪzəm] N racismo *m*

rack [ræk] N (for clothes) perchero *m*; (for luggage) baca *f*; (for spices) especiero *m*; (for towels) toallero *m*; (for torture) potro de tormento *m*; (breasts) *fam* tetamen *m*; **— and pinion** cremallera *fy* piñón *m*; VT **to be —ed with pain** estar transido de dolor; **to — one's brain** devanarse los sesos; **to — up** acumular

racket [rǽkɪt] N (sports) raqueta *f*; (noise of an impact) estrépito *m*, estruendo *m*; (noise of voices and movement) barahúnda *f*, batahola *f*; (swindle) estafa *f*; (extortion) extorsión *f*

racketeer [rækɪtír] N (swindler) trapacero -ra *mf*, estafador -ora *mf*; (extortionist) extorsionista *mf*; VI (swindle) estafar; (extort) extorsionar

radar [rédɑr] N radar *m*

radial [rédiəł] ADJ radial

radiance [rédiəns] N resplandor *m*, fulgor *m*

radiant [rédiənt] ADJ radiante, resplandeciente

radiate [rédiet] VI/VT irradiar, radiar

radiation [rediéʃən] N radiación *f*; **— sickness** enfermedad por radiación *f*; **— therapy** radioterapia *f*

radiator [rédiedɚ] N radiador *m*

radical [rǽdɪkəł] ADJ & N radical *mf*

radicalism [rǽdɪkəlɪzəm] N radicalismo *m*

radio [rédio] N (device, system of communication) radio *f*; **— announcer** locutor -ora *mf*; **— listener** radioescucha *mf*; **— station** radiodifusora *f*; **— telescope** radiotelescopio *m*; **— transmitter** radiotransmisor *m*; **by —** por radio; ADJ **—active** radiactivo, radioactivo; VT (broadcast) transmitir por radio; VI/VT (call) llamar por radio

radiologist [rediálədʒɪst] N radiólogo -ga *mf*

radiology [rediálədʒi] N radiología *f*

radish [rǽdɪʃ] N rábano *m*

radium [rédiəm] N radio *m*

radius [rédiəs] N radio *m*

radon [rédɑn] N radón *m*

raffle [rǽfəł] N rifa *f*, sorteo *m*; VI rifar, sortear

raft [ræft] N balsa *f*

rafter [rǽftɚ] N viga *f*

rag [ræg] N (piece of cloth) trapo *m*, guiñapo *m*; (on clothes) harapo *m*, andrajo *m*; **— doll** muñeca de trapo *f*

rage [redʒ] N ira *f*, rabia *f*, cólera *f*; **to be all the — estar de moda; VI enfurecerse; to — with**

anger bramar de ira

ragged [rǽgɪd] ADJ (ill-clothed) andrajoso, harapiento, desharrapado; (voice) ronco, roto; (on an edge) irregular, desigual; **to be on the — edge** estar al borde

raid [red] N (military) incursión *f*; (by police) allanamiento *m*, redada *f*; (by air) bombardeo aéreo *m*; VI/VT hacer una incursión; VT (attack) atacar; (rob) asaltar; (carry out a police operation on) allanar

raider [rédɚ] N empresa tiburón *f*

rail [reł] N (of a railroad track) riel *m*, carril *m*; (on a balcony) baranda *f*, barandilla *f*; **— fence** barrera *f*; **—road** ferrocarril *m*; **—road company** empresa ferroviaria *f*; **—road crossing** cruce de ferrocarril *m*; **—road employee** ferroviario -ria *mf*; **—way** ferrocarril *m*; **by —** por ferrocarril; VT **to —road** (goods) transportar por ferrocarril; (laws) hacer aprobar apresuradamente; (a person) condenar injustamente

railing [rélɪŋ] N (barrier) baranda *f*; (on a bridge) pretil *m*; (on a stairway) pasamano *m*

rain [ren] N lluvia *f*; **—bow** arco iris *m*; **—coat** impermeable *m*; **—drop** gota de lluvia *f*; **—fall** precipitación *f*; **— forest** selva tropical *f*; **— gauge** pluviómetro *f*; **—storm** temporal de lluvia *f*; **— water** agua llovediza *f*; VI/VT llover; **— or shine** llueva o truene; **to — cats and dogs** llover a cántaros

rainy [réni] ADJ lluvioso

raise [rez] VI/VT (voice, hand, a house, spirits) levantar[se]; VT (an alarm) dar; (funds) recaudar, captar; (a salary) aumentar; (a flag) izar; (crops) cultivar; (animals, children) criar; (money) recabar, recaudar; **to — a question** plantear una pregunta; **to — a racket** armar un alboroto; N aumento *m*

raisin [rézɪn] N pasa [de uva] *f*

rake [rek] N rastrillo *m*; VI/VT rastrillar; **to — in money** amasar dinero

rally [rǽli] VI/VT (reorganize troops) reunir[se], juntar[se]; (inspire) reanimar; VI (demonstrate) concentrarse; (recuperate) recuperarse; (reinvigorate) recobrar ánimo; (rise in value) repuntar; (in tennis) pelotear; **to — around someone** apoyar a alguien; N (demonstration) concentración *f*; (recovery) recuperación *f*; (rise in prices) subida *f*; (in tennis) peloteo *m*

RAM [random-access memory] [ræm] N RAM *m*

ram [ræm] N (male sheep) carnero *m*; (tool for battering) ariete *m*; (part of a ship) espolón *m*; VT chocar contra; **to — a boat** embestir un buque con el espolón

ramble [rǽmbəł] VI vagar; **to — on** divagar; N paseo *m*

ramp [ræmp] N rampa f
rampage [rǽmpedʒ] N **to go on a** — andar destrozando todo; VI andar destrozando todo
rampant [rǽmpənt] ADJ desenfrenado
ran [ræn] see run
ranch [ræntʃ] N hacienda f; Mex rancho m
rancid [rǽnsɪd] ADJ rancio
rancor [rǽŋkə-] N rencor m
random [rǽndəm] ADJ aleatorio, azaroso; **at** — al azar; — **access memory** memoria de acceso directo f
randomize [rǽndəmaɪz] VT aleatorizar
rang [ræŋ] see ring
range [rendʒ] N (of types) gama f; (of a gun) alcance m; (of variation) fluctuación f; (of mountains) cadena f; (for shooting) campo de tiro m; (of an aircraft) autonomía f; (grazing place) campo abierto m; (stove) cocina f; estufa f; — **finder** telémetro m; — **of vision** alcance visual m; VT (align) alinear; (of a gun) tener alcance; VI (vary) oscilar; (be found in an area) extenderse; **his children** — **in age between 2 and 10** sus hijos van en edad entre 2 y 10
ranger [réndʒə-] N (in a park) guardabosque[s] mf; (soldier) guardia de asalto m
rank [ræŋk] N (in a hierarchy) rango m, grado m; (line) fila f; — **and file** (of an army) tropa f sg; **the** —**s** (soldiers) la tropa; (union members) bases f pl; **a sculptor of the first** — un escultor de primer orden; VT (arrange) poner en orden de importancia; VI (rate) figurar; **to** — **high** tener alto rango; **to** — **second** estar clasificado en el segundo lugar; ADJ (smelly) hediondo; (growing vigorously) exuberante
ranking [rǽŋkɪŋ] N ránking m
ransack [rǽnsæk] VT saquear, desvalijar
ransom [rǽnsəm] N rescate m; VT rescatar
rant [rænt] VI/VT despotricar
rap [ræp] VI/VT (strike) golpear; (chat) charlar; VI (in music) rapear, cantar rap; N (blow) golpe m; (accusation) cargo m; **to take the** — ser el cabeza de turco; — **music** música rap f
rapacious [rəpéʃəs] ADJ rapaz
rape [rep] N (violation) violación f; (statutory) estupro m; (plant) colza f; (grape pulp) orujo m; VT violar
rapid [rǽpɪd] ADJ rápido; N —**s** rápidos m pl
rapidity [rəpídɪti] N rapidez f
rapport [rəpór] N relación f
rapt [ræpt] ADJ extasiado
rapture [rǽptʃə-] N éxtasis m, embeleso m; **to go into a** — arrobarse
rare [rɛr] ADJ (infrequent) raro, poco frecuente, extraño; (of gas, earth) raro; (thin, of air) enrarecido; (excellent) excepcional; (not well cooked) crudo; — **earths** tierras raras f pl
rarely [rérli] ADV raramente, raras veces
rarity [rérɪti] N rareza f; (of air)

enrarecimiento m
rascal [rǽskəł] N bribón m, bellaco m, pícaro m; Sp golfo m; **you little** —! ¡bandido! ¡sinvergüenza!
rash [ræʃ] ADJ (thoughtless) precipitado, temerario; N (on skin) sarpullido m
raspberry [rǽzbɛri] N frambuesa f; — **bush** frambueso m
raspy [rǽspi] ADJ ronco, áspero
rat [ræt] N rata f; **I smell a** — aquí hay gato encerrado; VT (one's hair) cardar; VI **to** — **on** delatar
ratchet [rǽtʃɪt] N trinquete m
rate [ret] N (charge) tarifa f; (unit charge for insurance) prima f; (pace) paso m, ritmo m; — **of exchange** tipo de cambio m; — **of interest** tasa de interés f; **at any** — en todo caso; **at this** — a este ritmo; **at the** — **of** a razón de; VT (estimate) valorar, estimar; (esteem) considerar; **he** —**s as the best** se le considera como el mejor; **he** —**s high** se le tiene en alta estima
rather [rǽðə-] ADV (somewhat) bastante; (more precisely) más bien; — **than** en vez de; **I would** — **die than** antes la muerte que; **I would** — **not go** prefiero no ir
ratification [rædɪfɪkéʃən] N ratificación f
ratify [rǽDəfaɪ] VT ratificar
rating [réDɪŋ] N (act of adjudging) calificación f; (for credit) clasificación f; (TV quotient) rating televisivo m, índice de audiencia m
ratio [réʃio] N razón f, proporción f
ration [rǽʃən] N ración f; VT racionar
rational [rǽʃənł] ADJ racional
rationale [ræʃənǽł] N motivo m
rationalize [rǽʃənłaɪz] VI/VT racionalizar
rationing [rǽʃənɪŋ] N racionamiento m
rattle [rǽdł] VI (bang) golpetear; (move noisily) traquetear; **to** — **on** parlotear; VT hacer sonar, sacudir; **to** — **off** recitar; N (banging) golpeteo m; (movement) traqueteo m; (toy) sonaja f, sonajero m; (of a rattlesnake) cascabel m; (of death) estertor m; —**snake** víbora de cascabel f
raucous [rókəs] ADJ (loud) estridente; (rowdy) escandaloso
ravage [rǽvɪdʒ] VI/VT asolar, arruinar; N estrago m
rave [rev] VI (rant) desvariar, delirar; VI/VT (roar) bramar; **to** — **about** deshacerse en elogios; N (theater review) crítica muy favorable f
raven [révən] N cuervo m; ADJ azabache
ravenous [rǽvənəs] ADJ voraz, famélico; **to be** — tener un hambre canina
ravine [rəvín] N quebrada f, barranco m, cañada f
raving [révɪŋ] ADJ delirante; (extraordinary) extraordinario; — **mad** loco de remate; N desvarío m
ravish [rǽvɪʃ] VT (kidnap) raptar, secuestrar;

(rape) violar

raw [rɔ] ADJ (uncooked, unprocessed, damp and cold) crudo; (of vegetables) fresco, crudo; (unadorned) descarnado; — **flesh** carne viva *f*; — **material** materia prima *f*; — **sugar** azúcar bruto *m*; N —**hide** cuero crudo *m*

ray [re] N (beam) rayo *m*; (stingray) raya *f*

rayon [réɑn] N rayón *m*

raze [rez] VT arrasar, asolar

razor [rézɚ] N (device with blade) maquinilla de afeitar *f*, rasuradora *f*; (barber's tool) navaja *f*; (electric) rasuradora electrica *f*; — **blade** hoja de afeitar *f*; **safety** — navaja de seguridad *f*

reach [ritʃ] VI/VT (extend) alcanzar; **to** — **for** tratar de agarrar; *Sp* tratar de coger; **to** — **into** meter la mano en; VT (arrive at) llegar a; (contact) ponerse en contacto con; **to** — **out one's hand** alargar la mano; N alcance *m*; **beyond his** — fuera de su alcance; **within his** — a su alcance; **far** —**es** zona remota *f*

react [riækt] VI reaccionar

reaction [riækʃən] N reacción *f*

reactionary [riækʃəneri] ADJ & N reaccionario -ria *mf*

reactor [riæktɚ] N reactor *m*

read [rid] VI/VT leer; VT (interpret) interpretar; (give as a reading, indicate) decir, indicar, marcar; **it** —**s easily** es fácil de leer; N lectura *f*; — **protect** protección contra lectura *f*; —/**write file** archivo de lectura/ escritura *m*

readable [rídəbəl] ADJ (legible) legible; (nice to read) ameno

reader [rídɚ] N (person who reads) lector -ora *mf*; (schoolbook) libro de lectura *m*, cartilla *f*; (anthology) antología *f*

readership [rídɚʃip] N lectores *m pl*

readily [rédli] ADV fácilmente

readiness [rédinis] N estado de preparación *m*; (willingness) buena disposición *f*; **to be in** — estar preparado, estar listo

reading [rídiŋ] N lectura *f*; (interpretation) interpretación *f*; — **room** sala de lectura *f*

readjust [riədʒʌst] VI/VT (improve fit) reajustar; (acclimate) readaptar

readjustment [riədʒʌstmənt] N (fitting) reajuste *m*; (acclimation) readaptación *f*

ready [rédi] ADJ (prepared) listo, preparado, pronto; (willing) dispuesto; (available) disponible; (quick) rápido; —-**made** de confección

reaffirm [riəfɝm] VT reafirmar

reagent [riédʒənt] ADJ & N reactivo *m*

real [ril] ADJ real, verdadero; — **estate** bienes raíces *m pl*, bienes inmuebles *m pl*; — **time** tiempo real *m*

realism [ríəlizəm] N realismo *m*

realist [ríəlist] N realista *mf*

realistic [riəlístik] ADJ realista

reality [riǽlɪɖi] N realidad *f*; — **check** ajuste de perspectiva *m*

realization [riəlɪzéʃən] N (making real) realización *f*; (understanding) comprensión *f*

realize [ríəlaɪz] VT (achieve) realizar; (comprehend) darse cuenta [de], comprobar, percatarse [de]

really [rili] ADV (extremely) realmente; (truly) verdaderamente; (as question) ¿de veras? ¿verdad? **he's not** — **a lawyer** en realidad, no es abogado / no es abogado de verdad; **it's** — **hot in Seville** hace mucho calor en Sevilla; **she's a** — **good colleague** es una colega superbuena / es una buenísima colega

realm [rɛlm] N (kingdom) reino *m*; (domain) terreno *m*, esfera *f*

realtor™ [ríəltɚ] N agente inmobiliario -ria *mf*

reap [rip] VI/VT (cut with sickle) segar; (harvest) cosechar; **to** — **a benefit** obtener beneficio, sacar provecho

reaper [rípɚ] N (person) segador -ora *mf*; (machine) segadora *f*; (death) la Parca, la Muerte

reappear [riəpír] VI reaparecer

rear [rir] ADJ trasero, posterior; —**guard** retaguardia *f*; N (space at the back) parte de atrás *f*, fondo *m*; (backside) trasero *m*, posaderas *f pl*; — **end** trasero *m*; —**view mirror** espejo retrovisor *m*; VT (raise) criar; VI (rise on back legs) encabritarse, empinarse

reason [rízən] N (faculty) razón *f*; (cause) motivo *m*, razón *f*; **by** — **of** por causa de; **it stands to** — es lógico; VT razonar; **to** — **out** resolver por medio de la razón; **to** — **with** hacer entrar en razón

reasonable [rízənəbəl] ADJ razonable; (in price) módico, moderado

reasoning [rízəniŋ] N razonamiento *m*, raciocinio *m*; ADJ racional

reassert [riəsɝt] VT reafirmar

reassure [riəʃúr] VT tranquilizar

rebate [ríbet] N reembolso *m*, reintegro *m*; VT reembolsar, reintegrar

rebel[1] [rébəl] ADJ & N rebelde *mf*, insurrecto -ta *mf*

rebel[2] [rɪbɛl] VI rebelarse

rebellion [rɪbéljən] N rebelión *f*

rebellious [rɪbéljəs] ADJ rebelde, insurrecto

rebelliousness [rɪbéljəsnis] N rebeldía *f*

reboot [ribút] VT reiniciar

rebound[1] [ríbaund] VI (bounce) rebotar; (catch a rebound) rebotear; (recover) recuperarse

rebound[2] [ríbaund] N (bounce) rebote *m*; (recovery) recuperación *f*; **on the** — de rebote

rebuff [rɪbʌf] N desaire *m*, repulsa *f*; VT desairar, rechazar

rebuild [ribíld] VI/VT reconstruir, reedificar; (car engine) reacondicionar

rebuke [rɪbjúk] VT reprender, reprochar; N
reproche *m*, reprimenda *f*
recall[1] [rɪkɔ́ł] VT (remember) recordar; (call
back) retirar; (remove from office) destituir
recall[2] [ríkɔł] N (memory) memoria *f*; (of a
diplomat, product) retirada *f*; (from office)
destitución *f*
recapitulate [rikəpítʃəlet] VI/VT recapitular
recast [rikǽst] VT refundir
recede [rɪsíd] VI retroceder; (of hairline) tener
entradas
receipt [rɪsít] N recibo *m*; **upon — of** al recibo
de; **—s** entradas *f pl*, ingresos *m pl*
receivable [rɪsívəbəł] ADJ a cobrar
receive [rɪsív] VI/VT recibir; (suggestions)
acoger, recibir; (a broadcast) captar, recibir
receiver [rɪsívɚ] N recibidor -ora *mf*; (of a
telephone) auricular *m*; (of a television or
radio, in football) receptor *m*; (in tennis)
restador -ora *mf*; (of a bankrupt business)
síndico *m*
recent [rísənt] ADJ reciente
receptacle [rɪséptəkəł] N receptáculo *m*
reception [rɪsépʃən] N (hotel, social event, TV)
recepción *f*; (act of receiving) recibimiento *m*,
acogida *f*; **— room** recibidor *m*
recess [rísɛs] N (niche) nicho *m*; (pause) descanso
m; (playtime) recreo *m*; **in the —es of** en lo
más recóndito de; VI/VT (a meeting)
interrumpir; VT (a wall) hacer un nicho en
recession [rɪséʃən] N (act of receding) retroceso
m; (economic) recesión *f*
recessive gene [rɪsésɪvdʒín] N gen recesivo *m*
recidivism [rɪsídəvɪzəm] N reincidencia *f*
recipe [résəpi] N receta *f*
recipient [rɪsípiənt] N destinatario -ria *mf*
reciprocal [rɪsíprəkəł] ADJ recíproco
reciprocate [rɪsíprəket] VI/VT corresponder [a],
Am reciprocar
recital [rɪsáɪdl] N recital *m*
recitation [rɛsɪtéʃən] N recitación *f*
recite [rɪsáɪt] VI/VT recitar
reckless [réklɪs] ADJ (driver) temerario,
imprudente; (speed) desenfrenado
recklessness [réklɪsnɪs] N temeridad *f*,
imprudencia *f*
reckon [rékən] VI/VT (calculate) calcular;
(consider) considerar; (think) suponer
reckoning [rékənɪŋ] N (computation) cálculo *m*;
(settlement of accounts) ajuste de cuentas *m*;
the day of — el día del juicio *m*
reclaim [rɪklém] VT (win back, recover)
recuperar; (make land usable) ganar, sanear
recline [rɪkláɪn] VI/VT reclinar[se], recostar[se]
recluse [réklus] ADJ & N solitario -ria *mf*,
ermitaño -ña *mf*
recognition [rɛkəgníʃən] N reconocimiento *m*
recognizable [rɛkəgnáɪzəbəł] ADJ reconocible
recognize [rékəgnaɪz] VT reconocer

recoil[1] [rɪkɔ́ɪł] VI (firearm) dar un culatazo;
(move back) retroceder
recoil[2] [ríkɔɪł] N (of a gun) culatazo *m*; (move
back) retroceso *m*
recollect [rɛkəlɛ́kt] VI/VT recordar
recollection [rɛkəlɛ́kʃən] N recuerdo *m*
recommend [rɛkəménd] VI/VT recomendar
recommendation [rɛkəmɛndéʃən] N
recomendación *f*
recompense [rékəmpɛns] VI/VT recompensar; N
recompensa *f*
reconcile [rékənsaɪł] VT (persons) reconciliar;
(statements) conciliar; **to — oneself to**
resignarse a, conformarse con
reconciliation [rɛkənsɪliéʃən] N reconciliación *f*
reconnoiter [rikənɔ́ɪDɚ] VT reconocer; VI hacer
un reconocimiento
reconsider [rikənsíDɚ] VI/VT reconsiderar
reconstruct [rikənstrʌ́kt] VT reconstruir
reconstruction [rikənstrʌ́kʃən] N
reconstrucción *f*
record[1] [rékɚd] N (account) registro *m*, asiento
m; (account of a meeting) acta *f*; (of criminal
acts) antecedentes *m pl*; (of past activities)
historial *m*, hoja de servicios *f*;
(phonographic) disco *m*; (best performance)
récord *m*, plusmarca *f*; **— player** tocadiscos
m sg; **off the** — extraoficialmente
record[2] [rɪkɔ́rd] VI/VT (write down) registrar,
apuntar; (cut a recording) grabar
recorder [rɪkɔ́rDɚ] N (archivist) archivero -ra
mf; (sound device) grabadora *f*; (musical
instrument) flauta dulce *f*
recording [rɪkɔ́rDɪŋ] N grabación *f*; —
company grabadora *f*
recount[1] [rɪkáʊnt] VT (tell) narrar, relatar
recount[2] [ríkaʊnt] VT (count again) recontar
recoup [rɪkúp] VI/VT recuperar
recourse [ríkɔrs] N recurso *m*; **to have — to**
recurrir a
recover [rɪkávɚ] VI/VT recobrar[se],
recuperar[se]; VI (lost health) restablecerse;
VT (lost time, property) recuperar; (damages)
obtener indemnización
recovery [rɪkávəri] N (from an illness)
recuperación *f*; (of investments) amortización
f; (through a lawsuit) indemnización *f*; —
room sala de recuperación *f*
recreation [rɛkriéʃən] N recreación *f*, recreo *m*,
esparcimiento *m*
recreational [rɛkriéʃənəł] ADJ recreativo, de
recreo; **— drug** droga de recreo *f*; **— vehicle**
caravana *f*
recriminate [rɪkrímənet] VI/VT recriminar
recruit [rɪkrút] N recluta *mf*; VI/VT reclutar
recruitment [rɪkrútmənt] N reclutamiento *m*,
recluta *f*
rectangle [réktæŋgəł] N rectángulo *m*
rectangular [rɛktǽŋgjəlɚ] ADJ rectangular

rectify [réktəfaɪ] VT rectificar
rector [réktə-] N rector -ora *mf*
rectum [réktəm] N recto *m*
recuperate [rɪkúpəret] VI/VT recuperar[se], recobrar[se]
recur [rɪkɜ́-] VI volver a ocurrir, repetirse
recurring [rɪkɜ́-ɪŋ] ADJ recurrente
recycle [risáɪkəl] VI/VT reciclar
recycling [risáɪklɪŋ] N reciclaje *m*
red [rɛd] ADJ & N rojo *m*, colorado *m*; — **blood cell** glóbulo rojo *m*; — **card** tarjeta roja *f*; — **-handed** *fam* in fraganti; —**headed** pelirrojo; —**-hot** candente, al rojo vivo; — **light** luz roja *f*; —**neck** granjero -ra blanco -ca pobre *mf*; — **pepper** pimienta de cayena *f*; — **prawn** carabinero *m*; — **snapper** pargo *m*; — **tape** trámites *m pl*; — **wine** vino tinto *m*; —**wood** secoya/secuoya *f*; **in the** — en números rojos; **to see** — enfurecerse
redden [rédn̩] VI/VT enrojecer, ruborizar[se]
reddish [rédɪʃ] ADJ rojizo, bermejo
redeem [rɪdím] VT (deliver from sin) redimir; (pay off a mortgage) cancelar; (buy back from pawnshop) desempeñar; (exchange) canjear; (fulfill) cumplir
redemption [rɪdémpʃən] N redención *f*; (of something pawned) desempeño *m*
redevelopment [ridɪvéləpmənt] N remodelación *f*
redness [rédnɪs] N rojez *f*; (inflammation) inflamación *f*
redress[1] [rídrɛs] N reparación *f*, desagravio *m*
redress[2] [rɪdrés] VT reparar, desagraviar
reduce [rɪdús] VI/VT reducir[se]; **she was** —**d to tears** se echó a llorar
reduction [rɪdʌ́kʃən] N reducción *f*
redundant [rɪdʌ́ndənt] ADJ (repetitive) redundante; (superfluous) superfluo
reed [rid] N caña *f*, junco *m*, carrizo *m*; (of a musical instrument) lengüeta *f*
reef [rif] N (underwater ridge) escollo *m*; (of coral) arrecife *m*
reek [rik] VI heder, apestar; N hedor *m*
reel [ril] N carrete *m*, bobina *f*; VT (on a spool) bobinar; VI tambalearse; **to** — **off** recitar; **to** — **in a fish** sacar un pez del agua
reelect [riɪlékt] VT reelegir
reelection [riɪlékʃən] N reelección *f*
reemployment [riɪmplɔ́ɪmənt] N reinserción laboral *f*
reestablish [riɪstǽblɪʃ] VT restablecer
refer [rɪfɜ́-] VI/VT referir; (direct to a source of information) remitir; (direct to a doctor) mandar; (mention) referirse a, aludir a
referee [rɛfərí] N árbitro *m*; VT (a game) arbitrar; (a submission) hacer el referato
reference [réfərəns] N (mention) referencia *f*; — **book** libro de consulta *m*; **with** — **to** con respecto a, respecto de

referendum [rɛfəréndəm] N referéndum *m*
referral [rɪfɜ́-əl] N **he gave me a** — **to a specialist** me mandó con/a un especialista
refill[1] [rifíl] VI/VT rellenar
refill[2] [rifíl] N (for a pen) repuesto *m*; (for a lighter) carga *f*; **may I have a** —? ¿me sirve más?
refinance [rifáɪnæns] VI/VT refinanciar
refine [rɪfáɪn] VT (purify) refinar; (polish) refinar, pulir
refined [rɪfáɪnd] ADJ refinado
refinement [rɪfáɪnmənt] N (of manners) refinamiento *m*, pulimento *m*; (of oil) refinación *f*
refinery [rɪfáɪnəri] N (of oil) refinería *f*; (of sugar) ingenio *m*
reflect [rɪflékt] VI/VT (mirror) reflejar; VI (ponder) reflexionar; **to** — **poorly on** desacreditar
reflection [rɪflékʃən] N (image) reflejo *m*; (consideration) reflexión *f*; (unfavorable observation) tacha *f*; **on** — pensándolo bien
reflector [rɪfléktə-] N reflector *m*
reflex [ríflɛks] ADJ & N reflejo *m*
reflexive [rɪfléksɪv] ADJ reflexivo
reflux [ríflʌks] N reflujo *m*
reform [rɪfɔ́rm] VI/VT reformar[se]; N reforma *f*
reformation [rɛfə-méʃən] N reforma *f*
reformatory [rɪfɔ́rmətɔri] N reformatorio *m*
reformer [rɪfɔ́rmə-] N reformador -ora *mf*, reformista *mf*
refraction [rɪfrǽkʃən] N refracción *f*
refractory [rɪfrǽktəri] ADJ (not malleable) refractario; (rebellious) rebelde
refrain [rɪfrén] VI abstenerse; N (of a song) estribillo *m*
refresh [rɪfréʃ] VI/VT refrescar[se]; (computer screen) actualizar, refrescar
refreshing [rɪfréʃɪŋ] ADJ (drink) refrescante; (sleep) reparador; (honesty) agradable
refreshment [rɪfréʃmənt] N (drink) refresco *m*; (food) refrigerio *m*
refrigerate [rɪfríʤəret] VT refrigerar
refrigeration [rɪfrɪʤəréʃən] N refrigeración *f*
refrigerator [rɪfríʤəreDə-] N frigorífico *m*, nevera *f*, refrigerador *m*; RP heladera *f*
refuge [réfjuʤ] N refugio *m*; **to give** — dar albergue
refugee [rɛfjuʤí] N refugiado -da *mf*
refund[1] [rífʌnd] N reembolso *m*
refund[2] [rɪfʌ́nd] VT reembolsar
refurbish [rɪfɜ́-bɪʃ] VT restaurar
refusal [rɪfjúzəl] N negativa *f*, rechazo *m*; **first** — opción *f*
refuse[1] [rɪfjúz] VI/VT (deny a request) negar[se] [a]; **to** — **to** rehusarse a, negarse a; VT (decline to accept) rechazar, no aceptar
refuse[2] [réfjus] N desechos *m pl*, desperdicios *m pl*

refute [rɪfjút] VT refutar, rebatir
regain [rɪgén] VT (recover) recobrar; (get back to) volver a
regal [rígəł] ADJ regio, real
regard [rɪgárd] VT (consider) considerar; (esteem) estimar; N (consideration) consideración f; (esteem) respeto m, estima f; —**s** recuerdos m pl, saludos m pl; **as** —**s** en cuanto a; **with** — **to** con respecto a
regarding [rɪgárdɪŋ] PREP con respecto a
regardless [rɪgárdlɪs] ADV LOC — **of** independientemente de
regenerate [rɪdʒénəret] VI/VT regenerar[se]
regent [rídʒənt] N regente -ta mf
reggae [rége] N reggae m
regime [rɪʒím] N régimen m
regiment [rédʒəmənt] N regimiento m
region [rídʒən] N región f
regional [rídʒənł] ADJ regional
register [rédʒɪstə-] N (recording, range of voice) registro m; (entry) asiento m; VI/VT (enter into a list) registrar[se]; (enroll) matricular[se], inscribir[se]; VT (indicate) indicar, registrar; (a letter) certificar; VI (appear) aparecer; **that didn't** — no cayó en la cuenta
registered [rédʒɪstə-d] ADJ registrado; — **mail** correo certificado m; — **nurse** enfermero -ra titulado -da mf; — **trademark** marca registrada f
registrar [rédʒɪstrɑr] N secretario -ria de admisiones mf
registration [rɛdʒɪstréʃən] N (of a car) matrícula f; (of a student) inscripción f
regret [rɪgrét] VT (feel sorry) lamentar; (feel rueful) arrepentirse de; N arrepentimiento m; **to send** —**s** enviar sus excusas
regretful [rɪgrétfəł] ADJ lleno de remordimientos
regrettable [rɪgrédəbəł] ADJ lamentable
regroup [rigrúp] VT reagrupar; VI reorganizarse
regular [régjələ-] ADJ (symmetrical, uniform) regular; (normal) normal; (habitual) habitual; **a** — **fool** un verdadero necio; **a** — **guy** un buen tipo; (habitual customer) parroquiano -na mf; (soldier) soldado de línea m
regularity [rɛgjəlǽrɪDi] N regularidad f
regulate [régjəlet] VT (control) regular; (make regular) regularizar
regulation [rɛgjəléʃən] N (act of regulating) regulación f; —**s** reglamento m, reglamentación f
regulator [régjəleDə-] N regulador m
regurgitate [rɪgɜ́dʒɪtet] VI/VT regurgitar
rehabilitate [rihəbílɪtet] VI/VT rehabilitar[se]
rehabilitation [riəbɪlɪtéʃən] N rehabilitación f
rehearsal [rɪhɜ́səł] N ensayo m
rehearse [rɪhɜ́s] VI/VT ensayar

reign [ren] N reino m, reinado m; VI reinar
reimburse [riɪmbɜ́s] VI/VT reembolsar
reimbursement [riɪmbɜ́smənt] N reembolso m
rein [ren] N rienda f (also control); VI **to** — **in** dominar, refrenar
reincarnation [riɪnkɑrnéʃən] N reencarnación f
reindeer [réndɪr] N reno m
reinforce [riɪnfɔ́rs] VT reforzar
reinforcement [riɪnfɔ́rsmənt] N refuerzo m, reforzado m
reinsertion [riɪnsɜ́ʃən] N reinserción f
reinstate [riɪnstét] VT reinstaurar
reiterate [riídəret] VT reiterar
reject[1] [rɪdʒékt] VT rechazar
reject[2] [rídʒɛkt] N (thing) cosa rechazada f, desecho m; (person) rechazado -da mf
rejoice [rɪdʒɔ́ɪs] VI regocijarse
rejoicing [rɪdʒɔ́ɪsɪŋ] N regocijo m
rejoin [rɪdʒɔ́ɪn] VT (come again into a group) reincorporarse a; VI/VT (reunite) volver a unir[se]
rejuvenate [rɪdʒúvənet] VI/VT rejuvenecer
relapse[1] [rɪlǽps] VI (into bad health) recaer; (into crime) reincidir
relapse[2] [rílæps] N (into bad health) recaída f, recidiva f; (into crime) reincidencia f
relate [rɪlét] VT (tell) relatar, narrar; (connect) relacionar; VI **to** — **to** relacionarse con
related [rɪléDɪd] ADJ (connected) relacionado; (kin) emparentado
relation [rɪléʃən] N (association) relación f; (act of narrating) narración f; (kinship) parentesco m; (relative) pariente -ta mf; **with** — **to** con respecto a
relationship [rɪléʃənʃɪp] N relación f
relative [réləDɪv] ADJ relativo; N pariente -ta mf, allegado -da mf; — **to** relativo a, referente a
relativity [rɛlətívɪDi] N relatividad f
relax [rɪlǽks] VI/VT relajar[se], distender[se]; VT (grip) aflojar
relaxation [rilækséʃən] N (recreation) esparcimiento m, recreo m; (loosening) relajamiento m, relajación f
relay[1] [ríle] N relevo m, posta f; (electrical) relé m; — **race** carrera de relevos/postas f
relay[2] [ríle, rɪlé] N transmitir; **to** — **a broadcast** transmitir un programa
release [rɪlís] VT (let go) soltar; (free prisoners) librar, poner en libertad; (energy) liberar; (news) divulgar; (discharge from hospital) dar de alta; N (liberation) liberación f; (permission) permiso m; (of film) estreno m; (of gas) escape m; (of energy) desprendimiento m
relegate [rélɪget] VT relegar
relent [rɪlént] VI aplacarse
relentless [rɪléntlɪs] ADJ implacable
relevant [réləvənt] ADJ pertinente
reliability [rɪlaɪəbílɪDi] N fiabilidad f,

confiabilidad*f*

reliable [rɪláɪəbəł] ADJ fiable, confiable; (a person) formal

reliance [rɪláɪəns] N (dependency) dependencia *f*; (trust) confianza*f*

relic [rélɪk] N reliquia*f*

relief [rɪlíf] N (ease) alivio *m*; (aid) ayuda*f*; (projection) relieve *m*; (soldier) relevo *m*; (in golf) alivio *m*; **in** — en relieve; — **map** mapa en relieve *m*

relieve [rɪlív] VT (alleviate) aliviar; (free) liberar; (replace) relevar; VI **to** — **oneself** orinar

reliever [rɪlívə] N (baseball) relevista *mf*

religion [rɪlíʤən] N religión*f*

religious [rɪlíʤəs] ADJ religioso

relinquish [rɪlíŋkwɪʃ] VT (give up) renunciar; (let go) soltar

relish [rélɪʃ] VT (to like the taste) saborear, paladear; (enjoy) disfrutar; N (enjoyment) gusto *m*; (condiment) condimento de pepinillos en vinagre *m*

relocate [rilóket] VI/VT trasladar[se]

reluctance [rɪlʌ́ktəns] N renuencia*f*

reluctant [rɪlʌ́ktənt] ADJ renuente, reacio

rely [rɪláɪ] VI **to** — **on** (trust) confiar en; (depend on) depender de

REM [rapid eye movement] [áríém] N REM *m*, MOR *m pl*

remain [rɪmén] VI (continue to be) seguir siendo; (stay) quedar[se], permanecer; (to be left) quedar, restar; (to be left over) sobrar; N —**s** restos *m pl*

remainder [rɪméndə] N (extra) sobrante; (other) restante

remake¹ [rimék] VT rehacer; (film) hacer de nuevo

remake² [rímek] N nueva versión*f*

remark [rɪmárk] VT (comment) comentar, observar; (notice) notar, observar; **to** — **on** comentar; N observación*f*, comentario *m*

remarkable [rɪmárkəbəł] ADJ notable

remedial [rɪmíDiəł] ADJ (rehabilitative) rehabilitador; (to improve skills) de recuperación

remedy [rémɪDi] N (solution) remedio *m*; (cure) cura*f*; VT (solve) remediar, subsanar; (heal) curar

remember [rɪmémbə] VI/VT recordar, acordarse [de]; — **me to him** mándale saludos míos

remind [rɪmáɪnd] VT recordar

reminder [rɪmáɪndə] N (of a date, deadline) recordatorio *m*; (warning) advertencia*f*

reminiscence [rɛmənísəns] N reminiscencia*f*, recuerdo *m*

remiss [rɪmís] ADJ negligente

remission [rɪmíʃən] N remisión*f*

remit [rɪmít] VI/VT remitir

remittance [rɪmítn̩s] N remesa*f*, giro *m*

remnant [rémnənt] N (remainder) resto *m*; (of fabric) retazo *m*, retal *m*; (vestige) vestigio *m*

remodel [rimádl̩] VI/VT remodelar

remodeling [rimádlɪŋ] N remodelación*f*

remorse [rɪmɔ́rs] N remordimiento *m*

remote [rɪmót] ADJ (far away) remoto, recóndito; (aloof) distante; (in kinship) lejano; — **access** acceso remoto *m*; — **control** control remoto *m*, mando a distancia *m*; — **login** acceso remoto *m*; — **server** servidor remoto *m*

removal [rɪmúvəł] N (dismissal) deposición*f*, alejamiento *m*; (elimination) eliminación*f*; (extirpation) extirpación*f*

remove [rɪmúv] VT (an obstacle) remover; (take away, take off) quitar; (dismiss) deponer; (eliminate) eliminar; (extirpate) extirpar; **to** — **from office** separar/apartar del cargo

remunerate [rimjúnəret] VT remunerar*f*, retribuir*f*

remuneration [rɪmjunəréʃən] N remuneración *f*, retribución*f*

renaissance [rénɪsɑns] N renacimiento *m*; — **architecture** arquitectura renacentista*f*

renal [rínł] ADJ renal; — **failure** insuficiencia renal*f*

rend [rɛnd] VI/VT desgarrar[se], rajar[se]

render [réndə] VT (give) dar; (cause to become) dejar; (depict) representar; (translate) traducir; (give homage, account) rendir; (provide services, assistance) prestar; (melt down fat) derretir; (deliver a verdict) pronunciar; **to** — **useless** inutilizar

rendition [rɛndíʃən] N (translation) traducción *f*; (interpretation) interpretación*f*, versión*f*

renegade [rénɪged] N renegado -da *mf*

renegotiate [rinɪgóʃiet] VI/VT renegociar

renegue [rɪníg] VI incumplir

renew [rɪnú] VT (vows, contract) renovar; (furniture) restaurar; (friendship, effort) reanudar; (a loan) prorrogar

renewable [rɪnúəbəł] ADJ renovable

renewal [rɪnúəł] N (of vows, contract) renovación*f*; (of furniture) restauración*f*; (of a city) remodelación*f*; (of friendship, effort) reanudación*f*; (of loan) prórroga*f*

renounce [rɪnáuns] VT (give up) renunciar a; (repudiate) repudiar, renegar de

renovate [rénəvet] VT renovar

renown [rɪnáun] N renombre *m*

renowned [rɪnáund] ADJ renombrado

rent [rɛnt] N (monthly payment) alquiler *m*, arrendamiento *m*; **for** — se alquila, se arrienda; (fissure) rajadura*f*, hendidura*f*; (tear) rasgadura*f*; VI/VT (lease) alquilar, arrendar

rent [rɛnt] *see* rend

rental [réntł] ADJ de alquiler; — **agreement** contrato de alquiler *m*; N alquiler *m*,

arrendamiento *m*
renter [réntə-] N inquilino -na *mf*
renunciation [rɪnʌnsiéʃən] N renuncia *f*
reopen [riópən] VI/VT (doors) reabrir[se];
(negotiations) reanudar[se]
reorganization [riɔrgənɪzéʃən] N
reorganización *f*
reorganize [riórgənaɪz] VI/VT reorganizar[se]
repaginate [ripǽdʒɪnet] VT repaginar
repair [rɪpér] VT (fix) reparar, arreglar,
componer; (shoes) remendar; **to — to** acudir
a; N (fixing) reparación *f*; (of shoes) remiendo
m, compostura *f*; **in good —** en buen estado;
—man técnico en reparaciones *m*
reparation [rɛpəréʃən] N reparación *f*,
indemnización *f*
repay [ripé] VT (return money, favor) devolver;
(pay off) pagar
repayment [ripémənt] N (of a sum) reembolso
m; (of a loan) pago *m*
repeal [rɪpíɫ] VT derogar, revocar, abrogar; N
derogación *f*, revocación *f*, abrogación *f*
repeat[1] [rípít] VI/VT repetir; N repetición *f*
repeat[2] [rɪpít] N repetición *f*
repeated [rɪpíDɪd] ADJ repetido
repel [rɪpéɫ] VI/VT repeler; (an attack) rechazar
repellent [rɪpélənt] ADJ & N repelente *m*
repent [rɪpént] VI/VT arrepentirse [de]
repentance [rɪpéntəns] N arrepentimiento *m*
repentant [rɪpéntənt] ADJ arrepentido, pesaroso
repercussion [rɛpə-kʌ́ʃən] N repercusión *f*; **to
have —s** repercutir
repertoire [répə-twar] N repertorio *m*
repetition [rɛpɪtíʃən] N repetición *f*
replace [rɪplés] VT (place again) volver a colocar;
(substitute for) sustituir, reemplazar;
(provide a substitute for) reponer
replaceable [rɪplésəbəɫ] ADJ reemplazable,
sustituible
replacement [rɪplésmənt] N (substitute,
substitution) sustituto *m*, reemplazo *m*;
(making up for) reposición *f*; **— parts** piezas
de repuesto *f pl*
replenish [rɪplénɪʃ] VI/VT (supply) reabastecer;
(fill again) rellenar
replete [rɪplít] ADJ repleto
replica [réplɪkə] N réplica *f*
replicate [réplɪket] VT reproducir, replicar
replication [rɛplɪkéʃən] N reproducción *f*,
replicación *f*
reply [rɪplái] VI replicar, contestar; N réplica *f*,
contestación *f*
report [rɪpórt] VT (recount) relatar; (make a
crime known, denounce) denunciar; (make
an accident known) dar parte de; VI hacer un
informe, informar; **to — for duty**
presentarse; **to — on** hacer un informe sobre;
to — sick dar parte de enfermo, reportarse
enfermo; **it is —ed that** se dice que; N

informe *m*, comunicado *m*; (rumor) rumor *m*;
(loud noise) estallido *m*; **— card** boletín de
calificaciones *m*
reportedly [rɪpórDɪdli] ADV según se informa
reporter [rɪpórDə-] N (news) reportero -ra *mf*;
(sports) cronista *mf*
repose [rɪpóz] VI/VT reposar, descansar; N
reposo *m*, descanso *m*
repository [rɪpázɪtɔri] N (object) depósito *m*;
(person) depositario -ria *mf*
repossess [ripəzés] VT retomar posesión de
represent [rɛprɪzént] VT representar
representation [rɛprɪzɛntéʃən] N
representación *f*
representative [rɛprɪzéntəDɪv] ADJ
representativo; N representante *mf*
repress [rɪprés] VI/VT reprimir
repression [rɪpréʃən] N represión *f*
repressive [rɪprésɪv] ADJ represivo
reprieve [rɪprív] VT (pardon) indultar;
(commute) conmutar; (delay) aplazar; N
(pardon) indulto *m*; (commutation)
conmutación *f*; (delay) aplazamiento *m*
reprimand [réprəmænd] N reprimenda *f*,
regaño *m*; VT reprender, regañar
reprint[1] [riprínt] VI/VT reimprimir
reprint[2] [ríprɪnt] N (action, result) reimpresión
f; (offprint) separata *f*
reprisal [rɪpráɪzəɫ] N represalia *f*
reproach [rɪprótʃ] VT reprochar; N reproche *m*
reproduce [riprədús] VI/VT reproducir[se]
reproduction [riprədʌ́kʃən] N reproducción *f*
reproof [rɪprúf] N reprobación *f*
reprove [rɪprúv] VT reprobar
reptile [réptaɪɫ] N reptil *m*
republic [rɪpʌ́blɪk] N república *f*
republican [rɪpʌ́blɪkən] ADJ & N republicano -na
mf
repudiate [rɪpjúDiet] VT repudiar
repugnance [rɪpʌ́gnəns] N repugnancia *f*
repugnant [rɪpʌ́gnənt] ADJ repugnante
repulse [rɪpʌ́ɫs] VT repeler, rechazar; N repulsa
f, rechazo *m*
repulsive [rɪpʌ́ɫsɪv] ADJ repulsivo
reputable [répjəDəbəɫ] ADJ reputado
reputation [rɛpjətéʃən] N reputación *f*, fama *f*
request [rɪkwést] N solicitud *f*, petición *f*,
requerimiento *m*; **at the — of** a solicitud de,
a instancias de; VT solicitar, pedir
require [rɪkwáɪr] VI/VT (need) requerir;
(demand) exigir
requirement [rɪkwáɪrmənt] N (demand)
requisito *m*; (need) necesidad *f*
requisite [rékwɪzɪt] ADJ requerido, necesario; N
requisito *m*
requisition [rɛkwɪzíʃən] N (taking over) requisa
f; (order) pedido *m*; VT (take over) requisar;
(order) pedir
rerun [rírʌn] N refrito *m*

rescind [rɪsínd] VT rescindir
rescue [réskju] VT rescatar, salvar; N rescate *m*, salvamento *m*; **to go to the — of** acudir al socorro de, salir al quite de
research[1] [rísətʃ] N investigación *f*
research[2] [rɪsə́tʃ] VI/VT investigar
researcher [rɪsə́tʃɚ] N investigador -ora *mf*
resell [risél] VT revender
resemblance [rɪzémbləns] N semejanza *f*, parecido *m*
resemble [rɪzémbəl] VT semejar, asemejarse a, parecerse a
resent [rɪzént] VT resentirse de
resentful [rɪzéntfəl] ADJ resentido, rencoroso
resentment [rɪzéntmənt] N resentimiento *m*
reservation [rezɚvéʃən] N reserva *f*; *Am* reservación *f*; **to have one's —s** tener reservas
reserve [rɪzɚ́v] VT reservar; N reserva *f*; (shyness) pudor *m*
reserved [rɪzɚ́vd] ADJ reservado
reservoir [rézɚvwɑr] N (tank) depósito *m*, alberca *f*; (artificial lake) embalse *m*, represa *f*
reset [risét] VT (computer, machine) reiniciar; **— key** tecla de reinicio *f*
reside [rɪzáɪd] VI residir
residence [rézɪDəns] N residencia *f*
resident [rézɪDənt] ADJ & N residente *mf*; (of a neighborhood) vecino -na *mf*
residential [rezɪdéntʃəl] ADJ residencial
residue [rézɪdu] N residuo *m*
resign [rɪzáɪn] VI/VT renunciar [a], dimitir [de]; **to — oneself to** resignarse a
resignation [rezɪgnéʃən] N (act of resigning an office) renuncia *f*, dimisión *f*; (accepting attitude) resignación *f*; **— letter** carta de renuncia *f*
resilience [rɪzíljəns] N (elasticity) elasticidad *f*; (adaptability) adaptabilidad *f*
resilient [rɪzíljənt] ADJ (elastic) elástico; (adaptable) adaptable
resin [rézɪn] N resina *f*
resist [rɪzíst] VT (a temptation) resistir; VI/VT (tyranny) resistirse [a]
resistance [rɪzístəns] N resistencia *f*
resistant [rɪzístənt] ADJ resistente
resolute [rézəlut] ADJ resuelto, decidido
resolution [rezəlúʃən] N resolución *f*
resolve [rɪzáɫv] VI/VT resolver[se]; **to — into** convertirse en; **to — to** decidir, resolver; N resolución *f*
resonance [rézənəns] N resonancia *f*
resonate [rézənet] VI/VT resonar
resort [rɪzɔ́rt] N (seaside) centro de veraneo *m*; (for skiing) estación de esquí *f*; **as a last —** como último recurso; VI **to — to** recurrir a
resound [rɪzáʊnd] VI/VT resonar; **—ing victory** victoria contundente *f*
resource [rísɔrs] N recurso *m*

resourceful [rɪzɔ́rsfəl] ADJ ingenioso
respect [rɪspékt] VT respetar; N (esteem) respeto *m*; (detail) aspecto *m*; **with — to** [con] respecto a, respecto de
respectable [rɪspéktəbəl] ADJ respetable
respectful [rɪspéktfəl] ADJ respetuoso
respective [rɪspéktɪv] ADJ respectivo
respiration [respəréʃən] N respiración *f*
respiratory [réspəətɔri] ADJ respiratorio; **— failure** insuficiencia respiratoria *f*
respite [réspɪt] N (pause) respiro *f*, tregua *m*; (postponement) prórroga *f*
resplendent [rɪspléndənt] ADJ resplandeciente, refulgente
respond [rɪspánd] VI/VT responder
respondent [rɪspándənt] N (to a lawsuit) demandado -da *mf*; (to a poll) encuestado -da *mf*
response [rɪspáns] N respuesta *f*
responsibility [rɪspɑnsəbílɪDi] N responsabilidad *f*, reivindicación *f*
responsible [rɪspánsəbəl] ADJ responsable
rest [rest] N (repose) descanso *m*, reposo *m*; (musical) pausa *f*; (support) apoyo *m*; (remainder) resto *m*; **— home** (for convalescents) casa de reposo *f*; (for the aged) casa de ancianos *f*; **— room** servicio *m*; *Sp* aseo *m*; **an object at —** un objeto en reposo; VI/VT descansar, reposar; VT (one's gaze) posar; (against a wall) reclinar; VI (stop) parar; **to — on** depender de; **let it —** déjalo en paz
restaurant [réstərɑnt] N restaurante *m*; *Am* restorán *m*
restitution [restɪtúʃən] N restitución *f*
restless [réstlɪs] ADJ (worried) inquieto; (fidgety) movedizo
restlessness [réstlɪsnɪs] N inquietud *f*, desasosiego *m*
restoration [restəréʃən] N restauración *f*
restore [rɪstɔ́r] VT restaurar
restrain [rɪstrén] VT (hold back) refrenar, contener, moderar; (bring under control) reducir; **—ing order** medida cautelar *f*
restraint [rɪstrént] N (self-control) compostura *f*, moderación *f*; (device) seguro *m*; **under —** bajo control
restrict [rɪstríkt] VT restringir; (someone's liberty) coartar
restriction [rɪstríkʃən] N restricción *f*
restructuring [ristrʌ́ktʃɚɪŋ] N reestructuración *f*
result [rɪzʌ́lt] VI resultar; **to — from** resultar de; **to — in** dar por resultado; N resultado *m*; **as a —** de resultas, como resultado
resume [rɪzúm] VI/VT (take up again) reasumir, volver a asumir; (continue) reanudar
résumé [rézume] N currículum *m*, historial personal *m*
resurrection [rezərékʃən] N resurrección *f*

resuscitate [rɪsʌ́sɪtet] VI/VT resucitar
resuscitation [rɪsʌsɪtéʃən] N resucitación f
retail [rítel] N venta al por menor f; — **store** tienda minorista f; — **trade** comercio minorista m; VI/VT vender al por menor; **at** — al por menor, al menudeo
retailer [rítelə-] N minorista mf, detallista mf
retain [rɪtén] VT (recall, confine, detain) retener; (keep) conservar, quedarse con; (hire) contratar
retainer [rɪténə-] N (device that holds back) retén m; (payment) honorarios pagados por adelantado m pl
retaliate [rɪtǽliet] VI vengarse
retaliation [rɪtæliéʃən] N venganza f
retard [rɪtárd] VI/VT retardar
retarded [rɪtárdɪd] ADJ retrasado
retention [rɪténʃən] N retención f
reticence [rédɪsəns] N reserva f
retina [rétṇə] N retina f
retinue [rétṇu] N séquito m, comitiva f
retire [rɪtáɪr] VI/VT (stop working) retirar[se], jubilar[se]; (withdraw) retirar[se]; (go to bed) acostarse; (withdraw money, troops, machines) retirar
retiree [ritaɪrí] N jubilado -da mf
retirement [rɪtáɪrmənt] N retiro m, jubilación f; — **of debt** retiro de deuda m
retort [rɪtɔ́rt] N (reply) réplica f; (vessel) retorta f
retouch [ritʌ́tʃ] VT retocar; N retoque m
retrace [ritrés] VT (mental steps) repasar; (one's route) volver sobre
retract [rɪtrǽkt] VT (a statement) retractar; (claws) retraer[se]; VI desdecirse, retractarse
retreat [rɪtrít] N (place of refuge, period of meditation) retiro m, refugio m; (military) retirada f, repliegue m; (bugle call) retreta f; VI batirse en retirada, retroceder, replegarse
retrench [rɪtréntʃ] VI economizar
retrieval [rɪtrívəl] N recuperación f
retrieve [rɪtrív] VT (game animals) cobrar; (something lost) recuperar
retriever [rɪtrívə-] N perro cobrador m
retro [rétro] ADJ retro
retroactive [retroǽktɪv] ADJ retroactivo
retrospect [rétrəspɛkt] ADV LOC **in** — mirando para atrás
retrovirus [rétrovaɪrəs] N retrovirus m
return [rɪtɜ́n] VI (come back) volver, regresar; VT (put back) devolver, retornar; (deliver a verdict) fallar; — **to sender** devolver al remitente; N (to a place) vuelta f, regreso m; (of a thing) devolución f; (of profit) ganancia f; (on a typewriter) retorno de carro m; (on a computer) retroceso m, salto de línea m; — **address** señas del remitente f pl; — **game** revancha f; — **key** tecla de retorno f, tecla de retroceso f; — **of service** (tennis) resto m; — **ticket** billete de vuelta m; **by** — **mail** a

vuelta de correo; **election** — **s** resultados electorales m pl; **in** — a cambio; **in** — **for** a cambio de; **income tax** — Sp declaración de la renta f; Am declaración de impuestos f
reunification [rijunɪfɪkéʃən] N reunificación f
reunion [rijúnjən] N reunión f
reunite [rijunáɪt] VI/VT reunir[se]
rev [rɛv] VI/VT acelerar en vacío
reveal [rɪvíl] VT revelar
revealing [rɪvílɪŋ] ADJ revelador; (neckline) atrevido
revel [rɛ́vəl] VI (enjoy) deleitarse, gozar; (party) parrandear; N parranda f
revelation [rɛvəléʃən] N revelación f; (book in Bible) Apocalipsis m sg
revelry [rɛ́vəlri] N parranda f, jarana f
revenge [rɪvɛ́ndʒ] N venganza f, revancha f
revengeful [rɪvɛ́ndʒfəl] ADJ vengativo
revenue [rɛ́vənu] N (of a government) rentas públicas f pl; (of a person) ingresos m pl; — **stamp** sello fiscal m
reverberate [rɪvɜ́bəret] VI reverberar; VT hacer reverberar
revere [rɪvír] VT reverenciar
reverence [rɛ́vəəns] N reverencia f, veneración f; VT venerar
reverend [rɛ́vəənd] ADJ & N reverendo -da mf
reverent [rɛ́vəənt] ADJ reverente
reverie, revery [rɛ́vəri] N ensueño m, ensoñación f
reverse [rɪvɜ́s] ADJ inverso, opuesto; **the** — **side** el revés; N (opposite) lo opuesto; (back of clothing, mishap) revés m; (back of a coin, medal) reverso m; (gear) marcha atrás f; (back of a piece of paper) dorso m; VI/VT invertir[se]; VT (a policy, a vehicle) dar marcha atrás; (a verdict) revocar
revert [rɪvɜ́t] VI revertir
review [rɪvjú] N (inspection of a military unit, periodical publication) revista f; (repetition of studied material) repaso m; (critique of a book, drama) reseña f, crítica f; (examination of a judicial case) revisión f; VI/VT (examine) repasar, revisar; VT (reexamine) revisar, examinar; (inspect troops) pasar revista a; (write a critique of) reseñar
revile [rɪváɪl] VT vilipendiar, denostar
revise [rɪváɪz] VT corregir, enmendar
revision [rɪvíʒən] N (action of revising) corrección f; (revised version) versión corregida f
revitalize [rɪváɪdḷaɪz] VT revitalizar
revival [rɪváɪvəl] N (of customs) retorno m; (of religious feeling) resurgimiento m, despertar m; (from unconsciousness) resucitación f; (of a play) reposición f, revisión f; (evangelical meeting) asamblea evangelística f
revive [rɪváɪv] VT (an unconscious person) reavivar, reanimar; (an apparently dead

person) resucitar; (an old play) reponer; (a custom) restablecer; VI revivir, reanimarse; (be reestablished) restablecerse

revocation [rɛvəkéʃən] N revocación f

revoke [rɪvók] VT revocar

revolt [rɪvóɫt] N revuelta f, sublevación f; VI rebelarse, sublevarse; **it —s me** me da asco

revolting [rɪvóɫtɪŋ] ADJ repugnante, asqueroso

revolution [rɛvəlúʃən] N revolución f

revolutionary [rɛvəlúʃənɛri] ADJ & N revolucionario -ria mf

revolve [rɪváɫv] VI/VT girar

revolver [rɪváɫvɚ] N revólver m

revolving credit [rɪváɫvɪŋ] N crédito rotativo m

revue [rɪvjú] N revista f

revulsion [rɪváɫʃən] N repugnancia f, asco m

reward [rɪwɔ́rd] N recompensa f; VT recompensar

rewind [riwáɪnd] VI/VT rebobinar

rewrite[1] [riráɪt] VI/VT reescribir

rewrite[2] [ríraɪt] N corrección f

rhea [ríə] N ñandú m

rhetoric [rɛ́Dɚɪk] N retórica f

rheumatic [rumǽDɪk] ADJ reumático; **— fever** fiebre reumática f

rheumatism [rúmətɪzəm] N reumatismo m, reuma m

rheumatoid [rúmətɔɪd] ADJ reumatoide

Rh factor [árétʃfæktɚ] N factor Rh m

rhinoceros [raɪnásərəs] N rinoceronte m

rhinoplasty [ráɪnoplæsti] N rinoplastia f

rhinovirus [ráɪnováɪrəs] N rinovirus m

rhododendron [roDədéndrən] N rododendro m

rhubarb [rúbɑrb] N (vegetable) ruibarbo m; (brawl) reyerta f

rhyme [raɪm] N rima f; **without — or reason** sin ton ni son; VI/VT rimar

rhythm [ríðəm] N ritmo m

rhythmical [ríðmɪkəɫ] ADJ rítmico; (breathing) acompasado

rib [rɪb] N (of person, animal) costilla f; (of umbrella) varilla f; (in garment) canalé m, cordoncillo m; **— cage** caja torácica f; VT burlarse de

ribbon [ríbən] N (of cloth) cinta f; (of land) franja f, faja f

rice [raɪs] N arroz m; **— field** arrozal m

rich [rɪtʃ] ADJ rico; (tasty) sabroso; (buttery) mantecoso; (colorful) vivo; **— text format** formato de texto enriquecido m; N **—es** riquezas f pl

rickety [ríkɪDi] ADJ (shaky) desvencijado; (affected with rickets) raquítico

ricochet [ríkəʃe] N rebote m; VI rebotar

rid [rɪd] VT librar, desembarazar; **to get — of** librarse de, deshacerse de

ridden [rídn̩] see ride

riddle [rídl̩] N (puzzle) acertijo m, adivinanza f; (something puzzling) enigma m; VI hablar en

enigmas; VT acribillar, perforar; **to be —d with graft** estar plagado de corrupción

ride [raɪd] VI (on a horse) cabalgar, jinetear; (on a bicycle) montar; (in a vehicle) andar/viajar/ir en; **this car —s well** este coche anda bien; **his hopes are riding on that** tiene las esperanzas puestas en eso; **just let it —** déjalo tranquilo; VT (travel on horse, bicycle) montar; (travel on bus) andar en; (harass) hostigar; **to — away** irse; **to — by** pasar; **to — out** capear; **to — up** subirse; N (in a vehicle) paseo m, viaje m; (at an amusement park) aparato m; **to give someone a —** llevar/acercar en coche; **to go on a —** dar un paseo

rider [ráɪDɚ] N (on a horse) jinete m; (on a bicycle) ciclista mf; (on an insurance policy) cláusula añadida f; (law) anexo m

ridge [rɪdʒ] N (back of an animal) espinazo m, lomo m; (chain of hills) cadena f; (of a roof) caballete m; (of cloth) cordoncillo m

ridicule [rídɪkjuɫ] N burla f, mofa f; VT ridiculizar, poner en ridículo

ridiculous [rɪdíkjələs] ADJ ridículo

riffraff [rífræf] N pej gentuza f, chusma f

rifle [ráɪfəɫ] N rifle m, fusil m; VT robar; **to — through** revolver

rift [rɪft] N (opening) grieta f, hendidura f; (disagreement) desavenencia f

rig [rɪg] VT (sails) aparejar, equipar; (an election) amañar; **to — up** armar; N (on a ship) aparejo m, equipo m; (apparatus) aparato m; (truck) camión m

rigging [rígɪŋ] N jarcia f

right [raɪt] ADJ (not left) derecho; (not wrong) correcto, acertado; (suitable) adecuado; **— angle** ángulo recto m; **—-hand** derecho; **—- hand man** brazo derecho m; **—-handed** diestro; **— justification** alineación a la derecha f; **—-to-life** antiaborto, pro vida; **— triangle** triángulo recto m; **—-wing** derechista, de derecha; **at the — moment** en el momento justo; **the — people** la gente indicada; **to be —** tener razón; **to be all —** estar bien; **he's not in his — mind** no está en sus cabales; **to turn out —** salir bien; ADV (straight) derecho, directamente; (correctly) correctamente; (to the right) a la derecha; **— after** justo después de; **—-face** media vuelta a la derecha; **— now** ahora mismo, ahorita; **— there** allí mismo; **it is — where you left it** está exactamente donde lo dejaste; **to hit — in the eye** darle de lleno en el ojo; **— click** pulsación en el botón derecho del ratón f; N (just claim) derecho m; (moral good) bien m; (direction, political persuasion) derecha f; **— of way** prioridad f, preferencia f; **— to work** derecho al trabajo m; **make a — at the corner** gira/dobla a la derecha; **to the —**

a la derecha; **to be in the** — tener razón; VI/VT (make upright) enderezar[se]; **to** — **click** pulsar el botón derecho del ratón; VT (correct) corregir

righteous [ráɪtʃəs] ADJ recto, justo; — **anger** rabia justificada f

righteousness [ráɪtʃəsnɪs] N rectitud f, superioridad moral f

rightful [ráɪtfəl] ADJ legítimo

rightist [ráɪdɪst] N derechista mf

rightly [ráɪtli] ADV con razón

rigid [rídʒɪd] ADJ rígido

rigidity [rɪdʒídɪti] N rigidez f

rigor [rígə-] N rigor m

rigorous [rígə-əs] ADJ riguroso

rim [rɪm] N (edge) borde m; (on a car) llanta f; Am rin m; (on a bicycle) aro m; (on a plate) filete m; (of glasses) montura f

rind [raɪnd] N (cheese) corteza f; (fruit) cáscara f

ring [rɪŋ] N (on finger, of smoke) anillo m; (for women only) sortija f; (under the eyes) ojeras f pl; (in the nose) argolla f; (circle) círculo m, redondel m, ruedo m; (in a circus) pista f; (for bullfights) plaza de toros f; (for boxing) cuadrilátero m; (for gymnastics) anillas f pl; (of criminals) banda f; (undertone) tono m; (sound of telephone) timbrazo m, telefonazo m; (sound of bells) retintín m, repique m; — **finger** anular m; —**leader** cabecilla mf; —**worm** tiña f; VT (surround) cercar; (make doorbell sound) tocar; (make bell sound) tañer; VI (of ears) zumbar; (make sound of a doorbell) sonar; (make sound of a bell) repicar, repiquetear; **to** — **the nose of an animal** ponerle una argolla en la nariz a un animal; **to** — **the hour** dar la hora; **to** — **true** parecer verdad; **to** — **up the sale** marcar la venta

ringlet [ríŋlɪt] N (curl) rizo m, bucle m, sortija f; (small ring) sortija pequeña f

rink [rɪŋk] N pista de patinaje f

rinkydink [ríŋkidɪŋk] ADJ de pacotilla

rinse [rɪns] VI/VT enjuagar, aclarar; N enjuague m, aclarado m

riot [ráɪət] N (uprising) motín m, tumulto m; (excess) exceso m; **he's a** — es un cómico; VI amotinarse

riotous [ráɪədəs] ADJ (wanton) desenfrenado; (funny) graciosísimo

rip [rɪp] VI/VT rasgar[se], rajar[se]; VT (something sewn) descoser; **to** — **away** desprender; **to** — **into** asaltar; **to** — **off** robar; **to** — **out a seam** descoser una costura; N rasgadura f, rajadura f; — **cord** cordón de apertura m; —**off** robo m

ripe [raɪp] ADJ maduro; **to be** — **for** estar preparado/listo para; — **old age** edad avanzada f

ripen [ráɪpən] VI/VT madurar[se], sazonar[se]

ripeness [ráɪpnɪs] N madurez f

ripening [ráɪpənɪŋ] N maduración f

ripple [rípəl] VI/VT (water) rizar[se]; (grass) agitar[se]; N ondulación f, rizo m

rise [raɪz] VI (go up) subir; (increase) aumentar; (get up, stand up) levantarse; (slope up) elevarse; (arise) surgir; (of mist) levantarse; (of the sun, moon) salir; (of dough) crecer, leudar; **to** — **up in rebellion** sublevarse, alzarse; **to** — **above** superar; **to** — **to the challenge** aceptar el desafío y triunfar; N (of prices, volume) subida f, aumento m; (of an empire, talent) surgimiento m; (slope upward) elevación f; **to get a** — **out of someone** provocar a alguien; **to give** — **to** ocasionar

risen [rízən] see rise

risk [rɪsk] N riesgo m; — **factors** factores de riesgo m pl; **at** — a riesgo; ADJ -**free** sin riesgo; VT arriesgar, aventurar; **to** — **defeat** correr el riesgo de perder, exponerse a perder

risky [ríski] ADJ arriesgado, aventurado

risqué [rɪské] ADJ subido de tono, atrevido, picante

Ritalin hydrochloride [rídəlɪnhaɪdrəklɔ́raɪd] N clorhidrato de Ritalina m

rite [raɪt] N rito m

ritual [rítʃuəl] ADJ & N ritual m

ritzy [rítsi] ADJ elegante

rival [ráɪvəl] ADJ & N rival mf; VT rivalizar con, competir con

rivalry [ráɪvəlri] N rivalidad f

river [rívə-] N río m; —**bank** orilla f, ribera f; — **transport** transporte fluvial m

rivet [rívɪt] N remache m; VT (put rivets) remachar; (fix) fijar, clavar

riveting [rívɪdɪŋ] N (action) remache m; ADJ (fascinating) fascinante

RNA [**ribonucleic acid**] [áréné] N ARN m

roach [rotʃ] N cucaracha f

road [rod] N (in the country) camino m; (highway) carretera f; **on the** — **to recovery** en vías de recuperación; — **map** mapa carretero m; — **rage** ira caminera f; —**side** borde del camino m; —**way** camino m

roam [rom] VI/VT vagar [por], errar [por], rodar [por]; VI vagabundear

roar [rɔr] VI/VT rugir, bramar; **to** — **with laughter** reír a carcajadas; N rugido m, bramido m; — **of laughter** risotada f, carcajada f

roast [rost] VI/VT (meat, potatoes) asar[se]; (coffee, nuts) tostar, torrar; (criticize) criticar; N (meat) asado m; (party) barbacoa f; — **beef** rosbif m

rob [rɑb] VI/VT robar; **to** — **someone of something** robarle algo a alguien

robber [rábə-] N ladrón -ona mf

robbery [rábəri] N robo m

robe [rob] N manto *m*, traje talar *m*, túnica *f*; (ceremonial dress) toga *f*; (bath wrap) bata *f*
robin [rábɪn] N petirrojo *m*
robot [róbɑt] N robot *m*
robotics [robáDɪks] N robótica *f*
robust [robÁst] ADJ (strong) robusto; (hearty) saludable; (solid) sólido
rock [rɑk] N roca *f*; (crag) peñasco *m*, peñón *m*; (diamond) diamante *m*; (music style) rock *m*; — **crystal** cristal de roca *m*; — **salt** sal de piedra *f*, sal gema/mineral *f*; **on the** — en las rocas; **to go on the** —**s** tropezar en un escollo; *Am* escollar; **to hit** —-**bottom** tocar fondo; VI/VT (move to and fro) mecer[se]; (stagger) sacudir, estremecer; **to** — **to sleep** arrullar
rocker [rákɚ] N (chair) mecedora *f*; (fan or performer of rock music) roquero -ra *mf*
rocket [rákɪt] N cohete *m*
rocketry [rákɪtri] N cohetería *f*
rocking [rákɪŋ] N — **chair** mecedora *f*; — **horse** caballito de madera *m*, caballito mecedor *m*
rocky [ráki] ADJ (with rocks) rocoso; (difficult) difícil
rod [rɑd] N (stick) vara *f*, varilla *f*; (in engine) vástago *m*; (measure of length) aproximadamente 5 metros *f*
rode [rod] *see* ride
rodent [róDənt] N roedor *m*
rodeo [róDio] N rodeo *m*
rogue [rog] N pícaro -ra *mf*, bribón -ona *mf*; ADJ solitario y bravo
roguish [rógɪʃ] ADJ (rascally) pícaro, bribón; (mischievous) travieso
role [roł] N (in a drama) papel *m*, rol *m*; — **model** modelo ejemplar *m*; —-**playing** improvisación *f*
roll [roł] VI (move on wheels, rotate) rodar; (rotate one's eyes) revolear; (sway) balancearse, bambolearse; (reverberate) retumbar; (flow as waves) ondular; VT (steel) aplanar; (cigarettes) liar; (a drum) redoblar; (one's r's) pronunciar la erre; **to** — **over** (physically) volcar, darse vuelta; (investments) reinvertir; **to get** —**ing** ponerse en marcha; N (of paper, fabric, etc.) rollo *m*; (of coins) cartucho *m*; (of a ship) balanceo *m*; (of thunder) retumbo *m*; (of a drum) redoble *m*; (of members) lista *f*; (of waves) ondulación *f*; (of a typewriter) carro *m*; (of bread) bollo *m*, panecillo *m*; (of dice) tiro *m*; ADJ —-**on** de bolita
roller [rólɚ] N (for painting, moving things) rodillo *m*; (hair) rulo *m*, rulero *m*; — **coaster** montaña rusa *f*; — **skate** patín de ruedas *m*

rolling [rólɪŋ] ADJ (countryside) ondulado; (wheel) rodante; — **pin** rodillo *m*, palote *m*
roly-poly [rólipóli] ADJ rechoncho
ROM [read-only memory] [rɑm] N ROM *f*, memoria de ROM *f*, memoria de sólo lectura *f*
Roman [rómən] ADJ & N romano -na *mf*; — **numeral** número romano *m*
romance [rómæns] N (love affair, story) romance *m*; (romantic atmosphere) romanticismo *m*; VT cortejar; ADJ (linguistic) romance, románico
romanesque [romənésk] ADJ románico
Romania [roméniə] N Rumania *f*
Romanian [roméniən] ADJ & N rumano -na *mf*
romantic [romǽntɪk] ADJ romántico
romanticism [romǽntəsɪzəm] N romanticismo *m*
romp [rɑmp] VI (frolic) retozar, brincar; (win easily) arrasar; N (frolic) retozo *m*; (victory) victoria fácil *f*
roof [ruf] N (ceiling) techo *m*, tejado *m*; (flat roof) azotea *f*; — **of the mouth** paladar *m*; **to hit the** — poner el grito en el cielo; VT techar
rookie [rúki] N novato -ta *mf*
room [rum] N (in building) cuarto *m*; (large) sala *f*; (in a hotel) habitación *f*; (space) lugar *m*, sitio *m*; — **and board** pensión completa *f*; —**mate** compañero -ra de cuarto *mf*; — **service** servicio a la habitación *f*; **to take up** — ocupar espacio; **the whole** — **laughed** todos los presentes se rieron; VI hospedarse, alojarse
roomy [rúmi] ADJ espacioso, amplio
roost [rust] N vara *f*; VI posarse [para dormir]
rooster [rústɚ] N gallo *m*
root [rut] N raíz *f*; — **canal** (part of tooth) canal radicular *m*, tratamiento de conducto *m*; — **directory** directorio de raíz *m*, directorio raíz *m*; **to take** — (a plant) echar raíces, prender; (an idea) arraigar[se]; VI (grow roots) arraigar[se], echar raíces; (dig) hozar; **to** — **for** animar; **to** — **out/up** (uproot) arrancar de raíz; (eradicate) erradicar
rope [rop] N (cord) soga *f*, cuerda *f*; (lasso) reata *f*, lazo *m*; (on a ship) cabo *m*; (thick) maroma *f*; **to be at the end of one's** — no dar más; **to know the** —**s** conocer el paño, sabérselas todas; VT enlazar; **to** — **off** acordonar; **to** — **someone in** agarrar a alguien
Rorschach test [rórʃɑk tɛst] N prueba de Rorschach *f*
rosary [rózəri] N rosario *m*
rose [roz] N rosa *f*; (color) rosa *m*; —**bud** capullo de rosa *m*, pimpollo de rosa *m*; —**bush** rosal *m*; ADJ —-**colored** de color rosa
rose [roz] *see* rise
rosemary [rózmɛri] N romero *m*
roseola [roziələ] N roséola *f*
roster [rástɚ] N lista *f*

rostrum [rástrəm] N tribuna f
rosy [rózi] ADJ (pink) rosado, color de rosa; (of cheeks) sonrosado; — **future** porvenir halagüeño m
rot [rɑt] VI/VT pudrir[se]; N podredumbre f
rotary [róDəri] ADJ rotatorio, rotativo
rotate [rótet] VI/VT rotar
rotation [rotéʃən] N rotación f, giro m
rotor [róDə-] N rotor m
rotten [rátn̩] ADJ (decomposing) podrido; (stinking) hediondo; (morally corrupt) corrupto; (despicable) odioso
rotund [rotánd] ADJ rollizo
rouge [ruʒ] N colorete m
rough [rʌf] ADJ (coarse) áspero, rugoso; (violent) violento; (rude) tosco; (approximate) aproximado; (bumpy) desigual, irregular; (rugged) agreste, bronco; (stormy) picado, revuelto; — **diamond** diamante en bruto m; — **draft** borrador m; — **estimate** aproximación f; — **weather** mal tiempo m; **he had a — time** le fue mal; VI **to — it** vivir sin lujos ni comodidades
roughly [ráfli] ADV (not smoothly) ásperamente; (rudely) groseramente, rudamente; (approximately) aproximadamente; **to estimate** — tantear
roughness [ráfnɪs] N (lack of smoothness) aspereza f; (rudeness) rudeza f; (unevenness) desigualdad f; **the — of the sea** lo picado del mar
roulette [rulét] N ruleta f
round [raUnd] ADJ redondo; — **number** número redondo m; — **trip** viaje de ida y vuelta m; N (of talks, drinks, dance) ronda f; (of cheese) rodaja f; (in cards, sports) vuelta f; (in boxing) round m, asalto m; (of golf) partido m, ronda f; (canon) canon m; — **of ammunition** carga de municiones f; — **of applause** aplauso m; —**up** (of cattle) rodeo m; (of criminals) redada f; **to make the —s** hacer la ronda; PREP & ADV —**about** indirecto; —**-the-clock** veinticuatro horas al día; **all year** — todo el año; **to come** — pasar; **to go — a corner** doblar una esquina; VT (a corner) doblar; (an edge, a number) redondear; **to — off/out** redondear; **to — up** juntar, reunir; **to — up cattle** juntar el ganado
roundness [ráUndnɪs] N redondez f
rouse [raUz] VI/VT (wake) despertar[se]; VT (instigate) incitar
rout [raUt] N (defeat) derrota aplastante f; (flight) huida en desbandada f; VT (defeat) derrotar, destrozar; (cause to flee) poner en fuga
route [raUt, rut] N ruta f, trayecto m, recorrido m; (of newspaper delivery) reparto m; VT dirigir
routine [rutín] N rutina f

rove [rov] VI/VT vagar [por], errar [por]
rover [róvə-] N vagabundo -da mf
row¹ [raU] N (fight) riña f, pelea f, bronca f
row² [ro] N (line) fila f, hilera f, ringlera f; **four times in a** — cuatro veces seguidas; VI/VT (propel with oars) remar, bogar; —**boat** bote de remos m, barca f
rowdy [ráUdi] ADJ (person) alborotador; (party) bullicioso; N camorrista mf
rower [róə-] N remero -ra mf
royal [rɔ́Iəł] ADJ real; — **blue** azul marino m; — **flush** escalera real f
royalty [rɔ́Iəłti] N (group) realeza f; (person) miembro de la realeza m; **royalties** derechos m pl, regalías f pl
RSVP [**répondez s'il vous plaît**] [árésvípí] LOC S.R.C.
rub [rʌb] VI/VT (apply friction) frotar[se]; (massage) friccionar; (spread on) aplicar frotando; (make sore) rozar; **to — off** quitar[se] frotando; **to — out** borrar; **to — shoulders with** codearse con; **to — the wrong way** peinar a contrapelo; **don't — it in!** ¡no me lo refriegues por la cara! N (act of rubbing) fricción f; (difficulty) dificultad f; (abraded area) roce m, frote m
rubber [rábə-] N caucho m, goma f; (condom) condón m, preservativo m; — **band** goma elástica f; —**s** chanclos m pl; — **stamp** sello de goma m; — **tree** gomero m; VT **to —-stamp** autorizar automáticamente
rubbing alcohol [rábɪŋ ǽłkəhɔ́ł] N alcohol para fricciones m
rubbish [rábɪʃ] N (trash) basura f; (nonsense) pamplinas f pl
rubble [rábəł] N (debris) escombros m pl; (stone fragments) ripios m pl, cascote m
rubella [rubélə] N rubéola/rubeola f, sarampión alemán m
rubric [rúbrɪk] N rúbrica f
ruby [rúbi] N rubí m
ruckus [rákəs] N barahúnda f, jaleo m
rudder [ráDə-] N timón m
ruddy [ráDi] ADJ rubicundo
rude [rud] ADJ (impolite) grosero; (uncouth, crude, simple) tosco; (harsh) rudo
rudeness [rúdnɪs] N (impoliteness) grosería f; (crudeness) tosquedad f; (harshness) rudeza f
rueful [rúfəł] ADJ (inspiring pity) triste; (repentant) arrepentido
ruffian [ráfiən] N rufián m
ruffle [ráfəł] VI/VT (gather cloth) fruncir[se]; (raise feathers) erizar[se]; (ripple water) agitar[se], rizar[se]; (muss hair) desgreñar[se]; (bother a person) molestar[se], fastidiar[se]; N (frill on clothes) volante m; (gathering in cloth) frunce m, pliegue m; (ripples in water) ondulación f, rizo m
rug [rʌg] N alfombra f; (hairpiece) peluquín m

rugby [rʌ́gbi] N rugby *m*

rugged [rʌ́gɪd] ADJ (terrain) escarpado, áspero, fragoso; (face) recio; (manners) tosco; (way of life) duro; (man) robusto

ruin [rúɪn] N ruina *f*; **to go to** — arruinarse, venirse abajo; VI/VT arruinar[se], estropear[se]; (spoil) echar[se] a perder

ruinous [rúɪnəs] ADJ ruinoso

rule [ruɫ] N (principle) regla *f*; (line separating newspaper columns) filete *m*; (government) mando *m*, gobierno *m*; —**s and regulations** reglamentos y disposiciones administrativas *m pl*; **the** — **of law** el imperio de la ley; **as a** — **of thumb** por regla general, a ojo de buen cubero; VI/T (govern) reinar, gobernar; (decree) fallar, dictaminar, sentenciar; (put lines on paper) rayar, poner renglones; **to** — **out** excluir; **to** — **over** reinar, gobernar

ruler [rúlɚ] N (governor) gobernante *mf*; (measuring instrument) regla *f*

ruling [rúlɪŋ] N (decision) fallo *m*, sentencia *f*, dictamen *m*; (line on paper) renglón *m*; ADJ (governing) gobernante, reinante

rum [rʌm] N ron *m*

rumba [rʌ́mbə] N rumba *m*; VI rumbear

rumble [rʌ́mbəɫ] VI (as thunder) retumbar; (as a stomach) hacer ruido; (fight) pelear; N (roar) retumbo *m*; (growl) ruido *m*; (fight) pelea *f*

ruminate [rúmənet] VI rumiar

rummage [rʌ́mɪʤ] VI/VT rebuscar, hurgar; N cachivaches *m pl*; — **sale** venta de beneficencia *f*

rumor [rúmɚ] N rumor *m*; VT murmurar; **it is** —**ed that** se rumorea que, corre la voz que

rump [rʌmp] N (of quadruped) anca *f*, grupa *f*; (of bird) rabadilla *f*; (of person) trasero *m*

run [rʌn] VI (person, tears, water) correr; (stockings, dyes) correrse; (machines) funcionar; (faucet) chorrear; (candidate) presentarse como candidato; (sore) supurar; VT (a mile, a risk) correr; (one object through another) pasar; (a business) manejar, dirigir; (a red light) comerse; (a news story) publicar; (a sum of money) costar; (a computer program) ejecutar; (a fever) tener; — **along now!** ¡vete! **to** — **across someone** encontrarse con alguien; **to** — **after** perseguir; **to** — **around with** andar con; **to** — **away** fugarse, escaparse; **to** — **down** (stop working) dejar de funcionar; (capture) aprehender; (criticize) hablar mal de; (run over) atropellar; (tire) cansar; **to** — **dry** secarse; **to** — **into** (encounter) tropezarse con, encontrarse con; (collide) chocar con; **to** — **out** salir corriendo; **to** — **out of money** quedarse sin dinero; **to** — **over** (spill) derramarse; (run down) atropellar, arrollar; (move along a surface) deslizar por; **to** — **through** (stab) atravesar; (squander)

despilfarrar; **to** — **up** acumular; **the play ran for three months** la obra estuvo en cartel durante tres meses; **it** —**s in the family** es un rasgo de familia; N (act of running) carrera *f*, corrida *f*; (point in baseball) carrera *f*, anotación *f*; (defect in stockings) carrera *f*, corrida *f*; (routine trip) recorrido *m*; (of newspapers) tirada *f*; (of a play) temporada en cartel *f*; (on a bank) pánico *m*, corrida *f*; —**away** fugitivo -va *mf*; —**away horse** caballo desbocado *m*; — **batted in** carrera impulsada *f*; — **of good luck** racha de buena suerte *f*; — **of the mill** del montón; —**way** (for planes) pista *f*; (for models) pasarela *f*; **to be on the** — estar huyendo; **in the long** — a la larga; **the** —**s** *vulg* cagalera *f*; **he gave me the** —**around** contestó con evasivas; **she gave us a** —**down** nos hizo un resumen; ADJ —-**down** desvencijado

rung [rʌŋ] N (of a chair) barrote *m*; (of a ladder) peldaño *m*

rung [rʌŋ] *see* ring

runner [rʌ́nɚ] N (one who runs) corredor -ora *mf*; (on a table) tapete *m*; (on a sled) patín *m*; (on a skate) cuchilla *f*; (on a plant) estolón *m*; (of drugs, contraband) contrabandista *mf*; —-**up** segundo -da *mf*

running [rʌ́nɪŋ] N (of a race) corrida *f*, carrera *f*; (of a business) manejo *m*, dirección *f*; (of water) flujo *m*; (of machines) funcionamiento *m*; (of a car) rodaje *m*; **to be out of the** — estar fuera de combate; — **board** estribo *m*; ADJ (sore) supurante; — **water** agua corriente *f*; **in** — **condition** en buen estado; **for ten days** — durante diez días seguidos

runt [rʌnt] N (animal) animal más pequeño de la camada *m*; (person) *pej* mequetrefe *m*

rupture [rʌ́ptʃɚ] N (of relations, internal organ) ruptura *f*; (of a tire) rotura *f*; (hernia) hernia *f*; VI/VT romper[se], reventar[se]

rural [rúrəɫ] ADJ rural

rush [rʌʃ] VI/VT (hurry) apresurar[se]; *Am* apurar[se]; VT (a parcel) llevar con prisa, llevar rápido; (an enemy) precipitarse, abalanzarse sobre; **to** — **by/past** pasar corriendo; **to** — **out** salir corriendo; N (haste) prisa *f*; *Am* apuro *m*; (attack) acometida *f*; (hurried activity) bullicio *m*; (plant) junco *m*; — **hour** hora punta *f*; — **of air** ráfaga *f*; — **of people** tumulto *m*; — **of water** torrente *m*; — **order** pedido urgente *m*

Russia [rʌ́ʃə] N Rusia *f*

Russian [rʌ́ʃən] ADJ & N ruso -sa *mf*

rust [rʌst] N (oxidation) herrumbre *f*, orín *m*; (disease) tizón *m*; ADJ —-**colored** color herrumbre; —-**proof** inoxidable; VI/VT herrumbrar[se]

rustic [rʌ́stɪk] ADJ rústico; N campesino -na *mf*,

paleto -ta *mf*

rusting [rÁstɪŋ] N oxidación *f*

rustle [rÁsəł] VI susurrar, crujir; VT hacer susurrar, hacer crujir; **to — cattle** robar ganado; N susurro *m*, crujido *m*

rusty [rÁsti] ADJ (oxidized) herrumbrado, oxidado; (rust-colored) color herrumbre; (out of practice) falto de práctica; **my German is — se me ha olvidado el alemán**

rut [rʌt] N (furrow) surco *m*; (of a wheel) rodada *f*; (routine) rutina *f*; (heat) celo *m*; **to be in a — ser esclavo de la rutina**; VI estar en celo

ruthless [rúθlɪs] ADJ despiadado

ruthlessness [rúθlɪsnɪs] N crueldad *f*

Rwanda [ruándə] N Ruanda *f*

Rwandan [ruándən] ADJ & N ruandés -esa *mf*

rye [raɪ] N centeno *m*; **— bread** pan de centeno *m*

Ss

saber [sébɚ] N sable *m*

sabotage [sǽbətaʒ] N sabotaje *m*; VT sabotear

sac [sæk] N bolsa *f*, saco *m*

saccharine [sǽkəɪn] ADJ empalagoso; N sacarina *f*

sack [sæk] N (bag) saco *m*, bolso *m*; (looting) saqueo *m*; (in football) captura *f*; **in the —** en la cama; VT (bag) embolsar, ensacar; (loot) saquear; (fire) despedir

sacrament [sǽkrəmənt] N sacramento *m*

sacred [sékrɪd] ADJ sagrado

sacrifice [sǽkrəfaɪs] N (also in baseball) sacrificio *m*; **at a —** con pérdida; VT sacrificar

sacrilege [sǽkrəlɪdʒ] N sacrilegio *m*

sacrilegious [sækrəlídʒəs] ADJ sacrílego

sacrum [sékrəm] N sacro *m*

sad [sæd] ADJ triste

sadden [sǽdn̩] VI/VT entristecer[se]; VT pesar

saddle [sǽdl̩] N (for horse) silla de montar *f*, montura *f*; (for bicycle) sillín *m*; **—bag** alforja *f*; **— horse** caballo de silla *m*; **— pad** carona *f*; **— tree** arzón *m*; VT ensillar; **to — up** ensillar; **to — someone with responsibilities** cargar a alguien de responsabilidades

sadism [sédɪzəm] N sadismo *m*

sadistic [sədístɪk] ADJ sádico

sadness [sǽdnɪs] N tristeza *f*

sadomasochism [seDOmǽsəkɪzəm] N sadomasoquismo *m*

safari [səfári] N safari *m*

safe [sef] ADJ (secure) seguro, salvo; (trustworthy) digno de confianza; (careful) precavido, prudente; **— and sound** sano y salvo; **— deposit box** caja de seguridad *f*; **—guard** salvaguarda *f*; **—keeping** custodia *f*; **— mode** modo a prueba de fallos/errores *m*; **— sex** sexo seguro *m*; N caja fuerte *f*; **—-conduct** salvoconducto *m*; ADV (in baseball) safe; VT **to —guard** salvaguardar

safely [séfli] ADV (without danger) sin peligro; (without incident) sin percances; **I can — say** puedo decir con toda seguridad

safety [séfti] N seguridad *f*; **— belt** cinturón de seguridad *m*; **— device** mecanismo de seguridad *m*, seguro *m*; **— glass** vidrio inastillable *m*; **— net** red *f*; **— pin** imperdible *m*

saffron [sǽfrən] N (spice) azafrán *m*; (color) color azafrán *m*

sag [sæg] VI/VT (wall) combar[se], pandear[se]; VI (stock market, breast) caer; (spirits) decaer; (rope) aflojarse; (pants) abolsarse; **his shoulders —** tiene las espaldas caídas; N (of a wall) pandeo *m*, comba *f*; (in prices) caída *f*

sage [sedʒ] ADJ sabio; N (wise person) sabio -bia *mf*; (plant) salvia *f*

said [sɛd] *see* say

sail [seł] N (part of a boat) vela *f*; (trip) viaje en barco *m*; **—boat** velero *m*; **—fish** pez vela *m*; **under full —** a toda vela; **to set —** zarpar; VI/VT (travel by boat) navegar; (set sail) zarpar; **to — along** deslizarse, navegar; **to — along the coast** costear; **to — through an exam** aprobar un examen con facilidad

sailor [sélɚ] N marinero -ra *mf*

saint [sent] N santo -ta *mf*; **— John** San Juan

saintly [séntli] ADJ santo, piadoso

sake [sek] N **for the — of** por; **for my —** por mí; **for pity's —** por el amor de Dios; **for brevity's —** para ser breve; **for the — of argument** por vía de argumento; **art for art's —** el arte por el arte

salad [sǽləd] N ensalada *f*; **— dressing** aderezo *m*

salamander [sǽləmændɚ] N salamandra *f*

salary [sǽləri] N sueldo *m*, retribución *f*; **— bracket** categoría salarial *f*; **— range** escala de sueldos *f*, escala salarial *f*

sale [seł] N (act of selling) venta *f*; (special sales event) liquidación *f*, saldo *m*; **—s clerk** dependiente -ta *mf*; **—s force** personal de ventas *m*; **—sperson** dependiente -ta *mf*; **—s tax** impuesto sobre las ventas *m*; **for —** en venta; **on —** con rebaja, rebajado

salient [séliənt] ADJ & N saliente *m*

saline [sélin] ADJ salino; **— solution** solución salina *f*

saliva [səláɪvə] N saliva *f*

sally [sǽli] N (sortie) salida *f*; (excursion) excursión *f*; VI salir, hacer una salida; **to — forth** salir

salmon [sǽmən] N salmón *m*

salmonella [sælmənélə] N salmonela *f*

salon [səlán] N salón *m*; (beauty parlor) salón de

belleza *m*, peluquería *f*
saloon [səlún] N salón *m*, taberna *f*, bar *m*
salt [sɔlt] N sal *f*; (for smelling) sales *f pl*;
—**cellar** salero *m*; — **lick** salegar *m*; — **mine**
salina *f*; —**peter** salitre *m*; —**shaker** salero
m; —**water** agua salada *f*; **old** — lobo de mar
m; **the** — **of the earth** la sal de la tierra; VT
salar; **to** — **away** ahorrar
salty [sɔ́lti] ADJ (food, water) salado; (soil, water)
salobre
salutation [sæljətéʃən] N saludo *m*
salute [səlút] N saludo *m*; (of guns) salva *f*; VI/VT
(greet) saludar; (acknowledge) reconocer
Salvadoran, Salvadorian [sælvədɔ́r[i]ən] ADJ
& N salvadoreño -ña *mf*
salvage [sǽlvɪʤ] N (recovery) salvamento *m*;
(objects recovered) objetos salvados *m pl*; VT
salvar
salvation [sælvéʃən] N salvación *f*
salve [sæv] N ungüento *m*, pomada *f*
salvo [sǽlvo] N salva *f*
same [sem] ADJ (identical) mismo; (similar)
igual; —-**day delivery** entrega el mismo día
f; —-**sex marriage** matrimonio
homosexual *m*; **it is all the** — **to me** me da
igual, me da lo mismo; **the** — **to you**
igualmente; **all the** — de todos modos
Samoa [səmóə] N Samoa *f*
Samoan [səmóən] ADJ & N samoano -na *mf*
sample [sǽmpəl] N muestra *f*; VT (try) probar;
(take samples) muestrear
sampling [sǽmplɪŋ] N muestreo *m*
sanatorium [sænətɔ́riəm] N sanatorio *m*
sanctify [sǽŋktəfaɪ] VT santificar
sanction [sǽŋkʃən] N sanción *f*; VT sancionar
sanctity [sǽŋktɪDi] N santidad *f*
sanctuary [sǽŋktʃueri] N (church auditorium,
place of refuge) santuario *m*; (game preserve)
reserva *f*
sand [sænd] N arena *f*; —**box** arenero *m*; —
dollar erizo de mar plano *m*; —**paper** papel
de lija *m*; **to** —**paper** lijar; —**stone** arenisca
f; —**storm** tormenta de arena *f*; —**trap**
trampa de arena *f*; VT lijar, pulir
sandal [sǽndl] N sandalia *f*
sandwich [sǽndwɪtʃ] N bocadillo *m*,
emparedado *m*; VT intercalar; **to be** —**ed**
between quedar apretado entre
sandy [sǽndi] ADJ (full of sand) arenoso,
arenisco; (yellowish red) rubio
sane [sen] ADJ cuerdo
sang [sæŋ] *see* sing
sanitary [sǽnɪteri] ADJ sanitario; — **napkin**
paño higiénico *m*
sanitation [sænɪtéʃən] N (sewers) saneamiento
m; (hygiene) salubridad *f*
sanity [sǽnɪDi] N cordura *f*
sank [sæŋk] *see* sink
San Marinese [sænmærəníz] ADJ & N

sanmarinense *mf*, sanmarinés -esa *mf*
San Marino [sænməríno] N San Marino *m*
Sanskrit [sǽnskrɪt] N sánscrito *f*
Santa Claus [sǽntəklɔz] N Papá Noel *m*, Santa
Claus *m*
São Tomean [saʊtoméən] ADJ & N santotomense
mf
São Tome and Principe [saʊtoméændprínsipe]
N Santo Tomé y Príncipe *m*
sap [sæp] N (juice) savia *f*; (fool) tonto -ta *mf*; VT
(exhaust) agotar
sapling [sǽplɪŋ] N (tree) árbol joven *m*; (person)
jovenzuelo -la *mf*
sapphire [sǽfaɪr] N zafiro *m*
sarcasm [sárkæzəm] N sarcasmo *m*,
socarronería *f*
sarcastic [sɑrkǽstɪk] ADJ sarcástico, socarrón
sarcoma [sɑrkómə] N sarcoma *m*
sarcophagus [sɑrkáfəgəs] N sarcófago *m*
sardine [sɑrdín] N sardina *f*
sardonic [sɑrdánɪk] ADJ sardónico
sash [sæʃ] N (around waist) faja *f*; (around
shoulder) banda *f*; (on window) marco *m*,
bastidor *m*
sassy [sǽsi] ADJ insolente
sat [sæt] *see* sit
satanic [sətǽnɪk] ADJ satánico
satchel [sǽtʃəl] N cartera *f*
satellite [sǽdlaɪt] N satélite *m*; — **dish** [antena]
parabólica *f*
satiate [séʃiet] VT saciar, hartar
satin [sǽtn̩] N raso *m*, satén *m*
satire [sǽtaɪr] N sátira *f*
satirical [sətírɪkəl] ADJ satírico
satirize [sǽdəraɪz] VT satirizar
satisfaction [sædɪsfǽkʃən] N satisfacción *f*
satisfactory [sædɪsfǽktəri] ADJ satisfactorio
satisfied [sǽdɪsfaɪd] ADJ satisfecho
satisfy [sǽdɪsfaɪ] VI/VT satisfacer
saturate [sǽtʃəret] VI/VT (impregnate)
saturar[se]; (soak) empapar[se]; —**d fat** grasa
saturada *f*
Saturday [sǽdɚDe] N sábado *m*
sauce [sɔs] N salsa *f*; —**pan** cacerola *f*; VT
aderezar con salsa
saucer [sɔ́sɚ] N platillo *m*
saucy [sɔ́si] ADJ (insolent) fresco, descarado,
insolente; (who talks back) respondón
Saudi Arabia [sɔ́Diərébiə] N Arabia Saudí *f*,
Arabia Saudita *f*
Saudi Arabian [sɔ́Diərébiən] ADJ & N saudí *mf*,
saudita *mf*
saunter [sɔ́ntɚ] VI pasearse, deambular
sausage [sɔ́sɪʤ] N (thick) chorizo *m*; (thin)
salchicha *f*; (cured) longaniza *f*; —-**making**
charcutería *f*
savage [sǽvɪʤ] ADJ (uncivilized) salvaje;
(furious) rabioso; (rugged) agreste; N salvaje
m; VT hacer trizas de

savagery [sǽvɪʤri] N salvajismo *m*, barbarie *f*
savannah [səvǽnə] N sabana *f*
save [sev] VT (a sinner, a person in danger) salvar;
(furniture) salvaguardar, proteger; (money,
time, energy) ahorrar, economizar; (data)
guardar; VI (lay up money, be economical)
ahorrar; (protect) salvaguardar; **to — from**
librar de; **— as** (on a computer) almacenar
como, guardar como; **to — one's eyes**
cuidarse la vista; N (in baseball) salvado *m*;
PREP salvo, menos
savings [sévɪŋz] N ahorros *m pl*; **— account**
cuenta de ahorros *f*; **— bank** caja de ahorros *f*
savior [sévjɚ] N salvador -ora *mf*
savor [sévɚ] N (taste) sabor *m*; (trace) dejo *m*; VT
saborear
savory [sévəri] ADJ (delicious) sabroso; (not
sweet) salado
savvy [sǽvi] N astucia *f*; ADJ astuto
saw [sɔ] N sierra *f*; **—horse** caballete *m*; VI/VT
aserrar[se]; **—dust** aserrín *m*, serrín *m*;
—mill aserradero *m*
saw [sɔ] *see* see
sawn [sɔn] *see* saw
saxophone [sǽksəfon] N saxofón *m*
say [se] VT (something interesting) decir; (a
prayer) rezar; VI (a clock) marcar; (a sign)
rezar, decir; **—!** ¡oye! **that is to —** es decir; **—
I bought it** supongamos que yo lo comprara;
it goes without —ing huelga decir[lo];
there's a lot to be said for es muy
recomendable; **when all is said and done**
al fin y al cabo; **you can — that again** tú lo
has dicho; N **the final —** la última palabra;
to have one's — dar su opinión; ADV **you
could earn, —, a million dollars** podrías
ganar, pongamos, un millón de dólares
saying [séɪŋ] N dicho *m*, refrán *m*
scab [skæb] N (of a wound) costra *f*; (on plants)
roña *f*; (strikebreaker) esquirol *m*, amarillo
-lla *mf*; VI (wound) formar una costra; (break
a strike) ser esquirol
scabby [skǽbi] ADJ (wound) costroso; (plant)
roñoso
scaffold [skǽfəld] N (in construction) andamio
m; (of a gallows) patíbulo *m*
scald [skɔld] VI/VT escaldar[se]; N escaldadura *f*
scale [skel] N (progression) escala *f*; (for
weighing) balanza *f*; (heavy-duty) báscula *f*;
(on fish, reptiles, human skin) escama *f*; **pair
of —s** balanza *f*; VT (climb) escalar; (remove
scales) escamar; VI/VT (adjust
proportionately) graduar, escalar; **to —
down** rebajar proporcionalmente
scallion [skǽljən] N cebollino *m*
scallop [skǽləp] N (mollusk) vieira *f*; (of beef)
escalope *m*; (of fabric) festón *m*; VT festonear
scalp [skælp] N cuero cabelludo *m*; VT (to skin)
arrancar la cabellera; (to resell) revender

scalpel [skǽlpəl] N bisturí *m*
scalper [skǽlpɚ] N revendedor -ora *mf*
scam [skæm] N timo *m*, estafa *f*
scamp [skæmp] N pícaro -ra *mf*, tunante -ta *mf*,
pillo -lla *mf*
scamper [skǽmpɚ] VI (run) escabullirse,
escaparse; (caper) cabriolar
scan [skæn] VT (horizon) escudriñar, escrutar;
(brain) hacer una tomografía; (page) echar un
vistazo a; (verse) escandir; (digitalize for
computer) escanear; N tomografía *f*
scandal [skǽndl̩] N escándalo *m*
scandalize [skǽndl̩aɪz] VT escandalizar
scandalous [skǽndl̩əs] ADJ escandaloso
scanner [skǽnɚ] N escáner *m*
scanning [skǽnɪŋ] N escaneado *m*
scant [skænt] ADJ escaso
scanty [skǽnti] ADJ (provisions) escaso; (skirt)
muy corto; (bikini) breve
scapegoat [sképgot] N chivo expiatorio *m*,
cabeza de turco *m*
scapula [skǽpjələ] N escápula *f*, omóplato *m*
scar [skɑr] N cicatriz *f*, lacra *f*; VT dejar una
cicatriz
scarce [skɛrs] ADJ escaso; **to be —** escasear
scarcely [skɛrsli] ADV (barely) apenas; **he's — a
genius** no es un genio ni mucho menos
scarcity [skɛrsɪɾi] N escasez *f*, pobreza *f*,
carestía *f*
scare [skɛr] VI/VT espantar[se], asustar[se]; **to —
away** ahuyentar; **to — up** reunir; N susto *m*,
sobresalto *m*; (of war, of a heart attack) amago
m; **—crow** espantapájaros *m sg*
scared [skɛrd] ADJ asustado; **I'm — of spiders**
tengo miedo de las arañas / las arañas me dan
miedo
scarf [skɑrf] N (woolen) bufanda *f*; (silk, cotton)
pañuelo *m*; VI **to — up** engullir
scarlet [skɑrlɪt] N escarlata *m*, grana *f*; **— fever**
escarlatina *f*
scary [skɛri] ADJ (causing fright) de miedo;
(easily frightened) asustadizo
scat [skæt] INTERJ ¡fuera!
scatter [skǽɾɚ] VI/VT (seeds) esparcir[se],
desparramar[se], desperdigar[se]; (crowd)
dispersar[se]; **—brained** atolondrado; N
—brain cabeza de chorlito *mf*
scattered [skǽɾɚd] ADJ disperso
scavenge [skǽvɪnʤ] VT recoger, rescatar; VI
hurgar
scenario [sɪnério] N guión *m*; **worst-case —** el
peor de los casos
scene [sin] N escena *f*; (sphere of activity)
ambiente *m*, ámbito *m*; **to make a —** montar
una escena; **behind the —s** entre bastidores
scenery [sínəri] N paisaje *m*; (on a stage)
decorado *m*
scenic [sínɪk] ADJ panorámico
scent [sɛnt] N (smell) olor *m*; (fragrance)

perfume *m*; (trace) pista *f*, rastro *m*; (sense of smell) olfato *m*; VI/VT (perceive through smell) olfatear; (intuit) presentir; (give fragrance to) perfumar

schedule [skédʒʊł] N (plan) calendario *m*; (timetable) horario *m*; (appendix) apéndice *m*; (list) lista *f*; **on** — al día, a la hora prevista; **ahead of** — adelantado; VT programar, fijar

scheme [skim] N (plan) plan *m*, proyecto *m*; (plot) ardid *m*, trama *f*; (of colors) combinación *f*; VI/VT maquinar, intrigar, tramar

schemer [skímɚ] N maquinador -ora *mf*, intrigante *mf*

scheming [skímɪŋ] ADJ intrigante; N maquinación *f*

schizophrenia [skɪtsəfréniə] N esquizofrenia *f*

schmuck [ʃmʌk] N *pej* pendejo -ja *mf*, *pej* gilipollas *mf sg*

scholar [skálɚ] N (student) alumno -na *mf*; (fellow) becario -ria *mf*; (erudite person) erudito -ta *mf*, estudioso -sa *mf*

scholarly [skálɚli] ADJ erudito

scholarship [skálɚʃɪp] N (erudition) erudición *f*; (award) beca *f*

school [skuł] N (primary) escuela *f*, colegio *m*; (secondary) secundaria *f*; *Sp* instituto *m*; (university) universidad *f*; (of law, etc.) facultad *f*; (of language, driving) academia *f*; (of thought) escuela *f*; (of fish) banco *m*, cardumen *m*; —**boy** escolar *m*; —**girl** escolar *f*; —**house** escuela *f*; —**master** maestro -tra *mf*; —**mate** compañero -ra de escuela *mf*; —**room** aula *f*, sala de clase *f*; —**teacher** maestro -tra *mf*; — **year** año lectivo *m*; VT instruir, entrenar

schooling [skúlɪŋ] N instrucción *f*

schooner [skúnɚ] N goleta *f*

sciatic nerve [saɪǽɒɪknɚv] N nervio ciático *m*

science [sáɪəns] N ciencia *f*; — **fiction** ciencia ficción *f*

scientific [saɪəntífɪk] ADJ científico; — **method** método científico *m*

scientist [sáɪəntɪst] N científico -ca *mf*

scintillate [síntlet] VI (diamonds) centellear, destellar; (stars) titilar

scissor [sízɚz] VT cortar con tijera; N —**s** tijera *f*, tijeras *f pl*; — **kick** tijera *f*, tijereta *f*

sclerosis [sklərósɪs] N esclerosis *f*

scoff [skɑf] N mofa *f*, burla *f*; VI mofarse; **to** — **at** mofarse de, burlarse de

scold [skołd] VI/VT reprender, regañar, reñir; N regañón -ona *mf*

scolding [skółdɪŋ] N regaño *m*, reprimenda *f*

scoliosis [skoliósɪs] N escoliosis *f*

scoop [skup] N (ladle) cucharón *m*; (spoon for ice cream) cuchara *f*; (shovel) pala *f*; (news item) primicia *f*; VT sacar con cuchara; (report first) adelantarse a; **to** — **in a good profit** sacar

buena ganancia; **to** — **out** (water) achicar; (a hole) cavar; **to** — **up** recoger

scoot [skut] VI (go fast) correr; (go away) largarse

scooter [skúDɚ] N (with motor) scooter *m*; (toy) monopatín *m*, patinete *m*

scope [skop] N (range) alcance *m*, ámbito *m*; (sphere) esfera *f*; VT observar

scorch [skɔrtʃ] VI/VT chamuscar[se], quemar[se]; N chamuscadura *f*; *Am* quemadura *f*

score [skɔr] N (partial result) tanteo *m*; (total result) resultado *m*; (on a test) calificación *f*; (scratch) arañazo *m*; (twenty) veintena *f*; (of music) partitura *f*; —**board** marcador *m*; **on that** — a ese respecto; **to keep** — llevar la cuenta; **to settle old** —**s** ajustar cuentas; **what is the** —? ¿cómo va el marcador? VT (grade) calificar; (orchestrate) orquestar; (scratch) arañar; VI/VT (make points) marcar, tantear; (hook up with someone) ligar; **to** — **a goal** marcar/meter un gol

scorn [skɔrn] N desdén *m*, menosprecio *m*; VI/VT desdeñar, menospreciar

scornful [skɔrnfəł] ADJ desdeñoso

scorpion [skɔrpiən] N escorpión *m*, alacrán *m*

Scotch [skɑtʃ] ADJ escocés; — **whisky** whisky escocés *m*

Scotland [skátlənd] N Escocia *f*

Scotsman [skátsmən] N escocés *m*

Scotswoman [skátswumən] N escocesa *f*

Scottish [skádɪʃ] ADJ escocés

scoundrel [skáʊndrəł] N bellaco *m*, infame *m*, truhán *m*

scour [skaʊr] VT (clean) fregar, restregar; (search an area) inspeccionar

scourge [skɚdʒ] N (affliction, means of affliction) azote *m*; VT azotar

scout [skaʊt] N (military) explorador -ora *mf*; (child explorer) explorador -ora *mf*, scout *mf*; (for talent) cazatalentos *mf sg*; **a good** — una buena persona; VI/VT explorar; VI **to** — **for** buscar

scowl [skaʊł] N ceño fruncido *m*; VI fruncir el ceño

scram [skræm] VI largarse

scramble [skrǽmbəł] VI (climb) subir a gatas; **to** — **for** pelearse por; **to** — **up** subir a gatas; VT (eggs) revolver; (numbers) mezclar; —**d eggs** huevos revueltos *m pl*; N (difficult climb) subida difícil *f*; (struggle for possession) arrebatiña *f*

scrap [skræp] N (fragment) fragmento *m*, pedacito *m*; (of truth) ápice *m*; (fight) riña *f*, reyerta *f*; —**book** álbum de recortes *m*; — **iron** chatarra *f*; — **paper** papel borrador *m*; —**s** sobras *f pl*, desperdicios *m pl*; VT (break apart) desguazar; (discard) desechar; VI (fight) pelearse, reñir

scrape [skrep] VI/VT (rub) raspar; (damage) arañar; **to** — **along** ir tirando, ir pasándola;

to — by arreglárselas; **to — together** reunir; **to bow and —** ser muy servil; N (act of scraping) raspado *m*; (injury) raspón *m*, raspadura*f*; (sound) chirrido *m*; (fight) pelea *f*; (difficult situation) aprieto *m*

scraper [skrépə-] N raspador *m*

scratch [skrætʃ] VI/VT (mark) arañar, rasguñar; (relieve itching) rascar[se]; (cancel from a race) retirar[se]; (cause itching) picar; VI (to dig, as a hen) escarbar; **to — out** (words) tachar; (eyes) sacar; N (injury) arañazo *m*, rasguño *m*; (sound) chirrido *m*; **to start from —** empezar de cero; **— test** examen dérmico de alergias *m*

scrawny [skrɔ́ni] ADJ esmirriado

scream [skrim] N grito *m*, alarido *m*; **he's a —** es un payaso; VI/VT gritar

screech [skritʃ] N (of brakes) chirrido *m*; (of voice) chillido *m*; **— owl** lechuza*f*; VI (of brakes) chirriar; (of voice) chillar

screen [skrin] N (movie, computer) pantalla*f*; (divider) biombo *m*; (on window) mosquitero *m*; (sifter) tamiz *m*; **— door** puerta con mosquitero*f*; **—ing test** prueba de detección *f*; **—pass** pase pantalla *m*; **—play** guión *m*; **— saver** protector de pantalla *m*, salvapantallas *m sg*; **—writer** guionista *mf*; VT (conceal) tapar; (sift) tamizar; (project) proyectar; (select) seleccionar

screw [skru] N (device) tornillo *m*; (one turn) vuelta*f*; (propeller) hélice*f*; (sexual intercourse) *fam* polvo *m*; **—driver** destornillador *m* (also cocktail); VT (turn) atornillar; (have intercourse) *Sp vulg* follar; *Am vulg* coger, culear; **to — on** enroscar; **to — up one's courage** cobrar ánimo; **to — around** (waste time) perder tiempo; (be promiscuous) ser promiscuo; **to — something up** *vulg* chingar algo, joder algo; **I —ed up** *vulg* la cagué; **to — with** *vulg* chingar

scribble [skríbəl] VI/VT garabatear, garrapatear; N garabato *m*

scrimp [skrImp] VI hacer economías

script [skrIpt] N (writing) escritura*f*; (screenplay) guión *m*

scripture [skrípt∫ə-] N escritura sagrada*f*

scroll [skroł] N (roll) rollo *m*; (adornment) voluta *f*; VI **to — down** bajar el cursor

scrotum [skróɒəm] N escroto *m*

scrub [skrʌb] VI/VT (rub) fregar, restregar; **to — up** lavarse las manos; VT (cancel) cancelar; N (cleaning) friega*f*, fregada*f*; (bushes) maleza *f*; (rough terrain) breña*f*; **— pine** pino achaparrado *m*; **— team** equipo suplente *m*; **—woman** fregona*f*

scruple [skrúpəl] N escrúpulo *m*

scrupulous [skrúpjələs] ADJ escrupuloso

scrutinize [skrútṇaIz] VI/VT escrutar, escudriñar

scrutiny [skrútṇi] N escrutinio *m*, examen minucioso *m*

scuba [skúbə] N escafandra*f*; VI **to —-dive** bucear

scuff [skʌf] VT (shoes) rayar; (floor) marcar; N (on shoes) raya*f*; (on floor) marca*f*

scuffle [skʌ́fəl] N refriega*f*, riña*f*; VI (fight) pelear, reñir; (shuffle) arrastrar los pies

sculptor [skʌ́lptə-] N escultor -ora *mf*

sculpture [skʌ́lpt∫ə-] N escultura*f*; VI/VT esculpir

scum [skʌm] N (in a glass) capa de suciedad*f*; (on a pond) verdín *m*; (people) *pej* escoria*f*; (vile person) *pej* canalla *mf*; **—bag** *pej* canalla *mf*; VI cubrirse de espuma; VT espumar

scurrilous [skɜ́ələs] ADJ (coarse) grosero

scurry [skɜ́i] VI correr; **to — away/off** escabullirse

scurvy [skɜ́vi] N escorbuto *m*

scuttle [skʌ́dł] VI (run) correr; **to — away/off** escabullirse; VT (sink a ship) hundir; (abandon a plane) abandonar

scythe [saIð] N guadaña*f*

sea [si] N mar *mf*; **— battle** batalla naval*f*; **—board** costa*f*, litoral *m*; **—coast** costa*f*, litoral *m*; **— cow** vaca marina*f*; **— current** corriente marina*f*; **—food** frutos del mar *m pl*; **— green** verdemar *m*; **—gull** gaviota*f*; **— horse** caballito de mar *m*; **— level** nivel del mar *m*; **— lion** léon marino *m*; **—man** marino *m*, marinero *m*; **—plane** hidroavión *m*; **—port** puerto de mar *m*; **— power** potencia naval*f*; **—shore** costa*f*; **—sickness** mareo *m*; **—side** costa*f*, litoral *m*; **— turtle** tortuga marina*f*; **— urchin** erizo de mar *m*; **—weed** alga [marina]*f*; **at —** (on the ocean) en el mar; (confused) perdido; **by —** por barco; **to put to —** hacerse a la mar; **on the high —s** en alta mar; ADJ marino; **—faring** marinero; **—sick** mareado; **to get —sick** marearse; **—worthy** marinero

seal [sił] N (stamp) sello *m*; (on a jar) precinto *m*; (animal) foca*f*; **to set one's — to** sellar; VT (put a seal on) sellar; (close with a seal) precintar; **—ing wax** lacre *m*; **to — one's fate** determinar el destino de uno; **to — off** acordonar; **to — in** cerrar herméticamente; **to — with wax** lacrar

seam [sim] N (sewing) costura*f*; (in rock) grieta*f*; (in ore deposits) veta*f*; VT coser

seamstress [símstrIs] N costurera*f*

seamy [sími] ADJ sórdido

sear [sir] VT chamuscar

search [sɜ˞tʃ] VI/VT (an area) rastrear, requisar; (a suitcase) registrar; (a person) cachear; **— me!** ¡a mí que me registren! ¡yo que sé! **to — for** buscar; N (for something) búsqueda*f*; (of baggage, ships) registro *m*; (of an area) rastreo *m*; — **and replace** buscar y reemplazar; — **engine** motor de búsqueda *m*, máquina de búsqueda *f*; — **function** función de búsqueda *f*; —**light** reflector *m*; — **warrant** orden de registro *m*; **in** — **of** en busca de

season [sízən] N (of the year) estación *f*; (period of time) temporada *f*, época *f*; (sports schedule) temporada *f*; **in** — en temporada/época; — **ticket** billete de abono *m*; **open** — temporada de caza/pesca *f*; **out of** — fuera de temporada/época; VT (to spice) sazonar, aderezar; VI (wood) secarse; **a** —**ed pilot** un piloto experimentado

seasonal [sízənəł] ADJ estacional

seasoning [sízənɪŋ] N condimento *m*, aliño *m*

seat [sit] N (furniture) asiento *m*; (of bicycle) sillín *m*; (in parliament) escaño *m*; (of government) sede *f*; (in the theater) localidad *f*; (buttocks) asentaderas *f pl*; (of clothes) fondillos *m pl*; **to take a** — sentarse, tomar asiento; — **belt** cinturón de seguridad *m*; VT (cause to sit) sentar; (accommodate with seats) tener capacidad para; (place) colocar; **to** — **oneself** sentarse

seborrhea [sɛbɔríə] N seborrea *f*

seclude [sɪklúd] VT aislar; **to** — **oneself from** recluirse de, aislarse de

secluded [sɪklúDɪd] ADJ apartado, aislado, recogido

seclusion [sɪklúʒən] N recogimiento *m*, aislamiento *m*

second [sékənd] ADJ segundo; — **base** segunda base *f*, intermedia *f*; — **baseman** segunda base *mf*, camarero -ra *mf*, intermediarista *mf*; — **child** segundón -ona *mf*; — **cousin** primo -ma segundo -da *mf*; — **fiddle** segundón -ona *mf*; — **floor** primer piso *m*; — **half** (sports) segundo tiempo *m*; —**hand** de segunda mano; — **lieutenant** subteniente *mf*; — **mortgage** segunda hipoteca *f*; — **nature** automático; —**-rate** mediocre, de segunda; **to get** —**s** repetir, servirse por segunda vez; — **serve** segundo servicio *m*; **on** — **thought** pensándolo bien; N (part of a minute) segundo *m*; (helper in a duel) padrino *m*; —**s** (inferior wares) artículos de segunda *m pl*; (additional helping) segunda ración *f*; **in a** — ahorita; **may I have** —**s?** ¿puedo repetir? VT (support) secundar, apoyar; (assist in duels) apadrinar; (support a motion) apoyar; **to** — - **guess** cuestionar

secondary [sékəndɛri] ADJ secundario; — **school** escuela secundaria *f*

secondly [sékəndli] ADV en segundo lugar

secrecy [síkrɪsi] N secreto *m*

secret [síkrɪt] ADJ & N secreto *m*

secretariat [sɛkrɪtǽriət] N secretaría *f*

secretary [sékrɪtɛri] N (assistant) secretario -ria *mf*; (government) ministro -tra *mf*; (furniture) escritorio *m*

secrete [sɪkrít] VT (discharge) secretar, segregar; (hide) ocultar

secretion [sɪkríʃən] N secreción *f*

secretive [síkrɪDɪv] ADJ hermético

sect [sɛkt] N secta *f*

section [sékʃən] N (component) sección *f*; (of a chapter) apartado *m*; (of a text) trozo *m*; (of a city) sector *m*; (incision) corte *m*; (of orange) gajo *m*; VT seccionar

sector [séktɚ] N sector *m*

sectorial [sɛktóriəł] ADJ sectorial

secular [sékjələ˞] ADJ secular; N (person) seglar *mf*, lego -ga *mf*

secure [sɪkjúr] ADJ (certain, safe) seguro; (firm) firme; VT (make certain, guarantee) asegurar, afianzar; (make firm) afirmar, cimentar; (obtain) obtener; (protect) proteger; (lock) cerrar con llave; (capture) capturar; (tie) amarrar

security [sɪkjúrɪDi] N (safety, freedom from worry) seguridad *f*; (guarantee) fianza *f*, garantía *f*; (guarantor) fiador -ora *mf*; — **deposit** depósito de garantía *m*; **securities** valores *m pl*

sedan [sɪdǽn] N sedán *m*

sedate [sɪdét] ADJ sosegado, tranquilo; VT sedar

sedation [sɪdéʃən] N sedación *f*

sedative [sédətɪv] ADJ & N calmante *m*, sedante *m*

sedentary [sédn̩tɛri] ADJ sedentario

sediment [séDəmənt] N sedimento *m*; (dregs) heces *f pl*

sedition [sɪdíʃən] N sedición *f*

seduce [sɪdús] VI/VT seducir [a]

seduction [sɪdʌ́kʃən] N seducción *f*

see [si] VI/VT (perceive, find out, meet, visit) ver; (understand) entender; (make sure) fijarse, asegurarse; (date) salir con; —**ing-eye dog** perro guía *m*; **let me** — a ver; **to** — **to** encargarse de, atender; **to** — **off** despedir; **to** — **through someone** calar a alguien; **to** — **about** ocuparse de; **to** — **out** acompañar a la puerta; N sede *f*

seed [sid] N (grains) semilla *f*; (semen) simiente *f*; (in tennis) cabeza de serie *f*; **to go to** — echarse a perder; — **bed** semillero *m*; VI/VT (sow) sembrar; VT (remove seeds) despepitar, quitar las semillas; (player) clasificar; VI producir semillas

seedy [síDi] ADJ sórdido

seek [sik] VT (search for) buscar; (ask for) pedir; **to** — **after** buscar; **to** — **to** tratar de, esforzarse por

seem [sim] VI parecer; **they** — **to be here** parece que están aquí; **it** —**s to me** me parece

seemingly [símɪŋli] ADV aparentemente

seen [sin] *see* see

seep [sip] VI/VT rezumar[se]

seer [sir] N vidente *mf*

seesaw [sísɔ] N balancín *m*, subibaja *m*; VI oscilar

seethe [sið] VI bullir, hervir; **he was seething** hervía de rabia

segment [ségmənt] N segmento *m*

segregate [ségrɪget] VI/VT segregar

seismic [sáɪzmɪk] ADJ sísmico

seize [siz] VT (grab) asir, agarrar; (take possession) apoderarse de; (take advantage of) aprovecharse de; (confiscate) embargar, incautarse de, secuestrar; **to — upon** asir; VI **to — [up]** (mechanism, motor) agarrotarse; **to — upon** valerse de

seizure [síʒɚ] N (of power) toma *f*; (of property) confiscación *f*; (of drugs, guns) incautación *f*, secuestro *m*; (epileptic) ataque *m*

seldom [séłdəm] ADV rara vez, raramente

select [sɪlékt] ADJ selecto; VI/VT elegir, seleccionar

selection [sɪlékʃən] N selección *f*, elección *f*

selective [sɪléktɪv] ADJ selectivo

self [sɛłf] N (ego) yo *m*; **—-assurance** desenvoltura *f*; **—-control** autocontrol *m*; **—-defense** defensa propia *f*; (juridical term) legítima defensa *f*; **—-denial** abnegación *f*; **—-determination** autodeterminación *f*; **—-discipline** autodisciplina *f*; **—-esteem** autoestima *f*; **—-government** autogobierno *m*; **—-help** autoayuda *f*; **—-image** autoimagen *f*; **—-improvement** mejora personal *f*; **—-interest** interés personal *m*; **—-made man** hombre que debe su éxito a sus propios esfuerzos *m*; **—-pity** autocompasión *f*; **—-reliance** independencia *f*, autosuficiencia *f*; **—-respect** amor propio *m*; **—-sacrifice** sacrificio *m*; **—-satisfaction** autosatisfacción *f*; **his better —** su lado bueno *m*; **his former —** lo que era antes; ADJ **—-assured** desenvuelto; **—-centered** egocéntrico; **—-composed** tranquilo; **—-confident** con confianza de sí mismo; **—-conscious** (shy) cohibido; (with complexes) acomplejado; **—-destructive** autodestructivo; **—-employed** que trabaja por cuenta propia; **—-evident** evidente; **—-explanatory** claro, fácil de entender; **—-propelled** autopropulsado; **—-righteous** que afecta superioridad moral; **—-satisfied** pagado de sí, satisfecho de sí; **—-service** autoservicio; **—-serving** interesado; **—-sufficient** autosuficiente

selfish [séłfɪʃ] ADJ egoísta

selfishness [séłfɪʃnɪs] N egoísmo *m*

selfless [séłflɪs] ADJ desinteresado, generoso

sell [sɛł] VI/VT vender[se]; **his books — well** se venden bien sus libros; **to be sold on** estar entusiasmado con; **to — off** liquidar; **to —**

out (dispose of) liquidar; (betray) traicionar, vender; (run out) agotarse; N **—-off** (liquidation) liquidación *f*; (decline) baja *f*; **—out** traición *f*

seller [sɛlɚ] N vendedor -ora *mf*

selling [sélɪŋ] N venta *f*

semantics [sɪmæntɪks] N semántica *f*

semblance [sémbləns] N apariencia *f*

semen [símɪn] N semen *m*

semester [səméstɚ] N semestre *m*

semicircle [sémɪsɚkəł] N semicírculo *m*

semicolon [sémɪkolən] N punto y coma *m*

semiconductor [semikəndÁktɚ] N semiconductor *m*

semifinal [sémifaɪnł] ADJ & N semifinal *f*

seminar [sémənar] N seminario *m*

seminary [sémənɛri] N seminario *m*

Semitic [səmíDɪk] ADJ semítico

senate [sénɪt] N senado *m*

senator [sénətɚ] N senador -ora *mf*

send [sɛnd] VT enviar, mandar; **that sent chills down my spine** me dio escalofríos; **to — away** hacer salir; **to — back** devolver; **to — for** mandar buscar a; **to — in** remitir; **to — out for** encargar; **to — word** mandar decir

sender [séndɚ] N remitente *m*

Senegal [sénɪgəł] N Senegal *m*

Senegalese [sɛnɪgəlíz] ADJ & N senegalés -esa *mf*

senile [sínaɪł] ADJ senil, chocho

senility [sɪnílɪDi] N senilidad *f*, chochera *f*, chochez *f*

senior [sínjɚ] ADJ (with more seniority) más antiguo; (in school) de cuarto año; (for the elderly) para ancianos; **John Smith —** John Smith padre; N (person of higher rank) superior *mf*; (fourth-year student) estudiante de cuarto año *mf*; (elderly person) persona de la tercera edad *f*; **to be somebody's —** ser mayor que alguien; **— citizen** persona de la tercera edad *f*; **— partner** socio -cia principal *mf*

seniority [sinjórɪDi] N antigüedad *f*

sensation [sɛnséʃən] N sensación *f*

sensational [sɛnséʃənł] ADJ sensacional

sense [sɛns] N (of humor, honor, direction) sentido *m*; (of pain, insecurity) sensación *f*; (meaning) significado *m*, sentido *m*; **— of hearing** sentido del oído *m*; **— of humor** sentido del humor *m*; **— of sight** sentido de la vista *m*; **— of smell** sentido del olfato *m*; **— of taste** sentido del gusto *m*; **— of touch** sentido del tacto *m*; **to make —** tener sentido; **to make — of something** entender algo; **in a —** en cierto sentido; **to take leave of one's —s** volverse loco; **to come to one's —s** (wake up) volver en sí; (be reasonable) recobrar el juicio; VT (perceive) percibir, sentir; (intuit) intuir

senseless [sénslɪs] ADJ (meaningless) sin

sentido; (unconscious) inconsciente
sensibility [sɛnsəbíllɪDi] N sensibilidad *f*
sensible [sɛnsəbəɬ] ADJ sensato, razonable,
   juicioso
sensitive [sɛ́nsɪDɪv] ADJ (to emotions) sensible;
   (to stimuli) sensitivo
sensitivity [sɛnsɪtívɪDi] N sensibilidad *f*
sensitize [sɛ́nsɪtaɪz] VT sensibilizar
sensor [sɛ́nsɔr] N sensor *m*
sensory [sɛ́nsəri] ADJ sensorial; — **overload**
   sobrecarga sensorial *f*
sensual [sɛ́nʃuəɬ] ADJ sensual
sensuality [sɛnʃuǽlɪDi] N sensualidad *f*
sensuous [sɛ́nʃuəs] ADJ sensual
sent [sɛnt] *see* send
sentence [sɛ́ntəns] N (to prison) sentencia *f*,
   condena *f*; (phrase) oración *f*; VT condenar,
   sentenciar
sentiment [sɛ́ntəmənt] N sentimiento *m*
sentimental [sɛntəméntl̩] ADJ sentimental;
   (excessively) sensiblero
sentimentality [sɛntəmɛntǽlɪDi] N
   sentimentalismo *m*; (excessive) sensiblería *f*
sentinel [sɛ́ntn̩əɬ] N centinela *m*
sentry [sɛ́ntri] N centinela *m*; — **box** garita *f*
separate[1] [sɛ́prɪt] ADJ (apart) separado
separate[2] [sɛ́pəret] VI/VT separar[se]
separation [sɛpəréʃən] N separación *f*
Sephardi [səfárdi] N sefardí *mf*, sefardita *mf*
September [sɛptɛ́mbə-] N septiembre *m*,
   setiembre *m*
sequel [síkwəɬ] N continuación *f*
sequence [síkwəns] N secuencia *f*; (of events)
   serie *f*; **in** — en orden; VT secuenciar
Serb [sɝb] N (person) serbio -bia *mf*
Serbian [sɝ́biən] ADJ serbio; N (language) serbio
   m; (person) serbio -bia *mf*
serenade [sɛrənéd] N serenata *f*, ronda *f*; VI/VT
   dar [una] serenata [a], rondar [a]
serene [sərín] ADJ sereno
serenity [sərɛ́nɪDi] N serenidad *f*
sergeant [sárdʒənt] N sargento *m*
serial [síriəɬ] N (novel) novela por entregas *f*; ADJ
   (published in installments) por entregas;
   (murder) en serie; — **bus** bus en serie *m*; —
   connector conector en serie *m*; — **killer**
   asesino -na en serie *mf*; — **mouse** ratón en
   serie *m*; — **number** número de serie *m*; —
   port puerto serie/serial *m*; — **printer**
   impresora en serie *f*
series [síriz] N serie *f*
serious [síriəs] ADJ serio; (illness) grave
seriously [síriəsli] ADV (consider) en serio;
   (injure) gravemente; —, **what do you
   want?** hablando en serio, ¿qué es lo que
   quieres?
seriousness [síriəsnɪs] N seriedad *f*; (of an
   illness) gravedad *f*
sermon [sɝ́mən] N sermón *m*

serpent [sɝ́pənt] N sierpe *f*, serpiente *f*
serrated [sɛ́rɛDɪd] ADJ serrado
serum [sírəm] N suero *m*
servant [sɝ́vənt] N sirviente -ta *mf*, criado -da *mf*
serve [sɝv] VI/VT (in a restaurant, in a store)
   servir, atender; (in tennis) sacar; **to** — **a
   term in prison** cumplir una condena; **to** —
   a warrant entregar una orden judicial; **to** —
   as servir de; **to** — **notice** advertir; **to** —
   one's purpose resultarle útil a alguien; **it**
   —s me right me lo merezco; N (in tennis)
   saque *m*; — **and volley** saque y volea *m*
server [sɝ́və-] N (one who serves) servidor -ora
   mf; (in a restaurant) camarero -ra *mf*; (for pie)
   utensilio para servir *m*; (computer) servidor
   m; (tennis player) sacador -ora *mf*
service [sɝ́vɪs] N servicio *m*; (in tennis) saque *m*,
   servicio *m*; (of a warrant) entrega *f*; — **break**
   rotura de servicio *f*; — **entrance** entrada de
   servicio *f*; —**man** (soldier) militar *m*; (for
   repairs) reparador *m*; — **station** gasolinera *f*,
   estación de servicio *f*; **at your** — a su
   servicio; VT (a car) revisar; (an industry)
   atender, servir; (a debt) pagar; **in**-—
   training capacitación para empleados; **out
   of** — (broken) averiado, fuera de servicio
serviceable [sɝ́vɪsəbəɬ] ADJ (practical) práctico;
   (durable) duradero
servile [sɝ́vaɪɬ] ADJ servil
servitude [sɝ́vɪtud] N servidumbre *f*
sesame [sɛ́səmi] N sésamo *m*, ajonjolí *m*
session [sɛ́ʃən] N (meeting) sesión *f*; (semester)
   semestre *m*; (of Congress) período de
   sesiones *m*
set [sɛt] VT (place) colocar; (fix) fijar, establecer;
   (sic) azuzar; (print) componer; VI (cement)
   fraguar; (jelly) cuajar; (sun) ponerse; (glue)
   endurecerse; **to** — **a bone** reducir un hueso
   dislocado; **to** — **a diamond** engastar un
   diamante; **to** — **an example** dar ejemplo; **to**
   — **a poem to music** ponerle música a un
   poema; **to** — **a precedent** establecer un
   precedente; **to** — **a trap** tender una trampa;
   to — **a watch** poner el reloj en hora; **to** —
   about disponerse a; **to** — **aside** (move an
   object) apartar; (money) ahorrar; (a claim)
   rechazar; (a verdict) anular; **to** — **back**
   (hinder, make earlier) atrasar; (cost) costar; (a
   clock) retrasar; **to** — **forth** exponer; **to** —
   forth on a journey ponerse en camino; **to**
   — **free** librar; **to** — **off** (make explode) hacer
   estallar; (start on a journey) ponerse en
   camino; (intensify) resaltar; **to** — **one's
   heart on** tener la esperanza puesta en; **to** —
   one's mind on resolverse a; **to** — **out for**
   partir para; **to** — **out to** proponerse; **to** —
   right rectificar; **to** — **the table** poner la
   mesa; **to** — **up** (assemble) armar; (set a trap
   for) tender; (establish) establecer; (a

computer program) instalar; **to — upon
someone** acometer a alguien; ADJ (fixed)
fijo; (ready) listo; (hard) duro; N (ensemble)
juego *m*; (group) conjunto *m*; (TV) aparato *m*;
(scenery) escenario *m*; (of tennis) set *m*,
manga *f*; **—back** revés *m*; **— of teeth**
dentadura *f*; **— point** punto de set/manga *m*;
—up (arrangement) arreglo *m*; (assembly)
montaje *m*; (installation) instalación *f*; (trap)
tongo *m*, timo *m*; **—up program** programa
de instalación *m*

setter [sɛ́Dɚ] N sétter *m*

setting [sɛ́DIŋ] N (act of putting down)
colocación *f*; (jewel) engaste *m*; (in theater)
escenario *m*; (of sun, moon) puesta *f*; (of dial)
posición *f*; **— sun** sol poniente *m*

settle [sɛ́dl̩] VT (a territory) colonizar, poblar;
(affairs) arreglar; (argument) zanjar; (lawsuit)
arreglar; (an estate) liquidar; (a bill) saldar,
solventar; (one's nerves) calmar; VI (end a
dispute) llegar a un arreglo; (take up
residence) establecerse; (alight) posarse; (sink
to bottom) depositarse; **to — down** (get
married) casarse; (mend one's ways) sentar
cabeza; (take up residence) instalarse;
(become calm) calmarse; **to — on a date**
fijar/señalar una fecha; **to — for** conformarse
con; **to — up** pagar

settlement [sɛ́dl̩mənt] N (community) colonia *f*,
población *f*; (act of establishing)
asentamiento *m*; (agreement) acuerdo *m*; (of a
lawsuit) arreglo *m*; (of a bill) pago *m*, finiquito
m; (final disposition) liquidación *f*

settler [sɛ́tlɚ] N colono -na *mf*, poblador -ora *mf*

settling [sɛ́dl̩Iŋ] N asentamiento *m*

seven [sɛ́vən] NUM siete; **— hundred**
setecientos

seventeen [sɛvəntín] NUM diecisiete

seventh [sɛ́vənθ] ADJ séptimo

seventy [sɛ́vənti] NUM setenta

sever [sɛ́vɚ] VT (an arm) cortar; (relations)
romper

several [sɛ́vəəl] ADJ varios

severance pay [sɛ́vəənspe] N indemnización
por despido *f*

severe [səvír] ADJ (criticism, standards) severo;
(winter, test) duro; (storm, heat) intenso;
(illness) grave

severity [səvérIDi] N (of criticism, standards)
severidad *f*; (of water, test) dureza *f*; (of
storm, heat) intensidad *f*; (of illness)
gravedad *f*

Sevillian [səvíłjən] ADJ & N sevillano -na; **—
dances** sevillanas *f pl*

sew [so] VI/VT coser

sewage [súIdʒ] N aguas negras *f pl*; **— system**
alcantarillado *m*

sewer [súɚ] N alcantarilla *f*, cloaca *f*, colector *m*

sewing [sóIŋ] N costura *f*; **— machine** máquina

de coser *f*

sewn [son] *see* sew

sex [sɛks] N sexo *m*; **— appeal** atractivo sexual
m; **— symbol** símbolo sexual *m*; **to have —**
tener relaciones [sexuales]; VT sexar

sexism [sɛ́ksIzəm] N sexismo *m*

sexist [sɛ́ksIst] ADJ & N sexista *mf*

sexton [sɛ́kstən] N sacristán *m*

sexual [sɛ́kʃuəł] ADJ sexual; **— assault** violación
f; **— discrimination** discriminación sexual
f; **— harassment** acoso sexual *m*; **—
intercourse/relations** relaciones sexuales
f pl; **—ly transmitted disease** enfermedad
de transmisión sexual *f*

sexuality [sɛkʃuǽlIDi] N sexualidad *f*

sexy [sɛ́ksi] ADJ sexy, morboso

Seychelles [seʃɛ́ł] N Seychelles *f pl*

shabby [ʃǽbi] ADJ (worn) gastado; (slovenly)
andrajoso; (tawdry) sórdido; (mean)
mezquino; **not too —** no está mal

shack [ʃæk] N casucha *f*, choza *f*

shackle [ʃǽkəł] N grillete *m*; **—s** cadenas *f pl*,
grillos *m pl*; VT (put in chains) engrillar;
(impede) estorbar

shad [ʃæd] N sábalo *m*

shade [ʃed] N (shadow) sombra *f*; (nuance) matiz
m; (for windows) persiana *f*; (phantom)
espectro *m*; (of a lamp) pantalla *f*; **a — longer**
un poco más largo; **in the —** a la sombra; **—s**
(sunglasses) *Am* lentes negros/oscuros *m pl*;
Sp gafas de sol *f pl*; VT (protect from sun)
sombrear, dar sombra

shadow [ʃǽdo] N (dark image, shade) sombra *f*;
(phantom) espectro *m*; **in the — of** a la
sombra de; **without a — of doubt** sin
sombra de duda; VT (darken) sombrear;
(make gloomy) ensombrecer; **to — someone**
seguirle la pista a alguien

shady [ʃéDi] ADJ sombreado, umbrío; **—
character** sospechoso -sa *mf*; **— dealings**
negocios turbios *m pl*

shaft [ʃæft] N (of a mine) pozo *m*; (of a feather)
cañón *m*; (of an elevator) hueco *m*; (of an
arrow) asta *f*

shaggy [ʃǽgi] ADJ peludo, lanudo

shake [ʃek] VI (tremble) temblar; VI/VT (move
back and forth) sacudir[se]; (in order to mix)
agitar[se]; (elude) deshacerse de; **to — hands**
darse la mano; **to — one's head** menear la
cabeza; **to — with cold** tiritar; **to — with
fear** temblar de miedo; **to — off** (a cold,
disappointment, etc.) deshacerse de;
(depression) librarse de; **to — up** (a liquid)
agitar; (a person) trastornar; N (violent)
sacudida *f*; (of milk) batido *m*; **hand—**
apretón de manos *m*; **the —s** escalofríos *m pl*;
— -up reorganización *f*

shaken [ʃékən] *see* shake

shaky [ʃéki] ADJ (hand) tembloroso; (start)

vacilante
shall [ʃæɫ] V AUX **I — come** vendré; **— I help
you?** ¿te ayudo? **thou shalt not steal** no
robarás
shallow [ʃǽlo] ADJ (plate) llano; (water) poco
profundo; (breathing) superficial;
(explanation) superficial, somero
shallowness [ʃǽlonɪs] N (of plate) lo llano; (of
water) poca profundidad f; (of person)
superficialidad f
sham [ʃæm] N (hoax) farsa f; (impostor)
impostor -ora mf; **— battle** simulacro de
batalla m
shambles [ʃǽmbəɫz] N desorden m, caos m
shame [ʃem] N (embarrassment) vergüenza f;
(dishonor) deshonra f; (pity) lástima f; **— on
you!** ¡qué vergüenza! **to bring — upon**
deshonrar; VT avergonzar
shameful [ʃémfəɫ] ADJ vergonzoso
shameless [ʃémlɪs] ADJ desvergonzado,
descarado
shamelessness [ʃémlɪsnɪs] N desvergüenza f
shampoo [ʃæmpú] N (product) champú m; (act
of washing) lavado del cabello m; VI/VT lavar
con champú
shamrock [ʃǽmrak] N trébol m
shank [ʃæŋk] N (part of leg) canilla f, espinilla f;
(cut of meat) pierna f, pata f
shanty [ʃǽnti] N casucha f; Sp chabola f; **—town**
suburbio m
shape [ʃep] N (form) forma f; (condition)
condición f; (silhouette) bulto m; **to be in
bad —** andar mal; **to get in —** ponerse en
forma; **to take —** configurarse; VT plasmar,
dar forma a; **to — up** reformarse
shapeless [ʃéplɪs] ADJ informe
share [ʃer] N (portion) parte f, porción f; (stock)
acción f; **—cropper** aparcero m; **—holder**
accionista mf; VI/VT compartir; **to — in**
participar en
shark [ʃark] N (fish) tiburón m; (swindler)
estafador -ora mf
sharp [ʃarp] ADJ (blade) afilado, filoso; (needle)
puntiagudo; (curve) cerrado; (contrast)
marcado, nítido; (smell) acre; (wind)
cortante; (pain) punzante; (remark) mordaz,
agudo; (mind) perspicaz; (musical note)
sostenido; (dresser) elegante; (cheese)
picante; (ear) fino; **— eye** vista aguzada f;
—shooter tirador -ora de primera mf; **—-
tongued** mordaz; **—-witted** agudo; N (in
music) sostenido m
sharpen [ʃárpən] VI/VT (knife) afilar[se]; VT
(pencil) sacar punta a; (skill) afinar
sharply [ʃárpli] ADV (contrast) marcadamente;
(respond) bruscamente, con aspereza; (turn)
bruscamente
sharpness [ʃárpnɪs] N (of a blade) lo afilado; (of
a needle) lo puntiagudo; (of a curve) lo

cerrado; (of a contrast) nitidez f; (of a smell)
acritud f; (of pain) intensidad f; (of a remark)
mordacidad f; (of a mind) perspicacia f,
agudeza f; (of cheese) lo picante
shatter [ʃǽDɚ] VI/VT (glass) astillar[se], hacer[se]
añicos; (nerves) destrozar[se]; (health)
quebrantar[se]; (hopes) frustrar
shave [ʃev] VI/VT (remove hair) afeitar[se],
rasurar[se]; VT (cut thin slices) cepillar;
(graze) rozar; **to — off** rapar; N afeitado m,
rasurado m; **he had a close —** se salvó por
poco
shaven [ʃévən] see shave
shaver [ʃévɚ] N afeitadora f
shavings [ʃévɪŋz] N virutas f pl
shawl [ʃɔɫ] N mantón m, chal m
she [ʃi] PRON ella; **— who** la que, quien; N **—-
bear** osa f
sheaf [ʃif] N (of corn) gavilla f; (of arrows) haz m;
(of paper) fajo m
shear [ʃir] VT esquilar, trasquilar; N **—s** (for
sheep) tijeras para esquilar f pl; (for plants)
tijeras para podar f pl; (for metal) cizallas f pl;
(for hair) tijeras de peluquero f pl
shearing [ʃírɪŋ] N esquila f, esquileo m
sheath [ʃiθ] N (of sword, peas) vaina f; (of knife,
umbrella) funda f
sheathe [ʃið] VT (a sword) envainar; (a knife)
enfundar
shed [ʃɛd] N cobertizo m, tinglado m, Am galpón
m; VT (tears) derramar; (light) arrojar;
(leaves) perder; (skin, hair) mudar, perder; VI
(be waterproof) ser impermeable; (lose hair)
pelechar; (lose leaves) deshojarse; (lose skin)
mudar la piel
sheen [ʃin] N brillo m
sheep [ʃip] N oveja f; **—dog** perro pastor m,
ovejero m; **—skin** (hide) piel de oveja f;
(leather) badana f; (parchment) pergamino m;
(diploma) diploma m
sheepish [ʃípɪʃ] ADJ vergonzoso, tímido
sheer [ʃir] ADJ (absolute) puro, total; (fine) fino;
(vertical) vertical, acantilado
sheet [ʃit] N (bedding) sábana f; (of ice) capa f; (of
paper) hoja f; (of glass) lámina f; (of rain)
cortina f; **— metal** chapa de metal f; **—
music** música en hojas de partitura f
shelf [ʃɛɫf] N estante m, repisa f, anaquel m; (of
rock) saliente f
shell [ʃɛɫ] N (turtles, snail) caparazón f; (of
mollusk) concha f; (of egg, nut) cáscara f; (of
peas) vaina f; (of a ship) casco m; (of a
building) armazón m; (of artillery) proyectil
m; (of a rifle) cartucho m; **—fish** mariscos m
pl; VT (nuts, eggs) pelar; (peas) desgranar;
(military target) bombardear
shelter [ʃéɫtɚ] N (refuge) refugio m, resguardo
m, abrigo m; **to take —** refugiarse,
guarecerse; VI/VT (take or give refuge)

refugiar[se], resguardar[se], abrigar[se]
shelve [ʃɛɫv] VT (place on a shelf) colocar en un estante; (defer) archivar
shepherd [ʃɛpə‑d] N pastor *m*; (dog) perro pastor *m*
sherbet [ʃɝbɪt] N sorbete *m*
sheriff [ʃɛrɪf] N alguacil *m*
sherry [ʃɛri] N jerez *m*
shield [ʃiɫd] N escudo *m*; VI/VT (protect) escudar[se]; VT (conceal) ocultar
shift [ʃɪft] VI/VT (gears) cambiar; **to — for oneself** arreglárselas solo; **to — the blame** echar la culpa a otro; N (of gears, of wind) cambio *m*; (dress) vestido suelto *m*; (of workers) turno *m*; **— key** tecla de [cambio a] mayúsculas *f*
shiftless [ʃɪftlɪs] ADJ holgazán
shimmer [ʃímə‑] VI titilar; N titileo *m*
shin [ʃɪn] N espinilla *f*, canilla *f*; VI **to — up** trepar
shine [ʃaɪn] VI brillar, relucir; VT (shoes) limpiar, lustrar; (furniture) lustrar; N brillo *m*, resplandor *m*; (of shoes) lustre *m*
shingle [ʃíŋgəɫ] N (on roof) teja *f*; (sign) chapa *f*; **—s** (skin disorder) culebrilla *f*, zona *f*; **to hang out one's —** abrir un consultorio; VT cubrir con tejas
shiny [ʃáɪni] ADJ (bright) brillante; (worn) brilloso
ship [ʃɪp] N (on water) buque *m*, navío *m*; (in air) avión *m*; **—builder** constructor -ora naval *mf*; **—mate** camarada de a bordo *mf*; **—wreck** naufragio *m*; **—yard** astillero *m*; ADJ **—shape** ordenado; VT transportar; **to — off** sacarse de encima; VI **to —wreck** naufragar
shipment [ʃípmənt] N cargamento *m*, remesa *f*
shipper [ʃípə‑] N (sender) expedidor -ora *mf*; (carrier) transportista *mf*
shipping [ʃípɪŋ] N envío *m*; **— charges** gastos de envío *m pl*; **— and handling** gastos de envío *m pl*
shirk [ʃɝk] VT evadir, esquivar, rehuir
shirt [ʃɝt] N camisa *f*; **in —sleeves** en mangas de camisa; **—tail** faldón *m*
shit [ʃɪt] N (excrement) *vulg* mierda *f*; (stuff) porquerías *f pl*; **the —s** *fam* cagalera; **that's a crock of —** y una polla [como una olla]; **he doesn't know —** *vulg* no sabe un carajo; **he's on my —list** estoy enojado con él; VI/VT (defecate) *vulg* cagar; (lie to) *vulg* joder; **to — bricks** *vulg* cagarse de miedo; INTERJ *vulg* carajo; *Sp vulg* joder
shitty [ʃídi] ADJ *vulg* de mierda
shiver [ʃívə‑] VI (from cold) tiritar; (from cold, fear, etc.) temblar; N temblor *m*; **—s** escalofríos *m pl*
shoal [ʃoɫ] N (sandbank) bajío *m*, banco de arena *m*; (school of fish) banco *m*, bandada *f*

shock [ʃɑk] N (impact, disturbance) choque *m*; (of electricity) sacudida *f*; (of wheat) hacina *f*; (physical convulsion) shock *m*, choque *m*; **— absorber** amortiguador *m*; **— of hair** guedeja *f*; **— therapy** terapia de electroshock *f*, terapia electroconvulsiva *f*; **— troops** tropas de choque *f pl*; **— wave** onda expansiva *f*; VT (bewilder) chocar, horrorizar; (discharge electricity) dar una descarga eléctrica; (make bundles of grain) hacinar, hacer gavillas de
shocking [ʃákɪŋ] ADJ chocante, escandaloso
shod [ʃɑd] *see* shoe
shoddy [ʃádi] ADJ chapucero
shoe [ʃu] N zapato *m*; (for brakes) zapata *f*; (for horses) herradura *f*; **—horn** calzador *m*; **—lace** cordón *m*; **—maker** zapatero -ra *mf*; **— polish** betún *m*; **— repairman** zapatero -ra remendón -ona *mf*; **— store** zapatería *f*; **—string** cordón *m*; **to live on a —string** vivir con poco dinero; **to tie one's —s** atarse los zapatos; VT (a person) calzar; (a horse) herrar
shone [ʃon] *see* shine
shoo-in [ʃúɪn] N favorito -ta *mf*
shook [ʃʊk] *see* shake
shoot [ʃut] VT (wound with a bullet) pegar un tiro; (discharge a firearm) disparar; (film a movie) rodar; (hit a soccer ball) chutar; VI (discharge bullet, arrow) disparar, tirar; (be discharged) dispararse; (hunt with a gun) cazar; (germinate) brotar; (throw) lanzar; (take a photo) fotografiar; (film) filmar; (try to score, in soccer) chutar; (try to score, in basketball) tirar; **to — at** disparar a, tirar a; **to — at goal** patear al arco; **to — by** pasar rápidamente; **to — down** (plane) derribar; (argument) refutar; **to — forth** brotar; **to — up** (grow) crecer rápidamente; (damage by shooting) tirotear; (inject drugs) chutar; N (new growth) yema *f*, retoño *m*, vástago *m*; (filming) rodaje *m*
shooter [ʃúDə‑] N (of guns) tirador -ora *mf*; (of balls, soccer) goleador -ora *mf*
shooting [ʃúDɪŋ] N (discharge of a gun) tiro *m*, disparo *m*; (exchange of shots) tiroteo *m*; (filming) filmación *f*; **— guard** escolta *mf*; **— match** concurso de tiro *m*; **— pain** punzada *f*; **— star** estrella fugaz *f*
shop [ʃɑp] N (store) tienda *f*; (artisan's place of business, carpentry course) taller *m*; (business) planta *f*; **—keeper** tendero -ra *mf*; **—lifter** ladrón -ona de tiendas *mf*; **—lifting** hurto en las tiendas *m*; **— window** escaparate *m*, vitrina *f*; **to talk —** hablar de negocios; VI ir de compras; **to — for** ir a comprar; **to —lift** hurtar [en las tiendas]
shopper [ʃápə‑] N cliente -ta *mf*, comprador -ora *mf*

shopping [ʃápɪŋ] N **to go** — ir de compras; — **center** centro comercial *m*
shore [ʃɔr] N costa *f*, ribera *f*; (of a lake) orilla *f*; VT **to** — **up** apuntalar
shorn [ʃɔrn] *see* shear
short [ʃɔrt] ADJ (not long in duration) corto, breve; (not long in length) corto; (not tall) bajo; (scanty) escaso; (curt) brusco; — **circuit** cortocircuito *m*; —**comings** limitaciones *f pl*; —**cut** atajo *m*, cortada *f*; —**fall** déficit *m*, insuficiencia *f*; —**hand** taquigrafía *f*; —-**handed** escaso de personal; —-**legged** pernicorto; —**sighted** miope, corto de vista; — **stop** torpedero -ra *mf*, campocorto *mf*; — **story** cuento *m*; —**wave** onda corta *f*; **in the** — **run/haul/term** a corto plazo; **for** — para abreviar; **in** — en resumen, en suma; **in** — **order** rápidamente; **to be** — **on** estar escaso de, estar alcanzado de; **to be** — **on something** faltarle a uno algo; **to cut** — interrumpir; **I'm running** — **on sugar** se me está acabando el azúcar; ADV **to stop** — parar de repente, parar en seco; **to come up** — quedarse corto; N (circuit) cortocircuito *m*; —**s** short *m*, pantalón corto *m*; VI/VT (a circuit) cortocircuitar[se]; (change) dar de menos; **to** —**change** dar de menos; **to** — **out** fundir
shortage [ʃɔrDɪʤ] N escasez *f*, penuria *f*
shorten [ʃɔrtn̩] VI/VT acortar[se]; VT recortar
shortening [ʃɔrtn̩ɪŋ] N (lard) manteca *f*; (abbreviation) acortamiento *m*
shortly [ʃɔrtli] ADJ (soon) en breve, pronto; (curtly) bruscamente, secamente
shortness [ʃɔrtnɪs] N (of length, height) cortedad *f*; (of time) brevedad *f*; (of breath) falta *f*; (of a reply) brusquedad *f*
shot [ʃat] N (discharge) tiro *m*, disparo *m*; (photograph) foto *f*; (pellet) perdigón *m*, plomo *m*; (ball in shot-putting) bala *f*; (injection) inyección *f*; (swallow) trago *m*; (throw) tirada *f*; (in soccer) tiro *m*, disparo *m*; —**gun** escopeta *f*; — **put** lanzamiento de bala *m*; **not by a long** — ni con mucho; **he is a good** — tiene buena puntería; **to take a** — disparar; **to take a** — **at** intentar
shot [ʃat] *see* shoot
should [ʃud] V AUX **I** — **think so** ya lo creo; **you** — **arrive before nine** deberías llegar antes de las nueve; **you** — **eat less** tendrías que comer menos; **you** — **have seen her** tendrías que haberla visto; **were he to come, I** — **be pleased** si viniera, me alegraría
shoulder [ʃóldə] N (of a person, coat) hombro *m*; (cut of meat) paletilla *f*; (of a road) arcén *m*; — **blade** (person) homóplato *m*; (animal) paletilla *f*; — **pad** hombrera *f*; **to turn a cold** — **to** hacerle el vacío a; **the responsibility**

is on your —**s** tú tienes la responsabilidad; VT (a load) cargar al hombro; (a task, an expense) cargar con, asumir; (a door) empujar con el hombro
shout [ʃaut] VI/VT gritar; N grito *m*
shove [ʃʌv] VI/VT empujar; **to** — **aside** echar a un lado; **to** — **off** (go away) largarse; (push off) desatracar; N empujón *m*, empellón *m*
shovel [ʃʌvəl] N pala *f*; VT echar con la pala
show [ʃo] VT (exhibit) mostrar, manifestar; (prove) demostrar; (indicate) indicar, marcar; (a film, a TV program) dar; VI (be visible) verse, asomar; (make an appearance) aparecerse; — **him in** hazle entrar; **to** —**case** presentar; **to** — **mercy** tener piedad; **to** — **off** hacer alarde, aparentar; **to** — **up** aparecer; **to** — **someone up** poner a alguien en evidencia; **to** — **the way** señalar el camino; N (exhibition) exposición *f*; (display) demostración *f*; (ostentation) ostentación *f*, alarde *m*; (performance) espectáculo *m*; (showing) función *f*; (on TV) programa *m*; (movie theater) cine *m*; — **business** farándula *f*; —**case** vitrina *f*; —**down** confrontación *f*; —-**off** fanfarrón -ona *mf*; **to go to the** — ir al cine; **for** — para impresionar
shower [ʃáuə] N (rain) aguacero *m*, chubasco *m*; (bath) ducha *f*; (for brides) fiesta para novias *f*; (of sparks, blows) lluvia *f*; VI (bathe) ducharse; (rain) llover; VT (with gifts) inundar; (with praise) colmar
shown [ʃon] *see* show
showy [ʃói] ADJ ostentoso; (attractive) vistoso
shrank [ʃræŋk] *see* shrink
shred [ʃrɛd] N (of paper) tira *f*; (of evidence) pizca *f*; **to be in** —**s** estar hecho jirones; **to tear to** —**s** hacer trizas; VI/VT (documents) triturar; (vegetables) rallar
shrew [ʃru] N (animal) musaraña *f*; (woman) arpía *f*
shrewd [ʃrud] ADJ astuto, sagaz
shriek [ʃrik] VI/VT chillar; N chillido *m*
shrill [ʃrɪl] ADJ chillón
shrimp [ʃrɪmp] N (animal) camarón *m*; (small person) renacuajo *m*; VI pescar camarones
shrine [ʃraɪn] N (chapel) capilla *f*; (altar) altar *m*
shrink [ʃrɪŋk] VI/VT (in size) encoger; VI (in value) reducirse; **to** — **from** retroceder; N (psychiatrist) *fam* loquero -ra *mf*; —**wrap** envoltura de plástico transparente *f*
shrinkage [ʃríŋkɪʤ] N (of clothes) encogimiento *m*; (of value) reducción *f*
shrivel [ʃrívəl] VI/VT secar[se], marchitar[se]
shroud [ʃraud] N mortaja *f*; VT (to wrap for burial) amortajar; (to hide) cubrir
shrub [ʃrʌb] N arbusto *m*
shrug [ʃrʌg] VI encogerse de hombros; VT encogerse de; **to** — **off** minimizar, ignorar; N

encogimiento de hombros *m*

shrunk [ʃrʌŋk] *see* shrink

shrunken [ʃrʌ́ŋkən] *see* shrink

shudder [ʃʌ́Dɚ] VI (from cold) tiritar; (from fear) temblar, estremecerse; N temblor *m*, estremecimiento *m*

shuffle [ʃʌ́fəł] VI/VT (cards) barajar; VT (mix) mezclar; VI (walk) arrastrar los pies; (dance) bailar arrastrando los pies; **to — along** ir arrastrando los pies; N (of cards) barajadura *f*; (of feet) arrastrapiés *m sg*

shun [ʃʌn] VT rehuir, evitar

shut [ʃʌt] VI/VT cerrar[se]; **to — down** cerrar; **to — off** cortar; **to — out** impedir la entrada de; **to — up** (close) cerrar bien; (lock up) encerrar; (be quiet) callarse; N **—down** cese de actividades *m*; **—eye** sueño *m*; **—in** enfermo -ma confinado -da a la casa *mf*

shutter [ʃʌ́Dɚ] N (of a window) postigo *m*, contraventana *f*; (of a camera) obturador *m*

shuttle [ʃʌ́dl] N (in loom) lanzadera *f*; (spaceship) transbordador espacial *m*; (airplane) puente aéreo *m*; (bus, train) servicio regular *m*; VI ir y venir; VT llevar y traer

shy [ʃaɪ] ADJ tímido, retraído; (wary) esquivo; (lacking) escaso; VI asustarse, respingar; **to — away** (start) asustarse, respingar; (avoid) esquivar

shyness [ʃáɪnɪs] N timidez *f*, retraimiento *m*

shyster [ʃáɪstɚ] N *fam* picapleitos *m sg*

sibling [síblɪŋ] N hermano *m*; hermana *f*; **— rivalry** rivalidad entre hermanos *f*

sic [sɪk] VT azuzar

sick [sɪk] ADJ (ill) enfermo; (deranged) enfermizo, morboso; (at heart) angustiado; **— and tired** harto; **to be — of** estar harto de; **to be — to one's stomach** tener náuseas; **to make —** (disgust) dar asco; (anger) dar rabia, enfermar; **— leave** licencia por enfermedad *f*

sicken [síkən] VI/VT (with illness) enfermar[se], poner[se] enfermo; (with disgust) dar asco; (with anger) dar rabia, enfermar

sickening [síkənɪŋ] ADJ repugnante

sickle [síkəł] N hoz *f*; **— cell anemia** anemia falciforme *f*

sickly [síkli] ADJ enfermizo, enclenque

sickness [síknɪs] N enfermedad *f*

side [saɪd] N lado *m*; (of a coin, piece of paper) cara *f*; (of a person) costado *m*; (of a hill) ladera *f*; (of beef) media res *f*; (of a boat) banda *f*; (team) equipo *m*; (garnish) acompañamiento *m*; **—arm** arma de mano *f*; **—bar** ladillo *m*; **—board** aparador *m*; **—burns** patillas *f pl*; **—glance** mirada de soslayo/reojo *f*; **—light** (illumination) luz lateral *f*; (detail) detalle incidental *m*; **—line** (in sports) banda *f*, línea de banda *f*; (in business) negocio suplementario *m*; **to sit on**

the —lines no intervenir; **—walk** acera *f*; *Carib* andén *m*; *Am* vereda *f*; *Mex* banqueta *f*; **—wall** flanco *m*; **—ways** (walk) de costado; (glance) de soslayo; **— by —** uno al lado del otro; **by his —** a su lado; **by the — of** al lado de; **on all —s** por todos lados; ADJ (on the side) lateral; (secondary) secundario; VI **to —step** evitar, esquivar; **to —track** (a train) desviar; (attention) distraer; **to — with** ponerse del lado de

siding [sáɪDɪŋ] N revestimiento *m*

SIDS [sudden infant death syndrome] [sídz] N síndrome de muerte súbita infantil *m*

siege [sidʒ] N sitio *m*, asedio *m*, cerco *m*; **to lay — to** sitiar

Sierra Leone [siérəlión] N Sierra Leona *f*

sieve [sɪv] N tamiz *m*, cedazo *m*

sift [sɪft] VT cerner, tamizar; **to — through** revisar

sigh [saɪ] VI suspirar; N suspiro *m*

sight [saɪt] N (sense) vista *f*; (attraction) punto de interés *m*; (ridiculous thing or person) adefesio *m*, mamarracho *m*; (on a gun) mira *f*; **—seeing** turismo *m*; **in —** a la vista; **on —** en el acto; **he is out of —** ya no se ve; **at first —** a primera vista; **to catch — of** divisar; **to lose — of** perder de vista; **you're a — for sore eyes** dichosos los ojos que te ven; VT (a ship) avistar, divisar; (a gun) apuntar

sign [saɪn] N (gesture) seña *f*, señal *f*; (indication) muestra *f*, señal *f*, indicio *m*; (placard) letrero *m*; (omen) agüero *m*, presagio *m*; (astrological, mathematical) signo *m*; (on road) cartel *m*, letrero *m*; **— language** lenguaje de signos *m*; VI/VT (write name) firmar; (signal) hacer señas [de]; VT (hire) contratar; (use sign language) hablar por señas; **to — off on** aprobar; **to — over property** ceder una propiedad; **to — up** (in a club) anotarse; (in the army) alistarse

signal [sígnl] N señal *f*; VI/VT señalar, hacer señas [a]; ADJ notable

signature [sígnətʃɚ] N firma *f*

signer [sáɪnɚ] N firmante *mf*, signatario -ria *mf*

significance [sɪgnífɪkəns] N significación *f*

significant [sɪgnífɪkənt] ADJ significativo; **my — other** mi media naranja *f*

significantly [sɪgnífɪkəntli] ADV (considerably) apreciablemente, considerablemente; **he looked at me —** me dio una mirada significativa/expresiva

signify [sígnəfaɪ] VT significar

silence [sáɪləns] N silencio *m*; VT (child, fears) acallar; (criticism) silenciar, enmudecer

silencer [sáɪlənsɚ] N silenciador *m*

silent [sáɪlənt] ADJ (machine) silencioso; (person) callado, silencioso; **— agreement** acuerdo tácito *m*; **— film** película muda *f*

silhouette [sɪluét] N silueta *f*; VT **to be —d**

against perfilarse contra

silicon [síllkən] N silicio *m*; — **chip** chip de silicio *m*

silk [sɪłk] N seda *f*; — **industry** industria sedera *f*; —**worm** gusano de seda *m*

silken [síłkən] ADJ (of silk) de seda; (like silk) sedoso

silky [síłki] ADJ sedoso

sill [sɪł] N alféizar *m*, antepecho *m*

silly [síli] ADJ necio, bobo, lelo

silo [sáilo] N silo *m*

silt [sɪłt] N cieno *m*, limo *m*

silver [síłvə-] N (metal, color) plata *f*; (tableware) cubiertos de plata *m pl*; ADJ (of silver) de plata; (silver-colored) plateado; — **anniversary** las bodas de plata *f pl*; —**-plated** bañado en plata; —**-plating** plateado *m*; —**smith** platero -ra *mf*; —**ware** cubiertos de plata *m pl*; VT platear; (a mirror) azogar

similar [símələ-] ADJ semejante, similar

similarity [sɪmələ́rɪDi] N semejanza *f*, similitud *f*

similarly [símɪlə-li] ADV de manera similar; —, **a mile is longer than a kilometer** del mismo modo, una milla es más larga que un kilómetro; **they were — surprised** quedaron igualmente sorprendidos

simile [síməli] N símil *m*

simmer [símə-] VI/VT hervir a fuego lento; **to — down** calmarse

simple [símpəł] ADJ (uncomplicated) simple, sencillo; (naive) simple; —**minded** simple, simplón

simpleton [símpəłtən] N simplón -ona *mf*, mentecato -ta *mf*

simplicity [sɪmplísɪDi] N (lack of complication) sencillez *f*, simplicidad *f*; (naiveté) simpleza *f*

simplify [símpləfaɪ] VI/VT simplificar

simplistic [sɪmplístɪk] ADJ simplista

simply [símpli] ADV (in a simple manner) con sencillez; (merely) simplemente; **it is — ridiculous** francamente, es ridículo

simulate [símjəlet] VI/VT simular

simulation [sɪmjəlé∫ən] N simulación *f*

simultaneous [saɪməłténiəs] ADJ simultáneo

sin [sɪn] N pecado *m*; VI pecar

since [sɪns] CONJ (continuously) desde que; (inasmuch as) puesto que, ya que; PREP (continuously) desde; (from a past time) a partir de; **we have been here — five** estamos aquí desde las cinco; ADV desde entonces; **ever —** desde entonces; **he died long —** murió hace mucho tiempo; **she has — agreed** después de eso consintió

sincere [sɪnsír] ADJ sincero

sincerity [sɪnsérɪDi] N sinceridad *f*

sine [saɪn] N seno

sinew [sínju] N tendón *m*

sinewy [sínjui] ADJ (full of tendons) nervudo;

(robust) membrudo; (chewy) estropajoso

sinful [sínfəł] ADJ (act) pecaminoso; (person) pecador

sing [sɪŋ] VI/VT cantar; N —**song** sonsonete *m*

Singapore [síŋəpɔr] N Singapur *m*

Singaporean [sɪŋəpórian] ADJ & N singapurense *mf*

singe [sɪnʤ] VT chamuscar, socarrar; N chamusquina *f*, socarrina *f*

singer [síŋə-] N cantante *mf*; intérprete *mf*

single [síŋgəł] ADJ (only one) solo, único; (for one person) individual; (unmarried) soltero; — **bed** cama de una plaza *f*; —**-entry bookkeeping** teneduría por partida simple *f*; —**-family home** vivienda unifamiliar *f*; — **file** fila india *f*; —**-handed** solo, sin ayuda; —**-minded** resuelto; —**-spacing** sencillo *m*; **every — one** cada uno; **not a — word** ni una sola palabra; N (bill) billete de uno *m*; (unmarried person) soltero -ra *mf*; (record) disco sencillo *m*; (in baseball) sencillo *m*; —**s** (in tennis) individuales *m pl*; VT **to — out** elegir

singular [síŋgjələ-] ADJ & N singular *m*

sinister [sínɪstə-] ADJ siniestro

sink [sɪŋk] VI/VT (ship) hundir[se]; VT (money) invertir; (a well) cavar; (a pipeline) enterrar; **it finally sank in** finalmente nos dimos cuenta de eso; **to — one's teeth into** clavar los dientes en; **to — to one's knees** caer de rodillas; **sunk in thought** absorto; **my heart sank** se me fue el alma al piso; **the sun was —ing** se iba poniendo el sol; N (in the kitchen) fregadero *m*; (in bathroom) lavabo *m*; (pond for sewage) pozo negro *m*; —**hole** socavón *m*, sumidero *m*

sinner [sínə-] N pecador -ora *mf*

sinuous [sínjuəs] ADJ sinuoso

sinus [sáɪnəs] N seno *m*

sinusitis [saɪnəsáɪDɪs] N sinusitis *f*

sip [sɪp] VI/VT sorber; N sorbo *m*

siphon [sáɪfən] N sifón *m*; VI/VT (liquid) sacar con sifón; (money) desviar

sir [sɝ] N señor *m*

siren [sáɪrən] N sirena *f*

sirloin [sɝ́lɔɪn] N solomillo *m*

sissy [sísi] ADJ & N afeminado *m*; *offensive* marica *m*, maricón *m*

sister [sístə-] N hermana *f*; —**-in-law** cuñada *f*; — **Mary** Sor María *f*

sit [sɪt] VI sentar[se]; (pose) posar; (be seated) estar sentado; (be located) estar situado; **to — down** sentarse; **to — in on a class** ir de oyente a una clase; **to — on** posponer; **to — out a dance** saltearse una pieza; **to — still** estarse quieto; **to — tight** mantenerse firme en su puesto; **to — up** incorporarse; **to — up all night** quedarse en vela; N —**-in** sentada *f*; —**-up** abdominal *m*

sitcom [sítkɑm] N comedia de situación *f*
site [saɪt] N (for construction) terreno *m*, solar *m*; (on the Internet) sitio *m*; — **license** licencia de sitio *f*; **on-** — **training** capacitación en el lugar de trabajo
sitter [síDɚ] N niñera *f*, *Sp* canguro *mf*
sitting [síDɪŋ] N sesión *f*; **in one** — de una sentada, de un tirón; ADJ — **duck** blanco fácil *m*; — **room** cuarto de estar *m*
situated [sítʃueDɪd] ADJ situado, ubicado
situation [sɪtʃuéʃən] N situación *f*
Sitz bath [síts bæθ] N baño de asiento *m*
six [sɪks] NUM seis; — **hundred** seiscientos; N —**-pack** paquete de seis *m*; —**-shooter** revólver de seis tiros *m*
sixteen [sɪkstín] NUM dieciséis
sixth [sɪksθ] ADV & N sexto *m*
sixty [síksti] NUM sesenta
size [saɪz] N tamaño *m*; (of clothing) talla *f*; VT clasificar según el tamaño; **to** — **up** juzgar
sizable, sizeable [sáɪzəbəl] ADJ de tamaño considerable
sizzle [sízəl] VI chisporrotear; N chisporroteo *m*
skate [sket] N patín *m*; —**board** monopatín *m*; VI/VT patinar
skein [sken] N madeja *f*
skeletal [skélɪdl] ADJ esquelético
skeleton [skélɪtən] N esqueleto *m*, osamenta *f*; (of a building) armazón *m*; — **key** llave maestra *f*
skeptic, sceptic [sképtɪk] N escéptico -ca *mf*
skeptical [sképtɪkəl] ADJ escéptico
skepticism [sképtɪsɪzəm] N escepticismo *m*
sketch [sketʃ] N (drawing) boceto *m*, croquis *m*; (outline) esbozo *m*, bosquejo *m*; (skit) sketch *m*; VI/VT (draw) dibujar; (outline) bosquejar
skew [skju] VT (cloth) sesgar; (data) tergiversar
skewer [skjúɚ] N brocheta *f*
ski [ski] N esquí *m*; — **jump** (sport) salto con esquís *m*; (course) pista de saltos *f*; — **lift** telesquí *m*; VI/VT esquiar [en]
skid [skɪd] N patinazo *m*; VI patinar
skiing [skíɪŋ] N esquí *m*
skill [skɪl] N destreza *f*, habilidad *f*, maña *f*
skilled [skɪld] ADJ diestro, habilidoso; — **worker** obrero -ra calificado -da *mf*
skillet [skílɪt] N sartén *f*
skillful, skilful [skílfəl] ADJ diestro, habilidoso
skim [skɪm] VT (milk) desnatar; (a broth) espumar; (pass near surface) rozar; VI/VT (read) leer por encima, repasar; **to** — **over** rozar; N — **milk** *Sp* leche desnatada *f*; *Am* leche descremada *f*
skimp [skɪmp] VI escatimar; **to** — **on** escatimar
skimpy [skímpi] ADJ (funds) escaso; (dress) corto; (bikini) pequeño
skin [skɪn] N piel *f* (also of animal, sausage, potato); (of the face) cutis *m*, tez *f*; (for carrying wine) pellejo *m*; (of boiled milk) nata

f; (of grapes) hollejo *m*; —**-deep** superficial; —**-diving** natación submarina *f*; — **flick** película pornográfica *f*; —**flint** roña *mf*; —**head** cabeza rapada *mf*; **to save one's** — salvar el pellejo; **to be saved by the** — **of one's teeth** salvarse por un pelo; VT (animal) despellejar, desollar; (fruit) pelar; (a person) quitarle a uno el dinero
skinny [skíni] ADJ flaco; **to** —**-dip** nadar desnudo
skip [skɪp] VI (jump) brincar, ir dando saltos; (omit) saltarse; (bounce) rebotar; VT (a page) saltar[se]; (class) faltar a; (a stone) hacer rebotar; **to** — **out** escaparse; N salto *m*, brinco *m*
skipper [skípɚ] N (captain) patrón -ona *mf*, capitán -ana *mf*; (jumper) saltador -ora *mf*
skirmish [skɚ́mɪʃ] N escaramuza *f*; VI escaramuzar
skirt [skɚt] N falda *f*; VT bordear; **to** — **an issue** evitar un tema
skit [skɪt] N sketch *m*
skull [skʌl] N cráneo *m*, calavera *f*; — **and crossbones** calavera *f*
skunk [skʌŋk] N mofeta *f*; *Am* zorrillo *m*
sky [skaɪ] N cielo *m*; — **blue** azul celeste *m*; —**diving** paracaidismo extremo *m*; —**-high** muy alto; —**lark** alondra *f*; —**light** claraboya *f*; —**line** horizonte *m*; —**scraper** rascacielos *m sg*; VI **to** —**rocket** subir vertiginosamente
slab [slæb] N (of wood) trozo *m*; (of stone) losa *f*, laja *f*; (of meat) tajada *f*
slack [slæk] ADJ (not taut) flojo; (careless) descuidado; (sluggish) lento; — **season** temporada baja *f*; **to take up the** — llenar el vacío; —**s** pantalones *m pl*; VI holgazanear; **to** — **off** holgazanear
slag [slæg] N escoria *f*
slain [slen] *see* slay
slalom [slálɔm] N slalom *m*
slam [slæm] VI/VT cerrar[se] de un golpe; VI (hit) chocar; VT (throw down) hacer golpear; (criticize) criticar; **to** — **on the brakes** dar un frenazo; **to** — **the door** dar un portazo; N (blow) golpazo *m*; (criticism) crítica *f*; (of a door) portazo *m*; —**-dunk** (easy decision) éxito seguro *m*
slander [slǽndɚ] N calumnia *f*, difamación *f*; VT calumniar, difamar
slanderous [slǽndɚəs] ADJ calumnioso, difamatorio
slang [slæŋ] N (jargon) jerga *f*; (argot) argot *m*
slant [slænt] N (orientation, bias) sesgo *m*; (of a roof) inclinación *f*; VI/VT (bias) sesgar; (slope) inclinar[se], ladear[se]
slap [slæp] N (to the body) palmada *f*; (to the face) bofetada *f*, torta *f*, cacheteada *f*; (with a glove) guantada *f*; —**-happy** aturdido; —**stick** de

golpe y porrazo; **a — in the face** un desaire;
a — on the wrist un tirón de orejas; **a — on
the back** una palmadita en la espalda; VT
abofetear; **to — down** reprimir
slash [slæʃ] VI/VT (cut) acuchillar; *Am* tajear; VT
(whip) azotar; (reduce) reducir, rebajar; N
(sweeping stroke, wound) cuchillada *f*, tajo *m*;
(typographical sign) barra *f*
slat [slæt] N tablilla *f*
slate [slet] N (rock, roofing) pizarra *f*; (color)
color pizarra *m*; (list of candidates) lista de
candidatos *f*; VT empizarrar; **this building
is —d for destruction** se ha programado la
demolición de este edificio
slaughter [slɔ́Dɚ] N matanza *f*; **—house**
matadero *m*; VT (animals) matar; (people,
opponents) masacrar
slave [slev] N esclavo -va *mf*; **—driver** capataz de
esclavos *m*; **— labor** (workers) mano de obra
esclava *f*; (work) trabajo de esclavos *m*; VI
trabajar como esclavo -va
slavery [slévəri] N esclavitud *f*
Slavic [slávɪk] ADJ eslavo
sleazy [slízi] ADJ (squalid) sórdido;
(contemptible) despreciable
sled [slɛd] N trineo *m*
sledgehammer [slédʒhæmɚ] N almádena *f*
sleek [slik] ADJ (hair) lustroso; (sports car)
elegante
sleep [slip] VI/VT dormir; **it —s three** tiene
espacio para que duerman tres personas; **to —
around** ser promiscuo; **to — in** dormir hasta
tarde; **to — it off** dormir la mona; **to —
something off** dormir para que desaparezca
algo; **to — over** dormir en casa ajena; **to —
together** acostarse juntos; **to — with**
acostarse con; **to — on it** consultarlo con la
almohada; N sueño *m*; **— apnea** apnea
obstructiva del sueño *f*; **— disorder**
trastorno del sueño *m*; **— mode** modo de
dormir *m*; **—walker** sonámbulo -la *mf*; **to go
to —** dormirse; **to put to —** (put to bed)
dormir a; (euthanize) sacrificar
sleeper [slípɚ] N (one who sleeps) persona que
duerme *f*; (beam) durmiente *m*; (on a train)
coche cama *m*; (unexpected success) éxito
inesperado *m*; (sofa bed) sofá-cama *m*
sleepily [slípili] ADV con somnolencia
sleepiness [slípinɪs] N sueño *m*, somnolencia *f*
sleeping [slípɪŋ] N sueño *m*; ADJ dormido; **—
bag** saco de dormir *m*; **— pill** píldora para
dormir *f*, somnífero *m*; **— sickness**
enfermedad del sueño *f*
sleepless [slíplɪs] ADJ (person) desvelado;
(night) en blanco
sleepy [slípi] ADJ somnoliento, adormilado; **to
be —** tener sueño
sleet [slit] N cellisca *f*; VI caer cellisca
sleeve [sliv] N manga *f*; **to have something up**

one's — tener algo en la manga
sleigh [sle] N trineo *m*; **—bell** cascabel *m*; VI
pasear en trineo
sleight of hand [sláɪD əvhǽnd] N
prestidigitación *f*
slender [sléndɚ] ADJ delgado, esbelto
slept [slɛpt] *see* sleep
sleuth [sluθ] N sabueso -sa *mf*
slew [slu] *see* slay
slice [slaɪs] N (of bread, cheese) rebanada *f*; (of
fruit) tajada *f*, raja *f*; (of meat) lonja *f*; (in
tennis) cortado *m*, golpe cortado *m*; VT cortar,
rebanar, tajar
slick [slɪk] ADJ (unctuous) untuoso; (sly) astuto;
(slippery) resbaladizo
slicker [slíkɚ] N impermeable *m*
slid [slɪd] *see* slide
slide [slaɪd] VI/VT deslizar[se]; **to — in** cerrar[se]
deslizando; **to — out** abrirse deslizando; **to
let something —** dejar pasar algo; N
deslizamiento *m*; (playground equipment)
tobogán *m*; (of a trombone) vara corredora *f*;
(photographic) diapositiva *f*; (for
microscopes) portaobjeto *m*
slight [slaɪt] N desaire *m*; VT (snub) desairar;
(neglect) descuidar; ADJ (slim) delgado;
(delicate) delicado, tenue; (small in degree)
leve, ligero
slightly [sláɪtli] ADV algo, un poco
slim [slɪm] ADJ delgado, esbelto; **a — chance**
una posibilidad remota
slime [slaɪm] N (in rivers) limo *m*, fango *m*; (of
snails) baba *f*; (despicable person) asqueroso
-sa *mf*
slimy [sláɪmi] ADJ (muddy) fangoso; (slobbery)
baboso, gomoso; (despicable) asqueroso
sling [slɪŋ] N (weapon) honda *f*; (for arm)
cabestrillo *m*; **—shot** (toy) tirachinas *m sg*,
tirador *m*; (weapon) honda *f*; VT lanzar; **to —
a rifle over one's shoulder** ponerse el rifle
en bandolera
slink [slɪŋk] VI (move furtively) andar
furtivamente; (move provocatively) caminar
provocativamente; **to — away** escurrirse
slip [slɪp] VI (slide) deslizarse; (slide accidentally)
resbalar[se]; (fail to engage) patinar;
(deteriorate) empeorar; VT (make slip) hacer
resbalar; (put) meter; **to — away** escaparse,
escabullirse; **to — by** correr; **to — in**
meter[se]; **to — one's dress on** ponerse el
vestido; **to — out** (leave) salir inadvertido;
(say inadvertently) escapársele a uno algo; **to
— up** meter la pata; **to let an opportunity
— by** dejar pasar una oportunidad; **it —ped
my mind** se me olvidó; **it —ped off** se zafó;
N (act of slipping) resbalón *m*, traspié *m*;
(mistake) equivocación *f*; (pillow cover) funda
f; (underskirt) viso *m*; (piece of paper)
papeleta *f*, tira de papel *f*; (space for boats)

embarcadero *m*; — **of the tongue** lapsus [linguae] *m*; —**knot** nudo corredizo *m*; **Freudian** — acto fallido *m*

slipper [slípɚ] N zapatilla *f*, pantufla *f*

slippery [slípəri] ADJ resbaloso, resbaladizo; (evasive) evasivo, escurridizo

slipshod [slípʃad] ADJ chapucero

slit [slɪt] VT cortar a lo largo; **to — someone's throat** degollar a alguien; **to — into strips** cortar en tiras; N raja *f*, hendidura *f*

slither [slíðɚ] VI serpentear, culebrear; N serpenteo *m*, culebreo *m*

sliver [slívɚ] N astilla *f*; VI/VT astillar[se]

slob [slab] N (unkempt) dejado -da *mf*; (uncouth) bruto -ta *mf*

slobber [slábɚ] N baba *f*; VI/VT babosear, babear[se]

slogan [slógən] N eslogan *m*, lema *m*

slop [slap] VT (splash) salpicar; (feed) dar de comer; N (pigswill) bazofia *f*; (mud) fango *m*

slope [slop] VI/VT inclinar[se]; N vertiente *f*, declive *m*, cuesta *f*, cortado *m*; (in math) pendiente *f*

sloppiness [slápinɪs] N chapucería *f*

sloppy [slápi] ADJ (muddy) fangoso; (splashed) salpicado; (slovenly) cochino; (poorly done) chapucero

slot [slat] N (for coins, letters) ranura *f*; (in a computer) bahía *f*, ranura *f*; (place in a series) casilla *f*; (job) puesto *m*; — **machine** tragamonedas *mf sg*, tragaperras *mf sg*; VT hacer una ranura

sloth [slɔθ] N (vice) pereza *f*; (animal) perezoso *m*

slouch [slaʊtʃ] N (posture) encorvamiento *m*; (inept person) torpe *mf*; (lazy person) holgazán -ana *mf*; VI/VT (crouch) andar agachado, encorvar[se]; (shuffle) andar caído de hombros

Slovakia [slovákiə] N Eslovaquia *f*

Slovakian [slovákiən] ADJ & N eslovaco -ca *mf*

Slovene [slóvin] ADJ & N esloveno -na *mf*

Slovenia [slovíniə] N Eslovenia *f*

slovenliness [slávənlinɪs] N (of a person) desaseo *m*, desaliño *m*; (of work) descuido *m*

slovenly [slávənli] ADJ (unclean) desaseado; (unkempt) desaliñado; (poorly done) descuidado

slow [slo] ADJ (not fast) lento, tardo; (running behind) atrasado; (sluggish) lerdo, torpe, pesado; **in — motion** en cámara lenta; ADV lentamente, despacio; VI/VT **to — down/up** andar más despacio, frenar; N **—down** (in business) disminución de actividades *f*; (in labor disputes) huelga de celo *f*

slowly [slóli] ADV despacio, lento, lentamente; — **but surely** lenta pero seguramente

slowness [slónɪs] N (of speed) lentitud *f*; (of intelligence) torpeza *f*

slug [slʌg] N (bullet) bala *f*; (coin) moneda falsa *f*;

(animal) babosa *f*; (swallow) trago *m*; (blow with fist) puñetazo *m*; VT aporrear; **to — it out** agarrarse a puñetazos

sluggard [slágɚd] N holgazán -ana *mf*

sluggish [slágɪʃ] ADJ (slow) lento; (torpid) aletargado, torpe

sluggishness [slágɪʃnɪs] N torpeza *f*

sluice [slus] N (channel with a gate) esclusa *f*; (channel) canal *m*; — **gate** compuerta *f*

slum [slʌm] N barrio bajo *m*; —**s** tugurios *m pl*; —**lord** propietario de tugurio *m*; VI visitar los barrios bajos; **to — it** divertirse en lugares de poca categoría

slumber [slámbɚ] VI dormir; N sueño *m*; — **party** fiesta de niñas que se quedan a dormir *f*

slump [slʌmp] VI (a person) desplomarse; (prices, markets) bajar repentinamente; N (in prices) baja repentina *f*; (in the economy) ralentización *f*; (in sports) mala racha *f*

slung [slʌŋ] *see* sling

slunk [slʌŋk] *see* slink

slur [slɚ] VT (pronounce indistinctly) pronunciar mal; (connect notes) ligar; N (connection of notes) ligado *m*; (insult) insulto *m*

slush [slʌʃ] N (melted snow) nieve a medio derretir *f*; (sludge) nieve fangosa *f*; (mud) fango *m*; (refuse) desperdicios *m pl*; — **fund** (illicit fund) cuenta para fines ilícitos *f*; (petty cash) caja chica *f*

slut [slʌt] N (slovenly woman) *pej* puerca *f*; (loose woman) *offensive* mujerzuela *f*, puta *f*

sly [slaɪ] ADJ astuto, taimado; **on the —** a escondidas

smack [smæk] N (taste) dejo *m*; Sp deje *m*; (kiss) beso ruidoso *m*; (loud eating) chasquido *m*; (slap) palmada *f*, sopapo *m*; (heroin) *fam* caballo *m*; VT (kiss) dar un beso ruidoso; (eat loudly) chascar, chasquear; (slap) dar una palmada; **to — of** tener un dejo de

small [smɔɫ] ADJ (not large) pequeño, chico; (of build) menudo; (narrow) estrecho; (lowercase) minúsculo; (petty) mezquino; — **caps** versalillas *f pl*, versalitas *f pl*; — **change** cambio suelto *m*; — **fry** gente menuda *f*; — **intestine** intestino delgado *m*; —**pox** viruela *f*; — **talk** cháchara *f*; **to feel** — avergonzarse; N (size) pequeño *m*; — **of the back** baja espalda *f*

smallness [smɔ́ɫnɪs] N pequeñez *f*

smart [smart] ADJ (intelligent) listo, inteligente; (astute) astuto; (stylish) elegante; — **aleck/ alec** sabihondo -da *mf*; —**ass** *fam* sabihondo -da *mf*; — **bomb** bomba inteligente *f*; — **card** tarjeta de circuito integrado *f*, tarjeta inteligente *f*; — **money** inversión inteligente *f*; — **remark** insolencia *f*; N (pain) escozor *m*; VI picar; **I'm —ing from his rude remarks** todavía me duelen sus groserías

smash [smæʃ] VT (destroy) estrellar, destrozar; (a rebellion) aplastar; **to — into** estrellarse contra; N (sound) estrépito *m*; (blow) choque violento *m*; (tennis shot) remate *m*; **a — hit** un exitazo

smear [smir] VT (daub) untar; (spot, vilify) manchar; (blur) correrse; (defeat) reventar; **to — with paint** pintorrear, pintarrajear; N (stain) mancha *f*; (culture) frotis *m*; — **campaign** campaña de difamación *f*

smell [smɛl] VI/VT oler; **to — of** oler a; **that —s** huele mal, apesta; **to — up** apestar; N (odor) olor *m*; (sense) olfato *m*; — **of** olor a

smelly [sméli] ADJ hediondo, apestoso

smile [smaɪl] VI sonreír[se]; N sonrisa *f*

smiling [smáɪlɪŋ] ADJ risueño, sonriente

smirk [smɚk] N sonrisa suficiente *f*; VI sonreír con suficiencia

smith [smɪθ] N herrero -ra *mf*

smitten [smítn̩] *see* smite

smog [smɑg] N smog *m*

smoke [smok] N humo *m*; (cigarette) cigarro *m*, cigarrillo *m*; — **detector** detector de humo *m*, detector de incendios *m*; — **inhalation** inhalación de humo *f*; — **screen** cortina de humo *f*; —**stack** chimenea *f*; **to have a —** fumar; VI (put off smoke) echar humo; (go fast) volar; VT (tobacco) fumar; (ham, fish, glass) ahumar; **to — out** (drive out) ahuyentar con humo; (expose) poner al descubierto

smoker [smókɚ] N fumador -ora *mf*; (train car) vagón de fumar *m*

smoking [smókɪŋ] ADJ humeante; — **car** vagón de fumar *m*; — **gun** prueba irrefutable *f*; — **room** cuarto de fumar *m*; N (use of tobacco) tabaquismo *m*, fumar *m*

smoky [smóki] ADJ humoso

smolder, smoulder [smółdɚ] VI arder

smooth [smuð] ADJ (surface) liso; (skin) suave, terso; (tire) gastado; (sea) sereno, tranquilo; (manners) agradable, fino; (flatterer) zalamero; VT (make surface even) alisar; (make easy) allanar; **to — away** hacer desaparecer; **to — one's hair** atusarse el cabello; **to — over** limar asperezas

smoothness [smúðnɪs] N (of a surface) lisura *f*; (of skin) tersura *f*, suavidad *f*; (of sea) tranquilidad *f*; (of manners) fineza *f*; (of a flatterer) zalamería *f*

smote [smot] *see* smite

smother [smʌ́ðɚ] VT (stifle) ahogar[se], sofocar[se], asfixiar[se]; (envelop) cubrir; (overprotect) sobreproteger

smudge [smʌʤ] N borrón *m*, mancha *f*; VI/VT borronear[se], manchar[se]

smug [smʌg] ADJ suficiente, petulante

smuggle [smʌ́gəl] VI/VT contrabandear, hacer contrabando; **to — in** entrar de contrabando;

to — out sacar de contrabando

smuggler [smʌ́glɚ] N contrabandista *mf*

smut [smʌt] N (soot) hollín *m*; (pornography) pornografía *f*; (parasite) tizon *m*

snack [snæk] N tentempié *m*, bocadillo *m*; — **bar** cafetería *f*, tizón *m*

snafu [snæfú] N relajo *m*

snag [snæg] N (branch) gancho *m*; (in fabric) enganchón *m*; (any obstacle) pega *f*, obstáculo *m*, contrariedad *f*; **to hit a —** tropezar con un obstáculo; VI/VT enganchar[se]; VT (a ball) agarrar

snail [snel] N caracol *m*; — **mail** correo regular *m*; —**'s pace** paso de tortuga *m*

snake [snek] N serpiente *f*; —**bite** mordedura de serpiente *f*; — **in the grass** víbora *f*; —**skin** piel de serpiente *f*; VI serpentear

snap [snæp] VI (make sound) chasquear, dar un chasquido; (lose control) estallar, perder los estribos; VT (take a photograph) sacar; VI/VT (break) quebrar[se]; **to — at** (try to bite) tirar un mordiscón; (speak harshly) ladrar; **to — one's fingers** chasquear los dedos, castañetear con los dedos; **to — out of** recuperarse de; **to — shut** cerrar[se] de golpe; **to — together** abrochar; **to — up** llevarse; N (sound) chasquido *m*; (fastener) broche *m*; (bite) tarascada *f*; **it's a —** es pan comido; — **judgment** decisión atolondrada *f*; —**dragon** dragón *m*; —**shot** instantánea, foto *f*

snappy [snǽpi] ADJ (biting) mordedor; (elegant) elegante; **make it —!** ¡date prisa!

snare [snɛr] N (trap) trampa *f*; — **drum** tambor con bordón *m*; VT atrapar

snarl [snɑrl] VI/VT (growl) regañar; (tangle) enmarañar[se], enredar[se]; N (growl) gruñido *m*; (tangle) maraña *f*, enredo *m*

snatch [snætʃ] VT (seize) arrebatar; (kidnap) secuestrar; VI **to — at** dar manotazos; N (act of snatching) arrebato *m*; (fragment) fragmento *m*

snazzy [snǽzi] ADJ llamativo

sneak [snik] VI andar furtivamente; **to — in** entrar a escondidas; **to — out** salir a hurtadillas; VT **to — something in** meter algo a escondidas; **to — something out** sacar a escondidas; **to — a cigarette** fumar a escondidas; N persona solapada *f*

sneakers [sníkɚz] N zapatillas [deportivas] *f pl*, tenis *m pl*

sneer [snir] VI (smile) sonreír con sorna; **to — at** mofarse de; N expresión de sorna *f*

sneeze [sniz] VI estornudar; **that's nothing to — at** no es nada desdeñable; N estornudo *m*

snicker [sníkɚ] VI reírse burlonamente; N risita burlona *f*

snide [snaɪd] ADJ malévolo

sniff [snɪf] VI/VT husmear, olfatear; **to — at**

husmear; (ridicule) menospreciar; N (act of sniffing) husmeo *m*, olfateo *m*; (smell) bocanada *f*

sniffle [snífəł] VI (with a cold) sorberse los mocos; (when crying) gimotear; N (when crying) gimoteo *m*; **the —s** un resfrío

snip [snɪp] VT tijeretear; **to — off** cortar de un tijeretazo; N (act of snipping) tijeretada *f*, tijeretazo *m*; (piece cut off) pedacito *m*, recorte *m*; — **of conversation** retazo de conversación *m*

sniper [snáɪpə·] N francotirador -ora *mf*

snitch [snɪtʃ] VI (tell on) chivar, chivatar; VT (rob) ratear; N soplón -ona *mf*, chivato -ta *mf*

snob [snab] N esnob *mf*

snoop [snup] VI fisgar, fisgonear; N fisgón -ona *mf*

snooze [snuz] VI dormitar; N siesta *f*; **to take a — echar un sueñecito / un sueñito / una siesta**

snore [snɔr] VI roncar; N ronquido *m*

snorkel [snɔ́rkəł] N esnórquel *m*

snort [snɔrt] VI resoplar, bufar; VI/VT (drugs) esnifar; N resoplido *m*, bufido *m*; (drink) trago *m*

snot [snat] N (mucus) *fam, vulg* moco *m*; (person) *pej* mocoso -sa *mf*

snout [snaʊt] N hocico *m*, jeta *f*, morro *m*; (nose) *fam* napias *f pl*

snow [sno] N nieve *f* (also cocaine, heroin); —**ball** bola de nieve *f*; —**board** monopatín de nieve *m*; —**drift** ventisquero *m*; —**fall** nevada *f*; —**flake** copo de nieve *m*; —**man** muñeco de nieve *m*; —**mobile** motonieve *f*; —**plow** quitanieves *m sg*; —**shoe** raqueta *f*; —**storm** ventisca *f*; VI nevar; **the airport was —ed in** cerraron el aeropuerto por nieve; **to — under** (cover in snow) cubrir de nieve; (overwhelm) abrumar; **to —ball** aumentar rápidamente

snowy [snói] ADJ nevado; (white) níveo

snub [snʌb] VT volverle la cara a, desairar, despreciar; N desaire *m*, desprecio *m*; —-**nosed** chato; *Am* ñato

snuck [snʌk] *see* sneak

snuff [snʌf] VI **to — out** apagar, extinguir; N (tobacco product) rapé *m*; **to be up to —** dar la talla

snug [snʌg] ADJ (tight-fitting) ajustado; (comfortable) cómodo

so [so] ADV (in this way) así; (to this degree) tan; (so much) tanto; — **am** I yo también; —-**and-** — fulano [de tal]; —-**called** llamado; — **as to** para; — **far as I know** que yo sepa; — **many** tantos; — **much** tanto; —-— regular; — **much the better** tanto mejor; — **that** de modo que; **I was — a beauty queen!** ¡sí que fui reina de belleza! — **long!** ¡hasta luego! **and — forth** etcetera, y así sucesivamente; **I believe —** creo que sí; **is that — ?** ¿en serio?

¡no me digas! **ten minutes or —** unos diez minutos; INTERJ (upon discovering a secret) ajajá; CONJ (in order that) de modo que; (consequently) así que, entonces

soak [sok] VI/VT (immerse) remojar[se]; (drench) empapar[se]; **to — through** colarse por; **to — up** absorber, embeber; **to be —ed through** estar empapado, estar calado hasta los huesos; N remojón *m*

soap [sop] N jabón *m*; (television show) telenovela *f*; — **bubble** pompa de jabón *f*; — **dish** jabonera *f*; VT enjabonar

soapy [sópi] ADJ jabonoso

soar [sɔr] VI/VT (airplane) elevar[se]; (kite) remontar[se]; (hopes) aumentar[se]; (prices) disparar[se]; (glider) planear[se]; VI (bird) volar

sob [sab] VI sollozar, hipar; N sollozo *m*, hipo *m*

SOB [**son of a bitch**] [ésóbí] N *offensive* hijo de puta *m, offensive* hijo de perra *m*

sober [sóbə·] ADJ (not drunk) sobrio; (temperate) moderado; (serious, subdued) serio, sobrio; VI **to — up** (get over drunkenness) despejarse; (become more serious) sentar cabeza

sobriety [səbráɪɪDi] N (not being drunk) sobriedad *f*; (moderation) moderación *f*; (seriousness) seriedad *f*

soccer [sákə·] N fútbol *m*, balompié *m*; — **ball** esférico *m*; — **field** campo de juego *m*, cancha *f*; — **player** futbolista *mf*; — **World Cup** Campeonato Mundial de Fútbol *m*

sociable [sóʃəbł] ADJ sociable

social [sóʃəł] ADJ (of society) social; (friendly) sociable; — **climber** arribista *mf*; — **science** ciencias sociales *f pl*; — **security** seguridad social *f*; — **welfare** asistencia social *f*; — **work** asistencia social *f*; N reunión social *f*

socialism [sóʃəlɪzəm] N socialismo *m*

socialist [sóʃəlɪst] ADJ & N socialista *mf*

socialize [sóʃəlaɪz] VT socializar; VI salir, tener trato social

society [səsáɪɪDi] N sociedad *f*; (companionship) compañía *f*

socioeconomic [sosioɛkənámɪk] ADJ socioeconómico

sociology [sosiáləʤi] N sociología *f*

sociopath [sósiəpæθ] N sociópata *mf*

sock [sak] N (garment) calcetín *m*; (blow) puñetazo *m*, zumbido *m*; VT pegar, zumbar; **to — away** ahorrar

socket [sákɪt] N (of eye) cuenca *f*; (electrical outlet) enchufe *m*; (for bulb) portalámparas *m sg*, casquillo *m*

sod [sad] N (lawn) césped *m*; (piece) tepe *m*; VT cubrir de césped

soda [sóDə] N (drink) gaseosa *f*; (sodium hydroxide) soda *f*, sosa *f*; — **fountain** bar de bebidas sin alcohol *m*; — **pop** gaseosa *f*; —

water agua con gas *f*
sodium [sóɒiəm] N sodio *m*
sodomy [sáɒəmi] N sodomía *f*
sofa [sófə] N sofá *m*; — **bed** sofá-cama *m*
soft [sɔft] ADJ (butter, bed, water, penalty)
blando; (life) fácil, cómodo; (hair, skin) suave;
(light) tenue; —**ball** softball *m*; —-**boiled**
eggs huevos pasados por agua *m pl*; — **coal**
carbón bituminoso *m*; — **drink** gaseosa *f*; —
page break salto de página suave/
automático *m*; — **palate** velo del paladar *m*;
— **return** salto de línea suave *m*; —**ware**
software *m*
soften [sɔfən] VI/VT (butter) ablandar[se]; (skin)
suavizar[se]; VT (a blow) amortiguar; (voice)
bajar
softly [sɔftli] ADV (talk) en voz baja; (walk) sin
hacer ruido
softness [sɔftnɪs] N (of butter) blandura *f*; (of
hair, skin) suavidad *f*; (of light) tenuidad *f*
soggy [sági] ADJ (clothes) empapado; (day)
húmedo
soil [sɔɪl] N suelo *m*, tierra *f*; VI/VT ensuciar[se],
manchar[se]
solace [sálɪs] N consuelo *m*; VT consolar
solar [sólɚ] ADJ solar; — **eclipse** eclipse de sol
m; — **energy** energía solar *f*; — **plexus**
plexo solar *m*; — **system** sistema solar *m*
sold [sołd] *see* sell
solder [sáɒɚ] VI/VT soldar[se]; N soldadura *f*;
—**ing iron** soldador *m*
soldier [sółdʒɚ] N (of low rank) soldado *m*; (of
any rank) militar *m*
sole [soł] ADJ solo, único; N (of a foot) planta *f*;
(of a shoe) suela *f*; (fish) lenguado *m*
solely [sółli] ADV solamente; **you are** —
responsible eres el único responsable
solemn [sáləm] ADJ solemne
solemnity [səlémnɪɒi] N solemnidad *f*
solenoid [sólənɔɪd] N solenoide *m*
solicit [səlísɪt] VT (aid) pedir; (a prostitute)
ofrecerse; VI (sell) vender, ofrecer productos
solicitor [səlísɪɒɚ] N abogado *m*; — **general**
subsecretario -ria de justicia *mf*
solicitous [səlísɪɒəs] ADJ solícito
solid [sálɪd] ADJ (firm) sólido; (dense) denso; —
blue azul liso *m*; — **geometry** geometría del
espacio *f*; — **gold** oro puro *m*; — **line** línea
continua *f*; —-**state** de estado sólido; **for**
one — **hour** por una hora entera; N sólido *m*
solidarity [salɪdǽrɪɒi] N solidaridad *f*
solidify [səlídəfaɪ] VI/VT solidificar[se]
solidity [səlídɪɒi] N solidez *f*
solitary [sálɪteri] ADJ solitario; **to be in** —
confinement estar incomunicado
solitude [sálɪtud] N soledad *f*
solo [sólo] N (in music) solo *m*
soloist [sóloɪst] N solista *mf*
Solomon Islander [sáləmənáɪləndɚ] N

salomonense *mf*
Solomon Islands [sáləmənáɪləndz] N Islas
Salomón *f pl*
solstice [sółstɪs] N solsticio *m*
soluble [sáljəbəł] ADJ soluble
solution [səlúʃən] N solución *f*
solve [sałv] VT resolver, solucionar
solvent [sáłvənt] N solvente *m*, disolvente *m*
Somalia [sómáljə] N Somalia *f*
Somalian [sómáljən] ADJ & N somalí *mf*
somber [sámbɚ] ADJ sombrío
some [sʌm] ADJ algún, alguno; **I worked for** —
time trabajé por un rato; **that is** — **dog!**
¡menudo perro! PRON algunos; **and then** —
y más todavía; ADV — **twenty people** unas
veinte personas; **I like it** — me gusta un poco
somebody [sámbaɒi] PRON alguien
someday [sámde] ADV algún día
somehow [sámhaʊ] ADV de alguna manera; —
or other de alguna manera u otra
someone [sámwʌn] PRON alguien, alguno
somersault [sámɚsɔłt] N (on ground) voltereta
f; (in air) salto mortal *m*; VI (on ground) dar
una voltereta; (in air) dar un salto mortal
something [sámθɪŋ] PRON algo *m*; — **else** otra
cosa; **thirty**— (age) treinta y tantos; (person)
treintañero -ra *mf*
sometime [sámtaɪm] ADV algún día, en algún
momento; —**s** a veces, de vez en cuando
somewhat [sámhwat] ADV algo
somewhere [sámhwer] ADV en alguna parte; —
else en alguna otra parte
son [sʌn] N hijo *m*; —-**in-law** yerno *m*; — **of a**
bitch *offensive* hijo de puta *m*; — **of a gun**
fam hijo de su madre *m*
sonar [sónɑr] N sonar *m*
song [sɔŋ] N canción *f*; (of a bird) canto *m*; — **and**
dance cuento chino *m*; —**writer** compositor
-ora *mf*; —**bird** ave canora *f*, pájaro cantor *m*;
to buy something for a — comprar algo
muy barato
sonic barrier [sánɪkbǽriɚ] N barrera del sonido *f*
sonnet [sánɪt] N soneto *m*
sonority [sənɔ́rɪɒi] N sonoridad *f*
sonorous [sánɚəs] ADJ sonoro
soon [sun] ADV pronto; — **after nine** poco
después de las nueve; **as** — **as** tan pronto
como, en cuanto; **see you** — hasta pronto;
how — **do you want it?** ¿para cuándo lo
necesitas? **he arrived** —**er** llegó antes; —**er**
or later tarde o temprano; **I'd** —**er stay**
here prefiero quedarme aquí
soot [sʊt] N hollín *m*, tizne *m*
soothe [suð] VT calmar, aliviar
soothsayer [súθseɚ] N agorero -ra *mf*
sooty [súɒi] ADJ tiznado
sop [sap] VT empapar; **to** — **up** absorber; **to be**
—**ping wet** estar empapado; N —**s** sopas *f pl*
sophisticated [səfístɪkeɒɪd] ADJ sofisticado

sophomore [sáfəmɔr] N estudiante de segundo año *mf*

soprano [səprǽno] N soprano *m*

sorcerer [sɔ́rsərə] N brujo *m*, hechicero *m*

sorceress [sɔ́rsəɪs] N hechicera *f*

sordid [sɔ́rdɪd] ADJ sórdido, escabroso

sore [sɔr] ADJ (painful) dolorido, doloroso; (grieved) dolorido; (angry) enojado; **—head** cascarrabias *mf*; **my arm is —** me duele el brazo; **to have a — throat** tener dolor de garganta; N llaga *f*, úlcera *f*

soreness [sɔ́rnɪs] N dolor *m*

sorority [sərɔ́rɪdi] N asociación femenina de estudiantes *f*

sorrow [sáro] N (sadness) pena *f*, pesar *m*, pesadumbre *f*; (cause of sadness) disgusto *m*

sorrowful [sárəfəł] ADJ triste, pesaroso

sorry [sári] ADJ **I am —** lo siento; **I am — about that** lo lamento; **I am — for her** la compadezco; **—?** ¿Cómo? **a — SOB** *pej* un desgraciado; **you'll be —** te arrepentirás; **he was in — shape** estaba en un estado lamentable

sort [sɔrt] N clase *f*, tipo *m*; **— of tired** algo cansado; **all —s of** toda clase de; **out of —s** (depressed) de mal humor; (ill) indispuesto; **— key** tecla de ordenación *f*; **— order** orden de clasificación *m*; VT (classify) clasificar; (put in order) ordenar; **to — out** separar, apartar; **to — out a problem** resolver un problema

SOS [ésoés] N SOS *m*

sought [sɔt] *see* seek

soul [soł] N alma *f*; **— music** música soul *f*; **not a —** nadie, ni un alma; **the — of tact** la imagen del tacto

sound [saʊnd] N sonido *m*; (inlet) brazo de mar *m*; **— barrier** barrera del sonido *f*; **— card** tarjeta de sonido *f*; **—proof** a prueba de sonido; **—track** banda sonora *f*; **— wave** onda sonora *f*; ADJ (healthy) sano; (sane) cuerdo; (well founded) bien fundado, lógico; **— advice** buen consejo *m*; **— sleep** sueño profundo *m*; **a — beating** una buena paliza; **of — mind** en su sano juicio; **safe and —** sano y salvo; VI sonar; VT (an alarm) tocar; (a channel) sondar; (opinion) sondear; **to — out** tantear, sondear

soup [sup] N sopa *f*; **— dish** plato sopero *m*; **—spoon** cuchara sopera *f*; **— tureen** sopera *f*

sour [saʊr] ADJ (acidic) agrio, ácido; (peevish) agrio, avinagrado; **to go —** (milk) cortarse, agriarse; (a relationship) estropearse; **— cream** *Sp* nata agria *f*; *Am* crema agria *f*; **— milk** leche cortada *f*; **—puss** cascarrabias *mf*, avinagrado -da *mf*; VI/VT agriar[se], avinagrar[se]; (milk) cortar[se]

source [sɔrs] N fuente *f*, origen *m*; **— code** código fuente *m*

sourness [sáʊrnɪs] N acidez *f*

souse [saʊs] VI/VT (plunge) zambullir[se]; (soak) empapar[se]; N borracho -cha *mf*, esponja *f*

south [saʊθ] N sur *m*, mediodía *f*; ADJ meridional, sureño; **— Africa** Sudáfrica *f*; **— African** sudafricano -na *mf*; **— America** América del Sur *f*, Sudamérica *f*; **— American** sudamericano -na *mf*; **—bound** con rumbo al sur; **—east** sureste, sudeste; **—eastern** sureste, sudeste; **— Korea** Corea del Sur *f*; **— Korean** surcoreano -na *mf*; **—paw** zurdo -da *mf*; **— pole** polo sur *m*; **—west** sudoeste, suroeste; **—western** sudoeste, suroeste; ADV hacia el sur

southern [sʌ́ðən] ADJ meridional, sureño

southerner [sʌ́ðənə] N sureño -ña *mf*, meridional *mf*, habitante del sur *mf*

southward [sáʊθwəd] ADV hacia el sur, rumbo al sur

souvenir [suvənír] N recuerdo *m*

sovereign [sávərɪn] ADJ & N soberano -na *mf*

sovereignty [sávərɪnti] N soberanía *f*

sow[1] [saʊ] N puerca *f*

sow[2] [so] VI/VT sembrar

sown [son] *see* sow[2]

soy [sɔi] N *Sp* soja *f*; *Am* soya *f*; **—bean** *Sp* semilla de soja *f*; *Am* semilla de soya *f*; **— sauce** *Sp* salsa de soja *f*; *Am* salsa de soya *f*

spa [spɑ] N balneario *m*

space [spes] N espacio *m*; **—-age** de la era espacial; **—bar** barra espaciadora *f*; **—craft** nave espacial *f*; **—ship** nave espacial *f*; **— shuttle** transbordador espacial *m*; **— station** estación espacial *f*; **— suit** traje espacial *m*; VT espaciar; **to — out** distraerse

spacious [spéʃəs] ADJ espacioso, amplio

spade [sped] N (shovel) pala *f*; (in cards) pica *f*; **to call a — a —** al pan, pan y al vino, vino

Spain [spen] N España *f*

spam [spæm] N correo electrónico basura *m*, spam *m*

span [spæn] N (of hand) palmo *m*; (of time) espacio *m*; (of attention) lapso *m*, período *m*; (of bridge) tramo *m*; (of wing) envergadura *f*; (of life) duración *f*; VT (time) abarcar; (a river) atravesar, salvar

Spaniard [spǽnjəd] N español -ola *mf*

Spanish [spǽnɪʃ] ADJ (of Spain) español; (Spanish-speaking) hispano; N (language) español *m*; **— America** Hispanoamérica *f*

spank [spæŋk] VT dar nalgadas; N palmada *f*, nalgada *f*

spanking [spǽŋkɪŋ] N zurra en las nalgas *f*; ADJ **— new** flamante

spare [spɛr] VT (embarrassment) ahorrar, evitar; (money) prestar; (an enemy) perdonar la vida a; (a worker) prescindir de; **— me!** ¡ten piedad de mí! **to — no expense** no escatimar gastos; **to have time to —** tener tiempo de sobra; ADJ (austere) austero; (extra) de sobra, de más; — **cash** dinero disponible *m*; — **parts** repuestos *m pl*; — **time** tiempo libre *m*; N (part) repuesto *m*; (tire) neumático de repuesto *m*

spark [spark] N chispa *f*; — **plug** bujía *f*; VI chispear, echar chispas; VT (a riot) desencadenar; (interest, criticism) provocar

sparkle [spárkəł] VI (diamond) centellear; (sparkler) chispear; (eyes) brillar; N (flashing) brillo *m*, centelleo *m*; (spirit) viveza *f*, animación *f*

sparkling [spárklɪŋ] ADJ (diamond) centelleante; (eyes) brillante; — **water** agua con gas *f*; — **wine** vino espumoso *m*

sparrow [spǽro] N gorrión *m*

sparse [spars] ADJ escaso; (hair) ralo

spasm [spǽzəm] N espasmo *m*

spasmodic [spæzmáDɪk] ADJ espasmódico

spastic [spǽstɪk] ADJ espástico

spat [spæt] N riña *f*

spat [spæt] *see* spit

spatial [spéʃəł] ADJ espacial

spatter [spǽDɚ] VI/VT salpicar; N salpicadura *f*

spatula [spǽtʃələ] N espátula *f*

spawn [spɔn] VI desovar; VT engendrar; N (of fish) huevas *f pl*; (of frogs) huevos *m pl*

spay [spe] VT esterilizar, castrar

speak [spik] VI hablar; VT (a language) hablar; (the truth) decir; (one's lines) recitar, decir; **so to** — por decirlo así, valga la expresión; **to** — **for** hablar en nombre de / a favor de; **to** — **one's mind** hablar sin rodeos; **to** — **out against** denunciar; **to** — **out for** defender; **to** — **up** hablar fuerte

speaker [spíkɚ] N orador -ora *mf*; (at a conference) conferenciante *mf*; (of a language) hablante *mf*; — **of the House** presidente -ta de la cámara de representantes *mf*; —**phone** teléfono con parlante *m*

spear [spir] N (weapon) lanza *f*; (for fishing) arpón *m*; (sprout) brote *m*; VT (a person, animal) alancear, herir con lanza; (a fish) arponear

spearmint [spírmɪnt] N mentaverde *f*

special [spéʃəł] ADJ especial; — **delivery** entrega inmediata *f*; — **education** educación especial *f*; — **effects** efectos especiales *m pl*; — **interest [group]** grupo de presión *m*; N (sale item) especialidad *f*; (TV program) especial *m*

specialist [spéʃəlɪst] N especialista *mf*

specialization [spɛʃəlɪzéʃən] N especialización *f*, especialidad *f*

specialize [spéʃəlaɪz] VI/VT especializar[se]

specially [spéʃəli] ADV especialmente, específicamente

specialty [spéʃəłti] N especialidad *f*

species [spíʃiz] N especie *f*

specific [spɪsífɪk] ADJ específico, determinado; — **gravity** peso específico *m*; N —**s** detalles *m pl*

specifically [spɪsífɪkli] ADV concretamente, específicamente

specify [spésəfaɪ] VI/VT especificar

specimen [spésəmən] N (representative) espécimen *m*, ejemplar *m*; (sample) muestra *f*

speck [spɛk] N (small dot) mota *f*, manchita *f*; (small amount) pizca *f*

speckle [spékəł] N manchita *f*, mota *f*; VT salpicar, motear; —**d** moteado

spectacle [spéktəkəł] N espectáculo *m*; —**s** gafas *f pl*, anteojos *m pl*; **to make a** — **of oneself** dar un espectáculo, ponerse en ridículo

spectacular [spɛktǽkjələ] ADJ espectacular

spectator [spéktɛDɚ] N espectador -ora *mf*

spectrum [spéktrəm] N espectro *m*

speculate [spékjəlet] VI/VT especular

speculation [spɛkjəléʃən] N especulación *f*

speculative [spékjələDɪv] ADJ especulativo

speculator [spékjələDɚ] N especulador -ora *mf*

sped [spɛd] *see* speed

speech [spitʃ] N (faculty of speaking) habla *f*; (formal) discurso *m*; (in a play) parlamento *m*; — **defect** defecto de pronunciación *m*; — **recognition** reconocimiento de habla *m*; — **synthesis** síntesis de habla *m*; **to make a** — pronunciar un discurso

speechless [spítʃlɪs] ADJ (dumb) mudo; (astonished) estupefacto

speed [spid] N (rapidity) velocidad *f*, rapidez *f*; (gear) velocidad *f*; (amphetamine) anfeta *f*; — **limit** límite de velocidad *m*; **at full** — a toda velocidad; VI (break speed limit) ir con exceso de velocidad; **to** — **by** pasar a toda velocidad; **to** — **off/away** irse a toda velocidad; **to** — **up** (a car, work) acelerar; (a delivery) hacer llegar a toda velocidad

speedometer [spɪdámɪDɚ] N velocímetro *m*

speedy [spíDi] ADJ veloz, rápido

spell [spɛł] N (charm) hechizo *m*, sortilegio *m*, conjuro *m*; (period) temporada *f*; (sickness) ataque *m*; **to put under a** — hechizar; ADJ —**bound** hechizado; VT (spoken) deletrear; (written) escribir; (represent) significar, representar; **to** —**-check** comprobar la ortografía; **I** —**ed it out for him** se lo dije con todas las letras

spelling [spélɪŋ] N ortografía *f*; — **bee** concurso de ortografía *m*

spend [spɛnd] VT (money) gastar; (time) pasar; —**thrift** derrochador -ora *mf*, gastador -ora *mf*, pródigo -ga *mf*

spending [spéndɪŋ] N gastos *m pl*; — **cut** recorte de gastos *m*; **to go on a** — **spree** salir a gastar dinero a lo loco

spent [spɛnt] *see* spend

sperm [spɝm] N esperma *mf*, semen *m*; — **bank**

banco de semen/esperma *m*; — **whale** cachalote *m*

spermicide [spɚ́məsaɪd] N espermicida *m*

sphere [sfir] N esfera *f*; — **of influence** esfera de influencia *f*

spherical [sférɪkəł] ADJ esférico

sphincter [sfíŋktɚ] N esfínter *m*

spice [spaɪs] N especia *f*; VT condimentar; **to —** **up** dar sal

spiciness [spáɪsɪnɪs] N lo picante

spick and span [spíkənspǽn] ADJ impecable

spicy [spáɪsi] ADJ picante

spider [spáɪDɚ] N araña *f*; — **monkey** mono araña *m*; —**'s web** telaraña *f*

spigot [spígət] N grifo *m*, espita *f*

spike [spaɪk] N (sprout) espiga *f*; (sharp object) púa *f*, pincho *m*; (on shoes) clavo *m*; —**s** zapatillas con clavos *f pl*; VT (impale) clavar; (add alcohol to) echar alcohol a; (hit a volleyball) picar

spill [spɪł] VI/VT volcar[se], derramar[se], verter[se]; VT (a rider) hacer caer; **to — the** **beans** descubrir el pastel; VI **to — over** (a liquid) desbordarse; (a conflict) extenderse; N (of water) derrame *m*; (of blood) derramamiento *m*; (fall) caída *f*

spilt [spɪłt] *see* spill

spin [spɪn] VT (wool) hilar; (a top, one's partner) hacer girar; VI dar vueltas, girar; **to — yarns** contar cuentos; N (turning) giro *m*, vuelta *f*; (of an airplane) barrena *f*; (political) sesgo *m*; **to take a —** dar una vuelta

spinach [spínɪtʃ] N espinaca *f*

spinal [spáɪnļ] ADJ espinal, vertebral; — **column** columna vertebral *f*, espina dorsal *f*; — **cord** médula espinal *f*

spindle [spíndļ] N (for weaving) huso *m*; (on machines) eje *m*

spine [spaɪn] N espina *f*, espinazo *m*

spinning [spínɪŋ] N (action) hilado *m*; (art) hilandería *f*; — **machine** máquina de hilar *f*; — **mill** hilandería *f*; — **top** trompo *m*, peonza *f*; — **wheel** rueca *f*

spinster [spínstɚ] N solterona *f*

spiral [spáɪrəł] ADJ & N espiral *m*; — **notebook** cuaderno de espiral *m*; — **staircase** escalera de caracol *f*

spire [spaɪr] N aguja *f*, chapitel *m*

spirit [spírɪt] N (ghost) espíritu *m*; (animation) ánimo *m*, brío *m*; (alcohol) alcohol *m*; **low** —**s** abatimiento *m*; **to be in good —s** estar de buen humor; VT **to — away** llevar como por arte de magia

spirited [spírɪDɪd] ADJ fogoso, brioso

spiritual [spírɪtʃuəł] ADJ & N espiritual *m*

spirituality [spɪrɪtʃuǽlɪDi] N espiritualidad *f*

spit [spɪt] VI/VT escupir; N (saliva) escupitajo *m*; (for roasting) asador *m*, espeto *m*, espetón *m*; (of sand) banco *m*

spite [spaɪt] N despecho *m*, inquina *f*; **in — of** a pesar de; **out of —** por despecho; VT contrariar

spiteful [spáɪtfəł] ADJ malicioso

splash [splǽʃ] VI/VT salpicar; VI chapotear, chapalear; N salpicadura *f*, chapoteo *m*; **to** **make a —** hacer olas

splatter [splǽDɚ] VI/VT salpicar; N salpicadura *f*

spleen [splin] N bazo *m*; (ill humor) mal humor *m*

splendid [spléndɪd] ADJ espléndido

splendor [spléndɚ] N esplendor *m*

splice [splaɪs] VT (tape, genes) empalmar, unir; N empalme *m*, unión *f*

splint [splɪnt] N tablilla *f*; VT entablillar

splinter [splíntɚ] N astilla *f*; VI/VT astillar[se]

split [splɪt] VI/VT (stone, wood) hender[se], rajar[se]; (candy bar) partir[se], dividir[se]; **to** **— hairs** hilar fino; **to — one's sides with** **laughter** desternillarse de risa; **to — the** **difference** partir la diferencia; ADJ (wood) partido, hendido; (a group) dividido; —-**level** en desnivel; — **personality** doble personalidad *f*; — **screen** pantalla dividida *f*; **— second** fracción de segundo *f*; N hendidura *f*, grieta *f*; (in a group) escisión *f*, división *f*

spoil [spɔɪl] VI (milk) cortar[se]; (food) echarse a perder; VT (vacation, performance) estropear, arruinar; (plans) desbaratar; (enjoyment) aguar; (child) malcriar, mimar demasiado; N —**s** botín *m*

spoiler [spɔ́ɪlɚ] N alerón *m*

spoke [spok] N rayo *m*

spoke [spok] *see* speak

spoken [spókən] *see* speak

spokesperson [spókspɚsən] N portavoz *mf*, vocero -ra *mf*

sponge [spʌndʒ] N (animal, utensil) esponja *f*; (parasite) gorrón -ona *mf*; — **bath** baño de esponja *m*; — **cake** *Am* bizcochuelo *m*; *Sp* bizcocho *m*; VI **to — off** (clean) quitar con esponja; (take advantage of) gorronear; **to —** **up** absorber con una esponja

sponger [spʌ́ndʒɚ] N gorrón -ona *mf*, parásito *m*

spongy [spʌ́ndʒi] ADJ esponjoso, espongiado

sponsor [spʌ́nsɚ] N (of the arts) mecenas *mf*; (of sports, TV program) patrocinador -ora *mf*; (of a bill) proponente *mf*; VT (a child) apadrinar; (arts, sports, TV show) patrocinar; (bill) proponer

sponsorship [spʌ́nsɚʃɪp] N patrocinio *m*

spontaneity [spɑntənéɪDi] N espontaneidad *f*

spontaneous [spɑnténiəs] ADJ espontáneo; — **abortion** aborto espontáneo *m*

spook [spuk] N (ghost) espectro *m*; (spy) espía *mf*

spool [spuł] N carrete *m*, carretel *m*; VT (wool) devanar; (tape) enrollar

spoon [spun] N cuchara *f*; VT cucharear, poner

con una cuchara; **to — -feed** dar de comer en la boca

spoonful [spúnfʉɫ] N cucharada f

spore [spɔr] N espora f

sport [spɔrt] N deporte m; **to be a good** — tener espíritu deportivo; **— utility vehicle** vehículo utilitario deportivo m; **—s car** coche deportivo m; **—s jacket** saco de sport m, americana f; **—sman** (hunter) cazador m; (in sports) hombre de espíritu deportivo m; **—smanship** espíritu deportivo m, deportividad f; **—swriter** cronista deportivo -va mf; ADJ deportivo; VT lucir

sporty [spɔ́rɒi] ADJ deportivo

spot [spɑt] N (stain) mancha f, mota f; (blemish) espinilla f; (insect bite) roncha f; (place) lugar m, paraje m; (difficult situation) aprieto m; **on the** — en el acto; **— -check** inspección al azar f; **—light** (in theater) foco m; (outdoors) reflector m; **to be in the —light** ser el centro de atención; **— remover** quitamanchas m sg; VI/VT (stain) manchar, ensuciar; VT (see in the distance) divisar; (notice) notar; (give advantage) dar como ventaja

spotless [spátlɪs] ADJ inmaculado

spotted [spádɪd] ADJ manchado, moteado

spouse [spaʊs] N cónyuge mf; **— abuse** abuso conyugal m

spout [spaʊt] VT (throw) arrojar chorros de; (talk) soltar tonterías; VI (flow out) salir a chorros; (talk) perorar; N (of a fountain) caño m; (of a gutter) canalón m; (of a teapot) pico m

sprain [spren] VT torcerse; N torcedura f

sprang [spræŋ] see spring

sprawl [sprɔɫ] VI (spread limbs) despatarrarse; (extend) extenderse; (fall) tumbarse; N postura despatarrada f

spray [spre] VI/VT rociar[se]; N (of liquid) rociada f; (foam) espuma f; (of flowers) ramillete m; **— can** aerosol m; **— paint** pintura en aerosol f

spread [sprɛd] VI/VT (arms, newspaper) extender[se]; (butter) untar[se]; (map) desdoblar[se]; (legs) abrir[se]; (seeds) esparcir[se]; (news) difundir[se], diseminar[se]; (odor) difundir[se], expandirse; (rumor) propalar; (panic) sembrar; VT (panic, news) sembrar; N (of ideas) difusión f; (of opinion) diseminación f; (of disease) propagación f; (of nuclear weapons) proliferación f; (for a bed) cubrecama m; (for bread) pasta f; (of food) festín m; (ranch) hacienda f; **—sheet** (paper) planilla de cálculo f; (program) planilla electrónica f

spree [spri] N parranda f, farra f; **to go on a —** ir de parranda/farra; **to go on a shopping —** gastar dinero desenfrenadamente

spring [sprɪŋ] VI saltar; **to — at** abalanzarse sobre; **to — from** nacer de; **to — open** abrir[se] de golpe; **to — to mind** venir a la mente; **to — up** surgir; VT **to — a leak** (boat) hacer agua; (pipe) comenzar a gotear; **to — news** dar una noticia de sopetón; N (season) primavera f; (coil) muelle m, resorte m; (elasticity) elasticidad f; (jump) salto m; (water) manantial m, fuente f; **—board** trampolín m; **— fever** fiebre de primavera f; **— mattress** colchón de muelles m; **—time** primavera f; **— water** agua de manantial f; **he's no — chicken** no se cuece en el primer hervor

sprinkle [sprɪ́ŋkəl] VT (with sugar) espolvorear; (with droplets) salpicar, rociar; (rain) gotear, chispear

sprint [sprɪnt] VI (run) echarse una carrera; (run a competitive race) [e]sprintar; N (run) corrida corta f; (race) [e]sprint m

sprocket [sprákɪt] N piñón m, rueda dentada f

sprout [spraʊt] VI (leaf) brotar, salir; (plants) retoñar; (seeds) germinar; (houses) surgir; VT echar; **he —ed horns** le salieron cuernos; N retoño m, brote m, renuevo m

spruce [sprus] N picea f; VI **to — up** arreglarse

sprung [sprʌŋ] see spring

spun [spʌn] see spin

spunk [spʌŋk] N agallas f pl, vulg cojones m pl

spur [spɝ] N (on stirrups) espuela f; (stimulus) aguijón m; (of a rooster) espolón m; (of a mountain) estribación f; (of a railroad track) ramal m; **on the — of the moment** espontáneamente; VT espolear; **to — on** animar

spurious [spjúriəs] ADJ espurio

spurn [spɝn] VT rechazar, desdeñar

spurt [spɝt] VI salir a chorros; N (of water) chorro m; (of a runner) esfuerzo repentino m; **in —s** por rachas

sputter [spʌ́də] VI (fire) chisporrotear; (person) refunfuñar; N (fire) chisporroteo m

sputum [spjúɒəm] N esputo m

spy [spaɪ] N espía mf; **—glass** catalejo m; VI espiar; **to — on** espiar

squabble [skwábəl] VI reñir; N reyerta f

squad [skwɑd] N (of police) patrulla f; (for execution) pelotón m; (of athletes) equipo m; (for guarding) retén m; **— car** [coche] patrullero m

squadron [skwádrən] N (in navy) escuadra f; (in army) escuadrón m

squalid [skwálɪd] ADJ escuálido

squall [skwɔɫ] N (rain) chubasco m, borrasca f; (sound) berrido m; VI berrear

squalor [skwálə] N miseria f, escualidez f

squander [skwándə] VT despilfarrar, derrochar, disipar

squanderer [skwándərə] N derrochador -ora mf

square [skwɛr] N (shape) cuadrado *m*; (on a pattern) cuadro *m*; (plaza) plaza *f*, *Mex* zócalo *m*; (tool in carpentry) escuadra *f*; (on chessboard) casilla *f*; — **brackets** corchetes *m pl*; — **dance** cuadrilla *f*; — **knot** nudo de rizo *m*; — **meal** comida completa *f*; — **root** raíz cuadrada *f*; **he is a** — es muy conservador; VT (make square) cuadrar; (draw squares on) cuadricular; (multiply by itself) elevar al cuadrado; **to** — **one's shoulders** erguirse; ADJ (in shape) cuadrado; (at ninety degrees) en ángulo recto; (tied) empatado; (frank) franco; **to be** — **with someone** estar a mano con alguien; ADV **right** — **between the eyes** justo entre los ojos

squash [skwɑʃ] N (gourd) calabaza *f*; (sport) squash *m*; VT (smash) aplastar, despachurrar

squat [skwɑt] VI (sit low) acuclillarse; (occupy) ocupar sin autorización; ADJ (sitting low) acuclillado; (thickset) rechoncho, achaparrado; N (nothing) nada; **he doesn't know**— no sabe un comino; **in a** — en cuclillas

squawk [skwɔk] VI (of chickens) cacarear; (complain) quejarse; N (of chickens) cacareo *m*; (complaint) quejido *m*

squeak [skwik] VI (door) rechinar, chirriar; (shoe) rechinar; (mouse) chillar; N (of door) rechinamiento *m*, chirrido *m*; (of shoe) rechinamiento *m*; (of mouse) chillido *m*

squeaky [skwíki] ADJ (door) chirriante; (shoes) rechinante

squeal [skwił] VI chillar; (complain) protestar; (snitch) chivatar, delatar; N chillido *m*

squeamish [skwímɪʃ] ADJ delicado

squeegee [skwídʒi] N escurridor de goma *m*, limpiavidrios *m sg*

squeeze [skwiz] VT apretar; (press very hard) estrujar; (an orange) estrujar, exprimir; (hug) abrazar; **to** — **into** meter[se] con dificultad en, encajar[se] en; **to** — **out** (an orange) exprimir; (a towel) escurrir; **to** — **through a crowd** abrirse paso entre la multitud; N (of hands) apretón *m*; (excessive squeeze) estrujón *m*; (hug) abrazo *m*; (lack) restricción *f*

squelch [skwɛltʃ] VT (revolt) aplastar, sofocar; (criticism) acallar

squid [skwɪd] N calamar *m*

squint [skwɪnt] VI (partially close eyes) entrecerrar los ojos; (look askance) mirar de soslayo; N (look with partially closed eyes) mirada con los ojos entrecerrados *f*; (side glance) mirada de soslayo *f*

squirm [skwɝm] VI retorcerse; **to** — **out of a difficulty** zafarse de un aprieto

squirrel [skwɝəl] N ardilla *f*

squirt [skwɝt] VT echar un chisguete en; VI salir a chorritos; N chisguete *m*, chorrito *m*; —

gun pistola lanzaagua *f*, pistola de agua *f*

Sri Lanka [srilɑ́ŋkə] N Sri Lanka *f*

Sri Lankan [srilɑ́ŋkən] ADJ & N cingalés -esa *mf*

stab [stæb] VI/VT apuñalar, acuchillar; **to** — **at** tirar puñaladas a; N (with a dagger) puñalada *f*; (with a knife) cuchillada *f*; (with a pocketknife) navajazo *m*; (of pain) punzada *f*, pinchazo *m*; **to take a** — **at** intentar; — **wound** cuchillada *f*

stability [stəbílɪDi] N estabilidad *f*

stabilization [stebəlɪzéʃən] N estabilización *f*

stable [stébəł] ADJ estable; N establo *m*, cuadra *f*; (for horses only) caballeriza *f*; VT poner en el establo

stack [stæk] N (ordered) pila *f*; (chaotic) montón *m*; (of a chimney) chimenea *f*; (in a library) estantería *f*; VT amontonar, apilar

stadium [stédiəm] N estadio *m*

staff [stæf] N (stick) cayado *m*; (of a flag) asta *f*; (personnel) personal *m*, plantel *m*; (of music) pentagrama *m*; — **of life** pan de cada día *m*; — **officer** oficial de estado mayor *m*; **editorial** — redacción *f*; **teaching** — cuerpo docente *m*; VT contratar personal para

stag [stæg] N (deer) venado *m*, ciervo *m*; (other animals) macho *m*; — **beetle** ciervo volante *m*; — **party** fiesta para hombres *f*

stage [stedʒ] N (showplace) escenario *m*; (for popular entertainment) tablado *m*; (theater) teatro *m*, las tablas *f pl*; (period) etapa *f*, estadio *m*; (distance) etapa *f*; —**coach** diligencia *f*; — **fright** miedo al escenario *m*, fiebre de candilejas *f*; —**hand** tramoyista *mf*; **by** —**s** por etapas; VT (a play) poner en escena; (an attack) organizar

stagger [stǽgɚ] VI (totter) tambalearse, dar tumbos; VT (hit hard) hacer tambalear; (overwhelm) dejar azorado; (alternate) escalonar; N tambaleo *m*

stagnant [stǽgnənt] ADJ estancado

stagnate [stǽgnet] VI estancarse

stagnation [stægnéʃən] N estancamiento *m*

staid [sted] ADJ envarado

stain [sten] N (spot) mancha *f*; (color) tinte *m*, tintura *f*; VI/VT (spot) manchar[se]; (color) teñir[se]; —**ed-glass window** vitral *m*

stainless [sténlɪs] ADJ sin mancha; — **steel** acero inoxidable *m*

stair [stɛr] N peldaño *m*, escalón *m*; —**case** escalera *f*; —**s** escalera *f*; —**way** escalera *f*

stake [stek] N (pole) estaca *f*; (investment) interés *m*; (bet) apuesta *f*; **at** — en juego; **to die at the** — morir en la hoguera; VT estacar; **to** — **out** vigilar

stalactite [stəlǽktaɪt] N estalactita *f*

stalagmite [stəlǽgmaɪt] N estalagmita *f*

stale [steł] ADJ (bread) duro; (air) viciado; (joke) viejo; —**mate** punto muerto *m*

stalk [stɔk] N tallo *m*; VT acechar

stall [stɔł] N (at a market) puesto *m*; (at a fair) caseta *f*, barraca *f*; (in a stable) compartimiento *m*; VI (airplane) entrar en pérdida; (talks) llegar a un punto muerto; (motor) pararse; **he is —ing** está arrastrando los pies; VT (airplane) hacer entrar en pérdida; (talks) paralizar; (motor) parar

stallion [stǽljən] N semental *m*

stamina [stǽmənə] N resistencia *f*, aguante *m*

stammer [stǽmɚ] VI balbucear; N balbuceo *m*

stamp [stæmp] VT (a letter) sellar; *Mex* timbrar; *Am* estampillar; (an official document) sellar, timbrar; (a coin) acuñar; VI (with foot) pisotear, patalear; (with hoof) piafar; **to — out** eliminar; N (on a letter) *Sp* sello *m*; *Mex* timbre *m*; *Am* estampilla *f*; (on an official document) sello *m*, timbre *m*; (instrument, character) sello *m*; (on the ground) pisotón *m*; (sound) paso *m*; **— tax** timbre *m*

stampede [stæmpíd] N estampida *f*; VI huir en estampida; VT hacer huir en estampida

stance [stæns] N posición *f*, postura *f*; (political) posicionamiento *m*

stanch, staunch [stɔntʃ] VT restañar; ADJ (strong) firme; (loyal) fiel

stand [stænd] VI (take a standing position) ponerse de pie, levantarse; *Am* parar[se]; (to be in a standing position) estar de pie; *Am* estar parado; (stop) detenerse; (withstand, tolerate) aguantar, tolerar, soportar; (remain valid) mantenerse; **to — aside** apartarse; **to — back** retroceder; **to — behind someone** respaldar a alguien; **to — by** (be uninvolved) mantenerse al margen; (be alert) estar alerta; (support) respaldar; **to — for** (denote) significar; (tolerate) tolerar; **to — one's ground** mantenerse firme; **to — out** destacarse, sobresalir; **to — up for** defender; **it —s to reason** es razonable; **it —s one meter tall** mide un metro de alto; **to — a chance of** tener posibilidad de; **where do you — on this issue?** ¿qué opinas al respecto? N (at a market) puesto *m*; (at a fair) caseta *f*; (of trees) bosque *m*; (opinion) posición *f*; (for music) atril *m*; (for taxis) parada *f*; **—by** recurso viejo *m*; **—by passenger** pasajero -ra en la lista de espera *mf*; **—off** empate *m*; **—point** punto de vista *m*; **to come to a —still** pararse; **to be at a —still** estar parado; ADJ **—alone** autónomo

standard [stǽndɚd] N (of behavior) norma *f*; (of living, performance) nivel *m*; (of weights) patrón *m*; (banner) estandarte *m*; **gold —** patrón oro *m*; **—-bearer** portaestandarte *mf*; **— deviation** desviación estándar *f*; **— of living** nivel de vida *m*; **— time** hora oficial *f*; **to be up to —** satisfacer los requisitos; ADJ (normal) normal; (standardized) estándar

standardization [stændɚdizéʃən] N

standardize [stǽndɚdaɪz] VT estandarizar, uniformar

standby [stǽndbaɪ] ADV **we're flying —** estamos volando standby

standing [stǽndɪŋ] N (position) posición *f*; (rank) rango *m*; (reputation) reputación *f*; ADJ (not seated) derecho, en pie; (permanent) permanente; (stagnant) estancado; **— order** pedido fijo *m*; **— ovation** ovación de pie *f*

stank [stæŋk] *see* stink

stanza [stǽnzə] N estrofa *f*

staple [stépəł] N (for paper) grapa *f*; (main product) producto principal *m*; (food) alimento básico *m*; ADJ (principal) principal; (basic) básico; VT engrapar

stapler [stéplɚ] N grapadora *f*

star [stɑr] N estrella *f* (also actor); (asterisk) asterisco *m*; **— attraction** atracción principal *f*; **—fish** estrella de mar *f*; **—light** luz de las estrellas *f*; **—-spangled** salpicado de estrellas; **a — student** un[a] estudiante sobresaliente; VT (act in) protagonizar; (put asterisk on) marcar con asterisco; (cover with stars) estrellar

starboard [stárbərd] N estribor *m*; ADV a estribor

starch [stɑrtʃ] N almidón *m* (also food); VT almidonar

stardom [stárDəm] N estrellato *m*

stare [stɛr] VI/VT mirar fijamente; N mirada fija *f*

stark [stɑrk] ADJ (landscape) yermo; (truth) descarnado, desnudo; (contrast) marcado; ADV **— naked** en cueros; **— raving mad** loco de remate

starling [stárlɪŋ] N estornino *m*

starry [stári] ADJ estrellado

start [stɑrt] VI/VT (begin) comenzar, empezar; (a car) poner[se] en marcha, arrancar; VT (a fire) provocar; VI (jump) sobresaltarse; **to — off/ out/up** empezar; **don't get him —ed** no le des cuerda; N (beginning) comienzo *m*, principio *m*; (of a race) salida *f*; (nervous jump) sobresalto *m*; (nervous jump of a horse) respingo *m*; **—-up** compañía recién establecida *f*; **—-up funds** capital inicial *m*; **— button** botón de inicio *m*; **— menu** menú de inicio *m*

starter [stárDɚ] N (on an automobile) arranque *m*; (for a race) juez de salida *mf*; **for —s** para empezar

startle [stárdl] VI/VT asustar[se], sobresaltar[se]

startling [stárdlɪŋ] ADJ asombroso, sorprendente

starvation [stɑrvéʃən] N inanición *f*

starve [stɑrv] VI/VT hambrear; VI morirse de hambre; VT matar de hambre; (for affection) privar de cariño

starving [stárvɪŋ] ADJ hambriento, muerto de

hambre

stash [stæʃ] VI **to — away** ir ahorrando; N alijo *m*

state [stet] N estado *m*; **— of the art** con los últimos avances; **—room** (on a ship) camarote *m*; (on a train) compartimiento *m*; **—-run company** compañía estatal *f*; **—sman** estadista *m*; **—swoman** estadista *f*; VT (declare) declarar, aseverar, manifestar; (describe) exponer

stately [stétli] ADJ majestuoso, imponente

statement [stétmənt] N (declaration) declaración *f*, aseveración *f*; (bill) estado de cuentas *m*

static [stǽDɪk] ADJ estático; N interferencia *f*; **— electricity** electricidad estática *f*; **don't give me any** — no me compliquen la vida

station [stéʃən] N estación *f*; (on the radio) emisora *f*; (on television) canal *m*; (social rank) condición *f*; **— wagon** camioneta *f*; VT (a sentry) apostar; (troops) estacionar

stationary [stéʃəneri] ADJ (not moving) estacionario; (stopped) detenido; (fixed) fijo

stationery [stéʃəneri] N (material) artículos de papelería *m pl*; (paper) papel de carta *m*

statistical [stətístɪkəl] ADJ estadístico

statistics [stətístɪks] N (science) estadística *f*; (data) estadísticas *f pl*

statue [stǽtʃu] N estatua *f*

stature [stǽtʃɚ] N (physical) estatura *f*; (moral) talla *f*

status [stǽDəs] N (prestige, rank) status *m*; (legal, financial) situación *f*; (marital) estado *m*; **— bar** (computer) barra de estado *f*; **— symbol** símbolo de status *m*

statute [stǽtʃut] N (bylaw) estatuto *m*; (law) ley *f*; **— of limitations** ley de prescripción *f*

statutory [stǽtʃətɔri] ADJ estatutario; **— rape** estupro *m*

stave [stev] N (of a barrel) duela *f*; VI **to — off** evitar

stay [ste] VI (remain) quedarse, permanecer; **to — away** mantenerse alejado; **to — in** quedarse en casa; **to — out of trouble** no meterse en líos; **to — up** quedarse levantado; VT **to — an execution** aplazar una ejecución; N (time spent) estancia *f*, estadía *f*, permanencia *f*; (support) sostén *m*, soporte *m*

STD [sexually transmitted disease] [éstídí] N ETS *f*

stead [sted] N **in her — en su lugar**; **to stand one in good —** ser de provecho para uno

steadfast [stédfæst] ADJ fijo, firme

steadiness [stéDɪnɪs] N (firmness) firmeza *f*; (of the hand) pulso *m*; (constancy) constancia *f*; (continuity) continuidad *f*

steady [stéDi] ADJ (not shaky) firme; (constant) constante; (continuous) continuo; **— boyfriend** novio formal *m*; **— customer** cliente -ta asiduo -dua *mf*; **— income** ingreso

fijo *m*; VI/VT (an object) asegurar; (nerves) calmar

steak [stek] N bistec *m*, churrasco *m*

steal [stil] VT (a thing, a base) robar, hurtar; (a girlfriend) soplar; VI **to — away/out** escabullirse, escaparse; N (bargain) ganga *f*

stealth [stɛlθ] N sigilo *m*; **by —** furtivamente

stealthy [stɛlθi] ADJ furtivo

steam [stim] N (evaporated water) vapor *m*; (arising from an object) vaho *m*; **— engine** máquina de vapor *f*; **— roller** apisonadora *f*, aplanadora *f*; **— ship** [buque de] vapor *m*; **— shovel** excavadora *f*; VT (cook) cocer al vapor; VI (give off steam) echar vapor; **to get —ed up** (angry) indignarse; (covered with vapor) empañarse

steamer [stímɚ] N buque de vapor *m*

steed [stid] N corcel *m*

steel [stil] N acero *m*; **— blue** azul acero *m*; **— industry** siderurgia *f*; **— mill** acería *f*; **— wool** lana de acero *f*; VT acerar; **to — oneself** prepararse

steep [stip] ADJ (hill) empinado, escarpado, acantilado; (decline) marcado; (price) excesivo; VT (tea) infusionar; VI (tea) estar en infusión, infusionarse

steeple [stípəl] N (spire) aguja *f*, chapitel *m*; (bell tower) campanario *m*

steer [stir] N (young bovine) novillo *m*; (grown bovine) buey *m*; VI/VT (a car) conducir, manejar; (a ship) gobernar, timonear; VI (turn) girar, doblar; **to — clear of** evitar; **to — a conversation** desviar una conversación; **the car —s easily** el coche es fácil de conducir; **—ing** dirección *f*; **—ing wheel** volante *m*

stellar [stélɚ] ADJ estelar

stem [stɛm] N (of a plant) tallo *m*; (of a leaf) pedúnculo *m*, rabo *m*; (of a glass) pie *m*; (of a pipe) cañón *m*; **— cell** célula estaminal/ embrional *f*; VT detener, contener, estancar; **to — from** provenir de

stench [stɛntʃ] N hedor *m*, hediondez *f*, tufo *m*

stencil [sténsəl] N plantilla *f*, matriz *f*

stenographer [stənágrəfɚ] N taquígrafo -fa *mf*

step [stɛp] N (in walking, dancing) paso *m*; (on stairs) peldaño *m*, escalón *m*; (in music) tono *m*; **— by —** paso a paso; **—ladder** escalera *f*; **to take —s** (walk) dar pasos; VI dar un paso; **— this way** pase por aquí; **to — aside** hacerse a un lado; **to — back** retroceder; **to — down** (descend) bajar; (resign) renunciar; **to — off** bajar; **to — off a distance** medir a pasos una distancia; **to — on** pisar, pisotear; **to — on the gas** pisar el acelerador; **to — out** salir; (act) tomar medidas; **to — up** subir; **in — with the music** al compás de la música

stepbrother [stépbrʌðɚ] N hermanastro *m*

stepdaughter [stépdɔDə-] N hijastra f
stepfather [stépfaðə-] N padrastro m
stepmother [stépmʌðə-] N madrastra f
steppe [stɛp] N estepa f
stepsister [stépsɪstə-] N hermanastra f
stepson [stépsʌn] N hijastro m
stereo [stério] ADJ & N estéreo m
stereotype [stériətaɪp] N estereotipo m
sterile [stérəł] ADJ estéril
sterility [stərílɪDi] N esterilidad f
sterilize [stérəlaɪz] VT esterilizar
stern [stɜn] ADJ austero, severo, adusto; N (of a ship) popa f
sternum [stɜnəm] N esternón m
steroid [stérɔɪd] N esteroide m
stethoscope [stéθəskop] N estetoscopio m
stew [stu] VI/VT (cook) estofar[se], guisar[se]; VI (worry) preocuparse; N estofado m, guiso m; **to be in a** — estar preocupado
steward [stúə-d] N (manager) administrador m; (on a ship) camarero m; (on an airplane) auxiliar de vuelo m
stewardess [stúə-DIs] N (on a ship) camarera f; (on an airplane) auxiliar de vuelo f, azafata f
stick [stɪk] N (of wood) palo m, vara f; (of firewood) raja f; (of dynamite) cartucho m; — **shift** palanca de cambios f; —-**up** atraco m, asalto m; VI/VT (adhere) pegar[se], adherir[se]; VT (place) poner, meter; (stab) clavar, pinchar; VI (become jammed) atascarse; — **'em up!** ¡arriba las manos! **to** — **out** salir, sobresalir; **to** — **out one's head** asomar la cabeza; **to** — **out one's tongue** sacar la lengua; **to** — **to a job** persistir en una tarea; **to** — **up** (point up) estar parado de punta; **to** — **up for** defender; **to** — **someone up** asaltar/atracar a alguien
sticker [stíkə-] N (thistle) abrojo m; (adhesive) etiqueta adhesiva f
sticky [stíki] ADJ pegajoso
stiff [stɪf] ADJ (leather, cardboard) tieso, duro; (drink) fuerte, cargado; (shirt) almidonado; (back) entumecido; (test) difícil; (breeze) fuerte; (personality) envarado; (climb) arduo; (price) alto; **to get** — entumecerse; N (cadaver) fam fiambre m
stiffen [stífən] VI/VT (leather) endurecer[se]; (back) entumecer[se]; (shirt) almidonar[se]; **to** — **up** agarrotar[se]
stiffness [stífnɪs] N (of leather) dureza f, tiesura f; (of one's back) entumecimiento m; (of one's personality) envaramiento m; (of resistance) firmeza f
stifle [stáɪfəł] VI/VT ahogar[se], sofocar[se]; **to** — **a yawn** contener un bostezo
stigma [stígmə] N estigma m
stigmatize [stígmətaɪz] VI/VT estigmatizar
still [stɪł] ADJ (not moving) quieto; (quiet) silencioso; —**born** nacido muerto; — **life**

naturaleza muerta f; VT acallar; ADV todavía, aún; **he's** — **here** todavía está [aquí]; CONJ de todos modos, en todo caso; —, **it's a good buy** en todo caso, es una ganga; N (for distilling) alambique m; (quiet) silencio m
stillness [stílnɪs] N (not moving) quietud f; (silence) silencio m
stilt [stɪłt] N (for walking) zanco m; (support) pilote m
stilted [stíłtɪd] ADJ (personality) envarado; (style) afectado
stimulant [stímjələnt] ADJ & N estimulante m
stimulate [stímjəlet] VT estimular
stimulation [stɪmjəléʃən] N estimulación f
stimulus [stímjələs] N estímulo m
sting [stɪŋ] VI/VT (insects, thorns) picar; (insects) aguijonear; VT (shampoo) hacer picar; (rain) azotar; (cheat) timar; N (pain) picadura f; (stinger) aguijón m; (confidence game) golpe m; — **of remorse** punzada de remordimiento f; —**ray** manta raya f
stinger [stíŋə-] N aguijón m
stinginess [stíndʒɪnɪs] N tacañería f, mezquindad f
stingy [stíndʒi] ADJ mezquino, tacaño
stink [stɪŋk] VI (smell bad) heder, apestar; **to** — **of** heder a; **to** — **up** dar mal olor a; **your performance** —**s** tu actuación es un desastre; N hedor m
stipend [stáɪpɪnd] N (fellowship) beca f; (salary) estipendio m
stipulate [stípjəlet] VT estipular
stipulation [stɪpjəléʃən] N estipulación f
stir [stɜ-] VI (move) bullir, rebullir; (awaken) despertar; VT (mix) revolver; (move emotionally) conmover; (stoke) atizar; **to** — **up** (trouble) provocar, suscitar; (an old grudge) remover; **to** —-**fry** saltear; N —-**crazy** claustrofóbico; **to give something a** — revolver algo; **to cause a** — causar revuelo
stirring [stɜ-ɪŋ] ADJ (moving) conmovedor
stirrup [stɜ-rəp] N estribo m
stitch [stɪtʃ] N (in sewing) puntada f; (on a wound) punto m; **to be in** —**es** desternillarse de risa; VI/VT coser
St. Kitts and Nevis [sentkítsənnívɪs] N San Cristóbal y Nieves m
St. Lucia [sentlúʃə] N Santa Lucía f
St. Lucian [sentlúʃən] ADJ & N santalucense mf
stock [stak] N (selection) surtido m; (reserves) existencias f pl; (livestock) ganado m; (lineage) estirpe f; (shares) acciones f pl, valores m pl; (in grafting) patrón m; (broth) caldo m; —**broker** corredor -ora de bolsa mf, bolsista mf; — **company** sociedad anónima f; — **exchange** bolsa de valores f; —**holder** accionista mf; — **market** mercado de valores m, bolsa de valores f; — **market trends** tendencias bursátiles f pl; — **options**

opciones *f pl*; **—pile** acopio *m*; **—room**
depósito *m*; **—size** tamaño ordinario *m*;
—yard corral *m*; **in**— en existencia; **out of**
— agotado; VT (sell) vender; (fill shelves)
abastecer; **to**— **up on** surtirse de, acumular;
to —pile acopiar; ADJ (trite) trillado
stockade [stɑkéd] N (fence) estacada *f*,
empalizada *f*; (prison) prisión militar *f*
stocking [stákɪŋ] N (hose) media *f*; (sock)
calcetín *m*
stocky [stáki] ADJ robusto
stoic [stóɪk] ADJ & N estoico -ca *mf*
stoke [stok] VT (fire) atizar; (engine) alimentar
stole [stol] (fur) estola *f*
stole [stol] *see* steal
stolen [stólən] *see* steal
stomach [stámək] N (organ) estómago *m*; (belly)
panza *f*, barriga *f*; **he has a big**— es
barrigón; **to lie on one's**— estar panza
abajo; VT (tolerate) aguantar
stomp [stɑmp] VI pisar fuerte; VT (crush)
pisotear; (defeat) aplastar
stone [ston] N (rock, gem) piedra *f*; (in fruit)
hueso *m*; (in kidneys) cálculo *m*; **within a**
—'s throw a tiro de piedra; **— Age** Edad de
Piedra *f*; ADJ **—-deaf** sordo como una tapia;
VT (a person) lapidar; (a fruit) deshuesar; **to**
—wall bloquear, ignorar; **to get —d** (get
high) *fam* volarse; *Sp fam* colocarse
stony [stóni] ADJ (made of stone) pétreo;
(driveway) pedregoso; (silence) sepulcral
stood [stʊd] *see* stand
stool [stuł] N (furniture) taburete *m*, banqueta *f*;
(excrement) materia fecal *f*; **— pigeon**
soplón -ona *mf*, chivato -ta *mf*
stoop [stup] VI (bend over) agacharse; (have bad
posture) encorvarse; **to — to** rebajarse a; N
(posture) encorvamiento *m*; (porch) entrada
f, porche *m*; **to walk with a**— andar
encorvado; ADJ **—-shouldered** encorvado,
cargado de espaldas
stop [stɑp] VI (halt) parar, detenerse;
(malfunction) parar[se]; VT (halt) parar,
detener; (cancel) cancelar; (suspend)
suspender; (plug) tapar; **to — at nothing** no
tener escrúpulos; **to — by/in** visitar; **to —**
from impedir; **to — over at** hacer escala en;
to — short parar en seco; **to — up** tapar,
atascar; **it —ped raining** paró/dejó de
llover; N parada *f*, detención *f*; (on organ)
registro *m*; **—gap** arreglo provisorio *m*;
—light semáforo *m*; **—over** escala *f*; **— sign**
Sp stop *m*; *Am* señal de pare *f*; *Mex* alto *m*;
—volley (tennis) dejada de volea *f*; **—watch**
cronómetro *m*; **to bring to a**— parar; **to**
make a— parar
stoppage [stápɪdʒ] N interrupción *f*; (strike)
huelga *f*
stopper [stápɚ] N tapón *m*

storage [stóridʒ] N almacenaje *m*,
almacenamiento *m*; (of electronic data)
almacenamiento *m*; **— battery** acumulador
m; **— device** dispositivo de almacenamiento
m; **to keep in**— almacenar
store [stor] N (shop) tienda *f*, almacén *m*; (supply)
reserva *f*, provisión *f*; **—house** (warehouse)
almacén *m*, depósito *m*; (source) mina *f*,
fuente *f*; **—keeper** tendero -ra *mf*,
almacenista *mf*; **—room** almacén *m*, depósito
m; **what is in — for us?** ¿qué nos espera? VT
(commercial goods) almacenar; (personal
effects) guardar; **to — up** acumular
stork [stɔrk] N cigüeña *f*
storm [stɔrm] N (on land) tormenta *f*; (at sea)
tempestad *f*, temporal *m*; (of protest) ola *f*; **—**
troops tropas de asalto *f pl*; VT (attack) tomar
por asalto; VI **to — in/out** entrar/salir en
tromba
stormy [stɔ́rmi] ADJ tormentoso, tempestuoso
story [stóri] N (tale) cuento *m*, historia *f*;
(newspaper article) artículo *m*; (lie) mentira *f*;
(information) información *f*; (plot)
argumento *m*, trama *f*; (floor) piso *m*
stout [staʊt] ADJ (fat) corpulento; (robust)
robusto, fornido; (strong) fuerte;
(courageous) valiente
stove [stov] N (for heating) estufa *f*; (for cooking)
cocina *f*; estufa *f*
stow [sto] VT (keep) guardar; (hide) esconder;
(put in cargo hold) estibar; **to — away on a**
ship viajar de polizón
stowaway [stóəwe] N polizón -ona *mf*
straddle [strǽdl̩] VI/VT estar a horcajadas; VT (a
fence) ponerse a horcajadas; (one's legs) abrir;
(not take sides) no comprometerse
strafe [stref] VT ametrallar
straggle [strǽgəl] VI **to — along/behind**
rezagarse; **to — in** entrar de a pocos
straight [stret] ADJ (not curved) recto; (not
tilted) derecho; (in succession) seguido; (hair)
lacio, liso; (teeth) parejo; (frank) franco;
(heterosexual) heterosexual; **— A's**
sobresaliente en todo; **—edge** regla *f*; **— face**
cara seria *f*; **— flush** escalera de color *f*; ADJ
—forward (honest) honesto; (simple)
sencillo, campechano; (clear) claro; ADV **—**
ahead todo derecho, todo recto; **for two**
hours— dos horas seguidas; **to come —**
home volver derecho a casa; **to leave —**
after lunch irse justo después de comer; **to**
set a person— aclararle algo a alguien; **tell**
me— dímelo francamente; **he can't think**
— no puede pensar con claridad; N (of a
racetrack) recta *f*
straighten [strétn̩] VI/VT enderezar[se];
(situation) arreglar[se]; VT (hair) alisar, *RP*
laciar; **to — out a child** enderezar a un niño
straightness [strétnɪs] N derechura *f*

strain [stren] VI (pull) tironear; (try hard) esforzarse; VT (exhaust) agotar; (hurt voice) forzar; (injure a joint) torcer; (injure a muscle) sufrir un tirón en; (hurt a relationship) crear una tirantez en; VI/VT (filter) colar[se]; N (effort) esfuerzo *m*; (injury) torcedura *f*; (pressure) presión *f*; (trouble in a relationship) tirantez *f*; (lineage) cepa *f*

strainer [strénə-] N colador *m*

strait [stret] N estrecho *m*; **in dire —s** en aprietos; **—jacket** camisa de fuerza *f*, chaleco de fuerza *m*; ADJ **—laced** puritano

strand [strænd] VI/VT (a ship) encallar, varar; VT (a person) dejar plantado; **to be —ed** (boat) estar encallado; (person) quedar plantado; N (beach) costa *f*, playa *f*; (of rope) ramal *m*; (of thread) hebra *f*; (of hair) mechón *m*

strange [strendʒ] ADJ (bizarre) extraño, raro; (unknown) desconocido

strangeness [strénʤnɪs] N (unusualness) lo extraño, rareza *f*; (unexpectedness) lo inesperado

stranger [strénʤə-] N (unknown person) extraño -ña *mf*, desconocido -da *mf*; (outsider) forastero -ra *mf*; **to be no — to something** tener experiencia con algo

strangle [strǽŋgəl] VI/VT estrangular[se]; VT (creativity) coartar; N **—hold** (in wrestling) llave al cuello *f*; (in markets) monopolio *m*

strap [stræp] N (leather band) correa *f*, tira *f*; (on a dress) tirante *m*; VT atar con correa; **to — in** amarrar[se], abrochar[se]

stratagem [strǽDəʤəm] N estratagema *f*

strategic [strətíʤɪk] ADJ estratégico

strategy [strǽDəʤi] N estrategia *f*

stratosphere [strǽDəsfir] N estratosfera *f*

stratum [strǽDəm] N estrato *m*

straw [strɔ] N paja *f* (also for drinking); **—berry** fresa *f*; **— man** testaferro *m*; **— vote** votación de prueba *f*; ADJ **—-colored** pajizo

stray [stre] VI (deviate, digress) desviarse; (get lost) perderse; (wander) vagar; (sin) descarriarse, perderse; ADJ extraviado, perdido; N perro/gato mostrenco *m*

streak [strik] N (line) raya *f*; (vein) vena *f*; (of luck) racha *f*; (of light) rayo *m*; VI (run naked) correr desnudo; (get discolored) aclararse

stream [strim] N (jet) chorro *m*; (river) río *m*; (brook) arroyo *m*; ADJ **—lined** (vehículo) aerodinámico; (business) racionalizado; VI (water) correr, fluir; (blood) derramar; **to — out** brotar, manar; **to — in** entrar a raudales

streaming [strímɪŋ] N corriente *f*, flujo *m*; **— audio** flujo continuo de datos de audio *m*; **— video** flujo continuo de datos de vídeo *m*

street [strit] N calle *f*; **—car** tranvía *f*; **—lamp** farol *m*, poste de alumbrado *m*; **— sweeper** barrendero -ra *mf*; **—walker** prostituta *f*

strength [strɛŋθ] N fuerza *f*; (spiritual) firmeza *f*;

on the — of en base a

strengthen [strɛ́ŋθən] VI/VT fortalecer[se], reforzar[se]

strengthening [strɛ́ŋθənɪŋ] N fortalecimiento *m*

strenuous [strénjuəs] ADJ arduo

strep throat [strépθrót] N infección por estreptococo *f*

stress [strɛs] N (tension) tensión *f*; (strain) estrés *m*; (pressure) esfuerzo *m*; (emphasis) énfasis *m*; (accent) acento *m*; **— test** prueba de esfuerzo *f*; VT (emphasize) enfatizar; (accentuate) acentuar; (exert force) someter a un esfuerzo; (put under pressure) estresar; **to — out** estresarse

stressful [strésfəl] ADJ estresante

stretch [stretʃ] VI/VT (make or become longer) estirar[se], alargar[se]; (extend) extender[se]; (exaggerate) exagerar; **to — oneself** estirarse, desperezarse; **to — out** (lengthen) extender[se]; (lie) tumbarse, tenderse; N (act of stretching) desperezo *m*; (segment of road) trecho *m*, tramo *m*; (period of time) período *m*; (exaggeration) exageración *f*; **— mark** estría *f*

stretcher [strétʃə-] N camilla *f*

strew [stru] VT esparcir

strewn [strun] *see* strew

stricken [stríkən] ADJ (with disease) aquejado; (by a flood) afectado, (with fear) aterrado

stricken [stríkən] *see* strike

strict [strɪkt] ADJ estricto; **in — confidence** en absoluta confianza

stridden [strídn] *see* stride

stride [straɪd] VI caminar a paso largo, dar zancadas; N (gait) paso *m*; (long step) zancada *f*, tranco *m*

strident [stráɪdənt] ADJ estridente

strife [straɪf] N conflictos *m pl*

strike [straɪk] VI/VT (hit) golpear, pegar; (stop work) hacer huelga [contra]; VT (find oil, etc.) dar con, encontrar; (occur to) ocurrírsele a uno; (cross out) tachar; (mark by chimes) dar; (light a match, etc.) encender; (make a coin) acuñar; **to — a compromise/deal** llegar a un acuerdo; **to — one's fancy** antojársele a uno; **to — out** (cross out) tachar; (set forth) encaminarse; (fail) fracasar; (in baseball) poncharse; **to — someone out** ponchar a alguien; **to — up a conversation** entablar conversación; **to — up a friendship** trabar amistad; **how does she — you?** ¿qué tal te parece? N (work stoppage) huelga *f*; (attack) ataque *m*; (finding of oil) descubrimiento *m*; (in baseball) strike *m*; **—breaker** esquirol *m*, rompehuelgas *m sg*; **—out** ponchado *m*, ponche *m*; **—through** tachado *m*; **— zone** zona de strike *f*; **called —** strike cantado *m*

striker [stráɪkə-] N (person on strike) huelguista *mf*; (of a bell) badajo *m*; (in soccer) artillero

-ra *mf*
striking [stráɪkɪŋ] ADJ (unusual, conspicuous) notable; (attractive) llamativo; (on strike) en huelga
string [strɪŋ] N (cord) cuerda *f*, cordel *m*; (of pearls, lies) sarta *f*; (of questions) serie *f*; (of data) secuencia *f*; (of beans) fibra *f*; (of garlic, peppers) ristra *f*; — **bean** habichuela *f*, judía verde *f*; —**s** (in an orchestra) cuerdas *f pl*; (on a tennis racket) cordaje *m*, encordado *m*; **no —s attached** sin condiciones; VT (beads) ensartar; (a musical instrument) encordar; **to — along** tener en ascuas; **to — out** extender[se], prolongar[se]; **to — up** colgar, ahorcar; **to be strung out** estar muy tenso
stringent [stríndʒənt] ADJ (law, need) riguroso; (time limit) estrecho, ajustado
strip [strɪp] VI/VT (make/get naked) desnudar[se]; VT (remove bark) descortezar; (remove leaves) deshojar; (remove sheets) deshacer; (remove varnish) quitar el barniz; (damage gears) estropear el engranaje; **to — search** registrar al desnudo; **to —-mine** explotar a cielo abierto; N (of a thing) tira *f*; (of land) faja *f*; — **mall** centro comercial *m*; — **search** registro al desnudo *m*; —**tease** strip-tease *m*
stripe [straɪp] N (band) raya *f*, lista *f*, banda *f*; (military insignia) galón *m*; (type) tipo *m*
striped [straɪpt, stráɪpɪd] ADJ listado, rayado
stripper [strɪpə-] N striptisero -ra *mf*
strive [straɪv] VI esforzarse por, luchar por
striven [strívən] *see* strive
strode [strod] *see* stride
stroke [strok] N (in golf, tennis, of luck, of genius) golpe *m*; (cerebral hemorrhage) derrame cerebral *m*; (movement in swimming) brazada *f*; (style in swimming) estilo *m*; (of a piston) carrera *f*; (of a painter's brush) pincelada *f*, trazo *m*; (of lightning) rayo *m*; **at the — of ten** al dar las diez; VT (pet) acariciar; (praise) halagar
stroll [strol] VI dar un paseo, pasearse; N paseo *m*, caminata *f*
stroller [strólə-] N cochecito de bebé *m*
strong [strɔŋ] ADJ fuerte; (husky) recio; (eyesight, probability) bueno; (protest) enérgico; (views, faith, support) firme; (features, resemblance) marcado; (argument) sólido; —**hold** (fortress) fortaleza *f*; (center of activity) baluarte *m*; —**-willed** (resolute) resuelto, decidido; (stubborn) terco; ADV **to be going** — seguir activo; VT **to —-arm** intimidar
strongly [strɔ́ŋli] ADV (argue, object) enérgicamente; (pull) con fuerza
strove [strov] *see* strive
struck [strʌk] *see* strike
structural [strʌ́ktʃərəl] ADJ estructural

structure [strʌ́ktʃə-] N (the way parts are arranged) estructura *f*; (thing constructed) construcción *f*; VT estructurar
structuring [strʌ́ktʃə-ɪŋ] N estructuración *f*
struggle [strʌ́gəl] VI (with difficulties) luchar, bregar; (with an assailant) forcejear; **she —s in math** la pasa mal en matemáticas; N lucha *f*; (of ideas) pugna *f*, lucha *f*; (fight) contienda *f*, forcejeo *m*; **it's a** — da mucho trabajo
strung [strʌŋ] *see* string
strut [strʌt] VI pavonearse; N pavoneo *m*; (support) tirante *m*, puntal *m*; (shock absorber) amortiguador *m*
strychnine [stríknaɪn] N estricnina *f*
stub [stʌb] N talón *m*; VT **to — one's toe** dar[se] un tropezón, reventarse el dedo
stubble [stʌ́bəl] N (of a crop) rastrojo *m*; (of a beard) barba de unos días *f*
stubborn [stʌ́bə-n] ADJ terco, testarudo
stubbornness [stʌ́bə-nnɪs] N terquedad *f*, testarudez *f*
stucco [stʌ́ko] N estuco *m*; VT estucar
stuck [stʌk] ADJ (unable to move) atascado; (adhering) pegado; **to be — on someone** estar loco por alguien; —**-up** estirado, presumido
stuck [stʌk] *see* stick
stud [stʌd] N (knob) tachuela *f*, tachón *m*; (earring) arete *m*; (cufflink) gemelo *m*; (on shirtfront) botón *m*; (horse, man) semental *m*; (horse) garañón *m*; VT tachonar
student [stúdn̩t] N alumno -na *mf*; (secondary, university) estudiante *mf*; — **body** alumnado *m*; ADJ estudiantil
studio [stúdio] N estudio *m*, taller *m*; — **apartment** estudio *m*
studious [stúdiəs] ADJ estudioso
study [stʌ́di] N estudio *m*; VT estudiar
stuff [stʌf] N (material) materia *f*, material *m*; (things) trastos *m pl*, bártulos *m pl*; (cloth) paño *m*, tela *f*; (affair) cosa *f*; (junk) cachivaches *m pl*; VT (mattress) rellenar; (dead animal) embalsamar, disecar; **to — into** meter en; **I'm —ed** estoy lleno
stuffing [stʌ́fɪŋ] N relleno *m*
stuffy [stʌ́fi] ADJ (person) envarado; (air) viciado; (nose) tapado
stumble [stʌ́mbəl] VI (trip) tropezar, trastabillar, dar un traspié; (stutter) balbucear; **to — out** salir a tropezones; **to — upon** tropezar con; **stumbling block** obstáculo *m*; N tropezón *m*, tropiezo *m*, traspié *m*
stump [stʌmp] N (of a tree) tocón *m*, cepa *f*; (of a tooth) raigón *m*; (of a limb) muñón *m*; **to be on the** — hacer una campaña electoral; VT (baffle) dejar perplejo; (remove stumps) arrancar los tocones de; **to — the country** recorrer el país haciendo campaña

stun [stʌn] VT (shock, surprise) dejar atónito, pasmar; (render unconscious) dejar sin sentido; — **gun** pistola tranquilizante *f*
stung [stʌŋ] *see* sting
stunk [stʌŋk] *see* stink
stunning [stʌ́nɪŋ] ADJ (shocking) pasmoso; (beautiful) elegante, bellísimo
stunt [stʌnt] VT (stop growth) atrofiar; (do acrobatic tricks) hacer acrobacia; N (feat) acrobacia *f*; (for publicity) maniobra *f*; —**man** doble *m*; —**woman** doble *f*; **to pull a** — hacerse el listo
stupefy [stúpəfaɪ] VT (make lethargic) atontar, embrutecer; (astonish) dejar estupefacto, alelar
stupendous [stupéndəs] ADJ estupendo
stupid [stúpɪd] ADJ tonto, estúpido, majadero
stupidity [stupídɪDi] N tontería *f*, estupidez *f*, majadería *f*
stupor [stúpɚ] N estupor *m*
sturdy [stɝ́Di] ADJ (person) fornido, fuerte; (construction) sólido, robusto
stutter [stʌ́Dɚ] VI tartamudear, tartajear; VT decir tartamudeando; N (act of stuttering) tartamudeo *m*; (speech defect) tartamudez *f*
stutterer [stʌ́Dərɚ] N tartamudo -da *mf*
stuttering [stʌ́Dərɪŋ] ADJ tartamudo; N (act of stuttering) tartamudeo *m*; (speech defect) tartamudez *f*
St. Vincent and the Grenadines [sentvínsəntəndəgrénədinz] N San Vicente y las Granadinas *m*
sty [staɪ] N (for pigs) pocilga *f*; (in eye) orzuelo *m*
style [staɪɫ] N estilo *m*; (type) modelo *m*; — **sheet** página de estilo *f*; **out of** — fuera de moda; **like it's going out of** — como loco; VT (a book) intitular; (hair) peinar; **he —s himself Professor Smith** se hace llamar Profesor Smith
stylish [stáɪlɪʃ] ADJ elegante, de moda
stylistic [staɪlístɪk] ADJ estilístico
stylistics [staɪlístɪks] N estilística *f*
stymie, stymy [stáɪmi] VT obstaculizar
Styrofoam™ [stáɪrəfom] N poliestireno *m*
suave [swav] ADJ urbano, educado
subcommittee [sʌ́bkəmɪDi] N subcomité *m*
subconscious [sʌbkánʃəs] ADJ subconsciente
subcontract [sʌbkántrækt] VT subcontratar
subdivide [sʌbdɪváɪd] VT subdividir
subdivision [sʌbdɪvɪʒən] N subdivisión *f*; (of land) parcelación *f*
subdue [səbdú] VT (overcome, vanquish) sojuzgar, someter, rendir; (repress) reprimir; (attenuate) atenuar
subdued [səbdúd] ADJ (atmosphere) tranquilo; (mood) deprimido; (lighting, color) tenue
subject[1] [sʌ́bdʒɪkt] N (of a king) súbdito -ta *mf*; (of a sentence, in an experiment) sujeto *m*; (in school) asignatura *f*, materia *f*; — **matter**

tema *m*; ADV LOC — **to** (changes, laws, conditions) sujeto a; (depression, earthquakes) propenso a
subject[2] [səbdʒékt] VT someter
subjection [səbdʒékʃən] N sometimiento *m*
subjective [səbdʒéktɪv] ADJ subjetivo
subjectivity [sʌbdʒektívɪDi] N subjetividad *f*
subjugate [sʌ́bdʒəget] VT sojuzgar, avasallar
subjunctive [səbdʒʌ́ŋktɪv] ADJ & N subjuntivo *m*
sublet [sʌ́blét] VI/VT subarrendar
sublime [səbláɪm] ADJ sublime
submarine [sʌbmərín, sʌ́bmərin] ADJ submarino; N submarino *m*
submerge [səbmɝ́dʒ] VI/VT sumergir[se]
submerged [səbmɝ́dʒd] ADJ inmerso, sumergido
submission [səbmíʃən] N (humility) sumisión *f*; (subjugation) sometimiento *m*, sumisión *f*; (sending) entrega *f*, envío *m*
submissive [səbmísɪv] ADJ sumiso
submit [səbmít] VI/VT someter[se]; (to a judge) elevar[se]; **to** — **a report** presentar un informe
subordinate[1] [səbórdn̩ɪt] ADJ & N subordinado -da *mf*, subalterno -na *mf*
subordinate[2] [səbórdn̩et] VT subordinar
subpar [sʌbpár] ADJ inferior
subpoena [səpínə] N citación *f*, orden de comparecencia *f*
subroutine [sʌ́brutin] N subrutina *f*
subscribe [səbskráɪb] VI (underwrite, sign) suscribir; (receive a magazine) abonarse, suscribirse; (agree with) adherirse a
subscriber [səbskráɪbɚ] N (to shares) suscriptor -ora *mf*; (to services) abonado -da *mf*; (to a magazine) suscriptor -ora *mf*, abonado -da *mf*; (to an idea) partidario -ria *mf*
subscript [sʌ́bskrɪpt] N subíndice *m*
subscription [səbskrípʃən] N suscripción *f*, abono *m*
subsequent [sʌ́bsɪkwənt] ADJ subsiguiente
subsequently [sʌ́bsɪkwəntli] N posteriormente, con posterioridad *f*
subservient [səbsɝ́viənt] ADJ servil
subside [səbsáɪd] VI (sediment) hundirse; (water level) bajar; (volcano, storm, anger) calmarse, aquietarse
subsidiary [səbsídiɛri] ADJ subsidiario; N sucursal *f*, filial *f*
subsidize [sʌ́bsɪdaɪz] VT subvencionar, subsidiar
subsidy [sʌ́bsɪDi] N subvención *f*, subsidio *m*
substance [sʌ́bstəns] N sustancia *f*; — **abuse** abuso de sustancias *m*
substandard [sʌbstǽndɚd] ADJ de calidad inferior
substantial [səbstǽnʃəɫ] ADJ (changes) sustancial; (food, lecture) sustancioso; (furniture) sólido; (amount) considerable, importante; **to be in** — **agreement** estar

básicamente de acuerdo
substantiate [səbstǽnʃiet] VT (verify) verificar; (prove) probar
substantive [sʌ́bstəntɪv] ADJ & N sustantivo *m*
substitute [sʌ́bstɪtut] VT sustituir, reemplazar; I **—d water for milk** usé agua en vez de leche, sustituí/reemplacé la leche por agua; VI **John —d for Mary** Juan sustituyó/ reemplazó a María; N (one who substitutes) sustituto *m*, reemplazo *m*; (teacher, athlete) suplente *mf*; (thing) sucedáneo *m*
substitution [sʌbstɪtúʃən] N sustitución *f*; **the — of water for milk** la sustitución de leche por agua
subterfuge [sʌ́btɚfjudʒ] N subterfugio *m*
subterranean [sʌbtərénɪən] ADJ subterráneo
subtitle [sʌ́btaɪdl̩] N subtítulo *m*
subtle [sʌ́dl̩] ADJ sutil
subtlety [sʌ́dl̩ti] N sutileza *f*
subtotal [sʌ́btodl̩] N subtotal *m*
subtract [səbtrǽkt] VT (deduct) restar; (take away) sustraer
subtraction [səbtrǽkʃən] N sustracción *f*, resta *f*
suburb [sʌ́bɚb] N barrio residencial periférico *m*
suburban [səbɝ́bən] ADJ (residential) residencial; (on the outskirts) periférico
subversive [səbvɝ́sɪv] ADJ subversivo
subway [sʌ́bwe] N metropolitano *m*, metro *m*, subterráneo *m*
succeed [səksíd] VI (be successful) tener éxito; (manage) lograr; **to — to** heredar; VT (follow) suceder a
success [səksés] N éxito *m*
successful [səksésfəl] ADJ (person) exitoso; (effort) productivo, satisfactorio; **to be —** tener éxito
succession [səkséʃən] N sucesión *f*
successive [səksésɪv] ADJ sucesivo
successor [səksésɚ] N sucesor -ora *mf*
succinct [səksíŋkt] ADJ sucinto, escueto
succor [sʌ́kɚ] N socorro *m*; VT socorrer
succumb [səkʌ́m] VI sucumbir
such [sʌtʃ] ADJ tal; **— as** tal como; **at — and — a place** en tal o cual lugar; **he's — an idiot!** ¡es tan idiota! **in — a case** en tal caso / en semejante caso; **there's no — thing** eso no existe; PRON **hobbies, pastimes, and —** hobbies, pasatiempos y cosas por el estilo; **a car — as yours** un coche como el tuyo; ADV **— nice neighbors** vecinos tan simpáticos
suck [sʌk] VI/VT chupar; (suckle) mamar; (vacuum, pump) aspirar; (perform fellatio) *vulg* mamarla; **to be —ed into** ser arrastrado a; VI **this book —s!** *vulg* ¡este libro es una cagada! **to — in air** aspirar; **to — up to someone** *vulg* lamerle el culo a alguien; N chupada *f*; (sexual) *vulg* mamada *f*
sucker [sʌ́kɚ] N (gullible person) primo -ma *mf*; (lollipop) *Sp* pirulí *m*; *Mex* paleta *f*; *RP*

chupetín *m*
sucrose [súkros] N sacarosa *f*
suction [sʌ́kʃən] N succión *f*, aspiración *f*
Sudan [sudǽn] N Sudán *m*
Sudanese [sudníz] ADJ & N sudanés -esa *mf*
sudden [sʌ́dn̩] ADJ súbito, repentino, brusco; — **death** (also in sports) muerte súbita *f*; — **infant death syndrome** síndrome de muerte infantil súbita *m*; **all of a —** de repente, de improviso
suddenly [sʌ́dn̩li] ADV de repente, repentinamente
suddenness [sʌ́dn̩nɪs] N brusquedad *f*, lo repentino
suds [sʌdz] N espuma *f*
sue [su] VI/VT demandar, poner pleito; **to — for** pedir, suplicar; **to — for damages** demandar por daños y perjuicios
suede [swed] N gamuza *f*, ante *m*
suffer [sʌ́fɚ] VI/VT (feel pain) sufrir, padecer; VT (tolerate) tolerar
sufferer [sʌ́fərɚ] N paciente *mf*
suffering [sʌ́fəɪŋ] N sufrimiento *m*, padecimiento *m*
suffice [səfáɪs] VI/VT bastar, ser suficiente
sufficient [səfíʃənt] ADJ suficiente, bastante
suffix [sʌ́fɪks] N sufijo *m*
suffocate [sʌ́fəket] VI/VT ahogar[se], sofocar[se]; (to die, kill) asfixiar[se]
suffocation [sʌfəkéʃən] N ahogo *m*, sofoco *m*
suffrage [sʌ́frɪdʒ] N sufragio *m*
sugar [ʃúgɚ] N azúcar *mf*; (endearment) cariño *m*; — **cane** caña de azúcar *f*; VT azucarar; **to — the pill** dorar la píldora
suggest [səgdʒést] VT (propose) sugerir; (hint) insinuar; **—ed retail price** precio sugerido *m*
suggestion [səgdʒéstʃən] N (proposal) sugerencia *f*; (in hypnosis) sugestión *f*
suggestive [səgdʒéstɪv] ADJ insinuante; **to be — of** evocar
suicide [súɪsaɪd] N (act) suicidio *m*; (person) suicida *mf*; **to commit —** suicidarse
suit [sut] N (clothes) traje *m*; (in cards) palo *m*, color *m*; (lawsuit) demanda *f*, pleito *m*, querella *f*; **—case** maleta *f*, valija *f*; VT (adapt) adaptar, ajustar; (satisfy) satisfacer; (look good) quedarle bien a, sentarle bien a; (be convenient, appropriate) convenir, venir bien; **— yourself** haz lo que te parezca
suitable [súɪəbəl] ADJ (appropriate) apropiado; (apt) apto
suitably [súɪəbli] ADV como corresponde
suite [swit] N (series) serie *f*; (series of rooms, musical composition) suite *f*; (furniture) juego *m*; (software) paquete de programas de productividad *m*
suitor [súɪɚ] N pretendiente *m*, galán *m*
sulfate, sulphate [sʌ́łfet] N sulfato *m*

sulfide, sulphide [sʌ́lfaɪd] N sulfuro *m*

sulfur, sulphur [sʌ́lfə-] N azufre *m*

sulfuric, sulphuric [sʌlfjúrɪk] ADJ sulfúrico

sulk [sʌlk] VI enfurruñarse; N **to be in a** — estar
enfurruñado

sulky [sʌ́lki] ADJ malhumorado, enfurruñado

sullen [sʌ́lən] ADJ hosco, huraño

sully [sʌ́li] VT mancillar, ensuciar

sultry [sʌ́ltri] ADJ (hot) bochornoso, sofocante;
(sensual) sensual

sum [sʌm] N suma *f*; **in** — en resumen; VI **to** —
up resumir, recapitular

summarize [sʌ́məraɪz] VI/VT resumir

summary [sʌ́məri] N resumen *m*; ADJ sumario

summer [sʌ́mə-] N verano *m*, *lit* estío *m*; —
resort balneario *m*, lugar de veraneo *m*; —
school cursos de verano *m pl*; **—time** verano
m; VI veranear

summit [sʌ́mɪt] N cumbre *f*, cima *f*

summon [sʌ́mən] VT (a witness) citar; (an
employee, the police) llamar; N **—s** citación
judicial *f*

sumptuous [sʌ́mptʃuəs] ADJ suntuoso

sun [sʌn] N sol *m*; **to —bathe** tomar el sol;
—beam rayo de sol *m*; **—block** protector
solar *m*; **—burn** quemadura de sol *f*; **—dial**
reloj de sol *m*; **—down** puesta de[l] sol *f*;
—flower girasol *m*; **—glasses** gafas de sol *f
pl*, anteojos de sol *m pl*; — **lamp** lámpara
solar *f*; **—light** luz del sol *f*; **—rise** salida de[l]
sol *f*, amanecer *m*; **—screen** protector solar
m; **—set** puesta de[l] sol *f*; **—shine** luz [del
sol] *f*; **—spot** mancha solar *f*; **—stroke**
insolación *f*; **—tan** bronceado *m*; **—up** salida
del sol *f*; VI **to** — **oneself** tomar el sol; **to**
—burn quemar[se] al sol

Sunday [sʌ́nde] N domingo *m*; — **school** escuela
dominical *f*

sundry [sʌ́ndri] ADJ diversos

sung [sʌŋ] *see* sing

sunk [sʌŋk] *see* sink

sunny [sʌ́ni] ADJ (day, patio) soleado;
(disposition) alegre

super [súpə-] N (of a building) conserje *m*,
portero -ra *mf*; ADJ (wonderful) súper,
bárbaro

superb [supɝ́b] ADJ excelente

supercharger [súpə-tʃɑɾdʒə-] N
sobrealimentador *m*

supercomputer [súpə-kəmpjuɾə-] N *Am*
supercomputadora *f*; *Sp* superordenador *m*

superego [supə-ígo] N superego *m*, superyó *m*

superficial [supə-fíʃəl] ADJ superficial

superfluous [supɝ́fluəs] ADJ superfluo

superhuman [supə-hjúmən] ADJ sobrehumano

superimpose [supə-ɪmpóz] VT superponer,
sobreponer

superintendent [supə-ɪnténdənt] N (of work)
superintendente *mf*, supervisor -ora *mf*; (of

building) conserje *mf*, portero -ra *mf*

superior [supíriə-] ADJ & N superior *mf*

superiority [supiriɔ́rɪdi] N superioridad *f*

superlative [supɝ́ləDɪv] ADJ & N superlativo *m*

supermarket [súpə-mɑrkɪt] N supermercado *m*,
súper *m*

supernatural [supə-nǽtʃə-əl] ADJ sobrenatural

superpower [súpə-paUə-] N superpotencia *f*

superscript [súpə-skrɪpt] N superíndice *m*

supersede [supə-síd] VT reemplazar

supersonic [supə-sánɪk] ADJ supersónico

superstar [súpə-stɑr] N superestrella *f*

superstition [supə-stíʃən] N superstición *f*

superstitious [supə-stíʃəs] ADJ supersticioso

superstore [súpə-stɔr] N hipermercado *m*

supervise [súpə-vaɪz] VI/VT supervisar, fiscalizar

supervision [supə-víʒən] N supervisión *f*,
fiscalización *f*

supervisor [súpə-vaɪzə-] N supervisor -ora *mf*

supine [súpaɪn] ADJ supino

supper [sʌ́pə-] N cena *f*

supplant [səplǽnt] VT suplantar

supple [sʌ́pəl] ADJ (flexible) flexible, elástico;
(agile) ágil, grácil

supplement[1] [sʌ́pləmənt] N (of a newspaper)
suplemento *m*; (of a book) apéndice *m*; (of
one's diet) complemento *m*

supplement[2] [sʌ́pləmənt] VT complementar,
suplementar

supplemental [sʌpləméntəl] ADJ
suplementario

supplier [səplaɪə-] N abastecedor -ora *mf*,
proveedor -ora *mf*

supply [səplaɪ] VT abastecer, suministrar; N (act
of supplying) abastecimiento *m*; — **and**
demand oferta y demanda *f*; **in short** —
escaso; **supplies** suministros *m pl*,
provisiones *f pl*; **office supplies** artículos de
oficina *m pl*; **military supplies** pertrechos
m pl

support [səpɔ́rt] VT (keep from falling) sostener,
soportar; (encourage) apoyar; (facilitate)
potenciar; (corroborate) corroborar; (help
with computers) soportar; **to be —ed by**
fundamentarse en/sobre; N (of a structure)
sostén *m*, soporte *m*; (of a family) sustento *m*;
(of a candidate, idea) apoyo *m*; (of a theory)
respaldo *m*; (for a computer) soporte *m*; —
group grupo de apoyo *m*

supporter [səpɔ́rDə-] N partidario -ria *mf*,
simpatizante *mf*; (in sports) hincha *mf*

supportive [səpɔ́rDɪv] ADJ solidario; **you've**
always been very — of us siempre nos has
apoyado

suppose [səpóz] VT suponer; **we are —d to go**
tenemos que ir

supposedly [səpózɪdli] ADV supuestamente

supposition [sʌpəzíʃən] N suposición *f*,
supuesto *m*

suppository [səpázɪtɔri] N supositorio *m*
suppress [səprés] VT (repress) reprimir; (eliminate) suprimir; (a revolt) sofocar
suppression [səpréʃən] N (repression) represión *f*; (elimination) supresión *f*; (of a revolt) sofocación *f*
supremacy [suprémǝsi] N supremacía *f*
supreme [suprím] ADJ supremo
surcharge [sɚtʃɑrdʒ] N recargo *m*, prima *f*
sure [ʃur] ADJ seguro; (judgment) certero; (hand) firme; **to make — of** asegurarse de; ADV **he — drinks a lot** es una esponja; **may I sit here? —!** ¿me puedo sentar? ¡cómo no!
surely [ʃúrli] ADV seguramente, ciertamente; **— you jest** no hablarás en serio; **he will — come** seguramente vendrá
surf [sɚf] N (breaking waves) rompientes *mf pl*; (foam) espuma *f*; (undertow) resaca *f*; **—board** tabla de surf *f*; VI/VT (on water) hacer surfing [en], surfear; (on the Internet) navegar, surfear
surface [sɚfɪs] N superficie *f*; (of a solid) cara *f*; VI (come to top) emerger; (turn up) salir a la luz; VT (a submarine) sacar a la superficie; (a road) revestir
surfeit [sɚfɪt] N (excess) exceso *m*; (feeling of fullness) hartazgo *m*; VI/VT hartar[se]
surfing [sɚfɪŋ] N (on water) surfing *m*; (on the Internet) navegación *f*
surge [sɚdʒ] N (of people, disgust) oleada *f*; (of waves) oleaje *m*; (of electricity) sobrecarga de voltaje *f*; **— protector** protector contra sobrecargas de voltaje *m*; VI (people) precipitarse; (current) subir
surgeon [sɚdʒən] N cirujano -na *mf*
surgery [sɚdʒəri] N cirujía *f*; (room) quirófano *m*
surgical [sɚdʒɪkəl] ADJ quirúrgico; **— dressing** vendaje quirúrgico *m*; **— instruments** instrumentos quirúrgicos *m pl*
Suriname, Surinam [súrɪnɑm] N Surinam *m*
Surinamese [surɪnɑmíz] ADJ & N surinamés -esa *mf*
surly [sɚli] ADJ malhumorado, hosco, arisco
surmise [sɚmáɪz] VT conjeturar, suponer; N conjetura *f*, suposición *f*
surmount [sɚmáʊnt] VT superar
surname [sɚnem] N apellido *m*
surpass [sɚpǽs] VT superar, sobrepujar
surpassing [sɚpǽsɪŋ] N superación *f*
surplus [sɚplʌs] N excedente *m*, sobrante *m*, sobra *f*; (of funds) superávit *m*
surprise [sɚpráɪz] N sorpresa *f*; VT sorprender
surprising [sɚpráɪzɪŋ] ADJ sorprendente
surprisingly [sɚpráɪzɪŋli] ADV sorprendentemente; **not —** como era de esperar
surreal [səríəl] ADJ surrealista
surrealism [səríəlɪzəm] N surrealismo *m*
surrealist [səríəlɪst] N surrealista *mf*

surrealistic [sərɪəlístɪk] ADJ surrealista
surrender [səréndɚ] VI (accept defeat) rendir[se], darse por vencido; (give oneself up) entregarse; VT entregar; N rendición *f*
surreptitious [sɚəptíʃəs] ADJ subrepticio
surrogate [sɚəgɪt] ADJ sustituto; **— mother** madre de alquiler *f*
surround [səráʊnd] VT rodear, circundar; (a city) sitiar
surrounding [səráʊndɪŋ] ADJ circundante; N **—s** alrededores *m pl*, inmediaciones *f pl*, entorno *m*
surtax [sɚtæks] N sobretasa *f*
surveillance [sɚvéləns] N vigilancia *f*
survey[1] [sɚvé] VT (evaluate) evaluar; (measure) medir; (contemplate) contemplar; (poll) encuestar
survey[2] [sɚve] N (inspection) reconocimiento *m*, inspección *f*; (measure) medición *f*; (overview) panorama *m*; (poll) encuesta *f*, sondeo *m*; **— course** curso general *m*
surveyor [sɚvéɚ] N agrimensor -ora *mf*
survival [sɚváɪvəl] N supervivencia *f*, sobrevivencia *f*; (subsistence) subsistencia *f*; **the — of the fittest** la supervivencia del más apto
survive [sɚváɪv] VI/VT sobrevivir (also live longer than); (subsist) subsistir
surviving [sɚváɪvɪŋ] ADJ superviviente
survivor [sɚváɪvɚ] N sobreviviente *mf*, superviviente *mf*
susceptible [səséptəbəl] ADJ susceptible; **to be — of proof** poderse demostrar; **to be — to pneumonia** ser propenso a la pulmonía
suspect[1] [sáspɛkt] N sospechoso -sa *mf*
suspect[2] [səspékt] VT sospechar, recelar
suspend [səspénd] VT suspender
suspenders [səspéndɚz] N tirantes *m pl*
suspense [səspéns] N (uncertainty) incertidumbre *f*; (in movie) suspenso *m*; Sp suspense *m*; **to keep in —** mantener en suspenso, tener en vilo
suspension [səspénʃən] N suspensión *f*; (of a ban) levantamiento *m*; **— bridge** puente colgante *m*
suspicion [səspíʃən] N sospecha *f*
suspicious [səspíʃəs] ADJ (causing suspicion) sospechoso; (experiencing suspicion) suspicaz, desconfiado
sustain [səstén] VT (weight) sostener, sustentar; (pretense, effort) mantener; (an injury) sufrir; (an objection) admitir; (a musical note) sostener
sustainable [səsténəbəl] ADJ sostenible, sustentable
sustenance [sástənəns] N sustento *m*, alimento *m*
suture [sútʃɚ] N sutura *f*
swab [swɑb] N bola de algodón *f*, RP hisopo *m*; VT

pasar un hisopo sobre

swagger [swǽgɚ] VI (walk) pavonearse, contonearse; (boast) fanfarronear; N (walk) pavoneo *m*, contoneo *m*; (bluster) fanfarronería *f*

swallow [swálo] N (drink) trago *m*; (bird) golondrina *f*; VI/VT tragar; **to — up** consumir

swallowing [swáloɪŋ] N deglución *f*

swam [swæm] *see* swim

swamp [swɑmp] N pantano *m*, ciénaga *f*; **—land** cenagal *m*; VI/VT (flood) inundar[se]; (overwhelm) abrumar[se], agobiar[se]

swampy [swámpi] ADJ pantanoso, cenagoso

swan [swɑn] N cisne *m*; **— dive** salto del ángel *m*; **— song** canto de cisne *m*

swap [swɑp] VT cambiar, canjear; N cambio *m*, canje *m*

swarm [swɔrm] N enjambre *m*; VI (of bees) salir en enjambre; (of people, tourists) pulular, hormiguear; **to be —ing with** ser un hervidero de, abundar en

swarthy [swɔ́rði] ADJ trigueño, moreno

swat [swɑt] VT (a person) pegar; (flies) aplastar; **to — at** manotear; N manotazo *m*

sway [swe] VI/VT (move to and fro) balancear[se], bambolear[se]; (move hips) menear[se]; (influence) influir [en]; N (movement) balanceo *m*, vaivén *m*, bamboleo *m*; (influence) influencia *f*; **to hold — over** dominar

Swazi [swázi] N suazi *mf*

Swaziland [swázilænd] N Suazilandia *f*

swear [swer] VI/VT (vow) jurar; (use profanity) decir palabrotas; *Sp* soltar tacos; **to — in** (give oath) juramentar; (take oath) prestar juramento; **she —s by canned peaches** para ella no hay nada como los duraznos enlatados; **to — off** renunciar a; **to — to** jurar por

sweat [swɛt] VI (perspire) sudar; (ooze) exudar, sudar; (worry) preocuparse; N sudor *m*; **— glands** glándulas sudoríparas *f pl*; **—shirt** sudadera *f*; **—suit** equipo deportivo *m*; *Sp* chándal *m*; **no — no** hay problema

sweater [swɛ́Dɚ] N suéter *m*, jersey *m*

sweating [swɛ́Dɪŋ] N sudor *m*, sudoración *f*, transpiración *f*

sweaty [swɛ́Di] ADJ sudoroso, sudado

Swede [swid] N sueco -ca *mf*

Sweden [swídn̩] N Suecia *f*

Swedish [swídɪʃ] ADJ sueco

sweep [swip] VI/VT (clean with broom, scan) barrer; (dredge) dragar; VT (touch) rozar; (search) rastrear; VI (spread) extenderse; **to — away** llevar, arrastrar; **to — down upon** caer sobre, asolar; **to — off** limpiar; **to — into** (enter majestically) entrar majestuosamente; (enter quickly) entrar rápidamente; **to — up** recoger; N (cleaning)

barrida *f*; (extension) extensión *f*; (movement) barrido *m*; (search) rastreo *m*

sweeper [swípɚ] N (for cleaning) barredora *f*; (in soccer) líbero *m*

sweeping [swípɪŋ] ADJ (statement) [demasiado] general; (victory) aplastante

sweet [swit] ADJ (in flavor, personality) dulce; (in smell) bueno, fragante; **—-and-sour** agridulce; **—heart** querido -da *mf*; **— pea** *Sp* guisante de olor *m*; **— potato** batata *f*, boniato *m*; *Mex* camote *m*; **to have a — tooth** ser goloso; N dulce *m*, golosina *f*; **my — mi** vida, mi alma; VT **to —-talk** halagar

sweeten [swítn̩] VI/VT (a food) endulzar[se]; (an experience) dulcificar[se]

sweetener [swítn̩ɚ] N endulzante *m*, edulcorante *m*

sweetness [swítnɪs] N (of personality) dulzura *f*; (of taste) dulzor *m*

swell [swɛl] VI/VT (limbs, with pride) hinchar[se], henchir[se]; VI (river) crecer; (population) crecer, engrosar[se]; VT (make grow) hacer crecer, hacer aumentar, engrosar; N (of ocean) oleaje *m*; ADJ regio, bárbaro

swelling [swɛ́lɪŋ] N hinchazón *f*

swelter [swɛ́ltɚ] VI sofocarse de calor

swept [swɛpt] *see* sweep

swerve [swɝv] VI/VT (in a car) virar; (from a goal) desviar[se]; N viraje *m*

swift [swɪft] ADJ ligero, veloz, raudo; N vencejo *m*

swiftness [swɪ́ftnɪs] N velocidad *f*, rapidez *f*

swim [swɪm] VI/VT nadar; (float) flotar; **to — across** atravesar nadando; **my head is —ming** me da vueltas la cabeza; **I love —ming** me encanta nadar; N *Mex* alberca *f*; **—suit** traje de baño *m*; **to take a —** ir a nadar, dar una nadada

swimmer [swɪ́mɚ] N nadador -ora *mf*; **—'s ear** otitis externa *f*

swimming [swɪ́mɪŋ] N natación *f*; **— pool** piscina *f*

swindle [swɪ́ndl̩] VT estafar; N estafa *f*, trapacería *f*

swine [swaɪn] N puerco *m*, cerdo *m*; (person) *offensive* puerco -ca *mf*, sinvergüenza *mf*

swing [swɪŋ] VI/VT (on a swing) columpiar[se]; (move to and fro) balancear[se], bambolear[se]; (baseball, golf) dar un swing [con]; VI (change) virar; **to — and miss** abanicar; **to — around** dar vueltas; **to — open** abrirse; VT (make turn) hacer girar; (influence) influir sobre; **to — a deal** concretar un negocio; **I can't — a new car** no me puedo dar el lujo de comprar un auto nuevo; N (playground toy) columpio *m*; (oscillation) balanceo *m*, vaivén *m*, bamboleo *m*; (in golf, baseball, music) swing *m*;

(change) cambio *m*; — **and a miss** abanico *m*; **in full** — en su apogeo; **to get into the** — **of things** agarrarle la onda a algo, cogerle el tranquillo a algo

swipe [swaɪp] VT (steal) afanar, sisar; (slide) deslizar; **to** — **a card** pasar una tarjeta por un lector; N (insult) insulto *m*; **to take a** — **at someone** (physical) tirarle un manotazo a alguien; (verbal) insultar

swirl [swɝl] VI/VT arremolinar[se]; (dancers) girar; N remolino *m*; (smoke) espiral *f*

Swiss [swɪs] ADJ & N suizo -za *mf*; — **cheese** queso suizo *m*

switch [swɪtʃ] N (change) cambio *m*; (electrical) interruptor *m*, llave *f*; (stick for whipping) varilla *f*; (on railways) agujas *f pl*; —**blade** navaja automática *f*; —**board** centralita *f*; —**man** guardagujas *m sg*; —**-hitter** (in baseball) bateador -ora ambidiestro *mf*; (bisexual) bisexual *mf*; VI/VT cambiar [de]; (train cars) desviar; **to** — **off** (current) cortar; (light, TV) apagar; **to** — **on** encender, prender

Switzerland [swítsɚlənd] N Suiza *f*

swivel [swívəl] N pivote *m*; — **chair** silla giratoria *f*

swollen [swólən] ADJ hinchado

swollen [swólən] *see* swell

swoon [swun] VI desvanecerse, desmayarse; **to** — **over someone** morirse por alguien; N vahído *m*

swoop [swup] VI **to** — **down upon** abalanzarse sobre; N descenso súbito *m*; **at one fell** — de un tirón

sword [sɔrd] N espada *f*; —**fish** pez espada *m*

swore [swɔr] *see* swear

sworn [swɔrn] *see* swear

swum [swʌm] *see* swim

swung [swʌŋ] *see* swing

sycamore [síkəmɔr] N sicomoro *m*

syllable [síləbəl] N sílaba *f*

syllabus [síləbəs] N programa [de estudios] *m*

syllogism [sílədʒɪzəm] N silogismo *m*

symbiosis [sɪmbiósɪs] N simbiosis *f*

symbol [símbəl] N símbolo *m*

symbolic [sɪmbálɪk] ADJ simbólico

symbolism [símbəlɪzəm] N simbolismo *m*

symbolize [símbəlaɪz] VT simbolizar

symmetrical [sɪmétrɪkəl] ADJ simétrico

symmetry [símɪtri] N simetría *f*

sympathetic [sɪmpəθéDɪk] ADJ (compassionate) compasivo; (understanding) comprensivo, solidario; (favoring) favorable; (nervous system) simpático

sympathize [símpəθaɪz] VI (be compassionate) compadecer[se]; (be understanding) comprender; (be in favor) favorecer; **to** — **with** estar a favor de

sympathizer [símpəθaɪzɚ] N simpatizante *mf*

sympathizing [símpəθaɪzɪŋ] ADJ simpatizante

sympathy [símpəθi] N (compassion) compasión *f*; (understanding) comprensión *f*; (condolence) condolencia *f*, pésame *m*; **to extend one's** — dar el pésame

symphony [símfəni] N sinfonía *f*; — **orchestra** orquesta sinfónica *f*

symposium [sɪmpóziəm] N simposio *m*

symptom [símptəm] N síntoma *m*

synagogue [sínəgɑg] N sinagoga *f*

synchronize [síŋkrənaɪz] VI/VT sincronizar[se]

synchronous [síŋkrənəs] ADJ sincrónico

syndicate[1] [síndɪkɪt] N sindicato *m*

syndicate[2] [síndɪket] VI/VT (form a syndicate) sindicar[se]; VT (sell rights) vender los derechos de

syndrome [síndrom] N síndrome *m*

synergy [sínɚdʒi] N sinergia *f*

synonym [sínənɪm] N sinónimo *m*

synonymous [sɪnánəməs] ADJ sinónimo

synopsis [sɪnápsɪs] N sinopsis *f*

syntax [síntæks] N sintaxis *f*

synthesis [sínθəsɪs] N síntesis *f*

synthesize [sínθəsaɪz] VI/VT sintetizar

synthesizer [sínθəsaɪzɚ] N sintetizador *m*

synthetic [sɪnθéDɪk] ADJ sintético

syphilis [sífəlɪs] N sífilis *f*

Syria [síriə] N Siria *f*

Syrian [síriən] ADJ & N sirio -ria *mf*

syringe [səríndʒ] N jeringa *f*

syrup [sírəp] N (food) almíbar *m*, jarabe *m*; (medicine) jarabe *m*

system [sístəm] N sistema *m*; — **crashes** caídas del sistema *f pl*

systematic [sɪstəmǽDɪk] ADJ sistemático

systematize [sístəmətaɪz] VI/VT sistematizar

systemic [sɪstémɪk] ADJ sistémico

systolic [sɪstálɪk] ADJ sistólico

Tt

tab [tæb] N (on a keyboard) tabulador *m*; (on index cards) pestaña *f*, ceja *f*; (bill) cuenta *f*; — **key** tecla de tabulación *f*; VI tabular

table [tébəl] N (furniture) mesa *f*; (list) tabla *f*; — **lamp** lámpara de mesa *f*; — **of contents** tabla de contenido *f*, índice *m*; **at** — a la mesa; VT posponer indefinidamente, dar carpetazo a; —**cloth** mantel *m*; —**spoon** (spoon) cuchara grande *f*; (measurement) cucharada *f*; —**spoonful** cucharada *f*; — **tennis** tenis de mesa *m*; —**ware** vajilla *f*, servicio de mesa *m*

tablet [tǽblɪt] N (pill) pastilla *f*, tableta *f*; (paper) bloc *m*; (stone) tabla *f*, lápida *f*; (portable writing surface) tablilla *f*

tabloid [tǽblɔɪd] N (paper size) tabloide *m*; (type of press) prensa amarilla/sensacionalista *f*

taboo [tæbú] N tabú *m*

tabulate [tǽbjəlet] VT tabular

tachometer [tækámɪDɚ] N tacómetro *m*

tacit [tǽsɪt] ADJ tácito

taciturn [tǽsɪtɜn] ADJ taciturno

tack [tæk] N (nail) tachuela *f*; (stitch) hilván *m*; (heading of a boat) rumbo *m*; (course of action) táctica *f*; (equipment for a horse) arreos *m pl*; VT (to nail) clavar con tachuelas; (to stitch) hilvanar; **to — on** agregar; VI virar, cambiar de rumbo

tackle [tǽkəł] N (for fishing, hoisting) aparejo *m*; (in rugby, football) placaje *m*, parada *f*; (person) atajador *m*; VT (a problem) enfrentar, abordar; (a task) emprender; (a horse) poner arreos; VI/VT (rugby, American football) placar, atajar

tacky [tǽki] ADJ (in bad taste) de mal gusto, chabacano; *Sp* hortera; (sticky) pegajoso

tact [tækt] N tacto *m*

tactful [tǽktfəł] ADJ que tiene tacto

tactics [tǽktɪks] N táctica *f*

tactile [tǽktl] ADJ táctil

tactless [tǽktlɪs] ADJ falto de tacto

tag [tæg] N (label) etiqueta *f*; (question) coletilla *f*; (nickname) apodo *m*; **to play — jugar al** pillapilla; VT etiquetar; (in the game of tag) pillar; **to — along** acompañar

tail [teł] N cola *f*, rabo *m*; (of a shirt) faldón *m*; (pursuer) perseguidor -ora *mf*; (buttocks) *vulg* culo *m*; **—bone** rabadilla *f*; **— end** (of a concert) final *m*; (of a procession) cola *f*; **—light** luz trasera *f*; **—pipe** tubo de escape *m*; **—s** (of a coin) cruz *f*; (of a tuxedo) frac *m*; **—spin** barrena *f*; **to —gate** seguir demasiado de cerca [a otro coche]

tailor [télɚ] N sastre *m*; **— shop** sastrería *f*; VT hacer a medida; (adapt) adaptar

taint [tent] N (stain) mancha *f*; (contamination) contaminación *f*; VI/VT (stain) manchar[se]; (contaminate) contaminar[se]

Taiwan [taɪwán] N Taiwán *m*

Taiwanese [taɪwɑníz] ADJ & N taiwanés -esa *mf*

Tajik [tɑdʒík] ADJ & N tayiko -ka *mf*

Tajikistan [tɑdʒíkɪstæn] N Tayikistán *m*

take [tek] VT (a load) llevar; (someone else's property) robar, llevarse; (one number from another) restar; (prisoner, medicine, measures, a course) tomar; (one of a set) elegir, coger; (a bribe) aceptar; (a prize) recibir; (advice) seguir; (a walk) dar; (a vacation) irse; (a trip) hacer; (a piece of news) recibir; (a photo) sacar; **to — a bath** bañarse; **to — after** parecerse a; **to — a look at** echar un vistazo a; **to — a notion to** ocurrírsele a uno; **to — apart** desarmar, desmontar; **to — aside** apartar; **to — away** (carry away)

llevarse; (steal) sustraer; **to — back** devolver; **to — back one's words** retractarse; **to — by surprise** tomar desprevenido; **to — care of** (a person) cuidar de; (a matter) atender a; **to — charge of** encargarse de; **to — down in writing** anotar, apuntar; **to — effect** entrar en vigencia; **to — exercise** hacer ejercicio; **to — in** (include) incluir; (observe) observar; (deceive) embaucar; (provide shelter for) albergar; (make smaller) tomar, achicar; **to — leave** despedirse; **to — off** (remove) quitar[se]; (conduct) llevar; (discount) rebajar; (start flight) despegar; **to — offense** ofenderse; **to — office** asumir un cargo; **to — on** (accept) asumir; (hire) tomar, contratar; (acquire) adquirir; **to — out** (withdraw) sacar; (carry out [food], take on a date) llevar; **to — over** hacerse cargo [de]; **to — place** tener lugar; **to — revenge** vengarse; **to — stock** hacer un balance; **to — stock in** tener confianza en; **to — the floor** tomar la palabra; **to — to heart** tomar a pecho; **to — to one's heels** poner pies en polvorosa; **to — to task** reprender, regañar; **to — up a matter** tratar un asunto; **to — up again** retomar; **to — up space** ocupar espacio; **I — it that** supongo que; **it —s ten minutes** lleva diez minutos; **the vaccination didn't — la vacuna no** prendió; N (profits) ingresos *m pl*; (of fish) pesca *f*, captura *f*; (of a film production) toma *f*; (opinion) opinión *f*; (approach) enfoque *m*; **—off** (of an airplane) despegue *m*; (parody) parodia *f*; **—over** (of a government) toma de poder *f*; (of a company) adquisición *f*

taken [tékən] *see* take

talcum [tǽłkəm] N talco *m*; **— powder** polvo de talco *m*

tale [teł] N (story) cuento *m*, relato *m*; (lie) mentira *f*

talent [tǽlənt] N talento *m*

talented [tǽləntɪd] ADJ talentoso

talk [tɔk] VI/VT hablar; (chat) charlar; VT (nonsense) decir; (a language) hablar; (politics) hablar de; **to — back** contestar con impertinencia; **to — down to** hablar con arrogancia a; **to — someone into something** convencer a alguien para que haga algo; **to — out of** disuadir de; **to — over** discutir; **to — up** alabar, hacer propaganda; N (formal speech) charla *f*; (gossip) habladurías *f pl*; (lingo) habla *f*; **— of the town** la comidilla del pueblo *f*; **— show** programa de entrevistas *m*

talkative [tɔ́kəDɪv] ADJ hablador, parlanchín, charlatán

tall [tɔl] ADJ alto; **— order** misión imposible *f*; **— tale** cuento chino *m*, patraña *f*; **six feet — de** seis pies de altura; **how — are you?** ¿cuánto mides?

tallow [tǽlo] N sebo *m*

tally [tǽli] N (account) cuenta *f*; VT llevar la cuenta; **to — up** sumar; **to — with** concordar con

tambourine [tæmbərín] N pandereta *f*

tame [tem] ADJ (docile) manso, dócil; (domesticated) domesticado; (dull) aburrido; VT (make docile) amansar, domar; (domesticate) domesticar

tamper [tǽmpə-] VI **to — with** (a jury) sobornar; (a lock) intentar forzar; (a document) alterar, amañar; ADJ —-**proof** a prueba de alteración

tampon [tǽmpɑn] N tampón *m*

tan [tæn] VI/VT (cure) curtir[se]; (darken skin) broncear[se], tostar[se]; VT (cure) adobar; (spank) zurrar; N color tostado *m*; (of skin) bronceado *m*; ADJ (car) color tostado; (skin) bronceado, tostado

tandem [tǽndəm] N tándem *m*; **in — with** en colaboración con

tangent [tǽndʒənt] ADJ & N tangente *f*; **to go off on a —** salirse por la tangente

tangerine [tændʒərín] N mandarina *f*; *Am* tangerina *f*

tangible [tǽndʒəbəl] ADJ tangible

tangle [tǽŋgəl] VI/VT enredar[se], enmarañar[se]; N enredo *m*, maraña *f*; (in hair) nudo *m*, enredijo *m*

tank [tæŋk] N tanque *m* (also military), depósito *m*; VT guardar en un tanque; VI **to — up** (with gasoline) llenar el tanque; (with alcohol) emborracharse

tannery [tǽnəri] N curtiduría *f*, tenería *f*; *Am* curtiembre *f*

tantalize [tǽntlaɪz] VT atormentar con tentaciones

tantamount [tǽntəmaʊnt] ADJ **to be — to** equivaler a

tantrum [tǽntrəm] N berrinche *m*, perrera *f*, rabieta *f*

Tanzania [tænzəníə] N Tanzania *f*

Tanzanian [tænzéniən] ADJ & N tanzano -na *mf*

tap [tæp] N golpecito *m*; (repeated) golpeteo *m*; (with the hand) palmadita *f*; (faucet) llave *f*; *Sp* grifo *m*; **— dance** claqué *m*; **— water** agua de llave *f*; VI/VT (once) tocar; (repeatedly) golpetear; (with fingers) tamborilear; (utilize) explotar; (draw off liquid) extraer; **to — a tree** sangrar un árbol; **to — a telephone** intervenir un teléfono

tape [tep] N (adhesive, magnetic) cinta *f*; **— measure** cinta métrica *f*; **— recorder** grabadora *f*, grabador *m*; **— recording** grabación *f*; —**worm** lombriz *f*, solitaria *f*; VT (affix) atar con cinta; VI/VT (record) grabar; **to —-record** grabar

taper [tépə-] N (diminished size) estrechamiento *m*; (candle) vela *f*, candela *f*; VI/VT afinar[se];

to — off (become smaller) afinar[se]; (diminish) ir disminuyendo

tapestry [tǽpɪstri] N (wall hanging) tapiz *m*; (art, industry) tapicería *f*

tapioca [tæpióka] N tapioca *f*

tapir [tépər] N tapir *m*

tar [tɑr] N alquitrán *m*, brea *f*; VT alquitranar; **to — and feather** emplumar

tarantula [tərǽntʃələ] N tarántula *f*

tardy [tárDi] ADJ **to be —** llegar tarde

target [tárgɪt] N blanco *m*; **— practice** tiro al blanco *m*

tariff [tǽrɪf] N tarifa *f*, arancel *m*

tarnish [tárnɪʃ] VI/VT (metal) deslustrar[se], empañar; (reputation) manchar[se]

tart [tɑrt] ADJ (fruit) agrio, ácido; (remark) mordaz; N (pie) tarta *f*; (woman) *pej* fulana *f*

tartar [tárDə-] N (in wine) tártaro *m*; (on teeth) sarro *m*; **— sauce** salsa tártara *f*

task [tæsk] N tarea *f*, labor *f*; **— bar** barra de tareas *f*; **— force** fuerza de tarea *f*; **—master** tirano -na *mf*; **to take to —** reprender, regañar

tassel [tǽsəl] N borla *f*

taste [test] VT (perceive) sentir el gusto/sabor de; (try) probar; (try wine) catar; VI **to — of onion** saber a cebolla; **it —s sour** tiene un sabor agrio; N (sense, aesthetic judgment) gusto *m*; (flavor) sabor *m*; (small amount of food) bocadito *m*; (small amount of drink) sorbo *m*; **— bud** papila gustativa *f*

tasteless [téstlɪs] ADJ (with no taste) soso, desabrido; (in bad taste) de mal gusto

tasty [tésti] ADJ sabroso

tatter [tǽDə-] N andrajo *m*, harapo *m*, pingajo *m*

tattered [tǽDə-d] ADJ harapiento, andrajoso

tattle [tǽdl̩] VI acusar; **to — on** acusar a; N **—tale** acusetas *mf sg*

tattoo [tætú] N tatuaje *m*; VI/VT tatuar[se]

taught [tɔt] *see* teach

taunt [tɔnt] VT provocar, burlarse de; N provocación *f*, pulla *f*

taut [tɔt] ADJ tenso, tirante

tavern [tǽvə-n] N taberna *f*, cantina *f*

tawdry [tɔ́dri] ADJ (affair) sórdido; (outfit) charro

tax [tæks] N impuesto *m*, contribución *f*, gravamen *m*; (burden) carga *f*; VT (a product) gravar; (a person) cobrarle impuestos a; (patience, resources) poner a prueba; **— attorney/lawyer** abogado -da tributarista *mf*; **— code** código impositivo *m*; **—-deductible** desgravable; **— deduction** deducción impositiva *f*; **— evasion** evasión de impuestos *f*; **—payer** contribuyente *mf*; **— return** declaración de impuestos *f*; **— shelter** abrigo impositivo *m*, refugio fiscal *m*; **— withholding** retención impositiva *f*; ADJ —-**exempt** no gravable, exento de

impuestos; — **-free** libre de impuestos
taxable [tǽksəbəl] ADJ imponible, tributable
taxation [tækséʃən] N (result of taxing)
impuestos *m pl*; (act of taxing) imposición de
contribuciones *f*
taxi [tǽksi] N taxi *m*; VI ir en taxi; (an airplane)
rodar por la pista; **—cab** taxi *m*
taxidermy [tǽksɪdɚmi] N taxidermia *f*
taxonomy [tæksánəmi] N taxonomía *f*
tea [ti] N té *m*; — **bag** bolsita de té *f*; **—cup** taza
de té *f*; **—kettle/pot** tetera *f*; — **party** té *m*;
—spoon (spoon) cucharita *f*, cucharilla *f*;
(measurement) cucharadita *f*; **—spoonful**
cucharadita *f*; **—time** hora del té *f*
teach [titʃ] VI/VT enseñar; **to** — **a class** dar clase
teacher [títʃɚ] N (primary school) maestro -tra
mf; (secondary school) profesor -ora *mf*; **—s**
college [escuela] normal *f*
teaching [títʃɪŋ] N enseñanza *f*; **—s** enseñanzas *f*
pl; — **activities** actividades pedagógicas *f pl*;
— **profession** magisterio *m*
team [tim] N equipo *m*; (of yoked animals) yunta
de bueyes *f*; (of horses) tiro *m*, enganche *m*;
—mate compañero -ra de equipo *mf*; VI **to** —
up unirse, formar un equipo
teamster [tímstɚ] N transportista *mf*,
camionero -ra *mf*
tear[1] [tir] N lágrima *f*; **—drop** lágrima *f*; — **gas**
gas lacrimógeno *m*; **to burst into —s**
romper a llorar
tear[2] [tɛr] VI/VT (rip) rasgar[se]; (rip a hole)
hacer[se] un siete; VT **to** — **along** ir a toda
velocidad; **to** — **apart** (rip up) romper,
destrozar; (separate) separar; **to** — **away**
apartar[se]; **to** — **down** (a building) demoler,
derribar; (a machine) desarmar, desmontar;
(a person) denigrar; **to** — **one's hair**
arrancarse los cabellos; N desgarrón *m*,
desgarradura *f*, rasgón *m*
tearful [tírfəl] ADJ (look) lloroso; (farewell) triste
tease [tiz] VT (make fun of a person) molestar,
fastidiar; (tantalize sexually) provocar; (comb
wool, hair) cardar; **to** — **out** sacar; N
provocadora *f*
teat [tit] N teta *f*
techie [téki] N *fam* experto -ta en computación
mf
technical [téknɪkəl] ADJ técnico; — **support**
soporte técnico *m*
technician [tɛkníʃən] N técnico -ca *mf*, perito -ta
mf
technique [tɛkník] N técnica *f*
technological [tɛknəládʒɪkəl] ADJ tecnológico
technology [tɛknálədʒi] N tecnología *f*, técnica *f*
tectonics [tɛktánɪks] N tectónica *f*
tedious [tíɾiəs] ADJ tedioso, aburrido
tedium [tíɾiəm] N hastío *m*
tee [ti] N (T-shirt) camiseta *f*; (golf ball support)
tee *m*; (start of hole in golf) punto de salida *m*

teem [tim] VI **to** — **with** abundar en, estar lleno
de
teen [tin] *see* teenager
teenager [tínedʒɚ] N adolescente *mf*
teens [tinz] N (teenage years) adolescencia *f*;
(numbers 13–19) números de trece a
diecinueve *m pl*
teethe [tið] VI **the baby is teething** al bebé le
están saliendo los dientes
teetotaler [títóɾl̩ɚ] N abstemio -mia *mf*
telecast [téləkæst] N teledifusión *f*
telecommunication [tɛlɪkəmjunɪkéʃən] N
telecomunicación *f*; **—s** telecomunicaciones *f*
pl
telecommuting [tɛlɪkəmjúɾɪŋ] N teletrabajo *m*
teleconference [télɪkɑnfɚəns] N
teleconferencia *f*
telegram [téləgræm] N telegrama *m*
telegraph [téləgræf] N telégrafo *m*; VI/VT
telegrafiar
telegraphic [tɛləgrǽfɪk] ADJ telegráfico
telemarketing [tɛləmárkɪɾɪŋ] N telemercadeo
m, telemarketing *m*
telepathy [təlépəθi] N telepatía *f*
telephone [téləfon] N teléfono *m*; — **book** guía
telefónica *f*; — **booth** cabina telefónica *f*; —
number número telefónico *m*; — **operator**
telefonista *mf*; — **receiver** auricular *m*, tubo
de teléfono *m*; VI/VT telefonear, llamar por
teléfono
telescope [télɪskop] N telescopio *m*; VI plegarse
televisable [tɛləváɪzəbəl] ADJ televisivo
televise [téləvaɪz] VT televisar
television [téləvɪʒən] N (medium) televisión *f*;
(device) televisor *m*; — **program** programa
televisivo *mf*; — **viewer** televidente *mf*
tell [tɛl] VI/VT (the truth) decir; (a story) contar;
to — **apart** distinguir; **to** — **on someone**
acusar a alguien; **to** — **someone off** regañar
a alguien; **to** — **time** decir la hora; **I can't** —
if he's old or young no sé si es viejo o joven;
his age is beginning to — se le comienza a
notar la edad; ADJ **a —tale sign** una señal
reveladora; **he is a —tale** es un acusica
teller [télɚ] N (narrator) narrador -ora *mf*; (in a
bank) cajero -ra *mf*
temerity [təmérɪɾi] N temeridad *f*
temp [tɛmp] N empleado -da temporal *mf*
temper [témpɚ] N (hardness) temple *m*; (bad
humor) mal genio *m*; **to keep one's** —
mantener la calma; **to lose one's** — perder
los estribos, encolerizarse; VT templar
temperament [témpɚəmənt] N temperamento
m, genio *m*, talante *m*
temperance [témpɚəns] N (moderation)
templanza *f*, temperancia *f*; (abstinence from
alcohol) abstinencia de bebidas alcohólicas *f*
temperate [témpɚɪt] ADJ (weather) templado;
(opinions, habits) moderado

temperature [témpəətʃur] N temperatura *f*; **to have a** — tener fiebre

tempest [témpɪst] N tempestad *f*

tempestuous [tɛmpéstʃuəs] ADJ tempestuoso

template [témplɪt] N plantilla *f*

temple [témpəl] N (church) templo *m*; (side of the forehead) sien *f*

temporal [témpəəł] ADJ temporal

temporary [témpərɛri] ADJ temporal, eventual

tempt [tɛmpt] VT tentar

temptation [tɛmptéʃən] N tentación *f*

tempting [témptɪŋ] ADJ tentador

ten [tɛn] NUM diez; N **—s of candidates** decenas de candidatos *f pl*

tenacious [tənéʃəs] ADJ tenaz

tenacity [tənǽsɪDi] N tenacidad *f*

tenant [ténənt] N inquilino -na *mf*, arrendatario -ria *mf*

tend [tɛnd] VT (care for) cuidar; **to** — **to** (take care of) ocuparse de; (lean toward) tender, inclinarse

tendency [téndənsi] N tendencia *f*

tender [téndəʳ] ADJ tierno; (painful) sensible; N (offer) oferta *f*; (legal currency) curso legal *m*; (person who tends) cuidador -ora *mf*, vigilante *mf*; VT presentar, ofrecer

tenderness [téndəʳnɪs] N (of feeling) ternura *f*; (of meat) terneza *f*, ternura *f*; (sensitivity to pain) sensibilidad *f*

tendinitis [tɛndənáɪDɪs] N tendinitis *f*

tendon [téndən] N tendón *m*

tendril [téndrəł] N zarcillo *m*

tenement [ténəmənt] N casa de vecindad *f*

tenet [ténɪt] N principio *m*

tennis [ténɪs] N tenis *m*; — **court** cancha de tenis *f*, pista de tenis *f*; — **elbow** codo de tenista *m*; — **player** tenista *mf*; — **shoes** tenis *m pl*

tenor [ténəʳ] N tenor *m*

tense [tɛns] ADJ tenso; N (grammatical) tiempo *m*

tension [ténʃən] N (stress) tensión *f*; (tautness) tirantez *f*

tent [tɛnt] N (camping) tienda de campaña *f*; (circus) carpa *f*; VI acampar

tentacle [téntəkəł] N tentáculo *m*

tentative [téntəDɪv] ADJ tentativo

tenth [tɛnθ] ADJ & N décimo *m*

tenuous [ténjuəs] ADJ (light, color, cloth) tenue; (peace) frágil

tenure [ténjəʳ] N (of professorship) titularidad *f*; (of an office) ocupación *f*

tepid [tépɪd] ADJ tibio

terabyte [térəbaɪt] N terabyte *m*

term [tɜʳm] N (word, mathematical expression) término *m*; (period) período *m*; (time in office) mandato *m*; (semester) semestre *m*; (trimester) trimestre *m*; (set date for payment) plazo *m*; — **life insurance** seguro de vida a término *m*; — **paper** trabajo final *m*; **—s** condiciones *f pl*; **at** — a término; **to be**

on good —s estar en buenas relaciones; **not to be on speaking —s** no hablarse; **to come to —s** aceptar; VT denominar

terminal [tɜʳmənł] ADJ terminal; N (of airport, computer) terminal *mf*; (electric) terminal *m*

terminate [tɜʳmənet] VI/VT terminar[se]

termination [tɜʳmənéʃən] N terminación *f*; (of an employee) despido *m*

terminology [tɜʳmənáləʤi] N terminología *f*

termite [tɜʳmaɪt] N termita *f*

terrace [térɪs] N terraza *f*, escalón *m*; VT poner terrazas en, escalonar

terrain [tərén] N terreno *m*

terrestrial [təréstriəł] ADJ terrestre

terrible [térəbəł] ADJ terrible, tremendo

terrier [tériəʳ] N terrier *m*

terrific [tərífɪk] ADJ estupendo

terrify [térəfaɪ] VT aterrar, aterrorizar, espeluznar

territory [térɪtɔri] N territorio *m*

terror [térəʳ] N terror *m*

terrorism [térəʳɪzəm] N terrorismo *m*

terrorist [térəʳɪst] N terrorista *mf*

terrorize [térəʳaɪz] VT aterrorizar

terse [tɜʳs] ADJ lacónico

test [tɛst] N (trial, experiment) prueba *f*; (of intelligence, multiple choice) test *m*; (examination) examen *m*, prueba *f*; — **market** mercado de prueba *m*; — **pilot** piloto de pruebas *m*; — **tube** tubo de ensayo *m*, probeta *f*; — **-tube baby** bebé de probeta *m*; **to undergo a** — someterse a una prueba: **to take a** — dar un examen; **to give a** — poner un examen; **to put to the** — poner a prueba; VT (put to the test) probar, poner a prueba; (give an exam) poner una prueba, examinar; **—ing** pruebas *f pl*; **to —-drive** probar; VI **girls** — **better than boys** en los exámenes salen mejor las niñas que los niños

testament [téstəmənt] N testamento *m*; (testimony) testimonio *m*

testicle [téstɪkəł] N testículo *m*

testify [téstəfaɪ] VI (serve as witness) testificar; (confirm) dar fe

testimony [téstəmoni] N testimonio *m*

testosterone [tɛstástəron] N testosterona *f*

tetanus [tétṇəs] N tétano[s] *m*

tetracycline [tɛtrəsáɪklin] N tetraciclina *f*

Teutonic [tutánɪk] ADJ teutónico

text [tɛkst] N texto *m*; **—book** libro de texto *m*; — **editor** editor de texto[s] *m*; — **message** mensaje de texto *m*; VT enviar mensajes de texto, *RP* textear

textile [tékstaɪł] ADJ textil; N textil *m*, tejido *m*; — **mill** fábrica de tejidos *f*

texture [tékstʃəʳ] N textura *f*

Thai [taɪ] ADJ & N (person) tailandés -esa *mf*; (language) tailandés *m*

Thailand [táɪlænd] N Tailandia *f*

than [ðæn] CONJ que; **I have more — you** tengo más que tú; **more — once** más de una vez

thank [θæŋk] VT dar las gracias, agradecer; **to have oneself to — for** tener la culpa de; INTERJ **— heaven!** ¡gracias a Dios! **— you** gracias; **—-you letter** carta de agradecimiento *f*; N **—s** gracias *f pl*

thankful [θǽŋkfəł] ADJ agradecido

thankfulness [θǽŋkfəłnɪs] N gratitud *f*, agradecimiento *m*

thankless [θǽŋklɪs] ADJ ingrato

thanksgiving [θæŋksgívɪŋ] N acción de gracias *f*; **— Day** día de acción de gracias *m*

that [ðæt] ADJ (something nearer the speaker) ese, esa; (something more remote from speaker) aquel, aquella; **— dog** ese/aquel perro *m*; **— one** (nearer) ese, esa; DEMON PRON (nearer to speaker) ese, esa; (more remote from speaker) aquel, aquella; (neuter) eso, aquello; **— is my daughter** esa/aquella es mi hija; **— was a nightmare** eso/aquello fue una pesadilla; REL PRON que; **the bike — disappeared** la bici que desapareció; **the pen — I was writing with** la lapicera con la que / la cual escribía; **— is** es decir; CONJ que; **she said — she would come** dijo que vendría; ADV tan; **it's not — far** no queda tan lejos; **— much** tanto; **she was — tall** era así de alta

thatch [θætʃ] N paja *f*; *Am* quincha *f*; VT techar con paja; *Am* quinchar; **—ed roof** techo de paja *m*; *Am* techo de quincha m

thaw [θɔ] VI/VT (food) descongelar[se]; (ice and snow) derretir[se]; (relations, refrigerator) deshelar[se]; N deshielo *m*

the [ðə, ði] DEF ART (singular) el *m*, la *f*; **— boy** el chico *m*; (plural) los *m*, las *f*; **— girls** las chicas *f pl*; **— good thing about that** lo bueno de eso; ADV **— more I work, — less I accomplish** cuanto más trabajo, menos consigo

theater, theatre [θíəDɚ] N teatro *m*

theatrical [θiǽtrɪkəł] ADJ teatral

theft [θɛft] N hurto *m*, robo *m*

their [ðɛr] POSS ADJ **this is — dog** este es su perro, este es el perro de ellos

theirs [ðɛrz] PRON **this book is —** este libro es suyo, este libro es de ellos/ellas; **these things are —** estas cosas son suyas / de ellos / de ellas; **— is bigger** el suyo / la suya / el de ellos / la de ellos es más grande; **a friend of —** un amigo suyo, un amigo de ellos

them [ðɛm] PRON los *m pl*, las *f pl*; **I see —** los/las veo; **I talk to —** les hablo a ellos; **I went with —** fui con ellos/ellas

thematic [θɪmǽDɪk] ADJ temático

theme [θim] N (topic) tema *m*; (essay) ensayo *m*, redacción *f*; **— park** parque temático *m*; —

song tema *m*

themselves [ðɛmsɛ́łvz] PRON **they — built their house** ellos mismos se construyeron la casa; **they are not — today** hoy no son los mismos de siempre; **they were sitting by —** estaban sentados solos; **they looked at — in the mirror** se miraron en el espejo; **they talk to —** hablan solos; **they bought — a yacht** se compraron un yate

then [ðɛn] ADV (at that time) entonces, en aquel tiempo; **it was cheaper —** era más barato en aquel tiempo; (after) luego, después; **from — on** a partir de entonces; **now and —** de vez en cuando; **until —** hasta entonces; **I ate, — I paid** comí, luego pagué; **now —** ahora bien; **are you sorry —?** ¿estás arrepentido pues? ADJ entonces; **the — president** el entonces presidente; CONJ entonces; **if not, — you should stay** si no, entonces deberías quedarte

theologian [θiəlódʒən] N teólogo -ga *mf*

theological [θiəládʒɪkəł] ADJ teológico

theology [θiáłədʒi] N teología *f*

theoretical [θiərɛ́Dɪkə ł] ADJ teórico

theory [θíəri] N teoría *f*; **in —** en teoría

therapeutic [θɛrəpjúDɪk] ADJ terapéutico

therapist [θɛ́rəpɪst] N terapeuta *mf*; (psychologist) psicólogo -ga *mf*

therapy [θɛ́rəpi] N terapia *f*

there [ðɛr] ADV ahí; *Am* allí; (more remote) allá; *Sp* allí; **—abouts** por ahí, más o menos; **—after** (later) después; (always subsequently) de allí en adelante; **—by** así, de ese modo; **— ensued a war** a continuación hubo una guerra; **—fore** por consiguiente, por lo tanto; **—in** en eso, allí; **— is/are** hay; **— goes the bus** ahí va el autobús; **— —** bueno, bueno; **—of** de eso; **—on** (on that) encima; (later) luego, después; **—upon** (after) luego, después; (for this reason) por consiguiente; (upon that) encima; **—with** (with that) con eso; (after that) luego, en seguida; **who's —?** ¿quién es? **is Mary —?** ¿está María? **we got — at 5** llegamos a las 5

thermal [θɝməł] ADJ termal; **— energy** energía térmica *f*

thermal [θɝməł] ADJ térmico

thermodynamic [θɝmodaɪnǽmɪk] ADJ termodinámico

thermometer [θɚmámɪDɚ] N termómetro *m*

thermonuclear [θɝmonúkliɚ] ADJ termonuclear

thermos [θɝməs] N termo *m*

thermostat [θɝməstæt] N termostato *m*

thesaurus [θɪsórəs] N (synonym dictionary) diccionario de sinónimos *m*; (large dictionary) diccionario *m*

these [ðiz] ADJ & PRON estos, estas

thesis [θísɪs] N tesis *f*

they [ðe] PRON ellos, ellas

thick [θɪk] ADJ (slice) grueso; (fog, soup) espeso; (accent) marcado; (wit) torpe; **one inch —** una pulgada de espesor; **— as thieves** como carne y uña; ADJ **—headed** estúpido; **—set** grueso; **—-skinned** insensible; N **the — of the fight** lo más reñido de la pelea; **through — and thin** pase lo que pase

thicken [θíkən] VI/VT espesar[se], trabar[se]; **the plot—s** la trama se complica

thicket [θíkɪt] N soto m, matorral m, boscaje m

thickness [θíknɪs] N (of paper, wood) espesor m, grosor m; (of soup) lo espeso; (of lips) lo grueso; (of a beard) lo tupido; (of hair) lo abundante

thief [θif] N ladrón -ona mf

thieve [θiv] VI/VT hurtar, robar

thigh [θaɪ] N muslo m

thimble [θímbəł] N dedal m

thin [θɪn] ADJ (ice, wire) delgado, fino; (person) flaco; (vegetation, beard, hair) ralo; (voice) tenue, fino; (air) enrarecido; (excuse) débil; (soup) aguado; VI/VT (paint, soup, sauce) diluir; (hair) entresacar; **to — out** (hair) ralear; (crowd) dispersarse

thing [θɪŋ] N cosa f; **there's no such —** eso no existe; **that is the — to do** eso es lo que hay que hacer; **the — about Mary** lo que pasa con María

thingamajig [θíŋəmədʒɪg] N chisme m, coso m

think [θɪŋk] VI/VT (reason) pensar, razonar; (believe) creer, opinar; **to — about** pensar en; **to — back** recordar; **to — it over/ through** pensarlo bien, reflexionar sobre; **I'm —ing of you** pienso en ti; **what do you — of Mary?** ¿qué piensas de María? **I thought of a plan** se me ocurrió un plan; **to — up an excuse** inventar/elucubrar una excusa; **I don't — so** no creo; **who does he — he is?** ¿quién se cree que es? **to — well of** tener buena opinión de; **she —s nothing of spending $1000** no le importa nada gastar $1000

thinking [θíŋkɪŋ] N **current —** la opinión actual f; **to my way of —** a mi parecer; ADJ pensante

thinner [θínɚ] N disolvente m

thinness [θínnɪs] N (of ice, person) delgadez f, flacura f; (of hair) escasez f; (of air) enrarecimiento m; (of soup) fluidez f

third [θɚd] ADJ tercer[o]; **— base** tercera base f, antesala f; **— baseman** tercero m, antesalista m; **— chapter** capítulo tercero m, tercer capítulo m; **— person** tercera persona f; **— rate** de poca categoría; **— World** Tercer Mundo m; ADV tercero; N tercio m; (gear, musical interval) tercera f; **the — of March** el tres de marzo

thirst [θɚst] N sed f; VI tener sed; **to — for** tener sed de, estar sediento de

thirsty [θɚ́sti] ADJ sediento; **to be —** tener sed

thirteen [θɚtín] NUM trece

thirty [θɚ́Di] NUM treinta; ADJ & N **—something** treintañero -ra mf

this [ðɪs] ADJ & PRON este m, esta f, esto (neuter); **— dog** este perro; **— is a disaster** esto es un desastre

thistle [θísəł] N cardo m

thong [θɔŋ] N (strip of leather) correa f; (garment) tanga mf; (shoe) chancleta f

thorax [θɔ́ræks] N tórax m

thorn [θɔrn] N (sharp growth) espina f; (plant) espino m

thorny [θɔ́rni] ADJ espinoso, escabroso

thorough [θɚ́o] ADJ (exhaustive) exhaustivo, minucioso, detenido; (conscientious) concienzudo; **—bred** ADJ de pura sangre; N purasangre m

those [ðoz] ADJ & PRON (nearer) esos m, esas f; PRON (more remote) aquellos m, aquellas f; **— of you** los de vosotros/ustedes; **— that/who** los/las que

though [ðo] CONJ aunque; **as —** como si; ADV sin embargo

thought [θɔt] N (act, product of thinking) pensamiento m; (idea) idea f; (opinion) opinión f; (concern) consideración f; **to be lost in —** estar abstraído; **to give it no —** no darle importancia; **the very —** la mera idea; **at the — of** ante la idea de; **on second —** pensándolo bien; **my —s are with you** te acompaño en el sentimiento

thought [θɔt] see think

thoughtful [θɔ́tfəł] ADJ (considerate) considerado, atento; (well thought out) bien pensado; (reflective) pensativo, reflexivo

thoughtfulness [θɔ́tfəlnɪs] N consideración f

thoughtless [θɔ́tlɪs] ADJ (inconsiderate) desconsiderado; (careless) descuidado; (not reflective) irreflexivo

thoughtlessness [θɔ́tlɪsnɪs] N (lack of consideration) desconsideración f; (carelessness) descuido m; (lack of reflection) falta de reflexión f

thousand [θáuzənd] NUM mil

thrash [θræʃ] VI/VT (whip, defeat) zurrar, vapulear, apalear; (thresh) trillar, desgranar; **to — around** revolverse, agitarse; **to — out a matter** ventilar un asunto

thread [θrɛd] N (in fabric) hilo m; (on a screw) rosca f; ADJ **—bare** raído; VT (a needle) enhebrar; (beads) ensartar; (a screw) enroscar; **to — one's way** abrirse paso

threat [θrɛt] N amenaza f

threaten [θrétn̩] VI/VT amenazar

threatening [θrétn̩ɪŋ] ADJ amenazador, amenazante

three [θri] NUM tres; **— hundred** trescientos;

ADJ —-**dimensional** tridimensional; —-**point basket** triple *m*; —-**point play** jugada de tres puntos*f*

thresh [θrɛʃ] VT trillar

threshold [θréʃhołd] N umbral *m*

threw [θru] *see* throw

thrift [θrɪft] N economía*f*

thrifty [θrífti] ADJ económico, ahorrativo

thrill [θrɪł] VI/VT emocionar[se], ilusionar[se]; N emoción*f*, ilusión*f*

thrive [θraɪv] VI (person, economy) prosperar, florecer; (plants) crecer mucho

throat [θrot] N garganta*f*

throb [θrɑb] VI latir, palpitar; N latido *m*, palpitación*f*

throes [θroz] ADV LOC **in the — of war** en plena guerra; **in the — of death** agonizando

throne [θron] N trono *m*

throng [θrɔŋ] N muchedumbre*f*, turbamulta*f*; VI apiñarse, llegar en tropel

throttle [θrádl] N (of a motor) válvula reguladora / de aceleración*f*, regulador *m*; (of a motorcycle) puño giratorio del gas *m*; VT ahogar, estrangular

through [θru] PREP por, a través de; (as intermediary) por medio de; **Monday — Friday** de lunes a viernes; **all — the night** toda la noche; ADV (completely) de un lado a otro; (from beginning to end) de principio a fin, de cabo a rabo; **loyal — and —** leal a toda prueba; **he's an aristocrat — and —** es un aristócrata de pura cepa; **to carry —** llevar a cabo; ADJ (ticket, train) directo; **to be —** (with a task) haber terminado; (in a profession) estar acabado; **we're —!** (with a boyfriend) ¡se acabó entre nosotros!

throughout [θruáʊt] PREP (all through) por todo; (during) a lo largo de, durante; ADV (duration) de principio a fin; (space) por todas partes

throw [θro] VI/VT (a ball) tirar, lanzar; (a light, voice) arrojar; (a switch) conectar; (a pot on a wheel) modelar; (a punch) lanzar; (a wrestler) tumbar; (a game for a bribe) dejarse perder; (a rider) desmontar; (a party) dar, organizar; **that really threw me** eso me confundió; **to — away** (dispose of) tirar, arrojar; (squander) malgastar; **to — down** tirar al suelo; **to — in** añadir; **to — into gear** engranar; **to — in the clutch** embragar; **to — out** (garbage) tirar, arrojar; (unruly guest) echar; **to — up** vomitar, devolver; N (act or instance of throwing) tiro *m*; (of dice) tirada*f*; (shawl) chal *m*; (blanket) manta*f*; —-**in** (soccer) saque de banda *m*; ADJ —**away** desechable

thrown [θron] *see* throw

thrush [θrʌʃ] N tordo *m*, zorzal *m*

thrust [θrʌst] VT (stab) clavar; (shove) empujar; **to — oneself upon** meterse en; **to — a task**

upon someone imponerle una tarea a alguien; **to — aside** echar a un lado; VI (push) dar un empujón; (stab at) lanzar una estocada; (push through) empujar para pasar; N (stab) estocada*f*; (force of a jet engine) empuje *m*; (shove) empujón *m*; (military assault) arremetida*f*, acometida*f*

thud [θʌd] N golpe sordo *m*; VI caer con un golpe sordo

thug [θʌg] N matón *m*

thumb [θʌm] N pulgar *m*; —**tack** chinche*f*, tachuela*f*; **under the — of** bajo la bota de; VT hojear; **to give a —s up** aprobar

thump [θʌmp] N golpe sordo *m*; VI hacer un ruido sordo

thunder [θʌ́ndɚ] N trueno *m*; —**bolt** rayo *m*; —**head** nubarrón *m*; —**storm** tormenta eléctrica*f*, tronada*f*; VI tronar

thunderous [θʌ́ndɚəs] ADJ atronador, estruendoso

Thursday [θɝ́zde] N jueves *m*

thus [ðʌs] ADV así; **— far** (space) hasta aquí; (time) hasta ahora

thwart [θwɔrt] VT frustrar

thyme [taɪm] N tomillo *m*

thyroid [θáɪrɔɪd] N tiroides *m sg*

Tibet [tɪbét] N Tíbet *m*

Tibetan [tɪbétn̩] ADJ & N tibetano -na *mf*

tic [tɪk] N tic *m*, manía*f*

tick [tɪk] N (sound of a clock) tic tac *m*; (cover of a pillow) funda*f*; (checkmark) marca*f*; (insect) garrapata*f*; VI hacer tic tac; **to — off** (check off) marcar; (anger) enojar

ticket [tíkɪt] N billete *m*; *Am* boleto *m*; (slate of candidates) candidatura*f*; (summons) multa *f*; (tag) etiqueta*f*; **— office** taquilla*f*; VT (give passage) vender billetes; (give summons) multar

tickle [tíkəł] VT (poke) cosquillear, hacer cosquillas; (amuse) dar ilusión; VI picar; N picazón*f*, cosquilleo *m*

ticklish [tíklɪʃ] ADJ (prone to tickling) cosquilloso; (delicate) delicado

tidal [táɪdl̩] ADJ **— wave** (tsunami) tsunami *m*, maremoto *m*; (large wave) marejada*f*

tidbit [tídbɪt] N (snack) golosina*f*; (gossip) chisme jugoso *m*

tide [taɪd] N marea*f*; (of opinion) corriente*f*; —**water** (water) agua de marea*f*; (land) marisma*f*; VT **to — over** cubrir

tidy [táɪdi] ADJ (orderly) ordenado; (large) considerable; VI/VT arreglar; **to — oneself up** arreglarse

tie [taɪ] VI (fasten) atarse; (make same score) empatar; VT (fasten) atar; (make a knot) hacer un nudo en; (make same score as) empatar con; **to — a record** empatar una marca; **to — down** atar; **to — in** cuadrar; **to — one on** emborracharse; **to — tight** atar fuerte; **to —**

up (bind) atar; (hinder) bloquear; (occupy) ocupar; (moor a ship) amarrar; N (cord) cuerda f; (relations) lazo m, vínculo m; (cravat) corbata f; (railway) durmiente m, traviesa f; (score) empate m; **—-break** (in sports) desempate m; (in tennis) muerte súbita f

tier [tir] N nivel m

tiger [táigə-] N tigre m

tight [tait] ADJ (knot, nut) apretado, ajustado; (clothes) ceñido, ajustado; (control) firme, estricto; (race) reñido; (stingy) tacaño, mezquino; (drunk) borracho; **— end** (football) receptor cerrado m; **—-fisted** agarrado; **—rope** cuerda floja f; **—wad** tacaño -ña mf; **to be in a — spot** estar en un aprieto; ADV bien, herméticamente; **to hold on —** agarrarse bien

tighten [táitṇ] VI/VT (knot, nut, belt) apretar[se]; (control) estrechar[se]

tightness [táitnis] N (narrowness) estrechez f; (stinginess) tacañería f

tilde [tíłdə] N tilde f

tile [tail] N (on a roof) teja f; (on a floor) baldosa f; (on a wall) azulejo m; **— roof** tejado m; VT (roof) tejar; (floor) embaldosar; (wall) azulejar

till [tił] PREP hasta; CONJ hasta que; VI/VT (plow) labrar, arar; N (cash drawer) caja f

tilt [tiłt] VI/VT ladear[se], inclinar[se]; N (act or instance of tilting) ladeo m, inclinación f; (incline) declive m; (joust) justa f; **at full —** a toda velocidad

timber [tímbə-] N (cut wood) madera [de construcción] f; (trees) árboles para madera m pl; (beam) viga f; **—line** límite de la vegetación arbórea m; **— wolf** lobo gris m

timbre [tímbə-] N timbre m

time [taim] N (past, present, future) tiempo m; (on the clock) hora f; (occasion) vez f; (period) período m, momento m, época f; **—-and-a-half pay** paga de tiempo y medio f; **— bomb** bomba de tiempo f; **— frame** plazo aproximado de tiempo m; **—keeper** cronometrador -ora mf; **— limit** límite de tiempo m; **— out** descanso m; **—piece** reloj m; **—share** tiempo compartido m; **— signature** compás m; **—table** horario m; **— zone** huso horario m; **at —s** a veces; **at the same —** a la vez, al mismo tiempo; **at this —** en este momento; **behind —** atrasado; **lunch—** hora del almuerzo f; **from — to —** de vez en cuando; **for the — being** por el momento; **in —** a tiempo; **in no —** en seguida; **it's about —** ya era hora; **on —** puntual; **to buy on —** comprar a plazo; **— after —** una vez tras otra; **to do —** cumplir una condena; **to have a good —** divertirse; **what — is it?** ¿qué hora es? VT (a race)

cronometrar; (a test) fijar la duración de; (one's arrival) fijar la hora de; **to — an attack well** atacar en el momento oportuno

timeless [táimlis] ADJ eterno

timely [táimli] ADJ oportuno

timer [táimə-] N (person) cronometrador -ora mf; (device) reloj m

timid [tímid] ADJ tímido, apocado

timidity [timídidi] N timidez f, apocamiento m

timing [táimiŋ] N (measurement) cronometraje m; (synchronization) sincronización f; **that was good —** lo hiciste en el momento oportuno

timorous [tímə-əs] ADJ timorato

tin [tin] N (metal) estaño m; (tin plate) hojalata f; **— can** lata f; **—foil** papel de estaño m, papel de aluminio m; VT estañar

tincture [tíŋktʃə-] N tintura f

tinder [tíndə-] N yesca f

tinge [tindʒ] VT (tint) teñir; (affect slightly) matizar; N (of color) tinte m, matiz m; (of taste) dejo m; (of irony) matiz m

tingle [tíŋgəł] VI sentir hormigueo, hormiguear; **to — with excitement** estremecerse de entusiasmo; N hormigueo m

tinker [tíŋkə-] VI ocuparse, entretenerse; **to — with** hacer ajustes

tinkle [tíŋkəł] VT (ring lightly) tintinear; (urinate) fam hacer pipí; N tintineo m

tinnitus [tináidəs] N tinitus m

tinsel [tínsəł] N (Christmas trim) espumillón m, guirnalda f; (tawdry decoration) oropel m

tint [tint] N (hue) matiz m; (for hair) tinte m, tintura f; (for glass) coloreado m; VT (hair) teñir; (glasses) colorear

tiny [táini] ADJ diminuto, chiquito

tip [tip] N (point) punta f; (gratuity) propina f; (piece of advice) consejo m; VI/VT (tilt) inclinar[se], ladear[se]; (give a gratuity) dar propina [a]; **to — a person off** advertir a alguien; **to — one's hat** sacarse/quitarse el sombrero; **to — over** volcar[se]

tipsy [típsi] ADJ alegre

tiptoe [típto] N punta del pie f; **on —s** de puntillas; VI andar de puntillas

tirade [táired] N diatriba f

tire [tair] N neumático m; Mex llanta f; Am goma f; VI/VT cansar[se], fatigar[se]; **to — out** cansar, fatigar

tired [taird] ADJ cansado, fatigado; **— out** agotado; **I'm — of your complaining** estoy harto de tus quejas

tireless [táirlis] ADJ incansable

tiresome [táirsəm] ADJ aburrido, pesado, plasta

tissue [tíʃu] N (cell aggregate) tejido m; (handkerchief) pañuelo de papel m; **— paper** papel tisú m

tit [tit] N (bird) paro m; (breast) vulg teta f

titanic [taitǽnik] ADJ titánico

titanium [taɪténiəm] N titanio *m*

tithe [taɪð] N diezmo *m*; VI pagar el diezmo

titillate [tídl̩et] VT (sexually) excitar; (interest) despertar interés

title [táɪdl̩] N título *m*; (of a painting) rótulo *m*; — **deed** título de propiedad *m*; — **page** portada *f*

TNT [tíéntí] N TNT *m*

to [tu] PREP **I gave it — you** te lo di a ti; **to count — ten** contar hasta diez; **I called — find out** llamé para averiguar; — **my surprise** para mi sorpresa; **a quarter — five** las cinco menos cuarto; **bills — be paid** cuentas por pagar; **things — do** cosas que hacer; **frightened — death** muerto de susto; **from house — house** de casa en casa; ADV — **and fro** de acá para allá; **to come —** volver en sí

toad [tod] N sapo *m*; —**stool** seta *f*, hongo no comestible *m*

toast [tost] VI/VT (brown) tostar[se]; VT (congratulate) brindar por; N (bread) tostada *f*; (congratulation) brindis *m*

toaster [tóstɚ] N tostadora *f*; — **oven** horno tostador *m*

tobacco [təbæko] N tabaco *m*

today [tədé] ADV hoy; (nowadays) hoy día

toddler [tádlɚ] N niño pequeño *m*, niña pequeña *f*

toe [to] N dedo del pie *m*; (of shoe, sock) punta *f*; —**nail** uña del dedo del pie *f*; VT (touch with toe) tocar con el dedo del pie; **to — the line** hacer buena letra, entrar en vereda

together [təɡéðɚ] ADV (in union) juntos; (at the same time) al mismo tiempo; — **with** junto con; **all —** todos juntos

Togo [tógo] N Togo *m*

Togolese [togəlíz] ADJ & N togolés -esa *mf*

toil [tɔɪl] VI trabajar, esforzarse, bregar; N trabajo *m*, esfuerzo *m*

toilet [tɔ́ɪlɪt] N (bowl) inodoro *m*; (lavatory) aseo *m*, lavabo *m*; — **paper** papel higiénico *m*; ADJ —-**trained** que ya no usa pañales

token [tókən] N (symbol) señal *f*; (keepsake) recuerdo *m*; (coinlike metal piece) ficha *f*; — **payment** pago nominal *m*; **as a — of friendship** en prenda de amistad

told [told] *see* tell

tolerance [tálɚəns] N tolerancia *f*

tolerant [tálɚənt] ADJ tolerante

tolerate [tálɚet] VT tolerar

toll [tol] N (of bells) tañido *m*; (payment) peaje *m*; (charges) tarifa *f*; (of victims) balance *m*; — **bridge** puente de peaje *m*; — **road** carretera de peaje *f*; ADJ —-**free** libre de cargos; VI/VT tañer [a muerto]

tomato [təméDo] N tomate *m*

tomb [tum] N tumba *f*, sepulcro *m*, sepultura *f*; —**stone** lápida *f*

tomboy [támbɔɪ] N marimacho *m*

tomcat [támkæt] N gato macho *m*

tomorrow [təmɔ́ro] ADV & N mañana *f*; — **morning** mañana por la mañana *f*

ton [tʌn] N tonelada *f*

tone [ton] N (pitch) tono *m*; (of a voice, instrument) sonoridad *f*; (of a speech) tono *m*, tónica *f*; VI **to — down** moderar, matizar

toner [tónɚ] N tóner *m*; — **cartridge** cartucho de tóner *m*

Tonga [tángə] N Tonga *m*

Tongan [tángən] ADJ & N tongano -na *mf*

tongs [tɔŋz] N tenazas *f pl*

tongue [tʌŋ] N (body part, language, of a flame) lengua *f*; (of a shoe) lengüeta *f*; — **depressor** depresor de lengua *m*; — **in cheek** irónicamente; — **twister** trabalenguas *m sg*; **on the tip of my —** en la punta de la lengua; **to hold one's —** callarse la boca; VI tocar con la lengua; **to —-lash** reprender; **to be —-tied** tener trabada la lengua

tonic [tánɪk] ADJ tónico; N (medicine) tónico *m*; (water, key note) tónica *f*; — **water** agua tónica *f*

tonight [tənáɪt] ADV esta noche

tonsil [tánsəl] N amígdala *f*

tonsillitis [tansəláɪDɪs] N amigdalitis *f*, anginas *f pl*

too [tu] ADV (in addition) también; (excessively) demasiado; — **bad!** ¡qué lástima! — **many** demasiados; — **much** demasiado

took [tʊk] *see* take

tool [tul] N herramienta *f*; —**bar** barra de herramientas *f*; —**box/kit** caja de herramientas *f*; —**shed** cobertizo para herramientas *m*

toot [tut] VI/VT (horn) sonar; (whistle) pitar; (trumpet) tocar; **to — one's own horn** darse autobombo; N (of horn, trumpet) toque *m*; (of horn) bocinazo *m*; (of whistle) pitido *m*

tooth [tuθ] N (front) diente *m*; (back) muela *f*; —**ache** dolor de muelas *m*; —**brush** cepillo de dientes *m*; — **decay** caries [dental] *f sg*; — **fairy** ratoncito Pérez *m*; — **mark** dentellada *f*; —**paste** pasta dental *f*, pasta dentífrica *f*; —**pick** mondadientes *m sg*, palillo de dientes *m*; **to fight — and nail** luchar a brazo partido; **to have a sweet —** ser goloso

toothed [tuθt] ADJ dentado

toothless [túθlɪs] ADJ desdentado

top [tɑp] N (of a mountain) cumbre *f*, cima *f*; (of a page) parte superior *f*; (of a jar) tapa *f*; (of a convertible) capota *f*; (of a table) superficie *f*; (of a tree) copa *f*; (toy) trompo *m*, peonza *f*; (blouse) blusa *f*; —**coat** abrigo *m*; — **dollar** precio exorbitante *m*; — **hat** sombrero de copa *m*; —**spin** liftado *m*; **at — speed** a velocidad máxima; **to be — dog** ir a la cabeza; **to be at the — of the class** ser el mejor de la clase; **at the — of one's voice** a voz en cuello; **filled up to the** — lleno hasta el tope; **from — to bottom** de arriba abajo; **on — of** encima de; ADJ (officer, floor) superior; (shelf, step) más alto; — -**flight** de primera; — -**heavy** desbalanceado; —**most** superior; — -**rated** de la más alta categoría; — -**secret** altamente confidencial; — -**notch** de primera; VT (a tree) desmochar; (a list) encabezar; (a performance) superar; (a level) exceder; **to — off** (an action) rematar; (a tank) llenar hasta el tope; **that —s everything!** ¡eso es el colmo!

topaz [tópæz] N topacio *m*

topic [tápɪk] N tema *m*, materia *f*, Am tópico *m*

topical [tápɪkəl] ADJ (of medicine) tópico; (current) de actualidad

topless [táplɪs] ADJ topless; — **swimsuit** monokini *m*

topple [tápəl] VT (knock over) derribar; (overthrow) derrocar; VI (fall) volcarse; (lose power) caer; **to — over** volcarse

topsy-turvy [tápsɪtɚvi] ADJ & ADV patas arriba

torch [tɔrtʃ] N antorcha *f*

tore [tɔr] *see* tear

torment[1] [tɔ́rmɛnt] N tormento *m*

torment[2] [tɔrmɛ́nt] VT atormentar, martirizar

torn [tɔrn] *see* tear[2]

tornado [tɔrnéɪ̃ɒ] N tornado *m*

torpedo [tɔrpíɪ̃ɒ] N torpedo *m*; — **boat** torpedero *m*; VT torpedear

torpid [tɔ́rpɪd] ADJ torpe

torpor [tɔ́rpɚ] N letargo *m*, torpor *m*

torque [tɔrk] N par de torsión *m*

torrent [tɔ́rənt] N torrente *m*

torrential [tɔrénʃəl] ADJ torrencial

torrid [tɔ́rɪd] ADJ tórrido

torsion [tɔ́rʃən] N torsión *f*

torso [tɔ́rso] N torso *m*, tronco *m*

tortoise [tɔ́rɒɪs] N tortuga *f*

tortuous [tɔ́rtʃuəs] ADJ tortuoso

torture [tɔ́rtʃɚ] N tortura *f*; VT torturar

torturous [tɔ́rtʃɚəs] ADJ torturante, torturador

toss [tɔs] VT (a ball, coin) tirar; (one's head) echar; (a salad) revolver; **to — aside** echar a un lado; VI (waves) cabecear; (a person in bed) dar vueltas; N (of coin, ball) tiro *m*; (of head) sacudida *f*

total [tódl] ADJ & N total *m*; — **amount** importe total *m*, montante *m*; — **loss** pérdidas totales *f pl*

totalitarian [totælɪtériən] ADJ totalitario

totter [tádɚ] VI tambalear[se], titubear

touch [tʌtʃ] VI/VT (have physical contact with) tocar; (move deeply) conmover, enternecer; (compare with) compararse con, igualar; (affect) afectar; **to — down** aterrizar; **to — off** provocar; **to — up** retocar; **to — upon** mencionar; N (contact) contacto *m*, roce *m*,

toque *m*; (sense) tacto *m*; (knack) mano *f*; (slight amount) poquito *m*; ; —**down** anotación *f*; —**down pass** envío de anotación *m*, pase de anotación *m*; — **screen** pantalla táctil *f*; — -**sensitive display** pantalla táctil *f*; —**stone** piedra de toque *f*; **a woman's** — un toque femenino; **finishing** — toque final *m*; **to keep in** — mantenerse en contacto; ADJ — -**and-go** precario; — -**tone** de botones

touching [tʌ́tʃɪŋ] ADJ conmovedor

touchy [tʌ́tʃi] ADJ hipersensible

tough [tʌf] ADJ (leather) fuerte, resistente; (fighter) duro, fuerte; (steak) duro, correoso; (situation) difícil; (neighborhood) bravo

toughen [tʌ́fən] VI/VT (leather) curtir[se]; (meat) endurecer[se]; (person) endurecerse

toughness [tʌ́fnɪs] N (of leather) resistencia *f*; (of a fighter, steak) dureza *f*; (of a situation) dificultad *f*; (of a neighborhood) lo bravo

toupee [tupé] N peluquín *m*

tour [tur] N (professional, artistic) gira *f*; (touristic) tour *m*, excursión *f*; (of a building) visita *f*; VI/VT (artistic, political) hacer una gira [por]; (touristic) hacer un tour

tourism [túrɪzəm] N turismo *m*

tourist [túrɪst] N turista *mf*; — **attraction** atracción turística *f*; — **class** clase turista/turística *f*

tournament [tɚ́nəmənt] N torneo *m*

tourniquet [tɚ́nɪkɪt] N torniquete *m*

tow [to] VT remolcar; N (pull) remolque *m*; (fiber) estopa *f*; —**rope** cuerda de remolque *f*; — **truck** remolque *m*, grúa *f*, Am guinche *m*; **in** — a cuestas

toward, towards [təwɔ́rd(z)] PREP (in the direction of) hacia; (for) para; — **four o'clock** a eso de las cuatro; **to feel angry** — estar enojado con

towel [táuəl] N toalla *f*

tower [táuɚ] N torre *f*; — **model** Am computadora torre *f*, Sp ordenador torre *m*; VI **to — over** elevarse sobre, dominar

towering [táuɚɪŋ] ADJ (tall) elevado, muy alto; (excessive) desmedido

town [taun] N (large) ciudad *f*; (small) pueblo *m*, localidad *f*; (downtown) centro *m*; — **hall** ayuntamiento *m*; **out of** — de viaje

toxic [táksɪk] ADJ tóxico; — **shock syndrome** síndrome de choque tóxico *m*

toxin [táksɪn] N toxina *f*

toy [tɔɪ] N juguete *m*; — **poodle** caniche enano *m*; VI **to — with** (fiddle with) juguetear con; (consider) considerar

trace [tres] N (path, mark, footprint) huella *f*; (mark) rastro *m*, traza *f*; (vestige) vestigio *m*; VT (a plan) trazar; (history) examinar; (an image) calcar; (a criminal) rastrear

trachea [trékiə] N tráquea *f*

tracheotomy [trekiáɒəmi] N traqueotomía *f*
track [træk] N (of a heel, animal) huella *f*; (of a
wheel) rodada *f*; (for racing) pista *f*; (path)
senda *f*, sendero *m*; (of a railroad) vía *f*; (on a
record) surco *m*; (on a CD) tema *m*, pista *f*; (of
study) orientación *f*; — **and field** atletismo
m; — **meet** encuentro de atletismo *m*; —
record trayectoria *f*; **to be off the** — estar
descarrilado; **to keep** — **of** seguir el hilo de;
VI/VT (a criminal) rastrear, seguir la pista de;
(an aircraft, a student, progress) seguir; VI
(wheels) estar alineado; (stylus) seguir los
surcos; **to** — **down** perseguir; **to** — **in mud**
traer lodo en los pies
tract [trækt] N (of land) terreno *m*; (political)
octavilla *f*; (digestive) tubo *m*
traction [trǽkʃən] N tracción *f*
tractor [trǽktɚ] N tractor *m*; —-**trailer**
tractocamión *m*
trade [tred] N (buying and selling) comercio *m*,
trato *m*; (industry) industria *f*; (swap) canje *m*,
cambio *m*; (manual labor) oficio *m*;
(profession) profesión *f*; (people in a business)
gremio *m*; —-**in** entrega como parte de pago
f; —-**off** compensación *f*; —**mark** marca
registrada *f*, marca de fábrica *f*; —
agreement acuerdo comercial *m*; —
balance balanza comercial *f*; — **barrier**
barrera comercial *f*; — **name** (of product)
nombre comercial *m*; (of company) razón
social *f*; — **school** escuela industrial *f*; —
union sindicato *m*; VI/VT (buy and sell)
comerciar, negociar; (exchange) canjear;
(traffic) traficar; **to** — **in** entregar
trader [trédɚ] N (dealer) comerciante *mf*; (at
fairs) feriante *mf*; (of slaves) tratante *mf*
trading [trédɪŋ] N transacciones *f pl*, comercio
m; — **partners** socios comerciales *m pl*
tradition [trədíʃən] N tradición *f*
traditional [trədíʃənəł] ADJ tradicional
traffic [trǽfɪk] N (of drugs) tráfico *m*; (of
vehicles) tránsito *m*, tráfico *m*; — **accident**
accidente de tránsito *m*; — **jam** atasco
circulatorio *m*; — **light** semáforo *m*; VI
traficar
tragedy [trǽdʒɪdi] N tragedia *f*
tragic [trǽdʒɪk] ADJ trágico
trail [treł] VI/VT (drag) arrastrar[se]; (follow in a
race) ir detrás [de]; (track) seguir la pista [de],
rastrear; VT (leave a trace) dejar una estela /
un reguero de; VI **to** — **off** desvanecerse,
apagarse; N (trace) rastro *m*, huella *f*; (path)
trocha *f*, sendero *m*, senda *f*; (of smoke) estela
f; (of blood) reguero *m*; — **bike** motocicleta
de trail *f*
trailer [trélɚ] N (of a truck) remolque *m*; (of a
film) sinopsis *f*, trailer *m*, avance *m*; (house)
caravana *f*
train [tren] N (railroad) tren *m*; (part of a dress)

cola *f*; — **of thought** hilo de pensamiento *m*,
VI/VT (worker) capacitar[se]; (troops, athlete)
adiestrar[se]; Am entrenar[se]; VT (an animal)
amaestrar; (a child) educar, formar; (a
cannon) apuntar; **to** — **on** (a camera, eye)
enfocar
trainee [trení] N aprendiz -iza *mf*, practicante *mf*
trainer [trénɚ] N (of animals) amaestrador -ora
mf; (of workers, troops, athletes) entrenador
-ora *mf*
training [trénɪŋ] N (of animals) amaestramiento
m; (of workers) capacitación *f*; (of troops,
athletes) entrenamiento *m*, adiestramiento
m; (of children) educación *f*
trait [tret] N rasgo *m*, seña *f*
traitor [tréɒɚ] N traidor -ora *mf*
trajectory [trədʒéktəri] N trayectoria *f*
tramp [træmp] VT (trample) pisar; VI andar con
pasos pesados; (roam, as a hobo)
vagabundear; N (hobo) vagabundo -da *mf*;
(promiscuous woman) *fam* fulana *f*; Sp *pej*
golfa *f*
trample [trǽmpəł] VT pisotear; **to** — **on/over**
pisotear, atropellar; **to** — **out** apagar de un
pisotón
trampoline [træmpəlín] N trampolín *m*, cama
elástica *f*
trance [træns] N trance *m*
tranquil [trǽŋkwɪł] ADJ tranquilo
tranquilizer [trǽŋkwɪlaɪzɚ] N tranquilizante *m*
tranquillity [trænkwflíɒi] N tranquilidad *f*
transact [trænzǽkt] VT llevar a cabo
transaction [trænzǽkʃən] N transacción *f*,
negocio *m*; —**s** actas *f pl*
transatlantic [trænzitlǽntɪk] ADJ
transatlántico
transcend [trænsénd] VI/VT trascender
transcendence [trænséndəns] N trascendencia *f*
transcendental [trænsendéntł] ADJ
trascendental, trascendente
transcribe [trænskráɪb] VT transcribir
transcript [trǽnskrɪpt] N transcripción *f*
transfer [trǽnsfɚ] VI/VT (on a bus, train)
trasbordar; (a prisoner, worker) trasladar[se];
VT (loyalty, rights, money, data) transferir;
(property) traspasar; N (on a bus, train)
trasbordo *m*; (of loyalty, rights, money, data)
transferencia *f*; (of a prisoner, worker)
traslado *m*; (of property) traspaso *m*; — **of
ownership** traspaso de propiedad *m*; —
rate velocidad de transferencia *f*
transferable [trænsfɚəbəł] ADJ transferible
transfix [trænsfíks] VT (impale) traspasar,
atravesar; (paralyze) paralizar
transform [trænsfɔ́rm] VI/VT transformar[se]
transformation [trænsfɚméʃən] N
transformación *f*
transformer [trænsfɔ́rmɚ] N transformador *m*
transfusion [trænsfjúʒən] N transfusión *f*; **to**

give a — dar una transfusión de sangre, poner sangre

transgress [trænzgrés] VT transgredir; **to** — **against** pecar contra; **to** — **the bounds of** traspasar los límites de

transgression [trænzgréʃən] N transgresión f, pecado m

transient [trǽnziənt] ADJ transeúnte, pasajero; N transeúnte mf, vagabundo -da mf

transistor [trænzístə˞] N transistor m

transit [trǽnzɪt] N tránsito m; **in** — en tránsito, de paso

transition [trænzíʃən] N transición f

transitive [trǽnzɪDɪV] ADJ transitivo

transitory [trǽnzɪtɔri] ADJ transitorio, pasajero

translate [trǽnzlet] VI/VT traducir

translation [trænzléʃən] N (rendering in different language) traducción f; (movement) translación f

translator [trǽnzleDə˞] N traductor -ora mf

transmission [trænzmíʃən] N transmisión f

transmit [trænzmít] VI/VT transmitir

transmitter [trænzmíDə˞] N transmisor m

transnational [trænznǽʃənəɫ] ADJ transnacional

transom [trǽnsəm] N travesaño m, montante m

transparency [trænzpéɹənsi] N transparencia f

transparent [trænspéɹənt] ADJ transparente; **to be** — traslucirse

transpire [trænspáɪr] VI (happen) ocurrir; (become known) descubrirse; VI/VT (perspire) transpirar

transplant[1] [trænsplǽnt] VI/VT trasplantar

transplant[2] [trǽnsplænt] N trasplante m

transport[1] [trænspórt] VT transportar, acarrear

transport[2] [trǽnspɔrt] N (moving) transporte m, acarreo m; (airplane) avión de transporte m; (rapture) éxtasis m; (of freight) flete m

transportation [trænspə˞téʃən] N transporte m

transpose [trænspóz] VI/VT (letters) transponer; (a song) transportar

transsexual [trænsékʃuəɫ] ADJ & N transexual mf

transverse [trænsvɝ́s] ADJ transversal; (flute) transverso

transvestite [trænzvéstaɪt] N travestí mf, travesti mf, travestido -da mf

trap [træp] N trampa f; (for hunting) trampa f, cepo m; (under a sink) sifón m; —**door** trampilla f; VI/VT (to capture animals) cazar con trampa, atrapar; VT (to pin) aprisionar

trapeze [træpíz] N trapecio m

trapezoid [trǽpəzɔɪd] N & ADJ trapezoide m

trash [træʃ] N basura f, desechos m pl; (people) pej gentuza f; — **can** cubo de basura m

trashy [trǽʃi] ADJ ordinario

trauma [trómə] N (physical) traumatismo m; (psychological) trauma m

traumatic [trəmǽDɪk] ADJ traumático

travel [trǽvəɫ] VI/VT viajar [por]; VI (sound waves) propagarse; (in basketball) caminar, hacer pasos; N viaje m; — **agency** agencia de viajes f; — **expenses** gastos de viaje m pl, gastos de desplazamiento m pl; —**s** viajes m pl

traveler [trǽvələ˞] N viajero -ra mf; —**'s check** cheque de viajero m

traverse [trəvɝ́s] VI/VT atravesar, cruzar; (skiing) bajar en diagonal; N (crossbar) travesaño m; (crossing) travesía f

travesty [trǽvɪsti] N farsa f

tray [tre] N bandeja f

treacherous [trétʃəəs] ADJ traicionero, alevoso

treachery [trétʃəri] N traición f, alevosía f

tread [trɛd] VI/VT (trample) pisar, pisotear; VI (walk) andar, caminar; N (step) paso m; (on tire) banda de rodadura/rodaje f; (on shoe) dibujo m; —**mill** cinta rodante f

treason [trízən] N traición f

treasure [tréʒə˞] N tesoro m; — **hunt** búsqueda del tesoro f; VT atesorar

treasurer [tréʒərə˞] N tesorero -ra mf

treasury [tréʒəri] N tesorería f, tesoro m; **secretary of the** — ministro -tra de hacienda mf

treat [trit] VI/VT (act toward, discuss in writing, give medical aid) tratar; **I** —**ed myself to ice cream** me di un festín de helado; N (pleasure) placer m; (gift) regalo m; **my** — yo invito

treatable [tríDəbəɫ] ADJ tratable

treatise [tríDɪs] N tratado m

treatment [trítmənt] N trato m, tratamiento m; (artistic handling) interpretación f

treaty [tríDi] N tratado m

treble [trébəɫ] ADJ (triple) triple; (of higher clef) de tiple; — **clef** clave de sol f; N tiple m; VI/VT triplicar

tree [tri] N árbol m; — **hugger** ecologista mf; —**top** copa de árbol f; **up a** — en aprietos

treeless [trílɪs] ADJ pelado, sin árboles

trek [trɛk] N expedición f; VI viajar con dificultad

tremble [trémbəɫ] VI temblar; N temblor m

tremendous [trɪméndəs] ADJ tremendo

tremor [trémə˞] N temblor m, sacudida f

tremulous [trémjələs] ADJ trémulo

trench [trɛntʃ] N (military) trinchera f; (for pipes) zanja f; (on sea floor) fosa f; — **coat** trinchera f, gabardina f

trend [trɛnd] N tendencia f

trendy [tréndi] ADJ de moda

trespass [tréspæs] N (illegal entry) entrada ilegal f; (religious) deuda f; VI (enter illegally) entrar ilegalmente; **to** — **against** (violate) violar; (sin) pecar; **no** —**ing** prohibido el paso

triage [triáʒ] N triaje m, clasificación f

trial [tráɪəɫ] N (testing) ensayo m, prueba f; (attempt) tentativa f; (affliction) aflicción f;

(in a court of law) juicio *m*, proceso *m*; —
balloon globo sonda *m*; — **by fire** prueba de
fuego *f*; — **flight** vuelo de prueba *m*; — **offer**
oferta de prueba *f*; — **period** período de
prueba *m*; — **run** ensayo *m*, prueba *f*; **by** —
and error por ensayo y error
triangle [tráiæŋgəl] N triángulo *m*
triangular [traiǽŋgjələ-] ADJ triangular
tribe [traib] N tribu *f*
tribulation [tribjəléʃən] N tribulación *f*
tribunal [traibjúnəl] N tribunal *m*
tributary [tríbjəteri] ADJ & N tributario *m*,
afluente *m*
tribute [tríbjut] N (tax) tributo *m*; (testimonial)
homenaje *m*
triceps [tráisɛps] N tríceps *m* sg
trick [trik] N (ruse) treta *f*, trampa *f*, trapisonda *f*;
(magician's) truco *m*; (prank) broma *f*; (in
cards) baza *f*; (of a prostitute) *fam* chapa *f*; **to
be up to one's old —s** hacer de las suyas; **to
play a — on someone** gastarle una broma a
alguien; **to turn —s** prostituirse; *slang* hacer
chapas; VT hacer trampa, engañar; **to —
someone into something** hacer que
alguien haga algo por medio de artilugios
trickery [tríkəri] N engaños *m pl*, argucias *f pl*
trickle [tríkəl] VI gotear; **to — in [out]** llegar
[irse] de a poco; N goteo *m*
trickster [tríkstə-] N embustero -ra *mf*
tricky [tríki] ADJ (artful) mañoso; (difficult)
complicado
tricycle [tráisikəl] N triciclo *m*
trifle [tráifəl] N (worthless thing) fruslería *f*,
nadería *f*, bobada *f*; (cheap purchase) bagatela
f; (small sum) miseria *f*; VI **to — with** jugar
con; **to — away** perder
trigger [trígə-] N gatillo *m*; VT desencadenar
trill [tril] VI/VT (birds) trinar; (musical
instrument) tremolar; (the *r* sound)
pronunciar con vibración; N (of birds, etc.)
trino *m*; (of the *r* sound) vibración *f*
trillion [tríljən] N billón *m*
trilogy [trílədʒi] N trilogía *f*
trim [trim] VT (adorn) adornar, guarnecer; (an
edge) bordear; (fingernails, hair, threads)
recortar; (hedge) podar; (airplane) equilibrar;
(a wick) despabilar; ADJ (neat) cuidado; (slim)
delgado; (fit) en buen estado físico; N
(embellishment) adorno *m*; (of sails)
orientación *f*; (cutting of hair) recorte *m*;
(cutting of hedge) poda *f*; (of an airplane)
equilibrio *m*
trimming [trímiŋ] N (act of cutting) recorte *m*;
(on a uniform) orla *f*, ribete *m*; —**s**
(embellishments) adornos *m pl*; (food)
guarniciones *f pl*; (parts cut off) recortes *m pl*
Trinidad and Tobago [trínidædəntəbégo] N
Trinidad y Tobago *f*
Trinidadian [trinidǽðiən] ADJ & N trinitense *mf*

trinket [tríŋkit] N chuchería *f*, baratija *f*
trio [trío] N trío *m*
trip [trip] N (journey, drug-induced condition)
viaje *m*; (experience) experiencia *f*;
(accidental stumble) tropezón *m*; (making
fall) zancadilla *f*; — **planner** planificador de
rutas *m*; VT (cause to stumble) hacer una
zancadilla a; (trip up) confundir; (release a
catch) soltar; (blow a fuse) hacer saltar; VI
(stumble) tropezar; (skip) andar con paso
ligero; (make a mistake) equivocarse;
(hallucinate) viajar; (blow a fuse) saltar
triphthong [trípθɔŋ] N triptongo *m*
triple [trípəl] ADJ & N (also in baseball) triple *m*;
VI (in baseball) pegar un triple; VT (multiply
by three) triplicar
triplet [tríplit] N trillizo *m*
tripod [tráipad] N trípode *m*
trite [trait] ADJ trivial, trillado
triumph [tráiəmf] N triunfo *m*; VI triunfar
triumphant [traiámfənt] ADJ triunfante,
triunfador
trivial [tríviəl] ADJ trivial, baladí, fútil
trod [trad] *see* tread
trodden [tradn] *see* tread
trolley [tráli] N (electric bus) trole *m*, trolebús *m*;
(on tracks) tranvía *m*
trombone [trambón] N trombón *m*
troop [trup] N (of scouts) tropa *f*; (of soldiers)
escuadrón *m*; (of tourists) horda *f*; —**s** tropas *f
pl*
trophy [trófi] N trofeo *m*
tropic [trápik] N trópico *m*
tropical [trápikəl] ADJ tropical
trot [trat] VI trotar; VT hacer trotar; **to — out**
sacar a relucir; N trote *m*; **the —s** *fam*
cagalera *f*
trouble [trábəl] VT (afflict) aquejar; (make
turbid) enturbiar; VI/VT (bother) molestar[se];
(disturb) preocupar[se]; **to —shoot**
solucionar problemas; N (problem) problema
m; (difficulty) dificultad *f*, sinsabor *m*;
(disturbance) disturbio *m*; (effort) molestia *f*;
(ailment) enfermedad *f*, trastorno *m*;
(mechanical breakdown) avería *f*, desperfecto
m; —**maker** agitador -ora *mf*, revoltoso -sa
mf; —**shooter** solucionador -ora *mf*,
localizador -ora de averías *mf*; **to be in —**
estar en un aprieto; **it is not worth the —**
no vale la pena; **to make — causar
problemas; **to take the —** tomarse la
molestia; ADJ —**-free** sin problemas
trough [trɔf] N (for food) pesebre *m*, comedero
m; (for water) abrevadero *m*, bebedero *m*; (of
weather, on ocean floor) depresión *f*
trousers [tráuzə-z] N pantalones *m pl*
trousseau [trúso] N ajuar *m*
trout [traut] N trucha *f*
trowel [tráuəl] N (for mortar) llana *f*, paleta *f*;

(for digging) desplantador *m*

truant [trúənt] N alumno -na que falta a clase sin permiso *mf*

truce [trus] N tregua *f*

truck [trʌk] N (vehicle) camión *m*; *Mex* troca *f*; (dealings) trato *m*; (vegetables) hortalizas *f pl*; — **driver** camionero -ra *mf*; *Mex* troquero -ra *mf*; VI/VT transportar en camión; *Mex* transportar en troca

trudge [trʌdʒ] VI andar con dificultad

true [tru] ADJ verdadero; (story) verídico; (copy, translation) fiel; (well) a plomo; (wheel) alineado, centrado; **—-blue** leal; **—-false test** prueba de verdadero o falso *f*; **his dream came —** su sueño se hizo realidad

truly [trúli] ADV (surprisingly) verdaderamente; (sincerely) sinceramente; (actually) en realidad, realmente; (accurately) fielmente; **very — yours** su seguro servidor, atentamente

trumpet [trʌmpɪt] N trompeta *f*; VI/VT (musician) trompetear; (elephant) barritar

trunk [trʌŋk] N (of tree, body) tronco *m*; (receptacle) baúl *m*; (of elephant) trompa *f*; (of a car) maletero *m*, *Mex* cajuela *f*; **—s** traje de baño *m*

trust [trʌst] N (confidence) confianza *f*; (charge) cargo *m*; (firm) trust *m*; (fund) fondo fideicomiso *m*; VI/VT (rely on) confiar en, fiarse de; VT (believe) creer; (hope) esperar

trustee [trʌstí] N (person holding property of another) fideicomisario -ria *mf*; (administrator) administrador -ora *mf*

trusteeship [trʌstíʃɪp] N (position of holding property) fideicomiso *m*; (administrative position) cargo de administrador *m*

trustful [trʌstfəl] ADJ confiado

trusting [trʌstɪŋ] ADJ confiado

trustworthy [trʌstwɝði] ADJ fidedigno, digno de confianza

trusty [trʌsti] ADJ leal

truth [truθ] N verdad *f*

truthful [trúθfəl] ADJ (account) verídico; (person) veraz

truthfulness [trúθfəlnɪs] N veracidad *f*

try [traɪ] VT (attempt) tratar de, intentar; (test, taste) probar; (strain) poner a prueba; (put on trial) procesar, enjuiciar; **to — on** probarse; **to — one's luck** probar fortuna; **to — and** tratar de; **to — out** (test) probar; (for a team) presentarse para; N intento *m*, tentativa *f*; **—out** prueba *f*

trying [tráɪɪŋ] ADJ penoso

tryst [trɪst] N cita romántica *f*

T-shirt [tíʃɝt] N camiseta *f*

tub [tʌb] N (for bathing) bañera *f*; (for butter) envase *m*; (for washing) tina *f*

tuba [túbə] N tuba *f*

tube [tub] N tubo *m* (also electronic); (television) televisor *m*

tuberculosis [tʊbɝkjəlósɪs] N tuberculosis *f*

tubular [túbjələ] ADJ tubular

tuck [tʌk] VT (stick in) meter; (make fold) alforzar; **to — in one's shirt** meter la camisa dentro del pantalón; **to — into bed** arropar; **to — something under one's arm** meterse algo bajo el brazo; N alforza *f*

Tuesday [túzde] N martes *m*

tuft [tʌft] N (of feathers) penacho *m*; (of hair) mechón *m*, copete *m*; (of plants) mata *f*

tug [tʌg] VI/VT (pull) tirar, jalar; (drag) arrastrar; **to — at** tironear; N (pull) tirón *m*; (boat) remolcador *m*

tuition [tuíʃən] N matrícula *f*

tulip [túlɪp] N tulipán *m*

tumble [tʌmbəl] VI (fall) caer; (collapse) venirse abajo; (do handsprings, etc.) dar volteretas; **to — down** rodar; **to — dry** secar en la secadora; **to — over** tropezarse; N (fall) caída *f*; (gymnastic trick) voltereta *f*

tumbler [tʌmblə] N (glass) vaso *m*; (person) acróbata *mf*

tummy [tʌmi] N barriguita *f*

tumor [túmə] N tumor *m*

tumult [túmʌlt] N tumulto *m*

tumultuous [tumʌltʃuəs] ADJ tumultuoso

tuna [túnə] N (fish) atún *m*, bonito *m*; (prickly pear) tuna *f*

tune [tun] N (melody) tonada *f*, aire *m*; (electronic adjustment) sintonía *f*; **—-up** afinación *f*; **to be in —** (in pitch) estar afinado; (adjusted) sintonizado; **to be out of —** estar desafinado; VT (engine) afinar; (musical instrument) afinar, templar; (radio) sintonizar; **to — in** sintonizar; **to — out** ignorar

tuner [túnə] N afinador -ora *mf*; (electronic) sintonizador *m*

tungsten [tʌŋstən] N tungsteno *m*

tunic [túnɪk] N túnica *f*

Tunisia [tunízə] N Túnez *m*

Tunisian [tunízən] ADJ & N tunesino -na *mf*

tunnel [tʌnəl] N túnel *m*; (for traffic) viaducto *m*; **— vision** visión en túnel *f*; VI cavar; VT hacer un túnel

turban [tɝbən] N turbante *m*

turbine [tɝbaɪn] N turbina *f*

turbocharger [tɝbotʃardʒə] N turbocompresor *m*

turbojet [tɝbodʒɛt] N turborreactor *m*

turbulence [tɝbjələns] N turbulencia *f*

turbulent [tɝbjələnt] ADJ turbulento

turd [tɝd] N *vulg* zurullo *m*, mojón *m*

turf [tɝf] N (lawn) césped *m*; (peat) turba *f*; (track for horse races) pista *f*; (territory) territorio *m*; VT cubrir con césped

Turk [tɝk] N turco -ca *mf*

turkey [tɝki] N pavo *m*; **— vulture** buitre

pavo *m*
Turkey [tɜ́ki] N Turquía *f*
Turkish [tɜ́kɪʃ] ADJ turco; — **bath** baño turco *m*
Turkmen [tɜ́kmən] ADJ & N turcomano -na *mf*
Turkmenistan [tɜkmɛnɪstǽn] N Turkmenistán *m*
turmoil [tɜ́mɔɪɫ] N confusión *f*, agitación *f*
turn [tɜn] VT (corner) doblar, dar vuelta; (wheel, key) girar, dar vuelta; (page) dar vuelta; (soil) labrar; (stomach) revolver; (ankle) torcer[se]; (a river) desviar; VI (change color) cambiar de color; (become) ponerse; (rotate) girar; (change direction) girar, dar la vuelta; **to — against** volverse en contra de; **to — around** dar la vuelta, girar; **to — away** (face) volver; (eyes) apartar; (person) rechazar; **to — back** (return) volver; (a clock) atrasar; **to — down** (offer, request) rechazar; (radio) bajar; **to — in** (hand in/over) entregar; (go to bed) acostarse; **to — inside out** dar vuelta al revés; **to — into** convertir[se] en; **to — off** (light) apagar; (faucet) cerrar; (a road) salir de; (person in general sense) disgustar; (person in sexual sense) quitarle las ganas a alguien; **to — on** (light) encender, prender; (faucet) abrir; (person) excitar; **to — out** (light) apagar; (people) expulsar; (product) producir; **to — out well** salir bien; **to — over** (car) volcar[se]; (engine) arrancar; (thought, idea, etc.) dar vueltas a; (criminal, weapon, etc.) entregar; —**table** plato giratorio *m*; **to — to** (have recourse to) acudir a, recurrir a; (become) volver[se]; **to — up** aparecer; **to — up one's nose** desdeñar; **to — up one's sleeves** arremangarse; **to — upside down** dar vuelta, N (rotation) vuelta *f*, revolución *f*; (change of direction) giro *m*, vuelta *f*; (change in condition) cambio *m*; (curve) recodo *m*, curva *f*; (opportunity) turno *m*; — **of mind** actitud *f*; —**off** (disgusting thing) asco *m*; (road exit) salida *f*; — **of phrase** giro *m*; —**out** concurrencia *f*; —**over** (of employees) renovación *f*; (of merchandise) volumen *m*; (in football) pérdida de balón *f*; (pastry) empanada *f*, pastelito *m*; (of a ball) pérdida *f*; —**pike** autopista *f*; —**stile** torniquete *m*, molinete *m*; — **signal** intermitente *m*; **at every** — a cada paso; **bad** — mala pasada *f*; **good** — favor *m*; **his bad teeth are a** —**off** sus feos dientes me dan asco / me repugnan; **his foreign accent is a** —**on** su acento extranjero me excita; **it's my** — me toca a mí; **to take** —**s** turnarse
turnip [tɜ́nɪp] N nabo *m*
turpentine [tɜ́pəntaɪn] N trementina *f*, aguarrás *m*
turquoise [tɜ́kɔɪz] N turquesa *f*
turret [tɜ́ɪt] N (small tower, gun tower) torreta *f*;

(on a ship) torre *f*
turtle [tɜ́dl] N tortuga *f*; —**dove** tórtola *f*; —**neck** cuello vuelto *m*
tusk [tʌsk] N colmillo *m*
tutor [túdɚ] N profesor -ora particular *mf*; VI/VT dar clases particulares
tutorial [tutóriəl] ADJ de tutoría; N (computer) tutorial *m*; (math, Spanish) cursillo *m*
Tuvalu [túvəlu] N Tuvalu *m*
Tuvaluan [tuvəlúən] ADJ & N tuvaluano -na *mf*
tuxedo [tʌksído] N esmoquin *m*
TV [television] [tiví] N *fam* tele *f*
twang [twæŋ] N (in music) tañido *m*; (of speech) nasalidad *f*; VI (vibrate) vibrar; VT hacer vibrar; VI/VT (speak nasally) ganguear
twangy [twǽŋi] ADJ gangoso
tweak [twik] VT (pinch) pellizcar; (adjust) ajustar; N (pinch) pellizco *m*; (adjustment) ajuste *m*
tweed [twid] N tweed *m*
tweezers [twízɚz] N pinzas *f pl*
twelve [twɛlv] NUM doce
twentieth [twɛntiɪθ] NUM vigésimo; **it's his** — **birthday** hoy cumple veinte años; **it's the** — **time I've told you** ya te lo dije veinte veces
twenty [twɛ́nti] NUM veinte; —**-five** veinticinco
twerp [twɚp] N idiota *mf*, papanatas *mf sg*
twice [twaɪs] ADV dos veces
twig [twɪg] N ramita *f*
twilight [twáɪlaɪt] N crepúsculo *m*, ocaso *m*; — **zone** zona gris *f*
twin [twɪn] ADJ & N (fraternal) mellizo -za *mf*; (identical) gemelo -la *mf*; — **bed** cama individual *f*
twine [twaɪn] N cuerda *f*; VI/VT (twist) enroscar[se]; (interlace) entrelazar[se]
twinge [twɪndʒ] N (of pain, remorse) punzada *f*
twinkle [twíŋkəl] VI (star) titilar, parpadear; (eyes) brillar; N (of stars) titileo *m*, parpadeo *m*; (of eyes) brillo *m*
twirl [twɚl] VI/VT girar, dar vueltas [a]; N giro *m*, vuelta *f*; (of ice cream) espiral *m*
twist [twɪst] VI/VT (wind, coil) torcer[se]; (distort) tergiversar[se]; (writhe) retorcer[se]; (coil) enroscar[se]; N (of an ankle) torcedura *f*; (distortion) tergiversación *f*; (in a road, coil) vuelta *f*; (unforeseen event) vuelta de tuerca *f*
twister [twístɚ] N tornado *m*
twitch [twɪtʃ] VI/VT crispar[se], mover[se]; N (tic) tic *m*; (pang) punzada *f*; (tug) tirón *m*
twitter [twídɚ] VI gorjear; N gorjeo *m*
two [tu] NUM dos; — **hundred** doscientos; —- **point conversion** conversión de dos puntos *f*; **my** — **cents' worth** mi opinión *f*; **to put** — **and** — **together** atar cabos; ADJ —- **bit** de chicha y nabo; —-**edged** de doble filo; —-**faced** (with two faces) de dos caras; (hypocritical) hipócrita, falso; —-**fisted**

pendenciero; —**-way** de dos sentidos
tycoon [taɪkún] N magnate *mf*
type [taɪp] N tipo *m*, índole *f*; —**face** tipo de letra
m; —**script** texto escrito a máquina *m*;
—**writer** máquina de escribir *f*; —**writing**
mecanografía *f*; VI/VT (a letter) escribir a
máquina, mecanografiar, digitar, teclear,
tipiar, tipear; VT (blood) determinar el grupo
sanguíneo; **to** —**set** componer; **to** —**write**
escribir a máquina; ADJ —**written** escrito a
máquina
typhoid [táɪfɔɪd] N tifoidea *f*; — **fever** fiebre
tifoidea *f*, tifus *m*
typhoon [taɪfún] N tifón *m*
typhus [táɪfəs] N tifus *m*
typical [típɪkəł] ADJ típico
typist [táɪpɪst] N mecanógrafo -fa *mf*
typo [táɪpo] N error tipográfico *m*
typographical [taɪpəgrǽfɪkəł] ADJ tipográfico;
— **error** error de imprenta *m*, errata *f*
typology [taɪpáləʤi] N tipología *f*
tyrannical [tɪrǽnɪkəł] ADJ tiránico
tyranny [tírəni] N tiranía *f*
tyrant [táɪrənt] N tirano -na *mf*

Uu

ubiquitous [jubíkwɪDəs] ADJ ubicuo
U-boat [júbot] N submarino alemán *m*
udder [ʌ́Dɚ] N ubre *f*
UFO [**unidentified flying object**] [júéfó] N
OVNI *m*
Uganda [jugǽndə] N Uganda *f*
Ugandan [jugǽndən] ADJ & N ugandés -esa *mf*
ugliness [ʌ́glɪnɪs] N fealdad *f*
ugly [ʌ́gli] ADJ feo; (incident) deplorable; (mood)
de perros
uh-huh [ʌhʌ́] INTERJ *fam* sí
Ukraine [jukrén] N Ucrania *f*
Ukrainian [jukréniən] ADJ & N ucraniano -na *mf*
ulcer [ʌ́łsɚ] N úlcera *f*
ulcerate [ʌ́łsəret] VI ulcerar
ulcerous [ʌ́łsɚəs] ADJ ulceroso
ulna [ʌ́lnə] N cúbito *m*
ulterior [ʌłtíriɚ] ADJ ulterior; — **motive**
segunda intención *f*
ultimate [ʌ́łtəmɪt] ADJ (destination) último,
final; (authority) final, máximo; (principle)
fundamental; (vacation) perfecto; N
súmmum *m*
ultimately [ʌ́łtəmɪtli] ADV en última instancia
ultimatum [ʌłtəméDəm] N ultimátum *m*
ultralight [ʌ́łtrəlaɪt] ADJ & N ultraligero *m*
ultramodern [ʌ́łtrəmádɚn] ADJ ultramoderno
ultrasound [ʌ́łtrəsaʊnd] N ultrasonido *m*; —

imaging imágenes por ultrasonido *f pl*
ultraviolet [ʌ́łtrəváɪəlɪt] ADJ & N ultravioleta *m*
umbilical cord [ʌmbílɪkəłkɔrd] N cordón
umbilical *m*
umbrella [ʌmbrélə] N paraguas *m sg*
umpire [ʌ́mpaɪr] N árbitro *m*; (in tennis) juez
-eza de silla *mf*; VI/VT arbitrar
unable [ʌnébəł] ADJ **to be** — **to** no poder
unabridged [ʌnəbríʤd] ADJ íntegro
unaccented [ʌnǽksɛntɪd] ADJ sin acento
unacceptable [ʌnɪkséptəbəł] ADJ inaceptable,
inadmisible
unaccustomed [ʌnəkʌ́stəmd] ADJ (not used to)
no acostumbrado; (uncommon) insólito
unadjusted [ʌnəʤʌ́stɪd] ADJ no ajustado
unadulterated [ʌnədʌ́łtəreDɪd] ADJ puro
unaffected [ʌnəféktɪd] ADJ (not affected) no
afectado; (sincere) natural, sincero;
(unpretentious) sin afectación
unaffiliated [ʌnəfílieDɪd] ADJ no afiliado
unanimity [junənímɪDi] N unanimidad *f*
unanimous [junǽnəməs] ADJ unánime
unarmed [ʌnɑ́rmd] ADJ desarmado
unassuming [ʌnəsúmɪŋ] ADJ modesto, sin
pretensiones
unattached [ʌnətǽtʃt] ADJ (piece of paper)
suelto; (person) soltero
unauthorized [ʌnɔ́θəraɪzd] ADJ no autorizado
unavailable [ʌnəvéləbəł] ADJ no disponible
unavoidable [ʌnəvɔ́ɪDəbəł] ADJ inevitable,
ineludible
unaware [ʌnəwér] ADJ inconsciente; ADV **to be**
— **of** ignorar; —**s** sin darse cuenta
unbalanced [ʌnbǽlənst] ADJ desequilibrado
unbearable [ʌnbérəbəł] ADJ inaguantable,
insoportable
unbeatable [ʌnbíDəbəł] ADJ imbatible
unbeaten [ʌnbítn̩] ADJ invicto
unbecoming [ʌnbɪkámɪŋ] ADJ (behavior)
impropio; (clothes) que no [le] luce
unbelief [ʌnbɪlíf] N incredulidad *f*,
descreimiento *m*
unbelievable [ʌnbɪlívəbəł] ADJ increíble
unbeliever [ʌnbɪlívɚ] N descreído -da *mf*
unbending [ʌnbéndɪŋ] ADJ inflexible
unbiased [ʌnbáɪəst] ADJ imparcial
unbounded [ʌnbáʊndɪd] ADJ ilimitado
unbridled [ʌnbráɪdl̩d] ADJ desenfrenado
unbroken [ʌnbrókən] ADJ (intact) intacto; (not
tamed) indomado; (uninterrupted)
ininterrumpido
unbuckle [ʌnbʌ́kəł] VT desabrochar
unbutton [ʌnbʌ́tn̩] VI/VT desabotonar,
desabrochar
uncalled-for [ʌnkɔ́łdfɔr] ADJ injustificado
uncanny [ʌnkǽni] ADJ inexplicable, misterioso
uncertain [ʌnsɚ́tn̩] ADJ incierto
uncertainty [ʌnsɚ́tn̩ti] N incertidumbre *f*
unchanged [ʌntʃénʤd] ADJ inalterado

uncharitable [ʌntʃǽrɪDəbəł] ADJ duro, poco caritativo

uncivilized [ʌnsívəlaɪzd] ADJ incivilizado

uncle [ʌ́ŋkəł] N tío *m*; **to say —** darse por vencido

unclean [ʌnklín] ADJ (dirty) sucio; (impure) impuro

uncollectable [ʌnkəléktəbəł] ADJ incobrable

uncomfortable [ʌnkʌ́mfɚɔəbəł] ADJ incómodo

uncommon [ʌnkámən] ADJ (unusual) poco común; (extraordinary) extraordinario

uncompromising [ʌnkámprəmaɪzɪŋ] ADJ (intransigent) intransigente; (unfailing) incondicional

unconcerned [ʌnkənsɚ́nd] ADJ indiferente

unconditional [ʌnkəndíʃənəł] ADJ incondicional

unconfirmed [ʌnkənfɚ́md] ADJ no confirmado

unconscious [ʌnkánʃəs] ADJ inconsciente

unconstitutional [ʌnkɑnstɪtúʃənļ] ADJ inconstitucional

uncontrollable [ʌnkəntróləbəł] ADJ (movement) incontrolable; (urge, laughter) incontenible

unconventional [ʌnkənvénʃənəł] ADJ poco convencional

uncouth [ʌnkúθ] ADJ tosco

uncover [ʌnkʌ́vɚ] VI/VT descubrir[se]; VI (remove bedcovers) destaparse

uncovered [ʌnkʌ́vɚd] ADJ descubierto

unctuous [ʌ́ŋktʃuəs] ADJ untuoso, zalamero

uncultivated [ʌnkʌ́łtəveDɪd] ADJ (person) inculto, no cultivado; (land) no cultivado

uncultured [ʌnkʌ́łtʃɚd] ADJ inculto

undaunted [ʌndɔ́ntɪd] ADJ impávido, intrépido

undecided [ʌndɪsáɪDɪd] ADJ indeciso

undeclared [ʌndɪklérd] ADJ no declarado

undefined [ʌndɪfáɪnd] ADJ indefinido

undelete utility [ʌndɪlít jutɪlɪDi] N programa para recuperar datos borrados *m*

undeniable [ʌndɪnáɪəbəł] ADJ innegable, indudable

under [ʌ́ndɚ] PREP (below) bajo, debajo de, abajo de; (in a ranking) por debajo de; (less) menos de; **— the Democrats** durante el mandato de los Demócratas; **— a pseudonym** bajo un pseudónimo; **— cost** a menos del costo/coste, por debajo del costo/coste; **— contract** bajo contrato; **— wraps** oculto; ADV (below) debajo, abajo; (less than) menos; **to be —** estar inconsciente

underage [ʌndəéʤ] ADJ menor de edad; **— drinking** consumo de alcohol por menores de edad *m*

underarm [ʌ́ndəɑrm] N axila *f*

underbrush [ʌ́ndɚbrʌʃ] N maleza *f*

undercharge [ʌndətʃárʤ] VI cobrar de menos

underclass [ʌ́ndəklæs] N subproletariado *m*

undercover [ʌndəkʌ́vɚ] ADJ clandestino, secreto

undercut [ʌndɚkʌ́t] VT (undermine) socavar; (sell for less) vender por menos que

underdeveloped [ʌndɚdɪvéləpt] ADJ subdesarrollado

underdog [ʌ́ndɚdɔg] N el de abajo *m*, la de abajo *f*

underemployed [ʌndɚɛmplɔ́ɪd] ADJ subempleado

underestimate [ʌndɚéstəmet] VT (person) subestimar; (price) subvaluar

underfed [ʌndɚféd] ADJ desnutrido

underfoot [ʌndɚfút] ADJ (beneath the feet) bajo los pies; (in the way) estorbando

undergird [ʌndɚgɚ́d] VT reforzar

undergo [ʌndɚgó] VT (an operation) someterse a; (a change) experimentar, sufrir

undergraduate [ʌndɚgrǽʤuɪt] N estudiante de pregrado *mf*; **— course** clase de pregrado *f*

underground¹ [ʌndɚgráund] ADV (under the earth) bajo tierra; (secretly) en secreto

underground² [ʌ́ndɚgraund] ADJ (under the earth) subterráneo; (secret) clandestino; N resistencia *f*, grupo clandestino *m*

underhanded [ʌndɚhǽndɪd] ADJ (secret) secreto, solapado; (illicit) ilícito

underlie [ʌndɚláɪ] VI/VT subyacer [a]

underline [ʌ́ndɚlaɪn] VT subrayar

underlying [ʌndɚláɪɪŋ] ADJ (inflation, racism) subyacente; (problems) de fondo

undermine [ʌndɚmáɪn] VT minar, menoscabar

underneath [ʌndɚníθ] PREP bajo, debajo de, abajo de; ADV debajo, abajo; N la parte inferior

undernourished [ʌndɚnɚ́ɪʃt] ADJ desnutrido

underpants [ʌ́ndɚpænts] N (for men) calzoncillos *m pl*; (for women) *Sp* bragas *f pl*; *Mex* pantaletas *f pl*; *RP* bombacha *f*

underrated [ʌndɚréDɪd] ADJ infravalorado

underscore [ʌndɚskór] N subrayado *m*; VT subrayar

undersecretary [ʌndɚsékrətɛri] N subsecretario -ria *mf*

undersell [ʌndɚséł] VT (to sell at a low price) malbaratar; (to sell cheaper) vender a menos precio

undershirt [ʌ́ndɚʃɚt] N camiseta *f*

underside [ʌ́ndɚsaɪd] N parte inferior *f*

undersigned [ʌndɚsáɪnd] N abajo firmante *mf*, infrascrito -ta *mf*

underskirt [ʌ́ndɚskɚt] N enaguas *f pl*

understaffed [ʌndɚstǽft] ADJ falto de personal

understand [ʌndɚstǽnd] VI/VT comprender, entender; **I — you're leaving** tengo entendido que te vas; **to — about** saber de/ entender de

understandable [ʌndɚstǽndəbəł] ADJ comprensible

understanding [ʌndɚstǽndɪŋ] N

(comprehension) comprensión f,
entendimiento m; (tolerance) comprensión
mutua f; (agreement) acuerdo m; ADJ
comprensivo

understate [ʌndə-stét] VT minimizar

understood [ʌndə-stúd] ADJ entendido;
(implicit) sobreentendido

understood [ʌndə-stúd] see understand

understudy [ʌndə-stʌdi] N suplente mf,
sobresaliente mf; VI/VT suplir [a], servir de
sobresaliente [para]

undertake [ʌndə-ték] VT emprender, acometer;
to — to comprometerse a

undertaken [ʌndə-tékən] see undertake

undertaker [ʌndə-tekə-] N director -ora de
funeraria / pompas fúnebres mf, funerario
-ria mf

undertaking [ʌndə-tékɪŋ] N empresa f

under-the-table [ʌndə-ðətébəł] ADJ ilícito, bajo
cuerda

undertone [ʌndə-ton] N (low voice) voz baja f;
(undercurrent) tónica f

undertook [ʌndə-túk] see undertake

undertow [ʌndə-to] N resaca f

undervalued [ʌndə-væljud] ADJ infravalorado

underwater [ʌndə-wɔtə-, ʌndə-wɔ́tə-] ADJ
submarino; ADV por debajo del agua

underwear [ʌndə-wɛr] N ropa interior f

underweight [ʌndə-wet] ADJ de peso
insuficiente

underworld [ʌndə-wɜ́łd] N (of criminals)
hampa f; (netherworld) el más allá

underwrite [ʌndə-raɪt] VI/VT (finance)
financiar; (sign) suscribir; (insure) asegurar

underwriter [ʌndə-raɪdə-] N (insurance)
asegurador -ora mf; (stock exchange)
suscriptor -ora mf

undesirable [ʌndɪzáɪrəbəł] ADJ indeseable

undetermined [ʌndɪtɝ́mɪnd] ADJ
indeterminado

undid [ʌndíd] see undo

undisclosed [ʌndɪsklózd] ADJ no divulgado

undisturbed [ʌndɪstɝ́bd] ADJ (unworried,
uninterrupted) tranquilo; (unspoiled) virgen

undivided [ʌndɪváɪdɪd] ADJ indiviso

undo [ʌndú] VT (reverse an action) deshacer,
anular; (unfasten) desabrochar, desabotonar;
(destroy) destruir; (loosen hair) soltar

undocumented [ʌndákjəmɛntɪd] ADJ
indocumentado

undoing [ʌndúɪŋ] N (reversal) deshacer m;
(destruction) destrucción f, perdición f; (of
buttons) desabrochar m

undone [ʌndÁn] ADJ (unfinished) sin terminar;
(ruined) perdido; (unfastened) desabrochado;
to come — (clothing) desabrocharse;
(person) desquiciarse

undone [ʌndÁn] see undo

undoubtedly [ʌndáʊdɪdli] ADV
indudablemente, sin duda

undress [ʌndrés] VI/VT desnudar[se],
desvestir[se]

undue [ʌndú] ADJ (inappropriate) indebido;
(excessive) excesivo

undulate [ʌndʒəlet] VI/VT ondular

undying [ʌndáɪɪŋ] ADJ imperecedero, eterno

unearned [ʌnɝ́nd] N inmerecido; **— run**
(baseball) carrera sucia f

unearth [ʌnɝ́θ] VT desenterrar

uneasiness [ʌnízinɪs] N (feeling) inquietud f,
desasosiego m, desazón f; Sp grima f; (of
peace) precariedad f; (of silence, situation)
incomodidad f; (of sleep) agitación f

uneasy [ʌnízi] ADJ (feeling) inquieto; (peace)
precario; (silence) incómodo; (situation)
molesto; (sleep) agitado

uneducated [ʌnédʒəkeDɪd] ADJ inculto,
ignorante

unemployable [ʌnɪmplɔ́ɪəbəł] ADJ inempleable

unemployed [ʌnɪmplɔ́ɪd] ADJ (jobless)
desocupado, desempleado, Sp parado;
(unused) ocioso

unemployment [ʌnɪmplɔ́ɪmənt] N
desocupación f, desempleo m, Sp paro m; —
compensation seguro de paro m; Sp paro m;
— rate Am tasa de desempleo f, Sp tasa de
paro f

unending [ʌnéndɪŋ] ADJ interminable

unequal [ʌníkwəł] ADJ desigual; **to be — to a
task** no ser capaz de cumplir una tarea

unequivocal [ʌnɪkwívəkəł] ADJ inequívoco,
tajante

unerase [ʌnɪrés] VT recuperar archivos borrados

unethical [ʌnéθɪkəł] ADJ no ético

uneven [ʌnívən] ADJ (rough) irregular,
accidentado; (inequitable) desigual; (not
uniform) desparejo; (odd, of numbers) impar

uneventful [ʌnivéntfəł] ADJ sin incidente

unexpected [ʌnɪkspéktɪd] ADJ inesperado

unexpressive [ʌnɪksprésɪv] ADJ inexpresivo

unfailing [ʌnfélɪŋ] ADJ (inexhaustible)
inagotable; (dependable) infalible

unfair [ʌnfér] ADJ (measure, price) injusto;
(competition) injusto, desleal

unfaithful [ʌnféθfəł] ADJ infiel

unfamiliar [ʌnfəmíljə-] ADJ (unknown) poco
familiar, desconocido; (unacquainted) poco
familiarizado

unfasten [ʌnfǽsən] VI/VT desabrochar[se],
desprender[se]

unfavorable [ʌnfévə-əbəł] ADJ desfavorable

unfeeling [ʌnfílɪŋ] ADJ insensible

unfettered [ʌnféDə-d] ADJ (untied) desatado;
(free) libre

unfinished [ʌnfínɪʃt] ADJ (matter) inacabado,
inconcluso; (business) pendiente; (wood) sin
terminar, sin barnizar; (task) inconcluso, sin
terminar

unfit [ʌnfít] ADJ (unsuitable) no apto; (incapable) incapaz

unfold [ʌnfóɫd] VT (open out) desdoblar, desplegar; VI (happen) desarrollarse; (reveal) revelarse

unforced error [ʌnfɔrst érɚ] N (tennis) error no forzado *m*

unforeseen [ʌnfɔrsín] ADJ imprevisto

unforgettable [ʌnfɚgéDəbəɫ] ADJ inolvidable

unfortunate [ʌnfɔ́rtʃənɪt] ADJ desgraciado, desafortunado, desventurado

unfortunately [ʌnfɔ́rtʃənətli] ADV desafortunadamente, lamentablemente

unfounded [ʌnfáʊndɪd] ADJ infundado

unfriendly [ʌnfréndli] ADJ (forces) hostil; (person) antipático

unfurl [ʌnfɚɫ] VI/VT desplegar[se]

unfurnished [ʌnfɚ́nɪʃt] ADJ sin amueblar, desamueblado

ungainly [ʌngénli] ADJ (ungraceful) desgarbado, desmadejado; (clumsy) torpe

ungrateful [ʌngrétfəɫ] ADJ ingrato, desagradecido

unguarded [ʌngárDɪd] ADJ (incautious) descuidado, desprevenido; (unattended) sin vigilancia; (defenseless) indefenso; **an — moment** un momento de descuido

unhappiness [ʌnhǽpɪnɪs] N infelicidad *f*

unhappy [ʌnhǽpi] ADJ (sad) infeliz, desdichado, desgraciado; (dissatisfied) insatisfecho; (infelicitous) poco afortunado

unharmed [ʌnhármd] ADJ ileso

unhealthy [ʌnhéɫθi] ADJ (climate, food, lifestyle) malsano, insalubre; (complexion, obsession) enfermizo

unheard-of [ʌnhɚ́Dɑv] ADJ inaudito, desconocido

unhinge [ʌnhíndʒ] VT desquiciar

unholy [ʌnhóli] ADJ (noise) infernal; (alliance) nefasto

unhook [ʌnhúk] VT (disentangle) desenganchar; (undo) desabrochar

unhurt [ʌnhɚ́t] ADJ ileso

uniform [júnəfɔrm] ADJ & N uniforme *m*

uniformity [junəfɔ́rmɪDi] N uniformidad *f*

unify [júnəfaɪ] VI/VT unificar[se]

unilateral [junəlǽDɚəɫ] ADJ unilateral

unimportant [ʌnɪmpɔ́rtn̩t] ADJ insignificante, sin importancia

uninhabited [ʌnɪnhǽbɪDɪd] ADJ deshabitado

uninhibited [ʌnɪnhíbɪʋɪd] ADJ desinhibido, desenfadado

uninspired [ʌnɪnspáɪrd] ADJ poco inspirado

uninstall [ʌnɪnstáɫ] VT desinstalar

uninsured [ʌnɪnʃúrd] ADJ sin seguro médico

unintelligible [ʌnɪntélɪdʒəbəɫ] ADJ ininteligible

uninterrupted [ʌnɪntərʌ́ptɪd] ADJ ininterrumpido

union [júnjən] N unión *f*; (labor) sindicato *m*,

gremio *m*; **— dues** cuotas sindicales *f pl*; **— labor** mano de obra sindicalizada/agremiada *f*; **— leader** dirigente sindical *mf*

unionize [júnjənaɪz] VI/VT sindicar[se], agremiar[se]

unique [juník] ADJ único, singular; **that feature is — to the South** ese rasgo es peculiar del sur

unisex [júnəsɛks] ADJ unisex

unison [júnəsən] ADV LOC **in —** al unísono

unit [júnɪt] N (part of a whole) unidad *f*; (part of a machine) módulo *m*

unitarian [junɪtériən] ADJ unitario

unitary [júnɪteri] ADJ unitario

unite [junáɪt] VI/VT unir[se]

United Arab Emirates [junáɪDɪdǽrəbémɚɪts] N Emiratos Árabes Unidos *m pl*

United Kingdom [junáɪDɪdkíŋdəm] N Reino Unido *m*

United States [junáɪDɪdstéts] N Estados Unidos *m pl*

unity [júnɪDi] N unidad *f*; (concord) unión *f*

universal [junəvɚ́səɫ] ADJ universal; **— donor** donante universal *mf*; **— joint** acoplamiento universal de cardán *m*

universe [júnəvɚs] N universo *m*

university [junəvɚ́sɪDi] N universidad *f*; **— degree** título universitario *m*

unjust [ʌndʒʌ́st] ADJ injusto

unjustifiable [ʌndʒʌstəfáɪəbəɫ] ADJ injustificable

unkempt [ʌnkémpt] ADJ (uncombed) desgreñado, despeinado; (messy) desaliñado

unkind [ʌnkáɪnd] ADJ antipático, poco amable

unknown [ʌnnón] ADJ desconocido; **— quantity** incógnita *f*; **it is —** se ignora

unlawful [ʌnlɔ́fəɫ] ADJ ilegal

unleaded [ʌnléDɪd] ADJ sin plomo

unleash [ʌnlíʃ] VT desatar

unless [ənlés] CONJ a menos que, a no ser que

unlicensed [ʌnláɪsənst] ADJ (without permission) sin permiso, ilícito; (without credentials) no acreditado

unlike [ʌnláɪk] ADJ distinto, diferente; **he is — me** es diferente de mí; PREP a diferencia de; **how — you to forget!** ¡me extraña que te hayas olvidado!

unlikely [ʌnláɪkli] ADJ (improbable) improbable; (not realistic) inverosímil; (exotic) exótico; **I am — to come** es improbable que venga

unlimited [ʌnlímɪDɪd] ADJ ilimitado

unload [ʌnlód] VI/VT (take cargo from) descargar; VI (pour out one's feelings) desahogarse; (sell) liquidar

unlock [ʌnlák] VI/VT abrir con llave

unlucky [ʌnlʌ́ki] ADJ (unfortunate) desafortunado; (ominous) aciago, funesto; **an — number** un número de mala suerte

unmanageable [ʌnmǽnɪdʒəbəł] ADJ (crisis, situation) inmanejable; (person) rebelde
unmanned [ʌnmǽnd] ADJ (deprived of courage) achicado; (with no crew) no tripulado
unmarked [ʌnmárkt] ADJ sin marcar
unmarried [ʌnmǽrid] ADJ soltero
unmask [ʌnmǽsk] VI/VT desenmascarar[se]
unmistakable [ʌnmɪstékəbəł] ADJ inconfundible
unmitigated [ʌnmídɪɡeDɪd] ADJ absoluto
unmoved [ʌnmúvd] ADJ (unflinching) impasible; (indifferent) indiferente
unnatural [ʌnnǽtʃəəł] ADJ (contrary to nature) no natural; (unloving) desnaturalizado; (monstrous) monstruoso; (affected) afectado
unnecessary [ʌnnésəseri] ADJ innecesario
unnoticed [ʌnnóDɪst] ADJ inadvertido, desapercibido
unobserved [ʌnəbzɝ́vd] ADJ inadvertido
unobtrusive [ʌnəbtrúsɪv] ADJ discreto
unoccupied [ʌnákjəpaɪd] ADJ (house) desocupado; (territory) no ocupado
unofficial [ʌnəfíʃəł] ADJ extraoficial, no oficial
unoriginal [ʌnərídʒənəł] ADJ poco original
unorthodox [ʌnɔ́rθədɑks] ADJ heterodoxo
unpack [ʌnpǽk] VT (a suitcase) deshacer, desempacar; (a carton) desembalar
unpaid [ʌnpéd] ADJ (debt) impagado, por pagar; (work) no remunerado
unplayable [ʌnpléəbəł] ADJ (golf) injugable
unpleasant [ʌnplézənt] ADJ desagradable
unpleasantness [ʌnplézəntnɪs] N (quality or state of being unpleasant) lo desagradable; (unpleasant episode) desavenencia f, disgusto m
unplug [ʌnplʌ́g] VI/VT desenchufar
unpopular [ʌnpápjələ˞] ADJ (decision) impopular; **she was — in school** tenía pocos amigos en la escuela
unprecedented [ʌnprésɪdentɪd] ADJ sin precedente, inaudito
unpredictable [ʌnprɪdíktəbəł] ADJ impredecible, imprevisible
unpremeditated [ʌnprɪméDɪteDɪd] ADJ impremeditado; (murder) sin premeditación
unprepared [ʌnprɪpérd] ADJ (surprised) desprevenido; (not ready) no preparado
unpretentious [ʌnprɪténʃəs] ADJ modesto, sin pretenciones
unprincipled [ʌnprínsəpəłd] ADJ sin escrúpulos, falto de principios
unprintable [ʌnpríntəbəł] ADJ impublicable
unproductive [ʌnprədʌ́ktɪv] ADJ improductivo
unprofessional [ʌnprəféʃənəł] ADJ poco profesional
unprofitable [ʌnpráfɪDəbəł] ADJ no rentable
unpublished [ʌnpʌ́blɪʃt] ADJ inédito, sin publicar
unpunished [ʌnpʌ́nɪʃt] ADJ impune

unqualified [ʌnkwáləfaɪd] ADJ (worker) Sp no cualificado; Am no calificado; (support) incondicional; (disaster) absoluto
unquestionable [ʌnkwéstʃənəbəł] ADJ incuestionable, indiscutible
unravel [ʌnrǽvəł] VI/VT (a rope) desenredar[se]; (a sweater) destejer[se]; (cloth) deshilachar[se]; (a plan) deshacer[se]; VT (a mystery) desentrañar
unreal [ʌnríəł] ADJ (not real) irreal; (unbelievable) increíble
unreasonable [ʌnrízənəbəł] ADJ (excessive) exagerado; (irrational) irracional, poco razonable
unrecognizable [ʌnrɛkəgnáɪzəbəł] ADJ irreconocible
unrefined [ʌnrɪfáɪnd] ADJ (oil, sugar) no refinado; (behavior) inculto, grosero
unrelated [ʌnrɪléDɪd] ADJ no relacionado
unreliable [ʌnrɪláɪəbəł] ADJ (person) informal; (machine, information) Sp poco fiable; Am poco confiable
unreported [ʌnrɪpɔ́rDɪd] ADJ sin declarar
unrest [ʌnrést] N malestar m, agitación f
unrestricted [ʌnrɪstríktɪd] ADJ no restringido
unroll [ʌnrół] VI/VT desenrollar[se]
unruly [ʌnrúli] ADJ (student) indisciplinado, revoltoso, díscolo; (country) ingobernable; (hair) rebelde
unsafe [ʌnséf] ADJ (risky) arriesgado; (dangerous) peligroso
unsanitary [ʌnsǽnɪteri] ADJ (behavior) antihigiénico, insalubre; (place, climate) insalubre
unsatisfactory [ʌnsæDɪsfǽktəri] ADJ no satisfactorio, insatisfactorio
unscrew [ʌnskrú] VT desatornillar, destornillar
unscrupulous [ʌnskrúpjələs] ADJ sin escrúpulos
unseasonable [ʌnsízənəbəł] ADJ impropio de la estación
unseat [ʌnsít] VT derribar
unsecured [ʌnsɪkjúrd] ADJ sin garantía
unseen [ʌnsín] ADJ invisible, oculto
unselfish [ʌnséłfɪʃ] ADJ desinteresado
unselfishness [ʌnséłfɪʃnɪs] N desinterés m
unsettled [ʌnsédłd] ADJ (situation) desordenado; (wilderness) sin colonizar; (case) pendiente; (weather) variable
unsightly [ʌnsáɪtli] ADJ feo, antiestético
unskilled [ʌnskíłd] ADJ (not trained) inexperto; (not qualified) Sp no cualificado; Am no calificado
unsolicited [ʌnsəlísɪDɪd] ADJ no solicitado
unsophisticated [ʌnsəfístɪkeDɪd] ADJ sencillo, no sofisticado
unsound [ʌnsáund] ADJ (argument) erróneo, falso; (body) enfermizo; (mind) demente; (foundation) poco sólido; (investment) poco

seguro
unspeakable [ʌnspíkəbəł] ADJ indecible
unspecified [ʌnspésɪfaɪd] ADJ no especificado
unsportsmanlike [ʌnspɔ́rtsmənlaɪk] ADJ
    antideportivo
unstable [ʌnstébəł] ADJ inestable
unsteady [ʌnstéDi] ADJ (walk) inseguro,
    inestable; (flame) tembloroso; (pulse)
    irregular
unsuccessful [ʌnsəksésfəł] ADJ sin éxito,
    infructuoso
unsuitable [ʌnsúDəbəł] ADJ (person) no apto;
    (place) inadecuado, inapropiado
unsuspected [ʌnsəspéktɪd] ADJ insospechado
untenable [ʌnténəbəł] ADJ insostenible
unthinkable [ʌnθíŋkəbəł] ADJ impensable
untidy [ʌntáɪDi] ADJ (dress) desaliñado,
    desastrado; (room) desordenado
untie [ʌntáɪ] VI/VT desatar[se], destrabar[se]
until [əntíł] PREP hasta; CONJ hasta que
untimely [ʌntáɪmli] ADJ (ill-timed) inoportuno;
    (premature) prematuro
untiring [ʌntáɪrɪŋ] ADJ incansable, denodado
untold [ʌntółd] ADJ (riches) incalculable;
    (suffering) inaudito
untouched [ʌntʌ́tʃt] ADJ (not injured) ileso; (not
    affected) no afectado; **he left his dessert —**
    no tocó el postre
untrained [ʌntrénd] ADJ (worker) *Sp* no
    cualificado; *Am* no calificado; (animal) no
    amaestrado; (eye) inexperto
untried [ʌntráɪd] ADJ (untested) no probado, no
    ensayado; (not taken to trial) no juzgado
untrue [ʌntrú] ADJ (incorrect) falso; (unfaithful)
    infiel; (disloyal) desleal
untutored [ʌntúDəˑd] ADJ (unschooled) sin
    instrucción; (unsophisticated) inculto
untwist [ʌntwíst] VT desenroscar
unused [ʌnjúzd] ADJ (no used) sin usar;
    (unaccustomed) no habituado
unusual [ʌnjúʒuəł] ADJ (infrequent)
    desacostumbrado, raro; (highly abnormal)
    inusitado, insólito
unvarnished [ʌnvárnɪʃt] ADJ (without varnish)
    sin barnizar; (straightforward) puro
unveil [ʌnvéł] VT (remove a veil) quitar el velo a;
    (reveal) descubrir
unwarranted [ʌnwɔ́rəntɪd] ADJ injustificado
unwelcome [ʌnwéłkəm] ADJ (untimely)
    inoportuno; (unpleasant) desagradable;
    (poorly received) mal recibido
unwholesome [ʌnhółsəm] ADJ malsano
unwieldy [ʌnwíłdi] ADJ poco manejable, difícil
    de manejar
unwilling [ʌnwílɪŋ] ADJ **to be — to** no estar
    dispuesto a
unwise [ʌnwáɪz] ADJ imprudente
unwonted [ʌnwɔ́ntɪd] ADJ inusitado,
    inacostumbrado

unworthy [ʌnwɝ́ði] ADJ indigno
unwrap [ʌnrǽp] VT desenvolver
unwritten [ʌnrítn̩] ADJ no escrito; (agreement)
    de palabra
unzip [ʌnzíp] VT abrir la cremallera
up [ʌp] ADV (position) arriba; (direction) hacia
    arriba; **—-front** (paid in advance) inicial;
    (frank) franco; **— and down** de arriba para
    abajo; **— against** enfrentado con; **he's —
    for reelection** se presenta para la
    reelección; **I'm feeling —** me siento
    optimista; **I'm — for golf** tengo ganas de
    jugar al golf; **prices are —** los precios han
    subido; **that is — to you** queda en tus
    manos, es cosa tuya; **the children are
    already —** ya se levantaron los niños; **the
    moon is —** salió la luna; **the wheat is —**
    germinó el trigo; **time is —** se terminó el
    tiempo; **to be — on the news** estar al
    corriente de las noticias; **to be — to one's
    old tricks** hacer de las suyas; **what's —?**
    ¿qué pasa? **he — and went** agarró y se fue;
    PREP **— the current** contra la corriente; **—
    the river** río arriba; **— the street** calle
    arriba; **— to now** hasta ahora; N **—s and
    downs** altibajos *m pl*; VI; ADJ (assembled)
    armado; (finished) terminado, concluido; **—-
    and-coming** prometedor; **—-to-date**
    actualizado
upbeat [ʌ́pbit] ADJ optimista
upbringing [ʌ́pbrɪŋɪŋ] N crianza *f*
update [ʌpdét] VT actualizar; N actualización *f*
upend [ʌpénd] VI/VT (stand on end) poner[se] de
    punta; (defeat) derrotar
upgrade [ʌ́pgred] VT (facilities) mejorar;
    (computer) actualizar; N (facilities) mejora *f*;
    (computer) actualización *f*
upheaval [ʌphívəł] N trastorno *m*
upheld [ʌphéłd] *see* uphold
uphill[1] [ʌ́phíł] ADV cuesta arriba
uphill[2] [ʌ́phíł] ADJ penoso, arduo
uphold [ʌphółd] VT sostener, apoyar; (legal
    decision) refrendar
upholster [ʌphółstɚ] VT tapizar
upholstery [ʌphółstəri] N tapicería *f*
upkeep [ʌ́pkip] N mantenimiento *m*
uplift [ʌplíft] VT (physically) elevar; (spiritually)
    edificar
upload [ʌ́plod] VT cargar, subir; N carga *f*
upon [əpán] PREP sobre, encima de; **— arriving**
    al llegar; **once — a time** érase una vez
upper [ʌ́pɚ] ADJ (higher) superior; (high) alto;
    to have the — hand dominar, llevar la
    ventaja; N (of shoe) pala *f*; (of berth) litera
    superior *f*; **— class** clase alta *f*; **— crust** flor y
    nata *f*; **—case** mayúsculo; **—cut** (in boxing)
    gancho al mentón *m*; **—most** (highest) de
    más arriba; (most important) mayor; **—
    respiratory infection** infección

respiratoria alta *f*; **—s** dentadura postiza superior *f*

uppity [ápɪDi] ADJ presumido

upright [ápraɪt] ADJ (posture) erecto, erguido; (position) vertical; (character) íntegro, recto, cabal; — **piano** piano vertical *m*; N (column) montante *m*; (piano) piano vertical *m*; (post) poste *m*

uprightness [ápraɪtnɪs] N (physical) verticalidad *f*; (moral) rectitud *f*

uprising [ápraɪzɪŋ] N alzamiento *m*, levantamiento *m*

uproar [áprɔr] N tumulto *m*, alboroto *m*, bulla *f*

uproarious [ʌprórɪəs] ADJ (tumultuous) tumultuoso; (funny) graciosísimo

uproot [ʌprút] VT arrancar de raíz, desarraigar

upscale [ápskɛɫ] ADJ de lujo

upset[1] [ʌpsɛ́t] VI/VT (overturn) volcar[se], tumbar; (distress) trastornar[se], perturbar[se], alterar[se]; VT (in sports) derrotar al favorito; ADJ (overturned) volcado; (ill) indispuesto; (distressed) disgustado, enojado

upset[2] [ápsɛt] N (overturning) vuelco *m*; (unexpected defeat) derrota inesperada *f*; (emotional state) trastorno *m*, disgusto *m*; (illness) malestar *m*

upshot [ápʃat] N consecuencia *f*

upside [ápsaɪd] N (upper part) parte superior *f*; (positive prospect) lo bueno; ADJ & ADV — **down** al revés, patas arriba

upstage [ʌpstɛ́dʒ] VT eclipsar

upstairs[1] [ʌpstɛ́rz] ADV (location) arriba, en el piso de arriba; (movement) [para] arriba

upstairs[2] [ápstɛrz] ADJ de arriba; N piso de arriba *m*

upstart [ápstɑrt] N advenedizo -za *mf*

uptake [áptek] N **quick on the** — listo; **slow on the** — duro de entendederas

uptight [ʌptáɪt] ADJ (nervous) nervioso; (conventional) estreñido

up-to-the-minute [áptəðəmínɪt] ADJ actualizado

upturn [áptɜn] N (prices) aumento *m*, subida *f*; (markets) tendencia alcista *f*

upward [ápwəd] ADV (toward a higher place) hacia arriba; — **of** más de; ADJ ascendente; — **mobility** ascenso social *m*; — **trend** tendencia al alza *f*

uranium [jurénɪəm] N uranio *m*

urban [ɜ́bən] ADJ urbano; — **blight** tugurización *f*; — **legend** leyenda urbana *f*; — **renewal** renovación urbana *f*; — **sprawl** expansión urbana *f*

urbanism [ɜ́bənɪzəm] N urbanismo *m*

urchin [ɜ́tʃɪn] N pilluelo -la *mf*, guaje -ja *mf*

urethra [juríθrə] N uretra *f*

urge [ɜdʒ] VT (exhort) exhortar, urgir; (beg) rogar; (propose) propugnar; **to — on** animar;

N impulso *m*, gana *f*

urgency [ɜ́dʒənsi] N urgencia *f*

urgent [ɜ́dʒənt] ADJ urgente

urinal [júrənɫ] N urinario *m*, mingitorio *m*

urinalysis [jurənǽlɪsɪs] N análisis de orina *m*

urinary [júrəneri] ADJ urinario; — **tract** vías urinarias *f pl*

urinate [júrɪnet] VI/VT orinar

urine [júrɪn] N orina *f*

URL [Uniform Resource Locator] [júárél] N URL *m*

urn [ɜn] N urna *f*

urologist [jurálədʒɪst] N urólogo -ga *mf*

Uruguay [júrəgwaɪ] N Uruguay *m*

Uruguayan [jurəgwáɪən] ADJ & N uruguayo -ya *mf*

us [ʌs] PRON nos; **she saw** — nos vio; **he came with** — vino con nosotros; **he gave it to** — nos lo dio [a nosotros]

USA [United States of America] [júésé] N EEUU *m sg/pl*

usable [júzəbɫ] ADJ utilizable, aprovechable

usage [júsɪdʒ] N uso *m*, costumbre *f*

USB [Universal Serial Bus] [júésbí] N USB *m*; — **port** puerto USB *m*

use[1] [juz] VT usar, utilizar (also exploit); (consume) gastar; (take advantage of) aprovecharse de; VI **to — up** gastar, agotar

use[2] [jus] N (application) uso *m*; (utilization) empleo *m*, utilización *f*, aprovechamiento *m*; (usefulness) utilidad *f*; **it is of no** — es inútil; **out of** — en desuso; **to have no** — **for** no soportar; **to make** — **of** usar, utilizar; **to put to** — utilizar; **what is the** — **of it?** ¿para qué sirve?

used[1] [juzd] ADJ usado

used[2] [just] VI **to be** — **to** estar acostumbrado a; **it** — **to be green** antes era verde

useful [júsfəɫ] ADJ útil

usefulness [júsfəlnɪs] N utilidad *f*

useless [júslɪs] ADJ inútil, inservible

uselessness [júslɪsnɪs] N inutilidad *f*

user [júzɚ] N usuario -ria *mf*; —-**friendly** fácil de utilizar; — **group** grupo de usuarios *m*; —**name** nombre del usuario *m*

usher [ʌ́ʃɚ] N acomodador -ora *mf*; VT conducir, acompañar; **to** — **in** (a person) acompañar; (an era) anunciar, marcar el comienzo de

usual [júʒuəɫ] ADJ (habitual) usual, habitual; (everyday) de todos los días; **as** — como siempre; **she wasn't her** — **self** no era la de siempre; **the** — **thing** lo normal; **more than** — más que de costumbre

usually [júʒuəli] ADV generalmente, normalmente; **he** — **doesn't mind** no suele importarle

usurp [jusɜ́p] VI/VT usurpar

usury [júʒəri] N usura *f*

utensil [juténsəɫ] N utensilio *m*, útil *m*

uterine [júDə‑ɪn] ADJ uterino
uterus [júDə‑əs] N útero *m*
UTI [**urinary tract infection**] [jútíáɪ] N infección del tracto urinario *f*
utilitarian [jutɪlɪtériən] ADJ utilitario
utility [jutílɪDi] N (usefulness) utilidad *f*; (public service) empresa de servicio público *f*, empresa de agua o electricidad *f*; — **furniture** muebles prácticos *m pl*; — **program** programa utilitario *m*; — **room** lavadero *m*
utilization [judlɪzéʃən] N utilización *f*
utilize [júdlaɪz] VT utilizar
utmost [Átmost] ADJ (extreme) sumo, extremo; (farthest) más distante; N máximo *m*; **he did his** — hizo cuanto pudo; **to the** — al máximo
utopia [jutópiə] N utopía *f*
utter [Áɒə‑] VT (emit) dar, proferir; (say) decir, pronunciar; (make circulate) poner en circulación; ADJ absoluto, completo
utterance [Áɒə‑əns] N (of words) enunciado *m*; (of money) emisión *f*
uvula [júvjələ] N campanilla *f*, úvula *f*
Uzbek [Úzbɛk] ADJ & N uzbeko ‑ka *mf*
Uzbekistan [Uzbékɪstæn] N Uzbekistán *m*

Vv

vacancy [vékənsi] N (job) vacante *f*; (room in hotel) habitación libre *f*; **no** — completo
vacant [vékənt] ADJ (position) vacante; (expression) vacío; (seat, room) libre
vacate [véket] VI/VT (a room) desalojar, desocupar; (a contract) anular; (a position) dejar vacante
vacation [vekéʃən] N vacaciones *f pl*; **on** — de vacaciones
vaccinate [væksənet] VI/VT vacunar
vaccination [væksənéʃən] N vacunación *f*
vaccine [væksín] N vacuna *f*
vacillate [væsəlet] VI vacilar
vacuum [vækjum] N vacío *m*; — **cleaner** aspiradora *f*; — **tube** tubo de vacío *m*; ADJ —‑**packed** envasado al vacío; VI/VT pasar la aspiradora
vagabond [vǽgəbɑnd] ADJ & N vagabundo ‑da *mf*
vagina [vədʒáɪnə] N vagina *f*
vaginal [vǽdʒənl] ADJ vaginal; — **bleeding** hemorragia vaginal *f*; — **discharge** flujo vaginal *m*; — **itching** escozor vaginal *m*
vaginitis [vædʒɪnáɪDɪs] N vaginitis *f*
vagrancy [végrənsi] N vagancia *f*
vagrant [végrənt] ADJ & N vagabundo ‑da *mf*
vague [veg] ADJ vago, indistinto

vain [ven] ADJ (futile) vano, hueco; (proud of appearance) vanidoso; **in** — en vano
Valencian [vəlénsiən] ADJ & N valenciano ‑na
valentine [vǽləntaɪn] N (card) tarjeta del día de San Valentín *f*; (person) querido ‑da *mf*; —'**s Day** día de San Valentín *m*, día de los enamorados *m*
valet [vælé] N (manservant) criado *m*; (in a hotel) mozo de habitación *m*; (car parker) aparcacoches *m sg*
valiant [vǽljənt] ADJ valiente
valid [vǽlɪd] ADJ válido, valedero; **to be/ become** — tener efectividad
validity [vəlíDɪti] N validez *f*
valise [vəlíz] N maleta *f*, valija *f*
valley [vǽli] N valle *m*
valor [vǽlə‑] N valor *m*, valentía *f*
valorize [vǽləraɪz] VT valorar
valorous [vǽlə‑əs] ADJ valeroso, valiente
valuable [vǽljəbəl] ADJ valioso, preciado; N —**s** objetos de valor *m pl*
valuation [væljuéʃən] N (value) valoración *f*; (appraisal) tasación *f*, valuación *f*
value [vǽlju] N valor *m*; VT valorar
valve [vælv] N válvula *f*; (on mollusks) valva *f*
vamp [væmp] N vampiresa *f*; VT seducir
vampire [vǽmpaɪr] N vampiro *m*
van [væn] N camioneta *f*
vandal [vǽndl] N vándalo *m*
vane [ven] N (for weather) veleta *f*; (of a fan, windmill) aspa *f*; (of propeller) paleta *f*
vanilla [vənílə] N vainilla *f*
vanish [vǽnɪʃ] VI desaparecer, esfumarse
vanity [vǽnɪDi] N vanidad *f*; — **table** tocador *m*
vanquish [vǽnkwɪʃ] VT vencer
vantage point [vǽntɪdʒpɔɪnt] N mirador *m*
Vanuatu [vɑnuátu] N Vanuatu *m*
Vanuatuan [vɑnuátuən] ADJ & N vanuatuense *mf*
vapor [vépə‑] N vapor *m*, humo *m*
vaporize [vépə‑aɪz] VI/VT vaporizar[se]
variable [vériəbəl] ADJ & N variable *f*; — **annuity** anualidad variable *f*
variance [vériəns] N discrepancia *f*, desacuerdo *m*; **to be at** — no concordar
variant [vériənt] N variante *f*, modalidad *f*
variation [veriéʃən] N variación *f*
varicose [vǽrɪkos] ADJ varicoso; — **veins** *Sp* varices *f pl*; *Am* várices *f pl*
varied [vérid] ADJ variado, vario
variegated [vériɪgeDɪd] ADJ variopinto
variety [vəráɪɪDi] N variedad *f*
various [vériəs] ADJ vario
varnish [várnɪʃ] N barniz *m*, charol *m*; VT barnizar, charolar
varsity [vársɪDi] N equipo universitario *m*
vary [véri] VI/VT variar
vascular [vǽskjələ‑] ADJ vascular
vase [ves] N jarrón *m*; (for flowers) florero *m*
vasectomy [vəséktəmi] N vasectomía *f*

Vaseline™ [vǽsəlín] N vaselina f
vast [væst] ADJ vasto, inmenso
vastly [vǽstli] ADV enormemente
vastness [vǽstnɪs] N inmensidad f
vat [væt] N tina f, barrica f
VAT [value-added tax] [víétí] N IVA m
Vatican City [vǽDɪkənsíDi] N Ciudad del Vaticano f
vaudeville [vɔ́dvɪɫ] N vodevil m
vault [vɔɫt] N (arched structure) bóveda f; (burial chamber) panteón m; (place for valuables) cámara acorazada f; (jump) salto m; VT (cover with a vault) abovedar; VI/VT (jump) saltar
VCR [videocassette recorder] [vísíár] N Am video m; Sp vídeo m
VD [venereal disease] [vídí] N [enfermedad] venérea f
veal [viɫ] N ternera f; — **cutlet** chuleta de ternera f
vector [vɛktɚ] N vector m
veer [vir] VI/VT virar; N virada f
vegan [vígən] ADJ & N vegan mf
vegetable [védʒtəbəɫ] N (food) verdura f, hortaliza f; (plant, comatose person) vegetal m; — **garden** huerto m; (large) huerta f; — **kingdom** reino vegetal m; — **oil** aceite vegetal m
vegetarian [vɛdʒɪtériən] ADJ & N vegetariano -na mf
vegetate [védʒɪtet] VI vegetar
vegetation [vɛdʒɪtéʃən] N vegetación f
vegetative [védʒɪteDɪv] ADJ vegetativo
vehemence [víəməns] N vehemencia f
vehement [víəmənt] ADJ vehemente
vehicle [víɪkəɫ] N vehículo m
veil [veɫ] N velo m; VT velar
vein [ven] N (blood vessel, style) vena f; (small deposit of ore) veta f; (large deposit of ore) filón m
veined [vend] ADJ (marble) veteado; (leaf) nervado
velocity [vəlásɪDi] N velocidad f
velvet [vélvɪt] N terciopelo m; ADJ (of velvet) de terciopelo; (like velvet) aterciopelado
velvety [vélvɪDi] ADJ aterciopelado
vendetta [vɛndéDə] N vendetta f
vending machine [véndɪŋməʃin] N expendedor automático m, máquina expendedora f
vendor [véndɚ] N vendedor -ora mf, proveedor -ora mf; (in a stall) puestero -ra mf
veneer [vənír] N (layer of wood) chapa f; (outward appearance) barniz m; VT chapar, enchapar
venerable [vénɚəbəɫ] ADJ venerable
venerate [vénɚet] VT venerar
veneration [vɛnɚéʃən] N veneración f
venereal [vəníriəɫ] ADJ venéreo; — **disease** enfermedad venérea f
venetian blind [vəníʃənbláɪnd] N veneciana f

Venezuela [vɛnɪzwélə] N Venezuela f
Venezuelan [vɛnɪzwélən] ADJ & N venezolano -na mf
vengeance [véndʒəns] N venganza f; **with a** — (violently) con furia; (energetically) con ganas
vengeful [véndʒfəɫ] ADJ vengativo
venison [vénəsən] N carne de venado f
venom [vénəm] N veneno m
venomous [vénəməs] ADJ venenoso
vent [vɛnt] N (outlet for air) ventilación f; (opening of a volcano) chimenea f; **to give** — **to anger** desahogar la ira; VI/VT desahogar[se], descargar[se]
ventilate [véntɫet] VI/VT ventilar[se]
ventilation [ventɫéʃən] N ventilación f
ventilator [véntɫeDɚ] N ventilador m
ventricle [véntrɪkəɫ] N ventrículo m
venture [véntʃɚ] N (adventure) aventura f; (business enterprise) empresa f; — **capital** capital de riesgo m; VI/VT aventurar[se], arriesgar[se]
venue [vénju] N lugar m
veranda [vərǽndə] N porche m, terraza f
verb [vɝb] N verbo m
verbal [vɝbəɫ] ADJ (linguistic, related to verbs) verbal; (not written) oral
verbatim [vɚbéDəm] ADJ textual; ADV textualmente
verbiage [vɝbiɪdʒ] N palabrerío m
verbose [vɚbós] ADJ verboso
verdict [vɝDɪkt] N veredicto m
verdure [vɝdʒɚ] N lit verdura f
verge [vɝdʒ] ADV LOC **on the** — **of** al borde de, a punto de; VI **to** — **on** rayar en, lindar con
verification [vɛrɪfɪkéʃən] N verificación f, comprobación f
verify [vérɪfaɪ] VT verificar, constatar, comprobar
veritable [vérɪDəbəɫ] ADJ verdadero
vermillion [vɚmíljən] ADJ & N bermellón m
vermin [vɝmɪn] N bichos m pl
vermouth [vɚmúθ] N vermú m
vernacular [vɚnǽkjəlɚ] ADJ vernáculo; N (plain language) lengua vernácula f
versatile [vɝsədɫ] ADJ versátil
verse [vɝs] N verso m; (stanza) estrofa f; (line of poem) verso m; (in Bible) versículo m
versed [vɝst] ADJ versado
version [vɝʒən] N versión f
versus [vɝsəs] PREP contra; (in sports) versus
vertebra [vɝDəbrə] N vértebra f
vertebrate [vɝDəbrɪt] ADJ vertebrado
vertical [vɝDɪkəɫ] ADJ vertical
vertigo [vɝDɪgo] N vértigo m
very [véri] ADV muy; — **many** muchísimos; — **much** muchísimo; **it is** — **cold today** hace mucho frío hoy; ADJ (same) mismo; (mere) mero

vessel [vésəl] N (container) vasija *f*; (duct) vaso *m*; (ship) nave *f*
vest [vɛst] N chaleco *m*; VT conferir; —**ed interests** intereses creados *m pl*
vestibule [véstɪbjuł] N vestíbulo *m*, zaguán *m*
vestige [véstɪʤ] N vestigio *m*
vet [vɛt] N (veterinarian) veterinario -ria *mf*; (veteran) veterano -na militar *mf*; VT evaluar
veteran [véɒəən] ADJ & N veterano -na *mf*
veterinarian [vɛɒəənériən] N veterinario -ria *mf*
veterinary [véɒəənɛri] ADJ veterinario; —**medicine** veterinaria *f*
veto [víto] N veto *m*; VT vetar
vex [vɛks] VT molestar, irritar
via [váɪə, víə] PREP (by way of) vía; (by means of) por
viability [vaɪəbílɪDi] N viabilidad *f*
viable [váɪəbəł] ADJ viable
vial [váɪəł] N ampolla *f*, frasco *m*
vibrate [váɪbret] VI/VT vibrar
vibration [vaɪbréʃən] N vibración *f*
vibrator [váɪbreɒə] N vibrador *m*
vicarious [vaɪkériəs] ADJ indirecto
vice [vaɪs] N vicio *m*
vice president [váɪsprézɪɒənt] N vicepresidente -ta *mf*
viceroy [váɪsrɔɪ] N virrey *m*
viceroyalty [vaɪsróɪəłli] ADJ virreinato
vice versa [váɪsəvɜ́sə] ADV viceversa
vicinity [vɪsínɪDi] N vecindad *f*, cercanías *f pl*, aledaños *m pl*
vicious [víʃəs] ADJ (violent) violento, sanguinario; (evil) maligno, perverso; (malicious) malicioso; —**circle** círculo vicioso *m*; —**dog** perro fiero *m*, perro bravo *m*
vicissitude [vɪsísɪtud] N vicisitud *f*, peripecia *f*
victim [víktɪm] N víctima *f*
victimize [víktəmaɪz] VT (make victim) victimizar; (dupe) estafar
victor [víktə] N vencedor -ora *mf*
victorious [vɪktóriəs] ADJ victorioso
victory [víktəri] N victoria *f*
video [vídio] N *Am* video *m*; *Sp* vídeo *m*; —**cassette** *Am* video *m*; *Sp* vídeo *m*; —**cassette recorder** videocasete *m*; —**conference** videoconferencia *f*; —**console** videoconsola *f*; —**game** videojuego *m*; —**portal** *Am* portal de videos *m*; *Sp* portal de vídeos *m*; —**tape** *Am* cinta de video *f*; *Sp* cinta de vídeo *f*; —**clip** videoclip *m*
vie [vaɪ] VI competir; **to —for power** disputarse el poder
Vietnam [vietnám] N Vietnam *m*
Vietnamese [viɪtnəmíz] ADJ & N vietnamita *mf*
view [vju] N (field of vision) vista *f*; (opinion) opinión *f*; (panorama) visión panorámica *f*; —**point** punto de vista *m*; **in —of** en vista

de; **to be within** — estar a la vista; **with a —to** con el propósito de; VT (see) ver; (consider) enfocar
viewer [vjúə] N telespectador -ora *mf*, televidente *mf*
vigil [víʤəł] N vigilia *f*, vela *f*; **to keep** — velar
vigilance [víʤələns] N vigilancia *f*
vigilant [víʤələnt] ADJ vigilante
vigor [vígə] N vigor *m*, pujanza *f*, dinamismo *m*
vigorous [vígəəs] ADJ vigoroso
vile [vaɪł] ADJ (evil) vil, ruin; (foul, bad) pésimo
villa [víłə] N quinta *f*, casa de campo *f*
village [víłɪʤ] N aldea *f*, villa *f*
villager [víłɪʤə] N aldeano -na *mf*
villain [víłən] N villano -na *mf*
villainous [víłənəs] ADJ vil, villano
villainy [víłəni] N villanía *f*, vileza *f*
vindicate [víndɪket] VT reivindicar, vindicar
vindication [vɪndɪkéʃən] N reivindicación *f*, vindicación *f*
vindictive [vɪndíktɪv] ADJ vengativo
vine [vaɪn] N (grapevine) vid *f*; (decorative) parra *f*; (stem) sarmiento *m*; (climbing plant) enredadera *f*
vinegar [vínɪgə] N vinagre *m*
vineyard [vínjəd] N viña *f*, viñedo *m*
vintage [víntɪʤ] N (act or season of gathering grapes) vendimia *f*; (harvest of grapes) cosecha *f*; (year) año *m*; ADJ (wine) añejo; (classic) excelente; (old) antiguo, de colección; (typical) típico
vinyl [váɪnł] N vinilo *m*
viola [vióła] N viola *f*
violate [váɪəlet] VT violar; (a law) violar, quebrantar
violation [vaɪəléʃən] N violación *f*; (traffic) infracción *f*
violence [váɪələns] N violencia *f*
violent [váɪələnt] ADJ violento
violet [váɪəlɪt] N (flower) violeta *f*; (color) violeta *m*; ADJ violeta
violin [vaɪəlín] N violín *m*
violinist [vaɪəlínɪst] N violinista *mf*
VIP [very important person] [víáɪpí] N & ADJ VIP *m*
viper [váɪpə] N víbora *f*
viral [váɪrəł] ADJ viral
virgin [vɜ́ʤɪn] ADJ & N virgen *f*; (uninitiated) no iniciado -da *mf*; —**Islands** Islas Vírgenes *f pl*
virginal [vɜ́ʤənł] ADJ virginal
virile [vírəł] ADJ viril
virility [vərílɪDi] N virilidad *f*
virology [vaɪráləʤi] N virología *f*
virtual [vɜ́tʃuəł] ADJ virtual; —**community** comunidad virtual *f*; —**reality** realidad virtual *f*; —**stores** tiendas virtuales *f pl*
virtually [vɜ́tʃuəli] ADV (remotely) virtualmente; (almost) prácticamente
virtue [vɜ́tʃu] N virtud *f*

virtuosity [vɜtʃuásɪDi] N virtuosismo *m*
virtuoso [vɜtʃuóso] ADJ & N virtuoso -sa *mf*
virtuous [vɜtʃuəs] ADJ virtuoso
virulent [vírələnt] ADJ virulento
virus [váɪrəs] N virus *m*; **—-free** libre de virus; **— protection software** programas de protección contra virus *m pl*
visa [vízə] N *Am* visa *f*; *Sp* visado *m*
vis-à-vis [vízəví] PREP con respecto a
visceral [vísəəł] ADJ visceral
viscous [vískəs] ADJ viscoso
vise [vaɪs] N tornillo de banco *m*
visibility [vɪzɪbílɪDi] N visibilidad *f*
visible [vízəbəł] ADJ visible
Visigoth [vízɪgəθ] N visigodo -da *mf*
vision [víʒən] N (sense, apparition) visión *f*; (eyesight) vista *f*
visionary [víʒənɛri] ADJ & N visionario -ria *mf*
visit [vízɪt] VT visitar; (afflict) infligir; VI estar de visita; **to — with** charlar con; N (stay) visita *f*; (chat) charla *f*
visitation [vɪzɪtéʃən] N (apparition) visitación *f*; (punishment) castigo *m*; (parental right) régimen de visita *m*
visiting [vízɪDɪŋ] ADJ (team) visitante
visitor [vízɪDɚ] N visita *f*, visitante *mf*
visor [váɪzɚ] N visera *f*
vista [vístə] N (visual) vista *f*; (mental) perspectiva *f*
visual [víʒuəł] ADJ visual; **— recognition** reconocimiento visual *m*
visualize [víʒuəlaɪz] VT visualizar, imaginar
vital [váɪdł] ADJ vital; **— signs** signos vitales *m pl*
vitality [vaɪtǽlɪDi] N vitalidad *f*
vitamin [váɪDəmɪn] N vitamina *f*
vituperation [vaɪtupəréʃən] N vituperación *f*, vituperio *m*
vivacious [vaɪvéʃəs] ADJ vivaz, vivaracho
vivacity [vaɪvǽsɪDi] N vivacidad *f*
vivid [vívɪd] ADJ vívido, vivo
vivisection [vívɪsɛkʃən] N vivisección *f*
vocabulary [vokǽbjələri] N vocabulario *m*
vocal [vókəł] ADJ (musical) vocal; (outspoken) vociferante; **— cords** cuerdas vocales *f pl*
vocalic [vokǽlɪk] ADJ vocálico
vocation [vokéʃən] N vocación *f*
vociferous [vosífɚəs] ADJ vociferante
vodka [vádkə] N vodka *m*
vogue [vog] N boga *f*, moda *f*; **in —** en boga, de moda
voice [vɔɪs] N voz *f*; **—mail** correo de voz *m*, contestador automático *m*; **— recognition** reconocimiento de voz *m*; **— synthesis** síntesis de voz *f*; VT expresar
voicing [vɔ́ɪsɪŋ] N sonoridad *f*
void [vɔɪd] ADJ (devoid, empty) vacío; (not binding) nulo, inválido; **— of** desprovisto de; N vacío *m*; VT (bowels) evacuar; (a check) anular; **—ed check** cheque anulado *m*

volatile [váləd] ADJ (liquid) volátil; (political situation) explosivo, conflictivo; (stock market) voluble; (temperament) cambiante
volcanic [vaɫkǽnɪk] ADJ volcánico
volcano [vaɫkéno] N volcán *m*
volition [vəlíʃən] N volición *f*; **of one's own —** por su propia voluntad
volley [váli] N (of firearms) descarga *f*; (of protests, arrows, stones) lluvia *f*; (of a tennis ball) volea *f*; **—ball** voleibol *m*, balonvolea *m*; VI/VT (shoot bullets) descargar; (hit tennis balls) volear
volt [voɫt] N voltio *m*
voltage [vóɫtɪdʒ] N voltaje *m*
volume [váljəm] N volumen *m*, tomo *m*
voluminous [vəlúmɪnəs] ADJ voluminoso
voluntary [váləntɛri] ADJ voluntario
volunteer [valəntír] ADJ & N voluntario -ria *mf*; VI/VT (offer) ofrecer[se], brindar[se]; *RP* comedir[se]; VI (do volunteer work) trabajar de voluntario -ria
voluptuous [vəláptʃuəs] ADJ voluptuoso
vomit [vámɪt] N vómito *m*; VI/VT vomitar
voodoo [vúDu] N vudú *m*
voracious [vəréʃəs] ADJ voraz
vortex [vórtɛks] N vórtice *m*
vote [vot] N (right, ballot) voto *m*; (act of voting) votación *f*; VI votar; VT (a bill) aprobar; (a political party) votar a/por; **to — against** votar en contra; **to — in favor** votar a favor; **to — for something** votar por hacer algo
voter [vóDɚ] N votante *mf*
voting [vóDɪŋ] N votación *f*
vouch [vautʃ] VI **to — for** dar fe de, salir de fiador a, fiar a; VT **to — that** dar fe de que
voucher [váutʃɚ] N (receipt) comprobante *m*; (coupon) vale *m*; (person) fiador -ora *mf*, garante *mf*
vow [vau] N voto *m*; **to take a —** prometer; VT jurar
vowel [váuəł] N vocal *f*
voyage [vɔɪɪdʒ] N (long trip) viaje *m*; (trip by sea) travesía *f*; VI viajar
voyeur [vɔɪɚ] N mirón -ona *mf*
VP [vice president] [vípí] N vice presidente -ta *mf*
vulgar [váɫgɚ] ADJ (rude) ordinario, grosero, soez; (popular, vernacular) vulgar
vulgarity [vaɫgǽrɪDi] N ordinariez *f*, vulgaridad *f*
vulnerable [váłnəəbəł] ADJ vulnerable
vulture [váɫtʃɚ] N buitre *m*
vulva [váɫvə] N vulva *f*

Ww

wacky [wǽki] ADJ (person) chiflado; (idea) descabellado

wad [wɑd] N (for artillery, for filling) taco *m*; (ball) pelota *f*, pelotón *m*; (of money) rollo *m*, fajo *m*; (of cotton) bola *f*; VI/VT (a firearm) atacar; (a piece of paper) hacer una pelota [con]

waddle [wádl] VT anadear, andar como un pato; N anadeo *m*

wade [wed] VI andar por el agua; **to — through a book** leer con dificultad un libro

wafer [wéfɚ] N (cookie) oblea *f*; (in Catholic ritual) hostia *f*; (computer) lámina/oblea de silicio *f*

waffle [wáfəl] ADJ *Sp* gofre *m*; *Am* wafle *m*; — **iron** *Sp* plancha para hacer gofres *f*; *Am* waflera *f*

waft [wæft] VI flotar; VT llevar por el aire; N (of air) ráfaga *f*; (of odor) ola *f*

wag [wæg] VI/VT menear[se], mover[se]; **to — the tail** colear; N (movement) meneo *m*, movimiento *m*; (joker) bromista *mf*

wage [wedʒ] N salario *m*; — **earner** asalariado -da *mf*; (paid daily) jornalero -ra *mf*; —**s** salario *m*; (daily) jornal *m*; — **scale** escala salarial *f*; VT (war) hacer; (battle) librar

wager [wédʒɚ] N apuesta *f*; VI/VT apostar

wagon [wǽgən] N (horsedrawn) carro *m*; (covered) carreta *f*; (toy) carrito *m*; **to fix someone's** — vengarse de alguien; **to be on the** — abstenerse de bebidas alcohólicas

wail [weł] VI lamentar; N lamento *m*

waist [west] N cintura *f*; (of garment) talle *m*; —**band** pretina *f*; —**coat** chaleco *m*; —**line** talle *m*, cintura *f*

wait [wet] VI/VT esperar; **to — for** esperar; **to — on** servir; **to — tables** trabajar de camarero -ra; N espera *f*; **to lie in — for** estar en/al acecho de

waiter [wédɚ] N camarero *m*, mozo *m*, mesero *m*

waiting [wéDɪŋ] N espera *f*; — **list** lista de espera *f*; — **room** sala de espera *f*

waitress [wétrɪs] N camarera *f*, moza *f*, mesera *f*

waive [wev] VT (rights) renunciar a; (a rule) hacer una excepción

waiver [wévɚ] N (of rights) renuncia *f*; (of rules) excepción *f*

wake [wek] VI/VT despertar[se]; **to — up** despertar[se]; N (at death) velatorio *m*; (of a ship) estela *f*, surco *m*; —**-up call** (in a hotel) llamada del servicio despertador *f*; (to action) llamada de atención *f*; **in the — of** después de, detrás de

wakeful [wékfəl] ADJ (awake) despierto; (insomniac) insomne

waken [wékən] VI/VT despertar[se]

Wales [wełz] N Gales *m sg*

walk [wɔk] VI andar, caminar; (to a place) ir a pie; (go away) marcharse; (in baseball) sacar una base por bolas *f*; **to — back** volver a pie; **to — down** bajar a pie; **to — in** entrar caminando; **to — out** (to go out) salir caminando; (to abandon) dejar; (to strike) declararse en huelga; **to — up** subir a pie; VT (to cause to walk) hacer caminar; (to trace on foot) recorrer; **to — the streets** callejear; **to — someone** (baseball) darle una base por bolas; N (period of walking) paseo *m*, caminata *f*; (pace) paso *m*; (gait) andar *m*; — **of life** condición *f*; —**out** huelga *f*; **to take a —** pasear, dar un paseo

walker [wɔ́kɚ] N (device to aid walking) andador *m*; (one who walks) caminante *mf*; (in sports) marchista *mf*

walking [wɔ́kɪŋ] ADJ andante; — **papers** despido *m*; — **stick** bastón *m*

wall [wɔł] N (interior) pared *f*; (garden) muro *m*, tapia *f*; (fort) muralla *f*; (of silence) barrera *f*; —**paper** papel de empapelar *m*; —**flower** alhelí *m*; —**-to-** de pared a pared; **to have one's back to the** — estar entre la espada y la pared; **to drive someone up the** — sacar a alguien de quicio; **I was climbing the —s** me moría de aburrimiento; **she was a —flower** no la sacaban a bailar; VT **to —paper** empapelar

wallet [wálɪt] N cartera *f*, billetera *f*

wallow [wálo] VI (roll) revolcarse; (indulge oneself) regodearse

walnut [wɔ́łnʌt] N nuez *f*; — **tree** nogal *m*

walrus [wɔ́łrəs] N morsa *f*

waltz [wɔłts] N vals *m*; VI valsar

wand [wɑnd] N (rod) vara *f*; (magic) varita *f*

wander [wándɚ] VI/VT vagar [por], errar [por]; **to — away** perderse; **my mind —s easily** me distraigo fácilmente

wanderer [wándərɚ] N vagabundo -da *mf*

wane [wen] VI menguar, flaquear; N **to be on the** — ir menguando

wannabe [wánəbi] N aspirante *mf*

want [wɑnt] VI/VT (desire) querer; **he —s judgment** le falta juicio; **he's —ed in Texas** se lo busca en Texas; N (desire) deseo *m*; (lack) falta *f*; (scarcity) escasez *f*; **to be in** — estar necesitado; — **ad** [anuncio] clasificado *m*

wanting [wántɪŋ] ADJ (lacking) falto; (deficient) deficiente

wanton [wántən] ADJ (immoderate) desenfrenado; (immoral) lascivo; (senseless, unprovoked) gratuito

war [wɔr] N guerra *f*; — **crime** crimen de guerra *m*; — **fare** guerra *f*; — **games** juegos de guerra *m pl*, simulacro de batalla *m*; —**head** ojiva *f*; —**ship** acorazado *m*; VI guerrear, hacer la guerra; —**like** bélico *f*

warble [wɔ́rbəl] VI gorjear; N gorjeo *m*

warbler [wɔ́rblɚ] N (European) curruca *f*; (American) arañero *m*

ward [wɔrd] N (district) distrito *m*; (of a hospital)

pabellón *m*; (of a tutor) pupilo -la *mf*; VI **to —
off** resguardarse de, conjurar
warden [wɔ́rdn̩] N (of prison) alcaide *m*
wardrobe [wɔ́rdrob] N (room) guardarropa *m*;
(furniture) armario *m*, ropero *m*; (garments)
vestuario *m*, guardarropa *m*
warehouse [wérhaʊs] N almacén *m*, depósito *m*
wares [wɛrz] N mercancías *f pl*
warm [wɔrm] ADJ (bath) caliente; (clothes)
abrigado; (weather) caluroso; (colors,
reception) cálido; **—-blooded** de sangre
caliente; **—hearted** de buen corazón; **it is —
today** hace calor hoy; N **—up**
precalentamiento *m*; VI/VT calentar[se]; **to —
over** recalentar; **to — up** calentar[se],
templar[se]; **it —s my heart** me alegra el
corazón; **she —ed to the idea** se entusiasmó
con la idea
warmth [wɔrmθ] N calor *m*, tibieza *f*
warn [wɔrn] VI/VT (advise of danger) advertir;
(urge to behave) amonestar
warning [wɔ́rnɪŋ] N (of danger) advertencia *f*;
(of punishment) amonestación *f*
warp [wɔrp] N (yarn) urdimbre *f*; (curve) comba
f, alabeo *m*; VI/VT (wood) combar[se],
alabear[se]; (character) deformar[se]; **he has
a —ed personality** tiene una personalidad
retorcida
warrant [wɔ́rənt] N orden *f*; **a — for his arrest**
una orden de arresto contra él; VT garantizar
warranty [wɔ́rənti] N garantía *f*; VT garantizar
warrior [wɔ́riɚ] N guerrero -ra *mf*
wart [wɔrt] N verruga *f*
wary [wéri] ADJ cauteloso, cauto; **to be — of**
desconfiar de
was [wɑz] *see* be
wash [wɑʃ] VI/VT lavar[se]; **to — out** (a bottle)
lavar; (a substance) quitar lavando; (a
creekbed) erosionar; **to — up** lavarse; **the
bottle was —ed up on the shore** la botella
fue traída por el mar; **he was —ed away by
the waves** fue arrastrado por las olas; **his
excuse won't —** su excusa no va a colar; N
(act of washing) lavado *m*; (clothes to be
washed) ropa para lavar *f*; (washed clothes)
ropa lavada *f*; **—cloth** toallita para lavarse *f*;
—out (erosion) derrubio *m*; (failure) fracaso
m; **—room** lavabo *m*, lavatorio *m*; ADJ **—-
and-wear** de lava y pon, de no planchar;
—ed-up fracasado; **—ed-out** desteñido
washable [wáʃəbəɫ] ADJ lavable
washer [wáʃɚ] N (washing machine) lavadora *f*,
máquina de lavar *f*; (metal ring) arandela *f*;
—woman lavandera *f*
washing [wáʃɪŋ] N lavado *m*; **— machine**
lavadora *f*, máquina de lavar *f*
wasp [wɑsp] N avispa *f*
WASP [White Anglo-Saxon Protestant]
[wɑsp] N persona blanca, anglosajona y

protestante *f*
waste [west] VI/VT (squander resources)
malgastar, desperdiciar; **to — away**
consumirse; VT (squander time) perder;
(murder) liquidar; N (of resources)
desperdicio *m*, malgasto *m*, derroche *m*; (of
time) pérdida *f*; (refuse) desperdicios *m pl*,
desechos *m pl*; (liquid refuse) vertido *m*;
—land tierra yerma *f*, páramo *m*; **— of time**
pérdida de tiempo *f*; **—paper basket**
papelera *f*; **— products** productos de
desecho *m pl*; **— treatment** tratamiento de
residuos *m*; **to go to —** desperdiciarse; **to lay
— to** asolar
wasted [wéstɪd] ADJ (squandered) desperdiciado;
(debilitated) consumido; (drunk) borracho
wasteful [wéstfəɫ] ADJ (person) despilfarrador,
gastador; (method) antieconómico
watch [wɑtʃ] VI (look) mirar; (be careful)
cuidarse; (be vigilant) vigilar; VT (view)
mirar, ver; (observe) observar; (tend) cuidar;
— out for the cars! ¡cuidado con los coches!
to — for estar a la espera de; **to — over**
proteger; N (timepiece) reloj *m*; (period of
wakefulness) vela *f*, vigilia *f*; (vigilant guard)
guardia *mf*; (duty shift) guardia *f*; (lookout)
centinela *m*; **—band** pulsera *f*; **—dog** (type of
dog) perro guardián *m*; (organization)
organismo de control *m*; **—maker** relojero
-ra *mf*; **—making** relojería *f*; **—man**
vigilante *m*, sereno *m*; **—tower** atalaya *f*,
torre de vigilancia *f*; **—word** (password)
contraseña *f*; (motto) consigna *f*, lema *m*; **to
be on the —** estar alerta; **to keep — on/
over** vigilar a
watchful [wátʃfəɫ] ADJ alerta, atento
water [wɔ́Dɚ] N agua *f*; **—bed** cama de agua *f*;
—bird ave acuática *f*; **— buffalo** búfalo de
agua *m*; **—color** acuarela *f*; **—cress** berro *m*;
—fall (small) cascada *f*; (large) catarata *f*;
—front muelles *m pl*; **—fountain** fuente *f*,
Mex, RP bebedero *m*; **— heater** calentador de
agua *m*; **— lily** nenúfar *m*; **—melon** sandía *f*;
— pistol pistola de agua *f*; **— power** energía
hidráulica *f*; **—shed** vertiente *f*; **— ski** esquí
acuático *m*; **— softener** ablandador de agua
m; **— sports** deportes acuáticos *m pl*;
—spout (pipe) tubo de desagüe *m*; (tornado)
tromba *f*; **— supply** abastecimiento de agua
m; **— table** capa freática *f*; **— vapor** vapor de
agua *m*; **—way** vía navegable *f*; **my — broke**
se me rompieron las aguas, se me rompió la
fuente; ADJ **—logged** empapado; **—proof**
(fabric) impermeable; (watch) sumergible;
—tight hermético; VT (irrigate) regar;
(dilute) aguar; VI/VT (animals) abrevar;
—ed-down (with water) aguado; (simplified)
simplificado; (softened) suavizado; **to
—proof** impermeabilizar; **to —-ski** hacer

esquí acuático; **my eyes are —ing** me lloran los ojos; **it makes my mouth —** se me hace agua la boca

watery [wɔ́Dəɾi] ADJ (watered-down) aguado; (like water) acuoso; (boggy) húmedo

watt [wɑt] N vatio *m*

wattage [wɑ́DIʤ] N vataje *m*

wave [wev] N (radio) onda *f*; (water, heat, fashion) ola *f*; (of disgust, of people) oleada *f*; (with the hand) saludo *m*; **—length** longitud de onda *f*; **on the same —length** en la misma onda, en sintonía; VI (flag) ondear; (hair) ondular[se]; VI (greet) saludar con la mano; **to — good-bye** decir adiós con la mano

waver [wévə‑] VI (hesitate) vacilar, titubear; (falter) flaquear

wavy [wévi] ADJ ondeado, ondulado

wax [wæks] N cera *f*; (for seals) lacre *m*; **— paper** papel encerado *m*; VT (cover with wax) encerar; (defeat) derrotar; VI (moon) crecer; **to — poetic** ponerse poético

way [we] N (road) camino *m*; (manner) modo *m*, manera *f*; **—farer** caminante *mf*; **— in** entrada *f*; **— out** salida *f*; **—s** costumbres *f pl*; **—side** borde del camino *m*; **— through** paso *m*, pasaje *m*; **a long — off** muy lejos; **by — of London** por Londres; **by — of comparison** a modo de comparación; **by the —** a propósito; **in no —** de ningún modo; **on the — to** rumbo a; **to get out of the —** apartarse; **to go out of one's — to** desvivirse por; **to look the other —** hacer la vista gorda; **to lead the —** ir a la cabeza; **to be in a bad —** hallarse mal de salud; **to give —** (yield) ceder; (break) quebrarse; **to get one's — salirse** con la suya; **to make — for** abrir paso para; ADJ **—-out** estrafalario; VT **to —lay** (wait in ambush) estar al acecho de; (attack) asaltar; (stop) detener

wayward [wéwə‑d] ADJ (disobedient) desobediente; (willful) porfiado

we [wi] PRON nosotros -as *mf*

weak [wik] ADJ débil; (deficient) flojo; **— force** fuerza débil *f*; **—-kneed** achicado; **— sister** (coward) cobarde *mf*; **— link** parte más delgada del hilo *f*

weaken [wíkən] VI/VT debilitar[se], quebrantar[se]

weakling [wíklIŋ] N alfeñique *m*

weakness [wíknIs] N debilidad *f*, flaqueza *f*; (deficiency) flojedad *f*

wealth [wɛłθ] N riqueza *f*

wealthy [wɛ́łθi] ADJ rico, adinerado, pudiente

wean [win] VT destetar; **to — oneself of** quitarse el vicio de

weapon [wépən] N arma *f*

wear [wɛr] VT (have on) llevar, tener puesto; (dress in habitually) usar; VI/VT (waste away) desgastar[se]; **to — away** gastar[se], desgastar[se]; **to — down** (a person) agotar; (a pencil) desgastar; **to — off** perder efecto; **to — on** prolongarse; **to — out** (make unfit) gastar[se], degastar[se], sobar[se]; (expend) agotar; **it —s well** es duradero; N (use) gasto *m*; (clothes) ropa *f*; (durability) durabilidad *f*; (deterioration) desgaste *m*; **— and tear** desgaste *m*

weariness [wírinIs] N cansancio *m*, fatiga *f*

wearing [wérIŋ] ADJ (causing wear) desgastante; (causing fatigue) cansado

wearisome [wírisəm] ADJ fastidioso

weary [wíri] ADJ cansado, fatigado; VI/VT cansar[se], fatigar[se]

weasel [wízəł] N comadreja *f*

weather [wéðə‑] N tiempo *m*; (storm) tempestad *f*; **—-beaten** desgastado/curtido por la intemperie; **— bureau** oficina meteorológica *f*; **— conditions** condiciones atmosféricas *f pl*; **—man** meteorólogo *m*; **— report** parte meteorológico *m*; **—vane** veleta *f*; **it is fine —** hace buen tiempo; **to be under the —** estar enfermo; ADJ **—proof** resistente a la intemperie; VI/VT (a surface) gastar[se]; (skin) curtir; (crisis, storm) capear

weave [wiv] VT (cloth, basket) tejer, entretejer; (to put together) urdir, tramar; **to — together/into** entretejer, entrelazar; **to — one's way** zigzaguear; N tejido *m*

weaver [wívə‑] N tejedor -ora *mf*

web [wɛb] N (of a spider) telaraña *f*; (of lies) sarta *f*; (membrane) membrana *f*; (Internet) web *f*; (animal) palmípedo *m*; **— browser** navegador [web] *m*; **—cast** transmisión por la web *f*; **—foot** pata palmada *f*; **— hosting** alojamiento web *m*; **—master** administrador -ora de un sitio web *mf*; **— page** página web *f*; **—site** sitio web *m*; VT; ADJ **—footed** palmípedo; VI/VT **to —cast** transmitir por la web

wed [wɛd] VI/VT casarse [con]; VT casar a

wedding [wédIŋ] N boda *f*, casamiento *m*; **— day** día de boda *m*; **— dress** traje de novia *m*; **— ring** anillo de boda *m*

wedge [wɛʤ] N cuña *f*; **to drive a — between** separar; VT acuñar, meter cuñas entre; **to be —d between** estar apretado entre

Wednesday [wénzde] N miércoles *m*

wee [wi] ADJ chiquito, pequeñito

weed [wid] N mala hierba *f*; (marijuana) hierba *f*; **—killer** herbicida *m*; VT deshierbar, escardar; **to — out** eliminar

week [wik] N semana *f*; **—day** día de semana *m*; **—end** fin de semana *m*; **a — from today** de aquí en una semana

weekly [wíkli] ADJ semanal; ADV semanalmente; N semanario *m*

weep [wip] VI llorar, lagrimear

weeping [wípɪŋ] ADJ lloroso; — **willow** sauce llorón *m*; N llanto *m*

weevil [wívəl] N gorgojo *m*

weigh [we] VI/VT pesar; (consider) ponderar, sopesar, barajar; **to — anchor** levar anclas; **to — down** agobiar, abrumar; **to — on one's conscience** pesar en la conciencia de uno

weight [wet] N (heaviness, importance) peso *m*; (for clocks, scales, barbells) pesa *f*; —**lifting /** —**training** levantamiento de pesas *m*, halterofilia *f*; —-**watcher** persona a dieta *f*; **to put on** — engordar; **to lose** — adelgazar; VT (add weight) añadir peso; (in statistics) ponderar; **to — someone down** agobiarle a uno

weightless [wétlɪs] ADJ ingrávido

weighty [wéɒi] ADJ importante

weird [wírd] ADJ (strange) extraño; (supernatural) misterioso

weirdo [wírdo] N bicho raro *m*, ente *m*

welcome [wéłkəm] N bienvenida *f*; ADJ bienvenido; — **mat** alfombrilla *f*, felpudo *m*; — **rest** descanso agradable *m*; **you are** — no hay de qué, de nada; **you are** — **here** estás en tu casa; **you are** — **to use it** a tus órdenes; VT dar la bienvenida a, acoger

weld [wɛld] VI/VT soldar[se]; N soldadura *f*

welfare [wéłfɛr] N (good fortune) bienestar *m*; (public assistance) asistencia social *f*; — **state** estado de bienestar *m*

well [wɛł] ADV bien; — **then** pues bien; —- **being** bienestar *m*; —-**nigh** casi, muy cerca de; **he is** — **over fifty** tiene mucho más de cincuenta años; **all is** — todo está bien; INTERJ ¡bueno! ADJ (healthy) bien de salud, sano; N (of water, oil) pozo *m*; (of staircase) caja *f*; —**spring** fuente *f*, manantial *m*; ADJ —-**bred** bien educado; —-**defined** bien definido; —-**done** (steak) bien cocido; (a task) bien hecho; —-**fed** bien alimentado; —- **founded** bien fundamentado; —- **groomed** bien arreglado, aseado; —- **heeled** adinerado; —-**informed** bien informado; —-**known** (of a fact) bien sabido; (of a person) bien conocido, notorio; —- **made** bien hecho; —-**meaning** bien intencionado; —-**off** adinerado, acomodado; —-**read** leído, educado; —-**rounded** completo; —-**spoken** bien hablado; —- **to-do** adinerado; VI **tears** —**ed up in his eyes** se le llenaron los ojos de lágrimas

wellness [wéłnɪs] N (health) salud *f*; (health care) medicina preventiva *f*

welsh [wɛłʃ] VI **to** — **on** (a debt) no pagar; (a promise) no cumplir

Welsh [wɛłʃ] ADJ & N galés -esa *mf*

welt [wɛłt] N verdugón *m*

went [wɛnt] *see* go

wept [wɛpt] *see* weep

were [wɝ] *see* be

west [wɛst] N (cardinal point) oeste *m*; (hemisphere) occidente *m*; — **Berlin** Berlín occidental *m*; — **Indies** Antillas *f pl*; ADJ — **wind** viento del oeste *m*; ADV (direction) hacia el oeste; (location) al oeste

western [wéstɚn] ADJ occidental, del oeste; N (movie genre) película del oeste *f*

westerner [wéstɚnɚ] N occidental *mf*

westward [wéstwɚd] ADV hacia el oeste; ADJ occidental

wet [wɛt] ADJ (drenched) mojado; (damp, rainy) húmedo; —**back** *offensive* espalda mojada *mf*, mojado -da *mf*; — **blanket** aguafiestas *mf sg*; — **dream** sueño húmedo *m*; —**land** humedal *m*; — **nurse** nodriza *f*; — **paint** pintura fresca *f*; — **suit** traje de buzo *m*; VI/VT (soak) mojar[se]; (dampen) humedecer[se]

wetness [wétnɪs] N humedad *f*

whack [hwæk] VI/VT (hit) golpear, pegar; (assassinate) *fam* liquidar; **to** — **off** (cut) cortar; (masturbate) *vulg* hacer[se] una paja; N (blow) golpazo *m*; *Sp vulg* hostia *f*; **to take a** — **at** hacer un intento de; **out of** — descompuesto, averiado

whale [hweł] N ballena *f*; VI pescar ballenas

wharf [hwɔrf] N muelle *m*, embarcadero *m*

what [hwɑt] INTERR PRON & N qué; — **did you say?** ¿qué dijiste? — **for?** ¿para qué? —'s **the matter?** ¿qué pasa? —'s **the score?** ¿cómo va el marcador? **and** —**not** y demás; REL PRON lo que; **come** — **may** venga lo que venga; **anyplace** —**soever** en cualquier lugar; **so** —? y qué? **take** — **you need** toma lo que necesites; ADJ qué; — **books did you want?** ¿qué libros querías? **take** — **books you need** toma los libros que necesites; INTERJ cómo, qué; — **happy children!** ¡qué niños más felices! — **luck!** ¡qué buena suerte!

whatever [hwɑtévɚ] PRON lo que; **do it,** — **happens** hazlo, pase lo que pase; — **you may think** pienses lo que pienses; — **do you mean?** ¿qué demonios quieres decir? **take** — **you need** toma lo que necesites; ADJ **any person** — una persona cualquiera / cualquier persona; **no money** — nada de dinero; INTERJ (anything) ¡lo que sea! (I give up) ¡lo que tú digas!

wheat [hwit] N trigo *m*; — **germ** germen de trigo *m*

wheel [hwił] N (disc) rueda *f*; (of cheese) horma *f*; (for pottery) torno *m*; (for steering a car) volante *m*; (for steering a ship) timón *m*; —**barrow** carretilla *f*; —**base** batalla *f*, paso *m*; —**chair** silla de ruedas *f*; —**s** (car) *fam* coche *m*; VT (a round object) hacer rodar; (a person, bicycle, wheelchair) empujar; VI **to** — **out** sacar rodando; **to** — **in** entrar rodando;

to — around girar sobre los talones

wheeze [hwiz] N resuello ruidoso *m*; VI resollar

when [hwɛn] ADV & CONJ cuando; INTERJ, ADV, & N cuándo

whenever [hwɛnévə-] CONJ — **I see him** (each time) cada vez que lo veo; ADV (at a future time) — **I see him** cuando lo vea

where [hwɛr] ADV, N, & INTERR PRON dónde *m*; (direction) adónde; CONJ donde; (direction) adonde

whereabouts [hwérəbaʊts] N paradero *m*; INTERR ADV dónde

whereas [hwɛrǽz] CONJ mientras que; (in preambles) visto que, considerando que

whereby [hwɛrbáɪ] ADV por lo cual

wherefore [hwérfɔr] ADV por lo cual

wherein [hwɛrín] ADV en donde

whereof [hwɛráv] REL PRON de que; INTERR PRON de qué

whereupon [hwɛrəpán] ADV después de lo cual

wherever [hwɛrévə-] ADV dondequiera que

wherewithal [hwérwɪðɔ̀ł] N medios *m pl*, fondos *m pl*

whet [hwɛt] VT (stimulate) estimular; (sharpen) afilar; **—stone** piedra de afilar *f*

whether [hwéðə-] CONJ — **we like it or not** nos guste o no nos guste; **I doubt — we can do it** dudo [de] que lo podamos hacer; **he asked — I was coming** me preguntó si venía

which [hwɪtʃ] INTERR PRON cuál[es]; — **do you want?** ¿cuál[es] quieres? REL PRON que; **the apple, — I just bought** la manzana, que acabo de comprar; **the book of — I spoke** el libro del que / del cual hablé; **that — you don't know can hurt you** lo que no sabes puede hacerte daño; INTERR ADJ qué, cuál[es] de; — **house is it?** ¿qué casa es? ¿cuál de las casas es?

whichever [hwɪtʃévə-] PRON & ADJ (no matter which) cualquiera [que]; — **you choose, you'll regret it later** elijas el que elijas, te arrepentirás después; (anyone that) el que / la que; **choose — you like** elije el que quieras

whiff [hwɪf] N (waft) soplo *m*; (odors, scandal) bocanada *f*, tufillo *m*; **to take a —** oler

while [hwaɪł] N rato *m*; **a short —** un ratito; **a short — ago** hace poco; CONJ (during) mientras; (whereas) mientras que; (even though) aunque; VT **to — away** pasar

whim [hwɪm] N capricho *m*, antojo *m*

whimper [hwímpə-] VI/VT lloriquear, gimotear; N lloriqueo *m*, gimoteo *m*

whimsical [hwímzɪkəł] ADJ caprichoso, antojadizo

whine [hwaɪn] VI (whimper) gemir; (complain) quejarse; N (whimper) gemido *m*; (complaint) quejido *m*; **stop whining!** ¡deja de quejarte!

whiner [hwáɪnə-] N llorón -ona *mf*, quejica *mf*

whiny [hwáɪni] ADJ quejoso, quejica

whip [hwɪp] N azote *m*, látigo *m*, rebenque *m*; VT (hit with a whip) azotar, fustigar; (spank) zurrar, dar una paliza; (beat to a froth) batir; (defeat) vencer; **to — out** sacar; **to — up** (prepare) preparar rápidamente; (incite) incitar

whipping [hwípɪŋ] N zurra *f*, paliza *f*; — **cream** crema para batir *f*

whir [hwɜ-] VI zumbar; N zumbido *m*

whirl [hwɜ-ł] VI girar; **to — around** arremolinarse; **my head —s** me da vueltas la cabeza; N (rotation) giro *m*; (of water) remolino *m*; **—pool** remolino *m*; **—pool bath** baño de remolino *m*; **—wind** torbellino *m*, remolino de viento *m*; **—wind tour** gira relámpago *f*; **my head is in a —** me da vueltas la cabeza; **to give it a —** probarlo

whisk [hwɪsk] VT (sweep) barrer; (beat) batir; **to — away** llevarse de prisa; VI **to — by** pasar rápidamente; N (broom) escobilla *f*; (beater) batidor *m*

whisker [hwískə-] N (hair of beard) pelo de la barba *m*; (sideburn) patilla *f*; (of animals) bigote *m*

whiskey, whisky [hwíski] N whisky *m*

whisper [hwíspə-] VI/VT (person) cuchichear, secretear; (leaves, water) susurrar; N (people) cuchicheo *m*; (leaves, water) susurro *m*; **to talk in a —** cuchichear

whistle [hwísəł] VI/VT silbar; (loud) chiflar; (in protest) rechiflar; VI (referee, train) pitar; **to — for someone** llamar a uno con un silbido; N (sound) silbido *m*; (loud sound) chiflido *m*; (of a referee) pitido *m*; (instrument) silbato *m*, pito *m*; **—-blower** acusador -ora *mf*

white [hwaɪt] ADJ (color, ethnicity) blanco; — **blood cell** glóbulo blanco *m*; — **bread** pan blanco *m*; **—caps** cabrillas *f pl*; **—-collar** administrativo, de cuello blanco; — **gold** oro blanco *m*; — **hair** cana *f*; — **lie** mentirilla *f*; — **noise** ruido blanco *m*; — **trash** *offensive* sureño -ña blanco -ca pobre *mf*; **—wash** (paint) lechada *f*; (cover-up) encubrimiento *m*; N blanco *m* (also ethnicity); (of egg) clara *f*; VT **to —wash** (paint) blanquear, enjalbegar; (cover up) encubrir

whiten [hwaɪtn̩] VI/VT blanquear[se], emblanquecer

whiteness [hwáɪtnɪs] N blancura *f*

whitish [hwáɪdɪʃ] ADJ blancuzco, blanquecino

whittle [hwídł] VI/VT tallar; **to — away** ir gastando; **to — down expenses** reducir los gastos

whiz [hwɪz] VI zumbar; **to — by** pasar zumbando; VT hacer zumbar; N (sound) zumbido *m*; (ace) as *m*; — **kid** niño -ña prodigio *mf*

who [hu] REL PRON quien[es]; INTERR PRON quién[es]; **he —** el que

WHO [World Health Organization]
[dábətjuétʃó] N OMS f
whoa [hwo] INTERJ (to express amazement) ¡jo!
(to stop a horse) ¡so!
whoever [huévə-] REL PRON (whatever person)
quienquiera que, el/la que; INTERR PRON
(who) quién
whole [hoł] ADJ (complete) completo, íntegro;
(unbroken) entero; (uninjured) ileso; — -
grain integral; —**hearted** sincero;
—**heartedly** de todo corazón; — **life
insurance** seguro de vida permanente m; —
milk leche entera f; — **note** redonda f;
—**sale** (in bulk) al por mayor; (massive)
masivo; —**sale slaughter** matanza f; —-
wheat integral; **the — day** todo el día; **to go
— hog** tirar la casa por la ventana; N todo m;
(for amounts) totalidad f; —**sale** venta al por
mayor f, mayoreo m; —**saler** comerciante al
por mayor mf, mayorista mf, almacenista mf;
as a — en su totalidad; **on the —** en general;
ADV —**sale** al por mayor; VI/VT **to —sale**
vender al por mayor
wholesome [hółsəm] ADJ sano
whom [hum] REL PRON a quien[es]; **for/to/
with —** para/a/con quien; INTERR PRON a
quién[es]
whoop [hwup] N (shout) grito m; (gasp)
respiración convulsiva f; VI (person) gritar;
(owl) ulular; **to — it up** armar jaleo
whopper [hwápə-] N (large thing) cosa enorme f;
(lie) mentira f, trola f
whopping [hwápɪŋ] ADJ enorme
whore [hor] N offensive puta f; —**house** vulg casa
de putas f
whose [huz] REL PRON cuyo; **the man — son is
here** el hombre cuyo hijo está aquí; INTERR
PRON de quién; — **book is this?** ¿de quién es
este libro?
why [hwaɪ] ADV & CONJ por qué; **that's the
reason — he left** es por eso que se fue; N
porqué m; INTERJ —, **of course!** ¡pero claro!
wick [wɪk] N mecha f, pabilo m
wicked [wíkɪd] ADJ malvado, perverso
wickedness [wíkɪdnɪs] N maldad f, perversidad f
wicker [wíkə-] N mimbre m; — **chair** silla de
mimbre f
wide [waɪd] ADJ (broad) ancho; (of great range)
amplio; (spacious) vasto, extenso; — **apart**
muy apartados; —-**awake** muy despierto,
despabilado; — **body** avión de fuselaje ancho
m; —-**eyed** ojiabierto, con los ojos bien
abiertos; — **of the mark** lejos del blanco; —-
open abierto de par en par; — **receiver**
receptor abierto m; —**spread** (over a wide
area) extendido; (among many people)
generalizado; **to open —** (a door) abrir de par
en par; (one's mouth) abrir bien; **two feet —**
dos pies de ancho

widely [wáɪdli] ADV **it is — known that** es bien
sabido que; **he is a — known artist** es un
artista muy conocido; **he is — read** es muy
leído; — **different versions** versiones muy
diferentes
widen [wáɪdn] VI/VT ensanchar[se], ampliar[se]
widow [wíDo] N viuda f
widower [wíDoə-] N viudo m
width [wɪdθ] N ancho m, anchura f
wield [wiłd] VT (power) ejercer; (tool) manejar;
(weapon) blandir, esgrimir
wife [waɪf] N esposa f, señora f, Sp mujer f
wifi [wireless fidelity] [wáɪfaɪ] N wifi f
wig [wɪg] N peluca f
wiggle [wígəl] VI/VT (hips) menear[se]; (toes)
mover[se]; N (of hips) meneo m; (of toes)
movimiento m; — **room** flexibilidad f
wigwam [wígwɑm] N tienda indígena f
wild [waɪld] ADJ (animal, savage) salvaje, bravío,
bronco; (plant) silvestre; (party)
desenfrenado; (conduct) alocado; (storm,
temperament) violento; (hair) desordenado;
(look) extraviado, desencajado; (enthusiasm)
delirante; — **boar** jabalí m; — **card** comodín
m; —**cat** gato montés m; —-**eyed** de mirada
extraviada, con los ojos desencajados; —**fire**
fuego arrasador m; —**flower** flor silvestre f;
— **goose chase** búsqueda inútil f; —**life**
fauna f; **I'm just — about Mary** estoy loco
por María; **not in your —est dreams** ni lo
pienses; **to drive someone —** volver loco a
alguien; **to talk —** decir disparates; N —**s**
regiones salvajes f pl
wilderness [wíłdə-nɪs] N (near mountains)
monte m; (desert) desierto m; (jungle) jungla f
wile [waɪł] N artimaña f, treta f
will [wɪł] VT (use willpower) conseguir a fuerza
de voluntad; (bequeath) legar, dejar; V AUX **if
you —** si quieres; **she — come** va a venir,
vendrá; **this motorcycle — go 100 mph**
esta motocicleta puede hacer 100 millas por
hora; **in spite of everything, he — not
stop complaining** a pesar de todo, no deja
de quejarse; **she — just sit for hours
doing nothing** se pasa horas sentada sin
hacer nada; **that — do** basta; N (wish)
voluntad f; (testament) testamento m;
—**power** fuerza de voluntad f; **at —** a
discreción, a voluntad
willful [wíłfəl] ADJ testarudo, porfiado
willies [wíliz] N escalofríos m pl
willing [wílɪŋ] ADJ dispuesto, voluntarioso
willingly [wílɪŋli] ADV de buena gana,
gustosamente
willingness [wílɪŋnɪs] N buena voluntad f,
buena gana f
willow [wílo] N sauce m
wilt [wɪłt] VI/VT (plant) marchitar[se]; VI (person)
languidecer

wily [wáɪli] ADJ astuto, artero

wimp [wɪmp] N pelele *m*

win [wɪn] VI/VT ganar; VT (support, fame, affection) ganarse; (victory) alcanzar, conseguir; **to — out** ganar, triunfar; **to — over** conquistar; **a —-— situation** una situación beneficiosa para ambas partes; N victoria *f*

wince [wɪns] VI hacer una mueca; N mueca *f*

winch [wɪntʃ] N cabrestante *m*, torno *m*, *Am* guinche *m*

wind[1] [wɪnd] N (air) viento *m*; (gas) gases *m pl*; **—bag** charlatán -ana *mf*; **—breaker**™ cazadora *f*; **—fall** ganancia inesperada *f*; **— instrument** instrumento de viento *m*; **—mill** molino de viento *m*; **—pipe** tráquea *f*; **— power** energía eólica *f*; **—shield** parabrisas *m sg*; **—shield wiper** limpiaparabrisas *m sg*; **—sock** manga de viento *f*; **—surfing** windsurf *m*; **— tunnel** túnel aerodinámico *m*; **to get — of** enterarse de; **to break —** ventosear; **to catch one's —** recobrar el aliento; ADJ **—ward** de barlovento; ADV **—ward** hacia/a barlovento

wind[2] [waɪnd] VT enrollar; (watch) dar cuerda a; VI (take a bending course) serpentear; **to — around** enrollarse; **to — down** (relax) tranquilizarse; (come to a conclusion) irse terminando; **to — up** (string) enrollar; (a clock) dar cuerda; (a project) completar; (in jail) acabar; N (turn) vuelta *f*; (bend) recodo *m*; **—up** conclusión *f*

winding [wáɪndɪŋ] ADJ sinuoso; **— staircase** escalera de caracol *f*

window [wíndo] N (in building, on screen) ventana *f*; (in building, large) ventanal *m*; (in car, plane) ventanilla *f*; (in a shop) escaparate *m*; *Am* vidriera *f*; **—pane** cristal *m*, vidrio *m*; **— shade** visillo *m*; **—sill** alféizar *m*

windy [wíndi] ADJ ventoso; **it is —** hace/hay viento

wine [waɪn] N vino *m*; **— cellar** bodega *f*; **—glass** copa *f*; **—grower** viticultor -ora *mf*, viñatero -ra *mf*; **— industry** industria vinícola *f*; **—skin** odre *m*; **— tasting** cata de vinos *f*

winery [wáɪnəri] N bodega *f*

wing [wɪŋ] N (of bird, plane, building, table) ala *f*; **— nut** tuerca [de] mariposa/palomilla *f*; **—span/—spread** envergadura *f*; **—tip** extremo del ala *m*; **in the —s** en los bastidores; **under one's —** al amparo de alguien; **to take — levantar vuelo; VI volar; VT (wound slightly) herir en el ala/brazo; to — it** improvisar

winger [wíŋə˞] N (in soccer) ala *mf*, extremo *mf*

wink [wɪŋk] VI/VT guiñar; **to — approval** guiñar en aprobación; **to — at** hacer la vista gorda; N guiño *m*, guiñada *f*; **I didn't sleep a**

— no pegué un ojo

winner [wínə˞] N ganador -ora *mf*, triunfador -ora *mf*

winning [wínɪŋ] ADJ (successful) ganador, vencedor; (charming) atractivo; **—s** ganancias *f pl*

wino [wáɪno] N *pej* borracho -cha *mf*

winter [wíntə˞] N invierno *m*; **— weather** clima invernal *m*; VI invernar

wintry [wíntri] ADJ invernal

wipe [waɪp] VT (sweat, tears) enjugar; (wet surfaces) secar; (dry surface) limpiar; **to — away** enjugar; **to — off** limpiar; **to — out** aniquilar; **to — up** limpiar

wiper [wáɪpə˞] N limpiaparabrisas *m sg*

wire [waɪr] N (filament) alambre *m*; (telegram) telegrama *m*; **— fence** alambrado *m*; **—tap** intervención del teléfono *f*, pinchazo *m*; **— transfer** transferencia electrónica *f*; **by —** por telégrafo; VT (an appliance) alambrar; (a house) electrificar; VI/VT (a message) telegrafiar; (money) girar; **to — together** atar con alambre; **to —tap** intervenir un teléfono, pinchar un teléfono

wired [waɪrd] ADJ (installed) alambrado; (tied) atado con alambre; (electrified) electrificado; (enthusiastic) sobreexcitado

wireless [wáɪrlɪs] ADJ inalámbrico; **— Internet** internet inalámbrico *m*

wiring [wáɪrɪŋ] N cableado *m*

wiry [wáɪri] ADJ (skinny) nervudo; (like wire) crespo

wisdom [wízdəm] N (moral) sabiduría *f*; (scholarly) saber *m*; **— tooth** muela del juicio *f*

wise [waɪz] ADJ (discerning) sabio; (prudent) sensato, prudente; (erudite) erudito; **—ass** sabihondo -da *mf*; **—crack** broma *f*, chiste *m*; **— guy** sabihondo *m*; **the Three — Men** los Tres Reyes Magos; N **in no —** de ningún modo; VI **to — up** avisparse

wish [wɪʃ] VT desear; **I — you were here** ojalá estuvieras aquí; **I — you the best** te deseo lo mejor; **to — for** pedir; **to — upon a star** pedir un deseo; N deseo *m*; **to make a —** pedir un deseo; **best —es** saludos

wishy-washy [wíʃiwɑʃi] ADJ indeciso

wistful [wístfəɫ] ADJ (pensive) pensativo; (nostalgic) nostálgico

wit [wɪt] N (intelligence) agudeza *f*, ingenio *m*; (verbal humor) gracejo *m*, sal *f*, chispa *f*; (person) persona aguda *f*, persona ingeniosa *f*; **to be at one's —s' end** no saber qué más hacer; **to live by one's —s** vivir de su ingenio; **to lose one's —s** perder el juicio; **to use one's —s** valerse de su ingenio

witch [wɪtʃ] N bruja *f*; **—craft** brujería *f*; **— hunt** cacería de brujas *f*

with [wɪθ, wɪð] PREP con; **— rice — chicken** arroz

con pollo *m*; **the man — glasses** el hombre de gafas; **I left my son —** Mary dejé a mi hijo al cuidado de María; **to be — it** está al día; — **me** conmigo; — **you** contigo, con usted

withdraw [wɪðdrɔ́] VI/VT retirar[se]

withdrawal [wɪðdrɔ́əɫ] N (of troops) retirada *f*; (from public office) alejamiento *m*; (from a bank) *Am* retiro *m*; *Sp* retirada *f*; — **[symptoms]** síndrome de abstinencia *m*

withdrawn [wɪθdrɔ́n] *see* withdraw

withdrew [wɪθdrú] *see* withdraw

wither [wíðɚ] VI/VT (of a plant) marchitar[se]; (of a person) consumir[se]; **she —ed him with a look** lo fulminó con la mirada

withheld [wɪθhɛ́ɫd] *see* withhold

withhold [wɪθhóɫd] VT (approval) negar; (funds) retener; (truth) ocultar

withholding tax [wɪθhóɫdɪŋtæks] N impuesto deducido del salario *m*

within [wɪðín] PREP dentro de; — **five miles** a menos de cinco millas; ADV dentro, adentro

without [wɪðáut] PREP sin; — **my seeing him** sin que yo lo vea; ADV fuera, afuera

withstand [wɪθstǽnd] VI/VT resistir

withstood [wɪθstúd] *see* withstand

witness [wítnɪs] N (person) testigo *mf*; (testimony) testimonio *m*; **to bear —** atestiguar; VT (see) presenciar; (sign) firmar como testigo

witticism [wídɪsɪzem] N ocurrencia *f*

witty [wídi] ADJ ocurrente, dicharachero

wizard [wízɚd] N (sorcerer) mago *m*, brujo *m*, hechicero *m*; (computer expert) experto -ta *mf*; (genius) genio *m*

wobble [wábəɫ] N tambaleo *m*, bamboleo *m*; VI/VT tambalear[se], bombolear[se]

woe [wo] N aflicción *f*; — **is me!** ¡pobre de mí!

woeful [wófəɫ] ADJ lamentable

wok [wɑk] N wok *m*

woke [wok] *see* wake

woken [wókən] *see* wake

wolf [wuɫf] N lobo *m*; — **spider** araña lobo *f*

woman [wúmən] N mujer *f*; *fam* tía *f*; **a —'s touch** un toque femenino; **women's lib[eration]** movimiento de liberación femenina *m*; **women's rights** derechos de la mujer *m pl*

womanhood [wúmənhʊd] N (condition) condición de mujer *f*; (all women) las mujeres *f pl*

womanizer [wúmənaɪzɚ] N mujeriego *m*

womankind [wúmənkaɪnd] N las mujeres *f pl*

womanly [wúmənli] ADJ femenino

womb [wum] N (uterus) útero *m*, matriz *f*; (insides of something) vientre *m*; (center) seno *m*

won [wʌn] *see* win

wonder [wándɚ] VI/VT preguntarse; **to — at**

admirarse de, maravillarse de; **I — what time it is** ¿qué hora será? N (marvel) maravilla *f*; (surprise) asombro *m*; (miracle) milagro *m*; **it's a — that** es asombroso que; **it's no — that** no es de extrañar que

wonderful [wándɚfəɫ] ADJ maravilloso, estupendo

woo [wu] VI/VT cortejar

wood [wʊd] N (material, also golf club) madera *f*; (firewood) leña *f*; **—cutter** leñador -ora *mf*; **—louse** cochinilla *f*; **—pecker** pájaro carpintero *m*; **—s** bosque *m*; — **shaving** viruta *f*; **—shed** leñera *f*; **—sman** leñador *m*; **—winds** maderas *f pl*; **—work** carpintería *f*, maderaje *m*; **to come out of the —work** salir de la nada

wooded [wʊ́dɪd] ADJ arbolado

wooden [wʊ́dn̩] ADJ (of wood) de madera; (lifeless) inexpresivo

woody [wʊ́di] ADJ (with trees) arbolado; (like wood) leñoso

woof [wʊf] N (of fabric) trama *f*; INTERJ (sound made by a dog) ¡guau!

wool [wʊɫ] N lana *f*; — **sweater** suéter de lana *m*

woolen [wúlən] ADJ de lana; N **—s** (fabric) tejido de lana *m*; (clothes) ropa de lana *f*

woolly [wúli] ADJ lanudo

word [wɚd] N (lexical unit) vocablo *m*, palabra *f*; (promise) palabra *f*; (news) noticia *f*, aviso *m*; (order) mandato *m*, orden *m*; — **for —** palabra por palabra; — **processing** procesamiento de textos *m*; *Sp* tratamiento de texto[s] *m*; **—s [of a song]** letra [de una canción] *f*; — **spacing** espaciado de palabras *m*; — **wrap** retorno de línea automático *m*; **I found out by — of mouth** me lo dijeron; **may I have a — with you?** ¿podemos hablar? **to eat one's —s** tragarse/comerse las palabras; VT (oral) expresar; (written) formular

wording [wɚ́dɪŋ] N formulación *f*

wordy [wɚ́di] ADJ verboso, prolijo

wore [wor] *see* wear

work [wɚk] N (effort) trabajo *m*; (employment) empleo *m*, trabajo *m*; (artistic product, fortification) obra *f*; **—book** cuaderno/libro de trabajo *m*; **—day** día laborable *m*; — **environment** entorno de trabajo *m*; — **flow** flujo de trabajo *m*; **—force** mano de obra *f*; **—load** cantidad/carga de trabajo *f*; **—man** obrero *m*; — **of art** obra de arte *f*; **—out** sesión de ejercicio *f*; — **permit** permiso de trabajo *m*; **—place** lugar de trabajo *m*; — **schedule** horario de trabajo *m*; **—sheet** planilla *f*, hoja de ejercicios *f*; **—shop** taller *m*; **—station** estación de trabajo *f*; — **stoppage** huelga *f*, paro laboral *m*; **—s** fábrica *f*; **the —s** todo; **—week** semana de trabajo *f*; **he's hard at —** está trabajando duro; ADJ —-**related** laboral; VI (labor) trabajar; (function) funcionar; VT (change) efectuar; (metal, land) trabajar; (a crowd) manipular; (a mine) explotar; (employees) hacer trabajar; **to — in[to]** introducir; **to — loose** soltar[se], aflojar[se]; **to — on** (repair) arreglar; (improve) tratar de mejorar; **to — one's way through college** pagarse los estudios trabajando; **to — one's way up** ascender a fuerza de trabajo; **to — out** (a plan) urdir; (a problem) resolver; **he —s out every day** hace ejercicio todos los días; **to — overtime** trabajar horas extras; **it all —ed out** al final todo salió bien; **to be all —ed up** estar sobreexcitado; **to get —ed up** agitarse

workaholic [wɝkəhálɪk] N adicto -ta al trabajo *mf*

worker [wɝkɚ] N trabajador -ora *mf*; (in a factory) obrero -ra *mf*; (in an office) oficinista *mf*

working [wɝkɪŋ] N (act of someone who works, shaping of metals) trabajo *m*; (operation) funcionamiento *m*, operación *f*; (of a problem) cálculo *m*; (of a mine) explotación *f*; ADJ (class) obrero, trabajador; (majority) suficiente; **— class** clase obrera/trabajadora *f*; **— lunch** comida de trabajo *f*; **—man** obrero *m*

workmanship [wɝkmənʃɪp] N (skill) habilidad *f*, destreza *f*; (quality of work) confección *f*

world [wɝld] N mundo *m*; **— Bank** Banco Mundial *m*; **— Cup** Copa del Mundo *f*; **—view** cosmovisión *f*; **— war** guerra mundial *f*; **— Wide Web** web *f*, red [mundial electrónica] *f*; ADJ —-**class** de categoría mundial; —-**famous** de fama mundial; —-**shaking** trascendental; —**wide** mundial

worldly [wɝldli] ADJ (mundane) mundano, temporal; (sophisticated) de mundo, corrido; (material) material

worm [wɝm] N gusano *m*; ADJ —-**eaten** comido por los gusanos, carcomido; VT desparasitar, quitar las lombrices; **to — a secret out of someone** extraerle/sonsacarle un secreto a alguien; **to — oneself into** insinuarse en

worn [wɔrn] ADJ desgastado, usado

worn [wɔrn] *see* wear

worrisome [wɝisəm] ADJ preocupante, inquietante

worry [wɝi] VI/VT preocupar[se], inquietar[se]; VT (harass) hostigar; VI **to — with** juguetear con; N preocupación *f*, inquietud *f*, zozobra *f*; —**wart** preocupón -ona *mf*

worse [wɝs] ADJ & ADV peor; **— and** — cada vez peor; **— than ever** peor que nunca; **from bad to** — de mal en peor; **so much the** — tanto peor; **to be — off** estar peor que antes; **to change for the** — empeorar[se]; **to get**

— empeorar[se]

worship [wɝʃɪp] N (act of worshiping) adoración *f*; (ceremony) culto *m*; VT (revere) adorar, venerar; VI (attend services) asistir al culto

worshiper [wɝʃɪpɚ] N (one who worships) adorador -ora *mf*; —**s** fieles *mf pl*

worst [wɝst] ADJ & ADV **the — one** el/la peor; **the — thing** lo peor; —-**case scenario** el peor de los casos; VT derrotar

worth [wɝθ] ADJ **to be — a dollar** valer un dólar; **to be — hearing** ser digno de oírse; **to be —while** valer la pena; **it's — doing** vale la pena hacerlo; N valor *m*, valía *f*; **ten cents' — of** diez centavos de; **to get one's money's — out of** aprovechar al máximo

worthless [wɝθlɪs] ADJ (useless) inútil; (despicable) despreciable; **— check** cheque sin fondos *m*

worthy [wɝði] ADJ (meritorious) digno, meritorio; (esteemed) benemérito; **— cause** causa noble *f*; **— of praise** digno de elogio; N persona ilustre *mf*

would [wʊd] V AUX **I — do it if I could** lo haría si pudiera; **— you please open the door?** ¿podrías abrir la puerta por favor? **he said he — do it** dijo que lo haría; **as a child, I — play all the time** de niño, jugaba todo el tiempo; **— that she were alive!** ¡ojalá estuviera viva!

wound[1] [wund] N herida *f*; VI/VT herir; (with an arrow) flechar

wound[2] [waund] *see* wind

wove [wov] *see* weave

woven [wóvən] *see* weave

wow [waʊ] VT impresionar; INTERJ ¡huy!

wrangle [ræŋgəl] VI/VT (quarrel) discutir; (obtain) agenciarse de; VT (herd) juntar; *Am* rodear; N riña *f*, pendencia *f*

wrangler [ræŋglɚ] N vaquero -ra *mf*

wrap [ræp] VT envolver; **to — up** (a present) envolver; (a baby) arropar; (a task) terminar; (against the cold) abrigar[se]; **to be —ped in** estar envuelto en; **to be —ped up in** estar absorto en; N (coat) abrigo *m*; (shawl) chal *m*; —-**up** (summary) resumen *m*; (end) final *m*; **keep under —s** mantener secreto

wrapper [ræpɚ] N envoltura *f*, envoltorio *m*

wrapping [ræpɪŋ] N envoltura *f*; **— paper** papel para envolver *m*

wrath [ræθ] N ira *f*, cólera *f*

wreak [rik] VT **to — havoc** hacer estragos

wreath [riθ] N corona *f*; **— of smoke** espiral de humo *f*

wreck [rɛk] N (building) ruina *f*; (car, plane) restos *m pl*; (a ship) pecio *m*; (shipwreck) naufragio *m*; (person) desastre *m*, ruina *f*; (accident) accidente *m*; VI tener un accidente; VT (a ship) naufragar; (a car, totally) destrozar; (a car, with minor damage) chocar;

(a building) demoler

wreckage [rékɪʤ] N (of a building) escombros *m pl*; (of a car, plane) restos de un accidente *m pl*; (of a ship) pecio *m*

wrecker [rékɚ] N (tow truck) grúa *f*, camión de remolque *m*; (worker) obrero -ra de demolición *mf*

wrench [rentʃ] N (twist) torcedura *f*; (pull) tirón *m*; (tool) llave de tuercas *f*; VT torcer, retorcer; **to — off/out** arrancar de un tirón, arrebatar

wrest [rest] VT (pull) arrancar; (take away) arrebatar

wrestle [résəl] VI/VT luchar [con/contra]; N lucha *f*

wrestler [réslɚ] N luchador -ora *mf*

wrestling [réslɪŋ] N lucha libre *f*

wretch [retʃ] N miserable *mf*, infeliz *mf*

wretched [rétʃɪd] ADJ (unfortunate) desdichado, infeliz; (despicable) vil, miserable, arrastrado; (inferior) pésimo

wriggle [rígəl] VI culebrear, serpentear; **to — out of** escabullirse de; VT menear, retorcer

wring [rɪŋ] VT (twist) torcer, retorcer; (extract) arrancar; **to — one's hands** retorcerse las manos; **to — out** escurrir

wrinkle [ríŋkəl] N arruga *f*, surco *m*; (problem) problema *m*; VI/VT arrugar[se]

wrist [rɪst] N muñeca *f*; **—watch** reloj [de] pulsera *m*

writ [rɪt] N auto *m*, mandato *m*

write [raɪt] VI/VT escribir; (transfer data) grabar; **to — back** contestar; **to — down** apuntar; **to — off** cancelar; **to — out** escribir en forma completa; **to —-protect** proteger contra grabación; **to — up** hacer un reportaje sobre; **it's written all over his face** se le ve en la cara; **she —s for a living** es escritora; N —-**up** reportaje *m*; **— protection** protección contra grabación *f*

writer [ráɪdɚ] N escritor -ora *mf*, literato -ta *mf*

writhe [raɪð] VI retorcerse

writing [ráɪdɪŋ] N (act of writing) escritura *f*; (handwriting) letra *f*, escritura *f*; (style) estilo *m*; **— desk** escritorio *m*; **— paper** papel de escribir *m*; **—s** obra *f*; **to put in —** poner por escrito

written [rítn] *see* write

wrong [rɔŋ] ADJ (incorrect) incorrecto, equivocado; (improper) inapropiado; **what's — with you?** ¿qué te pasa? **you are —** estás equivocado; **the — side of a fabric** el revés de una tela; **— side out** con lo de adentro para afuera; **to be on the — side of the road** ir a contramano / en sentido contrario; **that is the — book** ese no es el libro; **it is in the — place** está fuera de lugar; ADV mal; **to go —** salir mal; N (evil) mal *m*; (injustice) injusticia *f*; **to be in the —** (not be right)

estar equivocado; (be to blame) tener la culpa; **to do —** hacer mal; VT perjudicar

wrongful [rɔ́ŋfəl] ADJ injusto, injustificado

wrongly [rɔ́ŋli] ADV (reported) incorrectamente; (accused) injustamente

wrote [rot] *see* write

wrought [rɔt] ADJ forjado; **— iron** hierro forjado *m*

wrung [rʌŋ] *see* wring

wry [raɪ] ADJ (smile) torcido; (remark, humor) irónico; **to make a — face** torcer la cara

WTO [World Trade Organization] [dʌ́bəljutíó] N OMT *f*

WWW [World Wide Web] [dʌ́bəljudʌ́bəljudʌ́bəlju] N web *f*

Xx

xenophobia [zɛnəfóbiə] N xenofobia *f*

Xerox™ [zírɑks] N fotocopia *f*; VI/VT fotocopiar

x-rated [éksreDɪd] ADJ pornográfico

x-ray [éksre] N rayos X *m pl*, radiografía *f*; VI/VT radiografiar

xylophone [záɪləfon] N xilofón *m*, xilófono *m*

Yy

yacht [jɑt] N yate *m*; VI navegar en yate

y'all [jɔl] PRON *Am* ustedes *mf*; *Sp* vosotros -as *mf*

Yankee [jǽŋki] ADJ & N estadounidense del norte del país *mf*

yard [jɑrd] N (measure) yarda [0.9144m] *f*; (spar) verga *f*; (courtyard) patio *m*; (grassy area) jardín *m*; **—stick** (stick) vara de medida [de una yarda] *f*; (criterion) patrón *m*, norma *f*

yarn [jɑrn] N (material) hilo *m*; (story) cuento *m*

yawn [jɔn] VI bostezar; N bostezo *m*

yeah [jéə] ADV *fam* sí; *fam* **— right!** ¡de eso, nada! ¡qué va!

year [jir] N año *m*; **—book** anuario *m*; ADJ **—-end** de fin de año; **—-round** de todo el año; **—-to-date** del año hasta la fecha

yearling [jírlɪŋ] N animal de un año *m*; (of cows) añojo -ja *mf*

yearly [jírli] ADJ anual; ADV anualmente

yearn [jɚn] VI anhelar, suspirar por

yearning [jɚ́nɪŋ] N anhelo *m*

yeast [jist] N levadura *f*

yell [jɛl] VI/VT gritar; N grito *m*

yellow [jélo] ADJ (color) amarillo; (coward) cobarde; **— card** (in soccer) tarjeta amarilla *f*;

— **fever** fiebre amarilla f; — **jacket** avispa f;
— **pages** páginas amarillas $f pl$; N amarillo m;
VI/VT poner[se] amarillo, amarillear
yellowish [jéloɪʃ] ADJ amarillento
yelp [jɛłp] VI gañir, aullar; N gañido m, aullido m
Yemen [jémən] N Yemen m
Yemeni [jémәni] ADJ & N yemení mf
yen [jɛn] N (currency of Japan) yen m; (desire)
anhelo m; VI anhelar
yes [jɛs] ADV sí; —-**no question** pregunta de sí o
no f
yesterday [jéstә-de] ADV & N ayer m; **the day
before** — anteayer
yet [jɛt] ADV & CONJ **are they here** —? ¿ya
llegaron? **they aren't here** — todavía no
llegan, aún no han llegado; — **another** otro
más; **ugly** — **charming** feo pero
encantador; **as** — todavía, aún
yield [jiłd] VI/VT (surrender, give in) ceder;
(produce) rendir, redituar; **to** — **5 percent**
dar un cinco por ciento de interés; N
(production) rendimiento m, producción f;
(of stocks) rédito m
yodel [jódl] VI cantar a la tirolesa; N canto
tirolés m
yoga [jógә] N yoga m
yogurt [jógә-t] N yogur m
yoke [jok] N (crossbar) yugo m; (pair of animals)
yunta f; (on a shirt) canesú m; VT uncir
yolk [jok] N yema f
yonder [jándә-] ADJ aquel; ADV (location) allá;
(direction) hacia allá
yore [jɔr] N **in days of** — antaño
you [ju] SUBJ PRON (sg informal) tú; RP, Central
Am vos; (sg formal) usted; (pl informal) Sp
vosotros; Am ustedes; (pl formal) ustedes; **I
see** — (sg informal) te veo; (sg formal) lo veo;
(pl informal) Sp os veo; Am los veo; (pl
formal) los veo; **I talk to** — (sg informal) te
hablo; (sg formal) le hablo; (pl informal) Sp os
hablo; Am les hablo; (pl formal) les hablo; **I
went with** — (sg informal) fui contigo; (sg
formal) fui con usted; (pl informal) Sp fui con
vosotros; Am fui con ustedes; (pl formal) fui
con ustedes; **it's for** — (sg informal) es para
ti; (sg informal) RP, Central Am es para vos; (sg
formal) es para usted; (pl informal) Sp es para
vosotros; Am es para ustedes; (pl formal) es
para ustedes; **this is how** — **make bread**
así se hace el pan
young [jʌŋ] ADJ joven; — **man** joven m; —
people gente joven f; — **woman** joven f; N
(offspring) cría f
youngster [jáŋstә-] N muchacho -cha mf,
jovencito -ta mf
your [jɔr] POSS ADJ **this is** — **dog** (sg informal)
este es tu perro; (sg formal) este es su perro;
(pl informal) Sp este es vuestro perro, Am este
es su perro; (pl formal) este es su perro

yours [jɔrz] PRON **this book is** — (sg informal)
este libro es tuyo; (sg formal) este libro es
suyo / de usted; (pl informal) Sp este libro es
vuestro; Am este libro es suyo / de ustedes; (pl
formal) este libro es suyo / de ustedes; — **is
bigger** (sg informal) el tuyo / la tuya es más
grande; (sg formal) el suyo / el de usted / la
suya / la de usted es más grande; (pl informal)
Sp el vuestro / la vuestra es más grande; Am el
suyo / el de ustedes es más grande; (pl formal)
el suyo / el de ustedes es más grande; **a
friend of** — (sg informal) un amigo tuyo; (sg
formal) un amigo suyo / de usted; (pl
informal) Sp un amigo vuestro; Am un amigo
suyo / de ustedes; — **truly** atentamente
yourself [jɔrsɛłf] PRON **you** — **wrote the
letter** (sg informal) tú mismo escribiste la
carta; (sg formal) usted mismo escribió la
carta; **you yourselves wrote the letter** (pl
informal) Sp vosotros mismos escribisteis la
carta; Am ustedes mismos escribieron la
carta; (pl formal) ustedes mismos escribieron
la carta; **you are not** — **today** (sg informal)
hoy no eres el mismo de siempre; (sg formal)
hoy no es el mismo de siempre; **you are not
yourselves today** Sp hoy no sois los mismos
de siempre; Am hoy no son los mismos de
siempre; (pl formal) hoy no son los mismos
de siempre; **you were sitting by** — (sg
informal) tú estabas sentado solo; (sg formal)
usted estaba sentado solo; **you were sitting
by yourselves** (informal) Sp vosotros
estabais sentados solos; Am ustedes estaban
sentados solos; (pl formal) ustedes estaban
sentados solos; **you look at** — **at the
mirror** (sg informal) tú te miras en el espejo;
(sg formal) usted se mira en el espejo; **you
look at yourselves at the mirror** (pl
informal) Sp vosotros os mirais en el espejo;
Am ustedes se miran en el espejo; (pl formal)
ustedes se miran en el espejo; **you bought** —
a house (sg informal) te compraste una casa;
(sg formal) usted se compró una casa; **you
bought yourselves a house** (pl informal)
Sp os comprasteis una casa; Am se compraron
una casa; (pl formal) se compraron una casa
youth [juθ] N (person) joven m; (young age)
juventud m
youthful [júθfәł] ADJ juvenil
yo-yo [jójo] N yo-yo m
yuan [juán] N yuan m
yucca [jákә] N yuca f
yuck [jʌk] INTERJ puaj, puaf
Yugoslavia [jugoslávi ә] N Yugoslavia f
Yugoslavian [jugoslávi әn] ADJ & N yugoslavo
-va mf
Yuletide [júłtaɪd] N Navidad f
yummy [jámi] ADJ delicioso; INTERJ ¡qué rico!
yuppie [jápi] N yuppie mf

Zz

Zambia [zǽmbiə] N Zambia *f*
Zambian [zǽmbiən] ADJ & N zambiano -na *mf*
zany [zéni] ADJ loco, chiflado
zap [zæp] VT liquidar
zeal [ził] N celo *m*, fervor *m*
zealot [zélət] N fanático -ca *mf*
zealous [zéləs] ADJ celoso, fervoroso
zebra [zíbrə] N cebra *f*
zenith [zíniθ] N cenit *m*
zephyr [zéfɚ] N céfiro *m*
zeppelin [zépəlɪn] N zepelín *m*, dirigible *m*
zero [ziro] NUM cero *m*; **there's — possibility**
    that he'll come las posibilidades de que
    venga son nulas
zest [zɛst] N entusiasmo *m*
zigzag [zígzæg] N zigzag *m*; ADJ & ADV en zigzag;
    VI zigzaguear, andar en zigzag; VT hacer
    zigzaguear
Zimbabwe [zɪmbábwe] N Zimbabue *m*
Zimbabwean [zɪmbábweən] ADJ & N zimbabuo
    -bua *mf*
zinc [zɪŋk] N cinc *m*, zinc *m*
zip [zɪp] VI/VT cerrar/abrir con cremallera; **to —**
    by pasar volando; **to — over** ir corriendo; N
    cero *m*; **— code** código postal *m*
zipper [zípɚ] N cremallera *f*, cierre [relámpago]
    m
zirconium [zɚkóniəm] N circonio *m*
zodiac [zóDiæk] N zodíaco *m*
zombie [zámbi] N zombi *mf*
zone [zon] N zona *f*; **— defense** defensa en zonas
    f; VT dividir en zonas
zoning [zónɪŋ] N zonificación *f*
zoo [zu] N zoológico *m*; *Sp* zoo *m*; **—keeper**
    guardián -ana del zoológico *mf*
zoological [zoəládʒɪkəł] ADJ zoológico
zoology [zoálədʒi] N zoología *f*
zoom [zum] VI (make sound) zumbar; **to — in**
    ampliar una imagen; **to — off** salir
    zumbando; **to — out** achicar la imagen; N
    zumbido *m*; **— lens** teleobjetivo *m*, zoom *m*
zucchini [zukíni] N calabacín *m*
zygote [záɪgot] N cigoto *m*, zigoto *m*